CRITICAL SURVEY

OF

DRAMA

CRITICAL SURVEY
OF
DRAMA
Second Revised Edition

Volume 7
Giangiorgio Trissino - Arnold Zweig
Essays

Editor, Second Revised Edition
Carl Rollyson
Baruch College, City University of New York

Editor, First Editions, English and Foreign Language Series
Frank N. Magill

SALEM PRESS, INC.
Pasadena, California   Hackensack, New Jersey

Editor in Chief: Dawn P. Dawson
Managing Editor: Christina J. Moose
Developmental Editor: R. Kent Rasmussen
Project Editor: Rowena Wildin
Research Supervisor: Jeffry Jensen
Research Assistant: Michelle Murphy

Acquisitions Editor: Mark Rehn
Photograph Editor: Philip Bader
Manuscript Editor: Sarah Hilbert
Assistant Editor: Andrea E. Miller
Production Editor: Cynthia Beres
Layout: Eddie Murillo and William Zimmerman

Library of Congress Cataloging-in-Publication Data

Critical survey of drama / edited by Carl Rollyson.-- 2nd rev. ed.

    p. cm.

Previous edition edited by Frank Northen Magill in 1994.

"Combines, updates, and expands two earlier Salem Press reference sets: Critical survey of drama, revised edition, English language series, published in 1994, and Critical survey of drama, foreign language series, published in 1986"--Pref.

Includes bibliographical references and index.

ISBN 1-58765-102-5 (set : alk. paper) -- ISBN 1-58765-109-2 (vol. 7 : alk. paper) --

1. Drama--Dictionaries. 2. Drama--History and criticism--Dictionaries. 3. Drama--Bio-bibliography. 4. English drama--Dictionaries. 5. American drama--Dictionaries. 6. Commonwealth drama (English)--Dictionaries. 7. English drama--Bio-bibliography. 8. American drama--Bio-bibliography. 9. Commonwealth drama (English)--Bio-bibliography. I. Rollyson, Carl E. (Carl Edmund) II. Magill, Frank Northen, 1907-1997.

PN1625 .C68 2003

809.2'003—dc21

2003002190

Fourth Printing

CONTENTS

VOLUME 7

Complete List of Contents cxv

Trissino, Giangiorgio 3371
Tristan L'Hermite 3377
Turgenev, Ivan 3384
Tyler, Royall 3393

Udall, Nicholas 3400
Uhry, Alfred 3406
Unamuno y Jugo, Miguel de 3410
Usigli, Rodolfo 3416

Valdez, Luis Miguel 3422
Valle-Inclán, Ramón María del 3428
Vanbrugh, Sir John 3436
Van Druten, John William 3445
Vega Carpio, Lope de 3448
Verga, Giovanni 3457
Vicente, Gil 3464
Vilalta, Maruxa 3472
Villiers, George 3477
Vogel, Paula 3483
Voltaire 3486
Vondel, Joost van den 3494

Wakefield Master 3499
Walcott, Derek 3506
Walker, Joseph A. 3514
Walser, Martin 3518
Wasserstein, Wendy 3527
Webster, John 3533
Wedekind, Frank 3539
Weiss, Peter 3548
Weldon, Fay 3554
Werfel, Franz 3558
Wertenbaker, Timberlake 3565
Wesker, Arnold 3571
White, Patrick 3580

Whiting, John 3585
Wilde, Oscar 3592
Wilder, Thornton 3600
Willems, Paul 3610
Williams, Emlyn 3614
Williams, Tennessee 3621
Williamson, David 3635
Wilson, August 3644
Wilson, Lanford 3650
Wilson, Robert 3658
Witkiewicz, Stanisław Ignacy 3664
Wolf, Friedrich 3671
Wycherley, William 3679
Wyspiański, Stanisław 3687

Yeats, William Butler 3694

Zamyatin, Yevgeny 3700
Zangwill, Israel 3703
Zeami Motokiyo 3708
Zindel, Paul 3713
Zola, Émile 3721
Zorrilla y Moral, José 3731
Zuckmayer, Carl 3738
Zweig, Arnold 3744

AMERICAN DRAMA
American Drama 3751
Contemporary American Drama 3769
African American Drama 3775
Asian American Drama 3784
Latino Drama 3787
Native American Drama 3792
American Regional Theater 3797
New York Theater 3804
Obie Awards 3809
Pulitzer Prizes 3813
Tony Awards 3817

BRITISH DRAMA

British Medieval Drama 3823
Elizabethan and Jacobean Drama 3836
Restoration Drama 3857
Eighteenth Century British Drama 3874
Nineteenth Century British Drama 3898
Twentieth Century British Drama 3909
Contemporary British Drama 3926
Irish Drama 3931

COMPLETE LIST OF CONTENTS

VOLUME 1

Abe, Kōbō. 1
Abell, Kjeld 5
Adamov, Arthur 12
Addison, Joseph 18
Aeschylus 25
Aguirre, Isidora 33
Akalaitis, JoAnne 39
Aksyonov, Vassily 44
Albee, Edward 49
Alfieri, Vittorio 62
Almqvist, Carl Jonas Love 69
Álvarez Quintero, Serafín *and* Joaquín
    Álvarez Quintero 73
Anderson, Maxwell 79
Anderson, Robert 83
Andreyev, Leonid 91
Anouilh, Jean 97
Anzengruber, Ludwig 109
Apollinaire, Guillaume 115
Arden, John 120
Aretino, Pietro 127
Ariosto, Ludovico 134
Aristophanes 139
Arrabal, Fernando 146
Artsybashev, Mikhail 155
Asturias, Miguel Ángel 159
Auden, W. H. 163
Augier, Émile 170
Ayckbourn, Sir Alan 178

Baillie, Joanna 187
Baitz, Jon Robin 190
Baldwin, James 198
Bale, John 205
Baraka, Amiri 214
Barker, James Nelson 225
Barnes, Peter 232
Barrie, Sir James 240
Barry, Philip 249
Bataille, Félix-Henry 257

Beaumarchais, Pierre-Augustin
    Caron de 260
Beaumont, Francis 268
Beckett, Samuel 273
Becque, Henry 280
Behan, Brendan 285
Behn, Aphra 291
Behrman, S. N. 299
Belasco, David 307
Benavente y Martínez, Jacinto 315
Bergman, Hjalmar 321
Bernard, Jean-Jacques 328
Bernhard, Thomas 333
Bernstein, Henry 339
Besier, Rudolf 344
Betti, Ugo 349
Bird, Robert Montgomery 355
Bjørnson, Bjørnstjerne 364
Blessing, Lee 370
Blok, Aleksandr 375
Bogosian, Eric 379
Boker, George H. 383
Bolt, Robert 388
Bond, Edward 399
Bottomley, Gordon 407
Boucicault, Dion 414
Bracco, Roberto 421
Braun, Volker 427
Brecht, Bertolt 436
Brenton, Howard 447
Bridie, James 456
Brieux, Eugène 463
Brome, Richard 470
Browning, Robert 475
Bruckner, Ferdinand 482
Büchner, Georg 489
Buero Vallejo, Antonio 495
Bulgakov, Mikhail 504
Bullins, Ed 511
Bulwer-Lytton, Edward 520

Buzo, Alexander 526
Buzzati, Dino. 532
Byron, George Gordon, Lord 535

Calderón de la Barca, Pedro 548
Camus, Albert 557

VOLUME 2

Canth, Minna. 565
Čapek, Karel 571
Caragiale, Ion Luca . . . . : . . 580
Carr, Marina 585
Casona, Alejandro 589
Centlivre, Mrs. Susannah 595
Cervantes, Miguel de 601
Césaire, Aimé 606
Chapman, George 611
Chase, Mary 619
Chekhov, Anton 622
Chiarelli, Luigi. 633
Chikamatsu Monzaemon 639
Childress, Alice 645
Chin, Frank. 649
Churchill, Caryl 656
Cibber, Colley 661
Clark-Bekederemo, John Pepper 667
Clarke, Austin 673
Clarke, Martha 679
Claudel, Paul. 687
Cocteau, Jean 696
Colum, Padraic. 703
Congreve, William 713
Connelly, Marc. 726
Corneille, Pierre 733
Coward, Noël 743
Cristofer, Michael 749
Crowley, Mart 753
Crowne, John 759
Cruz, Sor Juana Inés de la 766
Csokor, Franz Theodor. 772
Cumberland, Richard 776
Curel, François de 784

D'Annunzio, Gabriele 790
Davenant, Sir William 796
Davies, Robertson 802
Davis, Owen 812

De Filippo, Eduardo 816
Dekker, Thomas 822
Delaney, Shelagh 831
Della Porta, Giambattista 836
Denison, Merrill 842
Diderot, Denis 850
Dietz, Steven 857
Dodson, Owen 861
Dorst, Tankred 865
Drinkwater, John. 871
Dryden, John 876
Dumas, Alexandre, *fils* 885
Dumas, Alexandre, *père* 894
Dunlap, William 905
Dunsany, Lord 911
Durang, Christopher 917
Duras, Marguerite 923
Dürrenmatt, Friedrich 930

Echegaray y Eizaguirre, José 938
Elder, Lonne, III 944
Eliot, T. S. 949
Encina, Juan del 960
Ennius, Quintus 967
Ernst, Paul 971
Ervine, St. John 978
Etherege, Sir George 982
Euripides 991
Evreinov, Nikolai 1002

Farquhar, George 1009
Ferber, Edna 1013
Ferreira, António 1020
Feydeau, Georges 1025
Fielding, Henry 1033
Fierstein, Harvey 1046
Fitch, Clyde 1050
Fleisser, Marieluise 1058
Fletcher, John 1071

Fo, Dario 1081
Fonvizin, Denis Ivanovich 1089
Foote, Horton 1098

Foote, Samuel 1103
Ford, John 1109
Foreman, Richard 1124

VOLUME 3

Fornes, Maria Irene 1133
Frayn, Michael 1136
Fredro, Aleksander 1143
Friel, Brian 1149
Frisch, Max 1158
Fry, Christopher 1166
Fugard, Athol 1174
Fuller, Charles 1186

Galsworthy, John 1193
Gambaro, Griselda 1199
Gao Ming 1207
García Lorca, Federico 1215
Garnier, Robert 1226
Gascoigne, George 1231
Gay, John 1239
Gelber, Jack 1244
Genet, Jean 1251
Ghelderode, Michel de 1263
Giacosa, Giuseppe 1269
Gibson, William 1277
Gilbert, W. S. 1283
Gilman, Rebecca 1293
Gilroy, Frank D. 1297
Giraldi Cinthio, Giambattista 1309
Giraudoux, Jean 1315
Glaspell, Susan 1322
Goethe, Johann Wolfgang von 1326
Gogol, Nikolai 1337
Goldoni, Carlo 1343
Goldsmith, Oliver 1349
Gombrowicz, Witold 1358
Gorky, Maxim 1366
Gozzi, Carlo 1374
Grabbe, Christian Dietrich 1381
Granville-Barker, Harley 1388
Grass, Günter 1395
Gray, Simon 1405

Gray, Spalding 1412
Green, Paul 1417
Greene, Graham 1424
Greene, Robert 1433
Gregory, Lady Augusta 1440
Griboyedov, Alexander 1447
Grillparzer, Franz 1452
Gryphius, Andreas 1460
Guare, John 1468
Guarini, Battista 1477
Gurney, A. R., Jr. 1482

Hacks, Peter 1490
Hagedorn, Jessica 1495
Hakim, Tawfiq al- 1501
Hall, Willis 1510
Handke, Peter 1516
Hansberry, Lorraine 1523
Hardy, Thomas 1531
Hare, David 1538
Hart, Lorenz 1548
Hart, Moss 1556
Hauptmann, Gerhart 1562
Havel, Václav 1570
Hebbel, Friedrich 1576
Heiberg, Gunnar 1581
Heiberg, Johan Ludvig 1585
Heijermans, Herman 1592
Hellman, Lillian 1597
Henley, Beth 1606
Henshaw, James Ene 1611
Heyward, DuBose 1618
Heywood, John 1622
Heywood, Thomas 1627
Hochhuth, Rolf 1634
Hochwälder, Fritz 1642
Hofmannsthal, Hugo von 1649
Holberg, Ludvig 1656

Horovitz, Israel 1662
Horváth, Ödön von 1670
Howard, Bronson 1677

Howard, Sidney 1683
Howe, Tina 1687

VOLUME 4

Hugo, Victor 1693
Hwang, David Henry 1700

Ibsen, Henrik 1708
Inchbald, Elizabeth 1719
Inge, William 1723
Innaurato, Albert 1730
Ionesco, Eugène 1738
Ives, David 1751

James, Henry 1756
Jarry, Alfred 1763
Jolley, Elizabeth 1770
Jones, Henry Arthur 1774
Jones, Preston 1780
Jonson, Ben 1785

Kaiser, Georg 1795
Kālidāsa 1803
Kane, Sarah 1809
Kantor, Tadeusz 1813
Kaufman, George S. 1818
Kennedy, Adrienne 1824
Kingsley, Sidney 1830
Kipphardt, Heinar 1837
Kirkland, Jack 1843
Kivi, Aleksis 1850
Kleist, Heinrich von 1858
Klopstock, Friedrich Gottlieb 1866
Knowles, James Sheridan 1870
Kohout, Pavel 1876
Kopit, Arthur 1883
Kops, Bernard 1893
Kotzebue, August von 1900
Kramer, Larry 1907
Krasiński, Zygmunt 1911
Kraus, Karl 1919
Kroetz, Franz Xaver 1927

Kushner, Tony 1937
Kyd, Thomas 1941

Labiche, Eugène 1950
La Chaussée, Pierre-Claude Nivelle de 1956
Lagerkvist, Pär 1960
Laurents, Arthur 1970
Lawler, Ray 1979
Laxness, Halldór 1985
Lee, Nathaniel 1990
Lenormand, Henri-René 1994
Lenz, Jakob Michael Reinhold 1998
Leonard, Hugh 2005
Lermontov, Mikhail 2012
Lesage, Alain-René 2019
Lessing, Gotthold Ephraim 2027
Lewis, Matthew Gregory 2041
Lillo, George 2052
Linney, Romulus 2059
Livings, Henry 2065
Lodge, Thomas 2070
Lonergan, Kenneth 2075
Lonsdale, Frederick 2078
Lovelace, Earl 2087
Lucas, Craig 2091
Ludlam, Charles 2095
Ludwig, Otto 2100
Lyly, John 2103

McCullers, Carson 2112
MacDonagh, Donagh 2119
McDonagh, Martin 2127
McGrath, John 2132
Machado, Antonio 2137
Machado, Eduardo 2142
Machiavelli, Niccolò 2150
MacLeish, Archibald 2156
McNally, Terrence 2165

Madách, Imre 2176
Maeterlinck, Maurice 2181
Maffei, Francesco Scipione 2187
Mairet, Jean 2190
Mamet, David 2196
Manrique, Gómez 2205

Marber, Patrick 2209
Margulies, Donald 2212
Marivaux 2216
Marlowe, Christopher 2225
Marston, John 2238

VOLUME 5

Martin, Jane 2245
Martínez de la Rosa, Francisco 2248
Martínez Sierra, Gregorio, *and*
    María Martínez Sierra 2255
Martyn, Edward 2262
Masefield, John 2267
Massinger, Philip 2274
Maugham, W. Somerset 2282
Mauriac, François 2290
Mayakovsky, Vladimir 2294
Medoff, Mark 2302
Medwall, Henry 2309
Menander 2315
Mercier, Louis-Sébastien 2322
Metastasio, Pietro 2328
Middleton, Thomas 2334
Millay, Edna St. Vincent 2342
Miller, Arthur 2346
Mishima, Yukio 2359
Molière 2366
Molnár, Ferenc 2375
Montherlant, Henry de 2381
Moratín, Leandro Fernández de 2387
Moravia, Alberto 2392
Moreto y Cabaña, Agustín 2396
Mortimer, John 2401
Mosel, Tad 2408
Mrożek, Sławomir 2412
Müller, Heiner 2421
Munk, Kaj 2429
Musset, Alfred de 2435

Naevius, Gnaeus 2446
Nashe, Thomas 2449
Nestroy, Johann 2456

Ngugi wa Thiong'o 2465
Niccolini, Giovanni Battista 2473
Nichols, Peter 2478
Norman, Marsha 2488
Norton, Thomas, *and* Thomas Sackville 2494

O'Casey, Sean 2503
Odets, Clifford 2511
Oehlenschläger, Adam Gottlob 2519
Olesha, Yury 2525
O'Neill, Eugene 2528
Örkény, István 2538
Orton, Joe 2543
Osborne, John 2550
Ostrovsky, Alexander 2558
Otway, Thomas 2565
Overmyer, Eric 2576
Owens, Rochelle 2581

Parks, Suzan-Lori 2589
Patrick, John 2593
Patrick, Robert 2600
Payne, John Howard 2607
Peele, George 2612
Pérez Galdós, Benito 2618
Phillips, Caryl 2626
Pinero, Arthur Wing 2629
Pinget, Robert 2639
Pinter, Harold 2644
Pirandello, Luigi 2654
Pixérécourt, Guilbert de 2661
Planché, James Robinson 2666
Plautus 2673
Pomerance, Bernard 2678
Ponsard, François 2682

Pontoppidan, Henrik 2686
Priestley, J. B. 2691
Purdy, James 2702
Pushkin, Alexander 2706

Quinault, Philippe 2713

Rabe, David 2718
Racine, Jean 2727
Raimund, Ferdinand 2736

Rattigan, Terence 2745
Reaney, James 2752
Regnard, Jean-François 2762
Reza, Yasmina 2770
Ribman, Ronald 2774
Rice, Elmer 2781
Riggs, Lynn 2788
Robertson, Thomas William 2794
Robinson, Lennox 2803

VOLUME 6

Romains, Jules 2811
Rostand, Edmond 2818
Rotimi, Ola 2825
Rotrou, Jean de 2833
Rowe, Nicholas 2840
Różewicz, Tadeusz 2846
Rudnick, Paul 2855
Rueda, Lope de 2859
Ruiz de Alarcón, Juan 2866
Ryga, George 2873

Saavedra, Ángel de 2882
Sachs, Hans 2887
Sackler, Howard 2893
Sánchez, Luis Rafael 2898
Sanchez, Sonia 2901
Sardou, Victorien 2905
Sargeson, Frank 2912
Saroyan, William 2916
Sartre, Jean-Paul 2921
Sastre, Alfonso 2932
Schenkkan, Robert 2940
Schiller, Friedrich 2944
Schisgal, Murray 2953
Schnitzler, Arthur 2958
Scribe, Eugène 2965
Seneca 2972
Shadwell, Thomas 2979
Shaffer, Peter 2986
Shakespeare, William: The Dramatist 2997

Shakespeare, William: The Man 3021
Shange, Ntozake 3026
Shanley, John Patrick 3032
Shaw, George Bernard 3036
Shaw, Irwin 3049
Shawn, Wallace 3053
Shelley, Percy Bysshe 3060
Shepard, Sam 3070
Sheridan, Richard Brinsley 3079
Sherriff, R. C. 3090
Sherwood, Robert E. 3097
Shirley, James 3107
Shvarts, Yevgeny 3117
Simon, Neil 3123
Slade, Bernard 3132
Słowacki, Juliusz 3141
Sondheim, Stephen 3154
Sophocles 3159
Soyinka, Wole 3168
Steele, Sir Richard 3179
Sternheim, Carl 3184
Stoppard, Tom 3191
Storey, David 3201
Strauss, Botho 3211
Strindberg, August 3215
Sudermann, Hermann 3224
Sukhovo-Kobylin, Alexander 3234
Sumarokov, Aleksandr Petrovich 3239
Swinburne, Algernon Charles 3245
Synge, John Millington 3252

Tabori, George 3260
Tagore, Rabindranath 3263
Tamayo y Baus, Manuel 3271
Tasso, Torquato 3280
Tennyson, Alfred, Lord 3287
Terence 3294
Terry, Megan 3299
Tesich, Steve 3305

Thomas, Dylan 3310
Tieck, Ludwig 3317
Tirso de Molina 3326
Toller, Ernst 3331
Torres Naharro, Bartolomé de 3343
Tourneur, Cyril 3349
Tremblay, Michel 3357
Trevor, William 3367

VOLUME 7

Trissino, Giangiorgio 3371
Tristan L'Hermite 3377
Turgenev, Ivan 3384
Tyler, Royall 3393

Udall, Nicholas 3400
Uhry, Alfred 3406
Unamuno y Jugo, Miguel de 3410
Usigli, Rodolfo 3416

Valdez, Luis Miguel 3422
Valle-Inclán, Ramón María del 3428
Vanbrugh, Sir John 3436
Van Druten, John William 3445
Vega Carpio, Lope de 3448
Verga, Giovanni 3457
Vicente, Gil 3464
Vilalta, Maruxa 3472
Villiers, George 3477
Vogel, Paula 3483
Voltaire 3486
Vondel, Joost van den 3494

Wakefield Master 3499
Walcott, Derek 3506
Walker, Joseph A. 3514
Walser, Martin 3518
Wasserstein, Wendy 3527
Webster, John 3533
Wedekind, Frank 3539
Weiss, Peter 3548
Weldon, Fay 3554
Werfel, Franz 3558

Wertenbaker, Timberlake 3565
Wesker, Arnold 3571
White, Patrick 3580
Whiting, John 3585
Wilde, Oscar 3592
Wilder, Thornton 3600
Willems, Paul 3610
Williams, Emlyn 3614
Williams, Tennessee 3621
Williamson, David 3635
Wilson, August 3644
Wilson, Lanford 3650
Wilson, Robert 3658
Witkiewicz, Stanisław Ignacy 3664
Wolf, Friedrich 3671
Wycherley, William 3679
Wyspiański, Stanisław 3687

Yeats, William Butler 3694

Zamyatin, Yevgeny 3700
Zangwill, Israel 3703
Zeami Motokiyo 3708
Zindel, Paul 3713
Zola, Émile 3721
Zorrilla y Moral, José 3731
Zuckmayer, Carl 3738
Zweig, Arnold 3744

AMERICAN DRAMA

American Drama 3751
Contemporary American Drama 3769
African American Drama 3775

Asian American Drama 3784
Latino Drama 3787
Native American Drama 3795
American Regional Theater 3797
New York Theater 3804
Obie Awards 3809
Pulitzer Prizes 3813
Tony Awards 3817

BRITISH DRAMA

British Medieval Drama 3823
Elizabethan and Jacobean Drama 3836
Restoration Drama 3857
Eighteenth Century British Drama 3874
Nineteenth Century British Drama 3898
Twentieth Century British Drama 3909
Contemporary British Drama 3926
Irish Drama 3931

VOLUME 8

EUROPEAN DRAMA

Preclassical Drama 3939
Classical Greek and Roman Drama 3949
Medieval Drama on the Continent 3988
Renaissance Drama 4009
Central and Southeastern European
    Drama 4045
French Drama Since the 1600's 4054
German Drama Since the 1600's 4074
Italian Drama Since the 1600's 4094
Russian Drama Since the 1600's 4109
Scandinavian Drama Since the 1600's 4120
Spanish Drama Since the 1600's 4134

WORLD DRAMA

Primitive Drama 4157
Postcolonial Theater 4161
Movements in Modern Drama 4165
English-Language African Drama 4174
French-Language African Drama 4185
Asian Drama 4192
Chinese Drama 4197
Indian Drama 4222
Islamic Drama 4230
Japanese Drama 4234
Korean Drama 4248
Southeast Asian Drama 4252
Australian Drama 4257
Canadian Drama 4264
Latin American Drama 4271
West Indian Drama 4281

DRAMATIC GENRES

Dramatic Genres 4291
Melodrama 4344
Vaudeville 4348
Musical Drama 4352
English-Language Opera 4366
Western European Opera 4374
Deaf Theater 4382
Experimental Theater 4386
Feminist Theater 4403
Gay and Lesbian Theater 4408
Political Theater 4414
Cinema and Drama 4420
Radio Drama 4425
Television Drama 4434

DRAMA TECHNIQUES

Acting Styles 4445
Monologue and Soliloquy 4455
Staging and Production 4459
Adapting Novels to the Stage 4483

RESOURCES

Bibliography 4491
Dramatic Terms and Movements 4512
Major Awards 4532
Time Line 4543
Chronological List of Dramatists 4552

INDEXES

Geographical Index of Dramatists III
Categorized Index of Dramatists IX
Subject Index XXI

CRITICAL SURVEY

OF

DRAMA

GIANGIORGIO TRISSINO

Born: Vicenza, Republic of Venice (now in Italy);
July 8, 1478

Died: Rome, Papal States (now in Italy); December
8, 1550

PRINCIPAL DRAMA

La Sofonisba, wr. 1515, pb. 1524, pr. 1562 (verse
play)

I simillimi, pb. 1548 (based on Plautus's
Menaechmi)

*Tutte le opere di Giovan Giorgio Trissino,
gentiluomo vicentino*, pb. 1729 (2 volumes)

OTHER LITERARY FORMS

The most distinguished *letterato* of his generation, Giangiorgio Trissino was a grammarian, critic, poet, and diplomat as well as a dramatist. His most serious literary endeavor stemmed from his desire to break the romance tradition in Italian literature and to replace it with the epic. Scorning Ludovico Ariosto's *Orlando furioso* (1516, 1521, 1532; English translation, 1591), he worked for twenty years on his national epic, *La Italia liberata da Gotthi* (1547-1548; Italy liberated from the Goths), in twenty-seven books. He took his story from Procopius's history of the war of Belisarius against the Goths in order to recapture Italy for the Byzantine Empire, and he strove to imitate Homer according to Aristotle's *De poetica* (c. 334-323 B.C.E.; *Poetics*, 1705). The epic, written in the blank verse of a medieval chronical, encumbered by intricate subplots and fulsome passages of praise for noble Italian families, and full of Lombardisms, failed to interest the Italian public, whose enthusiasms were more religious than heroic and would await Torquato Tasso's epic *Gerusalemme liberata* (1581; *Jerusalem Delivered*, 1600) some thirty years later. The fact that Trissino admitted pagan deities into the Christian hierarchy (such as the "Angel" Neptune) seemed to offend everyone. The topic lacked relevance for Italians: Italy delivered from the Goths was only Italy delivered to the Lombards, and Italians bore little or no hostility toward either of these invaders anyway. What Trissino had hoped would be a second *Iliad* (c. 750 B.C.E.; English translation, 1611) turned out to be a parody of the *Iliad*.

In addition to his epic, Trissino wrote many shorter Italian lyrics: three Pindaric odes, two eclogues, and the first Horatian ode in Italian, along with forty-seven sonnets and a variety of *canzoni*, *ballate*, *madrigali*, and *sirventesi*. One sonnet honors Trissino's first wife and begs her pardon as the sonneteer guiltily yields to the charms of another woman. Two sonnets convey sincere praise for Pope Paul III and Pietro Bembo. The sonnet to Bembo was answered in kind by the poet-cardinal, but this exchange of poetry seems to represent a truce perhaps effected by an intermediary rather than a rapprochement of their many political and intellectual differences.

There are also a few epigraphs in Latin written by Trissino: on the death of Bembo, for the tomb of his teacher Demetrius Chalcondyles, for his dead son Francesco, and the especially beautiful lines on the death of his friend Giovanni Rucellai ("You asked me, o learned Giovanni/ What I would do without you").

In 1529, Trissino published the first four divisions of his treatise *La Poetica*, which deal mainly with linguistic matters and Italian versification. The last two divisions, published posthumously in 1562, basically paraphrase Aristotle's *Poetics*, discussing poetry in general and drama in particular and stressing drama as an adjunct to morality: Tragedy teaches by means of pity and fear, and comedy teaches by deriding things that are vile.

With his *Epistola del Trissino de le lettere nuovamente aggiunte ne la lingua italiana* in 1524 and its sequel, *Il Castellano* (the chatelain), in 1529, Trissino entered the *questione della lingua* controversy and argued for the spelling reforms that he conscientiously put into practice in his works.

ACHIEVEMENTS

Giangiorgio Trissino's *La Sofonisba*, which was highly praised by his contemporaries, is considered by scholars to be the first tragedy of modern European literature and provided a model for many succeeding writers. The tragedy was imitated by Pierre Corneille and Voltaire in France, by Vittorio Alfieri in Italy, by Emanuel Geibel in Germany, and notably by Étienne Jodelle in *Cléopâtre captive* (1553). *La Sofonisba* was rendered into French prose in 1559 by Mellin de Saint-Gelais. Jean Mairet, whose *Sophonisbe* (1634; English translation, 1956) was the first tragedy written in French in accord with the neoclassical unities. This work followed more closely the rules of unity of time, place, and action than Trissino's had and owed much to the inspiration of Trissino's work. Trissino introduced the formal pattern of versification in Italian tragedy, and Giambattista Giraldi Cinthio confirmed it in both practice and theory: unrhymed verse for the greater part of the dialogue and rhyme for the chorus and the most important passages of the dialogue. This Italian legacy of blank verse reached as far as England and became the primary medium of Elizabethan tragedy.

By attributing so much importance to the love affair of the character Sofonisba, Trissino helped establish the importance of women in Renaissance tragedy; Giraldi Cinthio's emphasis on the cult of the feminine soul was an outgrowth of the example set in *La Sofonisba*.

La Poetica, in which Trissino reduced Horace and Aristotle to Italian prose and set down literary laws for poets and dramatists, had a lasting influence on his successors. Trissino formulated a more emphatic unity of time than had Aristotle; this he conceived as precisely the artistic principle that would help rescue the new dramatic poetry from the chaotic directions of medieval drama. Henceforth this unity was not only a dramatic law but also one whose observance could serve to distinguish the accomplished dramatic artist from the crude compiler of plays.

He maintained a friendly rivalry with Giovanni Rucellai, who dedicated his didactic poem "Le api" ("The Bees") to his friend Trissino and who inserted a tribute to him within the poem itself. Following Trissino, Rucellai wrote parts of his own plays *Rosmunda* (1525) and *Oreste* (wr. 1515-1520, pb. 1723) in blank verse. The gothic subject matter of

Rosmunda was doubtless influenced by Trissino's interest in the role of the Goths in Italian history. When Rucellai died in 1525, he bequeathed the manuscript of "The Bees" to Trissino, and it was Trissino who had the poem published at Venice in 1539.

Trissino's epic poem *La Italia liberata da Gotthi*, though dull and unread in modern times, exhibits a thorough knowledge of Roman tactics and topography. It was in the spirit of Trissino's title that Tasso's *Il Goffredo* was retitled (without the consent of Tasso) *Gerusalemme liberata* in 1581. Trissino's short poems are imitative of Petrarch; yet, significantly in an age so slavishly devoted to the Petrarchan ideal, Trissino also did much to revive interest in Dante and to establish him as equal with Petrarch. His attempts to reform Italian spelling by the addition of certain Greek letters met with derision, but he is credited with establishing the "x" and "z" of the Italian alphabet and with distinguishing between "u" and "v."

Trissino exerted a formative influence on the great architect Andrea Palladio, whom he discovered working as a mason on his villa at Cricoli outside Vicenza. He educated the young man in his academy, gave him the name Palladio in allusion to the Pallas Athena of Greek mythology and to a character in his own poem *La Italia liberata da Gotthi*, and took him on visits to Rome.

Trissino's greatest achievement stems from his translation of Dante's Latin treatise *De vulgari eloquentia*, which he discovered in the Biblioteca Trivulziana and which had an immediate impact. Dante's essay, to which modern philology can add little, is an attempt to identify the *volgare illustre*, the ideal norm that contemporaray Italian writers strove to perfect as they came to realize that Latin was no longer adequate for communication in Italy. After systematically examining the principal Italian dialects and refusing to identify the *volgare* with any of them, including his own native Tuscan dialect, Dante concludes that no specific part of Italy can claim to have nurtured the Italian literary standard and that, like a panther's scent, the *volgare* is present in every city but belongs to none.

By the first half of the sixteenth century, the question of how to identify the Italian literary standard came to absorb the energies of many Italian intellectuals. They divided into basically three camps: those who favored following the by then slightly archaic Florentine dialect used by Petrarch, Giovanni Boccaccio, and Dante; those who favored an eclectic solution; and those who favored using the current speech of Florence and Tuscany as the logical successor of the language enshrined by the triad of great Tuscan writers.

During one of Trissino's visits to Florence, probably in 1514, he discussed the contents of Dante's treatise with a group of literati who met in the Orti Oricellari, and he continued to speak of this during his sojourns in Rome from 1514 to 1518, in 1524, and in 1526. His lively conversations on language at Florence, remembered long afterward, inspired Niccolò Machiavelli to write on the subject. In November, 1524, Trissino published his *Epistola del Trissino de le lettere nuovamente aggiunte ne la lingua italiana*, in which he defended the new spelling he had introduced in *La Sofonisba* (employing the epsilon for open "e," the omega for open "o," and other substitutions to indicate phonemic distinctions not made in conventional spelling), which had been published in September of the same year. There, Trissino writes of an "Italian" language and develops a distinction between Tuscan/Florentine on one hand and what he calls the "courtly and common" language on the other. He claims to have used Tuscan dialect whenever feasible in *La Sofonisba* for the comprehension of his readers but admits using the courtly and common language when a Tuscan word would be unfamiliar to non-Tuscan readers. This essay created much controversy; much of the dissent came from Tuscans, such as Agnolo Firenzuola, who disliked Trissino's spelling reforms. Lodovico Martelli argued that the language should be called Florentine instead of Italian, and he also questioned whether Dante was the actual author of *De vulgari eloquentia*. Trissino responded with *Il Castellano*, written in 1528 and published the following year, in which a resurrected Rucellai, appointed keeper of the Castel Sant' Angelo in Rome by Pope Clement VII, upholds the theories of Arrigo Doria (Trissino). In this new dialogue, Trissino claims that Tuscan is in

fact synonymous with Italian, but that the great authors have always absorbed words from the other dialects when a Florentine word was unsuitable. The linguistic legacy of Dante, as Trissino interprets the crucial Dantean word *discretio* (even today translated variously as either "amalgamation" of the best elements or "elimination" of the worst elements), is the ideal of mingling the choicest words from the different dialects to supplement and enhance the lexical base of Tuscan.

In 1525, the Venetian Pietro Bembo published his *Prose della volgar lingua*, in which he claimed a tyrannical authority for the usage of Petrarch and Boccaccio, and—almost grudgingly—for Dante, whom he saw as a mingler of dialects and wielder of a coarse and imperfect medium. Ultimately the views of Bembo prevailed, and for many years the uniformity of Italian was achieved at the cost of repressing the natural interplay between the spoken and written language. As Jacob Burckhardt wrote in *Die Kulter der Renaissance in Italien* (1860; *The Civilization of the Renaissance in Italy*, 1878), "Literature and poetry probably lost more than they gained by the contentious purism which was long prevalent in Italy, and which marred the freshness and vigour of many an able writer."

The resultant language was called Italian as Trissino had argued, and his pleas that the vernacular as the common property of the Italian people be cultivated with a discretionary concession to local diction were not without effect. The Florentine Accademia della Crusca was never as hostile to the use of alternative forms as were, for example, the French and Spanish academies, and in modern times, with television and increased communications, the standard language of Italy has become receptive to lexical enrichments from its many dialects by a process not so very different from the ideal envisioned by Trissino.

BIOGRAPHY

Giangiorgio Trissino was born to patrician parents, Gaspare Trissino and Cecilia Bevilacqua, in Vicenza. From his family, he inherited vast estates. His education did not begin in earnest until 1506, when, already a widower with two children, he settled in Milan, where he became a student of Chalcondyles. At the home of Chalcondyles, he met Ippolita Sforza Bentivoglio and the beautiful Cecilia Gallerana, both of whom figure prominently in his letters and poetry.

In 1509, Vicenza was allotted to the Holy Roman Empire, and when the city gave itself back to the Venetian Republic a month later, Trissino's loyalty to Maximilian forced him into exile in Germany for some months and caused the temporary confiscation of his property. He returned to Italy the next year, settling in Ferrara, where he met Lucrezia Borgia. To escape the humidity of Ferrara, he moved on to Florence, where he frequented Machiavelli's literary circle, and then to Rome, where he associated with Bembo and enjoyed the friendship of Rucellai. Trissino and Rucellai composed their plays *La Sofonisba* and *Rosmunda* concurrently, meeting from time to time to recite verses and compare notes. In Rome, Trissino established himself as a capable diplomat, serving Popes Leo X, Clement VII, and Paul III. Leo X sent him on a mission to Bavaria and on his return effected his pardon from the Venetian Republic and the restitution of his property. At the time of the coronation of Charles V, Trissino was made knight and count.

Trissino always lived in magnificent style. When he traveled, he was accompanied by an elaborate retinue. Between 1530 and 1538, he rebuilt his villa at Cricoli in the ancient Roman style with lavish Italian gardens to house his La Trissiniana academy, the pupils of which lived a semimonastic life, studying mathematics, music, philosophy, and classical literature. The architecture of the villa derives from Trissino's interpretation of the ancient Roman architect Vitruvius, whom Andrea Palladio, himself a protégé of Trissino, would later credit as his greatest inspiration.

He spent the years from 1540 to 1545 on the island of Murano at another, more secluded villa, but despite his desire for solitude and his studious habits, the courtly life of the great cities never failed to reclaim his interest. While perfecting the last two sections of *La Poetica*, on a journey to Rome in 1550, he died in the arms of his student and friend Marco

Thiene and was buried near John Lascaris in the church of Sant'Agata in Suburra.

The last years of Trissino's life were plagued by his bad relations with his son Giulio. After the death of his first wife, he married a cousin, Bianca Trissino, by whom he fathered another child, Ciro, whom he openly preferred to his older son, Giulio. Father and son fought, lawsuits were undertaken, and the courts of Vicenza and Venice made judgments against the father, whereupon Trissino penned a series of acrid sonnets against the two cities. Trissino's revenge on his son was harsh. First he blackened his character under the name of Agrilupo in *La Italia liberata da Gotthi*, and then he disinherited him with a curse and accused him in his will of Lutheran heresy, for which Giulio was prosecuted, excommunicated, and thrown into prison, where he died a martyr to his Lutheranism in 1576.

ANALYSIS

Giangiorgio Trissino was a man of great intellect, erudition, and enterprise, who did not always choose well the topics and trappings for his creativity. He wished to be remembered as an innovator, but the innovations that he proposed were not always appropriate for his age. His epic poem, though born of the noblest goals, was a failure. Nevertheless, what was worthy of imitation in Trissino's work was recognized. *La Sofonisba* stands today as the first secular tragedy of modern European literature, and the pattern of versification that was thereby introduced was widely followed by subsequent dramatists.

LA SOFONISBA

Trissino completed his tragedy *La Sofonisba* in 1515. Galeotto Del Caretto had written a more traditional (that is, medieval) version of the story in rhyme in 1502, but Del Caretto's play was not printed until 1546. Petrarch had even used the story in one of his poems. Trissino's play, taken directly from Livy, proved more erudite than stageworthy. Although it was not staged until 1562, after the author's death, when it was lavishly produced by the Teatro Olimpico at Vicenza, it was printed at least ten times in Italy between 1524 and 1620 and was highly praised. In his dedication to Pope Leo X, Trissino, like Dante more than two centuries before him, felt it necessary to justify his having written in Italian rather than in Latin or Greek: He wanted to reach the common people.

Although Trissino liked to say that *La Sofonisba* was written according to Aristotelian theory, he was not yet so familiar with the theory at the time of the play's composition as he was to become. As Marvin T. Herrick observes, if Trissino had had a good understanding of the *Poetics* of Aristotle when he wrote *La Sofonisba*, he would not have chosen the story of Sofonisba in the first place, for Livy's original account does not lend itself to arrangement in the complex plot employing discovery and reversal of fortune that Sophocles and Euripides used in their best plays and that Aristotle recommended. In his *La Poetica*, Trissino confessed that the plot of *La Sofonisba* was not like that of Sophocles' tragedy *Oidipous Tyrannos* (c. 429 B.C.E.; *Oedipus Tyrannus*, 1715) or Euripides' *Iphigeneaē en Taurois* (c. 414 B.C.E.; *Iphigenia in Tauris*, 1782), but rather like that of Sophocles' *Aias* (c. 440 B.C.E.; *Ajax*, 1729), which Aristotle called a "tragedy of suffering."

Trissino wrote *La Sofonisba* in reaction against the vogue for Senecan tragedy. Following Greek models and eschewing the precedent of Horace and Seneca for a five-act drama, he arranged his play in episodes and choral odes, although if the prologue, incorporated as an integral part of the play as in the Greek fashion, is counted as an act, it and the episodes actually meet the five-act requirement. Although his followers preferred to continue using the traditional segmentation into five acts, Trissino did set a precedent when he chose to write *La Sofonisba*, not in the *terza rima* of Dante or the *ottava rima* of Boccaccio and the writers of the heroic romances, but in blank verse, which he deemed more appropriate for the poetry of tragedy, especially for a tragedy with a military setting. He used the eleven-syllable line, which bears some resemblance to the iambic trimeter of Greek tragedy. In a play as dependent on argument as *La Sofonisba*, Trissino did not abandon Seneca's penchant for *sententiae* (maxims such as Laelius's rebuke of Masinissa for his marriage, "The physician who sees that the disease needs a knife is unwise to use charms"), although in this, he probably saw himself as following Euripides rather than Seneca.

Although Trissino adhered strictly to the unities of action and of time, there is no strict unity of place. The setting opens in Cirta in Numidia and shifts in the third episode to the Roman camp. The chorus, which remains on stage throughout, must be transferred from the palace to the camp and then back to the palace.

The Carthaginian Sophonisba, in the company of her confidante Erminia, sets the tone of suffering in the first lines of the prologue. To Erminia she declares her intention to "speak at great length and to begin with fulsome words." This in fact she does, beginning with Dido and continuing through her own political marriage to Syphax, king of Numidia, when she was already betrothed to Masinissa. When, in the first episode, the page brings the queen bad tidings, Sophonisba exclaims "O harsh exordium," a word that underscores Trissino's concern for the rhetorical element in tragedy. When the page tells Sophonisba that her husband has been captured by the Romans, it becomes evident that the queen fears capture by the Romans more than she fears death. In anticipation of her suicide, the chorus argues against self-destruction, to which Sophonisba replies, "Our life is like a fine treasure, which ought not to be spent on base matter, nor should it shirk honorable enterprises, because a beautiful and glorious death makes our past life resplendent."

By now the Romans are approaching, and Masinissa, the Numidian ally of Rome, appears. When Sophonisba pleads with him, the chivalrous Masinissa promises to protect her. At this time, the chorus sings of the evils of war and invests its only hope in the compassion of Masinissa. In the second episode, the Roman general Laelius is informed that Masinissa has just married Sophonisba, and he later learns that the two had actually been betrothed before the marriage of Sophonisba to Syphax. The second episode ends with Laelius agreeing with Masinissa to consult Scipio about the propriety of their marriage, since Sophonisba herself may not be considered an enemy of Rome.

The chorus prays to God in His mercy to spare the queen and the people, a sentiment which, more Italian than pagan, reflects Trissino's design to write an essentially modern tragedy. In the third episode, an unhappy Syphax is shown as a prisoner well treated in the Roman camp by Scipio. Scipio is, however, unsympathetic to the new marriage and decrees that Sophonisba belongs to Rome. Masinissa does not demur: "I will contend no longer." The chorus intervenes, invoking the god of love for Sophonisba, betraying in this case Trissino's Petrarchism.

The suicide of the queen comes in the fourth and final episode. Masinissa sends Sophonisba a vial of poison, and she drinks it. Erminia is with the queen as she dies, and although she wishes to accompany her mistress in death, she must continue to live in order to care for the queen's two-year-old child, whom Erminia holds up for his mother to see in her dying moments. As the women of the chorus take charge of the body, Masinissa appears and promises an escort for the return of the funeral party to Carthage. The chorus closes with the philosophical lament, "The false hope of mortals, like a wave in a proud river, is seen one minute and then seems to be dissolved."

Although there is some attempt to develop character in Laelius, Scipio, and Masinissa, they do not ring true, and there is little real dramatic action in the play. The tone is more that of a monotonous elegy. Sophonisba is an automaton, marrying Masinissa without remorse for Syphax and drinking her poison like an obedient child. Masinissa, who has sent her the poison in the first place, is shocked when she takes it. Trissino repeated the facts of a well-known story, but in his slavish attention to rules, he failed to endow his characters with credible motivation. On the other hand, the play has in its favor its unified and relatively uncomplicated structure, the soaring poetic heights reached by the chorus in certain spots, and Sophonisba's farewell scene, which is not easily forgotten. *La Sofonisba* has been admired by critics as varied as Tasso (who annotated one of its editions), Alexander Pope, Voltaire, and Benedetto Croce, who called it a "moving tragedy entirely worthy of its pioneering position in the history of Italian tragedy."

I SIMILLIMI

I simillimi, also known as *I simillissimi*, is Trissino's attempt at comedy, but it lacks both the linear simplicity and the comic strength of Plautus, from whose *Menaechmi* (*The Twin Menaechmi*, 1595) Trissino borrowed his plot. Trissino, always wishing to be an innovator, modified the plot, added characters, changed the names, dispensed with the prologue, and added a choral role. Two centuries later, Carlo Goldoni used the same Plautine plot in his *I due gemelli veneziani* (1748; *The Venetian Twins*, 1968), but Trissino's play was not an influence on this more successful work. The sad but unavoidable truth is that Trissino wrote a comedy that is neither stageworthy nor amusing.

OTHER MAJOR WORKS

POETRY: *Le Rime*, 1529; *La Italia liberata da Gotthi*, 1547-1548.

NONFICTION: *I ritratti*, 1524; *Epistola de la vita, che dee tenere una donna vedova*, 1524; *Epistola del Trissino de le lettere nuovamente aggiunte ne la lingua italiana*, 1524; *Il Castellano*, 1529; *La Poetica*, 1529-1562; *Giangiorgio Trissino: O, Monografia di'un letterato nel secolo XVI*, 1878.

TRANSLATION: *De la volgare eloquenzia*, 1529 (of Dante's *De vulgari eloquentia*).

MISCELLANEOUS: *Giangiorgio Trissino: Scritti scelti*, 1950.

BIBLIOGRAPHY

Brand, Peter, and Lino Pertile, eds. *The Cambridge History of Italian Literature*. Rev. ed. New York: Cambridge University Press, 1999. Covers Italian literature from early to modern times. Discusses the development of theater in Italy. Bibliography and index.

Di Maria, Salvatore. *The Italian Tragedy in the Renaissance: Cultural Realities and Theatrical Innovations*. Lewisburg, Pa.: Bucknell University Press, 2002. Examines the early history of Italian theater. Bibliography and index.

Migliorini, Bruno. *The Italian Language*. Rev. ed. Boston: Faber, 1984. Migliorini examines the development of the Italian language, touching on

Trissino's part in its development. Bibliography and index.

Mulryne, J. R., and Margaret Shewring, eds. *Theatre of the English and Italian Renaissance.* New York: St. Martin's Press, 1991. This collection of essays from a seminar held at the University of Warwick in May, 1987, covers, among other subjects, the early Italian theater. Bibliography and index.

Wilkins, Ernest Hatch. *A History of Italian Literature.* Rev. ed. Cambridge, Mass.: Harvard University Press, 1974. Examines the history of Italian literature, including the early theater. Bibliography and index.

Jack Shreve

TRISTAN L'HERMITE

Born: Soliers, France; c. 1601
Died: Paris, France; September 7, 1655

PRINCIPAL DRAMA

La Mariane, pr. 1636, pb. 1637 (English translation, 1856)

Panthée, pr. 1638, pb. 1639

La Folie du sage, pr. 1643, pb. 1645

La Mort de Sénèque, pr. 1644, pb. 1645 (English translation, 1968)

La Mort de Chrispe, pr. 1644, pb. 1645

Osman, pr. 1647, pb. 1656 (English translation, 1968)

Amarillis, pr. 1652, pb. 1653

Le Parasite, pr. 1653, pb. 1654

Théâtre complet, pb. 1900-1904 (8 volumes)

OTHER LITERARY FORMS

Tristan L'Hermite was one of the most eclectic writers of the seventeenth century. His first published work, of 1626, was the scenario of a ballet, *Vers du ballet de Monsieur Frère du Roi.* An impressive ode, *La Mer*, followed in 1628, and his first collection of poetry, *Les Plaintes d'Acante*, in 1633. Numerous individual poems and collections of all types—erotic, heroic, religious, burlesque—followed in a fairly steady stream; the most notable of these are *Les Amours de Tristan* (1638), *La Lyre* (1641), *L'Office de la Sainte Vierge* (1646), and *Les Vers héroïques* (1648). It is principally for this poetic output that he is remembered today, but in addition to that—and to his multifaceted dramatic endeavors—he penned numerous letters (*Lettres mêlées*, 1642), a treatise on cosmography, *Principes de cosmographie* (1637), a fine picaresque novel, *Le Page disgracié* (1643), and a series of debates, *Plaidoyers historiques* (1643). With the exception of *Le Page disgracié*, which is receiving increasing critical attention, Tristan's prose works have fallen into a not-undeserved neglect. Such is not the case with his poetry, which was frequently edited and well-represented in every major anthology of his time. Neglected for two centuries, his poetry returned to the limelight at the time of the Symbolists (Claude Debussy set some of Tristan's best lines to music) and today, thanks in large part to the efforts of poets such as Amédée Madeleine and Carriat, he is universally recognized as the greatest lyric voice of the age of Louis XIII.

ACHIEVEMENTS

One of Cyrano de Bergerac's extraterrestrial travelers said of Tristan L'Hermite, "He is the only poet, the only philosopher, and the only free man that you have." The author who has been called the predecessor of Symbolism and the precursor of Jean Racine was basically an anachronism. His first play, *La Mariane*, was a huge success, artistically and critically. Though lyric and oratorical, it revealed to the audience of seventeenth century France what psychological drama could be and do. By the time he died, some twenty years later, he was already out of step with his time and ready for oblivion. Much the same can be said of his poetry, but it is precisely those qualities that made the classical age reject it that allow the modern reader to appreciate it fully. His poetry is replete with conceits, prolonged metaphors, and preciosity, but beyond these commonplaces of baroque expression lie a sensitivity and sensibility so universal as to reduce all artifice to subservience. All the thematic and metaphoric commonplaces of his day are to be found in his work, yet they are imbued with such a personal coloration and such deep conviction that they strike responsive chords in a modern reader. What first appears to be a mere rhetorical exercise is shown by careful scrutiny to be a sterling expression of profound sensibilities. A court poet, Tristan had to play a game, one that had to be played consciously and seriously. "The Muses have no brush that I cannot handle with some dexterity," he once said, and though his work is not of uniform merit, he was right. His poetry is once again finding its way into numerous anthologies, both academic and commercial, and his drama is being dusted off by academics and actors alike.

BIOGRAPHY

François L'Hermite was born in the old castle of Soliers in 1601. It was not until much later that he assumed the name "Tristan" to call attention to his illustrious ancestry. He was barely three when he was taken to Paris, and, sometime before 1609, he became the page of the duc de Verneuil, son of the king. One day, having wounded someone in a fit of anger, he ran away from the court, took refuge in England, and eventually returned to France by way of Scotland and Norway—if one is to believe his account in *Le Page disgracié*. In the years that ensued, he had many masters, including Nicolas de Sainte-Marthe, a poet and dramatist, and that man's more famous uncle, Scévole de Sainte-Marthe. Reader and librarian of Scévole, Tristan expanded his literary horizons and acquired a taste for poetry he was to keep the rest of his days. In 1620, he entered the royal household and one year later became attached to the person of Gaston d'Orléans, the rebellious young brother of Louis XIII, whose political embroilments and misfortunes he shared for nearly twenty-five years. His

steadfast loyalty to his volatile master was not reciprocated, and Tristan, an incorrigible gambler, was constantly buffeted by alternating waves of good and bad fortune. Add to that chronic bad health, and his vacillations between elation and despondency are easily understood.

During the first ten years at the court of Gaston, Tristan followed his master in and out of exile. In such turmoil, the composition of works of any breadth was out of the question. Tristan did, however, write some superior occasional poetry and, above all, *Les Plaintes d'Acante*, one of the finest lyric collections of the century and the nucleus of the later—and equally successful—*Les Amours de Tristan*.

By 1634, Gaston and Tristan were back in France, and the poet began to frequent the theaters, particularly that of his actor friend Mondory, the Théâtre du Marais. It is to this troupe that he gave his first play, *La Mariane*, the hit of the 1636 season. *Panthée*, produced in 1638, deservedly failed. Returning to his purely lyric tendencies, Tristan brought out in quick succession *Les Amours de Tristan*, *La Lyre*, and several major isolated poems. He also published his letters, many of them gems of pastoral fiction, and his autobiographical novel *Le Page disgracié*. In 1643, fate seemed to smile on him. Louis XIII had died, and Gaston had been made lieutenant-governor of the realm. Tristan gave his third tragedy, *La Mort de Sénèque*, to Molière's troupe; it was a hit. Once again, however, fate proved to be fickle: Gaston forgot his poet, and the success of the play was short-lived. Despondent, Tristan finally gave up his loyalty to Gaston. His next play, *La Mort de Chrispe*, was dedicated to his new patron, the duchesse de Chaulnes. That patronage did not last long, and knowing himself to be dying of consumption, Tristan went, although he hated so much to "lie like a dog at some lord's feet," to do just that at the court of the duc de Guise.

Tristan's last years were plagued by worsening health and frequent poverty but were fairly productive nevertheless. He compiled *L'Office de la Sainte Vierge*, a collection of religious poems interspersed with prose. *Osman*, another tragedy, was performed in 1647, though not published until after Tristan's death. The following year saw the appearance of his *Les Vers héroïques*, a collection of occasional poems reflecting an entire life spent as a courtier. In 1649, there was a single ray of light in his dark firmament, as he was elected to the Académie Française. In 1652, Tristan, despite his deteriorating health, brought out *Amarillis*, a reworking of Jean de Rotrou's pastoral, *La Célimène* (pr. 1631, pb. 1637), and in 1653, *Le Parasite*, a rowdy and vivacious comedy. He celebrated his patron's feats—a feat in itself—in his last long occasional poem, "La Renommée," but time and his health were running out. He had several projects in process, including a novel and the translation of the hymns of the Roman Breviary, when he died on September 7, 1655. He was buried in the church of Saint-Jean-en-Grève, which was destroyed during the Revolution. Of his native castle, only a mantel-stone survives, in a nearby barn.

ANALYSIS

Pierre Corneille and Jean Racine, whatever their differences, were very much attuned to a new social order that was moving toward order, decorum, and polish, one in which there was little room for the self-centered artist or hero. There are some vestiges of the feudal ideal in Corneille; there are none in Racine. The French have rightfully enshrined these two great dramatists, but in so doing, they have set them up as standards by which all other writers are to be judged, extrapolating from their dramas rules that are the essence of these works but that were never meant as universal guidelines. Tristan L'Hermite, as a man and as an artist, did not belong to, and could not enter, the new order. To treat him as an incomplete Racine, or a precursor, is to be deaf to the specific timbre and tonality of this great writer. In every way, Tristan was a stranger in his own time, in his own land. His plays are populated with reflections of himself, noble souls out of tune with their milieus—strangers.

The tragic hero is, almost by definition, an idealist—whether his ideal be one of good or evil—lost in a practical world of relative values. Such a conflict is obviously insoluble, and the only suspense possible is not centered on "what" but on "how," for it is only in

his rejection of facile contingencies and compromises that the hero can achieve greatness—that is, fulfill his destiny, his essence. The wrong sacrifices, the wrong choices predicated on false values, these are the dangers confronting tragic heroes, evils they must reject by rejecting the world of contingencies. Racine's heroes do reject the world but not its basic values. That is precisely what makes their farewells so long and agonizing. Tristan's protagonists, on the contrary, reject the world because they cannot abide its values. The crux of the action, then, is not the crisis leading to a decision, but the crisis resulting from one. Walls are erected to preserve the integrity of a spirit; these walls frustrate those who would possess and so destroy the strangers. Thus, destiny, imposed but not accepted, may well crush a mortal; it cannot triumph over his will. As Blaise Pascal states in his *Pensées* (1670; *Monsieur Pascal's Thoughts, Meditations, and Prayers*, 1688; best known as *Pensées*), at that fatal moment, the hero is triumphant, because he knows why he dies while the executioner lacks that understanding.

Tristan's heroes are unable—or unwilling—to communicate with their fellow human beings. The resulting isolation is the basis of their tragic situation. These rebels, with concentrated introspection, seek to establish their own identities, to find answers within themselves to basic ontological questions, hoping to derive viable or at least acceptable modi operandi. In short, the typical Tristanian protagonist seeks to establish an authentic and dynamic *moi* in a fundamentally unauthentic and static world, a situation that can only lead to a nauseous and noxious anxiety. The greatness of these characters—what makes them so attractive, even to the modern reader—resides in their painful lucidity: Fully aware of the absurdity of the world, they refuse the balms of unconsciousness no less than those of compromise. They die because they willfully choose not to live a lie. In that sense, they are active contributors to their destiny, succumbing because of their intransigence, proud witnesses of their foes' inferiority, and in the final analysis, they are victors over them because these foes must witness in turn the enshrinement of their victims' superiority made inviolate by death.

Tristan wrote only five tragedies; not all are of equal value. It cannot be said that his dramaturgy was ever set in a firm mold, for he constantly experimented. He failed at times, but he always learned a lesson from these attempts. Therefore, even these lesser plays shed some light on the better ones.

LA MARIANE

Performed in 1636, *La Mariane* is a landmark in the transition of French tragedy from the stiff, rhetorical style of the humanistic theater to what is now known as the classical period. It had an instant and lasting success that not even the appearance of Corneille's *Le Cid* (pr., pb. 1637; *The Cid*, 1637) some months later, was able to overshadow. Some have credited Mondory, creator of the role of Hérode, for the unusually large crowds that flocked to the theater, and indeed, some of the credit should go to that sterling actor who was struck down by apoplexy while playing this demanding role in 1637. It would be a mistake, however, to look no further, for his performance and following can in no way explain the ten editions of the play in the relatively few years remaining in Tristan's short life; nor could they explain the fact that Molière's troupe performed it more than thirty-four times between 1659 and 1680, while the Comédie-Française put it on more than thirty-eight times from 1680 to 1703. For the rest of the century, and well into the eighteenth, the play was very popular, both in France and abroad, as can be seen by the many translations that were published. A true psychological drama—the first theatrically viable one in France—it contains some of the best lines in French drama, and certainly the best before Corneille's *The Cid*, though it is perhaps too declamatory and lyrical for modern tastes.

The story of Hérode and Mariane was well known at the time, and several dramatists had treated it before Tristan, both in France and elsewhere. Tristan's innovation lies in that he readily understood what his predecessors had not—that a broad fresco of history, with a large cast of characters and a plethora of psychological entanglements, could not yield a cohesive and effective drama. He saw that the basic idea of two people misunderstanding each other, with others fostering that misunderstanding, was quite sufficient to give birth to an intensely dramatic nucleus. Critics weaned on less declamatory plays than those favored by pre-Cornelian spectators and readers often find the play static; there is some justification in this, but *La Mariane* is a dramatic poem of solitude, of estrangement. That is its limitation and also its beauty. It is to be fully enjoyed for its intrinsic merits, not compared to something it was never meant to be.

In the first act, Hérode declares his need for a physically absent yet psychologically omnipresent Mariane. The second act reverses the situation, and one readily realizes that Mariane and Hérode cannot live without each other. The tragedy resides precisely in the fact that Mariane, failing to see that Hérode is as necessary to her hatred as she is to his love, rejects all his overtures and makes communication impossible. For all of her words of rejection, her isolation is a posture: Her constant goading, as she taunts her husband with her moral superiority, cannot be aiming at isolation, but seeks a reaction, which eventually comes. When Hérode's mounting frustration makes him blurt out words of hate, she welcomes these manifestations of a sentiment he does not harbor but which she desperately needs to feel truly free. Mariane is an eminently moral being in an amoral, Machiavellian world. To find inner peace, she opts for values in which she can believe and which demand the reaction she seeks from Hérode as well as make any externally imposed verdict meaningless. By her decision and the position she assumes, she forces Hérode into an impasse from which he can exit only by murdering the unbearable witness to his debasement. His reaction—rather, the reaction she dictated—and the ensuing death of Mariane enshrine Hérode's impotence and dependence. Before he met her, he was nothing; without her, he goes mad.

PANTHÉE

Tristan's second play, *Panthée*, managed to maintain itself in the repertoire some twenty-five years, but it cannot be considered a success, either on stage or in print. Part of its failure has been ascribed to the fact that Tristan had intended the play specifically for Mondory, who was incapacitated before the play could be staged. It is true that this play, like its predecessor, has some beautiful tirades; unfortunately, it does not have *La Mariane*'s dramatic cohesiveness. Badly disjointed, it has no single dramatic focus, no smooth rise to the necessary climax. That too may be blamed on Mondory's apoplexy, but such considerations do not redeem the play.

In Xenophon's *Kurou Paideia* (*The Cyropaedia: Or, Education of Cyrus*, 1560-1567), the story of Panthea is a political footnote to the history of Cirus's reign. It deals with the reluctant betrayal of a cause by a husband desperately in love with a misguided wife and on the consequences of that betrayal. Tristan, in the employ of Gaston d'Orléans, could not keep that tack, since his master was frequently taking up arms against his royal brother for rather tenuous personal reasons. He therefore decided to reduce in importance the roles of the political figures, the husband and the king, and to center attention on the wife and a would-be lover, Araspe. An interesting political story was thus transformed into a drama of unhappy love. The problem does not stop there. Tristan had taken two episodes from Xenophon, but he failed to weld them together. The fault is perhaps not entirely his own: In the first three acts, Araspe plays a major role; in the last two acts, he has only twenty-eight lines. Most of the time, he is out of sight and out of mind, while the focus of the play changes radically. It is logical to surmise that the role, initially conceived for Mondory, was reduced when that actor suffered his stroke; it is equally logical to suggest that Tristan, ill and demoralized at the time, did not bother to revise what he had already written, and simply reduced that role in the acts he had yet to write. There is another, cardinal flaw. The three main characters function on three separate planes in such a way as to make dramatic intercourse impossible. They take turns expounding, but never exchange ideas. The results are frequent passages of great lyricism but no drama of any consequence. These beautiful lines are eminently worth reading; they will probably never be heard from a stage again.

LA MORT DE SÉNÈQUE

Molière's troupe first performed Tristan's third tragedy, *La Mort de Sénèque*, shortly after the death of Louis XIII. It was a success on stage and in print, but after 1647, there were no further editions and few performances, and the play soon fell into oblivion. That was to be expected: Certain technical demands of the play made it unsuitable for the classical stage, and the crudity of its tone made it unfit for the elite of the age of Louis XIV. The changes in dramatic conventions chased this powerful drama from the stage; the changes in taste kept it from returning. Here again, the critics have been blinded by extraneous considerations to what a modern audience could readily consider sterling dramatic qualities. These qualities caused the directorship of the Comédie-Française to return the play to the permanent repertory as of the 1984 season.

La Mort de Sénèque deals with a complex plot against the emperor Néron. Epicaris, a freedwoman, leader of the plot, and Sénèque, innocent but implicated because he stands in Néron's way, are accused, condemned, and put to death (Sénèque being allowed to commit suicide in a less painful way). The technical demands are many: a large cast, great mobility (for the sake of verisimilitude), and intricate staging. None of these is insurmountable today.

The main reasons for the play's eventual failure lie elsewhere. As France moved toward the age that was to be consecrated at Versailles, the tragic stage, along with the pulpit, became a prime instrument for the propagation of the new credo; tragedy was therefore expected to be decorous and unsullied by earthy or comic contacts. The label "Shakespearean," which has been attached to *La Mort de Sénèque* by French critics with derogatory intentions, refers to these impure, nonclassical traits of the play. Socially, Tristan had erred; artistically, he was right. The world of Nero was one in which values had been reversed and in which decorum was either trampled underfoot or used as a thin and easily cracked veneer. It was a world of the absurd, in which the grotesque invaded all realms of human endeavor. Tristan's genius resides precisely in his ability to capture this mood, to translate it into an artistic coherence, and to put it on stage. The earthy duels of wits between Sabine, the sister of Néron, and Epicaris, the freedwoman, or the teeth-grinding laughter that is evoked at the most horrendous moments are but contributors to a general feeling of disorientation, of loss and, eventually, of fear, that first grips the characters of the play and engulfs the spectator or the imaginative reader. Such a manic hell, from which there is no escape but death or madness, had never before been experienced on the French stage. Tristan was to refine the process for his last tragedy, *Osman*; it was Racine who adapted it to the new exigencies in masterpieces such as *Britannicus* (pr. 1669; English translation, 1714) and *Bajazet* (pr., pb. 1672; English translation, 1717).

LA MORT DE CHRISPE

The theme of *La Mort de Chrispe*—that of a young wife in love with her stepson—is one that had been frequently dealt with before Tristan; it was to yield one of the great masterpieces of all time, Racine's *Phèdre* (pr., pb. 1677; *Phaedra*, 1701). *Phèdre* was a success from the start, *La Mort de Chrispe* a failure; the public has been right in both cases.

Historically, Fausta, wife of the emperor Constantine, fell in love with her stepson, Chrispus; rebuffed, she accused the young man of making improper advances. Constantine had Chrispus arrested and put to death; informed of the truth, he ordered Fausta drowned. Such a barbaric father and wanton stepmother would have disgusted Tristan's public, and he decided to make some major changes; unfortunately, in trying to make history palatable, Tristan gutted it of any dramatic potential. The role of Constantin is episodic; that of Constance, beloved of Chrispe, is not sufficiently delineated to draw the reader's sympathy; Chrispe himself plays a rather limited role, in turn passive or impervious. Fauste is thus the only interesting character in the entire play, devoid of any worthy foil. Also, for the sake of propriety, Fauste is not allowed to declare her passion explicitly. Her inner turmoil, though touching, does not bear constant repetition. Chrispe's death is no longer imputed directly to either Fauste (the cause) or to Constantin (the agent), but is the result of a silly accident attributable only indirectly to Fauste. The expurgation diluted whatever dramatic intensity might have pervaded the play, a mistake that Racine was careful to avoid in his handling of the same theme.

OSMAN

In 1647, Tristan took out an unusually long copyright (twenty years; five to ten was the norm) for his last tragedy, *Osman*. For reasons that remain a mystery to this day, he then buried the play, which was published only after his death by his admirer and protégé, Philippe Quinault, himself a fairly good dramatist. The subject was taken from contemporary history: Osman had been raised to the throne of Turkey in 1618 at the age of fourteen, then strangled four years later by the same Janissaries who had brought him to power. In his play, Tristan remained quite faithful to history; for dramatic purposes, he altered the manner of the young sultan's death—he dies fighting in the streets rather than strangled in a cell. He also invented a character, Osman's sister, and gave prominence to an obscure historical figure, the Mufti's daughter, in love with Osman. In the play, it is the Mufti's daughter who, scorned, sets off the Janissaries' rebellion.

Tristan was also faithful to the well-entrenched unities, though he opted for a variation then coming into its own, one that Racine was to bring to full fruition: Instead of a single action, to which some minor side issues could be grafted, Tristan offers two parallel plots, the political struggle of Osman and the erotic one of the Mufti's daughter, both inseparably intertwined into a single entity that can only be loosened by death.

Like Mariane, Osman is a stranger in his own land. Proud of his station and of his worth, he is bitterly disappointed in all his human relations and, justifiably or not, rejects them. The Mufti's daughter tries repeatedly to enter into his world, but is rebuffed, just as the Janissaries, who demand only to be reassured about their role in governance, are denied a simple answer because the young prince feels it beneath his dignity to give an account to his soldiers. He rejects all the compromises—erotic and political—that are proffered. His values never change, his resolve never wavers. Cruelly truthful to the end, he accepts his assured death and exits like a sultan, his honor and his isolation intact.

This is Tristan's ultimate statement of his estrangement, so much so that it is often too dialectical to be consistently dramatic. With comparison inevitable, it is probably well that, with Racine's *Bajazet* permanently entrenched in the repertory, *Osman* never be performed, but the poetry, the magnificent pomp of the tirades, do not deserve to be buried and forgotten. Of even greater importance is the fact that, whether one wishes to see Tristan as a writer on his own terms or as a precursor of Racine, in *Osman*, he managed to create an atmosphere as no one had done before and as only Racine was to do after him. From the first line of the sultan's sister's nightmare to the dying gasp of the Mufti's daughter, the reader with imagination and sensitivity is immersed in a claustrophobic and stifling atmosphere such as the one that must have prevailed in the seraglio (palace). The barbaric grandeur echoed by the sonorous Alexandrines, the ominous mystery of court intrigues, the passions engendered by human beings who consider life an expendable commodity, all this is part of a mantle of psychological verisimilitude that covers the empathetic reader and grants him a deeper understanding of the human experience.

This Turkish atmosphere is a strange one, totally foreign to the norms of French classical tragedy. Honor and glory are replaced by stealth and deception, heroism by anxiety. Anxiety, in *Osman*, is a dual curse, both social, the result of a cleavage between one human being and others, and spatial, resulting when material obstacles keep people from realizing themselves. Almost by definition, a seraglio is inductive to claustrophobia, yet Osman is able to leave the confines of its walls. To be sure, his freedom is an illusion, a dramatically ironic one, but one under which he operates. The claustrophobia cannot therefore be predicated exclusively or even principally on spatial considerations. If Osman is unable to leave the city, it is not because of stone walls but because of psychological ones erected by his pride. Unable to communicate, people cease to trust relationships and each other. Walls, in such a milieu, do not contain; they conceal and separate personalities, all the while fostering physical proximity. In fact, one has here two sets of walls, the physical and the psychological. The former are meant to keep in; the latter are carapaces necessary to those confined. Ironically, these barriers so necessary to certain psyches are also lethal: In these confines, social anxiety can only lead to deadly explosions. In short, it is not enough to see that the seraglio presents a physical enclosure; one must also see that it has a dramatic function, which is not to keep the protagonists closely confined, in direct contact with each other but, reinforced by the psychological walls, to alienate them. In ancient tragedies, walls were meant to circumscribe the city—that is, civilization—to protect it from the beasts without; here, the walls, physical and psychological, turn the city into a madhouse and its inhabitants into beasts.

LA FOLIE DU SAGE

Tristan's only tragicomedy, *La Folie du sage*, was published in 1645, and seems to have achieved a certain success, both on stage and in print. Much of that success may be the result of its many allusions to notables and events of the day—or at least of what contemporaries viewed as such—and its heavy reliance on themes that could only appeal to a limited public for a limited time. Today, the play is of interest only to Tristan scholars.

AMARILLIS

In 1652, Tristan adapted Rotrou's *La Célimène*, made a pastoral of it, and thus contributed to a surprising renewal of the genre. The play, *Amarillis*, had a brief but definite success, both in the city and at court. It is quite likely that Molière tried his hand at pastoral comedy because he saw in the success of *Amarillis* and its imitations an ideal prototype for spectacular court entertainment. For all that—and in spite of a few witty scenes—the play deserves its subsequent obscurity.

LE PARASITE

That is not the case of *Le Parasite*, Tristan's last play. In 1653, just when the French were getting ready for great comedies of manners and of characters, Tristan—as Racine was to do with *Les Plaideurs* (pr. 1668; *The Litigants*, 1715)—deliberately turned to antiquity and the *commedia dell'arte* for the inspiration of a piece of pure buffoonery, which is perpetrated by caricature-like archetypes.

The plot of *Le Parasite*, a mere vehicle for the reincarnation of the spirit of the *commedia dell'arte*, is of no consequence. The verbal fantasy unleashed by its characters, the wit and élan, the old, anachronistic language deliberately abused by Tristan for its comic effect, all these ingredients of a gigantic burlesque feast for the mind make this play the delight that it is. The undeniable Italian influences are less those of specific plays than the broad joyous qualities brought to France by the Italian players. As a result, though the play deals with young love and its travails, its interest is centered on the movers of the comic action, the parasitic Fripesauces, the miles gloriosus Capitan, and the nurse Phenice. If the Capitan's bombastic tirades are witty parodies of the heroic ideal, those of the parasite are their equal in spoofing both lovers and heroes. It is in such delightful spoofs that Tristan is at his comic best. Unfortunately, Tristan's heavy reliance on archaisms and on puns that are no longer operative causes much of the humor to be lost to the modern reader or viewer. It is particularly the latter—who cannot seek the help of lexical notes—who is bewildered by the play today, and that is unfortunate, for this is an important work of art. Deliberately relying on a language and a framework both antiquated and base, Tristan used these elements as sources of laughter in a way unknown since François Rabelais (1494-1553) and which only Molière was to resurrect with such gusto. His contribution to comedy is undeniable. He easily outdistanced his predecessors in the relief of his caricature-like figures and the verve of his poetry. At a time when farce and serious comedy were finally to be merged, he gave verbal fantasy and burlesque its finest hour. The classical generation, by subduing burlesque, fixing the language, and demanding psychological depth even in comedy, made Molière inevitable and *Le Parasite* passé.

OTHER MAJOR WORKS

LONG FICTION: *Le Page disgracié*, 1643.

POETRY: *La Mer*, 1628; *Les Plaintes d'Acante*, 1633; *Les Amours de Tristan*, 1638; *La Lyre*, 1641; *L'Office de la Sainte Vierge*, 1646; *Les Vers héroïques*, 1648.

NONFICTION: *Principes de cosmographie*, 1637; *Lettres mêlées*, 1642; *Plaidoyers historiques*, 1643.

BIBLIOGRAPHY

Abraham, Claude. *Tristan L'Hermite*. Boston: Twayne, 1980. A basic biography examining the life and works of Tristan L'Hermite. Bibliography and index.

Grove, Laurence, ed. *Emblems and the Manuscript Tradition: Including an Edition and Studies of a Newly Discovered Manuscript of Poetry by Tristan L'Hermite*. Glasgow, Scotland: University of Glasgow, 1997. Although this discussion focuses on Tristan L'Hermite's poetry, it also provides information on his life and dramatic works.

Gude, Mary Louise. *Le Page disgracié: The Text as Confession*. University, Miss.: Romance Monographs, 1979. This publication, in discussing Tristan L'Hermite's autobiographical work, provides insights into his life. Bibliography.

Shepard, James Crenshaw. *Mannerism and Baroque in Seventeenth Century French Poetry: The Example of Tristan L'Hermite*. Chapel Hill: University of North Carolina Press, 2001. Through his examination of the poetry of Tristan L'Hermite, Shephard sheds light on the dramatic works of Tristan L'Hermite. Bibliography and indexes.

Claude Abraham

IVAN TURGENEV

Born: Orel, Russia; November 9, 1818
Died: Bougival, France; September 3, 1883

PRINCIPAL DRAMA

Neostorozhnost, pb. 1843 (*Carelessness*, 1924)

Bezdenezhe, pb. 1846, pr. 1852 (*A Poor
     Gentleman*, 1924)
Kholostyak, pr. 1849 (*The Bachelor*, 1924)
Zavtrak u predvoditelya, pr. 1849, pb. 1856 (*An
     Amicable Settlement*, 1924)
Nakhlebnik, wr. 1849, pb. 1857, pr. 1862 (*The
     Family Charge*, 1924)
Razgovor na bolshoy doroge, pr. 1850, pb. 1851 (*A
     Conversation on the Highway*, 1924)
Mesyats v derevne, wr. 1850, pb. 1855, pr. 1872 (*A
     Month in the Country*, 1924)
Provintsialka, pr. 1851 (*A Provincial Lady*, 1934)
Gde tonko, tam i rvyotsya, wr. 1851, pr. 1912
     (*Where It Is Thin, There It Breaks*, 1924)
Vecher v Sorrente, wr. 1852, pr. 1884, pb. 1891 (*An
     Evening in Sorrento*, 1924)
The Plays of Ivan Turgenev, pb. 1924
Three Plays, pb. 1934

OTHER LITERARY FORMS

Ivan Turgenev achieved literary renown predominantly through his novels and short stories, although
he also produced accomplished works in the genres
of poetry and drama. His first literary success came
with the publication of the long poem *Parasha*
(1843). Turgenev's next resounding success came
nearly a decade later with the publication of *Zapiski
okhotnika* (1852; *Russian Life in the Interior,* 1855;
better known as *A Sportsman's Sketches*, 1932), a
collection of short stories depicting life in nineteenth
century rural Russia. *A Sportsman's Sketches* met
with widespread acclaim both for its objective, realistic portrayal of rural characters and for its role in
arousing the indignation of the Russian intelligentsia
over the mistreatment of serfs by the Russian nobility. It is probable that this book had a significant effect on Czar Alexander II, who liberated the serfs in
1861.

In his novels, Turgenev continued to portray realistically the men and women who characterized his
society. He explored the concerns of the Russian intelligentsia by addressing specific problems, usually
through a love story. His most famous novel is also
the one which aroused the most controversy: *Ottsy i
deti* (1862; *Fathers and Sons*, 1867) angered both

conservatives and radicals in its depiction of the conflict between the older, reactionary generation and
the younger, revolutionary generation. The "nihilist"
hero, Evgeni Bazarov, pleased partisans of neither
side, and this work signaled Turgenev's demise as a
major contributing force in the Russian literature of
his age.

In addition to his poetry, drama, and fiction,
Turgenev was the author of essays, articles, autobiographical works, and opera librettos.

ACHIEVEMENTS

Ivan Turgenev's place among the luminaries of
Russian literature is ensured by both his artistic and
his historical importance. The outstanding characteristics of Turgenev's canon are his highly crafted style,
his psychological characterization, and his ability to
articulate the concerns of his age. The aesthetics of
his early efforts in poetry carried over into his prose
in its lyric grace and spare, lucid style. In the manner
of Jane Austen or Henry James, Turgenev held up a
mirror to his society by creating probing psychological portraits of representative members of that society. So accurate were his portraits that the terms he
used to describe them passed into the common currency of Russian literature. The "superfluous man"
embodied in the protagonist of his first novel, *Rudin*
(1856; English translation, 1873), was recognized by
Turgenev's audience as a type that abounded not only
on the pages of Turgenev's drama and fiction but also
on the pages of much nineteenth century Russian literature, and the "nihilist" hero of *Fathers and Sons*
embodied an entire generation determined to tear
down the foundations of Russian society rather than
slowly to reform it.

The plots of Turgenev's novels and plays are love
stories, but underlying his work throughout his literary career was his concern for the destiny of his country. Just as that concern influenced his writing, so
his writing influenced the intellectual thought of Russia. Turgenev believed that Russia's future lay in
assimilating the best of Western European culture
through intelligent, liberal reform. By portraying the
members of the Russian intelligentsia with an ironic
detachment that revealed the frequently ineffectual

Ivan Turgenev (Library of Congress)

the social importance of his themes ensure him a place in the annals of Russian literature. Yet he is also noteworthy as a pivotal figure in the transition from early nineteenth century Romanticism to late nineteenth century realism. Turgenev's early verse and drama were written during the heyday of Romanticism: His early protagonists are Byronic heroes. His early heroines are idealized, and his early plots are sentimental. Although Turgenev continued to employ love stories—usually centering on romantic triangles—in his later dramas and in his novels, the passionate, sentimental heroes and heroines gave way to the strong-willed women and superfluous men who more closely matched Turgenev's realistic view of society. By evolving from a Romantic subject and style to a realistic subject and style, Turgenev's drama and fiction provided both continuity for the Russian literary tradition and an early model for the realistic plays and novels that would follow.

Although Turgenev's accomplishments as a novelist and a writer of short stories were appreciated in his lifetime—he was one of the first Russian novelists of the nineteenth century to achieve international renown—his accomplishments as a dramatist were not widely appreciated until the turn of the century, when the innovative elements of his dramaturgy were recognized as presaging the psychological realism of Anton Chekhov's plays, which also depicted life in rural Russia and the relationships among members of the upper and lower classes. Yet, apart from his significance as a major novelist and as a transitional figure in nineteenth century Russian literature, Turgenev would be remembered as a dramatist in any case, on the strength of one play, *A Month in the Country*. This play was a unique contribution to Russian theater and was one of the outstanding Russian plays to be written during the mid-nineteenth century.

BIOGRAPHY

Ivan Sergeyevich Turgenev was born in Orel, Russia, on November 9, 1818, into a family of wealthy landed gentry. His childhood was spent on his mother's estate. His father, Sergey Turgenev, was a member of an impoverished noble family, and his fa-

nature of their liberalism and by portraying the peasantry as fully rounded characters, often superior to their masters in compassion and understanding, Turgenev did much to spur Russian society to address the problems of its oppressive feudal system.

When, in the late 1850's, political differences were polarizing Russian society, dividing it into revolutionaries and reactionaries, Turgenev again turned his ironic observation on representative members of society in the characterizations of the reactionary landowner and the nihilist hero in his novel *Fathers and Sons*. The anger with which this novel was met by revolutionaries and reactionaries alike attests the accuracy of Turgenev's depiction. In a nation that was already on the road to revolution, Turgenev's moderation and objectivity were no longer appreciated.

Turgenev's lyricism and clarity of style, the universality of his love stories and characterizations, and ther's marriage to the wealthy and domineering Varvara Petrovna Lutovinova was primarily one of convenience. Sergey Turgenev left the management of both the family and the estate to his wife, leaving himself free to pursue his lifelong passion—women. Both parents served as obvious models for many of the characters in Turgenev's plays and novels.

At an early age, young Turgenev witnessed the injustices and harsh punishments of Russia's feudal system, administered by his mother to the serfs on her estate. Such an environment aroused in him a strong compassion for the victims of his mother's tyranny. The ignorance and backwardness that Turgenev observed in this outdated rural society may in part have caused his preference for European civilization and his reluctance to spend much time either on his estate or indeed in any part of Russia. In spite of this, the beauty of his ancestral countryside ignited in him a lasting love of Russia's rural landscapes, such as the ponds, gardens, and lime groves on the estate, so lyrically depicted in many of his works.

As was typical of the nineteenth century Russian gentry, the education of the young Turgenev was entrusted to a series of foreign tutors until the family moved in 1827 to Moscow, where he was enrolled at the Weydenhammer Preparatory School. There he first came under the influence of the "pseudosublime" school of Russian literature when he began to read such Russian Romantics as the novelist-playwright Mikhail Zogoskin and the poet Vladimir Benediktov. In the fall of 1829, Turgenev and his brother Nikolai transferred to the Lazarevski Institute of Moscow to study English. Then, in 1833, after undergoing a rigorous period of intensive private tutoring, Turgenev at the age of fifteen was accepted into Moscow University, where, because of his democratic idealism and enthusiasm for the United States, he was nicknamed "the American." After one year, Turgenev moved with his mother to St. Petersburg and within months became a student of philosophy at the University of St. Petersburg, studying the Greek and Roman classics as well.

After completion of his degree in 1838, Turgenev traveled to Germany to continue the study of philosophy at the University of Berlin. There he became acquainted with Russian revolutionaries abroad, such as Nikolai Stankevich and Mikhail Bakunin, both of whom exerted considerable influence on him as he was drawn into their circle of Hegelian idealistic philosophy.

In 1841, Turgenev returned to Russia to enter the civil service but remained only two years, after which time he gave up his position for a career in literature. In the summer of 1843, Turgenev met the critic Vissarion Belinsky, and the two became almost inseparable for the next three years, carrying on heated discussions about literature, philosophy, and Russian society.

Through his great love of music, in 1843, Turgenev met the woman he was to love and pursue unflaggingly throughout his life: Pauline Viardot, the most famous opera singer in Europe at that time. Although she was already married to a middle-aged man twice her age and was cool toward Turgenev, after her St. Petersburg performance he followed her all over Europe, finally succeeding in becoming a close companion of the Viardot family. She encouraged his friendship, and he spent considerable time with her on her estate, Château de Courtevenal, forty miles east of Paris. During Turgenev's stay there, he produced plays by Jean Racine and Molière and wrote operettas and one-act plays.

Cut off from his mother's funds because of her disapproval of his decision to leave the civil service, Turgenev was for some time forced to live a rather bohemian life (as does the protagonist in his play *A Poor Gentleman*), often at the expense of Pauline Viardot. Judging by some scenes from his play *The Family Charge*, this interim was at times a most trying and humiliating existence.

In 1850, Turgenev returned to Russia to be with his dying mother and after her death received a substantial inheritance. Turgenev spent the remainder of his life traveling back and forth between Russia and Western Europe. He eventually settled in Paris and became an intimate of French literary circles. After many infrequent short trips back to his native countryside, he died in France, in the home of Pauline Viardot, on September 3, 1883.

ANALYSIS

Ivan Turgenev wrote his ten plays between 1842 and 1852, before the publication of his first major prose work, *A Sportsman's Sketches*, and before the publication of his first novel, *Rudin*. Four of his plays, however, were not performed or published until several years after they were written. For example, *The Family Charge*, written in 1849, was banned by the censors because it was critical of the nobility and was not published until 1857.

Like many other dramatists of his time, Turgenev often patterned his dramas after the vaudevilles imported from France. The vaudevilles were light comedies, focusing on domestic situations, which were popular with audiences. They usually escaped censorship because of their innocuous subject matter and because their humor was based on witty dialogue rather than on social satire. In contrast, the humor in Turgenev's comedies often comes from the devastating irony in his characterizations of the ruling class, which reveal an implicit criticism beneath the sentimental plots.

As does his entire canon, Turgenev's plays reflect the movement in Russian literature away from the dominant forces of the mid-nineteenth century, including Romanticism and the theater of Nikolai Gogol, toward the naturalism that would dominate European and Russian literature during the late nineteenth century. His first play, *Carelessness*, is typically Romantic in its exotic setting, stock Romantic characters, and flowery language, and the influence of Gogol's comic theater is clear in Turgenev's second play, *A Poor Gentleman*. Yet in his efforts to portray realistically the characters and characteristics of his society, Turgenev inevitably moved toward naturalism, although his lyricism and sentimental plots precluded the grimmer naturalism of the French writer Émile Zola.

In the course of his dramatic development, Turgenev delineated the techniques, major character types, and themes that would shape his later fiction. In his playwriting, he depended on dialogue rather than on description or narration to define his characters, and this technique carried over into his fiction, as did the main character types that he portrayed. His heroes usually fell into one of two categories, which he described in the essay "Gamlet i Don Kikhot" ("Hamlet and Don Quixote," 1930), first presented in a public lecture in 1860. Turgenev described the Hamlet character type as cold and aloof, a man who intellectualizes life and who is motivated only by irony directed at himself. His constant self-analysis results in paralysis of the will. The hero of *Where It Is Thin, There It Breaks* is an example of the Hamlet type. The Quixote character type is spontaneous and exuberant, directing his energies toward an external goal that is usually beyond his grasp. Vasilij Kuzovkin in *The Family Charge*, Mikhail Moskin in *The Bachelor*, and Rakitin in *A Month in the Country* exemplify the Quixote type. These character types, which recur in his drama and fiction, offer both universal insights into human nature and criticism of the ineffectual intellectuals among the nobility, who dreamed and talked of reform endlessly but who accomplished very little. Turgenev perceived both these character types as incomplete human beings. In his plays, such heroes usually fail to accomplish their goals. Turgenev's heroines, on the other hand, are often strong-willed women who know what they want, and sometimes manage to obtain it. Darja in the comedy *A Provincial Lady* is one such heroine. She uses her feminine charms to climb the social ladder by beguiling a childhood friend, Count Valerian Nikolaevic Lubin, who, flattered by her feigned affection, promises to obtain for her a husband with a position in the city.

While social criticism, subtly revealed through ironic characterization, is present in much of Turgenev's work, the themes of his plays also derive from his personal experiences. The recurrence of love triangles throughout his work can be ascribed largely to the central relationship of his own life, his love for the married Pauline Viardot. Turgenev's adult life before receiving his inheritance was often marked by the need to subsist on his wit and charm, depending on affluent friends to support him, and this experience is reflected in his superfluous men—both Hamlets and Quixotes—who are often long-term houseguests and who often lack the iron will of their female counterparts. The domineering figure of his mother and the assertive personality of Pauline Viardot are reflected in his many decisive heroines. Finally, Turgenev's hatred of the injustices of serfdom was first aroused during the periods when he lived with his mother on her provincial estate, an estate that is similar to the setting of Turgenev's masterpiece, *A Month in the Country*.

Although Turgenev's plays were usually well received by audiences when he managed to get them produced, they were not outstanding successes, and the critics often reacted coolly. Time has proved the critics of Turgenev's age correct regarding most of his plays. His plays are significant primarily because they demonstrate the development of his literary concerns and abilities, which he would later employ in his fiction, and because they presage his important play *A Month in the Country*.

CARELESSNESS

Turgenev's first play, *Carelessness*, is a short comedy that was published in the periodical *Annals of the Fatherland* in 1843. It did not receive positive reviews and was not produced. It is significant, however, as an example of Turgenev's early movement away from Romanticism and of his developing use of irony. The plot recalls the love triangle so typical of Romanticism as well as of Turgenev's own style: A bold, handsome young hero, Don Rafael de Luna, scales the walls of a country house at night to woo the beautiful, dark-eyed Dona Dolores, who pines away in a melancholy trance, longing for some heroic warrior to save her from the boredom of her mismatched marriage to a wealthy Spanish nobleman twice her age, Don Balthazar d'Esturiz.

It is clear from the beginning of the play that, even in this early work, Turgenev is gently mocking the conventions of Romanticism. For example, the image of the pure, young heroine, trying to resist certain "sinful desires," is comically deflated by her wistful but somewhat ludicrous attempt to imagine her fat, balding, and boring husband as a nonexistent hero, fashionably dressed with a white, feathered hat, a velvet mantle, spurs, and a sword. This mock-heroic portrayal of Don Balthazar is only one of the many humorous moments in the play that illustrate Turgenev's love of subtle irony. The multiplicity of tones

characteristic of Rafael's speech is another. When addressing Dona Dolores, Rafael plays the role of artful, passionate courtier, reciting flowery bits of poetry and song, which he constantly undercuts with biting, sarcastic asides to himself and the audience. In the same vein, while he feigns extraordinary courage in the face of possible discovery, he makes certain that no one is around before he in fact descends into the shadows of Dona Dolores's garden. His true cowardly nature is revealed by his very unheroic retreat on discovery in her bedroom.

Don Pablo Sangrè, Balthazar's close and trusted friend, is typical of a later stage of Romanticism. He has grown to middle age brooding in silent disenchantment, his hopes and beliefs long ago shattered. Don Pablo cynically mocks the sentimentality and eloquent phrases of his young rival, Don Rafael de Luna, whose very name (Luna) suggests the romantic realm of night and dreams. The manipulative and self-possessed Don Pablo has himself long been nurturing a secret passion for his good friend's young bride. Unlike his effusive, enamored young competitor, he has stood apart in "eloquent silence" in order to analyze his love, which, he quite openly recognizes, is only a desire to control a proud young woman whom he has not been able to influence.

In turn, Dona Dolores shows unusual perception and understanding of human nature as she sees through Don Pablo's declaration of love. She deflates his exaggerated heroic stance, ironically mocking his speech: "Two years of eloquent silence. . . . 'Eloquent!' I like that word." When she refuses to submit to his embraces, Don Pablo kills her without remorse because she has seen him in a moment of weakness, in his "tears and feelings." Cold-hearted egoism, which causes only pain and suffering for others, had already become a dominant character trait for the Russian literary hero before the writings of Turgenev and was to become a dominant motif in the later works of this author.

Turgenev abruptly ends his play with a brief epilogue stating that Don Pablo has gone on to secure a position in "the office of an important official." This final cryptic note dispels any illusion of idealism or Romanticism, signaling Turgenev's own gradual disassociation from his earlier dreams of the "sublime and the beautiful." Although *Carelessness* is a charming and witty work, it also offers a sad commentary on the wasted and misguided strength of the younger generation, which once channeled its talents and energies in quest of golden dreams but which ultimately turned to a self-centered, mundane pursuit of power and material wealth.

A Poor Gentleman

Turgenev's second one-act comedy, *A Poor Gentleman*, represents a marked shift from the sentimentality of a balmy evening in Spain in *Carelessness* to the mundane reality of contemporary Russian life. This most Gogolian work by Turgenev recalls several scenes in Gogol's *Revizor* (pr., pb. 1836; *The Inspector General*, 1890), in which a young, pampered nobleman lies idly around, verbally abusing his old and devout servant. Like the nobleman in *The Inspector General*, the central figure in Turgenev's plays, Timofei Petrovic Zazikov, has squandered all of his money on frivolous living and can no longer afford the items indispensable for his self-respect, such as tea and firewood. He hurls a steady stream of invective at Matvei, his servant, blaming him for his predicament. Quoting from Alexander Pushkin's *Evgeny Onegin* (1825-1832, 1833; *Eugene Onegin*, 1881), Zazikov bemoans his lost youth and tries to set himself down to some serious work, which amounts to merely opening up a French book at random or singing before a mirror.

Like Gogol, Turgenev presents a whole sector of the lower classes in the figures of the creditors coming for their money—a shoemaker, a merchant, a sixteen-year-old girl who works for a washerwoman, and a driver. Although Turgenev offers only brief sketches of these types, the overall effect of their appearance colors the play with a certain sense of realism. The language of these common people is down-to-earth, colloquial, and truncated. Characterized by crude insults and folk humor, their speech is sharply distinguished from the flowery, romantic language of Turgenev's first play and indicates his swing toward naturalism in this period.

In *A Poor Gentleman*, Turgenev satirizes the strange combination of affection and abuse inherent in the strained relationship between Russian master and servant. Zazikov's servant, Matvei, is compassionately and positively depicted: He shows great concern for his master's well-being and possesses a certain intuitive wisdom that allows him to see the proximate cause of Zazikov's ruin: his exodus from the countryside (where he could have led a productive and useful life) to the empty whirlwind of city society. This positive characterization is qualified by Matvei's submissive acceptance of his master's verbal thrashings. Ultimately, Matvei's concern has little effect on Zazikov, who does not possess the strength of character to take an active, responsible role in life. Instead, Zazikov is enticed by a wealthy, protective friend back into the empty social life of St. Petersburg, attending balls, plays, and restaurants and continuing his pampered, indolent lifestyle. The play ends with the forlorn words of Matvei as he laments the demise of the nobility: "Gone are the good days. How changed is the nobility." Fifty-eight years later, Chekhov concluded his masterpiece *Vishnyovy sad* (pr., pb. 1904; *The Cherry Orchard*, 1908) in a similar fashion, with the melancholy monologue of the old servant Firs, who sees himself as a discarded remnant of a bygone age.

Where It Is Thin, There It Breaks

Turgenev's one-act comedy *Where It Is Thin, There It Breaks* was written in 1851, at the end of his Romantic period. In this play, Turgenev adapts the image of the "superfluous" hero to a setting that reflects Turgenev's own environment: the estate of a wealthy female Russian landowner in France. In spite of this location, the play portrays Russian, not French, country life. Paving the way for the subsequent full-length plays, the number of the characters in this short play has increased, and the nature of their interaction is much more complex. As in *Carelessness*, the nexus of the story lines is a love triangle in which Turgenev's two types of heroes are pitted against each other in a competition for the hand of the landowner's nineteen-year-old daughter, Vera Nikolaevan Libanova.

The dominant male protagonist bears the first name of Pushkin's classic hero—Evgeny Andreevič Gorsky—and represents Turgenev's Hamlet type. He has the reputation of being "a strange, cold-blooded man," who calculatingly treats his pursuit of Vera as a fencing match to be either won or lost. Deriving from the root "bitter," the name "Gorsky" suggests the pose of an alienated man who stands back skeptically, calculating his every step, never giving in to his emotions.

Central to this play are Gorsky's frequent monologues on the merits of personal freedom and the practicality of realism. He negates the euphoric states of love and fantasy, stating that for him, "a lobster or an oak tree is more meaningful than imagination or the tales of Hoffmann." Ironically, Gorsky's rival, Stanitsyn, arrives on stage at the moment when Gorsky is about to seal his fate by proposing to Vera. Stanitsyn's timely appearance prevents Gorsky from uttering such decisive words.

Finding himself in such a precarious position, Gorsky compares himself to Podkolyosin in Gogol's play *Zhenit'ba* (wr. 1835, pr., pb. 1842; *Marriage: A Quite Incredible Incident*, 1926), who, when faced with the certainty of marriage, throws himself comically from a "not so high window." Despite Gorsky's attempt not to follow in Podkolyosin's cowardly footsteps, he commits the equally unheroic act of "running," not walking, away from the scene. By contrast, Stanitsyn's straightforward declaration of his intentions seems to solicit the audience's approval, but his excessive naïveté and simplicity make him an equally easy target for mockery.

A CONVERSATION ON THE HIGHWAY

The action of *A Conversation on the Highway*, consisting of only one scene, centers on one of the most popular images in nineteenth century literature (particularly in the works of Gogol)—the carriage on an open road, which has been interpreted as a symbol for a not only personal but also historical state of flux. In the style of the naturalists, Turgenev prefaces his comic scene with a detailed description of the physiognomy of the three characters riding in the carriage: a young landowner, his serf driver, and a rural officer of low rank. The depiction of individual negative features such as "pudgy fatness," "piggish eyes," and "heavy" asthmatic breathing recalls similar details in character descriptions by Gogol. Here, more

than in any other Turgenev play, the author calls attention to facial expressions, body dynamics, and peculiarities of speech. The use of many pauses and silences, interspersed throughout the scene, mimes the excruciatingly slow pace of the horses, suggesting the stagnancy of all provincial Russia. As in Turgenev's other works, the serf driver, Efrem, shows the greatest vitality and strength of character. Efrem chatters away almost nonstop, expanding his views of life, which take the scrambled form of superstitions mixed with a certain simple, intuitive wisdom. His dream of traveling along a hilly, vacant highway without purpose or direction underscores the slumbering mood of his environment. In the end, only Efrem's voice can be heard, singing a folk song with a healthy, "high voice."

AN EVENING IN SORRENTO

Turgenev's last play, *An Evening in Sorrento*, satirizes members of the Russian nobility living abroad in Europe, where they are entertained in their hotels by a series of second-rate artists, musicians, and singers who flock to them for their money. The relationship between the two main characters, the middle-aged Sergey Plantonovic Avakov and the younger widow, Nadezda Pavlovna Eleckaja, bears a resemblance to the long and at times difficult relationship between Pauline Viardot and Turgenev. In this play, however, it is portrayed without the earlier romantic overtones so apparent in Turgenev's earlier plays. Dreaming of his distant homeland, a sleepy, stodgy Avakov awakens in disgust to find himself in these foreign surroundings, where he patiently endures Nadezda Pavlovna's quick temper, mocking laughter, and coquettish flirtations with her young entourage of artists. In the end, it is the seasoned, middle-aged Avakov, rather than the flamboyant, dashing Belsky, who proves to be Nadezda's true and devoted friend. It is apparent in this last experiment in theater that in his decade of writing plays, Turgenev had succeeded in drastically pruning his work; in place of his earlier excessive sentimentality, he had established ironic understatement as his chief comic device.

A MONTH IN THE COUNTRY

Turgenev's one outstanding drama, *A Month in the Country*, was written in 1850, toward the end of his brief playwriting career. It was immediately banned and was not published until 1855; it was not produced until 1872. On its first publication and performance, it was not recognized as the significant work that later critics have realized it to be. It was not until 1909, when the great Soviet director Konstantin Stanislavsky realized its importance and staged it at the Moscow Art Theatre, that it attained a permanent place in Soviet dramatic repertoire.

Stanislavsky, as well as other critics of his day, recognized that in *A Month in the Country* were the roots of the dramaturgy of Anton Chekhov, particularly the principle of "undercurrent action," in which the flow of everyday life merges with the subtle disclosure of the characters' emotions. Turgenev's concentration on the tone of this play also links it with Chekhov's sober country dramas.

A Month in the Country displays a far greater psychological depth than do Turgenev's earlier works; the characters who would populate Turgenev's major novels appear more clearly delineated in this play, and, as noted above, the portrayal of the inertia of rural life in nineteenth century Russia equals that found in Chekhov's *Dyadya Vanya* (pb. 1897; *Uncle Vanya*, 1914) or *The Cherry Orchard*. Like Chekhov's plays, *A Month in the Country* is a psychological drama with universal appeal. The inevitable love triangle is more complex in this play. Natalya Petrovna is loved by her husband and by her devoted and doting friend Rakitin, but she falls in love with her son's young tutor, Belsky. Natalya's teenage ward, Vera, also falls in love with the tutor. Two less serious courtships also complicate the plot, that of the doctor and that of the servant. Natalya first vents her feelings by abusing her longtime admirer Rakitin, then tries to marry Vera off to a middle-aged neighbor. Natalya relents and does not press the match, but she cannot resist trying to humiliate Vera by informing Belsky of Vera's love. Vera retaliates by telling the tutor of Natalya's feelings. The tutor is rather astonished, although gratified, by all this adoration. Before the situation can progress further, however, Natalya's husband discovers her in the arms of Rakitin, who is comforting her in her lovesick state. Rakitin explains that he is merely comforting his friend's wife, but it is

suggested that perhaps he should leave the estate. He does so, but before he goes, he manages to convince the young tutor that he should leave as well. Vera has become both embittered and matured in her first foray into the world of adult emotions, and she decides to marry the middle-aged neighbor in order to escape Natalya's household. At the end of the play, Natalya is left alone with her husband, whom she does not love.

In *A Month in the Country*, Turgenev abandoned Romanticism and Gogolian farce to depict as realistically as possible the life that he lived and the social class to which he belonged. There are obvious echoes of Turgenev's own often unhappy relationship with Pauline Viardot in this play, and perhaps it was in personal rather than in social concerns that Turgenev excelled as a dramatist. Turgenev wrote only three more plays after *A Month in the Country* before turning to the novels and short stories that would earn for him the standing of a major figure in Russian literature. His plays were, in a way, his apprenticeship. Yet in these early works, he transcended mid-century Romanticism and the dominating influence of Gogol to pave the way for the Chekhovian drama of the future, and he created one play that is still being performed more than a century after it was first produced. *A Month in the Country* remains one of the major plays of nineteenth century Russian literature.

OTHER MAJOR WORKS

LONG FICTION: *Rudin*, 1856 (*Dimitri Roudine*, 1873; better known as *Rudin*, 1947); *Asya*, 1858 (English translation, 1877); *Dvoryanskoye gnezdo*, 1859 (*Liza*, 1869; also as *A Nobleman's Nest*, 1903; better known as *A House of Gentlefolk*, 1894); *Nakanune*, 1860 (*On the Eve*, 1871); *Pervaya lyubov*, 1860 (*First Love*, 1884); *Ottsy i deti*, 1862 (*Fathers and Sons*, 1867); *Dym*, 1867 (*Smoke*, 1868); *Veshniye vody*, 1872 (*Spring Floods*, 1874; better known as *The Torrents of Spring*, 1897); *Nov*, 1877 (*Virgin Soil*, 1877); *The Novels of Ivan Turgenev*, 1894-1899 (15 volumes).

SHORT FICTION: *Zapiski okhotnika*, 1852 (*Russian Life in the Interior*, 1855; better known as *A Sportsman's Sketches*, 1932); *Povesti i rasskazy*, 1856.

POETRY: *Parasha*, 1843; *Senilia*, 1882, 1930 (better known as *Stikhotvoreniya v proze*; *Poems in Prose*, 1883, 1945).

NONFICTION: "Gamlet i Don Kikhot," 1860 ("Hamlet and Don Quixote," 1930); *Literaturnya i zhiteyskiya vospominaniya*, 1880 (*Literary Reminiscences and Autobiographical Fragments*, 1958); *Letters*, 1983 (David Lowe, editor); *Turgenev's Letters*, 1983 (A. V. Knowles, editor).

MISCELLANEOUS: *The Works of Iván Turgenieff*, 1903-1904 (6 volumes).

BIBLIOGRAPHY

Allen, Elizabeth Cheresh. *Beyond Realism: Turgenev's Poetics of Secular Salvation.* Stanford, Calif.: Stanford University Press, 1992. A critical analysis of Turgenev's works. Bibliography and index.

Costlow, Jane T. *Worlds Within Worlds: The Novels of Ivan Turgenev.* Princeton, N.J.: Princeton University Press, 1990. Although this work focuses on Turgenev's novels, it sheds light on his dramatic works. Bibliography and index.

Knowles, A. V. *Ivan Turgenev.* Boston: Twayne, 1988. A basic biography of Turgenev that includes critical analysis of his literary works. Bibliography and index.

Lowe, David A., ed. *Critical Essays on Ivan Turgenev.* Boston: G. K. Hall, 1989. A collection of essays on Turgenev's literary works. Bibliography and index.

Schapiro, Leonard Bertram. *Turgenev, His Life and Times.* 1978. Reprint. Cambridge, Mass.: Harvard University Press, 1982. A basic biography of Turgenev, covering his life and works. Bibliography and indexes.

Seeley, Frank Friedeberg. *Turgenev: A Reading of His Fiction.* New York: Cambridge University Press, 1991. This study provides a critical analysis of Turgenev's fictional works. Bibliography and index.

Worrall, Nick. *Nikolai Gogol and Ivan Turgenev.* New York: Grove Press, 1983. Worrall compares and contrasts the dramatic works and lives of the two Russian playwrights.

Jane E. Knox

ROYALL TYLER

Born: Boston, Massachusetts; July 18, 1757
Died: Brattleboro, Vermont; August 16, 1826

PRINCIPAL DRAMA

The Contrast, pr. 1787, pb. 1790

Four Plays by Royall Tyler, pb. 1941 (includes *The Island of Barrataria*, *Joseph and His Brethren*, *The Judgement of Solomon*, and *The Origin of the Feast of Purim: Or, The Destinies of Haman and Mordecai*)

OTHER LITERARY FORMS

Royall Tyler is recalled in contemporary anthologies of American literature principally as the author of the first professionally performed comedy by an American; this play, *The Contrast*, is one of five extant plays by Tyler. Readers of his own day, however, probably knew Tyler best as the witty and energetic author of the Spondee essays and poems, which he, along with his longtime friend Joseph Dennie, known as Colon, submitted for several years to various journals, gentlemen's magazines, and newspapers. In these Spondee pieces, collected by Marius B. Péladeau in *The Prose of Royall Tyler* (1972), Tyler addressed himself to such contemporary subjects as current artistic tastes or preferences, social mores, slavery (to which he was vehemently opposed), his staunch support of Federalist politics, and attacks on the French experiment in democracy. His position in regard to these subjects was almost invariably that of the satirist. Tyler and Dennie, as Spondee and Colon, carried on a compatible, if sometimes strained (by geographic separation), literary partnership from 1794 until 1811. The pair often found themselves imitated by other literary partners who assumed such arresting signatures as "Messrs. Dactyl and Comma," "Quip, Crank and Co.," "Messrs. Verbal and Trochee," and "The Shop of Messrs. Anapoestic and Trochee."

Among Tyler's other works is the two-volume *Reports of Cases in the Supreme Court of Vermont* (1809-1810); these volumes resulted from Tyler's tenure as chief justice of Vermont's supreme court. Tyler also published a single novel, *The Algerine Captive* (1797), which enjoyed a modicum of success and became one of the first novels by an American to be reprinted in London (in 1802 and again in *Lady's Magazine* in 1804).

Tyler also wrote quite a few poems, collected by Marius B. Péladeau in *The Verse of Royall Tyler* (1968). Such poems as "Ode Composed for the Fourth of July," "Spondee's Mistresses," "Choice of a Wife," and "The Chestnut Tree" display Tyler's penchant for witty satire. At the same time, these poems, especially "The Chestnut Tree," demonstrate the poet's underlying serious concerns.

ACHIEVEMENTS

Although Royall Tyler is remembered today almost exclusively as the author of *The Contrast*, the first American comedy to be professionally produced (on April 16, 1787, at the John Street Theatre in New York City), his achievements as a literary artist were much more extensive than is currently recognized. Four others of Tyler's estimated nine or ten plays have been published in the twentieth century, and several of the lyrics of his no longer extant *May Day in Town: Or, New York in an Uproar* (pr. 1787)— perhaps the first musical written and produced by an American—were discovered and published in 1975. Tyler's contribution to American literature, however, does not end with his dramas. *The Algerine Captive* was one of America's first native novels, as well as one of its first to be printed abroad, and Tyler's collaborative efforts with Joseph Dennie on the Spondee

and Colon pieces constitute one of the first American newspaper columns. Certainly his poetry, which is both witty and serious, deserves to be more extensively studied and anthologized. An all-around man of letters, Tyler distinguished himself as one of America's first authors who self-consciously wrote as an American.

BIOGRAPHY

Born William Clark Tyler on July 18, 1757, in Boston, Massachusetts, Royall Tyler adopted his father's name on the latter's death in 1771. Tyler's older brother, John Steele Tyler, had fallen out of favor with both parents and was disinherited; hence, most of the Tyler estate reverted to the young Royall. In 1772, Royall Tyler entered Harvard, from which he was graduated in 1776, the year of the Declaration of Independence. Tyler and his classmates were much caught up in the rhetoric and ideas of revolt that led to independence.

Tyler's days at Harvard were hardly, then, devoted entirely to disputation, to the study of the Latin and Greek authors, or to the pursuit of philosophy, theology, and mathematics. Indeed, at one point in his

Royall Tyler (Hulton Archive by Getty Images)

Harvard studies, Tyler, along with his roommate, was suspended for relieving the college president of his wig by means of a book dropped from their dormitory window. This incident did not mark the end of Tyler's collegiate escapades. During the period of his attendance at Harvard, the college had a strict rule that, on penalty of expulsion, no student could have anything to do with directing, staging, or acting in plays. Certain incidents related in the autobiographical *The Bay Boy*, concerning the clandestine performance of drama in Boston, suggest that the future dramatist violated this restriction as well.

Shortly after Tyler began to pursue his vocation as a lawyer, he struck up a courtship with the young Abigail Adams, daughter of Abigail and John Adams, who were later to become the first family of the United States. Evidently, the father of seventeen-year-old Abigail heard rumors of the enthusiastic young Tyler (who in 1777 was accused of wayward conduct), for not too long after Tyler let Abigail know of his intention to marry her, John Adams demanded that his wife and daughter join him in London, where the future second president of the United States was negotiating the peace treaty between America and Britain.

Tyler's abortive romance with Abigail, who was nicknamed "Nabby," also has its irony. While Nabby was in London with her parents, she met and eventually married a Colonel William Stephens Smith, an attaché of the American contingency and one of George Washington's protégés. While Adams was president, he remarked of his son-in-law, "All the actions of my life and all the conduct of my children have not yet disgraced me as much as this man. His pay will not feed his dogs; and his dogs must be fed if his children starve. What a folly!"

Tyler went on to wed Mary Palmer of Boston in 1794, to adopt the state of Vermont as his permanent residence, and subsequently to become one of that state's leading citizens. Probably, President Adams would not have been disappointed in having Tyler as his son-in-law. Tyler's activities before his marriage to Mary Palmer, however, most likely would have disappointed Adams. In 1787, while on a diplomatic mission on behalf of his future state, Tyler was in New York, where he not only flouted the old Harvard restrictions concerning association with plays but also enacted total rebellion against those restrictions by writing *The Contrast*, performed on April 16. This success Tyler immediately followed with *May Day in Town*, produced on May 19. *May Day in Town* was America's first musical comedy; regrettably, only the lyrics of the musical numbers survive.

Later, in Vermont, Tyler established a prosperous legal practice. He was elected an assistant judge of Vermont's supreme court and in 1807 was elected Chief Justice of the Vermont supreme court. These distinctions were followed in 1811 by his appointment as professor of jurisprudence at the University of Vermont. Tyler's middle years of success were also marked by his collaboration with Joseph Dennie on the Colon and Spondee series of newspaper and magazine articles, by the publication in 1797 of the novel *The Algerine Captive*, by the production in that same year of *The Georgia Spec: Or, Land in the Moon* (a play now lost), and by the publication of several poems on public events and prose works of legal commentary.

Shortly after 1820, however, Tyler's fortunes began to decline rather rapidly. About this time, Tyler began to develop a cancerous growth on his face. This health problem and his advancing age limited his capacity to practice. Eventually, he and his wife became totally dependent on the benevolence of their children and neighbors. It is to Tyler's credit that he attempted, during these declining years, to return to his pen. Between 1824 and his death on August 16, 1826, he wrote (usually with the assistance of amanuenses) three biblical dramas, as well as *The Bay Boy*, "The Chestnut Tree," and "Utile Dulci," which is a collection of miscellaneous writings devoted to moralistic instruction (intended for children) and to an explication of his ideas on marriage. It is also to Tyler's credit that certain passages among these last works are among his best and his most intense.

ANALYSIS

Although Thomas Godfrey's *The Prince of Parthia* (pr. 1767) must be acknowledged as the first American play to be produced on an American stage,

Royall Tyler's *The Contrast* remains a play whose production on April 16, 1787, marked several firsts. The first American comedy, it also introduced to the American stage the prototype of the Yankee in the character of Jonathan and featured the first stage singing of "Yankee Doodle." *The Contrast* was also the first American drama to receive a press review. Finally, Tyler's play was, before 1916, the most commercially successful play written by an American.

Several of Tyler's other dramatic works have survived, including one farce, *The Island of Barrataria*, and three biblical closet dramas. Some of the lyrics of Tyler's *May Day in Town*, perhaps America's first comic opera, have been found; when these lyrics are combined with information Tyler wrote in a letter to James Madison wherein a performance of the play is described, its plot can be almost wholly reconstructed. Three additional plays of which no copies are known to exist have been attributed to Tyler; these include *The Medium: Or, The Happy Tea-Party* (pr. 1795), *The Farm House: Or, The Female Duellists* (pr. 1796), and *The Georgia Spec*. Therefore, Tyler is the author of at least nine plays.

Tyler's unfinished autobiographical work, *The Bay Boy*, which remained in manuscript until Péladeau's publication of it in *The Prose of Royall Tyler*, provides two brief descriptions of his experiences with dramatic performances attempted within Puritan Boston's unsympathetic boundaries. One details a homespun attempt to render Joseph Addison's *Cato* (pr. 1713) into dramatic representation, and the other records the witnessing of a "forlorn fragment of monkish mysteries." Addison's *Cato* was performed under cover of night in a store emptied of all merchandise "excepting one or two counters and several empty hogsheads, barrels and boxes which served as pit, box and gallery for the spectators"; Tyler's description suggests a makeshift Globe Theatre. Actors and spectators stealthily assembled after "Mater, Pater or guardian" were all safely asleep. Tyler next describes the exact procedure for securing the "theater" from unsympathetic passersby:

> The front door of the store was closed and every crack and keyhole carefully stopped with paper or cotton that no glimmering light might alarm the passing watchman. The entrance was through a bye lane into a door in the backyard, and such was the caution observed that but one person was admitted at a time, while two, one at each end of the lane, were on the watch to see if the person to be admitted had been noticed. No knocking was permitted but a slight scratch announced the approach of the initiated.

Tyler then says that the thrill of this sort of performance was never equaled by public performances in New York's public theaters.

Tyler's depiction of the "monkish mystery" is a bit less spectacular, but it does express a persistent need for the dramatic despite puritanical restrictions. On a certain Christmas Eve during the Boy's youth, the house wherein he found himself was visited quite suddenly by a group of traveling players who enacted a brief dueling scene that was most realistic but for the grotesque attire and masks of the players. Tyler calls this representation a "masque" and at the same time somewhat satirically refers to it as reminiscent of early church mystery plays. Tyler's early familiarity with mystery plays, as well as with such a contemporary drama as Addison's *Cato*, suggests a dramatic background of some sophistication, belying the myth that Tyler wrote *The Contrast* some two weeks after having been initiated into the English comedy of manners during a brief stay in New York, when he was an adult of almost thirty. In these two instances, Tyler also gives present-day readers a rare glimpse of how drama exerted itself even in a period during which it had been outlawed (stage plays in Boston, the place of Tyler's birth and youth, were forbidden by a law enacted in March of 1750).

THE ISLAND OF BARRATARIA

Of Tyler's five extant plays, *The Island of Barrataria* is, next only to *The Contrast*, the most appealing and the most actable. The three blank-verse closet dramas are based closely on stories from the Old Testament; though too constrained and formal for performance, they contain some of Tyler's best poetry. By far the most significant of these five plays is *The Contrast*, and it is this drama which most clearly demands the attention of critics.

THE CONTRAST

Indeed, *The Contrast* remains so popular that it not only appears in nearly every standard collection of early American literature but also has enjoyed the distinction of being adapted as a musical. On November 27, 1972, *The Contrast: A Musical*, adapted by Anthony Stimac, premiered at New York City's Eastside Playhouse. Don Pippin composed the music, and the lyrics were by Steve Brown. Tyler's play itself can hold the interest of today's readers and audiences because of its steadfast censure of affectation at all social levels, because of its avowed concern to emphasize the corrective function of Thalia (the Comic Muse), because of its intelligent yet humorous depiction of human behavior in terms of seemingly interminable contrasts, and because of its refusal to fit easily within the bounds of a single comedic genre.

Commentators on *The Contrast* frequently emphasize the charge of the play's opening lines: "Exult, each patriot heart!—this night is shown/ A piece, which we may fairly call our own." To be sure, Tyler is, in many of his works, pointedly moved to encourage the quest for American literary independence. In their attempts to ferret out the play's "patriotic gore," however, commentators often obfuscate many other possible themes. Indeed, the prologue asserts other intentions for the play. Investigation of these additional intentions reveals that Tyler endeavored to produce not simply a play by an American or a distinctly American play but rather a play that bears the signature of Royall Tyler.

Throughout Tyler's prose and poetry runs the forceful strain of a moralist—though it must be observed that he stops just short of adopting the role of a didactic prescriber of conduct. In *The Contrast*, Tyler most clearly manifests this moral strain in his summary condemnation of affectation and insincerity at all levels of human behavior. In the ninth couplet of the verse prologue, the playwright asserts that "our free-born ancestors" despised the "arts" of the fashions or follies of their age: "Genuine sincerity alone they priz'd." The major theme of the play is the playwright's desire to reject the behavior of "modern youths, with imitative sense,/ [who] Deem taste in dress the proof of excellence" and to reclaim the re-

fined, though unadorned, "native worth" which is the "solid good" of the virtuous American's heritage. Tyler condemns what he sees as the corrupting influx of European affectation and strongly endorses the "honest emulation" of the behavior and customs that characterized those who struggled for American independence.

Billy Dimple, whose effete-sounding name signals his character, most fully embodies the postrevolutionary American who has embraced the European "Vice," which "trembles, when compell'd to stand confess'd." To such an extravagant expression have Dimple's affectations brought him that he stoops to all manner of deceit in order to dupe the young, desirable, and wealthy Maria Van Rough into a marriage of convenience—so that Dimple can carry on in his excessive and profligate manner, thereby avoiding bankruptcy yet experiencing no interruption of his many affairs of lust. When Dimple attempts to seduce Charlotte, sister of Colonel Manly, Dimple's antithesis, he and his "Vice" do indeed tremble before Manly's capable sword. The insipidity of insincere affectation, whether European, American, or extraterrestrial, is vividly "confess'd" by Jessamy, Dimple's valet, to Jonathan, Manly's "waiter." In a lively and hilarious scene derived from the classical subplot of the servants whose behavior both mirrors and comments on the behavior of their "betters," Jessamy presumes to instruct Jonathan in the "art" of proper display of amusement at the theater. Jessamy even points out how his master has clearly marked the texts of plays as to the precise juncture when the spectator should titter a "piano" or laugh a "fortissimo."

This sort of affected behavior Tyler aspires gently to correct by means of Thalia, the Comic Muse: "the wisdom of the Comic Muse/ Exalt your merits, or your faults accrue./ But think not, 'tis her aim to be severe." Tyler does not intend to offend his audience; rather, he hopes to "amend" human foibles. Throughout the history of the drama, the intention of the writer of serious comedy has always been constructive and corrective.

Tyler's seriocomic intentions are much in evidence in the first scene of act 2. Charlotte and her friend Letitia, who is another of Dimple's targets, are engaging in prattling banter about the nature of insincerity in friendship. Charlotte seizes this opportunity to expound her theory of the virtues of scandal. After admonishing Letitia not "to turn sentimentalist," Charlotte continues, "Scandal, you know, is but amusing ourselves with the faults, foibles, and reputations of our friends." Ironically, the process Charlotte describes strikingly parallels the action of the play itself; that is, Tyler's audience is engaged in the process of amusing itself "with the faults, foibles, follies, and reputations" of these characters on the stage. Charlotte has further suggested that such a process cannot attend the sentimentalist. She then reinforces her judgment by making this antisentimentalist remark: "Indeed, I don't know why we should have friends, if we are not at liberty to make use of them."

This remark is indeed hardly that of a sentimentalist; neither is it that of a moralist. Within comedic limits, Charlotte's assertion of immorality—wanton abuse of one of the most sacrosanct of human institutions, friendship—is simply too ludicrous to be taken seriously; hence, the audience's response is inevitably one of amusement. Within the constraints of Tyler's avowed hope to correct such foibles, however, his motive is at its most serious. Tyler's implicit acknowledgment here of the value of sincere friendship is intensely moral, yet his casting of this moral instruction within the mold of comedy prevents its becoming oppressively didactic.

No less instructive but, happily, more amusing are the many contrasts that pervade the play. Tyler has created the foppish Dimple, who appears to have much in common with the insidious Charlotte. Charlotte, as does Dimple, contrasts dramatically and often according to her own words with her somber, painfully moral brother, Colonel Manly. Maria Van Rough, who is betrothed to Billy Dimple, ironically seems perfectly fitted to become the partner in life to Colonel Manly. Charlotte recognizes the affinity of Maria for Manly when she exclaims to Letitia, "Oh! how I should like to see that pair of penserosos together." Tyler quite cleverly includes a subplot in which the servants of Dimple and Manly imitate somewhat questionably the actions of their masters. This scene, which opens the fifth act, strongly sug-

gests that the playwright recommends, as preferred conduct, neither Manly's melancholic disposition nor the foppishness of Dimple. Rather, Tyler bridges these two extremes when he holds up each for ridicule, thereby advancing a golden mean between them.

The scene opens as Jessamy and Jonathan discuss the success (or lack of it) that Jonathan has experienced in his endeavor to seduce Jenny, waitress to Maria. Much as would her mistress, Jenny has soundly rebuffed Jonathan's advances. Jessamy's promise to Jonathan of "cherubim consequences" has, alas, been shattered. Jessamy appears at a loss as to how to explain Jonathan's failure to seduce Jenny, much as Dimple is later dumbfounded that his consistent exercise of all of his arts, prescribed for him in Lord Chesterfield's letters to his son, gets him nowhere but in a court of law for bankruptcy and in a possible duel with Manly for his lustful intemperance. In a state of consternation (one that typifies much of the play), Jessamy concludes that Jonathan's failure can only be attributed to his lack of "the graces." Significantly, Jonathan misunderstands the use of the word "graces" and exclaims, "Why, does the young woman expect I must be converted before I court her?" In this exclamation, Jonathan reveals that, though he is certainly familiar with the rhetoric of Protestant conversion, he has not himself capitulated to it. Hence, Jonathan is every inch an American, who, though schooled in the doctrines of John Calvin, has refused to allow himself to become a saint; rather, he retains the proverbial Yankee independence.

Jessamy next attempts to instruct Jonathan in the art of acting natural—that is, appearing sophisticated while at the same time behaving with artless grace. First, Jessamy reproves Jonathan for having laughed too naturally at the theater. Jonathan retorts with a most sensible rhetorical question, "What does one go to see fun for if they can't laugh?" Undaunted, Jessamy explains to Jonathan, whom he perceives to be a sort of country bumpkin, that he must affect "natural motions . . . regulated by art." The explicit contradiction here is hardly lost on the not-so-dumb Jonathan. Then Jessamy details so unnatural a gamut of "artful" audience response to comedic action that, if such descriptions were drawn out on the stage, they would approach some of the distorted, contorted figures of Dante's *Inferno*. Picture an entire audience with mouths twisted "into an agreeable simper." How does one "twist" oneself into an agreeable anything?

Nevertheless, so misshapen is Jessamy's conception here that he sees such a scene to resemble a "chorus of Handel's at an Abbey commemoration." Jonathan, however, is not persuaded; he responds much as the audience of Tyler's own time doubtless did: "Ha, ha, ha! that's dang'd cute, I swear." As Colonel Manly is not at all convinced by the pseudo-sophisticated behavior both of his sister and of Dimple, Jonathan does not for a moment seriously consider adopting Jessamy's counsel concerning the proper response to comedy. Indeed, he has allowed himself to be advised by Jessamy in his approach to Jenny, which has proved most unrewarding. Now he joins the audience, and the comic spirit, in his gentle but definitely unapproving laughter at poor Jessamy, who is diseased with most foolish affectation.

This scene exposes affectation for what it is, insincere behavior that only the most lamentably foolish can long sustain in a world that always prefers reality to falsehood. It also predicts Dimple's inevitable exposure, Charlotte's reform, and Manly's triumph. One essential difference between Jonathan and his master, however, must be pointed out. Unlike Jonathan, who achieves a measure of disinterestedness and aloofness from the action and who learns not to be so gullible, Manly remains relatively static. Even before the action of the play begins, Charlotte tells Letitia that her brother once instructed her that "the best evidence of a gentleman" was that he "endeavor in a friendly manner to rectify [the] foibles" of his lady. At the crucial moment when he realizes that he loves Maria and she loves him but her betrothal to Dimple prevents their happiness, he finds solace in his injunction to Maria and to himself that their respective virtues merit that "we shall, at least, deserve to be" happy. Maria and Manly overcome this obstacle. The point here, however, is to emphasize the difference between master and servant; in keeping with the Roman comedies of Plautus and Terence, the servant is actually the superior of the master. Jonathan's

gentle laughter at Jessamy's specious logic firmly grounds *The Contrast* in the real world, while Colonel Manly continues to reside within a world of morose idealism.

Though virtue wins and vice pays the price of depravity, the Comic Spirit who instructs by means of gentle laughter appears still to have the upper hand in *The Contrast*. In good-naturedly correcting excessive behavior, Tyler has created comedy of neither manners nor sentiment nor of morals. What he has created is a play that bears his own signature—one characterized by an easily recognizable morality but stamped with the gentle judgment of a comedic spirit that anticipates that of George Meredith.

OTHER MAJOR WORKS

LONG FICTION: *The Algerine Captive*, 1797.

POETRY: *The Verse of Royall Tyler*, 1968 (Marius B. Péladeau, editor).

NONFICTION: *Reports of Cases in the Supreme Court of Vermont*, 1809-1810 (2 volumes); *The Prose of Royall Tyler*, 1972 (includes *The Bay Boy*; Marius B. Péladeau, editor).

BIBLIOGRAPHY

Carson, Ada Lou, and Herbert L. Carson. *Royall Tyler*. Boston: Twayne, 1979. This volume offers the most convenient and available account of this early American lawyer, law professor, judge, and scholar.

Silverman, Kenneth. *A Cultural History of the American Revolution: Painting, Music, Literature, and the Theatre in the Colonies and the United States from the Treaty of Paris to the Inauguration of George Washington, 1763-1789*. Reprint. New York: Columbia University Press, 1987. The most comprehensive survey of Tyler's life and times. Silverman places Vermont's first scholar in a historical and cultural context.

Tanselle, G. Thomas. *Royall Tyler*. Cambridge, Mass.: Harvard University Press, 1967. This volume has become the standard source on this early American playwright, poet, and novelist.

John C. Shields,
updated by Peter C. Holloran

U

NICHOLAS UDALL

Born: Southampton, England; December, 1505(?)
Died: London, England; December, 1556

Ralph Roister Doister, pr. c. 1552, pb. 1566(?)

OTHER LITERARY FORMS

Nicholas Udall is known today almost exclusively as the author of the first regular English comedy, *Ralph Roister Doister*. He was better known in his own time, however, as a scholar and translator. Aside from a few occasional verses and a medical book (*Compendiosa totius anatomie delineatio*, 1552), the balance of Udall's work consists of translations of Latin authors. In 1534, he published *Floures for Latine Spekynge*, a translation into idiomatic English of selected parts of Terence. Two translations of the great Humanist Desiderius Erasmus followed, *Apophthegmes* in 1542 and *The Paraphrase of Erasmus upon the New Testament* in 1549. Finally, in 1550, Udall published a translation of Peter Martyr's Protestant disputation with Roman opponents, *Tractatie de Sacramente* (1549); Udall's work is entitled *A Discourse or Tractise of Petur Martyr*.

ACHIEVEMENTS

Nicholas Udall's literary efforts are almost exclusively connected to his work as a scholar and teacher. Except for a few verses written to celebrate the coronation of Anne Boleyn, the famous second wife of Henry VIII and mother of Queen Elizabeth, the translations and plays credited to him were produced to aid him in his profession. Even the play that secured his reputation, the innovative and delightful *Ralph Roister Doister*, was most likely composed as a Christmas comedy for a boys' school in London.

The *Floures for Latine Spekynge* is a work written by a schoolmaster for schoolchildren. Udall's work was used in a Latin-English dictionary published in 1548 by Thomas Cooper: *Bibliotheca Eliotae*. Cooper praises "the learned man Udall, by whose scholarly annotations our labors have been lightened in many places, give deserved praise and gratitude."

Udall's purpose in *Floures for Latine Spekynge* was to give students selected Latin passages from Terence Rattigan as exercises. Udall best explains his intent on the title page:

> *Floures for Latine Spekynge* selected and gathered out of Terence, and the same translated into Englyeshe, together with the exposition and settynge forthe as welle of such latyne words, as were thought nedeful to be annoted, as also of dyvers grammatical rules, very profytable and necessary for the expedite knowledge in the latine tongue: Compiled by Nicholas Udall.

In his preface, Udall notes, "I have added wherever it seemed necessary certain scholia as it were, in which both the sense of the poet is explained and the words themselves not a little more clearly declared." The "scholia" were intended to help the neophyte student understand not only the ideas of Terence but also the difficult task of translating those ideas from Latin into English. Instead of translating idioms literally, Udall uses equivalent English idioms, so that the resulting translation is both faithful to the sense of the Latin and at the same time a good English composition. The work was used by hundreds of English schoolchildren to gain an understanding of and an appreciation for classical ideas and language.

More important than *Floures for Latine Spekynge* for Udall's reputation, for both his own generation and the succeeding generation, was his *The Paraphrase of Erasmus upon the New Testament*. Erasmus had popularized scholarly annotations on the New

Testament, maintaining the scholarly quality of the commentaries while omitting the jargon and apparatus peculiar to scholarship. Udall employed his skills as an accomplished translator to provide for English readers a clear, lively rendering of the important commentaries.

So important was Udall's translation thought to be to the Protestant clergy, many of whom were ill-prepared as scholars, that royal injunctions in 1547 and 1559 insisted "that every parson, vicar, curate, chantry-priest, and stipendary, being under the degree of bachelor of divinity, shall provide and have of his own . . . the New Testament both in Latin and English, with the Paraphrase upon the same of Erasmus, and diligently study the same, conferring the one with the other."

Whether Udall's *Ralph Roister Doister* was as important and influential as his translations is a question not easily answered. The play clearly cannot be considered in the same category as comedies by Ben Jonson or William Shakespeare. Udall's comedy does not develop a complete plot, analyze a significant idea, or probe the psychology of human emotions or foibles, but it does blend classical Roman and native English elements in an English comedy in a way that forms a foundation for the author's more famous successors. Udall is not unreasonably considered the father of English comedy.

BIOGRAPHY

Nicholas Udall (or Udal, Owdall, Uvedale, Owdale, Dowdall, Woodall, Woddell, or Yevedale) was born during the Christmas season, probably of 1505, in Southampton, Hampshire, England. Little is known of his family, but some scholars speculate that the future playwright was a member of the prominent Uvedale family in Hampshire. No record exists of Udall's ever having been married.

In 1517, Udall can be placed in residence at St. Mary's College, Winchester, a school noted for rigorous studies, long days, and few holidays. At Winchester, where Latin was the language both of studies and of daily life, Udall would have studied the works of Vergil, Cicero, Terence, and other Latin authors, but especially Terence, whose subjects and Latin style are accessible to students. Udall's later devotion to the works of Terence can reasonably be traced to his early days at Winchester.

In 1520, Udall was admitted to Corpus Christi College, Oxford, the center for Humanistic studies. Under the tutelage of Thomas Lupset, lecturer and friend of the Humanists Sir Thomas More and Erasmus, the young Udall, in company with his friend John Leland, embraced Humanistic ideas and skills to such an extent that Udall and Leland are usually considered to be "second-generation Humanists." It was at Corpus Christi College also that Udall met Edward Wotton, lecturer in Latin and Greek and a scholarly English physician. Udall's later *Compendiosa totius anatomie delineatio*, an illustrated digest of anatomy, may be traced to his association with Wotton.

At Oxford, Udall most likely studied under the Spanish Humanist and Latin lecturer Juan Luis Vives. From Vives, Udall would have been introduced to such Humanistic concepts as the importance of education for women, the importance of the vernacular, and reasonable arguments for morality. Although Vives adopted Plato's opinion of poetry, especially of drama, the Humanistic principles he espoused can be found in Udall's *Ralph Roister Doister*. A clearly English play, written in the vernacular, it has a strong, well-educated heroine in Dame Christian Custance. Furthermore, it is free of the more earthy, obscene, and immoral thoughts, actions, and language of Latin comedies.

The exciting intellectual atmosphere at Oxford might well have led the young scholar-author close to his first scrape with the law. He had received his bachelor of arts degree in 1524 and immediately became a probationary fellow of the college. By 1526, he was a full fellow and lecturer in Greek. In 1527, the English authorities arrested several Oxford men for circulating Lutheran works and the outlawed Tyndale Bible. Apparently Udall was one of several men who were admonished to avoid even the appearance of heresy. Surely the curiosity of these young men, thriving in the center of Humanistic learning, had been drawn to the ideas of the Protestant Reformation.

Udall's whereabouts from 1529, when he left Oxford, until 1533 are not known. Some evidence exists to suggest that he may have traveled in France and Germany, where school drama enjoyed great popularity. By 1533, he was in London, where he and John Leland, his friend from Oxford, wrote verses for the coronation of Anne Boleyn. Using the "Judgment of Paris" theme from Homer and Ovid, Udall and Leland praise the new queen as more beautiful than the three goddesses Hera, Athene, and Aphrodite. The verses are at once hyperbolic and rather dull.

In 1534, Udall turned his attention from polite flattery to scholarship with his *Floures for Latine Spekynge*, a work used for many years to teach Latin to English schoolboys. In June, 1534, soon after the publication of this pedagogical work, Udall was appointed headmaster of Eton. A stern master, one who did not spare the rod, Udall was nevertheless praised for his devotion to the subjects he taught and for his effectiveness as a teacher.

Udall's tenure as headmaster at Eton, however, was not without problems. Although his work as a scholar and teacher was without blemish, he did run afoul of the law in his personal life. In 1541, he was charged with complicity in the theft of "certain images of silver and other plate" (according to *Proceedings and Ordinances of the Privy Council of England*, 1834-1837; Harris Nicolas, editor) and was sent to Marshalsea. The *Proceedings* also reports that while "Nic. Vuedall, Schoolmaster of Eton" was being questioned about "other felonious trespasses," he confessed "that he did commit buggery with the said Cheney," Thomas Cheyney, an Eton scholar.

Certainly conviction of such crimes, especially that of buggery, would have been more than serious enough to end the career of any scholar-teacher. Whether it was a case of an error in the records ("buggery" written for "burglary") or of Udall's having powerful friends (namely, Thomas Wriothesley, on the Privy Council) or of his having written a moving letter of apology addressed to "Right Worshipfull and My Singular Good Master," Udall was soon released from custody.

Udall continued his scholarship, publishing in 1542 *Apophthegmes*, a translation of the oral sayings of the ancients collected by Erasmus. That he was, in 1543, appointed to direct a group of scholars in translating *The Paraphrase of Erasmus upon the New Testament* indicates that Udall had escaped the stigma of his conviction and suggests that it was not, after all, buggery for which he was convicted. After devoting several years to this translation and several more years working in a scholarly fashion for the Protestant government, Udall was, in 1549, appointed tutor to Edward Courtenay, then a royal prisoner in the Tower. By 1552, Udall's career was fully recovered from his earlier troubles. He had, during the previous year, been appointed canon of St. George's Chapel at Windsor Castle, and when Edward VI was in residence at Windsor during September of 1552, Udall very likely presented his play *Ralph Roister Doister* for the first time.

When Mary came to the throne in 1553, Udall's work as a Protestant-Humanist scholar ended. By June of 1554, he was replaced as canonary at Windsor, and no more translations of the great Humanists appeared. Extant records show that his reputation as a dramatist was still good: Warrants from Queen Mary indicate that Udall received payment for dramatic entertainment performed in the royal presence.

In December of 1555, Udall was appointed headmaster of St. Peter's Grammar School, Westminster. The year he spent in residence at Westminster seems to have been uneventful; in any case, there are no records of translations, plays, or lawsuits during this period. Udall was never able to resume his important scholarly activities, perhaps because of the Catholic reign of Queen Mary or perhaps because he was ill. What is known is that slightly more than a year after his appointment as headmaster at Westminster, Udall died. Under the name "Nicholas Yevedale," he is listed as having been buried on December 23, 1556, at St. Margaret's Church, Westminster.

ANALYSIS

Nicholas Udall would almost certainly have seen mystery and morality plays presented in his community as he was growing up. Traveling companies brought English drama to communities throughout England, including Southampton. When, beginning at the age of twelve, he attended St. Mary's College, Winchester, he most likely would have studied Aristotle's *De poetica* (c. 334-323 B.C.E.; *Poetics*, 1705), the major plays of the Greek dramatists, and the Roman comedies of Plautus and Terence, especially those of Terence. Although no records exist to indicate specifically which plays might actually have been performed at Winchester while Udall was a student, it is known that Greek and Roman plays were presented at other grammar schools in England at that time, and later in his life Udall demonstrated an analytical knowledge of the works of Terence. Further familiarity with the elements of drama would have come from his participation in, or at least his knowledge of, the ceremony of the Festival of the Boy Bishop, which was celebrated annually at Winchester. The ceremony involved having students take the parts of ecclesiastical officials in presenting divine services at the school. If Udall did not actually participate in such ceremonies, he would certainly have observed them.

Udall probably wrote a number of plays presented during and after his lifetime both in the schools as pedagogical exercises and at court for entertainment. John Bale, the notable Protestant spokesperson, credits Udall with *commaediae plures* (many comedies). The only play that, in addition to *Ralph Roister Doister*, can definitely be attributed to Udall is *Ezechias* (c. 1546), a play acted before Queen Elizabeth at Cambridge in 1564, but no longer extant. In this play, which perhaps belonged to Udall's Eton period, Hezekiah was portrayed as a reformer sent by God "to roote up al Idolatry," as Udall wrote in *The Paraphrase of Erasmus upon the New Testament*, comparing King Henry VIII to Hezekiah in that regard.

Two other plays are sometimes thought to be by Udall, but inadequate evidence exists to make such an assertion: *Thersites* (1537), an interlude whose title character is a braggart soldier in the vein of *Ralph Roister Doister*, and *Respublica* (wr. 1553, pb. 1866), a piece of dramatic propaganda illustrating how Roman Catholicism is beneficial to a nation. Still two more plays are occasionally mentioned in connection with Udall, mainly because the authors are unknown and because the plays resemble *Ralph Roister*

Doister in some ways. In *Jacob and Esau* (entered in the Stationers' Register in 1557), the household servants of Esau are reminiscent of those in the household of Dame Christian Custance in *Ralph Roister Doister*. In *Jack Juggler* (pb. 1562), a Plautine plot is given English dress, again as in *Ralph Roister Doister*.

RALPH ROISTER DOISTER

Most scholars believe that *Ralph Roister Doister* was written in 1552, at the time the author was canon of St. George's Chapel at Windsor Castle. Udall's purpose was apparently to provide a Christmas comedy for the students of some London school. The plot of the play is simple enough. Ralph Roister Doister is a roistering, bullying coward who, like William Shakespeare's Sir Andrew Aguecheek in *Twelfth Night: Or, What You Will* (pr. c. 1600-1602) is nothing but bluster. He is constantly in love with some woman or another. As the play opens, he is infatuated with Dame Christian Custance, a rich and virtuous widow betrothed to Gawin Goodluck, a merchant who is away on business. Ralph sees himself, quite inaccurately, as God's gift to women and sees no reason why Dame Christian should not be delighted to wed him. In his misapprehension, Ralph is aided by the sycophantic Matthew Merrygreek, who avows that people often mistake Ralph for Launcelot, Guy of Warwick, Hector of Troy, Sampson, Alexander, and others. Merrygreek assures Ralph that he is indeed "the tenth worthy." Thus encouraged, Ralph sends a love letter to Dame Christian.

Using flattery and promises of gifts, Ralph persuades Dame Christian's servant Madge Mumblecrust to take the letter to her mistress. Dame Christian refuses even to open the letter, however, and chastises Madge, ordering her to bring "no mo letters for no man's pleasure." When Dobinet Doughty, Ralph's servant, brings a ring as a present for Dame Christian, Madge, therefore, refuses to deliver it. Dobinet turns to other servants: Tom Truepenny, Tibet Talkapace, and Annot Alyface, who are anxious to take the gift to their mistress. Their reward, however, is a severe scolding from Dame Christian.

Sent by Ralph to learn the effects of his letter and gifts, Merrygreek praises Ralph to Dame Christian, who rejects Ralph utterly, calling him "a very dolt and lout." When he hears of the rejection, the courtly lover Ralph insists that he will surely die. Merrygreek holds a mock funeral, with Ralph interrupting from time to time. Merrygreek advises Ralph "for a while to revive again," in order to get even with Dame Christian, who has caused his death.

When Ralph meets Dame Christian, he again declares his love for her. The virtuous widow, angered at being pestered, tells him plainly: "I will not be served with a fool in no wise; When I choose a husband, I hope to take a man." Reminded that Ralph has sent her tokens of his love and a true love letter, the widow produces the letter and allows Merrygreek to read it. The parasite so alters the punctuation that the letter consistently says the opposite of what Ralph intended it to say. Ralph threatens to avenge himself on the scrivener who wrote the letter for him, but when the scrivener arrives, he so bullies the cowardly Ralph that no revenge is attempted. Merrygreek agrees to explain the misunderstanding to Dame Christian.

Sim Suresby, servant to Goodluck, arrives to see how Dame Christian is getting along. As he and the widow talk, Ralph and Merrygreek come back to explain the love letter. Sim hears enough to arouse his suspicions and leaves to report to his master. Angered at having her good reputation stained, Dame Christian sends Ralph and the mischievous Merrygreek packing; Ralph threatens to burn down her house. Dame Christian sends for her Tristram Trusty to protect her and arms her servants with brooms, clubs, and distaffs to defend herself against the threat. Trusty arrives and assures her that she has nothing to worry about from the cowardly Ralph and the practical joker Merrygreek. When Merrygreek returns, they enlist him as an ally against Ralph.

Ralph returns ready to battle the woman who spurned him and is advised by Merrygreek to show Dame Christian that he is a real man. When she sees Ralph, the widow, as agreed, runs away pretending to be afraid. Even so, Ralph decides to retreat, claiming that he has forgotten his helmet, but Merrygreek gives him a stewpot for his head and urges him forward. With drums beating and flags waving, Ralph inches his way into battle. Dame Christian returns to take on Ralph, while her servants take revenge on Dobinet for his earlier behavior.

Merrygreek, arguing that he is protecting his valiant friend by striking at the widow, actually pummels Ralph with every blow. Thoroughly battered and defeated, Ralph swears that Dame Christian is an Amazon and wagers that she must have killed her first husband. Shouting "Away, away, away! She will kill us all," Ralph drops ceremony and runs for his life.

In the meantime, Sim Suresby has reported his suspicions to his master, who has returned home. After talking with his friend Tristram, Gawin Goodluck is reconciled with Dame Christian. To celebrate, Goodluck invites all of his friends to supper. After Merrygreek apologizes for his mischief, Goodluck asks both the parasite and the braggart soldier to join the party. The play ends with a song in praise of the queen.

The plot of *Ralph Roister Doister* is clearly based on the classical Roman model of comedy that Udall knew well from his study of Plautus and Terence. The unities of place and action are strictly adhered to, and the unity of time is not much warped. The scene is consistently simple, a village street. The action, occurring in only slightly more than a day, has a clear beginning, middle, and end.

The character of Ralph Roister Doister is easily traceable to the third century B.C.E. *Miles Gloriosus* (*The Braggart Warrior*, 1767) of Plautus and Terence's Thraso in *Eunuchus* (pr. 161 B.C.E.; *The Eunuch*, 1598). Ralph's opinion of himself as a great man, one whom love has weakened, is established early in the play and developed consistently throughout the work. Matthew Merrygreek is also a character suggested by the traditional parasite of Roman comedy. Like Diccon of *Gammer Gurton's Needle* (pb. 1575), Merrygreek is an opportunist who depends on his wit for his livelihood.

As dependent as both Ralph and Merrygreek are on their Roman models, however, both are also distinctively English. Plautus's braggart soldier is brasher, less sociable than Ralph. Terence's Thraso is overweening in his pride; Ralph is merely stupid—agonizingly, painfully, pitifully stupid. Terence's parasite fools Thraso more to further his own interests than in an attempt to increase the festivities of the play. Merrygreek, on the other hand, intends no lasting harm. More important than his own gain is the intrinsic humor of the situation of the blockhead, Ralph, in love with a woman whose name he cannot even remember. Merrygreek says early in the play,

> But such sport have I with him as I would not leese,
> Though I should be bound to live with bread and
>   cheese.

He is more nearly the father of the buffoons who appear in the later English comedies than the son of Roman parasites; in truth, he is both.

Dame Christian Custance can also be traced to Roman comedy. Terence regularly presents heroines in distress who are rescued from dire financial, physical, or social straits. Such a woman is Dame Christian Custance. At the same time, she recalls Geoffrey Chaucer's Constance in "The Man of Law's Tale": Both are women in distress, and both pray to the God who "didst help Susanna wrongly accused." Udall's Custance is distinctive, however, as an English woman beset with local problems and surrounded with English servants.

Perhaps Dame Christian's servants are the most English element in the play. Unlike the servants of Roman comedy, who can never be anything but servants, no matter if they be wiser than their masters, Udall's servants are all pretenders to the middle class. Dame Christian's servants are clearly not wiser than their mistress, as she often explains to them, but they have a kind of independence unknown to Roman servants. Madge Mumblecrust does not hesitate to kiss Ralph, who she thinks has come to woo her mistress. Tibet and Annot leap at the chance to take Ralph's love tokens to their mistress because they believe that as soon as Dame Christian is married,

> . . . we shall go in our French hoods every day,
> In our silk cassocks, I warrant you, fresh and gay.

In sum, Udall did not merely translate Plautus and Terence, as Sir Thomas Wyatt and Henry Howard, earl of Surrey, sometimes did Petrarch; rather, Udall added to his classical models elements of native En-

glish drama and of life on sixteenth century English streets. All English comedies that followed—those by Shakespeare, Ben Jonson, Thomas Dekker, and even *Gammer Gurton's Needle* (written shortly after *Ralph Roister Doister*)—show great improvements in the genre, but *Ralph Roister Doister* established the type by combining Roman and English elements into a new formula whose total is greater than the sum of its parts.

Because *Ralph Roister Doister* has a secure place in history as the first regular English comedy, scholars sometimes give it more credit than it is due. Although it provided the foundation for the later great English comedies, no one can reasonably discuss it alongside the significant plays of Jonson, Shakespeare, and others. Udall's purpose, as the prologue declares, was to use "mirth with modesty." Who, the audience is asked, would not like to have a story told

> Wherein all scurrility we utterly refuse,
> Avoiding such mirth wherein is abuse,
> Knowing nothing more commendable for man's
>   recreation
> Than mirth which is used in an honest fashion?

OTHER MAJOR WORKS

NONFICTION: *Compendiosa totius anatomie delineatio*, 1552.

TRANSLATIONS: *Floures for Latine Spekynge*, 1534 (of Terence); *Apopthegmes*, 1542 (of Erasmus); *The Paraphrase of Erasmus upon the New Testament*, 1549 (of Erasmus); *A Discourse or Tractise of Petur Martyr*, 1550 (of Peter Martyr's *Tractatie de Sacramente*).

BIBLIOGRAPHY

Boas, Frederick F. *An Introduction to Tudor Drama.* Reprint. New York: AMS Press, 1978. An attractive reprint of the 1933 original edition. Contains basic facts about Udall and his works, including his relationship with Queen Mary and a lawsuit against him in the early 1500's. Offers a comment on the classical influences on Udall, the "most representative" English playwright in the three decades between John Heywood and the major Inns of Court dramas of the 1560's.

Cartwright, Kent. *Theatre and Humanism: English Drama in the Sixteenth Century*. New York: Cambridge University Press, 1999. Cartwright examines the influence of Humanism on English drama in the 1500's. Udall followed Humanism and received instruction in it. Bibliography and index.

Edgerton, William. *Nicholas Udall.* New York: Twayne, 1965. The biographical sections are enlarged by references to major historical events. *Respublica* is dismissed as probably not by Udall. The longest chapter is devoted to *Ralph Roister Doister*, with emphasis on the dating problem and on the presence of Latin influence in the comedy. *Ezechias*, though now lost, is examined for its importance to Tudor England. Annotated bibliography.

Walker, Greg. *The Politics of Performance in Early Renaissance Drama*. New York: Cambridge University Press, 1998. Walker examines the theater of Great Britain, focusing on the writers Udall, David Lindsay, John Heywood, and Thomas Norton. Bibliography and index.

Eugene P. Wright,
updated by Howard L Ford

ALFRED UHRY

Born: Atlanta, Georgia; December 3, 1936

PRINCIPAL DRAMA

Here's Where I Belong, pr. 1968 (lyrics; book by Alex Gordon; music by Robert Waldman; adaptation of John Steinbeck's *East of Eden*)

The Robber Bridegroom, pr. 1975, pb. 1978 (lyrics and libretto; music by Waldman; adaptation of Eudora Welty's novella)

Chapeau, pr. 1977

Swing, pr. 1980 (lyrics; book by Conn Fleming; music by Waldman)

Little Johnny Jones, pr. 1982 (adaptation of George M. Cohan's musical)

America's Sweetheart, pr. 1985 (lyrics and libretto; adaptation of John Kobler's novel)

Driving Miss Daisy, pr. 1987, pb. 1988

The Last Night of Ballyhoo, pr. 1996, pb. 1997

Parade, pr. 1998

OTHER LITERARY FORMS

Alfred Uhry has written for television and film. His screenplays include *Mystic Pizza* (1988; written with others), *Driving Miss Daisy* (1989; adapted from his play), and *Rich in Love* (1993).

ACHIEVEMENTS

Alfred Uhry has received several honors. He was awarded the 1988 Pulitzer Prize and the 1988 Outer Critics Circle Award for Best Off-Broadway Play for *Driving Miss Daisy*. Uhry's film adaptation of *Driving Miss Daisy* also won the 1989 Academy Award for Best Adapted Screenplay. He won the 1997 Tony Award and the 1997 Outer Critics Circle Award for *The Last Night of Ballyhoo* in 1997. The Drama League Award and the American Theater Critics Association Award also went to *The Last Night of Ballyhoo* in 1997. *Parade* won the 1999 Tony Award for Best Book of a Musical and was named Best New Musical in the 1999 Drama Desk Awards and Best Musical in the 1999 New York Drama Critics Circle Awards.

BIOGRAPHY

Alfred Fox Uhry was born on December 3, 1936, in Atlanta, Georgia, the son of Ralph K. Uhry, a furniture designer and artist, and Alene Fox Uhry, a social worker. He graduated from Druid Hills High School in Atlanta in 1954. Uhry received his B.A. from Brown University in 1958. There he first teamed up with Robert Waldman to write two student-

From left to right, producer Nina Kenealy, playwright Alfred Uhry, producer Jane Harmon, and producer Liz Oliver, holding their Tony Awards for Best Play for The Last Night of Ballyhoo *in 1997. (AP/Wide World Photos)*

produced musicals. In 1959 he married Joanna Kellogg. They had four daughters.

From 1960 to 1963, Uhry worked with composer Frank Loesser. He taught high school English and drama at Calhoun High School in New York City from 1963 to 1980. He struggled to find his place in theater. He worked as a lyricist and a librettist on several shows. He finally had moderate success with *The Robber Bridegroom*, a musical adaptation of Eudora Welty's novella set among the lively characters of the Natchez Trace in early Mississippi. It is performed in the style of Paul Sills's *Story Theatre*. First produced by John Houseman's Acting Company in 1975, it later ran for 157 performances on Broadway and received a 1976 Tony nomination. Uhry continued to work in musical theater. He was affiliated with the Goodspeed Opera House from 1980 to 1984 and taught lyric writing at New York University from 1985 to 1988.

In 1987 greater recognition came to Uhry with his play, *Driving Miss Daisy*, a drama based on his memories of his grandmother and others of her generation who were part of Atlanta's Jewish community. It ran for 1,195 performances Off-Broadway. Uhry successfully adapted the play to film. His screenplay won a Writers Guild Award and an Oscar. Uhry worked on other screenplays, including *Mystic Pizza* and *Rich in Love*.

The Alliance Theatre Company of Atlanta commissioned *The Last Night of Ballyhoo*, a play set in the Atlanta Jewish community in 1939 at the time of the premiere of *Gone with the Wind*. It was first presented by the Atlanta Committee for the Olympic Games, Cultural Olympiad for the 1996 Olympic Arts Festival. It later had a run of 580 performances on Broadway.

Uhry's 1998 musical *Parade* has as its unlikely subject Leo Frank, a Brooklyn Jew who was lynched in 1915 by a mob because he had allegedly murdered a thirteen-year-old factory worker whom he supervised. Uhry had long known of the case because his great-uncle had owned the pencil factory run by Leo Frank and had helped to raise money for Frank's defense. Harold Prince, who directed the show, worked with Uhry to develop the story into a musical. The musical ran for eighty-four performances on Broadway.

In 1999, Uhry was honored by his alma mater, Druid Hills High School in Atlanta, which renamed its seventy-year-old auditorium the Alfred Uhry Theater.

ANALYSIS

Alfred Uhry's contribution to American theater has been to bring southern Jewish life to the stage. The stresses on this community from within and from without form the conflicts in *Driving Miss Daisy*, *The Last Night of Ballyhoo*, and *Parade*. They all focus on issues of self-identity and assimilation as well. In each play, characters try to balance their Jewish heritage and their southern heritage, but sometimes that proves impossible. Although Uhry's emphasis in these three works is on the southern Jewish community, his theme relates to the question of the role that background and heritage play in anyone's search for identity.

DRIVING MISS DAISY

Driving Miss Daisy, a three-person play, shows the slow unfolding of a relationship between Daisy Werthan, a wealthy Jewish widow, and Hoke Coleburn, her African American chauffeur. Boolie Werthen, Daisy's son, is a minor character. Although the principal focus in the play is on character revelation, the historical change in race relations in the South is also subtly disclosed in the background.

The play does not follow conventional structure but rather progresses in a series of scenes with no break. The events flow from one to another, covering the time from 1948 to 1973. The arc of the relationship between Miss Daisy and Hoke begins with resentment and even hostility on her part and develops into acceptance, respect, and trust. Miss Daisy gradually sees Hoke more as an individual. Much later in

the play, she finally acknowledges that Hoke is her best friend.

The issue of prejudice within Daisy herself and in the society beyond is addressed. Although Daisy asserts that she is not prejudiced, she has some stereotypical opinions about blacks and what "they" do. Daisy herself experiences the effects of prejudice when her temple is bombed. This incident is one of the things that helps her to see some common ground with African Americans, for later Daisy buys tickets to a United Jewish Appeal dinner for Martin Luther King, Jr.

The effects of prejudice are also revealed through Hoke's life. At the beginning of the play, he talks about the difficulty he is experiencing, as an older black man, in finding a job. On a long trip to Mobile, Alabama, the demeaning effects of segregation laws are evident when Hoke and Miss Daisy have an argument about his having to stop on the road in the middle of nowhere to urinate because he could not use the bathroom at the service station. Later, the temple bombing prompts him to speak of having seen a friend's father lynched when he was a boy.

While Daisy gradually becomes less prejudiced, her son Boolie follows a different route. In his efforts to be accepted as a Jewish businessperson in the southern Christian community, he and his wife gradually become more assimilated to the point, for example, of celebrating Christmas. After successfully becoming part of the business community, Boolie will not go with his mother to the Martin Luther King, Jr., dinner because of what some of his white colleagues might think. He would rather conform than stand out.

Another issue in the play is the difficulty of growing old with dignity. Part of Daisy's resentment at having a chauffeur is that she must give up some of her independence. She proudly asserts her self-sufficiency. Because of the trust she builds up with Hoke, she gradually accepts her dependence on him. Touchingly, at the end of the play, she allows Hoke to feed her some pumpkin pie.

THE LAST NIGHT OF BALLYHOO

A romantic comedy, *The Last Night of Ballyhoo* is set in Atlanta in December, 1939, at the time of the premiere of *Gone with the Wind*. Looming in the background is the beginning of World War II in Europe. The Freitag family is the center of the play. Ostensibly, the plot is about Lala's rivalry with her cousin Sunny, as both cousins consider attending the dance on the last night of Ballyhoo, a holiday party of several days, at which young Jewish Atlantans have fun and look for the right partners. Lala's mother, Boo, is determined that Lala go to Ballyhoo with an appropriate date and perhaps find her future husband.

A social issue in the play is the prejudice of the German Jews, longtime southerners, against the Eastern European Jews, relative newcomers to the United States and frequently from the North. The Freitags, one of whose ancestors was the first white child born in Atlanta, have become so well assimilated into southern culture that they seem more southern than Jewish to Joe Farkas, a young Jewish northerner of Eastern European descent who has been hired by Adolph Freitag, Sunny and Lala's uncle.

One theme of the play is that of the search for self-identity. This theme plays out principally through the characters of Lala, Sunny, and Joe. Lala has been away to college at the University of Michigan, but she abruptly returned in the middle of the semester when she did not receive a bid from the sorority that usually accepted her kind—German Jews. This rejection humiliated her. She sets out to achieve social success by modeling herself on Scarlett O'Hara. This model represents the fact that she prefers a southern identity to a Jewish one. Not very interested in religion anyway, she dismisses the Passover ceremony she once observed as boring. Like Lala, Sunny too has experienced rejection, but from Christians, not from other Jews. When she was a girl, she went swimming at a private club with some friends and was asked to leave the pool because Jews were not allowed to swim there. Sunny tells Joe that he cannot understand what it was like to grow up as a minority among the Christian majority. However, as a sociology major, she now believes that religion is not that important in the modern world. Sunny is more thoughtful than the superficial Lala, but she too rejects her Jewish heritage as insignificant. She sees herself as a modern young woman. In contrast, as Sunny observes, Joe has had the experience of growing up in a large Jewish community and thus being accepted as part of the larger group. He has a much stronger sense of his Jewish identity than the Freitags do, and he is comfortable with who he is. He is surprised at how little they know about their faith.

Although strongly attracted to each other, Sunny and Joe find their different attitudes toward their heritage to be an obstacle in their relationship. Matters reach a crisis when Joe, who has escorted Sunny to the Ballyhoo dance at the Standard Club, abruptly leaves when he learns that "his kind" would not be invited to join the exclusively German Jewish club. Joe accuses Sunny of hating her Jewishness. This being a romantic comedy, Joe and Sunny later reconcile. The last scene shows an idealized celebration of the Sabbath as Sunny and Joe lead the others in the ceremony, bringing them into the Jewish tradition.

PARADE

A much darker story than *Driving Miss Daisy* or *The Last Night of Ballyhoo*, *Parade* directly confronts violent anti-Semitism in its recounting of the real-life case of Leo Frank, who was convicted of the murder of a thirteen-year-old girl and lynched by a mob in 1915. In this play, once again southern and Jewish backgrounds come into conflict. Leo Frank, a Brooklyn Jew, feels discomfort at his work supervising southern factory workers and with his wife, Lucille, a southern Jew. Conscious of being an outsider, he feels alienated.

Leo is convicted and condemned to death because the jury members find their own prejudice against Leo confirmed by witnesses who lie because they were threatened or because they embellish the facts in the glare of the media sensationalism. Ironically, Leo and Lucille's relationship becomes closer as he finally accepts her help in his efforts to file appeals. Lucille manages to convince the governor to review the case, and although the governor hesitates to make the decision because he knows it will cost him his political career, he finally commutes Leo's death sentence to life in prison. At that point, mob justice takes over, and Leo is dragged from prison and lynched when he refuses one last time to say he is guilty. Much of the blame for the conviction and for the lynching lies with the newspapers, which make every effort to report any and all lurid details with little effort to discern the truth. They willingly confirm negative stereotypes. Frank's trial and murder are object lessons in what can occur when ignorance and prejudice rule.

OTHER MAJOR WORKS

SCREENPLAYS: *Mystic Pizza*, 1988 (with others); *Driving Miss Daisy*, 1989; *Rich in Love*, 1993 (adaptation of Josephine Humphreys' novel)

BIBLIOGRAPHY

Bordman, Gerald. "*Driving Miss Daisy.*" In *The Oxford Companion to American Theatre*. 2d ed. New York: Oxford University Press, 1992. Brief account of production information, plus a plot summary and critical commentary. Sees the play as involving but inconsequential.

Evans, Eli. *The Provincials: A Personal History of Jews in the South*. Rev. ed. New York: Free Press Paperbacks, 1997. Brief discussion of Uhry's depiction of southern Jewish life. Sets the plays in their historical context.

Gussow, Mel. Review of *Driving Miss Daisy. The New York Times*, April 16, 1987, p. C22. Remarks on the humanity and humor of the play. Miss Daisy and Hoke come to perceive that they have much in common, but they will never be able to say so.

Uhry, Alfred. "A Sorry Chapter, A Source for Song." *The New York Times*, December 13, 1998, sec. 2, p. 7. Uhry discusses his interest in the Leo Frank case. Mentions his family's connections to the case. Reflects on his southern roots but says that the Frank case reminded all Georgia Jews that no matter how long they had been in Georgia, they were still outsiders.

Winer, Laurie. "*Ballyhoo* Emerges as a Powerful Southern Family Drama." *Los Angeles Times*, February 28, 1997, p. F3. Review of the Broadway production. The contrast between Lala and Sunny—their looks, personalities, and self-images—sets up the conflict. Another conflict is between the family and its fear of Jewishness.

Witchel, Alex. "Remembering Prejudice, of a Different Sort." *The New York Times* February 23, 1997, sec. 2, p. 5. In this interview Uhry discusses the prejudice of Jews against other Jews that he writes about in *The Last Night of Ballyhoo*. He also reviews some of his accomplishments.

Carol Luther

MIGUEL DE UNAMUNO Y JUGO

Born: Bilbao, Spain; September 29, 1864
Died: Salamanca, Spain; December 31, 1936

PRINCIPAL DRAMA

La esfinge, wr. 1898, pr. 1909, pb. 1959
La venda, wr. 1899, pb. 1913, pr. 1921
La difunta, pr. 1910
El pasado que vuelve, wr. 1910, pr. 1923, pb. 1959
Fedra, wr. 1910, pr. 1918, pb. 1921 (*Phaedra*, 1959)
La princesa doña Lambra, pb. 1913
Soledad, wr. 1921, pr. 1953, pb. 1954
Raquel encadenada, wr. 1921, pr. 1926, pb. 1953
El otro, wr. 1926, pr., pb. 1932 (*The Other*, 1947)
El hermano Juan: O, El mundo es teatro, wr. 1927, pb. 1934
Sombras de sueño, pr., pb. 1930
Teatro completo, pb. 1959, 1973

OTHER LITERARY FORMS

Miguel de Unamuno y Jugo is known primarily for his philosophical essays, most notably *En torno al casticismo* (1902; on authentic tradition), *Vida de*

Don Quijote y Sancho según Miguel de Cervantes Saavedra, explicada y comentada por Miguel de Unamuno (1905; *The Life of Don Quixote and Sancho According to Miguel de Cervantes Saavedra Expounded with Comment by Miguel de Unamuno,* 1927), *Mi religión y otros ensayos breves* (1910; my religion and other short essays), *Del sentimiento trágico de la vida en los hombres y en los pueblos* (1913; *The Tragic Sense of Life in Men and in Peoples,* 1921), and *La agonía del Cristianismo* (1931; *The Agony of Christianity,* 1928, 1960).

Unamuno was, however, active in many other genres; his fiction in particular has been the subject of increasing critical interest. His novels include *Paz en la guerra* (1897; *Peace in War,* 1983), *Niebla* (1914; *Mist: A Tragicomic Novel,* 1928), *Abel Sánchez: Una historia de pasión* (1917; *Abel Sánchez,* 1947), *Tres novelas ejemplares y un prólogo* (1920; *Three Exemplary Novels and a Prologue,* 1930), and *La tía Tula* (1921; *Tía Tula,* 1976). The novella *San Manuel Bueno, mártir* (1933; *Saint Manuel Bueno, Martyr,* 1956) is one of his finest works. Unamuno is also noted for his short stories.

Unamuno's poetry includes *Poesías* (1907; poems), *El Cristo de Velázquez* (1920; *The Christ of Velázquez,* 1951), and *Rimas de dentro* (1923; rhymes from within). His travel books include *Paisajes* (1902; landscapes) and *Por tierras de Portugal y de España* (1911; through regions of Portugal and Spain).

ACHIEVEMENTS

Though recognized as the leading philosophical thinker of the distinguished group of Spanish writers known as the Generation of 1898, Miguel de Unamuno y Jugo spurned rigorous methodology in his passionate probing of what he regarded as humanity's deepest and primary concern: to know what becomes of individual consciousness after death, whether it is immortal or ends in nothingness. Unable or unwilling to accept the Catholic Church's doctrine on this central issue and yet obsessed with a tremendous desire for personal immortality, he struggled throughout his adult life to build his defenses against what he regarded as the final void. Though reason and the science of his day seemed to deny the Christian belief

in personal immortality, man's transcendental desires and aspirations, what Unamuno often called his "heart," demanded such immortality. This conflict between logic and sentiment is best expressed in his key work, *The Tragic Sense of Life in Men and in Peoples,* and reflected in one way or another throughout his writings in different literary genres. For Unamuno, literature was primarily a vehicle for anguished philosophical-religious probings of the final reality of humankind's being and destiny, and differences among literary genres were insignificant. Anarchic and deeply personalistic in his thinking, Unamuno habitually employed paradox or the opposing of contraries, often through anguished dialogues between personages or within an individual.

Though very much interested in the theater throughout his professional life, Unamuno was never successful as a dramatist. His drama is important, however, because to some extent it anticipated in its themes and in its unadorned stagecraft, or "naked theater," many of the characteristics of more recent European theater.

Unamuno stands with José Ortega y Gasset, a systematic philosopher nineteen years his junior, as one of the two most powerful Spanish thinkers of the twentieth century. Whereas Ortega cultivated only the essay, Unamuno wrote superbly in several genres, leaving his pronounced and indelible stamp on all, and he is therefore, in a strictly literary sense, the greater of the two.

BIOGRAPHY

Miguel de Unamuno y Jugo, the third of six children, was reared as a strict Catholic in Bilbao. His father died when he was six. Deeply religious as a child and adolescent, he began in 1880 his studies at the University of Madrid. There, under the influence of the skepticism in vogue at the time, he lost faith in some of his most cherished religious beliefs. The bulk of his vast literary production during the rest of his life stems from his anguished efforts to recapture the comfort and strength of his earlier faith through his own powers of reason rather than through humble acceptance of the Church's dogma. Fiercely rejecting all positivistic modes of thinking that denied tran-

Miguel de Unamuno y Jugo (Library of Congress)

scendental meaning in life, he nevertheless maintained open conflict with the Catholic Church until his death.

In 1883, Unamuno received his licentiate degree from the University of Madrid; in 1884, his doctorate. In 1891, he married and assumed the chair of Greek at the University of Salamanca, becoming rector of the University nine years later, a post in which he remained until 1914. In 1924, the Primo de Rivera dictatorship exiled him to the Canary Islands. From there, he fled to France, where he remained until 1930, when he returned to Spain. In 1931, he was reappointed rector of Salamanca, being granted lifelong tenure as rector when he retired from the faculty in 1934. Yet, his lifelong tenure was short-lived: He was dismissed because of his criticism of Francisco Franco. Unamuno died in his home on December 31, 1936.

Analysis

Miguel de Unamuno y Jugo wrote only eleven dramatic pieces. His first five dramas, three of which were one-act plays, are generally regarded as belong-

ing to his formative period as a playwright. *Phaedra*, written in 1910 though not staged until 1918 (in the Ateneo in Madrid), is the first of the six major plays of his maturity as a dramatist. Using Euripides' *Hippolytos* (428 B.C.E.; *Hippolytus*, 1781) as his starting point, Unamuno developed its plot differently and set the action in contemporary Spain.

Phaedra

In harmony with his own ideas about the theater, expounded in various essays on the theater but especially in *La regeneración del teatro español* (the regeneration of the Spanish theater) and *Teatro de teatro* (theater of theater), *Phaedra* is an example of simple or "naked" theater: no staging except for a sheet in the background, a table and chairs; the six characters (called "persons," not personages, by the author) in street clothes; no makeup or special lighting; and total unity of place in its three acts. In short, Unamuno believed in a return to simplicity with almost total reliance on dialogue. Anything seen onstage, including action, Unamuno insisted, should be avoided unless it reinforces what is heard. At the end of the play, for example, even Phaedra's death is communicated to the audience through dialogue.

In the first act, Phaedra reveals to Hipólito (Hippolytus), her stepson by virtue of her recent marriage to Pedro, her passionate carnal love for him. Hipólito rejects her. In the second act, after an interval during which Hipólito has carefully managed to avoid the desperate Phaedra, he is again approached by her. Again he rejects her despite her threat to accuse him falsely to Pedro of making amorous advances to her. When she carries out her threat, Hipólito nobly declines to defend himself, thus creating a rift between him and his father. The act ends with Phaedra's desperate contemplation of suicide.

In act 3, Phaedra, having attempted suicide, lies dying. Hipólito, who had left home, is summoned. He arrives in time to talk alone briefly with Phaedra before she expires. She leaves for Pedro a written confession of her false accusation of Hipólito. Thus, the play ends with the reconciliation in grief of father and son.

Through avoidance of sentimentality and of excessive intellectualization (so common in Unamuno's work); through great naturalness of dialogue and the creation of a lifelike situation; through the avoidance of explicit moralizing; and through sensible utilization of the mythological theme, *Phaedra* becomes convincingly realistic in its impact. A staunch believer in the implicit didactic purpose of art, Unamuno insisted that art, if truly representative of reality, teaches its own moral lesson. Unamuno proposed to write not traditional theater but theater directed at the inner consciousness, the inner reality of the spectator (or reader). *Phaedra* and the five full-length dramas that followed belong to what Iris M. Zavala (*Unamuno y su teatro de conciencia*, 1963) calls "theater of consciousness"—that is, a theater of "inner reality." Following the author's custom of not allowing publication of his plays until after they had been staged, *Phaedra* was not published until 1921.

SOLEDAD

After 1910, Unamuno, apparently disheartened by the poor reception accorded his plays by both the critics and the theatergoing public, temporarily abandoned the theater, turning instead to lyric poetry. Eleven years elapsed before he wrote his next play, *Soledad* (solitude), like *Phaedra* a three-act drama set in contemporary Spain. Although written in 1921, it was not staged until 1953, long after the author's death; it was published in 1954.

In act 1, Agustín, an idealistic dramatist who strongly resembles Unamuno, discusses the "world" of the theater in contrast to that of politics. Pressured by his wife, Soledad, who is jealous of Gloria, the actress who plays the leading feminine roles in her husband's plays, and by Pablo, a local politician, Agustín decides at the end of the act to enter politics. The setting for this act is Agustín's home: A picture of the couple's dead infant son is prominently placed on a desk, while the son's playhorse occupies a corner of the room. Childless since her son's death, Soledad is obviously obsessed with the desire to be a mother.

The setting for act 2 is the same as for act 1. An indefinite period of time has passed between acts, enough for Agustín to have failed totally in politics. He is now regarded as a political criminal and is in hiding in his own home. Obsessed with the problem of reality, Agustín rants and raves about the world of

politics being a farce, less "real" than the life of the theater he forsook for it. Fact and fiction become utterly confused in his mind, and he regresses to a kind of childhood in which he desires only Soledad ("solitude"). To him, she represents reality. Meanwhile, Sofía, his mother, who has suffered a severe stroke between acts, sits throughout act 2 speaking incoherent phrases that fit into the dialogue of others, creating a hilarious tragicomic mood; the act ends with Sofía's death.

In the final act, the setting is divided into two rooms: a bedroom (in which the son's playhorse and picture again appear) on the left and a reception room to the right. Since act 2, Agustín has suffered imprisonment. Now, however, he is again home. His mental confusion has worsened; Soledad is the only reality left to him. His regression to infancy (and a kind of innocence before the effects of "original sin," a Christian concept that is ever present in Unamuno) is complete. Its corollary is that Soledad has become his mother. The play ends with her singing him a lullaby and calling him "son of mine."

As is characteristic of Unamuno's theater, dialogue predominates in *Soledad*, dialogue full of anguished philosophical concerns with which the Spanish theatergoing public had little sympathy. Departing slightly from his concept of naked theater, Unamuno divided the stage in act 3 and made effective use of concrete props—the playhorse and the son's picture—throughout the play. Agustín's passion for probing the true nature of reality is an exaggeration of the author's own agonized spirit, a deformation of reality rather than its full-bodied incarnation, yet what Unamuno sought was the inner drama or "inner realism" of his personages, their struggles with or agonizing over deep inner conflicts. Both Agustín and Soledad are examples of Unamunian "agonists" (*agonistas*); they are agonists more than protagonists of external action.

RAQUEL ENCADENADA

The most extreme case of the woman-mother in all of Unamuno's works is Raquel in *Raquel encadenada* (Rachel in chains), written (as was *Soledad*) in 1921. It was first staged in Barcelona in 1926 under the title *Raquel*. In this four-act drama set in contemporary times, Raquel is a concert violinist married to Simón, her business manager. Because of his miserliness, Simón denies motherhood to her while using her simply as an instrument for making money.

Having married the miser Simón not for love but out of a desire to have a secure home in which to bear and rear children, Raquel abandons him for a former suitor, Aurelio, whose illegitimate child she had nursed back to health and whose children she will bear. She does this in open defiance of Spanish social conventions.

The play, despite its exaggeration of the maternal instinct in Raquel, has considerable merit. Its appeal lies in its freedom from Unamuno's typical philosophical-intellectual verbiage, its concentration on a believable (although unusual) situation, and its theme of frustrated motherhood (so easily understood in Spanish society). Unamuno preached loudly that drama must appeal not to the current theatergoing public in Spain but to the people, the *pueblo* (a term he refused to define but which generally means the great mass of relatively unschooled Spaniards). Yet his drama failed with the *pueblo* as well as with the critics of his time. He persistently refused to make concessions to the demands or realities of the Spanish theater—to write roles for specific actors or actresses, or to give in to the prevailing taste for visual effects. Indeed, from 1921 on, he dubbed his plays "drumas," not dramas, in his desire to emphasize, as Zavala states, that he wrote them not for the critics nor for the theatergoing public nor for actors or actresses but for the soul of the individual spectator or reader.

THE OTHER

The mystery of the final reality of the self was of consuming interest to Unamuno. One of his major explorations of this theme is *The Other*, written while he was in exile in Hendaya, France, in 1926. The play was not staged until 1932, the year in which it was first published. Subtitled "Mystery in Three Acts and an Epilogue," *The Other* probes the problem, the mystery, of one's final identity: A mystery cannot be understood by mere reasoning; only by participating in it can one come to a kind of understanding.

The setting throughout *The Other* is a room in the home of Cosme and his wife, Laura. While Laura

was out of the house, a murder was committed: Either Cosme killed his identical twin Damián, or Damián killed Cosme. The surviving twin now identifies himself as simply the "Other," refusing to admit which of the twins he is. In fact, he apparently no longer knows. Both Laura and Damiana, Damián's wife, claim him as their own, apparently indifferent both to his crime and to his real identity. He will accept neither woman, though Laura, Cosme's wife, finally yields him to Damiana, who is pregnant. At the end of act 3, the "Other" kills himself. In the epilogue, the "mystery" is discussed by Don Juan, the family doctor; Ernesto, Laura's brother; and "El Ama," the old family servant who was the twins' wet nurse. Though the "Ama" has known the twins since their infancy and must, therefore, surely know the identity of the assassin, she professes not to know, poetically philosophizing that no one knows who he or she really is.

The Unamunian theme that one must individualize one's self, be one's self, which means being different from others, is clearly here in central position. To be another, to be the "Other," is to fail to be oneself; the "Other" had no real existence and therefore committed suicide. Secondary to the theme of being one's true self (though that self cannot finally or fully be known in this life) is the Cain and Abel motif, which preoccupied Unamuno throughout his life. It was one twin's frustration in having no social identity or "self" separate from that of his twin that drove him to hate his brother and finally to murder him.

Though *The Other* is one of the two plays by Unamuno most available to readers and most often discussed in criticism (the other one being *El hermano Juan*), it is not at all his best play, at least not from the point of view of its effectiveness on the stage. Although its philosophical meaning is rich, the situation portrayed in it is in itself quite unreal or unbelievable. It should not, however, be judged too harshly because of its lack of realism; essentially, it was written as an allegory.

EL HERMANO JUAN

Although never staged, *El hermano Juan: O, El mundo es teatro* (brother John: or, the world is a stage), which was written in 1927, is one of Unamuno's best-known and most easily obtainable plays, primarily because it dramatizes the author's peculiar conception of the popular Don Juan theme and not because of its merits as theater per se. A long three-act drama set in contemporary Spain, *El hermano Juan* presents Don Juan as impotent (an anti-Don Juan) and a prisoner of the social image or legend of himself foisted on him by others; he merely plays the role expected of him by his creators, those who imagine him. In a long soliloquy in act 2, John questions even his own existence. In the final act, having become a Franciscan brother, he dies in a convent; his prolonged death scene is one of the best features of the play. Death, in fact, is a powerful theme well presented throughout the work.

Although the Don Juan theme still has enormous vitality in the Spanish-speaking world and especially in Spain, it is not at all surprising that Unamuno's version of the theme has never been staged: An impotent Don Juan is unappealing. The play's chief merit lies in its portrayal of life as theater, a frequent theme with Unamuno; Don Juan can do no other than enact on the stage of life the role assigned to him by his creators—by those who through the centuries have imagined him into existence.

OTHER MAJOR WORKS

LONG FICTION: *Paz en la guerra*, 1897 (*Peace in War*, 1983); *Amor y pedagogía*, 1902; *Niebla*, 1914 (*Mist: A Tragicomic Novel*, 1928); *Abel Sánchez: Una historia de pasión*, 1917 (*Abel Sánchez*, 1947); *Tres novelas ejemplares y un prólogo*, 1920 (*Three Exemplary Novels and a Prologue*, 1930); *La tía Tula*, 1921 (*Tía Tula*, 1976); *San Manuel Bueno, mártir*, 1931 (*Saint Manuel Bueno, Martyr*, 1956); *Dos novelas cortas*, 1961 (James Russell Stamm and Herbert Eugene Isar, editors).

SHORT FICTION: *El espejo de la muerte*, 1913; *Soledad y otros cuentos*, 1937.

POETRY: *Poesías*, 1907; *Rosario de sonetos líricos*, 1911; *El Cristo de Velázquez*, 1920 (*The Christ of Velázquez*, 1951); *Rimas de dentro*, 1923; *Teresa*, 1924; *Romancero del destierro*, 1928; *Poems*, 1952; *Cancionero: Diario poético*, 1953 (partial translation as *The Last Poems of Miguel de Unamuno*, 1974).

NONFICTION: *De la enseñanza superior en España*, 1899; *Nicodemo el fariseo*, 1899; *Tres ensayos*, 1900; *En torno al casticismo*, 1902; *De mi país*, 1903; *Vida de Don Quijote y Sancho según Miguel de Cervantes Saavedra, explicada y comentada por Miguel de Unamuno*, 1905 (*The Life of Don Quixote and Sancho According to Miguel de Cervantes Saavedra Expounded with Comment by Miguel de Unamuno*, 1927); *Recuerdos de niñez y de mocedad*, 1908; *Mi religión y otros ensayos breves*, 1910; *Soliloquios y conversaciones*, 1911 (*Essays and Soliloquies*, 1925); *Contra esto y aquello*, 1912; *Del sentimiento trágico de la vida en los hombres y en los pueblos*, 1913 (*The Tragic Sense of Life in Men and in Peoples*, 1921); *La agonía del Cristianismo*, 1925 (*The Agony of Christianity*, 1928, 1960; in French *L'Agonie du Christianisme*, 1931); *Cómo se hace una novela*, 1927 (*How to Make a Novel*, 1976); *La ciudad de Henoc*, 1941; *Cuenca ibérica*, 1943; *Paisajes del alma*, 1944; *La enormidad de España*, 1945; *Visiones y commentarios*, 1949.

MISCELLANEOUS: *Obras completas*, 1959-1964 (16 volumes).

BIBLIOGRAPHY

Ch'oe, Chae-Sok. *Greene and Unamuno: Two Pilgrims to La Mancha*. New York: Peter Lang, 1990. This comparison of the Christian fiction of Unamuno and Graham Greene sheds light on the religious themes employed by Unamuno in his dramatic works. Bibliography and index.

Ellis, Robert Richmond. *The Tragic Pursuit of Being: Unamuno and Sartre*. Tuscaloosa: University of Alabama Press, 1988. This work compares and contrasts the existentialism revealed in the works of Unamuno and Jean-Paul Sartre. Bibliography and index.

Hansen, Keith W. *Tragic Lucidity: Discourse of Recuperation in Unamuno and Camus*. New York: Peter Lang, 1993. A comparison of the political and social views of Unamuno and Albert Camus, as evidenced in their literary works. Bibliography.

Nozick, Martin *Miguel de Unamuno*. New York: Twayne, 1971. A basic biography of Unamuno that covers his life and works. Bibliography.

Round, Nicholas G., ed. *Re-reading Unamuno*. Glasgow, Scotland: University of Glasgow Department of Hispanic Studiies, 1989. This collection of papers from a conference on Unamuno provides literary criticism of his works. Bibliographies.

Sinclair, Alison. *Uncovering the Mind: Unamuno, the Unknown, and the Vicissitudes of Self*. New York: Manchester University Press, 2002. An ex-amination of the fictional works of Unamuno in respect to his portrayal of the self. Bibliography and index.

Wyers, Frances. *Miguel de Unamuno, the Contrary Self*. London: Tamesis, 1976. A look at the image of self in the literary works of Unamuno. Bibliography.

Charles L. King

RODOLFO USIGLI

Born: Mexico City, Mexico; November 17, 1905
Died: Mexico City, Mexico; June 18, 1979

PRINCIPAL DRAMA

El niño y la niebla, wr. 1936, pr., pb. 1951
Estado de secreto, pr. 1936, pb. 1963
Medio tono, pr. 1937, pb. 1938 (*The Great Middle Class*, 1968)
La mujer no hace milagros, pr. 1939, pb. 1949
La familia cena en casa, pr., pb. 1942
El gesticulador, pb. 1944, pr. 1947
Otra primavera, pr. 1945, pb. 1947 (*Another Springtime*, 1961)
Corona de sombra, pr., pb. 1947 (*Crown of Shadows*, 1946)
Jano es una muchacha, pr., pb. 1952
Un día de éstos, pr. 1954, pb. 1957 (*One of These Days*, 1971)
Corona de fuego, pr., pb. 1960
Corona de luz: La virgen, pr. 1963, pb. 1965 (*Crown of Light*, 1971)

OTHER LITERARY FORMS

Although Rodolfo Usigli is recognized principally as a playwright, he has worked in other genres as well. His theoretical works on the theater, in general, and the Mexican theater, in particular, include: *México en el teatro* (1932; *Mexico in the Theater*, 1976), *Caminos del teatro en México* (1933; paths of the theater in Mexico), *Itinerario del autor dramático y otros ensayos* (1940; itinerary of a dramatist), and *Anatomía del teatro* (1966; anatomy of the theater). He has also produced two theoretical essays on the theater titled "Ensayo sobre la actualidad de la poesía dramática" (essay on the actuality of dramatic poetry) and "Epílogo sobre la hipocresía del Mexicano" (epilogue on the hypocrisy of the Mexican). Usigli's poetry is collected in a volume entitled *Conversación desesperada* (1938; desperate conversation). He has also produced a novel, *Ensayo de un crimen* (trial of a crime), which was published in 1944.

ACHIEVEMENTS

Rodolfo Usigli has been hailed as the father of Mexican theater. He introduced authentic dramatic representations of Mexico through works that addressed its history, its politics, and the psychological makeup of its people. The psychological factor is the core of his theater.

Usigli does not merely criticize the Mexican people and their society: Rather, he seeks to ennoble them by offering them models of their own potential greatness. Usigli accomplishes this by introducing the concept of myth formation. The concept of myth formation has its roots in Georg Wilhelm Friedrich Hegel's conception of the historical process as a series of syntheses that revolve around transcendental historical figures such as Maximilian and Montezuma, who represent superior cultural symbols. From a cultural and theatrical perspective, a myth is a transcendental synthesis embodied in one of these figures that offers a new perspective, a positive direction for the country's future growth. Its direct appeal to the faith of the Mexican audience causes them to reevaluate their mythical past and to experience a catharsis of nationality with those national sentiments and values that most ennoble it. In recognition of his efforts to create a Mexican national theater, Usigli was awarded the Premio Nacional de Letras in 1972.

Usigli's determination to forge a sense of national identity for Mexico, his sense of the Mexican spirit and the originality with which he expresses it in his plays, and the increased awareness he offers Mexican audiences of their national identity, culture, history, and values constitute his most important achievements.

BIOGRAPHY

Rodolfo Usigli was born in Mexico City, Mexico, on November 17, 1905, the product of Italian, Austrian, and Polish ancestry. Usigli demonstrated his interest in the theater at an early age. When he was eleven years old, he worked as an extra in the Castillo-Taboada troupe at Mexico's Teatro Colón. He wished to study drama, but there were no established schools of drama in Mexico at that time. Therefore, he designed his own curriculum whereby he read and analyzed on a daily basis six plays by well-known dramatists. He then attended local performances, at which he compared the dramas he studied with the actual stage productions. His commentaries were published in Mexican newspapers. By the time he reached the age of twenty, he had become a respected theater critic.

Usigli met with little success in finding producers for his first dramatic attempts. His difficulties with managers, producers, and critics may perhaps be traced to unhappy childhood experiences. Usigli was born with slightly crossed eyes, a person the Spaniards call *bizco*. His classmates punned on the word and nicknamed him *Visconde* (Viscount), which also alluded to his conviction of being superior to them. He later underwent corrective surgery for his eyes but never lost his conviction about his superiority, which often expressed itself in an arrogance and

defensiveness that theater authorities found unappealing.

From 1932 to 1934, Usigli offered courses in the history of the Mexican theater at the University of Mexico and served as director of the Teatro Radiofónico, which broadcast plays in conjunction with the Ministry of Education. During this period, he was also associated with the Teatro Orientación, which was created to introduce Mexico to the masterpieces of world theater, performing plays translated from French, Italian, English, German, and Russian. Usigli prepared the Spanish versions for the stage. In 1935, Usigli was awarded a scholarship to study dramatic composition at Yale University. During this period, he wrote *El gesticulador* (the pretender), one of his greatest works. On his return to Mexico, he was appointed director of the school of drama and theater and director of the department of fine arts at the University of Mexico. In 1940, he founded his own theater, the Teatro Media Noche, to produce his Mexican plays, but ongoing problems with producers soon ended this venture.

During the period from 1943 to 1946, Usigli served Mexico in a diplomatic capacity, becoming the cultural attaché at the Mexican embassy in Paris. During his tenure in Europe, he had the opportunity to meet his idol, playwright George Bernard Shaw. Also during this period, he completed another of his great works, *Crown of Shadows*, part of a trilogy about the three Mexican myths of sovereignty. (The other works in the trilogy are *Corona de fuego*—crown of fire—and *Crown of Light*.) After completing his tour of duty, Usigli returned to Mexico and offered courses at the University of Mexico in the history of the theater and playwriting. He completed The Corona Trilogy and several other plays.

Usigli resumed his diplomatic career from 1956 until 1962, serving as Mexico's ambassador to Lebanon and Norway. During this period and after his return to Mexico, he continued to produce dramatic works.

ANALYSIS

Mexico and its people have furnished the material for almost all of Rodolfo Usigli's dramatic works.

Psychology is the essential component of his writing and the soul of his interpretations. Usigli's dramatic works can be classified into two major categories: the social satire of contemporary Mexico, and the treatment of certain historically significant figures or periods in the development of Mexico. The themes most frequently treated are insanity, hate, love, hereditary illness, stagnant lifestyle, cruelty, sex from a Mexican perspective, and culminating moments in Mexican history.

There are four elements that constantly recur in Usigli's plays: fantasy, myth, family types, and humor. Fantasy is present in all of his works. Through examples that illustrate his philosophy, he sets the course that propels the action and motivates the characters: madness, absurdity, dreams, superstition, double identity, and illusions. The element of the fantastic is reinforced by dramatic techniques such as the play of lights, visions, flashbacks, and anonymous voices. Myth is of utmost importance in Usigli's works. He sees Mexico as an outstanding example of a fusion of two cultures, the indigenous and the Hispanic, both of which are myth-oriented. Within the framework of Usigli's Hegelian view of history, the central characters become transcendental myth figures. He uses myth to reinterpret historical events, clarifying their significance and offering a new and positive direction for Mexico's future. Another recurring element found in Usigli's dramatic productions is the character types based on members of the family. He treats all social levels—lower, middle, upper, and aristocratic—to portray segments of Mexican society. Usigli's acute awareness of the inconsistencies in Mexican life and culture are often expressed in witty dialogue and amusing episodes.

The Great Middle Class, *El gesticulador*, and *Crown of Shadows* are considered to be Usigli's finest works. Each portrays a conflict that tests the spirit. Human emotions are presented so as to diminish the distance between the public and the stage. Ridicule is not provoked from pathetic situations; rather, the audience feels a sense of spiritual elevation at the conclusion of each of these dramas.

Usigli dedicated his life to the creation of a Mexican national theater. He combined practical experi-

ence, a keen sense of the Mexican spirit, a thorough knowledge of the theater, stylistic creativity, and a new ideology to establish the basis for a new Mexican theater. His dramas are neither didactic nor doctrinal, but objective in their thematic treatment. Usigli's desire was to bring the past and the present into harmony, to see them in a positive light, and to appeal to the faith of the Mexican people to overcome their weaknesses and gain a new and optimistic perspective on their country's future. Through his acting, translating, teaching, and writing, he played a decisive part in the creation of a Mexican national theater.

THE GREAT MIDDLE CLASS

In the sociological drama *The Great Middle Class*, the mundane Sierra family is transformed by Usigli into a universal symbol of middle-class family life. This play depicts the problems that beset a typical middle-class family, not only in Mexico but anywhere in the world. Each family member has his own particular problem. The father has lost his job with the government because of his political affiliation and has taken refuge in pursuing other women. The mother's overwhelming religious character prevents her from seeing that anything is wrong. Their sons also have problems. David, the eldest son and moderator of the family, suffers from tuberculosis. Victor is unhappy because he has no money with which to court a girl whom he has just met. Julio finds that everyone is hostile to him because of his Communist sympathies. Martin, the youngest son, is interested only in animals and is unhappy because animals are not allowed in their apartment. The daughters are also unhappy with their situations. Gabriela is frustrated because she cannot find a political party compatible with her beliefs; Enriqueta is suffering from the banalities of married life and from grave financial problems after the bankruptcy of her husband's store; Sarah is in love with someone of whom the family does not approve. David alone realizes that the only form of salvation is unity. Still, it seems that each one must find his way by himself or herself because each finds the others to be incapable of understanding and showing compassion. An atmosphere of dissension, pessimism, confusion, and egotism prevails. Unknowingly, however, the family members share a sense of unity that will surface during a grave crisis.

At the end of the drama, the circumstances are much more serious than at the beginning. The father moves the family, which is very poor, to another province, and he must sell much of the family furniture in order to pay the rent. The mother is able to recognize and acknowledge her family's difficulties and suffers much, knowing that Gabriela spent the night in jail for attending a Communist rally. David enters the hospital to seek help for his illness. Julio leaves for Spain to fight against the forces of Francisco Franco and the Fascists, and Sarah is pregnant. The difference, however, lies in the sense of consolidation and unity among the members of the family and their attempts to rescue one another. They feel a new freedom in thought and action, born of the now-prevailing atmosphere of mutual love and respect.

The Sierra family is a typical example of the trials and tribulations of any middle-class family anywhere in the world. The value of this drama lies in the fact that Usigli, by presenting the life of the Sierra family in a universal light, successfully transcended national boundaries and won the empathy of other frontiers. Psychologically, Usigli appealed to a fundamental element of Mexican society: the clan instinct, the overpowering desire of family members to overcome their personal differences, no matter what the sacrifice or price, in order to ensure the continuation of their line.

EL GESTICULADOR

El gesticulador, like *The Great Middle Class*, deals with conflict and the psychology of human emotions. They are presented from a political perspective, however, and involve the concept of myth formation. *El gesticulador* is the story of a professor of revolutionary history, César Rubio, who loses his job for political reasons and returns with his family to his native province. He realizes that his life has been a failure and is afraid that he has been a sorry example to his children. During a chance meeting with a historian from the United States, César, on a promise of secrecy, assumes the identity of a glorified revolutionary general of the same name whose fate had been a mystery. César then uses his acquired identity to run for provincial governor. He is assassinated and

dies a famous man. César's son finally learns the truth but is powerless to proclaim it. If he exposes his father as an impostor and is believed, it would arouse little indignation; if he is not believed, he would be incarcerated as an insane political agitator.

In the structure of *El gesticulador*, there is a clear progression toward the formation and propagation of a myth. The work is divided into three acts. Act 1 introduces César and the character he assumes, General César Rubio. The arrival of Bolton, the historian from the United States, looking for information about the general, causes a psychological change in the personality of César, who almost instantly believes himself to be the general. This enables Usigli to introduce the element of predestination, which is made manifest in three ways: by the arrival of the failed professor and his family in his native town, where, coincidentally, two men share the same name and one is a hero; by the attitude of the other family members toward César; and by the arrival of the American historian Bolton. César, desperate because of his family's rejection of him, acts solely on his instincts in an effort to save himself.

Act 2 traces the development of the myth, César's assumption of the false identity that permits him to overcome his sense of inadequacy. His family plays a large part in this. The family functions as a chorus— they serve as César's conscience and externalize his inner conflict. His wife represents the part of his conscience that wants to liberate itself from the lie. His precocious son suspects that something is amiss and becomes very disgusted. His daughter, however, represents the other side of his conscience. She shares her father's sense of failure because she believes that she is ugly and socially unacceptable. Because she aspires to be loved and to live well, she sees something positive in her father's new lifestyle and encourages him. Finally, César accepts the lie, the past becomes the present, the myth begins to take root, and optimism becomes the prevailing mood of the play.

Act 3 presents the propagation of the myth. At the beginning of the act, César is converted into the universal candidate who has reached the peak of glory. He is respected and loved by his people. Yet the confrontation between César and his colleague Navarro interrupts the euphoria. The meeting between the two rivals illustrates the theme of truth against illusion. Navarro wants to denounce him as a fraud to all the people. The most important event of act 3 is César's assassination. With his death, the myth will never be separated from the man. Navarro immediately changes his attitude toward César and proclaims him a true hero. The myth is engraved in the public mind; it is stronger than reality.

In this work, Usigli uses the Revolution to focus on Mexico and its people. The false César Rubio is not regarded in a negative light. Rather, he is revered as a hero for assuming a new identity to affirm his faith in the Revolution and ultimately to die for it. Psychologically, the Mexican concept of heroism is infantile. A hero is not expected to perform only one great deed but rather constantly to provide examples of heroism during his lifetime. Mexico had no such heroes. The hero César Rubio evolved because a conflict arose that created a need for one of these heroes in a historical event that was purely Mexican. Thus, Usigli was able to save the intention of the Revolution, metamorphose it, and convert it into a positive growth symbol for Mexico. It is interesting to note that Usigli dedicated *El gesticulador* to his hypocritical countrymen because of their tendency to hide from reality and avoid the truth by putting on other faces. By exposing this character flaw, Usigli hoped to chide his countrymen out of this weakness.

CROWN OF SHADOWS

Crown of Shadows shares with *The Great Middle Class* and *El gesticulador* the theme of conflict and an acute psychological analysis of the Mexican people and their ideologies. Like *El gesticulador*, it deals with myth. It is part of a trilogy devoted to three fundamental Mexican myths: political sovereignty (*Crown of Shadows*: Benito Juárez versus Maximilian), territorial or national sovereignty (*Corona de fuego*: Cuauhtémoc versus Hernán Cortés), and spiritual sovereignty (*Crown of Light*: the synthesis of paganism and Catholicism).

Crown of Shadows is a reinterpretation of the history of Maximilian and Carlota presented as a modernized version of an Aristotelian tragedy. In this set-ting, the psychological projection of his characters, rather than the action, is emphasized. This drama involves the conflict between fate and justice. Maximilian and Carlota abide by completely opposite moral codes yet share an adverse fate. Maximilian is a novice in the political world and dies, without ever having committed any wrongdoing, for a country that never accepted him. He is sacrificed for the deeds of another politician, namely Napoleon Bonaparte. Carlota, on the other hand, is driven by a strong sense of ambition for which she is punished by the death of her husband and seventy years of madness.

This play has been widely lauded for its innovative theatrical techniques. The stage is divided, which helps to evoke and reconstruct the past and allows for rapid shifts of space, simultaneous action, and the juxtaposition of time using flashbacks. Some psychological symbols are presented by crossing planes of reality. For example, in the first scene, when the doorman is guiding Erasmo Ramírez, the Mexican historian, through Carlota's home, visible reality, such as the terrace and the garden, is described using the verb "to seem." An unreal environment as well as a sense of atemporality is constructed. Another example occurs when Carlota becomes confused and believes that she is speaking to Juárez, her husband's rival. The error establishes the symbolism present in the title: It alludes to her insanity and her illusion of power. Her constant demands for more light symbolize a brief recovery of her reason, during which time she clarifies historical reality to her listener.

Usigli's purpose in writing *Crown of Shadows* was to justify the misfortune suffered by Maximilian and Carlota by suggesting its ultimate positive significance. He classifies the play as antihistorical, treating his characters as human beings rather than historical figures. Thus, he was able to present them at various levels: husband and wife, rulers, foreigners. He succeeded in ennobling this period of Mexican history through Erasmo Ramírez, the Mexican historian: His name recalls the Dutch scholar who sought reforms from within. The audience, and the historian, are able to review and reconcile themselves to the past. They are able to see that Maximilian loved Mexico and sensed the essence of the nation—its ancient symbols and bloody upheavals—and that his death was in fact a catalyst for the birth of Mexican nationalism.

OTHER MAJOR WORKS

LONG FICTION: *Ensayo de un crimen*, 1944.

POETRY: *Conversación desesperada*, 1938.

NONFICTION: *México en el teatro*, 1932 (*Mexico in the Theater*, 1976); *Caminos del teatro en México*, 1933; *Itinerario del autor dramático y otros ensayos*, 1940; *Anatomía del teatro*, 1966.

BIBLIOGRAPHY

Beardsell, Peter R. *A Theatre for Cannibals: Rodolfo Usigli and the Mexican Stage*. Rutherford, N.J.: Fairleigh Dickinson University Press, 1992. A study of the dramatic works of Usigli and of the Mexican theater of his times. Bibliography and index.

Jones, Willis Knapp. Introduction to *Two Plays: "Crown of Light," "One of These Days,"* by Rodolfo Usigli. Translated by Thomas Bledsoe. Carbondale: Southern Illinois University Press, 1971. In his introduction to the translation of two of Usigli's plays, Jones provides information on Usigli's life and dramatic works.

Savage, Ronald Vance. "Rodolfo Usigli's Idea of Mexican Theatre." *Latin American Theatre Review* 4, no. 2 (1971): 13-20. This essay examines the Mexican theater according to the viewpoint of Usigli.

Tilles, Solomon H. "Rodolfo Usigli's Concept of Dramatic Art." *Latin American Theatre Review* 3, no. 2 (1970): 31-38. A discussion of drama as conceived by Usigli.

Anne Laura Mattrella

V

LUIS MIGUEL VALDEZ

Born: Delano, California; June 26, 1940

PRINCIPAL DRAMA

The Theft, pr. 1961
The Shrunken Head of Pancho Villa, pr. 1965, pb. 1967
Las dos caras del patroncito, pr. 1965, pb. 1971
La quinta temporada, pr. 1966, pb. 1971
Los vendidos, pr. 1967, pb. 1971
Dark Root of a Scream, pr. 1967, pb. 1973
La conquista de México, pr. 1968, pb. 1971 (puppet play)
No saco nada de la escuela, pr. 1969, pb. 1971
The Militants, pr. 1969, pb. 1971
Vietnam campesino, pr. 1970, pb. 1971
Huelguistas, pr. 1970, pb. 1971
Bernabé, pr. 1970, pb. 1976
Soldado razo, pr., pb. 1971
Actos, pb. 1971 (includes *Las dos caras del patroncito*, *La quinta temporada*, *Los vendidos*, *La conquista de México*, *No saco nada de la escuela*, *The Militants*, *Vietnam campesino*, *Huelguistas*, and *Soldado razo*)
Las pastorelas, pr. 1971 (adaptation of a sixteenth century Mexican shepherd's play)
La Virgen del Tepeyac, pr. 1971 (adaptation of *Las cuatro apariciones de la Virgen de Guadalupe*)
Los endrogados, pr. 1972
Los olivos pits, pr. 1972
La gran carpa de los rasquachis, pr. 1973
Mundo, pr. 1973
El baille de los gigantes, pr. 1973
El fin del mundo, pr. 1975
Zoot Suit, pr. 1978, pb. 1992
Bandido!, pr. 1981, pb. 1992, revised pr. 1994
Corridos, pr. 1983

"I Don't Have to Show You No Stinking Badges!," pr., pb. 1986
Luis Valdez—Early Works: Actos, Bernabé, and Pensamiento Serpentino, pb. 1990
Zoot Suit and Other Plays, pb. 1992
Mummified Deer, pr. 2000

OTHER LITERARY FORMS

Although Luis Miguel Valdez is known primarily for his plays, his writing on Chicano culture has had a significant impact. In a number of essays initially in the 1960's and 1970's ("Theatre: El Teatro Campesino," "Notes on Chicano Theatre," and several others), he elaborated an aesthetic based on what he believed to be the special features of Chicano reality: bilingualism, *mestizaje* (mixed race), and cultural disinheritance. Valdez's commitment to Chicano nationalism is reflected in two important works of nontheatrical writing—*Aztlan: An Anthology of Mexican American Literature* (1972; coedited with Stan Steiner), whose lengthy introduction recounts the history of the Chicano people as the original inhabitants of "Aztlan" (the contemporary American Southwest), and *Pensamiento Serpentino: A Chicano Approach to the Theatre of Reality* (1973), which explores the influence of Aztec and Mayan spirituality on Chicano art and thought. It is in this latter book that all of Valdez's published poetry can be found.

ACHIEVEMENTS

Without Luis Miguel Valdez, the Chicano theater would not exist in its present vibrant form. At the age of twenty-five, in the fields of rural California, without financial backing and using farm laborers as actors, Valdez single-handedly created a movement that has since become international in scope, leading to the founding of Chicano theater troupes from Los

Angeles, California, to Gary, Indiana. Although not usually mentioned in the company of revered American playwrights of his generation, such as Sam Shepard, David Mamet, and Richard Foreman, he is in many ways as distinguished and as well known internationally, both in Europe and in Latin America.

In one respect especially, Valdez has accomplished what no other American playwright has: the creation of a genuine workers' theater, completely indigenous and the work of neither university intellectuals nor producers of a commercialized "mass culture." He has made "serious" drama popular, political drama entertaining, and ethnic drama universal.

Valdez has won acclaim in two parallel but distinct artistic communities. If his early career fits neatly within the contours of the cultural nationalism of the Civil Rights movement (whose Chicano forms in the American Southwest are perhaps less well known than the African American forms of the South), he found a hearing also in more established circles. One of the original organizers for the United Farm Workers Union, a tireless propagandist for Chicano identity, and a founder of an annual cultural festival in Fresno, California, he has also been a founding member of the California Arts Council. In addition to this, he served on a congressional subcommittee of the National Endowment for the Arts and on the board of directors of the Theatre Communications Group, and he acted in teleplays and films based on his own work. Winning an honorary Obie Award in 1968 for his work on the West Coast, he appropriately was the first, ten years later, to produce a Chicano play on Broadway, the highly acclaimed *Zoot Suit*.

He cannot, however, be seen simply as a major playwright. His fortunate position as a public figure at the first serious outbreak of Chicano nationalism, in the mid-1960's—which he helped articulate and which helped articulate him—makes him also an emblematic representative of American cultural politics, especially as it regards the important (and often forgotten) Latino community.

Crucial in this respect is his groundbreaking book, *Aztlan*, which brings together writings from the pre-Columbian period to the late twentieth century, sketching a picture of Chicanos as a distinct people

with a long tradition and an active history. Valdez's passionate commitment to Chicano nationalism must be seen as a driving force of his art. If *Aztlan* defiantly underlines the uniqueness of the Chicano in an alienating landscape of oppressive Anglo institutions, his next book, *Pensamiento Serpentino*, emphasizes the evils of artificially separating peoples on the basis of race and culture; it argues for a common North American experience in a spirit of forgiveness and mutual cooperation and derives its moral approach to contemporary social problems from Aztec and Mayan teachings.

The rarity of someone from Valdez's background and interests finding so distinctive a public voice cannot be underestimated. Nevertheless, his greatest work is probably the legacy he leaves to Chicano culture itself. The Centro Campesino Cultural, a non-profit corporation he founded in Del Rey, California, in 1967, became a clearinghouse for Chicano artists around the country and operated film, publishing, and musical recording facilities for their use. Inspired by the success of El Teatro Campesino, many other groups have come into being. Some of the most important are Teatro Urbano, Teatro de la Esperanza, El Teatro de la Gente, and El Teatro Desengañó del Pueblo. It is the pioneering work of Valdez that has allowed these vital regional theaters to operate in a coordinated and organized fashion under a national network known as TENAZ (Teatro Nacional de Aztlan), a direct offshoot of the Centro Campesino Cultural.

BIOGRAPHY

Luis Miguel Valdez was born on June 26, 1940, in Delano, California, the second of ten brothers and sisters. His father and mother were migrant farmworkers. Already working in the fields by the age of six, Valdez spent his childhood traveling to the harvests in the agricultural centers of the San Joaquin Valley. Despite having little uninterrupted early schooling, he managed to win a scholarship to San Jose State College in 1960.

Soon after his arrival at college, he won a regional playwriting contest for his first one-act play, *The Theft*. Encouraged by his teachers to write a full-length work, Valdez complied with *The Shrunken Head of Pancho Villa*, which was promptly produced by the San Jose State drama department. Graduating with a bachelor's degree in English in 1964, Valdez spent the next several months traveling in Cuba; on his return, he joined the San Francisco Mime Troupe under Ron Davis, where he worked for one year, learning from the troupe's *commedia dell'arte* techniques, which he was later to adapt in new ways.

Partly as a result of the sense of solidarity that he gained from his experiences while in Cuba, Valdez returned home to Delano, where the United Farm Workers Union was then being formed under the leadership of César Chávez. Amid a strike for union recognition, the union officials responded enthusiastically to Valdez's offer to create an educational theater group. Using volunteer actors from among the strikers, he formed El Teatro Campesino in 1965. Traveling on a flatbed truck from field to field, the troupe produced a series of one-act political skits dubbed *actos* (actions, or gestures), performing them in churches, storefronts, and on the edges of the fields themselves.

Enormously successful, the plays soon won outside attention and led to a United States tour in the summer of 1967. Later that year, Valdez left the fields to found the Centro Campesino Cultural in Del Rey, California. Similar recognition followed, with an Obie Award in New York in 1969 for "creating a workers' theater to demonstrate the politics of survival" and an invitation to perform at the Theatre des Nations festival in Nancy, France—one of four tours to Europe between 1969 and 1980. Later in 1969, Valdez and the troupe moved to Fresno, California, where they founded an annual Chicano theater festival, and Valdez began teaching drama at Fresno State College.

The Centro Campesino Cultural relocated once again in 1971 to San Juan Bautista, a small rural California town, where it would stay for the next several years, rooting itself in the community and transforming its dramaturgy to reflect local concerns—particularly through its adaptations of earlier devotional drama dating from the Spanish occupation. El Teatro Campesino there underwent a fundamental

transformation. Living more or less in a commune, the group began increasingly to emphasize the spiritual side of their work, as derived not only from the prevalent Christianity of the typical Chicano community but also from their own newfound Aztec and Mayan roots. This shift from the agitational *actos* to a search for spiritual solutions was met with anger by formerly admiring audiences at the Quinto Festival de los Teatros Chicanos in Mexico City in 1974.

From its base in San Juan Bautista, the Centro Campesino Cultural continued to flourish, touring campuses and communities on a yearly basis; giving financial support, training, and advice to other theater troupes; and hosting visitors such as English director Peter Brook, who brought his actors from the International Centre of Theatre Research in 1973. After a career of refusing to participate in the commercial theater, Valdez determined finally, in 1978, to try reaching a middle-class audience. The result was *Zoot Suit*, a polished, full-length dance-musical based on the Sleepy Lagoon murder trial of 1943. It premiered at the Mark Taper Forum in Los Angeles in 1978 and ran for eleven months. The play opened at the Wintergarden Theatre on Broadway in 1979 but was forced to close after a month because of bad reviews. A film version of the play was made in 1981. In 1985, *Soldado razo* and *Dark Root of a Scream* were performed for the first time in New York at the Public Theatre as part of a Latino theater festival.

Valdez brought Tony Curiel into El Teatro Campesino in 1985 to help run the company. Valdez's play *"I Don't Have to Show You No Stinking Badges!"* (a famous line from the 1948 film *The Treasure of the Sierra Madre*) was coproduced with the Los Angeles Theatre Center in 1986. The film *La Bamba* (1987), written and directed by Valdez, was the first major release to celebrate the urban Hispanic youth lifestyle.

In 1991, a trio of *actos* from earlier El Teatro Campesino projects were presented in Dallas at the South Dallas Cultural Center; reviewers noted that they remained "remarkably fresh and quick-witted." *Soldado razo*, a 1970's play of protest about Chicano involvement in the Vietnam War, was revived in San Jose, California, in 1991.

El Teatro Campesino began the process of restructuring in 1988, learning to work more independently of Valdez, although his commitment to it remained substantial. On July 29, 1990, in a retrospective in the *Los Angeles Times* in celebration of Valdez's fiftieth birthday ("Luis Valdez at Fifty: The Rage Has Cooled"), the playwright, firmly established in Hollywood, admitted: "I couldn't turn around and kiss the teatro good-bye . . . without ruining my chances in Hollywood . . . my roots would dry up. I need to be true to what I set out to do."

In 2001, in a keynote address for the American Society for Theatre Research, with a new play in production and a forthcoming anthology, Valdez reaffirmed his commitment to El Teatro Campesino, Chicano Theatre, politicization and his work.

ANALYSIS

Luis Miguel Valdez's genius was to reach an audience both Chicano and working-class, not only with political farces about strikers, "scabs," and bosses in a familiar street-theater concept but also by incorporating the popular theatrical forms of Latin America itself: the *carpas* (traveling theater shows), *variedades* (Mexican vaudeville), *corridos* (traditional Mexican folk ballads), and others. It is a unique combination to which Valdez added his own distinctive forms. Appraising Valdez's work is, however, different from appraising that of most other playwrights of his stature. By political conviction and by necessity, much of his œuvre is a collective product. Although he has always been El Teatro Campesino's major creative inspiration and although entire passages from the collective plays were written by him alone, Valdez's drama is largely a joint project under his guidance—a collective political and religious celebration.

The starting point for all of Valdez's work is his evocation of what he calls *la plebe, el vulgo,* or simply *La Raza,* that is, the Chicano people. It is from this outlook that the first *actos* were created—a genre very close to the Brechtian *Lehrstück* (teaching piece), with its episodic structure, its use of broad social types, its indifference to all but the most minimal of props and scenery, and its direct involvement of the audience in the solving of its dramatized social problems. In Valdez's words, the *actos* "must be popular, subject to no other critics except the pueblo itself, but it must also educate the pueblo toward an appreciation of *social change,* on and off the stage."

According to various accounts, the form was first developed in a Delano storefront, where Valdez had assembled his would-be performers from among the strikers. He hung signs around their necks that read: *huelguista* (striker), *esquirol* (scab), and *patroncito* (little boss) and then simply asked them to show what had happened that day on the picket line. After some hesitation, the actors performed an impromptu political play, alive with their own jargon and bawdy jokes and inspired by the passions of the labor dispute within which they found themselves.

Valdez's theatrical vision is inseparable from the conditions under which he founded El Teatro Campesino in the farmworkers' strike of 1965. Born in struggle, his early plays all have a vitality, directness, and urgency that cannot be divorced from their lasting appeal. His achievement blossoms finally with his successful incorporation of the deep cultural roots of the Chicano nation, which are found in the religious imagery of the *indio* past. Both facets of his career have been widely copied by other Chicano directors and playwrights and admired widely outside the Chicano community as well.

LAS DOS CARAS DEL PATRONCITO

One exemplary early *acto* is *Las dos caras del patroncito* (the two faces of the boss), in which a typical undocumented worker, recruited fresh from Mexico by a California landowner in order to scab on the strike, exchanges roles with his *patroncito*. Dressed in a pig mask and speaking in an absurd Texas drawl, the *patroncito* playfully suggests that he temporarily trade his own whip for the *esquirol*'s pruning sheers. The two quickly assume the inner reality of these symbolic outward forms. The climactic moment occurs when the owner removes his mask, at which point the *esquirol* has the revelation that worker and boss look (and therefore are) the same. Calling now for help, the boss is mistaken by the police for a troublemaker and is hauled off-stage, shouting for César Chávez and declaring his support for *La huelga* (the strike). The social tensions and contradictions of this role-reversal are central to all the *actos*. If the boss is brought down to a vulnerable stature and the worker is shown to be capable of leadership, there is no simplistic identification of one or the other as totally good or evil.

BERNABÉ

In the next stage of his career, Valdez explored the legends and myths of the Chicano's *indio* past. *Bernabé* is perhaps Valdez's most fully realized *mito* (myth-play). The hero is a thirty-one-year-old village idiot who has never had sexual relations with a woman. At the same time, he is a symbolic embodiment of the Chicano who possesses what Valdez calls "divinity in madness." After a series of taunts by the village toughs and an embarrassing encounter with Consuela, the local prostitute, Bernabé flees to a favorite hiding place in the countryside, where he has dug a gravelike hole in which he frequently masturbates in a kind of ritual copulation with *La Tierra* (the earth).

The climactic scene occurs when the elemental surroundings take on the forms of an Aztec allegory. *La Luna* (the moon) appears dressed as a *pachuco* (an urban Chicano zoot-suiter), smoking marijuana and acting as a go-between for his sister *La Tierra*, who then enters in the costume of a Mexican revolutionary camp follower (the proverbial "Adelita"). In the interchange, *La Tierra* questions the extent of Bernabé's love for her—whether he is "Chicano" enough to kill and to die for her. It is precisely his status as *loco* (crazy) that gives him the courage finally to say yes, and *El Sol* (the sun), as father, is pleased. As if mimicking the sacrifices to the Aztec sun god, Huitzilopochtli, Bernabé offers his physical heart to *La Tierra* and immediately ceases being the village idiot he was before, buried now within the earth but living on as a lesson to his people.

Valdez was to refine further this allegorical (and less immediately political) approach to Chicano identity in his plays throughout the 1970's, particularly in *La gran carpa de los rasquachis* (the great tent of the underdogs) and *El fin del mundo* (the end of the world), which further developed the use of the Mexican *corrido* (musical ballad), the split-level staging

designed to evoke a mythical and suprahistorical realm of action, and the traditional images from Latino religious drama—particularly the *calavera* (skeleton) costume. In *El fin del mundo*, his play had become a full-scale allegorical ballet—a great dance of death.

ZOOT SUIT

With his first deliberate turn to the commercial theater in 1978, Valdez incorporated the *mito*, *acto*, and *corrido* in the unlikely framework of a play about the urban Chicano of the 1940's. *Zoot Suit*—filled with stylized scenes from the Los Angeles barrio—was a drama about a celebrated murder trial and the racist hysteria surrounding it. A panorama of American life of the time, the play deliberately adopted many of the outward features of the "professional" theater, while transforming them for its purposes. It displayed immense photographic projections of newspaper headlines, slickly choreographed dances and songs, and the overpowering central image of the narrator himself, dressed in a zoot suit—the mythical *pachuco*. To an extent greater than in any other of his plays, the work addressed Americans as a whole, reviving for them a historical moment of which they had never been aware and bringing them face-to-face with their latent prejudices.

"I DON'T HAVE TO SHOW YOU NO STINKING BADGES!"

"I Don't Have to Show You No Stinking Badges!" Valdez's most celebrated play, concerns a middle-class Chicano family's attempts to blend into the American cultural mainstream. The family's parents, Buddy and Connie Villa, are middle-aged bit-part actors who play stereotyped Latino roles in television and films; their son, Sonny, is a law student who disapproves of his parents' work, which he finds demeaning. The play's mixture of the themes of generational and cultural conflict drew wide praise, and the work confirmed Valdez's standing as an important contemporary dramatist.

MUMMIFIED DEER

Mummified Deer is Valdez's first play after a gap in playwriting of almost fifteen years. It reaffirms his status as the "father of Chicano drama" and continues his exploration of his heritage through the juxtaposition of ritual and realism. The play takes its inspiration from a newspaper article Valdez read concerning the discovery of a sixty-year-old fetus in the body of an eighty-four-year old woman. According to scholar Jorge Huerta, in his unpublished paper, "For Valdez the mummified fetus became a metaphor for the Chicanos' Indio heritage, seen through the lens of his own Yaqui blood." A Yaqui deer dancer serves as the alter-ego to the old woman, Mama Chu, and is visible only to her. A present-day narrative is established, and the gathering of Mamu Chu's relatives around the old woman provides the play's central image. The play's major dramatic action, however, operates in the historical/fictional past. Through the representation of Cajeme, the deer dancer, Valdez deftly divides his characters' philosophies into two distinct camps— revolutionaries and colonizers. The deer dancer "is, to Mama Chu, above all, a son, a man, a symbol of freedom, purity and preconquest liberation," according to actress Alma Martinez, who originated the role of Mama Chu. When Mama Chu dies, "Cajeme dances to a climax at the foot of the bed. With his deer head up in triumph, he collapses, lifeless," thus commenting on the past versus the present, cultural heritage versus assimilation.

OTHER MAJOR WORKS

SCREENPLAYS: *Zoot Suit*, 1982; *La Bamba*, 1987.

TELEPLAYS: *Fort Figueroa*, 1988; *La Pastorela*, 1991; *The Cisco Kid*, 1994.

EDITED TEXT: *Aztlan: An Anthology of Mexican American Literature*, 1972 (with Stan Steiner).

MISCELLANEOUS: *Pensamiento Serpentino: A Chicano Approach to the Theatre of Reality*, 1973.

BIBLIOGRAPHY

Broyles-Gonzales, Yolanda. *El Teatro Campesino: Theater in the Chicano Movement*. Austin: University of Texas Press, 1994. This study uses previously unexamined materials such as production notes and interviews with former ensemble members to demystify the roles Valdez and El Teatro Campesino played in the development of a Chicano theatre aesthetic. Broyles-Gonzales employs a cultural studies methodology and reexamines the company in terms of class, race, and gender. Provides an "alternative reading" to the accepted El Teatro Campesino narrative.

Elam, Harry J., Jr. *Taking It to the Streets: The Social Protest Theatre of Luis Valdez and Amiri Baraka*. Ann Arbor: University of Michigan Press, 2001. Noted African American Theatre scholar Harry Elam explores the political, cultural, and performative similarities between El Teatro Campesino and Baraka's Black Revolutionary Theater. An intriguing examination of the political theater of these two marginalized groups, Chicanos and African Americans, and their shared aesthetic.

Flores, Arturo C. *El Teatro Campesino de Luis Valdez*. Madrid: Editorial Pliegos, 1990. This five-chapter study examines the importance, gradual development, theoretical considerations, touring, and "return to identity," and the "steps to commercialization (1975-1980)" represented by *Zoot Suit*. A strong study with a bibliography. In Spanish.

Huerta, Jorge A. *Chicano Theatre: Themes and Forms*. Ypsilanti, Mich.: Bilingual Press, 1982. This well-written and well-illustrated study begins with Valdez's experiences in Delano in 1965. It contains an excellent immediate description with dialogue of these first energies and is written in the present tense for immediacy and energy. Provides some discussion of the beginnings of the San Francisco mime troupe and strong description of the *actos* and their literary history in Europe. Highly descriptive and lively. Valuable bibliography and index.

_____. "Labor Theatre, Street Theatre, and Community Theatre in the Barrio, 1965-1983." In *Hispanic Theatre in the United States*, edited by Nicolas Kanellos. Houston: Arte Publico Press, 1984. Placed at the end of a longer study of Hispanic theater history, this essay takes on more importance by indicating that Valdez's contribution belongs in a continuum of history. Under the wing of César Chávez's farm labor union, the playwright used the workers in a manner reminiscent of Clifford Odets's *Waiting for Lefty* (pr., pb. 1935). Good on contemporaries of El Teatro Campesino; strong bibliography.

Kanellos, Nicolas. *Mexican American Theater: Legacy and Reality*. Pittsburgh: Latin American Literary Review Press, 1987. Begins with an examination of Valdez's transformation from director of El Teatro Campesino, in league with the rural farm worker, to the urban commercial playwright of *Zoot Suit* in 1978, "an attempt at addressing a mass audience on a commercial basis." Cites Valdez's contribution to the "discernible period of proliferation and flourishing in Chicano theatres" from 1965 to 1976, then moves on to examine other offshoots of the impulse.

Morales, Ed. "Shadowing Valdez." *American Theatre* 9 (November, 1992): 14-19. An excellent essay on Valdez, his followers, his film plans, his shelved Frida Kahlo project (he was criticized for casting an Italian American in the role of Kahlo), and later productions in and around Los Angeles, with production stills. Includes an essay entitled "Statement on Artistic Freedom" by Valdez, in which he defends his nontraditional casting: "My first objective is to create mutual understanding between Americans and Mexicans, not to provoke more mistrust and suspicion."

Orona-Cordova, Roberta. "*Zoot Suit* and the Pachuco Phenomenon: An Interview with Luis Valdez." In *Mexican American Theatre: Then and Now*, edited by Nicolas Kanellos. Houston: Arte Publico Press, 1983. The opening of the film version of *Zoot Suit* in 1982 prompted this interview, in which Valdez reveals much about his motives for working, his view of Chicano literature and art, and his solutions to "the entrenched attitude" that will not allow Chicano participation in these industries. Much on Pachuquismo from an insider's point of view.

Pottlitzer, Joanne. *Hispanic Theater in the United States and Puerto Rico: A Report to the Ford Foundation*. New York: Ford Foundation, 1988. This volume provides a brief history to 1965 and discusses the Hispanic theater during the upheaval of the Vietnam War. Also examines the theater's activities and budget and pays homage to the inspiration of El Teatro Campesino and Valdez. Supplemented by an appendix and survey data.

Timothy Brennan, updated by Thomas J. Taylor, Robert McClenaghan, and Anne Fletcher

RAMÓN MARÍA DEL VALLE-INCLÁN

Born: Villanueva de Arosa, Spain; October 28, 1866
Died: Santiago de Compostela, Spain; January 5, 1936

PRINCIPAL DRAMA

Cenizas, pr., pb. 1899
El marqués de Bradomín, pr. 1906, pb. 1907
Águila de blasón, pb. 1907, pr. 1960
Romance de lobos, pb. 1908 (*Wolves! Wolves!*, 1957)
El yermo de las almas, pb. 1908
Cuento de abril, pr., pb. 1910
La cabeza del dragón, pr. 1910, pb. 1914 (*The Dragon's Head*, 1918)
Voces de gesta: Tragedia pastoríl, pb. 1911, pr. 1912
La marquesa Rosalinda, pr. 1912, pb. 1913
El embrujado, pb. 1913, pb. 1931
Farsa de la enamorada del rey, pb. 1920
Divinas palabras, pb. 1920, pr. 1933 (*Divine Words*, 1968)
Luces de Bohemia, pb. 1920, pr. in French 1963, pr. in Spanish 1971 (*Bohemian Lights*, 1967)
Los cuernos de don Friolera, pb. 1921, pr. in Italian 1934, pr. in Spanish 1936 (*The Grotesque Farce of Mr. Punch the Cuckold*, 1991)
Farsa y licencia de la reina castiza, pb. 1922, pr. 1931

Cara de Plata, pb. 1922

Las galas de difunto, pb. 1926

Retablo de la avaricia, la lujuria y la muerte, pb. 1927

La hija del capitán, pb. 1927

Obras completas de don Ramón del Valle-Inclán, pb. 1944 (2 volumes)

Las "comedias bárbaras": Historicismo y expresionismo dramático, pb. 1972 (includes *Águila de blasón*, *Wolves! Wolves!*, and *Cara de Plata*)

Plays, pb. 1993

Savage Acts: Four Plays, pb. 1993

OTHER LITERARY FORMS

Ramón María del Valle-Inclán is well known for work in other genres, especially prose fiction. Among his most important works are his cycle of four novels, published between 1902 and 1905, known as the *Sonatas*. In this cycle are *Sonata de otoño* (1902; *Autumn Sonata*, 1924); *Sonata de estío* (1903; *Summer Sonata*, 1924); *Sonata de primavera*, 1904 (*Spring Sonata*, 1924); *Sonata de invierno* (1905; *Winter Sonata*, 1924). The *Sonatas* were published together in English in 1924 as *The Pleasant Memoirs of the Marquis de Bradomín: Four Sonatas*. Among his other cycles are *La guerra carlista*, published between 1908 and 1909, which consists of *Los cruzados de la causa* (1908), *El resplandor de la hoguera* (1909), and *Gerifaltes de antaño* (1909), and *El ruedo ibérico*, published between 1927 and 1958, which consists of *La corte de los milagros* (1927), *Viva mi dueño* (1928), and *Baza de espadas*, serialized in 1932 and published as a book in 1958.

Other noteworthy works by Valle-Inclán are his aesthetic treatise *La lámpara maravillosa* (1916; *The Lamp of Marvels*, 1986), his collection of poetry *La pipa de kif* (1919; the marijuana pipe), and his novel *Tirano Banderas: Novela de tierra caliente* (1926; *The Tyrant: A Novel of Warm Lands*, 1929).

ACHIEVEMENTS

Ramón María del Valle-Inclán's mature plays, now considered to be among his finest and most innovative works, were largely unappreciated during his own lifetime. Much of his theater was deemed impossible to stage, and the avant-garde nature of his post-1920 works puzzled and outraged his contemporaries. The note of social and aesthetic rebellion and the distortions associated with expressionism and with Valle-Inclán's favored artistic mode, the grotesque, help to explain this response to his work. The merits of his dramaturgy have been recognized by numerous modern critics, however, and advances in staging techniques have enabled directors and designers to mount productions of his most demanding plays with considerable success. As a critical perspective on avant-garde drama has evolved, Valle-Inclán's importance as an innovator in technique and as a playwright whose thematic concerns are at once universal and illuminative of a fascinating period in Spanish history has been firmly established.

BIOGRAPHY

The task of presenting an objective biography of Ramón José Simón Valle Peña (later Ramón María del Valle-Inclán) is complicated by his extravagant appearance and his mania for projecting a distorted anecdotal view of his own life. His noble origin exerted a strong influence on his social views, and the folklore, superstitions, and natural beauty of his native Galicia provided him with the material for many of his works. His life in that province, in combination with a sophisticated, intellectual orientation developed through reading and frequenting Madrid's literary cafés while he resided in the capital, helped to shape his artistic vision. The young Valle-Inclán soon abandoned the requisite study of law for a literary career. Journalistic endeavors provided income in periods of economic hardship. By 1895, Valle-Inclán was living in Madrid, where he led a bohemian existence. His interest in theater, a reflection of the theatricality of his own lifestyle, led him to attempt acting and playwriting. His marriage to the actress Josefina Blanco helped solidify his contact with the world of theater; he was to write more regularly in that genre than in any other. In 1912, Valle-Inclán returned to Galicia, where he found the inspiration for his finest works in all genres. He twice ran for political office—once as an archtraditionalist and later as a radical—but was unsuccessful each time. The turmoil of the Primo de Rivera dictatorship and of the Second Republic that followed was echoed in his personal life. The 1930's were marked by his separation from his wife, by economic straits, and by ill health. He spent some time as director of the Spanish Academy of Fine Arts in Rome but had to relinquish that post because of medical problems. He returned again to his native Galicia, where he died in 1936.

ANALYSIS

As the primary creator of the legend of his own life, Ramón María del Valle-Inclán thrived on controversy, and the polemics that characterize the critical appraisal of his work would unquestionably have delighted him. The principal source of debate concerns the relationship between his early, Modernist works, with their focus on pure aesthetics, and his mature endeavors (most notably the *esperpentos*, his expressionist visions of reality, with their emphasis on political and social issues). Several perceptive critics have identified some of the essential ingredients of his esperpentic dramas in several of his pre-World War I plays, in which there is a clear note of estrangement and a suggestion of expressionistic distortion. These qualities are heightened in the *esperpentos*; the grotesque emerges as Valle-Inclán's central aesthetic, and the motif of the puppet produces a strong sense of alienation.

Valle-Inclán's association with the Modernist movement, with its cultivation of art for art's sake, has caused some critics to accuse him of ignoring social and political concerns in his work. Others detect a sensitivity to such matters in even his earliest plays and novels that is intensified and developed in his *esperpentos*. The theme of the decline of an aristocracy characterized not only by lust and immorality but also by nobility and charity as well as the subsequent emergence of a decadent and dissolute bourgeoisie dominates his early play *Wolves! Wolves!* The *esperpentos*, most notably Valle-Inclán's masterpiece, *Bohemian Lights*, present a scathing vision of the turmoil and perversity rampant in post-World War I Spain. Valle-Inclán may offer no constructive solutions for Spain's ills, but his vision of his native land

as a grotesque deformation of modern civilization communicates a genuine sense of outrage, frustration, and existential pain that can only be endured by the adoption of an ironic perspective. His aesthetic and evolving dramatic technique functioned harmoniously to produce the optimal form for the expression of his social and political concerns.

Certain features of Valle-Inclán's theater demand attention in presenting an overview of his œuvre. His ability to create visual images through the use of languages obliges critics to allude to specific artists and paintings in evaluating his poetic stage descriptions and his grotesqueries. The Spanish artist Francisco de Goya has clearly exerted a strong influence on his aesthetic. Goya's use of black humor, bitter social satire, and irony are all echoed in Valle-Inclán's work. The panoramic sweep of his settings, his sensitivity to light and color, and the epic dimension and medieval flavor of his dramatic trilogy *Las "comedias bárbaras"* are suggestive of Henrik Ibsen's early theater and of Bertolt Brecht's epic theater. Valle-Inclán's theater at its best incorporates all the arts in a manner reminiscent of Richard Wagner's *Gesamtkunstwerk*. The musicality of his finest works, reflected both in language and in rhythmic structure, is another of the salient characteristics of Valle-Inclán's dramatic art.

Although the nature of Valle-Inclán's stage directions changed during the course of his career, their demands on stage designers pose a continuing challenge, and their cinematographic quality remains a constant feature of his theater. Some critics have viewed his plays as novels in dialogue that are unsuited for actual production. Others insist that improved lighting techniques and new ideas in the area of stage design have already confirmed the efficacy of Valle-Inclán's dramatic vision as realized in the theater. As Lyon notes, Valle-Inclán "disclaimed any connection with the theater not because he thought his works were unsuitable for the theater as he conceived it could become, but because he thought the theater as it existed was unsuitable for his works." The pioneering nature of Valle-Inclán's work and his independence of spirit, sense of adventure, and awareness of his image as a bohemian "legend" and aristocratic romantic all aided him in his quest for genuine innovation in the theater.

Valle-Inclán's dramaturgy produced a highly original corpus of work that has proven its effectiveness in theater productions. From the extremely visual, stylized, and archaic presentation of humankind's base instincts in *Wolves! Wolves!* to the coarse, earthy naturalism of *Divine Words*, Valle-Inclán's skill with dialogue and ability to integrate all of the arts into dramatic rhythms is manifest. Although aesthetic concerns, ranging in character from the Romantic to the expressionistic and the grotesque, are of paramount importance throughout his dramatic production, social and political issues also receive attention, particularly in such *esperpentos* as *Bohemian Lights* and *The Grotesque Farce of Mr. Punch the Cuckold*. The diversity of his themes and techniques and the originality of his dramatic vision ensure Valle-Inclán a prominent place among modern European playwrights.

WOLVES! WOLVES!

Wolves! Wolves! constitutes the final chapter in the epic saga of Don Juan Manuel Montenegro, Valle-Inclán's Don Juanesque alter ego who is the subject of the trilogy *Las "comedias bárbaras."* It was not the last of the three plays to be written (the first was *Águila de blasón*). *Cara de plata*, the opening drama from the point of view of plot, was not completed until 1922, during Valle-Inclán's esperpentic period. *Wolves! Wolves!* is generally considered to be the playwright's finest drama of his early period. Highly representative of Valle-Inclán's art at that stage of his career, it contains some of the elements of Modernism while also anticipating a number of the features that would be developed more fully in his *esperpentos*. The most authentically epic of the trilogy, the play features a protagonist who is larger than life and in confrontation with supernatural forces. Thematically, *Wolves! Wolves!* presents Don Juan Manuel Montenegro's quest for spiritual absolution, a quest that is paralleled by the collapse of the aristocratic world that he represents. In the opening scene of the play, Montenegro encounters a funeral procession. The *santa campaña* (the souls of the departed), which in Galician folklore appears to announce death, alerts him to his own impending demise while preparing him for the news of his wife's death. The rest of the play constitutes Montenegro's attempts, both overt and unconscious, to save his soul from perdition.

Wolves! Wolves! contains a number of elements associated with the Romantic movement. Montenegro's witnessing his own funeral in the initial scene is certainly one such element. The original title of the work contains the word *romance* (ballad), which suggests both the medieval flavor of the piece as well as its musical, poetic component. The stage descriptions are replete with depictions of the violence of nature used to parallel the inner, emotional states of the characters. Romantic situations abound; Montenegro's valiant effort to open his wife's grave in order to embrace her remains, constitutes one quintessential example. The work as a whole, however, transcends traditional Romanticism in its recourse to distortion and the surreal, in its note of social protest, and in the sense of irony inherent in its opposition between form and content, producing dissonances that disturb the harmony of its musical structure.

The drama is divided into three acts of six scenes each. The symmetry in structure clashes with the violence of the work: Sexual lust, greed, and hypocrisy characterize Montenegro's five sons, who represent the new order of Galician society. They are the wolves of the play. Allusions to animals and descriptions of people in terms of various creatures of the night underscore the dramatist's vision of his region's immorality. Hints of the grotesque recur throughout. The influence of Goya is quite apparent in the grafting of animalistic traits and features onto human characters. Montenegro, ridden with guilt caused by his incessant infidelities over the years, seeks death through starvation after returning to his home by boat to discover that his wife has already died. His emotional state is described by an acquaintance in terms of the image of a worm gnawing at his intestines. That image, which refers to the announcement of his own death in the play's opening scene, obliterates ordinary chronological time while introducing yet another destructive creature of the animal world. This nightmarish vision of life is suggestive of Surrealism;

here Valle-Inclán's worldview, like Goya's, clearly transcends the realm of Romanticism.

Wolves! Wolves! echoes William Shakespeare's *King Lear* (pr. c. 1605-1606, pb. 1608) in a variety of ways. Like Lear, Montenegro suffers the pain caused by unloving and greedy children. His sons are thoroughly despicable; they fight with one another over their father's possessions, defile the chapel and their mother's own grave to steal objects of value, and deny charity to the servants and beggars who had been dependent on the Montenegros. Juan Manuel adopts those beggars as his true sons, and it is on their behalf that he finally confronts his sons and is killed by one of them (Mauro). Before that final encounter, Juan Manuel is wandering through the streets in search of death and redemption and encounters a former mistress, who asks him the following question (which also links him with King Lear): "Where are you wandering with your white head exposed to the rain?" His night in the fields with the mad, demonic beggar, Fuso Negro, represents a clear reference to Lear's fool. The beggars constitute a sort of Greek chorus that interjects a note of irony by linking the world of classical theater to the moral dissolution of Galicia. Montenegro's genuine sympathy for the poor and the suffering is his most admirable virtue; it provides him with the stature necessary for a tragic hero.

Valle-Inclán constructed his drama with precision, and despite its Romantic excesses, it is tightly structured. Visually, its vast expanses, the incorporation of a voyage by ship, the sound effects, and the chiaroscuro lighting clash with that structure. In the theater, the use of projections and propitious lighting would be crucial if the panoramic sweep of the work were to be preserved. Darkness and shadows are necessary to underscore the element of superstition and the supernatural that is critical to the ambience of the play. The final scene, with its act of patricide, is lit by the light of a fireplace and becomes the visual as well as the dramatic climax of the piece. The rich language of the stage directions, the archaic quality of the dialogue, and the musicality of the structure are the play's salient virtues as a written text. In the hands of an imaginative designer, *Wolves!*

Wolves! should provide a visceral dramatic experience for a modern audience.

DIVINE WORDS

Written in 1920, *Divine Words* was the first of Valle-Inclán's mature masterpieces. It occupies a unique position among his post-World War I dramas. Although it does have a few of the features of the *esperpentos* that follow, it does not belong to the genre that the playwright was to create and define later that same year with *Bohemian Lights*. *Divine Words*, like *Wolves! Wolves!*, uses the dramatist's native Galicia as its setting. The differences between the two plays in aesthetic, worldview, and dramatic technique, however, are striking and serve to underscore the significant evolution of the playwright's craft.

In *Divine Words*, Valle-Inclán chooses to focus on the ordinary peasants of Galicia. The archaic, eloquent language of Don Juan Manuel Montenegro has been replaced by the coarse, earthy, colorful utterances of this radically different segment of society. The play is essentially naturalistic in style. Periodic recourse to expressionistic deformation and stylization occurs throughout with telling effect, but the overall objectivity of the dramatist's vision dominates. Valle-Inclán continues to evoke the plastic arts in his stage directions, but these are of a more limited scope than was the case with *Wolves! Wolves!* Moreover, the aesthetic of those visual images is now clearly the grotesque. Problems of staging remain but have changed in nature. Instead of the constant challenge of capturing the panoramic sweep of natural surroundings, here Mari-Gaila's flight through space with a goat-devil, her husband's leap off a tower, and the convincing depiction of a hydrocephalic pose are what have been demonstrated to be surmountable difficulties for a stage designer.

The plot and structure of *Divine Words* are the very essence of simplicity. The unifying focus of the drama is the hydrocephalic dwarf, Laureano. He is exhibited for profit by the unscrupulous characters who populate the play's rural microcosm. When Juana la Reina dies, her sister Marica del Reino and sister-in-law Mari-Gaila finally agree to alternate caring for the child and to profit from his grotesqueness.

The creature is present onstage throughout the work, even after his death from an overdose of alcohol. The other plot line concerns Mari-Gaila's affair with Séptimo Miau, the dilemma of her husband, Pedro Gaila, when he realizes that he has been cuckolded, and his final act of mercy, prompted by fear, when he rescues a naked Mari-Gaila from the townspeople, who are bent on stoning her.

Divine Words is divided into three acts of five, ten, and five scenes, respectively. Several critics have pointed out the irony of that structure, with its suggestion of a religious tryptich. The title of the play echoes the ironic undercurrent present throughout. When Pedro Gailo, a sacristan, attempts to dissuade the hypocritical mob from killing his wife, he pronounces in Spanish the words of Christ: "Let he who is without sin cast the first stone." His words have no effect on the populace, but those very same words spoken in Latin miraculously serve to calm the group and allow Pedro to lead Mari-Gaila to safety. The magical, ceremonious quality of the Latin, which they do not comprehend, ironically succeeds where the clearly understood message of Christ fails. The fact that Mari-Gaila mockingly refers to her husband as "Latin" adds yet another dimension to Valle-Inclán's irony.

The dramatist's sensitivity to juxtapositions is central to both the structure and the aesthetic of the play. The lust and voluptuousness of the lovemaking between Mari-Gaila and Séptimo Miau, summarized by the latter's incisive comment "We entered, we sinned and we went on our way," is followed by Pedro Gailo's drunken, incestuous advances toward his daughter in the next scene. The aesthetic of the grotesque, which has been defined as the uneasy union of the horrifying and the comic, utilizes such juxtapositions and antitheses. Much that is grotesque in the work relates to Laureano. One visceral example, which demonstrates Valle-Inclán's continued sensitivity to the plastic arts, is the description of the child after he has died and his face has been devoured by pigs. Valle-Inclán's attention to detail in portraying the delicately embroidered shroud and the flowers on the child's forehead creates the kind of clash between form and content that is encountered in German expressionist painters such as George Grosz. Ironic juxtapositions and dialectics support the grotesque, which proves to be a most propitious aesthetic for this work.

Hypocrisy, lust, and cruelty dominate *Divine Words*. Marica del Reino's and later the entire town's outrage over Mari-Gaila's immorality is clearly tinged by jealousy and personal frustration. Pedro Gailo's failure to avenge his honor by killing his wife does not constitute a moral repudiation of the conventional code associated with Spanish theater and society; rather, it is motivated by his fear of the gallows. Mari-Gaila's sensuousness and undaunted search for the fulfillment of her desires makes her a strong and, in some ways, an admirable character. All of the personages that populate Valle-Inclán's dramatic milieu, however, are ultimately condemned by their callous and mercenary treatment of the repulsive, pathetic hydrocephalic, whose physical presence is a visual reminder of the playwright's nihilistic view of his country's moral state.

BOHEMIAN LIGHTS

The supreme expression of Valle-Inclán's tortured vision of his country, *Bohemian Lights* is clearly his finest work for the theater. It is also well known for its presentation of the concept of the *esperpento*, a term that has come to refer to the author's style and artistic technique during the final period of his work (from 1920 on). Máximo Estrella, the play's protagonist, identifies Goya as the true originator of the *esperpento*, which he then defines as the reflection of the classical hero given by a concave mirror. He further notes that Spain is a grotesque deformation of European civilization. That observation elucidates and justifies both the theme and the aesthetic of the drama. *Bohemian Lights* is set in Madrid in 1920, the year it was written. Its sixteen episodes present the final day in the life of the blind poet Max, using as a background the growing violence in strife-torn Spain. Max becomes progressively drunker throughout the work, and the drama's perspective reflects his alcoholic, clouded vision of the horrors of reality. The motif of the mirror serves to reinforce the basic concept of the *esperpento*. In combination with Max's inner vision, a cubist image is produced, especially in the depiction of the café that Max and his cohort Latino enter in the ninth scene. Paradoxically, the more violent the play's distortions become, the more accurately Max and the audience perceive the true essence of the drama's milieu.

The unity of time (one day in Max's life) constitutes an ironic allusion to the form of classical tragedy, and Max emerges as a parody of the classical hero. It is his growing insight into ontological questions, rather than the traditional unity of action, that provides the unifying focus for the work. As Max's understanding of reality deepens, the irony implicit in his name ("Maximum Star") dissipates, and his blindness evolves into a higher vision. When he becomes able to laugh, albeit bitterly, at the absurdity of his endeavors within the context of his environment, he grows in stature.

The central episode of the drama is the arrest, imprisonment, and mistreatment of Max by the police. His friends manage to have him freed, and the minister, a friend and former poet himself, offers him a salary. However, Max fails to find what he really wants: justice. While in prison, he enters into dialogue with a Catalonian anarchist who shares his views of Spain and who perceptively anticipates his own execution under the *ley de fugas* (he is shot in the back while attempting to "escape"). The realization of that anticipation, as well as Max's encounter with a woman bemoaning the senseless slaying of her small child by a stray bullet, drives the poet to the edge of despair.

In the drama's climactic episode, Max is abandoned to die in a doorway by the novelist Don Latino. Allegedly Max's friend, Latino also takes his wallet and later drinks up the winnings from Max's lottery ticket. That he is the artistic successor to Max becomes a sad commentary on the state of literature as well as of life in the Spain of 1920. The transition from one to the other parallels the rise to power of Montenegro's sons in *Wolves! Wolves!* The change in aesthetic, the heightened use of the grotesque, and the political and philosophical dimension of *Bohemian Lights* all confirm the advances in Valle-Inclán's art from his earlier work. The dramatist clearly identified with Montenegro in the earlier play, in keeping with

his desire to cultivate the legend of his own life. His identification with Max is equally apparent; here, however, the identification is honest rather than pretentious.

Valle-Inclán's perspective on his protagonist provides the justification for his inclusion of three scenes after the poet's death. They serve to underscore the grotesque nature of existence (an absurd journalist, Soulinake, insists that Max is only in a cataleptic state and tests his theory by burning the dead man's finger) and to reveal the unremittingly bleak nature of life in Madrid in the absence of Max's wit and insights. The efficacy of the play results at least in part from the author-protagonist's *angst* coupled with his ability to mock all of his own pretenses and to come to grips with the absurdity of his own existence. It is that dimension of the drama that elevates *Bohemian Lights* above all of Valle-Inclán's other plays in theme and dramatic impact.

THE GROTESQUE FARCE OF MR. PUNCH THE CUCKOLD

The Grotesque Farce of Mr. Punch the Cuckold is Valle-Inclán's quintessential *esperpento*. The work lacks the emotional impact and social realism of *Bohemian Lights* but uses multiple perspectives in a complex and significant manner, making *The Grotesque Farce of Mr. Punch the Cuckold* the playwright's most intriguing drama from a structural standpoint. More absurd than grotesque, *The Grotesque Farce of Mr. Punch the Cuckold* employs the figure of the puppet and numerous allusions to animals in a lighter manner than previous works considered, producing a more farcical, comic grotesque. The play is essentially a literary parody that incorporates an oblique but telling satire of Spanish society and its conventions.

The Grotesque Farce of Mr. Punch the Cuckold consists of a prologue, the drama proper, containing a dozen scenes, and an epilogue. Each portion of the work is presented from a different perspective. (In *La lámpara maravillosa*, Valle-Inclán wrote of the three perspectives that a writer can adopt in creating characters: true to life, larger in status, and smaller in status than their author). The prologue presents the story of the cuckolded Lieutenant Friolera in the form of a puppet show. The action is viewed from above. The puppet-master, author, and audience all perceive the characters as smaller than life. The drama proper encourages the audience to view the characters as ordinary human beings. Echoes and resonances of the puppets in the prologue and elements of farce interject a note of irony and function to project the interplay of illusion and reality in a manner reminiscent of Luigi Pirandello. Finally, the epilogue presents Friolera as a mock-epic hero, simultaneously aggrandized and dismissed as hollow and absurd. Valle-Inclán mocks himself and a number of literary conventions, most notably the Golden Age honor play, in his presentation of the classic tale of infidelity and revenge. The comments of the two intellectuals, Don Estarfalario and Don Manolito, about the literary works contained in the prologue and the epilogue further complicate the drama's shifting perspectives; the discussion culminates with Estrafalario's suggestion that they purchase the epic ballad of the play's final section so that they can burn it.

Friolera's puppetlike gestures, his constant repetition of "Pim-Pam-Pum" to simulate the manner in which he will slay his wife and her lover, and his mistaken assertion that he has shot them when in reality he has killed his daughter instead—all contribute to the farcical grotesque that dominates the play's aesthetic. Another grotesque touch is the description of Lieutenant Rovirosa, whose glass eye is often on the verge of falling out, especially when he gestures vehemently in expressing his concern over Friolera's predicament and its impact on the company. There are also numerous allusions to animals in reference to Friolera and to the devout *beata*, or traditional spinster, who makes his dishonor known to him and to the entire town.

The play's satiric targets include the military and the concept of honor: Both are ridiculed in this nihilistic view of Spanish literary and social conventions. Friolera is Spain's Othello, an inane puppet whose gestures fail to ring true. He is also a loving father and husband who suffers and truly laments having to cope with the obligation of cleansing his honor. Tragedy and farce combine at the end of the central portion of the work when Friolera, faced with the reality

that his "revenge" was really the accidental murder of his beloved daughter, asks if he can be sent to a hospital rather than to prison. Valle-Inclán's greatest achievement in this play is his success in interweaving a multiplicity of perspectives and paradoxes so that Friolera's ambivalence as a simultaneously ludicrous and admirable character is affirmed in the work as a whole.

OTHER MAJOR WORKS

LONG FICTION: *Cara de Dios*, 1899; *Sonatas*, 1902-1905 (*The Pleasant Memoirs of the Marquis de Bradomín: Four Sonatas*, 1924; includes *Sonata de otoño*, 1902 [*Autumn Sonata*]; *Sonata de estío*, 1903 [*Summer Sonata*]; *Sonata de primavera*, 1904 [*Spring Sonata*]; *Sonata de invierno*, 1905 [*Winter Sonata*]); *Flor de santidad*, 1904; *La guerra carlista*, 1908-1909 (includes *Los cruzados de la causa*, 1908; *El resplandor de la hoguera*, 1909; and *Gerifaltes de antaño*, 1909); *Tirano Banderas: Novela de tierra caliente*, 1926 (*The Tyrant: A Novel of Warm Lands*, 1929); *El ruedo ibérico*, 1927-1958 (includes *La corte de los milagros*, 1927; *Viva mi dueño*, 1928; and *Baza de espadas*, 1958 [serialized 1932]).

SHORT FICTION: *Femeninas*, 1895; *Corte de amor*, 1903; *Jardín umbrío*, 1914.

POETRY: *Aromas de leyenda*, 1907; *La pipa de kif*, 1919; *El pasajero*, 1920; *Claves líracas*, 1930 (includes the three earlier collections).

NONFICTION: *La lámpara maravillosa*, 1916 (*The Lamp of Marvels*, 1986); *La media noche*, 1917.

MISCELLANEOUS: *Opera omnia*, 1913-1930; *Obras completas*, 1944.

BIBLIOGRAPHY

Almeida, Diane M. *The Esperpento Tradition in the Works of Ramón del Valle-Inclán and Luis Buñuel.* Lewiston, N.Y.: Edwin Mellen Press, 2000. Almeida takes a close look at *esperpento* in the works of Valle-Inclán and Luis Buñuel. Bibliography and index.

Andrews, Jean. *Spanish Reactions to the Anglo-Irish Literary Revival in the Early Twentieth Century: The Stone by the Elixir.* Lewiston, N.Y.: Edwin Mellen Press, 1991. Andrews examines the works of Valle-Inclán and Juan Ramón Jiménez and contrasts them to contemporary Irish works. Bibliography and index.

Flynn, Gerard C. *The Aesthetic Code of Don Ramón del Valle-Inclán*. Huntington, W.Va.: University Editions, 1994. An extensive analysis of the aesthetics of Valle-Inclán's works. Bibliography and index.

Lima, Robert. *Valle-Inclán: The Theater of His Life*. Columbia: University of Missouri Press, 1988. A

full-length biography of Valle-Inclán, covering his life and works. Bibliography and index.

LoDato, Rosemary C. *Beyond the Glitter: The Language of Gems in Modernista Writers Rubén Darío, Ramón del Valle-Inclán, and José Asunción Silva*. Lewisburg, N.Y.: Bucknell University Press, 1999. LoDato examines the works of Modernista writers Valle-Inclán, Rubén Darío, and José Asunción Silva. Bibliography and index.

Peter L. Podol

SIR JOHN VANBRUGH

Born: London, England; January 24, 1664 (baptized)
Died: London, England; March 26, 1726

PRINCIPAL DRAMA

The Relapse: Or, Virtue in Danger, pr., pb. 1696
Aesop, Part I, pr. 1696, pb. 1697, *Part II*, pr., pb. 1697 (based on Edmé Boursault's play *Les Fables d'Ésope*)
The Provok'd Wife, pr., pb. 1697
The Country House, pr. 1698, pb. 1715 (based on Florent Carton Dancourt's play *La Maison de Campagne*)
The Pilgrim, pr., pb. 1700 (based on John Fletcher's play *The Pilgrim*)
The False Friend, pr., pb. 1702 (based on Alain-René Lesage's play *Le Traître puni*)
Squire Trelooby, pr., pb. 1704, (with William Congreve and William Walsh; adaptation of Molière's play *Monsieur de Pourceaugnac*)
The Confederacy, pr., pb. 1705 (based on Florent-Carton Dancourt's play *Les Bourgeoises à la mode*)
The Mistake, pr. 1705, pb. 1706 (based on Molière's play *Le Dépit amoureux*)
The Cuckold in Conceit, pr. 1707 (adaptation of Molière's play *Sganarelle: Ou, Le Cocu imaginaire*)

A Journey to London, pb. 1728 (unfinished; also as *The Provok'd Husband*, pr., pb. 1728, with revisions by Colley Cibber)

OTHER LITERARY FORMS

Sir John Vanbrugh also wrote *A Short Vindication of "The Relapse" and "The Provok'd Wife"* (1698). The standard edition of Vanbrugh's dramatic and nondramatic works is the four-volume edition prepared by Bonamy Dobrée and Geoffrey Webb (1927-1928).

ACHIEVEMENTS

Despite his numerous translations and adaptations of others' plays, Sir John Vanbrugh's fame rests on his two complete original plays, *The Relapse* and *The Provok'd Wife*. These comedies reflect the transition from the Restoration comedy of manners to the sentimental comedy that dominated the theater of the eighteenth century. Vanbrugh's plays are transitional only in a very limited sense, however, because the species of comedy Vanbrugh developed, a comedy that presents problems realistically but rejects both cynicism and simplistic solutions to complex problems, did not prosper.

Vanbrugh's primary interest was in the treatment of serious moral issues through careful and consistent characterization. His plays focus primarily on problems that can arise after marriage rather than on those of courtship, and they explore the relationship between marital incompatibility and infidelity. Although Vanbrugh's comedies neither approve nor excuse adultery, they indicate the ways in which husbands can unintentionally encourage their wives to be unfaithful. Although Vanbrugh employs many of the stock character types of the comedy of manners, he endows them with a new freshness and significance by combining types and by presenting these types in new contexts. Moreover, in Vanbrugh's plays, in contrast to Restoration comedy, characters may be evaluated according to their exercise of charity and common sense rather than simply according to the quality of their wit. Although wit provides much of the humor in Vanbrugh's plays, the dialogue is remarkable more for realism and vigor than for aphoristic polish. Characters also express emotion, especially sexual passion, physically as well as verbally onstage, and this physical element provides some additional humor in the form of farce.

Although some characters in *The Relapse* and *The Provok'd Wife* experience genuine moral struggles and speak of virtue with veneration and without cynicism, Vanbrugh's plays cannot be classified as sentimental comedies. Unlike sentimental comedies, Vanbrugh's plays do not present a facile reformation of immoral characters; rather, they maintain consistency of characterization and thus fail to offer entirely happy conclusions. *The Provok'd Wife* and *The Relapse* are criticized most often for their failure to resolve all the problems each raises.

BIOGRAPHY

Sir John Vanbrugh's parents were Giles Vanbrugh, a prosperous London sugar refiner, and Elizabeth Barker Carleton, a wealthy heiress and widow. His exact birth date is not known; however, he was baptized January 24, 1664. Vanbrugh was probably educated at the King's School in Chester, and, in 1683, he visited France, possibly to study architecture. He did not immediately start his architectural career but obtained a commission in the earl of Huntingdon's Regiment of Foot. He resigned this commission in August of the same year, and his whereabouts for the

Sir John Vanbrugh (Hulton Archive by Getty Images)

next five years are uncertain. In September, 1688, Vanbrugh was arrested in France for his support of William of Orange. He remained imprisoned in France on charges of espionage until 1692, spending the last seven months of his captivity in the Bastille, where he composed an early draft of *The Provok'd Wife*.

On his release from the Bastille in November of 1692, Vanbrugh returned to England, where he briefly resumed a military career, only to abandon it again, this time for dramatic pursuits. Encouraged by the success of *The Relapse*, the first of his plays to be produced, he brought to the stage *Aesop, Part I* in December, 1696; *Aesop, Part II* in March, 1697; and *The Provok'd Wife* in April, 1697. *The Provok'd Wife* was the last original play Vanbrugh completed. After responding in an essay to the attacks made on his plays by Jeremy Collier's *A Short View of the Immorality and Profaneness of the English Stage* (1698), Vanbrugh directed his dramatic gifts toward translating and adapting the plays of others. The one additional original comedy he attempted, *A Journey to London*, was unfinished at the time of his death. After Vanbrugh's death, his old friend Colley Cibber revised and completed the play, which was presented in 1728 as *The Provok'd Husband.*

At about the same time as Collier launched his attack, Vanbrugh's career in architecture suddenly blossomed. By 1700, Vanbrugh was already at work on his first commission, Castle Howard, which Charles Howard, third earl of Carlisle, commissioned him to build. Vanbrugh's work so pleased Carlisle that he helped Vanbrugh become comptroller of the Board of Works in 1702. Vanbrugh was thus involved in the building of many public buildings as well as country homes, and he became one of the foremost English architects of the eighteenth century. His most famous architectural achievement is Blenheim Palace, a project that was a source of great political, legal, and financial trouble for him. Vanbrugh also designed and, with William Congreve, managed the Queen's Theatre in Haymarket, which opened in 1705. The theater was not a success, largely because Vanbrugh's massive design caused serious acoustical problems, making it unsuitable for the production of either plays or operas, which Vanbrugh had vainly hoped to popularize in England. In 1708, Vanbrugh sold his interests in this enormous drain on his spirit and pocketbook.

Vanbrugh married Henrietta Yarborough in 1719. On March 26, 1726, in the Whitehall home that he had designed and that Jonathan Swift had dubbed Goose-Pie House, Vanbrugh died of a bacterial infection.

ANALYSIS

Sir John Vanbrugh's *The Relapse* and *The Provok'd Wife* are important in theatrical history because they were among the main targets of Jeremy Collier's famous attack on contemporary theater, *A Short View of the Immorality and Profaneness of the English Stage.* Vanbrugh drew Collier's fire not only because of his treatment of adultery but also because of his satire on the clergy, which appears both in the plays and in their prefatory material. Collier accused Vanbrugh of both moral and artistic irresponsibility, humorlessly condemning Vanbrugh's presentation of flawed characters. Vanbrugh argues in his response, *A Short*

Vindication of "The Relapse" and "The Provok'd Wife," that Collier understands neither the nature nor the function of satire but wrongly assumes that to present behavior onstage is to recommend it. Nevertheless, Collier does offer some valid criticism of *The Relapse*: The blank verse is indeed poor, the plot is improbable, and the play's awkward structure does obscure its focus.

Collier's attack is important, however, not so much because he provided literary insight into the plays but because his attitude reflected the shift in public taste away from Restoration comedy and Vanbrugh's more realistic comedy toward sentimental comedy. Gradually, Vanbrugh's audience came to share Collier's disapproval of the character types, dialogue, and plots that were typical of Restoration comedy and to demand a more morally self-conscious theater.

THE RELAPSE

Although *The Provok'd Wife* was the first play that Vanbrugh wrote, the first of his comedies to be produced was *The Relapse.* Written in six weeks as part response, part sequel, to Colley Cibber's *Love's Last Shift* (pr. 1696), *The Relapse* was an immediate popular and critical success. The play was performed by the Drury Lane Company, the same company that had presented *Love's Last Shift*; the original cast included John Verbruggen (as Loveless), Susanna Verbruggen (as Berinthia), George Powell (as Worthy), and, in a "breeches part," Mary Kent as Young Fashion. The choice role of Lord Foppington went to Cibber, who had acted as well as created Lord Foppington's original, Sir Novelty Fashion. Although Vanbrugh adopted Cibber's double-plot structure, he retained only the main characters from the original play. Young Fashion and Lord Foppington (in Cibber, Sir Novelty Fashion) appear in *Love's Last Shift*, but Young Fashion's personality and the relationship between the brothers bear very little resemblance to those of the corresponding characters in *The Relapse.*

In writing *The Relapse*, Vanbrugh explored the comic and psychological possibilities suggested by the sudden reformation of the rake Loveless at the end of *Love's Last Shift. The Relapse* does not ridicule the idea that a rake can reject vice because of the influence of a virtuous woman—indeed, *The Relapse* itself presents such a rapid reformation in the rake Worthy. Rather, Vanbrugh's play explores the extent to which one's attempt to be virtuous, however sincere, can withstand temptation. Further, in *The Relapse*, the moral complexity of the situation is deepened, for Amanda, too, experiences real temptation and undergoes a genuine moral struggle.

Like most English comedies, *The Relapse* presents not one but two plots: Scenes focusing on the concerns of Loveless and Amanda alternate with scenes centering on Lord Foppington and Young Fashion. These two plots are very tenuously connected by a single visit from Lord Foppington to Loveless and Amanda. Because each plot seems to be afforded equal emphasis and development, readers have not always accepted Vanbrugh's assertion in *A Short Vindication of "The Relapse" and "The Provok'd Wife"* that the Loveless-Amanda plot is the central concern of the play.

The Relapse opens with the reformed Loveless expounding in irregular blank verse his contentment with his wife and his quiet, virtuous life in the country. Although Amanda is pleased by her husband's dedication to virtue, she is apprehensive at his insistence that he is capable of withstanding any temptation the city may offer during their forthcoming visit. Her fears deepen after they arrive in London, when Loveless confesses his attraction to a young woman he noticed at the playhouse. Although Loveless's strong sexual appetite is typical of the rake-hero of Restoration comedy, his pride in his chastity (however short-lived) and his verse panegyric to virtue certainly are not.

Whereas in Restoration comedy, the wife who contemplates adultery typically concerns herself only with pragmatic considerations and is an object of derisive laughter, Amanda undergoes a real moral struggle and elicits the audience's sympathy and admiration. Unaware that her cousin is the object of her husband's desire, she confesses to Berinthia her contrary emotional responses to Lord Foppington's and Worthy's unsuccessful attempts to seduce her. In response to Berinthia's inquiry whether she will remain chaste should Loveless again betray her, Amanda predicts that, despite her consequent loss of love for him, she will retain her virtue. Amanda vehemently rejects Berinthia's suggestion that she avenge herself on a straying Loveless by cuckolding him, innocently dismissing Berinthia's wholly serious suggestion as mere wit. In the scenes in which Berinthia—not, as in Restoration comedy, a potential lover—tries to persuade Amanda to allow herself to be seduced, Berinthia's cynicism concerning love and marriage becomes evident. Berinthia's wit and her cynical and exploitative conception of human relationships align her with the characters of Restoration comedy, just as Amanda's implicit faith in her husband and often vocalized dedication to virtue anticipate the qualities of the heroine of sentimental comedy.

Eager to conceal the affair she wishes to have with Loveless, Berinthia agrees to Worthy's scheme to distract Amanda by entangling her in an affair with Worthy. Aware that Amanda will be more receptive to Worthy's attentions if she feels abused and betrayed by Loveless, Berinthia offers to confirm Amanda's suspicions concerning Loveless's fidelity by enabling Amanda to observe him meeting his mistress. In addition to informing Amanda of Loveless's betrayal, Berinthia also repeatedly tells her of Worthy's devotion.

Amanda's convictions are put to the test when she sees Loveless meet his mistress (whom she never recognizes as Berinthia) for a rendezvous. Although she knows that Loveless truly cares for her, that he only "runs after something for variety," Amanda is so deeply disturbed at finding him relapsed into rakehood that she momentarily considers duplicating his sin. Immediately, however, Amanda rejects such moral relativism, declaring in a lengthy verse speech that her husband's fall would in no way excuse her own. Though her love for him has died, her love for virtue is unaltered. Thus, despite Amanda's intense attraction to him, Worthy's advances fail utterly. Resisting his attempts to seduce her at first with words and later with force, she insists that the only proof of Worthy's love that she will accept is his not tempting her virtue. Amanda leaves the awed Worthy alone onstage to confess the profundity of his admiration and love for Amanda and for virtue. As Loveless once had, he now dedicates himself to virtue, though he realistically prefaces his announcement of his reformation with "How long this influence may last, heaven knows."

This last section of the Loveless-Amanda plot, like the first, is written entirely in blank verse, perhaps to emphasize the high seriousness of the ideas. Nevertheless, the conclusion of this plot is at best partial, for several serious problems remain unresolved: Loveless has not reformed, and there is no suggestion that he will reform or that Amanda's love for him will be rekindled; even at the moment of his repentance, Worthy admits the fragility of his love for virtue; and Amanda's only reward for her chastity is her not being raped by Worthy. Worthy's attempted rape of Amanda, like Loveless's mock-rape of the softly protesting Berinthia, is also significant in that in these scenes, passion is presented onstage in an overtly physical rather than in a detached, intellectualized manner, as was the case in Restoration comedy.

Like the Loveless-Amanda plot, the Lord Foppington-Young Fashion plot also employs and adapts the elements of Restoration comedy. The humor in this plot, unlike that of the other, comes largely from farce, though Lord Foppington also provides humor of wit. Having expended his small inheritance, Young Fashion unsuccessfully appeals for money to his wealthy, wasteful, and selfish brother, Lord Foppington, and ultimately relieves his financial distress by stealing his brother's bride, Miss Hoyden. Although Young Fashion shares the Restoration rake-hero's refined tastes and insight into human nature, he has a more fully developed conscience than does the rake, for he gives his brother several opportunities to avert being duped by exercising even minimal generosity.

Young Fashion's brother, Lord Foppington, is unquestionably the wittier of the pair, but it is clearly not he with whom the audience is intended to sympathize. In Lord Foppington, Vanbrugh transforms the intellectually deficient, self-deluded fop of Restoration comedy into a heartless yet self-aware egotist. Unlike his predecessors, Lord Foppington is not a fop because he lacks sufficient wit to establish proper values. An intelligent but unscrupulous man, he deliberately adopts contemptible values and displays ludicrous behavior because he knows that those who do so prosper most in society. Cruelly selfish, he advises his brother to become a highwayman and thus obtain relief from his problems through theft or hanging. Lord Foppington's awareness of and indifference to the consequences of his distorted priorities provide a novel and serious undercurrent to the traditional fop scenes. Such concern with the moral implications of a fool's actions, rather than mere laughter at the fool's expense, indicates Vanbrugh's movement away from the Restoration comedy ethos and toward that of sentimental comedy.

Another character who is based on a Restoration comedy type is Miss Hoyden, a virginal but sexually precocious country girl. Hoyden's virtue is merely technical, having been preserved only by the watchfulness of her overly protective father, also a Restoration comedy country type. Moral questions do not trouble Hoyden: Unconcerned about committing bigamy, she readily marries the real Lord Foppington after having just married an impostor. Hoyden ultimately rejects her second spouse and retains her first not because of any promptings of conscience or affection but because she finds Young Fashion more attractive physically and because she expects he will be less likely to restrict her spending than would his brother.

Though Young Fashion is pleased to have stolen Miss Hoyden for himself, he is aware of her moral shortcomings, including the likelihood that, once in London, she will be successfully pursued by young beaux. Young Fashion does not contemplate his imminent cuckoldom with much distress, however, assuring himself that the size of Hoyden's estate will provide him with sufficient consolation. Certainly in this plot, unlike the other, marriage and adultery are not weighty concerns, and marital compatibility and virtue are of no importance to either party. The ultimate priority for these characters is financial. Thus, though Young Fashion's reluctance to deceive his brother suggests that he has a conscience, he is nevertheless not a typical hero of sentimental comedy. His complacency about marrying and being cuckolded solely for money indicates that he does not share their veneration of virtue.

THE PROVOK'D WIFE

From its opening at the Lincoln's Inn Fields playhouse early in 1697 through the middle of the eighteenth century, *The Provok'd Wife* enjoyed even more frequent production than did *The Relapse*. Sir Thomas Betterton, the head of the company, was the first actor to play Sir John Brute, a role that became a favorite of eighteenth century actors, including Colley Cibber and David Garrick. Because of its occasional coarseness in dialogue and action and its ambiguous moral stance concerning adultery, the popularity of *The Provok'd Wife* declined during the latter half of the eighteenth century, despite the revision of material that the new audience would have found objectionable. Even more than *The Relapse*, *The Provok'd Wife* is concerned with problems between couples after marriage, but whereas *The Relapse* focuses on the effects of adultery, *The Provok'd Wife* focuses on its causes. In *The Provok'd Wife*, as in *The Relapse*, there is a secondary plot involving a courtship, but the more carefully unified structure of *The Provok'd Wife* makes it evident that the Sir John-Lady Brute-Constant plot rather than the Heartfree-Bellinda-Lady Fancyfull plot is the main concern of the play.

The Provok'd Wife opens with Sir John Brute voicing in soliloquy his contempt for marriage and for his wife. Despite his awareness of her attractiveness and virtue, he never loved Lady Brute but married her only in order to satisfy his sexual desire for her. His irrational hostility in response to Lady Brute's polite inquiry whether he will be dining at home is typical of his treatment of her throughout the play. Although antipathy toward marriage typifies the Restoration rake-hero, Sir John's poor manners, his disregard for his appearance, his belligerence, cowardice, coarse language, and lack of wit and self-control certainly are not. Thus, with Sir John, Vanbrugh put the cynical sentiments of the Restoration comedy rake-hero into the mouth of a despicable character.

Although, like Amanda, Lady Brute is a mistreated wife who elicits the sympathy of the audience, unlike Amanda, she is partly to blame for having entangled herself in such an unhappy match, as she admits in her soliloquy. Though forewarned of the problems that would arise between them, she married Sir John not for love but for money, vainly assuming that she could control his behavior through her sexual charms. Nevertheless, it is she who most earns sympathy because, unlike Sir John, she tries to make the best of this unfortunate union and struggles to remain a pleasant and virtuous companion to her husband. Despite her unwillingness to cuckold Sir John, Lady Brute does not derive the same degree of satisfaction from maintaining her virtue that Amanda does, nor does she always discuss virtue with Amanda's deep seriousness. For Lady Brute, chastity is a source of frustration rather than of comfort, and though she fails to convince herself of the justice of discarding her marriage vows, she cynically questions accepted assumptions about the rewards of virtue. Lady Brute is thus not the model of self-restraint Amanda is, but she is decidedly the more human of the two women.

At the end of her soliloquy, Lady Brute is joined by her cousin and confidante, Bellinda, who is aware of the mutual attraction between Lady Brute and Constant. Unlike Amanda's confidante, Berinthia, Bellinda is virtuous and does not try to manipulate her friend into committing adultery. Lady Brute's and Bellinda's witty discussion of sexual matters is reminiscent of Restoration comedy, but here, as in *The Relapse*, the discussion is between two women rather than between a woman and her would-be lover. Unlike Amanda's, Lady Brute's wit is as sharp as is that of her confidante, and throughout their conversation, the intelligence, perceptiveness, and fundamental virtuousness of both women are emphasized.

Attention is next directed to Lady Fancyfull, a female fop also drawn from the Restoration comedy tradition, whose vanity and affectation emphasize by contrast Lady Brute's and Bellinda's self-awareness and naturalness. Like that of Lord Foppington of *The Relapse*, Lady Fancyfull's foolishness is the result of conscious effort. So adamant is Lady Fancyfull in her self-delusion that she rejects without reflection the constructive criticism Heartfree offers her as a prerequisite for his love, despite her attraction to him.

Having failed to rescue Lady Fancyfull from her vanity, Heartfree wittily examines woman's nature with his friend Constant, who has been attempting to seduce Lady Brute since he first met her at her wedding two years earlier. Half rake and half sentimental comedy lover, Constant simultaneously praises Lady Brute for her virtue and complains that she will not commit adultery with him. After accepting the unsuspecting Sir John's invitation, Heartfree encourages Constant to persist in his seduction, believing that Sir John's ill usage may prompt Lady Brute to cuckold him to gain revenge.

Awaiting his visitors, Sir John deliberately annoys Lady Brute and Bellinda by smoking his pipe. Determined not to allow him to force them from the room, Lady Brute and Bellinda wittily tease him about its unpleasant smell. When Bellinda suggests that men who deliberately offend their wives deserve to be cuckolded, the enraged Sir John hurls his pipe at them and chases them out of the room; while running from her husband, Lady Brute runs, symbolically, into Constant's arms. The emphasis on physical action and the violence in this scene mark another departure from the detached intellectualism of Restoration comedy.

Having drunk with Heartfree and Constant, Sir John departs to carouse with his friends, leaving the young men alone with Lady Brute and Bellinda. After some witty banter between the couples in the manner of Restoration comedy, Lady Fancyfull arrives, and she mockingly reviews Heartfree's criticisms of her. To make Lady Fancyfull jealous, Bellinda flirts with Heartfree, inviting him to offer criticism of her character. Charmed by Bellinda, Heartfree ignores Lady Fancyfull, who follows Constant and Heartfree out as they leave, vowing vengeance on Bellinda.

Once Lady Fancyfull has gone, Constant reenters and, encountering Lady Brute alone, assures her that he left only to safeguard her reputation. Like the Restoration comedy rake, he attempts to seduce her with witty sophistry, and like a Restoration comedy heroine, Lady Brute exposes the fallaciousness of

every argument he offers until, feeling her resistance abate, she terminates the conversation. The essential difference between this wit-battle between the sexes and that found in the typical Restoration comedy is, of course, that this witty, virtuous lady is married.

With mutual trust not usually found between women in Restoration comedy, Lady Brute and Bellinda wittily discuss men's and women's mutual deception and abuse. They agree that men are the ultimate source of pleasure in all arenas of a woman's life, and they laugh at the affectation and folly that they themselves cultivate, along with the rest of their sex. Although many women in both Restoration and sentimental comedy are self-aware, only the former are likely to find an assessment of their faults and virtues a source of amusement. In the course of their conversation, Lady Brute also tells Bellinda that she is weakening toward Constant. Aware of Sir John's abuse of her cousin, Bellinda sympathizes with Lady Brute and neither criticizes her for contemplating adultery nor sermonizes about the rewards of virtue. At the end of their conversation, Bellinda and Lady Brute devise a stratagem typical of Restoration comedy: In order to meet Heartfree and Constant again, they will invite the men anonymously to a rendezvous in Spring Garden and meet them there in disguise.

The scene then shifts to Sir John and his friends, who drunkenly lament that a man whom they have attacked is not dead; they next threaten a tailor and steal the parson's gown he carries, which Sir John puts on, adding to the farce. When the Constable comes to investigate the disturbance, Sir John swears and strikes the Constable and, as his friends run off, is taken into custody. Once again, the violence and coarseness of the scene mark a departure from the comedy of manners. Because Sir John has donned the parson's gown, his captors assume that he is a clergyman and thus lock him up not in jail but in the Constable's roundhouse. Later, when he is brought before the justice of the peace, he remains sullen and abusive but is again given preferential treatment and released without penalty because he wears the garb of a cleric. Anticipating an unfavorable response to the satire on the clergy in this scene at the 1726 revival of the play, Vanbrugh revised it extensively, refining Sir John's coarse language and eliminating the clerical satire by substituting one of Lady Brute's dresses for the cleric's gown.

When the anonymous invitation to a rendezvous arrives, Heartfree, now in love with Bellinda, very reluctantly agrees to accompany Constant. On their way to Spring Garden, they are followed by Mademoiselle and Lady Fancyfull, who conceal themselves in order to eavesdrop on the conversation between the men and Lady Brute and Bellinda. The ladies are forced to reveal their identities to the men when Heartfree and Constant agree to Sir John's request of the favors of their two "whores." After Sir John leaves, angered by his friends' apparent selfishness, Lady Brute and Bellinda express their gratitude, and then each speaks privately with her suitor. With the reluctance to wed typical of a Restoration wit, Heartfree confesses to Bellinda that he could love her "even to—matrimony itself a'most." Bellinda's response is, likewise, in the Restoration comedy tradition: She inquires of him whether he would continue to love her after they were married.

While Bellinda and Heartfree go off for a walk alone, Constant continues his efforts to seduce Lady Brute, reminding her of Sir John's cruelty and of his own constancy. In another scene that departs from Restoration comedy in its emphasis on the physical aspects of love and in its use of physical action onstage, Constant kisses Lady Brute repeatedly and tries to pull her into the arbor to complete his seduction. Unlike Amanda, Lady Brute is saved not by her virtue but by her fear for her reputation, when Lady Fancyfull and Mademoiselle noisily make their presence known. Terrified that she has been recognized, Lady Brute insists that Heartfree and Constant bring her and Bellinda home.

On their return to Sir John's house, Lady Brute invites the men to play cards with her and Bellinda because she does not expect Sir John for hours. When Sir John suddenly arrives, however, Heartfree and Constant conceal themselves in the closet. Unaware of their presence, the filthy, blood-covered Sir John makes coarse, drunken sexual advances toward Lady

Brute, her revulsion only augmenting his desire. Distracted momentarily by his thirst, Sir John insists on drinking some of the tea in the closet before having sexual relations with Lady Brute, and, kicking in the jammed closet door, he discovers Heartfree and Constant. Although Sir John assumes that Lady Brute has cuckolded him, his drunkenness prevents him from taking any action, and after a few coarse remarks, he passes out.

To avert Sir John's wrath, Lady Brute and Bellinda agree that, if Constant and Heartfree are willing, they will tell Sir John that Constant had merely accompanied Heartfree on a visit to Bellinda, whom he wishes to marry; Bellinda will readily break off the engagement, if Heartfree wishes, once Lady Brute's good name has been restored. Despite her awareness that she could find a wealthier husband than this younger brother, Bellinda is nevertheless willing to marry Heartfree. Unlike the heroines of sentimental comedy, Bellinda does not romanticize suffering. She assures Lady Brute that she would not join Heartfree to live in utter poverty on love alone. Bellinda is, nevertheless, an idealist in that love is her highest consideration in choosing a spouse. She prefers to marry a man of moderate means whom she loves than a wealthy man whom she does not. As a realist, Bellinda acknowledges the truth of Lady Brute's warning that she may end up unhappy and poor rather than unhappy and rich, but she resolves to trust to Heartfree's sense of honor and good nature.

When the ladies' proposal arrives, Heartfree is very reluctant to marry Bellinda despite his love for her, for he fears that some man may eventually cuckold him just as his friend Constant intends to cuckold Sir John. Although Heartfree and Constant agree that women usually remain faithful to their husbands unless they are abused, Heartfree fears that he might indeed turn into a Sir John in time, arguing that men, not women, are the more likely to change. Agreeing with Constant that marriage is "the only heaven on earth," Heartfree expresses the very unrakish sentiment that "to be capable of loving one, doubtless is better than to possess a thousand." Still questioning his capacity for love, he does not decide to marry

Bellinda until, wielding the wit he has found so attractive, she asks his intentions, drawing her imagery from warfare.

Despite Heartfree's engagement to Bellinda, Sir John remains convinced that he has been cuckolded; he hypocritically declares love for and trust in Lady Brute only to avoid fighting a duel for her honor with Constant. Just as Lady Brute's honor is being restored, however, Lady Fancyfull enters in disguise, intending to sully Bellinda's and Heartfree's reputations and thus to prevent their marriage. Lady Fancyfull informs Bellinda that she is Heartfree's wife whom, she says, he married for money (thus playing on one of Bellinda's fears) and whom he has reduced to poverty and threatened with murder. Meanwhile, Lady Fancyfull has also sent a letter to Heartfree, informing him that Bellinda has already had one illegitimate child and that she is anxious to marry because she is pregnant with another. Both Bellinda and Heartfree are thoroughly deceived, and each hurls veiled accusations at the other until Rasor, Heartfree's servant, confesses his part in the plot and forces Lady Fancyfull and Mademoiselle to admit theirs. Having begged each other's pardon, Heartfree and Bellinda once again agree to marry, and the play ends with Bellinda warning Heartfree of the fate of surly husbands.

In *The Provok'd Wife*, as in *The Relapse*, Vanbrugh does not resolve the questions that he raises; he does not employ a facile happy ending at the expense of the consistency of the characterization. Sir John and Lady Brute remain yoked together with no suggestion that their relationship will improve; Lady Brute can—and probably will—find physical and emotional satisfaction only through an extramarital affair; and although Heartfree and Bellinda will marry, the readiness with which they believe profound ill of each other does not bode well for their future happiness.

A JOURNEY TO LONDON

Although Vanbrugh never completed another original play, he did draft a little more than three acts of *A Journey to London*. Here, again, Vanbrugh employs a double-plot structure but does not adequately integrate the elements of the two plots. The play's minor plot satirizes the Headpieces, a family of country bumpkins who visit London, while the main plot focuses on the incompatibility of Lord and Lady Loverule. In *A Journey to London*, however, unlike *The Relapse* and *The Provok'd Wife*, the husband rather than the wife is the more sensible and sympathetic character, and gambling, not adultery, is the main source of conflict. Although Vanbrugh did not complete this play—with Cibber's revisions, it became *The Provok'd Husband*—he told Cibber that the main plot would conclude with Lord Loverule's turning out Lady Arabella for her refusal to mend her ways. Thus, Vanbrugh intended once more to reject the unrealistic fifth-act reformation and falsely happy ending of sentimental comedy.

OTHER MAJOR WORKS

NONFICTION: *A Short Vindication of "The Relapse" and "The Provok'd Wife,"* 1698.

MISCELLANEOUS: *The Complete Works of Sir John Vanbrugh*, 1927-1928 (4 volumes; Bonamy Dobrée and Geoffrey Webb, editors).

BIBLIOGRAPHY

Berkowitz, Gerald M. *Sir John Vanbrugh and the End of Restoration Comedy*. Amsterdam: Rodopi, 1981. Berkowitz examines the works of Vanbrugh in the context of the transition from Restoration comedy to new forms of comedy. Bibliography and index.

Bull, Jon. *Vanbrugh and Farquhar*. New York: St. Martin's Press, 1998. Bull analyzes the work of Vanbrugh and George Farquhar in the context of English drama in the seventeenth and eighteenth centuries. Bibliography and index.

Downes, Kerry. *Sir John Vanbrugh: A Biography*. New York: St. Martin's Press, 1987. Downes examines the life and works of this dramatist and architect. Bibliography and index.

McCormick, Frank. *Sir John Vanbrugh: The Playwright as Architect*. University Park: Pennsylvania State University Press, 1991. McCormick provides both critical analysis of Vanbrugh's works and discussion of his role as architect. Bibliography and index.

Ridgway, Christopher, and Robert Williams. *Sir John Vanbrugh and Landscape Architecture in Baroque England, 1690-1730*. Stroud, England: Sutton in association with the National Trust, 2000. Although this work focuses on Vanbrugh as an archi-

tect, it provides valuable insights into his life and the times in which he lived. Bibliography and index.

Laurie P. Morrow,
updated by Howard L. Ford

JOHN WILLIAM VAN DRUTEN

Born: London, England; June 1, 1901
Died: Indio, California; December 19, 1957

PRINCIPAL DRAMA

The Return Half, pr. 1923
Young Woodley, pr. 1925, pb. 1926
Chance Acquaintance, pr. 1927
Return of the Soldier, pr., pb. 1928 (adaptation of Rebecca West's novel)
Diversion, pr., pb. 1928
After All, pr., pb. 1929
Sea Fever, pr. 1931 (with Auriol Lee)
Hollywood Holiday, pr., pb. 1931 (with Benn Levy)
London Wall, pr., pb. 1931
There's Always Juliet, pr., pb. 1932
Behold We Live, pr., pb. 1932
Somebody Knows, pr., pb. 1932
The Distaff Side, pr., pb. 1933
Flowers of the Forest, pr., pb. 1934
Most of the Game, pr. 1935, pb. 1936
Gertie Maude, pr., pb. 1937
Leave Her to Heaven, pr. 1940, pb. 1941
Old Acquaintance, pr., pb. 1941
Solitaire, pr. 1942
The Damask Cheek, pr. 1942, pb. 1943 (with Lloyd Morris)
The Voice of the Turtle, pr. 1943, pb. 1944
I Remember Mama, pr. 1944, pb. 1945 (adaptation of Kathryn Forbes's *Mama's Bank Account*)
The Mermaids Singing, pr., pb. 1946
The Druid Circle, pr., pb. 1948
Make Way for Lucia, pr., pb. 1949
Bell, Book, and Candle, pr. 1950, pb. 1951

I Am a Camera, pr. 1951, pb. 1952 (adaptation of Christopher Isherwood's *Berlin Stories*)
I've Got Sixpence, pr. 1952, pb. 1953

OTHER LITERARY FORMS

John William Van Druten was primarily a dramatist but also a prolific screenwriter. In addition, he published a body of literary reviews, poems, and short stories. His letters and papers are housed in the New York Public Library.

ACHIEVEMENTS

John William Van Druten's most successful plays were light comedies that modernized the drawing-room comedy genre. He specialized in small-cast, one-setting plays that emphasized character and witty dialogue over plot or action. Beginning with *Young Woodley* in 1925, Van Druten wrote five plays that were selected among the top ten plays of their respective years, and *I Am a Camera* received the New York Drama Critics Circle Award in 1951. He usually directed his own plays and also directed *The King and I* (pr. 1951) for Richard Rodgers and Oscar Hammerstein. He was nominated for an Academy Award for best screenplay for *Gaslight* (1944). It was not unusual to find two of Van Druten's plays running simultaneously on Broadway. Although he was a successful playwright, his pleasant comedies were not great plays. His sentimental script for *I Remember Mama*, based on family values and situations, may well prove to be his most enduring work. Van Druten's *I Am a Camera* was adapted into the musical *Cabaret* (1966) by John Kander and Fred Ebb.

Van Druten wrote when the Broadway theater and films were especially alive and vibrant. There was an audience for every genre of theater and drama. His five most successful plays (*Young Woodley*; *The Voice of the Turtle*; *I Remember Mama*; *Bell, Book, and Candle*; and *I Am a Camera*) made him known on Broadway.

BIOGRAPHY

John William Van Druten was born to a Dutch banker in London on June 1, 1901. Although Van Druten's mother was English by nationality, she was Dutch by heritage. Van Druten, a sickly infant, had one brother, Harry, who was eight years older. Neither physically strong nor athletically gifted, Van Druten preferred to spend his time in the world of books and imagination, avoiding sports and games. This avoidance of sports caused others to tease and make fun of him. In return, he developed a vitriolic turn of phrase as self-protection.

Both of the Van Druten parents had received continental educations and saw the arts as a way of life as well as a cultural experience; consequently, the family regularly attended art exhibitions, concerts, and theatrical performances. In addition to his books, Van Druten's favorite possession was a miniature theater, and early in life, he began writing plays to perform with his toy.

Van Druten would come to see 1914 as a turning point in the life of Europe, as well as a turning point in his own life. He felt World War I destroyed an era of gentleness and innocence, never again allowing the population of Europe to feel secure and in control of its destiny. Certainly, World War I changed Van Druten from a rather carefree child to a more mature thinker, even though he never was nor would ever become any kind of activist.

Van Druten always wanted to be a writer. He believed that his destiny was poetry, but he was unable to find a publisher for his poems even though he slavishly imitated the work of the poets that he admired. He graduated from University College School at age seventeen. Ready to conquer the literary world, Van Druten suffered a disappointment when his father insisted that he should prepare for a real profession.

Choosing law as a field for advanced study, Van Druten passed his exams in 1923 and became a solicitor. He chose, however, to become a lecturer rather than a practitioner and accepted a post at a Welsh college. This position left him free time to work at his writing. An interview with the editor of *Mercury* magazine resulted in the publication of one of his poems after Van Druten was advised to write what he felt rather than what he admired. He also wrote columns for an obscure English newspaper published in Switzerland.

Van Druten's first play, *Young Woodley*, optioned for production in London and the United States, premiered in New York after being banned by the London censor. Only twenty-three at the time, Van Druten resigned from his lecturer's post and devoted himself to writing full time. Although his major emphasis remained playwriting, he also received favorable notices for several novels: *A Woman on Her Way* (1931) and *And Then You Wish* (1936). He novelized *Young Woodley* for British publication in 1929.

A string of Van Druten's British productions were optioned for film treatments, which led him into a second career as screenwriter. From the 1930's until World War II, Van Druten split his time between England and the United States. With the onset of World War II and fighting in Europe, Van Druten decided to make the United States his permanent home and became a naturalized citizen in 1944.

More than fifteen years before his death, Van Druten purchased a large ranch in Indio, California, and settled there with his manager and partner, although he continued to spend six months of each year in New York. Frequently in ill health, Van Druten died at home on his ranch on December 19, 1957.

ANALYSIS

Arriving on the scene of a massive theater boom in both London and New York, John William Van Druten's sophisticated comedies filled a space between the serious dramas and typical comedies of the time. Although Van Druten's plays were driven by character rather than plot, he more than mastered the devices of effective theater. His use of telephone conversations to establish characters who never appeared on the stage helped to flesh out small casts and created a world beyond the one-setting interiors.

Later, in the late 1940's and 1950's, when the economics of theater became problematic, Van Druten's use of small casts in single settings made him commercially viable without sacrificing quality. As the commercial theater began to dry up and the only plays audiences cared to see were musicals, Van Druten's plays continued to attract playgoers.

Taking his cue from the drawing room comedies of an earlier age, Van Druten never descended into low comedy or farce. His was the high comedy of British plays, remodeled for modern times and American people. As Van Druten often repeated, he wrote about people. His audiences recognized the people he wrote about and responded. He was never issue minded and wrote to change neither society nor the theater. Van Druten's plays exist to amuse. In his memoirs, Van Druten seldom mentions his novels or screenplays: He was a playwright, first and foremost, and he reveled in that fact.

YOUNG WOODLEY

Van Druten's first professional play failed to pass the British censor because it was deemed to be critical of the British school system. The discussion of sex between the schoolboy characters also raised objections. George Tyler arranged for the American rights to *Young Woodley* with Basil Dean, the British producer. The production started in Boston and, in November of 1925, moved to New York, where it played to full houses and critical praise.

American audiences took exception to neither the subject matter nor the dialogue of the play. The three-act comedy with a cast of nine is set in a boys' school. The conflict is between the title character, a romantic, imaginative, eighteen-year-old poet and a staid, prosaic, controlling, and dour schoolmaster who has no time or sympathy for poets or poetry. Indeed, this headmaster stifles all attempts at creativity and is also stifling his pretty, young wife, who encourages Woodley's poetry. In their affinity for one another, the wife and Woodley commit a slight indiscretion. As a result, and with the support of his understanding father, Woodley leaves the school, having learned something about the differences between love and lust.

THE VOICE OF THE TURTLE

Although Van Druten authored a number of plays between 1925 and 1943, *The Voice of the Turtle* was his next unqualified success. Critics were amazed that he had created such a complete and believable play with a cast of only three characters and one interior set. The title is from the Song of Solomon, and "turtle" refers to turtle dove, symbolizing the arrival of spring, a new beginning.

The story is a romance: Boy finds girl, boy loses girl, boy gets girl, or vice versa. The time is World War II, and the sense of urgency inherent in wartime makes (or seems to make) sex without marriage acceptable to the audience. A sophisticated soldier and a young actress are thrown together by circumstance and fall in love. Finally, her objections are overcome, and she is united with her soldier. Had the setting been anything other than wartime, moral sensibilities would have probably rebelled at the situation. However, the time and circumstances combined to make audiences less morally judgmental.

I REMEMBER MAMA

Rodgers and Hammerstein approached Van Druten about dramatizing Kathryn Forbes's book and formed a production company expressly to produce the sentimental comedy. *I Remember Mama* is a series of character sketches and vignettes involving a family of Norwegian immigrants. Papa is a good man, but Mama is the fiber that holds the family together and on course.

Later, Van Druten felt that the character of Mama was probably an idealized portrait of his own mother and that the characters of the aunts, her sisters, gave him a chance to poke fun at his own aunts, whom he disliked as a child. The wholesome, loving, and secure nature of the family unit appealed to audiences almost universally. In fact, the script holds a kind of timeless and universal appeal and is frequently revived, even though it borders on sentimentality at times. The script was adapted to film, a television series, and later on, an unsuccessful musical.

BELL, BOOK, AND CANDLE

This stylish bit of fluff captured the imagination of audiences. The fact that Rex Harrison and Lili Palmer enacted the leads brought in an audience eager to see the famous British husband and wife team perform live on the stage. The major characters are modern, urbane witches. Once again, with a small cast and one interior setting, Van Druten takes a weak plot furnished with outstanding characters, witty situations, and dialogue reminiscent of Noël Coward to produce a sparkling high comedy. Although the plot was weak, Van Druten's frequently used theme about the sacrifices made for love was evident.

I AM A CAMERA

With this play, Van Druten, who had a string of successful plays to his credit, finally won a New York Drama Critics Circle Award. When interviewed about his play, Van Druten said that he had great difficulty with plots, and his plays were about people rather than action. In *I Am a Camera*, an adaptation of Christopher Isherwood's *Berlin Stories* (1945), Van Druten concentrates on the character of Sally Bowles. Set in pre-World War II Germany, the play deals peripherally with the Nazi-Jewish issue, but the focus of the comedy is on Sally, a repressed Londoner, seeking to liberate herself from an overbearing mother. Later, the script was to form the basis for the musical *Cabaret*.

OTHER MAJOR WORKS

LONG FICTION: *Young Woodley*, 1929 (adaptation of his play); *A Woman on Her Way*, 1931; *And Then You Wish*, 1936; *The Vicarious Years*, 1955.

SCREENPLAYS: *Young Woodley*, 1930 (adaptation of his play); *Night Must Fall*, 1937; *Parnell*, 1937; *Raffles*, 1940; *Lucky Partners*, 1940; *My Life with Caroline*, 1941; *Forever and a Day*, 1943; *Johnny Come Lately*, 1943; *Gaslight*, 1944; *Voice of the Turtle*, 1947 (adaptation of his play).

NONFICTION: *The Way to the Present*, 1938; *Playwright at Work*, 1953; *The Widening Circle*, 1957 (memoir).

BIBLIOGRAPHY

Chapman, John, ed. *Best Plays of 1950-1951* and *Best Plays of 1951-1952*. New York: Dodd, Meade, 1951, 1952. These two volumes, which include plays by Van Druten, contain production facts, interviews, statistics, critical responses, and summaries of the featured plays for the year.

Mantle, Burns, ed. *Best Plays of 1925-1926*, *Best Plays of 1943-1944*, and *Best Plays of 1944-1945* New York: Dodd, Meade, 1927, 1944, and 1945. These three volumes, which include plays by Van Druten, contain production facts, interviews, statistics, critical responses, and summaries of the selected plays of the year.

Weber, Bruce. "A Play Outside the Mainstream of Its Time and Ours." Review of *The Voice of the Turtle*, by John William Van Druten. *New York Times*, September 14, 2001, p. E3. This review of the revival of Van Druten's *The Voice of the Turtle* by the Keen Company at the Blue Heron Arts Center in New York examines how its 1940's sentiments translate into modern times.

H. Alan Pickrell

LOPE DE VEGA CARPIO

Born: Madrid, Spain; November 25, 1562
Died: Madrid, Spain; August 27, 1635

PRINCIPAL DRAMA

Los comendadores de Córdoba, wr. 1596-1598, pb. 1609

El nuevo mundo descubierto por Cristóbal Colón, wr. 1596-1603, pb. 1614 (*The Discovery of the New World by Christopher Columbus*, 1950)

El mayordomo de la duquesa de Amalfi, wr. 1599-1606, pb. 1618 (*The Majordomo of the Duchess of Amalfi*, 1951)

El anzuelo de Fenisa, wr. 1602-1608, pb. 1617

La corona merecida, wr. 1603, pb. 1620

La noche toledana, wr. 1605, pb. 1612

Los melindres de Belisa, wr. 1606-1608, pb. 1617

El acero de Madrid, wr. 1606-1612, pb. 1618
   (*Madrid Steel*, 1935)
Castelvines y Monteses, wr. 1606-1612, pb. 1647
   (English translation, 1869)
La niña de plata, wr. 1607-1612, pb. 1617
Peribáñez y el comendador de Ocaña, wr. 1609-
   1612, pb. 1614 (*Peribáñez*, 1936)
La buena guarda, wr. 1610, pb. 1621
Las flores de don Juan, y rico y pobre trocados, wr.
   1610-1615, pb. 1619
El villano en su rincón, wr. 1611, pb. 1617 (*The
   King and the Farmer*, 1940)
Fuenteovejuna, wr. 1611-1618, pb. 1619 (*The
   Sheep Well*, 1936)
Lo cierto por lo dudoso, wr. 1612-1624, pb. 1625
   (*A Certainty for a Doubt*, 1936)
El perro del hortelano, wr. 1613-1615, pb. 1618
   (*The Gardener's Dog*, 1903)
El caballero de Olmedo, wr. 1615-1626, pb. 1641
   (*The Knight from Olmedo*, 1961)
La dama boba, pb. 1617 (*The Lady Nit-Wit*, 1958)
Amar sin saber a quién, wr. 1620-1622, pb. 1630
El mejor alcalde, el rey, wr. 1620-1623, pb. 1635
   (*The King, the Greatest Alcalde*, 1918)
Los Tellos de Meneses I, wr. 1620-1628, pb. 1635
El premio del bien hablar, wr. 1624-1625, pb. 1636
La moza de cántaro, wr. 1625-1626, pb. 1646?
El guante de doña Blanca, wr. 1627-1635, pb.
   1637
El castigo sin venganza, pb. 1635 (based on Matteo
   Bandello's novella; *Justice Without Revenge*,
   1936)
Las bizarrías de Belisa, pb. 1637
Four Plays, pb. 1936
Five Plays, pb. 1961

OTHER LITERARY FORMS

Lope de Vega Carpio was an incredibly prolific writer. In addition to his plays, which number in the hundreds, he wrote poems, such as *La Dragontea* (1598; Drake the pirate), *El Isidro* (1599), *La hermosura de Angélica* (1602; Angélica's beauty), *Jerusalén conquistada* (1609; Jerusalem regained), and *La gatomaquia* (1634; *Gatomachia*, 1843). He also wrote several prose works, including *La Arcadia*

(1598), *El peregrino en su patria* (1604; *The Pilgrim: Or, The Stranger in His Own Country*, 1621), *Los pastores de Belén* (1612; the shepherds of Bethlehem), *Novelas a Marcia Leonarda* (1621; stories for Marcia Leonarda), and *La Dorotea* (1632). His *Égloga a Claudio* (1637; eclogue to Claudio), published after his death, contains autobiographical and critical material on his life and work.

ACHIEVEMENTS

Lope de Vega Carpio, "the father of Spanish theater," is generally credited with establishing the norms for the drama of Spain's Golden Age and is recognized as one of its most accomplished dramatists as well as its most prolific. His *El arte nuevo de hacer comedias en este tiempo* (1609; *The New Art of Writing Plays*, 1914), presented to a Madrid literary society, sets out the norms that Lope de Vega followed in writing his dramas. These norms are not entirely original with him but represent instead his synthesis of a long process of development in which many dramatists participated. It is significant, however, that once this style of theater received Lope de Vega's endorsement, it became fixed in the Spanish canon. Thus, *The New Art of Writing Plays* provides a fairly accurate description of most Spanish drama from that time until the death of the last great Golden Age dramatist, Pedro Calderón de la Barca, in 1681.

The full extent of Lope de Vega's dramatic production remains unknown and is the subject of scholarly debate. He is the undisputed author of 316 surviving full-length plays and the probable or reputed author of many more. In 1609, in *The New Art of Writing Plays*, he claimed to have authored 483 dramas, and, toward the end of his life, he elevated that number to 1,500. His first biographer, Juan Pérez de Montalbán, who was also a close friend, credited him with more than 1,800 dramatic works. Both sources, however, are suspect. Lope de Vega is certainly not noted for his modesty, and there is some evidence indicating that he never intended the figures he cited to be taken literally; Pérez de Montalbán's biography is an exaggerated encomium that deliberately suppresses the various scandalous incidents in Lope de

Vega's life that would have damaged his reputation. Therefore, more cautious critics have suggested that Lope de Vega's total dramatic production probably did not exceed 800 full-length plays.

Lope de Vega also produced a number (estimates run as high as 400, a tenth of which remain) of *autos sacramentales*—short, allegorical, religious dramas that were used in the Corpus Christi celebrations. His contribution to this genre, however, has been overshadowed by that of Calderón.

BIOGRAPHY

Lope Félix de Vega Carpio was born in Madrid on November 25, 1562, to Félix de Vega Carpio and Francisca Fernández Flores, humble Asturian (northern Spanish) parents, who had moved to Madrid less than a year earlier. Very little is known about his childhood and early youth. His biased biographer, Pérez de Montalbán, claims that Lope de Vega studied at the prestigious Jesuit school the Colegio Imperial de San Pedro y San Pablo, but court records indicate that he studied at the smaller Colegio de los Teatinos. He attended the University of Alcalá de Henares (as did Miguel de Cervantes, Calderón, and Tirso de Molina), and he may have studied at the Uni-

Lope de Vega Carpio (Hulton Archive by Getty Images)

versity of Salamanca as well. He enlisted in the armed forces in 1583 and fought in the Azores.

On returning to Madrid, Lope de Vega engaged in a love affair with Elena Osorio, the married daughter of a theater manager for whom he wrote plays. This affair lasted until 1587, when Elena (apparently at her parents' instigation) rejected him in order to establish a liaison with a wealthier man. Lope de Vega reacted violently, circulating anonymous poetry in which he insulted Elena and her family. He was consequently accused and convicted of criminal libel and was sentenced to eight years of exile from Madrid. It was apparently at this time that he recorded in *La Dorotea* his impressions of this, the first of many amorous affairs that were subsequently reflected in his writing; this novel, however, was not published until 1632.

During his exile, which he apparently violated on several occasions, Lope de Vega lived first in Valencia and then in Toledo, where he was in the service of the duke of Alba. In 1588, he was married by proxy to Isabel de Urbina (the Belisa of his poetry), by whom he had a daughter, Antonia, and who died giving birth to another, Teodora, in 1594. Neither daughter lived to maturity. In the same year as his marriage, Lope de Vega may also have participated in the ill-fated expedition of the Spanish Armada against England.

Lope de Vega returned to Madrid in 1596 and was indicted the same year for concubinage with Antonia Trillo de Armenta, a wealthy widow in her early thirties who was noted for her easy virtue. Shortly afterward, he began a more lasting (until 1608) affair with Micaela de Luján, an actor's wife, whom he referred to in his writings as Lucinda or Camila Lucinda. In 1598, apparently motivated by the promise of a huge dowry (which he never received), he married Juana de Guardo, the daughter of a wealthy fish and meat merchant. Through his writings, he managed to maintain two households, moving both wife and mistress with him to Seville and Toledo before finally returning to Madrid. Both Juana and Micaela bore him children. Those born to Micaela were baptized in the name of her husband until his death in 1603; those born afterward were listed in the baptismal registry as being of unknown parents. Only two of his children by Micaela lived to maturity: One, a son named Lope Félix, joined the armed forces and died in a pearl-hunting expedition toward the end of his father's life; the other, a daughter, Marcela, became a nun at the age of sixteen. Lope's wife, Juana, bore him three daughters and a son before her death in 1613; of these children only one, a daughter, Feliciana, reached maturity.

On a visit to Madrid in 1605, Lope de Vega met Luis Fernández de Córdoba, the twenty-three-year-old duke of Sessa, and established with him a friendship that was as remarkable as it was enduring. The duke used Lope de Vega to write letters to his paramours and prevailed on him to give him letters that he had written to his own mistresses—at least one of whom the duke may have shared. Because of the duke's fondness for Lope de Vega and his penchant for collecting anything that the writer's pen had produced, a substantial amount of Lope de Vega's correspondence as well as the manuscripts of a number of his plays have survived to the present.

In 1614, a year after his second wife's death, Lope de Vega decided to enter the priesthood. His religious vocation, however, did not involve a conversion to chastity. He had already replaced Micaela with another mistress, a friend of hers and, like her, married and an actress, Jerónima de Burgos. Jerónima—whom he called *la señora Gerarda* ("Mrs. Gerarda") in his letters to the duke of Sessa—was with Lope de Vega when he was ordained in Toledo, and she continued to live with him until he rejected her because of her increasing obesity and her chronic alcoholism. He then engaged in a brief but passionate fling with Lucía de Salcedo, whom he refers to as *la loca* ("the crazy girl").

The last great love of Lope de Vega's life was Marta de Nevares (Amarilis in his writing), the wife of the highly unattractive (if Lope de Vega's description of him can be trusted) Roque Hernández de Ayala, the scribe who copied Lope de Vega's plays for the duke of Sessa. A daughter, Antonia Clara, was born to Marta in 1617 and was baptized as the daughter of Hernández, though it was common knowledge that Lope de Vega was her father. After a number of difficulties—including an attempt by Hernández to

have Lope de Vega killed—Marta obtained a separation decree from her husband. He appealed but died suddenly, leaving both Marta and Lope de Vega ecstatic. A few years later, however, when Marta began to lose her sight, Lope de Vega was seized by the fear that her misfortune was divine retribution for their sin. As he grew increasingly repentant, scourging himself every Friday, new calamities arrived. Marta lost her sight completely and suffered periodic bouts of insanity, from which she recovered only briefly before her death in 1632; Lope Félix drowned during a pearl-hunting expedition; and Antonia Clara was abducted by a Madrid nobleman. Lope de Vega continued to write in spite of these misfortunes and produced some of his most admirable works in the final years of his life. He died on August 27, 1635, and was buried in the Church of Saint Sebastian in Madrid after an elaborate nine-day funeral arranged by the duke of Sessa.

ANALYSIS

The theater of Lope de Vega Carpio is so varied that it eludes generalizations. Indeed, its rich variety is probably its most defining trait, and it would seem that Lope de Vega intended this to be so. Commenting in *The New Art of Writing Plays* on his decision to mix comic and tragic elements in the same drama, he noted that this choice is based on his imitation of nature, which is beautiful because of its variety. Their diverseness explains why virtually all of Lope de Vega's plays are referred to as *comedias*, or "comedies." This designation does not mean that his plays are not often serious. Indeed, they frequently concern subjects (such as rape, murder, and political intrigue) that can scarcely be treated humorously. Rather, the designation "comedy" implies only that the plays are not tragedies; they usually end with a restoration of order rather than a catastrophe, and their principal characters are generally common people rather than the nobility whom classical norms deemed appropriate for tragedy. Moreover, humor is an important element in all of Lope de Vega's plays, no matter how serious they are. Even those few that are designated tragedies include a buffoonlike character known as a *gracioso* ("funny one"), usually a servant, whose lack of dignity provides occasion for laughter in spite of the generally serious tone of these works.

By mixing comic and tragic elements in the same work, Lope de Vega was intentionally ignoring the classical dramatic precepts established by Aristotle and Horace. He also deliberately disregarded the classical unities, which sought to limit a play's setting to a single place and decreed that its action should occur in a single day. For all these reasons, Lope de Vega's drama (and Spanish Golden Age drama in general) bears a closer resemblance to the theater of Elizabethan England than to the more classically oriented theater of seventeenth century France. His theater differs from its English counterparts in other ways, however, such as following a three-act rather than a five-act format and employing polymetric verse. In *The New Art of Writing Plays*, Lope de Vega recommended accommodating the verse form used in each passage to the material being treated—a principle based on Spanish poetic tradition. Therefore, Lope de Vega recommended that exposition be written in one of the two standard verse forms used for narrative poetry: Normal exposition may be handled in the popular *romance* or ballad form, but special cases should be rendered in the more elegant Italianate *octava real*, used for the polished epic poetry of the day. Lope de Vega also recommended accommodating each character's speech to his station and to the material being treated, using figurative language in key discussions, for example, while rendering everyday conversations in more prosaic speech.

In spite of its varied nature, Lope de Vega's theater is characterized by a few constants. Among these are an interest in nature, an affection for the common people, an ability to discover poetic beauty in the everyday life of sixteenth and seventeenth century Spain, a penchant for reflecting his own experiences in his drama, and—above all—an abiding interest in the theme of honor or reputation. Lope de Vega recommended this theme in *The New Art of Writing Plays* because of its ability to elicit a strong emotional response from the audience, and he followed his own recommendation by including this theme in

the overwhelming majority of his plays, where his treatment of it ranges from the humorous to the tragic.

PERIBÁÑEZ

Probably no play illustrates all that is typical of Lope de Vega better than does *Peribáñez*, a drama about a common Spanish farmer who kills the noble commander of the town's military forces in order to defend his wife (and his own honor) against the commander's unwelcome advances—and who is pardoned by King Enrique III for this offense. Much of the play's appeal is its poetic treatment of life in the town of Ocaña, where Peribáñez and his wife live. The play's opening scene shows a simple and joyful wedding celebration in Peribáñez's house following his marriage to Casilda, and other scenes concern the town's celebration of its patron saint's day and farm laborers who sing in the fields as they work. Not only do these scenes paint an appealing picture of rural Spanish life, but also they advance the play's action. The town's commander passes by the wedding celebration and—appropriately, for a man who cannot control his passions—is thrown from his horse, so that he must be taken to recuperate in Peribáñez's house, where he sees Casilda. The scenes centering on the celebration of the patron saint's day and the singing farm laborers similarly contribute to the play's development. It is because of his involvement in the preparations for the festival of San Roque that Peribáñez is obliged to visit Toledo and accidentally sees there a portrait of Casilda, which the commander has ordered painted surreptitiously. He learns of the commander's attempt to seduce Casilda and of her refusal when, on returning from Toledo, he overhears a song that the farm laborers have composed celebrating the incident.

Probably the most discussed passage in the play is a statement by a minor character, Belardo—a name that Lope de Vega frequently used as a pseudonym for himself—that he has taken refuge in the Church. Because *Peribáñez* was first published in 1614, the same year that Lope de Vega became a priest, some critics have believed that this passage is a reflection of that event. The current consensus, however, is that the play was written four years earlier and that this passage actually reflects Lope de Vega's joining the Congregation of the Calle del Olivar in 1610. A far more interesting reflection of Lope de Vega's life can be found in the play's evocation of the biblical story of David and Bathsheba when the commander has Peribáñez sent to war (just as David did Uriah) so that he may satisfy his lust for his subject's wife. Lope de Vega evoked the story of David in many of his works, and it is likely that he felt a special affinity for this biblical king whose great sin was lust and who enjoyed divine forgiveness for that sin. In this light, it is interesting to note that Lope de Vega has the commander, who is stabbed by Peribáñez, live long enough to receive absolution, but that the commander's servant and Casilda's treacherous friend Inés—both of whom are motivated by greed—are not so fortunate.

The most noteworthy aspect of the play is its treatment of the theme of honor. In the commander's opinion, honor is the prerogative of the nobility. This view was probably a commonly held one at the time of the play's composition. Therefore, Peribáñez is obliged to defend his slaying of the commander on the grounds that, when the commander ordered him to fight the Moors, he also made him a knight—thereby endowing him with honor and the obligation to defend it. It is clear, however, that in the author's view, the common man possesses honor and dignity as an inalienable birthright, and it is significant that the play closes with the king's pronouncement that his pardoning of Peribáñez is not an act of grace but of justice.

THE SHEEP WELL

The right of the common man to defend his honor was a popular theme that reappeared in the work of Lope de Vega's followers as well as in several other plays by Lope de Vega himself. Probably the most notable of these is his most frequently anthologized work, *The Sheep Well*, which is based on a rebellion that occurred in 1476 in the Spanish town of Fuente Ovejuna ("Sheep Well"). Like *Peribáñez*, this play dramatizes the murder of a town's military commander. In the case of *The Sheep Well*, however, the commander's offense is against the entire town. The commander believes that all of the town's women are

obligated to satisfy his sexual appetite, and it is thus appropriate that his death occurs because of the united action of the entire populace rather than at the hands of a single individual.

Initially, *The Sheep Well* may impress a modern reader as a rather disjointed work in which several independent episodes—the town's vindication of its honor, the love and marriage of two of the town's young people, and the war between Queen Isabel and her half sister Juana—are not satisfactorily united into an aesthetically pleasing whole. Closer inspection, however, reveals that Lope de Vega has established a thematic unity based on a proper understanding of love and of the relationship between love and harmony. He thus carefully develops in the play a connection between the broken political order in Spain and in Fuente Ovejuna and a perverted understanding of love as appetite, and he shows that the restoration of this broken harmony depends on a self-sacrificing love evident in the willingness of the citizens to risk their individual security because of their love for their neighbors.

As with *Peribáñez*, much of the charm of *The Sheep Well* comes from its poetic portrayal of the simple townspeople and of their customs and festivals. By including music and dancing in these and by having this music interrupted by the commander, Lope de Vega emphasizes even in these scenes the central theme of the relationship between love and harmony. This theme is based largely on the Neoplatonic view of love that had become popular in Spain during the sixteenth century.

THE KING, THE GREATEST ALCALDE

A third important play revolving around the common man's right to honor and a nobleman's abuse of that right is *The King, the Greatest Alcalde*, which dramatizes the abduction, during her wedding, of an attractive peasant girl, Elvira, by a nobleman, Don Tello. In this case, Elvira's intended husband, Sancho, does not avenge his honor himself but relies instead on King Alfonso VII, whom he implores to send a mayor. Rather than do this, the king comes himself. On learning that Don Tello has already raped Elvira, the king commands him to marry her and endow her with half his estate and then has Tello put to death for his offense. Elvira, with her lost honor thus restored by her marriage to the man who raped her, is then able to marry Sancho and to bring to her marriage a large dowry. This ending inevitably seems unconvincing to modern readers, and it is unlikely that any amount of discussion could change this impression. However, seventeenth century Spanish audiences apparently found it quite satisfactory, and various other plays of this period end in a similar manner.

The King and the Farmer

It is clear that in Lope de Vega's view, society functions best if it is a harmonious whole in which each member assumes a place appropriate to his station. Plays such as *Peribáñez*, *The Sheep Well*, and *The King, the Greatest Alcalde*, show how the social balance is broken when aristocrats abuse their position of authority. *The King and the Farmer* gives a contrasting and complementary view by illustrating the presumption of a peasant, Juan Labrador ("John Worker"), who fails to recognize his dependence on the aristocracy. Living in a comfortable rural world in which nature's bounty seems to respond generously to all human needs, Juan is proud of his isolation from the court and presumes to build, before his death, his tomb, which he inscribes with the boast that he lived and died without having seen the king. The folly of this boast becomes evident when the king visits Juan's town on a hunting trip, sees the tomb, and visits Juan without revealing his identity. Juan receives him hospitably but in a series of comic scenes issues to him a series of arrogant commands, which the king obligingly obeys before eventually revealing his identity.

Although this play is one of Lope de Vega's most curious works, its main point seems evident enough: In spite of their apparent isolation from each other, the world of the court and the world of the peasant (the worlds of government and of the people) are mutually dependent. The marriage at the end of the play between Juan's daughter Lisarda and Otón, the king's marshal, is an expression of this complementary relationship.

Los melindres de Belisa

The theme of honor, which is treated seriously in *Peribáñez*, *The Sheep Well*, and *The King, the Great-*

est Alcalde, is handled in a humorous manner in *Los melindres de Belisa* (the caprices of Belisa). This work is typical of a genre referred to as *comedias de capa y espada* or cape and sword plays, a name derived from the costume worn by the actors playing the leading male roles. These plays have complicated plots revolving around the courtship of one or more sets of middle-class youths who devise ingenious measures to overcome the obstacles to their love. The young people frequently resort to deceptions or disguises that lead to a confusion of identities and threaten to cause a loss of honor, but cape and sword plays inevitably have happy endings each involving at least one wedding. Though duels are frequently an ingredient of these plays, they are never serious, merely contributing an additional element to the prevailing atmosphere of confusion and misunderstanding.

Thus, in *Los melindres de Belisa*, it is Felisardo's and his sweetheart Celia's mistaken belief that Felisardo has killed a man in a duel, which causes them to hide in their friend Elisio's house and to disguise themselves as slaves. As is usual in cape and sword plays, their seemingly logical deception backfires, and they are seized by the authorities as payment of a debt that Elisio owes the mother of the flighty and finical Belisa, who has rejected many suitors because she can find none refined enough for her. Ironically, this finical girl and her widowed mother both fall in love with Felisardo, whom they believe to be a slave, and Belisa's brother Don Juan falls in love with Celia. In a treatment that pokes fun at the hypocrisy underlying the Spanish concept of honor, Lope de Vega has each family member express outrage when he or she suspects that one of the others may damage the family's reputation by loving a social inferior.

The Lady Nit-Wit

The Lady Nit-Wit is a relatively simple cape and sword play that lacks the disguises and the intricate complications of *Los melindres de Belisa*. Nevertheless, it has most of the standard ingredients of the genre, including a humorous duel that ends harmlessly when the two contenders realize that each of them prefers the girl whom the other is supposed to be courting. This ironic treatment of dueling is typical of the tone of the entire play, which dramatizes a scheme by which the supposedly stupid Finea outsmarts her brilliant sister Nise in order to win Nise's suitor for herself. The play also shows how Finea—so naïve and illiterate in the beginning that she requests help from her father in deciphering a love letter that her sister's suitor has smuggled to her—is transformed by love into an intelligent and discreet person. The theme that love could change people for the better is part of the same Neoplatonic tradition, which, as has been noted, provided the background for understanding *The Sheep Well*.

LAS BIZARRÍAS DE BELISA

Lope de Vega cultivated the cape and sword drama all his life. Written the year before he died, *Las bizarrías de Belisa* continues to be typical of the genre. The plot concerns Belisa's contest—involving various misunderstandings—with her rival Lucinda for the affection of Don Juan de Cardona (who is involved twice in dueling in the course of the play). The work closes with a passage in which Lope de Vega addresses the public through Belisa, informing them that the author's desire to serve them caused him to leave retirement to write this play. Because of this statement, critics believed until recently that this was the last play he wrote. Though that conclusion has been questioned, it is probable that Lope de Vega himself expected that this would be the case. Therefore, throughout the play, he mixes references to the phoenix (evoking his own nickname "the Phoenix of Spain") and the swan (who, according to tradition, sings before his death).

THE GARDENER'S DOG

Because one of its principal characters, the Countess Diana, belongs to the nobility rather than the middle class, *The Gardener's Dog* is not a cape-and-sword play in the strictest sense. It is generally linked with this genre, however, because it treats humorously an ingenious scheme that allows two lovers—the countess and her secretary Teodoro—to overcome the obstacle to their love caused by their differing social stations. This obstacle is a serious one, and the countess struggles with it through most of the play, refusing to recognize openly her love for Teodoro but refusing also to allow him to marry one of her servants. Her behavior is thus like that of the proverbial dog in the manger, who neither eats nor allows others to eat. The solution to Teodoro's and Diana's dilemma is provided by Teodoro's servant, the *gracioso* Tristán, who devises a scheme that convinces everyone that Teodoro is the lost son of a wealthy nobleman, Ludovico—and who begs the audience in the last lines of the play not to reveal Teodoro's secret. This request emphasizes the artificiality of the play, and it is possible that this is Lope de Vega's way of underscoring the artificiality of the restricting social conventions of his day. It is also possible that the audience might have felt threatened by the play's violation of its social conventions had it not been reminded that this was only fiction after all.

THE KNIGHT FROM OLMEDO

Though he wrote very few tragedies, two of Lope de Vega's finest works belong to this genre. The first of these, *The Knight from Olmedo*, dramatizes the murder of the protagonist, Alonso, a handsome and courageous knight, by Rodrigo, a man whose life Alonso saves but who is his rival for the love of Inés. The play establishes tragic expectations from the beginning by evoking in its title a well-known song (sung in the last act) about the murder of a knight described as "the flower of Olmedo" (Alonso's birthplace) and "the glory of Medina" (the town in which Alonso courted Inés), and these expectations are reinforced by parallels between the play's action and passages in the song describing the knight from Olmedo as being warned by ghosts of the danger that awaits him. In spite of this, much of the first part of the play strikes the modern reader, who is unfamiliar with the song evoked by the title, as being inappropriately light for tragedy—evidence that Lope de Vega is following his customary practice of mixing tragic and humorous elements in the same work.

Alonso's employment of the witch Fabia's services in order to win Inés led a number of critics to interpret this play moralistically and to view the protagonist's death as a form of divine punishment. This reading has been corrected, however, and the current view of the play recognizes it as a poetic evocation of the thanatos-eros theme—of the inherent connection between love and death.

JUSTICE WITHOUT REVENGE

Another tragedy, *Justice Without Revenge*, is more consistent in its tone than *The Knight from Olmedo* and is generally acknowledged as the equal of the great tragic dramas of the ancient Greeks and of William Shakespeare. Because of its tragic tone, it is probably the least typical of all of Lope de Vega's plays, but one still finds among its characters the customary *gracioso* (whose jokes are in this case often related to the play's serious theme). Lope de Vega's abiding interest in nature is also evident in a number of passages that extol—perhaps ironically—the virtues of rural life.

The play's plot, taken from a novella by Matteo Bandello, concerns a scheme by which the Italian duke of Ferrara tricks his illegitimate son Federico into unwittingly murdering Casandra, the duke's young bride, with whom Federico has had an adulterous affair. The duke then has Federico put to death for killing his stepmother. Because of its bloody and startling denouement, this play is typical of the Senecan tragic style that was popular in Spain and sought to dazzle or amaze the audience with the spectacular. It is also typical of a peculiarly Spanish genre referred to informally as the "wife-murder play," because it dramatizes a husband's need to defend his honor by murdering his wife. Calderón is a more noted writer of this type of drama, but Lope de Vega had experimented with it as early as 1596-1598, when he wrote *Los comendadores de Córdoba* (the commanders of Cordoba). However, until the composition of *Justice Without Revenge* in the final years of his life, he did not produce a masterpiece in the genre, and it is probable that the work's tragic tone reflects the author's own circumstances at the time he wrote it.

The most striking feature of *Justice Without Revenge* is its ambiguity, which is not limited to the dialogue but also extends to the characters and the theme. For this reason, the play has been the subject of many conflicting interpretations, in which scholars have tried to assign the blame for the final catastrophe to one or another of the characters. As with *The Knight from Olmedo*, however, it is probably best to avoid moralistic interpretations of this work. Rather, the play's ambiguity seems designed to evoke the ultimate ambiguity of life, and all three of the main characters seem caught in a dilemma for which they are not entirely responsible. The work's basically pessimistic tone is attentuated, however, by a complex series of images in which Lope de Vega—apparently now taking his religious vocation seriously—evokes the Christian doctrine of the Atonement. Thus, even in his final, despairing years, he was unable to view life without hope.

OTHER MAJOR WORKS

LONG FICTION: *La Arcadia*, 1598; *El peregrino en su patria*, 1604 (*The Pilgrim: Or, The Stranger in His Own Country*, 1621); *Los pastores de Belén*, 1612; *Novelas a Marcia Leonarda*, 1621; *La Dorotea*, 1632.

POETRY: *La Dragontea*, 1598; *El Isidro*, 1599; *La hermosura de Angélica*, 1602; *Rimas*, 1602; *El arte nuevo de hacer comedias en este tiempo*, 1609 (*The New Art of Writing Plays*, 1914); *Jerusalén conquistada*, 1609; *Rimas sacras*, 1614; *La Circe*, 1621; *La filomena*, 1621; *Triunfos divinos*, 1625; *La corona trágica*, 1627; *Laurel de Apolo*, 1630; *Amarilis*, 1633; *La gatomaquia*, 1634 (*Gatomachia*, 1843); *Rimas humanas y divinas del licenciado Tomé de Burguillos*, 1634; *Filis*, 1635; *La Vega del Parnaso*, 1637.

NONFICTION: *Égloga a Claudio*, 1637.

BIBLIOGRAPHY

Fox, Diane. *Refiguring the Hero: From Peasant to Noble in Lope de Vega and Calderón*. Penn State Studies in Romance Literature series. University Park: Pennsylvania State University Press, 1991. Fox examines the image of the hero and class status in the works of Lope de Vega and Pedro Calderón de la Barca. Bibliography and index.

McKendrick, Melveena. *Playing the King: Lope de Vega and the Limits of Conformity*. Rochester, N.Y.: Tamesis, 2000. An examination of Lope de Vega's portrayal of the monarchy in his works. Bibliography and index.

Morrison, Robert R. *Lope de Vega and the Comedia de Santos*. New York: Peter Lang, 2000. This study examines the religious drama of Lope de Vega. Bibliography and index.

Ostlund, DeLys. *The Re-creation of History in the Fernando and Isabel Plays of Lope de Vega*. New York: Peter Lang, 1997. Oslund examines the historical aspects of the dramas of Lope de Vega. Bibliography and index.

Smith, Marlene K. *The Beautiful Woman in the Theater of Lope de Vega: Ideology and Mythology of Female Beauty in Seventeenth Century Spain.*

New York: Peter Lang, 1998. A discussion of the feminine beauty as portrayed in the works of Lope de Vega. Bibliography and index.

Wright, Elizabeth R. *Pilgrimage to Patronage: Lope de Vega and the Court of Philip III, 1598-1621*. Lewisburg, Pa.: Bucknell University Press, 2001. This study focuses on the patronage system and the interactions between politics and the life and work of Lope de Vega. Bibliography and index.

Currie K. Thompson

GIOVANNI VERGA

Born: Catania, Kingdom of the Two Sicilies (now in Sicily, Italy); September 2, 1840
Died: Catania, Sicily, Italy; January 27, 1922

PRINCIPAL DRAMA

Cavalleria rusticana, pr., pb. 1884 (based on his short story; *Cavalleria Rusticana: Nine Scenes from the Life of the People*, 1893)

In portineria, pb. 1884, pr. 1885 (based on his short story "Il canario del N. 15")

La Lupa, pr., pb. 1896 (based on his short story)

La caccia al lupo, pr. 1901, pb. 1902 (based on his short story; *The Wolf Hunt*, 1921)

La caccia alla volpe, pr. 1901, pb. 1902

Dal tuo al mio, pr. 1903, pb. 1952

Teatro, pb. 1912

Rose caduche, pb. 1928 (wr. 1873-1875)

OTHER LITERARY FORMS

Giovanni Verga is best known as a novelist and a short-story writer and is generally considered Italy's greatest novelist, after Alessandro Manzoni, and the father of the contemporary Italian novel, especially that of the neorealist school. His name is closely associated with the term *Verismo*, which was the Italian manifestation of French naturalism. *Verismo*, or Verism, as explicated by Verga's close friend Luigi Capuana, like naturalism, rejected the current artistic

trends that preferred historical and Romantic subjects, extraordinary events, aristocratic characters, sentimentality, and elegant and sophisticated language, in favor of contemporary subjects dealing with contemporary individuals and social problems of middle-class and working-class people, in a rational and straightforward style. Yet while naturalism primarily considered the problems of an urban and industrial society, related by narrators equipped with positivistic explanations, *Verismo* concentrated on the problems of rural and small-town life in the provinces, particularly of southern Italy, and emphasized the practice of the "impersonality of the author"— that is, that the characters should speak for themselves.

Verga's youthful works were still very much in the Romantic tradition. His first published work, *I carbonari della montagna* (1861-1862; the mountain Carbonari), is a historical novel based on the Italian Risorgimento. He established his reputation as a successful novelist with *Storia di una capinera* (1871; *Sparrow: The Story of a Songbird*, 1994), a sentimental novel whose protagonist is forced to live in a convent. This was followed by a series of novels, *Eva* (1873), *Eros* (1874), and *Tigre reale* (1875; royal tigress), dealing with the erotic passions of various femmes fatales and young attractive artists from the provinces. Verga's first veristic work was "Nedda"

(1874), a short story based on the life of a poor and desperate peasant girl. This work was followed by other short stories in which the author both theorized and practiced veristic principles and which were published in the volume *Vita dei campi* (1880; *Under the Shadow of Etna*, 1896). These preparatory works culminated in Verga's masterpiece, *I Malavoglia* (1881; *The House by the Medlar Tree*, 1890, 1953; a complete translation was published in 1964), the story of the misfortunes of a family of fishermen. *The House by the Medlar Tree* was intended as the first of a series of five novels with the collective title "I vinti" (the defeated), each of which would illustrate, on a different societal level, the theme that individuals, in responding to the natural impulse to improve their condition, are inevitably subject to defeat. Only the second of the series, *Mastro-don Gesualdo* (1889; English translation, 1893, 1923), the story of an enriched laborer's aspirations and defeat and considered Verga's second masterpiece, was published.

Giovanni Verga (Library of Congress)

ACHIEVEMENTS

Because his theater is generally considered a minor aspect of his total opus, there is some irony in the fact that Giovanni Verga achieved his greatest popular triumph with his theatrical version of his short story "Cavalleria rusticana," and that his enduring international fame is supported by the popularity of Pietro Mascagni's opera based on the same story. Nevertheless, there is evidence that, from his earliest years, Verga had the ambition of becoming a successful playwright. His motivation may also have been partly materialistic because in the latter decades of the nineteenth century, the theater represented to a young writer some of the same economic temptations as the cinema does in the twenty-first century. That Verga apparently conceived of the theater as an adaptation of narrative literature, without adequately considering the fundamental differences between the two genres, may have been the cause of his general lack of theatrical success. There is even reason to speculate on the extent to which external factors may have been responsible for the surprising and extraordinary success of *Cavalleria Rusticana*. Certainly the ad-

vance publicity given to the debate over its probable failure and a newspaper article appealing for openness and objectivity on the part of the audience, published the day before the opening, contributed to an atmosphere of tense expectation.

According to a newspaper critic's eyewitness account, the beauty and distinction of the set significantly contributed to the positive attitude with which the audience then received the play. For whatever reason, the enormous success of *Cavalleria Rusticana* opened the door to *Verismo* and contemporary realism in the theater. The traditional historical themes, the exaggerated gestures, the rhetorical language, the spectacular, and the marvelous would be increasingly replaced by the contemporary, the sincere, the vivid, the humble, and the straightforward. A successful playwright such as Guiseppe Giacosa would attempt to change from historical themes to contemporary middle-class themes. More important, Verga's theatrical revolution would have a direct effect on fellow Sicilian Luigi Pirandello, from whose theater most important contemporary European theater derives.

BIOGRAPHY

When Giovanni Verga was born in Catania on September 2, 1840, into a well-to-do landowning family of aristocratic background, Italy was not yet united, and Sicily belonged to the Kingdom of the Two Sicilies, governed by Bourbon monarchs from their capital in Naples. Catania remained very distant, therefore, from the cultural centers of Milan and Florence. Verga's father deserves credit for wanting his son to have the most liberal education possible in his culturally provincial society, and for this purpose, he enrolled him, at age ten, in the private school of Antonino Abate. The teacher, who shared the liberal and pro-Italian sentiments of the younger generation, had the attitude and enthusiasm, if not the talents, of a Romantic poet and as such inspired his pupils, including the young Verga, to try their hands at writing. At age seventeen, Verga wrote his first novel, *Amore e patria* (1857; love and fatherland), inspired by the American Revolution and full of teenage enthusiasm for patriotic ideals, although not worthy of publication.

In 1858, Verga enrolled in the Faculty of Law at the University of Catania, but instead of studying, he worked on his second novel, *I carbonari della montagna*, another historical novel imbued with patriotic fervor, which, with his father's consent, he published, using the money intended for his last two years of university study. Although the second novel was little better than the first, it was given a favorable review in the Florentine periodical *Nuova Europa*. Encouraged by this success, Verga submitted a third novel, *Sulle lagune* (1863; on the lagoon), to the same periodical, which published it in serial form (it was published in book form in 1975). In the meantime, he had become involved in various Sicilian journalistic enterprises, but the combination of his publication in Florence and the transfer to Florence of the capital of the now independent and united Italian Kingdom made that city irresistibly attractive to him. After several visits, he established residence there in 1869 and was befriended by the temporary capital's intellectual, artistic, and social elite. These were Verga's most intensely lived years, full of the experiences that inspired the series of novels of passion from *Una peccatrice* (1866; *A Mortal Sin*, 1995) to *Eros*, as well as the play *Rose caduche* (fading roses).

With the exception of Florence's brief heyday as a capital city, Milan was Italy's leading center of culture in the nineteenth century, and soon afterward, the capital was transferred to newly annexed Rome. Verga moved to Milan in 1872, where he quickly took up with the leading cultural figures of the Lombard city. In addition to its own traditional culture, Milan has always been the Italian city most receptive to cultural influences originating beyond the Alps, and the most tolerant of unorthodox styles. Thus, it was here that Verga came into contact with both the *Scapigliati* and French naturalism. The *Scapigliati* (that is, the disheveled) were a group of young intellectuals and artists who, as the epithet coined by one of their own number suggests, explicitly rejected the high ideals and heroic tension that characterized the Risorgimento, embracing instead all that was abnormal, irregular, and antibourgeois. Most important for Verga, this group attempted to express itself in everyday language, a practice that would become characteristic of Verga's masterpieces. It was also here that Verga became more familiar with the work of Honoré de Balzac, Gustave Flaubert, and particularly Émile Zola. Verga maintained a residence in Milan until 1885, but after the death of his sister in 1877, and his mother in 1878, he spent increasingly longer periods in Sicily.

The period of Verga's greatest literary production began in 1880 with the publication of *Under the Shadow of Etna* and ended in 1889 with *Mastro-don Gesualdo*. In 1884, he enjoyed his only theatrical success with *Cavalleria Rusticana*. For practical purposes, he made a tactical error by not following it immediately with another Sicilian drama. Instead, he tried a Milanese working-class background in *In portineria* (the doorkeeper's house), which had a lukewarm reception in Milan in 1885.

The satisfaction he received from the success of *Cavalleria Rusticana* was soon spoiled by the litigation that he had to undertake in an attempt to gain a larger share of author's royalties from the very profitable operatic production of his play. This, and his general disillusionment with society, caused him to lead an increasingly isolated life during his last two decades. On the occasion of his eightieth birthday, he was honored by an official celebration but refused to attend. In the same year, he was named Senator of the Italian Republic. Attended by his lifelong friend Frederico De Roberto, he died on January 27, 1922.

ANALYSIS

Among Giovanni Verga's earliest youthful writings was a play entitled "I nuovi tartufi" (the new Tartuffes), which, according to Frederico De Roberto, he submitted to a competition held in Florence. The play did not win any prizes for him nor has its manuscript survived. A second comedy written in Florence was also unsuccessful and has since been lost. The first play that has survived, *Rose caduche*, written sometime between 1873 and 1875, was never produced, but was published posthumously in 1928.

ROSE CADUCHE

Like the novels of passion that Verga wrote during this same period, *Rose caduche* is set in the atmosphere of the elegant but superficial and frivolous society in which the author was living. By the time he wrote the play, he had apparently decided to emphasize the more negative aspects of this society, particularly the shallowness of the romantic relationships between the sexes. For this purpose, he created four couples and assigned to each the role of a different attitude toward this relationship. Act 1 brings the eight still-unattached individuals together at an elegant garden party in the villa of Countess Baglini. Each of the characters has the opportunity to reveal his or her personality. The countess is egotistical and conniving; Irma Scotti is passionate and defenseless; Lucrezia is sincere and rational; Signoria Merelli is practical and domineering; Luciano De-Galiani is a romantic poet; Paolo Avellani is a levelheaded lawyer; Cavalier Falconi is a charming hypocrite; and Commendatore Gaudenti is a bumbling lecher. This analysis reflects the simplicity of the play itself, whose meager plot involves the mixing and matching of the couples, complicated only by some momentary jealousies and misunderstandings caused primarily by the characters' inability or unwillingness to speak directly and clearly. Indeed, if *Rose caduche* has any artistic value,

it is in the author's virtuosity in representing the circuitous speech patterns of his characters. Yet even this virtuosity is compromised by the necessity of too frequently used stage directions such as "ironic," "ironic with significant accent," and "with double meaning," which reveal the failure of the dialogue to convey attitudes by itself.

By the end of act 2, which is set in another elegant gathering in the home of Irma Scotti, the couples have been matched. After sacrificing his right to a duel and promising to leave, Irma cannot resist Luciano's passionate desire for her. When Lucrezia, who was infatuated by Falconi, realizes that he has only dishonorable intentions, she accepts Paolo's offer of marriage based on sincere admiration and friendship. The countess, who had desired Luciano, ends up with Falconi, and Signora Morelli and Commendatore Gaudenti come together by default.

Act 3, which takes place sometime later at Irma's country home, dramatizes the outcome of these pairings. Only Lucrezia and Paolo are happy, because only their relationship is not based on passion and sexual gratification, which are doomed to grow pale, but rather on real love, which is directed toward family unity. Luciano, who still claims to love Irma but no longer feels passion for her, is sent away by her, and as the play ends, she shows signs of incipient madness. *Rose caduche* fails as a play because it is an illustration rather than a representation. The play's characters never move beyond the function of role-playing in the literal sense. Because they do not successfully conceal the fact that they are acting, they, and the play, fail to create the illusion of real life.

CAVALLERIA RUSTICANA

Verga's first produced play was the one-act tragedy, *Cavalleria Rusticana*, and it proved to be an enormous success. By 1883, having fully developed the narrative potential of *Verismo*, he believed that the theatergoing public was ready to accept it as well. Rather than create a new plot, he decided to transform one of his published short stories into a play, emphasizing the more dramatic aspects of the story. Turiddu Macca, after returning to his Sicilian village from military service, finds that Lola, whom he had intended to marry, is instead married to Alfio, a hard-working and prosperous carter. In order to make Lola jealous, he seduces Santuzza. Lola then invites him to her bed while Alfio is away. These background facts are revealed through dialogue. The action of the play begins with Santuzza looking for Turiddu at his mother's wine shop. She begs him not to abandon her, but after his refusal, in anger and desperation, she reveals the truth to Alfio, who then challenges Turridu to mortal combat, resulting in the latter's death.

The realism of the plot must be understood in terms of the traditional Sicilian code of honor, according to which every wrong must be revenged by the victim against the victimizer; in particular, a cuckold must kill the adulterer in order to regain his honor. Verga correctly believed that this kind of primitive action would fascinate the sophisticated audiences of northern Italy, who were weary of the vacuousness of the current Romantic and neoclassical theater. Everything that happens in *Cavalleria Rusticana* seems to happen, as in Greek tragedy, out of predetermined necessity. In contrast to a play such as *Rose caduche*, here the characters never seem to be posing or acting. Instead, they appear to be living out their destinies with no possibility of doing otherwise. The audience has the illusion of being an unobserved observer of the unavoidable suffering of the characters. This illusion is created by the rapidly moving action, the decisiveness of the characters, the directness of the language, and the lack of discussion. No one attempts to dissuade Alfio and Turiddu from their duel, and there are no second thoughts on their parts. This primitive fatalism renders all the more effective the hint of regret that Turiddu expresses about the ruined reputation of Santuzza as he goes off to the duel.

Cavalleria Rusticana was an enormous success despite the negative predictions of friends whom Verga had asked to read the manuscript. With the help of the prestigious playwright Giuseppe Giacosa, he persuaded Italy's best director-actor, Cesare Rossi, to put on the play in Turin, but only on condition that Verga pay for the scenery and the costumes. Rossi's company included the brilliant young actress Eleanora Duse, for whom the role of Santuzza was given in-

creased importance in the final version of the play. Opening night was January 14, 1884. The author was deliberately not present, but the following night the audience insisted that he receive their ovation from the stage. The play's reputation was clearly established, and it went on to continued success in Milan and elsewhere.

IN PORTINERIA

Encouraged by this success, Verga decided to use another of his published veristic short stories as the basis for his next play. *In portineria*, a two-act drama presented in Milan for the first time on May 16, 1885, was adapted from the short story "Il canario del N. 15" (the canary of No. 15). Like its predecessor, the play deals with humble folk and simple lives, but in contrast to the Sicilian village setting of *Cavalleria Rusticana*, *In portineria* takes place in a squalid working-class neighborhood of Milan. Màlia, affectionate, warmhearted, generous, and self-sacrificing, but sickly and dying of consumption, is secretly in love with Carlini, who works in the printing shop across the street. He, however, asks for the hand of Gilda, Màlia's beautiful but capricious and ambitious sister, who, after a brief period of flirtation, rejects him. Even after Gilda leaves home, Carlini, who has become an intimate of the sisters' parents, spends much time talking to Màlia, expressing his feelings about Gilda. The dramatic tension of the play is in Màlia's inner suffering, forced as she is to suppress her own emotions in order to comfort Carlini and her parents. In the end, she dies almost unnoticed, as Gilda, who has come home for the occasion, and Carlini seem to be rekindling their relationship before her eyes.

The fact that only one year after the great success of *Cavalleria Rusticana*, *In portineria* proved a failure, raises some questions about the acceptance of *Verismo* among Italian theatergoers of the time. The two plays are similar in the low societal level of their characters, the simplicity and explicitness of their events, and their direct and colloquial language. Yet for a middle-class Milanese audience, the problems of Màlia and her family were undoubtedly all too familiar and may even have seemed similar to their own problems, only reduced to their essential form and thus without the Romantic trappings that make them appear heroic and worthy. What could be worse for a typical bourgeois than to see himself reflected in a proletarian character? The problems of Sicilian peasants, however, were distant, unrelated to the lives of the audience, and therefore fascinating and allowing for feelings of compassion. In short, it may have been merely the exotic aspects of *Verismo* that appealed to the audiences of the time, an appeal that Verga did not exploit.

La Lupa

By 1896, it may have been too late: *La Lupa*, adapted from the celebrated short story of the same name, although returning to the Sicilian setting, met with little success. Pina, thirty-five years old, described in the list of characters as still beautiful and provocative, is obsessed by sexual desire for Nanni Lasca, who is described as tender with women, but even more tender with his own (economic) interests. The necessity to describe the characters in this and more detail reveals a fundamental weakness in the play: the ineffectiveness of the dialogue in expressing the personality of the characters. Although Nanni does tell Pina that he needs to marry a girl with a dowry, he does not dwell on this necessity, and it does not seem to be a determining factor in his decision to marry Pina's daughter, Mara, who is younger and more beautiful. Pina arranges the marriage and gives the young couple her house, but her intention is to seduce Nanni. The economic theme, so effectively expressed and so central to other important works such as his novel *Mastro-don Gesualdo*, here only detracts from the main theme of irrational and inevitable sexual desire. Nanni cannot resist Pina's temptations, and this sin dooms to failure his otherwise idyllic relationship with Mara. Every attempt at mediation on the part of the townspeople fails, and in the end, provoked by Pina, Nanni kills her with an ax.

Whereas in *Cavalleria Rusticana* Verga wisely emphasized the dramatic episodes at the expense of narrative, concentrating on the elements of the story essential for expressing the tragedy, in *La Lupa* he apparently felt the need for a longer, two-act play and achieved this length by adding elements to it,

such as the joking and dancing of the peasants that occupies a large part of act 1. While providing the local color that Verga probably imagined his audiences would want, these elements detract from and dilute the dramatic tension provided by Pina's obsession. They also create a lack of coherence between the two acts. Through most of act 1, Pina does not really seem like anything more than a middle-aged woman unfortunately infatuated with a younger man. It is only in act 2 that she is presented as depraved, despicable, and irrational. Mara, who in act 2 displays an aggressive sense of right and wrong and fights passionately against her mother, hardly speaks a word in act 1.

The Wolf Hunt

Much later, in 1901, Verga made another attempt at playwriting, this time using the short story "La caccia al lupo" (the wolf hunt) as the basis for the one-act play *The Wolf Hunt*. In effect, he did little more than change the narrative of the short story into the stage directions of the play. The shepherd Lollo comes home unexpectedly on a rainy night and finds his wife, Mariangela, looking nervous and acting suspiciously. Lollo tells her of his plan to trap a wolf that has been seen in the area by using a lamb as bait. As he describes his plan, the double meaning of his words soon becomes apparent to Mariangela and to the reader, who begins to suspect that the wolf is really a man, that Mariangela is the lamb, and that the house is the trap. In fact, as soon as Lollo leaves, locking his wife inside, Bellamà comes out of the inner room. The rest of the play dramatizes the struggle of the two lovers, now turned against each other, against imminent death. Too short for production, *The Wolf Hunt* may be favorably compared to *Cavalleria Rusticana* for its dramatic intensity.

La caccia alla volpe

La caccia alla volpe (the fox hunt) was apparently intended as a companion piece for *The Wolf Hunt*, whose theme it parallels in high society. By feigning an injury, Di Fleri persuades Artale to go for a doctor, thus giving him the opportunity to seduce Donna Livia, who is Artale's lover. Di Fleri is unsuccessful and is exposed, but Donna Livia becomes angry with Artale for his rather uninspired defense of their relationship. The contrast between the sincere emotion of the primitive shepherds and the superficiality of the aristocrats is obvious, but like its characters, *La caccia alla volpe* is completely lacking in substance and is at best favorably compared to *Rose caduche* because of its brevity.

DAL TUO AL MIO

Verga's last play was his longest, and it was his only produced play that was not based on a short story. On the contrary, after staging the three-act *Dal tuo al mio* (what is yours is mine) in 1903, he later adapted it as a novella. The easy transition between the two genres confirms Verga's basic inability to distinguish between narrative and dramatic art. The theme here is economic, with love being relegated to a secondary role. Baron Navarra, because of the failing productivity of his sulfur mine, is forced to ask his daughter Nina to forgo her love for Lucio and instead marry the son of Rametta, a lower-class person who has become rich through hard work in the mines and wise investment. When the mines are flooded, however, Rametta calls off the wedding. In act 2, when Rametta demands repayment of the loans that he has given Navarra at high interest, the baron resists the proposed assignment to Rametta of the profits of the mine for fifteen years until an affair between Lisa, his second daughter, and Luciano, the foreman, is revealed. In act 3, the problem of labor unrest, presented, but downplayed in acts 1 and 2, assumes primary importance. The miners, incited and led by Luciano, have been on strike for three weeks, demanding higher wages which both Navarra, who is unable, and Rametta who is unwilling, refuse to pay. Reduced to hunger, the miners turn to violence and threaten to burn the mine. At the last minute, Luciano turns against the miners and defends the mine, which is the property of Lisa, who is now his wife. At this moment, Navarra embraces Luciano and Lisa, whom he had earlier disowned. Still, all would be lost were it not for the last-minute arrival of the army, announced by a bugle call. This stirring finish, too much like the traditional arrival of the cavalry, confirms one's suspicions about the quality of the play.

One major problem is the abundance of stage directions, which serve the purpose of what would later become the narrative of the novella and without which the dialogue would not cohere. Another problem is the lack of coherence in tone. Act 1 has the atmosphere of a situation comedy with elements of melodrama. The plot revolves around Nina's unfortunate situation and her self-sacrificing acceptance of it. The most effective part of the play is the aborted attempt at negotiation, in act 2, between Navarra and Rametta. Yet here, too, the play seems undecided between its comic and its serious intentions. Meanwhile, Nina has become a rather practical and aggressive businesswoman, a transformation that jars with her behavior in act 1. In act 3, she has virtually no function at all, as attention is focused on Lisa and Luciano, whose final decision is not based on anything they have previously said or done. In the preface to the narrative version of the play, Verga declared that he had no intention of expounding any political position but sought only to represent objectively an aspect of life. Nevertheless, the play ends with the uncompromising owners being protected by the army while the starving miners will apparently be punished and forced to return to the mines at survival wages. Luciano's traitorous act is rewarded as one based on tardy, but nevertheless solid, wisdom—the protection of one's property.

OTHER MAJOR WORKS

LONG FICTION: *Amore e patria*, 1857; *I carbonari della montagna*, 1861-1862 (also as *I carbonari della montagna: Sulle lagune*, 1975; includes *Sulle lagune*); *Una peccatrice*, 1866 (*A Mortal Sin*, 1995); *Storia di una capinera*, 1871 (*Sparrow: The Story of a Songbird*, 1994); *Eva*, 1873; *Eros*, 1874; *Tigre reale*, 1875; *I Malavoglia*, 1881 (*The House by the Medlar Tree*, partial translation, 1890, 1953; complete translation, 1964); *Il marito di Elena*, 1882; *Mastro-don Gesualdo*, 1889 (English translation, 1893, 1923).

SHORT FICTION: *Primavera ed altri racconti*, 1876; *Vita dei campi*, 1880 (*Under the Shadow of Etna*, 1896); *Novelle rusticane*, 1883 (*Little Novels of Sicily*, 1925); *Per le vie*, 1883; *Vagabondaggio*, 1887; *I ricordi del capitano D'Arce*, 1891; *Don Candeloro e C'.*, 1894; *Dal tuo al mio*, 1905 (adaptation of his play); *Cavalleria Rusticana and Other Stories*, 1926; *The She-Wolf and Other Stories*, 1958.

NONFICTION: *Lettere al suo traduttore*, 1954; *Lettere a Dina*, 1962, 1971; *Lettere a Luigi Capuana*, 1975.

BIBLIOGRAPHY

Alexander, Alfred. *Giovanni Verga: A Great Writer and His World*. London: Grant and Cutler, 1972. A basic biography of Verga that covers his life and works. Bibliography.

Alexander, Foscarina. *The Aspiration Toward a Lost Natural Harmony in the Work of Three Italian Writers: Leopardi, Verga, and Moravia*. Lewiston, N.Y.: Edwin Mellen Press, 1990. Alexander compares and contrasts the works of Verga, Giacomo Leopardi, and Alberto Moravia with emphasis on their treatment of the concepts of harmony, nature, and alienation. Bibliography and index.

Cecchetii, Giovanni. *Giovanni Verga*. Boston: Twayne, 1978. A basic biography of Verga that covers his life and works. Bibliography and index.

Patruno, Nicholas. *Language in Giovanni Verga's Early Novels*. Chapel Hill: University of North Carolina Press, 1977. This study of Verga's early novels focuses on his use of language, which can also be seen in his dramatic works. Bibliography and index.

Woolf, D. *The Art of Verga: A Study in Objectivity*. Sydney: Sydney University Press, 1977. A critical analysis of the literary works of Verga, with emphasis on his technique. Bibliography and index.

Peter N. Pedroni

GIL VICENTE

Born: Portugal; c. 1465
Died: Portugal; c. 1537

PRINCIPAL DRAMA

Monólogo do vaqueiro, pr. 1502, pb. 1562

Auto pastoril castelhano, pr. 1502, pb. 1562

Auto dos reis magos, pr. 1503, pb. 1567 (*The Three Wise Men*, 1960)

Quem tem farelos?, pr. 1509, pb. 1562 (*Serenade*, 1960)

Auto da India, pr. 1509, pb. 1562 (*The Sailor's Wife*, 1960)

Auto da fé, pr. 1510, pb. 1562

O velho da horta, pr. 1512, pb. 1562

Auto dos fisicos, pr. 1512, pb. 1562

Exhortação da guerra, pr. 1513, pb. 1562 (*Exhortation to War*, 1920)

Auto da sibila Cassandra, pr. 1513, pb. 1562 (*The Play of the Sibyl Cassandra*, 1921)

Auto de la fama, pr. 1515, pb. 1562

Auto dos quatro tempos, pr. 1516, pb. 1562

Auto da barca do inferno, pr. 1516, pb. 1562 (*The Ship of Hell*, 1929)

Auto da barca do purgatório, pr. 1518, pb. 1562 (*The Ship of Purgatory*, 1929)

Auto da alma, pr. 1518, pb. 1562 (*The Soul's Journey*, 1920)

Auto da barca da glória, pr. 1519, pb. 1562 (*The Ship of Heaven*, 1929)

Comedia do viuvo, pr. c. 1521, pb. 1562 (*Widower's Comedy*, 1960)

Amadis de Gaula, pr. 1523, pb. 1562 (*Amadis of Gaul*, 1959)

Farsa de Inês Pereira, pr. 1523, pb. 1562

Auto das ciganas, pr. 1525, pb. 1562

Auto da festa, pr. 1525, pb. 1906

Tragicomédia de dom Duardos, pr. 1525; pb. 1562 (English translation, 1942)

O juiz da Beira, pr. 1525, pb. 1562

Dialógo sobre a ressurreição, pr. 1526, pb. 1562

Nao de amores, pr. 1527, pb. 1562

Farsa dos almocreves, pr. 1527, pb. 1562 (*The Carriers*, 1920)

Tragicomédia pastoril da Serra da Estrella, pr. 1527, pb. 1562 (*The Pastoril Tragicomedy of the Serra da Estrella*, 1920)

Auto da feira, pr. 1528, pb. 1562

O triunfo do inverno, pr. 1529, pb. 1562

Romagem de agravados, pr. 1533, pb. 1562

Auto da Mofina Mendes, pr. 1534, pb. 1562

Floresta de enganos, pr. 1536, pb. 1562

Copilação de todalas obras de Gil Vicente, pb. 1562

Four Plays of Gil Vicente, pb. 1920

Obras completas, pb. 1942-1944 (6 volumes)

OTHER LITERARY FORMS

Many of Gil Vicente's songs have been extracted from his plays and included in poetry anthologies such as *The Penguin Book of Spanish Verse* (1960), edited by J. M. Cohen. Vicente is often, but not always, considered a Spanish writer; as he also wrote in Portuguese, his lyrics are only sometimes available in Spanish-language anthologies of verse.

In the *Copilação de todalas obras de Gil Vicente* of 1562, commonly called the *Copilação*, is a section entitled "Trovas e Cousas Miúdas" (verses and small things), containing twelve miscellaneous works. Of these, the most literary is "Pranto de Maria Parda" ("Maria Parda's Lament"), and the most significant biographically is an untitled "Letter for Tolerance." In addition, there is an epistolary dedication for the *Copilação*, which demonstrates that Vicente was planning, if not implementing, the publication of his complete works during his lifetime. In this two-page Portuguese prose piece, the author evinces the proper humility before the fact of his own success and claims that he would not think of publishing his works if it were not for the king's request that he do so. As many of his plays are works of devotion, he reasons, their publication will not only serve the king but also work in the service of God.

Among the other pieces are a sermon, a paraphrase in Portuguese of Psalm 50 ("Have mercy on me, O God, according to Thy great mercy"), a lament on the passing of Manuel I, a poem on the subsequent

coronation of his son John III, and sundry verses addressed to a variety of persons.

Vicente's "Letter for Tolerance," sent to John III in January, 1531, helped to allay a burst of anti-Semitic hysteria in the wake of an earthquake that had shaken Portugal on January 26, 1531. To charges that the earthquake was caused by the wrath of God for the sins of the nation, which apparently included Portuguese toleration of newly converted Jews whose practice of Christianity was less than convincing, Vicente replied that earthquakes are typical phenomena of a natural world characterized by sudden changes. Furthermore, he advised that if some of the Portuguese people (namely, the converted Jews) were still not devout Christians, perhaps it was for the greater glory of God. He suggested that perhaps if they were treated gently, their eventual conversion would follow. Unfortunately, Vicente's tolerance did not extend to the material he incorporated into his plays. In *Dialógo sobre a ressurreição*, for example, it is the three rabbis in their rejection of the Resurrection who bear the brunt of the play's ridicule.

"Maria Parda's Lament," one of Vicente's most fascinating works, is a 369-line poem in Portuguese about how a drunkard named Maria Parda copes with a wine shortage in Lisbon. After traversing Lisbon from end to end to no avail (she names the streets) in hopes of slaking her thirst, she decides that she is about to die and composes her last will and testament, commending her soul to Noah, who first planted the vine. Despite the morbid nature of the subject, Vicente's characterization of Maria Parda is remarkably sympathetic.

ACHIEVEMENTS

Gil Vicente created the national drama of Portugal one generation before the Spanish Golden Age and two generations before the Elizabethans. From 1502 to 1536, he was virtually poet laureate of Portugal in the capacities of musician, actor, lyric poet, and playwright, and the royal court did not plan any celebration without asking for his help. He has been called a Lusitanian Plautus, a medieval Aristophanes, and a Portuguese William Shakespeare. His light touch and singing verses reminded John Dos Passos of Theocritus. Observing the dramatic vitality generated by Vicente in tiny, isolated Portugal, Richard Garnett in his *History of Italian Literature* (1898) laments that there was no one of Vicente's caliber among the Italians of the sixteenth century.

As a result of censorship, the changing tastes brought in with the Renaissance, and imitators who were simply unworthy of their master, the tradition of Vicente had little continuation within Portugal (although glimmers of his influence can be detected in the theatrical works of Luís de Camões, Antonio Prestes, and Antonio Ribeiro Chiado). However, his influence can be found in the playwrights of the Spanish Golden Age. Lope de Rueda was acquainted with Vicente, as was Miguel de Cervantes. Vicente's compression of history and abandonment of chronology as seen in *The Play of the Sibyl Cassandra* were later a distinguishing feature in the great sacramental plays of Pedro Calderón de la Barca. Various critics have suggested a direct or indirect influence on William Shakespeare.

Erasmus is said to have wished that he knew Portuguese in order to read Vicente's plays in the original. The eschatological Ship Trilogy, with its angel laying bare the souls in judgment, is unsurpassed in the literature of the Iberian Peninsula in the sixteenth century. Vicente's *Auto das ciganas* is the first piece of European theater dealing professedly with the Gypsy race. Dámaso Alonso calls him one of the finest lyric poets of the Spanish language, and indeed some modern Spanish poets, such as Rafael Alberti (in whose poem "Arión," Vicente, alongside Rubén Darío, and Charles Baudelaire, is one of eight poets whom Alberti acknowledges as his masters), have been inspired by his poetic example. If, as is widely assumed, Vicente the dramatist and poet was indeed the same person as Gil Vicente the goldsmith who made the monstrance for the Hieronymite monastery in Belem, then, as Dos Passos observes, he was one of the most versatile artists who has ever lived.

In 1838, the Portuguese romantic dramatist Almeida Garrette published *Um Auto de Gil Vicente*, in which he portrayed Vicente as the actor-director of a theatrical company at the court of King Manuel. This same nineteenth century writer translated Vicente's "Ballad of Flérida" from *Tragicomédia de dom Duardos* into Portuguese (from Spanish) and included it in his *Romanceiro* (1843). About the same time, in the United States, Henry Wadsworth Longfellow helped acquaint American readers with Vicente's name by including English renderings of his poems "How Fair the Maiden" (from *The Play of the Sibyl Cassandra*) and "If Thou Art Sleeping, Maiden" (from *Quem tem farelos?*) in his *The Poets and Poetry of Europe* (1845).

BIOGRAPHY

Gil Vicente was born in about 1465, possibly in Guimarães, in northern Portugal, or in the western province of Beira, whose dialect he occasionally employs in his plays and which is adjacent to the area of Spain whose dialect, called *sayagués*, he employs in his Spanish plays. His education is a matter of conjecture, and his learning seems to have stemmed more from devotional books than from humanistic study. His knowledge of the Bible was undeniably extensive. There is even some doubt about exactly who he was, although it seems reasonably certain that Gil Vicente the playwright of the Portuguese royal court was the same person as Gil Vicente who was Queen Leanor's goldsmith.

In June, 1502, Vicente, in the guise of a herdsman, accompanied some thirty courtiers dressed as herdsmen and bearing such rustic gifts as eggs, milk, cheese, and honey. They presented themselves in Queen Maria's bedchamber to congratulate their sovereigns on the birth of their first-born son, later John III. Vicente in his skit related how the palace guards tried to keep his group from entering and explained how their village had sent them to verify if indeed the royal birth had taken place. The composition, written in Castilian as a compliment to the young Spanish-speaking queen, was called *Monólogo do vaqueiro* (the herdsman's monologue).

Before 1502, Vicente had been in the service of the Dowager Queen Leanor; after this "new thing," she was so pleased that she asked for a repeat performance the following Christmas, whereupon Vicente wrote another play, *Auto pastoril castelhano*. The dowager queen was again delighted and asked for another play for Twelfth Night. This was *The Three Wise Men*, and after that, no court function was complete without a dramatic production by Vicente. Following the court from palace to palace, Vicente wrote plays that provided court members with distraction in times of difficulty and in times of rejoicing gave expression to the jubilation of the people.

After the composition of his first four plays, there was a five-year lull that is generally explained as time that Vicente devoted to his activities as a goldsmith. In September, 1503, Vasco da Gama returned from his second voyage to India with two thousand *miticaes* of gold, and King Manuel ordered that a monstrance be crafted of it for the service of the altar. By 1506, Vicente finished his glorious monstrance for the Monastery of the Jerónimos at Belém (on display today at the National Museum of Ancient Art in Lisbon), and from 1512 to 1516, he was master of the Royal Mint.

Vicente married twice, first to Branca Bezerra, who died in about 1512 and who bore him two sons, and then, in 1517, to Melicia Rodrigues, by whom he had three more children. Of these three, two were involved in their father's dramatic activities: Paula as an actress and Luis as the compiler of his father's works in the *Copilação*.

The dramatist's last play, *Floresta de enganos*, was performed at Évora in 1536. Vicente belonged both to the Middle Ages and to the Renaissance; he loved the traditional themes of the Middle Ages, but his natural curiosity, his tolerance of others, and his love of life belonged more to the Renaissance. His versatility has already been noted; in addition to poetry, drama, and goldsmithing, he dabbled in astrology and witchcraft and wrote music for some of his lyrics.

Vicente was a profoundly religious dramatist who believed that prayers do not suffice without a "clean" soul and that people are judged by their works. He had a mystical and pantheistic bent and loved humble flowers—chicory, chamomile, honeysuckle, and wild roses—and those human beings closest to nature, such as children and peasants. Of city folk, he was less enamored, as when he speaks of "*a desvairada opinião do vulgo*" ("the confused thoughts of the

masses"), and he abhorred the general slackness of the times. In his religious plays, he frequently satirizes the clergy for their hypocrisy and lack of commitment. The first edition of Vicente's plays survived without mutilation by the Inquisition as a result of the support of Queen Mother Catarina, but the second edition of 1586 was severely bowdlerized and was the last printed for 250 years. This apparent irreverence, however, was not directed at the Church, but rather at its unworthy ministers. Unlike Martin Luther, he wished to reform the Church from within, and he directed his wrath and satire at abuses, not at doctrine.

ANALYSIS

Gil Vicente divided his plays into farces, religious pieces (elaborated from medieval mimes and mysteries), comedies, and tragicomedies, but his categories overlap. For example, nothing separates some of the comedies and tragicomedies from the farces, and some of the farces are religious. The tragicomedies, or aristocratic pieces, were the result of his contact with the royal court and are more often spectacular than dramatic, depending more on music, songs, and dances, and on the lyricism of their versification. It is rather in his comedies and farces that he displays his dramatic skill, his keen powers of observation, and his generous human sympathy. Brilliant character sketches, clever dialogue, and comic situations occur in the farces *Quem tem farelos?*, *The Sailor's Wife*, *Farsa de Inês Pereira*, *O velho da horta*, and in other plays that are devoid of conventional plot, such as *The Carriers* and *O juiz da Beira*, which are more like modern revues than any dramatic genre. The vitality of Vicente's humorous and satiric studies is especially remarkable if indeed they lacked the stimulus of popular audiences.

Most of the plays are written in the national *redondilha* verse of eight-syllable lines and are introduced by rubrics stating the date, the place, the audience, and the occasion of each performance. Most of them were staged at the various royal palaces, although some were played in hospitals; Aubrey Bell believed that some were also produced in private homes, but this does not appear to be documented. The liturgical plays were performed at the great festivals of Christmas, Epiphany, and Maundy Thursday. Many of the plays contain songs, either written and set to music by the author or collected from popular sources, and often the characters leave the stage singing and dancing, as in the medieval comedies. The plays of Vicente also contain a wealth of folklore in the form of proverbs, listed by Bell at the end of his *Four Plays of Gil Vicente*: "*Nam se toman trutas a bragas enxutas*" ("One does not catch trout without getting wet"), "*Grão a grão gallo farta*" ("Many a mickle makes a muckle"), and "*A amiga e o amigo mais aquenta que bom lenho*" ("A pair of lovers makes more heat than good wood").

One of Vicente's most remarkable skills was his capacity to portray a type so well in so few lines, a skill that Bell compares to that of a master goldsmith accustomed to setting jewels. Vicente's gallery of priests is unforgettable: Frei Paço, who minces with his velvet cap and gilt sword "like a very sweet courtier"; Frei Narciso, who starves and studies and stains his face an artificial yellow in hopes that his phony asceticism will win for him a bishopric; the city priest who feasts on rabbits and sausages and good red wine; and the country priest who resembles a kite pouncing on chickens. Many of Vicente's other creations are as memorable as his priests: the witch busy at night over a hanged man at the crossroads; the chattering *saloia* (rustic woman) who sells watered milk and overpriced eggs; *alcouviteiras* (procuresses) such as Ana Dias, who promises a squire the favors of a Moorish slave and takes his money without producing results; the plowman who does not forget his prayers and is charitable to tramps but who skimps his tithes; the Jew who had been prosperous in Spain but now as a new Christian is a poor cobbler in Lisbon; and the poor farmer's daughter who is brought to be a court lady while still stained from the winepress.

Of Vicente's forty-four surviving plays, sixteen are in Portuguese, eleven are in Spanish, and seventeen are in both languages. Although Vicente apparently never journeyed outside Portugal, the Spanish connections of the Portuguese court and the belief that the two countries would soon be united under one throne because of a series of royal marriages be-

tween their respective ruling houses encouraged his use of the closely related—but nevertheless distinct—Spanish language. His Spanish is often peculiar; he uses the Portuguese "personal infinitive" when he writes in Spanish, and his rhymes in Spanish are often imperfect (such as *parezca* and *cabeza*, based on their Portuguese cognates *pareça* and *cabeça*). In his earliest plays, his shepherds speak the *sayagués* "dialect" invented or elaborated by Juan del Encina and Lucas Fernández of the Salamancan school of Spanish drama. *Sayagués*, erroneously associated with Sayago to the north of Salamanca, is more correctly associated with the province of Salamanca itself, adjacent to the Portuguese province of Beira, possibly Vicente's native area, which in turn allows the possibility of a childhood intimacy with a dialect very closely related to the *sayagués* that he placed in the mouths of his rustics.

Vicente uses language to distinguish many of his characters. While his shepherds speak *sayagués*, his blacks chatter in pidgin Portuguese, his Gypsies lisp, and in *Auto de la fama*, in which Fame is courted successively by a Frenchman, an Italian, and a Spaniard before she decides to pledge her troth to Portugal, Vicente makes an attempt to have each foreign suitor speak in his own language.

Although he picked up foreign words and mannerisms with ease, Vicente does not appear to have had much acquaintance of or even liking for fashions from beyond the Pyrenees. If he introduced a French song into one of his plays, he probably did so out of deference to the taste of the Portuguese court. Vicente was unaffected by the innovations of Giangiorgio Trissino and other Italian dramatists, and with his medieval appreciation of folkways and folk wisdom, he stood unswayed against the inevitable literary artificiality that followed the return to Portugal of Francisco Sá de Miranda with the hendecasyllabic line from Italy in 1526.

Although Vicente's work lacks psychological depth by today's standards, his plays reveal a grasp of characterization vastly superior to that of the medieval dramatists who preceded him. Indifferent to the rules of Aristotle, as a playwright he combined disparate elements in a way more faithful to life than to any theory of drama. Himself a man of the people, he refused to imitate the products of classical theater, choosing to absorb the critical spirit of the fast-approaching Renaissance without its erudition. In his religious toleration, he was spokesperson for the better men of his age and society. The embryonic genius in the drama of Vicente provides the modern critic with a strong temptation to hypothesize: Had he written fifty years later in the requisite Renaissance environment of freedom and sophistication, he might have surpassed Calderón and equaled Shakespeare.

EARLY PLAYS

After his first short plays, which were written between 1502 and 1504 in the pastoral manner of the Spaniards Encina and Fernández, several years passed before Vicente's next work was staged. His first attempt at allegory, in which Faith, speaking Portuguese, explains the meaning of Christmas to peasants speaking Spanish, occurs in *Auto da fé* and is still much in the pastoral style of Encina and Fernández. Although his earlier plays are largely derivative, his distinctive personality soon began to emerge in his works. In 1512, Vicente wrote two plays with characters inspired by those in the Spanish play *Comedia de Calisto y Melibea* (1499, rev. ed. 1502 as *Tragicomedia de Calisto y Melibea*; commonly known as *La Celestina*; *Celestina*, 1631): *O velho da horta* (the farce of the old man in the orchard), which ridicules an old man who is in love with a young girl he sees in his orchard and who engages the services of the procuress Branca Gil, and the rather hilarious *Auto dos físicos* (play of the doctors), which shows a love-stricken priest at the mercy of a series of outrageous doctors and a procuress, Brasias Dias. They give up on their patient and leave him to a priest-confessor, who confesses that he himself has been in love for many years and argues that since love is ordained by God, no shame need be felt for it. Later Vicente introduced other procuresses into his plays, such as Brigida Vaz in *The Ship of Hell* and Ana Gil of *O juiz da Beira*.

THE PLAY OF THE SIBYL CASSANDRA

In 1513 or 1514, while he was under the influence of his Salamancan masters (lexically, especially Encina), Vicente wrote what is considered one of his masterpieces, *The Play of the Sibyl Cassandra*, which was probably performed before Queen Leanor after Christmas matins in the Convent of Enxobregas in Lisbon. In this work, Vicente skillfully blended peasant scenes and religious rhapsodies as well as love passages and biting satire, and interspersed refreshing *letras para cantar* (popular songs) in the play to signal dancing scenes.

Vicente's immediate source was a fifteenth century Italian novel of chivalry, *Guerin meschino* (1473), translated into Spanish by Andrea da Barberino in 1512. The title translates as "Guerrino the wretched," in reference to the hero's wretched childhood slavery, above which he rises to discover his royal parentage, marry a princess, and die a saintly death. Cassandra, the name of one of the sibyls whom Guerrino encounters—but not the one sibyl in the Italian story intent on saving her virginity to become the mother of Christ—was a name already well-known to Vicente. The Erythean sibyl Erutea had appeared as well in a well-known pseudo-Augustinian sermon as one who foretold the coming of the Messiah, and in Vicente's play, this Erythean sibyl recites a version of the Fifteen Signs of Judgment Day.

In Vicente's version, Cassandra does not want to renounce her freedom for marriage. She is importuned by her handsome admirer Salomon; by her three aunts, the sibyls Erutea, Peresica, and Cimeria; and by Salomon's three uncles, the prophets Abraham, Isaiah, and Moses. There is satire in Cassandra's haughty disdain of marriage, as there is in Salomon's presumption that Cassandra has no better choice than to marry him. She gives as her reason for spurning marriage the quarreling and the difficulties inherent in such a relationship, and it is only later that she discloses the real reason: She wants to be the virgin who bears the Son of God. At length, after the scriptural prophecies made by her aunts, a curtain is drawn aside and the real Virgin is revealed in the manger. Appropriately humbled, Cassandra begs to be forgiven for her presumption. The play ends with a *cantiga* (song) about the real Virgin's beauty ("Tell me, sailor/ you who live in ships,/ if the ship or the sail or the star/ is as beautiful") and, enigmatically for the modern reader, a *terreiro*, or call to arms ("To war,/ Ye gallant knights,/ Since the angels from heights/ Come to help us upon earth./ Go forth!"). This *terreiro* may be interpreted literally (especially in consideration of Portugal's involvement in the North African religious wars) or allegorically, as symbolizing Cassandra's acceptance of her role as both bride and soldier for Christianity. Another work written by Vicente at about the same time and continuing the theme of this final *terreiro*, *Exhortation to War* was probably performed for King Manuel I in Lisbon as a Portuguese expedition set out for Azamor in North West Africa in August, 1513.

SHIPS TRILOGY

Vicente's Ships Trilogy represents an apex in his dramatization of religious themes and indeed has been compared with Dante's *La divina commedia* (c. 1320; *The Divine Comedy*, 1802). The first play of the trilogy, *The Ship of Hell*, in Portuguese, was presented to Queen Maria on her deathbed in 1516. This was followed by *The Ship of Purgatory*, also in Portuguese, which was performed on Christmas morning, 1518, before the new Queen Eleanor (who had married Manuel I), in the Hospital de Todos os Santos in Lisbon. The third, *The Ship of Heaven*, in Spanish, was presented to the Portuguese monarchs during Holy Week, 1519, at Almeirim. The first two ship plays are full of Aristophanic humor and irony and treat the fates of peasants and persons of middle rank as they are rewarded or punished on Judgment Day, and *The Ship of Heaven* deals with men of only the highest rank, representatives of church and state, including an emperor and a pope. This last play of the trilogy is the one based most clearly on the Spanish *Dance of Death*, an anonymous seventy-nine-stanza poem dating from approximately 1400, which achieves significant dramatic import by its antiphonal alternating of the victims' pleas with Death's implacable words of condemnation. The theme of death was a source of obsession in the European Middle Ages and in Vicente's own century—a time of short life expectancy, apocalyptic visions, and millenarian yearnings—and had apparently evolved from a literal dance of the dying during the time of the Black Death to a dance-of-death motif in both art and literature, in which Death is grotesquely personified.

In Vicente's version, the transgressions of each high-ranking person are tirelessly enumerated by the boatman of Hell, who presides as prosecutor, and their futures look bleak indeed until the Redeemer arrives to accept them. The Pope especially has been welcomed by the Devil as one of his own kind, one who has shone for his practice of simony and lust, and all of his repentant acts are ineffectual until the arrival of the Redeemer.

AUTO DA FEIRA

The Papacy is again the target of Vicente's satire in *Auto da feira* (play of the fair), written in Portuguese in 1528. At a fair, Time sets up a booth to sell virtuous wares (such as the fear of God). The Devil is there as well, hawking his evil wares (such as deceits of all kinds and hypocrisy). The Church of Rome appears and, as is her wont, goes first to the Devil's booth. When she stops at Time's booth, she tries to sell Time her indulgences: "Sell me the place of heaven, since I have power here below." At length the Church of Rome repents of her errors, and the play ends optimistically as a group of dancing people praise the Virgin. As noted above, Vicente's open contempt for the hypocrisy of the clergy should not be equated with the reforming spirit of Luther; rather, it reflects an elemental hostility long in evidence throughout medieval Europe toward a privileged class of men, the clergy, who, while disdainful of the ways of ordinary men, more than occasionally embraced those very ways in secret.

FARSA DE INÊS PEREIRA

Another play generally considered one of Vicente's best is *Farsa de Inês Pereira*, performed in Portuguese before John III in the Monastery of the Knights of Christ in Tomar, in 1523, and inspired by the proverb, "*Mais quero asno que me leve, que cavalo que me derrube*" ("I prefer a donkey which will carry me to a horse which will throw me"). A woman named Inês marries the more impressive of two suitors, the stately horse rather than the solid donkey—a poor choice from which fate delivers her when her husband perishes at war, leaving her free to marry her first and more reliable suitor. The play is distinguished by its fine characterizations, its superior versification, and a unity of action that is rare in Vicente's drama.

TRAGICOMÉDIA DE DOM DUARDOS

Vicente realized before other writers the dramatic potential present in the romances of chivalry. Written entirely in Spanish, probably in 1522, and based on the Spanish novel *Primaleon* (1512), *Tragicomédia de dom Duardos* is Vicente's longest play (2,054 lines) and displays the subtlest development and sustained lyricism to be found in his works. The play chronicles an English prince's successful wooing of Princess Flérida of Constantinople by the ruse of his disguising himself as her gardener. When she falls in love with him after drinking from an enchanted cup which he has given her, she asks him to reveal his identity, but, romantically, he refuses to abandon his humble station until she accepts him as he is. The happy ending is punctuated by a ballad that has won the highest praise from all critics: Flérida bids a tender farewell to her homeland ("God keep you all, my flowers,/ Which once my glory were:/ I go to foreign lands/ Since fate has called me there") and as she falls asleep in the arms of Dom Duardos to the gentle sound of rowing, the audience is cautioned, "All men who now draw breath/ Learn wisdom from my tale:/ O'er power of love and death/ There's none that can prevail."

AMADIS OF GAUL

In *Amadis of Gaul*, performed at Évora before John III in 1523, Vicente elaborated on one of the best episodes of the chivalric novel of the same name and converted it into a moving drama with characters that are more skillfully portrayed than those in the novel. The play deals with Oriana's rejection of Amadis, and although in the novel Oriana does this heartlessly, Vicente gives to her an insightful soliloquy in which she wavers, so that when she revises her opinion, an immediate rapprochement is possible. Some critics have insisted on the ironic and satiric nature of Vicente's treatment of the Amadis story, but at least one critic views it as a straight dramatization of a well-known story in which Vicente revivifies the conventions of courtly love, showing his audience that in this case these courtly lovers are dealing with deeply felt emotions. The satirization of Amadis would have to wait for the appearance of a Miguel de Cervantes.

OTHER MAJOR WORKS

POETRY: "Pranto de Maria Parda," 1522; *Lyrics of Gil Vicente*, 1914, 1921.

BIBLIOGRAPHY

Garay, René Pedro. *Gil Vicente and the Development of the Comedia*. Chapel Hill: University of North Carolina Department of Romance Languages, 1988. A study of Vicente and of Portuguese and Spanish drama in the Classical period. Bibliography and index.

Hart, Thomas R. *Gil Vicente, Casandra and Don Duardos*. London: Grant & Cutler in association with Tamesis Books, 1981. A study of Vicente that focuses on *The Play of the Sibyl Cassandra* and *Tragicomédia de dom Duardos*. Bibliography.

Stathatos, Constantine C. *A Gil Vicente Bibliography, 1975-1995: With a Supplement for 1940-1975*. Cranbury, N.J.: Associated University Presses, 1997. An extensive bibliography of materials related to Vicente.

_____. *A Gil Vicente Bibliography, 1995-2000*. Kassel: Edition Reichenberger, 2001. A continuation of the bibliography also prepared by Stathatos.

Suárez, José I. *The Carnival Stage: Vicentine Comedy Within the Serio-comic Mode*. Rutherford, N.J.: Fairleigh Dickinson University Press, 1993. A look at Vicente's comedic works. Bibliography and index.

Jack Shreve

MARUXA VILALTA

Born: Barcelona, Spain; September 23, 1932

PRINCIPAL DRAMA

Los desorientados, pb. 1959, pr. 1960 (adaptation of her novel)

Trio, pr. 1964, pb. 1965 (includes *Un país feliz*, *Soliloquio del tiempo*, and *La última letra*)

El 9, pr. 1965, pb. 1966 (*Number 9*, 1973)

Cuestión de narices, pr. 1966, pb. 1967

Esta noche juntos, amándonos tanto, pr., pb. 1970 (*Together Tonight, Loving Each Other So Much*, 1973)

Nada como el piso 16, pr. 1975, pb. 1977 (*Nothing Like the Sixteenth Floor*, 1978)

Historia de Él, pr. 1978, pb. 1979 (*The Story of Him*, 1980)

Una mujer, dos hombres, y un balazo, pr. 1981, pb. 1984 (*A Woman, Two Men, and a Gunshot*, 1984)

Pequeña historia de horror (y de amor desenfrenado), pb. 1984, pr. 1985 (*A Little Tale of Horror [and Unbridled Love]*, 1986)

Una voz en el desierto: Vida de San Jerónimo, pb. 1990, pr. 1991 (*A Voice in the Wilderness: The Life of Saint Jerome*, 1990)

Francisco de Asís, pr. 1992, pb. 1993 (*Francis of Assisi*, 1993)

Jesucristo entre nosotros, pr. 1994, pb. 1995

El barco obrio, pb. 1995

En blanco y negro: Ignacio y los jesuitas, pr., pb. 1997

1910, pr. 2000, pb. 2001

OTHER LITERARY FORMS

Although Maruxa Vilalta is known primarily as a playwright, she is the author of three novels and one collection of short stories.

ACHIEVEMENTS

Maruxa Vilalta is known at home and abroad as an experimentalist, a playwright who with every new work further explores the possibilities of the theatrical medium. Her plays have been showcases for significant theatrical innovations since the mid-twentieth century, and they have been associated with names such as Eugène Ionesco, Samuel Beckett, Harold Pinter, and Bertolt Brecht. Vilalta has been concerned with the most pressing issues of the twentieth century, such as the loss of direction in a seemingly absurd world, humankind's horrifying capacity for cruelty, and the corrupting allure of power. Given these concerns, it is not surprising that Vilalta's plays are themselves often violent and shocking and that her characters are dehumanized grotesques.

Vilalta's work, like much experimental theater since the 1960's, means to assault rather than comfort audiences, and has a definite political intent while not being allied with any specific ideology. Instead, it makes a statement with a broad application, regardless of geography or culture. As a result, Vilalta has won audiences throughout Latin America, in the United States, Canada, and numerous European countries. In Mexico itself, Vilalta has three times received that country's most prestigious drama award, the Alarcón Prize of the Mexican Critics Association—for *Together Tonight, Loving Each Other So Much*, *Nothing Like the Sixteenth Floor*, and *The Story of Him*. *Number 9* was selected for publication in the United States as one of the best short plays of 1973. Vilalta's major plays have been published in English as well as in French, Italian, Catalan, and Czech.

Vilalta won the Sor Juana Inés de la Cruz award for best play in 1976 for *Nothing Like the Sixteenth Floor*. That same year, she was awarded the El Fígaro award for best play for *The Story of Him*. In 1991, she received the award for best play for *A Voice in the Wilderness: The Life of Saint Jerome* from the Agrupación de Periodistas Teatrales. The drama also won the Claridades award for best play of the year. The Asociación Mexicana de Críticos de Teatro gave the drama *Francis of Assisi* its award for the best creative research.

BIOGRAPHY

Maruxa Vilalta was born in Barcelona, Spain, on September 23, 1932. Her family, exiles from the Spanish Civil War, emigrated in 1939 to Mexico, where Vilalta has continued to reside. After completing her primary and secondary education at the Liceo Franco Mexicano in Mexico City, Vilalta studied Spanish literature at the college of philosophy and letters of the Autonomous National University of Mexico. She was married in 1951 and has two children.

Vilalta began her writing career as a novelist in 1957, with *El castigo* (the punishment). When, in 1959, she adapted her second published novel, *Los desorientados* (1958; the disoriented ones), for the stage, Vilalta was so impressed by the immediacy of the theatrical medium and the concrete life it gave to her characters that she dedicated herself thereafter almost exclusively to playwriting. While her early plays, especially *Number 9*, won for her considerable critical attention, it was in 1970, with *Together Tonight, Loving Each Other So Much*, that she really established herself as one of Mexico's leading experimental dramatists. This was the first of three plays that would win for her the coveted Alarcón Prize for the best play of the year; in 1978, *The Story of Him* won that prize on a unanimous vote, something rather rare in the award's history.

In 1975, with the prizewinning *Nothing Like the Sixteenth Floor*, Vilalta began directing her own plays, and as a director, she has been closely associated with the National Autonomous University of Mexico, which is considered the major locus for experimental play production in Mexico. Vilalta is also a noted essayist and theater critic for Mexico's leading daily newspaper, *Excelsior.*

ANALYSIS

Maruxa Vilalta's playwriting fits within a universalist trend in Latin American theater, and for this reason, her plays are not peculiarly Mexican, either in their language, their characters, or their setting. This goes hand in hand with Vilalta's rejection of more realistic stage conventions, which she considers too much associated with a local theater of customs or manners, what in Spanish is called *costumbrismo*. Instead, Vilalta usually prefers a nonrepresentational theater, whose characters belong to no specific country. When she does place them geographically, as in *Nothing Like the Sixteenth Floor*, it is in Manhattan, New York, and not in Mexico City.

Vilalta's conscious effort to avoid things typically Mexican clearly places her on one side of a longstanding debate among fellow playwrights about how indigenous their art should be and the degree to which it should be valued based on international appeal. A similar debate has been waged by artists in most Latin American countries, who recognize the necessity to deal with their own reality but also do not want to be potentially isolated from world audiences. Many have chosen the same solution as Vilalta, which is to write plays that can be read as allegories. Thus, while on one level they may not have anything overtly Mexican about them, the issues with which they deal—the dehumanization of the labor force, the cruelty individuals inflict on one another, the institutionalization of violence—most certainly do. It is by indirection, then, that Vilalta makes a powerful commentary on the specific world in which she lives, while not actually having to place her characters there.

Vilalta often expresses her thematic concerns through the theatrical metaphor of game playing. Usually she keeps the number of players at two or three, and the intensity of the games may well explain her preference for one-act plays. The rules for the games her characters play are not always easy to follow, because they do not necessarily adhere to everyday logic. Their logic resides in the games themselves, which should be interpreted as metaphors and not concrete depictions of reality offstage.

Vilalta represents a considerable presence in Mexican experimental drama, and her plays show the clear influence of many major theater innovators of the twentieth century. Vilalta is not merely derivative, however, for she adapts these influences to her own ends. The result is a very personal theater, one that is not particularly Mexican in any obvious way but that still manages to make an indirect commentary on the social and political realities of Mexican culture.

Moreover, although the vision of humankind that Vilalta paints is bleak in the extreme, critical and audience enthusiasm for her plays, both in Mexico and abroad, would seem to indicate playgoers' recognition that, by emphasizing the negative, Vilalta ultimately hopes to provoke change for the better.

NUMBER 9

Vilalta's first important play, *Number 9*, takes place in a small yard behind a large factory. Everything there, which is not much—a wall, a bench, a trash can, some barbed wire—is a depressing, prisonlike gray color; the workers, themselves dressed in dull gray overalls, are the inmates of this dehumanized workplace. The game here is an unevenly matched one—the powerful forces of capitalism against the ordinary men and women who keep its machinery running. The violence done to them is camouflaged behind a smokescreen of cleanliness, order, and paternalism. The workers for Sunshine of Your Life, Ltd., labor with the most modern conveniences and under employers who care about their well-being, or so they are constantly told by a throaty female voice blaring at them over the loudspeaker in the yard. They supposedly have a spotless cafeteria, immaculate working areas, a complaints bureau—everything a labor force could ask for.

What this disembodied voice fails to mention, however, is that the workers to whom and of whom she speaks have no names, only numbers; they have become automatons, indistinguishable from the machines they operate, and their lives are as anesthetized as the colorless surroundings at the factory. The workers are cogs in a superefficient system that does not even stop to mourn the death of Number 9, who, in desperation to assert his individuality, has allowed himself to be mangled to death by the very machine that made his life intolerable. Only then does Number 9 regain an identity and his name—José.

In writing this play, Vilalta certainly felt the influence of the Theater of the Absurd, which gained popularity in the early 1960's. The dominant mood of *Number 9*, with its often disjointed dialogue, sense of a repetitive action leading nowhere, schematic characters, and the gloomy picture painted of a pointless existence, is that of absurdism, but with one funda-

mental difference. Unlike the European variety, absurdism here is not an ontological or existential dilemma but a specifically socioeconomic one instead. Number 9 and his fellow workers are the playthings not of a disinterested or irrational god but rather of the cruel demigods of exploitative capitalism. Vilalta's adaptation of the Theater of the Absurd was not an unusual one among Latin American playwrights of the period, many of whom emulated the movement's theatrical innovations while not necessarily embracing its philosophical premises.

TOGETHER TONIGHT, LOVING EACH OTHER SO MUCH

This same kind of adaptation takes place in Vilalta's next important play, *Together Tonight, Loving Each Other So Much*, except that in this case the game playing is a much more salient motif, and her mastery of the stage is more evident. Whereas *Number 9* sometimes seems safe and unimaginative, with its obvious, if not clichéd, symbolism (the gray walls, the characters' mechanical movements and speech patterns, Number 9's suicide), here Vilalta is far bolder and more innovative. The principal characters in this play, Rosalía and Casimiro (also referred to as Her and Him), are a vicious old couple who have barricaded themselves behind the walls of their filthy apartment, where they delight in playing a humiliating game of one-upmanship. They cackle with glee as they debase each other, all the while congratulating themselves on the love they share and on their generous hearts, an ironic self-appraisal that explains the play's title and that is reinforced by the way Rosalía and Casimiro refuse to aid a dying neighbor and by the nearly erotic pleasure they take in reading all the bad news about what is going on in the real world outside of their wretched little apartment.

In *Together Tonight, Loving Each Other So Much*, Vilalta once again writes the kind of illogical, sometimes quirky dialogue that is associated with the Theater of the Absurd. In many ways, Rosalía and Casimiro are rather nastier versions of the old couple in Eugène Ionesco's *Les Chaises* (pr. 1952; *The Chairs*, 1957), but they are also reminiscent of two other famous absurdist couples. Like Didi and Gogo in Samuel Beckett's *En attendant Godot* (pb. 1952, pr. 1953; *Waiting for Godot*, 1954), Rosalía and Casimiro live a routinized life of waiting. She spends her days knitting and he smoking his pipe, always in anticipation of a dinner hour that never comes. Like George and Martha in Edward Albee's *Who's Afraid of Virginia Woolf?* (pr., pb. 1962), Vilalta's husband and wife fill their time with cruel and maiming verbal games.

As in *Number 9*, however, Vilalta molds aspects of the Theater of the Absurd to her own purposes. In this instance, she combines them with multimedia techniques and methods that were popularized by the German playwright Bertolt Brecht in the creation of his so-called epic theater. A notable example of this is when Vilalta has Rosalía and Casimiro read the newspaper, while other characters appear onstage—a General, a Dictator, a Hangman—at the same time that slides depicting real events having to do with war, famine, torture, and repression are projected onto a screen. In this way, Vilalta is able to connect her characters' private, domestic horror with the public horrors of twentieth century life, without ever having to verbalize it.

NOTHING LIKE THE SIXTEENTH FLOOR

In *Nothing Like the Sixteenth Floor*, the theatrical kinship is closer to the English dramatist Harold Pinter, who writes seemingly realistic plays that are in fact quite strange and offbeat. The stage set in this Vilalta play is meant to be a realistic depiction of an elegant apartment in Manhattan. The three characters—Max, Stella, and Jerome—are not such obvious abstractions as Number 9 or Him and Her. Jerome, a young electrician, is called to the apartment by Max, who has actually tampered with the electrical systems in order to lure him there. Max insults Jerome because of his working-class background and then bullies him into having sex with his live-in prostitute, Stella. During the following months, Stella shares her favors with both men and their *ménage à trois* becomes a power struggle with shifting roles of dominance. At first, Jerome is repulsed by the game, but he finds that he cannot resist the allure of sex, power, and material goods with which Max and Stella entice him. By the end of the play, he is no different from his tormentors, and it is only then, with the three

characters equally matched, that they can play their games for even higher stakes.

While there is nothing obviously unrealistic about this play, the subtle undercurrents in its mood signal that these characters are not quite what they appear to be. Vilalta manages to create this mood mostly through the dialogue, which sounds very ordinary but which, on closer inspection, proves to be too loaded with double meanings, sinister innuendos, ambiguities, and symbolism to be simple, everyday talk. Characterization is also deceptive, for although the characters at first seem the sort to be readily defined by their surface, there is something not quite concrete about them. This is especially true of the woman, who changes her name from Jane to Stella to Samantha, depending on her male partner, and is actually more a product of masculine wishful thinking than a real person, rather like Ruth in Pinter's *The Homecoming* (pr., pb. 1965). Similarly, the characters in *Nothing Like the Sixteenth Floor*, despite superficial touches of realism, are more (and less) than they appear to be. The play is not a psychological exploration of the sexual games that a few people play; the characters represent what could become of all human society. As one of them says, "Three on the sixteenth floor, or a million all over the world."

THE STORY OF HIM

The Story of Him marks a notable change in both the form and content of Vilalta's plays. The story it tells is of a lowly bank clerk named simply Él (Him) and his rise through the world of finance into the political arena and, ultimately, the highest office of an unspecified country. In the process, he leaves behind a trail of broken hearts and bodies, only to end up a hollow shell of a man, a twisted tyrant who blabbers about revolution while tyrannizing his people.

Because this is such a familiar tale in Latin American history, *The Story of Him* is easily Vilalta's most overtly political play and marks the first time that she makes repeated reference or allusion to Mexico. Whereas before she relied on a single setting and casts of two or three, here there are eighty-seven characters and at least thirteen different settings in seventeen different scenes that are given continuity by one character—The Reader—who functions as a narrator and commentator. The rapid set changes and broadly sketched characters give the play a cartoonlike quality that is very effective in ridiculing the madness of power politics without ever trivializing it. In fact, even though he is a caricature, the central character has an emotional depth that makes him the most human and pathetic of Vilalta's creations and *The Story of Him* the most satisfying of her plays.

A WOMAN, TWO MEN, AND A GUNSHOT

The broad brushstrokes used to render the cast of characters in *The Story of Him* become even broader in *A Woman, Two Men, and a Gunshot* and *A Little Tale of Horror (and Unbridled Love)*, where Vilalta tries her hand at humor. *A Woman, Two Men, and a Gunshot* consists of four brief one-acts that parody certain theatrical styles: melodrama, Theater of the Absurd, Surrealism, and Broadway musicals. Because Vilalta herself has used some of these styles, she is also poking fun at herself; one of these playlets, "In Manhattan That Night," is in many ways a humorous rendition of *Nothing Like the Sixteenth Floor.*

A LITTLE TALE OF HORROR (AND UNBRIDLED LOVE)

A Little Tale of Horror (and Unbridled Love) is more farce than parody and revolves around mistaken identities, gender confusions, a murder, and the inevitable sinister butler. With these plays, Vilalta explores new territory without leaving behind her usual thematic concerns, although these do seem secondary to her preoccupation with humorous effect—a shift in emphasis that might explain why these plays have not received the degree of critical success that her others have enjoyed.

FRANCIS OF ASSISI

In her play about Saint Francis of Assisi, Vilalta searched for authenticity in her depiction of the legendary saint. She sought to demystify his image and reveal him as a man who followed the teaching of the Gospel as steps guiding him toward consciousness of God. Vilalta researched historical records for years in order to approach her topic as accurately as possible with documented sources. The dramatic action results in a fascinating biographical study of a complex figure.

A VOICE IN THE WILDERNESS

Saint Jerome's internal conflicts are explored in *A Voice in the Wilderness: The Life of Saint Jerome*. The drama reconstructs the visionary world of the saint as it blends history with fiction. The biographical study takes shape as a journey that gradually reveals the mysteries of a life devoted to the quest for wisdom.

EN BLANCO Y NEGRO

In *En blanco y negro: Ignacio y los jesuitas* (in black and white, Saint Ignatius and the Jesuits), the last segment of her trilogy devoted to the lives of saints, Saint Ignatius of Loyola exemplifies the contradictions of the Catholic Church. The play dramatizes the conflicts among Jesuits as Saint Ignatius embodies the condition of Jesuits in contemporary Latin America. Vilalta's play examines the Theology of Liberation in action and the negative repercussions of its practice. The plot dramatizes the reality of priests murdered for defending the rights of minorities and supporting others who fight for liberty and human dignity.

1910

1910 won Vilalta critical acclaim. The epic dramatizes the commoners' experience of the Mexican Revolution. As director as well as playwright, she intended to demonstrate how theater was the perfect medium for the Mexican Revolution, which played out as the history of passions. Vilalta's 168 characters portray anonymous townspeople and farmers, not famous military or governmental figures. She intended to demythicize the revolution. Rather than political heroics or the official story of history, *1910* portrays child soldiers, women *guerrilleras* fighting among the men, violence inflicted by the campesinos on themselves, and thoughtless yet pure acts of heroism. Vilalta's Mexico reveals the realities of all wars.

Like most of Vilalta's plays, *1910* exposes sociopolitical problems that extend beyond Mexico. She denounces governments that practice dictatorial abuses behind a facade of democracy while they dehumanize their citizens. Power in interpersonal relations is examined in all its facets and degrees, from the abuser to the abused.

OTHER MAJOR WORKS

LONG FICTION: *El castigo*, 1957; *Los desorientados*, 1958; *Dos colores para el paisaje*, 1961.

SHORT FICTION: *El otro día, la muerte*, 1974.

BIBLIOGRAPHY

Bearse, Grace, and Lorraine E. Roses. "Maruxa Vilalta: Social Dramatist." *Revista de estudios hispánicos* 43 (October, 1984): 399-406. An analysis of Vilalta's role as a social dramatist.

Cajiao Salas, Teresa, and Margarita Vargas. *Women Writing Women: An Anthology of Spanish American Theater of the 1980's*. Albany: State University of New York Press, 1997. The authors analyze Vilalta's dramaturgy and provide detailed biblio-graphical information. They include an English translation by Kirsten F. Nigro of *A Woman, Two Men, and a Gunshot*.

Gladhart, Amalia. *The Leper in Blue: Coercive Performance and the Contemporary Latin American Theater*. Chapel Hill: University of North Carolina Press, 2000. This study explores contemporary controversial playwrights with sociopolitical messages. Gladhart examines several of Vilalta's plays.

"Maruxa Vilalta." In *Dictionary of Mexican Literature*. Westport, Conn.: Greenwood Press, 1992. A concise biographical treatment of Vilalta.

Kirsten F. Nigro,
updated by Carole A. Champagne

GEORGE VILLIERS

Born: London, England; January 30, 1628
Died: Kirkby Moorside, England; April 16, 1687

PRINCIPAL DRAMA

The Chances, pr. 1667, pb. 1682 (revision of John Fletcher's play)

The Rehearsal, pr. 1671, pb. 1672

The Battle of Sedgmoor, wr. 1685, pb. 1704

The Militant Couple: Or, The Husband May Thank Himself, wr. 1685(?), pb. 1704

The Restauration: Or, Right Will Take Place, wr. 1685, pb. 1704 (revision of Francis Beaumont and Fletcher's play *Philaster*)

OTHER LITERARY FORMS

George Villiers left his mark on English literature solely with his contribution to drama; his remaining miscellaneous works are obscure. His letters have not been collected, although Tom Brown, Villiers's editor, included a number of them in *The Works of His Grace, George Villiers, Late Duke of Buckingham* (1715). The published letters appear to hold more interest for the biographer and historian than for the student of literature.

Only a few of Villiers's poems were published during his lifetime, and his total poetic output is small. Brown's edition includes twenty-odd poems, largely occasional verses, songs, verse epistles, satires, prologues, and epilogues. The verses reveal that Villiers never achieved the smoothness and polish found in the works of the best courtier poets during the reign of Charles II. Poets such as the earls of Dorset and Rochester, taking to heart the maxims of Horace and following the example of Ben Jonson, produced verses of lyric smoothness and elegance. Villiers lacked either the ear to detect or the patience to produce pleasing rhythm, and his poems do not achieve memorable figures of speech or scintillating wit. Therefore, editors of anthologies of his period omit his poems from their collections.

ACHIEVEMENTS

Time has not dealt kindly with either George Villiers's life or his works. In his public and private life, he is remembered more for his eccentricities than for his achievements, and only one of his literary works is read today. One reason for this is that he took only a passing interest in literature. Another reason is that he possessed a talent narrow and ill-suited to some of the projects he undertook. Defending his ministry before the House of Commons in 1674, Villiers declared that he could hunt the hare as well as any man with a pack of hounds "but not with a brace of lobsters," a reference to the king and the duke of York. This preposterous comparison proved more shocking than effective, but it indicates his ready wit, his willingness to take risks for a jest, and his sense of the ridiculous. This talent for oblique wit enabled him to produce brilliant parody. It represents one gift that can lead to brilliant satire, yet more is required—knowledge and skill in the craft of poetry, balance, an idealistic vision or a sense of a norm, and a genuine desire to reform. Villiers achieved the full potential of his limited talent only in *The Rehearsal*.

BIOGRAPHY

George Villiers, second duke of Buckingham, devoted little of his active and irregular life to literature, a matter to him of amateur interest. Instead, he turned his major efforts to the pursuits of pleasure and statecraft, two interests that came naturally to him because of his birth and rearing. He was the oldest son of the first duke of Buckingham, who was a favorite courtier of James I and Charles I. Assassinated by a fanatic at the height of his power and fame, the duke left three children—two sons and a daughter. Out of respect for the father, King Charles I took the two boys as his wards and reared them as his own, allowing them to spend much of their time with the royal princes. Provided with the best education and with financial security, Villiers developed a strong attachment to the house of Stuart. From his father he inherited vast estates, treasures of art, and other properties. After the Restoration, his estates made him for a time the wealthiest man in England, ensuring him a base of support for his ambitions and his pleasures.

After the death of Charles I, Villiers attached himself closely to Prince Charles, sharing with him the adventures and dangers involved in his attempts to advance his claim to the throne. Villiers's military exploits were marked by audacity, gallantry, and a total disregard of his own safety. During the period when he was assuming the role of military commander, he was also developing his political abilities. In the role of adviser to the prince, he revealed his mercurial nature, his intelligence, a certain instability, and a penchant for intrigue. Further, in some of his exploits, he showed himself a master of mimicry and disguise.

When the hopes of toppling the government of Oliver Cromwell collapsed following the Battle of Worcester, the prince and Villiers sought refuge on the Continent. Villiers, restless in inactivity, returned to England and there married Mary Fairfax, daughter of the parliamentary general Lord Fairfax. This alliance failed to reassure Cromwell of Villiers's loyalty, and he had the duke imprisoned in the Tower of London, where he remained until Cromwell's death. Following his release, he involved himself in intrigues intended to restore the Stuart monarchy and stood among the first to greet Charles II on his return in 1660.

The king appointed Villiers to the ruling Privy Council, a group of thirty ministers then under the leadership of the Lord Chancellor, the earl of Clarendon. Jealousies, rivalries, and intrigues among the king's ministers proved the order of the day, and Villiers allied himself with those ministers opposed to Clarendon. After the fall of the Lord Chancellor, Villiers became one of the five ministers known as the Cabal—Lord Clifford, Lord Arlington, Villiers, Anthony Ashley Cooper, and Lord Lauderdale—who led in matters of state for seven years. During much of the period, Villiers remained the most powerful among them. He was entrusted with important foreign affairs and missions, carrying on negotiations in France and Holland, yet the king did not repose his entire trust in his childhood companion, for in his public career, Villiers consistently pressed two important principles that did not always suit the king's purposes—religious freedom and English sea power. It was Villiers's private life, however, that proved to be the pretext for his fall from power.

While serving as a minister of state, Villiers pursued a variety of interests and avocations. A frequenter of the theater and an amateur musician, he pursued numerous other interests as well—the manufacture of glass, chemistry, astrology, and architecture. His usual associates were the king, the ladies of

George Villiers (Hulton Archive by Getty Images)

the court (through whom he exerted influence), and the Court Wits, the brilliant and profligate young lords who attached themselves to the king after the Restoration. Frequently seen in the theater, Villiers, like the other Court Wits, became the subject of gossip, anecdotes, and scandal. Having been reared as a royal ward, he seemed not to understand that the degree of license in behavior tolerated in the king did not apply equally to him.

Villiers's duchess, Mary Fairfax, fell far short of the beauty and charm that Andrew Marvell praised so highly in his poem "Upon Appleton House," though what she lacked in these qualities she made up for in her patience with and endurance of her philandering husband. Like the queen, she was barren, a fact that Villiers took as an excuse for his numerous infidelities. In 1667, he fell passionately in love with Anna Maria, countess of Shrewsbury, whose languid and voluptuous beauty lives today in her portraits by Sir Peter Lely. They appeared in public together on numerous occasions, and one evening at the theater,

Harry Killigrew, her previous lover, insulted the countess. When Villiers sought an apology, Killigrew struck Villiers across the head with the flat of his sword, whereupon the enraged duke drove Killigrew from the theater, creating a furor. The earl of Shrewsbury, husband of the countess, took this public display as an insult and felt compelled to issue Villiers a challenge, Killigrew having fled to France. In the ensuing duel, Villiers ran the earl through, not killing him outright but causing his death some three months afterward. Thereafter, Villiers installed the widowed countess in his London home as his mistress for seven years, a situation accepted by his duchess. When the countess bore him an illegitimate son, Villiers managed to obtain for him the hereditary title earl of Coventry. Following the death of his son during his first year of life, Villiers had the infant interred with ceremony and pomp in Westminster Abbey. This flagrant disregard of convention was remembered when Villiers's enemies grew strong enough to topple him from power. In 1674, Parliament forced him to resign all of his offices and swear never to cohabit with the countess again. She married another man shortly after the duke's fall, and the duke joined the opposition to the court party, led by Anthony Ashley Cooper, first earl of Shaftesbury, with whom he had served on the Cabal. For the next few years, his efforts in politics were devoted to the vain attempt to exclude James, duke of York, from the throne.

In an exceptionally active and eventful life, literature represented for Villiers only one interest among many. He associated with poets and dramatists and became the patron of a few, though he did not rank as one of the great literary patrons of the age. Abraham Cowley enjoyed his support and hospitality for a time, as did Thomas Sprat, who wrote the history of the Royal Society. Although Villiers could match the brilliance of his fellow Court Wits in conversation, he was not their equal in poetry. It is remarkable that John Dryden, whom he satirized so effectively in *The Rehearsal*, left in response verses on Villiers that capture, strikingly and somewhat unfairly, the contradictions inherent in his character. In his political satire *Absalom and Achitophel* (1681), Dryden produced a character based on Villiers named Zimri. By a cruel irony, these lines usually represent what students of literature remember about George Villiers, if they take note of him at all:

> A man so various that he seem'd to be
> Not one, but all mankind's epitome.
> Stiff in opinions, always in the wrong,
> Was everything by starts and nothing long,
> But in the course of one revolving moon,
> Was chemist, fiddler, statesman, and buffoon;
> Then all for women, painting, rhiming, drinking,
> Besides ten thousand freaks that di'd in thinking.
> Blest madman, who could every hour employ
> With something new to wish or to enjoy!
>
> . . . .
>
> Begger'd by fools, whom still he found too late,
> He had his jest, and they had his estate.

During the final period of Villiers's life, King Charles was reconciled to his old companion, and Villiers spent many enjoyable hours with the king, but he was not trusted to wield power. With the accession of James II, shunned by his former allies and no longer able to pay his debts or appeal to his friends, Villiers left London and established himself at one of his remaining estates, the ruined Helmsly Castle in Yorkshire, where he spent most of his time racing and riding to the hounds. Following one outing, he grew suddenly ill and took refuge in Kirkby Moorside, an obscure village near York, where he died quietly within two days. His debts consumed his entire estate at his death. King James II, his old adversary, boasted that the duchess of Buckingham would have been destitute without his support, but the king's boast was not entirely correct, for the duchess retained her father's estate, Nun Appleton, in her own right.

ANALYSIS

George Villiers's restless, unstable nature urged him to live at a fast pace and to play for high stakes. He would no doubt have justified his risk taking with the potential rewards, yet despite a few successes, notably the manufacture of glass in England, he lost in most of his ventures. His achievements in statecraft and literature, with the exception of *The Rehearsal*, do not rise above mediocrity.

THE CHANCES

During the Restoration, scores of plays by Elizabethan dramatists, including William Shakespeare, Ben Jonson, and Francis Beaumont and John Fletcher, were revised for theater audiences. Villiers's first significant effort as a playwright, *The Chances*, was a revision of Fletcher's comedy of the same name, which saw a successful production in 1667. Villiers retouched Fletcher's first three acts and rewrote entirely the final two acts, rendering the blank verse of the original into prose while leaving the first three acts largely in blank verse.

The play features a tangled plot that turns on coincidence and confusion of identities. Two women named Constantia, one a duke's mistress and the other the unwilling mistress of an older lover who proves to be impotent, decide to leave their lovers at the same time. Both seek help from Don John, a young rake, and his friend Don Frederick. Meanwhile, Petruchio, brother of the duke's mistress, seeks to avenge her loss of honor and sends the duke a challenge, only to learn that the duke has married her. After confused brawling in the street and several mistakes in efforts to straighten matters out, the play ends with the first Constantia restored to the duke and with the younger Constantia beginning a relationship with the reformed rake Don John, after her lover Antonio has reclaimed the money she took from him in order to flee.

The play features a number of witty exchanges and maintains a realistic tone throughout, successfully avoiding sentimentality, but it relies too heavily on confused identity and improbable circumstances in the plot, and it lacks the brilliant repartee of the later Restoration comedies of manners. Oddly, very few of the speeches are between the paired lovers. Villiers ties up the loose ends of the plot and sets a moral tone regarding love somewhat above that of the comedy of manners, yet apart from the lively character Don John, the play holds little attraction.

THE REHEARSAL

The only drama by Villiers well known today is *The Rehearsal*, a burlesque of the theater first produced in 1671. In its composition he probably had the assistance of Samuel Butler, Martin Clifford, and

Thomas Sprat. The work achieved enormous popularity during its day. It belongs in the literary tradition of such drama burlesques as Beaumont and Fletcher's *The Knight of the Burning Pestle* (pr. 1607), Henry Fielding's *Tom Thumb: A Tragedy* (pr. 1730), and Richard Brinsley Sheridan's *The Critic* (pr. 1779). The object of its satiric attack is the heroic play, a dramatic genre that developed following the Restoration, and its most successful practitioner, John Dryden.

Largely influenced by French tragedy, which attracted the king's interest during his exile, the heroic play originated in England during the early 1660's. Dramas of this type were written in rhymed heroic couplets, a distinctive feature that rendered the dialogue artificial. The speeches were often long, consisting of debate and ratiocination, often marked by bombastic language. The dramas typically presented a swashbuckling hero drawn into a conflict between love and his sense, or code, of honor; his task was to resolve the conflict without compromising either emotionally charged value. He was surrounded by a group of stock characters drawn primarily from the drama of Beaumont and Fletcher—characters such as the weak king, the faithful friend, the sentimental maiden, the evil woman, and the Machiavellian villain. The plays usually had remote or exotic settings, strange names, violent action, somewhat disjointed plots, and elaborate scenery and costuming.

As a counterweight to the excesses of the heroic play, *The Rehearsal* introduces two characters who might be considered naïve observers. Smith, who has just arrived at the theater from the country, seeks out Johnson, a city man who can explain to him the current fashion and taste of the city. They create a kind of commonsense perspective that illuminates the absurdities of the popular drama. As they are talking, John Bayes, a dramatist, walks across the stage, and they engage him in conversation about the theater. He invites them to remain for a rehearsal of his new play, *The Two Kings of Brentford*.

Although Bayes is something of a composite, reflecting certain qualities of Sir William Davenant and using speech mannerisms of Edward Howard, he is intended chiefly as a caricature of John Dryden. Villiers himself coached the actor John Lacy, who played the role, so that he might accurately mimic Dryden's mannerisms and speech. Often the dialogue incorporates brief passages from Dryden's critical writings, and some of the expressions—"nick," used as a verb, and "igad"—were habits of speech identified with Dryden. As a character, Bayes comes alive, proving himself interesting and memorable, if not well-rounded. One finds Smith and Johnson reacting with incredulity and bewilderment to the absurd parodies and dramatic conventions of the play being "rehearsed," yet Bayes takes the two into his confidence and proudly explains all that is going on with genuine and naïve enthusiasm. With disarming candor, he reveals his tricks of plotting, which amount to plagiarism, unaware that they will be viewed with disfavor. Frequently he praises his work without waiting for response, commenting to the observers after one scene, "I'm afraid this scene had made you sad, for, I must confess, when I writ it, I wept myself." The only explanation that occurs to him for the failure of some to appreciate his work is that they lack taste, and when the actors refuse to continue the rehearsal, Bayes threatens to sell his work to a rival theater. Throughout, he maintains a kind of irrepressible optimism and oblivious good humor.

In its multiple parodies and wide-ranging allusions, *The Rehearsal* satirizes at least seventeen plays, the majority being heroic plays, though not all by Dryden. The primary vehicle for satire is the play-within-a-play, Mr. Bayes's *The Two Kings of Brentford*. The chaotic and disjointed plot concerns the deposing of the two kings by their physician and a gentleman usher. Following the deposition, Prince Pretty-man, Prince Volscius, and the swashbuckling hero Drawcansir appear, each in his turn, and introduce separate and unrelated themes. The "heroines," Chloris, Parthenope, Lardella, and Amaryllis, provide opportunities for developing the theme of love. Following an elaborate procession involving four cardinals, the two kings are restored, descending from the clouds, and the usurpers steal away. Then a battle takes place, stopped suddenly by an eclipse. Afterward, the fighting resumes and Drawcansir enters slaying all the participants, friend and foe alike. This devastation concludes the fourth act of the play-within-a-play. For the final act, Bayes reads a synopsis, a digression involving a tragic ending to the love of Chloris and Prince Pretty-man. Before the reading, Smith and Johnson steal away, and afterward the actors follow their example, leaving Bayes to express his frustration to the stage keeper.

To appreciate fully the exquisite parody found in *The Rehearsal,* one needs to recognize the echoes from now obscure heroic plays. With only slight changes of phrasing, it was possible to reduce the exaggerated and artificial expressions of emotion in heroic couplets to absurdity. In Dryden's *The Conquest of Granada by the Spaniards* (pr. 1670, 1671), the hero Almanzor steals to the queen's chamber to profess his love for her. When asked his identity, he explains: "He, who dares love, and for that love must die,/And, knowing this, dares yet love on, am I." Villiers parodies this episode by having Drawcansir, a similar hero, enter on a banquet held by the two usurping kings and identify himself in the following manner:

> KING PHYSICIAN: What man is this that dares disturb our feast?
> DRAWCANSIR: He that dares drink, and for that drink dares die;
> And, knowing this, dares yet drink on, am I.

In numerous other passages, the bombast of the heroic play is captured with withering effect. A lieutenant general addresses the eclipse that has stopped the battle: "Foolish Eclipse, thou this in vain hast done;/ My brighter honour had eclips'd the sun./ But now behold eclipses two in one." At times, the prosaic content of the heroic couplets, when expressed in heightened style, produced bathos, an effect parodied in this speech by the first king as he seeks safety from the battle: "Let us for shelter in our cabinet stay;/ Perhaps these threat'ning storms will pass away." More often, however, the inflated and sometimes impenetrable language of the heroic plays forms the target, as in Prince Pretty-man's lament: "The blackest ink of fate was sure my lot,/ And when she writ my name she made a blot." Prince Volscius,

smitten by love for Parthenope, experiences the love-honor conflict, a thematic commonplace, when he is called to meet his army outside town. Putting on one boot, he sees that leg as representative of honor—the bootless one symbolizing love. His will being paralyzed by the conflict, he hobbles out wearing only one boot.

The gaiety, energy, and mirth of burlesque and parody are sustained throughout Villiers's comic masterpiece. He refrains from satirizing those elements of the heroic play that would detract from the lighthearted parody. There are no Machiavellian plotters or evil women—even his villains are comic. Although the work achieved acclaim and had an unusually successful run in the theater, it did not drive the heroic play from the stage. London audiences laughed at the absurdities with Villiers, yet they enjoyed the pageantry, liveliness, novelty, and variety of the heroic drama until the vogue wore itself out approximately a decade later.

OTHER MAJOR WORKS

MISCELLANEOUS: *The Works of His Grace, George Villiers, Late Duke of Buckingham*, 1715 (2 volumes; Tom Brown, editor); *Buckingham, Public and Private Man: The Prose, Poems and Commonplace Book of George Villiers, Second Duke of Buckingham (1628-1687)*, 1985 (Christine Phipps, editor).

BIBLIOGRAPHY

Dharwadker, Aparna. "Class, Authorship, and the Social Intertexture of Genre in Restoration Theater." *Studies in English Literature, 1500-1900* 37, no. 3 (Summer, 1997): 461-462. An analysis of the relation between class and genre in Restoration theater. Provides an analysis of Villiers's *The Rehearsal.*

Lockyer, Roger. *Buckingham: The Life and Political Career of George Villiers, First Duke of Buckingham, 1592-1628.* New York: Longman, 1981. This biography of Villiers, while centering on his political life, provides many insights into the writer. Bibliography and index.

O'Neill, John H. *George Villiers, Second Duke of Buckingham.* Boston: Twayne, 1984. A basic biography that covers the lives and literary works of Villiers. Bibliography and index.

Treadwell, V. *Buckingham and Ireland, 1616-1628: A Study in Anglo-Irish Politics*. Portland, Ore.: Four Courts Press, 1998. An examination of the relations between Ireland and England, particularly Villiers's views on Ireland. Bibliography and index.

Yardley, Bruce. "George Villiers, Second Duke of Buckingham, and the Politics of Toleration." *The Huntington Library Quarterly* 55, no. 2 (Spring, 1992): 317. Although the author focuses on Villiers's support of religious toleration, the essay sheds some light on the man behind the plays.

Stanley Archer

PAULA VOGEL

Born: Washington, D.C.; November 16, 1951

PRINCIPAL DRAMA

Meg, pr., pb. 1977
Apple Brown Betty, pr. 1979
Desdemona: A Play About a Handkerchief, pr. 1979, pb. 1994
The Last Pat Epstein Show Before the Reruns, pr. 1979
The Oldest Profession, pr. 1981, pb. 1996
Bertha in Blue, pr. 1981
And Baby Makes Seven, pr. 1986, pb. 1996
The Baltimore Waltz, pr., pb. 1992
Hot 'n' Throbbing, pr. 1993, pb. 1996
The Baltimore Waltz and Other Plays, pb. 1996
How I Learned to Drive, pr., pb. 1997
The Mineola Twins, pr. 1997, pb. 1998
The Mammary Plays, pb. 1998

OTHER LITERARY FORMS

Paula Vogel is known only for her plays.

ACHIEVEMENTS

Paula Vogel has received numerous awards for her work. In 1975 and again in 1976 she won the Heerbes-McCalmon Playwrighting Award, and in 1978 she won the American National Theater and Academy-West Award. She received a Guggenheim Fellowship in 1995 and a Pew/TCG senior residency award from 1995 to 1997. She has also received the Rhode Island Pell Award in the Arts, the Robert Chesley Award in Playwrighting, the Pew Charitable Trusts Senior Residency Award, an AT&T New Plays Award, the Fund for New American Plays, and several National Endowment for the Arts fellowships

Vogel's plays have also been honored. In 1977, as a student at Cornell she won the American College Theater Festival Award for best new play for *Meg*. *The Baltimore Waltz* won the 1992 Obie Award for Best Play. In addition she won the Fund for New American Plays Award in 1995 for *Hot 'n' Throbbing*. *How I Learned to Drive* is clearly Vogel's most honored play. It won the Best Play honors in 1997 from Lortel Awards, the Drama Desk Awards, the Outer Critics Circle Awards, The New York Drama Critics Awards, and the Obie Awards. In 1998 it was awarded the Pulitzer Prize in Drama.

After writing *How I Learned to Drive*, Vogel has become one of the most influential feminist playwrights in the United States and in the world. Her work has been produced at theaters across the country including the American Repertory Theater, the Circle Repertory Theatre, the Juilliard School, Theater Rhinoceros in San Francisco, Actors Theatre of Louisville and many others. She is helping to create a feminist aesthetic that calls for deeply flawed female characters. She also has managed to successfully write plays that deal with complex issues that would normally be considered taboo for a self-identified feminist playwright.

BIOGRAPHY

Paula Anne Vogel was born to a Jewish father and a Roman Catholic mother, Donald and Phyllis Vogel, in Washington, D.C., in 1951. Her parents divorced when she was thirteen, and she lived with her mother and brother in working-class apartments in Washington, D.C., and Baltimore, Maryland. Her mother moved their family to a new apartment every year or so. At age seventeen, she came out as a lesbian. She received her B.A. from Catholic University of America in 1974. She spent three years in graduate school at Cornell before leaving without writing her dissertation in 1977. Vogel worked for the American Place Theater from 1978 to 1979 before joining the staff of Cornell, where she worked from 1979 to 1982. In 1985 she began working as the director for the M.F.A. in Playwrighting Program at Brown University in Rhode Island.

In addition to her work as a teacher, Vogel had several plays given full productions beginning with *Meg*, which was produced by the Kennedy Center in Washington, D.C., in 1977 and *Apple Brown Betty*, which was produced by the Actors Theatre of Louisville in 1979. She labored in relative obscurity until 1992 when she had her first big success with *The Baltimore Waltz*, which she wrote following her brother's death from AIDS (acquired immunodeficiency syndrome). The play won the Obie Award for best play that year. Her next major New York opening was the critically panned *And Baby Makes Seven*. The play, which follows a lesbian couple, their gay roommate, and their three imaginary children, is considered by many to be Vogel's most comedic play. Both *The Baltimore Waltz* and *And Baby Makes Seven* dealt with issues of homosexuality and powerful women, establishing Vogel as a major playwright in both the feminist and gay and lesbian communities.

Vogel continued to write feminist plays, and her next New York production was *Desdemona: A Play About a Handkerchief* in 1993. The rethinking of William Shakespeare's *Othello, the Moor of Venice* (pr. 1604) drew both applause and cynicism from feminist theater critics. In 1994 the American Repertory Theater in Cambridge, Massachusetts, produced her *Hot 'n' Throbbing*, although because of its controversial subject matter (domestic abuse), it received no other productions in the United States until after the success of *How I Learned to Drive*. That play would win virtually every award possible, including the Obie Award for best play and the Pulitzer Prize in Drama and would establish Vogel as a major mainstream playwright. *How I Learned to Drive* has been produced all over the United States after its success in New York City, where it ran for four hundred performances. In 1998 *How I Learned to Drive* was the most produced new play in the country.

Vogel has worked closely with director Anne Bogart, who directed productions of *Hot 'n' Throbbing* at the American Repertory Theater and *The Baltimore Waltz* at the Circle Repertory Theatre. Vogel resides in Providence, Rhode Island, and is a professor-at-large at Brown University.

ANALYSIS

Paula Vogel's work, which covers such topics as AIDS, pedophilia, domestic abuse, and female sexuality, takes an aggressive view of the way theater has typically portrayed women. She tries to create characters that fly in the face of her audiences' expectations. Her work is sometimes considered unsettling because she raises questions without answering them. She deconstructs both classic works and socially held beliefs in her plays. She often expects her audience to be familiar with works that she is parodying. Her plays are nonlinear and episodic in their construction, often using Brechtian elements such as slides or a chorus. Fiercely political, Vogel's dramas are meant to get a rise out of both her audience and her sponsors. Although she considers herself a feminist, Vogel's plays do not necessarily show women in a positive light. To the contrary, Vogel creates complex female characters who are often deeply flawed. She believes that only by creating unsavory female protagonists can women begin to be treated equally on the stage and in the world.

THE BALTIMORE WALTZ

Vogel's first successful show was written after the death of her brother Carl from AIDS. In the introduction to the play, Vogel includes a letter from Carl that she urges all productions to include in their programs.

This letter is the first indicator for the audience of the personal nature of this play. Opening at the height of the AIDS crisis, Vogel's play attempts to both call attention to and universalize the disease by deconstructing the homosexual stigma that had become associated with it.

The play tells the story of Anna (Vogel's actual middle name), a schoolteacher who is diagnosed with acquired toilet disease (ATD), a fatal illness. In search of a possible cure, she and her homosexual brother Carl travel across Europe, where Anna has sex with all of the men whom she encounters. At the end of the play, it is revealed that it was Carl who had a fatal disease, AIDS, and that the two never did manage to take Carl's dream trip across Europe. Anna's sexual conquests are used to show her independence from both societal norms (as dictated, often, by her brother) and the devastation of her AIDS-like illness. (Anna shows no ill-effects from the disease, and her doctor assures her that she poses no risk to her sexual partners.)

The Baltimore Waltz makes use of many Brechtian techniques. The characters act to title each of the scenes (for example, "Medical Straight Talk: Part One" and "Lesson Five: Basic Dialogue"). Also, one character, known as the Third Man, plays all of the people whom Carl and Anna encounter, including Anna and Carl's doctor, Harry Lime (a character from the film *The Third Man*), and all of Anna's sexual partners. Finally the seemingly harmless acquired toilet disorder also serves as a way to make light of the serious illness that it clearly represents. These elements constantly remove the audience from the light-hearted action of the play and act as a reminder of Carl's (and Vogel's brother's) affliction with AIDS and their inevitable death.

DESDEMONA

Desdemona deconstructs Shakespeare's *Othello, the Moor of Venice*. Vogel's play retells the story from the tragic heroine's point of view. Vogel's Desdemona is not the innocent victim depicted in Shakespeare's tragedy. On the contrary, she is a mean-spirited harlot who, when her husband is away, works at the brothel run by Bianca, who in this text is trying to be Cassio's lover. There are only three characters in the show:

Desdemona, her scullery maid Emilia, and Bianca. The play is broken down into what Vogel refers to as "thirty cinematic 'takes'" that create a filmlike feel to the piece.

As the audience hears about Desdemona's sexual exploits and sees her learn the "tricks of the trade" from Bianca, the audience grows ever more aware of the inevitable death that awaits her at the hands of her husband. By taking advantage of the audience's familiarity with the original Shakespearean text, Vogel does not need to reveal her characters' final ends. Despite the great changes made to the title character, her fate remains the same. Vogel intends this to call into question the ability that women have to control their lives. Vogel's play also serves to illustrate that Shakespeare's play could be read as an extreme case of spouse abuse rather than a noble tragedy.

HOT 'N' THROBBING

Vogel deals directly with the issue of spouse abuse in her play *Hot 'n' Throbbing*. The piece tells the story of a woman who has escaped an abusive husband and makes her living writing scripts for female erotic films. Her daughter may or may not work as a stripper and her son may or may not be masturbating while thinking of his sister or his mother. When the woman's husband breaks into the house, she shoots him in the buttocks. While he is recovering, he manages to get ahold of the gun and the play ends with his strangling her to death.

The playwright admitted to writing this show to test the bounds of acceptability for a nation in which the National Endowment for the Arts (NEA) was forcing artists to sign a pledge against offensiveness. Her use of pornographic imagery, underage stripping, suggestions of incest, masturbation, and violence certainly pushed the limits of what would be considered inoffensive to potential audience members. Much like her other plays, *Hot 'n' Throbbing* makes a typically offensive character, in this case an abusive husband, a sympathetic one, and even a victim. Vogel claimed that the piece was meant to confront the realities of domestic abuse. Despite her deliberate challenging of the NEA guidelines, she has suggested that she is outraged and troubled by the lack of productions of the play.

How I Learned to Drive

Vogel had no troubles in 1997 and 1998 getting *How I Learned to Drive* produced. The 1998 Pulitzer Prize winner tells the story of Lil' Bit, a woman aged eleven to forty, who is sexually molested by Uncle Peck until she is eighteen. One of the elements that makes the drama interesting is how complicit in her abuse the girl is and, also, how sympathetic her molester seems. The play unfolds in a series of flashbacks and fastforwards about Lil' Bit's sexual awakening at the hands of her uncle. Through her molestation, Bit learns to become stronger and protect herself by anticipating the moves of others. This self-protection, however, ultimately serves to sever her from any meaningful relationships in her life.

In addition to using Brechtian elements similar to those in her earlier plays, Vogel includes three "Greek choruses": Male, Female, and Teenage. These characters, in addition to playing the other characters in the play with whom Bit and Peck interact, serve to comment on the action of the story. The chorus gives drivers' education-type titles, such as "idling in the neutral gear" to each scene. The play uses these titles to draw the connections between Bit's learning how to drive and her sexual awakening/deadening at the hands of her uncle. By feminizing the automobile in which Bit is "educated," Vogel questions the gender role of her protagonist, suggesting that because of her early exposure to sexuality, Bit has become more masculine, living in her head instead of her body. This fragmentation of the body is a continual image in the play and adds to the alienation of the audience.

Bibliography

Novy, Marianne. "Saving Desdemona and/or Ourselves: Plays by Ann-Marie MacDonald and Paula Vogel." In *Transforming Shakespeare: Contemporary Women's Re-Visions in Literature and Performance*, edited by Marianne Novy. New York: St. Martin's Press, 1999. Compares Vogel's *Desdemona* with MacDonald's *Goodnight Desdemona, Good Morning Juliet* to discuss feminist reclamations of Shakespearean heroines.

Savran, David. Introduction to *The Baltimore Waltz and Other Plays*, by Paula Vogel. New York: Theatre Communications Group, 1996. Savran's introduction, as well as Vogel's preface to the plays, offers interesting ways of approaching the works and helps to shed light on the writer's intentions.

Sinfield, Alan. *Out on Stage: Lesbian and Gay Theatre in the Twentieth Century*. New Haven, Conn.: Yale University Press, 1999. Although he only touches briefly on *The Baltimore Waltz*, Sinfield tries to group Vogel and many other gay and lesbian dramatists into categories that can serve as a starting point for comparisons between works.

Vogel, Paula. "Driving Ms. Vogel." Interview by David Savran in *American Theatre* (October, 1998). The most extensive published interview with Vogel. More about her writing style and personal life than any of her plays. Great insight into the personality of Vogel.

Matthew J. Kopans

VOLTAIRE
François-Marie Arouet

Born: Paris, France; November 21, 1694
Died: Paris, France; May 30, 1778

Principal drama

Œdipe, pr. 1718, pb. 1719 (*Oedipus*, 1761)
Artémire, pr. 1720
Mariamne, pr. 1724, pb. 1725 (English translation, 1761)
L'Indiscret, pr., pb. 1725 (verse play)
Brutus, pr. 1730, pb. 1731 (English translation, 1761)
Ériphyle, pr. 1732, pb. 1779

Zaïre, pr. 1732, pb. 1733 (English translation, 1736)

La Mort de César, pr. 1733, pb. 1735

Adélaïde du Guesclin, pr. 1734

L'Échange, pr. 1734, pb. 1761

Alzire, pr., pb. 1736 (English translation, 1763)

L'Enfant prodigue, pr. 1736, pb. 1738 (verse; prose translation, *The Prodigal*, 1750?)

La Prude: Ou, La Grandeuse de Cassette, wr. 1740, pr., pb. 1747 (verse; based on William Wycherley's play *The Plain-Dealer*)

Zulime, pr. 1740, pb. 1761

Mahomet, pr., pb. 1742 (*Mahomet the Prophet*, 1744)

Mérope, pr. 1743, pb. 1744 (English translation, 1744, 1749)

La Princesse de Navarre, pr., pb. 1745 (verse play; music by Jean-Philippe Rameau)

Sémiramis, pr. 1748, pb. 1749 (*Semiramis*, 1760)

Nanine, pr., pb. 1749 (English translation, 1927)

Oreste, pr., pb. 1750

Rome sauvée, pr., pb. 1752

L'Orphelin de la Chine, pr., pb. 1755 (*The Orphan of China*, 1756)

Socrate, pb. 1759 (*Socrates*, 1760)

L'Écossaise, pr., pb. 1760 (*The Highland Girl*, 1760)

Tancrède, pr. 1760, pb. 1761

Don Pèdre, wr. 1761, pb. 1775

Olympie, pb. 1763, pr. 1764

Le Triumvirat, pr. 1764, pb. 1767

Les Scythes, pr., pb. 1767

Les Guèbres: Ou, La Tolérance, pb. 1769

Sophonisbe, pb. 1770, pr. 1774 (revision of Jean Mairet's play)

Les Pélopides: Ou, Atrée et Thyeste, pb. 1772

Les Lois de Minos, pb. 1773

Irène, pr. 1778, pb. 1779

Agathocle, pr. 1779

OTHER LITERARY FORMS

In addition to his plays, Voltaire wrote many poems, especially odes. Some of his most important longer poems are *Poème sur la religion naturelle* (1722); *La Henriade* (1728), an epic poem initially entitled *La Ligue* (*Henriade*, 1732); *Le Temple du goût* (1733; *The Temple of Taste*, 1734), on literary criticism; *Discours en vers sur l'homme* (1738-1752; *Discourses in Verse on Man*, 1764); *Poème sur le désastre de Lisbonne* (1756; *Poem on the Lisbon Earthquake*, 1764); and *La Pucelle d'Orléans* (1755, 1762; *The Maid of Orleans*, 1758, also as *La Pucelle*, 1785-1786).

Voltaire's main historical works are *Histoire de Charles XII* (1731; *The History of Charles XII*, 1732); *Le Siècle de Louis XIV* (1751; *The Age of Louis XIV*, 1752); and *Essai sur les mœurs* (1756, 1763; *The General History and State of Europe*, 1754, 1759).

Voltaire's current reputation is based on his *contes philosophiques* (philosophical tales), of which three of the principal ones are: *Zadig: Ou, La Destinée, Histoire orientale* (1748; originally as *Memnon: Histoire orientale*, 1747; *Zadig: Or, The Book of Fate*, 1749), *Candide: Ou, L'Optimisme* (1759; *Candide: Or, All for the Best*, 1759), and *La Princesse de Babylone* (1768; *The Princess of Babylon*, 1769).

Voltaire wrote numerous philosophical treatises, essays, polemics, and brochures, and he left behind a voluminous correspondence, compiled in *The Complete Works of Voltaire* (1968-1977; 135 volumes, in French).

ACHIEVEMENTS

Voltaire dominated the eighteenth century theater by the number of his plays alone. He wrote fifty-two in all, of which twenty-seven are tragedies. He was the most popular dramatist of his time and the principal author for the Comédie-Française, which now only occasionally performs his plays. In his own time, Voltaire was regarded as one of the masters of French drama. More of his plays were performed than those of Pierre Corneille and Jean Racine together. Today, he is best known for his philosophical works, especially his tales, but during his lifetime he believed his immortality would rest on his dramatic accomplishments. Although he wrote most of his plays rapidly, he constantly reworked them and revised the failures, often bringing them to success, as with *Mariamne*.

Voltaire (Library of Congress)

Voltaire was the literary and philosophical bridge between the classical theater of the seventeenth century and the Romantic theater of the nineteenth century. It was he who kept the classical theater alive, both in subject matter (one-third of his tragedies are based on classical themes) and in form. He insisted on adherence to the Aristotelian unities of action, time, and place, and on verse, propriety, and verisimilitude. His style, though sometimes declamatory, is in accurate French *alexandrins*, elegant and frequently excellent poetry in the style of Corneille. Yet, as dedicated as he was to the values of French classicism in the drama, Voltaire was intrigued, if torn, by contemporary literary theories and foreign dramatic works, and at times he violated his own precepts in introducing into his plays—and into France—dramatic elements of the coming age.

Thus, while Voltaire kept French classical theater alive, he distinctly widened its frontiers. Voltaire's trip to England from 1726 to 1729 brought him into contact with the English theater, and especially with the plays of William Shakespeare. Critic Admad Gunny maintains that Voltaire also came to know and was influenced by the works of John Dryden, Alexander Pope, Jonathan Swift, Joseph Addison, John Milton, Laurence Sterne, Samuel Richardson, and Henry Fielding. Their influence can be seen in many plays, among them *Brutus* and *La Mort de César*, based on Shakespeare's *Julius Caesar* (pr. c. 1599-1600); *Ériphyle*, *Semiramis*, *Oreste*, and *Tancrède*, all inspired by Shakespeare's *Hamlet, Prince of Denmark* (pr. c. 1600-1601); *Zaïre*, inspired by Shakespeare's *Othello, the Moor of Venice* (pr. 1604); and *Alzire*, inspired by Dryden's *The Indian Emperor: Or, The Conquest of Mexico by the Spaniards* (pr. 1665, pb. 1667). Although Voltaire was most influenced by Shakespeare, and his numerous literary essays on the English dramatist helped to make Shakespeare known on the Continent, Voltaire did not unreservedly accept Shakespearean drama, as is especially evident in his "Lettre à l'Académie Française" (1776). Yet his contributions in incorporating English dramatic theory into the French theater are the most significant of the eighteenth century and prepared the way for the Romantic drama of the nineteenth century as described in Victor Hugo's preface to *Cromwell* (1827), particularly in the emphasis on action rather than introspection.

Voltaire did not limit his subjects to classical sources, but widened the geographical boundaries of the tragedy. *Zaïre* is situated in Jerusalem, *Alzire* in Peru, *Zulime* in Africa, *Mahomet the Prophet* in Mecca, *The Orphan of China* in China, *Les Scythes* in Scythia, and *Les Guèbres* in Syria. There is, however, very little local color in these plays other than the settings and the names. Heralding Romanticism years before it would flourish, Voltaire used French national themes and names for his inspiration. *Zaïre* recalls the illustrious family of Lusignan; *Adélaïde du Guesclin* is based on fourteenth century Breton history; and *Tancrède*, in the style of historical romance, returns to the courtly love theme. The critic Thurston Wheeler Russel maintains that one of Voltaire's greatest literary innovations was his development of the heroic romance in the manner of Dryden; Voltaire's plays in this genre, especially *Zaïre*, *Alzire*, *Tancrède*, and *Mérope*, almost operatic in nature, remain among his most popular.

Less successful in comedy than in tragedy, Voltaire, who greatly admired Molière, declared that comedy exists mainly to provoke laughter among the spectators. He did, however, allow tearful situations in his comedies, and his best comedies are sentimental in the vein of the *comédie larmoyante* ("weeping comedy"), as in, for example, *The Prodigal* and *The Highland Girl*. Voltaire intended comedy to be a faithful portrayal of manners and to rest on mistaken identity, historically two of the most important comic devices. His own plays illustrate these techniques and thus were rather successful in continuing the tradition of Molière and the classical comedy of Plautus and Terence. Critic Raymond Navès sees caricature as Voltaire's main accomplishment in comedy, and the use of prose in *The Highland Girl* as more effective than his ten-syllable verses in *The Prodigal* and *Nanine*.

BIOGRAPHY

François-Marie Arouet, known to his contemporaries and to posterity as Voltaire, was born on November 21, 1694, very likely in Paris, though there is some evidence for Châtenay. His father, a former notary, was a well-to-do bourgeois. Like Jean-Jacques Rousseau, Voltaire grew up without a mother, whom he lost when he was seven years old. From 1704 to 1711, he attended the aristocratic Collège Louis-le-Grand, where he received an excellent classical formation from the Jesuits. Despite his later anticlericalism, Voltaire maintained several attachments to his Jesuit teachers, among them Father Thoulié, who received him into the Académie Française in 1746. Voltaire also formed lasting bonds with his companions, especially Charles Augustin Feriol, comte d'Argental, his lifelong friend.

Voltaire's father envisioned a career in law for his son, who felt no attraction to it, and preferred writing. He frequented the frivolous Society of the Temple, and in 1713 was exiled to Holland by his father, beginning a series of travels and romantic liaisons that were to characterize his life. At the same time, he began his literary career with an ode to commemorate the construction of Notre-Dame, soon to be followed by a play that was declared insulting to the Regent

Philippe of Orléans, for which he was imprisoned in the Bastille in 1718. An expert in the art of flattery, he soon learned to court royal favor, and was well received until an argument with Gui Auguste de Rohan-Chabot, who had him beaten, necessitated exile in England. Thedore Besterman is of the opinion that this upsetting experience fueled Voltaire's lifelong passion for social justice.

Voltaire's three years in England, from 1726 to 1729, were important in his intellectual development. He became acquainted with new ideas on political economy and literary theory through association with Lord Henry St. John Bolingbroke, already his friend in France, Lord Charles Mordaunt Peterborough, Swift, Pope, John Gay, Edward Young, George Berkeley, and Samuel Clarke. He was later to popularize the new trend in thought in his *Lettres philosophiques* (1734; originally published as *Letters Concerning the English Nation*, 1733, also as *Philosophical Letters*; 1961). On his return he became acquainted with Mme Émilie du Châtelet, with whom he maintained an erratic liaison until her death in 1749. He lived most of the time at her château of Cirey, and there, under her influence, became interested in experimental science and Isaac Newton's physics. After her death, he spent two years, from 1750 to 1752, at the court of Frederick II of Prussia. Frederick had previously received Voltaire warmly, but gradually their relationship cooled, and it ceased in 1757.

From 1743 until his death, Voltaire's companion and mistress was his niece Mme Denis, with whom he settled at the estate of Les Délices, and at Ferney, near Geneva, from 1755 to 1778. The Calvinist pastors were not anxious to receive him among them, particularly since his anticlericalism was strongest at this time. He won his battles with them and with Rousseau on the theater, and in 1765 successfully rehabilitated the name of Jean Calas, who had been wrongly executed, and later the family Sirven and the Chevalier de la Barre (who was also killed), all victims of religious fanaticism. Voltaire created a model village at Ferney and became its provident patriarch. In 1778, he returned in triumph to Paris for the performance of his last tragedy, *Irène*. He died there on May 30, 1778, after having received the Sacraments of the Church. His nephew Father Mignot gave him secret Christian burial near Troyes. In 1791, the revolutionaries carried his remains in triumph to Paris, where they were placed in the Pantheon.

ANALYSIS

Voltaire's theater is characterized both by innovation and by certain recurring themes. He draws primarily on the French classical theater, and uses techniques popularized by his contemporaries, such as Denis Diderot's bourgeois drama and heroic romance, and his rival Prosper Jolyot de Crébillon's recognition scenes. Voltaire's sources of inspiration include exotic settings such as China in *The Orphan of China*, America in *Alzire*, and French national history, as in *Adélaïde du Guesclin*. At the same time, he uses Greek sources in five plays: *Oedipus*, *Ériphyle*, *Mérope*, *Semiramis*, and *Oreste*. In these plays, the ancient theme of the avenging deity is uppermost, yet as early as *Oedipus* (1718), Voltaire displays his humanism in showing the hero as an innocent victim who protests his independence. Voltaire wrote four plays of Roman inspiration: *Brutus*, *La Mort de César*, *Rome sauvée*, and *Le Triumvirat*. Less successful than his Greek-inspired plays, they extol a patriotic and republican theme, to which Voltaire himself was not very committed.

In the classical tradition, Voltaire kept alive the three unities as well as *vraisemblance* (verisimilitude), and *bienséance* (propriety). Yet his innovative emphasis on action, the influence of Shakespeare, and his use of recognition scenes evidence his inexact observance of the classical rules of theater. Many plays fail in unity of action, as in, for example, his first play, *Oedipus*: The addition of yet one more character to the action, Jocasta's former lover Philoctetes, overdoes an already complex plot. The classical unity that Voltaire most frequently violates is that of place, as in *Mahomet the Prophet*, *Mérope*, and *Alzire*. In these plays, to give an appearance of exactness, Voltaire brings unlikely characters together in one location. Influenced by the English theater, at times Voltaire disregards the classical and contemporary French taboo against violence onstage, as in the murder scene in *Mahomet the Prophet*.

(Such a case is an exception, however, since Voltaire generally preserves the French sense of delicacy with the classical device of a messenger who reports an act of violence.) Voltaire often fails in verisimilitude: The sudden change in Genghis Khan (in *The Orphan of China*) from a barbarous destroyer to a benevolent protector is unlikely; Semiramis's failure to recognize Assur as her husband's murderer is equally unbelievable; Mérope's blindness to her son's presence is improbable.

This lack of strict adherence to classical rules reflects Voltaire's changing dramatic theories. Although in many ways he resembles Racine, unlike that pillar of French classicism Voltaire subordinates psychological analysis to action, which in turn gives rise to an emphasis on staging and decoration—all highly untraditional at that time. Voltaire's later plays often resemble operatic performances. With *Tancrède*, Voltaire succeeded in eliminating spectators from the stage, where they had been accustomed to sit and witness characters discuss action that had taken place previously or offstage. The action in Voltaire's plays depends mainly on the *coup de théâtre* (an abrupt turn of events), surprise, and unexpected recognition scenes. Most frequently a child lost in early years is reunited with his or her parents. For example, in *Mahomet the Prophet*, Séïde and Palmire, who plan on marrying, learn that they are brother and sister, the children of Mahomet's rival, Zopire. In *Mérope*, a suspected murderer is discovered to be Egisthe, Mérope's lost child, and Zaïre, about to renounce her religion for her lover, discovers that she is Lusignan's daughter. Even Voltaire's comedies use this device; the impoverished Miss Lindon in *The Highland Girl* is really Montross's daughter, who was taken from him at age five.

Although Voltaire made action primary in his plays, and used a variety of sources for his inspiration, he actually rewrote the same play again and again and shows a pattern in his themes. Some are hardly distinguishable: *Ériphyle* and *Semiramis*; *Zaïre*, *Alzire*, and *Mahomet the Prophet*; *Mérope* and *Mahomet the Prophet*. Because of Voltaire's belief in the theater as a moralizing device, he intended his plays to instruct spectators. In the theater, as elsewhere, Voltaire directed all his efforts against intoler ance in religion and injustice in government. As early as *Oedipus*, Voltaire cited the danger in the power of priests. *Alzire* and *Zaïre* show the superiority of natural religion. In *Alzire*, the uninstructed Zamore is more compassionate than the inflexible Gusman, who compels the Indians to accept Christianity. *Mahomet the Prophet* is itself a fanatic apology for tolerance, falsifying history to present Muḥammad as a merciless murderer and adulterer. Although Voltaire dedicated his play to Pope Benedict XIV, its anticlerical intent was not lost on the critics, among them Voltaire's rival Crébillon, at that time a censor, who outlawed the play.

Voltaire's character analysis is for the most part rather superficial; his characters develop through action rather than through expression of their thoughts or through conversation. They resemble one another from play to play, usually revealing only one side, so that each character represents a human quality: Mérope and Idamé are maternal love; Alzire and Zaïre, romantic love; Zamti, patriotism; Mahomet and Polyphonte, tyranny. Yet owing to Voltaire's genius, his characters manage to be human and touching. They are usually victims of love, be it maternal or romantic, and are often on the verge of committing incest before the recognition scene. In many cases, Voltaire the humanist prevents his tragedy from becoming tragic (in the classical sense), for he spares the innocent victim, as in *The Orphan of China*. René Pomeau sees *Oedipus* as marking the end of traditional French tragedy, as the victim accuses the gods. In fact, it is for this humanizing dimension that Voltaire's plays are best appreciated, for he brought into a theater dominated by classical *reason* the Romantic trait of feeling, *sensibilité*, that was to characterize it in future years.

OEDIPUS

Oedipus, says Pomeau, is important because it is Voltaire's first tragedy, and among his best. In it, Voltaire announced the themes that he would spend his life proclaiming: justice and tolerance. Voltaire had begun the play before his imprisonment in the Bastille in 1718 and finished it there. It enjoyed a run of forty-five performances and featured two of the best-

known actors of the time in the leading roles: Dufresne as Oedipus and Mlle Demarès as Jocasta. The play is obviously based on Sophocles' *Oidipous Tyrannos* (c. 429 B.C.E.; *Oedipus Tyrannus*, 1715), though at the actors' insistence Voltaire added the love scenes. The play was an enormous success, yet was attacked by critics as a plagiarism of Corneille, to which it does have strong resemblances. Voltaire responded to critics with several *Lettres philosophiques*, which form an excellent documentation of his literary views at the time.

Although Voltaire uses the story of Oedipus's search for the truth as narrated by Sophocles, like Corneille (whom he imitated), he complicates the plot with extraneous events. Such is the introduction of Philoctetes into the action of the story. Jocasta's former lover is accused of killing Laius but denies the charge. Although he still loves Jocasta, he is not jealous of Oedipus, who is noble and has saved the city. Oedipus in turn respects Philoctetes and even wishes to have him as his successor. Oedipus learns his identity from Phorbas, originally Laius's companion, and from Icarus, his former guardian. As in Sophocles' play, Oedipus blinds himself and Jocasta commits suicide.

Voltaire shows his anticlerical tendencies in act 2, scene 5, in which he points out the dangerous effects of priestly power. Voltaire also shows his humanism, differing from Sophocles in presenting an Oedipus who is not submissive to fate but assertive in protesting his innocence. Jocasta, too, defends Oedipus in act 4, scene 3; her suicide at the end is less convincing than her belief in justice. According to Pomeau, Voltaire's *Oedipus* is a new dimension in the theater, actually bringing to an end the traditional concept of tragedy.

ZAÏRE

Zaïre has always been one of the most popular of Voltaire's plays, with thirty-one performances in its first season alone and a long time in the repertory of the Comédie-Française. Voltaire's aim was that there should be "nothing so Turkish, nothing so Christian, so full of love, so tender, so furious," as *Zaïre*. He added the love element lacking in the unsuccessful *Ériphyle*; in fact, as Jean-Baptiste Rousseau commented, passion seems to triumph over grace. Set in Jerusalem, it shows the widening geographical frontiers of Voltaire's drama.

Zaïre is a captive of the sultan Orosmane, who loves her and wishes to marry her. She has abandoned her Christian faith for him and has forgotten Nerestan, who returns with her ransom. Orosmane, however, refuses to part with her or with the aged Lusignan. Lusignan, about to die, recognizes Nerestan and Zaïre as his lost children and as his last request wants to see Zaïre convert to Christianity. She accepts, though she does not wish to abandon Orosmane. He intercepts a letter that seems to indicate that Zaïre has betrayed him for Nerestan, and following a secret rendezvous, unknowingly stabs Zaïre. When he discovers his error, Orosmane frees Nerestan and then kills himself.

Zaïre's Deistic overtones were immediately perceived by the critics. Orosmane is as virtuous as Nerestan because Voltaire wished to show the equality of all beliefs. Zaïre herself states the relativity of religion: Had she been brought up along the Ganges, she would have been a "heathen"; in Paris, a Christian; she is a Muslim in Jerusalem. The play, however, is touching and very human; hence, Voltaire's daring ideas did not prevent its success.

ALZIRE

Alzire also treats the question of true religion, and has always been among the most popular of Voltaire's plays. In *Alzire*, for the first time in the French theater, the scene was set in America—in Peru—and according to critic Theodore Besterman it remains one of the most modern of Voltaire's plays because it deals with the problem of colonization and of "the relations between an occupying power and a subject people." Besterman believes that Voltaire does not solve this problem, but rather shows the triumph of force. This may be the de facto answer, but it is not necessarily the ideal proposed by Voltaire. The play is preceded by a lengthy preface, in which Voltaire declares his purpose: "to discover to what extent the true spirit of religion is superior to the natural virtues." For Voltaire, to harbor this true spirit is not to practice useless rituals, but rather "to consider all men as brothers, to do good and to forgive evil."

The brutal Spanish conqueror Gusman receives the governorship of Peru from his gentle father, Alvarez. Gusman is in love with Alzire, the Aztec king Montezuma's daughter, who refuses the man responsible for the death of her lover Zamore. Zamore, however, is not dead; in fact, he has saved Gusman's father, Alvarez, and returns to avenge the wrong done by Gusman. When Zamore arrives, Alzire has just been married to Gusman to appease the Spaniards. Alzire, though faithful to Gusman, pleads for mercy for Zamore, who in turn attacks Gusman. Both Alzire and Zamore are condemned, but are saved by Gusman's pardon of Zamore. Zamore, inspired by Gusman's gesture of forgiveness, accepts the Christian religion and will live to marry Alzire.

Although Voltaire extolled the virtue of forgiveness, he did not make a convincing case for Gusman's superiority. In fact, Zamore is equally virtuous, and Gusman's sudden change of heart is highly improbable. D'Argental, Voltaire's constant friend, found fault with the unconvincing ending, as do more modern critics, among them Pomeau and Besterman. Once again, however, Voltaire's play has charm because of the touching love story it recounts and the deeply human character of Alzire.

MÉROPE

The popular subject of *Mérope* is based on a nonextant tragedy of Euripides. Voltaire used the play by Francesco Scipione Maffei (*Mérope*, 1713), performed in Paris in 1717, as his main source. First planning a translation, Voltaire worked on the tragedy from 1736 to 1743, and dedicated it to Maffei. It was the best received of all Voltaire's plays, and broke all records in its proceeds. This was surprising, as the play has no love element other than maternal affection directly inspired by Racine's *Andromaque* (pr. 1667; *Andromache*, 1674). *Mérope* also repeats the theme of *Mahomet the Prophet* in Polyphonte, tyrant of Messène, who insists on blind obedience and fear in his followers. Besterman notes a Rousseauian element in Egisthe, "the virtuous man brought up far from cities and courts in an atmosphere of rustic simplicity."

Polyphonte, tyrant of Messène, wishes to marry Mérope, widow of the slain Cresphonte. She, howcvcr, dctcsts Polyphontc and yearns only for the return of her lost son Egisthe. Egisthe has in fact returned, but his identity is unknown both to him and to Mérope, and he is accused of being the murderer of Mérope's lost son. Although Mérope wishes to punish Egisthe, the alleged murderer, at the same time she feels tenderness for him. The mystery of his identity is solved by Narbas, Egisthe's guardian; Polyphonte insists on punishing the young stranger, but on learning the truth, Polyphonte agrees to spare Egisthe on the condition that Mérope marry him and Egisthe swear homage to him. Egisthe kills the tyrant and becomes king in his place.

The critic Fernand Vial ascribes the popularity of this tragedy to its simplicity. Voltaire's contemporaries also hailed it as a model of true classical drama, although in fact it is not tragic, since the innocent triumph over the guilty. It is free from Voltaire's usual complications, however, though it does violate unity of place and has several improbable situations, such as the delays in recognition. Nevertheless, it is human and touching, and shows Voltaire's greatest merit as a dramatist: a sense of warmth and feeling, *sensibilité.*

OTHER MAJOR WORKS

LONG FICTION: *Zadig: Ou, La Destinée, Histoire orientale,* 1748 (originally as *Memnon: Histoire orientale,* 1747; *Zadig: Or, The Book of Fate,* 1749); *Le Micromégas,* 1752 (*Micromegas,* 1753); *Histoire des voyages de Scarmentado,* 1756 (*The History of the Voyages of Scarmentado,* 1757; also as *History of Scarmentado's Travels,* 1961); *Candide: Ou, L'Optimisme,* 1759 (*Candide: Or, All for the Best,* 1759; also as *Candide: Or, The Optimist,* 1762; also as *Candide: Or, Optimism,* 1947); *L'Ingénu,* 1767 (*The Pupil of Nature,* 1771; also as *Ingenuous,* 1961); *L'Homme aux quarante écus,* 1768 (*The Man of Forty Crowns,* 1768); *La Princesse de Babylone,* 1768 (*The Princess of Babylon,* 1769).

SHORT FICTION: *Le Monde comme il va,* 1748 (revised as *Babouc: Ou, Le Monde comme il va,* 1749; *Babouc: Or, The World as It Goes,* 1754; also as *The World as It Is: Or, Babouc's Vision,* 1929); *Memnon: Ou, La Sagesse humaine,* 1749 (*Memnon: Or, Human*

Wisdom, 1961); *La Lettre d'un Turc,* 1750, *Le Blanc et le noir,* 1764 (*The Two Genies,* 1895); *Jeannot et Colin,* 1764 (*Jeannot and Colin,* 1929); *L'Histoire de Jenni,* 1775; *Les Oreilles du Comte de Chesterfield,* 1775 (*The Ears of Lord Chesterfield and Parson Goodman,* 1826).

NONFICTION: *An Essay upon the Civil Wars of France . . . and Also upon the Epick Poetry of the European Nations from Homer Down to Milton,* 1727; *La Henriade,* 1728 (*Henriade,* 1732); *Histoire de Charles XII,* 1731 (*The History of Charles XII,* 1732); *Le Temple du goût,* 1733 (*The Temple of Taste,* 1734); *Letters Concerning the English Nation,* 1733; *Lettres philosophiques,* 1734 (originally published in English as *Letters Concerning the English Nation,* 1733; also as *Philosophical Letters,* 1961); *Discours de métaphysique,* 1736; *Éléments de la philosophie de Newton,* 1738 (*The Elements of Sir Isaac Newton's Philosophy,* 1738); *Discours en vers sur l'homme,* 1738-1752 (*Discourses in Verse on Man,* 1764); *Vie de Molière,* 1739; *Le Siècle de Louis XIV,* 1751 (*The Age of Louis XIV,* 1752); *Essai sur les mœurs et l'esprit des nations,* 1756, 1763 (*The General History and State of Europe,* 1754, 1759); *Traité sur la tolérance,* 1763 (*A Treatise on Religious Toleration,* 1764); *Dictionnaire philosophique portatif,* 1764, enlarged 1769 (as *La Raison par alphabet,* also known as *Dictionnaire philosophique; A Philosophical Dictionary for the Pocket,* 1765; also as *Philosophical Dictionary,* 1945, enlarged 1962); *Commentaires sur le théâtre de Pierre Corneille,* 1764; *Avis au public sur les parracides imputés aux calas et aux Sirven,* 1775; *Correspondence,* 1953-1965 (102 volumes).

MISCELLANEOUS: *The Works of M. de Voltaire,* 1761-1765 (35 volumes), 1761-1781 (38 volumes); *Candide and Other Writings,* 1945; *The Portable Voltaire,* 1949; *Candide, Zadig, and Selected Stories,* 1961; *The Complete Works of Voltaire,* 1968-1977 (135 volumes; in French).

BIBLIOGRAPHY

Besterman, Theodore. *Voltaire.* 3d ed. Chicago: University of Chicago Press, 1976. This biography by a Voltaire scholar provides coverage of the writer's life and works. Bibliography and index.

Bird, Stephen. *Reinventing Voltaire: The Politics of Commemoration in Nineteenth Century France.* Oxford, England: Voltaire Foundation, 2000. An examination of the critical response to Voltaire, particularly in the nineteenth century. Bibliography and indexes.

Carlson, Marvin A. *Voltaire and the Theatre of the Eighteenth Century.* Westport, Conn.: Greenwood Press, 1998. An examination of the French theater in the eighteenth century and Voltaire's role. Bibliography and index.

Gray, John. *Voltaire.* Great Philosophers 19. New York: Routledge, 1999. A biography of Voltaire that covers his life and works, while concentrating on his philosophy. Bibliography.

Knapp, Bettina Liebowitz. *Voltaire Revisited.* New York: Twayne, 2000. A basic biography of Voltaire that describes his life and works. Bibliography and index.

Mason, Haydn, ed. *Studies for the Tercentenary of Voltaire's Birth, 1694-1994.* Oxford, England: Voltaire Foundation, 1994. Contains essays on Voltaire's works and life, including one on the French theater in the 1690's. Bibliography.

Irma M. Kashuba

JOOST VAN DEN VONDEL

Born: Cologne, Germany; November 17, 1587
Died: Amsterdam, the Netherlands; February 5, 1679

PRINCIPAL DRAMA

Het Pascha, pr. 1610, pb. 1612
Hierusalem verwoest, pb. 1620
Palamedes of Vermoorde Onnoselheit, pr., pb. 1625
Gijsbrecht van Aemstel, pb. 1637, pr. 1638 (English translation, 1991)
Maeghden, pb. 1639
Gebroeders, pb. 1640
Joseph in Dothan, pr. 1640
Joseph in Egypten, pr. 1640
Maria Stuart, pb. 1646 (Mary Stuart, 1996)
De Leeuwendalers, pb. 1647, pr. 1648
Lucifer, pr., pb. 1654 (English translation, 1917)
Jeptha, pb. 1659
Samson of Heilige wraeck, pb. 1660 (*Samson: Or, Holy Revenge*, 1964)
Adam in ballingschap, pb. 1664 (*Adam in Exile*, 1952)
Noah, pb. 1667
Zungchin of Ondergang der Sinesche Heerschappye, pb. 1667

OTHER LITERARY FORMS

Joost van den Vondel mastered numerous other genres besides drama, including sonnets, odes, elegies, epics, and a great volume of religious and occasional poetry. Vondel's great strength as lyricist profoundly influenced the writing of Dutch poetry. He also became renowned for his biting political satire. Besides writing religious polemics, hagiography, and literary criticism, Vondel translated many classics, including works by Sophocles, Ovid, and Vergil.

ACHIEVEMENTS

Although no formal national or international book awards existed in Joost van den Vondel's time, his achievements were widely recognized. The emergent Dutch nation regarded him as its national poet. He was as much in demand as a poetic dispenser of public praise as he was feared for his caustic satires. As the leading author of Amsterdam theater, he sometimes had as many as three of his plays in performance during the same year. Of the thirty-three tragedies he wrote, eighteen were presented onstage. The performance of *Gijsbrecht van Aemstel* became an annual tradition until 1968.

Vondel's authority as critic was seldom challenged. He applied the most modern views on drama theory of his time to his art and represents a culmination of dramatic achievement in a genre that, according to sixteenth century humanist thought, reflected an ideal balance between aesthetic and religious goals.

The esteem of the artistic community for this great Dutch poet and playwright of the Golden Age was dramatically demonstrated when on October 20, 1653, at the age of sixty-six, Vondel was honored at a dinner by more than one hundred painters, poets, architects, sculptors, and lovers of the arts and in a splendid ritualistic ceremony was crowned with a laurel wreath as King of the Feast. After his death, he was eulogized as the first poet of his age, "the oldest and the greatest."

BIOGRAPHY

Joost van den Vondel was born in Cologne on November 17, 1587. His parents had moved there shortly before from Antwerp, a predominantly Calvinist city that had become unsafe for Mennonites. After some years, Roman Catholic Cologne also became uncomfortable for the Vondels. In 1596, the family settled in Amsterdam, where the father became a prosperous hosier. Little is known of Joost's early years and education. Apparently he was largely self-taught. His inclination toward poetry came to expression in his teenage years, his first known poem dating from 1605. Five years later, Vondel married Mayken de Wolff. His wife assumed responsibility for the daily management of the family hosiery business, which Joost had taken over from his father. This allowed the young husband to devote much of his time to the study of the classics and the writing of poetry and plays. In fact, Vondel lived primarily for his art and studies; to him, poetry was as basic as breathing.

In 1610, Vondel's first dramatic work, *Het Pascha* (the passover), was performed. This tragicomedy on the Exodus from Egypt had obvious parallels to the Dutch liberation from Spain. More plays and much poetry soon followed. In the 1620's, Vondel suffered a prolonged period of depression. Still he managed to publish *Hierusalem verwoest* (Jerusalem destroyed)

and *Palamedes of Vermoorde Onnoselheit* (Palamedes of murdered innocence), the latter a Greek tragedy about the conflict between Ulysses and Palamedes but with such undisguised insinuations about the power politics of the local centralized government that it was quickly seized. Vondel was fined by the court, but his play went through seven more editions within the year. His fame grew rapidly in the 1630's, even as Vondel suffered the deaths of three of his five children, followed by the death of his beloved wife in 1635. These heartbreaking losses confronted Vondel as never before with the religious question of life's ultimate purpose and value. He emerged from this valley of darkness a more mature artist, as though his technical and moral vision had been refined in the crucible of suffering, demonstrated amply in his celebrated *Gijsbrecht van Aemstel*.

At the age of fifty-four, Vondel converted to Roman Catholicism. He had found Calvinism too tyrannical in its orthodoxy and often hostile to the aesthetic beauty of art and freedom of expression. It was a courageous decision in a time when Calvinism dominated and the Catholic Church was officially forbidden. However, joining the universal church gave Vondel a much-needed peace of mind. His poetry had always conveyed a mystical longing for the divine, but now it also celebrated the joy of life. His drama in this decade included *De Leeuwendalers* in 1647, a pastoral play and a glorification of the Peace of Munster; it was designated as "the most perfect drama that our poet has left us."

Still, Vondel was more than sixty years old when he wrote some of his best poems, remarkable works of prose, and his greatest plays. *Lucifer* was published in 1654 and is a masterpiece of lyrical power. Other magnificent biblical tragedies followed, closely patterned after classical models.

Personal tragedy struck again when Vondel's son mismanaged the family business, then died at sea while sailing for the East Indies. To pay off the debts his son left behind, Vondel gave up all his savings and, at the age of seventy, took a salaried job as a clerk in a pawnshop. During the ten years of his employment, he still managed to write an impressive number of lyric, dramatic, and didactic verses.

Interest in his plays, however, declined at a time when some of his best dramatic work was still to be written. Popular interest shifted away from sacred drama to the livelier romantic tragedies and social satires of Vondel's contemporaries. Today, none of Vondel's plays is performed, and the author, despite his artistic achievements, is seldom seriously studied.

Vondel had outlived all his children when he died at age ninety-one, on February 5, 1679. He was carried to his grave by fourteen poets and lovers of poetry, a fitting tribute to this prolific and supremely gifted Dutch poet and dramatist.

ANALYSIS

Though Joost van den Vondel ranks higher perhaps as a poet than as a dramatist, his unique contribution to seventeenth century religious drama ensured his renown. Renaissance drama was steeped in the Senecan tradition, practiced also by Vondel's contemporaries, P. C. Hooft and Hugo Grotius. Vondel's early works, especially the highly pictorial *Hierusalem verwoest*, show the influence of the French theater's Senecan religious tragedy. However, Vondel, following the Renaissance tradition of adapting religious drama to the form and language of classical theater, found himself increasingly attracted to the Aristotelian concept of tragedy, coming to expression already in his Joseph plays of 1640. His maturing religious view of human beings' sinful nature and people's yearning for goodness while being unable to attain it found a good fit in the Greek or Sophoclean depiction of the tragic hero. The later plays, such as *Lucifer* and *Jeptha*, demonstrate Vondel's significant contribution: As a neoclassicist, he transformed the humanist religious drama from a celebration of a virtuous hero and the educability of humankind to a more provocative portrayal of a fallen, tragic hero in need of divine redemption. His heroes changed from innocent victims of injustice to fatally flawed protagonists who caused their own destruction. Vondel went beyond the more idealized depiction of the sixteenth century to complicate the relationship between a holy God and sinful humankind, holding up for a more thoughtful contemplation the universal human dilemma.

The influence of the Bible on Vondel's art and drama was both extensive and comprehensive. From early in his writing career, Vondel saw the Scriptures as ideal and significant subject matter for tragic drama. Only a handful of Vondel's plays (*Palamedes, Gijsbrecht van Aemstel, Maeghden, Mary Stuart, De Leeuwendalers*) deal with nonbiblical subject matter. In particular, the Old Testament stories provided him with a continuous source of inspiration and insight into what matters most in the Christian's life. They also supplied the recurring theme for his religious works, the tension between human beings' will to rebel and their quest for God. The conflict between right and wrong, Christ and Satan, obedience and revolt, God and humanity, faith and reason, and redemption and despair was at the center of nearly every dramatic work Vondel produced. However, Vondel, a profound man of faith, never failed to affirm the mystery and hope of Redemption and the presence of the grace of God.

Thus Vondel assimilated his intellectual admiration of non-Christian Greek and Roman culture into his devout Christian faith and the creation of his art. As a follower of Aristotle, Vondel strictly observed the classical unities of action, place, and time in his tragedies. He strove for simplicity and dignity, though he could also soar to extravagant Baroque exuberance. For he had the gift of a verbal artistry that seemed effortless and spontaneous, setting the highest of standards for Dutch diction in the seventeenth century. Still, Vondel's true genius might have found greater fulfillment in the writing of epics than in drama. His greatness lies in the power of his poetry rather than in his drama, which too often substitutes description for action. Perhaps his very strength as lyricist weakened his achievement as dramatist.

GIJSBRECHT VAN AEMSTEL

Vondel wrote this play in honor of the opening of the new Amsterdam Performance Hall in 1637. Its strong appeal to civic pride ensured its success from the beginning; it enjoyed more than one hundred productions in Vondel's own lifetime. In contrast to most of Vondel's plays, it had staying power: It was the annual New Year's selection of choice for more than three hundred years.

The play describes the siege and burning of Amsterdam by the partisans of Count Floris V in revenge of his death. Gijsbrecht, unjustly accused, is forced to go into exile, but the angel Raphael comforts him with the promise that one day Amsterdam will be reborn and rise to international greatness, a prophecy well on the way to fulfillment in the Golden Age of the seventeenth century.

This play marks the first time that Vondel acknowledges the Greeks as his models and masters. He emulates their qualities of naturalness and freedom of movement while observing the classic conventions of five acts, the use of the chorus, the classic unities, and Alexandrine verse; moreover, in closely following the second book of Vergil's *Aeneid* (c. 29-19 B.C.E.; English translation, 1553), he makes the similarity to the fall of Troy obvious. However, here, too, Vondel integrates his Christian convictions into the political and social fabric of the subject matter. God's providence guides those who suffer adversity if they in humility submit to God's leadership, symbolized by Gijsbrecht's submission to Rafael.

LUCIFER

This play marks Vondel's greatest poetic achievement. Along with *Adam in Exile*, the continuation of the Lucifer story, *Lucifer* represents the full-blown maturity of Vondel's art. It is of course high celestial and earthly drama: the fall of the rebellious angels, the fall of the first man Adam, and the promise of salvation. It premiered in the Amsterdam theater on February 2, 1654, and immediately unleashed both praise and protest. The praise endured, the protest did not. In fact, the banning of the play by the religious community only served to make *Lucifer* an instant best seller, though the criticism hurt Vondel deeply. The rejection of the conservative Christian leaders was purportedly because of the presence of angels onstage but was in essence a rejection of Vondel's avoidance of the heavy moralism and transparent meanings of traditional religious drama. Vondel's Lucifer, though ultimately God's fallen rebel, has moments of magnificence as a tragic hero; the anguish of his inner conflict in act 4 forms the poignant climax of the whole play.

Published thirteen years before John Milton's *Paradise Lost* (1667, 1674), *Lucifer* pulsates with the turbulent passions and lofty dreams of the Golden Age, here wrapped around the main theme of unchecked ambition. Revolt, freedom, and individualism constitute the tensions in the conflict and allude to the struggle between the Netherlands and Spain. However, Vondel did not write this as political but rather as cosmic allegory: the moral struggle of the soul for its rightful place in the universe. The interplay of majesty, malignity, and mercy comes to riveting expression through an artful blending of characters, chorus, and action. However, since much of the action cannot be staged, perhaps *Lucifer* might better have been cast as an epic than as a drama.

JEPTHA

Vondel found the story of the biblical judge, Jeptha, ideal for a Sophoclean tragedy. Jeptha, in a rash moment, vows to God that he will sacrifice whoever first comes to meet him after God grants him victory in battle. When his daughter is the first one, Jeptha becomes an instant tragic hero.

Vondel wrote this play specifically to demonstrate that a biblical topic could easily be adapted to neoclassic form. He succeeded admirably. It is remarkable for its simplicity, restraint, close adherence to the classic unities, and use of iambics rather than Alexandrines. Moreover, Vondel continued to develop his notions of humankind's fallibility, influenced by his study of Greek tragedy. As exemplified in *Jeptha*, human beings are irreversibly prone to such sins as pride and self-serving piety, to a misguided faith and understanding of God, to terrible action and the anguish of its consequences. However, as in all of his tragedies, Vondel ends on a note of hope: Recognition leads to contrition, and contrition to the reaching out for grace and forgiveness.

OTHER MAJOR WORK

MISCELLANEOUS: *De complete werken van Joost van den Vondel*, 1870.

BIBLIOGRAPHY

Barnouw, A. J. *Vondel*. New York: Charles Scribner's Sons, 1925. A complete discussion of Vondel's life and works, with emphasis on the major works, especially drama. Also places Vondel in the context of his contemporaries and the political and cultural currents of the time.

Kirkconnell, Watson. *The Celestial Cycle: The Theme of Paradise Lost in World Literature with Translation of the Major Analogues.* Toronto: University of Toronto Press, 1952. Includes a discussion and translation of *Lucifer* and *Adam in Exile.*

_____. *That Invincible Samson.* Toronto: University of Toronto Press, 1964. Includes his translation, *Samson: Or, Holy Revenge.*

Meijer, Reinder P. *Literature of the Low Countries: A Short History of Dutch Literature in the Netherlands and Belgium.* New York: Twayne, 1971. Includes a section on Vondel's life and a number of his major dramas.

Noppen, Leonard Charles van. *Vondel's "Lucifer."* Greensboro, N.C.: Charles L. van Noppen, 1917. A superb translation of Vondel's masterpiece, as well as an analytical discussion of the play and of Vondel's life and times.

Henry J. Baron

W

WAKEFIELD MASTER

Born: Wakefield, England; c. 1420
Died: Unknown; c. 1450

PRINCIPAL DRAMA

Mactacio Abel (commonly known as *The Killing of Abel*)

Processus Noe cum Filiis (commonly known as *Noah*)

Prima Pastorum (commonly known as *The First Shepherds' Play*)

Secunda Pastorum (commonly known as *The Second Shepherds' Play*)

Magnus Herodes (commonly known as *Herod the Great*)

Coliphizacio (commonly known as *The Buffeting*)

The Wakefield Pageants in the Towneley Cycle, pb. 1958 (includes all the above among the 32 surviving pageants of the Towneley, or Wakefield, mystery cycle; A. C. Cowley, editor)

OTHER LITERARY FORMS

A few scholars have perceived a relationship between the style of verse used in the plays of the Wakefield Master and the fifteenth century poems *The Northern Passion* and *The Turnament of Totenhamm*. The relationship is tenuous, however, and most scholars believe it to be specious.

ACHIEVEMENTS

The mystery pageants of medieval Europe did not follow classical dramatic form. They were indigenous Western European plays that evolved out of religious ritual. The plays of the Wakefield Master are the finest surviving examples of this genre. His work is notable for its humor, its structural sophistication, its unusually fine use of dialect, and its finely developed character. In the mystery pageants of the Wakefield Master, one can find the elements of a uniquely English drama that blossomed in the works of the great Elizabethan and Jacobean playwrights. The dramatic force of his plays, the exuberance of his language, and the insight of his characterizations make the Wakefield Master a significant contributor to the development of Western drama.

BIOGRAPHY

The Wakefield Master is a mysterious figure, and the high literary value of his work has enticed many scholars into speculating about who he may have been. The dialects used by the Wakefield Master are from the general area of Wakefield, England, and the Master's plays also refer to places in and around Wakefield. Therefore, he probably wrote while living in or near the town. Evidence that the town staged mystery pageants indicates that the Master's work was composed specifically for Wakefield. The signs of his style in revisions of various portions of the cycle as well as the neatness with which his plays fit into the cycle have led some scholars to conclude that all the plays in the Towneley manuscripts were performed in Wakefield. Such a conclusion is reasonable and accounts for many scholars calling the cycle the "Wakefield Mystery Plays."

Drawing on what is known of the York and Chester cycles, scholars have speculated that the Wakefield Master was a cleric, perhaps a monk. He was probably a man, although not necessarily so. Custom and known practice indicate that women were excluded from participation in the writing of such works as the Wakefield pageants. He almost certainly had an occupation other than writing; his plays were probably commissioned, as was his editing of other plays in the Towneley Cycle. Learned members of the clergy were often expected to be able to contribute writings to public religious activities. The variety of dialects in his plays indicates that the Wakefield Master may have traveled in the Midlands area of England; the dominant dialect indicates that he was native to the Wakefield area.

ANALYSIS

The Wakefield Master was an unusually talented playwright. He used tradition and the Bible to create plays that make insightful comments on humanity. Although he was very much a medieval Christian, his authorial techniques presaged the outburst of English Humanism that occurred only two or three generations after he wrote. Notable for his wit and skill with language, he was also a highly skilled dramatist who took best advantage of what the form of the mystery pageant offered him. Characterization, format, theme, and staging—in these and the other major facets of drama he was superbly accomplished. He was therefore not only a good writer of mystery plays, nor only a good medieval dramatist, but also a great dramatist for any age. Perhaps the strongest impression retained after reading his plays is that of a writer who knew people and knew how to show them truthfully onstage, one who understood the problems that afflict every generation.

To appreciate the Wakefield Master's work, one needs to understand the nature of the mystery pageants, which were specialized religious dramas with staging and format requirements different from those of modern drama. Part of what elevates the Wakefield Master's plays above the ordinary is his manipulation of the limitations of his dramatic form to obtain sophisticated dramatic effects. His actors were shopkeepers and laborers, his employers undoubtedly expected him to follow carefully the well-known biblical stories, and his stage was limited in the props and scenery it could contain. The Wakefield Master made these limitations into assets, using them to heighten the effect on his audience of the characters and events in his plays.

MYSTERY PLAYS

A medieval mystery pageant is a play that deals with the Christian concept of the universe. The creation of the world, the sacrifice of Christ, and the Judgment are parts of the mystery, with the life of Christ being central to all the events. Thus, in a mystery cycle, the creation of the world is related to the life of Jesus, as are the biblical events that precede his birth; events that follow his ascension to heaven are shaped by his life, with the end of the world coming as a logical consequence of Christ's life. The word "cycle" has a double meaning: It refers to the medieval Christian concept of God's creation as a unified whole, which the mystery cycle portrays with plays depicting Christian history beginning with God before the act of creation and ending with the final judgment. "Cycle" also refers to the medieval tradition of viewing life as cyclical. Therefore, a mystery cycle is a dramatic representation of the medieval Christian's view of the universe. The mystery cycle presents the beginning and end of the world, unified and given their meanings by Jesus Christ.

Mystery plays are sometimes called Corpus Christi pageants because of their association with the spring Corpus Christi festival. The mystery cycles seem to have evolved as part of the public celebrations held after Easter, but their performances were held not only during Corpus Christi celebrations but also at other times, notably during Whit week. Regardless of whether they coincided with the Corpus Christi observances, these plays were springtime events and were profoundly religious in purpose. Their origins were both religious and secular, a blend that resulted in the mysteries of God's work becoming powerfully accessible to lay audiences. Liturgical drama began in the early Middle Ages as a way to teach biblical ideas to illiterate audiences who could neither read their vernacular languages nor understand Latin. Such early plays probably were staged inside churches and were part of significant religious holidays. Late medieval performances of the Lincoln Corpus Christi plays were probably still staged at the Lincoln cathedral—although outside—long after liturgical drama had evolved into the complex mystery cycles and miracle plays (the miracle plays focused on the lives of saints, not on Christ). By the time the Wakefield Master wrote his plays, mystery cycles were well-established religious celebrations, with rules and audience expectations that he had to fulfill. The rules involved inclusion of important aspects of Christian faith, and the expectations were based not only on the biblical accounts themselves but also on Christian tradition. For example, tradition had it that the wife of Noah was a shrew: She was anticipated comic relief in the mystery cycle.

Indeed, extrabiblical tradition played a large role in the development of the mystery cycles and was an important influence on the Wakefield Master. The medieval audience rarely read the Bible; it developed embellishments and twists for biblical stories. Some of the embellishments linger in modern tradition: Satan with horns, hooves, and a tail; the Apostle John as Jesus's closest friend; the apple as the forbidden fruit of which Adam and Eve eat in the Garden of Eden. The satire and ribald humor in the Wakefield Master's plays reflect the influence of folk dramas such as the Feast of Fools, in which Church ritual was mocked. In addition to popular biblical traditions and folk dramas, the mystery cycles reflected some of Western Europe's most significant secular—sometimes even pagan—myths. The death and rebirth of Christ is informed by old myths of hero-gods of the pre-Christian era; the legends of King Arthur and Roland reflect the old myths of heroes rising from their graves to help their people in times of peril. Christ was thus a secular hero-figure as well as a messianic one.

The Wakefield Master had to fulfill the basic purposes of the mystery plays, the foremost of which was to teach the audience about fundamental Christian doctrines. In *Noah*, he must communicate the idea of the Great Flood as God's response to the sins of humanity and must be sure to tell his audience how animals and the human race were preserved. In the shepherds' plays, he must convey the importance of the birth of Christ. In *The Buffeting*, the belief that Christ suffered as a surrogate for all people, past and future, is important.

STAGING AND PRESENTATION

In addition to meeting such expectations, the Wakefield Master had to work within the peculiar stage conventions of the mystery pageant. No one knows exactly how the Towneley Cycle was staged in the era in which the Wakefield Master flourished, although many scholars assume that the Wakefield plays were staged in a manner similar to the staging of the York Cycle, about which more is known. There were crucial differences between York and Wakefield that make some of the York practices unlikely for Wakefield, but York represents the broad pageant tradition in which the Wakefield Master worked. York was a relatively large and prosperous medieval city, with a large mercantile class. The mercantile class was divided into trades, and each trade was represented by a guild. Each guild was responsible for the performance of a particular play in the York Cycle. The effect of this is a fragmentation in the cycle; each play had to suit the available players in a given guild and would be altered to suit changes in the membership of the guild. Therefore the continuity found in the Towneley Cycle is not found in the York Cycle. Further, the cycles were associated with a processional tradition that was part of the Corpus Christi celebrations. The procession, a kind of parade, would involve an entire community; the guild actors would participate in their roles. Eventually the procession and the performances split because the cycles became too complex to be performed on the same day as the procession. In York, twelve to sixteen stations were designated along a processional route; at each station, a single audience could see all the plays. The stages were on large carts that were pulled by horses or oxen, and each stage belonged to a particular guild that was responsible for a particular play. Thus, Jesus, who would appear in several plays, would be performed by a different actor in each play; there was no continuity of actors from one play to the next. The York Cycle grew so long that it probably had to be performed on two or three consecutive days because of the time needed to move the stages from one station to the next.

The manner of the York Cycle's presentation is generally believed by literary historians to be the standard one for mystery cycles, but Wakefield differed from York in ways that might have made the presentation of the Towneley Cycle significantly changed from that of the York Cycle. Wakefield was relatively small; it probably did not have the large number of guilds that York had. The Towneley Cycle is believed to have included at least thirty-two known plays; missing numbered leaves from its manuscript indicate that it consisted of even more plays in the Wakefield Master's day. The city of Wakefield may have been too small to have the necessary number of guilds; it might even have had trouble finding enough actors for the multitude of roles if its plays were to have separate companies as in the York performances. In *The Wakefield Mystery Plays*, published in 1961, Martial Rose suggests that the Towneley Cycle was performed on one stage with the same actors playing the major roles throughout.

There is much to recommend the theory that the Wakefield plays were performed in a single location, probably in a theater-in-the-round. The Towneley Cycle was edited, perhaps by the Wakefield Master himself, to give it a continuity in structure and theme not found in the York Cycle. A continuity of actors and a minimum of guild plays would allow for such consistency. Also, the few records that exist indicate that the plays began and ended in one day; if they were performed in one place, they could have fit into the dawn-to-dusk schedule required by daylight performances (dusk was customarily the legal curfew). The Church, as with the Corpus Christi procession, could have had principal responsibility for staging the cycle, instead of the guilds, although there is evidence that, after the Wakefield Master's day, at least a few guilds were given specific plays. This would explain the consistent editing that is evident throughout the cycle; the plays could have been the responsibility of a central group rather than many.

The theater-in-the-round was used by traveling companies. *The Castle of Perseverance* (c. 1440), one of the great medieval morality dramas, was roughly contemporaneous with the Towneley Cycle and was performed in an outdoor theater. The use of such a theater by traveling troupes indicates that this kind of stage could be quickly set up in a field. An easily set up outdoor theater would have been well suited to the needs of Wakefield and the annual nature of the performances of its cycle. The stage would enable the Wakefield Master to use multiple exits and entrances, to and from which his actors would pass through their audience. The stage's limitations would resemble those of the York Cycle's processional arrangement. There would be no curtains and thus no changes of scenery during a given play, the actors would be surrounded on all sides by their audience, and the actors would be local people, not professionals. The Wakefield Master may have solved some of his problems by designating different areas of his stage as different dramatic locales; when an actor moved from one area of the stage to another, he moved from one imagined locale to another. The Wakefield Master also handled his staging problem by implying much of the action. Unable to build an ark onstage in *Noah*, he has the action take place in Noah's home with references to the work on the ark.

TIME IN THE CYCLES

Like many medieval writers, the Wakefield Master did not view time as linear. It was, instead, eternal; in the Christian universe of his day, God was everywhere in time as well as space. Therefore, it was reasonable that the shepherds should be like local ones and that Cain should speak of being buried locally; the Wakefield Master would have perceived little incongruity in having English tradesmen portray biblical figures. Part of the message of the cycles, indeed, was that Christ's sacrifice involved people from all eras. This treatment of time based on the universality of human experience enhances the appeal of the Wakefield Master's plays to modern readers.

THE KILLING OF ABEL

The Killing of Abel was probably edited and rewritten by the Wakefield Master. His typical nine-line stanza—found in his other plays—is possibly uniquely his; elements of the stanza have been detected by some researchers among the couplets of *The Killing of Abel*. The play also shares themes of human and divine relationships and a distinctive comic style with his other plays. The Wakefield Master has in common with other great playwrights the ability to mix pathos and humor; as in William Shakespeare's plays, tragedy is leavened with humor, and comedy with the tragic.

The plot of *The Killing of Abel* is that of the familiar biblical story: A jealous Cain commits the first murder by slaying his brother Abel. After lying to God about his deed, he is exiled by God. In this story, the Wakefield Master incorporates themes of the relationships between masters and servants, the nature of good and evil, and the universality of sin. Some critics assert that the themes of the play are too complex for its intended audience of farmers, tradespeople, and the general citizenry of Wakefield; others note that the play is loose and disorganized. Neither negative criticism is fair to the play. The first one underestimates the audience; the middle and lower classes of medieval England were deeply inculcated with religious doctrine. Nearly everything they did could have religious significance. One critic points out that the intended audience of *The Killing of Abel* would have been able to recognize in Cain, the plowman, the symbol of "the assiduous Christian." The audience would have understood the Christian symbolism and much of the basic theology. Medieval England of the Wakefield Master's day was not untouched by the Humanist revolution—as the secular themes of the Master's plays indicate—but religion still gave life and its events their meanings for the Towneley Cycle's audience. Such an audience would have perceived, for example, in the relationship between Garcio and his master Cain the relationship between God and Christian, and Satan and sinner. If Garcio is understood to be a demon, then *The Killing of Abel*'s seemingly confused structure may make sense. Simply put, if Garcio is a demon and servant of Cain, then Cain is the servant of Satan, although he may not know whom he serves. The role of Garcio need not be demoniac, though, to serve its purpose. He remarks early in the play that "Som of you ar his [Garcio's master's] men." If Garcio's master is taken to be not only Cain but also Satan, it would make members of the audience servants of Satan. Although this is a good reading, it is not one that would be readily picked up by an audience during the rush of the play's events. Cain's entrance is enough to lend meaning to Garcio's assertion; he enters while driving a plow team before him. The comparison of men with animals was common in medieval literature, and like the animals, some of the audience would be servants of sin—of the first murderer, Cain. Such an image is consistent with the Wakefield Master's work; its wit is biting. Cain is the focus of the play, the representative of the universality of sin. The sophistication of imagery and theme in *The Killing of Abel* is typical of the Wakefield Master's work. That he should turn the story of Cain and Abel into one that involves his audience typifies his efforts to stretch the subjects of his plays to encompass universal truths.

NOAH

Noah continues the themes of master-and-servant relationships, with the relationship between God and Noah opposed to that between Noah and Uxor. Noah is a near-perfect servant: God commands, and he obeys. In his role as servant of God, Noah is Christlike—a notion that would have been immediately comprehended by a medieval audience because Noah was commonly used as a Christ figure in religious teachings. The serious theme of Noah as a type of Christ is wonderfully blended with Noah's comic relationship with Uxor, his wife. Like Christ, Noah gathers his flock from the world. The ark was often treated as a symbol of the body of Christ by medieval biblical commentators, and thus Noah gathers the world to the symbol of the body of Christ, much as the Word of Christ is supposed to do. When Noah deals with Uxor, he is sometimes confounded by her cantankerous refusals to cooperate with him. When the great storm comes, she sits at her spinning wheel and ignores all entreaties to board the ark until the water rises near her. Her behavior at home and in the ark is amusing; it also represents the cantankerous, mulish, and foolish behavior with which Christ must contend in his Christian servants. The Wakefield Master blends biblical story, Christian tradition, and earthy humor into a play that tells Noah's story, shows the relationship between human beings and God, and presages the coming of Christ later in the cycle.

THE FIRST SHEPHERDS' PLAY

The Wakefield Master contributed two plays about the coming of Christ to the Towneley Cycle, *The First Shepherds' Play* and *The Second Shepherds' Play*. Some scholars suggest that *The First Shepherds' Play* was meant to end a day's series of performances and that *The Second Shepherds' Play* was meant to begin the next day's performances. Another possible explanation for two shepherds' plays is that the first one gave the Wakefield Master inspiration for the second, better play, and he chose to preserve both. *The First Shepherds' Play* focuses on three pastors or shepherds who begin as comic figures incapable of understanding the spiritual world and who end with enough wisdom to perceive the divine nature of the Christ child. One critic sets forth a persuasive argument that the play's farcical elements represent Old Jerusalem, body, and earth, and that the coming of understanding represents New Jerusalem, spirit, and heaven. A less traditional view is taken by another critic, who asserts that the play portrays the growth of imagination—that the shepherds begin by perceiving their world only in literal terms and that, as their imaginations grow, they come to perceive the greater reality of the spirit. *The First Shepherds' Play* is impressive in the sophistication of the readings it allows; the Wakefield Master grapples with difficult and important questions about the human spirit and humanity's ability to comprehend the divine. The play also is good entertainment. One critic compares the shepherds to the twentieth century's Marx Brothers, and when one reads the shepherds' argument over nonexistent sheep, the comparison seems apt.

THE SECOND SHEPHERDS' PLAY

The Second Shepherds' Play is the Wakefield Master's best play and is one of the masterpieces of world drama. It exhibits the Wakefield Master's control of form and is carefully structured to reflect the Holy Trinity, containing three shepherds, three gifts to the Christ child, and three dramatic movements, among other sets of three. The characters of the shepherds—Coll, Gyb, and Daw—are well defined and realistic. In fact, the realism of the characters, combined with the realistic earthiness of their humor, has encouraged some critics to discuss *The Second Shepherds' Play* as if it were a modern play instead of the medieval pageant it is. The Wakefield Master's genius is revealed in the combination of realistic characterization and tone with medieval Christian traditions. He anticipates the sophistication of later English drama but remains rooted in the concerns natural to the subject of the play.

The three shepherds are oppressed by misbehaving gentry and a cold and almost barren world. Their joking and singing are intended to fend off despair. When Mak enters the stage, the shepherds have shown their spiritual unreadiness to know of the birth of Christ. The subsequent farcical scenes with Mak prepare them for seeing the Christ child. Mak, dressed as if one of the gentry, dupes the shepherds and steals one of their sheep. In order to hide his crime, he and his wife, Gyll, hide the sheep in a cradle. When the shepherds come to look for their sheep, Mak claims that the cradle holds his new child. The shepherd Daw's anger changes to friendly interest; he likes children. Coll and Gyb are similarly moved. They are willing to set aside their suspicions. The discovery of the sheep and the tossing up and down of Mak are moments of boisterous comedy that might distract from the significance of what has happened. The shepherds have matured from complainers to doers—from uncharitable people to ones who wanted to visit kindnesses on Mak's putative son. The parallel between the sheep in the cradle and Christ, the Lamb of God, is obvious, and the three shepherds' readiness to offer gifts to the sheep-child represents their preparedness to give to Christ. Less obvious is the notion put forward by some scholars that Mak is an anti-God figure. Perhaps the Wakefield Master intended Mak and the stolen sheep to be antitheses of God and Christ, but their roles make good sense without heavily allegorical interpretations: Mak, Gyll, and the sheep provide a rehearsal for the three shepherds.

The play lends itself to allegorical interpretations that enhance its literary sophistication, but its dramatic success is the growth of the shepherds, and the careful development of events and form is wonderful. The play is not, as some might contend, two plays: one of Mak and the shepherds and another one attached, like a coda, of the shepherds visiting Christ. It is a careful rendering of three steps in the lives of Coll, Gyb, and Daw. They begin as lost souls in a universe whose order they do not understand. They move into the world of disorder, in which sheep are babies, in which the wife, Gyll, rules the man, Mak, and good and evil are confused. Then they mature to an understanding of the importance of the birth of Christ, to whom they bring with open hearts gifts they can happily give. Christ is the restoration of

God's order and the negation of oppression, disorder, evil, and despair. *The Second Shepherds' Play* is a blend of comedy and pathos worthy of a great playwright; it is a dramatic gem that speaks of hope.

HEROD THE GREAT

Herod the Great is possibly the Wakefield Master's best allegory. Herod, the slaughterer of the Innocents, was traditionally a satanic figure. Some critics view the Wakefield Master's Herod as a satanic parody of God; Herod is called "kyng of kyngys" and is ruler over all the world. He and his court are ostentatious and loud; he is prone to claiming powers for himself that are God's alone. He represents the old order—the world before the new age Christ brings to Earth. As such, he represents satanic perversion of order and virtue: Bragging substitutes for deeds, the master rules by fear instead of love, and courage is manifested by the butchering of infants. The Wakefield Master's comedy, open and earthy in the shepherds' plays, is dark and terrible in *Herod the Great*. The strutting Herod and his moronic sycophants are ridiculous and their absurdity laughable, yet the results of their hellish views of the world are awful. The absurd Herod becomes a monster when, onstage, his troops pull babies from their mothers and stab the infants: "His hart-blood shall thou se," declares a soldier to a mother. The language indicates that the audience is shown stage blood; swords are reddened and babies are then displayed to their mothers. Rarely in literature is humor so turned in on itself; the silly king arrogates to himself the prerogatives of God in a contest between himself and the Lord. Thematically, Herod is Satan lashing out at the newborn Christ.

The Wakefield Master is admired by many critics for his comedy rather than for his other dramatic traits, perhaps because his comedy presages modern dramatic techniques and was innovative for his era. His comedy can provide a modern reader with an exciting sense of seeing postmedieval drama being invented. Often, however, critics ignore his other achievements because of their interest in his comedy, missing the pathos in *The Killing of Abel* and the shepherds' plays. His skill encompassed the major elements of good drama, and in *Herod the Great* he ac-

tually turned his comic skills into evocations of horror and palpable evil.

THE BUFFETING

In *The Buffeting*, he used his talent for creating lively, bantering dialogue to convey not comedy but brutal insensitivity. Christ is tried by Cayphas and Anna in a mockery of a trial. One of His torturers says "wychcraft he mase" (he makes witchcraft), accusing Christ of witchery. *The Buffeting* features another of the Wakefield Master's reversals: The evildoers accuse Christ of evil. They derogate his teachings and subject him to an insane trial and to torture. The play seems peopled by madmen, with Christ like a rock of serenity in the middle of a world gone crazy. Some critics interpret Jesus's silence as a sign of the Wakefield Master's genius, suggesting that the Wakefield Master turns Christ's silence into words, that in the context of the cycle as a whole, the play's audience would speak Christ's words for him as they helplessly watched lying witnesses try to degrade him. The easy conversation of the torturers, Cayphas, and Anna, with their smiles and jokes and their almost serene confidence in merciless law, is disquieting, not amusing. Christ's silence provides answers to their gibes and accusations; these are people who are out of touch with the new world Christ has brought with him. Christ is sanity amid the insane; the lies of his accusers attest his truth. They answer themselves by revealing the emptiness of their beliefs. *Herod the Great* is disquietingly horrific; *The Buffeting* is disquieting through the contrast between worldly values and heavenly ones. Christ need not even speak. His presence alone answers his enemies.

BIBLIOGRAPHY

Beadle, Richard, ed. *The Cambridge Companion to Medieval English Theatre*. New York: Cambridge University Press, 1994. This reference guide covers English theater from around 500 to 1500, including discussion of the Wakefield pageants and mystery plays. Bibliography and index.

Helterman, Jeffrey. *Symbolic Action in the Plays of the Wakefield Master*. Athens: University of Georgia Press, 1981. In this full-length study of the playwright, Helterman states his belief that the Wakefield Master rewrote existing plays in the final third (the "passion group") of the cycle and that the success led to the composition of six new plays (including *Mactacio Abel*), each of which is discussed in a substantial chapter. Bibliography.

Robinson, J. W. *Studies in Fifteenth Century Stagecraft*. Early Art, Drama, and Music Monograph series. Kalamazoo: Western Michigan University, 1991. Among the topics covered in this volume are the Wakefield Master, the Towneley plays, the York plays, and the Wakefield pageants. Bibliography and index.

Stevens, Martin. *Four Middle English Mystery Cycles*. Princeton, N.J.: Princeton University Press, 1987. Stevens considers the Wakefield Cycle to have been constructed as a unit and asserts that the Wakefield Master was the guiding mind in the creation of this unit. Evidence for this interpretation is found in the "Wakefield Stanza." Illustrations.

Kirk H. Beetz,
updated by Howard L. Ford

DEREK WALCOTT

Born: Castries, St. Lucia, West Indies; January 23, 1930

PRINCIPAL DRAMA

Henri Christophe: A Chronicle, pr., pb. 1950
The Sea at Dauphin, pr., pb. 1954
The Wine of the Country, pr. 1956
Ione, pr., pb. 1957
Ti-Jean and His Brothers, pr. 1957, revised pr. 1958, pb. 1970 (music by Andre Tanker)
Drums and Colours, pr. 1958, pb. 1961
Malcochon: Or, Six in the Rain, pr. 1959, pb. 1970
Dream on Monkey Mountain, pr. 1967, pb. 1970
Dream on Monkey Mountain and Other Plays, pb. 1970
In a Fine Castle, pr. 1970
The Charlatan, pr. 1974
The Joker of Seville, pr. 1974, pb. 1978 (adaptation of Tirso de Molina's *El burlador de Sevilla*; music by Galt MacDermot)
O Babylon!, pr. 1976, pb. 1978
Remembrance, pr. 1977, pb. 1980
The Joker of Seville and O Babylon!: Two Plays, pb. 1978
Pantomime, pr. 1978, pb. 1980
Marie LaVeau, pr. 1979
"Remembrance" and "Pantomime," pb. 1980
Beef, No Chicken, pr. 1981, pb. 1986
The Isle Is Full of Noises, pr. 1982
The Last Carnival, pr. 1982, pb. 1986
A Branch of the Blue Nile, pr. 1983, pb. 1986
The Haitian Earth, pr. 1984, pb. 2001
Three Plays, pb. 1986
To Die for Grenada, pr. 1986
Ghost Dance, pr. 1989, pb. 2002
Viva Detroit, pr. 1990
Steel, pr. 1991 (music by MacDermot)
The Odyssey: A Stage Version, pr. 1992, pb. 1993
Walker, pr. 1992, revised pb. 2002
The Capeman: A Musical, pr. 1997, pb. 1998 (music by Paul Simon)
The Haitian Trilogy, pb. 2001

OTHER LITERARY FORMS

Derek A. Walcott began writing poetry and poetic drama as a teenager. First on street corners in Castries, then in regional journals, and ultimately through major publishing houses in England and the United States, his poetry gathered a following, eventually earning him international recognition. His early affinity for the Metaphysical poets is abundantly clear in his collection, *In a Green Night: Poems, 1948-1960* (1962). Since then, his travels and his interest in a variety of cultures have added considerable variety and depth to successive volumes: *The Castaway and Other Poems* (1965), *The Gulf and Other Poems*

(1969), the semi-autobiographical *Another Life* (1973), *Sea Grapes* (1976), *The Star-Apple Kingdom* (1979), *The Fortunate Traveller* (1981), and *Midsummer* (1984). In addition to his duties as founding director of and chief writer for the Trinidad Theatre Workshop from 1959 to 1977, Walcott contributed steadily as a columnist on the arts to the *Trinidad Guardian*. Selections of his journalistic prose are collected in his *What the Twilight Says: Essays* (1998). A recording of Walcott reading selections from his own work may be found on Caedmon's *Derek Wolcott Reads* (1994); Semp Studios Ltd. (Port of Spain) has recorded the sound track for Walcott's play *The Joker of Seville* (score by Galt MacDermot in 1975). The poetry selected for *Collected Poems, 1948-84* (1986) and his verse narrative *Omeros* (1990), based on canonical Western epics from Homer to James Joyce, were instrumental in his winning the Nobel Prize in Literature in 1992. His narrative poem *Tiepolo's Hound* (2000), loosely drawn from the life of Camille Pissaro, is illustrated with twenty-six of Walcott's own watercolor and oil paintings.

ACHIEVEMENTS

Recognition of Derek Walcott's promise as a playwright came early, in 1958, when he received a Rockefeller Foundation grant to work with theater in New York. What was to have been an extended period of study was cut short, however, when the scarcity of serious plays with major parts for black actors drove him to return to the West Indies, where he established the Trinidad Theatre Workshop in 1959. In the short time that he had been away, he had been selected to write a play (*Drums and Colours*) to commemorate the opening of the first Federal Parliament of the West Indies on April 23, 1958. The Negro Ensemble Company performance of his *Dream on Monkey Mountain* garnered an Obie Award in 1971. The Royal Shakespeare Company commissioned Walcott to write two adaptations: first, of Tirso de Molina's *El burlador de Sevilla* (wr. 1625?, pb. 1630; *The Trickster of Seville*, 1923), which became *The Joker of Seville*; then of Homer's *Odyssey* (c. 725 B.C.E.; English translation, 1614), which became *The Odyssey*.

Walcott's poetry has also been well received, winning a number of awards: the Guinness Award for Poetry in 1961, the Royal Society of Literature Award for *The Castaway and Other Poems* in 1965, the Cholmondeley Award for *The Gulf and Other Poems* in 1969, the Jock Campbell New Statesman Award for his autobiographical *Another Life* in 1973, the Welsh Arts Council's International Writer's Prize in 1980, and a John D. and Catherine MacArthur Award in 1981. He won the Queen Elizabeth II Gold Medal for Poetry in 1988 and the Nobel Prize in 1992.

BIOGRAPHY

In Castries, capital of the small Caribbean island of St. Lucia, Derek Alton Walcott and his twin brother, Roderick, were born January 23, 1930. Their mother, Alix, was a teacher in a Methodist primary school, while their father, Warwick, was a civil official and a gifted artist. Although Walcott lost his father when he was hardly a year old, fatherly guidance was provided by the St. Lucian painter Harold Simmons, the

Derek Walcott (Virginia Shendler)

mentor commemorated in Walcott's autobiographical poem *Another Life*.

Being of mixed blood—his grandfathers were white Dutch and English, his grandmothers black—and the son of Protestants in a predominantly Catholic island, Walcott experienced from an early age the schizophrenia of New World blacks and mulattoes in an alien environment. While childhood in a colonial backwater island might seem disadvantageous, Walcott believes that his classroom exposure to traditional Western culture—Greek, Roman, and British—was vitally enriching. Combining this with his informal contact with African slave tales and life in the streets, he learned to admire both currents of his dual heritage. Early evidence of his gift for cultural synthesis appears in one of Walcott's first plays, *Henri Christophe*. This dramatization of the famous black rebel general is couched in the poetic images and the elaborate language of Elizabethan England.

In order to provide an outlet for his drama, Walcott and his brother founded the St. Lucia Arts Guild in 1950, the same year in which Walcott was awarded a scholarship to pursue advanced education at the University of the West Indies in Mona, Jamaica. His graduation in 1953 was followed in 1954 by his marriage to Faye Moyston. Four years later, as a result of a Rockefeller Foundation grant to study theater in New York, Walcott reached a major turning point in his career.

Two specific influences in New York seem to have given Walcott the impetus to launch his professional career. First was his discovery, through Bertolt Brecht, of Asian theater. In Brecht there were precedents for using the ritual, mime, symbolic gestures, rhythmic movement, and music of Walcott's native background. Second was Walcott's realization that there were precious few major roles for black actors in the standard repertoire. Thus, he resolved to return to the islands and create a style of drama that would be suited to the multifarious elements of the West Indian character: an indigenous drama.

Walcott's creation of the Trinidad Theatre Workshop came in 1959, the same year as his divorce from his first wife, after which he remarried, went through a second divorce, and married again. From the first two marriages there are three children, two daughters and a son. Indications of his struggle to maintain himself as a creative writer and continue living in the Caribbean may be seen in many of the articles he wrote for the *Trinidad Guardian* in the 1960's and early 1970's. His column often served as a forum for arguing the cause of a national theater. After resigning from the Trinidad Theatre Workshop in 1976, a second divorce, and marriage to his third wife, Walcott began dividing his time between the United States and the Caribbean. While he taught during semesters at Yale, Columbia and Harvard, he devoted vacations to engagements with his newly created theatrical company, Warwick Productions, in various Caribbean islands. Following his decision to teach at Boston University, a third divorce in 1982, and the Nobel Prize in 1992, Walcott began to spend as much time as he could in St. Lucia, where he owned a seaside estate. Aside from occasional academic appointments, he continued to lecture internationally, write, direct plays, and devote time to painting.

In 1992, for his lifelong achievements in the drama from *Henri Christophe* and the breakthrough poetry of *In a Green Night* to his monumental Caribbean epic *Omeros*, Walcott was honored with the Nobel Prize in Literature. The Swedish Academy said of Walcott: "In him West Indian culture has found its great poet."

ANALYSIS

Because drama is performed live before an audience, its impact is more immediate and of a more communal nature than that of fiction and poetry. Derek A. Walcott's major contribution to West Indian literature may be his dramatic re-creation of the scenes, the people, and the language of his native region. On a larger scale, his Trinidad Theatre Workshop tours, as well as performances of his plays by foreign companies, have brought West Indian life to the attention of audiences on virtually every continent.

Drawing from St. Lucia, Trinidad, Jamaica, and other islands, Walcott uses the patchwork history of his Caribbean people to focus on problems that relate to all humankind. The child of mixed blood, he embodies the cultural heritage of Europe and the New World. Translating this legacy to the stage, he re-creates conquistadors, slaves, indentured servants, colonialists, and the unheralded common men and women who may be the most interesting figures of all—for their ingenuity in simply surviving.

The culture of Western Europe lends a shaping hand to Walcott's polyglot material. Over the years, he has been indebted to sources as diverse as the Jacobean dramatists, the Spanish Golden Age, John Millington Synge, T. S. Eliot, Bertolt Brecht, the Japanese Nō theater, and the Greek classics. Conveniently for Walcott, Trinidad's fabulous carnival provides the raw material and inspiration he needs— masquerades, pantomime, satiric calypso, massive choreography, the meeting of disparate cultures in one gigantic bacchanal—for blending all the disparate ingredients of his New World background.

Prior to his formative experience in New York in 1958, Walcott's playwriting suffered from his failure to integrate his folk subjects with borrowed European forms. Alongside *Henri Christophe*'s Elizabethan verse is *The Sea at Dauphin*, with deliberate echoes of John Millington Synge's *Riders to the Sea* (pb. 1903): peasant fishermen enduring their fate with unassuming nobility. *Drums and Colours*, with its extensive pageantry and broad range of characters (from the days of discovery up to the 1958 West Indian Federation) may be said to have settled any debt Walcott owed to West Indian history. In the year of the initial performance of *Drums and Colours*, he also put into production *Ti-Jean and His Brothers*, his first stylized West Indian play.

In a 1970 article titled "Meanings," Walcott explained the type of dynamic fusion that West Indian drama requires. Studying Brecht in New York, he came to the conclusion that the besetting sin of most Caribbean theater was its self-indulgent exuberance. Brecht's adaptation of highly ritualized Oriental techniques offered the model Walcott needed. Without stifling the vitality of West Indian folk spirit, he sought to instill discipline. Because his culture is an amalgam of the African, the Oriental, and the Occidental, Walcott draws from them all. From Europe, he takes classical conventions of language and structure; from Africa and parts of the East, he adopts ritual ceremonies involving dance, mime, and narrative traditions; from the Kabuki and Nō plays, he takes expressive power and beauty in restrained gesture and formalized rhythm.

TI-JEAN AND HIS BROTHERS

In *Ti-Jean and His Brothers*, a St. Lucian folktale with vestiges of African animal fable provides the story of Ti-Jean, a young black man who outsmarts the plantation-master devil. Dialogue is spiced with fast-paced puns, metaphors, and verbal play. Movement is carried by music, dance, mime, abrupt pauses, asides to the audience, and intervals of conversation among the animal chorus about human affairs. Pleased as Walcott was with the blend of discipline and folk life in *Ti-Jean and His Brothers*, this work was but a prelude to the more profound and highly imaginative *Dream on Monkey Mountain*.

DREAM ON MONKEY MOUNTAIN

Completed especially for the Trinidad Theatre Workshop's first tour outside the Caribbean, *Dream on Monkey Mountain* appeared in Toronto in 1967. Subsequent productions in the United States and on NBC television in 1970 garnered the prestigious Obie Award for the best foreign play of 1970-1971. Multiple themes and the dream framework account for only a fraction of the play's complexity. Characters exchange parts, glide into symbols, and are revived from death; the plot develops in fragments as the hero, Makak, tries to explain his vision of a white goddess. The very names of characters imply allegory: Makak, the monkey, is an ugly charcoal burner who must come to grips with his awareness of being black; the mulatto Lestrade, neither black nor white, is an ambivalent straddler.

Lestrade's stereotypical house-Negro prejudices surface in the prologue, when he ridicules Makak's apelike appearance and his obsessive dream of a white woman. The first scene is a flashback to Makak's first vision, where he reveals that he has been called back to Africa, to his true place as a lion-king. Armed with his new racial identity, Makak is able to heal the sick while crowds pour in to hear his words. Unfortunately, Moustique, his traveling companion, is quick to exploit opportunity; like many a trickster character of West Indian folklore, he turns faith and trust into profitable enterprise. When his tricks are discovered, he is killed by a mob, only to return to life again in later scenes.

Although the play is cast in terms of black consciousness, the action continually pushes the meaning of the narrative to a broader plane. In his dream, Makak escapes and establishes his African throne. Corporal Lestrade, in pursuing the rebels, goes native and ultimately becomes Makak's most fanatic convert, a blind advocate of black supremacy. Caught up in the frenzy for power and revenge, Makak is helpless to avert the internecine bloodletting and the execution of all symbols of whiteness that follow.

Paradoxically, Makak's beheading of the white goddess finally frees him from his obsession with blackness. By doing away with his illusion, Makak is free to become himself; he completes the journey by recognizing the possibility of beauty in his own black body. In his introduction to *Dream on Monkey Mountain and Other Plays*, Walcott argues that once blacks have given up the wish to be white, they assume the longing to be black; the difference is clear, but both pursuits are careers.

In the epilogue, then, Walcott leads his protagonist to his essential being through the act of understanding. On his release after the night that he has spent in jail, Makak determines to establish himself on his mountain and fulfill his chosen destiny—neither white nor black, but a West Indian. Thus, the final image of *Dream on Monkey Mountain* is not the beheading of a white goddess but rather a hopeful vision of a man's accommodation to his environment, a fact easily overlooked by critics seeking racial conflict.

THE JOKER OF SEVILLE

Because of the vital Spanish background of Trinidad's culture and because of the society's predilection for the flamboyant male, Walcott may seem well-suited to revive the ancient legend of Don Juan. This, at any rate, was the decision of the Royal Shakespeare Company when it commissioned him in 1974 to write a modern version of Tirso de Molina's *El burlador de Sevilla*. Don Juan the aristocratic violator of maidenhood is a departure from Walcott's peasant

heroes, yet he is a rich vehicle for some of Walcott's primary themes. Juan is the archetypal lover, the arch-rebel, the trickster, the Dionysian liberator, and, in Walcott's version, the sacrificial god. Rather than alter these dimensions, Walcott preferred to amplify certain characteristics and expand the field of action to include the New World.

While Tirso places Juan's second scene of seduction (of Tisbea) in a Spanish coastal village, Walcott's *The Joker of Seville* sends him across the Atlantic to a Caribbean island. Whether in the Old or New World, however, Juan's adventures lead to death and immortal legend. He embodies an irrational force— the subconscious impulse to defy the prohibitions that were first imposed in Eden and then in society. As it turns out, the men he outwits learn to see vicarious fulfillment, through him, of their own suppressed drives. While they despise him and the dark elements their consciences attempt to keep under control, they secretly relish his freedom. Ironically, having selected his inhuman role, Juan denies himself all the pleasures of ordinary life. He admits that he cannot feel love. Instead, like Dionysus, he presents to humankind the possibility of uninhibited pleasure and pain, but he ultimately suffers and returns to the cold earth.

Death, nevertheless, does not have the final word. Juan's corpse is carried off to the insistent calypso beat of a song of resurrection. Juan's compensation, like Makak's in *Dream on Monkey Mountain*, is to attain the status of a dream image. Unlike Makak, however, Juan does not have the privilege of descending from the realm of legend to the earthly plane of day-to-day living.

O BABYLON!

The lively music and expressive dance that animate *The Joker of Seville* again attest Walcott's inventive use of West Indian culture. The same may be said of his next major play, *O Babylon!*—the music in the play is based on the reggae of Jamaica's Rastafarian cult. This cult also is the logical source of the play's ritualistic elements: the "four horsemen of the apocalypse" and the visions. At the center of the plot is a conflict between the temptations of material gain and human beings' yearning for spiritual fulfillment.

Land developers with Mafia ties plan to acquire an area settled by a Rastafarian community. The corporation buys the support of politicians, social workers, and weaker members of the settlement. Aaron, the protagonist, and Sufferer, one of the older brethren, hold out against official harassment, physical abuse, and bribery. Matters are forced to a climax by the news that the Rastafarians' god in the flesh, Haile Selassie, is arriving. (The play is set in 1966 to coincide with Selassie's actual visit to Jamaica.)

Ultimately, when a few are chosen to return with Selassie to Ethiopia, Aaron and the brethren left behind must choose between misery in the Babylon of Kingston and beginning anew in the mountains. Despite the losses, Walcott concludes with a triumphant vision of a heavenly Zion. The final scene is rescued from escapism by explicit passages that show Aaron gaining a sense of his own belonging. In two days of meditation in the quiet mountains, Aaron finds peace with his homeland and within himself—the place, Walcott implies, where one must seek one's authentic identity.

REMEMBRANCE

Remembrance and *Pantomime* seem subdued in comparison with the exuberant music and action of their immediate predecessors. *Remembrance* was first performed in St. Croix in April, 1977. Albert Jordan, a retired schoolteacher, reminisces for a local newspaper reporter about the independence and Black Power movements that swept through Trinidad and interfered with the life he would have preferred to live peacefully.

At first recalling only mistakes, Jordan contends that his efforts as teacher, husband, father, and amateur writer have been futile. Students called him "Uncle Tom" because of the standards he asserted in the classroom. His wife constantly chided him about his get-rich-quick lottery tickets. The police killed one son during a Black Power confrontation. His younger son is risking a slower death by undertaking the life of an artist in the lost and forgotten colony of Trinidad.

Contrary to his own assessment, Jordan is worthy of the credit he only grudgingly allows himself for having raised his students' consciousness to the point

where Black Power found receptive imaginations. Both sons' independent choices might seem futile to him, yet they reveal the strength of character to undertake ambitious destinies. Others who know Jordan—his wife and son, the editor of the *Belmont Bugle*—respect what he stands for in spite of his own self-criticism. Had he really been a weakling, he would not have called for reason against the furious rhetoric and blind revolutionary action that surrounded him. Jordan's life is the stable factor blending the episodes reenacted on the stage. At the close of the final curtain, he has come to terms with himself and he is ready to begin the review of his eventful career.

PANTOMIME

Pantomime involves no reverie, but it draws on history to accomplish an enlightening as well as entertaining tour de force. The action involves an agreement—between Harry, an Englishman managing a second-rate tourist hotel, and Jackson, a struggling calypsonian—concerning a skit to be performed before the hotel's patrons. After much argument about the propriety of the skit, the two undertake a reversal of the Robinson Crusoe and Friday roles.

Harry tries to play his part at first but balks at the extreme idea of having African culture and gods imposed on a civilized Christian. Jackson, who is quick to convert to the inversion, seizes the opportunity to note that Harry's refusal is precisely the history of colonialism. At the point when a native asserts equality with his master, the dominant power wants to revert to the old order.

In act 2, Harry is more willing to pursue the implications of racial and cultural equality, and Jackson instructs him in the characteristics of a more mature version of Robinson Crusoe. His West Indian Crusoe would be a practical man, not Harry's lonely romanticist yearning for his distant wife and son. The New World Crusoe would come to grips with the raw material of his environment. Jackson sees him as the original Creole because of his faith and effective action. The immediate application of this new version is to Harry's personal situation. With Jackson's encouragement, he acts out some of his frustrations over his failures as an actor and as a husband. Living through the experience, Harry gains deeper understanding, and both men achieve a more equitable relationship.

THREE PLAYS

Between publication of *"Remembrance"* and *"Pantomime"* in 1980 and *Three Plays* in 1986, Walcott wrote five plays: *Beef, No Chicken*; *The Last Carnival*; *The Isle Is Full of Noises*; *A Branch of the Blue Nile*; and *The Haitian Earth*. Of these, *Three Plays* brings together *The Last Carnival*; *Beef, No Chicken*; and *A Branch of the Blue Nile*. *The Last Carnival* is placed first in the collection because it is a significantly revised version of *In a Fine Castle* from 1970. The earlier *In a Fine Castle*, influenced by the 1970 Black Power disturbances in Trinidad, balances emphases between a radical minority of activists and descendants of an aristocratic French family who are losing influence in this newly independent island.

By 1982, when *The Last Carnival* was first performed, Walcott had become more interested in the declining fortunes of the De La Fontaine family. Employing Jean Antoine Watteau's Rococo masterpiece *Embarkation for Cythera* for atmospheric reference, Walcott risks nostalgic dramatization of a passing era. Despite the indisputable inequities of the old order, Europeans who have settled in the colony for generations must adapt or abandon the only home they have ever known. Next in order of printing, *Beef, No Chicken* is no less serious in intent but takes the form of a lively farce concerning one man's unsuccessful attempts to prevent the Kentucky Fried, McDonald's-ized modernization of the little village of Couva in Trinidad.

In aesthetic scope, the most ambitious of the three plays, *A Branch of the Blue Nile*, draws on William Shakespeare's *Antony and Cleopatra* as a play-within-a-play to reflect on the trials suffered by a colonial theater troupe. Much as the storied love between Roman Antony and Egyptian Cleopatra entails a cultural divide, whereby provincial actors contend over the efficacy of repeating canonical classics as opposed to performing locally generated scripts in their own dialect. Chris, the male lead, eventually writes a hybridized manuscript based on the personal and professional story of their lives that turns out to be "A

Branch of the Blue Nile" itself. The intertextuality of the multiple plots and palimpsests of meaning is compounded for anyone recognizing the semi-autobiographical traces of Walcott's estrangement from the Trinidad Theatre Workshop since his resignation from the company in 1976.

THE ODYSSEY

In the 1990's Walcott saw through production *To Die for Grenada*, *The Haitian Earth*, *Viva Detroit*, and *Steel*, and published *The Odyssey: A Stage Version* and *The Capeman: A Musical*. In his dramatization of *The Odyssey*, Walcott modernizes Homer's epic. His Polyphemus suggests both linguistic parallels with Jamaica's Rastafarian culture and political repression in modern Greece under the "grey colonels" (1967-1974). Odysseus's Hades is reconfigured for London's underground system. Inclusion of Caribbean rhythms, patois, and a more assertive Penelope simultaneously reinforces the international dimensions of the original and asserts its continued timeliness in the light of postmodern views on intercultural fermentation and the emergence of feminist awareness.

THE HAITIAN TRILOGY

Prominent as European classics have been in Walcott's recent work, in 2001 he resurrected his life-long fascination with Haiti and Caribbean history with publication of two of his earliest plays, *Henri Christophe* and *Drums and Colours*, together with the more recent *The Haitian Earth* in a collection titled *The Haitian Trilogy*. *Drums and Colours* is a historical pageant with many Brechtian affinities. Carnival revelers representing the racial gamut of Caribbean society provide a chorus to link major plot segments centered on four periods: discovery, conquest, rebellion, and constitutional independence. While historically significant figures such as Christopher Columbus, Sir Walter Ralegh, Toussaint L'Ouverture, and George William Gordon occupy center stage, characters from the peasant chorus participate in the action, create comic relief, and ensure the folk dimension of the play.

Whereas *Henri Christophe* depicts the sordid bloodletting among racial factions following Haiti's successful slave rebellion against Napoleonic France in 1803, *The Haitian Earth* goes back to the insurrection itself, starting in 1791. In both plays, blacks (slave and free) are pitted against their white oppressors; but a third group, the mulatto segment of the population, has its own interests to protect. Walcott brings to life remarkable natural leaders such as Toussaint L'Ouverture, Jean Jacques Dessalines, Henri Christophe, and Alexander Pétion who could withstand European armies but were unable to reach accommodation among themselves. As Walcott makes clear in both plays, no race may claim a monopoly on noble causes nor the basest inhumanity to humankind.

OTHER MAJOR WORKS

POETRY: *Twenty-five Poems*, 1948; *Poems*, 1951; *In a Green Night: Poems, 1948-1960*, 1962; *Selected Poems*, 1964; *The Castaway and Other Poems*, 1965; *The Gulf and Other Poems*, 1969; *Another Life*, 1973; *Sea Grapes*, 1976; *The Star-Apple Kingdom*, 1979; *The Fortunate Traveller*, 1981; *Midsummer*, 1984; *Collected Poems, 1948-1984*, 1986; *The Arkansas Testament*, 1987; *Omeros*, 1990; *Poems, 1965-1980*, 1992; *The Bounty*, 1997; *Tiepolo's Hound*, 2000.

NONFICTION: "Meanings: From a Conversation with Derek Walcott," 1970 (in *Performing Arts*); *The Antilles: Fragments of Epic Memory*, 1993 (Walcott's Nobel lecture); *Homage to Robert Frost*, 1996 (with Joseph Brodsky and Seamus Heaney); *What the Twilight Says: Essays*, 1998.

BIBLIOGRAPHY

Baer, William. *Conversations with Derek Walcott.* Jackson: University Press of Mississippi, 1996. Collection of previously published interviews, spanning 1966-1993.

Burnett, Paula. *Derek Walcott: Politics and Poetics.* Gainesville: University of Florida Press, 2000. A valuable survey of the author's work. Includes extensive coverage of Walcott's unpublished plays.

Hamner, Robert D., ed. *Critical Perspectives on Derek Walcott.* Boulder, Colo.: Lynne Rienner, 1993. This frequently cited collection offers eight essays by Walcott along with forty-four interviews, reviews, and critical articles spanning Walcott's career through early responses to *Omeros*.

_____. *Derek Walcott: Updated Edition.* Boston: Twayne, 1993. An analytical appreciation of the poet and dramatist in mid-career. This revision of a 1981 text remains valuable for the balance of poetic discussion and dramatic analysis, and for the placement of Walcott in Caribbean literature as well as Third World literature in general. Includes a strong discussion of *Dream on Monkey Mountain*, a chronology, a good bibliography, and an index.

King, Bruce. *Derek Walcott: A Caribbean Life.* Oxford, England: Oxford University Press, 2000. This meticulously documented biography provides information on the background of a poet and dramatist whose work is often based on personal experience. Also provides images of Walcott's paintings and drawings.

_____. *Derek Walcott and West Indian Drama.* Oxford, England: Clarendon, 1995. This thoroughly researched study of the development of Walcott's Trinidad Theatre Workshop is valuable for its historical data, illustrations, and calendar of performances from the 1950's through 1993.

Ross, Robert L., ed. *International Literature in English: Essays on the Major Writers.* New York: Garland, 1991. Robert D. Hamner contributes an essay on Walcott, taking his biography up to the Catherine MacArthur Award in 1981. Counts fourteen books of poetry (to *The Arkansas Testament*) and four volumes of plays, and discusses the "chiaroscuro" of Walcott's aesthetic choices, which "creates the illusion of bulk and depth for three-dimensional objects in a two-dimensional plane."

Terada, Rei. *Derek Walcott's Poetry: American Mimicry.* Boston: Northeastern University Press, 1992. Although this book primarily concentrates on the poetry, Terada touches on several plays in discussing Walcott's creative use of ideas and elements assimilated from the many cultural strands running through the New World.

Thieme, John. *Derek Walcott.* Manchester, England: Manchester University Press, 1999. Thieme's is a twofold undertaking: first, examination of Walcott's evasion of polarities in favor of a cohesive cultural vision on both his poetry and drama; and second, the contention that Walcott's multinational fusions provide a model appropriate for a Caribbean aesthetic.

Walcott, Derek. "Meanings." *Savacou* 2 (1970): 45-51. Walcott discusses his plays through *Dream on Monkey Mountain* and his vision of an authentic Caribbean dramatic form.

Robert D. Hamner,
updated Thomas J. Taylor

JOSEPH A. WALKER

Born: Washington, D.C.; February 23, 1935

PRINCIPAL DRAMA
  The Believers, pr., pb. 1968 (with Josephine Jackson)
  The Harangues, pr. 1969, revised pb. 1971 (as *Tribal Harangue Two*)
  Ododo, pr. 1970, pb. 1972
  Yin Yang, pr. 1972
  The River Niger, pr. 1972, pb. 1973
  Antigone Africanus, pr. 1975
  The Lion Is a Soul Brother, pr. 1976
  District Line, pr. 1984

OTHER LITERARY FORMS

Joseph A. Walker's reputation rests almost exclusively on his dramatic works, but he has made numerous successful forays into the television and film industries. Primarily a stage dramatist, he expanded his literary horizons during the 1970's and the 1980's by regularly contributing essays to *The New York Times*, including "Broadway's Vitality" (1973), "The Hiss" (1978), "Black Magnificence" (1980), and "Themes of the Black Struggle" (1982). In 1976, he rewrote his three-act play *The River Niger* into a screenplay for New Line Cinema. The resulting film, starring Cicely Tyson and James Earl Jones, received considerable critical acclaim both at the time and in subsequent years.

ACHIEVEMENTS

Joseph A. Walker began his association with the stage as an actor in theater productions of *The Be-* *lievers*, *Cities of Beziques*, *Once in a Lifetime*, *A Raisin in the Sun*, and *Purlie Victorious*; then appeared on the screen in *April Fools* (1969) and Woody Allen's *Bananas* (1971); and acted in the television series *N.Y.P.D.* The lessons he learned as an actor helped him understand the fundamentals of dramatic production. In 1969, Walker became playwright, director, and choreographer for the Negro Ensemble Company in New York City. He served as playwright-in-residence for Yale University for 1970-1971 and as an instructor of advanced acting and playwriting for Howard University.

Walker has won a number of prestigious awards, many of them for his *The River Niger*, which was recognized with an Obie Award (1973), an Antoinette Perry (Tony) Award (1973), the Dramatist Guild's Elizabeth Hull-Kate Award (1973), the first Annual Audelco Award (1973), a John Gassner Award from Outer Circle (1973), a Drama Desk Award (1973), and the Black Rose Award (1973). This remarkable outpouring of critical approval culminated, also in 1973, with Walker being awarded a Guggenheim Fellowship. Also, in recognition for his years of work in drama, Walker was granted a Rockefeller Foundation grant (1979).

BIOGRAPHY

Joseph A. Walker was born in Washington, D.C., in 1935. Although his father, Joseph Walker, was a house painter and his mother, Florine Walker, a housewife, Walker had higher aspirations. He graduated from Howard University in 1956 with a B.A. in philosophy and a minor in drama, having acted in several student productions (he portrayed Luke in James Baldwin's *Amen Corner* in May of 1955). Although he had realized that his real love was the theater, his fear of poverty drew him, after graduation, to the United States Air Force, where he enlisted as a second lieutenant and reached the rank of first lieutenant by the time of his discharge in 1960. His desire to become a high-ranking officer caused Walker to initially pursue navigators' training, but he later quit when he found himself spending more time writing poetry than studying for his navigator's exams. This dramatic shift of career was the source for a famous scene in *The River Niger* when navigator school student Jeff Williams is belittled by a white airman for his poetry writing in exactly the same way as Walker himself has described being insulted during his military career. Trying to establish a balance between his fear of financial dependence and his inner desire to compose poetry, Walker decided to devote his full attention to the study of drama and poetry rather than to achieving high rank in the military. Further education gave him time to clarify his goals. Walker received an M.F.A. from Catholic University in 1963 and began teaching in a Washington, D.C., high school.

Walker followed this teaching position with one at City College of New York. He combined the role of instructor and playwright during his year as a playwright-in-residence at Yale University and then returned to Howard University, where he became a full professor of drama. While teaching, Walker continued his study of the stage and film by continuing to act. This personal line of study had a profound effect on the young actor-playwright. In 1969, the Negro Ensemble Company produced *The Harangues*. This was a personal milestone for the young Walker, who had, at this point, been studying other people's dramatic work for more than a decade. In 1970, Walker and his second wife, Dorothy Dinroe, started the acting troupe The Demi-Gods, a professional music-dance repertory company with Walker serving as artistic director. Walker's play *Ododo*, which The Demi-Gods later presented at Howard University in 1973, opened the Negro Ensemble Company's 1970 season. This work further examined racial strife and prepared audiences for the African American history

that would be so vehemently elucidated in *The River Niger* and his later writings.

After the 1970's, Walker continued to write, albeit infrequently, about minority issues derived from his own, personal experiences. One play, *District Line*, used his personal experience as a cab driver to demonstrate universal themes of racial strife and harmony. Essays submitted to *The New York Times* ("Themes of the Black Struggle," and "Black Magnificence," for example) and interviews conducted during the 1980's have documented more recent difficulties that minorities have faced in the mainstream world of the theater. Walker has said that mainstream theaters are not willing to produce works from minority authors and there has not been adequate funding of minority-interest theater companies to make up for the lack of mainstream interest. According to Michele DiGirolamo in *Afro-American*, Walker stated that he had little success in getting his plays produced in the 1980's and 1990's because of shrinking budgets and an apathetic public. In 1995, he made an appearance at the National Black Theatre Festival in Winston-Salem, North Carolina, to encourage more young African American authors to write for the stage in the hope that the number of minority-run theater groups would continue to grow and present greater numbers of minority-interest plays.

ANALYSIS

Like many other African American authors, Joseph A. Walker examines issues close to the black community and, in particular, those dealing with black American men. Issues of personal identity, relationship strife, and racism play dominant roles in influencing both the thinking and the actions of the black male characters portrayed in his dramas. Lacking a homeland and history, repressed by both whites and assimilationist blacks, and dissociated from the comforts of stable male-female relationships, Walker's black protagonists lead desperate and often destructive lives.

Walker's critical success has derived from his realistic portrayals of African American men. Working from his own, personal experiences as a black man in the United States, Walker examines interracial relationships, conflicts between people and society, and the struggle that many blacks have in achieving inner peace and acceptance.

THE HARANGUES

The Harangues is made up of two closely paired one-act plays, each introduced by an episode designed purely to serve as the media for the author's invective. In the first episode, a fifteenth century West African man observes the presence of slave traders' ships sitting in the nearby harbor and, foreseeing a life of slavery for his newborn son, chooses to drown him rather than have him captured by the traders.

The one-act that follows this violent episode presents the story of a young interracial couple. A young black man wishes to marry a young white woman who has fallen deeply in love with him and become pregnant with his child. Because the woman's wealthy father opposes the match and threatens to disinherit his daughter, the young man decides that he and his fiancée must kill her father. Seemingly lacking any familial feeling, the white woman agrees to assist her lover in the murder of her father. However, the plan backfires while still in the planning stages. A traitorous black "friend" reveals the couples' intentions to the girlfriend's father and causes the death of the young black man, bringing an end to his plan to marry his white girlfriend and, with her, inherit her father's estate.

The second episode, echoing in theme and purpose the first, presents a contemporary black American revolutionary who, depressed by his vision of the repression inherent in modern society, decides that he has no future. Knowing that he himself will die, he nevertheless convinces his wife not to die with him but to live on to raise their son as a freedom fighter.

The one-act play that follows centers on a deranged, black man in a bar who has taken captive three people—a white liberal man, a black conservative man sympathetic to white society, and the black man's white girlfriend—and has threatened to kill them unless they can justify their existence. After the captives are subjected to numerous humiliations, it becomes apparent that, according to the protagonist's ideas of "worthiness," only the white woman may be

allowed to live. When the "executions" take place, however, the woman takes a bullet meant for her black lover. In the ensuing struggle, the black conservative gains control of his captor's gun and kills him. Once again, Walker demonstrates that the black man who resorts to violence to achieve his goals is destroyed by his own violence.

YIN YANG

Walker's next play, *Yin Yang*, is his least traditional. First produced in 1972, Walker designed the play to represent the age-old struggle between good and evil. In an article published in *The New York Times*, Walker says that "Good is represented by God, a hip swinging, fast-talking black mama . . . in conflict with Miss Satan, who is also a black female swinger." Although the play may seem to have been directed for a children's audience, with its reliance on archetypical figures and simple language, Walker claims that the play draws on the biblical books of Job and Revelation. Walker has long seen a symbolic parallel between Job and blacks because, he says, both believe in their society and their religion even when such institutions seemingly cause them to suffer.

Yin Yang operates on the Chinese philosophy that everything in existence is the result of the combination of two opposing principles: the yin, the feminine, "evil," passive principle; and the yang, the masculine, "good," active principle. Thus, the characters of *Yin Yang* themselves represent the balance of good and evil, masculine and feminine.

THE RIVER NIGER

Walker wrote four major plays before writing *The River Niger*, but it is this work that brought Walker nationwide recognition and revealed both his strengths and weaknesses as a playwright. *The River Niger*, rather than being an entirely original work, is more a reworking and refinement of the ideas and issues developed in his earlier plays for a broader audience.

Although the plot and themes of *The River Niger* deal with African American life and issues, the play has been seen as having a far more universal relevance. Mel Gussow, in *Time* magazine, said that the play was powerful and compassionate and has an appeal beyond the borders of black experience. Both the play's realism and this global appeal arise from the fact that it is derived in part from Walker's own experiences and family—experiences that many outside the black community can also appreciate. As Gussow noted, "The playwright knows his people and we grow to know them, too, to understand their fears, appetites, frustrations, and vulnerabilities."

In *The River Niger*, Jeff Williams, who has dropped out of U.S. Air Force navigators' school because of the racist comments of a colleague, returns home to determine what to do with the rest of his life. Everyone has a different opinion on the direction he should take. His friends demand that he join them in defying the established order of white society and take part in the "revolution," while his family is disappointed that he ended his promising military career (his father's first question is "Where is your uniform?") and wants him to continue becoming an officer. Williams, however, is starting to recognize his own, inner desire to become a lawyer. Williams's hesitation and ambivalence can be readily understood by anyone who has had to make dramatic changes in his or her life.

DISTRICT LINE

District Line is an interesting discussion of how individuals of differing viewpoints and backgrounds can find common ground. A Washington, D.C., taxi stand serves as the setting for *District Line*, which depicts a day in the lives of six cab drivers: two white men, three black men, and one black woman. Each of the drivers comes from a different background, but each has similar hopes for the future and similar reactions to his or her past experiences. The issues and concerns of the black male characters, however, dominate this play, as they have most of Walker's earlier plays. The scenes concerning two of the black drivers (who are, by far, the most developed characters)—Doc, a moonlighting Howard University professor, another of Walker's alter egos, and Zilikazi, an exiled South African revolutionary—are the ones that receive the greatest amount of attention. Despite this focus on black men's issues, in *District Line*, Walker's presentation of the white characters—the two white drivers—seems more balanced. These white men, compared with white characters in Walker's earlier

plays, are complex individuals rather than stereotypical white liberals or oppressors.

OTHER MAJOR WORKS

SCREENPLAY: *The River Niger*, 1976 (adaptation of his play).

NONFICTION: "Broadway's Vitality," 1973; "The Hiss," 1980; "Themes of the Black Struggle," 1982.

BIBLIOGRAPHY

Barthelemy, Anthony. "Mother, Sister, Wife: A Dramatic Perspective." *Southern Review* 21, no. 3 (1985). Barthelemy compares and analyses the dysfunctions of male-female relationships in three of Walker's plays. He presents Walker's repetitive use of stereotypical female roles in defining the positions and roles forced on black women by both their families and society in general.

Clurman, Harold. "The River Niger." *The Nation* 215, no. 21 (1972): 668. Although Clurman praises Walker's technique in *The River Niger*, he finds fault with Walker's use of symbolism in *Ododo*. He suggests that Walker is not sure which historical truths about black-white relationships he wants to tell, so he tries to make the play tell them all. This lack of focus, Clurman states, distorts and creates internal contradiction within both plays.

Kauffmann, Stanley. "The River Niger." *The New Republic* 169, no. 12 (1973): 22. Kauffmann criticizes many of Walker's techniques in *The River Niger*, in particular his lack of subtlety with character motivations and dialogue, but appreciates both the real affection shown by his characters for one another and the recognition with which black audiences have responded to the play.

Lee, Dorothy. "Three Black Plays: Alienation and Paths to Recovery." *Modern Drama* 19, no. 4 (1975): 397-404. Lee argues that the alienation theme, when addressed in the context of African American concerns, is also a metaphor for the human condition. Lee describes Walker as seeking definitions of a sense of community or its telling absence both uniquely black and universally relevant.

Julia M. Meyers

MARTIN WALSER

Born: Wasserburg, Germany; March 24, 1927

PRINCIPAL DRAMA

Der Abstecher, pr., pb. 1961 (*The Detour*, 1963)

Eiche und Angora, pr., pb. 1962 (*The Rabbit Race*, 1963)

Überlebensgross Herr Krott: Requiem für einen Unsterblichen, pr. 1963, pb. 1964

Der schwarze Schwan, pr., pb. 1964

Die Zimmerschlacht, pr., pb. 1967 (*Home Front*, 1971)

Wir werden schon noch handeln, pr. 1968 as *Der schwarze Flügel*, pb. 1968

Ein Kinderspiel, pb. 1970, pr. 1972

Aus dem Wortschatz unserer Kämpfe, pb. 1971

Ein reizender Abend, pr. 1971

Das Sauspiel: Szenen aus dem 16. Jahrhundert, pr., pb. 1975

In Goethes Hand: Szenen aus dem 19. Jahrhundert, pr., pb. 1982

Die Ohrfeige, pr. 1984, pb. 1986

Ein fliehendes Pferd, pr., pb. 1985 (adaptation of his novel)

Das Sofa, pb. 1992, pr. 1994

Kaschmir in Parching, pb. 1995, pr. 1997

OTHER LITERARY FORMS

Martin Walser's earliest literary efforts resulted in several radio plays, written while he was employed by the South German Radio Network. His real breakthrough as a writer of serious fiction came with the publication of his first book of short stories, *Ein Flugzeug über dem Haus und andere Geschichten* (1955; an airplane over the house and other stories), and his first novel, *Ehen in Philippsburg* (1957; *The Gadarene Club*, 1960; also known as *Marriage in Philippsburg*). Walser's place as one of the most important, most controversial, and most talented West German prose writers was clearly established through his trilogy of novels, *Halbzeit* (1960; half-time), *Das Einhorn* (1966; *The Unicorn*, 1971), and *Der Sturz* (1973; the crash). The protagonist of all three works,

Anselm Kristlein, is the prototypical main character for virtually all of Walser's writing.

Walser's other notable fiction works include *Jenseits der Liebe* (1976; *Beyond All Love*, 1982), *Ein fliehendes Pferd* (1978; *Runaway Horse*, 1980), *Seelenarbeit* (1979; *The Inner Man*, 1984), *Das Schwanenhaus* (1980; *The Swan Villa*, 1982), *Brandung* (1985; *Breakers*, 1987), *Dorle und Wolf* (1987; *No Man's Land*, 1989), *Die Verteidigung der Kindheit* (1991), *Ohne Einander* (1993), *Ein springender Brunnen* (1998), and *Der Lebenslauf der Liebe* (2001). The reception of Walser's prose works in general, by critics and the public alike, has been more favorable than that of his plays. The critical acclaim, for example, of such a work as *Runaway Horse* has been as positive as that accorded virtually any other single literary work in West Germany in the postwar period. Even among those critics who have been quite negative about Walser's plays, there are several who have praised his prose works both for their content and for their form. Probably the nontraditional qualities of Walser's writing find greater acceptance as prose fiction than they do as drama, but that says more about the inclinations of several German theater critics, perhaps, than it does about Walser's talent as a dramatist.

Walser has established himself as a leading essay writer in West Germany. His topics range from literary criticism to cultural, political, and social criticism in general. The most important of his publications are *Erfahrungen und Leseerfahrungen* (1965; experiences and reader-experiences), *Heimatkunde* (1968; home-arts), *Wie und wovon handelt Literatur* (1973; how and what literature concerns), *Wer ist ein Schriftsteller?* (1979; who is an author?), *Über Deutschland reden* (1988; speaking about Germany), *Vormittag eines Schriftstellers* (1994; a writer's afternoon), *Deutsche Sorgen* (1997; German worries), *Ansichten, Einsichten: Aufsätze zur Zeitgeschichte* (1997; opinions, insights: essays on contemporary history), *Erfahrungen beim Verfassen einer Sonntagsrede: Friedenspreis des Deutschen Buchhandels*

(1998; experiences while composing a Sunday speech: Peace Prize of the German Publishing Industry).

ACHIEVEMENTS

One of the most important authors of post-World War II German literature, Martin Walser has distinguished himself with an extensive output of plays, novels, short stories, and essays. Like others in his generation of (West) German authors, such as Günter Grass and Siegfried Lenz, Walser was born at the end of the 1920's, grew up in Germany during the Third Reich, and then, once he began writing in the 1950's, directed his literary efforts at forcing his fellow Germans to confront rather than suppress their history and to recognize that their recent, terrible past is a part of their present, whether they are willing to admit it, and it cannot and must not be conveniently, uncritically, and irresponsibly swept under the rug. In all Walser's works, he has retained that critical sensibility toward his society, analyzing in particular the power structures in both private and public, historical and contemporary realms, and exposing how those structures oppress individuals as well as keep genuine social progress from occurring. He grants a certain amount of sympathy and understanding to his protagonists, virtually all of whom come from the middle and lower-middle classes, yet they are anything but heroic and, in fact, usually end up as failures—in their occupations, in their private and political lives, and in their attempts to find lasting meaning or realize their aspirations. Walser's dramas and prose works alike, despite all their variety, consistently display these basic thrusts.

Although the critical and popular acclaim for Walser's literary and dramatic creations has not been unanimous, he has attracted considerable scholarly attention and has been awarded numerous prestigious literary prizes, including the Prize of the Gruppe 47 (1955), the Hermann Hesse Prize (1962), the Gerhart Hauptmann Prize (1962), the Georg Büchner Prize (1982), and the Peace Prize of the German Publishing Industry (1998).

BIOGRAPHY

Martin Walser was born the son of relatively poor innkeepers in the small but picturesque south German town of Wasserburg on Lake Constance, on March 24, 1927. He claims that he was shielded from the most blatant Nazism by his very Catholic family, but there were other kinds of hardship in his youth, especially after the death of his father in 1938. His schooling was often interrupted, particularly toward the end of the war when he was forced into civilian and then military service. He was captured by Allied troops but was released at war's end. He then resumed his schooling, receiving his diploma in 1946. Walser studied initially at the Theological-Philosophical College in Regensburg; in 1948, he transferred to the University in Tübingen. He completed his studies in literature, history, and philosophy with an important Ph.D. dissertation on Franz Kafka in 1951. Both as a student and afterward, between 1949 and 1957, Walser worked for the South German Radio Network, and it was during that time that he began his career as an author, writing numerous radio plays.

Martin Walser in 1977. (Hulton Archive by Getty Images)

After the critical success in 1957 of his first novel, *Marriage in Philippsburg*, Walser and his wife moved to Lake Constance, where they took up permanent residence, rearing four artistically talented daughters. Walser's literary productivity has been prolific and steady, as has his production of significant work in the areas of literary and social criticism. Even though Walser "withdrew" to the idyllic shores of Lake Constance, he has remained a committed and frequently extremely controversial public figure since the days of his radio work. During the 1960's, he spoke out frequently and consistently for social and political progress, moved steadily toward the political Left, and championed many of the causes associated with the student movement of those turbulent years. Walser's political engagement, evident in his literary works only indirectly and never dogmatically, has never been undertaken for a specific political party, such as was the case with Günter Grass's well-publicized engagement for the Social Democrats. For a time, some observers placed Walser close to the Communists; yet, even though his social and economic analyses are definitely informed by certain Marxist principles, Walser did not join, nor would he have been at home in, the small and rather dogmatic West German Communist Party. The "revolutionary" momentum of the late 1960's and early 1970's slowed and then halted, in West Germany as well as in the United States, and Walser's direct engagement decreased in a corresponding fashion; although his political activism is never altogether absent, his works and public statements in the later 1970's indicated an increased pessimism with regard to hopes for lasting social and political change.

Walser's reputation as a writer was solidified by the success of novels and dramas alike, particularly that of the novel trilogy (which had begun with *Halbzeit* in 1960, continued with *The Unicorn* in 1966, and culminated in *Der Sturz* in 1973), as well as the plays *The Detour* in 1961, *The Rabbit Race* in 1962, and *Home Front* in 1967. The reception of Walser's works in general has been marked by vocal disagreements, contradiction, and controversy. In certain of Walser's works, most directly in the play *Wir werden schon noch handeln* (we're going to get to the plot soon), he turns the reception of his works into a literary theme. Although the balance between the positive and negative reactions to Walser's works has varied with the individual works, it can be asserted that politically and aesthetically conservative critics have tended to be more negative in their assessment than have those whose politics are more liberal and whose artistic expectations are less traditional. In any case, Walser and his works continue to inspire lively commentary from scholars, critics, and reviewers across the political-cultural spectrum. The one work which has elicited virtually universal praise from critics and readers is the novella *Runaway Horse*, which Walser later adapted into a stage version that was first performed in 1985.

The main protagonist of that novella appears later as the central figure in the novel *Brandung*. This novel is an anomaly among Walser's works in that it is not set primarily in Germany, but in California. This is a reflection of the fact that Walser has spent considerable time, particularly during stints as a visiting professor (at universities in West Virginia, New Hampshire, Texas, and California) in the United States. The novel is based largely on those experiences. Walser continues to live in Nussdorf on Lake Constance, but makes frequent trips to teach and lecture, both in Europe and abroad.

During the late 1980's and through the 1990's, Walser wrote almost exclusively prose, both fiction and essays. Drama appears to have been relegated to a secondary role in his literary production in this latest phase of his work. Within the context of this later prose work, Walser's interest has rested most clearly, on one hand, with the awkward and, for him, pressing "German question" (*No Man's Land*) and, on the other, with the difficulties surrounding memory and narrative (*Ein springender Brunnen*).

Always a controversial writer and public intellectual, Walser was at the center of two major cultural debates in Germany, in the late 1980's and again in the late 1990's. The first was ignited by his 1988 speech titled "Über Deutschland reden," in which he expressed a rather strong criticism for the divided German status quo and thereby broke a long-standing taboo among the West German left and liberal establishment. Given the surprising turn of events in 1989 and the subsequent reunification of the two Germanies a year later, Walser's thoughts proved quite prescient. The second major controversy resulted from comments Walser made in his acceptance speech for the Peace Prize of the German Publishing Industry, a major German-language literary prize, in 1998. Once again scratching at long-held taboos, Walser suggested that he had grown rather weary of hearing about Auschwitz uninterruptedly and that the entire Holocaust complex was frequently being used or "instrumentalized" for questionable political purposes. In both cases, there arose a legitimate question about the extent to which Walser had abandoned his earlier, impeccable "left-leaning" political and cultural ideas, if at all. Regardless of the answer to that question, Walser was quickly chastised by former friends and colleagues for appearing to have done so.

ANALYSIS

Critics have frequently, and correctly, claimed that Martin Walser writes the story of the everyday. The characters that populate his plays are not the movers and shakers of history, but rather singularly unexceptional individuals. These antiheroes are generally struggling, somewhat neurotic types who display middle-class, even lower-middle-class, sensibilities and behavior. Often the larger moments of history are evident in the background, but the protagonists are usually far too passive and acquiescent to be major actors on that level. Walser's perspective on history as well as on contemporary society is thus from below rather than from above, and although it is obvious that he is highly critical of his unheroic figures, it is also obvious that he identifies with them.

Several main topics run throughout Walser's dramatic works, whether these focus specifically on dealing with Germany's immediate past (*The Rabbit Race, Der schwarze Schwan*), on its more distant past (*Das Sauspiel, In Goethes Hand*), or on contemporary domestic (*The Detour, Home Front, Ein Kinderspiel*) or artistic situations (*Wir werden schon noch handeln, In Goethes Hand*). In all of his plays, Walser is concerned with power structures, master-servant relationships, and the tensions that are inherent in

such structures and relationships. The tensions usually have a deleterious, even crippling effect on the protagonists, who struggle but never quite succeed in getting out of the dependent positions in which they find themselves. Exploitation, opportunism, and subservience are all important catchwords. Walser is consistently critical of those who abuse their power as well as of those who acquiesce and allow such abuse to occur. He is concerned as well with the German past, not for its own sake, even in his history plays, but because of the shadows it casts on the German present. Whether it is the Germany of the sixteenth century (*Das Sauspiel*), the nineteenth century (*In Goethes Hand*), or the Nazi era (*The Rabbit Race, Der schwarze Schwan*) that is in question, it is the patterns of behavior, the attitudes, and the traditions developed in those eras yet still present in Walser's Germany, usually in infelicitous ways as far as he is concerned, that command his attention. The third major topical category found in Walser's plays is that of the artist and intellectual—his (they are all men) status in society, responsibility (and irresponsibility) to society, and use of his position and talent either to legitimize or to challenge and criticize the reactionary and oppressive structures and characteristics of society.

The major literary influences on Walser, especially early in his career, were Franz Kafka, Samuel Beckett, and Bertolt Brecht. Although these writers may seem to make rather strange bedfellows, one thing they have in common is their break with traditional literary forms. Walser has followed their lead and, with few exceptions, has rejected traditional dramatic form, choosing instead a loosely connected, open, or epic (in the Brechtian sense) structure instead. As the individual scenes or sections of the play have gained in importance, the significance of overall plot or character development has decreased, at times becoming even minimal, as is the case, for example, in *Wir werden schon noch handeln*. The subtitle to *Das Sauspiel*, *Szenen aus dem 16. Jahrhundert*, which means "scenes from the sixteenth century," and the subtitle to *In Goethes Hand*, *Szenen aus dem 19. Jahrhundert*, which means "scenes from the nineteenth century," also point up the relative autonomy of the individual scenes over the general, chronological plot. Furthermore, where any substantial changes occur in the protagonists, it is clearly as disintegration or diminution rather than any positive growth.

Some of Walser's earliest plays, particularly *The Detour* and *Überlebensgross Herr Krott*, display some elements of the Theater of the Absurd and, hence, the influence of Beckett and existentialism. Most of Walser's plays, however—even though they can be read on one level as parables or allegories, and even though symbols play a very significant role—are far more grounded in clearly recognizable reality. Other significant features of Walser's style are his strong sense of irony, a satirical bent, wit and witticisms, love of wordplay, and an inclination toward lightly grotesque situations and figures.

In his uncompromising attempts to confront his fellow Germans with critical portrayals of the past they consistently try to suppress, of the relationship of that past to the present, and of traits and developments in private and public behavior that inhibit progress toward liberation of all kinds, Walser is one of the most vociferous spokespeople in contemporary German letters for honesty, openness, and critical thinking. And even though some of his plays do show weaknesses in structure and consistently convincing style, others are masterpieces of postwar German drama. Walser's refusal to follow trends in modern drama, to cave in to criticism of his unconventional dramatic forms, is one of his greatest strengths, even though it sometimes means that his plays, because of their experimental nature, fall short of "masterpiece" status. Although Walser's major literary work during the 1980's and 1990's has been in the areas of fiction, for which he is rightfully regarded as one of the three or four most important German writers of the entire post-World War II era, his contributions to the body of German drama and theater during that same extensive period remain substantial and very significant. It is unfortunate that most of Walser's plays, some of which are still performed on German stages, are still inaccessible in English to theatergoers and interested parties.

THE DETOUR

The Detour, Walser's first play, enjoyed an enthusiastic response from West German theatergoers following its premiere in 1961, and it was staged in numerous theaters in the following few years. The play is divided into three parts: a prologue, the main section, and an epilogue. The prologue and epilogue consist of conversations between the now-successful West German businessman Hubert Meckel and his subservient chauffeur Berthold. More or less on a whim, Hubert has decided to take a short detour from the freeway and visit his former lover, now married, in Ulm. At the beginning of the main section, he has found her at home, but as Frieda responds to his lighthearted flirtation with accusations of shabby treatment earlier, the mood of the play gradually becomes tense, frightening, and even rather grotesquely absurd. When Frieda's husband arrives home, the two of them decide to put Hubert "on trial" for the way he had treated Frieda several years before. A sense of terror arises when they bind Hubert and conclude that he should be put to death. Ultimately, however, this terror subsides, as Frieda's husband shifts positions and aligns himself instead with Hubert against Frieda, in a show of a kind of "good old boys" solidarity.

The surrealistic, absurd atmosphere of the "trial" is thus abandoned, only to be replaced, however, by the rather grotesque and cruel irony of the men (in this case, the oppressors) joining forces against the woman (the victim). "Everyday reality" returns, Hubert bids adieu and rejoins his chauffeur, and they drive off. During the ensuing conversation between them, as well as in parts of their discussion in the prologue, the same kind of master-servant, oppressor-oppressed, exploiter-victim structures, attitudes, and behavior patterns become evident in the relationship between boss and chauffeur. Walser's intent is to analyze various kinds of power structures and the negative tensions that are inherent in them, both in the more private realm of male-female relationships and in the more public, capitalistic business world.

The didactic thrust of the play is illuminated during the "trial" when Hubert, scared out of his wits, is forced to recognize the corruption of his behavior and the abuse of power that he exerted and exerts through his position and attitudes. For the reader or viewer, he clearly becomes a symbol of the system he represents. The fact that he is to remain a "negative hero," however, whose cathartic moment of insight is only fleeting, is evident when he dismisses the whole episode as a "joke" as he and Berthold drive off, back into their everyday routines. Walser thus poses the challenge to repressive structures, but the reality of his society will not allow him to portray, optimistically, any real changes in that society, its structures, and attitudes. It is not possible to overlook the fact that Walser's play can be read, on one level, as a kind of parable of how West German society, seduced into amnesia and a false sense of righteous security by its overwhelming "economic miracle" of the 1950's, refused to deal honestly, openly, and self-critically with its own shabby past, even though the attitudes that prevailed in that past remain visible in the present for those who dare to look.

THE RABBIT RACE

In Walser's next play, *The Rabbit Race*, he attacked this topic more directly. Divided into three main parts set in 1945, 1950, and 1960, respectively, the play follows Alois Grubel through his ill-timed political transformations. The audience learns that, during the Nazi period, Alois was a communist and was sent to a concentration camp for his views. While in the camp, he was castrated and, in a rather grotesque twist, became converted to Nazism and was released. At the war's end, where the play begins, Grubel and his acquaintances in the small southern German town where they live attempt to shed the signs of their Nazism as the Allies approach. The others do so successfully, even though only the signs and rhetoric change, certainly not the attitudes. These are not shown to be mean people; they are not real Nazi criminals, but they embody the banality of evil in their subservience, their gullibility, and their petty opportunism. Grubel, though, does not make the transformation from one ideological setting to another, and in 1950 he is still making statements that reveal Nazi sentiments. He is sent to an asylum, betrayed by those who had shared his sentiments earlier. Grubel is a pathetic figure, powerless and easily manipulated, both by ideologies and by other people. The fact, however, that his ultimate failure to survive in his society derives not from his views but from his

timing is a clear indictment of a German society that has survived by its timing and opportunism, rather than by any real changes in attitudes and behavior. Walser's criticism of his fellow West Germans for their smug righteousness while they steadfastly refuse to look hard and deep at the relationship between their past and present is perhaps nowhere expressed as strongly as in this play.

ÜBERLEBENSGROSS HERR KROTT

Walser's next play, *Überlebensgross Herr Krott*, whose subtitle, *Requiem für einen Unsterblichen*, means "requiem for an immortal," is one of his most allegorical. Set in a rather surrealistic Alpine hotel, the play abounds in deaths, but Mr. Krott, the immensely wealthy industrialist who actually wants to die, cannot. Krott is an insatiable power broker who uses everything and everyone around him for his own gain, convenience, and enjoyment. It is hinted that Krott's alienation from all others and even from any human decency has its roots in the Nazi years, including war experiences, but that is not offered as an excuse. Krott is far more representative than a flesh-and-blood character, standing for an aggressive and brutal capitalistic system that, even though corrupt and inhumane, remains "alive" while causing the death, literal and metaphorical, of countless others.

DER SCHWARZE SCHWAN

Walser's play from 1964, *Der schwarze Schwan* (the black swan), marks an intensification of his attempt to confront German society with its terrible, recent past and its efforts to suppress or deny its responsibility, even guilt, for that past. The timing of the play coincided with the Frankfurt trials of Nazi criminals, trials that pointed up very clearly the need for Germans to deal with the unfinished business of their Nazi past. This was also the time when serious generational conflicts in Germany began to show themselves, not least of all because teenagers and young adults began to ask their parents about their roles, activities, and attitudes during the Third Reich. Forthright answers to such questions were infrequent, and youth began to criticize and rebel against the older generation. That, in fact, becomes the main focus of Walser's *Der schwarze Schwan*.

Walser sets the play in a postwar insane asylum, which is directed by a former Nazi doctor. This doctor, Professor Libere, has withdrawn to the asylum for two seemingly contradictory reasons: to atone for his role in the medical atrocities that occurred, but also to invent an imaginary past, for himself and his family, in which he had no part in the Third Reich. Libere's rather schizophrenic manner of dealing with guilt appears to be representative, for Walser, of the way his society has dealt with it. There is more of a plot in this play than in most other Walser plays, and it starts with the arrival of Rudi Goothein, a young man about twenty years old, who claims that he is a former SS man. His father, also a former Nazi doctor, brings him to the asylum, thinking his son has had a nervous breakdown. Rudi demands a "trial" for his own "imagined" crimes, during which he wants to confront his father with the latter's unacknowledged crimes. Rudi has discovered a letter in which his father's responsibility for atrocities is evident. The "trial," which takes place in the asylum as a kind of play-within-a-play, suggests comparison with William Shakespeare's *Hamlet, Prince of Denmark* (pr. c. 1600-1601). It leads to outrage on the part of Libere and Rudi's father when they are forced to recognize themselves, their guilt, and their elaborate attempts to deny and suppress their true pasts, but they refuse, nevertheless, to abandon their false masks and claims of innocence. Realizing that he has failed to force his father to confess and recognizing that the foundation for his own life and future is therefore corrupt, Rudi commits suicide rather than live with this lie. He views his death as a protest and symbolic statement about the futility and impossibility of building a sound future on a mendacious past. Rudi's situation, then, is clearly meant to be allegorical for that of postwar German youth in general. It is also a bitter admonition to the older members of German society to come clean and face their past honestly, if not for their own sake, then at least for that of their children.

HOME FRONT

Walser's fifth play, *Home Front*, was written about the same time as *Der schwarze Schwan* but was not performed or published until 1967. By this time, a pattern for Walser's dramatic works had begun to reveal itself: his movement back and forth from more public questions and situations to those of a more private nature. The themes tend to be similar but are emphasized differently in each kind of play. *Home Front* presents a kind of domestic nightmare, somewhat in the mode of August Strindberg's marriage plays or Edward Albee's *Who's Afraid of Virginia Woolf?* (1962). The only two characters, Felix and Trude, have been married for many years and, by suppressing feelings and expectations, have managed to coexist with a certain degree of innocuous harmony. On the evening that is the focus of the play, however, aided by too much alcohol, they both let down their guard and begin to speak honestly with each other. The result is disastrous, for their pseudoharmony is unmasked as a lie, as a kind of ritual to cover the genuine sadomasochistic nature of their relationship. Walser is not asserting that glossing over the truth is better, however, for it is obvious that they could not have lived this lie much longer, with or without alcohol. Once again, then—although in a much different situation from those he posited before—Walser focused on the theme of truth, the difficulty of confronting it openly, but the necessity, regardless of the consequences, of doing so.

WIR WERDEN SCHON NOCH HANDELN

In Walser's next play, *Wir werden schon noch handeln*, he very cleverly and ironically presents a self-conscious analysis of the contemporary German world of theater, performances, and reviewers. It is a play that attacks and satirizes those critics who expect and demand traditional form even for radically nontraditional, contemporary topics. It is also, therefore, a defense, though not without self-irony, of Walser's own theatrical style and attitudes about contemporary drama.

EIN KINDERSPIEL

The last play that Walser wrote before taking a significant break was *Ein Kinderspiel*, written and performed in 1970. The title is bitterly ironic, for this play is anything but a "children's game." The topic is once again the conflict between the generations, a conflict that was virtually everywhere in evidence in Germany, as in many other places, during the late

1960's. What the play actually portrays as black, psychological comedy is an almost absurdly dysfunctional family. The mother in the family has recently died, and Asti, the twenty-year-old son, his twenty-three-year-old sister Bille, their estranged father, and his new, young wife, come to the family cottage for a kind of reunion. There are hints of incest between mother and son, as well as between brother and sister, and the plot thickens as Asti tries to enlist his sister's help in killing their father upon his arrival. Asti plans patricide not only because he believes that his father is responsible for his mother's death but also because he holds him "responsible" for his own *birth* and his sister's. The murder never occurs, as the father unwittingly calls Asti's bluff, but the rest of the play teems with intensely bizarre and cruel provocations. This is private drama, psychological drama of consciousness, and Walser seems to be highly critical of everyone. One can sense not only Walser's criticism of the older generation but also his growing disenchantment with the younger one that appears, at least in Asti, to engage in infantile and destructive self-indulgence. The question presents itself whether Walser sees before him, reflected in such dysfunctional domestic situations, the end of bourgeois, capitalistic society.

DAS SAUSPIEL

Three years after *Ein Kinderspiel*, Walser presented his first genuine history play, *Das Sauspiel* (pig-play). In a series of loosely connected scenes, Walser concentrates on the post-Reformation, post-revolutionary situation in Nuremberg in the years 1525 to 1527. The city is now Lutheran, free of the oppressive control of the Catholic Church and the bishop of Bamberg. It is governed by those who had revolted, an illustrious group of artisans, merchants, teachers. Many of their names are famous, either from Albrecht Dürer's paintings or from historical and fictional sources, including Hans Sachs and Dürer himself. Walser does not place them in the key roles, however, and the protagonist is a poor street-singer who feigns blindness in order to increase donations, Jörg Graf. This device allows Walser to portray the events, characters, and historical dilemmas from the perspective of those who are less the shapers of history than its victims. Walser uses much documentary material in the play, but it is not a documentary drama in the well-known style of Rolf Hochhuth, Peter Weiss, or Heinar Kipphardt.

Walser is interested in what happens *after* a revolution has apparently succeeded, and he concludes that, if not inevitably, then certainly often, a reaction sets in whereby the revolutionaries of old, now in power, become reactionary and distance themselves from their old ideals in order to establish their power and position. In this play, Walser shows how these former revolutionaries begin to persecute those former allies who are not yet satisfied with what has happened and who want to extend the benefits of the successful revolution to others. Representative of these former allies are the Anabaptists, the so-called radical reformers, who not only were persecuted but also, according to Walser and numerous progressive historians, have been unjustly maligned by historical, fictional, and theological accounts up to the present day.

Walser is thus keen on challenging traditional interpretations of these historical events and characters, but he is equally intent on exploring post-revolutionary patterns in general. The disappointment that Walser felt over the return of what he viewed as reactionary patterns in West German society after the "revolutionary" changes in the progressive 1960's is certainly in evidence here, as well as his attempts to find explanations for that reaction. In *Das Sauspiel*, he is critical not only of idealists-turned-establishment-politicians but also of opportunistic artists and intellectuals who abandon their "ideals" when the wind changes directions, as does Jörg Graf.

Das Sauspiel, which was performed in numerous German theaters, both West and East, elicited a genuine controversy among reviewers and critics, in part because Walser had challenged both the legitimacy of Nuremberg's legendary humanistic tradition and the traditional ways of interpreting the events, characters, and results of the Reformation. During the next seven years, until 1982, Walser focused most of his literary energy on novels and other prose forms, and this was a period in which he firmly established himself, even in the eyes of critics who had been former detractors, as a novelist of international significance. In 1982, however, his next play appeared, and it, too, caused much controversy.

IN GOETHES HAND

The play *In Goethes Hand* (in Goethe's hand), like *Das Sauspiel*, is a history play, which, despite its title, concentrates not directly on the famous title character but on his rather subservient assistant, Eckermann, and on what Walser views as the negative, inhibitory, and even reactionary legacy of the "Goethe legend" for the subsequent development of German culture.

Once again, Walser's interest in history is not merely for its own sake but for the ways in which it still informs and affects the present. Walsert criticizes not Goethe's literary works but rather his ego, monumental posing, and later conservative views toward politics and art. Eckermann, with whom Walser's sympathies partially reside, also is subject to criticism for his subservience and his part in perpetuating a bigger-than-life image of Goethe. There is no doubt that Goethe is the central figure in modern German literature, and Walser would not dispute that, but he does want to view the man and his legacy critically. *In Goethes Hand* is a play about the tensions between traditional and modernist art, about the reception of culture, and about history and its sometimes burdensome relationship to the present. It is also, however, a play about the venerable German problem of subservience, about dependence and exploitation.

DIE OHRFEIGE

Walser's 1984 play *Die Ohrfeige* (the slap in the face) takes up once again with the theme of the master-servant relationship, this time in very satirical and rather comic fashion. Specifically, the play revolves around a dramatist (clearly based on the Austrian writer Thomas Bernhard) and his rather surprising turn from nihilist to Pollyanna following an incident during which he is mistaken for a factory owner, is slapped across the face, and falls backward, resulting in his becoming a paraplegic. One has the sense that Walser is having fun parodying certain kinds of writers, overbearing publishers, and know-it-all critics, while also getting in some pretty good licks at members of those groups who had caused him, in various ways, pain.

KASCHMIR IN PARCHING

In *Kaschmir in Parching*, Walser addresses once more the unavoidable connections between the private and public realms, the present and the past. This mingling of alleged opposites occurs here during a mayoral campaign in a small town (Parching) near Munich, during which the town's long-suppressed past during the Nazi period is exposed by one candidate, a teacher, who is, however, opposed by industry's candidate who "represents," by contrast, the future and has no time for or interest in the past, especially that past.

OTHER MAJOR WORKS

LONG FICTION: *Ehen in Philippsburg*, 1957 (*The Gadarene Club*, 1960; also known as *Marriage in Philippsburg*); *Halbzeit*, 1960; *Das Einhorn*, 1966 (*The Unicorn*, 1971); *Die Gallistl'sche Krankheit*, 1972; *Der Sturz*, 1973; *Jenseits der Liebe*, 1976 (*Beyond All Love*, 1982); *Ein fliehendes Pferd*, 1978 (*Runaway Horse*, 1980); *Seelenarbeit*, 1979 (*The Inner Man*, 1984); *Das Schwanenhaus*, 1980 (*The Swan Villa*, 1982); *Brief an Lord Liszt*, 1982 (*Letter to Lord Liszt*, 1985); *Brandung*, 1985 (*Breakers*, 1987); *Dorle und Wolf*, 1987 (*No Man's Land*, 1989); *Jagd*, 1988; *Die Verteidigung der Kindheit*, 1991; *Ohne Einander*, 1993; *Finks Kreig*, 1996; *Ein springender Brunnen*, 1998; *Der Lebenslauf der Liebe*, 2001.

SHORT FICTION: *Ein Flugzeug über dem Haus und andere Geschichten*, 1955; *Liebegeschichten*, 1964; *Selected Stories*, 1982; *Gesammelte Geschichten*, 1983; *Messmers Gedanken*, 1985; *Fingerübungen eines Mörders: 12 Geschichten*, 1994.

NONFICTION: *Beschreibung einer Form: Versuch über Franz Kafka*, 1961; *Erfahrungen und Leseerfahrungen*, 1965; *Heimatkunde*, 1968; *Wie und wovon handelt Literatur*, 1973; *Wer ist ein Schriftsteller?*, 1979; *Selbstbewusstsein und Ironie*, 1981; *Liebeserklärungen*, 1983; *Variationen eines Würgegriffs: Bericht über Trinidad und Tobago*, 1985 (travel); *Heilige Brocken*, 1986; *Über Deutschland reden*, 1988; *Vormittag eines Schriftstellers*, 1994; *Ansichten, Einsichten: Aufsätze zur Zeitgeschichte*, 1997; *Deutsche Sorgen*, 1997; *Erfahrungen beim Verfassen einer Sonntagsrede: Friedenspreis des*

Deutschen Buchhandels 1998, 1998; *Ich vertraue— Querfeldein*, 2000.

MISCELLANEOUS: *Werke in zwölf Bänden*, 1997 (12 volumes).

BIBLIOGRAPHY

Fetz, Gerald A. "Martin Walser, Germany, and the 'German Question.'" In *Leseerfahrungen mit Martin Walser*, edited by Heike Doane and Gertrud Bauer Pickar. Munich: Fink, 1995. An examination of Walser and his attitude toward Germany.

_____. "Martin Walser's *Sauspiel* and the Contemporary German History Play." *Comparative Drama* 12, no. 3 (1978): 249-265. A look at Walser's *Das Sauspiel* and other German history plays.

Pilipp, Frank, ed. *New Critical Perspectives on Martin Walser*. Columbia, S.C.: Camden House, 1994. An examination of contemporary critiques of Walser's works. Bibliography and index.

Schlunk, Jürgen E., and Armand E. Singer, eds. *Martin Walser: International Perspectives*. New York: Peter Lang, 1987. A collection of papers presented at the International Martin Walser Symposium at the West Virginia University in April, 1985. Bibliographies.

Waine, Anthony Edward. *Martin Walser: The Development as Dramatist, 1950-1970*. Bonn: Bouvier, 1978. Waine traces Walser's development as a playwright until 1970. Bibliography and index.

Gerald A. Fetz

WENDY WASSERSTEIN

Born: Brooklyn, New York; October 18, 1950

PRINCIPAL DRAMA

Any Woman Can't, pr. 1973
Happy Birthday, Montpelier Pizz-zazz, pr. 1974
When Dinah Shore Ruled the Earth, pr. 1975 (with Christopher Durang)
Uncommon Women and Others, pr. 1975 (one act), pr. 1977 (two acts), pb. 1978
Isn't It Romantic, pr. 1981, pr. 1983 (revised version), pb. 1984
Tender Offer, pr. 1983, pb. 2000 (one act)
The Man in a Case, pr., pb. 1986 (one act; adaptation of Anton Chekhov's short story)
Miami, pr. 1986 (musical)
The Heidi Chronicles, pr., pb. 1988
The Heidi Chronicles and Other Plays, pb. 1990
The Sisters Rosensweig, pr. 1992, pb. 1993
An American Daughter, pr. 1997, pb. 1998
Waiting for Philip Glass, pr., pb. 1998 (inspired by William Shakespeare's Sonnet 94)
The Festival of Regrets, pr. 1999 (libretto)
Old Money, pr. 2000, pb. 2002
Seven One-Act Plays, pb. 2000

OTHER LITERARY FORMS

Wendy Wasserstein, though best known for her plays, is the author of several teleplays, including *The Sorrows of Gin* (1979), an adaptation of John Cheever's short story, and *An American Daughter* (2000), an adaptation of her play. She also has written several unproduced film scripts. Her essays, which have appeared in numerous periodicals, including *Esquire* and *New York Woman*, have been published in two collections, *Bachelor Girls* (1990) and *Shiksa Goddess* (2001).

ACHIEVEMENTS

Wendy Wasserstein has been hailed as the foremost theatrical chronicler of the lives of women of her generation. Her plays, steeped in her unique brand of humor, are moving, sometimes wrenching explorations of women's struggle for identity and fulfillment in a world of rapidly shifting social, sexual, and political mores. Most often against the backdrop of the burgeoning feminist movement, her characters navigate through obstacle courses of expectations—those of their parents, their lovers, their siblings, their friends, and, ultimately, themselves. They seek answers to fundamental questions: how to find meaning in life and how to strike a balance between the need to connect and the need to be true to oneself. Wasserstein's works, which deftly pair wit and pathos, satire and sensitivity, have garnered numerous honors, including the Pulitzer Prize, the Tony (Antoinette Perry) Award, the New York Drama Critics Circle Award, the Outer Critics Circle Award, and the Susan Smith Blackburn Prize.

BIOGRAPHY

Wendy Wasserstein was born on October 18, 1950, in Brooklyn, New York. She was the fourth and youngest child of Morris W. Wasserstein, a successful textile manufacturer, and Lola (Schleifer) Wasserstein, a housewife and nonprofessional dancer, both Jewish émigrés from central Europe. When she was thirteen, Wasserstein's family moved to Manhattan, where she attended the Calhoun School, an all-girl academy at which she discovered that she could get excused from gym class by writing the annual mother-daughter fashion show. Some years later, at Mount Holyoke, an elite Massachusetts women's college, a friend persuaded Wasserstein, a history major, to take a playwriting course at nearby Smith College. Encouraged by her instructor, she devoted much of her junior year, which she spent at Amherst College, performing in campus musicals before returning to complete her B.A. degree at Mount Holyoke in 1971.

Upon graduating, Wasserstein moved back to New York City, where she studied playwriting with Israel Horovitz and Joseph Heller at City College (where she later earned an M.A.) and held a variety of odd jobs to pay her rent. In 1973, her play *Any Woman Can't* was produced Off-Broadway at Playwrights Horizons, prompting her to accept admission to the Yale School of Drama and to turn down the Columbia Business School, which had simultaneously offered her admission.

It was at Yale University, where she earned her M.F.A. degree in 1976, that Wasserstein's first hit play, *Uncommon Women and Others*, was conceived as a one-act. Ultimately expanded, it was given a workshop production at the prestigious National Playwrights Conference at the O'Neill Theater Center in Connecticut, a well-known launching pad for many successful playwrights. Indeed, in 1977, the Phoenix Theater's production of *Uncommon Women and Others* opened Off-Broadway at the Marymount Manhattan Theater. Although some critics objected to the play's lack of traditional plot, most praised Wasserstein's gifts as a humorist and a social observer.

By 1980, Wasserstein, established as one of the United States' most promising young playwrights, was commissioned by the Phoenix Theater to write *Isn't It Romantic* for its 1980-1981 season. The play's mixed reviews prompted Wasserstein to rework it under the guidance of director Gerald Gutierrez and André Bishop, artistic director of Playwrights Horizons. There, with a stronger narrative line and more in-depth character development, it opened in 1983 to widespread praise.

In the meantime, Wasserstein had been at work on several new pieces—among them a one-act play, *Ten-*

Wendy Wasserstein (AP/Wide World Photos)

der Offer, which was produced at Ensemble Studio Theater, and, collaborating with Jack Feldman and Bruce Sussman, a musical, *Miami*, which was presented as a work-in-progress at Playwrights Horizons in 1986. In 1988, one of Wasserstein's most ambitious works, *The Heidi Chronicles*, which had been previously performed in workshop at the Seattle Repertory Theatre, had its New York premiere at Playwrights Horizons. It moved quickly to the larger Plymouth Theater on Broadway, where it opened to mostly positive critical response. The play earned for Wasserstein the Pulitzer Prize, the Tony Award, and virtually every New York theater award. Wasserstein's eagerly awaited *The Sisters Rosensweig* opened at the Mitzi E. Newhouse Theater at Lincoln Center in the fall of 1992. Receiving widespread critical acclaim, the piece augmented her already prominent presence on the American dramatic scene.

Wasserstein has branched out from her typical output to participate in several innovative theater events. In 1998 she was one of seven playwrights contributing one-act plays based on Shakespearean sonnets to the production of *Love's Fire*. In 1999, she was one of three playwrights creating librettos for *Central Park*, a New York City Opera production presented at Glimmerglass Opera and Lincoln Center. Her libretto, "The Festival of Regrets," was scored by Deborah Drattell, composer-in-residence for New York City Opera and Glimmerglass Opera.

At the age of forty-eight, Wasserstein became a single mother after treatment with fertility drugs. Her daughter, Lucy Jane, weighed only one pound, twelve ounces at birth. Wasserstein's essay about her struggle to conceive and her daughter's birth is one of the most moving pieces in *Shiksa Goddess*.

ANALYSIS

Wendy Wasserstein's plays are, for the most part, extremely consistent in their emphasis on character, their lack of classical structure, and their use of humor to explore or accompany serious, often poignant themes. Throughout her career, Wasserstein's central concern has been the role of women—particularly white, upper-middle-class, educated women—in contemporary society. Though her plays are suffused

with uproarious humor, her typical characters are individuals engaged in a struggle to carve out an identity and a place for themselves in a society that has left them feeling, at worst, stranded and desolate and, at best, disillusioned. This is not to say that Wasserstein's worldview is bleak. Rather, the note of slightly skewed optimism with which she characteristically ends her works, along with her prevailing wit, lends them an air of levity and exuberance that often transcends her sober themes.

These themes—loneliness, isolation, and a profound desire for meaning in life—are examined by Wasserstein chiefly through character. One of the playwright's great strengths is her ability to poke fun at her characters without subjecting them to ridicule or scorn. Her women and men, with all their faults and foibles, are warmly and affectionately rendered. They engage their audience's empathy as they make their way through the mazes of their lives, trying to connect and to be of consequence in the world.

Wasserstein is a unique and important voice in contemporary American theater. As a woman writing plays about women, she has been a groundbreaker, though never self-consciously so. Despite her often thin plot lines, she finds and captures the drama inherent in the day-to-day choices confronting the women of her generation. As a humorist, too, Wasserstein is unquestionably a virtuoso. Her ability to see the absurdity of even her own most deeply held convictions, and to hold them deeply nevertheless, is perhaps the most engaging and distinctive of her writing's many strengths.

Wasserstein is best known for her four full-length, professional plays, *Uncommon Women and Others*, *Isn't It Romantic*, *The Heidi Chronicles*, and *The Sisters Rosensweig*. The first three plays have in common their episodic structure and non-plot-driven narrative. In each of the three, scenes unfold to reveal aspects of character.

UNCOMMON WOMEN AND OTHERS

Uncommon Women and Others begins with five former college friends assessing their lives as they reunite six years after graduation. The body of the play is a flashback to their earlier life together at a small women's college under the often conflicting influences of the school's traditional "feminine" rituals and etiquette and the iconoclasm of the blossoming women's movement. In each of the two time frames, events are largely contexts for discussions in which Wasserstein's women use one another as sounding boards, each one testing and weighing her hopes, fears, expectations, and achievements against those of her friends.

Isn't It Romantic

Similarly, in *Isn't It Romantic*, two former college friends, Janie Blumberg, a freelance writer, and Harriet Cornwall, a corporate M.B.A., move through their postcollege lives, weighing marriage and children against independence and the life choices of their mothers against their own. The play climaxes at the point where the two women diverge: Harriet, who has formerly decried marriage, accepts a suitor's proposal out of fear of being alone, and Janie chooses to remain unattached and to seek happiness within herself.

The Heidi Chronicles

The Heidi Chronicles, though more far-reaching in scope, is also a character-driven play. Here, Wasserstein narrows her focus to one woman, Heidi Holland, but through her reflects the changing social and political mores of more than two decades. From the mid-1960's to the late 1980's, Heidi, like Wasserstein's earlier characters, struggles to find her identity. Moving through settings ranging from women's consciousness-raising meetings and protests to power lunches in trendy restaurants and Yuppie baby showers, Wasserstein's Heidi functions as, in her words, a "highly-informed spectator" who never quite seems to be in step with the prescribed order of the day. In a pivotal scene, Heidi, now an art-history professor, delivers a luncheon lecture entitled "Women, Where Are We Going?" Her speech, which disintegrates into a seeming nervous breakdown, ends with Heidi confessing that she feels "stranded": "And I thought the whole point was that we wouldn't feel stranded," she concludes, "I thought the whole point was that we were in this together."

Isolation and loneliness and, contrastingly, friendship and family are themes that run throughout these three earlier plays. Heidi's wish, expressed in that luncheon speech, is for the kind of solidarity that exists among the women in *Uncommon Women and Others*, who, while constantly comparing their lives, are not competitive in the sense of putting one another down. On the contrary, they are fervent in their praise and support of one another, a family unto themselves. Janie and Harriet, in *Isn't It Romantic*, share a relationship that is much the same until something comes between them, Harriet's decision to marry a man she hardly knows because he makes her feel "like [she has] a family." Heidi, on the other hand, at the point when she makes her speech, has no close women friends. Presumably, they are all off having babies or careers. Her decision, at the play's end, to adopt a Panamanian baby girl, thereby creating a family of her own, is much akin to Janie Blumberg's decision finally to unpack her crates in her empty apartment at the end of *Isn't It Romantic* and make a home for herself.

This desire on the part of Wasserstein's characters for a family and a place to belong has at its root the desire for self-affirmation. It is evident in the refrain that echoes throughout *Uncommon Women and Others*, "When we're twenty-five [thirty, forty, forty-five], we're going to be incredible," as well as in Janie Blumberg's invocation, "I am," borrowed from her mother, Tasha. Though failures by the standards of some, Janie, Heidi, and the others can be seen as heroic in their resilience and in the tenacity with which they cling to their ideals—however divergent from the reality at hand.

Wasserstein's tendency to create characters who resist change can exasperate audiences, as her critics have noted. The women, in particular, who people her plays are often, like Janie with her unpacked crates of furniture, in a state of suspension, waiting for life to begin. In *Uncommon Women and Others*, there is a constant look toward the future for self-substantiation, as there is, to some extent, in Heidi's persistent state of unhappiness. Still, Heidi does ultimately make a choice—to adopt a baby, a step toward the process of growing up, another of Wasserstein's recurrent themes.

One of Wasserstein's greatest gifts is her ability to find and depict the ironies of life. This is evident in each of the three plays' bittersweet final images: the "uncommon women," their arms wrapped around one another, repeating their by now slightly sardonic refrain; Janie, tap-dancing alone in her empty apartment; and Heidi, singing to her new daughter "You Send Me," the song to which she had previously danced with her old flame, Scoop, at his wedding reception. These images are pure Wasserstein. In the face of disappointment, even the disillusionment, of life, her characters manifest a triumph of the spirit and a strength from within that ultimately prevails.

THE SISTERS ROSENSWEIG

Wasserstein's *The Sisters Rosensweig* is a departure from her earlier plays in a number of ways. Most overt among these differences are the play's international setting (the action takes place in Queen Anne's Gate, London) and its concern with global issues and events. Also of note is the playwright's uncharacteristic use, here, of classical, nonepisodic structure, maintaining unity of time and place: in this case, several days' events in the sitting room of Sara Goode, the play's main character and the eldest of the three sisters for whom the play is named.

Sara shares many of the characteristics of Wasserstein's earlier protagonists—that is, her gender (female), ethnic group (Jewish), social class (upper-middle to upper class), and intelligence quotient (uncommonly high). She is, however, considerably older than her forerunners. *The Sisters Rosensweig* centers on the celebration of Sara's fifty-fourth birthday. This is significant in that Sara, a hugely successful international banker who has been married and divorced several times, does not share the struggle for self-identity carried out by such Wasserstein heroines as Heidi Holland and Janie Blumberg. With a lucrative, challenging career (noteworthily, in a male-dominated field) and a daughter she loves, Sara has achieved, to some degree, the "meaning" in her life that those earlier characters found lacking and sought.

As the play progresses, however, it is revealed that Sara, despite her self-confidence and seeming self-sufficiency, shares with Heidi, Janie, and the others a deep need to connect—to find, create, or reclaim a family. As she fends off and at last gives in to a per-

sistent suitor, Merv Kant, a fake-fur dealer, and plays hostess to her two sisters (Pfeni Rosensweig, a socio-political journalist turned travel writer, and "Dr." Gorgeous Teitelbaum, who hosts a radio call-in show), Sara manages, at last, to peel back the layers of defense and reserve that have seen her through two divorces and the rigors of her profession and to rediscover the joys of sisterhood and the revitalizing power of romantic love.

It is not Sara alone who serves Wasserstein in her exploration of her characteristic themes of loneliness, isolation, and the search for true happiness. Pfeni, forty years old, the play's most seemingly autobiographical character, a writer who has been temporarily diverted from her true calling, has been likewise diverted from pursuing "what any normal woman wants" by remaining in a relationship with Geoffrey, a former homosexual. Jilted and distraught over the havoc that acquired immunedeficiency syndrome (AIDS) has played with the lives of his friends, Geoffrey has wooed and won Pfeni, only to leave her in the end to follow his own true nature. Pfeni's ceaseless "wandering" as well as her self-confessed need to write about the hardships of others to fill the emptiness in her own life is much akin to Heidi Holland's position as a "highly-informed spectator," waiting for her own life to begin.

The Sisters Rosensweig harks back to Wasserstein's *Isn't It Romantic* in its concerns with the profound role that both mothers and Judaism play in shaping women's lives. Here, Sara rejects, and attempts to cast off, the influences of both. An atheist expatriate in London, she has reinvented her life, purging all memories of her Jewish New York upbringing and her deceased mother's expectations as firmly as she has embraced the habits and speech patterns of her adopted home. Sara's eventual acquiescence to Merv, a New York Jew, along with the rekindling of her emotional attachment to her sisters, represents, at the play's end, an acceptance and embracing of the past that she has worked so hard to put behind her.

Like all Wasserstein's works, *The Sisters Rosensweig* presents characters whose spirit triumphs over their daily heartaches and heartbreaks. While they long to escape the tangled webs of their lives ("If I could only get to Moscow!" Pfeni laments, in one of the play's several nods to Anton Chekhov's *Tri sestry*, pr., pb. 1901, rev. pb. 1904; *Three Sisters*, 1920), they manage to find within themselves and in one another sufficient strength not only to endure but also to prevail.

As in *Uncommon Women and Others*, *Isn't It Romantic*, and *The Heidi Chronicles*, there is a scene in *The Sisters Rosensweig* in which women join together to share a toast, affirming and celebrating their sisterhood and themselves. Be they biological sisters, sorority sisters, or sisters of the world, Wasserstein has made sisters her province. With *The Sisters Rosensweig*, she adds three more portraits to her ever-growing gallery of uncommon women, painted, as always, with insight, wit, and compassion.

OTHER MAJOR WORKS

NONFICTION: *Bachelor Girls*, 1990; *Shiksa Goddess: Or, How I Spent My Forties*, 2001.

SCREENPLAY: *The Object of My Affection*, 1998 (adaptation of Stephen McCauley's novel).

TELEPLAYS: *The Sorrows of Gin*, 1979 (from the story by John Cheever); *"Drive," She Said*, 1984; *The Heidi Chronicles*, 1995 (adaptation of her play); *An American Daughter*, 2000 (adaptation of her play).

CHILDREN'S LITERATURE: *Pamela's First Musical*, 1996.

BIBLIOGRAPHY

Bennetts, Leslie. "An Uncommon Dramatist Prepares Her New Work." *The New York Times*, May 24, 1981, p. C1. Written as *Isn't It Romantic* was being previewed, this piece provides a look at Wasserstein's entry into writing and theater during her high school and college years. Wasserstein discusses feminism and women's difficulty in making choices in life. Contains photographs of Wasserstein and Steven Robman, the director of *Isn't It Romantic*.

Berman, Janice. "The Heidi Paradox." *Newsday*, December 22, 1988. This article, in which Wasserstein defines herself as a "feminist," discusses the male and female characters in *The Heidi Chronicles* and refers to Wasserstein's earlier plays. Contains photographs of the playwright, of Joan Allen in *The Heidi Chronicles*, and of Christine Rose and Barbara Barrie in *Isn't It Romantic*.

Nightingale, Benedict. "There Really Is a World Beyond 'Diaper Drama.'" *The New York Times*, January 1, 1984, p. C2. This two-page piece discusses *Isn't It Romantic* in the context of plays that focus on adult children struggling to sever ties with their parents. It compares Wasserstein's play with those of Tina Howe and Christopher Durang. Includes a photograph of the "mothers" in *Isn't It Romantic*.

Rose, Phyllis Jane. "Dear Heidi—An Open Letter to Dr. Holland." *American Theatre* 6 (October, 1989): 26. Written in letter form, this essay is a provocative, in-depth feminist critique of the images of women as presented in *The Heidi Chronicles*. Rose emphasizes Heidi's complicity in surrendering her independence to men, referring to Aeschylus's *Oresteia* (458 B.C.E.; English translation, 1777) as a means of furthering her point. Contains numerous photographs of scenes from *The Heidi Chronicles*.

Shapiro, Walter. "Chronicler of Frayed Feminism." *Time*, March 27, 1989, 90-92. Written shortly after *The Heidi Chronicles* moved to Broadway, this article provides insight into Wasserstein's impetus for writing the play. Shapiro offers a brief look at the feminist subtext throughout Wasserstein's work, as well as a more lengthy examination of her New York roots and family. Contains a full-page photograph of Wasserstein.

Wallace, Carol. "A Kvetch for Our Time," *Sunday News Magazine*, August 19, 1984, 10. Wallace focuses on *Isn't It Romantic* as a chronicle of the women of Wasserstein's generation. She also discusses Wasserstein's overachieving siblings, her New York youth, and her years at Mount Holyoke College. Includes a photograph of the playwright.

Anne Newgarden,
updated by Irene Struthers Rush

JOHN WEBSTER

Born: London, England; c. 1577-1580
Died: London, England; before 1634

PRINCIPAL DRAMA

Westward Ho!, pr. 1604, pb. 1607 (with Thomas Dekker)
Northward Ho!, pr. 1605, pb. 1607 (with Dekker)
The White Devil, pr. c. 1609-1612, pb. 1612
The Duchess of Malfi, pr. 1614, pb. 1623
The Devil's Law-Case, pr. c. 1619-1622, pb. 1623
Monuments of Honour, pr., pb. 1624
A Cure for a Cuckold, pr. c. 1624-1625, pb. 1661 (with William Rowley)
Appius and Virginia, pr. 1634(?), pb. 1654 (with Thomas Heywood)

OTHER LITERARY FORMS

John Webster wrote a few short poems, including commendatory verses to accompany publications by other poets and an elegy on the death of Prince Henry, heir to the English throne, entitled "A Monumental Column." In prose, he is believed to have written the thirty-two new character sketches that appeared in Sir Thomas Overbury's sixth edition of *New and Choice Characters of Several Authors* in 1615, including the famous one entitled "Excellent Actor." He also wrote a pageant, "Monuments of Honor," for the procession of John Gore, the lord mayor of London, in 1624.

ACHIEVEMENTS

John Webster is known for two powerful tragedies, *The White Devil* and *The Duchess of Malfi*, which have sufficiently impressed readers to rank him second only to William Shakespeare as a writer of English Renaissance tragedy. Each play presents an intense penetration into a world of evil, fully displaying Webster's genius for horror in scenes in which characters are tortured to the limits of endurance. Webster's deep psychological studies of ambition, lust, and revenge turn the morbid and macabre into great art. Webster's title characters, unusual for Renaissance tragedy, are women who are different in nature. In *The White Devil*, the murderous intent of Vittoria and her impassioned defense of herself at her trial contrast with *The Duchess of Malfi* with the kind, loving nature of the Duchess and the quiet nobility with which she ultimately faces death. Webster's poetry creates passages of great beauty and power, which in the Duchess's death scene combine to create one of the great moments in world drama.

BIOGRAPHY

In the late 1970's, new information was learned about a family named Webster that lived in London in the parish of St. Sepulcher-Without-Newgate and is believed to have been the family of John Webster, the tragic dramatist. The head of this family, also named John, was a member of the Merchant Taylors' Company; this information accords with a statement written by the playwright, which mentions that he had been "born free" of the Merchant Taylors', meaning that at the time of his birth his father was an actual member of that guild. The senior Webster became free in 1577 and, most likely with the expectation of a sufficient income to allow him to have a family, married Elizabeth Coates that same year. The future playwright, believed to be the eldest son because he bears his father's name, was most likely born within the years 1577-1580. The father later became a prosperous coach maker, whose coaches frequently carried the dead to burial. This may explain the playwright's preoccupation with death, which began at an early age.

No records prove that the young Webster went to the famous Merchant Taylors' School, but such an assumption is reasonable. Since his plays show knowledge of the law, it has always been thought that he attended law schools. Records do show, however, that on August 1, 1589, a John Webster was admitted to the Middle Temple from the New Inn.

The earliest record about the playwright's theatrical career comes from 1602, when he, along with four other writers including Thomas Dekker, received commission from the Lord Admiral's Company to write a play to be known as *Two Shapes*, probably the same play as *Caesar's Fall*, now lost, for which the company paid the playwrights five pounds on May 22. Later that year Webster collaborated on two other plays, being paid in October for *Lady Jane*, which may have been published under a different title, and in November for *Christmas Comes but Once a Year*, now lost. In 1602 and 1604, he wrote minor poems, prefatory verses for works by other poets, among whom was Thomas Heywood. Webster also worked with John Marston, penning the induction to his *The Malcontent* (pr., pb. 1604). He collaborated with Dekker on several plays over the next few years, the most notable being *Westward Ho!* and *Northward Ho!*, both performed by the boy actors at St. Paul's, probably in 1604 and 1605, respectively, and both published in 1607 along with *The Famous History of Sir Thomas Wyatt*, which may be, at least in part, the same play as *Lady Jane*.

Webster married Sara Peniall, probably on March 18, 1605, and their first child, John, was baptized on May 8, 1606. Shortly thereafter, Webster decided to write without collaborators. His first independent play was *The White Devil*, written in 1609 and performed that winter by the Queen's Company at the Red Bull theater. According to Webster, this play was not well received. In 1613, Webster published his elegy on the death of Henry, prince of Wales. Webster's other major play, *The Duchess of Malfi*, was performed before the end of 1614 by Shakespeare's company, the King's Men, at both the Blackfriars and the Globe theaters. Around this time, Webster staged a tragedy entitled *The Guise*, now lost.

Webster's father died in 1614 or 1615. By this time, the playwright had at least four other children. Definite biographical information comes from 1615: On June 19, Webster paid a fee to gain membership in the Merchant Taylors' Company, perhaps so that he could become the official poet of the guild. Also in 1615, the sixth edition of *New and Choice Characters of Several Authors* appeared, containing thirty-two new character sketches believed, on stylistic evidence, to have been written by Webster. In 1617, Webster was attacked in print by a figure of no literary importance, the satiric portrait describing Webster unfavorably and calling his work "obscure."

His last independent play, *The Devil's Law-Case*, was probably performed by the Queen's Men around 1620. He may have collaborated on a few other plays in the next few years, with an old acquaintance, Thomas Middleton, on *Anything for a Quiet Life* (pr. c. 1621, pb. 1662), and with William Rowley on *A Cure for a Cuckold* around 1624-1625. He assuredly collaborated with Dekker, Rowley, and John Ford on *The Late Murder in Whitechapel: Or, Keep the Widow Waking* in 1624. Later that year, Webster wrote a show for the lord mayor, a member of the Merchant Taylors' Company; it was in his dedication to this work that Webster stated he was "born free" of that company. Webster's name appears frequently in the records of the organization around 1623-1625. One other extant play is attributed to Webster, *Appius and Virginia*, of uncertain date and not published until 1654.

Webster probably died before 1634, because Heywood spoke of him in the past tense in *The Hierarchy of the Blessed Angels* (1635). The dramatist, however, may have been the John Webster whose burial was recorded on March 3, 1638, at St. James, Clerkenwell, where Dekker and Rowley were also buried.

ANALYSIS

John Webster's two greatest plays are *The White Devil* and *The Duchess of Malfi*. They have many points in common. Both are tragedies based on events that occurred in Italy in the sixteenth century. Both carry the audience into a dark and grim world in which evil characters are capable of virtually any atrocity and in which good characters are all too frequently destroyed by murderous plotters, many of whom are of their own family. Bonds of kinship and marriage are not enough to protect the innocent from the greed, jealousy, and ruthlessness of husbands, wives, and brothers. The bases of order seem in question. Church and state are both corrupt; evil seems rampant everywhere.

Webster's characters are memorable, particularly the women. Webster creates tragic heroines, Vittoria and the Duchess, women whose lives and deaths make them capable of drawing the admiration and sympathies of author and audience. The three major villains—Brachiano, the Cardinal, and Duke Ferdinand, men of rank in church and state—are creatures of immense selfishness whose will is law. What they desire they must have, even if innocents have to die. Both plays contain melancholics, Flamineo in *The White Devil* and Daniel de Bosola in *The Duchess of Malfi*, and much of Webster's sarcasm appears in their speeches. Both of them are poor, having been scholars who could find no preferment except by joining the service of cruel noblemen. Their low birth and poverty doom them to serve as tools to be used in the iniquity of others. Flamineo takes some pleasure in the villainies he commits, but Bosola is pained by the tortures he is forced to inflict.

THE WHITE DEVIL

The opening word in *The White Devil* catches attention immediately: "Banish'd!" The speaker is Count Lodovico, who is being banished for his many crimes, including several murders. He indicates the lack of moral value in his diseased world by calling his killings flea bites. He reveals more about his world by naming the gods that rule it: reward and punishment at court.

The evil master whom Flamineo serves is the Duke of Brachiano, who has been smitten by the great beauty of Vittoria, Flamineo's sister. Flamineo has no qualms about pandering to his own sister; her allure can help him to advance in Brachiano's service. Early in *The White Devil*, Brachiano meets secretly with Vittoria, whom he desires as a mistress. Vittoria indicates her willingness to become his lover, but unfortunately she sees two problems: his wife and her husband. Without ever saying so directly, she indicates that Brachiano should kill both of them. She tells him of a dream in which she was attacked by both of their spouses. Her situation was desperate until a limb from a yew tree fell and crushed both of her attackers. She has let Brachiano know that he is the "you" who must kill to get her. Flamineo, eavesdropping, appreciates the cunning of her invitation to murder.

In staging his plays, Webster greatly favored the device of the dumb show. The deaths of both un-

wanted spouses are depicted in this way. The murder of Brachiano's wife, Isabella, who loves her husband devotedly, is silently acted out onstage as Brachiano, with the aid of a conjurer who has supplied him with a magic cap, happily watches from a distance. Isabella prepares for bed, saying her prayers and then kissing, as she always does, her husband's picture, which has been anointed with a powerful poison. She dies immediately. Brachiano continues to watch as Vittoria is freed from her unwanted husband, Camillo, in a second show provided by the conjurer. The ambitious and unscrupulous Flamineo commits the murder himself, breaking the neck of his brother-in-law but making the injury appear to be the tragic result of a fall from a vaulting horse. Webster characterizes Brachiano deftly as he praises his henchmen; they provided a good show, and he enjoyed it. Vittoria is his.

Although the death of Isabella is not immediately known, the murderers have made dangerous enemies of two potent figures in church and state. Camillo was a nephew of Cardinal Monticelso, who will become the pope before the play ends. Isabella was a Medici, sister to Francisco, the great duke of Florence, who resents Vittoria's adultery with his sister's husband. These powerful men prosecute their revenge. Vittoria is brought to trial, and Webster's training in the law creates an impressive scene. Vittoria defends herself against all charges; she is neither a whore nor a murderess. Her spirited defense and her magnificent beauty win over many of the judges but show her to be the white devil of the title, for one meaning of the term is "hypocrite" and the other, something of external beauty that is ugly within. In either case, Vittoria seems a "white devil." She is sentenced to confinement in a religious house.

After the trial, Francisco learns of his sister's murder and plans his revenge. A book exists that contains the names of criminals who would be available for a price. Francisco borrows it from its owner, Cardinal Monticelso, soon to be pope. The next step in Francisco's revenge is to make Brachiano think that he has a rival for Vittoria's love. Brachiano rages at Vittoria, who turns away from him. Afraid of losing her, he takes her away from her house of confinement and marries her. Francisco chortles: He has tricked Brachiano into the disgrace of marrying his whore. Now he will kill him. As Brachiano prepares for a tournament, his assassins put poison inside his helmet. Heat and perspiration activate the poison, which surges through him. His agony is terrible, and his murderers delight in his suffering.

The duke's death is hard for Flamineo to bear. He has risked everything for Brachiano, but the new duke, Brachiano's son, banishes Flamineo from his court. Unless Vittoria, his sister, can rescue him, Flamineo has lost everything. Vittoria will not help him because one of his victims was their own brother, Marcello. The angry dispute between the two is interrupted by the assassins. Flamineo, furious with his sister, volunteers to kill her for them, but the killers strike both together. Vittoria dies bravely, regaining the admiration of her brother. Vittoria's last words voice Webster's view of nobles and their corrupt courts: Those who have never seen a court and have never known a nobleman are truly fortunate.

THE DUCHESS OF MALFI

The Duchess of Malfi is favored above the earlier play by many. The second play does have flaws, but its language is superb, its characterization rich, its themes immensely significant, and its story, from Italian history, well chosen to give Webster frequent opportunity to display his talent for creating horror.

At the court of the Duchess Giovanna of Malfi, five truly interesting characters appear, three of them villains. The coldest of them is the older brother of the Duchess, the Cardinal. The younger brother, Duke Ferdinand, is fiery. Again, Webster shows evil and corruption in the great positions that control power in the state and the church. The third figure is Bosola, the tool villain, used by the other two to carry out their crimes.

The victims of these men are the Duchess herself and Antonio Bologna. At the beginning of the play, Antonio, steward to the Duchess, wins a prize for his equestrian skill. Webster has thus indicated Antonio's worth. In an age that values good horsemanship exceedingly, Antonio, though not of noble birth, has excelled. From such a man, serving as Webster's choric commentator, come the statements that begin the

characterization of the other major figures. The Cardinal employs spies and panders to do his bidding; he has even tried to bribe his way into the papal chair. The Duke is like a spider, using the law like a cobweb to entrap his victims. The Duchess, however, is far different from her brothers; she is a gracious lady. As for Bosola, he is too melancholic, but Antonio has sympathy for him, believing that he has been used badly by the brothers and that he will be used by them again.

The situations that create the later crises begin with the brothers instructing their recently widowed sister not to remarry. Although the Duchess promises to obey their wishes, she immediately calls Antonio to her, and in a very affecting scene she tells him that she recognizes his great worth and wishes him to be her new husband. For the Duchess—as for Webster the iconoclast—there are measures of a person's worth other than birth or titles. They wed immediately in a ceremony that is binding because it occurs in the presence of a witness, her maid Cariola. The Duchess obviously demands to live her own life; for that, many readers admire her. She is acting in a very willful way, however, creating a situation of great danger for all present in the chamber and for any children born from this union; for that, many readers believe that she is at fault.

Her dangers are real and immediate because her brothers hire Bosola to stay at Malfi and spy on her. The Cardinal chooses Bosola, but he persuades Duke Ferdinand to do the actual hiring because the Cardinal does not want his involvement to be known by anyone else. The Cardinal is the Machiavellian villain in the play, preferring to let others do his evil work for him. The scene between Duke Ferdinand and Bosola is remarkably rich. When Duke Ferdinand suddenly offers gold coins to Bosola, he refuses them. Bosola knows that a nobleman would not come to him and offer riches without expecting much in return, and there are some things Bosola is not willing to do for money. Bosola is a villain with a conscience and a soul. Therefore, Duke Ferdinand announces nonchalantly that he has also secured a position for Bosola. Perhaps Bosola has not heard the news yet— Bosola is to be the master of the horse at the castle of

Malfi. Again, the value placed by the age on the horseman is emphasized; the honor just paid to Bosola is, as Bosola fully knows, an incredibly great one. For a nobleman to single out a poor man such as Bosola and gain for him a prestigious court position shocks Bosola. He cannot turn down such a benefactor, but he does not hesitate to give vent to his anguish:

> I would have you curse yourself now, that your bounty
> (Which makes men truly noble) e'er should make me
> A villain.

The next few scenes cover several years. The Duchess has had children. Bosola thinks her foolish and lustful, but he never considers the possibility that Antonio, a man far below the Duchess in rank, could be her husband; the only possibility that occurs to him is that Antonio is the bawd to the Duchess. When he learns that Antonio and the Duchess are actually married, he is amazed to realize that a man may succeed by virtue alone. His virtue will not save either of them now.

The Duchess's death scene, one of the superbly crafted scenes of English drama, constantly shows Webster's theatricality. By this time, the Duchess believes that Antonio and the children, who had stayed with him, are dead. Life is almost more than she can bear. As the scene opens, hideous noises come from outside her chamber; her brother tries to increase her torments by bringing madmen to scream and howl within her hearing. Ironically, this helps her retain her sanity. It is silence that she cannot stand because it gives her time to think and remember the depth of her loss.

The madmen are described as Webster mixes satire into even the most tragic of his scenes: One of the madmen is an English tailor who lost his mind by trying to keep up with changing fashions; another is an astrologer who predicted that the world would end on a certain day, and when it did not, he went mad from disappointment. Eight madmen enter and sing, the stage directions calling for "a dismal kind of music." The macabre stage business continues with their dance, "with music answerable thereunto," performed right in front of the suffering woman.

Bosola enters. His shame prevents him from coming to her without disguise; he appears as an old man, telling her, "Thou art a box of wormseed, at best but a salvatory of green mummy." The Duchess speaks of her rank; Bosola says that he knows she is a woman of high authority because her hair has turned gray many years before it should have. She proudly insists: "I am Duchess of Malfi still!" The response comes quickly: "Glories, like glowworms, afar off shine bright, But, looked to near, have neither heat nor light." Bosola knows the Duchess is shortly to die; Ferdinand will have it so. The unexpected element in the scene is that Bosola is concerned that she face death without pride in her position, for her title will not go with her in her passing. Her soul is Bosola's concern. The Duchess learns the lesson. As her assassins approach, she asks only for time to kneel:

> Yet stay. Heaven gates are not so highly arched
> As princes' palaces; they that enter there
> Must go upon their knees.

Earlier in the play, when the Duchess was tricked into believing her loved ones to have been murdered, she wished to die. Bosola would not let her die in despair. Now he relieves her soul of its burden of pride. She faces death not as a great Italian lady but as a simple mortal being. Never has she shown more nobleness than in her final moments.

The scene is not yet ended. Duke Ferdinand enters to see his murderers' handiwork. The Duchess's children have been killed also, but their deaths are of no interest to him: "The death/ Of young wolves is never to be pitied." It is his sister's body that holds his gaze: "Cover her face! Mine eyes dazzle; she died young." Then, to Bosola's consternation, Duke Ferdinand turns against him; the duke will give him no reward for his service. Bosola protests, but Duke Ferdinand cannot be brought to reason. He speaks of wolves digging up the grave; his sanity is going. Bosola has participated in Duke Ferdinand's atrocities for nothing; he has served a madman.

Commentary on this scene is important. Only here do readers learn that Duke Ferdinand and the Duchess are twins. Realization of their physical closeness reminds readers of earlier lines in which he spoke of her body and of the fury that erupted from him on Bosola's first report that she had a lover. Duke Ferdinand's incestuous desires for his sister explain many of his earlier actions.

The frequent references to wolves and howling in this and earlier scenes build to a grotesque consequence in act 5. Duke Ferdinand becomes a lycanthrope. He is found coming from a graveyard with a dead man's leg. The man whose cruelties seemed beastly has become a beast.

Many scholars object that the fifth act is anticlimactic because the Duchess plays no part in it. Bosola, however, has been as important a character as Giovanna, and his role continues to develop. He discovers that the Cardinal has been involved in the death of his sister, and he witnesses the Cardinal murder his mistress, having her swear her loyalty to him by kissing a Bible, which he has poisoned. As is true for Isabella in *The White Devil*, the woman literally kisses death. Bosola resolves that this churchman must die. He wounds him but is kept from killing him by the entrance of the mad Duke Ferdinand, who kills the Cardinal himself, just before Bosola kills him. There is symmetry and poetic justice at the end, as Duke Ferdinand turns on and slays the one who has manipulated him and then is slain in turn by Bosola, the one he has used, abused, and then fatally wounded. Bosola lives long enough to see the brothers die.

The ways in which his characters face death reveal much about Webster's moral views. The evil characters are not certain what will happen to their souls. Vittoria compares her soul to a ship on a stormy sea, driven she knows not where. Flamineo's end comes wrapped in mist. The Cardinal wishes to be buried and then forgotten. Duke Ferdinand's madness continues also to the very end; then he recognizes that what he has done to his sister is the cause of his own destruction. Bosola, like Vittoria, is about to make a voyage; like Flamineo, he finds a mist before his eyes. Bosola, however, has tried to atone; he can accept death. The dignity of the Duchess when facing death contrasts vividly with all the others. Webster still views life in terms of good and evil, sin and redemption, damnation and salvation. For the Duchess,

thanks to Bosola, death merely brings her to her home.

A human touch appears in the Duchess's concern for her children. She knows she must die shortly, but she asks her maid Cariola to be sure to give her "little boy/ Some syrup for his cold" and have the little girl say her prayers before she sleeps. A small flaw in the play involves one of her children. Webster has mentioned a son by her previous marriage, but then he is forgotten. The existence of this heir makes Duke Ferdinand's statement that he hoped to gain a great fortune by his sister's death implausible.

The echo scene in *The Duchess of Malfi* is famous. Shortly before his death, Antonio walks near an old fortification. He wonders about his wife: "Shall I never see her more?" The echo catches his words and mournfully returns: "*Never see her more.*" Within moments Antonio will be dead, killed in the darkness by accident.

Webster's language is often magnificent. His prose in the satiric passages of his melancholics is caustic and brutal. The slow cadences of his poetry create passages of great beauty, even though sometimes touched with morbidity, as in the scenes of the Duchess's torture and death. In those scenes, the relationship between Bosola and the Duchess is most memorable. He admires his victim, her greatness shows through her pain, and he must not let her despair. When she wishes to curse the heavens, Bosola responds with the famous "Look you, the stars shine still." His message is that even though she is a great duchess, her curses will have no effect on the stars. Duchesses, in their mortality, are slight things when compared with the order of the heavens.

Webster is greatly concerned with order. In the very opening lines of *The Duchess of Malfi*, Antonio, again serving as a chorus, speaks for Webster in lines praising the order being brought to France by the young French king. At the end of both of Webster's tragedies, with evil having been destroyed, young heirs to the power of Brachiano and Malfi appear to symbolize the hope for a better world. In Malfi, the Duchess's eldest son by Antonio is brought in by Delio, one of the few righteous characters in the play, so that he may be established in his mother's authority. In the other play, Brachiano's son, Giovanni, succeeds his father. His first act is to banish Flamineo from his presence, his next to capture four of the assassins, including Lodovico, and send them to prison, threatening punishment for all who have participated in the murders in his court. The courts have been purged, at a heavy price to be sure, but purged nevertheless. Just as Webster saw a new order coming in France, the reader may see a new order dawning at Fortress Brachiano and at the castle of Malfi.

BIBLIOGRAPHY

Aughterson, Kate. *Webster: The Tragedies.* New York: Palgrave, 2001. An analysis of the tragic works of Webster. Bibliography and index.

Cervo, Nathan A. "Webster's *The White Devil.*" *The Explicator* 57, no. 2 (Winter, 1999): 73-75. Cervo examines Webster's *The White Devil,* focusing on Brachiano's reference to Saint Anthony's fire.

Goldberg, Dena. *Between Worlds: A Study of the Plays of John Webster.* Waterloo, Ontario, Canada: Wilfrid Laurier University Press, 1987. Webster, born into the Elizabethan world, spoke frequently of its institutions and laws. That world was crumbling during the early years of Webster's maturity. The second world is that of revolutionary fervor in the 1640's; Webster, dead before 1640, is a pre-revolutionary. He is an iconoclast, but he sees potential for a new order.

Oakes, Elizabeth. "The Duchess of Malfi as a Tragedy of Identity." *Studies in Philology* 96, no. 1 (Winter, 1999): 51-67. This essay examines the Duchess of Malfi's behavior as a widow, placing it within the context of the society in which she lived.

Ranald, Margaret Loftus. *John Webster.* Boston: Twayne, 1989. This brief, general, and quite readable overview of Webster's life and work contains basic information about dating, sources, and texts. Critical sections are distinguished by the absence of esoteric argument. Lengthy annotated bibliography.

Waage, Frederick O. *"The White Devil" Discover'd: Backgrounds and Foregrounds in Webster's Tragedy.* New York: Peter Lang, 1984. Extremely close readings of the play (the foreground) follow the action carefully. Knowledge of historical events and contemporary publications (the background) contribute to interpretation.

Wymer, Rowland. *Webster and Ford.* New York: St. Martin's Press, 1995. Wymer compare and contrasts the works of English dramatists John Ford and Webster. Bibliography and index.

Howard L. Ford

FRANK WEDEKIND

Born: Hanover, Kingdom of Hanover (now in Germany); July 24, 1864
Died: Munich, Germany; March 9, 1918

PRINCIPAL DRAMA

Der Schnellmaler, pb. 1889, pr. 1916
Frühlings Erwachen, pb. 1891, pr. 1906 (*Spring Awakening*, 1909)
Der Erdgeist, pb. 1895, pr. 1898 (*Earth Spirit*, 1914)
Der Kammersänger, pr., pb. 1899 (*The Tenor*, 1946)
Die junge Welt, pb. 1900, pr. 1908
Der Marquis von Keith, pr., pb. 1901 (*The Marquis of Keith*, 1955)
Die Büchse der Pandora, pr., pb. 1904 (*Pandora's Box*, 1918)
Hidalla: Oder, Karl Hetmann der Zwergriese, pb. 1904, pr. 1905
Tod und Teufel, pb. 1905, pr. 1912 (revision of his play *Totentanz*; *Death and Devil*, 1952)
Musik, pr., pb. 1908
Die Zensur, pb. 1908, pr. 1909

Oaha, pb. 1908, pr. 1911

König Nicolo: Oder, So ist das Leben, pb. 1911, pr. 1919 (*Such Is Life*, 1929)

Schloss Wetterstein, pb. 1912, pr. 1917 (*Wetterstein Castle*, 1952)

Franziska, pr., pb. 1912, revised pr. 1914 (verse play; English translation, 1998)

Simson, pr., pb. 1914

Bismarck, pb. 1916, pr. 1926

Herakles, pb. 1917, pr. 1919

Die Kaiserin von Neufundland, pb. 1924 (ballet scenario)

Five Tragedies of Sex, pb. 1952

The Lulu Plays, pb. 1967

OTHER LITERARY FORMS

In addition to giving public readings of his own and of Henrik Ibsen's works, Frank Wedekind wrote poetry, fiction, and essays defending his ideas on sexuality and morality. Working as a journalist, as an advertising agent, and in various secretarial capacities, he contributed to many literary as well as nonliterary genres. His *Lautenlieder* of 1920 includes traditional ballads, many of which he sang in cabarets, along with other songs and verses. His views on education are included in *Mine-Haha: Oder, Über die körperliche Erziehung der jungen Mädchen*, published in 1903. His novellas, the most notable of which is *Feuerwerk* (1906), are colorful stylistically yet economic in their use of background material; they illustrate the tautness that came to characterize his style in general.

ACHIEVEMENTS

Frank Wedekind was in many ways a forerunner of modern drama, in terms of both dramatic style of presentation and "revolutionary" content. He consequently had to fight censorship as well as lack of understanding on the part of the audience.

Although Wedekind's œuvre is indebted to naturalism, which was the reigning literary movement when he started writing, his own style turned away from the meticulous mimesis of naturalist description and psychology. Most of his characters are not true-to-life human beings; their features are often dis-

torted and their behavior patterns exaggerated to the point that they appear to be marionettes rather than real people. They are representatives of ideas or types. This is why psychological criteria fail in the attempt to understand them and why they often speak in a stilted manner.

As a dramatist, Wedekind paved the way for expressionism, which practiced a similar antimimetic style of literary presentation, although its philosophical views were more comprehensive than those of Wedekind. Both Wedekind and German expressionism (which established itself around 1910) were hostile to modern industrial civilization. Although Wedekind's criticism focused primarily on the role of women and sexuality in modern middle-class society, expressionism went far beyond those issues, painting a grim picture of commercialism (only a minor theme in Wedekind's plays), modern technology, and war. Nevertheless, expressionist dramatists such as Georg Kaiser and Carl Sternheim learned much from Wedekind, as did a younger playwright whose international reputation was firmly established only after World War II: Bertolt Brecht. One dramaturgical device of Wedekind that Brecht adapted to his own intentions is the use of songs that are integrated into the text of the play.

Wedekind's fight for a more liberated attitude vis-à-vis eros and sexuality was a courageous one; it helped to initiate the long process of challenging and ultimately changing a repressive morality. Today, after the "sexual revolution," Wedekind's message seems to have lost its sting and its urgency. Its provocative flavor is gone. Still, even though it has become dated, Wedekind's work remains an important document of the cultural development of late nineteenth century and early twentieth century Germany.

BIOGRAPHY

Benjamin Franklin Wedekind was born on July 24, 1864, in Hanover. His father, a physician, had been one of the German liberals who, in 1848, fought for a democratic Germany and for constitutional reform. Disillusioned after the failure of the liberal cause, he emigrated to the United States, where he practiced medicine in San Francisco and Oakland, California.

It was during a visit of the Wedekinds to Hanover in 1864 that Frank Wedekind was born as the second son of Dr. Friedrich Wilhelm and Emilie Wedekind. Frank's father never returned to the United States. As his liberalism could not be reconciled with the repressive and reactionary political climate in Germany, he decided to settle in Switzerland.

During the 1870's, Frank Wedekind, through an intensive correspondence with his aunt Olga Plümacher, became acquainted with the pessimistic philosophy of Eduard von Hartmann (1842-1906) and the writings of Romantics Nikolaus Lenau and Heinrich Heine as well as with the works of the German dramatists Christian Dietrich Grabbe and Georg Büchner.

After having attended high school in Aarau, Switzerland, Wedekind went to Munich, where—according to his father's wishes—he was to prepare himself at the university for the career of a lawyer. In the Munich literary circles, Wedekind encountered the theories of naturalism as the German followers of Émile Zola propagated them. Wedekind, however, never approved of or felt at ease with the pseudoscientific methods of this literary school, which demanded of the writer a faithful reproduction of observed reality in a "realistic" mode. He did share, though, the naturalists' outrage against social injustice.

After a violent argument with his father, Wedekind had to find a way to support himself and found work as chief of the advertising bureau of the Swiss manufacturer of bouillon cubes, Maggi, in Zurich. Half a year later, he ended his brief involvement with the business world in order to try his luck as a freelance writer for the *Neue Zürcher Zeitung*. In Zurich, he also made the acquaintance of Gerhart Hauptmann, the leading German naturalist playwright. Hauptmann's example once more convinced Wedekind that his own credo and aspirations were not at all in line with the reigning literary viewpoints.

In the fall of 1888, Wedekind's father died. His inheritance gave Wedekind temporary financial security. After a brief stay in Berlin, he went back to Munich in 1891, having been forced to leave Berlin because his claim of American citizenship could not be substantiated and was not recognized by the authorities. He wrote a number of plays but failed to gain any recognition as a writer. Disenchanted, he left for Paris late in 1891. There he discovered his fascination with the world of the circus and befriended clowns and other circus personnel. After an eight-month visit to England, Wedekind, who had by now used up his inheritance money, returned to Paris, where he made the acquaintance of Lou Andreas-Salomé (Friedrich Nietzsche's and Rainer Maria Rilke's friend) and of August Strindberg. The friendship between the two playwrights proved to be short-lived, however, ending after less than half a year. Having worked as the personal secretary of Willi Gretor, an art forger, Wedekind returned to Berlin in 1895, hoping in vain to get his plays performed on a German stage.

In the summer of 1895, Wedekind was offered the job of senior editor of what was to become Germany's leading satiric magazine, *Simplizissimus*. Wedekind accepted the position and became one of the major contributors to the magazine. His texts, which often ridiculed the German establishment, including the kaiser, finally provoked a lawsuit for libel, brought against him by the German government. In 1899, he was sentenced to six months imprisonment.

In the meantime, his plays *Spring Awakening* and *Earth Spirit* had been performed in Leipzig and Munich with Wedekind himself as a member of the cast. Beginning in 1901, Wedekind also performed in a Munich cabaret theater with the group Die elf Scharfrichter (The Eleven Hangmen), singing grotesque ballads.

The year 1902 marked the beginning of Wedekind's lasting fame. Max Reinhardt, who was to become an internationally acclaimed producer and director, produced *Earth Spirit* at a Berlin theater. This was Wedekind's breakthrough. From then on, his plays were performed all over Germany, and he became the most controversial playwright of his time. Conservatives labeled his writings obscene and claimed that they were weakening and undermining the morality of the German nation. Many of Wedekind's plays were consequently banned from the stage, and the censors demanded that certain "dangerous" passages be stricken from the text of those plays that could still be staged. Until his death in 1918, Wedekind was relentlessly hounded by a reactionary press (which had support in high government circles) and denounced as an undesirable and morally depraved individual because he dared to criticize the moral values of middle-class society.

ANALYSIS

In many of his plays, Frank Wedekind championed a new, liberated attitude toward humankind's instincts and drives, especially in the sphere of sexuality. He attempted in his own way what Sigmund Freud achieved in a more detached scientific manner: to lift sexual taboos and to integrate sexuality into a modern enlightened image of humanity, to interpret it as a positive life force. In his mission to tear down repressive and outdated moral standards for the sake of a new morality that would do more justice to the role of women in society, Wedekind was supported by many of the great liberal writers and critics, such as Alfred Kerr, Karl Kraus, and Thomas Mann. In Wedekind's later works, however, there is an increasingly stronger undercurrent of skepticism. The nagging doubt arises whether "life" in its untamed and "raw" instinctual power and beauty (as it manifests itself in sexuality) would really guarantee a happier form of existence than that shaped by civilization.

SPRING AWAKENING

This liberated attitude is unmistakably present in *Spring Awakening*, which established his fame and is still considered by many critics to be his finest play. Its major characters are youths of high school age in late nineteenth century Germany. They are the innocent victims of adults (parents and teachers) who impose a meaningless system of "higher learning" on them. Their young minds are crammed with factual knowledge that has little, if anything, to do with the real world. So harsh is the discipline in school and so heavy the pressure to achieve and succeed that failure to be promoted to a higher grade often results in the suicide of the unfortunate student who failed. A case in point is Moritz Stiefel, who shoots himself because his teachers refuse to promote him.

Far worse than this excessively rigorous and disciplinarian system is the failure of the adult world to help the adolescents cope with the emotional bewilderment caused by the first stirrings of awakening sexuality. Sex in this society is taboo: One does not talk about it, and it is evil. Stifled by this outdated moral code, the youngsters are forced to fall back on a confusing and tantalizing conglomerate of half-truths, falsehoods, and the fabrications of overheated imaginations in their desperate efforts to explain "the facts of life." In one instance, middle-class puritanism coupled with timid bashfulness destroys the life of a young girl, Wendla Bergmann. When Wendla asks her mother about conception, she receives the answer that in order to have children one must love the man to whom one is married "as much as one can love a man." Wendla becomes pregnant by a young fellow student, Melchior Gabor. To her, her first love and pregnancy are totally natural and emotionally uplifting experiences, a viewpoint that is shattered when her parents force her into an abortion from which she dies.

Melchior, who has—through his reading and observation of animal behavior—gained some unbiased and undistorted knowledge about human sexuality, writes a treatise "On Cohabitation," which is found among the belongings of the deceased Moritz Stiefel. The writing of this pamphlet is interpreted by Melchior's teachers as an act of utter depravity and an assault on the established moral code, and the unfortunate author is expelled from school without being granted a chance to defend himself.

In a grotesque and surrealistic scene at the graveyard, the dead Moritz Stiefel appears carrying his head under his arm. As an emissary from the realm of death, he tries to lure Melchior away from life. Another mysterious emissary appears, however, a gentleman whose face is covered by a mask and who appeals to Melchior's desire to live. The masked gentleman prevails; Melchior will not take his own life.

The adult characters in the play are almost without exception reduced to absurd caricatures who lack any love or understanding of their children. The satiric portrayal of the authoritarian parents and teachers reveals that Wedekind is taking sides, that his play is intended as a bitter indictment of a generation of unfeeling citizens whose "respectability" and "morality" vilify the beauty and dignity of sexuality. The need to expose and criticize engenders a style that, by means of distortion and exaggeration, goes far beyond the tenets of naturalism or realism. On the other hand, the need to present an exact and sympathetic image of the victims (the children) calls for a style still akin to realism. The fact that the portrayal of the children contains comic elements (intended by the author) does not diminish their positive status as pitiful victims. In the graveyard scene, which is neither satiric nor realistic, a third (and, once again, nonrealistic) mode of presentation can be observed: the grotesque. Combining in a unique way the features of comedy, satire, tragedy, and the grotesque, *Spring Awakening* does not fit the naturalistic mold typical of late nineteenth century literature in Germany.

EARTH SPIRIT

In *Earth Spirit* and its sequel, *Pandora's Box*, Wedekind's fight against traditional morality takes on the form of an antagonism between society and a mysterious force that threatens the moral code from a position outside the social structure. The central character of both plays is Lulu, a young woman of obscure origin who is rescued from misery by Dr. Schön, a wealthy newspaper publisher. Lulu turns out to be a creature of instinct, blissfully ignorant of any moral taboos, a product of nature untamed by civilization and its mechanisms of sublimation. Whenever she becomes involved with "respectable" members of bourgeois society, Lulu causes disaster. Her animal innocence and her totally amoral way of entering and breaking relationships with male members of middle- and upper-middle-class society clash violently with established values. Virtues such as honesty and faithfulness mean nothing to her. She is the "archwoman" (*das Urweib*), a nymphlike creature whose presence spells scandal and death. While enjoying the power she has over men, she feels happiest when her behavior provokes her male companions to beat her. Paradoxically, physical punishment enhances her self-esteem and adds to her triumph over the bourgeois world. She personifies undomesticated female eros.

Her quasi-mythical role elevates her above the social status of a whore. Rather than a negotiable "commodity," she is a menace to those who want to protect their social respectability. Wedekind invented the figure of Lulu in order to deal a blow to the puritanism and the smug self-complacency on which that "respectability" is based. Confronted with the pure and original force of eros, civilization reveals not only its "dissatisfaction" (as Freud later taught) but also its loss of vitality, primeval happiness, untamed instinctual gratification, psychic health, and emotional freedom.

Lulu's first husband, Dr. Goll, becomes her first victim when he surprises her in the arms of the painter Schwarz. Her only comment about Goll's subsequent suicide is: "He left me in the lurch." Dr. Schön, who himself feels threatened by Lulu's erotic spell, marries her off to Schwarz. When Schwarz learns through Dr. Schön that Lulu's past does not measure up to accepted moral standards, he, too, takes his own life. The prompt suicides of Goll and Schwarz tragicomically reveal the power of the established moral code. Lulu's next victim is Dr. Schön, who totally succumbs to her eroticism and is forced by her to write a letter to his fiancée in which he is to inform her that he will break the engagement.

In a tragicomic scene at the end of *Earth Spirit*, Dr. Schön, in utter despair, tries to persuade Lulu to kill herself while several other suitors are hiding in the same room. When their presence is revealed in a moment of turmoil and confusion, Lulu, panic-stricken, points the revolver given to her by Dr. Schön toward him and kills him.

PANDORA'S BOX

The ending of *Earth Spirit* represents both the climax of Lulu's power over society and the beginning of her downfall. In *Pandora's Box*, she in turn becomes the victim, the hunted creature. Her power and her mythic, demoniac inspiration decline. Her mysterious strength as an opponent of civilization vanishes. Lulu, who serves a prison term for the murder of Dr. Schön, manages to escape to Paris with the help of Countess Geschwitz, a lesbian who is in love with her. By this time, Lulu has lost her independence, since anybody who knows about her escape can threaten to report her to the police. The marquis of Cast-Piani, a procurer, wants to sell her to a high-class bordello in Egypt, a proposition that Lulu finds utterly insulting. In order to escape all the scheming and manipulation surrounding her, she flees with Dr. Schön's son Alwa, the Countess Geschwitz, and old Schigolch, a beggarlike father figure, to London, where she is forced to live in abject poverty in a Soho attic. Lack of financial resources brings further humiliation on her: She must sell her body as a prostitute and is finally murdered by Jack the Ripper, the infamous London murderer. Thus one social outcast becomes the victim of another, who indirectly represents society striking back at the creature who dared to provoke it.

The tragic meaning of the two plays lies in the incompatibility of nature, in the guise of precivilized eros, and civilized society. Here, Wedekind's viewpoint is a pessimistic one. Since the time seems not yet ripe for sexual and other moral reforms, the collision of untamed eros and society leads to death. Both Lulu, the provoker, and the provoked become the victims of this collision.

THE TENOR

The fate of the performing artist and the relationship of art (in the broadest sense) and life constitute the central theme of Wedekind's *The Tenor*. The singer Gerardo personifies the artist whose life is totally absorbed by his professional (or "contractual," as Gerardo likes to point out) obligations. The performing of roles leaves no room for a private life. Gerardo has pledged to remain unmarried and is also forbidden by contract to travel in the company of women. His own view of his life is a very sober, almost cynical one: Art is nothing but a luxury article for the use of the bourgeoisie. Gerardo does not experience his extremely tight schedule, which accounts for every minute and second of his life, as a burden, and he willingly submits to it in order to satisfy the public and to live up to his own fame.

While preparing to catch a train to Brussels, where his next performance will take place (he uses the time before his departure to rehearse a part in his hotel room), three intruders disturb him. First, a sixteen-year-old English girl brings him a bunch of roses and begs for his love. Gerardo, after having spoken some fatherly words to her, calms her down and ushers her out, presenting her with an autographed photograph of himself. Next enters Professor Dühring, an old composer who has devoted his entire life to writing an opera that, as he insists, he must now play for the famous singer at the piano. While Dühring's agitated performance makes the singer doubt whether the work really deserves to be staged and published, Dühring expresses his own lofty philosophy of art, which is completely at odds with Gerardo's disillusioned and cynical one. Told by the singer that contractual obligations will not allow him to intercede on the composer's behalf, the disappointed Dühring finally leaves.

Finally, Helene Marowa, a beautiful married woman, storms in, demanding Gerardo's love. Helene must be his or she will kill herself. Like the English teenager, she confuses the roles played by the singer with the almost nonexistent private person. When Gerardo insists that he must sacrifice all his time to his career, Helene shoots herself. For a few moments, Gerardo is confused. He seems ready to break his contract and miss his next performance because Helene's death constitutes, as he puts it, an act of a "force majeure" that overrides contractual obligations. In the end, however, he slips back into the role of the total artist who ruthlessly brushes any private concerns aside. As no policeman can be found and since there is still time to catch his train, he abruptly abandons the dying Helene and stumbles out of his room. Fame in the world of the performing arts must be bought at the price of isolation from "normal" life. This is the message of the singer Gerardo, a caricature rather than a realistic portrait of the artist as prisoner of his calling.

THE MARQUIS OF KEITH

Although the artist Gerardo is part of society and yet at the same time isolated from it, the main character in *The Marquis of Keith* presents the struggle of another outsider for material wealth, social recognition, and *Lebensgenuss* (enjoyment of the pleasures of life). Keith, the son of a village schoolmaster and a gypsy, has lead a restless life, wandering all over the earth. Now, in the year 1899, he has come to Munich pretending to be the "Marquis of Keith," firmly determined to become part of Munich high society and to acquire material wealth. Keith is portrayed as the archcharlatan, a man of willpower and determination, sly, witty, without moral scruples, utterly self-centered. His never failing self-confidence carries him to the brink of success. He proposes to build a gigantic entertainment hall and manages to win the financial backing of some of Munich's wealthiest entrepreneurs. His manipulations include fraud: Keith forges the signature of the city's richest financier, Consul Casimir, on a congratulatory telegram that arrives at a party thrown by Keith for the investors of the project. When his associates find out that Keith keeps no records of his shady financial dealings and that his contribution to the project has been intellectual (it was his idea) and not financial, they promptly cut him out. Keith is given ten thousand marks and told to leave the city immediately. For a brief moment, he considers suicide as a way out of his failure, but very quickly his love of life and his indestructible determination to chase Lady Luck once more win out. He will take the money, accept the fact that life has its ups and downs, and leave the city.

As a counterpoint to Keith, Wedekind designed the character of Ernst Scholz. Both Keith and Scholz feel excluded from society, but for radically different reasons. While Keith is of common origin and poor, Scholz comes from an extremely wealthy aristocratic family. He deliberately changes his name in order to gain access to the life of the middle class. Plagued by a paranoid, overly sensitive conscience that tells him that he has not yet "earned" his right to exist, he desperately wants to become "a useful member of society." As a supervisor in the administration of a railway company, he was responsible (not through negligence but through bad judgment) for an accident that cost twenty people their lives, and this incident never ceases to haunt him. In his desperate attempt to become an accepted human being (he once states that he considers himself to stand "outside the human race"), the moralist Scholz selects his old friend Keith, the immoralist, to be his teacher. In a most paradoxical move, he decides to adopt a hedonistic, sensual lifestyle, which he will endure as a self-imposed

penitence in order to prepare himself for a morally acceptable middle-class life. When he realizes that his efforts have failed, he chooses a clinic for the mentally ill as his last refuge. Keith refuses Scholz's invitation to join him there.

It has often been pointed out that there are autobiographical elements in both Keith and Scholz. Wedekind himself might have wrestled with conflicting forces within his own personality: the adventurer, the man who coveted a respectable place in his society, versus the would-be reformer and moralist. Such autobiographical references have only limited validity, since both Keith and Scholz are not naturalistic imitations of real individuals but "constructions" in the sense that they embody extreme types of behavior such as would never be found in real life. Most of the minor characters, especially the two women closely attached to Keith, are also "types": the petty bourgeois Molly who adores Keith and acts like his slave and who ends up drowning herself because she cannot cope with Keith's ambitious charades, and Anna, the countess of Werdenfels (a counterpoint to Molly), who proves to be even more ambitious and calculating than Keith. She leaves him for Consul Casimir as soon as Keith's downfall becomes inevitable. In the end, bourgeois society prevails over the outsider, whether he is a morally questionable charlatan or an eccentric moralist.

DEATH AND DEVIL

Wedekind's play *Death and Devil* again takes up the theme of radical moral reform, focusing especially on the role of women in society and on the meaning of sensual pleasure. Elfriede von Malchus, a member of the "International Association for the Fight against Procurers," appears at a bordello run by the Marquis of Casti-Piani in order to rescue a young girl she knows and to express her moral outrage to the marquis. Her scorn abruptly turns into admiration and even love (a typically Wedekindian psychological tour de force) once the marquis presents his moral philosophy to her. He accuses the bourgeoisie of having turned prostitution into a disreputable trade. To give sensual pleasure is—in his view—an inalienable and natural gift that women possess. Consequently, they ought to take pride in selling their erotic "commodities" to the highest bidder. Those middle-class women who secretly break their marriage vows in order to fulfill their sexual desires (without taking money for their favors) are really degrading prostitution, which ought to be the celebration of sensuality. Therefore, argues Casti-Piani, the bourgeois institution of marriage should be abolished. As a procurer, he believes that there is only one thing in life immune to suffering and bitterness: the sanctity of sensuality.

When both Elfriede and Casti-Piani overhear the disillusioned and bitter account that the young prostitute Lisiska (the girl whom Elfriede is trying to rescue) gives of her experiences, their views and ideas on womanhood, sensuality, and prostitution are shattered. Lisiska, who confesses that she is driven by an insatiable lust for sensual gratification, tells her customer that the sexual drive is "hellish," that it will never be satiated, that lust torments the senses without ever yielding lasting pleasure. If life is in essence suffering, prostitution offers no relief. On the contrary: Prostitution means endless martyrdom.

As is so often the case in Wedekind's plays, the female characters (in this play both Elfriede and Lisiska) beg their male partners to beat them. This reveals both the presence of masochistic leanings as part of the female personality structure and the lack of respect for women on the part of a society that "breeds" women to be subservient to men, to play the role of "dogs" rather than "tigers." Casti-Piani, who (like Wedekind) calls himself a "moralist," now knows only one way out of his painful life: suicide. Elfriede, on the other hand, wants to assume the martyrdom of the life of a prostitute. This is the bizarre method through which she, a virgin with a strong intellect but weak sensual desire, hopes to find fulfillment in life.

The unquestioned belief in eros as a life force and a potential source of happiness, as expressed in many of Wedekind's earlier plays, now appears to have been eroded and undermined. Does Wedekind's new morality offer any positive values at all?

DIE ZENSUR

The answer given in *Die Zensur*, one of Wedekind's last plays, remains ambivalent. This is the playwright's most "confessional" play. The writer Buri-

dan lives with the beautiful young singer/dancer Kadidja and strives in vain toward a philosophy and a form of existence that reconcile the world of the senses and the instincts, of sexuality and beauty, with the lofty world of the spirit, of moral values, and, ultimately, the world of reason as it is revealed through God. Kadidja represents only one of these two dimensions: the sensual, instinctual one. Buridan, who has indulged too much in the pleasures offered him by Kadidja (a Lulu-figure without Lulu's demoniac features), has lost his *Genussfähigkeit*, the ability to enjoy sensual experiences. He now longs for spiritual satisfaction. Unless (and until) the balance of the two "worlds" mentioned above is restored, Buridan will not regain his sensibility and receptiveness in matters concerning the senses, and accordingly he pleads with Kadidja to leave him for two weeks.

In the midst of Buridan's animated argument with the girl, there appears Dr. Prantl, a priest who is the secretary to the father confessor of the emperor. Dr. Prantl is one of the censors who helped ban Buridan's play *Pandora*, and although Buridan requested Dr. Prantl's help in legalizing his relationship with Kadidja by means of marriage, the two gentlemen soon find themselves discussing the merits or shortcomings of Buridan's works. Dr. Prantl lashes out at Buridan, calling him a *Menschenverächter* (a misanthrope) and accusing him of deriving a cynical pleasure from the presentation of human suffering onstage. Buidan counters by giving a highly emotional and solemn account of his credo as a writer. He claims to write about the eternal laws of life and the necessary consequences of human interactions. Although this must include the presentation of suffering, it is also true that his plays celebrate the joys of human existence. Combining his defense with a proud proclamation of his artistic goals, he takes up once again the matter of his quest for a reconciliation of the senses and the spirit. Interpreting his artistic mission as an attempt toward the reunification of the sacred and the beautiful, he even sees this quest as a longing for religious fulfillment. Buridan, author of a play entitled *Pandora*, seems clearly to be an autobiographical character who articulates Wedekind's defense of his own plays.

As is often the case in Wedekind's later works, the seriousness with which certain positions and values are professed is undermined by a skeptical attitude. The song about the weather vane that Kadidja sings emphasizes the transitoriness of love and sensual pleasure. Furthermore, the idea of establishing a special bordello "as an institute for moral education," where young people are to be oversatiated with instinctual gratification so that they will long for the "pleasures" of toil and suffering, borders on the absurd. On one hand, Buridan (Wedekind) acknowledges that the arts have the special privilege to present erotic situations that in "real life" would violate the established moral code. (This is shown by the parable of the tightrope dancer who may take off her clothes with impunity while she is dancing. The moment she steps down from the rope, she must conceal her body in a coat.) On the other hand, Buridan, having been too long under the spell of Kadidja, now resolutely turns away from aesthetic sensuality and desires "bad taste," "unfathomable souls," and "ugliness." Those represent the somewhat perverted and therefore questionable "spiritual" antidotes to an excessive cult of eroticism and beauty. At the end of the play, Kadidja commits suicide (not without tragicomic overtones) because Buridan insists on her departure. Sensual pleasure is thus revealed as the wrong prescription to cure human suffering. Its happy marriage to lofty spirituality remains at best a utopian dream.

OTHER MAJOR WORKS

LONG FICTION: *Mine-Haha: Oder, Über die körperliche Erziehung der jungen Mädchen*, 1903.

SHORT FICTION: *Feuerwerk*, 1906.

POETRY: *Die vier Jahreszeiten*, 1905; *Lautenlieder*, 1920; *Ich habe meine Tante geschlachtet*, 1967.

NONFICTION: *Schauspielkunst*, 1910.

MISCELLANEOUS: *Die Fürstin Russalka*, 1897; *Prosa, Dramen, Verse*, 1960-1964 (2 volumes).

BIBLIOGRAPHY

Boa, Elizabeth. *The Sexual Circus: Wedekind's Theatre of Subversion*. New York: B. Blackwell, 1987. An analysis of Wedekind's works that focuses on his portrayal of sexuality. Bibliography and index.

Chick, Edson. *Dances of Death: Wedekind, Brecht, Dürrenmatt, and the Satiric Tradition*. Columbia, S.C.: Camden House, 1984. Chick examines the use of satire by the German dramatists Wedekind, Bertolt Brecht, and Friedrich Dürrenmatt. Bibliography and index.

Izenberg, Gerald N. *Modernism and Masculinity: Mann, Wedekind, Kandinsky Through World War I*. Chicago: University of Chicago Press, 2000. Izenberg looks at Modernism and masculinity in the pre-World War I works of Wedekind, Thomas Mann, and Wassily Kandinsky. Bibliography and index.

Jones, Robert A., and Leroy R. Shaw, comps. *Frank Wedekind: A Bibliographic Handbook*. 2 vols. New Providence, R.I.: K. G. Saur, 1996. A bilingual bibliography on the playwright. Includes indexes.

Lewis, Ward B. *The Ironic Dissident: Frank Wedekind in the View of His Critics*. Columbia, S.C.: Camden House, 1997. Lewis analyzes Wedekind's dramatic works, focusing on the comments of critics over the years. Bibliography and index.

Skrine, Peter N. *Hauptmann, Wedekind, and Schnitzler*. New York: St. Martin's Press, 1989. Skrine provides criticism and interpretation of the modern German dramatists Wedekind, Gerhart Hauptmann, and Arthur Schnitzler. Bibliography and index.

Christoph Eykman

PETER WEISS

Born: Nowawes, near Berlin, Germany; November
8, 1916
Died: Stockholm, Sweden; May 10, 1982

PRINCIPAL DRAMA

Der Turrm, pr. 1949 (radio play), pb. 1963, pr.
1967 (staged; *The Tower*, 1966)

Die Versicherung, wr. 1952, pr. 1966, pb. 1967

Nacht mit Gästen, pr., pb. 1963 (*Night with Guests*,
1969)

*Die Verfolgung und Ermordung Jean Paul Marats,
dargestellt durch die Schauspielgruppe des
Hospizes zu Charenton unter der Anleitung des
Herrn de Sade*, pr., pb. 1964 (*The Persecution
and Assassination of Jean-Paul Marat as
Performed by the Inmates of the Asylum of
Charenton Under the Direction of the Marquis
de Sade*, 1965, better known as *Marat/Sade*)

Die Ermittlung, pr., pb. 1965 (*The Investigation*,
1966)

Gesang vom lusitanischen Popanz, pr., pb. 1967
(*Song of the Lusitanian Bogey*, 1970)

*Wie dem Herrn Mockingpott das Leiden
ausgetrieben wird*, pr., pb. 1968 (*How Mister
Mockingpott Was Cured of His Suffering*,
1971)

*Diskurs über die Vorgeschichte und den Verlauf des
lang andauernden Befreiungskrieges in Viet
Nam als Beispiel für die Notwendigkeit des
bewaffneten Kampfes der Unterdrückten gegen
ihre Unterdrücker sowie über die Versuche der
Vereinigten Staaten von Amerika die
Grundlagen der Revolution zu vernichten*, pr.,
pb. 1968 (better known as *Viet Nam Diskurs*;
*Discourse of the Progress of the Prolonged War
of Liberation in Viet Nam and the Events
Leading Up to It as Illustration of the Necessity
for Armed Resistance Against Oppression and
on the Attempts of the United States of America
to Destroy the Foundations of Revolution*, 1970,
better known as *Vietnam Discourse*)

Dramen in zwei Bänden, pb. 1968 (2 volumes)

Trotski im Exil, pr., pb. 1970 (*Trotsky in Exile*,
1972)

Hölderlin, pr., pb. 1971

Der neue Prozess, pr. 1982, pb. 1984 (adaptation of
Franz Kafka's novel *Der Prozess*; *The New
Trial*, 2001)

OTHER LITERARY FORMS

Peter Weiss wrote essays and experimental novels
as well as drama. He gained recognition as a novelist
in 1960 with *Der Schatten des Körpers des Kutschers*
(1960; *The Shadow of the Coachman's Body*, 1969).
Much of his nondramatic prose is semiautobiographical, including the novels *Abschied von den
Eltern* (1961; *The Leavetaking*, 1966) and *Fluchtpunkt* (1962; *Vanishing Point*, 1966). The three-
volume *Die Ästhetik des Widerstands* (1975-1981),
completed the year before Weiss's death, is often
considered to be Weiss's *Bildungsroman*, because it
presents his aesthetic and political philosophies.

ACHIEVEMENTS

Simply because of the tendentious nature of most
of what he wrote, Peter Weiss will always remain
a controversial figure in the history of German letters. Although hailed by some in the 1960's as a second Bertolt Brecht, he was seen by others as essentially derivative and as an offensively blatant
disseminator of Marxist propaganda. Value judgments aside, however, it must be acknowledged that
Weiss was an inventive playwright, except, perhaps in
his documentary pieces. He burst onto the German
dramatic scene with the premiere of *Marat/Sade* in
West Berlin's Schiller Theater on April 29, 1964, and
the play was, overall, enthusiastically received. It remained popular for several years and was even filmed
in 1967.

Weiss's subsequent documentary phase, which
mirrored explicitly his "final conversion" to Marxist
theory and socialist systems (announced by Weiss in
Swedish and German newspapers in 1965), drew less
and less critical attention as his works grew more stri-

dent. Although many had sensed in *Marat/Sade* a dramatist who would take his genre in new directions, these hopes were soon dampened by Weiss's docudramas, which seemed simply patterned after the sociopolitical avant-grade theater of the 1920's and 1930's. Weiss was nevertheless very popular in Eastern Bloc countries, at least until he revised somewhat his political opinions as a result of the Soviet intervention in Czechoslovakia. With *Hölderlin*, Weiss returned to a more creative concept of drama, but he devoted the decade from 1970 to 1980 almost exclusively to epic concerns. *The New Trial*, a dramatization of Franz Kafka's novel *Der Prozess* (1925; *The Trial*, 1937), premiered in Stockholm a few weeks before Weiss's death. Weiss received numerous literary awards, among which were the Lessing Prize in 1965 and the Heinrich Mann Prize in 1966.

BIOGRAPHY

Peter Ulrich Weiss was born on November 8, 1916, in Nowawes, near Berlin, the son of a Swiss mother and a Czechoslovak father. Weiss's Jewish fa-

Peter Weiss in 1966. (AP/Wide World Photos)

ther had converted to Christianity, so Weiss was reared as a Lutheran, attending school in Nowawes and Berlin. In 1934, the rise to power of National Socialism forced the Weiss family to emigrate to Great Britain, where Weiss studied photography. Two years later, Weiss returned to the Continent to study at Prague's Academy of Art, but because he was intensely unhappy there, he moved to Switzerland in 1938. In 1939, he finally settled in Sweden, where he met and married Gunilla Palmstierna, an artist who designed the costumes for his plays. In Stockholm, Weiss began to shift his attention away from painting. After producing a series of documentary and surrealistic short films—as well as one feature-length work entitled *The Mirage* (1959)—Weiss began, in the late 1950's, to concentrate his energies on writing. A meeting with his boyhood guru, Hermann Hesse, in Montagnola was most encouraging to the young writer, and other acknowledged influences on the early Weiss were Kafka, Alfred Kubin, and the Surrealists. Primary among the specifically dramatic influences were August Strindberg, Bertolt Brecht, and Samuel Beckett.

Weiss's early dramatic efforts met with only scant success and were not accepted in German theaters until after the success of *Marat/Sade*, when Weiss was already in his late forties. Although he eventually became a Swedish citizen, Weiss continued to write in German until his death in Stockholm, in May of 1982.

ANALYSIS

Peter Weiss once said that every written word is a political statement, and he always insisted on being regarded as a "political" writer. In defining exactly what this meant, Weiss was fond of quoting the expressionist Ernst Toller, who wrote that "the basic prerequisite of the political writer is to feel responsible for himself and every one of his brethren in the human community." Throughout his career as a writer, this sense of commitment and engagement remained a constant for Weiss. Obvious in all but his earliest writings is an involvement with political and social events, a collective concern expressed in the confrontation of ideological prototypes, of oppressors versus oppressed, of good against evil, of statement and dialectically modifying counterstatement. Manifest in Weiss's literary art is not only this political sensitivity but also an aesthetic one, a clear feeling for the means of communication, for the visual and graphic possibilities of a creative and forceful employment of words. The problem with such didactic political writing, however, is that it is easier to write interesting dramatic fare about individual conflicts than about the issues underlying political and economic world events. A related pitfall is that didactic writing can easily degenerate into dogmatic preaching that fails to allow its audience the freedom to arrive at an autonomous decision regarding the matter at hand. This charge has often been leveled against Weiss's documentary dramatic pieces.

EARLY PLAYS

Although not his first effort, *Marat/Sade* was Weiss's stage breakthrough, the piece that vaulted him to immediate international fame. Its three dramatic predecessors have never become popular and remain relatively unknown. *The Tower* was written in 1948 but was not staged until 1967. The work is a heavily symbolic psychological allegory about an escape artist who longs for but fears freedom. *Die Versicherung*, written in 1952 and produced in 1966, but not produced in Germany until 1969, is a surrealistic critique of bourgeois customs and standards. *Night with Guests*, staged in the Berlin Schiller Theater in 1963, is another one-act allegory based on the interplay of light and darkness. The play's gruesome fairy-tale atmosphere is reminiscent of the Brothers Grimm, and the use of doggerel underscores this impression. The characters in the play act in a rigid, stylized manner, even as they murder one another with rhythmic exclamations.

MARAT/SADE

It was in this same theater, one year later, however, that Weiss's *Marat/Sade* was performed. Not the least imposing aspect of this work is its full title: *The Persecution and Assassination of Jean-Paul Marat as Performed by the Inmates of the Asylum of Charenton Under the Direction of the Marquis de Sade*. Although not intended to be a historical or factual documentary, this two-act, baroquely titled work

is indeed a play about historical events and their twentieth century implications.

The historical setting for the play is the insane asylum at Charenton, France, on July 13, 1808. In essence, the drama is a play-within-a-play, as the historical director of the Charenton Asylum, M. Coulmier, did in fact frequently allow his inmates to perform plays for therapeutic reasons. Beyond this, he even invited the dignitaries of Parisian society to view these performances for their entertainment. The play-within-a-play is a work under the direction of the Marquis de Sade, who actually was an inmate at Charenton. This fictional play (which the historical marquis did not write) dramatizes the bathtub murder of Jean-Paul Marat, whose assassination had taken place some fifteen years earlier.

The plot of Sade's play deals with the murder of Marat by Charlotte Corday, a young woman who was greatly disturbed by the heavy toll of bloodshed that the French Revolution was exacting under the left-wing rule of the Jacobins. By killing Marat, she attempted to put a stop to the bloodshed. The real meat of the play, however, is not as much the murder of Marat as it is the latter's ideological confrontation with the Marquis de Sade, who uses the play to stage an imaginary debate about the Revolution with an imaginary Marat. The debate is witnessed by M. Coulmier and his family, who are sitting on an elevated dais and who are the inner play's audience. As such, they possess an affinity to the outer play's audience—those in the theater itself, who are, by implication, asked to judge the winner of the Marat-Sade debate.

The philosophical-political confrontation of the two men is a clash of polar opposites, of radical social commitment and collective anarchism (Marat) versus extreme individualism, disillusionment with reality, and the desire to be left alone with private illusions (Sade). The two debate the nature of life and death, of justice and revolution, with Marat emerging as a precursor of Marx, and Sade as a pre-Freudian who is convinced that humankind is inherently selfish and incapable of establishing a society based on equality. A third position is espoused by Charlotte Corday and her Girondist lover, Duperret, who share the goals of Marat but who reject his methods. They idealistically desire freedom and equality but find bloodshed intolerable.

In the end, however, all positions seem to be canceled out because the play terminates in a most ambiguous manner. The asylum inmates surge forward in a violent outbreak, shouting senselessly as one of them screams, "When will you learn to take sides?" As the curtain falls, the marquis laughs cynically at the entire scene. Weiss does not take sides with this ending. The viewer is left with three positions, all of which have exponents in the play: the Marat thesis, which insists that violence is necessarily part of lasting social change because the empowered will never willingly divest themselves for the sake of the powerless; the Sade contention, which states that revolution and political violence simply serve as an outlet for base and dangerous human impulses, and that humankind is incapable of attaining the chimera of the classless society; and the third position, which acknowledges the human weakness described in the Sade thesis and therefore advocates the goals of Marat without violent means.

The diffidence and indecision suggested by the ending to *Marat/Sade* sparked much discussion and, in socialist countries especially, brought Weiss a good measure of criticism. To this point Weiss had been unable to espouse wholeheartedly a variety of political systems. In the year following the premiere of *Marat/Sade*, however, Weiss committed himself publicly to a political ideology and concern with the fate of the underprivileged, which his play associated with Marat. After several visits to the German Democratic Republic, Weiss published his *Arbeitspunkte eines Autors in der geteilten Welt* (1965), a polemic against capitalism, ideological neutrality, and detachment and in favor of socialism. It is therefore Marat and not Sade who was to have the last laugh, and Weiss's work was soon to register the effect of his decision.

THE INVESTIGATION

The premiere of *The Investigation* was held on October 19, 1965, simultaneously in some twenty theaters through Europe and, as this fact would imply, it had a tremendous impact. Erwin Piscator wrote

in *Die Zeit* of the occasion that it was "a serious attempt to restore to the theater within a larger, supraregional framework its position as a moral institution."

The Investigation, subtitled "an oratorio in eleven cantos," deals with the theme of the Auschwitz concentration camp and its absolute horror. The play also reflects pointedly Weiss's newfound Marxist perspective because, as Weiss stated, "it deals with the role of German big industry in exterminating the Jews; I want to brand capitalism, which benefited from the experiments of the gas chambers." The material of the drama is, except for a few lines of the text, taken directly from testimony in the 1964 Frankfurt trial of former Auschwitz SS men. Each of the work's eleven cantos possesses three parts, and the formal link to Dante's *La divina commedia* (c. 1320; *The Divine Comedy*, 1802) is unmistakable. The titles of the cantos mirror the unrelieved degradation and inhumanity that the play examines: "The Loading Ramp," "The Camp," "The Swing," "The Possibility of Survival," "The End of Lili Tofler," "S.S. Corporal Stark," "The Black Wall," "Phenol," "The Bunker Block," "Cyclone B," and "The Fire Ovens."

It has been estimated that four million human beings were murdered in the Auschwitz concentration camp between 1941 and 1945, and the absolute, incomprehensibly stupendous horror of this fact is beyond communication in words. For this reason, perhaps, Weiss consciously underdramatizes in *The Investigation*, making no attempt to shape his material dramatically. The material of the play is presented in the fashion of documentary theater. The dialogue is lifted from the actual testimony of the accused and the accusers in the Frankfurt trial. These accounts of Auschwitz procedures—the gas chambers, cremations, starvations, and wanton cruelties—create a terrifying picture, and a devastating indictment gradually forms. It forms, however, in an unemotional manner, reflecting the numbing of the senses, the dulling of human impulses that invaded the lives of both perpetrators and victims at Auschwitz. The defendants on trial in this play are not presented entirely unsympathetically. They were, they contend, only doing their duty, and they had little choice but to obey orders. The question implicitly raised, therefore, is whether they, like those who suffered and died, were not also victims of an ideological system.

Although it had powerful and worldwide reverberations, *The Investigation* was also criticized. The play's rapid repetition, some critics contended, inundated and blunted the receptive ability of its audience. Too much horror, especially if dispassionately presented, ceases, after a time, to horrify. Whom, therefore, would the play convince? Still others felt that *The Investigation* was a powerful enough statement, but they noted that it added nothing aesthetically to its genre or to the literature of the Holocaust. A reviewer in the *Times Literary Supplement* of April 24, 1969, stated that "*The Investigation* virtually wrote itself," and another critic in the *New York Review of Books* of November 3, 1966, acidly remarked that "If one were to want the transcript of the Frankfurt trials he would better be sent to the publication of them in book form . . . than to a rapid selection offered in a theater."

SONG OF THE LUSITANIAN BOGEY

Criticism notwithstanding, both *Marat/Sade* and *The Investigation* were, by any definition, provocative and successful productions. It was at this point in Weiss's dramatic career, however, that his shift to a Marxist and radically committed notion of literature (as an instrument of socialist education and as a catalyst to societal change) began to impinge somewhat on this success. Weiss's next dramatic offering was a piece of agitprop called *Song of the Lusitanian Bogey*. This "political musical" in two acts is an indictment of the Portuguese colonial system in Angola and Mozambique from the time of the first Portuguese explorers until the Africans' abortive revolt in March of 1961. Highlighted is the contrast between the wealth of the white imperialists and the parasitic European and American firms, and the destitution and humiliation of the Africans.

VIETNAM DISCOURSE

Another work with a similar concept is Weiss's *Vietnam Discourse*, whose full title is even longer than that of *Marat/Sade*; it is *Discourse of the Progress of the Prolonged War of Liberation in Viet Nam and the Events Leading Up to It as Illustration of the Necessity for Armed Resistance Against Oppression and on the Attempts of the United States of America to Destroy the Foundations of Revolution*. This two-part documentary traces eleven stages in the historical development of Vietnam, beginning with 500 B.C.E. and continuing on through the French and U.S. presences in the country.

HOW MISTER MOCKINGPOTT WAS CURED OF HIS SUFFERING

The publication of *Vietnam Discourse* coincided with the stage production of another piece by Weiss, a "drama for a clown" entitled *How Mister Mockingpott Was Cured of His Suffering*. The work differs from the above mentioned political dramas because it was written earlier, in 1963. It is, as its subtitle suggests, an admixture of slapstick and Kafka. Mr. Mockingpott is imprisoned without reason, released into a world stood on its head, and confronted by absurdity on every side. The play concludes with its Chaplinesque protagonist railing against God, who is portrayed as a cigar-smoking, indifferent businessman.

TROTSKY IN EXILE

Trotsky in Exile, however, published in 1970, is another example of Weiss's "theater of commitment." The drama is based on historical documents, and although it is in Weiss's words "a play about socialism for socialists," it is decidedly anti-Soviet in its depiction of Leon Trotsky's exile and later assassination. The essential conflict of the play is between international socialism as envisioned by Trotsky, and the nationalistic, brutal Communism practiced by Joseph Stalin. This standpoint opened the author to censure from socialist colleagues in the Soviet Union and its ideological satellites, but it was indicative both of independent thinking on the part of Weiss and of his sincerity as a Socialist. The work also prefigured Weiss's next—and last—major dramatic work, *Hölderlin*, which, like *Trotsky in Exile*, was revisionist in eschewing one-sided dogmatics.

HÖLDERLIN

The underlying central idea of Weiss's *Hölderlin* was a new conception of the mad poet, namely as a revolutionary and direct precursor to Karl Marx. Just as *Trotsky in Exile* is a depiction of a political writer and man of action, so *Hölderlin* is a drama—almost a melodrama—of a creative writer who is socially committed. This presentation of Friedrich Hölderlin traces his progression to madness not as a personal problem but rather as the consequence of adhering to political convictions even if doing so means increasing isolation, self-imposed exile, and apparent insanity. The protagonist here is not the traditional Hölderlin of German letters, usually categorized as a fragile individual whose artistic visions and hopeless illusions finally pushed him over the brink. This Hölderlin is a revolutionary aesthetically and politically, and his enemies are his contemporaneous intellectual peers (Johann Wolfgang von Goethe and Friedrich Schiller), who refuse to dedicate themselves to the practical reification of a "humanity," preferring instead simply to preach to people in their writing.

In the face of this artistic and political estrangement, *Hölderlin*'s eight scenes depict, in a language that in diction and orthography is patterned after the speech of the late eighteenth century, the protagonist's deepening frustrations, the onslaught of hypersensitivity, and the retreat to a final and symbolic enclosure, the tower. Encircled by confusion and isolation, only the young Karl Marx is able, in the play's dramatic final scene, to reach the now pathetic figure. Learning of Marx and seeing in him something of himself, Hölderlin attempts to shed his self-imposed paralysis and to act, to work for the revolution. He does so in vain, however, because he is by now incapable of throwing off the shackles of his catatonic self-imprisonment.

Soon after its Stuttgart premiere in 1971, *Hölderlin* became a stage success in both the East and the West, but it also came under heavy attack (especially in the West) for being historically inaccurate on several counts. This criticism may well explain why Weiss decided to abandon the dramatic genre and to spend the 1970's working on his three-volume *Die Ästhetik des Widerstands*, a kind of fictive autobiography that functions both as monomaniac self-analysis and as essayistic confrontation with contemporary social and political phenomena. The first volume appeared in 1975, the last in 1981.

OTHER MAJOR WORKS

LONG FICTION: *Der Schatten des Körpers des Kutschers*, 1960 (*The Shadow of the Coachman's Body*, 1969); *Abschied von den Eltern*, 1961 (*The Leavetaking*, 1966); *Fluchtpunkt*, 1962 (*Vanishing Point*, 1966); *Das Gespräch der drei Gehenden*, 1963 (*The Conversation of the Three Wayfarers*, 1970); *Die Ästhetik des Widerstands*, 1975-1981 (3 volumes).

NONFICTION: *Arbeitspunkte eines Autors in der geteilten Welt*, 1965; *Rapporte*, 1968-1971 (2 volumes); *Notizen zum kulturellen Leben der Demokratischen Republik Vietnam*, 1968 (*Notes on the Cultural Life of the Democratic Republic of Vietnam*, 1970); *Notizbücher, 1971-1980*, 1981; *Notizbücher, 1960-1971*, 1982.

BIBLIOGRAPHY

Cohen, Robert. *Understanding Peter Weiss*. Columbia: University of South Carolina Press, 1993. Cohen presents the life and analyzes the work of Weiss. Bibliography and index.

Ellis, Roger. *Peter Weiss in Exile: A Critical Study of His Works*. Theater and Dramatic Studies 37. Ann Arbor, Mich.: UMI Research Press, 1987. Ellis examines the political and social views of Weiss and how they manifested themselves in his work. Bibliography and index.

Herman, Jost, and Marc Silverman, eds. *Rethinking Peter Weiss*. New York: Peter Lang, 2000. The essays in this work are revised versions of lectures presented in November, 1998, at the University of Wisconsin. Bibliography.

Vance, Kathleen A. *The Theme of Alienation in the Prose of Peter Weiss*. Las Vegas: Peter Lang, 1981. Vance provides a critical analysis of Weiss's works, focusing on the theme of alienation. Bibliography.

Nicholas J. Meyerhofer

FAY WELDON

Born: Alvechurch, Worcestershire, England;
   September 22, 1931

PRINCIPAL DRAMA

   Permanance, pr. 1969, pb. 1970
   Time Hurries On, pb. 1972
   Words of Advice, pr., pb. 1974
   Friends, pr. 1975
   Moving House, pr. 1976
   Mr. Director, pr. 1978, pb. 1984
   Action Replay, pr. 1979, pb. 1980 (also pb. as *Love
      Among the Women*)
   After the Prize, pr. 1981 (also pr. as *Woodworm*)
   I Love My Love, pr. 1981, pb. 1984
   Tess of the D'Urbervilles, pr. 1992 (adaptation of
      Thomas Hardy's novel)
   The Four Alice Bakers, pr. 1999
   The Reading Group, pb. 1999, pr. 2001

OTHER LITERARY FORMS

   Fay Weldon is a prolific writer, best known for her
numerous novels, which focus on the same issues as
her drama—the lives and communities of women, the
politics of marriage, and the ways that sexual politics
affect relationships between women. Her novels are
popular both in Britain and the United States and
have been translated into many languages. Besides
her fiction for adult readers, she has published several
children's books.

   Weldon has also written television and radio plays
including original work, episodes of series, and adaptations of existing works such as Jane Austen's *Pride
and Prejudice* (1813). In addition, she has published
nonfiction books including ones on writers Jane
Austen and Rebecca West and essays on writing.

ACHIEVEMENTS

   Fay Weldon's drama is notable for its humorous
treatment of women's issues. Her subject matter echoes feminist concerns since the mid-1960's, and
Weldon's humor encourages the audience to be receptive to her messages.

   Weldon's awards include a 1973 Writers Guild
Award, the Giles Cooper Award for best radio play
for *Polaris* in 1978, nomination for the Booker
McConnell Prize in 1979, the Society of Authors
Traveling Scholarship in 1981, and the *Los Angeles
Times* Award for fiction in 1990.

BIOGRAPHY

   The reported facts of Fay Weldon's biography vary
among sources, apparently depending on Weldon's
motive in providing the information. Her life story
echoes a theme of her fiction—the power of and extent to which women can re-create themselves as a
form of control over their lives. Despite the uncer-
tainties, most sources agree on a few facts about
Weldon's life.

   Fay Weldon was born in 1931 in the village of
Alvechurch in Worcestershire, England, and was
named Franklin Birkinshaw, a name apparently selected by her mother based on numerology. The family moved to New Zealand while Weldon was young,
and her parents divorced when she was five years old.
Weldon has claimed that living in New Zealand allowed her to experience a less class-conscious society
than England's, an experience that has influenced her
thinking and her writing. Because of her parents' divorce, she grew up surrounded by women: Her
mother, grandmother, and sister made up the rest of
the household. Weldon has said that she was around
men so little until she went to college that she did not
realize that most of the world was not run by women.
The focus on communities of women is clear in her
drama. Weldon grew up in a family of writers. Her
mother wrote fiction under the pen name Pearl
Bellairs; her grandfather wrote articles for *Vanity
Fair* and published adventure novels. She was a vora-
cious reader from childhood.

   Weldon moved to London with her mother when
she was a teenager. After high school, she attended
St. Andrews University in Scotland, where she claims
she was admitted and allowed to study economics
only because the administration thought she was a

Fay Weldon (© Miriam Berkley)

man because of her name. After graduation, she returned to London where she held various writing jobs, married briefly, and gave birth to a son. Whether the son was born before or during the marriage is uncertain based on various biographical accounts. Weldon's experience as a single mother supporting herself and her child through low-paying jobs influenced her politics and her later writing.

In the early 1960's, she married Ronald Weldon, with whom she had three sons. After working as an advertising copywriter, she began publishing plays and novels in the mid-1960's. Weldon separated from Ronald Weldon in the late 1970's; he died during their divorce proceedings, and Weldon married Nicholas Fox in the 1990's.

ANALYSIS

Fay Weldon's drama is notable more for its political content than for formal innovations. Her plays focus on women characters and their lives. They are feminist in that they explore issues that concern women and the ways that women communicate with other women and with men; however, despite raising awareness of women's problems, they do not suggest major political change and, in fact, usually affirm the status quo. For example, one of Weldon's major themes is the sexual politics of marriage, yet she repeatedly reaffirms that institution, ending her plays with marriage or with couples reunited after solving their problems. So while Weldon's work contains feminist content, it is not politically radical.

Weldon's drama contains humorous situations and dialogue, which make the plays enjoyable and the content palatable to a wide audience. Her characters speak in realistic, non-stylized language. Many plays contain scenes in which the dialogue or action concerns the ability of the characters to communicate; the words themselves become subject matter for the plays. The plays do not require elaborate sets, allowing the attention to focus on the interactions between the characters.

PERMANANCE

Permanance was Weldon's contribution to a series of short plays by various playwrights performed and published together under the title *Mixed Doubles: An Entertainment on Marriage*. Weldon was the only female playwright of the nine who wrote for the production, simultaneously pointing to the barriers to women's success as playwrights and to the mainstream quality of Weldon's work in that her play does not stand out politically in the middle of a production written mainly by male playwrights.

The sequence begins with a play about a bride and groom and ends with one about an elderly couple contemplating headstones in a cemetary; Weldon's play, in the middle, presents a forty-year-old man and woman vacationing for the first time without their only child. The transition to the next stage of life offers an opportunity to explore what middle age means for men and women and what the sexes want from marriage.

Throughout the play, the characters sit in a tent. The tent, which they have vacationed in together for many years, serves as a symbol for their marriage thus far. The couple's ability to communicate is a crucial theme. Although the husband seems cold at first, not wanting to stop reading to have a conversation and being unsympathetic about his wife's wasp sting and broken glasses, by the end he is the one who affirms the importance of the marriage. At the end of the play, he suggests a villa in Italy for their next vacation; their marriage will change to meet the needs of both.

ACTION REPLAY

Action Replay borrows a technique from sportscasting—the replay. However, as the scenes are replayed, lines are changed and the outcomes differ in the various versions. In one scene, the characters discuss whether what happens to them is fate or the result of turns their conversations take. The play, overall, sides with the notion that language forms reality.

The play's time range, from 1952 to 1977, shows the changed roles of women during that period. At the beginning, the three young women sharing an apartment fit three stereotypes available to women of the early 1950's—one is a whore, one is a plain woman interested in domestic matters and seeking marriage, and one is a beautiful woman who is more interested in a man's money than in domesticity.

By the end, all have been married at least once and are roommates again. Weldon deploys stereotypes of women current in the late 1970's to contrast the earlier versions of these characters. The former whore has developed an interest in mysticism, the domestic woman has become a lesbian, and the beautiful woman has changed the least. In the final scene, she is with the same man as in the opening scene of the play, again deciding whether to invite him into her apartment or not. Minimal scenery is indicated for the play, focusing the attention on the characters and on their language.

I LOVE MY LOVE

I Love My Love explores the politics of marriage, a common theme of Weldon's drama. In its presentation of spouse swapping, it raises the issues of what makes men and and women happy with their marriages as well as the effect that being with a certain partner has on the behavior of each member of a couple. The play also examines the effect of the media on marriage and sexual politics. The two couples begin with very different views of marriage: Mark and Cat have an open marriage, while Derek and Anne have a traditionally monogamous one. Their daily activities contrast as well: Cat models for her husband's advertising work while Anne cooks, cleans, and cares for farm animals. The couples are paid to swap partners so that a journalist from the magazine *Femina* can write a story on them. While the questioning of values caused by the media spotlight causes each couple temporary confusion, the new ideas the couples encounter ultimately benefit them. By the end of the play, all four main characters have seen advantages in the opposing marriage styles. When the women return to their husbands, the behaviors of the two couples are much more similar than they were before. By concluding with the return of the wives to their husbands in an affirmation of marriage, the play follows the formula of traditional comedy. As in much of Weldon's work, the message has feminist leanings but is strongly tempered by conventional elements.

THE READING GROUP

The Reading Group was written for a drama contest for plays about women's lives. The committee rejected it because it contained male characters. Weldon explains in the introduction to the published script that the men could easily be written out of the play. The main action of the play takes place at a women-only reading group (book discussion club). The discussion of novelistic heroines by the characters not only offers a way to delve into the characters' personalities but also opens a discussion of whether literature reflects on life or is an escape from it. The play focuses on the need women have for community with other women and the ease with which women communicate when men are not present. However, although the male characters could be kept offstage, they cannot be forgotten. Even when the female characters are in an all-woman group, their thoughts and conversation center on men and, especially, on marriage.

On one hand, the play presents a positive view of the community of women in that the women openly discuss their lives and concerns even though they have not met before. They see an all-women group as a way to do something enjoyable for themselves. On the other hand, the women cannot stop talking about men and cannot even agree on a novel they all want to read. In the play's climax, it is revealed that one woman has come to the group because she is trying to lure away the husband of one of the others. The play ends with the women reunited with their appropriate men; the married man tells his wife he wants to stay with her, and the unmarried couple decide to get married. Despite the play's traditional ending, the women characters reject traditional feminine roles: Oriole has resisted marrying her much younger boyfriend despite his pleas, and Avril has attempted to seduce her clients. In both cases, the women behave in ways conventionally defined as masculine.

OTHER MAJOR WORKS

LONG FICTION: *The Fat Woman's Joke*, 1967 (pb. in U.S. as . . . *And the Wife Ran Away*, 1968); *Down Among the Women*, 1971; *Female Friends*, 1974; *Remember Me*, 1976; *Words of Advice*, 1977 (pb. in England as *Little Sisters*, 1978); *Praxis*, 1978; *Puffball*, 1980; *The President's Child*, 1982; *The Life and Loves of a She-Devil*, 1983; *The Shrapnel Academy*, 1986; *The Rules of Life*, 1987; *The Heart of the Country*, 1987; *The Hearts and Lives of Men*, 1987; *Leader of the Band*, 1988; *The Cloning of Joanna May*, 1989; *Darcy's Utopia*, 1990; *Growing Rich*, 1992; *Life Force*, 1992; *Affliction*, 1993 (pb. in U.S. as *Trouble*, 1993); *Splitting*, 1995; *Worst Fears*, 1996; *Big Women*, 1997 (pb. in U.S. as *Big Girls Don't Cry*, 1997); *Rhode Island Blues*, 2000; *The Bulgari Connection*, 2001.

SHORT FICTION: *Watching Me, Watching You*, 1981; *Polaris and Other Stories*, 1985; *Moon over Minneapolis: Or, Why She Couldn't Stay*, 1991; *Angel, All Innocence and Other Stories*, 1995; *Wicked Women: A Collection of Stories*, 1997; *A Hard Time to Be a Father*, 1998.

TELEPLAYS: *Wife in a Blonde Wig*, 1966; *The Fat Woman's Tale*, 1966; *What About Me*, 1967; *Dr. De Waldon's Therapy*, 1967; *Goodnight Mrs. Dill*, 1967; *The Forty-fifth Unmarried Mother*, 1967; *Fall of the Goat*, 1967; *Ruined Houses*, 1968; *Venus Rising*, 1968; *The Three Wives of Felix Hull*, 1968; *Hippy Hippy Who Cares*, 1968; *£13083*, 1968; *The Loophole*, 1969; *Smokescreen*, 1969; *Poor Mother*, 1970; *Office Party*, 1970; *On Trial*, 1971 (in *Upstairs,*

Downstairs series); *Old Man's Hat*, 1972; *Comfortable Words*, 1973; *Desirous of Change*, 1973; *In Memoriam*, 1974; *Poor Baby*, 1975; *The Terrible Tale of Timothy Bagshott*, 1975; *Aunt Tatty*, 1975 (adaptation of Elizabeth Bowen's story); *Act of Rape*, 1977; *Married Love*, 1977 (in *Six Women* series); *Life for Christine*, 1980; *Pride and Prejudice*, 1980 (adaptation of Jane Austen's novel); *Little Miss Perkins*, 1982; *Loving Women*, 1983; *Redundant! Or, The Wife's Revenge*, 1983.

RADIO PLAYS: *Spider*, 1972; *Housebreaker*, 1973; *Mr. Fox and Mr. First*, 1974; *The Doctor's Wife*, 1975; *Polaris*, 1978; *Weekend*, 1979 (in *Just Before Midnight* series); *All the Bells of Paradise*, 1979; *I Love My Love*, 1981.

NONFICTION: *Letters to Alice on First Reading Jane Austen*, 1984; *Rebecca West*, 1985; *Sacred Cows: A Portrait of Britain, Post-Rushdie, Pre-Utopia*, 1989; *Godless in Eden*, 1999; *Auto da Fay*, 2002.

CHILDREN'S LITERATURE: *Wolf the Mechanical Dog*, 1988; *Party Puddle*, 1989; *Nobody Likes Me*, 1997.

EDITED TEXT: *New Stories Four: An Arts Council Anthology*, 1979 (with Elaine Feinstein).

BIBLIOGRAPHY

Barreca, Regina, ed. *Fay Weldon's Wicked Fictions*. Hanover, N.H.: University Press of New England, 1994. Barreca has collected essays by literary scholars and writers on various aspects of Weldon's work. Essays range from those on themes common in Weldon's work to those on aspects of individual writings. The collection as a whole gives a good sense of Weldon's place in literature as well as the connections between her work and contemporary intellectual strains. Also includes a section of essays about fiction written by Weldon.

Dowling, Finuala. *Fay Weldon's Fiction*. Madison, Wis.: Fairleigh Dickinson University Press, 1988. Although Dowling's analysis focuses on Weldon's novels, her discussion of the author's works in terms of important philosophies of the time, particularly postmodernism and feminism, is useful for understanding the drama as well. Contains a listing of Weldon's work in various genres as well as a bibliography.

Faulks, Lana. *Fay Weldon*. New York: Twayne, 1998. Faulks provides an overview of Weldon's work, written for the general reader. The analysis touches on thematic and formal aspects of the work, with examples primarily from Weldon's novels. Faulks also discusses the social context of Weldon's writing. Contains a chronology and a brief biographical section.

Haffenden, John. "Fay Weldon." In *Novelists in Interview*. London: Methuen, 1985. Weldon discusses her life and her inspirations for and attitudes toward writing. The topic discussed at the greatest length is Weldon's feminism; she explains that what she writes is feminist because she is a feminist. Contains a selected bibliography of the author's works at the time of publication.

Zylinska, Joanna. "Nature, Science, and Witchcraft: An Interview with Fay Weldon." *Critical Survey* 12, no. 3 (2000): 108-122. Weldon discusses her writing and the inspirations for it. While the interview primarily concerns Weldon's novels, her comments are helpful for understanding the themes of her drama as well.

Joan Hope

FRANZ WERFEL

Born: Prague, Bohemia, Austro-Hungarian Empire (now in Czech Republic); September 10, 1890
Died: Beverly Hills, California; August 26, 1945

PRINCIPAL DRAMA

Der Besuch aus dem Elysium, pb. 1912, pr. 1918
Die Versuchung, pb. 1913
Die Troerinnen des Euripides, pb. 1915, pr. 1916 (a free adaptation of Euripides' *The Trojan Women*)
Die Mittagsgöttin, pb. 1919, pr. 1925
Spiegelmensch, pb. 1920, pr. 1921
Bocksgesang, pb. 1921, pr. 1922 (*Goat Song*, 1926)
Schweiger, pb. 1922, pr. 1923 (English translation, 1926)
Juárez und Maximilian, pb. 1924, pr. 1925 (*Juárez and Maximilian*, 1926)
Paulus unter den Juden, pr., pb. 1926 (*Paul Among the Jews*, 1928)
Das Reich Gottes in Böhmen, pr., pb. 1930 (*The Kingdom of God in Bohemia*, 1931)
Der Weg der Verheissung, pb. 1935, pr. 1937 (*The Eternal Road*, 1936)
In einer Nacht, pr., pb. 1937

Jacobowsky und der Oberst, pr. 1944, pb. 1945 (*Jacobowsky and the Colonel*, 1944)

OTHER LITERARY FORMS

Franz Werfel's sudden and dramatic explosion into international preeminence after the publication of the novel *Das Lied von Bernadette* (1941; *The Song of Bernadette*, 1942) tended to obscure the fact that this versatile author had already established an extraordinary reputation as an expressionist poet and playwright. In fact, it might perhaps be said that, with the possible exception of the American author Robert Penn Warren, no other modern writer has so firmly established his position in all three genres: poetry, drama, and the novel.

Apparently poetry was Werfel's first love: He produced four volumes before 1919, and it was his concern with the expressionist lyric and his connection with the expressionist publication *Der jüngste Tag* (the Judgment Day) that led to his consideration of drama as a vehicle of expressionist thought. Indeed, there are many critics who hold that Werfel's primary achievement lay in his contribution to the early development of expressionist poetry. It must also be remembered that much of Werfel's drama is highly poetic; for example, in the original German, *The Eternal Road* is written in a dactylic-trochaic descending rhythm of Werfel's own invention, a rhythm that Ludwig Lewisohn successfully reproduces in the English translation.

It was, however, the novel that established him as a popular writer. His first novel, *Nicht der Mörder* (1920; *Not the Murderer*, 1937), although brief enough to be called a novella by Werfel in the subtitle, is nevertheless considered to be a novel by most critics because of its depth and complexity. In *Not the Murderer*, Werfel explores, through the relationship of the protagonist to his father, the father-son relationship as it influences all forms of authority.

Werfel's second (and first full-length) novel, *Verdi: Roman der Oper* (1924; *Verdi: A Novel of the Opera*, 1925), established him as a serious contender in that genre. This work was followed by five others: *Der Tod des Kleinbürgers* (1927; *The Man Who Conquered Death*, 1927), *Der Abituriententag: Die Geschichte einer Jugendschuld* (1928; *Class Reunion*, 1929), *Barbara: Oder, Die Frömmigkeit* (1929; *The Pure in Heart*, 1931), *Die Geschwister von Neapel* (1931; *The Pascarella Family*, 1932), and *Kleine Verhältnisse* (1931; *Poor People*, 1937).

In 1933, however, *Die vierzig Tage des Musa Dagh* (*The Forty Days of Musa Dagh*, 1934), with its combination of fast-paced action and deep philosophical idealism, established Werfel in the top ranks of twentieth century novelists, and although his next two novels, *Höret die Stimme* (1937; *Hearken unto the Voice*, 1938) and *Der veruntreute Himmel* (1939; *Embezzled Heaven*, 1940), were not quite so successful, with the publication of *The Song of Bernadette*, Werfel was catapulted into a totally unexpected fame. He had written the book because of a vow he had taken at Lourdes and had never considered the possibility of it becoming a best-seller. Two more novels, the Utopian/anti-Utopian *Stern der Ungeborenen: Ein Reiseroman* (1946; *Star of the Unborn*, 1946) and *Cella: Oder, Die Überwinder* (1954; *Cella: Or, The Survivors*, 1989), were published after his death.

Werfel was also very adept at short fiction. These shorter works can be found in several collections,

Franz Werfel in 1940. (Library of Congress)

such as *Geheimnis eines Menschen* (1927; *Saverio's Secret*, 1937) and *Erzählungen aus zwei Welten* (1948-1952; *Twilight of a World*, 1937).

In addition, Werfel wrote numerous prose tracts, such as the early essay to Kurt Hiller, *Die christliche Sendung: Ein offener Brief an Kurt Hiller* (1917). According to his own testimony, Werfel had a great many of these tracts, but in fleeing the Nazis in 1940, he lost not only most of his unpublished manuscripts but also many of his minor writings that had been published between 1910 and 1938 in periodicals and annuals in Germany, Austria, and other European countries. Consequently, when, in 1944, Werfel gathered his philosophical, religious, and political works into a volume, he had to rely on those of his writings that were available in the United States, some lectures that he had given in Germany between 1930 and 1937, and what prose he had written in the United States between 1942 and 1944. This situation also resulted in the book coming out first in English translation in 1944 under the title *Between Heaven and Earth*: It did not appear in German until after the war, in 1946, under the title *Zwischen Oben und Unten*. Also interesting from a literary standpoint in Werfel's miscellaneous writings are his translations of several of Giuseppe Verdi's operas and his editing (with Paul Stefan) of Verdi's letters.

ACHIEVEMENTS

In the judgment of many critics, Franz Werfel's achievements as a dramatist are the most significant in a career notable for its diversity. Had he done nothing else, his contributions as a leader in the expressionist drama would ensure his place in literary history. Not only were Werfel's plays successful in Europe, but they also were almost immediately transported to London and New York, where they were produced by such men as Max Reinhardt and given generally fine reviews by such publications as *The New York Times*—although Brooks Atkinson was obviously confused by both *Goat Song* and *Schweiger*, and found them to be nearly incomprehensible.

In drama, just as he had in novels, Werfel crowned his rounded career with a change to a realistic straightforward style; his last dramatic work was a comedy filled with hope and optimism, so that even if Werfel's reputation as an expressionist had not been well secured he might have secured some level of recognition through his final dramatic masterpiece, *Jacobowsky and the Colonel*.

BIOGRAPHY

Franz Werfel was born into a wealthy Jewish family of Prague, Bohemia, Austro-Hungarian Empire, on September 10, 1890. His father, the owner of a large glove factory, played the piano, collected fine paintings, and, most of all, possessed a great love for the opera—a trait that Franz was to imitate. Franz did not, however, imitate his father in the love or aptitude for business. Franz began composing poetry while still in high school and had one poem published in 1908 before he was graduated. After very brief employment with a Hamburg shipping firm and a period studying philosophy at the German University of Prague, Werfel was called to compulsory military training in 1911, the year his first book of poetry, *Der*

Weltfreund (the world's friend), was published. Partly because of the success of this first book, Werfel obtained a position in the publishing house of Kurt Wolff in Leipzig.

During this period, Werfel became friends with Willy Haas, Max Brod, Franz Kafka (who admired Werfel greatly, although he found the play *Schweiger* to be mysteriously repugnant), and Otkar Březina. Later Werfel helped organize a pacifist society with Martin Buber, Gustav Landauer, and Max Scheler.

In June, 1914, Austrian archduke Francis Ferdinand was assassinated; and in July, 1914, Werfel was called back into military service for the beginning of World War I. On his way from Leipzig to his regiment in Prague, he was injured in a railway accident and was hospitalized at Bozen for two months. While convalescing, he was sent to the front, where he observed the Austrian retreat at Jezierna, the first wave of the Russian Revolution, and the Kerensky offensive of 1917—scenes that were to influence his later work, especially *Goat Song* and *The Kingdom of God in Bohemia*.

Meanwhile, in 1915, a collection called *Einander* (to one another) had appeared, which contained some of Werfel's pacifist poems; and in 1916, *Die Troerinnen des Euripides*, Werfel's free adaptation of Euripides' *Trōiades* (415 B.C.E.; *The Trojan Women*, 1782) ran for fifty days in Berlin, followed by a very successful tour of Germany and Austria.

In August of 1917, Werfel was transferred to the war press service in Vienna, where other writers such as Peter Altenberg, Franz Blei, Hugo von Hofmannsthal, Robert Musil, and Rainer Maria Rilke were also employed. In Vienna, also, Werfel met the woman he was later to marry, Alma Mahler, widow of the composer Gustav Mahler.

The next twenty years, from 1918 to 1938, were very fulfilling ones for Werfel. Although his poems *Der Gerichtstag* (1919; Judgment Day) and *Beschwörungen* (1923) were well received, Werfel turned increasingly toward drama and the novel. He wrote a series of highly successful and critically acclaimed plays including the expressionist *Speigelmensch* (in three parts), as well as *Goat Song*, *Schweiger*, *Juárez and Maximilian*, *Paul Among the Jews*, *The King-*

dom of God in Bohemia, and *The Eternal Road*. In the same period, he published eight novels, seven of which appeared in English translation; among these were the highly successful *Verdi: A Novel of the Opera*, *Class Reunion*, and *The Forty Days of Musa Dagh*.

Meanwhile, during this period of individual success but general political unrest, Werfel toured the cities and towns of Germany to speak out against the dangers he saw in the growing specter of National Socialism and the increasing general acceptance of right-wing or left-wing political doctrines with an unthinking religious fervor. By and large, however, his arguments fell on deaf ears. Once, in the industrial town of Insterburg in East Prussia, students claimed that Werfel's contention that "humanity could not live without faith in God and without Christianity" was "a Jewish Communist trick," and he was forced to abandon the lecture hall amid "howling and booing" and with "the derisive protection of the police."

Fortunately, when Adolf Hitler annexed Austria in 1938, Werfel was in Italy. He did not return to Austria but traveled to Zurich and then to Paris, where he finished *Embezzled Heaven*, which was published in Stockholm by the émigré publishing firm of Bermann-Fischer. The book was later to be published in the United States and become a Book-of-the-Month Club selection. In Paris, Werfel suffered the first of a series of heart attacks. He moved to the fishing village of Sanary-sur-Mer, then to Marseilles, then to Lourdes.

It was at Lourdes that Werfel made the vow that if he succeeded in reaching the United States he would write the story of Bernad Soubirous (Saint Bernadette), whose vision had resulted in Lourdes becoming a shrine. His exit being made somewhat easier by the Nazis having reported him dead, Werfel managed to reach Portugal and, finally, late in 1940, the United States.

On arriving in California, Werfel immediately began working on *The Song of Bernadette*, which much to his surprise became a best-seller. It was a Book-of-the-Month Club selection, was abridged by *Reader's Digest*, and in 1943 was made into a highly success-

ful motion picture with Jennifer Jones, Linda Darnell, Charles Bickford, and Vincent Price.

In the drama also, Werfel achieved a crowning success. His last play, *Jacobowsky and the Colonel*, opened successfully in New York, won the New York Drama Critics Circle Award, was published in both the original version and the stage adaptation—both of which received wide acclaim—and appeared in a screen version in 1958 entitled *Me and the Colonel*. Werfel died on August 26, 1945, at his home in Beverly Hills, California.

ANALYSIS

Although the plays of Franz Werfel cover a wide range of subjects and styles, certain motifs and themes run throughout his works from the earliest experiments to his last realistic drama. Werfel's primary assumptions about life are as follows: The most important thing in the world is people's relationship to God, other people, and nature. Faith in God is necessary, and humanity's highest calling is to effect a mystical union with the rest of humankind, a kind of brotherhood of man, but any attempt to impose a faith or, worse yet, to impose a materialistic-realistic interpretation of life on other people, is evil. The "isms" that have frequently been substituted for religion by the modern age are, in reality, merely vast materialistic superstitions that are bound to fall. Furthermore, evil does exist in the world and in the soul of humanity; to deny the existence of this evil, or to attempt to control it through force, might unleash it. Bureaucracy, technology, orthodoxy, and methodology tend to separate people and dehumanize them; faith, love, art, drama, music, and poetry tend to bring people together. Finally, although the effort to warn one's fellow humans of the presence of evil often results in estrangement, one has an obligation to give such warnings.

When these major concerns of Werfel are considered, it can be seen that his dramas present consistent patterns of image, symbol, character, and theme. Werfel's works are marked by the bringing together of people of very divergent views and backgrounds and the clash between the ideal and the mundane, between faith and orthodoxy, and between imposed

Utopianism and the hardship of freedom. For example, in his preface to *Die Troerinnes des Euripides*, his free adaptation of Euripides' *The Trojan Women*, Werfel states: "There is an essential tragedy in the world—a break—an original sin, wherein all participate, and from which the understanding soul suffers most."

SPIEGELMENSCH

In the three-part expressionist drama *Spiegelmensch* (mirror man), almost all these themes are encountered. In this play, Thamal is turned away from an Oriental monastery. Discovering a mystical looking glass, he tries to destroy his mirror image, thinking by that method to kill the evil side of nature. He succeeds, however, only in freeing the "mirror man," who then persuades Thamal to become a leader of men.

After causing the death of his father, eloping with his best friend's bride, Ampheh, and then deserting her while she is pregnant with his child, Thamal hears of a people suffering under the rule of Anathas, the snake god. Thamal fights and defeats Anathas, who then prophesies that Thamal will rule only if he remains pure. The mirror man then declares Thamal to be a god, but Thamal is deposed and must flee.

Alone in the wilderness, Thamal again meets Ampheh, who refuses to go back to him. Ampheh's child has died, as has Thamal's best friend. In the end, Thamal judges himself guilty and takes poison. The mirror man returns to the looking glass, which becomes a window of purity, and Thamal transmigrates again to the monastery, where he is free of falsity and can embrace true values.

In this drama, the true values of friendship and love clash with the false values of Utopian idealism. The struggle against oppression leads again to oppression because of the lack of spiritual values: People's lives must be more than mere reflections of themselves.

GOAT SONG

Goat Song employs similar themes. In this play, Stevan, the leader of a village, has fathered a monster, half man and half goat, which is kept in a stone house, a secret from all but Stevan, his wife, and the doctor. Somehow, however, the creature breaks loose ("the animal in us takes possession") and ravages the countryside, bringing death and destruction. The beast is eventually captured by Juvan, the leader of a peasant revolt. The peasants worship the creature as a kind of god of violence and revolution. The beast is finally destroyed, and Juvan is led away to be hanged, but not before Stevan has been forced to acknowledge that he fathered the beast and not before he loses Mirko, his human son, to suicide. In the final scene, Mirko's beloved Stanja reveals that she is carrying within her the child of the beast.

Again in this play, although symbolic structure is very profound, one can recognize Werfel's recurring themes. The sins of the father, Stevan, are visited on his sons, Mirko and the monster. Also, Stevan's attempt to hide evil and his failure to warn others cause a greater catastrophe to be loosed on the countryside, and the peasants worship of that which is half-man-half-beast leads, finally, to the cyclic perpetuation of evil.

SCHWEIGER

In *Schweiger*, on the other hand, the symbolism of the "animal in us" (rather than being presented in a literal and physical manner such as the beast in *Goat Song*) is presented as a form of psychosis. Franz Schweiger, a man of such spiritual values that he is asked to stand for election, turns out to have been, in reality, Franz Foster, who in a fit of insanity had brutally murdered several children. Schweiger has been cured of his schizophrenic rages, but the memory of his crimes is intolerable to him; even though he later, at great risk to himself, rescues several children from a burning ship, receiving severe burns on his face and hands, he still feels alienated by guilt. He puts his faith and his hope of redemption in the love of his wife and the prospects of a child. Unfortunately, his wife, after receiving the physician's report of his criminal insanity, deserts him, and Schweiger commits suicide.

In *Schweiger*, Werfel's usual themes and patterns are again present: the need for human love, for understanding, for family ties, for permanent values. The obvious symbolism of putting one's faith for redemption in the birth of a child lets the audience see that Schweiger is a kind of Everyman of the modern world: Humans cannot achieve grace merely through understanding the inherent nature of the evil within them or by explaining this evil in psychological terms; they must receive redemption or they are doomed to self-destruction.

JUÁREZ AND MAXIMILIAN

Juárez and Maximilian is also a play of values gone awry. Maximilian is presented as a man of extraordinary nobility (but not strength) of character. In the pattern of the ancient Greek tragedy, his downfall is brought about by a sin of pride—not pride in himself, for he is presented as an unselfish idealist, but pride in a kind of Utopian idealism that is bound to backfire. His hopes of establishing a benevolent rule are thwarted by his corrupt compatriots, who not only undercut his liberal policies but who also demand the death of Juárez. Maximilian, who is willing to compromise, becomes angry when Juárez refuses to negotiate. Maximilian then signs the order calling for the death of enemies of the state and (like Oedipus when he demanded vengeance on Laius's slayer) seals his own doom. The ensuing bloodshed turns the people against Maximilian, who, betrayed by friends and enemies alike, is captured, sentenced, and executed.

In the end, however, Maximilian does obtain a measure of redemption by writing a letter admitting his guilt and acknowledging Juárez as the true leader of Mexico's future—a letter, which, had it been written earlier under duress as a condition for pardon, might have saved Maximilian's life, but not his soul.

Juárez and Maximilian is not simply classical tragedy, but classical Werfel. Here again Werfel demonstrates the tragedy of putting faith in utopian schemes, the unleashing of the forces of destruction through failure to acknowledge the presence of evil in the world, and the fundamental evil of imposed utopianism—all interwoven with the theme of humanity's basic need for individual redemption.

THE KINGDOM OF GOD IN BOHEMIA

This theme of the fundamental evil of imposed utopianism is seen again in *The Kingdom of God in Bohemia*. In this case, it is a communistic utopia based on the teaching of the Bible that the protagonist

Propkop, a former priest, wishes to establish. Like Maximilian, however, Propkop is doomed to failure. His wife deceives him, his best friend betrays him, and part of his army mutinies. In the end, he is defeated and dies from his wounds.

PAUL AMONG THE JEWS

A more complex study of the clash between the old order and a new one is found in *Paul Among the Jews*. Paul, unlike Maximilian and Propkop, is not interested in imposing a new order—but he is committed to a mission to expand people's conception of the soul and their relationship to God. Paul encounters, however, a stultifying hierocracy; constant bickering between reactionaries, fanatics, and moderates; and a general tendency for each group to view religion, devotion, loyalty, and love within very strict confines of a narrow worldview. Paul, however, represents a broadening of humanity's soul—a religion that reaches out to all people.

THE ETERNAL ROAD

Serving in a sense as a kind of sequel to *Paul Among the Jews* is *The Eternal Road*. This play takes place during the "timeless night of Israel's persecution." The Jews are gathered at the synagogue. As they discuss the persecutions being perpetrated without and their own inner turmoil, the rabbi unrolls the Torah and begins to read from the sacred scroll; as he reads, pageants of patriarchs, kings, prophets, and others appear onstage to act out their own stories.

The Eternal Road is more than a rendition of the trials of the Jewish people and the strength of the Jewish faith. Werfel makes certain that the audience understands that what is being presented is the common heritage of Jew and Christian alike. For example, he works language from the New Testament into the tapestry of the Old, and one sees finally a growing, expanding concept of love and the brotherhood of humankind rooted in the ever-widening circles emanating from humanity's common heritage.

JACOBOWSKY AND THE COLONEL

Werfel's last play, considered by some to be his masterpiece, is a comedy about the fall of France to the Nazis in 1940. This "comedy about a serious subject," as Werfel called it, is *Jacobowsky and the Colo-*

nel. In spite of this play's departure from his usual style and methods, one sees here the same basic themes and symbols that characterize Werfel's earlier dramas.

The plot is straightforward and fast-paced. Jacobowsky, a persecuted Jew, who is accustomed to the trials and tribulations of a refugee, is very much at home in the disorder and chaos of the fall of France. Finding the only available car in town is no problem for him—he secures it, even though he cannot drive. He simply teams up with Colonel Stjerbinsky, a Polish officer who must convey certain papers to England, and the colonel's French mistress, Marianne. There is much humor and much sentiment that springs from the clash (and the growing sympathy toward one another) of the characters. Jacobowsky represents the persecuted and alienated individual but also the man with the expanded concept of humankind. The colonel is a representative of the status quo; Marianne represents the spirit of France; the brigadier, a minor character, comes to represent both the essence of bureaucracy and the man of good will. Altogether, the play presents an optimistic and positive statement of the main points that Werfel had established earlier in his darker and more complex dramas: In the chaos of this world, filled with the forces of evil and darkness, human beings' salvation lies not in institutions and ideologies but in a positive faith in God and their fellow humans.

OTHER MAJOR WORKS

LONG FICTION: *Nicht der Mörder,* 1920 (*Not the Murderer,* 1937); *Verdi: Roman der Oper,* 1924 (*Verdi: A Novel of the Opera,* 1925); *Der Tod des Kleinbürgers,* 1927 (novella; *The Man Who Conquered Death,* 1927; also known as *The Death of a Poor Man,* 1927); *Der Abituriententag: Die Geschichte einer Jugendschuld,* 1928 (*Class Reunion,* 1929); *Barbara: Oder, Die Frömmigkeit,* 1929 (*The Pure in Heart,* 1931; also as *The Hidden Child,* 1931); *Die Geschwister von Neapel,* 1931 (*The Pascarella Family,* 1932); *Kleine Verhältnisse,* 1931 (novella; *Poor People,* 1937); *Die vierzig Tage des Musa Dagh,* 1933 (*The Forty Days of Musa Dagh,* 1934); *Höret die Stimme,* 1937 (*Hearken unto the Voice,* 1938); *Twilight of a World,* 1937 (novellas); *Der veruntreute Himmel: Die Geschichte einer Magd,* 1939 (*Embezzled Heaven,* 1940); *Das Lied von Bernadette,* 1941 (*The Song of Bernadette,* 1942); *Stern der Ungeborenen: Ein Reiseroman,* 1946 (*Star of the Unborn,* 1946); *Cella: Oder, Die Überwinder,* 1954 (wr. 1937-1938; *Cella: Or, The Survivors,* 1989).

SHORT FICTION: *Geheimnis eines Menschen,* 1927 (*Saverio's Secret,* 1937); *Erzählungen aus zwei Welten,* 1948-1952 (part of *Gesammelte Werke*).

POETRY: *Der Weltfreund,* 1911; *Wir sind,* 1913; *Einander,* 1915; *Der Gerichtstag,* 1919; *Poems,* 1945 (Edith Abercrombie Snow, translator); *Gedichte aus den Jahren 1908-1945,* 1946.

NONFICTION: *Die christliche Sendung: Ein offener Brief an Kurt Hiller,* 1917; *Verdi: The Man in His Letters,* 1942 (with Paul Stefan); *Zwischen Oben und Unten,* 1946 (*Between Heaven and Earth,* 1944).

MISCELLANEOUS: *Gesammelte Werke,* 1948-1975 (16 volumes).

BIBLIOGRAPHY

Everett, Susanne. *The Bride of the Wind: The Life and Times of Alma Mahler-Werfel.* New York: Viking, 1992. This biography of Werfel's wife describes their life together and depicts twentieth century Austria. Bibliography and index.

Heizer, Donna K. *Jewish-German Identity in the Orientalist Literature of Else Lasker-Schüler, Friedrich Wolf, and Franz Werfel.* Columbia, S.C.: Camden House, 1996. Heizer compares and contrasts the works of Werfel, Else Lasker-Schüler, and Friedrich Wolf, paying particular attention to the issue of Jewish-German identity. Bibliography and index.

Huber, Lothar, ed. *Franz Werfel: An Austrian Writer Reassessed.* New York: St. Martin's Press, 1989. A collection of papers presented at an international symposium on Werfel, discussing his life and works. Bibliography.

Jungk, Peter Stephan. *Franz Werfel: A Life in Prague, Vienna, and Hollywood.* New York: Grove Weidenfeld, 1990. A biography of Werfel that covers his life and works. Bibliography and indexes.

Michaels, Jennifer E. *Franz Werfel and the Critics.* Columbia, S.C.: Camden House, 1994. An examination of the critical reaction to Werfel's literary works. Bibliography and index.

Wegener, Hans. *Understanding Franz Werfel.* Columbia, S.C.: University of South Carolina Press, 1993. A critical analysis and interpretation of the works of Werfel. Bibliography and index.

Glenn R. Swetman

TIMBERLAKE WERTENBAKER

Born: United States; 1946(?)

PRINCIPAL DRAMA

This Is No Place for Talullah Bankhead, pr. 1978

Breaking Through, pr. 1980

Case to Answer, pr. 1980

Second Sentence, pr. 1980

The Third, pr. 1980

New Anatomies, pr. 1981, pb. 1984

Home Leave, pr. 1982

Inside Out, pr. 1982

Abel's Sister, pr. 1984

The Grace of Mary Traverse, pr., pb. 1985

The Love of the Nightingale, pr. 1988, pb. 1989

Our Country's Good, pr., pb. 1988 (based on Thomas Keneally's *The Playmaker*)

Three Birds Alighting on a Field, pr. 1991, pb. 1992

The Break of Day, pr., pb. 1995

Plays One, pb. 1996

After Darwin, pr., pb. 1998

The Ash Girl, pr. 1999, pb. 2000 (adaptation of *Cinderella*)

Credible Witness, pr., pb. 2001

Plays Two, pb. 2002

OTHER LITERARY FORMS

Timberlake Wertenbaker is acclaimed for her translations and adaptations of French and classical Greek dramatic works into English. Her notable contributions in this area include her translations and stage adaptations of plays by Marivaux, *False Admissions* and *Successful Strategies*, both produced in London in 1983 and published along with a radio play as *False Admissions, Successful Strategies, La Dispute: Three Plays* (1989). *La Dispute*, a radio play that she created from a play by Marivaux, was broadcast in 1987. Wertenbaker also translated Jean Anouilh's play *Léocadia* (pr. 1940, pb. 1942), which she adapted for radio in 1985, and *Mephisto* (1986), Ariane Mnouchkine's theatrical adaptation of a novel by Klaus Mann. Her translations of classical Greek plays include *The Thebans: "Oedipus Tyrannus," "Oedipus at Colonus," and "Antigone"* (1992) from Sophocles' *Oidipous Tyrannos* (c. 429 B.C.E.), *Oidipous epi Kolōnōi* (401 B.C.E.), and *Antigonē* (441 B.C.E.) as well as *Hecuba* (1996), from Euripides' *Heklabē* (425 B.C.E.).

ACHIEVEMENTS

Timberlake Wertenbaker has received a number of prestigious awards for her plays, beginning with the *Plays and Players* Most Promising Playwright Award (1985) for *The Grace of Mary Traverse*. Perhaps her best-known play, *Our Country's Good*, won both the Laurence Olivier Play of the Year award and the *Evening Standard* Play of the Year Award (1988); in its American run, the play also earned Wertenbaker the New York Drama Critics Circle Award for Best Foreign Play (1990-1991). *The Love of the Nightingale* won the Eileen Anderson Central Television Drama Award (1989), and *Three Birds Alighting on a Field* won the Critics Circle Best West End Play (1991) as well as the Writers' Guild Best West End Play and the Susan Smith Blackburn Prize (both 1992).

BIOGRAPHY

Timberlake Wertenbaker is reluctant to discuss three aspects of her life: her name, her birthplace, and her birthdate. Born Lael Louisiana Timberlake in the United States, she is the daughter of Charles Wertenbaker (a foreign correspondent for *Time* magazine and a novelist) and his third wife, Lael Tucker Wertenbaker, a prolific author of both fiction and nonfiction. It is no surprise that the daughter of such literary parents chose to pursue a writing career herself.

When she was a young child, Wertenbaker's family moved to the Spanish Basque Provinces, and she was educated at schools near St. Jean-de-Luz, France. Wertenbaker's experience as an American who was reared in Europe and settled in London points to a recurring theme in her work: displacement. In her plays, characters are often removed from the familiarity of home and are forced to live in new cultures, sometimes defined by national boundaries, other times by cultural and class divisions. From this central theme emerge related themes, including isolation, dispossession, and the problem of forging an identity within a new cultural milieu. In her work, individuals often seem to assume roles, as if identity were a matter of persons performing themselves. Wertenbaker's work also demonstrates a keen awareness that communication occurs through language that often inadequately expresses experience. Her consciousness of language gives her work a lyricism that is antinaturalistic, a style served by the episodic structure of her plays, in which the narrative emerges from precisely crafted moments rather than from causally developed plots.

After her youth in Europe, she returned to the United States to attend St. John's College in Annapolis, Maryland, graduating in 1966. After a brief career as a journalist in New York and London, she taught French in Greece for one year. During the 1970's, she moved to London, where she settled. It was there that she began her career as a playwright, initially working in the fringe theaters. By 1984-1985, her eminence was recognized by her serving as the resident writer at the prestigious Royal Court Theatre, where many of the original plays for which she is acclaimed—notably *The Grace of Mary Traverse*, *Our Country's Good*, and *Three Birds Alighting on a Field*—have been produced.

In 1995, Wertenbaker accepted a commission from former Royal Court artistic director Max Stafford-Clark, then working with the Out of Joint theater company, to write a contemporary companion piece for their production of Anton Chekhov's *Tri sestry* (pr., pb. 1901, revised pb. 1904; *The Three Sisters*, 1920); the play resulting from this commission was *The Break of Day*.

Over the years since she began her career, Wertenbaker's output of both original and translated plays has been steady and, in general, very well received. As her plays, most particularly *Our Country's Good*, have been increasingly performed in regional, community, and college theaters worldwide and included in anthologies and on college syllabi, it would seem that Wertenbaker's place in the canon of contemporary drama is secure. The publication by Methuen of two collections of her major works, as well as the continuing publication of many of her single plays and translations, also suggests a popular interest in her work.

ANALYSIS

At its best, Timberlake Wertenbaker's work engages with large questions of philosophy and politics and explores the complex pressure of history on the present without ever losing sight of the individual humanity of the characters. Along with fellow playwright Caryl Churchill, with whom (for reasons of both politics and gender) her name is often paired, Wertenbaker has become recognized as one of the most important women writing for the contemporary British stage.

It is interesting to note Wertenbaker's role as a translator and adapter, and her complex relationship with her source materials. Since the mid-1980's, she has adapted a variety of works for the contemporary English stage. These include most notably classical Greek tragedies of Sophocles and Euripides and the modern French works of Anouilh (who himself became most famous for his World War II adaptation of Sophocles' *Antigone*). Even many of her original plays find their basis in earlier works of literature and drama. *Our Country's Good* takes its story from Thomas Keneally's novel *The Playmaker* (itself not simply an "original" work of fiction but an imaginative interpretation of real historical events), and *The Love of the Nightingale* is based on ancient Greek myth. Expanding still further the range of her source materials, *The Ash Girl* is a fanciful retelling of the Cinderella fairy tale. In each case, though, Wertenbaker has not simply created yet another more-or-less faithful translation of an original text. New characters are often added, old ones developed in new directions, and plot events altered to suit thematic development. Her adaptations must be acknowledged as true re-seeings, intended to give insight into the problems of here and now through an examination of those existing in other places and times. While her subjects and strategies have continued to evolve, Wertenbaker's concerns with dislocation, exile, the power of language, and the nature of the theater itself continue to be central to her work, whether original pieces or adaptations.

NEW ANATOMIES

The focus of Wertenbaker's plays is often a woman who has been radically dislocated from the culture into which she was born. This preoccupation is evident in Wertenbaker's first published play, *New Anatomies*, which dramatizes the life of Isabelle Eberhardt, a French woman who, in the early part of the twentieth century, disguised herself as an Arab man and lived among the Algerians as Si Mahmoud. The movement of the narrative between France and Algeria allows Wertenbaker not only to explore the cultural difference within the specific context of colonization but also to examine the relations between men and women as reproducing the colonial relations between imperial center and colony. By disguising herself as a man, Eberhardt appears to escape the constraints imposed on women by European ideals of femininity, and although she achieves a certain kind of freedom through her disguise, she faces tremendous physical risks, which eventually lead to her death.

Her disguise as an Arab man raises important questions about the European "exoticization" of non-Western cultures, which the play explores in a scene set in a Parisian salon catering to a lesbian clientele.

The women in the salon regard Eberhardt with fascination, as if she has overthrown the social constraints that doubly marginalize them as women and lesbians. One of the women, Verda Miles, is fascinated by Eberhardt's non-Western, male clothes. This fascination implies a relationship between the women of the salon and men from countries that Europe has colonized, as if the sexuality of each group not only is exoticized but also disrupts the conventional codes of gender: French lesbians appear as masculine, while Algerian men appear as feminine.

Miles's identification of Eberhardt's clothes as costume raises the possibility of gender as a performative act that can be altered by the individual refusing to play the socially sanctioned role appropriate to his or her sex. Eberhardt denies this position by stating that she is not "costumed' as a man and that these are her clothes. Her distinction makes clear that within the space of the salon, gender is theatricalized so that a woman dressing as a man emphasizes gender as the construct. In contrast, Eberhardt, traveling in Algeria, is received as a man, not as a woman in male attire.

THE GRACE OF MARY TRAVERSE

Like Isabelle Eberhardt, Mary Traverse, the central character in *The Grace of Mary Traverse*, attempts to escape the limitations imposed by the social codes of femininity and class. Mary is born into a life of privilege in eighteenth century London, where, as a young woman, her only acceptable option is to become the wife of a socially prominent man. The play opens with her father teaching her to make conversation in such a way that she provides opportunities for a man to display his brilliance. By nature a curious young woman who is unsuited to the passive role assigned to women, Mary asks the family's housekeeper, Mrs. Temptwell, to take her into the streets so that she might see life. Quickly, she realizes that the streets of London are brimming with a vitality that, although often violent, is more attractive to her than her life within her father's home. The world outside the home, however, is masculine and decidedly hostile toward women. One of her first experiences in the streets of London is witnessing Lord Gordon raping a young woman by first raising her skirts with his sword and then sexually violating her. (Men's violence against women as a demonstration of their power is explored again by Wertenbaker in two later plays, *Our Country's Good* and *The Love of the Nightingale*.)

Unlike Isabelle Eberhardt, who disguises herself as a man to escape the constraints of European womanhood, Mary Traverse does not disguise herself but rather models her behavior after that of men, demanding, for example, sexual satisfaction from a male prostitute. The social milieu of eighteenth century London cannot accommodate this woman who behaves as a man. Disowned by her father and unmarried, she can support herself only by becoming a prostitute. Once outside her father's home, Mary becomes acutely aware of the intersection of gender and class, particularly in terms of social privilege. The society is hierarchical, with upper-class men, regardless of whether they are worthy, enjoying power, while working-class women, who are at the bottom end of the social strata, are powerless. Without a radical restructuring of the world, Mary realizes that, as a woman, she will never enjoy the prerogatives of men, and therefore she sets out to refashion the world by politicizing the working class. Her attempt is a tragic failure, ending with the Gordon Riots, in which hundreds of people die.

The Grace of Mary Traverse, like *New Anatomies*, deals with a woman's attempt to break the constraints of gender, an image for the larger endeavor of creating a new world in which individuals are free. In *The Grace of Mary Traverse*, Wertenbaker begins to address the problematic nature of this endeavor. While Mary is the agent of change, her motives for wanting change are not altruistic but are apparently motivated by her own desire for power. The problem raised by the play is the following: If the motives of the agent of political change are tainted by her experience of oppression, can she envision a Utopian future? Although the play ends optimistically—with Mary standing with her daughter and father, an image of the future that has reconciled with its past—the terms of that future remain unspoken.

THE LOVE OF THE NIGHTINGALE

Like both *New Anatomies* and *The Grace of Mary Traverse*, *The Love of the Nightingale* is about a woman who is radically displaced from her homeland. The play retells the Greek myth of Procne, daughter of the Athenian king Pandion, who is married to the Thracian king Tereus. Alone in the strange land, unable to comprehend the nuances of a foreign language and culture, Procne lives in isolation. Tereus offers to go to Athens and return with Procne's sister, Philomele, so that Procne will have company. On the voyage back, however, he falls in love with Philomele, whom, after she refuses his advances, he rapes; to silence her, he then cuts out her tongue. As in *The Grace of Mary Traverse*, male power is exercised through the violent subjugation of women. In the context of the play, this point is reiterated through a monologue by an older woman, Niobe, who has been sent from Athens to attend Philomele on her journey. Hearing Philomele's screams during the rape, she comments that this is an experience common to women during times of war, since soldiers conquering a nation brutalize women as the spoils of war.

Also like the two earlier plays, *The Love of the Nightingale* explores the possibility of creating a new world. When Procne realizes that Itys, her son by Tereus, has been socialized to equate masculinity with violence, she decides to end Tereus's line by holding their son while her sister cuts his throat. Whereas *The Grace of Mary Traverse* attempts, although unsuccessfully, to envision a new world free of violence, the somber tone of *The Love of the Nightingale* implies that only an act of violence will rid the world of violence.

OUR COUNTRY'S GOOD

Like *The Love of the Nightingale*, *Our Country's Good* is also about a new beginning. An adaptation of Thomas Keneally's novel *The Playmaker*, *Our Country's Good*, which is set in 1788-1789, deals with a group of convicts being transported by ship to what is now Australia, where they mount the country's first theatrical production, *The Recruiting Officer* by George Farquhar. *Our Country's Good* opens with Lieutenant Ralph Clark overseeing the flogging of one of the convicts, Robert Sideway. The next scene, set in the hull of the ship, is a monologue by another convict, John Wisehammer. He expresses the despair of the convicts who have been ejected forcibly from England and their desire to be returned to their homeland. The speech establishes radical dislocation as a thematic preoccupation of this play; unlike Wertenbaker's earlier plays, however, *Our Country's Good* is a decidedly optimistic piece.

Although the play begins grimly with the flogging of Sideway and Wisehammer's articulation of loss, a sense of community begins to develop during the rehearsal for the production of *The Recruiting Officer*. The therapeutic effects of theater are felt in two ways: The convicts realize that each has a responsibility to others in the group if the production is to be mounted, and so a sense of community, built on the interdependence of its various members, develops; and, in this production, which is directed by Lieutenant Ralph Clark (who also takes the male lead), social difference is overcome because, in the community of actors, the distinctions between the convicts and their jailer are erased. Further, by playing the roles of upper-class characters in *The Recruiting Officer*, the convicts begin to imagine that they, too, might be capable of this refined language and behavior.

The humanistic spirit of the play (which posits that all people, when stripped of their social roles, are equal) is realized in two ways. First, through the experience of community in the rehearsal and through performing Farquhar's characters, the convicts and Clark realize that despite their social inequity within the colony, each is a person of inherent dignity and worth. When two officers interrupt a rehearsal and begin systematically to humiliate the women convicts by asking one of them to drop to her knees and bark like a dog and then asking another to raise her skirts, two of the other convicts resist this exercise of masculine authority by rehearsing the scene that includes the line "I shall meet with less cruelty among the most barbarous nations than I have found at home." This moment demonstrates not only the solidarity among the convicts but also the effectiveness of theater as a tool of political resistance and empowerment.

A second manifestation of the humanism underlying *Our Country's Good* is the love affair between Ralph Clark and one of the convict women, Mary Brenham, who is playing Silvia to Clark's Captain Plume. One evening, Clark approaches Mary, who is alone on the beach rehearsing a scene in which Plume indirectly declares his love for Silvia. Clark joins Mary, using the lines from *The Recuiting Officer* to declare his love for her. He, claiming never to have seen the body of a woman, asks her to undress, which she agrees to do but only if he, too, will undress. The image created by Wertenbaker is one of two people who stand before each other stripped of their social roles, signified by the uniform of an officer and the rags of a convict. On the beach, the two are simply a man and a woman who love each other.

While the humanism of *Our Country's Good* is attractive, the production of the play does serve the interests of the ruling class. The governor of the penal colony believes that theater teaches the convicts to be good citizens not only by exposing them to the fine language of great drama but also by making them into an audience that requires patient attentiveness, a social virtue. In short, the governor believes that theater is a tool in building a homogeneous, stable society.

THREE BIRDS ALIGHTING ON A FIELD

Three Birds Alighting on a Field was the first major published work of Wertenbaker's to be set in contemporary London rather than in the past. The play, like her earlier ones, explores a woman's sense of isolation and her desire to forge an authentic identity for herself. It deals with a woman named Biddy who, divorced from her first husband, is married to her second husband, a tremendously rich Greek nicknamed Yo-yo. As a Greek, Yo-yo believes that he is not fully accepted by the elite of British society and seeks to secure his position by becoming an art collector. While it is his capital that finances the collection, it is Biddy's responsibility to establish it, even though she knows nothing about art.

In some sense, Biddy is an updated version of the woman whom Mary Traverse might have become had she not left her father's house. Biddy's identity initially is based solely on her being the wife of a wealthy man. As Biddy moves through, and learns about, the world of art, Wertenbaker satirizes this world as one in which value is measured only in economic terms, which becomes an image of the bourgeois ethos of Margaret Thatcher's 1980's England. In the course of learning about art and establishing her own sense of what constitutes good art, Biddy gains a sense of herself and, in the process, realizes how much of herself she had to relinquish to maintain her identity as someone's wife. After her marriage to Yo-yo fails, she falls in love with Stephen, the one artist in the play who has retained a sense of integrity, even if it means his refusing to allow his work to circulate as a commodity.

Given Wertenbaker's interest in the ways in which a society's culture defines women as secondary to men, the ending of *Three Birds Alighting on a Field* is curious. While Wertenbaker seems to suggest that Biddy's two marriages denied her a chance to be herself because she was defined as someone's wife, her love affair with Stephen is problematic. She becomes his model, his inspiration. The play ends with her proclaiming that her body is beautiful and then Stephen, who has been painting her, moving from behind his easel and fondling her breasts. The idea of Biddy, a woman, as the object of male desire seems somewhat at odds with Wertenbaker's earlier explorations of women who desire knowledge and agency in the world.

AFTER DARWIN

Even those works of Wertenbaker's set entirely in the past are, of course, more than escapist meditations on distant times. Her work, whenever and wherever it may be set, deals with contemporary issues and, most often, with the effect of history on life in the present. One particularly clear example of this is *After Darwin*, a play that also deals with another of Wertenbaker's favorite theatrical themes, theatricality itself. The play centers around rehearsals for a modern day performance based on the 1831 Galapagos voyage of Charles Darwin aboard the *Beagle*. Though both Darwin and the ship's captain, Robert Fitzroy, are Christians, the naturalist's evolving theory of human evolution by natural selection troubles Fitzroy deeply as it threatens to shake the foundations of his faith and tear apart the relationship of the two men. As Ian and Tom, the actors portraying Darwin and Fitzroy, work under the tutelage of their director Millie on interpreting their characters, it becomes appar-

ent that the philosophical and religious climate of the past continues to haunt the present. To understand where we are and where we are going, indeed even *who* we are, Wertenbaker insists we must take into account where we, as a species and a culture, come from.

CREDIBLE WITNESS

Similarly, Wertenbaker's play *Credible Witness* is set in the present—indeed it is highly topical—yet the characters of this work are also haunted by the ghosts of history. The story follows a Macedonian mother's journey from Greece to a London detention center for asylum seekers as she looks for her missing son. Far more than a condemnation of bureaucratic indifference to refugees (though there is certainly a large helping of this as well), the play becomes a meditation of the role that historical forces play in the creation of the self, as mother and son disagree violently over identity politics. How important are nationality, religion, language, politics? Can these abstractions be so powerful that they will break even the bonds of family love? These are big issues, but critics of the original production of *Credible Witness* were generally pleased to find a powerful strain of optimistic humanism amid the topical politics and difficult philosophical questions.

OTHER MAJOR WORKS

SCREENPLAY: *The Children*, 1990

RADIO PLAYS: *Léocadia*, 1985 (translation and adaptation of a play by Jean Anouilh); *La Dispute*, 1987 (translation and adaptation of a play by Marivaux); *Dianeira*, 2002.

TRANSLATIONS: *Mephisto*, 1986 (of Ariane Mnouchkine's stage adaptation based on a novel by Klaus Mann); *False Admissions, Successful Strategies, La Dispute: Three Plays*, 1989 (of Marivaux's plays); *The Thebans: "Oedipus Tyrannus," "Oedipus at Colonus," and "Antigone,"* 1992 (of Sophocles' plays); *Hecuba*, 1996 (of Euripides' play).

BIBLIOGRAPHY

Carlson, Susan. "Language and Identity in Timberlake Wertenbaker's Plays." In *The Cambridge Companion to Modern British Women Play-*

wrights, edited by Elaine Aston and Janelle Reinelt. Cambridge, England: Cambridge University Press, 2000. Carlson discusses Wertenbaker's complex explorations, in several of her major plays, of the interplay between language and the formation of personal identity, particularly as it relates to gender.

Davis, Jim. "Festive Irony: Aspects of British Theatre in the 1980's." *Critical Survey* 3, no. 3 (1991): 339-350. Davis discusses the original production of *Our Country's Good* in the context of contemporary British drama. He concludes that the play is an apology for theater as a medium that can empower, liberate, and educate both practitioners and audience.

Dymkowski, Christine. "'The Play's the Thing': The Metatheatre of Timberlake Wertenbaker." In *Drama on Drama: Dimensions of Theatricality on the Contemporary British Stage*, edited by Nicole Boireau. New York: St. Martin's Press, 1997. Dymkowski explores Wertenbaker's use of plays and the discourse of theater within her plays. Major works treated include *Our Country's Good* and *The Love of the Nightingale*.

Rabey, David Ian. "Defining Difference: Timberlake Wertenbaker's Drama of Language, Dispossession, and Discovery." *Modern Drama* 33 (December, 1990): 518-528. Rabey analyzes a range of Wertenbaker's plays, suggesting that crisis in her work is a consequence of an individual not being able to fit within a defined code and the resulting quest for meaning.

Taylor, Val. "Mothers of Invention: Female Characters in *Our Country's Good* and *The Playmaker*." *Critical Survey* 3, no. 3 (1991): 331-338. Taylor compares Thomas Keneally's depiction of women characters in *The Playmaker* to Wertenbaker's representation of them in *Our Country's Good*. Concludes that Keneally's women are created from a paternalistic male perspective, whereas Wertenbaker's female characters, written from a feminist perspective, subvert the patriarchal representation of women evident in her source text.

Wilson, Ann. "*Our Country's Good*: Theatre, Colony, and Nation in Wertenbaker's Adaptation of *The Playmaker*." *Modern Drama* 34, no. 1 (March, 1991): 23-35. In this comparison of Wertenbaker's play to its source, Thomas Keneally's *The Playmaker*, Wilson argues that in the novel, the personal relationships of the officers with the convicts essentially extend their roles as agents of colonization, whereas in the play, these relationships allow each to recognize the other's humanity.

Ann Wilson,
updated by Janet E. Gardner

ARNOLD WESKER

Born: London, England; May 24, 1932

PRINCIPAL DRAMA

Chicken Soup with Barley, pr. 1958, pb. 1959
The Kitchen, pr. 1959, pb. 1960, revised pr., pb. 1961
Roots, pr., pb. 1959
I'm Talking About Jerusalem, pr., pb. 1960
The Wesker Trilogy, pb. 1960 (includes *Chicken Soup with Barley*, *Roots*, *I'm Talking About Jerusalem*)

Chips with Everything, pr., pb. 1962
The Nottingham Captain: A Moral for Narrator, Voices and Orchestra, pr. 1962, pb. 1971 (libretto; music by Wilfred Josephs and David Lee)
The Four Seasons, pr. 1965, pb. 1966
Their Very Own and Golden City, pr. 1965, pb. 1966
The Friends, pr., pb. 1970
The Old Ones, pr. 1972, pb. 1973
The Wedding Feast, pr. 1974, pb. 1980 (adaptation of Fyodor Dostoevski's story)

The Journalists, pb. 1975, pr. 1977

Love Letters on Blue Paper, pr. 1976 (televised), pr. 1977 (staged), pb. 1977 (adaptation of his short story)

The Merchant, pr. 1976, pb. 1980, pb. 1985 (revised; based on William Shakespeare's play *The Merchant of Venice*)

The Plays of Arnold Wesker, pb. 1976, 1977 (2 volumes)

Caritas, pr., pb. 1981

Four Portraits of Mothers, pr. 1982, pb. 1987

Annie Wobbler, pr. 1983, pb. 1987 (staged version of the radio play *Annie, Anna, Annabella*)

The Sullied Hand, pr. 1984

Yardsale, pr. 1984 (radio play), pr. 1987 (staged), pb. 1987

One More Ride on the Merry-Go-Round, pr. 1985, pb. 1990

Whatever Happened to Betty Lemon, pr. 1986, pb. 1987

Badenheim 1939, pr. 1987, pb. 1994 (adaptation of Aharon Appelfeld's novel)

Beorhtel's Hill, pr. 1989, pb. 1994

Little Old Lady, pr. 1989 (for children)

The Mistress, pb. 1989, pr. 1991

One-Woman Plays, pb. 1989

Shoeshine, pr. 1989 (for children)

When God Wanted a Son, pr. 1989, pb. 1990

The Kitchen and Other Plays, pb. 1990

Lady Othello and Other Plays, pb. 1990

Shylock and Other Plays, pb. 1990

Letter to a Daughter, pr. 1992, pb. 1994

Three Women Talking, pr. 1992, pb. 1994

Blood Libel, pb. 1994, pr. 1996

Wild Spring and Other Plays, pb. 1994

Break, My Heart, pr. 1997

Denial, pr. 2000

OTHER LITERARY FORMS

Although known mainly for his stage plays, Arnold Wesker has also written poetry, short stories, articles and essays, television plays, and film scripts. His poems have appeared in various magazines. Collections of his short fiction include *Six Sundays in January* (1971), *Love Letters on Blue Paper* (1974),

Said the Old Man to the Young Man: Three Stories (1978), and *Love Letters and Other Stories* (1980). A number of his articles, essays, and lectures have been published; representative collections include *Fears of Fragmentation* (1970), *The Journalists: A Triptych* (1979), and *Distinctions* (1985). His autobiography, *As Much as I Dare*, was published in 1994.

Two of Wesker's television plays have been presented by British Broadcasting Corporation television: *Menace* (1963) and *Love Letters on Blue Paper* (1976, adapted from his short story). Wesker also wrote the script for the film version of *The Kitchen* (1961).

ACHIEVEMENTS

Arnold Wesker presents the disheartening spectacle of a playwright who was an immense success at first but has since fallen from grace—a socialist angel with clipped wings, at least in his own country. With John Osborne, Harold Pinter, John Arden, and others, Wesker was a leading figure in the New Wave (or New Renaissance) of English drama centered on London's Royal Court Theatre in the late 1950's and early 1960's. The New Wave quickly swept the provinces and universities. Wesker was a star, for example, of the 1960 *Sunday Times* Student Drama Festival at Oxford University, where he gave an enthusiastic talk and where there was a rousing performance of *The Kitchen*. Wesker was the theatrical man of the political moment—a playwright of impeccable working-class origins whose naturalistic, socialistic drama seemed to define the true essence of the New Wave. In Wesker, a dynamo of commitment incarnate, there was no suspicious vagueness or wishy-washy wavering: The conditions, dreams, and frustrations of the working class were clearly laid out in *The Kitchen* and in subsequent dramas that rolled off Wesker's pen.

A quieter presence at the 1960 *Sunday Times* festival was Arden, a dominating presence at the next year's festival in Leeds, where a Leeds University production of Arden's *Serjeant Musgrave's Dance* (pr. 1959) won the first prize. Students were beginning to discover Arden, Bertolt Brecht, and even William Shakespeare; Wesker was already fading from memory. As for Wesker himself, his commitment began to take the form of direct social action, ranging from demonstrations against nuclear weapons to management of vast projects to bring the arts to the working class. When new plays finally came from him in the mid-1960's—*The Four Seasons* and *Their Very Own and Golden City*—the old Wesker, who served *Chips with Everything*, had disappeared. Critics and audiences alike were shocked at not being able to recognize Wesker in these works; Wesker's very own and golden moment had ended. The final indignity was Malcolm Page's 1968 article entitled "Whatever Happened to Arnold Wesker? His Recent Plays."

In the mid-1960's, Wesker began struggling to recapture his original success. He tried various kinds of plays—first, plays about interpersonal relationships such as *The Four Seasons*, *The Friends*, and *The Old Ones*, and later, plays based on other literary works such as *The Wedding Feast*, *The Merchant*, and *Love Letters on Blue Paper*. At times he had trouble getting his plays produced in the British professional theater, although productions on the Continent, where his reputation has grown, have usually taken up the slack. He seems to have made a modest comeback in the English-speaking theater with *The Wedding Feast*, *The Merchant*, and *Caritas*. *Caritas*, about a fourteenth century anchoress who has herself immured in a cell, could be a harrowing allegory of Wesker's own career as a committed playwright.

Despite the ups and downs of Wesker's reputation, there is more continuity in his work than at first appears. He has been both the beneficiary and the victim of theatrical and political fashions. As a new, young playwright, he was at first overpraised, though some early critics, noting his autobiographical material and kitchen-sink realism, accused him of lacking imagination. His writing and stagecraft were also

Arnold Wesker and his wife at the Odeon Cinema in Leicester Square, London, for the world premiere of This Sporting Life *in 1963.*
(Hulton Archive by Getty Images)

called awkward. Ironically, by the time Wesker developed his imagination, writing, and stagecraft, his reputation had diminished. Wesker has continued to survey the working class in modern Britain, but a working class dissipated and fragmented by the consumer society. He has also continued to explore questions of class conflict and commitment, but with more subtlety—or with a subtlety that was always there, although earlier audiences did not recognize it.

Many of Wesker's major awards came early in his career. In 1959 he won the London *Evening Standard* Award for the most promising playwright and also an *Encyclopedia Britannica* award. In 1962, *Chips with Everything* was voted the best play of the year, while *Their Very Own and Golden City* won the Premio Matzotto Drama Award in 1964. There was a long gap until, in 1987, a production of *Roots* won the Goldie award for the best play of the year in New York, presented by the Congress of Jewish Culture. In 1990, *Four Portraits of Mothers* and *Yardsale* won the Georges Bresson Prize.

Although Wesker is reported to have turned down the civil award of a companion of the British Empire (CBE), he did consent to becoming a fellow of the Royal Society of Literature (FRSL) and received an honorary doctor of letters (Litt.D.).

BIOGRAPHY

Arnold Wesker was born May 24, 1932, in Stepney, a working-class neighborhood of sweatshops and immigrants in London's East End. His parents were Joseph Wesker, a Russian-Jewish tailor, and Leah Perlmutter Wesker, a Hungarian-Jewish communist who often had to work in kitchens to support the family. *Chicken Soup with Barley* draws on this background. Like other London children, Wesker was evacuated during periods of World War II, living with foster parents in various sections of England and Wales. Failing his eleven-plus examination, which was given to determine whether eleven-year-olds went on to an academic or vocational secondary school, he did some amateur acting.

He left school in 1948 and worked at assorted jobs—as a furniture maker's apprentice, carpenter's mate, and bookseller's assistant. From 1950 to 1952,

he was in the Royal Air Force, where he organized an enlisted men's drama group and started writing. A series of letters, which he originally meant to turn into a novel, later provided material for *Chips with Everything*.

From 1952 to 1958, he worked at another string of jobs—bookseller's assistant and plumber's mate in London, farm laborer, seed sorter, and kitchen porter in Norfolk, then as a pastry cook in London and Paris. With his savings, he studied in 1956 at the London School of Film Technique. He had also continued writing, and in 1957 he showed his work to film director Lindsay Anderson, who sent *The Kitchen* and *Chicken Soup with Barley* to George Devine at the Royal Court Theatre. *Chicken Soup with Barley* was produced in 1958 at the Belgrade Theatre, Coventry, then transferred to the Royal Court. *Roots* and *The Kitchen* followed in 1959, *I'm Talking About Jerusalem* in 1960.

Wesker won immediate recognition for his work. In 1958, he received an Arts Council grant of three hundred pounds, on the strength of which he married Doreen Cecile "Dusty" Bicker, whom he had met when they worked together in a Norfolk hotel (she is the prototype of Beatie Bryant in *Roots*). They had three children, two sons and one daughter, and the family has grown to include several grandchildren.

With recognition also came social involvement. In 1961, Wesker, with philosopher Bertrand Russell and others, demonstrated against nuclear weapons and was sentenced to a month in prison. Also in 1961, Wesker became the founding director of Centre 42, a cultural movement or coalition of artists, trade unionists, and other prominent citizens who hoped to bring the arts to the working class. During the 1960's, with staging of regional arts festivals and management of the Round House (the London performance center), the movement consumed a considerable amount of Wesker's time and energy. The movement also required efforts to raise funds: When the cost of sustaining it became too great, Centre 42 was finally terminated in 1970. In addition to his writing, Wesker has also directed some of his own plays.

In 1975 he spent six weeks in the offices of the London *Sunday Times*. The outcome of this was a "triptych," *The Journalists*. The play was perhaps more notorious for the seven-year lawsuit Wesker brought against the Royal Shakespeare Company on the refusal of their actors to perform *The Journalists*. He has tried to recapture his East End of London beginnings in other literary forms. *Say Goodbye, You May Never See Them Again* is a text for paintings by John Allinn recording a social history of the East End. His autobiography, *As Much as I Dare*, also concerns itself primarily with this early period of his life. In 1999, University of Texas at Austin purchased ninety boxes of archival material as the basis for an Arnold Wesker collection.

ANALYSIS

Arnold Wesker's central concern has been the fate of the working class in modern Britain, and the developments in his work have by and large grown from this concern. In his early plays, which form a saga of the working class through two generations in city and country, the concern is obvious and so is Wesker's commitment. A second group of plays examines interpersonal relationships, which were certainly not neglected in the early plays. Most of the characters in this group are of working-class origin. Some of Wesker's plays have dealt with a variety of subjects and themes—journalism, class divisions, responsibility to one's community, commitment. These issues, however, were first raised in Wesker's early work. Wesker has merely shifted the focus of his concern from direct treatment of the working class to treatment of issues closely affecting it.

Besides indicating Wesker's personal growth, the developments in his work also reflect changes in the modern British working class. In Wesker's early plays, the working class is shown in its traditional role: serving the needs of the higher classes and worrying about where its next meal is coming from. Already, though, changes are occurring. With socialism comes more power, better living conditions, and greater opportunity, but these changes bring new problems. The old class solidarity dissipates. Some working people cannot escape their traditional role and grasp the opportunity for richer, fuller lives. Others grasp the opportunity but still find themselves searching for meaning. The Wesker trilogy introduces this stage of socialism, and his plays treating interpersonal relationships explore it further. In an epilogue to *The Four Seasons*, Wesker explicitly connects socialism and interpersonal relationships and defends his shift in emphasis:

> There is no abandoning in this play of concern for socialist principles nor a turning away from a preoccupation with real human problems; on the contrary, the play, far from being a retreat from values contained in my early writing, is a logical extension of them. . . .

In short, building the New Jerusalem is not merely a simple matter of seizing power and satisfying basic material needs.

Food, however, is quite obviously the main symbol in Wesker's plays, changing its meaning from context to context. In *Roots*, the farmers are sweating to grow it, while in *The Kitchen* the cooks are sweating to cook it—they represent the traditional role of the working class. In *Chicken Soup with Barley*, sharing food (particularly the archetypal chicken soup) symbolizes compassion and working-class solidarity. On the other hand, in *Roots* consuming food symbolizes the mindless animal contentment of the welfare state. In *Chips with Everything* (as in fish and chips), the "chips with everything" note on the greasy East End restaurant menu suggests not only familiar working-class identity but also—to the upper-class snob "Pip" Thompson—the indiscriminate potato-like nature of that identity. Throughout Wesker's plays people are constantly preparing food or tea for one another, usually as a token of love, respect, or fellowship. For example, onstage in *The Four Seasons* Adam makes Beatrice an apple strudel, the recipe for which Wesker kindly shares in a note to actors.

THE WESKER TRILOGY

The basic introduction to Wesker's work is *The Wesker Trilogy*, consisting of *Chicken Soup with Barley*, *Roots*, and *I'm Talking About Jerusalem*. They do not constitute a trilogy in the strictest sense (the three plays have separate actions and settings and do not follow in entirely chronological order), for each can easily stand alone. They are, however, united by their characters, two generations of the city Kahns and the country Bryants, and by the same general subject: the conditions, aspirations, and frustrations of the British working class. Thematically they are also tied together in a loose thesis-antithesis-synthesis relationship.

Covering the most history is *Chicken Soup with Barley*, which stretches over three decades of life in London's East End. The bustling first act shows militant workers, led by the communist Sarah Kahn, putting down a Fascist march during the 1930's. Later, one of the young workers, Dave Simmonds, leaves to continue fighting the Fascists in the Spanish Civil War. Even here, however, the idealized solidarity is not complete: A prominent shirker is Sarah's own husband, Harry Kahn, who in the thick of the fight runs off to hide at his mother's home. The second act is set in the 1940's, shortly after World War II, and change is apparent. Deterioration of the one-time solidarity is occurring: Tired out by political activity and war, sick of industrial urban society, Dave Simmonds and Ada, the Kahns' daughter, get married and withdraw to a quiet life in the country. Despite a new Socialist government, capitalists are still finding ways to exploit the workers. By act 3, set in the mid-1950's, the deterioration is complete. The Soviet Union's behavior has exploded Communist ideals, Sarah is now fighting welfare-state bureaucracy, and the old comrades have dispersed. One example is agitator-turned-businessman Monty Blatt, who expresses the prevailing "I'm all right, Jack" philosophy: "There's nothing more to life than a house, some friends, and a family—take my word." Ronnie, the Kahns' son, likewise disillusioned and searching, is embarrassed by the old language of solidarity; words such as "comrade" now seem unreal.

The most interesting characters in *Chicken Soup with Barley* are Sarah and Harry Kahn. Apparently held up for admiration, Sarah is a spunky Mother Courage figure who expounds the play's chicken-soup philosophy and who persists in her ideals even as her world crumbles around her: "you've got to care or you'll die." At the same time, she is a pushy wife and mother and something of a shrew. Poor Harry is already demoralized enough, as a breadwinner who

has trouble finding work (it is, after all, the Depression), and Sarah finishes the job of emasculating him. Finally, her nagging gives him a stroke, and thereafter his deterioration mirrors the decline of working-class solidarity, until he becomes the ultimate case of the uninvolved person, paralyzed and unable to control even his bladder and bowels. It is too bad that Sarah does not practice her chicken-soup philosophy more on Harry.

Picking up thematically where *Chicken Soup with Barley* leaves off, *Roots* at the same time provides a strong contrast in setting and characters. It is still welfare-state Britain, now 1959, but the place has switched to the Norfolk countryside, where the rural working class is presented in the persons of the Bryant family. The Bryant men work as pigmen, tractor drivers, and garage mechanics, and the women are housewives. Although the men are still subject to a mysterious "guts ache" and to being sacked at work, the Bryants are generally fat and complacent. Uneducated, unaware, and conservative, they take no interest in affairs outside their own little circle. Their conversation is about the weather, food, and family, or gossip about the neighbors. They enjoy popular culture (they can hardly wait to get television), but books and classical music are "squit." They represent the members of the working class who have trouble breaking out of the traditional mold and for whom Wesker's Centre 42 project was perhaps intended. They are little better off than poor Harry except that they can move.

There is one exception among the Bryants, the twenty-two-year-old daughter Beatie, who has benefited from living with young Ronnie Kahn for three years in London. Besides cohabiting with him, she has kept his interest by pretending to listen to his ideas, a necessity with which she can dispense once they are married and she starts having babies. The slim plot of *Roots* consists of waiting—while Beatie sings his praises and continuously quotes him—for the great Ronnie to appear and meet the other Bryants. He never does. They prepare a feast for him, but he does not show up. Instead, he sends a letter of regret breaking off his affair with Beatie because she is so uncultured. Ironically, Beatie is not destroyed but is instead shocked into the fluent awareness that Ronnie had always tried to develop in her. Meanwhile, the other Bryants wade into the food lest it go to waste.

Beatie represents the younger generation that is moving to the city and developing "roots" in working-class concerns; she is an embodiment of Sarah Kahn's continuing hope. She also anticipates the concerns of women's liberation, which might partly explain why her role has been a favorite in the modern theater. As for Ronnie, he takes after his mother: Politically and culturally correct, he is personally something of a snob and a heel (there is a bit of the father here too). Ronnie gets off too easily in *Roots*, while Wesker is too hard on the country folk. Unfortunately, though Wesker admires D. H. Lawrence, he does not seem to share Lawrence's appreciation for the animal vitality of country people (though it must be admitted that Lawrence wrote about an earlier generation that perhaps was more vital).

Wesker's *I'm Talking About Jerusalem* suggests that his mentor was not D. H. Lawrence but nineteenth century socialist William Morris, who envisioned a Jeffersonian democracy of independent craftsmen. Picking up a loose end from *Chicken Soup with Barley*, *I'm Talking About Jerusalem* goes to the country with Dave and Ada Kahn Simmonds, who settle a few miles from the Bryants in Norfolk. Their dream is to leave the problems of urban clutter behind and build their own private Jerusalem in the country, where Dave will support them by creating beautiful handmade furniture. He will thereby realize William Morris's vision of the independent craftsman who has a meaningful relationship with his work instead of merely filling a place on a factory assembly line. The Simmondses do enjoy their spacious country freedom, but, after thirteen years, a growing family and economic pressures force them back to the city. The throwaway consumer society does not sufficiently appreciate the worth of handmade items. The point seems to be that people cannot be uninvolved, cannot escape the problems of society, but must work together to bring about the New Jerusalem for everyone.

THE OLD ONES

The annals of British socialism continue in an example of Wesker's later work, *The Old Ones*. From *The Old Ones* it is clear that as the problems of subsistence are solved, the problems of existence come more to the fore. At times *The Old Ones* evokes the Theater of the Absurd as two old brothers, the optimist Emanuel ("Manny") and the pessimist Boomy, quote blasts at one another from William Butler Yeats, Thomas Carlyle, Voltaire, Martin Buber, John Ruskin, the Zohar, and Ecclesiastes. Other characters have similar problems: For example, old Jack goes around ringing a bell and sounding like a mad scene from William Shakespeare's *King Lear* (pr. c. 1605-1606). Yet the setting and characters are realistic enough—recognizable as contemporary Britain, from the youths who drop out of school and beat up old ladies in the street, to members of the next generation who are approaching middle age and still searching for a career choice, to the old folks who live in comfortable retirement but puzzle over the meaning of it all. It is clear that socialism has not yet solved the problems of old age, death, and the generation gap, much less the meaning of existence.

What is required is a Socialist theology, and Wesker attempts to provide it in the form of the old people's fellowship and Jewish custom. Through their own histories of failed relationships, the old ones have mellowed into tolerance of one another's eccentricities and appreciation of one another's company (even the quarreling brothers seem to need each other). They spend their time calling and visiting back and forth: At this stage, one needs all the moral support one can get. Their fellowship culminates in a revived celebration of Succoth, the Jewish harvest festival. Succoth calls for a symbolic hut in the room (in remembrance of frail humankind's vulnerability and need for God's help) and for a joyful countenance. Although marred by a few quarrels, the old ones' Succoth feast is indeed joyful, ending in a stirring Hasidic dance. Thus, ritual solidarity is achieved in the face of the universe.

As *The Old Ones* suggests, the movement from solidarity to religious fellowship is not as far as it might seem. In the epilogue to *The Four Seasons*,

Wesker argues that love must undergird all human interaction, at whatever level: Men and women "need to know and be comforted by the knowledge that they are not alone in their private pain. You can urge mankind to no action by intimidating it with your eternal condemnation of its frailties." In his work, Wesker does not commit the ideological fallacy committed by his characters Sarah and Ronnie Kahn, who voice their love for humankind in the abstract but seem uncaring toward those closest to them. Socialism, so to speak, begins at home.

THE WEDDING FEAST

The Wedding Feast picks up the theme of socialism, returning to Norfolk to do so. The Jewish show manufacturer, Louis Litvanov, tries to put his socialism to work through paternalism, deciding to attend the wedding reception of one of his employees. The often slapstick comedy does not hide his thwarted idealism. Wesker seems to be suggesting that equality is a necessary socialist fiction, rather than an ideal, since, in fact, class divisions need maintaining. Trying to collapse them merely leads to disorientation and disharmony.

THE JOURNALISTS

In *The Journalists* and *The Merchant*, Wesker moves away from working-class settings and concerns. *The Journalists* works rather like *The Kitchen* in showing the pressures of a hectic working environment undermining the possibility of idealism. The Sunday newspaper staff seem motivated by the need to cut public figures down to size. The central character is a star columnist who was once perhaps an idealist but now adopts a calculated cynicism as a defense against her disillusionment.

THE MERCHANT

In *The Merchant*, Wesker strikes out in a new direction: He takes a Shakespeare play (as did Edward Bond and Tom Stoppard) and rewrites it. He states that he has always found *The Merchant of Venice* (pr. c. 1596-1597) insupportable in its anti-Semitism. In his version, Wesker shows Shylock as an idealist, committed to open inquiry, a lover of books, a true Renaissance figure. In opposition to him are Christian "fundamentalists" who attack both the free-market forces of Venice and its toleration of Jews,

however limited. The Venetian establishment, holding the political power, is more subtle: It takes a foolish gesture (the signing of the bond between Shylock and his close Gentile friend Antonio) and exploits it to deprive Shylock of his priceless collection of books. His idealism is further shattered by the flight of his daughter, who eventually loses both family and lover.

The play contains rather more plot than is usual for Wesker—the constraints of the original play dictated this. For the play to work, a good knowledge of the original is needed, because it is in the differences that the real force of the play is felt. *The Merchant* is a play in which Jewishness is most obviously analyzed for what it is in its most enlightened forms, rather than as a paradigm for social cohesion and motivation.

LATER PLAYS

After critical neglect, the production of *The Merchant* brought Wesker back somewhat into critical focus. The plays that followed, however, did not build on this, showing little clear direction. *Annie Wobbler*, the stage version of an earlier radio play, was a one-woman stage piece written specifically for the actress Nichola McAulife. Wesker was careful to deny these were monologues, however. Other one-woman plays followed: *Four Portraits of Mothers* and *The Mistress*. *Letter to a Daughter* was the last in the cycle, about a doubt-ridden single mother. It had been written for Norwegian jazz singer Susanne Fuhr, based on her biographical notes, though it received an early production in Tokyo, Japan. The most successful of these plays was *Yardsale*. Another, contrasting exploration of the female psyche was in *Caritas*, about a fourteenth century young nun.

By contrast, *One More Ride on the Merry-Go-Round* shows a somewhat biographical but ultimately unsuccessful shift to middle-class, middle-age domesticity. Its shocking openings of a middle-aged lover romping around with a younger partner, making love barely offstage, do little to relieve a caricatured and stereotypical bedroom comedy. A Jewish mother is thrown in de rigeur. *Lady Othello* is a similar middle-aged jaunt, this time in New York.

A more promising development seemed to open up in an incursion into children's theater with *Shoeshine* and *Little Old Lady*, two plays for young people. In the same year, *The Kitchen* was produced by the National Youth Theatre. However, compared to the commitment to youth theater by his contemporary British playwright, Edward Bond, the incursion seemed dilettante.

DENIAL

Because of Wesker's failure to recapture his early success, most critics began writing Wesker off as a contemporary dramatist. However, Wesker himself has remained a committed and energetic playwright whose supply of plays shows no signs of dropping off, and the performance of a recent play, *Denial*, has challenged the received opinion of his superannuation.

The ninety-minute play deals with a controversial contemporary issue, False Memory Syndrome, especially in the sense that it can undermine family cohesiveness with its unprovable charges of sexual abuse. In this play, the triangle of daughter-father-therapist forms the dramatic foundation on which a hard-hitting set of speeches is based. Wesker refuses to demonize either the therapist as an implanter of false memories in an attempt to "solve" her client's problems or the father, as the supposed perpetrator of the original sexual abuse. Both have genuine cases to make. In the end, the parents' plea for normal touch and physical play to bond families emerges as Wesker's, thus linking the play to his earlier plays about family bonding, however dysfunctional the family might seem.

The one part of the play that drew criticism was the introduction of a Holocaust survivor, still dealing with (very real) memories, as a sort of counterbalance to hidden memories. The handling of this part was too mechanical to be credible. Whether Wesker can repeat this undoubted success remains to be seen.

OTHER MAJOR WORKS

SHORT FICTION: *Love Letters on Blue Paper*, 1974; *Said the Old Man to the Young Man: Three Stories*, 1978; *Love Letters on Blue Paper and Other Stories*, 1980.

SCREENPLAY: *The Kitchen*, 1961.

TELEPLAY: *Menace*, 1963.

RADIO PLAYS: *Annie, Anna, Annabella*, 1983; *Bluey*, 1985.

NONFICTION: *Fears of Fragmentation*, 1970; *Journey into Journalism*, 1977; *The Journalists: A Triptych*, 1979; *Distinctions*, 1985; *As Much as I Dare*, 1994 (autobiography); *The Birth of Shylock and the Death of Zero Mostel*, 1997.

CHILDREN'S LITERATURE: *Fatlips: A Story for Young People*, 1978.

MISCELLANEOUS: *Six Sundays in January*, 1971 (stories and plays).

BIBLIOGRAPHY

Alter, Iska. "'Barbaric Laws, Barbaric Bonds': Arnold Wesker's *The Merchant*." *Modern Drama* 31 (December, 1988): 536-547. Traces some of the intertextual ambiguities, especially concerning the insistent use of the law by Shylock. Wesker's historical research is noted to shift the play from Romance to political realism.

Brown, John Russell. *Theatre Language: A Study of Arden, Osborne, Pinter, and Wesker*. London: Allen Lane, 1972. Brown analyzes the language of *Roots*, *The Kitchen*, and *Chips with Everything*, dealing particularly with the way Wesker maintains theatricality by substituting talk for action in his drama. He also shows how he manages to hold theatrical discourse parallel to interpersonal talk in order to make explicit impact didactically. Short bibliography and index.

Dornan, Reade W., ed. *Arnold Wesker*. New York: Garland, 1998. One of the Casebook series, it consists of eighteen essays on various aspects of Wesker's plays by an international array of critics.

Hayman, Ronald. *Arnold Wesker*. London: Heinemann, 1970. This volume in the Contemporary Playwrights series includes chapters on each of the plays through *The Four Seasons*, in addition to two interviews with Wesker. A clearly written informative introduction to the earlier Wesker. Bibliography, biographical outline, and photographs.

Leeming, Glenda. "Articulacy and Awareness: The Modulation of Familiar Themes in Wesker's Plays of the Seventies." In *Contemporary English Drama*, edited by C. W. E. Bigsby. New York: Holmes and Meier, 1981. Leeming reviews the development of Wesker's drama from *The Old Ones* through *The Merchant*. She sees particularly an interiorization of a number of themes. The protagonists' awareness of their own suffering is located as the axis for the development.

_____, ed. *Wesker on File*. New York: Methuen, 1985. This invaluable small collection consists both of reviewers' and Wesker's own comments on his plays as well as on his work in general. Chronology and select bibliographies.

_____. *Wesker the Playwright*. New York: Methuen, 1983. This volume is probably the fullest account of Wesker's work written up to the date of its publication. Contains a chapter on each of his plays, an appendix, a select bibliography, an index, and photographs.

Wilcher, Robert. *Understanding Arnold Wesker*. Columbia: University of South Carolina Press, 1991. An analysis of the plays and stories. Originally a series of lectures by the Senior Lecturer at the University of Birmingham, England.

Harold Branam,
updated by David Barratt

PATRICK WHITE

Born: London, England; May 28, 1912
Died: Sydney, Australia; September 30, 1990

PRINCIPAL DRAMA
Return to Abyssinia, pr. 1947
The Ham Funeral, wr. 1947, pr. 1961, pb. 1965
The Season at Sarsaparilla, pr. 1962, pb. 1965
A Cheery Soul, pr. 1963, pb. 1965
Night on Bald Mountain, pr. 1963, pb. 1965
Four Plays, pb. 1965, revised and enlarged 1985-
    1994 as *Plays* (2 volumes)
Big Toys, pr. 1977, pb. 1978
Signal Driver, pr. 1982, pb. 1983
Netherwood, pr., pb. 1983
Shepherd on the Rocks, pr. 1987, pb. 1995

OTHER LITERARY FORMS
Patrick White is best known for his novels. In addition, he published numerous short stories and an autobiographical volume that he called a "self-portrait." He also wrote a screenplay based on one of his short stories, "The Night of the Prowler."

ACHIEVEMENTS
In 1973, Patrick White received the Nobel Prize in Literature for his fiction. Thereafter he wrote several more novels, short stories, and plays, which have been staged along with revivals of his earlier plays. Because his dramatic works are not widely known outside Australia, White's international reputation rests on his fiction, which constitutes an astounding achievement. In its grandeur and metaphysical use of the Australian landscape and character, it altered the course of that country's literature, previously marked, for the most part, by self-conscious realism and nationalism. Although many critics in Australia scoffed at his complex philosophical work before he received the Nobel Prize, White had steadily built a following abroad, beginning with the publication of *The Aunt's Story* in 1948. He has often been credited with setting Australian literature into the mainstream, as well as freeing and influencing an entire generation of writers in Australia whose work is now highly esteemed among those bodies of literature written in English. Whether White is a major dramatist may be open to argument; he does, however, deserve attention for a limited but solid achievement in plays characterized by originality in structure, powerful language, and expression of universal concerns. Although a number of Australian dramatists have achieved widespread recognition, White remains one of the first to experiment on the Australian stage. His exam-

Patrick White (© The Nobel Foundation)

ple posed a challenge in the 1960's, when realistic and provincial plays constituted the few native works that appeared in a country where theatergoers most often looked to Great Britain and the United States for "real plays."

In addition to his Nobel Prize in Literature in 1973, White also was the recipient of the Australian Literary Society gold medal in 1940 for *Happy Valley* (1939) and in 1956 for *The Tree of Man* (1955). He also earned the Miles Franklin Award in 1958 for *Voss* (1957) and in 1962 for *Riders in the Chariot* (1962). *Voss* also won the W. H. Smith and Son Literary Award in 1959, while *Riders in the Chariot* received the brotherhood award from the National Conference of Christians and Jews in 1962.

BIOGRAPHY

Although born in London, Patrick Victor Martindale White was the son of wealthy, third-generation Australian landowners, who were visiting England in 1912 but sailed for home six months after their son's birth. He spent his first thirteen years in and around Sydney, then left for Great Britain to attend school in Cheltenham. Returning to Australia in 1929, he worked for three years at a sheep station in the New England area northwest of Sydney before entering King's College, Cambridge. After he took his degree in modern languages, he remained in London to pursue his theatrical and writing ambitions. Travel through Europe and the United States followed, and in 1939 his first novel, *Happy Valley*, appeared. With the outbreak of World War II, he joined the Royal Air Force, serving in North Africa, Alexandria, the Middle East, and Greece. He returned to London after the war and there saw his first play, *Return to Abyssinia*, produced; the manuscript, lost (or destroyed), was never published. At this time, he wrote another play, *The Ham Funeral*, which did not receive a production until 1961. He returned to Australia in 1947 and except for brief trips abroad remained there.

For the next twenty-five years, he wrote novel after novel, all of which gained for him more recognition in Great Britain and the United States than in Australia. Following the award of the Nobel Prize in Literature in 1973 for his impressive achievement as a novelist, he emerged as something of a public figure in Australia, often criticizing his compatriots, voicing his opinion—at one time or another—on politics and politicians, literary criticism and its practitioners, the Australian involvement in the Vietnam War, preservation of natural resources, nuclear disarmament, and the treatment of Aborigines. He invested his Nobel Prize money in a fund to assist other Australian writers, established scholarships for Aboriginal students, and donated paintings from his extensive private collection to the New South Wales Art Gallery in Sydney. He continued to write both fiction and drama, although he once vowed never to write for the stage again. In 1986, one of his most famous novels, *Voss* (1957), was turned into an opera; another Australian novelist, David Malouf, wrote the libretto for the production, which enjoyed tremendous success in Australia. After a long illness, White died at his home in Sydney on September 30, 1990.

ANALYSIS

Patrick White's plays address the same thematic concerns as his novels: the role of the artist, the conflict between the visionary and the materialist, and the moral desolation and decay prevailing in modern life. Their language and structure intensify and heighten experience by combining the poetic with the mundane, the experimental with the traditional, the events of ordinary life with the metaphysical quest for truth. In general, the plays owe much to the European tradition of expressionism, which depends on the use of antinaturalistic stage devices, compression of language, symbolic picture sequences achieved through short unrealized scenes, lofty themes of spiritual regeneration or renewal, and a declamatory tone.

Although White's plays will not gain the kind of recognition his fiction has achieved, they should not be discounted or ignored. They stand as accomplished works in their own right, especially in their author's original handling of techniques that made expressionism so vital a force in twentieth century theater. An understanding of the dramas will lead to a richer appreciation of the novels, for both literary forms show how the artist can meld opposites: symbolism that employs the trivial to clarify the universal; characters who emerge as both real human beings and metaphysical abstractions; settings that rely on the tangible, which are microcosmic, but suggest the elusive, the universal.

THE HAM FUNERAL

The best known of the plays, *The Ham Funeral*, illustrates these points. The Young Man, the only name given to its major character, reveals in the prologue that he is a poet and, like all poets, knows too much but never enough. He proceeds to explain that the audience must enter with him into the house before which he stands and there learn what it means to be a poet. The scenes that follow bring together the disparate parts of The Young Man's psyche and give him direction as an artist. In the first scene, he lies on his bed in silence, considering "the great poem," when the Landlady interrupts to tell him that her husband has died. He assists in preparation for the funeral, at which the relatives eat the ham the widow has provided to give the funeral class. Later, the Landlady at-

tempts, unsuccessfully, to seduce The Young Man, who returns to his room and carries on a long conversation with The Girl, actually his anima. At the end of the play, The Young Man leaves the house—its back wall dissolving, the stage directions say—and walks into the "luminous night."

Through this fluid series of fragmented scenes, the self-absorbed artist has learned to identify himself with the raw stuff of life: love and lust, hate and compassion, the beautiful and the ugly. Henceforth his poetry will no longer resemble "self-abuse in an empty room" but a discovery of the human condition in all of its forms.

THE SEASON AT SARSAPARILLA

If *The Ham Funeral* may be taken as an autobiographical statement—and there exist substantial grounds for such an interpretation—then The Young Man (White) set his hand to the novel, forsaking poetry altogether and not returning to the drama for almost fifteen years. When he did, he took up in *The Season at Sarsaparilla* the plight of the visionary thrust into a world that is mundane, respectable, conventional, materialistic—but altogether lacking in awareness. An imaginary Sydney suburb, Sarsaparilla, comes to life on the stage through a setting that represents the kitchens and backyards of three adjoining houses. As the action moves from house to house, the families' lives intertwine in the most ordinary of ways, thus giving the outward texture of the play a deceptive air of naturalism. A dog in heat, or in season, interrupts the quiet lives of the three families when she goes under one of the houses, pursued by a pack of excited dogs. This ironic use of "season" in the title extends to the growing awareness of the central character, Pippy, a young girl on the verge of womanhood, who learns through the dogs' natural actions that life embraces passion, violence, birth, and death, that it goes through its seasons, as she will hers.

A CHEERY SOUL

A Cheery Soul takes for its setting the Sundown Home for Old People and centers its action on Miss Docker. This at once comic and bitter portrayal of a cheery soul, the very soul of suburban respectability and morality, offers a superbly drawn character in Miss Docker, who destroys herself and others as she goes about doing good and remaining cheerful in the face of every disaster. The destructive force, which she manifests unknowingly, stems from an absolute belief in the rightness of her actions, an attitude so pervasive that it leaves no room for sensitivity toward other people.

NIGHT ON BALD MOUNTAIN

Probably the least successful of all the plays, *Night on Bald Mountain* sets out to portray the disintegration of Western civilization. The means it uses, however, fail to rise to the loftiness of its theme: A woman more devoted to a herd of goats than to humankind, an embittered professor, his alcoholic wife, and a young woman with incestuous longings lack the universal appeal to make convincing so significant a message. Still, the play's artistry in language and structure and its striking use of setting lend it a pure theatrical excitement in spite of the defects.

BIG TOYS

Disheartened by the reception of his plays, White left the drama for the novel and shunned playwriting for fourteen years. Some critics believe, though, that his early plays, so different from anything native ever produced on the Australian stage, sowed the seeds for the new theater movement that got under way there in 1967, when several young writers demanded that Australian theater make room for the country's linguistic vigor, concern itself with matters contemporarily Australian, and liberate the imagination to experiment with new forms. Whereas these playwrights moved in directions different from White, they surely benefited from his earlier attempts to establish a distinctly Australian drama.

In 1977, *Big Toys* opened in Australia to a new breed of theatergoers, ones who not only took Australian drama seriously but also accepted work that ignored the conventions of theatrical realism. Set in a fashionable Sydney suburb, *Big Toys* depicts the empty lives of Mag and Ritchie Bosanquet, who have what should make life full—wealth, beauty, social position, every imaginable material possession, indeed all the "big toys." As they rise in the material realm, they are actually rushing to their downfall: In White's world, outward success leads to inward failure. *Big Toys* employs the elegant form of comedy of

manners and relies on a conflict created by industrial exploitation to draw this bleak picture. Yet the realistic conflict and the stylized form that frames it expand in such a way that they merge into White's earlier devotion to the expressionistic mode. The three characters—as real as those who appear in the daily newspaper with their personal, social, and business connivances—move into abstract and symbolic dimensions to declaim the moral bankruptcy that dominates the lives of those who determine the course of the late twentieth century.

SIGNAL DRIVER

Signal Driver is White's purest dramatic venture into expressionism and one of his most impressive plays. Taking its title from Sydney bus signs that instruct potential riders to "signal driver," the play follows Theo and Ivy Volkes from youth to old age, the telling of their stories amplified by two music-hall characters who serve as the Volkeses' alter egos. The entire action takes place at a bus stop, its environs and conditions changing to show the passage of time. Buses go by, but the Volkeses never board; when old age levels them, they realize that they have metaphorically missed the bus of life. Simplistic though the concept might sound, the talented application of the expressionistic techniques governing language, character development, staging, and handling of theme turns the play into a powerful and memorable statement on the desolate human condition.

NETHERWOOD

Netherwood follows theatrical conventions more closely than *Signal Driver*, at least on the surface. The action takes place in a once-grand Australian country house, called Netherwood, where a group of half-comic, half-mad characters live together on parole from the local mental institution, Bonkers Hall, under the supervision of a couple who are determined to do good. During act 1, the events unfold on a believable level and suggest that this play might be an Australian version of the English manor-house comedy. In the second act, however, all pretense toward representation of reality vanishes. Characters take on multiple identities and serve as one another's alter egos, thereby revealing to the audience their sexual repressions and perversions, their hidden failures, suppressed fears, and inability to grasp life's meaning. When the personal struggles of the characters cannot be solved by a tidy plot, the play ends on an apocalyptic note. Amid gratuitous gunfire, one of the characters says: "Comical bastards, us humans. Seems like we sorter *choose* ter shoot it out . . . to find out who's the bigger dill." At the end, White appears to voice his rising concern with nuclear armament through this statement, so very Australian in its syntax and diction. In Australia, a "dill" is a fool—a condition that suggests White's view of humankind.

SHEPHERD ON THE ROCKS

White's final play, *Shepherd on the Rocks*, was given a Sydney production in 1987. In the play, described as an "epic religious revue," the action follows the adventures of a priest named Danny Shepherd, who serves an Australian parish called Budgiwank. Through his "Budgiwank Experiment," he plans to convert prostitutes and junkies, then move them to his suburban parish so they can mix with the virtuous parishioners. Shepherd loses his position and moves to Jerusalem, where he becomes a performer in the Jerusalem Easter Show. Although not up to the standards of the earlier plays, *Shepherd on the Rocks* elaborates once more a theme that runs through all White's work when the ruined priest says: "At the gates of death—which is not hell, . . . I hope to shed my doubts, fears, obstinacy, lust. I do not expect an easy transition." So the young poet in the play *The Ham Funeral* has come to the end of his experience in the "luminous night," still knowing too much but never enough.

OTHER MAJOR WORKS

LONG FICTION: *Happy Valley*, 1939; *The Living and the Dead*, 1941; *The Aunt's Story*, 1948; *The Tree of Man*, 1955; *Voss*, 1957; *Riders in the Chariot*, 1961; *The Solid Mandala*, 1966; *The Vivisector*, 1970; *The Eye of the Storm*, 1973; *A Fringe of Leaves*, 1976; *The Twyborn Affair*, 1979; *Memoirs of Many in One*, 1986.

SHORT FICTION: *The Burnt Ones*, 1964; *The Cockatoos: Shorter Novels and Stories*, 1974; *Three Uneasy Pieces*, 1987.

POETRY: *The Ploughman and Other Poems*, 1935.
SCREENPLAY: *The Night of the Prowler*, 1976.

NONFICTION: *Flaws in the Glass: A Self-Portrait*, 1981; *Patrick White Speaks*, 1989; *Patrick White: Letters*, 1996 (David Marr, editor).

BIBLIOGRAPHY

Akerholt, May-Brit. *Patrick White*. Amsterdam: Rodopi, 1988. Provides extensive background material on White's published plays, including details on premiere dates, casts, directors, and set designers, as well as plot summaries and information on the plays' origins. Addresses recurrent themes in the plays, comments on their technical innovations, and stresses their satiric bent.

Bliss, Carolyn. *Patrick White's Fiction: The Paradox of Fortunate Failure*. New York: St. Martin's Press, 1986. Although not addressing the drama directly, this study offers an excellent introduction to White's overall thematic concerns. Argues that all White's writing stems from a paradox—that is, the failures so often experienced by the characters can in fact lead to their successful redemption.

Carroll, Dennis. "Patrick White." In *Australian Contemporary Drama, 1909-1982*. New York: Peter Lang, 1985. Focuses on White's use of symbolism, expressionism, and surrealism, and discusses the plays' techniques and stage conventions (through *A Cheery Soul*). Argues that White's work broke with the realistic Australian drama prior to the 1960's. Sees younger playwrights moving in new directions after White introduced such experimentation.

Collier, Gordon. *The Rocks and Sticks of Words: Style, Discourse, and Narrative Structure in the Fiction of Patrick White*. Amsterdam: Rodopi, 1992. Deconstructs White's themes and techniques in his fiction.

During, Simon. *Patrick White*. New York: Oxford University Press, 1996. Explores the life and works of White.

Marr, David. *Patrick White: A Life*. New York: Alfred A. Knopf, 1992. A lengthy biography covering all facets of White's life, from childhood to death. Provides extensive information on White's lifelong fascination with the theater, the writing and production of the plays, and their origins. Offers a more personal view of White as a playwright than do the formal studies devoted to his drama.

Whitman, Robert F. "The Dream Plays of Patrick White." *Texas Studies in Literature and Language: A Journal of the Humanities* 21, no. 2 (1979): 240-259. Sets out to define White's purpose in the early plays, discover their sources, and examine their themes. Concludes that they are all dream plays: They rely on distorted theatrical conventions, and in this way they uncover elements from the viewers' unconsciousness.

Williams, Mark. *Patrick White*. New York: St. Martin's Press, 1993. Includes many chapters that explore White's fiction titles in depth as well as discussions centered on the themes and contexts of his works. Bibliography and index.

Wolfe, Peter, ed. *Critical Essays on Patrick White*. Boston: G. K. Hall, 1990. Provides criticism and interpretation of White.

Robert Ross

JOHN WHITING

Born: Salisbury, Wiltshire, England; November 15, 1917

Died: Duddleswell, Sussex, England; June 16, 1963

PRINCIPAL DRAMA

Paul Southman, pr. 1946 (radio play), pr. 1965 (staged)

A Penny for a Song, pr. 1951, pb. 1957, revised pr. 1962

Saint's Day, pr. 1951, pb. 1952

Marching Song, pr., pb. 1954

The Gates of Summer, pr. 1956, pb. 1969

The Devils, pr., pb. 1961 (adaptation of Aldous Huxley's book *The Devils of Loudun*)

No Why, pb. 1961, pr. 1964

Conditions of Agreement, pr. 1965, pb. 1969

The Nomads, pr. 1965, pb. 1969

The Collected Plays of John Whiting, pb. 1969 (2 volumes)

No More A-Roving, pb. 1975, pr. 1979 (radio), pr. 1987 (staged)

Plays: One, pb. 1999

Plays: Two, pb. 2001

OTHER LITERARY FORMS

In 1945, John Whiting completed a novel entitled "Not a Foot of Land," but it was not published. His radio plays, *Paul Southman Eye Witness* (1949), *The Stairway* (1949), and *Love's Old Sweet Song* (1950) were broadcast by the British Broadcasting Corporation (BBC). In 1951, he began writing screenplays that were adaptations of others' works. These screenplays include *The Ship That Died of Shame* (1955, with Michael Relph and Basil Dearden), *The Good Companions* (1957, with T. J. Morrison and J. L. Hodgson), *The Captain's Table* (1959, with Bryan Forbes and Nicholas Phipps), and *Young Cassidy* (1965). His television play, *A Walk in the Desert*, aired in 1960 and was later published in *The Collected Plays of John Whiting*.

ACHIEVEMENTS

John Whiting sharply divided British audiences with his controversial departure from naturalistic drama. Labeled self-indulgent and obscure by critics, Whiting's work was championed by practical men and women of the theater. Actors, directors, and young playwrights found Whiting's structural and thematic density fertile ground for creativity and experimentation, but Whiting's work could not be easily understood in the immediacy of a production, so he alienated his audiences and baffled his critics. In the early 1950's, London audiences were not ready to depart from the standard theatrical diet of plays that were basically reproductions of life and its everyday conflicts. Whiting's way of looking at the world and dramatizing it was too different and too uncompromising to allow him success at the box office. Nevertheless, Whiting's departure from the traditional rules of drama, which require that motive, action, and consequence follow a clearly developed line, significantly expanded the range of drama, and thus he helped prepare the modern audience for such experimental playwrights as Harold Pinter and Samuel Beckett.

In the late 1940's, British drama was in the throes of a poetic renaissance. T. S. Eliot brought accessible verse to the stage and in *The Cocktail Party* (pr. 1949, pb. 1950) dramatized a vague spiritual optimism. Christopher Fry's *The Lady's Not for Burning* (pr. 1948, pb. 1949) entertained the audience with its whimsical poetry and affirmation of life, and the widely popular plays of Terence Rattigan provided the audience with evenings of well-made plays with easily accessible plots and characterizations. Whiting's work exhibits influences from all three playwrights, but his intellectual vision developed their poetry, comedy, and characterizations into plays with statements the audience did not care to comprehend.

Whiting's plays do not have easily labeled themes and preoccupations. He believed that while the purpose of entertainment was to reassure, the purpose of art was to raise doubts. Whiting claimed allegiance to the tradition of the intellectual elite whose concern was to write difficult plays for a discriminating audience. His recurrent concern with the nature of violence and the limits of personal responsibility anticipated the interests of a younger generation of playwrights who chose to write about similar conflicts, and although Whiting's originality was not recognized until the last years of his life, he is now considered a pioneer of contemporary drama. In 1965, an annual award of one thousand pounds was established—to be awarded to promising young playwrights—in memory of John Whiting.

BIOGRAPHY

Born in Salisbury, Wiltshire, England, John Robert Whiting was the son of an army officer who later became a lawyer. Whiting was educated at Taunton, a public school at Somerset, where he was considered an unremarkable student. When the time came to choose a career, a university education was not even considered an option because his academic standing, as well as his interest, was too low. On the advice of his father and his headmaster, Whiting decided to train to be an actor. As a student at the Royal Academy of Dramatic Art, Whiting was painfully self-conscious and shy, and thus his work suffered in the beginning. While on vacation from school, he was cast in a small part in a provincial theater, and he returned to the academy with much more skill, self-confidence, and determination. He completed his training in 1937 with a positive report of his abilities and chances as an actor. Although acting jobs were scarce, Whiting survived with occasional jobs in radio plays until World War II interrupted his career.

Originally, Whiting registered as a conscientious objector. Shortly after he registered, however, he changed his mind, having been exposed to pacifist groups that he regarded as collections of snobs and aggressive intellectuals. Whiting was also torn by the conflict between loyalty to his father's soldiering tradition and loyalty to his own feeling of repugnance toward war. Finally, Whiting became a reluctant soldier. When he registered in the army, he requested an infantry regiment because his father had been an infantry officer, but the army ignored his preference and put him in artillery. He often told his wife, Asthore Lloyd Mawson, whom he had married in 1940, that the guns he helped fire would never hit anything.

In the army, Whiting began writing as a hobby when he discovered Frederick Rolfe, an author who, under the name Baron Corvo, wrote strange tales in an elaborate pseudomedieval script. The slow, painstaking process of imitating Rolfe's calligraphy influenced more than Whiting's handwriting. The moments of concentration gave Whiting opportunities to think and to absorb an archaic style and a recondite vocabulary. He developed a love for language. Initially, Whiting wrote poems and stories, but his instinctive need for an audience led him to write plays. Several of his early radio plays were broadcast by the BBC, but much of his drama for the stage was kept private or was rejected by theaters.

In March, 1951, his comic *A Penny for a Song* opened at Haymarket Theatre. The much grimmer

Saint's Day was produced the following September and won first prize in the Festival of Britain play competition. *Saint's Day* angered critics and was labeled incomprehensible, but the contest judges remained firm in their support of Whiting as a talented and original playwright. Simple bad luck plagued many of Whiting's plays. Fires, accidents, and illnesses often spoiled premiere productions, and he was rarely well received by audiences and critics.

Finally, in 1961, *The Devils* brought Whiting long-awaited praise from critics. Although his late success brought him many calls for work from major companies and theaters, *The Devils* was his last completed play. In November, 1962, he was diagnosed as having cancer. After years of struggling to support a family, his last year of life was eased by financial and critical success, but his attempts at revisions and new plays were left incomplete when he died in June of 1963.

Like many of his characters, Whiting was forced to accept death when success was just within reach. He became terminally ill just as he was looking forward to a successful and creative future in a theater he could finally call his own. Unlike Pinter and Beckett, who had time to develop an audience, Whiting's audience was just beginning to understand him when his life ended.

ANALYSIS

Deeply influenced by the plays of T. S. Eliot, who had brought philosophical thought as well as verse to the stage, John Whiting showed that heightened prose was more viable than verse. He believed that the easiest way of communicating with an audience was direct speech. Unlike Pinter, who later exploited the colloquialisms of daily speech to the point of absurdity, Whiting combined common language with heightened intelligence and insight, and such a combination often confused his audience. Whereas Eliot never made his characters as interesting as what they said, Whiting created distinctive characters who were articulate, sensitive, and often pathetic in their extreme vulnerability.

The turning points in Whiting's plays involve personality changes that are so basic that they are better labeled conversions. Whiting's characters do not simply change their minds about a person or decision; they dramatically alter their views on life and death. In addition, Whiting never directly dramatizes how his characters change. The audience sees only the beginning and the end of a process, and the actual moments of decision are left obscure. Whiting chooses to dramatize conversions indirectly because to dramatize them too completely would invite didacticism or melodrama.

Whiting's position on the morality of his characters often baffles his audiences even more than do his plots. It is futile for the audience to look for motivation or to try to identify with Whiting's characters because they dramatize ideology in action rather than an easily identifiable human need. For example, in *Marching Song*, audiences resist identifying with a former army general who brutally killed children as a part of military strategy. When the general is strongly advised to commit suicide to avoid being a further embarrassment to his country, few in the audience care to share in his philosophical dilemma or try to understand Whiting's position. Rather than simple morality, Whiting is concerned with why characters behave the way they do and how their actions affect their worlds. The intellect is Whiting's playground, rather than the emotions, and one can best understand his plays by considering how they raise questions rather than how they stimulate emotions.

Whiting's vision is essentially tragic. Of his six full-length plays, three end in violent death, and each death is directly or indirectly the fulfillment of self-destruction. Whiting's characters are torn by dual motives to redeem themselves from and to damn themselves for their moral failure. Self-destruction becomes a twisted redemption that also fails. In his plays, the refusal to recognize responsibility leads to a tragic conclusion. The apocalyptic quality of much of Whiting's work, the sense of mortality, and the fear of inconsequence suggest a world that is run by a cruel god who uses death as a practical joke. At best, this awareness of death encourages human beings to grasp at the honest, loving moments of life; at worst, it invites them to enact their own destruction—if only to prove that they have some small measure of control over their lives.

A PENNY FOR A SONG

Whiting wrote *A Penny for a Song* during a happy period in his life, and the farcical action and the life-loving characters dramatize an optimistic perspective on the world. Set in the garden of the country home of Sir Timothy Bellboys, the tone suggests summer ease and festivities, although the threat of war hovers just beyond the garden: Napoleon and his army are expected to invade. The central characters all have delightfully complicated strategies for survival, and their energy and enthusiasm elevate the farce. The play suggests that war threatens everyday life and therefore that simple domestic moments of peace are fragile and precious.

From the opening moments of the play, when Humpage, the sleeping family lookout, spills his cakes from his post high in a tree and a dignified visitor becomes lost while looking for an outhouse, the audience knows that in this play about war, no one will be harmed. The ineffective, bungling characters with their candid feelings and good intentions charm the audience. Although they caricature a nation of simple people under the threat of war, they invite the audience to share in the real quirks and whims of humankind. The members of this respectable group of family and friends exhibit a childlike innocence in their plans for coping with invasion, and like imaginative children, they accept one another's fantastic schemes. Sir Timothy plans to defeat the French by impersonating Napoleon, tunneling his way to the rear of the invading troops and leading them in a retreat. The audience immediately understands that Sir Timothy does not exhibit a sound method of warfare; rather, he represents the noble human drive to take responsibility for one's countrymen.

In the comic tradition, Whiting's plot is based on confused messages and mistaken identities. When Sir Timothy does not receive the message that the home guard is engaging in a military exercise, he mistakes them for the French, and his potentially dangerous little war is on. Cannons fire, alarms sound, and it appears that real danger threatens these characters who are so intent on preserving life that they might hurt someone. Following the traditional comic plot, however, Whiting contrives timely revelations before serious damage is done.

The theatricality of the action—the sheer entertainment of the clownish characters and slapstick action—prevents the audience from questioning the play's sense. The garden bustles with strangers and relatives coming, going, and getting lost. Doors and windows open and close constantly as servants and family go about their business. In the distance, Sir Timothy flies through the air in a hot-air balloon. His brother Lamprett exhibits his fire-fighting equipment, and Lamprett's wife appears in full armorial regalia as she announces her plans to join the East Anglian Amazon Corps. Throughout the play, Humpage roosts in his tree and, amid the surrounding chaos, tries to hold on to his telescope and cakes.

Hardly a logical argument against war, the play is an affirmation of life and the human will to survive. The implausible plot staggers along as the characters refuse to let logic interfere with their plans to save one another: Whenever a character's ideas are challenged by reasonable remarks, he or she spontaneously transforms doubt into optimism, or simply changes the subject entirely. Therefore, the conversations are often incoherent. For these characters, however, reason stems from a serious perspective, and to be serious would be to admit that Napoleon might win. In a tragic play, such as *Saint's Day*, self-deception leads to self-destruction: In Whiting's serious plays, self-deception always involves the abdication of responsibility to others, and then shame and self-inflicted punishment. In contrast, in *A Penny for a Song*, the characters joyfully assume responsibility for the happiness and safety of others, so their self-deception is redeemed. Still, Whiting did not design the play to end happily simply because the characters have good intentions; many of his tragic characters have good intentions as well. Indeed, the happy resolution depends on inconsequence and implausibility. Disaster is always a possibility in *A Penny for a Song*, and the audience is constantly reminded that the characters survive because Whiting is writing a farce and wants their struggle to end in harmony.

Whiting uses the blind veteran, Edward Sterne, to articulate his view that self-deception is necessary for survival. Sterne comments on the outrageous schemes of the Bellboyses and their visitors:

> And so we escape, childlike, into the illusion. We clown and posture but not to amuse others—no—to comfort ourselves. The laughter is incidental to the tragic spectacle of each man attempting to hide his intolerable self.

Through Sterne, Whiting also comments subtly on the power of the dramatic illusion. While Sterne suggests that he knows the motivations for his own illusions, the playwright insists on a deeper human need to create and participate in dramatic artifice. Edward Sterne knows that his mission to walk to London and tell a mad king to stop the war is futile. He knows that he is deluding himself into believing that his small will can affect the world. Nevertheless, Whiting suggests that purposeful action has a kind of redemptive power, whatever the outcome. When Sir Timothy outlines his ridiculous and dangerous plan to save Britain, he refuses to let reasonable comments intimidate him. He speaks for the playwright when he says, "I may fail—but what of that? It is what we attempt that matters."

Whiting himself remarked that *A Penny for a Song* was simply about Christian charity. In a time of war, a chaotic household of eccentric characters meets, with individual passions ranging from fire fighting to reading a good poem, but in spite of vast differences, harmony prevails. The characters' cross-purposes never result in genuine conflict; the mock war ends with little damage done, and all the self-made soldiers retire to the kitchen to eat and talk of cricket. The successful actions of these charitable characters suggest that the only way to survive the violent onslaught of the world is to throw oneself into it imaginatively and cheerfully.

SAINT'S DAY

In *Saint's Day*, Whiting shows a very different response to a world that threatens the individual. The characters respond with self-righteousness, and their cynicism toward others results in self-destruction. They deliberately alienate themselves from family and community. The play's action symbolizes a death wish, with death the ultimate withdrawal into self.

Here, Whiting violently dramatizes the dangers of irresponsibility. The characters become so involved in using others for selfish goals that they lose sight of the larger human purpose of survival, and they are destroyed by the inevitable chaos of irresponsible action. After the first scene, set in the living room of the play's main character, Paul Southman, the audience knows that this is no standard drawing-room drama. In his stage directions, Whiting describes Southman's living room as an "architectural freak," noting that the elegant furniture has been neglected and abused. Dirty dishes are piled on an ornate yet filthy tray, and a bicycle lies upstage. The set suggests that normal life has suddenly and radically been interrupted. The audience is uncertain about the tone of the play, and thus Whiting prevents them from assigning labels or drawing neat conclusions.

Whiting uses dialogue to jolt the audience into viewing the play as a symbolic philosophical statement rather than an evening's dramatic illusion. Whereas the drawing-room setting parodies those of popular plays, the dialogue often parodies that of Eliot's poetic drama. Whiting does not use verse, but the audience is forced to perceive language as more than simple communication that moves the plot forward. For sophisticated audiences attuned to his intentions, Whiting's dialogue is dense with meaning, but the casual theatergoer may find it cryptic.

The opening of the play suggests possibilities for fulfillment: Aging writer Paul Southman is about to be honored for his literary achievements; his granddaughter, Stella, is pregnant; and her unsuccessful husband may sell some paintings in town. These possibilities, however, are but glimmers of hope. Images of death and decay permeate the play: The strong old trees outside the house are dying, the family dog mysteriously dies, and young Stella's hair is graying.

Southman himself, once a respected poet and radical pamphleteer, is approaching senility after twenty-five years of self-imposed exile. His literary attacks on society have been reduced to an irrational feud with the nearby villagers, who in turn despise him for his eccentricities. Southman's selfish withdrawal from the world has atrophied his emotions and his intellect. He is cynical about the celebration to be held in his honor. When soldiers terrorize the village, he wants them to be his allies so he can better continue his one-man war. When his granddaughter is killed, he places her death in the context of a bad joke, and when he is finally led to his own hanging, he is so far removed from reality that he believes he is going to his celebration, and therefore goes without a struggle. Symbolically, he is dead from the beginning of the play; his execution simply finalizes a process that began when he started his personal war on the world.

For an audience that expects coherent action and characters with identifiable motivations, Whiting's play offers some shocking surprises. The set is confusing; the dialogue, incoherent; and the actions, symbolic. The sequence of events in the play is implausible, but Whiting's purpose is not to present a logical world. Dramatizing the dangerous interrelationships of actions, Whiting illustrates how one careless act can lead to outrageous and deadly consequences.

When the pompous scholar Robert Procathren stupidly and accidentally shoots Stella, Whiting does not intend for the audience to feel sympathy or outrage: The characters are too symbolic and the action too contrived to warrant such emotions. Whiting contrives the shooting to make a statement about the inability of individuals to control themselves and their world. Although Procathren is innocent of malicious intent, he is guilty of both insensitivity and carelessness.

The audience is forced to consider each character's responsibility as a philosophical problem. Because each action has far-reaching ramifications, the audience must consider how responsible individuals are for their own actions as well as for the actions of others. The accident leads Procathren to alter his view of the value of life, for Stella's death suggests a world in which violence is random, in which death not only is inevitable but also often occurs as a grim practical joke. He suddenly links to a violent world, and as a result he begins a course of self-destruction as a way of getting revenge on the world and on himself. When Procathren's plan involves the deaths of Southman and Stella's husband, Whiting suggests that all three are indirectly responsible for Stella's death.

Whiting goes on to show that Procathren's careless act has ramifications beyond the corrupt Southman household. After the accident, Procathren becomes a militant cynic. He takes his bitter revelations to town and convinces the minister that theological books are deceptions and that faith is a lie. Totally convinced, the minister burns his books in a bonfire that rages out of control and destroys the entire town. Following the same logic, the closing scene of the play suggests that no one is innocent. A child from the village who, with her family, seeks refuge in Southman's home, closes the play by ignorantly dancing to music that heralds three hangings just beyond the door. She is immediately shamed when she realizes the impropriety of her actions. The audience learns that the girl's name is Stella, and the link with the dead Stella implies that even the young and innocent are doomed by the irresponsible actions of others and themselves.

THE DEVILS

In his last completed play, *The Devils*, Whiting even more violently dramatizes the destructive power of human beings' irresponsibility. In the program to the original production, Whiting offered his view of the historical incident that inspired the play—in Whiting's account, the tragedy of a talented and intelligent priest whose downfall was ultimately the result of his own actions. Here Whiting employs Bertolt Brecht's alienation effects to force the audience to consider the horrors that can result from selfishness and vengeful hypocrisy. The play's episodic structure is useful for conveying a wide range of information quickly, but it also continually reminds the audience that they are watching a play, an artifice designed to make a statement.

One of Whiting's typical characters, Grandier the priest, is a sensitive man who is driven toward self-destruction. His struggle toward his own death is a consciously sought redemption for his inability to feel tenderness in physical love. His frequent illicit relationships with women are weak attempts to disguise his sensuality with affection. He romantically enacts a mock marriage to his youngest and most innocent lover, and he says that her naïveté shames him, yet in another scene, when she reveals that she is pregnant, he harshly says that he is finished with her.

Throughout the play, Whiting dramatizes the conflict between human beings' basest drives and their noblest impulses. The nuns are guilty of debasing spiritual passion into lust and vengeance, while Grandier, the great theologian and orator, similarly debases his priestly office by reveling in a sensual life. An almost omnipresent character, the Sewerman, punctuates each act with his presence and reminds the characters and the audience that sewers run through the most official and noble places. Aspirations to love and spiritual redemption are graphically debased by the Sewerman's presence.

Through the destructive hysteria of the nuns, Whiting not only comments on the animalistic drives of people but also raises questions concerning the nature of evil. The sexually frustrated prioress, Sister Jeanne, seeks revenge on the object of her desire, and she incites the nuns to charge that Grandier is a demon who possesses them. As the play progresses, however, the audience sees that Sister Jeanne is not simply pretending. A scene in which she and the demon that possesses her converse and laugh suggests that evil is a real force, but a force made by human beings. The demon is Sister Jeanne's own creation, now all too real, no mere figment of the imagination.

OTHER MAJOR WORKS

SCREENPLAYS: *The Ship That Died of Shame*, 1955 (with Michael Relph and Basil Dearden); *The Good Companions*, 1957 (with T. J. Morrison and J. L. Hodgson); *The Captain's Table*, 1959 (with Bryan Forbes and Nicholas Phipps); *Young Cassidy*, 1965.

TELEPLAY: *A Walk in the Desert*, 1960.

RADIO PLAYS: *Eye Witness*, 1949; *The Stairway*, 1949; *Love's Old Sweet Song*, 1950.

MISCELLANEOUS: *The Art of the Dramatist and Other Pieces*, 1969 (short fiction, criticism, lectures; Ronald Hayman, editor).

BIBLIOGRAPHY

Demastes, William W., and Katherine Kelly, eds. *British Playwrights, 1956-1995: A Research and Production Sourcebook*. Westport, Conn.: Greenwood Press, 1996. An essay on Whiting discusses his life and works and provides an assessment of the playwright's career. Also provides a bibliography.

Goodall, Jane. "*The Devils* and Its Sources: Modern Perspectives on the Loudun Possession." In *Drama and Philosophy*, edited by James Redmond. New York: Cambridge University Press, 1990. The essay shows how Whiting shifts the emphasis from Grandier's villainy to his inner struggle. It also compares the play with Henry de Montherlant's *Port-Royal* (pr., pb. 1954; English translation, 1962) and Jean Genet's *Le Balcon* (pb. 1956; *The Balcony*, 1957).

_____. "Musicality and Meaning in the Dialogue of *Saint's Day*." *Modern Drama* 29 (December, 1986): 567-579. This essay defends the play against the early charges of abstruseness by demonstrating its underlying logic. It seeks to show the dramatic elements of this logic in terms of the search for revelation. Looks particularly at the play's dialogue.

Robinson, Gabrielle. *A Private Mythology: The Manuscripts and Plays of John Whiting*. Cranbury, N.J.: Associated University Press, 1988. Robinson examines myth as it is manifested in the works of Whiting. Bibliography and index.

Salmon, Eric. *The Dark Journey: John Whiting as Dramatist*. London: Barrie and Jenkins, 1979. Probably the fullest account of Whiting's complete œuvre. It traces in particular Whiting's obsession "with the innate tendency of the sensitive towards self-destruction." Four appendices, a bibliography, and an index.

Jane Falco,
updated by David Barratt

OSCAR WILDE

Born: Dublin, Ireland; October 16, 1854
Died: Paris, France; November 30, 1900

PRINCIPAL DRAMA

Vera: Or, The Nihilists, pb. 1880, pr. 1883
The Duchess of Padua, pb. 1883, pr. 1891
Lady Windermere's Fan, pr. 1892, pb. 1893
Salomé, pb. 1893 (in French), pb. 1894 (in
   English), pr. 1896 (in French), pr. 1905 (in
   English)
A Woman of No Importance, pr. 1893, pb. 1894
An Ideal Husband, pr. 1895, pb. 1899
*The Importance of Being Earnest: A Trivial
   Comedy for Serious People*, pr. 1895, pb. 1899
A Florentine Tragedy, pr. 1906, pb. 1908 (one act,
   completed by T. Sturge More)
La Sainte Courtisane, pb. 1908

OTHER LITERARY FORMS

Oscar Wilde's character and conversation were in themselves striking enough to gain for him the attention of the reading public, but in addition to playwriting, he practiced all the other literary forms. He began writing poetry at an early age, commemorating the death of his sister Isola with "Requiescat" in 1867 and winning the Newdigate Prize for Poetry at Oxford with *Ravenna* in 1878. Wilde's *Poems* appeared in 1881; *The Sphinx* in 1894; and *The Ballad of Reading Gaol*, his last literary work, in 1898. His efforts in fiction include "The Canterville Ghost" (1887), which was made into a movie in 1943; *The Happy Prince and Other Tales* (1888); *Lord Arthur Savile's Crime and Other Stories* (1891); *A House of Pomegranates* (1891); and his novel, *The Picture of Dorian Gray* (serialized in *Lippincott's Monthly Magazine* in 1890, published in book form in 1891). Oscar Wilde's best-known essays and literary criticism appear in *Intentions* (1891). *De Profundis*, the long letter the imprisoned Wilde wrote to Lord Alfred Douglas, was published in 1905; his collected letters, edited by Rupert Hart-Davies, appeared in 1962.

ACHIEVEMENTS

To accuse Oscar Wilde of anything so active-sounding as "achievement" would be an impertinence that the strenuously indolent author would most likely deplore. Yet it must be admitted that Wilde's presence, poses, ideas, and epigrams made him a potent influence, if not on the English literary tradition, at least on the artistic community of his own day. More visibly than any British contemporary, Oscar Wilde personified the doctrines of turn-of-the-century aestheticism—that art existed for its own sake and that one should live so as to make from the raw materials of one's own existence an elegantly finished artifice. Wilde's aestheticism, caricatured by W. S. Gilbert and Sir Arthur Sullivan in their operetta *Patience: Or, Bunthorne's Bride* (1881) and in Robert Smythe Hichens's novel *The Green Carnation* (1894), mingled ideas from his two very different Oxford mentors, John Ruskin and Walter Pater, with the influence of the French Symbolists and, for a time, certain theories of the American painter James McNeill Whistler. However, Wilde's Irish wit and eloquence made the articulation of this intellectual pastiche something distinctively his own.

Wilde's literary works are polished achievements in established modes rather than experiments in thought or form. His poems and plays tend to look across the English Channel to the examples of the Symbolists and the masters of the *pièce bien faite*, though his *Salomé*, a biblical play written in French after the style of the then acclaimed dramatist Maurice Maeterlinck, was to engender a yet more significant work of art, Richard Strauss's opera of the same title. If they are not intellectually or technically adventurous, however, Wilde's works are incomparable for their talk—talk that tends to be Wilde's own put into the mouths of his characters. The outrageous, elegant, paradoxical conversation volleyed by Wilde's languid verbal athletes have given English literature more quotable tags than have the speeches of any other dramatist save William Shakespeare.

BIOGRAPHY

Oscar Fingal O'Flahertie Wills Wilde was born on October 16, 1854, in Dublin, Ireland, to parents who were among the most colorful members of the Irish gentry. His father, Sir William Wilde, one of the foremost Victorian oculists and surgeons, numbered crowned heads of Europe among his patients. He was equally famed for his archaeological research and his amorous adventures. Oscar Wilde's mother was no less remarkable. Born Jane Francesca Elgee, she gained public notice for the patriotic pieces she published under the pseudonym Speranza. When one of Speranza's essays brought Sir Charles Gavan Duffy, leader of the Young Ireland party, to trial for high treason and sedition, the tall and dramatic authoress rose in court, proclaimed "I alone am the culprit," and on the spot became one of the heroines of Ireland.

This colorful background and his mother's doting attention must have fostered young Wilde's imagina-

Oscar Wilde (Library of Congress)

tion. His mind received more discipline and direction when, through good fortune, he was brought into contact with a series of fine teachers. At Trinity College in Dublin, Wilde's Greek tutor, the Reverend John Pentland Mahaffy, inspired him with a love of Hellenic culture and, by his own witty example, honed and polished the younger man's conversational talents. Next, having won a demyship to Magdalen College, Oxford, in 1874, Wilde encountered Ruskin (then Slade Professor of Art), whose social conscience, love of medieval architecture, and belief in the necessary connection between art and life were to become part of Wilde's own creed. Even more important to Wilde's development was Pater, the skeptical latter-day Epicurean famed for his *Studies in the History of the Renaissance* (1873). In the light of Pater's intellectual advice to the youth of the day, most memorably distilled in his observation that "to burn always with this hard, gemlike flame, to maintain this ecstasy, is success in life," the Oxonian Wilde's famous ambition, "Oh, would that I could live up to my blue china!" seems a less frivolous objective.

In 1879, Wilde went to London, where, sharing rooms with the artist Frank Miles, he became one of the central figures of the aesthetic movement and made the acquaintance of many of the celebrities of the day, particularly the lovely Lily Langtry, whose career as a professional beauty had been launched by Miles's drawings. The tall, heavy, epigrammatic young Wilde was soon known in society for his eccentric dress and his paradoxical wit. Caricatured as Reginald Bunthorne in Gilbert and Sullivan's *Patience*, he became the epitome of aestheticism for the wider public as well. The shrewd producers of the comic opera, which was to go on an American tour, realized that the presence of Bunthorne's prototype would fan the flames of interest, so with their sponsorship, Wilde embarked on an extended tour of the United States that permitted him to see the notable places, to meet the notable people, and having done so, to conclude, "When good Americans die they go to Paris. When bad Americans die they stay in America."

On his return to England after a short stay in Paris, Wilde launched himself on what was to be his period of eminence. He made friends with the painter Whistler and became engaged to the pretty but conventional daughter of an Irish barrister, Constance Lloyd, whom he married in 1883. They had two sons, Cyril and Vyvyan. In need of funds to finance his luxurious mode of life, he cultivated his literary career, if not in earnest, then at least with more enterprise than he would have wished to acknowledge. He lectured, reviewed books, and for a time edited *The Woman's World*. His prose works appeared in rapid succession: short stories (*Lord Arthur Savile's Crime and Other Stories*, *The Happy Prince and Other Tales*, *A House of Pomegranates*), a novel (*The Picture of Dorian Gray*), and a collection of critical essays (*Intentions*).

With his fiction, Wilde solidly established his reputation in the world of letters, but his great period of financial success began only when he turned to writing for the popular theater. Although he found the enforced discipline of playwriting difficult and never regarded his social comedies as anything more than well-crafted potboilers, Wilde managed in a span of three years to write four plays that paid him exceedingly well and made him even more famous. *Lady Windermere's Fan* (premiering in February, 1892) was followed by *A Woman of No Importance* (April, 1893), *An Ideal Husband* (January, 1895), and *The Importance of Being Earnest* (February, 1895). After completing *Lady Windermere's Fan*, Wilde went to France, where he wrote *Salomé*, a poetic drama intended to make his artistic reputation on the Continent and at home. Wilde offered the title role in that play to Sarah Bernhardt, who accepted and began rehearsals for a London production that was never staged: The Lord Chamberlain banned it for violating the old law forbidding the theatrical representation of biblical characters.

Having reached its zenith, Wilde's star rapidly sank to oblivion in the spring of 1895. Since 1891, Wilde had been friends, and more than friends, with the handsome, talented, spoiled, unstable Lord Alfred Douglas, a younger son of the eighth marquess of Queensbury. The relationship was not discreet. Lord Alfred took pleasure in flaunting himself in the role of minion to the celebrated Wilde and in flouting the authority of his father. As his letters reveal, Wilde in his turn expressed his feelings for the elegant youth whose "slim gilt soul walks between passion and poetry" with his customary extravagance. Finally, in what was to be one of the most perverse and distasteful interludes in the history of English jurisprudence, Wilde was provoked to sue the ferocious marquess for criminal libel when that rash peer had culminated a campaign of harassment by leaving at Wilde's club a card bearing the words "to Oscar Wilde posing as a somdomite [sic]." For his defense, Queensbury collected a small parade of blackmailers and male prostitutes to testify to the accuracy of his epithet. Unwisely persisting in his suit, Wilde failed, on Queensbury's acquittal, to seize his chance to flee the country. Having lost his battle with the marquess, Wilde in turn was arrested, tried, and ultimately convicted for practicing "the love that dares not tell its name." He was sentenced to two years at hard labor.

Wilde's twenty-four months of imprisonment were a continuous mortification of body, mind, and spirit. He had lost his honor, his position, his fortune, and his family. Although he was to write one more fine work, *The Ballad of Reading Gaol*, his life was behind him. Released from prison on May 19, 1897, he left England behind as well. Under the name Sebastian Melmoth, Wilde resided abroad, principally in France and Italy, until his death in Paris in 1900.

ANALYSIS

Oscar Wilde completed seven plays during his life, and for the purpose of discussion, these works can be divided into two groups: comedies and serious works. The four social comedies Wilde wrote for the commercial theater of his day, *Lady Windermere's Fan*, *A Woman of No Importance*, *An Ideal Husband*, and *The Importance of Being Earnest*, brought him money and prestige but not artistic satisfaction. There were three plays intended as serious works of art: *Vera*, *The Duchess of Padua*, and *Salomé*. None of these three plays gained popular regard, critical acclaim, or theatrical success in Wilde's lifetime. One can disregard the first two and lose little by the omission. *Vera*, published when Wilde was only twenty-five, is an apprentice piece that unsuccessfully mingles revolutionary Russian politics (particularly ill-timed, for Czar Alexander II had recently been assassinated, and the consort of his successor was sister to Alexandra, wife of the prince of Wales), improbable psychology, creaky melodrama, and what was already Wilde's dramatic forte: witty, ironic speech. *The Duchess of Padua* is a derivative verse drama in the intricate, full-blown style that worked so well in the hands of the Jacobeans and has failed so dismally for their many and often talented imitators. When read, the play has its fine moments, but even at its best, it is nothing more than a good piece of imitation. In *Salomé*, however, Wilde offered the world a serious drama of unquestionable distinction, a work that further enriched Western culture by providing a libretto for Richard Strauss's fine opera of the same title.

SALOMÉ

The English-speaking public, to whom Wilde's four comedies are familiar enough, is less likely to have read or seen performed his *Salomé*, yet this biblical extrapolation, with its pervasive air of overripe sensuality, is of all of his plays the one most characteristic of its age and most important to the European cultural tradition. Wilde wrote his poetic drama in France, and in French, during the autumn of 1891. Wilde's command of the French language was not idiomatic but fluent in the schoolroom style. This very limitation became an asset when he chose to cast his play in the stylized, ritualistic mold set by the Belgian playwright Maeterlinck, whose works relied heavily on repetition, parallelism, and chiming effect—verbal traits equally characteristic of a writer who thinks in English but translates into French. Like the language, the biblical source of the story is bent to Wilde's purposes. In the New Testament accounts of the death of John the Baptist (or Jokanaan, as he is called in the play), Salomé, the eighteen-year-old princess of Judea, is not held responsible for John's death; rather, blame for the prophet's death is laid on Salomé's mother, Herodias. Furthermore, as Wilde's literary executor, Robert Ross, and a number of other critics have observed, Wilde's Herod is a synthesis of

a handful of biblical Herods and tetrarchs. Although Wilde's license with the language and sources of his play is sometimes deprecated, it should not be faulted. As a poetic dramatist, a verbal contriver of a symbolic ritual, his intention was not to transcribe but to transfigure.

The action of Wilde's *Salomé* takes place by moonlight on a great terrace above King Herod's banquet hall. The simple setting is deftly conceived to heighten dramatic effects. On this spare stage, all entrances—whether Salomé's, and later Herod's and Herodias's by the great staircase of Jokanaan's from the cistern where he has been imprisoned—are striking. In addition, the play's ruling motifs, moonlight and the recurrent contrasts of white, black, and—with increasing frequency as the play moves toward its grisly climax—red, emerge clearly.

As the play begins, a cosmopolitan group of soldiers and pages attendant on the Judean royal house occupy the terrace. Their conversation on the beauty of the Princess Salomé, the strangeness of the moon, and the rich tableau of the Tetrarch and his party feasting within sets a weird tone that is enhanced by the sound of Jokanaan's prophesies rising from his cistern prison. Salomé, like "a dove that has strayed . . . a narcissus trembling in the wind . . . a silver flower," glides onto the terrace. The prophet's strange voice and words stir the princess as deeply as her beauty troubles the young Syrian captain of the guard, a conquered prince now a slave in Herod's palace. At her command, the Syrian brings forth Jokanaan from his prison. The prophet's uncanny beauty—he seems as chaste and ascetic as she has just pronounced the moon to be—works a double charm of attraction and repulsion on Salomé. His body like a thin white statue, his black hair, his mouth "like a pomegranate cut with a knife of ivory" all kindle the princess's desire. His disgusted rejection of her love only fans the flames of lust. She must have him: "I will kiss thy mouth, Jokanaan," she chants, as the Syrian who adores her kills himself at her feet and the prophet who despises her descends once more to his cistern.

At this point, Herod and Herodias, attended by their court, enter. Their comments on the moon (to

Herod, "She is like a mad woman, a mad woman who is looking everywhere for lovers"; to Herodias, "the moon is like the moon, that is all") introduce the significant differences in their equally evil natures. Herod is superstitious, cowardly, obliquely cruel, a tyrannical yet vacillating ruler; Herodias is brutal with the callous directness of an utterly debased woman. Salomé's strange beauty tempts Herod just as Jokanaan's tempts Salomé. Despite Herodias's disapproval and Salomé's reluctance, Herod presses the princess to dance. He offers her whatever reward she may request, even to the half of his kingdom. Having exacted this rash promise of the infatuated despot, Salomé performs her famous dance of seven veils and for her reward requires the head of Jokanaan on a silver charger. As horrified by this demand as his ghoulish consort is delighted, the superstitious Herod offers Salomé a long and intricate catalog of alternative payments—the rich, rare, curious, and vulgar contents of an Oriental or *fin de siècle* treasure chest. With the sure instincts of the true collector, Salomé persists in her original demand. Unable to break his vow, the horrified king dispatches the Nubian executioner into the cistern. Presently, in a striking culmination of the play's color imagery, the Nubian's arm rises from the cistern. This ebony stem bears a strange flower: a silver shield surmounted by the prophet's bloody head. Delirious with ecstasy, Salomé addresses her passion to the disembodied lover-prophet she has asked for, silenced, and gained. "I have kissed thy mouth, Jokanaan," she concludes as a moonbeam falls on her. At Herod's cry, "Kill that woman!" the soldiers rush forward, crushing her beneath their shields.

Even so brief an account as that above demonstrates that the play has potential in sheer dramatic terms, as the great Sarah Bernhardt realized when, though much too old for the title role, she agreed to play the role of Salomé in a proposed London production that was not to be. *Salomé* is a richly fashioned tapestry. The play's prevailing mode, presentation of typically talkative Wildean characters articulating rather than acting on their emotions, gives way at three powerful moments—when Salomé dances, when the arm bearing Jokanaan's head rises from the cistern, and when the silver shields crush the dancer and her reward—to pure act, unsullied by words.

The play's psychological and symbolic suggestiveness are equally rich. One of Wilde's great contributions to the Salomé story was to provide psychological underpinnings for the sequence of events. To Wilde's invention are owed Salomé's spurned love for the prophet and the mutual hostility that counterbalances the sensual bond between Herod and Herodias. As an expression of love's ambivalence, *Salomé* is "the incarnate spirit of the aesthetic woman," a collector who (much in the spirit of Robert Browning's duke of Ferrara, it would seem) does not desire a living being but a "love object" handsomely mounted. Richard Ellmann finds something more personally symbolic in the tragedy. Jokanaan, says Ellmann, presents the spirit-affirming, body-negating moral earnestness of Wilde's "Ruskinism"; Salomé, who collects beauty, sensations, and strange experiences, who consummates her love for the prophet in "a relation at once totally sensual and totally 'mystical,'" stands for the rival claims of Pater. Herod, like his creator, vainly struggles to master these opposing impulses both within and outside himself.

LADY WINDERMERE'S FAN, A WOMAN OF NO IMPORTANCE, AND AN IDEAL HUSBAND

Wilde's first three comedies, although each has its particular charms and defects, are sufficiently similar to one another, and sufficiently inferior to his fourth, *The Importance of Being Earnest*, to be discussed as a group rather than individually. Always lazy about writing (which was an arduous process for a verbal artist with his high standards) but perpetually in need of money to pay for the great and small luxuries that were his necessities of life, Wilde agreed in 1891 to write a play for George Alexander, the actor-manager of St. James's Theater. The result was *Lady Windermere's Fan*, a modern drawing-room comedy set in high society and frankly aimed to engage the interest of the London playgoing public. The financial results were gratifying enough to encourage Wilde to write three more plays in the same vein, though he never much respected the form or the products. Only in *The Importance of Being Earnest* was he to overcome the inherent weaknesses of the well-made society play, but each of the other three pieces is fine enough to win for him the title of best writer of British comedies between Richard Brinsley Sheridan and George Bernard Shaw.

Lady Windermere's Fan, A Woman of No Importance, and *An Ideal Husband* all center, as their titles suggest, on relationships between men and women, or more precisely between gentlemen and ladies. The plays were up-to-the-minute in providing fashionable furnishings and costumes to charm both segments of their intended audience. Late Victorian society people enjoyed seeing themselves reflected as creatures of such style and wit, while the middle classes delighted at being given a glimpse into the secret rites of the world of fashion. In fact, one might suspect that Wilde's stated concern for the Aristotelian unity of time in these plays springs less from belief in that classical standard than from the opportunity (or even necessity) that placing three acts of high life in a twenty-four-hour period provides for striking changes of costume and set.

In each of these elaborate "modern drawing-room comedies with pink lamp shades," as Wilde termed them, one finds recurrent character types: puritanical figures of virtue (wives in *Lady Windermere's Fan* and *An Ideal Husband,* an heiress soon to be a fiancé in *A Woman of No Importance*), mundanely fashionable hypocrites, and exceptional humanitarians of two types—the dandified lord (Darlington, Illingworth, and Goring) and the poised and prosperous "fallen woman," two of whom (Mrs. Erlynne in *Lady Windermere's Fan* and Mrs. Chevely in *An Ideal Husband*) go in for wit and the other of whom (Mrs. Arbuthnot of *A Woman of No Importance*), though equally unrepentant, specializes in good works. Clever, epigrammatic conversation is what these characters do best; guilty secrets and the situational intricacies they weave are the strings for Wilde's verbal pearls.

In *Lady Windermere's Fan,* the initial secret is that Mrs. Erlynne, the runaway mother of whose continued existence Lady Windermere is utterly ignorant, has returned to London to regain a place in society and is blackmailing Lord Windermere, who seeks to protect his wife from knowledge of the blot on her pedigree. Misinterpreting her husband's patronage of a mysterious lady with a hint of a past, Lady Windermere is led to the brink of unconsciously repeating her mother's error by eloping with another man, thereby prompting Mrs. Erlynne to the one maternal gesture of her life: The older and wiser woman sacrifices her own reputation (temporarily, it turns out) to save that of her daughter.

In *A Woman of No Importance,* Gerald Arbuthnot, a youth reared in rural seclusion and apparent respectability by his mother, happens to encounter the man who is his father: worldly Lord Illingworth, who when young and untitled had seduced Gerald's mother and, on learning of her pregnancy, refused to marry her. This complex situation allows Wilde to expose several human inconsistencies. Previously uninterested in the child he had begotten and also unwilling to marry the beautiful young mother, Lord Illingworth is now so full of paternal feeling that he offers to marry the middle-aged woman to retain the son. Gerald, who has just vowed to kill Lord Illingworth for attempting to kiss a prudish American girl, on hearing of Illingworth's past treachery to his mother wants her to let the offender "make an honest woman" of her. Mrs. Arbuthnot professes selfless devotion to her son but begs Gerald to forgo the brilliant prospects Illingworth can offer and remain with her in their provincial backwater.

In *An Ideal Husband,* the plot-initiating secret is a man's property rather than a woman's, and political intrigue rather than romantic. Sir Robert Chiltern, a high-principled politician with a rigidly idealistic young wife, encounters the adventuress Mrs. Chevely, who has evidence that Chiltern's career and fortune were founded on one unethical act—the selling of a political secret to a foreigner—and who attempts to use her knowledge to compel him to lend political support to a fraudulent scheme that will make her fortune. Acting against this resourceful woman is Chiltern's friend Lord Goring, an apparently effete but impressively capable man who can beat her at her own game. In brief, then, all three of these plays are formed of the highly theatrical matter that, in lesser hands, would form the stuff of melodrama.

Wilde's "pink lamp shade" comedies are difficult to stage because of the stylish luxury demanded of the actors, costumes, and sets, but the plays are not weaker for being so ornate: They accurately mirror a certain facet of late Victorian society. Similarly, the pervasive wit never becomes tiresome. The contrived reversals, artful coincidences, predictably surprising discoveries, and "strong curtains" may seem trite— but they work onstage. The defect that Wilde's first three comedies share is the problem of unreconciled opposites, implicit in *Salomé*. In *Lady Windermere's Fan*, *A Woman of No Importance*, and *An Ideal Husband*, part of Wilde is drawn to admire wit, style, vitality, and courage regardless of where they may be found, and part of him has a serious social or moral point to make. Even with this divided aim, Wilde wrote good comedies. When he solved the problem, he wrote a masterpiece: *The Importance of Being Earnest*.

THE IMPORTANCE OF BEING EARNEST

What makes *The Importance of Being Earnest*, unlike the three Wilde comedies that preceded it, a masterpiece of the theater rather than merely an eminently stageable play? Perhaps a good clue to the answer can be found in the play's subtitle, *A Trivial Comedy for Serious People*. This typically Wildean paradox has been variously interpreted. Whatever the author may have intended by it, one thing the phrase suggests to readers is that *The Importance of Being Earnest* is worth the attention of "serious people" because it, unlike Wilde's other three comedies, succeeds in being utterly trivial and thereby attains pure comic excellence. Eric Bentley has remarked of the play that "what begins as a prank ends as a criticism of life." Here at last Wilde offers witty wordplay and exuberant high spirits in an undiluted form. There are no melodramatic ambiguities or dark, complex emotions in *The Importance of Being Earnest*, where the chief events are flirtations that lead to engagements and prodigious consumption of tea, cucumber sandwiches, and muffins. Whereas *Lady Windermere's Fan*, *A Woman of No Importance*, and *An Ideal Husband* take place in the stylized but recognizably real world of contemporary London society, this play unfolds in a world apart, one that, despite its containing

a Mayfair flat and a Herefordshire manor, is as perfectly artificial yet completely valid as are Shakespeare's Forest of Arden in *As You Like It* (pr. c. 1599-1600) and Athens in *A Midsummer Night's Dream* (pr. c. 1595-1596).

The Importance of Being Earnest contains some of the stock theatrical devices Wilde relied on to galvanize his previous three comedies. There is mysterious parentage: Jack Worthing confesses to having been found in a handbag in Victoria Station. Characters run away from responsibility: Jack, in order to escape the country and get to town, has invented a wicked younger brother, Ernest, who lodges at the Albany; and Algernon Moncrieff, to escape from London to the country, has concocted an imaginary rural friend, the perennial invalid Bunbury. The comedy contains false identities: Both Jack and Algernon propose to and are accepted by their respective loves, the Honorable Gwendolyn Fairfax and Cecily Cardew, under the name "Ernest Worthing." There are misplaced possessions as significant as Lady Windermere's fan: Finding a cigarette case inscribed "From little Cecily, with her fondest love to her dear Uncle Jack," enables Algernon to discover his friend's double identity. The governess Miss Prism's unexpected, happy, eloquent reunion with the handbag she had mislaid twenty-eight years before brings the climactic revelation of the play: Through this recovery of the long-lost handbag, Jack, a comic Oedipus, discovers his true parentage. In all these cases, the dramatic machines of potential tragedy or melodrama are operated in the spirit of burlesque. There are no lapses or incongruities to drag down the lighthearted mood.

Similarly, the emotional developments, reversals, intrigues, and deceptions that were threatening in Wilde's other comedies are harmless in *The Importance of Being Earnest*, chiefly because the play is not about established relationships. It does not present married people with domestic differences; former lovers who should have married but failed to do so; present lovers already yoked to other people; parents, who through love, guilt, selfishness, or honor, influence the behavior of their children; or children who similarly manipulate their parents. The four principal characters—Jack Worthing, Gwendolyn

Fairfax, Algernon Moncrieff, and Cecily Cardew— are all young, single, and, with the exception of Gwendolyn, parentless. The Reverend Dr. Chasuble and Miss Prism are, to use their own words, "ripe" but "celibate." Early in the play, Lane, Algernon's manservant, admits that, with regard to marriage, he has had "very little experience of it myself up to the present." Of all the characters, only the marvelous Lady Bracknell is mature, married, and encumbered with children. Even so, Lord Bracknell is completely under her control; that pitiful peer, who dines upstairs at her command, does and knows only what she prescribes. Her daughter Gwendolyn, on the other hand, is completely free from her domination; the poised young lady listens politely to her dogmatic mother and then acts precisely as she chooses. As a consequence, Lady Bracknell's personal essence and the behavior it determines are modified by neither spouse nor child.

With this array of singularly unfettered characters, *The Importance of Being Earnest* is not about domestic complications but about the act of committing oneself to domesticity. The social comedy of the play parallels the movement of a Jane Austen novel: Characters who exist as pure potential define and place themselves by choosing to marry and by selecting their particular mates. The choreography of this matrimonial ballet is exceptionally elegant, particularly in the commonly known three-act version. (The original four-act version, first staged by the New Vic in 1980, contains material that is not essential, though not uninteresting.) The dialogue is so uniformly delightful that it is impossible to single out a high point or two for quoting. For the first time, Wilde's comedy is a brilliant whole rather than a series of sparkling effects. Indeed, the play's final interchange between Lady Bracknell and her newfound nephew (soon-to-be son-in-law) Jack could be the dramatist talking to himself, for by taking comedy seriously enough to stay within its bounds, Wilde the dramatist finally achieved his goal of creating a play not merely well-made but perfect of its kind:

> LADY BRACKNELL: My nephew, you seem to be displaying signs of triviality.

> JACK: On the contrary, Aunt Augusta, I've now realized for the first time in my life the vital Importance of Being Earnest.

OTHER MAJOR WORKS

LONG FICTION: *The Picture of Dorian Gray*, 1890 (serial), 1891 (expanded).

SHORT FICTION: "The Canterville Ghost," 1887; *The Happy Prince and Other Tales*, 1888; *Lord Arthur Savile's Crime and Other Stories*, 1891; *A House of Pomegranates*, 1891.

POETRY: *Ravenna*, 1878; *Poems*, 1881; *Poems in Prose*, 1894; *The Sphinx*, 1894; *The Ballad of Reading Gaol*, 1898.

NONFICTION: *Intentions*, 1891; *De Profundis*, 1905; *Letters*, 1962 (Rupert Hart-Davies, editor).

MISCELLANEOUS: *Works*, 1908; *Complete Works of Oscar Wilde*, 1948 (Vyvyan Holland, editor); *Plays, Prose Writings, and Poems*, 1960.

BIBLIOGRAPHY

Belford, Barbara. *Oscar Wilde: A Certain Genius*. New York: Random House, 2000. An examination of Wilde's life with a somewhat revisionist view of Wilde's post-prison years.

Ellmann, Richard. *Oscar Wilde*. London: Hamish Hamilton, 1987. A richly detailed, sympathetic account of Wilde's life and art, with balanced views of his accomplishments and significance for modern culture. Ellmann presents a forceful analysis of the events that caused Wilde's trial, imprisonment, and eventual early death. Contains many illustrations, notes, a select bibliography, two appendices of books by Wilde's parents, and an index.

McCormack, Jerusha Hull. *The Man Who Was Dorian Gray*. New York: Palgrave, 2000. A scholarly scraping together of the life of Wilde's model.

McGhee, Richard D. "Elizabeth Barrett Browning and Oscar Wilde." In *Marriage, Duty, and Desire in Victorian Poetry and Drama*. Lawrence: Regents Press of Kansas, 1980. Comparing the art of Wilde and Browning, this study focuses on their contrasting emphases on duty and desire, with some similarity in their motives for attempting to reconcile the opposition between such values. Wilde's dramas are closely examined along with his lyric poems and critical essays. Notes and index.

Small, Ian. *Oscar Wilde: A Recent Research, A Supplement to "Oscar Wilde Revalued."* Greensboro, N.C.: ELT Press, 2000. A follow-up to Small's earlier work on Wilde that surveys new biographical and critical materials. Bibliography.

Peter W. Graham,
updated by Richard D. McGhee

THORNTON WILDER

Born: Madison, Wisconsin; April 17, 1897
Died: Hamden, Connecticut; December 7, 1975

PRINCIPAL DRAMA

The Trumpet Shall Sound, pb. 1920, pr. 1927

The Angel That Troubled the Waters and Other Plays, pb. 1928 (includes 16 plays)

The Happy Journey to Trenton and Camden, pr., pb. 1931 (one act)

The Long Christmas Dinner, pr., pb. 1931 (one act; as libretto in German, 1961; translation and music by Paul Hindemith)

The Long Christmas Dinner and Other Plays in One Act, pb. 1931 (includes *Queens of France*, *Pullman Car Hiawatha*, *Love and How to Cure It*, *Such Things Only Happen in Books*, and *The Happy Journey to Trenton and Camden*)

Lucrece, pr. 1932, pb. 1933 (adaptation of André Obey's *Le Viol de Lucrèce*)

A Doll's House, pr. 1937 (adaptation of Henrik Ibsen's play)

The Merchant of Yonkers, pr. 1938, pb. 1939 (adaptation of Johann Nestroy's *Einen Jux will er sich machen*)

Our Town, pr., pb. 1938

The Skin of Our Teeth, pr., pb. 1942

The Matchmaker, pr. 1954, pb. 1956 (revision of *The Merchant of Yonkers*)

A Life in the Sun, pr. 1955, pb. 1960 (in German), pb. 1977 (in English; commonly known as *The Alcestiad*; act four pb. 1952, pr. 1957 as *The Drunken Sisters*)

Plays for Bleecker Street, pr. 1962 (3 one-acts: *Someone from Assisi*; *Infancy*, pb. 1961; and *Childhood*, pb. 1960)

The Collected Short Plays of Thornton Wilder, pb. 1997-1998 (2 volumes)

OTHER LITERARY FORMS

Thornton Wilder came to national prominence in 1927 with what has remained his best-known novel, *The Bridge of San Luis Rey*, which won for him the first of his three Pulitzer Prizes. The year before, his first published fiction, *The Cabala* (1926), had appeared, and in 1930 came his third novel, *The Woman of Andros*. These works were followed in 1934 by *Heaven's My Destination*—his first fictional work about the American experience—and, at lengthy intervals, by three additional novels. *The Ides of March*, the story of Caesar told from fictional diaries, letters, and records, and quite probably Wilder's most significant novel, appeared in 1948; *The Eighth Day*, winner of the National Book Award, was published in 1967; and his last novel, the semiautobiographical *Theophilus North*, was published in 1973. In 1942, Wilder cowrote the screenplay for Alfred Hitchcock's motion picture *Shadow of a Doubt* (1943). Over the years, Wilder wrote a number of essays, including several that develop his theory of drama; some that introduce works by other writers as varied as Sophocles, Gertrude Stein, James Joyce, and Emily Dickinson; and a few scholarly articles on the Spanish playwright Lope de Vega Carpio. These works have been collected posthumously in *American Characteristics and Other Essays* (1979).

ACHIEVEMENTS

Thornton Wilder was a true man of letters, equally accomplished and highly regarded at various points in his career as both a novelist and a dramatist. None of his works of fiction, however, seems likely to endure as a classic in the way that two of his plays, *Our Town* and *The Skin of Our Teeth*, most assuredly will. Wilder admittedly has always been, as the foreword to *The Angel That Troubled the Waters* insists, a decidedly and deliberately religious playwright, not in any parochial sense of espousing a specific body of theological doctrine but in the larger sense of consistently posing moral and metaphysical questions. As he makes clear in that preface, however, if the religious artist today is to reach a sizable and responsive audience, that artist generally must couch his or her views "in that dilute fashion that is a believer's concession to a contemporary standard of good manners." By birth, Wilder was a Christian; by education and training, he was a humanist. By his own reading and intellectual inquiry later in life, he became an existialist. Several of the playlets in his first volume reveal the intersection of pagan and Christian myth, showing how the former is implicit in and fulfilled by the latter. Continually, Wilder emphasizes the "presentness" of the past and how the best that has been thought and said throughout the ages continues to be of value. Always he asserts the importance of reason even in ages of faith.

Wilder was one of the most learned and erudite of all American dramatists. Throughout his life, he was a teacher as well as a writer, and his plays teach effortlessly, engagingly, and entertainingly. Much of American drama centers on the family, and Wilder's plays are no exception. His family, though, is the Family of Man, the human community throughout history. Because of the allegorical and parabolic nature of his plays, Wilder's works might appear at first to be lacking in subtlety and complexity, yet, through the simple means he employs, they touch on the most vital of ideas. The timeless rituals in which his families participate are the universal ones of birth and growth, love and marriage, sickness and death. If Wilder perhaps reflects Henri Bergson and Marcel Proust in his own philosophy of time as duration and memory as a simultaneous coexistence of all past experiences, he is a child of Ralph Waldo Emerson and Walt Whitman in his vague transcendentalism and almost religious belief in the value of democracy. Wilder insists that life has a purpose and a dignity, so it must be lived and cherished and nurtured. If this purpose and worth have become increasingly clouded, that simply makes artists all the more vital, for on them rests the task of revealing the divinity within human beings yet of showing them that they can become divine only by first being fully human.

He received numerous awards during his lifetime, beginning with the Pulitzer Prize in Fiction in 1928 for his novel *The Bridge of San Luis Rey*. He was awarded the Pulitzer Prize in Drama in 1938 for *Our Town* and in 1943 for *The Skin of Our Teeth*. He received the National Book Award for *The Eighth Day* in 1968. Among the many honors that came to Wilder late in life were the Gold Medal for Fiction of the American Academy of Arts and Letters, the United States Presidential Medal of Freedom, and the National Medal for Literature.

BIOGRAPHY

Thornton Niven Wilder was born on April 17, 1897, in Madison, Wisconsin, into a family with a strong New England Protestant background: Congregationalist on his father Amos's side, Presbyterian on his mother Isabella's. An older brother, Amos, became a professor of theology and commentator on religious poetry, and among Wilder's three younger sisters was Isabel, with whom he would later make his home and share the closest emotional attachment of his life. When their father was appointed consul general to Hong Kong and later to Shanghai in the first decade of the new century, the family lived with him for brief periods in each city, though the young Wilder was educated mostly in California. After he was graduated from Berkeley High School in 1915, Wilder went to Oberlin College in Ohio, later transferring to Yale, from which he received his bachelor of arts degree in 1920. While in college, he wrote numerous "three-minute plays," some of which would be included among the sixteen somewhat precious and pretentious closet dramas that reached print as *The Angel That Troubled the Waters and Other Plays*, as well as his first full-length effort, *The Trumpet Shall Sound*. Somewhat similar to Ben Jonson's *The Alchemist* (pr. 1610) in its incidents and thematic emphasis on justice, this early play was finally produced by the American Laboratory Theatre in New York in 1927.

While studying archaeology at the American Academy in Rome after college, Wilder began writing fiction. After returning to the United States, he taught French at the Lawrenceville School for Boys in New Jersey for much of the 1920's, staying there—with time out to attend Princeton for a master of arts degree and for a stint writing at the MacDowell Colony in New Hampshire—until after the critical acclaim of his second novel, *The Bridge of San Luis Rey*, which was awarded the Pulitzer Prize in Fiction in 1928. In 1930, Wilder began lecturing for part of each academic year in comparative literature at the University of Chicago, where

Thornton Wilder (Library of Congress)

he made the acquaintance of Gertrude Stein, whose theories of time and language exercised a powerful influence on all of Wilder's subsequent writing for the theater. During the 1930's, Wilder published six additional one-act plays in his volume entitled *The Long Christmas Dinner and Other Plays in One Act*. In 1961, the title play became the libretto for an opera with music by Paul Hindemith. In addition, Wilder adapted both André Obey's *Le Viol de Lucrèce* (1931) and Henrik Ibsen's *Et dukkehjem* (pr., pb. 1879; *A Doll's House*, 1880) for Broadway before writing his most famous work, *Our Town*, which won for him the Pulitzer Prize in Drama in 1938. The same year saw the unsuccessful production, under the direction of Max Reinhardt, of *The Merchant of Yonkers*, later revised as *The Matchmaker* for performance at the Edinburgh Festival in Scotland in 1954 and in New York in 1955; in a still later transformation (1964), dressed up with a musical score by Jerry Herman, *The Matchmaker* became *Hello, Dolly!*, one of the greatest successes in the history of American musical comedy. In

1943 while serving in the United States Army Air Corps during World War II, Wilder won his second Pulitzer Prize for *The Skin of Our Teeth*, perhaps one of the most original and inventive of all American comedies.

At the beginning of the 1950's, Wilder was Charles Eliot Norton Professor of Poetry at Harvard, lecturing on the American characteristics in classic American literature. In 1955, his last full-length drama, *A Life in the Sun*, was performed at the Edinburgh Festival. In 1962, it, too, became the libretto for an acclaimed German opera, *Die Alkestiade*, with music by Louise Talma. At the time of his death on December 7, 1975, he left incomplete two cycles of plays on which he had been working for more than a decade, "The Seven Deadly Sins" and "The Seven Ages of Man," whose titles suggest the allegorical and mythic nature of Wilder's best work for the theater. Perhaps the cumulative effect of the complete cycles would have been greater than the sampling of their parts that reached Off-Broadway production in

1962 under the collective title *Plays for Bleecker Street*. The three one-act plays, *Someone from Assisi*, *Infancy*, and *Childhood*, were Wilder's last original works produced for New York audiences.

ANALYSIS

Thornton Wilder's contributions in style and technique to American drama are akin to the innovations that Alfred Jarry in France, Luigi Pirandello in Italy, and Bertolt Brecht in Germany made to world drama in the twentieth century. Basically, Wilder was an antirealistic playwright, reacting against the tenets and presuppositions underlying the type of drama that held sway during the nineteenth century and continues to be a potent force even today. During a play that, as part of its attempt to create the absolute illusion of reality, employs a box set so that the audience sees the action through an imaginary fourth wall, there is a complete separation between actors and audience, stage space and auditorium. The audience, even though it implicitly knows it is in a theater watching a play, pretends for the duration that it is seeing reality on the stage; in short, the audience makes believe that it is not making believe. On the other hand, in theater that makes no attempt at achieving such an absolute illusion of reality, the audience readily accepts that what it is seeing is make-believe or pretense. In his important essay "Some Thoughts on Playwriting" (1941), Wilder argues that the theater in its greatest ages—Periclean Athens and Elizabethan England, for example—has always depended heavily on conventions, what he calls "agreed-upon falsehoods" or "permitted lies." Such accepted conventions help to break down the artificial boundary between play and audience by inviting a fuller imaginative participation in the action; by increasing the audience's awareness of itself as audience; and by emphasizing the communal and ritualistic nature of the theatrical experience. In Wilder's view, the traditional box set, because it localizes the action to a particular place and restricts it to a definite time, renders the action less universal and hinders its ascent into the desirable realms of parable, allegory, and myth. In contrast, Wilder sought a theater in which the large, recurrent outlines of the human story could be told through particular examples less important in themselves than the universal truths they stand for and embody.

THE HAPPY JOURNEY TO
TRENTON AND CAMDEN

Wilder's brand of minimalist theater can be illustrated by looking at *The Happy Journey to Trenton and Camden*, which the dramatist himself regarded as the best of his one-act plays. The action is simple: The Kirby family (father, mother, son, and daughter) takes a brief automobile trip to visit a married daughter/sister, whose baby died shortly after birth. Because the literal journey is less important than the metaphoric one, it is appropriate that the bare brick walls of the backstage remain visible; that the automobile is merely suggested by four chairs and a platform, with Dad Kirby working an imaginary gearshift and steering wheel in pantomime; that the towns through which the family travels (including Lawrenceville, where Wilder once taught) are simply mentioned in the dialogue; and that a Stage Manager is available to serve as property man, to read the parts of all the minor characters, and to act the role of service station attendant. When the car must stop for an imaginary funeral procession to pass, it allows the family an opportunity to recall their son and brother Harold, who died in the war, and to remember that every human being must be ready for death. As is typical in Wilder, the central female figure carries the weight of the play's meaning and expresses the dramatist's simple faith. Ma Kirby is the Eternal Mother, preserver of the family, who is close to God and to the nature that shadows forth the divine. She understands the process-oriented quality of existence: All things are born and they die; some, in fact, are born only to die. Further, she maintains her confidence in a providential order at work in the universe. Although human beings cannot know the ways of God, they must continue in faith that all things in life are for the best. What tempers Wilder's optimism and often prevents it from becoming sentimental is that he always keeps before his audience the dark side of human nature—human beings' myopic vision that limits them from being all that they might become—and the dark side of human existence—the fact of death, especially of dying without ever having really lived.

OUR TOWN

When the Stage Manager steps out onto the stage at the beginning of *Our Town* and locates the mythical and microcosmic New England village of Grover's Corners, New Hampshire, firmly in time and space, he creates a place so palpably present to the American imagination that most people in the audience might expect to be able to find it on a map. This is, truly, anyone's and everyone's town, and the people who are born and grow up and live and marry and suffer and die there are clearly Everyman and Everywoman. Wilder's opening stage directions specify "No curtain. No scenery." The absence of a curtain conveys the timeless quality of elemental experiences; the action has no specific beginning, because these daily events have been occurring since time immemorial and will continue to go on, despite an ever-changing cast on the world's stage. The almost complete lack of scenery, with only "two arched trellises" permitted as a concession to the unimaginative and literal-minded in the audience, indicates that the action is unlocalized and not tied to only one place at one time, but could, and does, happen everywhere. The pantomimed actions—perhaps influenced by the style of the Chinese theater, with which Wilder was well acquainted—achieve the same effect. The audience has no difficulty recognizing them, precisely because they are common actions (such as getting meals) that everyone performs.

The play's action is as basic, and yet as universal, as the setting: neither more nor less than the archetypal journey of man and woman through life to death and beyond. In this respect, the title play from *The Long Christmas Dinner and Other Plays in One Act* serves as a precursor to *Our Town*. In that short work, Wilder presented ninety years in the life of the Bayard family. Characters enter through a portal on one side of the stage, which symbolizes birth; partake of a Christmas dinner over the years that symbolizes the feast of life; and then exit through a portal, on the opposite side of the stage, that symbolizes death. One generation replaces another, even uttering many of the same lines of dialogue. Act 1 of *Our Town*, called

"Daily Life," focuses on the ordinary, day-to-day existence of two neighboring families: Editor Webb, his wife, older daughter, and younger son; and Doc Gibbs, his wife, older son, and younger daughter. In act 2, called "Love and Marriage," the playwright shows the courtship and wedding of George Gibbs and Emily Webb; the audience becomes an extension of the church congregation as the young couple enter and leave the ceremony via the theater aisles. Act 3, which is left untitled, is set in a cemetery with chairs for graves and an umbrella-protected group of mourners; it is the funeral of Emily, who died in childbirth and has been united in eternity with something like an Oversoul.

Although the action literally begins in May, 1901 (the hopeful springtime of a new century), *Our Town* is, unlike a play such as Eugene O'Neill's *Ah, Wilderness!* (pr. 1933), more than simply a nostalgic recollection of a bygone era of American democratic egalitarianism. Nor is the picture of life from the dawn of the twentieth century to the outbreak of World War I as sentimentally one-sided and limited in its awareness of evil and the darker forces of existence as has sometimes been charged. Along with Simon Stimson, the town drunk and eventual suicide, Wilder portrays petty gossip and backbiting, even among the church choir ladies; lack of communication between husband and wife and parent and child; the pain of separation and loss through death; and war (looking forward, since the action per se ends in 1913). The continuing importance of *Our Town*, however, should not be looked for on so basic a level as that of its story. Rather, it is a philosophical examination of time and the proper way of seeing, stressing the necessity for escaping from the narrow, myopic view of existence that human beings ordinarily take and embracing, with the poet's help, a God's-eye view of human history.

Wilder's attitude toward time as a continuum is made concrete in the way he conveys events that occurred before or will happen after the twelve-year scope of the action. Not only does the local expert, a college professor, Willard, provide a lengthy report about the geological formation of the region and the anthropological data of the area, but also the Stage

Manager, in his casual shifting of verb tenses from present to future or future to past, points to a perspective that is both inside secular time and outside time, transcending it. Wilder's laconic Stage Manager, with his understated and homespun New England manner, performs several functions: He is narrator, bridging shifts in time and place, setting the scene for the audience; he is actor of minor roles, including drugstore owner and preacher at George and Emily's wedding; he is property man, constructing the soda fountain from a few boards; he is chorus, philosophizing for the audience; and he is destroyer of the theatrical illusion, reminding the audience that they are in a theater watching a play. Distanced from the action that is filtered through his eyes, the audience begins to see with his sometimes ironic perspective. He possesses a Godlike omniscience, overseeing the progression of human history as God would. It is this kind of sight and insight that the audience, too, must develop.

In a seemingly inconsequential exchange of dialogue (perhaps influenced by a similar passage in James Joyce's *A Portrait of the Artist as a Young Man*, 1916), Wilder hints at the idea on which the entire work pivots. George Gibbs's sister Rebecca tells about a letter that a minister sent to a sick friend; included as the final words of the address on the envelope was the location, "the Mind of God." Wilder, who himself acted the role of the Stage Manager in the Broadway production, tells his audience that if it could only plumb the mind of God, where everything—from least to most, from smallest to largest, past, present, and to come—exists simultaneously as part of a purposive, providential order, then they would live life wholly and even be able to cope with death.

The tension and tragedy of the human condition, however, arise because, paradoxically, it is possible to gain the perspective necessary for seeing life steadily and seeing it whole only after death. Emily dies giving birth, a poignant image not only of mutability but also of the way in which life and death are inextricably bound in nature's cycle. Only after she dies and is given the opportunity to relive the most "unimportant day" in her life does she see that even the most ordinary and banal of life's experiences is full of wonder and learn to treasure more what she has lost. Sadly, only the "saints and poets" seem to recognize this wonder and beauty while they are still alive. The end of a human life, union with some larger spirit, is in its beginning hinted at even in the most common events of daily living—if only that person, like the poet, could see.

THE SKIN OF OUR TEETH

While *Our Town* displays some affinities with medieval morality plays, *The Skin of Our Teeth* is influenced by the medieval mystery cycles in its structure: In capsule form (and stylistically akin somewhat to a comic strip), it recounts human history from the beginning of time to the present and on into the future. The Antrobuses, Wilder's Family of Man in this play, begin each of the three acts on the upswing, feeling positive about themselves and the human race; see their fortunes descend to a nadir, through either a natural disaster or human culpability; yet finally finish each act—and the play as a whole—having narrowly muddled through "by the skin of their teeth." In each instance, temptation is overcome, sinful action somehow compensated for. In act 1, with its echoes of the Garden of Eden story from Genesis, son Henry's killing of the neighbor boy (he earlier killed his brother, for which he received the mark of Cain) prompts Mr. Antrobus to despair, but daughter Gladys' ability to recite in school a poem by Henry Wadsworth Longfellow restores his faith. In act 2, with its underpinning of the Noah tale, the father's lack of faithfulness to Mrs. Antrobus sends shock waves through the family, as Gladys dons red stockings and Henry attacks a black person with a slingshot. Yet Mr. Antrobus, unlike the other conventioneers at Atlantic City who writhe in a snakelike dance, is among the remnant of faithful ones saved from the Deluge. Act 3 finds the family returning to normalcy after the war (any war), but the anarchic Henry threatens the stability of the family unit just as the forces of totalitarianism almost destroyed the world, until he is finally reconciled with his father, who puts his confidence in the best ideas from the past to sustain the human race. The overall structure, therefore, embodies Wilder's concept of cyclic time, with one result being that time can be handled anachronistically. The play, which began with a slide of the sun rising, ends with the equivalent lines from Genesis: "And the Lord said let there be light and there was light."

In its techniques, which extend the nonillusionistic style adopted in *Our Town*, *The Skin of Our Teeth* reflects the influence of Surrealism and even points forward to the multimedia effects of the 1960's and 1970's. The scenery, with its angles askew, the dozen lantern slides projected onto the set, the talking dinosaur and mammoth, the cardboard cutouts and flats, the lighting and noises—all contribute to a carnival atmosphere, anticipating the playful techniques of some Absurdist drama while also suggesting a dream happening without conscious control. Mr. Fitzpatrick, Wilder's director/stage manager here, not only stops the play so that he can rehearse volunteers taking over the parts of sick actors, but also is mildly satirized for his literal-mindedness and prosaicism; even Ivy, the costumer, understands the meaning of the play better than he does. Significantly, the substitute actors are needed to play the hours of the night who cross the stage; that they recite passages from Benedict de Spinoza, Plato, Aristotle, and the Bible (as similar characters also had in *Pullman Car Hiawatha*) demonstrates that the enduring ideas of the past are not out of reach of the common man. The illusion of reality is further destroyed when Lily Sabina Fairweather, a compound of temptress, mistress, camp follower, and maid, steps out of character and, as the actress Miss Somerset, speaks directly to the audience, requesting that they send up their chairs for firewood during the Ice Age of act 1 and, at the end of the play, sending them home to do their part in completing the history of the human race on earth.

Within the framework of his comic allegory of humankind's journey, Wilder's characters assume an archetypal dimension; each member of the Antrobus family, whom Wilder calls "our selves," seems to stand for an aspect of the archetypal man or woman's personality. Mr. Antrobus—the former gardener (Adam), self-made man, inventor of the wheel, the lever, gunpowder, the singing telegram, the brewing of beer and of grass soup—represents the power of the intellect, which can be a force for both creation and destruction. Appreciating the importance of the wis-

dom of past ages, he will not tolerate the burning of William Shakespeare's works even to provide life-sustaining warmth. Mrs. Antrobus, inventor in her own right of the apron, the hem, the gore and the gusset, and frying in oil, is humankind's affective side; her watchword is the family and the promise of love between husband and wife that helps them endure and makes even suffering worthwhile. As one who insists that women are not the subservient creatures the media make them out to be, she stresses woman's role as transmitter of the Life Force.

Lily Sabina (Lilith), with her philosophy of enjoying the present moment, embodies the hedonistic pleasure principle. The Antrobuses' daughter Gladys, who appears after the war with a baby, symbolically conveys hope for the future. Their son Henry is a representation of the strong, unreconciled evil that is always with humankind; though he is the enemy during the war and in general refuses to accept responsibility, he is still taken along on the ark at the end of act 2.

In act 3, the actors playing Mr. Antrobus and Henry break out of their roles, moving from stereotypes to more rounded human beings as they reveal the tension between themselves as men rather than as characters. Something in the attitude of the actor playing Antrobus reminds the one portraying Henry of how authority figures have always blocked and hindered him, and so they clash personally. Through this tension, the actor playing Antrobus recognizes that there must indeed exist some lack within himself that triggered this negative response in the other, and so he promises to change. He ends confident that humanity, always on the edge of chaos and disaster, will ultimately endure and prevail, if only people accept the chance to do the hard work that Providence demands of them.

Wilder, like George Bernard Shaw, has often been criticized for his romantic optimism, which seems out of keeping with the darker facts of human history—*The Skin of Our Teeth* opened, after all, only a year after Pearl Harbor and found its greatest success in post World War II Germany. Whether Wilder's optimistic belief in humanity's "spiral progression through trial and error" is found congenial or not, *The*

Skin of Our Teeth remains a richly imaginative work and the seminal text of deliberately self-conscious art in the American theater.

THE MATCHMAKER

Wilder's *The Matchmaker*—a revision of his *The Merchant of Yonkers*, an adaptation of Johann Nestroy's 1842 Viennese comedy *Einen Jux will er sich machen* (pr. 1842, pb. 1844; *The Matchmaker*, 1957; which, in turn, was based loosely on John Oxenford's 1835 English comedy *A Day Well Spent*)—belongs to that most venerable of dramatic traditions, the genre of romantic comedy. As such, it is characterized by a repressive authority figure who tries to thwart young love; mistaken identities and confusion between the sexes, including boys disguised as girls; and a ritualized dance to foreshadow the multiple marriages that resolve the plot. Along with these appear elements of good-natured, boisterous farce, including inopportune entrances and exits; hiding behind a screen, in closets, and under tables; and exploding cans of tomatoes shooting up through a trapdoor in the floor. What marks all of this traditional, even stereotypical material with Wilder's own signature are the themes and the manner in which he breaks down the illusion of stage reality.

A further alteration from the norm in romantic comedy is that in this play, the older couple, rather than the young ones, are the hero and heroine. Horace Vandergelder, the sly, miserly merchant from Yonkers (he seems a direct descendant of Ben Jonson's Volpone, the fox) forbids his sentimental young niece and ward Ermengarde to marry the penniless artist Ambrose Kemper. They ultimately circumvent his authority through the agency of two older women: Miss Flora Van Huysen, the spinster fairy godmother in the play, and Mrs. Dolly Gallager Levi, the inimitable matchmaker herself. Miss Van Huysen refuses to permit her own loneliness to be extended to others through the destruction of young love, and so she acts as the presiding deity over the three marriages: Ermengarde's to Ambrose; Cornelius Hackl's to Irene Molloy, the Irish widow and milliner; and Barnaby Tucker's to Minnie, Mrs. Molloy's assistant.

Dolly, who all along has her eyes on Horace for herself, is the only character among a cast of types permitted enough depth to probe into herself and her motives. In the manner in which she arranges the relationships of others and herself, there is something of the artist in Dolly Levi; her vocation is to make life interesting, to make people less selfish, to spread enjoyment, to see that the community renews and fructifies itself. She must, first of all, tutor Horace in adopting a proper attitude toward money; for her, money must "circulate like rain water" among the people and be "spread around like manure" if it is to encourage life and growth. She must also, however, tutor herself into giving up her widow's weeds, so to speak, and completely rejoining the human community. Ever since the death of her first husband, Ephraim, she has allowed herself to become like a dying leaf and now must cure her underactive heart through marriage to Horace. For both Dolly and Horace, lonely old age is only narrowly averted. This emphasis on full participation in life and life's processes, of seeing that to everything there is a season and of not rushing before one's time toward death and decay, is peculiarly Wilder's. Also distinctively Wilder's is the emphasis on the need for "adventure" and "wonder," which are two of the key words spoken by nearly every one of the play's characters and are direct echoes of the attitudes espoused in *Our Town*.

The settings for the four acts of *The Matchmaker* are the most elaborately realistic box sets prescribed for any Wilder play. Precisely because they do form such a realistic background, replete with "obtrusive bric-a-brac," they make the several instances of direct address to the audience by the major characters all the more startling. The disjunction between the realistic sets and the very nonrealistic goings-on calls the audience's attention to the fact that it is watching a play and turns stage realism on its ear. *The Matchmaker* becomes, indeed, a playful and affectionate parody of the way that stage realism stifles life. To be doubly sure that the audience does not miss this point, Miss Van Huysen even repeats several times some variation of the line "Everything's imagination," which is another way of saying that all is make-believe and pretense: exactly what Wilder strives to provide for his theater audiences.

A LIFE IN THE SUN

Wilder's *A Life in the Sun* is, both in form and content, linked closely to the Greek drama of the fifth century B.C.E. Its form, a play in three acts (each of which could almost stand alone as a self-contained episode) and a satyr play, replicates that of the Greek trilogies, which were followed with a comic parody of the tragic action. Here, the satyr play (entitled *The Drunken Sisters*, which tells how Apollo tricked the vain Fates into allowing Admetus to live) is added by Wilder to make the point that the tragic and comic experiences are incomplete in and of themselves; in life, the two kinds of perceptions must coexist. The content of Wilder's powerful retelling of the Alcestis story for modern man is religious and mythological in nature, with his act 2 corresponding closely to the material found in Euripides' original. Unlike T. S. Eliot's *The Cocktail Party* (pr. 1949), which uses the same myth allusively as a vague underpinning for a contemporary parable, or Eugene O'Neill's *Mourning Becomes Electra* (pr. 1931), which takes the outlines and psychology of the Orestes and Electra stories and redresses them at a different time and place, Wilder creatively adjusts the myth to reflect contemporary philosophical currents, especially existentialism, as Jean-Paul Sartre had done in *Les Mouches* (pr., pb. 1943; *The Flies*, 1946).

Act 1 begins with a confrontation between Apollo, the force of light, and Death, the force of darkness, who introduce the issues that inform the entire play: the relationship between the divine and the human and the problem of discovering a meaning to life. Although Apollo admits that there exists much that human beings are incapable of understanding, he insists that what meaning does exist flows from him. Death, on the other hand—and later Tiresias, the wizened seer, will echo him—argues that it is the gods who cause human torment. By meddling in human affairs, the gods make people unhappy and distraught. On her wedding day, Alcestis decides not to marry the King of Thessaly unless she receives a clear sign from the gods; she will forsake humans, finite and of this world, to love only God, infinite and other-worldly. Alcestis desires absolute certainty and the assurance that the gods have not abandoned humankind; with-

out that, life is reduced to meaningless nonsense, and humankind is left in a condition similar to that of the absurdists, with life made all the more unbearable because human beings have been given hope of some meaning only to see that hope dashed. The God Apollo, by becoming human in the form of one of Admetus's herdsmen, must save Alcestis by forcing her to recognize that God is within each and every person, that the divine can be found within the human, the infinite within the finite. When Admetus enters wearing a blue cloak like Apollo's, the sight is an epiphany for Alcestis, who pledges to marry him and live totally for him, ready even to die for him.

Act 2, which occurs twelve years later, finds Admetus at the point of death and Alcestis finally favored with the long-sought-for message from Delphi, which indicates that the gods do demand the difficult. The message challenges her to do what she was prepared to do at the close of act 1: die in place of Admetus. The Watchman, the old nurse Aglaia, and the Herdsman all offer to sacrifice themselves so that Admetus might live, but Alcestis insists that the role fall to her. It is not that Alcestis has no hesitation, for she dreads to cease to be, to leave the sunlight, and she still craves the right to understand the ways of God to humankind that would make human beings more than animals. Finally, though, her love for Admetus dominates her love for life; she will die for him and, what is perhaps even harder, die from him, believing a divinity shapes her end. Yet, as Apollo intervenes in act 1, here Hercules, though in fear and trembling, descends into the Underworld to bring back from the dead the all-forgiving Alcestis, the "crown of women." The last image of the resurrected Alcestis led forth from Hell provides a further instance for the audience of the way in which classical and Christian myth and iconography fuse in Wilder: Apollo/Christ became man; Alcestis/Christ died and rose so that others might live.

If act 2 forms a meditation on death, act 3 is a metaphysical inquiry into the existence of human suffering, with Death taunting Apollo to explain why so many innocent in Thessaly have died in the pestilence: Do the gods make human beings suffer only so that people will remember rather than reject them?

Admetus is now dead, and Alcestis is an old slave under King Agis. Epimenes, the only surviving son of the former queen, returns to what has become a wasteland, vowing butchery and revenge, only to have his hand stopped by his mother. Rejecting all of those who see God's influence only in the evil in the world and never in the good, Alcestis says that the gods' ways are not human ways; they do not love one minute and then turn against the loved one in the next. She counsels Agis, whose daughter Laodamia dies in the plague, that evil does have a purpose within the divine scheme and that suffering can make him open his eyes and learn wisdom. Her final visionary pronouncement recalls that of Emily in *Our Town*: Human beings should despair at the point of death only if they have not really lived, if they have failed to experience fully and treasure the here and now. The meaning of life is in the living of life. Alcestis herself becomes the sign that life does possess a meaning in and of itself, and, freed from the grave by the grace of Apollo, she experiences an apotheosis as her reward.

A Life in the Sun, as much a paean to woman and her role in the cosmic order as are *The Happy Journey to Trenton and Camden* and *The Skin of Our Teeth*, provides a dramatic summation of much of Wilder's philosophy: To become divine, human beings must first be fully human; the extraordinary is to be discovered in the ordinary; the power of myth is timeless, cutting across cultures and religions, synthesizing the past and the present, making the past ever new and vital. The Watchman's words in act 1 of *A Life in the Sun*, a play that is essentially an undiscovered country for all but ardent enthusiasts of Wilder, might be paraphrased as an epigraph for all Wilder's dramatic works: The essential facts of human life do not change, nor should humankind expect them to, from millennium to millennium, from year to year, from minute to minute. What must change is human beings' way of seeing.

OTHER MAJOR WORKS

LONG FICTION: *The Cabala*, 1926; *The Bridge of San Luis Rey*, 1927; *The Woman of Andros*, 1930; *Heaven's My Destination*, 1934; *The Ides of March*, 1948; *The Eighth Day*, 1967; *Theophilus North*, 1973.

SCREENPLAYS: *Our Town*, 1940 (with Frank Craven and Harry Chantlee); *Shadow of a Doubt*, 1943 (with Sally Benson and Alma Revelle).

NONFICTION: *The Intent of the Artist*, 1941; *American Characteristics and Other Essays*, 1979; *The Journals of Thornton Wilder, 1939-1961*, 1985.

TRANSLATION: *The Victors*, 1948 (of Jean-Paul Sartre's play *Morts sans sépulture*).

BIBLIOGRAPHY

Blank, Martin, ed. *Critical Essays on Thornton Wilder*. New York: G. K. Hall, 1996. A collection of essays on the works of Wilder. Bibliography and index.

Blank, Martin, Dalma Hunyadi Brunauer, and David Garrett Izzo, eds. *Thornton Wilder: New Essays*. West Cornwall, Conn.: Locust Hill Press, 1999. A collection of essays containing critical analysis of the literary works of Wilder. Bibliography and index.

Bryer, Jackson R., ed. *Conversations with Thornton Wilder*. Jackson: University Press of Mississippi, 1992. A collection of interviews with Wilder, presenting interesting perspectives on the man and his literary works. Index.

Burbank, Rex J. *Thornton Wilder*. 2d ed. Boston: Twayne, 1978. In this updated version of the 1962 edition, Burbank traces the history of critical controversy surrounding Wilder's work, offers insights into his methods of fictional and dramatic composition, and assesses his work's relative merits. Chronology, bibliography.

Castronovo, David. *Thornton Wilder*. New York: Ungar, 1986. This biography of Wilder focuses on critical analysis and interpretation of his literary works. Bibliography and index.

Harrison, Gilbert A. *The Enthusiast: A Life of Thornton Wilder*. New Haven, Conn.: Ticknor & Fields, 1983. A biography of Wilder that covers his life and works. Bibliography and index.

Lifton, Paul. *Vast Encyclopedia: The Theatre of Thornton Wilder*. Westport, Conn.: Greenwood Press, 1995. An examination of the contribution that Wilder made to American theater. Bibliography and index.

Walsh, Claudette. *Thornton Wilder: A Reference Guide, 1926-1990*. A Reference Guide to Literature. New York: G. K. Hall, 1993. An annotated bibliography of works on or by Wilder. Indexes.

Wilder, Amos Niven. *Thornton Wilder and His Public*. Philadelphia: Fortress Press, 1980. An interesting account of the relationship between Wilder

and his critical and reading public, written by Wilder's older brother, a theologian. His aim is to offer a sophisticated discrimination, both aesthetic and sociological, of his brother's work in the light of contemporary American reality, particularly its symbolism, dynamics, creative modes, and registers of meaning. Bibliography and appendix.

Thomas P. Adler,
updated by Genevieve Slomski

PAUL WILLEMS

Born: Edegem, Belgium; April 4, 1912
Died: Edegem, Belgium; November 28, 1997

PRINCIPAL DRAMA

Le Bon Vin de Monsieur Nuche, pr. 1949, pb. 1954
Lamentable Julie, pr. 1949
Peau d'ours, pr., 1951, pb. 1958
Air barbare et tendre, pr. 1952
Off et la lune, pr. 1955, pb. 1995
Histoire du garçon qui voulait décrocher la Lune, wr. 1956, pb. 1996
Le Petit Chat vert, wr. 1957, pb. 1996
Il pleut dans ma maison, pr. 1958, pb. 1963 (*It's Raining in My House*, 1986)
La Neige, wr. 1959, pb. 1996
La Plage aux anguilles, pr. 1959, pb. 1963
Marceline, wr. c. 1960, pb. 1995
Warna: Ou, Le Poids de la neige, pr. 1962, pb. 1963 (*The Weight of the Snow*, 1992)
Le Marché des petites heures, pr. 1964, pb. 1983
La Ville à voile, pr., pb. 1967 (*The Sailing City*, 1992)
Le Soleil sur la mer, pr. 1970
Les Miroirs d'Ostende, pr., pb. 1974
Nuit avec ombres en couleurs, pr., pb. 1983
Elle disait dormir pour mourir, pr., pb. 1983 (*She Confused Sleeping and Dying*, 1992)
La Vita breve, pr. 1991, pb. 1989 (English translation, 1994)

OTHER LITERARY FORMS

Paul Willems began his literary career with novels that bear the imprint of his family chateau, the Rousseau-like retreat Missembourg. Like his mother, poet Marie Gevers, Willems celebrated intense sensory experiences that open a passage to lost paradise, a recurring theme in his work. Paradise, for Willems, resembled an Edenic garden of childhood innocence, unsullied by modern civilization and humankind's inhumanity. He also published numerous articles and prefaces, two collections of short stories, and *Un arrière-pays: Rêveries sur la création littéraire* (1989), a book of lectures on his creative process that he delivered during his year's appointment as poetry chair at the University of Louvain-la-Neuve.

ACHIEVEMENTS

Because of changing linguistic politics in Belgium, Paul Willems was the last of the great Belgian dramatic poets, such as Maurice Maeterlinck and Fernand Crommelynck, who were Flemings by birth but who conducted their literary life in French. Willems's plays have been translated into more than twelve languages and performed all over the world. He was particularly popular in Germany, with more than a hundred productions (some plays premiering before their Belgian openings). His musical comedy *Le Marché des petites heures* was written on commission for the Saltzberg Festival. *The Sailing City* won the international Marzotto prize for drama in 1966 and (like Willems's novel *Blessures*, 1945) was published by the prestigious French publishing house Gallimard.

Willems's plays were also produced in his home country. The Belgian government awarded the playwright its Triennial Prize for Dramatic Literature in 1963 and 1966, followed by the Quinquennial Prize for the body of his work in 1980. The Rideau de Bruxelles revived *It's Raining in My House* eight times over the years following the play's Belgian premiere (1962), always to sold-out houses.

Perhaps one of Willems's greatest contributions is the opportunity his plays offer actors, as well as audiences, to experience poetic fantasies that explore deep human truths. Following his death, one actress spoke her appreciation for "the precious gift of Paul Willems' words [that] allowed me to enter the mystical world of a waking dream which gives voice to the secrets of our souls."

BIOGRAPHY

Paul Willems was born on April 4, 1912, the son of revered Belgian poet Marie Gevers. He spent his childhood on the family estate, Missembourg, located in Edegem, near the seaside city Antwerp. The old country house had been bought by Willems's grandfather, a disciple of Rousseau, as a retreat from modern civilization. It was said to be haunted by the ghost of a famous highwayman, forever searching for his lost treasure.

Young Paul did not attend school until the age of twelve. His maternal grandmother gave him lessons in French and Latin in the mornings, and in the afternoons he was sent out into the gardens to learn from the greatest teacher: nature. The estate's gardener, who claimed to be a wizard, also taught the child respect for the tools of one's trade. Willems's novels and plays reflect his childhood love for nature, especially water: lakes, ponds, the sea, and the ever-present Belgian rain. A fatalistic pessimist who rejected religious orthodoxy, Willems nonetheless meditated with both irony and mystical delight on the nameless beauty of the ephemeral.

Willems received his law degree from the Free University of Brussels in 1936 and practiced maritime law in Antwerp from 1937 to 1940. In addition to pursuing an active writing career, Willems entered the Palais des Beaux Arts de Bruxelles in 1946, where he served as director general (1947-1984). He continued to reside at Missembourg, however, with his wife, Elza, and commuted to work. In search of artistic events for the Palais, he traveled all over the world, including the United States, Japan, China, and the Soviet Union.

After having published three novels, Willems was persuaded to write for the theater by Claude Etienne, director of the Rideau de Bruxelles. In 1949, the Rideau produced his first play, *Le Bon Vin de Monsieur Nuche*, which was also performed in English in New York City the following year. The Rideau continued to be an artistic home for Willems's drama.

Belgium is a dual-language country which contains two competing language groups, the Germanic (Flemish/Dutch) and Latin (Walloon/French). Literature became a weapon, as the Flemings sought to assert their identity against the dominant French culture. Although ethnically Flemish, in the tradition of the Belgian educated classes, Willems was raised as a French-speaker, and so wrote in French. As the Fleming/Walloon cultural battles heated up, Willems found himself ostracized by the Flemish and only marginally tolerated by the Walloons. Literary friends suggested that, like Belgian predecessors such as Maeterlinck, he should move to Paris to win French acceptance. Willems chose to remain at Missembourg, and his plays were never well received in France. On the other hand, his drama won considerable popularity in Germany, until eclipsed there by the vogue for political theater.

In the 1970's, Willems found an artistic soul mate in Belgian director Henri Ronse, who eventually staged five of his plays, including revised versions. After his retirement from the Palais, Willems turned full time to writing, publishing a novella, a play, a short-story anthology, and a collection of lectures. When struck by his final illness, he was working on another novel, *Le voleur d'eau* (the water thief).

ANALYSIS

Although the intersection of Germanic and Gallic cultures enriched his dramatic imagination, Paul Willems became caught in a cultural no-man's-land when it became "politically incorrect" for Flemish authors to write in French. Language itself was a recurring preoccupation in his drama, and he depicted numerous characters suffering from mutilated speech. However, Willems also played with language, delighting in rhythms, rhymes, puns, and invented words. His poetic dialogue weaves a magical spell to enchant the audience into entering a dream world that coexists with what is called "reality."

Willems's work reveals the allegorical tendencies and blend of earthiness and mysticism characteristic of Belgian literature. Other influences cited by critics include German Romanticism, Surrealism, and Magical Realism. Willems, however, refused to ally himself with any literary movement, citing his belief in freedom of thought.

Turning to the theatre with *Le Bon Vin de Monsieur Nuche*, Willems translated into theatrical terms the rhythmic musicality and sensory imagery of his novels. Like *Le Bon Vin de Monsieur Nuche*, his third play, *Peau d'ours*, was adapted from a fairy tale by the Brothers Grimm. Initially misled by the whimsy of Willems's early plays, critics only later recognized the underlying irony and cruelty characteristic of his mature drama. Underneath the humor and fanciful word-play of Willems's theatrical fairy tales lurked the darkness of the Brothers Grimm, as Willems sardonically watched the world lurch toward a fate described by the name he gave his feline narrator of *Nuit avec ombres en couleurs*: Cat Astrophe.

PEAU D'OURS

For *Peau d'ours* (bearskin), Willems adapted the Grimm tale of a soldier who must wear a bearskin for seven years as a result of a deal with the devil. In Willems's version, the devil is transformed into a pair of matchmaking woodpeckers, and the soldier's goal is no longer wealth but purification through love. Certainly, the allegory of a soldier's soul healed of war guilt helps to explain the popularity of *Peau d'ours* in postwar Germany, where it underwent more than nine hundred performances.

IT'S RAINING IN MY HOUSE

Produced by the Rideau de Bruxelles in 1962, the play became a perennial favorite, with numerous revivals. The actor who played the gardener considered the character the role of his lifetime and slept with the script beside his bed. A musical score performed live by composer Ralph Darbo drew the audience under the spell of nature with enchanting sounds for the buzzing of bees, the falling of rain. With its tree growing in the living room, the old house Grand'Rosière (modeled on Missembourg) sets an image of lost paradise onstage. Those who love the old house try to save it from its new owner, who wants to sell it and buy a condo in town. On one level, then, the play reflects its author's environmental concerns and his suspicion of modernization

In a lighthearted vein, *It's Raining in My House* demonstrates Willems's preoccupation with language. Man and woman, city dweller and country dweller, seem to speak different languages, making communication problematic. *It's Raining in My House* also includes a recurring Willems image: the double. Madeleine, the heir, is the exact double of Aunt Madeleine, the house's original owner. The reconciliation of the ghost couple, Aunt Madeleine and her fiancé, leads to Madeleine making up with her own fiancé and deciding not to sell Grand'Rosière, thus restoring lost paradise: The world of the living and the world of the dead appear as mirror reflections.

THE SAILING CITY

Through metaphors of mirrors, doubles, and life-sized dolls, Willems's mature plays reflect a narcissistic world in which the individual is trapped in his own consciousness, unable to love. The sailing city is Antwerp, which in Willems's fantasy sports sails from its rooftops. Willems traced the image to a day when, looking at Antwerp from the dock, he seemed to see the city gliding away under sails of billowing clouds.

Old and ill but rich, the protagonist of *The Sailing City* returns to Antwerp to buy happiness, equated with the shop window mannequin he had worshiped as a child. Although his real childhood sweetheart still loves him, he spurns her. Instead, he marries a young woman, the mannequin's double, but she disappoints him. He realizes that, like the sailing city, the lost past is drifting out of his grasp. Dreams cannot be captured but only adored from afar.

As in so many of Willems's plays, characters suffer from mutilated language. The shop owner's sexually repressed wife cannot finish her sentences, and the half-wit servant has been taught to repeat courteous formalities three times. Willems also treats language playfully, as the shop owner invents words to describe the fanciful flotsam and jetsam that crowd his curio shop.

LA VITA BREVE

Willems's last—and cruelest—play probes the paradoxical intertwining of guilt and innocence, sexuality and violence. The shipboard setting embarks the audience on a voyage into a dark night of the soul. A haunting musical score was composed for the Belgian première by Thanos Mikroutsikos, who later became minister of culture for Greece.

An erotic sailor's doll (played by an actress), a replica of a Neopolitan courtesan, serves as a focus for a reenactment of her murder. All the characters are unmasked as capable of brutal sexual jealousy, including the deranged young man who made the doll. Wounded language plays a role here, too, as the young man has lost his ability to speak but sings with the voice of an angel. Like the waves of Willems's beloved sea, the play rocks the audience back and forth between guilt and innocence and between beauty and horror. Refusing any simplistic interpretation, the play calls its audience to confront the mysterious contradictions of the ebb and flow of life, of death.

OTHER MAJOR WORKS

LONG FICTION: *Tout est réel ici*, 1941; *L'Herbe qui tremble*, 1942; *Blessures*, 1945; *La Chronique du cygne*, 1949; *Le Pays noyé*, 1990 (*The Drowned Land*, 1994).

SHORT FICTION: *La Cathédrale de brume*, 1983; *Le Vase de Delft*, 1995.

POETRY: *Douze couplets et un poème pour les treize mois de l'anée*, 1953.

TELEPLAY: *L'Écho*, 1963.

RADIO PLAY: *Plus de danger pour Berto*, 1966.

NONFICTION: *Un arrière-pays: Rêveries sur la création littéraire*, 1989.

BIBLIOGRAPHY

Burgoyne, Suzanne. "Belgian/American Theatre Exchanges: Reflections and Bridges." In *New Theatre Vistas: Modern Movements in International Theatre*, edited by Judy Lee Oliva. New York: Garland, 1996. Author's description of rehearsals for a revival of *It's Raining in My House* at the Rideau de Bruxelles and her own production of the play in the United States.

Burgoyne, Suzanne, and Shirley Huston-Findley. Forward to *Paul Willems' The Drowned Land and La Vita Breve*, translated by Donald Flanell Friedman and Suzanne Burgoyne. Belgian Francophone Library 1. New York: Peter Lang, 1994. Jungian analysis of *La Vita Breve* and comparison of the play with E. T. A. Hoffman's story "The Sandman." Volume also contains a discussion of Willems's novella, *The Drowned Land*.

Burgoyne Dieckman, Suzanne. Introduction to *Four Plays of Paul Willems: Dreams and Reflections*, edited by Suzanne Burgoyne Dieckman. New York: Garland, 1992. Analysis of the plays in the anthology: *It's Raining in My House*, *The Weight of the Snow*, *The Sailing City*, and *She Confused Sleeping and Dying*. Includes production photographs and a bibliography of Willems's published work, including major articles.

Emond, Paul, Henri Ronse, and Fabrice van de Kerckhove, eds. *Le monde de Paul Willems: Textes, entretiens, études* (the world of Paul Willems: texts, interviews, studies). Brussels: Éditions Labor, 1984. Contains important analyses of Willems's plays and novels by contributing scholars, as well as excerpts from Willems's writings and numerous photos. In French.

Friedman, Donald F. "Spaces of dream, protection, and imprisonment in the Theater of Paul Willems." *World Literature Today* 65 (1991): 46-48. Analysis of the ambiguous nature of seclusion in *The Weight of the Snow*, *Les Miroirs d'Ostende*, and *She Confused Sleeping and Dying*.

Otten, Michel, and Pierre Halen, eds. "Lectures de Paul Willems." *Textyles; Revue des Lettres Belges de Langue Française* 9 (1988). An international array of scholars interpret Willlems's work. Of particular interest are Michel Otten's treatment of the role of the reflection in the search for lost paradise and Alberte Spinette's study of the structural evolution of *La Vita breve*. In French.

Quaghebeur, Marc. Introduction to *Four Belgian Playwrights*. *Gambit International Theatre Review* 11, no. 42-42 (1986): 9-24. Belgian scholar Quaghebeur puts the work of Willems and three other playwrights into the context of the Belgian theater tradition. This special issue also contains a translation of *It's Raining in My House*, translator's notes on Willems, and a bibliography on Belgian theater.

Suzanne Burgoyne

EMLYN WILLIAMS

Born: Mostyn, Wales; November 26, 1905
Died: London, England; September 25, 1987

PRINCIPAL DRAMA

Vigil, pr. 1925, pb. 1954 (one act)
Full Moon, pr. 1927
Glamour, pr. 1928
A Murder Has Been Arranged, pr., pb. 1930
Port Said, pr. 1931, revised pr. 1933 (as *Vessels Departing*)
The Late Christopher Bean, pr., pb. 1933 (adaptation of a work by Sidney Howard)
Spring 1600, pr. 1934, revised pr. 1945, pb. 1946
Night Must Fall, pr., pb. 1935
He Was Born Gay: A Romance, pr., pb. 1937
The Corn Is Green, pr., pb. 1938
The Light of Heart, pr., pb. 1940
The Morning Star, pr. 1941, pb. 1942
Pen Don, pr. 1943
The Druid's Rest, pr., pb. 1944
The Wind of Heaven, pr., pb. 1945
Thinking Aloud: A Dramatic Sketch, pr. 1945, pb. 1946
Trespass: A Ghost Story, pr., pb. 1947
Accolade, pr. 1950, pb. 1951
Someone Waiting, pr. 1953, pb. 1954
Beth, pr. 1958, pb. 1959
The Collected Plays, pb. 1961
Cuckoo, pb. 1986

OTHER LITERARY FORMS

In addition to his stage and radio plays, Emlyn Williams wrote plays for television: in 1968, *A Blue Movie of My Own True Love*, about a love affair that results in murder; and in 1976, *The Power of Dawn*, about the final moments in the life of Leo Tolstoy.

Williams wrote the screenplays or provided dialogue for several motion pictures, including his *Friday the Thirteenth* (1933; with G. H. Moresby-White and Sidney Gilliat), *Evergreen* (1934; with Marjorie Gaffney), *The Man Who Knew Too Much* (1934; with A. R. Rawlinson and Edwin Greenwood), and *The Last Days of Dolwyn* (1949). His script for *The Citadel* (1938; with Frank Wead, Ian Dalrymple, Elizabeth Hill, and John Van Druten), based on the 1937 A. J. Cronin novel, was published in *Foremost Films of 1938*.

Williams also wrote two volumes of memoirs: *George: An Early Autobiography* (1961) and *Emlyn: An Early Autobiography, 1927-1935* (1973). The first tells the story of his childhood and youth in rural and urban Wales; the second chronicles his attempts to make a name for himself on the London stage as actor and playwright. Williams's interest in the psychology of killers, a concern of several of his plays, led to his account of the 1963-1964 Moors murders in England, *Beyond Belief: A Chronicle of Murder and Its Detection* (1967).

In his youth, Williams wrote several novels, but it was not until he was seventy-five that he actually published a novel, *Headlong* (1980), a variation of the "if I were king" theme. Its hero, Jack Green, who is an actor struggling to achieve success on the London stage, turns out to be the only living heir to the English throne when the entire royal family is wiped out in a catastrophe.

ACHIEVEMENTS

When one thinks of Wales in terms of theater, one thinks of Emlyn Williams, not only because he came from Wales but also because so many of his plays are filled with Welsh scenes and people. *The Corn Is Green*, his most popular play, is a hymn to the glory of life and to the distinctive virtues of the Welsh people. The play also won critical acclaim, receiving the New York Drama Critics Circle Award for Best Foreign Play of 1941.

Williams's studies of psychopathology are notable: His particularly chilling portrait of Dan in *Night Must Fall* was one of the first, and remains one of the most frightening, portraits of psychopathic killers who stalk their victims across countless reels and pages of twentieth century movies and books.

Williams has also been acclaimed for his acting ability, enjoying particular success for his impersonation of Charles Dickens reading his works and for his one-man show based on the works of Dylan Thomas. For his distinguished career in the theater, Williams was named Commander of the Order of the British Empire in 1962.

BIOGRAPHY

George Emlyn Williams was born on November 26, 1905, in the village of Mostyn, Wales, the first surviving child of Richard and Mary Williams. Like most other children of his village, the young George spoke only Welsh until he was eight, and like most boys in that part of Wales, he could look forward to a life in the mines.

Williams was an imaginative child, however, and when he was ten, he won a scholarship to the Holywell County School, where he came to the attention of Miss Grace Cooke, a London social worker

and the model for Miss Moffat in *The Corn Is Green*. Recognizing his talents—especially his facility with languages—she helped him secure a scholarship to Oxford, where he went in 1923. His choice of theater as a vocation was not surprising: As a child, he would cut characters from illustrated catalogs and create plays by inventing stories for them with himself as hero.

At Oxford, Williams—now using Emlyn as his first name—appeared in 1923 in his first play, a French farce. In 1924, he wrote his first play, a bittersweet version of Cinderella, never produced or published, and the following year, his first play was produced by the Oxford University Drama Society. *Vigil* is a one-act thriller about a cruel master who lures men to their deaths and who in turn is killed by his servant. As with so many of Williams's plays, there was a role in it for its author.

The year Williams received his M.A., 1927, was also the year the Drama Society, under the direction of J. B. Fagan, produced Williams's first full-length play, *Full Moon*, a story of conflict between romantic and possessive love. Fagan, a playwright as well as a producer, thought enough of Williams as an actor to give him a role in his own play *And So to Bed*, in which Williams made his London debut in April, 1927, and his New York debut in November, 1927. During the New York run, Williams wrote *Glamour*, which in 1928 became his first play to be seen in London. Not until 1930 and *A Murder Has Been Arranged*, however, did he gain the attention of the critics. A murder mystery with supernatural overtones, it features a protagonist, Maurice Mullins, whose surface charm conceals his ruthlessness, anticipating Dan in *Night Must Fall* and Fenn in *Someone Waiting*. Reviews were good, but business was not.

The two plays that followed—*Port Said* (revised in 1933 as *Vessels Departing*) and *Spring 1600* (revised in 1945)—were neither critical nor popular successes. If Williams's career as playwright seemed at a standstill, however, his career as actor was flourishing, with roles in plays by Émile Zola, Sean O'Casey, Luigi Pirandello, Georg Kaiser, and Edgar Wallace.

The year 1935 was an important one for Williams. He married Molly O'Shann, and his first child, Alan

Emlyn, was born. It was also the year in which *Night Must Fall* was produced. This psychological thriller ran for a year in London, provided Williams with one of his best roles, and established him as an important playwright. (Interestingly, 1935 is also the year in which the action of his novel *Headlong* occurs.)

He Was Born Gay, appearing two years later, did nothing to solidify Williams's reputation. Despite the presence in the cast of John Gielgud and Williams—his role of Lambert was another characterization in evil—the play barely lasted two weeks. Although its subtitle is *A Romance*, Williams could not decide whether the play was a romance, a comedy, or a tragedy.

The Corn Is Green, produced in 1938, is, with *Night Must Fall*, Williams's best work as a dramatist. An autobiographical comedy-drama about the efforts of an English schoolteacher to bring education to a small Welsh village, it was a success onstage in London with Sybil Thorndike and in New York with Ethel Barrymore, on-screen with Bette Davis, and on television with Katharine Hepburn.

The Light of Heart, Williams's next play, was written with an insider's knowledge of the theater. The character Maddoc Thomas, a Shakespearean actor in decline, is another of Williams's compelling portraits of an utterly self-absorbed, if charming, man, but the play is marred by sensationalism and lack of plausibility; it is difficult for the audience to believe that Thomas is as good an actor as Williams claims him to be.

Even less believable and more contrived is *The Morning Star*, a potboiler that served as the playwright's tribute to the courage of Londoners during the Blitz. Williams's heart was in the right place, but the incredible plot makes it difficult to take the play seriously. It was, however, a huge success in London. More significant contributions to the war effort were Williams's 1941 patriotic film, *This England*; his radio broadcasts, including readings from Charles Dickens; and his tours of various theaters of war to perform *Night Must Fall*, among other plays.

In *Pen Don*, Williams turned to medieval Wales for his setting and Welsh mythology for his subject matter. As far removed as *Pen Don* is from Williams's realistic plays, its theme—the conflict between innocence and experience—is a familiar one in his work.

Wales was also the setting for Williams's next two plays. *The Druid's Rest*, a comedy of misunderstanding, is steeped in local color. *The Wind of Heaven* is an ambitious play on the theme of the return of the Messiah in the guise of a boy during the time of the Crimean War. Ambrose Ellis, a Welsh apostate who tries to buy the boy for his circus, is another Williams protagonist caught between idealistic and materialistic motives. Save for him, however, the characters lack depth, and the conventions of the well-made play are at odds with the subject matter.

In comparison with the "kitchen sink" plays of the Angry Young Men that were setting the London theater on its heels with their scathing protests at the genteel Britain of yesteryear, Williams's postwar plays were tired and contrived: *Trespass*, a ghost story; *Accolade*, which fails to come to grips with its subject—the right of the artist to be free; *Someone Waiting*, a complicated mystery peopled with unpleasant characters; and *Beth*, his last play for the stage, which features a retarded heroine.

If these works added little to Williams's reputation as a playwright, he was, however, winning accolades as an actor, both in standard plays such as Henrik Ibsen's *Vildanden* (pb. 1884; *The Wild Duck*, 1891) and William Shakespeare's *The Merchant of Venice* (pr. c. 1596-1597) and in new works such as Terence Rattigan's *The Winslow Boy* (pr., pb. 1946), which gave him one of his most acclaimed roles, as Sir Robert Morton. This seemingly heartless lawyer, who is revealed as a man with a caring heart, is much like those divided selves Williams created in his own plays.

Williams's career in films, which began in 1932, was also flourishing; among his works in this medium were *The Citadel*, for which he wrote dialogue; *Major Barbara* (1941), based on George Bernard Shaw's play; *The Last Days of Dolwyn*, an evocation of Welsh village life, which he wrote and directed; and *Ivanhoe* (1952), based on the novel by Sir Walter Scott.

Williams's greatest success in the theater came in 1951, not with a play but with a triumphant one-man show, his impersonation of Charles Dickens reading from his works. Williams assumed the characters' personas and recreated the storytelling genius of Dickens. He toured all over the world with this show, performing it more than two thousand times. In 1955, he turned to the work of a fellow Welshman, Dylan Thomas, for another one-man show, *Dylan Thomas Growing Up*, which also proved popular. A third program of solo readings, based on the work of H. H. Munro (Saki) and entitled *The Playboy of the Wicked World* (1978), was less successful.

ANALYSIS

In genre, Emlyn Williams's plays range from fantasy to historical drama to psychological thriller to comedy; in time, from the days of King Arthur to Shakespeare's London to nineteenth century Wales to World War II London during the Blitz. Despite this variety and range, a majority of Williams's plays share common concerns: Wales, the theater, and the divided personality.

Seven of Williams's plays have Welsh settings; six others, though set elsewhere, feature Welsh characters, including Gwenny, Williams's first successful Welsh character, in his adaptation of Sidney Howard's *The Late Christopher Bean* (pr. 1932, pb. 1933). Dan, the psychopathic killer in *Night Must Fall*, is Welsh. Mason, the heir to the throne of Louis XVI in *He Was Born Gay*, was smuggled out of France as a child and reared in Wales.

In Williams's plays, Welsh characters, such as Rhys Price Morris in *Glamour*, often affirm positive values. Ambrose Ellis, the expatriate Welshman in *The Wind of Heaven*, regains his religious faith at the same time as he regains his command of the Welsh language. *The Corn Is Green* and *The Druid's Rest* depict Welsh village life as hard but healthy and unrelenting but uncomplicated. These plays celebrate the lives and loving hearts of Welsh men and women. They are hearts filled with music, recalling the plays of Irish life of John Millington Synge and Sean O'Casey.

Theater is the subject matter of *Glamour*, *Spring 1600*, and *The Light of Heart*. The dramatic sketch *Thinking Aloud* records the thoughts and feelings of an actress who has murdered her husband. The stage of a theater is the setting for *A Murder Has Been Arranged*. Ambrose Ellis of *The Wind of Heaven* and Saviello of *Trespass* are showmen, one a circus owner, the other a medium.

If not actors by vocation, some Williams protagonists—Maurice Mullins in *A Murder Has Been Arranged* and Dan in *Night Must Fall*—constantly, even compulsively, act. Indeed, Dan cannot remember a time when he was not acting. These coldhearted killers mask their true nature under a veneer of charm.

Dan and Maurice are also studies in abnormal psychology, a preoccupation of Williams from *Vigil*, his first produced play, to *Beyond Belief*, his study of the Moors murders. Another example is Fenn in *Someone Waiting*. This ineffectual, insignificant tutor is actually a man of insane cunning, who nurtures and pursues revenge without remorse. Although no killer, Saviello in *Trespass* belongs with this group. This Italian medium is exposed as a sham, a draper from Cardiff. In a stunning reversal, however, he turns out to be, much against his will, a genuine and natural medium.

A variant on this theme of split personality is the dual life many of Williams's artists lead and the choices they must make. The genius of the painter in *The Late Christopher Bean* has gone unrecognized during his lifetime because of the very private life he has chosen to lead. Both Jill in *Glamour* and Ann Byrd in *Spring 1600* must decide between a life of rural innocence and a career in the theater. Maddoc Thomas in *The Light of Heart* is torn between the desire to hold on to his daughter and the equally strong pull to reestablish his career in the theater. Will Trenting, the prizewinning novelist about to be knighted in *Accolade*, has been leading a Jekyll-and-Hyde existence. Ambrose Ellis is a man at war with himself. Saint and sinner, he struggles between the attraction of worldly success as an impresario and his sense of divine mission.

The persistence in Williams's plays of characters with divided personalities or characters faced with the choice of two ways of life reflects, perhaps, Williams's own dual role as actor and playwright and his own dual existence as George, the hero of his first volume of autobiography recording his life in Wales, and as Emlyn, the hero of the second volume, covering the years during which he was making his way in the London theater.

NIGHT MUST FALL

Williams's interest in crime and in murder trials was heightened in 1934 by accounts in London newspapers of recent and past killers who had left their victims' corpses in trunks and of one killer, termed the "Butcher of Hanover," a seemingly nice young man who had set his mother on fire in order to get her insurance money. These stories of murder became the basis for *Night Must Fall*.

As Williams worked on his script, he decided that his victim could not possibly be his young man's mother. In real life, sons do kill their mothers, but such a situation onstage would, Williams believed, prove too horrible for an audience to accept. Even so, Dan, the young man, tells his prospective victim that she reminds him of his own mother—he even calls her Mother—and she treats him indulgently, like a son.

Night Must Fall is set in a cottage on the edge of a forest in Essex, occupied by Mrs. Bramson, an overbearing invalid constantly demanding attention. Although she has a maid, a cook, and a visiting nurse, much of the burden of her care falls on her niece, Olivia, a lonely, repressed young woman.

Into the household comes Dan, a bellboy from a nearby hotel. A former seaman, blackmailer, and pimp, he has now taken up murder—that of a woman guest from the hotel who has vanished and whose decapitated body turns up several days later. We are led to believe that Dan carries the severed head around with him in a hatbox.

With his childlike, innocent airs and his good humor, Dan is most beguiling and quickly wins Mrs. Bramson over. Olivia initially distrusts him, yet she feels drawn to him, even when, to her horror, she knows he has murdered. Dan, compelled to show off, takes pleasure in almost confessing his guilt to her. Although he is not subject to remorse, he does suffer sudden panics during which he confides in her. Playing on her obvious attraction to him, he is able to keep her from giving him away.

Dan soon finds the opportunity he is seeking—to kill Mrs. Bramson and make off with her cashbox before the police become too suspicious of him. Reading to her one night from the Bible, he reminisces about mornings at sea when he was conscious of only the sun and himself. As the old lady reminds him, however, it is now night. Echoing Mrs. Bramson's remark, he loudly shuts the Bible and, singing a snatch of the same song heard before his first murder, picks up a cushion and smothers her.

In the play's final scene, Dan elatedly confesses to Olivia both the murder and his intention to burn the cottage with the body and Olivia in it. A beam from a police flashlight outside momentarily unnerves him, and Olivia, seeing him as an unprotected child, reaches out to him, but he soon regains his cocky self-assurance. As the police lead him off, he is looking forward to the attention women will give him at his trial, and he promises to give the spectators their money's worth. He passionately kisses Olivia, lights up a cigarette, and, with the same jauntiness that marked his first entrance, leaves.

Night Must Fall is no ordinary thriller. The audience knows from the prologue, set in the Court of Criminal Appeals, that the protagonist has been found guilty and condemned to death, a sentence with which the Lord Chief Justice finds no reason to interfere. Moreover, although the play provides a good deal of suspense, its emphasis is not on the twists and turns of plot but on the character of Dan.

Dan is a study in contrasts: raffish but ruthless, charming but callous, disarming but dangerous. Emotionally impregnable though he is, women find in him a vulnerability that fascinates them. He lives in the world of his imagination. There, nothing can touch him; there, everyone is under him. His masquerade feeds his vanity, and his vanity accounts for his constant desire to talk of himself.

There are enough chilling moments in the play to make palms sweat and pulses race. Williams places these moments most strategically at the end of each of the play's five scenes: Dan's singing "Mighty Lak a Rose" a few moments after we have learned the song was heard before the first victim disappeared; Olivia's look of horror as she stares into Dan's face at the news of the body's discovery; the murder of Mrs. Bramson as the lights dim and the music rises in crescendo; and Dan's final exit. No scene is more taut than the act 2 curtain. As the police inspector, suspicious of Dan, goes to open the hatbox, Dan sits drumming his fingers against the sofa and then wildly beats his fists against his head. Olivia claims the box as hers and walks off with it. The danger passed, Dan, left alone, crumples to the floor in a faint as the curtain quickly falls.

Night Must Fall is a tightly written play. Nowhere is this more evident than in Williams's handling of time. Although the action covers two weeks, each scene takes place just a little later in the day than the preceding one. The overall effect is that the play occurs in a single day, from morning to night. This telescoping of time adds to the play's growing suspense and tension. Also effective is the casual tone and banter of the opening scene and Williams's skillful use of humor. Both serve as a contrast to the dawning horror and lengthening shadows as night falls and envelops the cottage in darkness.

Night Must Fall ran in London for 435 performances with Dame May Whitty and the author in the leading roles. The play has been filmed twice, once in 1937 with Robert Montgomery and again in 1963 with Albert Finney.

THE CORN IS GREEN

The Corn Is Green tells the story of how a determined and dedicated schoolteacher in Wales discovers a literary talent among the local miners and exerts all of her power to make a success of him. A middle-aged English spinster, Miss Moffat, comes to a small Welsh village in the latter part of the nineteenth century to found a school for the children of Welsh miners. Though there is initial skepticism and resistance from some of the villagers and from the English Squire, who dominates the community through his ownership of the land, Miss Moffat perseveres, especially after she discovers a young boy, Morgan Evans, of great intellectual promise. She is resolved to release him into the world of enlightenment. She even plays up to the Squire to win his support.

Miss Moffat prepares Morgan well enough so that he can compete for an Oxford scholarship, but in the process she forgets that he is a human being. He rebels against her authority, turns to a local harlot, Bessie Watty, and gets her pregnant. Months later, Morgan learns of Bessie's baby at the same time that he learns of winning the scholarship. Out of a sense of duty, he is ready to give up Oxford to marry Bessie, who does not love him and does not want the baby. Miss Moffat agrees to adopt the child, freeing Morgan to take the scholarship. When another promising youngster comes along, she will not be as clumsy as she was with Morgan. As the school bell rings clearly and confidently, marking the beginning of another term, the curtain falls.

The Corn Is Green is a deeply felt play whose power derives in part from its autobiographical content. Because the material was too close to real life, Williams placed the action back in time. Morgan is the author's adolescent alter ego, although the playwright claimed that Morgan was not a self-portrait. Interestingly, Williams created the role of Morgan onstage. Certainly the relationship between teacher and pupil is autobiographical.

That relationship is the core of the play and accounts for the play's most dramatic and moving scenes: Miss Moffat's reading of Morgan's first essay, a lyric evocation of life in the mines; her impersonal treatment of him; his determination to climb over the stone wall behind which he has been a prisoner all his life and his acknowledgment that she has given him a leg up; his excited description to her of the Oxford examination; and their final confrontation and farewell, where they come together not as teacher and pupil, adult and youngster, but as two friends. Through her wisdom and understanding, Morgan now has the courage to become someone of whom Wales can be proud.

Miss Moffat is Williams's most surely drawn character and as close to a true heroine—or hero—as is any character in his plays. A woman of unbounded vitality, she will not be deterred from her goals—her pursuit of them makes her authoritative and tenacious—yet she is endowed with a genuine feeling for other people.

Morgan, the play's second major character, is also well conceived; his growth from crude youngster to self-conscious rebel to serious scholar is most convincing. An impudent young man, he desperately wants to learn, but in his understandable distrust of the ways and means of learning, he resents the domineering hand of Miss Moffat.

The minor characters are winning, if stereotyped: the no-nonsense Cockney mother; her trollop daughter; a genteel English lady; the Squire who prides himself on not reading but who accepts the poet Alfred, Lord Tennyson because Tennyson attended Cambridge, the Squire's school. Williams mines the rich comic vein of such characters as Old Tom, who all of his life thought Shakespeare a place, and the volcanic John Gorowny Jones, harmless even while erupting.

The Corn Is Green is a ringing affirmation of education, an unusual theme for a contemporary play, but one that Williams invests with sincerity and excitement. At the same time, one might question whether an Oxford education is worth the sacrifice of personal responsibility and self-identity. The play takes up several social concerns as well: the plight of children sent to the mines, the status of women, and the relationship of the Welsh people and language to the English people and language.

If there is a weakness, it is in Williams's reliance on melodrama to bring matters to a climax—in this case, the illegitimate baby. In a play in which for two acts characterization shapes plot, it is disappointing to find, in the final scenes, plot molding characters. Still, Williams handles the mechanics of plot with a sure hand, and the play's theatrical quality never falters.

When Miss Cooke, the real-life prototype of Miss Moffat, received a copy of the script for her approval, she wrote to her former pupil that she did not believe audiences would want to see a play about education. Wrong as she was about the play's appeal, she was right when she told Williams that in his earlier plays she found the characters "a little out of focus." She added, though, that the people in *The Corn Is Green* were "straight from life. So it was, and so it is written."

Night Must Fall and *The Corn Is Green* are Williams's most satisfying plays, distinguished by strong characterization, a simple but effective narrative line, expert control of suspense and atmosphere, and an artful blend of pathos and humor. Because of these solid dramatic virtues, they continue to have a place on the international stage.

OTHER MAJOR WORKS

LONG FICTION: *Headlong*, 1980; *Dr. Crippen's Diary: An Invention*, 1987.

SCREENPLAYS: *Friday the Thirteenth*, 1933 (with G. H. Moresby-White and Sidney Gilliat); *Evergreen*, 1934 (with Marjorie Gaffney); *The Man Who Knew Too Much*, 1934 (with A. R. Rawlinson and Edwin Greenwood); *The Divine Spark*, 1935 (with Richard Benson); *Broken Blossoms*, 1936; *The Citadel*, 1938 (with Frank Wead, Ian Dalrymple, Elizabeth Hill, and John Van Druten; based on A. J. Cronin's novel); *This England*, 1941 (with Bridget Boland and Rawlinson); *Major Barbara*, 1941 (based on George Bernard Shaw's play); *The Last Days of Dolwyn*, 1949; *Ivanhoe*, 1952 (based on Sir Walter Scott's novel).

TELEPLAYS: *A Month in the Country*, 1947; *Every Picture Tells a Story*, 1949; *In Town Tonight*, 1954; *A Blue Movie of My Own True Love*, 1968; *The Power of Dawn*, 1976.

RADIO PLAYS: *Pepper and Sand*, 1947; *Emlyn*, 1974 (adaptation of his autobiography).

NONFICTION: *George: An Early Autobiography*, 1961; *Beyond Belief: A Chronicle of Murder and Its Detection*, 1967; *Emlyn: An Early Autobiography, 1927-1935*, 1973.

BIBLIOGRAPHY

Brantley, Ben. "A Killer Just Loaded with Charm." Review of *Night Must Fall*, by Emlyn Williams. *The New York Times* March 9, 1999, p. 1. This favorable review of a 1999 staging of a *Night Must Fall* by the Tony Randall's National Actors Theater remarks on how well the play works more than sixty years after its premiere. The discussion of the production and the plot shed light on Williams's well-known work.

Dale-Jones, Don. *Emlyn Williams*. Cardiff: University of Wales Press, 1979. This monograph focuses on how Williams's Welsh background, including his studies in psychology and foreign literatures, determined his interest in the theater and influenced his plays. A thorough study of Williams. Bibliography.

Harding, James. *Emlyn Williams: A Life*. London: Weidenfeld and Nicholson, 1993. This biography of Williams looks at his life and works. Provides a listing of his works, bibliography, and index.

Stephens, John Russell. *Emlyn Williams: The Making of a Dramatist*. Chester Springs, Pa.: DuFour Editions, 2000. Stephens's biography traces the development of Williams as a dramatist and examines his works. Bibliography and index.

Richard B. Gidez,
updated by Irene Gnarra

TENNESSEE WILLIAMS

Born: Columbus, Mississippi; March 26, 1911
Died: New York, New York; February 25, 1983

PRINCIPAL DRAMA

Fugitive Kind, pr. 1937, pb. 2001
Spring Storm, wr. 1937, pr., pb. 1999
Not About Nightingales, wr. 1939, pr., pb. 1998
Battle of Angels, pr. 1940, pb. 1945
This Property Is Condemned, pb. 1941, pr. 1946 (one act)
I Rise in Flame, Cried the Phoenix, wr. 1941, pb. 1951, pr. 1959 (one act)
The Lady of Larkspur Lotion, pb. 1942 (one act)
The Glass Menagerie, pr. 1944, pb. 1945
Twenty-seven Wagons Full of Cotton, pb. 1945, pr. 1955 (one act)
You Touched Me, pr. 1945, pb. 1947 (with Donald Windham)
Summer and Smoke, pr. 1947, pb. 1948
A Streetcar Named Desire, pr., pb. 1947
American Blues, pb. 1948 (collection)
Five Short Plays, pb. 1948
The Long Stay Cut Short: Or, The Unsatisfactory Supper, pb. 1948 (one act)
The Rose Tattoo, pr. 1950, pb. 1951
Camino Real, pr., pb. 1953
Cat on a Hot Tin Roof, pr., pb. 1955
Orpheus Descending, pr. 1957, pb. 1958 (revision of *Battle of Angels*)
Suddenly Last Summer, pr., pb. 1958

The Enemy: Time, pb. 1959
Sweet Bird of Youth, pr., pb. 1959 (based on *The Enemy: Time*)
Period of Adjustment, pr. 1959, pb. 1960
The Night of the Iguana, pr., pb. 1961
The Milk Train Doesn't Stop Here Anymore, pr. 1963, revised pb. 1976
The Eccentricities of a Nightingale, pr., pb. 1964 (revision of *Summer and Smoke*)
Slapstick Tragedy: The Mutilated and The Gnädiges Fräulein, pr. 1966, pb. 1970 (one acts)
The Two-Character Play, pr. 1967, pb. 1969
The Seven Descents of Myrtle, pr., pb. 1968 (as *Kingdom of Earth*)
In the Bar of a Tokyo Hotel, pr. 1969, pb. 1970
Confessional, pb. 1970
Dragon Country, pb. 1970 (collection)
The Theatre of Tennessee Williams, pb. 1971-1981 (7 volumes)
Out Cry, pr. 1971, pb. 1973 (revision of *The Two-Character Play*)
Small Craft Warnings, pr., pb. 1972 (revision of *Confessional*)
Vieux Carré, pr. 1977, pb. 1979
A Lovely Sunday for Creve Coeur, pr. 1979, pb. 1980
Clothes for a Summer Hotel, pr. 1980
A House Not Meant to Stand, pr. 1981
Something Cloudy, Something Clear, pr. 1981, pb. 1995

OTHER LITERARY FORMS

Besides his plays, Tennessee Williams produced essays, letters, memoirs, music lyrics, original screenplays, poetry, short stories, and novels.

ACHIEVEMENTS

By critical consensus, Tennessee Williams ranks second after Eugene O'Neill among American dramatists. He was greatly influenced by Anton Chekhov in his ability to universalize strongly realized local settings, in his portrayal of frail characters in a cold and alien world, in his frequently superb use of symbol and in his development of a natural structure that does not call attention to itself. Like Chekhov's best works, Williams's best plays appear to unfold as naturally as life itself. Williams has been accused at times of "purple" writing, sentimentality, and an overemphasis on violence and depravity. Although such criticism may occasionally be justified, Wil-

liams remains one of the most dramatically effective and profoundly perceptive playwrights of the modern theater.

BIOGRAPHY

Tennessee Williams was born Thomas Lanier Williams in 1911 in Columbus, Mississippi, the son of Cornelius Coffin Williams and Edwina Dakin Williams. He lived his early years in the home of his grandparents, for whom he felt great affection. His grandfather was a minister, and Williams's father was a traveling salesperson, apparently at home infrequently. In about 1919, his father accepted a nontraveling position at his firm's headquarters in St. Louis. The move from a more or less traditional southern environment to a very different metropolitan world was extremely painful both for Williams and for his older sister, neither of whom ever really recovered from it.

The Glass Menagerie is clearly a play about the Williams family and its life in St. Louis, though Williams's *Memoirs* (1975) and other known facts make it clear that the play is by no means a precise transcription of actuality. On the other hand, *The Glass Menagerie* is not the only Williams play that has biographical elements. His father, his mother, and his sister (who became mentally ill) are reflected in his characters in various plays. Williams's homosexuality, which he examines in some detail in his *Memoirs*, is also an important element in a number of his plays, including *A Streetcar Named Desire*, *Cat on a Hot Tin Roof*, and *Suddenly Last Summer*.

Williams attended the University of Missouri and Washington University and was graduated in 1938 from the University of Iowa. His adult life involved considerable wandering, with periods in such places as Key West, New Orleans, and New York. After various attempts at writing, some of which gained helpful recognition, Williams first won acclaim with *The Glass Menagerie*. Most of his plays from that point through *The Night of the Iguana* were successful, either on first production or later. He won Pulitzer Prizes for *A Streetcar Named Desire* and *Cat on a Hot Tin Roof*, and New York Drama Critics Circle Awards for those two and for *The Glass Menagerie*

Tennessee Williams (Sam Shaw, courtesy of New Directions)

and *The Night of the Iguana*. The many plays that he wrote in the last twenty years of his life, however, achieved almost no success, either in the United States or abroad. Depending on one's point of view, either Williams's inspiration had run out, or he was writing a kind of play for which neither the public nor most critics were yet ready. Williams died in New York on February 25, 1983, having choked on a foreign object lodged in his throat.

ANALYSIS

If the weight of critical opinion places Tennessee Williams below Eugene O'Neill as America's premiere dramatist, there should be no question that the later playwright is without peer either in the diversity of genres in which he wrote or his impact on the cultural consciousness of mid-twentieth century America. In the course of his long career, Williams wrote essays; letters; memoirs; music lyrics; original screenplays, including that for the controversial *Baby Doll*; poetry; short stories; and novels, one of which, the bittersweet *The Roman Spring of Mrs. Stone*, was made into a major motion picture. However, it is as a playwright that Williams's genius shines most brightly, particularly from the early 1940's to the early 1960's, a period comprising *The Glass Menagerie*, *Summer and Smoke*, *A Streetcar Named Desire*, *The Rose Tattoo*, *Cat on a Hot Tin Roof*, *Orpheus Descending*, *Suddenly Last Summer*, *Sweet Bird of Youth*, and *The Night of the Iguana*. These plays encompass an unrelenting exploration of the dark underbelly of human experience: frigidity and nymphomania, impotence and rape, pedophilia and fetishism, cannibalism and coprophagy, alcohol and drug addiction, castration and syphilis, violence and madness, and aging and death. These themes place Williams squarely in the gothic tradition and reflect his early interest in the bizarre and grotesque. As a child he was fed large doses of Edgar Allan Poe by his grandfather. Tormented by a sense of existential loneliness, Williams was able to sublimate his dark vision into plays that bring to life such iconic characters as Big Daddy, Stanley Kowalski, Blanche Dubois, and Amanda Wingfield in language that has been compared favorably with William Shakespeare's. Wil-

liams is second to none among American writers whose works have been successfully made into major films. His plays have been translated into more than a score of languages and continue to be performed in theaters throughout the world.

THE GLASS MENAGERIE

Williams's *The Glass Menagerie* was regarded when first produced as highly unusual; one of the play's four characters serves as commentator as well as participant; the play itself represents the memories of the commentator years later, and hence, as he says, is not a depiction of actuality; its employment of symbolism is unusual; and in the very effective ending, a scrim descends in front of mother and daughter, so that by stage convention one can see but not hear them, with the result that both, but especially the mother, become much more moving and even archetypal. The play is also almost unique historically, in that it first opened in Chicago, came close to flopping before Chicago newspaper theater critics verbally whipped people into going, and then played successfully for months in Chicago before finally moving to equal success in New York.

One device that Williams provided for the play was quickly abandoned: A series of legends and images flashed on a screen, indicating the central idea of scenes and parts of scenes. This device provides a triple insight into Williams: first, his skill at organizing scenes into meaningful wholes; second, his willingness to experiment, sometimes successfully, sometimes not; and third, his occasional tendency to spell out by external devices what a play itself makes clear.

The Glass Menagerie opens on a near-slum apartment, with Tom Wingfield setting the time (the Depression and Spanish-Civil-War 1930's); the play's method as memory, with its consequent use of music and symbol; and the names and relationships of the characters: Tom, his sister Laura, his mother Amanda, and an initially unnamed gentleman caller. A fifth character, Tom says, is his father, who, having deserted his family years before, appears only as a larger-than-life photograph over the mantel, which on occasion—according to Williams's stage directions, but rarely in actual production—lights up.

Tom works in a shoe warehouse, writes poetry, and feels imprisoned by the knowledge that his hateful job is essential to the family's financial survival. Apparently, his one escape is to go to the movies. His relationship with his mother is a combination of love, admiration, frustration, and acrimony, with regular flare-ups and reconciliations. His relationship with his sister is one of love and sympathy. Laura is physically crippled as well as withdrawn from the outside world. She is psychologically unable (as one learns in scene 2) to attend business college and lives in a world of her phonograph records and fragile glass animals. Amanda, a more complex character than the others, is the heart of the play: a constantly chattering woman who lives in part for her memories, perhaps exaggerated, of an idealized antebellum southern girlhood and under the almost certain illusion that her son will amount to something and that her daughter will marry; yet she also lives very positively in the real world, aware of the family's poverty, keeping track of the bills, scratching for money by selling magazine subscriptions, taking advantage of her membership in the Daughters of the American Revolution. She is aware, too, that she must constantly remind her son of his responsibility to his family and that if her daughter is ever to marry, it must be through the machinations of mother and son. Yet, on the other hand, she is insufficiently aware of how her nagging and nostalgia drive her son to desperation and of how both son and daughter act on occasion to protect her illusions and memories.

Scene 1 provides a general picture of this background; scene 2 is a confrontation between mother and daughter. Amanda has discovered that, rather than attending business college, Laura has simply left and returned home at the proper hours, spending her time walking in the park, visiting the zoo, or going to the movies. Amanda must accept the fact that a job for Laura is out of the question, and she therefore starts planning for the other alternative, marriage. The scene introduces a second symbol in a nickname that Laura says a boy gave her in high school: "Blue Roses." Roses are delicate and beautiful, like Laura and like her glass menagerie, but blue roses, like glass animals, have no real existence. Scene 3 shows Amanda trying unsuccessfully to sell magazine subscriptions on the telephone and ends in a shockingly violent quarrel between mother and son, concluding with Tom throwing his overcoat across the room in his rage and unintentionally destroying some of Laura's animals. One of Williams's most notable uses of lighting occurs in this scene. A pool of light envelops Laura as Tom and Amanda quarrel, so that one becomes aware without words that the devastating effect on Laura is the scene's major point. Scene 4 shows Laura talking Tom into an apology and reconciliation, and Amanda taking advantage of Tom's remorse to persuade him to invite a friend from the warehouse home to dinner, in the hope that the "gentleman caller" will be attracted to Laura.

Scene 5 is long, building up suspense for Amanda and for the audience. Tom announces to his mother that he has invited a warehouse friend, Jim O'Connor, to dinner the next evening. Amanda, pleased but shocked at the suddenness of this new development, makes elaborate plans and has high expectations, but Tom tries to make her face the reality of Laura's physical and psychological limitations. Scene 6 shows the arrival of the guest and his attempt to accept Amanda's pathetic and almost comical southern-belle behavior and elaborate "fussing," and Laura's almost pathological fright and consequent inability to come to the dinner table. Dialogue between Tom and Jim makes clear Jim's relative steadiness and definite if perhaps overly optimistic plans for a career. It also reveals Tom's near failure at his job, his frustration over his family's situation, and his ripening determination to leave home: He has joined the merchant seamen's union instead of paying the light bill. The scene ends with the onset of a sharp summer storm. Laura, terrified, is on the sofa trying desperately not to cry; the others are at the dinner table and Tom is saying grace: a combination remarkable for its irony and pathos.

At the beginning of scene 7, the lights go out because of Tom's failure to pay the light bill, so the whole scene is played in candlelight. It is the climactic scene, and in it, Williams faced a problem faced by many modern playwrights: What kind of outcome does one choose, and by what means, in a situation where if things go one way they might seem incredible, and if they go the other, they might seem overly obvious? It is perhaps not a wholly soluble situation, but Williams did remarkably well in handling it. By Amanda's inevitable machinations after dinner, Jim and Laura are left alone. Jim—who has turned out to be the "Blue Roses" boy from high school, the boy with whom Laura was close to being in love—is a sympathetic and understanding person who, even in the short time they are alone together, manages to get more spontaneous and revealing conversation out of Laura than her family ever has, and even persuades her to dance. Clearly, here is a person who could bring to reality Amanda's seemingly impossible dreams, a man who could lead Laura into the real world (as he symbolically brought her glass unicorn into it by unintentionally breaking off its horn), a man who would make a good husband. For the play to end thus, however, would be out of accord with the facts of Williams's family life, with the tone of the whole play up to that point, and with modern audience's dislike of pat, happy endings in serious plays. Jim tells Laura that he is already engaged, a fact made more believable by Tom's unawareness of it. Laura's life is permanently in ruins. What might have happened will never happen. When Amanda learns the truth from Jim just before he leaves, the resulting quarrel with Tom confirms Tom in his plans to leave home permanently, abandoning his mother and sister to an apparently hopeless situation. Yet as he tells the audience—who are watching a soundless Amanda hovering over Laura to comfort her by candlelight—his flight has been unsuccessful. The memories haunt him; Laura haunts him. Speaking to her from a far-off world, he begs her to blow her candles out and thus obliterate the memory. She does, and the curtain falls.

A STREETCAR NAMED DESIRE

Williams's next successful play, *A Streetcar Named Desire*, is generally regarded as his best. Initial reaction was mixed, but there would be little argument now that it is one of the most powerful plays in the modern theater. Like *The Glass Menagerie*, it concerns, primarily, a man and two women and a "gentleman caller." As in *The Glass Menagerie*, one

of the women is very much aware of the contrast between the present and her southern-aristocratic past; one woman (Stella) is practical if not always adequately aware, while the other (Blanche) lives partly in a dream world and teeters on the brink of psychosis; the gentleman caller could perhaps save the latter were circumstances somewhat different; and the play's single set is a slum apartment.

Yet these similarities only point up the sharp differences between the two plays. *A Streetcar Named Desire* is not a memory play; it is sharply naturalistic, with some use of expressionistic devices to point up Blanche's emotional difficulties. Blanche is not, as is Laura, a bond between the other two family members; she is, rather, an intolerable intruder who very nearly breaks up her sister's marriage. A more complex creation than anyone in *The Glass Menagerie*, she is fascinating, cultured, pathetic, vulgar, admirable, despicable: a woman who, unlike Amanda, cannot function adequately outside the safe, aristocratic world of the past, but who, like Amanda, can fight almost ferociously for what she wants, even when it is almost surely unattainable. Her opponent, Stella's husband, Stanley Kowalski, is also a much sharper figure than Tom Wingfield.

One of the major critical problems of *A Streetcar Named Desire* has been whose side one should be on in the battle between Blanche and Stanley. The answer may be one that some critics have been unable to accept: neither and both. Blanche's defense of culture, of the intellectual and aesthetic aspects of life, may be pathetic coming from one who has become a near-alcoholic prostitute, but it is nevertheless genuine, important, and valid. Life has dealt her devastating blows, to which she has had to respond alone; her sister has offered no help. Yet she herself is partly responsible for the horrible world in which she finds herself, and her attempts to find a haven from it are both pitiable and (because she is inadequately aware of the needs of others) repellent. Stanley, the sort of man who might, in later years, be called "macho," uncultured and uninterested in culture, capable (as Blanche also is in her own way) of violence, is nevertheless an intelligent man, a man who functions more capably than do any of his friends in the world in which he finds himself, a man who loves his wife and would be pathetically lost without her. Stanley would find any intrusion into his happy home intolerable, but he finds it doubly so when the intruder is a woman who stays on indefinitely, a woman with Blanche's affectations, her intolerance of any lifestyle other than that of her own childhood, her obvious dislike of her sister's marriage, and her corrupt sexual past, which makes her attempts to attract one of Stanley's best friends more than Stanley can tolerate.

It is ironic that the play should end on a "happily-ever-after" note for Stanley and Stella (though surely Blanche can never be wholly forgotten), but this is life, not a model of life. Indeed, the life that both find, apparently, wholly satisfying and sufficient is itself a sort of irony. Stella has had to give up everything that Blanche believes in, everything from her own past, in order to accept it and welcome it.

The setting of *A Streetcar Named Desire* is the street and outdoor stairs of the building in which the Kowalskis live, and the interior of their two-room apartment. As scene 1 opens, neighbors are out front talking. Stanley and Mitch come in, prepared to go bowling. Stanley is carrying a package of meat. Stella comes out. Stanley throws the meat to her, and even the neighbors are amused at the symbolism. Stanley and Mitch proceed to the bowling alley, and Stella follows. Then Blanche comes around the corner, with her suitcase, dressed all in white—another ironic symbol—in a fashion appropriate to an upper-class garden party. In a stage direction, Williams compares her to a moth, and throughout the play, she fears the alluring but destructive light. She fears people seeing how she really looks. She fears facing the truth or having other people learn it. As she later says, she fibs because fibs are more pleasant; symbolically, she covers the overhead light bulb in the apartment with a paper lantern. Paper, indeed, is a recurring symbol throughout the play. For example, two of the melodies one hears from a distance are "Paper Doll" and "Paper Moon."

Blanche has never before seen Stella's apartment or met her sister's husband. To mark her progress through New Orleans to get to the apartment, Williams took advantage of actual New Orleans names (or former names); Blanche has to transfer from a streetcar called Desire to one called Cemeteries in order to arrive in the slum, called Elysian Fields. While the first of the streetcars gives the title to the play, Williams wisely makes use of the names only once after the opening scene. Blanche's progress in the play is from a wide range of desires (for culture, security, sex, and money) to a sort of living death, and while the slum may be an Elysian Fields for Stanley and Stella, it is a Tartarus for her. Williams also, like many earlier dramatists, gave some of his characters meaningful, and in this case, ironic names. Blanche DuBois is by no means a White Woods (though the name is a reminder of Anton Chekhov's *Vishnyovy sad*, pr., pb. 1904; *The Cherry Orchard*, 1908, and hence of the sort of life she has lost), and Stella is no Star. Such devices can be overdone: The name of their lost plantation, Belle Reve, may be an example.

A neighbor who owns the building lets Blanche into the apartment, and another neighbor goes for Stella. Blanche is alone. Like Laura on the night of the dinner, she is skittish, but her reaction is different: She spots a bottle of whiskey and takes a slug. Stella rushes in and, as is common in plays that begin with an arrival, the audience learns a great deal about both sisters as they talk—learns about their past, about Blanche's hostile attitude toward her environment, about the grim string of family illnesses and deaths, about the loss of the plantation. The sisters love each other but are obviously at odds in many respects. Blanche has been a schoolteacher, but one may doubt the reason she gives, a sort of sick leave, for being in New Orleans in early May while school at home is still in session. Stanley comes in with Mitch and another friend. Williams's description of him here, as the gaudy, dominant seed bearer, is famous. With Stella in the bathroom and his friends gone, Stanley encounters Blanche alone. He is surprised, but he tries to play the friendly host. Presently, he asks Blanche if she had not once been married. Blanche says that the boy died, promptly adding that she feels sick. The scene ends.

A prominent feature of this first scene, one that continues throughout the play, is the use of sound effects. There are sound effects in *The Glass Menagerie*, too, such as the glass menagerie thematic music and the music from the nearby dance hall, but in *A Streetcar Named Desire*, the sound effects are much more elaborate. As the curtain rises, one hears the voices of people passing and the sound of the "Blue Piano" in the nearby bar, and the piano becomes louder at appropriate points. Twice a cat screeches, frightening Blanche badly. As the subject of her husband and his death comes up, one hears—softly here but louder when Blanche reaches a crisis—the music of a polka, clearly a sound inside Blanche's head and hence an expressionistic device. At the end of scene 2, in which Blanche and Stanley have had a conversation that is both hostile and covertly sexual, a tamale vendor is heard calling "Red-hot!" Similar effects, notably of trains roaring past, occur throughout the play.

Scene 2 begins with a dialogue between Stanley and Stella. It is the next evening. Stella is taking Blanche out to dinner in order not to interfere with the poker night Stanley has planned. Stanley learns of the loss of the plantation and is angry, especially after he examines Blanche's trunk and finds it full of expensive clothes and furs. Stella has postponed telling Blanche that she is pregnant. Blanche enters and, seeing the situation, sends Stella on an errand so that she can have it out with Stanley. Stanley must accept the fact that the plantation has been lost because it was heavily mortgaged, and the mortgage payments could not be made. Blanche grows playful with him, and Stanley implies that she is being deliberately provocative. Stanley comes across Blanche's love letters from her dead husband, and Blanche becomes almost hysterical. Stanley tells Blanche of the coming baby. The men begin to arrive for poker. Stella returns and leads Blanche away.

Scene 3, entitled "The Poker Night," opens on a garish and, Williams says, Van Gogh-like view of Stanley and his three friends playing poker. Stanley has had too much to drink and is becoming verbally violent. The women return from their evening out. Blanche encounters Mitch at the bathroom door—she wants to take another of her endless hot baths—and they are clearly attracted to each other. Stanley, hating the presence of women during a poker game, becomes physically violent, and (offstage) hits Stella. The other men, who are familiar with this behavior but feel great affection for Stanley, subdue him and leave. Blanche, horrified, has taken Stella to the upstairs apartment. Stanley realizes what has happened, sobs, and screams for Stella, who presently joins him on the outside stairs. They fall into a sexual embrace, and he carries her inside. Clearly, this series of events has occurred before; clearly, this is the usual outcome, and is one of the attractions that Stanley has for Stella. Blanche comes down the stairs, even more horrified, and Mitch returns and comforts her.

In scene 4, Blanche returns from upstairs the next morning and is shocked to learn that Stella accepts all that has happened and wants no change in her marital situation. With some justice, Blanche describes Stanley as an uncultured animal in a world in which culture is essential—a speech that Stanley overhears. He comes in, and to Blanche's horror, Stella embraces him. It is in this scene that Blanche, uselessly and desperately, first thinks of an old boyfriend, now rich, as a source of rescue from her plight, a futile idea that she develops and tries harder and harder to believe in as her plight worsens. Scene 5 contains an example of Williams's occasionally excessive irony: Stanley asks Blanche her astrological sign, and it turns out that his is Capricorn and hers is Virgo. The major import of the scene is that Stanley confronts Blanche with stories he has heard about her life back home and afterward Blanche admits to Stella that some of them are true. Blanche and Stella agree that marrying Mitch is the solution to Blanche's problem, and Blanche is left alone. A young newsboy comes to collect money, and Blanche comes very close to trying, consciously and cynically, to seduce him. Clearly, sex, like alcohol, has been both a cause of and a response to her situation. Mitch arrives for a date, holding a bunch of roses, and the scene ends. Scene 6 opens with the return of the two from their date. Its major import is Blanche's telling Mitch about her dead husband, whom she encountered one evening in an embrace with an older man. Later that evening, while they were dancing to the polka she now keeps hearing, Blanche, unable to stop herself, told him he disgusted her. A few minutes later, he went outside and shot himself. Telling the story is a catharsis for Blanche and deeply enlists Mitch's sympathy. They are in each other's arms, and he suggests the possibility of marriage.

In scene 7, several months later, with Blanche still there and with the marriage idea apparently no further advanced, Stanley tells Stella of his now detailed and verified knowledge of Blanche's sordid sexual past, including her having seduced a seventeen-year-old student. As a result of this last action, Blanche lost her job, and Stanley, as he explains to Stella, has told Mitch the whole story. Stella is horrified, both at the facts themselves and at their revelation to Mitch. It is Blanche's birthday, there is a birthday cake, and Mitch has been invited. Scene 8 shows the women's mounting distress as Mitch fails to show up for the party; Stanley gives Blanche a "birthday present," a bus ticket back home for the following Tuesday; he makes it clear that Blanche's presence all this time has been almost too much to endure. Stella develops labor pains and leaves with Stanley for the hospital. Scene 9, later that evening, shows Mitch coming in with very changed intentions, tearing the paper lantern off and turning on the light to see Blanche plainly for the first time, telling her she is not clean enough to take home to his mother, and trying to get her to bed. She reacts violently, and he runs out.

In scene 10, the climactic scene, Stanley comes back. Blanche has been drinking and is desperately upset. With Stanley, she tries to retreat into fanciful illusions—Mitch has returned and apologized, her rich boyfriend has invited her on a Caribbean tour. Stanley exposes her lies, and her desperation grows, as indicated by lurid, darting shadows and other expressionistic devices. Their confrontation reaches a climax, and after she tries to resist, he carries her off to bed. In scene 11, some weeks later, one learns that Blanche has told Stella that Stanley raped her, that Stella must believe that the rape is merely one of Blanche's psychotic illusions if her life with Stanley is to survive, and that Stella has made arrangements to place Blanche in a state institution. A doctor and nurse come to get her. Blanche is terrified. The nurse is cold and almost brutal, but the doctor gains

Blanche's confidence by playing the role of a gentleman, and she leaves on his arm, clearly feeling that she has found what she has been seeking, a man to protect her. All this occurs while another poker game is in progress. The play ends with Stella in Stanley's arms, and with one of the other men announcing, "This game is seven-card stud."

The brutes have won, and Stella has permanently denied her heritage, yet one must remember that the "brutes" are not without redeeming qualities. Stanley has displayed intense loyalty to his friends, genuine love for his wife, and a variety of insecurities beneath his aggressive manner. The other men have displayed loyalty to Stanley, and Mitch has shown much sympathy and understanding. As Blanche has said early in the play, Stanley may be just what their bloodline needs, and that point is emphasized when, near the end of the final scene, the upstairs neighbor hands Stella her baby. Life must go on; perhaps the next generation will do better; but long before the play opens, life has destroyed a potentially fine and sensitive woman.

CAT ON A HOT TIN ROOF

Of Williams's four plays analyzed here, *Cat on a Hot Tin Roof*, his next big success, is the only one that falls into a special Williams category: plays that at some stage or stages have been heavily revised. Williams has said that, because of advice from Elia Kazan, the director of the first Broadway production, he made changes in the third act. The changes include the appearance of one of the main characters, Big Daddy, who had been in the second act only, and adjustments changing the bare possibility of an affirmative ending to a probability. Revisions of considerably greater scope than this were made by Williams in other plays, including plays that were completely rewritten long after their original productions (*Summer and Smoke* into *The Eccentricities of a Nightingale*, and *Battle of Angels* into *Orpheus Descending*).

Cat on a Hot Tin Roof is famous for its somewhat expressionistic set, the bedroom of Brick and Margaret (Maggie) Pollitt. The two major pieces of furniture, both with symbolic value, are a large double bed and a combination radio-phonograph-television-liquor cabinet. The walls are to disappear into air at the top, and the set is to be roofed by the sky, as though to suggest that the action of the play is representative of universal human experience. The powerful expressionistic psychology of the play recalls the theater of August Strindberg, but *Cat on a Hot Tin Roof* is deeply embedded in revealed reality, with one major exception: One does not know the truth, one cannot know the truth, behind the crucial relationship between Brick and his dead friend Skipper; the degree (if any) of Brick's responsibility for Skipper's decline and death; or of Maggie's responsibility.

The bedroom, outside of which is a gallery running the length of the house, is in the plantation mansion of Brick's father, Big Daddy, on his twenty-eight thousand-acre estate in the Mississippi delta. The first act is largely a monologue by Maggie, talking to a mostly inattentive and uninterested Brick, and interrupted only by brief appearances of Brick's mother, Big Mama, and his sister-in-law Mae and two of her five, soon to be six, children. Maggie, like Amanda and Blanche before her, is a loquacious and desperate woman who may be fighting for the impossible; unlike her predecessors, she lives entirely in the present and without major illusions, and hence fights more realistically. She wants Brick to return to her bed: She is a cat on a hot tin roof, sexually desperate but interested only in her husband. As the largely one-sided conversation continues, one learns the circumstances underlying Brick's loss of interest in her. Maggie tells Brick the news that his father is dying of cancer. Brick and Maggie have been living in the house for several months. Formerly an important athlete, a professional football player, and then a sports announcer, he has given up everything and lapsed into heavy drinking. He is on a crutch, having broken his ankle attempting, while drunk the previous night, to jump hurdles on the high school athletic field. Mae and her husband, Brick's older brother Gooper, a lawyer in Memphis, are visiting in hope, as Maggie correctly guesses, of Big Daddy's signing a will in Gooper's favor, because, while Brick is Big Daddy's favorite, he will want the estate to go to a son who has offspring. Maggie is from a society background in Nashville, though her immediate family had been poor because of her father's alcoholism. Big Daddy himself is a Mississippi redneck who has worked his way to great wealth. Brick and Maggie met as students at the University of Mississippi. Formerly, according to Maggie, an excellent lover, Brick has made Maggie agree that they will stay together only if she leaves him alone. Unable to bear the frustration, Maggie is ready to break the agreement and fight to get Brick back.

The roots of Brick and Maggie's conflict are fitfully revealed when Maggie begins to speak of Skipper, their dead friend, any mention of whom greatly upsets Brick. In Maggie's version of the story, from college on, Brick's greatest loyalty was to Skipper. She says that Brick's standards of love and friendship were so pure as to have been frustrating to both Skipper and Maggie; that on an out-of-town football weekend when Brick had been injured and could not go, Maggie and Skipper, out of their common frustration, went to bed together; that Skipper could not perform, and that Maggie therefore, but in no condemnatory sense, assumed that he was unconsciously homosexual, though she believes that Brick is not. Maggie told Skipper that he was actually in love with her husband, and she now believes that it was this revelation that prompted Skipper to turn to liquor and drugs, leading to his death. Maggie now tells Brick that she has been examined by a gynecologist, that she is capable of bearing children, and that it is the right time of the month to conceive. Brick asks how it is going to happen when he finds her repellent. She says that that is a problem to be solved.

Act 2 is famous for consisting almost entirely of a remarkably effective and revealing dialogue between Brick and Big Daddy. The act opens, however, with the whole family there, as well as their minister, the Reverend Mr. Tooker. The minister is there ostensibly because of Big Daddy's birthday, and there is to be cake and champagne. From the family's point of view, he is also there because after the birthday party (which is as big a failure as Blanche's), they are going to tell Big Mama the truth about Big Daddy's cancer, and they want his help in the crisis. From his own point of view, he is there to hint at a contribution, either now or in Big Daddy's will or both, for ornamentation for his church. He is totally useless in the crisis and is therefore, in spite of Williams's deep affection for his own minister grandfather, typical of Williams's ministers.

The birthday party will take place in Brick and Maggie's bedroom because Brick is on a crutch: an ingenious pretext for limiting the play's action to a single setting. Big Daddy is one of Williams's most complex characters, and the contradictions in his nature are never fully examined, any more than they are with Blanche, because, as Williams says in a stage direction in act 2, any truly drawn characters will retain some mystery. Big Daddy is a loud, vulgar, apparently insensitive man who was originally a workman on the estate, then owned by a pair of homosexual men. He is now in a position of power and worth many millions. Desperately afraid to show any real feelings, he pretends to dislike his whole family, although in the case of Gooper and Mae and their children, the dislike is genuine and deep. One never learns his real attitude toward Maggie. Near the end of his talk with Brick, with great difficulty, Big Daddy expresses the love he has for him. His real attitude toward Big Mama remains uncertain. He has always teased her, made gross fun of her, and in his ostensibly frank conversation with Brick, he says that he has always disliked her, even in bed. He is clearly moved, however, when at the end of the family-scene part of the act, she, who is in her own way both as gross and as vulnerable as he, yells that she has always loved him. The conversation with Brick reveals his sensitivity in another direction: his distress over the intense poverty he has seen while traveling abroad and particularly an instance in Morocco when he saw a very small child being used as a procurer.

The motivation for the long father-and-son talk is that Big Daddy, hugely relieved at having been told, falsely, that he does not have cancer, wants to find out why Brick has given up working, given up Maggie (as everyone knows, because Gooper and Mae have listened in their bedroom next door), and turned to heavy drinking. Apparently, he has attempted frank talks with Brick in the past, with no success, even though each clearly loves and respects the other, and because of Brick's lack of interest and determined reticence, it would appear that that is how the conver-

sation is going now. Having just gone through a severe life crisis himself, however, Big Daddy is determined to help his son. He gets the beginning of an answer out of Brick by taking away his crutch so he cannot get at his liquor. Brick's answer is that he is disgusted with the world's "mendacity." Finding that answer insufficient, Big Daddy finally brings himself to make the climactic statement that the problem began when Skipper died; he adds that Gooper and Mae think the Brick-Skipper relationship was not "normal." Brick, at last unable to maintain his detachment, is furious.

In a stage direction, Williams says that Skipper died to disavow the idea that there was any sexual feeling in the friendship, but whether Skipper did have such feelings is necessarily left uncertain. Brick himself, in his outrage, makes painfully clear that the very idea of homosexuality disgusts him. The relationship, he believes, was simply an unusually profound friendship, though he is finally forced to grant the likelihood that, from Skipper's point of view, though emphatically not his own, sexual love existed. (Whether Brick is himself bisexual is left uncertain, but it is clear that he could not face this idea if it were true.) He grants that liquor has been his refuge from a fact that Big Daddy (who has no prejudice against homosexuals) makes him face: that Brick's unwillingness to believe in the possibility of a homosexual reaction in Skipper, and to help Skipper recognize and accept it, is the major cause of Skipper's death. In a statement strongly reminiscent of some situations in the plays of O'Neill, Brick says that there are only two ways out: liquor and death. Liquor is his way, death was Skipper's. Then, in a state of strong emotional upheaval, Brick makes his father face the truth as his father has made him face it: He is dying of cancer. There is justice in Brick's remark that friends—and he and his father are friends—tell each other the truth, because the truth needs to be faced. As the act ends, Big Daddy is screaming at the liars who had kept the truth from him.

In the original version, as act 3 opens, the family and the Reverend Mr. Tooker enter. Big Daddy, one must assume, has gone to his bedroom to face his situation alone. The purpose of the gathering is to have the doctor, who presently comes in with Maggie, tell Big Mama the truth. Brick is in and out during the scene, but—in spite of appeals from Maggie and from Big Mama—he remains wholly aloof and is still drinking. If the shock of his conversation with Big Daddy is going to have an effect, it has not yet done so. After much hesitation, the doctor tells Big Mama the truth, to which she reacts with the expected horror. He tells her that Big Daddy's pain will soon become so severe as to require morphine injections, and he leaves a package.

Big Mama wants comfort only from Brick, not from Gooper. The Reverend Mr. Tooker leaves promptly, and the doctor soon follows. Gooper tries to get Big Mama to agree to a plan he has drawn up to take over the estate as trustee. Big Mama will have it run by nobody but Brick, whom she calls her only son. She remarks what a comfort it would be to Big Daddy if Brick and Maggie had a child. Maggie announces that she is pregnant. Whether this lie is planned or spontaneous, one has no way of knowing, but Brick does not deny it. Gooper and Mae, whose behavior throughout the scene has been despicable, are shocked and incredulous. Big Mama has run out to tell Big Daddy the happy news. Gooper and Mae soon follow, but just before they go, a loud cry of agony fills the house: Big Daddy is feeling the pain the doctor has predicted. Maggie and Brick are left alone. Maggie thanks Brick for his silence. Brick feels the "click" that results from enough liquor and that gives him peace, and he goes out on the gallery, singing. Maggie has a sudden inspiration and takes all the liquor out of the room. When Brick comes in she tells him what she has done, says she is in control, and declares that she will not return the liquor until he has gone to bed with her. He grabs for his crutch, but she is quicker, and she throws the crutch off the gallery to the ground. Big Mama rushes in, almost hysterical, to get the package of morphine. Maggie reiterates that she is in charge and tells Brick she loves him. Brick, in the last speech of the play, says exactly what Big Daddy had said earlier when Big Mama said she loved him: "Wouldn't it be funny if that was true." Apparently, he has yielded. The curtain falls.

The ending is dramatically effective, but in a different way from Williams's earlier endings. *The Glass Menagerie*'s ending is final in one way, because it is all in the past, and *A Streetcar Named Desire*'s in another, because Blanche is escorted off, and Stanley and Stella are reconciled. In *Cat on a Hot Tin Roof*, one can only assume that Brick will "perform," that the result will be a pregnancy, and that the eventual effect of Maggie's use of force and of Big Daddy's shock tactics may be Brick's return to normality. Even in its original form, as here described, that is what the ending suggests, and Williams's instinct to leave an element of uncertainty seems correct.

THE NIGHT OF THE IGUANA

The Night of the Iguana was Williams's next (and last) unmistakably successful play, after a series of plays of varying degrees of stage success but with more or less serious flaws. Unlike all of his earlier plays except *Camino Real*, *The Night of the Iguana* is set outside the United States and does not in any significant sense concern Southerners. It also differs from almost all the plays after *The Glass Menagerie* in being free of serious violence. Besides *A Streetcar Named Desire*, with the suicide of Blanche's husband, Williams had used castration, murder by blowtorch, death by cannibalism, and other extreme acts of violence, prompting the accusation, at times with some justice, of sensationalism.

The Night of the Iguana takes place on the veranda of a third-rate, isolated hotel in Mexico, in a rain forest high above the Pacific. Like several other Williams plays, it grew out of what was originally a short story. Unlike any of the others, except possibly the expressionistic *Camino Real*, its ending is affirmative, suggesting hope not only for the three major characters but also for humanity in general. The central male character, a minister who has been locked out of his church because of fornication and what was regarded as an atheistic sermon, may be prepared in the end for a life of self-sacrifice—which may turn out to be richly fulfilling, because the woman to whom he may "sacrifice" himself is a woman who knows what genuine love means. The other woman, who is the central character, is Blanche's opposite: a

New Englander instead of a quintessential Southerner, she is in no sense handicapped by the past; she retains a sense of humor; she sees things clearly; and she accepts her situation. She is tied to an elderly relative in a wheelchair but she is not bitter about it; the relative is neither a frustration nor an embarrassment. Finally, she uses whatever weapons she must to keep her grandfather and herself able, if sometimes only barely, to survive. Without being an obviously fierce fighter like Amanda, Blanche, or Maggie, she has come to terms with her circumstances and has prevailed. She is the first and only Williams character to do so, a new conception in his gallery of characters.

At the opening of act 1, Lawrence Shannon, the former minister, arrives at the hotel with a busload of female teachers and students on a Mexican tour for which he is the guide. He is in one of his periodic emotional breakdowns and has chosen to bring his tour party to this hotel in violation of the itinerary in order to get emotional support from his friends, the couple who run the hotel. It turns out, however, that the husband has recently drowned. The wife, now the sole owner, the brassy Maxine Faulk, clearly wants Shannon as a lover and may well be genuinely in love with him. Throughout the tour, and indeed on some previous tours, Shannon has ignored the announced tour route and facilities, leading the group where he chooses. He has also, and not for the first time, allowed himself to be seduced by a seventeen-year-old girl. The women are in a state of rebellion. Their leader, another of Williams's homosexuals, though an unimportant one, knows of the sexual liaison and later in the play reports the whole story to the tour company for which Shannon works, with the result that in act 3, he is replaced on the spot with another guide. He has the key to the tour bus, however, and refuses to relinquish it, so the passengers (most of whom never come up to the hotel) are helpless.

Shannon's situation is in some ways similar to, although milder than, Blanche's: He was pushed out of the church as Blanche was dismissed as a teacher; he is seriously distraught, and confused in his sexual orientation, he is attracted to young girls, as Blanche was to boys. Presently, there is another arrival at the hotel, Hannah Jelkes and her ninety-seven-year-old grandfather, whom she calls Nonno. She has pushed him up the hill and through the forest in his wheelchair. They are without funds, and she is desperate for a place for them to stay. Maxine, for all her rough exterior, cannot turn them away in their plight, but she is upset over their literal pennilessness. She is also upset over Hannah's desire to earn money, as she has done all over the world, by passing through hotel dining rooms so that, on request, her grandfather may recite his poetry or she may make sketches of guests. The only other guests at the hotel, because it is the offseason, are a group of Nazis, whose presence in the play may seem puzzling, as they have nothing to do with the plot. They are in and out at various points, a raucous group, delighted with radio news of German successes in bombing Britain. Totally without feeling, they are probably in the play for contrast; their lack of feeling contrasts with Hannah's genuine sympathy for anything human except unkindness, with Nonno's sensitive artistry as a recognized minor poet, with Maxine's apparent ability to love, and with the growing evidence, as the play develops, of Shannon's potential for overcoming his self-centered and almost uncontrollable desperation.

The major focus in both act 2 and act 3 is on the dialogues between Hannah and Shannon, which, in revelation of character and effect on character, resemble the dialogue between Big Daddy and Brick. Indeed, act 2 and act 3 are so intertwined as to make it difficult to separate them. One learns about Hannah's past, about her having suffered from emotional problems similar to Shannon's, from which she recovered by sheer determination. In a sense, she has sacrificed her life to caring for her grandfather; she feels only pride and love for him, and concern over his age, his periods of senile haziness, and his inability to finish his first poem in twenty years. In a moment of symbolism, one sees that she is capable of lighting a candle in the wind. Seeking for God, she has so far found him only in human faces. In sharp contrast, Shannon's view of the world is summed up in a memory of having seen starving persons searching through piles of excrement for bits of undigested food. Hannah's insight into Shannon's problem is deep, and she is adept in techniques, from sympathy to shock, to help bring him out of his somewhat self-indulgent despair. At one point in act 2, the Mexican boys who work for Maxine bring in an iguana and tie it to a post, planning to fatten it and eat it: a normal occurrence in their world. It escapes once and is recaptured. Maxine threatens to evict Hannah and Nonno but relents when Hannah makes her understand that she is not a rival for Shannon. Nonno provides embarrassing evidence of his intermittent senility. The act ends in the early evening with a heavy thunderstorm.

Early in act 3, later in the evening, Shannon's replacement arrives, and the bus key is taken from him by force. Shannon, growing more and more hysterical, tries to pull the gold cross from his neck and threatens to go down to the ocean and swim straight out to sea until he drowns. Maxine and her Mexican boys tie him in the hammock. Maxine tells Hannah that Shannon's behavior is essentially histrionic, and Hannah soon sees for herself that he is deriving a masochistic pleasure from the situation. She tells him, in a key speech, that he is enjoying an ersatz crucifixion, thus denying Shannon the role of Christ-figure that Williams had tried unsuccessfully to give his central male characters in certain earlier plays. Hannah as model and as psychiatrist begins to have an effect. He releases himself from the ropes, as she has told him all along he is able to do, and their conversation reveals enough about Hannah's past to make him admire her stamina, her hard-won stability, and her love of humanity, and to make him want, perhaps, to emulate her. He learns of the minimal, pathetic encounters she has had with male sexuality—in one instance, a man with a fetish for women's undergarments—and while they in no way disgusted her, since nothing does except cruelty, she is nevertheless a permanent virgin who is comfortable with her virginity.

Shannon suggests that they should travel together, platonically. She rightly refuses, and puts in his mind the idea that Maxine needs him, as Nonno needs her, and that he needs to be needed in order to achieve stability. Hannah persuades Shannon to free the iguana, which is, as he has been, "at the end of its rope."

Nonno wheels himself out of his room, shouting that he has finished his poem. He reads it, and they find it moving. Maxine persuades Shannon to stay with her permanently, though Williams seems undecided as to whether one should regard Shannon's acquiescence as a sacrifice. In any case, however, it is evidence that he may no longer be sexually askew and that he may be capable of living a life that has some kind of meaning.

The change is quicker than the change that may occur in Brick in *Cat on a Hot Tin Roof*, though both plays take place in a few hours, and though Williams says in a stage direction in *Cat on a Hot Tin Roof* that even if events have occurred that will result in changing a person, the change will not occur quickly. Perhaps one may say that the difference is justified in that Big Daddy, for all his love and honesty, is no Hannah—there are very few Hannahs in the world. Hannah's own trials are not over: After Maxine and Shannon go off together, as Hannah prepares to take Nonno back to his room, he quietly dies. Hannah is left alone. No one needs her any more. The curtain falls.

The play is notable for its atmosphere, its memorable characters, its compassion, its hard-won optimism. The ending of *The Glass Menagerie* is devastating. The ending of *A Streetcar Named Desire* may represent the best solution for Blanche and happiness for Stanley and Stella, but there is nevertheless a sense in which all three are victims. In *Cat on a Hot Tin Roof*, it is possible that the future will bring happiness to Brick and Maggie, but it is far from certain; the future means a horrible death from cancer for Big Daddy, a life deprived of much of its meaning for Big Mama, and wholly meaningless and despicable lives for Gooper and Mae. The contrast with *The Night of the Iguana* is enormous. With his poem, Nonno has at last, like his granddaughter, "prevailed," and one must assume that he is ready for death, a death that, in contrast to Big Daddy's, is swift and peaceful. Maxine is no longer alone and has someone to love. Shannon seems on the road to psychological recovery and a useful and satisfying life. Hannah, to be sure, is left alone, as Tom and Blanche are alone in their worlds, but the contrast between her and those others is sharp and unmistakable. She has faced previous crises, survived, prevailed. Happy endings in modern drama are rarely successful at a serious level. In *The Night of the Iguana*, Williams wrote that rare modern dramatic work: a memorable, affirmative play in which the affirmation applies to all the major characters and in which the affirmation is believable.

OTHER MAJOR WORKS

LONG FICTION: *The Roman Spring of Mrs. Stone*, 1950; *Moise and the World of Reason*, 1975.

SHORT FICTION: *One Arm and Other Stories*, 1948; *Hard Candy: A Book of Stories*, 1954; *The Knightly Quest: A Novella and Four Short Stories*, 1967; *Eight Mortal Ladies Possessed: A Book of Stories*, 1974; *Collected Stories*, 1985.

POETRY: *In the Winter of Cities*, 1956; *Androgyne, Mon Amour*, 1977; *The Collected Poems of Tennessee Williams*, 2002.

SCREENPLAYS: *The Glass Menagerie*, 1950 (with Peter Berneis); *A Streetcar Named Desire*, 1951 (with Oscar Saul); *The Rose Tattoo*, 1955 (with Hal Kanter); *Baby Doll*, 1956; *The Fugitive Kind*, 1960 (with Meade Roberts; based on *Orpheus Descending*); *Suddenly Last Summer*, 1960 (with Gore Vidal); *Stopped Rocking and Other Screenplays*, 1984.

NONFICTION: *Memoirs*, 1975; *Where I Live: Selected Essays*, 1978; *Five O'Clock Angel: Letters of Tennessee Williams to Maria St. Just, 1948-1982*, 1990; *The Selected Letters of Tennessee Williams*, 2000.

BIBLIOGRAPHY

Bloom, Harold, ed. *Tennessee Williams*. Modern Critical Views series. New York: Chelsea House, 1987. This collection of critical essays carries an introduction by Bloom that places Williams in the dramatic canon of American drama and within the psychological company of Hart Crane and Arthur Rimbaud. Authors in this collection take traditional thematic and historical approaches, noting Williams's "grotesques," his morality, his irony, his work in the "middle years," and the mythical qualities in his situations and characters.

Kolin, Philip, ed. *Tennessee Williams: A Guide to Research and Performance*. Westport: Greenwood Press, 1998. A helpful collection of twenty-three essays devoted to individual plays except the last three, which are devoted to Williams's fiction, poetry, and films respectively. Contains three indices that allow the reader easily to locate specific information.

Lyle, Leverich. *Tom: The Unknown Tennessee Williams*. New York: Crown Publishers, 1995. This is a sympathetic and meticulous study of Williams's life and work concluding with the theatrical triumph of *The Glass Menagerie* in 1945. Divided into five parts, this massive work contains a detailed genealogy of Tennessee Williams; numerous photographs of Williams, his ancestors and friends; and a useful index. Although Leverich felt that writing a biography of someone as sensitive and prickly as Williams was akin to "performing an autopsy on a living person," he admirably fulfills Williams's request to "report, in truth, his cause aright" even as he presents divergent views of this complex man. Of particular interest are the opening pages on the writer's death by strangulation in New York's Hotel Elysee and his convoluted relations with his parents and sister, Rose.

Rader, Dotson. *Tennessee: Cry of the Heart*. Garden City, N.Y.: Doubleday, 1985. The title and opening, explaining the author's first encounter with a "flipped out" Williams, give a flavor to this chatty biography. Although it does not have the virtue of notes or a scholarly biography, it does have the appeal of a firsthand account, filled with gossip and inside information, to be taken for what it is worth.

Rondane, Matthew C., ed. *The Cambridge Companion to Tennessee Williams*. Cambridge, England: Cambridge University Press, 1997. A collection of fourteen essays using a variety of critical approaches with an introduction by the editor summarizing each. Particularly useful are Jaqueline O'Connor's survey of Williams scholarship, "Words on Williams: A Bibliographic Essay," and R. Barton Palmer's "Hollywood in Crisis: Tennessee Williams and the Evolution of the Adult

Film." Contains a chronology from Williams's birth in 1911 to 1996, seven photographs of major actors in scenes from stage productions of the plays and a selected bibliography.

Spoto, Donald. *The Kindness of Strangers: The Life of Tennessee Williams.* Boston: Little, Brown, 1985. Spoto's literary biography begins with a description of Williams's parents, Cornelius and Edwina. Beginning with early separation, the Williams couple gave their children a stormy beginning in life. Spoto's lively chronicle details in ten chapters Williams's encounters with such diverse influences as the Group Theatre, Frieda and D. H. Lawrence, Senator Joseph R. McCarthy, Fidel Castro, Hollywood stars, and the homosexual and drug subcultures of Key West. Forty-two pages of notes, bibliography, and index.

Williams, Dakin, and Shepherd Mead. *Tennessee Williams: An Intimate Biography.* New York: Arbor House, 1983. One of the more bizarre duos in biographical writing, Williams (Tennessee's brother) and Mead (Tennessee's childhood friend) produce a credible biography in a highly readable, well-indexed work. Their account of the playwright also helps to capture his almost schizophrenic nature. A solid index and extensive research assist the serious scholar and general reader.

Windham, Donald. *As if. . .* Verona, Italy, 1985. This reminiscence of Williams's one-time friend portrays the writer as a man of bizarre contradictions and reveals in telling vignettes the downward spiral of his self-destructive lifestyle.

Jacob H. Adler, updated by Rebecca Bell-Metereau
and Robert Blake

DAVID WILLIAMSON

Born: Melbourne, Australia; February 24, 1942

PRINCIPAL DRAMA
The Coming of Stork, pr. 1970, pb. 1974
The Removalists, pr. 1971, pb. 1972
Don's Party, pr. 1971, pb. 1973
Jugglers Three, pr. 1972, pb. 1974
What If You Died Tomorrow, pr. 1973, pb. 1974
The Department, pr. 1974, pb. 1975
A Handful of Friends, pr., pb. 1976
The Club, pr. 1977, pb. 1978 (U.S. title, *Players*)
Travelling North, pr. 1979, pb. 1980
Celluloid Heroes, pr. 1980
The Perfectionist, pr. 1982, pb. 1983
Sons of Cain, pr., pb. 1985
Emerald City, pr., pb. 1987
Top Silk, pr., pb. 1989
Siren, pr. 1990, pb. 1991
Money and Friends, pr., pb. 1992
Brilliant Lies, pr., pb. 1993
Sanctuary, pr., pb. 1994

Dead White Males, pr., pb. 1995
Heretic, pr., pb. 1996
After the Ball, pr., pb. 1997
Third World Blues, pr., pb. 1997 (revision of *Jugglers Three*)
Corporate Vibes, pr., pb. 1999
Face to Face, pr., pb. 1999
The Great Man, pr., pb. 2000
Up for Grabs, pr., pb. 2000
Soulmates, pr. 2002

OTHER LITERARY FORMS

David Williamson has written numerous screenplays for Australian and American films. Some he has adapted from his own work: *Stork* (1971), *The Removalists* (1974), *Don's Party* (1976), *The Club* (1980), *Travelling North* (1986), *Emerald City* (1988), *Sanctuary* (1995), and *Brilliant Lies* (1997). Others are original: *Petersen* (1974), *Eliza Frazer* (1976), *Partners* (1981), and *Pharlap* (1984). Two screenplays known internationally are *Gallipoli*

(1981) and *The Year of Living Dangerously* (1982). He has also written the screenplays for *A Dangerous Life* (1988), the television miniseries *The Four-Minute Mile* (1988), and (with Kristin Williamson) other Australian-produced television programs including *The Last Bastion* (1984), *Princess Kate* (1988), and *Dogs Head Bay* (1999).

ACHIEVEMENTS

Early in his career, David Williamson gained recognition of the kind often considered most important to an Australian artist: the British George Devine Award in 1972 for his second play, *The Removalists*, while it was still onstage in Sydney. In 1973, the London *Evening Standard* conferred on him the Most Promising Playwright Award for the London production of *The Removalists*.

At home, Williamson received in 1972 his first two "Awgies" (Australian Writers Guild Award) for *The Removalists*; in the next few years, he took additional Awgies for *Don's Party, The Club*, and *Travelling North*, as well as the Eric Award from Melbourne Critics for *Jugglers Three* in 1974. In subsequent years he has picked up six more Awgies. Williamson has won the Australian Film Institute Script Award three times, for *Petersen, Don's Party*, and *Gallipoli*. He has also been active in various Australian arts organizations, including the Australian Writers Guild, the Australia Council, and the Theatre Board of the Council. In 1983 he was honored by the government with the Order of Australia, and in 1988, he received an honorary doctorate from the University of Sydney and another in 1990 from Monash University. The Australian National Trust in 1998 named him as one of the country's "100 Living National Treasures." Williamson's plays, especially, have gained acceptance abroad, even though each one stands firmly rooted in the Australian experience. Possibly, then, his greatest achievement lies in the talent to make universal that experience peculiar to Australians.

BIOGRAPHY

On the surface, David Keith Williamson's family background and early life hold little to suggest that he would someday help to revolutionize the Australian theater and in so doing emerge as one of Australia's major playwrights. Born in Melbourne in 1942, during the dark days of wartime Australia, this son of a bank official was reared and received his education for the most part in the small town of Bairnsdale, northeast of Melbourne. He was graduated from Monash University in 1964 with an engineering degree, then took postgraduate work in psychology at the University of Melbourne. From 1966 until 1972, he lectured on thermodynamics and social psychology at Swinburne College of Technology. He married Carol Cranby in 1965, but seven years later he ended both his marriage and his teaching career, determined to fulfill his promise as a writer. In 1974, he remarried, this time to a journalist, Kristin Green; they moved to Birchgrove, an inner Harborside suburb of Sydney. As the twenty-first century began, they made their residence in Queensland, the tropical state north of New South Wales.

Although concentrating on engineering and psychology, Williamson showed interest in the theater during his university years, writing for campus production several satiric reviews and a short play. His first full-length work, *The Coming of Stork*, was produced in 1970 for "a short weekend season" by the Café La Mama Theatre in Melbourne. After this modest start, Williamson established himself the following year as a fresh and original voice in Australian theater when two more of his plays had successful seasons in Melbourne and Sydney. Both written in 1971, these two plays, *The Removalists* and *Don's Party*, moved in 1973 to London and New York, where they received attention rarely accorded Australian theatrical offerings, at least not since the 1950's, when Ray Lawler's steamy drama *Summer of the Seventeenth Doll* (pr. 1955, pb. 1957; commonly known as *The Doll*) was produced; Lawler's account of Australian canecutters and barmaids in a Melbourne slum bore little resemblance, however, to the sophisticated and infinitely more universal plays Williamson sent abroad.

At home, Williamson continued to produce new work. That he was commissioned in 1973 to write a play to open the Drama Theatre of the new Sydney

Opera House shows how far he had come in three years, from out-of-the-way coffeehouse and storefront theaters such as Café La Mama and The Pram Factory to the establishment's center of culture.

Not to be outdone, the officials of the South Australian Theatre Company in Adelaide commissioned a Williamson work to open the Playhouse at the new Adelaide Festival Centre in 1974; Williamson wrote *The Department* for that occasion. Two years later, the Playhouse introduced another of Williamson's plays, *A Handful of Friends*.

In 1978, Williamson's play *The Club* was produced at the Kennedy Center in Washington, D.C., followed by a Broadway production (both productions were under the title *Players*). In 1980, *Travelling North* was produced in London. Although both plays had premiered earlier in Australia, their quick transport to England and the United States holds significance, for Australian artists are too often not taken seriously by many of their compatriots until they prove themselves abroad. Williamson had fulfilled that requirement, so those Australian critics still dubious about a writer whom some had called a "flash in the pan" were forced to accept their new playwright, one whose work had shaken the staid foundations of Australian theater much as Patrick White had, a few years earlier, altered the course of the Australian novel.

Even if Williamson had not established himself abroad as a playwright, he would have done so eventually as a screenwriter. In 1971, he adapted his first play, *The Coming of Stork*, into the film *Stork*, which was followed by several other adaptations and original screenplays. Not until 1981, though, did his screenwriting receive much attention outside Australia; the worldwide popularity of *Gallipoli* and *The Year of Living Dangerously* brought his work to millions, even though they may not have realized that the screenwriter was one of Australia's foremost playwrights. *Gallipoli* was based on various accounts of the Australian army landing on Gallipoli during World War I, an event that holds prominence in Australian history, while *The Year of Living Dangerously* was adapted from Australian novelist C. J. Koch's account of revolution in Indonesia. Intrigued by the events that led to the overthrow of the Ferdinand Marcos regime in the Philippines, Williamson wrote the screenplay for the Home Box Office (HBO) production about the revolution, *A Dangerous Life*. It showed in Australia, the United Kingdom, and the United States, and it was voted by American newspapers as one of the ten best television productions of 1988.

Williamson has said that writing for the film and television industries is not an especially "literary" activity, given the interference and whims of producers, directors, and financial backers. He has explained that he turned to these mediums because they provide opportunities, not possible on the stage, to address "epic" themes derived from historical and political events. He became involved in canceled projects considered too politically sensitive for general production, even though they were both based on true stories: one, the story of an American prisoner of war who was brainwashed by the Koreans, then accused by the McCarthy committee of collaborating with the Chinese; the other, an account of white South Africans who became victims of apartheid laws.

In the fall of 1984, Williamson's first major television effort, a miniseries titled *The Last Bastion*, aired in Australia. The highly praised series, on which Williamson and his wife had worked for two years, chronicles the American presence in Australia during World War II. Other television projects include *Princess Kate*, a children's drama, and *The Four-Minute Mile*, which retells John Landy's triumph in breaking the record for running the mile.

Unlike many Australian artists in the past, Williamson has not left his native land for the supposedly superior artistic environment he might find in Europe or the United States. Despite extensive travels and a growing international reputation, he continued to consider Australia his home. The screenplays may move into areas outside his native land, but the plays remain fixed in Australia. When a new production opens, which happens every two years or so, it always succeeds at the box office all across Australia, followed by productions abroad. Williamson once told an interviewer that he had ideas for at least ten new plays. He is not likely to quit writing drama that both entertains and challenges its audiences.

ANALYSIS

The early honors marking the achievements of so young a playwright must have been gratifying and encouraging to David Williamson as he battled against the established Australian theater. He comments on that battle's victorious outcome in an article that appeared in *Meanjin* (1974), a journal that has long challenged Australia's traditional approach to art. Although titled "*The Removalists:* A Conjunction of Limitations," the article includes, in addition to commentary on the play, some frank observations regarding the state of Australian theater when Williamson and his contemporaries decided that the country needed and deserved its own dramatic literature.

Theater in Australia, Williamson noted, has always flourished but only as an import business that considered its sole purpose the presentation of what was good from Europe and that would therefore educate and uplift "the barbarous beer-swilling populace" of Australia by showing them Europe's "more refined and sensitive values." Until the early 1970's, Williamson pointed out, plays by Australians about Australians held low priority, relegated as they were to coffeehouse theaters and small audiences. Such had been the fate of his first works.

By 1974, however, attitudes had changed so wholly that he could write: "As far as drama is concerned, the battle has been won." General audiences and the administrators of the large state-subsidized theaters had recognized at last the need to explore Australia on the stage and to support those dramatic explorations. Not many years earlier, when plays like Williamson's *The Coming of Stork* were enjoying "short weekend seasons" in small theaters before meager audiences, such a reassuring outcome to such a long-standing conflict must have seemed unlikely. The work of Williamson and other playwrights who came into their own during the late 1960's and early 1970's now holds a secure place in Australian theatrical repertory. That their work has been made available in reader's editions also shows that the literary value of these dramas is appreciated and recognized.

The plays of Williamson are distinguished by their naturalism, which they attain through disciplined structure, exact sense of place, honest and sympathetic treatment of characters, vivid language, and comedy. In each play, these elements combine to reveal believable characters caught up in familiar human conflicts. Yet the dramas consistently reach beyond the limitations of specific incidents, time, and place; in this reaching, however, they sidestep moralizing or didacticism, relying instead for their meaning on the mundane actions and often muddled responses of ordinary people.

In stage directions, Williamson stresses that the plays are "naturalistic" and should be produced accordingly. What he means by naturalistic critics have debated, but notes from directors who have worked with Williamson reveal that naturalistic to the playwright means exactly what it says: The plays should be performed in a natural manner. The scripts, even when read, do display a remarkable degree of naturalness, an outcome dependent in part on their disciplined structure.

Until *Travelling North* and *The Perfectionist*, Williamson followed the dictates of the well-made play, which makes his work more like George Bernard Shaw's, Henrik Ibsen's, or Anton Chekhov's than like that of many contemporary playwrights, who rely on fragmentary scenes, unpredictable shifts of time and place, role doubling, and so on. Williamson constructed these two plays with a series of short scenes set in varied places, but he did not permit this departure from his usual method to shatter the sense of reality for which he strives. Whether the action takes a few minutes or an hour, he maintains the tension and conflict essential to his kind of drama. Believable characters come into conventional rooms, carry out everyday activities—eating, drinking, smoking, fighting, and entering into conversations that may lead nowhere, that may be interrupted, or that may erupt in anger—and then leave the stage to continue their lives elsewhere. Rarely does a resolution take place.

Williamson has accepted the maxim that writers should write about what they know. He knows urban Australia, especially the two major cities, Melbourne and Sydney; he knows Australians, too, particularly the middle-class, educated, city-dwelling ones; and he understands and sympathizes with their ambitions, frustrations, and quirks. He has put this thorough knowledge and understanding to good use in each of his plays.

Whether the action of a Williamson play takes place in a suburban living room or in a cluttered engineering laboratory at a technical college, the setting for that action is exact, made so by street names, references to climate, distance, city districts, commercial names, and so on. Many people outside Australia know only of the country's Outback—those vast stretches of land sparsely inhabited by sheep, kangaroos, weathered bushmen, and Aborigines; few realize that 70 percent of Australians live in its five large cities. In part, this misconception stems from the tendency of Australian dramatists and fiction writers, until the 1970's or so, to set their works in the Outback, thereby giving the impression that Australia lacked an urban life. Williamson has helped to dispel that myth.

Australians have often been depicted by both their own writers and those abroad as bumptious colonials bragging and swaggering to hide their innate sense of insecurity. Williamson avoids such parody and stereotypical portrayals. Granted, his characters often swear and drink excessively, display crassness and greed, treat women as chattel, praise and indulge in violence, mouth racist slogans, and display all the other attitudes purported to be the mark of an Australian. Those characters caught up in the conflict of a Williamson play, however, never suffer unabated ridicule, for Williamson shows sympathy toward them in spite of the disagreeable habits and attitudes he takes such pains to reveal. He makes it evident, first, that such qualities are not peculiar to Australia alone but typical of many Western nations. Second, he lends characters more than one dimension, so that they emerge as troubled and pained humans striving to grasp their predicament, a predicament shared by all men and women at some time or another.

The plays' language, like their structure, settings, and characters, never veers from the naturalistic tone Williamson demands of his art. The dialogue abounds in Australianisms, such as "poofter" for homosexual, "daks" for trousers, "uni" for university, and so on. An uninformed playgoer or reader might at first long for a glossary, but these words meld so perfectly into the dialogue that their meaning becomes evident in context. The words add color and capture the unique rhythm of Australian speech, which Williamson reproduces so splendidly.

Profanity, too, is excessive, almost at times to the point of annoyance, which may well be the purpose of all the "bloodies" and four-letter words. In *The Coming of Stork*, the play's namesake is notably foulmouthed, and after he suggests that one of his friends "piss off," that character analyzes the command: "There you are," he says. "Piss, a simple colloquial word meaning 'to urinate' and off, another simple word suggesting movement, but put them together and there's a rather telling forcefulness about the phrase." When in anger Stork shouts the words again, his friend replies: "Yes that's, er, very good Stork, but if you say it too often it does tend to lose its impact."

Australian critic Roslyn Arnold sees this profane and abusive language as more than superficial; in her 1975 article "Aggressive Vernacular: Williamson, Buzo and the Australian Tradition," she observes that the language "strikes down into the preoccupations and motivations of the characters, sheds light on social rituals, and raises questions about contemporary Australian life and the traditions informing it." At the conclusion of her discussion, however, Arnold finds it a "pity" that the new playwrights do not "extend that language to explore the possible depths" of relationships rather than their "width." Williamson seems to have done exactly that, for his later plays depend less on the "aggressive vernacular" and more on language that leads its speakers to probe the mysteries of the human involvements with which they wrestle.

Although comedy may not seem appropriate for naturalistic theater, it remains a staple in Williamson's plays, to the extent that critics have accused him of relying on cheap gags, one-liners, and farcical situations. Disputing this charge, Williamson has said again and again that his work may be humorous but should neither be played for laughs nor taken as purely comic. The disparity between Williamson's subject matter and his comic treatment of it is best illustrated by the comments of a reviewer for the *International Herald Tribune*. He describes *The Removalists* as "a brutal play and also a hilarious one, an extraordinarily funny treatment of violence"; he then admits that "a comedy in which a man is beaten to a bloody and lifeless pulp" might seem "unlikely or contradictory," but the reviewer concludes that the play is neither. Williamson is certainly not the first writer to discover comedy as a weapon with which to bludgeon the unfunny people around him, but he has used the weapon with originality, proving once more that a playwright can be serious while being funny.

Williamson's work has shown steady progress over the years. He has continued to refine the striking qualities that set apart even the defective first play, *The Coming of Stork*. To an extent, all of Williamson's work for the stage has focused on a single theme: the perfection of relationships, a goal that forever eludes the characters. The plays are always open-ended, the suggestion left that the characters will continue their search and in so doing meet disappointments, make blunders, face defeat and humiliation, and, on occasion, succeed: In other words, they will continue to live out their lives. This view Williamson has explored in a variety of ways, so that the plays, although each an entity, may be placed in three groups: those about family and marriage, those about social relationships outside the family, and those about interactions in the larger world.

PLAYS ABOUT FAMILY AND MARRIAGE

Jugglers Three, *What If You Died Tomorrow*, *Travelling North*, *The Perfectionist*, *After the Ball*, and *Top Silk* take up the problems and the conflicts stemming from what Williamson perceives as the tyranny of family relationships and the fragility of marriage.

Set during the Vietnam War, *Jugglers Three* shows in part the adverse role that the war played in the lives of young Australians, but the work concerns itself more with marriage. A veteran returns to his home in Melbourne to discover that his wife has a lover, who

is also married. This well-worn plot moves along at rapid pace and provides for a series of both comic and sad scenes from which social commentary and an examination of marriage emerge. As the play closes, the lover departs, and the veteran and his wife engage in a ferocious game of table tennis, which turns into an allegory of marriage. Whether they will reunite remains indefinite—and unimportant. In 1997 Williamson revised *Jugglers Three*, which was staged under the title *Third World Blues*.

What If You Died Tomorrow dramatizes the havoc that fame can exert on both marriage and family relationships. Again set in Melbourne and focusing on a broken marriage and lovers, this play comes closest to farce of any of Williamson's work. A recently successful novelist, who has left his wife and children in order to live with a journalist, meets in the course of an evening an unlikely array of characters, including some literary types, his middle-class Australian parents just back from the requisite European tour, and a German afloat in Australia. By bedtime, not much has been settled, but much has been said about the artist and about the ordinary human struggle.

In *Travelling North*, the parent-child relationship comes into play when two older Australians engage in a twilight love affair, leaving their grown children, all unhappily married and generally alienated, to fend for themselves. Williamson reveals here a striking sensitivity toward the aging process with its accompanying physical deterioration, disappointment over failure, and crankiness. The title comes from the direction toward which the two aging lovers head: the Australian North, which is the equivalent of Florida.

The Perfectionist offers a microscopic examination of marriage and family and their consequent entanglements. Denmark is the setting for the first part of the play, which consists throughout of scenes that revive fragments of memory introduced by various characters. An Australian professor, serving as a visiting lecturer in a Danish university, and his wife engage in a quest to learn not only what marriage means but also what their independent lives mean. Once they have returned to Australia, the layers of protective illusions, jarred by their time abroad, begin to fall away, and they both face their denuded selves: the husband, whose striving for perfection has led him into pomposity, sycophancy, and isolation, and the wife, whose struggle against her helpmate role has led her into bitterness, an unsuccessful love affair, and dilettantism. They eventually separate, and at the play's closing, the possibility of their reunion remains indefinite. Yet the action has reached a more forceful kind of completion, for the major characters have discarded many of their illusions and admitted the need to reconstruct their lives. Whether that reconstruction will be accomplished remains as conjectural as their reunion.

After the Ball examines the relationship between a brother and sister who reunite at their mother's deathbed, only to dredge up painful family memories. One has lived overseas for years in a sophisticated milieu, the other has remained in suburban Australia, so their values and lifestyles have diverged sharply. Through their memories of family conflicts and the marital warfare they experienced as children, Williamson analyzes Australian suburban life during the social upheaval that marked the period from the 1960's to the 1990's. Many critics consider *After the Ball*, first produced in 1997, one of Williamson's best plays.

Top Silk focuses on a family as well, this one consisting of a husband and wife who are well-established lawyers with a son who is a potential dropout. Not an altogether successful play, *Top Silk* follows both the conflicts within the home and the parallel ones outside, as the lawyers engage in politics, bribery, and other chicanery, while trying to figure out what to do about their marriage and son.

PLAYS ABOUT SOCIAL RELATIONSHIPS

The Coming of Stork and *Don's Party* suggest that social relationships outside the family are equal in their complexity and delicacy to those within the family. *The Coming of Stork* carries all the excesses characteristic of plays of the 1960's and early 1970's; there is too much drinking, sex, and obscenity. Nevertheless, once the excesses are sifted out, what remains is a vivid series of vignettes depicting a group of educated, urban, young men and women seeking to establish themselves, not only in their professions

but also in the larger task of being part of a social structure.

Don's Party bears a similarity to *The Coming of Stork*, but it handles the theme far more confidently and skillfully. Set during an Australian election night, with actual television coverage reproduced, the play at first appears to be about the election, but as the action unfolds, Australian politics recede and the ugly traits of Don's guests take the foreground—their fears, sexual repression, ambition, pettiness, selfishness, pretense, and lechery. The only definite resolution in the plot is the election results. Although unsatisfactory to most of Don's guests, the results produce little disappointment, so fully immersed are the revelers in their own problems. They leave the party unchanged—drunk, tired, frustrated by interrupted sexual liaisons—to resume their careers. Each may have approached some kind of epiphany but failed to recognize the moment.

Again depending on a party for its structure, *Money and Friends* depicts nine professionals sharing a weekend at the beach. One man is in dire financial trouble, but his friends find good reasons for not helping, even as they profess their devotion to him. Although the threat of financial ruin evaporates, the friends expose their weaknesses through the way they react to the request for assistance. A comedy of contemporary manners, the play ends as Williamson's plays always do: The personal engagements have not visibly altered the participants, and they revert to their muddled lives.

PLAYS ABOUT THE WORLD AT LARGE

The theme of the individual interacting in the larger world provides the basis for *The Department*, *The Club*, *A Handful of Friends*, *Celluloid Heroes*, and *The Removalists*. The first two plays, one about a departmental meeting in a technical college, the other about behind-the-game politics in a Melbourne football club, spin out a web of forces that place all men and women on a common plane—that is, the forces of bureaucracy, compromise, and personal ambition. To escape may or may not be possible; the plays offer no solutions, only the dilemma. In *A Handful of Friends*, a film director, a journalist, an actress, a professor—all successful—meet and talk, and in so doing prove that outward attainment in the larger world does not assure personal security. *Celluloid Heroes* focuses on the Australian film industry.

Among this group of plays, *The Removalists* stands out. The principal action of the play is simple enough: A man is slowly and methodically beaten to death. The plot is set in motion when two sisters ask for police protection from the husband of one of the sisters, claiming that he is violent. A corrupt police veteran and an idealistic new officer offer to assist when the removalists (furniture movers) come to the couple's apartment. In an absurd, cruel, yet casual and hilarious way, the two sisters, the police officers, the husband, and a removalist complete the action, which, for no particular reason, seems inevitable. The police officers beat the husband while the mover takes out furniture, the sisters argue, and the older police officer intermittently attempts seduction. Once the others have left the apartment and the husband has died, the two officers engage in an orgy of violence, and the play ends.

Because of Australia's historical record of violence, a nation founded as a convict colony, critics there have tended to view the play as an expression of the country's lingering attraction to and acceptance of violent action. The play, however, has spoken in other historical contexts as well; it met with success in Poland when performed as a protest against oppressive rule before the fall of communism.

Sons of Cain, constructed in forty or so scenes, blends comedy, moralism, and documentary realism to condemn corruption in high places and the media's inability—or refusal—to expose it. More direct in its condemnation of corruption than *The Removalists*, which relies heavily on metaphor, this play offers no solutions, only the hope that the righteous few will continue to battle the entrenched power. *Siren* also ostensibly focuses on public corruption as it follows a task force's attempt to compromise a bribe-taking mayor. The siren is the woman whom the force has hired to entrap the mayor in a motel. While waiting for their victim's arrival, the siren and her employers engage in exchanges that lead to personal revelations unrelated to their original quest. As the play ends, the characters know more about themselves, but it is not clear whether that newfound knowledge will change them.

Sydney serves as the setting and inspiration for *Emerald City*, a place that will do its best to seduce the artist into greed—in this case, a naïve scriptwriter. The sometimes comic play about personal corruption leads its protagonist through a series of moral dilemmas as he tries but fails to become rich and powerful. He concludes finally that he has succeeded in preserving at least a shred of moral integrity—and that is about all the artist or anyone can hope for in such a society.

PLAYS ABOUT ACADEMIC LIFE

Both *Heretic* and *Dead White Males* depart from Williamson's typical focus on family conflicts and social relationships. Like *The Department*, written twenty years earlier, these two plays examine aspects of academic life. *Dead White Males* satirizes the upsurge of cultural studies in universities and the critical establishment's commitment to poststructural literary theory and political correctness. More than a mockery of intellectual pretensions, however, the play offers a biting critique of attitudes in Australian society toward the feminist movement, multiculturalism, and other contemporary orthodoxies. *Heretic* tells the story of the New Zealand professor Derik Freeman, who dared to undermine the highly regarded American anthropolgist Margaret Mead. In his books, he disputed and contradicted her celebrated studies of sexual mores in Samoa, thereby earning the title "Heretic." Through this exploration of an academic controversy, Williamson manages to blend in a commentary on the sexual revolution of the 1960's.

SANCTUARY

Sanctuary marks another departure for Williamson, who in this two-character play examines the power of the international media to influence and manipulate the way people think. The drama pits the two principals against each other to develop the theme. Robert "Bob" King, an Australian and a highly successful anchorman in the United States, returns to his native land to live in a luxurious sanctuary. For his amusement, he allows a sanctimonious and moralistic young student to question him about how he sold out to his media overlords. What starts out as a game turns into a dramatic confrontation that lambasts the current state of the media and reveals truths to and about the pair of intellectual combatants.

PLAYS ABOUT CURRENT EVENTS

In the 1990's several of Williamson's plays ventured into the world at large to investigate what might be called current events. *Face to Face* looks at a recent development in Australian justice called "community conferencing." This system brings the perpetrator and the victim face to face to work out their differences in an atmosphere that is less restricted and threatening than a traditional courtroom. Williamson stages such a conference between a fired employee and his former boss whose Mercedes he has damaged. *Brilliant Lies* focuses on sexual harassment and the difficulties involved in proving or disproving such charges. *The Great Man* recounts the history of a mythical politician, who has betrayed his principles to get ahead. For Australians, the play would immediately bring to mind their own political developments over the past fifty years. Yet such politicians are no rarity in any nation.

In *Corporate Vibes*, as its title suggests, Williamson moves into the modern business world and shows how management theory and day-to-day practices often contradict one another. The play's conflict arises from the way traditional, autocratic management and modern idealistic methods interact. Williamson offers no solution for the conduct of business, in this case real estate, but instead provides an incisive look at both sides of the question. *Up for Grabs* delves into another kind of business, that of dealing in artwork. The background for this play is the booming international art business, which has experienced its share of scandals over the years. The play follows a fledgling art dealer who is willing to forsake ethics to establish herself at "the big end of town" by negotiating a two-million-dollar sale of a painting by a famous Australian artist.

OTHER MAJOR WORKS

SCREENPLAYS: *Stork*, 1971 (adaptation of *The Coming of Stork*); *Petersen*, 1974; *The Removalists*, 1974 (adaptation of his play); *Don's Party*, 1976 (ad-

aptation of his play); *Eliza Frazer*, 1976; *The Club*, 1980 (adaptation of his play); *Gallipoli*, 1981; *Partners*, 1981; *The Year of Living Dangerously*, 1982; *Pharlap*, 1984; *Travelling North*, 1986 (adaptation of his play); *A Dangerous Life*, 1988; *Emerald City*, 1988 (adaptation of his play); *Sanctuary*, 1995 (adaptation of his play); *Brilliant Lies*, 1997 (adaptation of his play).

TELEPLAYS: *The Department*, 1980; *The Last Bastion*, 1984 (miniseries); *The Club*, 1986; *The Four-Minute Mile*, 1988 (miniseries); *Princess Kate*, 1988 (miniseries); *The Perfectionist*, 1995; *Dogs Head Bay*, 1999.

NONFICTION: "*The Removalists*: A Conjunction of Limitations," 1974 (in *Meanjin*); "The Australian Image," 1981 (in *Counterpoint*); "Men, Women, and Human Nature," 1996 (in *Double Take: Six Incorrect Essays*).

BIBLIOGRAPHY

Carroll, Dennis. "David Williamson." In *Australian Contemporary Drama, 1909-1982*. New York: Peter Lang, 1985. Focuses on Williamson's depiction of the "ocker"—the stereotypical Australian male proud to be a colonial bumpkin, loud, rude, uncouth, uncultured, and generally obnoxious. A limited discussion. Although many of the plays before the 1980's portray the "ocker," later ones have moved in other directions.

Fitzpatrick, Peter. "Styles of Love: New Directions in David Williamson." In *Contemporary Australian Drama*. Sydney: Currency Press, 1987. As well as discussing Williamson's early plays, the article also explores the playwright's reputation and the criticism that his work is repetitious and slick, charges made against him all through his career.

_____, ed. *Williamson*. North Ryde, Australia: Methuen Australia, 1987. Describes Williamson as a "storyteller to the tribe" and "a shaper of cultural images." Uses this approach to analyze the plays to *The Perfectionist*, focusing on their handling of "ockerism," meaningful human relationships, and public institutions. The appendices provide a chronology of Williamson's career and a survey of the plays in performance. Select bibliography.

Kiernan, Brian. "David Williamson: Satiric Comedies." In *International Literature in English: Essays on the Major Writers*, edited by Robert Ross. New York: Garland Press, 1991. Contains a biographical sketch, an essay on the plays through 1989, a primary bibliography, and an annotated secondary bibliography. Kiernan argues that while the plays are highly "accessible" on any level, they exceed both satire and comedy to combine those forms into an original drama with a rare "human dimension."

_____. *David Williamson: A Writer's Career*. Melbourne, Australia: Heinemann, 1990. Rev. ed. Sidney: Currency Press, 1996. Called a "critical biography," this comprehensive study chronicles Williamson's personal life along with his development as a writer. Discusses each of the plays, providing background on productions as well as interpretation. Provides extensive information on Williamson's film and television career. Bibliographical materials. Most complete work on Williamson.

Montesano, A. P. "A Dangerous Life." *American Film* 13 (November, 1988): 8. Examines "A Dangerous Life," the documentary about the fall of the Ferdinand Marcos regime, and compares it to Williamson's screenplay *The Year of Living Dangerously*.

Zuber-Skerritt, Ortrun, ed. *David Williamson*. Amsterdam: Rodopi, 1988. Offers excerpts from selected talks and articles by, and interviews with, Williamson. Provides an extensive bibliography of newspaper and magazine articles as well as international reviews.

Robert Ross

AUGUST WILSON

Born: Pittsburgh, Pennsylvania; April 27, 1945

PRINCIPAL DRAMA

Ma Rainey's Black Bottom, pr. 1984, pb. 1985
Fences, pr., pb. 1985
Joe Turner's Come and Gone, pr. 1986, pb. 1988
The Piano Lesson, pr. 1987, pb. 1990
Two Trains Running, pr. 1990, pb. 1992
Three Plays, pb. 1991
Seven Guitars, pr. 1995, pb. 1996
Jitney, pr. 2000, pb. 2001
King Hedley II, pr. 2001

OTHER LITERARY FORMS

Although August Wilson is known primarily for his plays, some of his poetry was published in black literary journals, such as *Black World*, in 1969. He published a teleplay, *The Piano Lesson*, in 1995, and a nonfiction work, *The Ground on Which I Stand*, in 2000.

ACHIEVEMENTS

Critics have hailed August Wilson as an authentic voice of African American culture. His plays explore the black experience historically and in the context of deeper metaphysical roots in African culture. Since 1984, his major plays have been successfully produced by regional theaters and on Broadway; in fact, he is the first African American playwright to have had two plays running on Broadway simultaneously.

Wilson has received an impressive array of fellowships, awards, and honorary degrees: the Jerome Fellowship in 1980, the Bush Foundation Fellowship in 1982, membership in the New Dramatists starting in 1983, and the Rockefeller Fellowship in 1984. He has also been an associate of Playwrights Center, Minneapolis, and received the McKnight Fellowship in 1985, the Guggenheim Fellowship in 1986, six New York Drama Critics Circle Awards from 1985 to 2001, the Whiting Foundation Award in 1986, the Pulitzer Prize in Drama in 1987 (for *Fences*) and 1990 (for *The Piano Lesson*), the Tony Award by the League of New York Theatres and Producers (for *Fences*), the American Theatre Critics Award in 1986, the Outer Circle Award in 1987, and the Drama Desk Award and John Gassner Award in 1987.

Wilson's goals are "to concretize the black cultural response to the world, to place that response in loud action, so as to create a dramatic literature as powerful and sustaining as black American music." While the form of his plays breaks no new ground, the substance and language produce powerful emotional responses. Rooted in the black experience, Wilson's plays touch universal chords.

BIOGRAPHY

August Wilson was born in Pittsburgh, Pennsylvania, on April 27, 1945, in the Hill District, a black neighborhood. He was one of six children born to Daisy Wilson from North Carolina, and a German baker, Frederick August Kittel, who eventually abandoned the family. Wilson left school at fifteen when a teacher refused to take his word that a twenty-page paper on Napoleon was his own work. He spent the next few weeks in the library, pretending to be at school. It was through reading, especially all the books he could find in the "Negro" subject section, that Wilson educated himself.

Later, he worked at odd jobs and spent time on street corners and at a cigar store called Pat's Place, listening to old men tell stories. Coming into adulthood during the Black Power movement of the 1960's, Wilson was influenced by it and participated in the Black Arts movement in Pittsburgh, writing and publishing poetry in black journals. With longtime friend Rob Penny, he founded the Black Horizons Theatre Company in Pittsburgh in 1968. He produced and directed plays, but his efforts at playwriting in those years failed, he later recalled, because he "didn't respect the way blacks talked" so he "always tried to alter it." He formed a connection with the Penumbra company in St. Paul and moved there in 1978. It was in this much smaller black community that he learned to regard the "voices I had been brought up with all my life" with greater respect.

August Wilson in 1989. (AP/Wide World Photos)

Married in 1981 to Judy Oliver (he has a daughter, Sakina Ansari, from an earlier marriage), Wilson began to write scripts for the children's theater of a local science museum. This effort led him to submit his scripts to the National Playwrights Conference at the Eugene O'Neill Center in Waterford, Connecticut. His work caught the attention of conference director Lloyd Richards, who was also the dean of the Yale School of Drama and the artistic director of the Yale Repertory Company. Under Richards's direction, a staged reading of *Ma Rainey's Black Bottom* was performed in 1982 at the Eugene O'Neill Center, followed by a production at Yale and a Broadway success. The succeeding plays by Wilson followed the same pattern, with intervening production at regional theaters. Wilson eventually dissolved his relationship with Richards and turned to director Marion McClinton to stage *Jitney* and *King Hedley II.*

Divorced in 1990, Wilson moved to Seattle, Washington, where he continued to write his cycle of plays. He also participated as a dramaturge at the Eugene O'Neill Center when one of his own works was not being produced. After *Seven Guitars*, Wilson and his co-producer, Ben Mordecai, formed a joint venture called Sageworks, which gave Wilson artistic and financial control of his plays both as a writer and producer. Wilson refined his plays through a series of separate productions, writing and editing through each production's rehearsal process. Before reaching its New York run, *King Hedley II* received six regional productions. Wilson married Constanza Romero, and they had a daughter, Azula.

ANALYSIS

Each of August Wilson's major plays dramatizes the African American experience in a different decade of the twentieth century, and the action of each play is driven by the arrival or presence of a character who has what Wilson calls the "warrior spirit," the quality that makes a man dissatisfied and determined to change or disrupt the status quo. Each of the plays is affected by Wilson's feeling for the blues, music that he calls the "flag bearer of self-definition" for African Americans. Characters sing the blues, music is called for in scene transitions, and the rhythms of the dialogue reflect the blues. His plays are written to be performed on a single setting with action that is chronological. While he writes within the genre of psychological realism, each play displays a different degree of adherence to structure and plotting. His characters, mostly men, are African Americans uncertain of their own places in the world.

One of Wilson's greatest strengths is with language: The authenticity and rhythms of the dialogue and the colorful vitality of metaphor and storytelling connect him to the oral tradition of the African American and African cultures. He discussed in an interview the indirect quality of black speech, with its circling of issues and answers that are not answers. Characters answer the question they think is intended, not necessarily the one that is expressed. This language, in fact, often becomes the unique poetry of his drama. The language is full of implied meanings and dependent on tonal quality for interpretation. Wilson also places increasing emphasis with each play on the superstitions and beliefs that affect his characters. These superstitions seem to come from a mixture of Christianity, ancient African religions, and street wisdom.

MA RAINEY'S BLACK BOTTOM

In *Ma Rainey's Black Bottom*, Wilson uses a historical figure, "Mother of the Blues" singer Ma Rainey, and invents a story around her. The setting is a simultaneous representation of a 1927 recording studio and a band-rehearsal room. Overlooking the studio from the control booth are Ma's white producer and white agent, their presence and location a graphic symbol of white society's control over black music.

The dialogue seems to meander through silly and inconsequential matters. The underlying seriousness of these matters becomes apparent as the characters reveal their ways of coping with the white world. Ma Rainey plays the prima donna (note the pun in the play's title) while she acknowledges to her band that, like all black artists, she is exploited. Her music is her "way of understanding life." Wilson centers her in the play, a dynamic and colorful presence, but the character central to the action is Levee.

Levee has that warrior spirit. The tragic irony is that when he lashes out and kills, he kills the only educated band member in the play. His urge for self-sufficiency (to have his own band and make his own music) becomes self-destructive. By application, Wilson suggests that the misplaced rage of his race can result in self-destruction. The grimly serious resolution to this play does not describe the tone of lightness and humor in much that precedes it. It is Levee's appetite that drives the play, sometimes comically, and it is his frustrated hunger that causes an unnecessary death.

FENCES

Wilson's second major work, *Fences*, won a Pulitzer Prize in Drama as well as Tony Awards for Wilson, the director, and two actors. It centers on the dynamic, volatile character Troy Maxson and takes place primarily in 1957. Troy is the warrior character whose spirit disrupts his own life as well as those of his sons and wife. Often inviting comparison with Arthur Miller's *Death of a Salesman* (pr., pb. 1949), the play dramatizes the life of a baseball player prevented from realizing his big-league dreams by the color barrier, overcome too late for him. *Fences* is about a man's battle with life and his emotional, sometimes irrational way of facing unfairness, pain, love, and hate. The fence that Troy built around his life, like that built around his home, could neither shut out the world's injustice nor protect his family or himself from his shortcomings. The final scene occurs after Troy's death in 1965, when others can express feelings about Troy that were not articulated before. This scene provides a quietly emotional contrast to the intensely alive Troy of the previous eight scenes. It is a necessary scene and yet points up the failure of father and son to express directly what they felt in their earlier confrontation.

Troy's brother, Gabriel, whose head injury from the war has made him believe himself to be God's angel Gabriel, provides a kind of mystical presence. Wilson uses his madness for a theatrically effective closing to the play. When Gabriel discovers that his horn will not blow to open the gates of heaven for Troy, he performs a weird "dance of atavistic signature and ritual" and howls a kind of song to open the gates. This marks the beginning of Wilson's increasing use of ritual, myth, and superstition in his plays.

JOE TURNER'S COME AND GONE

In *Joe Turner's Come and Gone*, Wilson reaches farther back into the historical black experience. As in the old blues song of the same title, the brother of the governor of Tennessee, Joe Turner, found and enslaved groups of black men. Herald Loomis, the mysterious central character in this play, was so enslaved in 1901 and not released for seven years. The play dramatizes his search for his wife, which is actually a search for himself. His arrival at a Pittsburgh boardinghouse in 1911 disrupts and disturbs, creating the tension and significance of the drama.

Another boardinghouse resident, Bynum, establishes his identity as a "conjure man" or "rootworker" early in the play. Bynum's search for his "shiny man" becomes a thematic and structural tie for the play. At the end of the first act, during a joyous African call-and-response dance, Loomis has a sort of ecstatic fit, ending with his being unable to stand and walk. Some kind of dramatic resolution must relate Bynum's vision and Loomis's quest. It comes in the final scene when wife Martha returns and Loomis learns that his quest is still unrealized. Wilson describes Loomis's transformation in actions rather than words. His wife does not restore him, nor does her religion restore him. In desperation, he turns a knife on himself, rubs his hands and face in his own blood, looks down at his hands, and says, "I'm standing. My legs stood up! I'm standing now!" It is at this point that he has found his "song of self-sufficiency." Wilson's rather poetic stage directions articulate a redemption that Loomis cannot verbalize, risking audience misinterpretation.

Bynum's final line of the play recognizes Loomis as a shiny man, the shiny man who can tell him the meaning of life. The suggestion of a Christ figure is unmistakable, and yet Loomis's soul is not cleansed through religious belief. He has denied the Christ of the white man, despite Martha's pleading. His epiphany is in finding himself. Joe Turner has come but he has also gone. Herald Loomis finds his identity in his own African roots, not in the slave identity that the white Joe Turner had given him.

THE PIANO LESSON

With his fourth major play, Wilson crafts a more tightly structured plot. In fact, *The Piano Lesson* is stronger thematically and structurally than it is in character development. The characters serve to dramatize the conflict between the practical use of a family heritage to create a future, and a symbolic treasuring of that heritage to honor the past. The piano, which bears the blood of their slave ancestors, is the focus of the conflict between Boy Willie and his sister, Berniece. Its exotic carvings, made by their great grandfather, tell the story of their slave ancestors who were sold in exchange for the piano. Its presence in the northern home of Berniece and her Uncle Doaker represents the life of their father who died stealing it back from Sutter.

Berniece is embittered and troubled not only by the piano and her father's death but also by her mother's blood and tears that followed that death and by the loss of her own husband. In contrast, Boy Willie is upbeat and funny, an optimistic, ambitious, and boyish man who is sure he is right in wanting to sell the piano to buy Sutter's land. He has the warrior spirit. Throughout the play, the presence of Sutter's ghost is seen or felt. Sutter's ghost seems to represent the control that the white man still exerts over this family in 1937. Boy Willie chooses to ignore the ghost, to accuse his sister of imagining it, but ultimately it is Boy Willie who must wrestle with the ghost.

Wilson has said that this play had five endings because Berniece and Boy Willie are both right. The conflict is indeed unresolved as Boy Willie leaves, telling Berniece that she had better keep playing that piano or he and Sutter could both come back. The lesson of the piano is twofold: Berniece has learned that she should use her heritage, rather than let it fester in bitterness, and Boy Willie has learned that he cannot ignore the significance of this piano, which symbolizes the pain and suffering of all of his ancestors. There is little in the play that deviates from the central conflict. The skill of Wilson's writing is seen in the interplay of characters bantering and arguing, in the indirect quality of questions that are not answered, and in the storytelling. While characters may serve primarily as symbols and plot devices, they are nevertheless vivid and credible.

TWO TRAINS RUNNING

The disruptive character in Wilson's fifth play is Sterling, but the theme of *Two Trains Running*, set in 1969, is found in the character Memphis, the owner of the restaurant in which the action occurs. Memphis came north in 1936, driven away by white violence. He has always meant to return and reclaim his land. In the course of the play, he learns that he has to go back and "pick up the ball" so as not to arrive in the end zone empty handed. He must catch one of those two trains running south every day. He must not surrender.

The major characters in the play represent varying degrees of tenacity. Wilson skillfully builds a plot around two threads: Memphis's determination to get the city to pay his price for his property, and Ster-

ling's determination to find a place for himself and gain the love of Risa. Hambone is a crazy character, driven mad almost ten years ago when the butcher Lutz across the street refused to pay him a ham for doing a good job of painting his fence. Hollaway, a commentator character, observes that Hambone may be the smartest of them all in his refusal to give up—each day going to Lutz and asking for his ham. The unfortunate fact is, though, that his life has been reduced to this one action; all he can say is "I want my ham. He gonna give me my ham." Risa, a woman determined not to be dependent on a sexual attachment, has scarred her own attractive legs to make herself less desirable. In spite of herself, she is attracted to the vitality and optimism of Sterling, and Sterling is most tenacious of all. His warrior spirit has landed him in prison and may do so again, but his zeal and good humor are compelling.

The constant reminders and presence of death give resonance to the lives and efforts of these people. When the play opens, the Prophet Samuel has already died and the offstage mayhem surrounding the viewing of his body is evident. Characters talk about several other deaths, and no sooner is Prophet Samuel buried than Hambone is discovered dead (again offstage). The reactions to his death make up the ending of the play. Memphis and Sterling, trusting in the prophecies of the 322-year-old seer Aunt Ester, both triumph. Sterling runs across the street, steals a ham, and presents it to Mr. West, the undertaker, to put in Hambone's coffin. This final flourish of the play is an assertion of character identity and life. *Two Trains Running* may be Wilson's most accomplished work in blending character, plot, and theme.

SEVEN GUITARS

Two Trains Running was followed in 1995 by *Seven Guitars*. Set in the 1940's, it tells the tragic story of blues guitarist Floyd Barton, whose funeral opens the play. The action flashes back to recreate the events of Floyd's last week of life. Floyd had arrived in Pittsburgh to try to get his guitar out of the pawn shop and to convince his former lover, Vera, to return with him to Chicago. A record he made years earlier has suddenly gained popularity, and he has been offered the opportunity to record more songs at a studio in Chicago.

The play's central conflicts are Floyd's struggle to move forward in his musical career and his personal strife with Vera and his band mates. A subplot centers on Floyd's friend Hedley and his deteriorating physical and mental health as his friends attempt to place him in a tuberculosis sanitarium. The play contains some of Wilson's familiar character types, including the mentally aberrant Hedley; the troubled-by-the-law young black male protagonist, Floyd; the capable and independent woman, Louise; and the more needy, younger woman, Ruby. It also contains elements of music, dance, story telling, violence, and food.

JITNEY

Wilson reworked an earlier, short play *Jitney*. Becker, a retired steel-mill worker, runs a jitney station, serving the unofficial taxi needs of the black community of Pittsburgh's Hill district during early autumn of 1977. The jitney drivers are a rich collection of troubled but hard-working men. The station offers the men a living and a sense of independence that is threatened by the city's plans to tear down the neighborhood in the name of urban renewal. Becker also faces a personal crisis. His son, Booster, is about to leave prison after serving twenty years for murdering his well-to-do white girlfriend. Father and son have not spoken for two decades. Becker is bitter that his son threw away a promising career, and Booster sees his father's lifetime of hard work and submissiveness to white landlords and bosses as demeaning. Father and son never reconcile, but they indirectly attempt to redeem themselves to each other. Becker decides to organize the jitney drivers and fight the urban renewal. Yet, just as Becker begins the move to resistance, he falls victim to his rigorous work ethic and dies unexpectedly. As the dispirited drivers praise his father, Booster begins to respect his father's accomplishments and prepares to carry on Becker's mission to save the jitney station.

KING HEDLEY II

King Hedley II takes place in the back yard of a few ramshackle houses in the Hill District of Pittsburgh in 1985. Its protagonist, King Hedley II, is a petty thief and a former convict engaged in selling stolen refrigerators. Believing that he is being held back while everybody else is moving forward, Hedley dreams of a better life. His partner in crime is a shady character named Mister. Hedley's wife, Tonya, is pregnant with a child she does not want to raise in the rough life she knows. Hedley's mother, Ruby, is a former jazz singer who is reunited with an old lover, the con man Elmore. The next-door neighbor, Stool Pigeon, is a crazy old man who stacks old newspapers in his hovel. He is the play's mystic messenger who buries a dead cat in the backyard and brings to its grave various tokens that he believes will bring the animal back to one of its nine lives. The yard, barren except for weeds and garbage, is a major symbol. Hedley tires to raise plants in it, even fencing off a small patch with barbed wire. However, like Hedley's efforts to better himself, the attempt to grow something is doomed.

OTHER MAJOR WORKS

NONFICTION: *The Ground on Which I Stand*, 2000.
TELEPLAY: *The Piano Lesson*, 1995 (adaptation of his play).

BIBLIOGRAPHY

Bigsby, C. W. E. *Modern American Drama, 1945-1990*. Cambridge, England: Cambridge University Press, 1992. The author interviewed Wilson for pertinent biographical data and includes some in-depth analysis of the first four plays.

Bogumil, Mary L. *Understanding August Wilson*. Columbia: University of South Carolina Press, 1999. Bogumil provides readers with a comprehensive view of the thematic structure of Wilson's plays, the placement of his plays within the context of American drama, and the distinctively African American experiences and traditions that Wilson dramatizes.

Brustein, Robert. *Reimagining American Theatre*. New York: Hill and Wang, 1991. Brustein, critic and former artistic director of the Yale Repertory Theatre before Lloyd Richards, is one of the few negative voices criticizing Wilson's drama. He finds particular fault with the mechanisms and symbols of *The Piano Lesson* and hopes that Wilson will work to develop the poetic rather than historical aspects of his talent.

Elkins, Marilyn, ed. *August Wilson: A Casebook.* New York: Garland, 1994. The essays investigate such thematic, artistic, and ideological concerns as Wilson's use of the South and the black human body as metaphors; his collaboration with Lloyd Richards; the influences of the blues and other writers on his work; his creative method; and his treatment of African American family life.

Herrington, Joan. *I Ain't Sorry for Nothin' I Done: August Wilson's Process of Playwriting.* New York: Limelight Editions, 1998. Herrington traces the roots of Wilson's drama to visual artists such as Romare Bearden and to the jazz musicians who inspire and energize him as a dramatist. She goes on to analyze his process of playwriting—how he brings his experiences and his ideas to stage life—by comparing successive drafts of his first three major plays.

Hill, Holly. "Black Theatre into the Mainstream." In *Contemporary American Theatre*, edited by Bruce King. New York: St. Martin's Press, 1991. Hill's analysis of the plays sets them in the context of their period.

Nadel, Alan. *May All Your Fences Have Gates.* Iowa City: University of Iowa Press, 1994. Nadel deals individually with five major plays and also addresses issues crucial to Wilson's canon: the role of history, the relationship of African ritual to African American drama, gender relations in the African American community, music and cultural identity, the influence of Romare Beardern's collages, and the politics of drama.

Theater 9 (Summer/Fall, 1988). This special issue includes the script of *The Piano Lesson* with an earlier version of the ending, production photographs, and two informative essays. The articles "Wrestling Against History" and "The Songs of a Marked Man" explore Wilson's themes, especially the importance of myths and superstitions.

Wolfe, Peter. *August Wilson.* London: Macmillan, 1999. A comprehensive analysis of Wilson's theater. Wolfe sees the dramatist as exploding stereotypes of the ghetto poor, through his juxtapositions of the ordinary and the African American surreal, which evoke anger, affection, and sometimes hope.

Sally Osborne Norton,
updated by Rhona Justice-Malloy

LANFORD WILSON

Born: Lebanon, Missouri; April 13, 1937

PRINCIPAL DRAMA

So Long at the Fair, pr. 1963 (one act)

Home Free!, pr. 1964, pb. 1965 (one act)

The Madness of Lady Bright, pr. 1964, pb. 1967 (one act)

No Trespassing, pr. 1964 (one act)

Balm in Gilead, pr., pb. 1965 (two acts)

Days Ahead: A Monologue, pr. 1965, pb. 1967 (one scene)

Ludlow Fair, pr., pb. 1965 (one act)

The Sand Castle, pr. 1965, pb. 1970 (one act)

Sex Is Between Two People, pr. 1965 (one scene)

This Is the Rill Speaking, pr. 1965, pb. 1967 (one act)

The Rimers of Eldritch, pr. 1966, pb. 1967 (two acts)

Wandering: A Turn, pr. 1966, pb. 1967 (one scene)

Untitled Play, pr. 1967 (one act; music by Al Carmines)

The Gingham Dog, pr. 1968, pb. 1969

The Great Nebula in Orion, pr. 1970, pb. 1973 (one act)

Lemon Sky, pr., pb. 1970

Serenading Louie, pr. 1970, pb. 1976 (two acts)

Sextet (Yes), pb. 1970, pr. 1971 (one scene)

Stoop: A Turn, pb. 1970

Ikke, Ikke, Nye, Nye, Nye, pr. 1971, pb. 1973

Summer and Smoke, pr. 1971, pb. 1972 (libretto; adaptation of Tennessee Williams's play; music by Lee Hoiby)

The Family Continues, pr. 1972, pb. 1973 (one act)

The Hot l Baltimore, pr., pb. 1973

Victory on Mrs. Dandywine's Island, pb. 1973 (one act)

The Mound Builders, pr. 1975, pb. 1976 (two acts)

Brontosaurus, pr. 1977, pb. 1978 (one act)

Fifth of July, pr., pb. 1978 (two acts)

Talley's Folly, pr., pb. 1979 (one act)

A Tale Told, pr. 1981 (pb. as *Talley and Son*, 1986; two acts)

Thymus Vulgaris, pr., pb. 1982 (one act)

Angels Fall, pr., pb. 1982 (two acts)

Balm in Gilead and Other Plays, pb. 1985

Say deKooning, pr. 1985, pb. 1994

Sa-Hurt?, pr. 1986

A Betrothal, pr., pb. 1986 (one act)

Burn This, pr., pb. 1987

Dying Breed, pr. 1987

Hall of North American Forests, pr. 1987, pb. 1988

A Poster of the Cosmos, pr. 1987, pb. 1990 (one act)

Abstinence: A Turn, pb. 1989 (one scene)

The Moonshot Tape, pr., pb. 1990

Eukiah, pr., pb. 1992

Redwood Curtain, pr. 1992, pb. 1993

Twenty-one Short Plays, pb. 1993

Collected Works, pb. 1996-1999 (3 volumes; Vol. 1, *Collected Plays, 1965-1970*; Vol. 2, *Collected Works, 1970-1983*; Vol. 3, *The Talley Trilogy*)

Lanford Wilson: The Early Plays, 1965-1970, pb. 1996

Day, pr., pb. 1996 (one act)

A Sense of Place: Or, Virgil Is Still the Frogboy, pr. 1997, pb. 1999

Sympathetic Magic, pr. 1997, pb. 2000

Book of Days, pr. 1998, pb. 2000

Rain Dance, pr. 2000

OTHER LITERARY FORMS

Besides stage plays, Lanford Wilson has written works in a number of other dramatic forms: several teleplays, *The Migrants* (1973, with Tennessee Williams), *Sam Found Out: A Triple Play* (1988), and *Taxi!* (1978, not to be confused with the television series *Taxi*); two unproduced screenplays, "One Arm," written in 1969 and based on a Williams story, and "The Strike," based on the book *Last Exit to Brooklyn* (1988), by Hubert Selby, Jr.; and the libretto for Lee Hoiby's opera *Summer and Smoke* (1971), adapted from the Williams play.

ACHIEVEMENTS

Lanford Wilson's plays have been produced throughout the United States and abroad; several have appeared on television, and *The Hot l Baltimore* was adapted as a television series. Wilson is the winner of numerous awards: a Vernon Rice Award (1967); Obies for *The Hot l Baltimore*, *The Mound Builders*, and *Sympathetic Magic*; a Pulitzer Prize and a New York Drama Critics Circle Award (as best-of-best) for *Talley's Folly*; the American Theater Critics Award for best play for *Book of Days*; the Brandeis University Creative Arts Award, and fellowships from the Rockefeller and Guggenheim foundations. He was admitted to the Theatre Hall of Fame in 1995, and the Missouri Writers Hall of Fame in 1997.

BIOGRAPHY

Lanford Eugene ("Lance") Wilson was born April 13, 1937, in Lebanon, Missouri, the son of Ralph Eugene and Violetta Tate Wilson. When he was five years old, his parents separated (and later divorced), his father leaving for California, his mother taking Lanford to Springfield, Missouri, where she worked in a garment factory and he attended school. When he was thirteen, his mother married again—a dairy inspector from Ozark, Missouri—and they moved to a farm. Wilson attended Ozark High School, where he painted, acted, and was on the track team.

Although his childhood was relatively happy, Wilson never quite recovered from his parents' marital breakup. At eighteen, after a term at Southwest Missouri State College, he headed for California for a reunion with his father, by then a San Diego aircraft-factory worker with a new wife and two younger sons. The reunion, painfully mirrored in Wilson's autobiographical play *Lemon Sky*, was unsuccessful: Wilson and his father were thoroughly incompatible. After a year in his father's household, during which he worked at his father's factory and attended San Diego State College, Wilson left for Chicago. He lived for six years in Chicago, where he worked as an artist in an advertising agency, studied playwriting at the University of Chicago, and wrote his first plays (none produced).

In 1962, Wilson moved to New York, worked as an office clerk—in a furniture store, at the Americana Hotel, and in the subscription office of the New York Shakespeare Festival—and surveyed the theatrical scene. He was disgusted by Broadway but stunned by an Off-Off-Broadway performance of Eugène Ionesco's *The Lesson* at Caffé Cino, a coffeehouse theater in Greenwich Village. Soon Wilson began waiting tables and writing plays for Caffé Cino: His first play produced was *So Long at the Fair*, in 1963, and he achieved his first success in 1964 with *The Madness of Lady Bright* (which was given 250 performances Off-Off-Broadway). In 1966, Wilson had his first Off-Broadway success with *The Rimers of Eldritch*.

Wilson's rise had been swift, but then he began experiencing some setbacks. In 1967, he lost his home base at Caffé Cino when Joe Cino, the owner-manager, committed suicide; in 1968, *The Gingham Dog* failed on Broadway, followed in 1970 by *Lemon Sky*. After the failure of *The Gingham Dog*, Wilson became so despondent that he stopped writing for a time. He got back into playwriting by first doing mundane jobs for the Circle Repertory Company, which he had recently cofounded with actress Tanya Berezin, actor Rob Thirkield, and director Marshall W. Mason. In 1973, that company produced *The Hot l Baltimore*, and Wilson's career was back on track. All of his major plays during the following decade were initially produced by them and directed by Mason.

Over his career, Wilson has collaborated with Mason on nearly forty productions, and he has continued to prefer working with regional theater companies, even after the Broadway success of *Talley's Folly*. In the late 1990's he accepted a commission to write a play for former Circle Repertory Company member Jeff Daniels, executive director of the Purple Rose Theatre in Chelsea, Michigan. That play, *Book of Days*, was called his best in twenty years and was followed in 2001 with *Rain Dance*, also produced at the Purple Rose.

ANALYSIS

During his first period of playwriting (1963-1972), Lanford Wilson struggled to learn his trade—mainly in the convivial atmosphere of Off-Off-Broadway, where it did not matter if sometimes audiences did not show up. His plays from this period, mostly one-act dramas, are clearly apprentice work. They contain echoes of Tennessee Williams, Arthur Miller, and the Theater of the Absurd. Experiments include the use of overlapping and simultaneous speeches, free-floating time sequences, and characters who are figments of the main character's imagination. Perhaps the most effective of the plays from this decade are *Home Free!*, about a bizarre, incestuous relationship between brother and sister; *The Madness of Lady Bright*, about "a screaming preening queen" losing his beauty to middle age; and two impressionistic "montage" works that draw on Wilson's small-town Missouri background: *This Is the Rill Speaking* and *The Rimers of Eldritch*.

With the exception of *The Rimers of Eldritch*, a two-act play, Wilson had trouble sustaining longer plays during his apprentice decade; his longer works of this period tend to be uneven, diffuse, almost plotless. Their subject matter provides the main interest. *Balm in Gilead*, set in and around an all-night café on Upper Broadway, pictures the New York City subculture of pimps, prostitutes, pushers, and users. *The Gingham Dog*, financially unsuccessful but favorably reviewed when it opened on Broadway, portrays the rancorous breakup of an interracial marriage. *Lemon Sky* is autobiographical—about a young man's efforts to reunite with his father, who fled years before and is rearing a second family in Southern California.

As he gained experience, Wilson's work became more substantial in every sense: His mature plays are generally longer, more conventional, more realistic, and more successful than those of the decade of his apprenticeship. Wilson's breakthrough was with *The Hot l Baltimore*, an Off-Broadway success (with 1,166 performances) produced in 1973. *The Hot l Baltimore* shows the playwright in control of his material, displays his sense of humor, and illustrates the format on which Wilson has relied (in lieu of plot) with repeated success—an updating of the old parlor or weekend drama that brings together a group of disparate characters in an interesting setting (usually threatened, usually around a holiday) and allows them to interact. Other plays falling into this format are *The Mound Builders*, *Fifth of July*, *Angels Fall*, *Talley and Son* (a revised version of the 1981 *A Tale Told*), *Burn This*, and *Book of Days*. Even the Pulitzer Prize-winning *Talley's Folly*, a romantic tour de force with only two characters, repeats the format on a smaller scale. Wilson reveals one source of this recurring device in his 1984 translation of Anton Chekhov's *Tri sestry* (pr., pb. 1901; *Three Sisters*, 1920).

The public has been accurate in judging *The Hot l Baltimore*, *Talley's Folly*, and *Burn This* the best of Wilson's plays: They are the most tightly knit and evenly written, though some critics find them marred by sentimentality. *The Mound Builders*, his most ambitious work, is Wilson's favorite, but it shares, with *Fifth of July* and *Angels Fall*, a tendency toward rambling, uneven dialogue that is witty one moment and dull the next. *Angels Fall*, in particular, is burdened with intellectual baggage, something not found in Wilson's early work.

One simply does not look for highly structured, suspenseful plots from Wilson (the description "tightly knit," used above, is only relative), though his plays usually rise to a climax, even if it is sometimes forced or artificial. Rather, Wilson's work is significant for its characters and themes. His plays contain the greatest menagerie of characters in contemporary American drama—drag queens, freaks, prostitutes, academics, priests—for the most part likable because Wilson has a special sympathy for the losers and lost of society (a category that, in his work, includes almost everybody). Wilson does not really need intellectual baggage, because his characters carry his themes much more powerfully: In the world of Wilson's plays, only "angels fall" because his characters are already down—but never out. This sense of humanity is Wilson's most sterling quality.

HEARTLAND DRAMAS

Wilson represents the most recent stage of an American cultural phenomenon that could be aptly termed "the heartland drama." Wilson's predecessor and fellow Missourian Mark Twain celebrated American innocence; Wilson mourns its loss. The loss occurred precisely on August 6, 1945, when Harry S. Truman, the presidential Huck Finn, ordered that the atomic bomb be dropped on Hiroshima. The United States had been trying hard for a long time to lose its innocence, but once it was gone, the nation regretted its loss. Apparently, the famed innocence had been the source of American wholeness, of Fourth of July optimism, of childlike wonder.

Wilson centered his version of this American heartland drama on the family, where, according to Sigmund Freud, all the history of the world is played out. It is in the family, once the bastion of American innocence, that signs of the disintegration are most noticeable and its effects most far-reaching, and it is there that wholeness must be restored. Longing for the old innocence is expressed in Wilson's plays through titles that sound as if they are from nursery rhymes or children's games (some are). It is also expressed through the constant efforts to mend splintered families or to construct surrogate families. Yet the longing and the efforts are mostly in vain: The nursery-rhyme titles are mockeries, and the versions of home and family depicted are little better than cruel parodies.

Extreme examples can be found in *Home Free!*, in which a brother and sister, huddled in their apartment in an attempt to shut out the world, play husband-wife and father-mother; in *The Madness of Lady Bright*, in which the fading drag queen Lady Bright, lonely in his apartment, reminisces about former lovers (whose autographs are on the wall), talks with an imaginary "Boy" and "Girl," and waits in vain for a phone call; and in *The Hot l Baltimore*, in which the condemned urban hotel of the title is the home of prostitutes and poor retirees. Unfortunately, in late-twentieth century America, these bizarre examples are only too real. For those seeking a substitute for the American family's lost wholeness, Wilson has some news: There is very little balm in Gilead, especially if one locates Gilead in such places as the New York City subculture of prostitutes and drug addicts.

Ultimately, in Wilson's work, the American heartland drama is not only played out in the family but also the family itself—real or surrogate—mirrors and becomes a metaphor for the whole society. Such is the case in *Fifth of July*, where the extended Talley family and its holiday guests mirror the post-Vietnam state of the nation. The older generation is blessedly dead or slightly dotty; the middle generation, now over thirty, is burnt out, subsisting on drugs and memories of Berkeley idealism and sexual entanglements; and the younger generation has a precocious vocabulary and sophistication that leaves little doubt that the era of old-fashioned Fourth of July innocence is finished. Similarly, the surrogate family group (including real families) gathered for an archaeological dig in *The Mound Builders* mirrors the larger tensions in American society, particularly the tensions between preservation and development. In both plays, the sense of America's loss—of its values, its history—is acute.

THE RIMERS OF ELDRITCH

In dramatizing America's loss, Wilson occasionally takes on the tones of an Old Testament prophet. Nowhere is this more the case than in *The Rimers of Eldritch*, the best example of Wilson's early experimental work. Reminiscent of Thornton Wilder's *Our Town* (pr., pb. 1938) and Dylan Thomas's *Under Milk Wood: A Play for Voices* (pr. 1953, pb. 1954), though with a different emphasis, *The Rimers of Eldritch* treats a somewhat worn subject, now a television standard—the hypocrisy of a small town. Just one big down-home family, the town's citizens close ranks to heap their evil on a poor scapegoat and thereby preserve their appearance of innocence, but the town's evil remains, its corruption confirmed. Appropriately,

the printed play has the following epigraph from Jeremiah (the reference to balm in Gilead appears two verses later): "The harvest is past, the summer is ended, and we are not saved" (Jeremiah 8:20). *The Rimers of Eldritch* takes place during one spring, summer, and fall, but the play skips backward and forward in time, from one conversation to another, creating a montage effect rather than presenting a chronological sequence. Less confusing than it sounds, the montage dresses the worn subject in mystery and suspense, ironic juxtapositions, different versions of what happened (thereby mimicking small-town gossip), and a memory-like quality.

The town is named Eldritch and, true to the meaning of its name, Eldritch displays a weird collection of small-town characters, descendants of Sherwood Anderson's midwestern grotesques: farmers; a garage mechanic; a trucker; Cora Groves, owner of the Hilltop Café, who is carrying on with her young and transient lover; Patsy Johnson, prettiest girl at Centerville High, who gets pregnant by the transient lover and arranges a quick marriage to a hometown boy; Skelly Mannor, the town hermit, who goes about peeping into people's windows and who is suspected, according to an old rumor, of bestiality (boys follow him in the street shouting "Baaa!"); the town hero, a stock-car driver, now deceased, who was impotent and beat women; and a group of gossips who could substitute for the Eumenides. What characterizes the town, however, is not only its individual members but also its collective mentality. As Skelly says, the town's citizens see what they want to see and think what they want to think, all in the name of good Christian living.

The play's slight, makeshift plot dramatizes this observation. The plot revolves around an innocent fourteen-year-old crippled girl, who dreams of flying like Peter Pan and sowing autumn rime over the town. She compares the rime to sugar, but it turns out to be more like salt. Out of her sexual curiosity, she provokes her equally innocent boyfriend to try to rape her. Skelly happens on the scene and prevents the rape, but a nearby neighbor emerges with his gun and, naturally thinking that Skelly is the molester, kills him. The two "innocents" tell the Skelly-the-molester story to the judge and jury—a story the town is only too ready to believe. As the preacher (who doubles as judge) points out to the accompaniment of hymn singing, the town is to blame for not shooting the fellow sooner.

THE HOT L BALTIMORE

Wilson's roots in the Bible Belt make him sound like the prophet Jeremiah in such plays as *Balm in Gilead* and *The Rimers of Eldritch*, but, in his *The Hot l Baltimore*, they also lead him to discover Mary Magdalene, whom he immediately forgave. An example of Wilson's mature work and his most popular play, *The Hot l Baltimore* is a warm and witty comedy—bittersweet, to be sure, but farcical at times. Apparently tired of turning his audiences into pillars of salt straining back toward the lost past, Wilson set out deliberately to entertain in *The Hot l Baltimore*—and happily succeeded with a realistic, conventional play that even observes the classical unities.

The play is set during one twenty-four-hour period ("a recent Memorial Day") in the lobby of a seedy Baltimore hotel. Once an ornate showplace of the railroad era, the Hotel Baltimore is now scheduled for demolition. It is the home of the expected motley assortment of Wilson characters: hotel workers, retirees, transients, and—most notably—three warmhearted prostitutes. Like an extended family, from grandparents down to teenagers, they gather in the lobby to share each other's company and experiences. The prostitutes, in particular, share some ribald experiences concerning their clients. April observes, "If my clientele represents a cross section of American manhood, the country's in trouble," citing as one of the representative samples the fellow who scalds himself in the bathtub. Occasionally these scenes obtrude onstage, as at the hilarious end of act 1, when the outraged but otherwise unhurt Suzy, beaten and locked out of her room by a client, creates a commotion in the lobby by appearing wrapped in her towel and then nude.

Beneath the repartee and rough sexual humor, the audience is constantly reminded of the parallel between a troubled United States and the rundown hotel. The hotel's residents will be losing their home, the workers, within a month, their jobs, and other

people with troubles appear: Mrs. Bellotti, whose crazy, thieving, alcoholic son Horse has been kicked out of the hotel and whose diabetic husband has had his leg amputated; Paul Granger III, a refugee from a reform school who is searching for his lost grandfather; and Jackie and Jamie, a sister and brother who bought salty desert land in Utah and now lack money to get their car on the road. All represent typical cases of the American blues, just as the hotel setting represents the transience of American values and society in general.

Presiding over this scene, ministering to the troubled in spirit, is the trinity of prostitutes, Suzy, April Green, and the Girl. These angels of mercy provide not only sex but also therapy, laughter, and sympathy. Significantly, they, among all the characters, show the most concern about family ties—about Mr. Bellotti disowning Horse, about Paul Granger III giving up the search for his namesake grandfather, about Jackie's abandonment of Jamie; they also have the strongest feelings about the scheduled demolition of the hotel and the dispersal of its workers and residents. "We been like a family, haven't we?" says Suzy. "My family." She is so broken up that she moves in with a rotten pimp, because she needs "someone; . . . I need love!" The prostitutes have lost their illusions along with their innocence, but they retain their sense of values, their humanity. As the Girl says, "I just think it's really chicken not to believe in anything!" For Wilson, still mourning the loss of American innocence, the prostitutes were an important discovery: One takes one's balm, however little there is, wherever one can get it.

TALLEY'S FOLLY

This philosophy of balm, discovered in *The Hot l Baltimore*, prevails in *Talley's Folly*, Wilson's Pulitzer Prize-winning work. *Talley's Folly* introduces two mature misfits who have about given up on love but finally find solace in each other's arms. As this simple plot suggests, *Talley's Folly*, like *The Hot l Baltimore*, observes the unities, only more so: Matt's wooing of Sally takes place entirely in an old boathouse (an ornate Victorian structure called Talley's Folly), and the time required coincides with the playing time (ninety-seven minutes, no intermission).

Family is a particularly important consideration in *Talley's Folly*, one of an ongoing series of Wilson plays about the Talley family of Lebanon, Missouri (the other plays are *Fifth of July* and *Talley and Son*). As in so many Wilson plays, however, here again the families depicted experience friction or breakup. Thirty-one-year-old Sally Talley is the family outcast, first because tuberculosis left her sterile and thus unfit to seal the Talley-Campbell family business partnership by marrying Harley Campbell, and second because her political views are anathema to the family, with its conservative small-town values (she sides with the union against the family's garment factory and is fired from teaching Sunday School). Forty-two-year-old Matt Friedman, a radical Jewish accountant, seems a likely mate for Sally, satisfying even her family's exacting requirements (though her brother Buddy runs Matt off with a shotgun). Matt does not even want children: Because the rest of his own family was wiped out in the Holocaust, he has resolved never to be responsible for bringing a child into this world.

Before the two can come together, they have to break down each other's solitary defenses. Matt has been melted down by Sally the summer before, with a few sessions in the boathouse, so now he takes the initiative. The play consists of their love sparring—Matt's persistence, Sally's attempts to chase him away, their anger, their jokes and repartee, their reminiscences, and finally their confessions—until Matt wins her hand. A fine vehicle for two good actors, *Talley's Folly* shows that, even in a bleak and hurtful world—no place to raise children—one can still find some balm in personal relationships.

TALLEY AND SON

The third play in the Talley family cycle, *Talley and Son*, a revision of the 1981 *A Tale Told*, is set in Lebanon, Missouri, on July 4, 1944, precisely the same evening as in *Talley's Folly*. A darker play than *Talley's Folly*, this play is about the financial and other machinations of three generations of Talleys, who, together with the Campbells, have run two of the most profitable businesses in Lebanon: the clothing factory and the bank. Because of the liberal use of plot devices, this story of meanness and greed has often been compared with Lillian Hellman's *The Little Foxes* (pr., pb. 1939).

ANGELS FALL

Lest Wilson be accused of recommending retreat from the world, it should be added that in *Angels Fall*, he has used his family metaphor to extend the possibilities of reconciliation and hope. In *Angels Fall*, the surrogate family is a group of travelers taking shelter in a New Mexico mission church from a nearby nuclear accident. The play's title, perhaps implying that only angels stand tall enough to fall, suggests that Wilson has become reconciled to the loss of American innocence. Here the characters are all forgivably flawed and, in their mutual danger, in their mutual need, lean on one another and show a caring attitude. (Whether a nuclear accident is necessary to bring this about is unclear.) Even if the traditional American family is a dying institution, the play suggests, some of its values are still preserved in the bigger family of humankind—or perhaps in the family of God: What Wilson considers to be the fountainhead of these positive possibilities is implied in the setting (a church) and its presiding official, the genial Father Doherty.

BURN THIS

Burn This, which premiered in January, 1987, is shocking, outrageous, and larger than life. It presents Wilson's views on art, human sexuality, and love. Like Sally and Matt of *Talley's Folly*, the characters Anna and Pale conclude the play as a couple, but here the union may be a mistake. It is a poetic and cataclysmic work, in which art is seen as a sacrament, as an outward sign for inward, often chaotic but exhilarating truths. *Redwood Curtain*, a disturbing yet compassionate drama that depicts Vietnam veterans eking out primitive lives in the forests of Northern California, is perhaps equally powerful.

BOOK OF DAYS

Book of Days was heralded as Wilson's "comeback" play, his most significant production in two decades, or perhaps in his entire career. The play is set in the small town of Dublin, Missouri, a spiritual sister city to Lebanon, the setting of the Talley family plays. When a Hollywood director named Boyd Middleton arrives in town to direct a community theatcr production of George Bernard Shaw's *St. Joan*, he sets off a chain reaction of events that upset the quiet lives of the other characters. The biblically named Ruth, cast in the role of Joan of Arc, stands up to evil in the form of big business after the mysterious murder of the owner of the local cheese factory.

Wilson has returned throughout his career to thinking about the Midwest where he was born. In the Talley family plays and *The Mound Builders*, he explored Midwest family dynamics, creating families that survived or unraveled after meeting outside forces. In *Book of Days*, Wilson moves beyond the family unit to ask serious questions about how towns, especially in the Midwest, can preserve their values against the threats of the Christian right and corporate greed.

Book of Days echoes elements found in Wilson's earlier work. Small towns such as Dublin, Missouri, marred by hidden corruption, have appeared in Wilson's plays since *The Rimers of Eldritch*. Ruth and Len, who manage to stay happily married because they are loyal to each other and because they have simple and honest dreams, are reminiscent of Sally and Matt of *Talley's Folly*. Doubts about the roles of art and artists in healing individuals and communities are raised in *Burn This*. What is intriguing in *Book of Days* is the combination of these elements, and the unusual political nature of the underlying conflict.

OTHER MAJOR WORKS

TELEPLAYS: *One Arm*, 1970; *The Migrants*, 1973 (with Tennessee Williams); *Taxi!*, 1978; *Sam Found Out: A Triple Play*, 1988; *Lemon Sky*, 1988; *Burn This*, 1992; *Talley's Folly*, 1992.

TRANSLATION: *Three Sisters*, 1984 (of Anton Chekhov's play *Tri sestry*).

BIBLIOGRAPHY

Barnett, Gene A. *Lanford Wilson*. Boston: Twayne, 1987. The most valuable general study of Wilson. This book carries chapters on all the major plays through *Talley and Son*. It also includes a family genealogy and a family chronology for the entire Talley clan.

Bryer, Jackson R. *Lanford Wilson: A Casebook*. New York: Garland, 1994. This collection includes ten critical articles, covering plays through *Burn This*. Also includes an introduction and chronology, and two interviews with Wilson.

Busby, Mark. *Lanford Wilson*. Boise, Idaho: Boise State University, 1987. Busby's brief monograph focuses on how Wilson's own family history has influenced his dramatic themes of longing for the past and conflict between generations. Literary influences, including Franz Kafka, and the influence of Wilson's early theater-going experiences, are also explored.

Dean, Anne M. *Discovery and Invention: The Urban Plays of Lanford Wilson*. Rutherford, Md.: Fairleigh Dickinson University Press, 1995. Written with the cooperation of Wilson, Marshall Mason, and other members of the Circle Repertory Company, this passionately affirming book examines Wilson's themes and the use of realistic yet poetic language, particularly in *Balm in Gilead*, *The Hot l Baltimore*, and *Burn This*.

Herman, William. "Down and Out in Lebanon and New York: Lanford Wilson." In *Understanding Contemporary American Drama*. Columbia: University of South Carolina Press, 1987. Herman's chapter includes explications of Wilson's major plays. He praises Wilson for the "delicate poetic language at the heart of his style" and for his "epic encompassment of American experience and mythologies."

Robertson, C. Warren. "Lanford Wilson." In *American Playwrights Since 1945*, edited by Philip C. Kolin. New York: Greenwood Press, 1989. An accessible reference to primary and secondary sources through 1987. Robertson provides a complete primary bibliography of Wilson's works and brief discussions entitled "Assessment of Wilson's Reputation" and "Production History." The article also includes an informative survey of secondary sources and a complete secondary bibliography.

Harold Branam,
updated by James W. Robinson, Jr.,
and Cynthia A. Bily

ROBERT WILSON

Born: Waco, Texas; October 4, 1941

PRINCIPAL DRAMA

Dance Event, pr. 1965

Solo Performance, pr. 1966

Theater Activity, pr. 1967

Spaceman, pr. 1967 (with Ralph Hilton)

ByrdwoMAN, pr. 1968

The King of Spain, pr. 1969, pb. 1970

The Life and Times of Sigmund Freud, pr. 1969

Deafman Glance, pr. 1970

Program Prologue Now, Overture for a Deafman,
    pr. 1971

Overture, pr. 1972

*Ka Mountain, GUARDenia Terrace: a story about
    a family and some people changing*, pr. 1972

king lyre and the lady in the wasteland, pr. 1973

The Life and Times of Joseph Stalin, pr. 1973

*DiaLOG/A MAD MAN A MAD GIANT A MAD
    DOG A MAD URGE A MAD FACE*, pr. 1974

The Life and Times of Dave Clark, pr. 1974

Prologue to a Letter for Queen Victoria, pr. 1974

A Letter for Queen Victoria, pr. 1974, pb. 1977
    (with Christopher Knowles)

To Street, pr. 1975

$ Value of Man, pr. 1975

DiaLOG, pr. 1975 (with Knowles)

Einstein on the Beach, pr., pb. 1976 (music by
    Philip Glass)

*I Was Sitting on My Patio This Guy Appeared I
    Thought I Was Hallucinating*, pr. 1977, pb. 1978

Prologue to the 4th Act of Deafman Glance, pr.
    1978

DiaLOG/NETWORK, pr. 1978

Death Destruction and Detroit, pr. 1979

DiaLOG/Curious George, pr. 1979

Edison, pr. 1979

Medea, pr. 1981

The Golden Windows, pr. 1982

*the CIVIL warS: a tree is best measured when it is
    down*, partial pr. 1983 and 1984 (includes *Knee
    Plays*)

Alcestis, pr. 1985 (based on Euripides' play)

Knee Plays, pr. 1986

Parzifal, pr. 1987, pb. 1990 (with Tankred Dorst
    and Christopher Knowles)

Cosmopolitan Greetings, pr. 1988

The Forest, pr. 1988

The Black Rider: The Casting of the Magic Bullets,
    pr. 1990 (with Tom Waits and William S.
    Burroughs)

When We Dead Awaken, pr. 1991 (adaptation of
    Henrik Ibsen's play *Naar vi døde vaagner*)

Lohengrin, pr. 1991, revision pr. 1998 (adaptation
    of Richard Wagner's opera)

Alice, pr. 1992 (with Tom Waits, Kathleen
    Brennan, and Paul Schmidt; adaptation of
    Lewis Carroll's *Alice in Wonderland*)

Dr. Faustus Lights the Lights, pr. 1992 (adaptation
    of Gertrude Stein's story)

Hamlet: A Monologue, pr. 1995

The Magic Flute, pr. 1995

Time Rocker, pr. 1996 (with Lou Reed and Darryl
    Pinckney)

A Dream Play, pr. 1998 (adaptation of August
    Strindberg's play *Ett drömspel*)

Das Rheingold, pr. 2000 (adaptation of Richard
    Wagner's opera)

POEtry, pr. 2000 (with Lou Reed)

Woyzeck, pr. 2000 (with Waits and Brennan;
    adaptation of Georg Büchner's play)

Siegfried, pr. 2001

Doctor Caligari, pr. 2002

Osud, pr. 2002

OTHER LITERARY FORMS

Although Robert Wilson has produced some artwork, generated from his stage designs and exhibited
in various galleries, no substantial literary works
other than plays are attributed to him.

ACHIEVEMENTS

An experimental performing artist whose major
work has been compared to Pablo Picasso's painting

Guernica and Igor Stravinsky's ballet *The Rite of Spring* (1913), and who has been characterized by Surrealist Louis Aragon as "a miracle," Robert Wilson is considered by many to be the single most gifted and creative theater artist of the twentieth century. In scope, vision, imagination, and sheer size, Wilson's marathon "operas" (as he insists on calling them) are giant panoramas of all the possibilities of the stage, physical and temporal (one environmental event in Iran lasted a whole week). His reputation in Europe as the modern theater's most significant avant-garde director/playwright is not so universally acknowledged in his native country, the United States, but with the performance of major works on Broadway and at the Metropolitan Opera House, as well as the Brooklyn Academy of Music and the studios of Wilson's theater group, the Byrd Hoffman School of Byrds, his place in the history of American contemporary theater, especially the strong and widespread experimental movement of the 1960's and 1970's, is assured.

Wilson has won several distinguished European awards for his work, including the Grand Prize for *Einstein on the Beach* at the International Festival of Nations in Belgrade in 1977. Others include the Premio Abbiati from the Italian Music Critic Association, two Italian Premio Ubu awards, and the German Theater Critics Award. Undoubtedly the greatest acknowledgement of Wilson's artistry and global influence was his nomination for the Pulitzer Prize for *the CIVIL warS*. In the United States, an Obie Special Award Citation for Direction was presented to Wilson in 1974; he has held numerous Guggenheim and Rockefeller Foundation Fellowships. He was awarded the Dorothy and Lillian Gish Prize for lifetime achievement in 1996 and the Harvard Excellence in Design Award (1998).

BIOGRAPHY

Born in Waco, Texas, to white, middle-class, Protestant and southern parents, Robert Wilson attended high school in his hometown. A gangly, shy, but likable young man, he had a speech impediment that was "cured" by a dance teacher, Mrs. Byrd Hoffman, who simply made Wilson realize that he could "take his time" to express himself. Following his early impulse to be a visual artist, Wilson studied at the University of Texas and privately in Paris, graduating from Pratt Institute in Brooklyn in 1965. During these years, his patience with and sympathy for learning disabilities led him to work with autistic and disturbed children in Texas, where he discovered not only a unique talent for helping them but also a personal metaphor for his own anguish at the virtually universal inability to communicate that is part of the existential condition.

After several striking visual projects such as "Poles" (an "installation" of more than six hundred telephone poles in rural Ohio) and the creation of giant puppets for Jean-Claude van Itallie's experimental play *America Hurrah* (1966), Wilson found that performance art offered the best medium for self-expression. Several small works in which Wilson was the primary performer were followed by increasingly ambitious projects, incorporating more and more "actors" (many of whom were untrained laypersons drawn to Wilson's charismatic personality) and more

Robert Wilson in New York City in 1997. (Hulton Archive by Getty Images)

and more special effects, stage props, and scenery. By 1967, he had gathered a group of friends and theater experimenters into the Byrd Hoffman School of Byrds (named in honor of the woman who helped Wilson in high school) and began an impressive series of long performance works, first in the modest studios of downtown New York, then at the Brooklyn Academy of Music, and finally throughout Europe, where the combination of his genius and the more benign attitude of political and cultural institutions toward the support of experimental art allowed Wilson to create his best work.

Wilson began his experimental career with theater pieces, "demonstrations," workshops, and other alternative theater activities; often he tried "sound" pieces, whose function was to experience pure sound rather than the contextual tyranny of words. After his early "sound" works gained acceptance, Wilson tried an actual opera, *The Life and Times of Joseph Stalin*, with music by Alan Lloyd, Igor Demjen, and others. It previewed in Copenhagen as a production of the Byrd Hoffman School of Byrds but premiered at the Brooklyn Academy of Music in December of 1973. Truncated versions of the opera were subsequently performed, along with his next opera, *A Letter for Queen Victoria*. The following years continued Wilson's collaborations with his team of composers, choreographers, visual artists, and actors: *Einstein on the Beach*, one of the most successful of this series of works, with music by Philip Glass, premiered in France. The return of his work to the United States met with both unreserved acclaim and scathing criticism, culminating in the financial failure of the monumental multinational project *the CIVIL warS*, rehearsed and also performed, in part, in six separate countries and scheduled to be performed during the Olympics in Los Angeles in 1984. The only surviving portion of that work, the American connective sections known as *Knee Plays*, has toured the United States in truncated form. The concept of the "knee play" continues as a production element throughout Wilson's later works, serving as a sort of alienation device, used even in such "classics" as *When We Dead Awaken*, Wilson's adaptation of Henrik Ibsen's *Naar vi døde vaagner* (pb. 1899; *When We Dead Awaken*, 1900), adding a popular entertainment idiom, often a comic spirit, to traditionally serious drama.

Wilson has continued to produce work for the stage and the opera fields into the twenty-first century, often revising earlier material and producing it in an entirely different way from the original concept. His imaginative direction of the plays of other playwrights has always included strongly experimental design elements, choreography, and alterations of the original text material to suit his unique style. Some later works are *Cosmopolitan Greetings*, based on the poems of Allen Ginsberg; *The Forest*, Wilson and David Byrne's version of the Gilgamesh legend; and a video piece, *La Femme à la Cafetière* (1989), dealing with the painting of that name by Paul Cézanne.

In 1992, Wilson founded the Watermill Center, on Long Island, for the express purpose of developing new works and subsequently affording an opportunity for the next generation of young artists to experiment. He continues to mount exhibits of his visual art, often, but not exclusively, in New York. His "14 Stations" installation most clearly illustrates the relationship between theatre and visual art, as it was originally commissioned by the city of Oberammergau in conjunction with the Passion Play 2000.

ANALYSIS

Robert Wilson's "Theatre of Visions" can best be described as a series of stage tableaux and slowly moving, apparently nondramatic activities which, in the individual minds of the witnesses, connect to form a nonreductive, nonrhetorical, nonnarrative but subjectively unified theatrical experience. This experience may or may not bear a relationship to the piece's title, often referring to a famous person, as in *The King of Spain*, *The Life and Times of Sigmund Freud*, *A Letter for Queen Victoria*, and *Edison*. In the course of the performance (always extremely long by traditional standards), the witness is presented with an opportunity to form whatever subjective connections the images suggest, either intellectually or subconsciously, during which process new "bisociations" are created. Although appearing arbitrary and unrehearsed, the activities are carefully arranged for maximum visual effect. Wilson, however, does not prescribe that effect; it remains for the witnesses to make what they will of the series of "visions," adding to the mix the private experiences and perceptions each one brings to the theatrical event.

All of his productions explore the relationship between time and space, onstage, and *vis-à-vis* the audience. He is most noted and often criticized for his "slow motion" technique in which, it has been said, he attempts to create a sort of "mythic time." One critic, Brigid Grauman in the *Wall Street Journal*, took Wilson to task, saying, "His actors in *Aida* in fact look more like fish swimming slowly in an aquarium, or people performing Tai Chi." As a "concept" director, Wilson opens himself up to such criticism. His choices are bold and he often deconstructs texts—perhaps one reason why he steers clear of published scripts by living playwrights and works exclusively on collaborative projects with living authors, classic dramas, or opera.

Nevertheless, no discussion of modern opera or experimental theater can be complete without taking Wilson's work into account. He is a writer, designer, and director whose avant-garde, multifaceted works combine operatic size and musical complexity with the visual possibilities of the stage and the meditative concentration of philosophical speculation. Wilson's imaginative and demanding productions have forced opera to expand its self-definition to include works as far removed from nineteenth century notions as his collaborators—Meredith Monk, David Byrne, Allen Ginsberg, Christopher Knowles, Laurie Anderson, Richard Foreman, and many others—are different from their classical counterparts in dance, theater, and dramaturgy; he has claimed his place in theater and opera history. His theatrical vision has no limitations of size or duration, and he will be satisfied only when the world stages itself.

THE LIFE AND TIMES OF JOSEPH STALIN

The Life and Times of Joseph Stalin, performed first in Denmark, then at Brooklyn Academy of Music, provides access to Wilson's prevailing imagery, because it is in large part a retrospective of all of his work up to that time. In seven acts, each with its own prologue, the piece lasted twelve hours (from 7:00 P.M.

to 7:00 A.M.) and survived four performances in December of 1973. The actors cross and move in seven planes parallel to the proscenium arch; objects hang from the flies against a sky backdrop; silent, immobile figures fill the stage (act 2 alone, originally part of *The King of Spain*, contains "a boy who stands on a stool for the entire act, a blind man and two other men who play chess, Freud, Anna, Stalin, a photographer who takes their picture, a piano player, and a walrus," as well as the King of Spain himself). Processions, choruses, minstrel-show performers, historically costumed, nude, and white-draped figures troop on and off; a cave, a pyramid, "two-dimensional trees and a three-dimensional house" are among the stage scenery; the menagerie includes four turtles with a pool on their backs, wooden fish that swim in it, a bull (beheaded during act 4), nine apes, and twenty dancing ostriches. Yet the huge size of the stage and the unimaginably long duration of the performance dwarf the props, performers, and action, and virtually every activity seems to take place in slow motion. The witness, partly lulled by the slow pace and absence of dramatic intensification, and partly prompted by its uniqueness to perceive everything with a new "vision," eventually succumbs to the rhythms of the performance, coming away from the experience freed from stale habits of passive receptivity and reenergized by the aesthetic euphoria of visual stimulation.

The dialogue passages in this monumental retrospective point to a transition in Wilson's work about this time. Earlier pieces (such as *Deafman Glance*) were essentially silent, with occasional songs, incomprehensible utterances, or sounds, but after the ambitious outdoor piece entitled *Ka Mountain, GUARDenia Terrace*, Wilson turned in another direction, marked by an increasingly concentrated examination of language as partial, failed, or desensitized communication. The spoken word, often in the form of seemingly meaningless phrases repeated and repeated, begins to draw the focus of the work. In stark contrast to the virtual silence of his early work, Wilson now exhaustively examined the nature of the word onstage.

A LETTER FOR QUEEN VICTORIA

A Letter for Queen Victoria is the best illustration of this new concern. The "text," edited by Bonnie

Marranca with her introductory essay and a preface by Wilson, immediately identifies the nonnormative nature of Wilson's language experiments during this period. Although the spoken word transliterates theoretically into the written word, no simple recitation of the "text" could reproduce the immediacy of the spoken performance, especially taking into account the participation of Christopher Knowles, a young man who shares authorship in the piece, clinically "autistic" but, according to Wilson, possessing perceptual powers different from but not inferior to normal perceptions. Knowles's and Wilson's "performance" of the phrases, neither linked nor "meaningful," reduces the text to "architectonic" sounds that express the actors' personal relationship in untranslatable ways.

From the backdrops of projected sound-words to the concrete layout of the poetry of the script page, Wilson's main arena of theatrical inquiry during this period becomes the word, the script, and its tenuous relationship to the spoken aspect of theatrical experience. For example, a "press conference" in Yugoslavia consisted of Wilson's repeating the word "dinosaur" for twelve hours while cutting an onion. A thwarted radio project called for actors to say "Hmm," "O.K.," and "There" for five hours. When a word is repeatedly uttered in this fashion, it loses its denotative meaning, resurfacing in the consciousness as pure sound, and, according to Wilson, helping to reestablish emotional responses which have been dulled by the everyday use of language. Wilson's close association with Knowles, Raymond Andrews, and other children with limited hearing and speech has inspired him to experiment with language as "weather," that is, as atmospheric pressures that alter accompanying movements and gestures, transforming them into highly subjective but effective personal communications.

The difficulties of "reading" a Wilson text should serve as a reminder: It is important to understand his work as performance art rather than primarily as literary expression. Although the "scripts" of Wilson's works are sometimes available, often in obscure and out-of-print formats, the complexity and visuality of the experiences are best captured in the form of "performance documentation." This genre, originating in such journals of experimental theater as *The Drama Review* and *Performing Arts Journal*, seeks to record nonscripted or partially scripted theatrical events by means of carefully detailed description of the nature, sequence, and duration of those events, told from the standpoint of a neutral, informed witness who avoids as much as is humanly possible any evaluative or subjective interpretations of those events. Necessarily, some interpretation is inevitable, but the reader can re-create, however imperfectly, some of the visual "semiotics" of the original performance. In Wilson's case, the German critic Stefan Brecht has reported all the significant performance pieces of the Byrd Hoffman Studio up to 1978 in his exhaustively comprehensive study, *The Theatre of Visions: Robert Wilson* (1978), a title that is descriptive of Wilson's whole aesthetic approach.

THE CIVIL WARS

After a very successful European tour of *Einstein on the Beach* (a collaboration with experimental music composer Philip Glass) in 1976, culminating in sold-out performances at the Metropolitan Opera House in New York City, Wilson found himself with increasingly complex production difficulties, brought on by his limitless vision and his refusal to compromise it with the petty realities of financial exigency. Forced to try smaller works such as *I Was Sitting on My Patio This Guy Appeared I Thought I Was Hallucinating*, Wilson seemed to be gathering his energy for his masterpiece, *the CIVIL warS*, a work that was to combine the most striking scenes and activities from earlier work with new visions on a grand scale. Yet after years of preparation in six countries and countless fund-raising trips and meetings, Wilson was forced to abandon his epic cycle, expressly designed in scope and theme for the Olympic Arts Festival in 1984. Efforts to mount it in Austin, Texas, in 1986 fell to financial realities as well; American audiences could only glimpse the tattered fragments of the Wagnerian vision in a tour of the diminutive *Knee Plays*, whose original purpose was to link the larger segments together.

LATER WORKS

Perhaps the most prolific of contemporary directors, Wilson's work in the 1990's and 2000's extends itself across geographic boundaries and continues to readdress the classics. His adaptations of classic works include *Alice*, *Hamlet: A Monologue*, *Das Rheingold*, and *Woyzeck*. His creative processes remain largely unchanged, although enhanced by the Watermill Center facility, where, in his own space, with his own company, he can first storyboard his productions and then choreograph the painstaking movements.

BIBLIOGRAPHY

Bigsby, C. W. E. *Beyond Broadway*. Vol. 3 in *A Critical Introduction to Twentieth Century American Drama*. Cambridge, England: Cambridge University Press, 1985. A full chapter on Wilson covers his life, his early work with speech-impaired individuals, and his association with the Byrd Hoffman School of Byrds, and describes *Ka Mountain*, *GUARDenia Terrace*, *$ Value of Man*, and other stage pieces. Behind his work, Bigsby says, "there lies a romantic conviction about continuity, a touching faith about the possibility of communication and the essentially holistic nature of experience."

Byrne, David. "*The Forest*: A Preview of the Next Wilson-Byrne Collaboration." Interview by Laurence Shyer. *Theater* 19 (Summer/Fall, 1988): 6-11. This interview with David Byrne discusses the nature of his collaboration with Wilson and contains many indirect Wilson quotations. Much on Wilson's forming a Berlin company in the fall of 1987 to make this Gilgamesh version (*The Forest*). Includes a seven-act breakdown of images in photographs and text.

Croyden, Margaret. *Lunatics, Lovers, and Poets: The Contemporary Experimental Theatre*. New York: McGraw-Hill, 1974. A description of the Byrd Hoffman School of Byrds, its "aesthetic of the Beautiful," and Wilson's experiences with brain-damaged children who "responded to dance and movement therapy." Much of the theater of silence is wordless, Croyden notes, "and in some of his later workshop pieces, where words are uttered, the effect is that of silence nonetheless." Deals at length with *Deafman Glance*.

Deak, Frantisek. "Robert Wilson." In *The New Theatre: Performance Documentation*, edited by Michael Kirby. New York: New York University Press, 1974. A reprint of an article originally appearing in *The Drama Review* (June, 1974), unique in its fully illustrated (with photographs by Carl Paler) white-on-black pages. Gives a strong impression of the performance itself, in an act-by-act visual description accompanied by striking production shots.

Holmberg, Arthur. *The Theatre of Robert Wilson*. New York: Cambridge University Press, 1997. Holmberg, who was associated with Robert Wilson at the American Repertory Theatre and beyond, examines Wilson's vast production corpus and organizes his material thematically. His explication serves as an invaluable tool for anyone interested in Wilson, novice and scholar alike.

Quadri, Franco and Franco Bertoni, Robert Stearns. *Robert Wilson*. New York: Rizzoli, 1998. A coffee-table book in the traditional sense of size and photographs, this book is enhanced by its critical essays and its detailed chronology of Wilson's work.

Shyer, Laurence. *Robert Wilson and His Collaborators*. New York: Theatre Communications Group, 1989. The most complete and authoritative record of Wilson's busy artistic life and his relationships with his collaborators (arranged by artistic specialty). This indispensable volume is illustrated with photographs and drawings of most of Wilson's productions and is complemented by a strong chronology (with comments by contemporaries) and a select bibliography.

Zurbrugg, Nicholas. "Post-Modernism and the Multi-Media Sensibility: Heiner Muller's *Hamletmachine* and the Art of Robert Wilson." *Modern Drama* 31 (September, 1988): 439-453. Zurbrugg finds that "Wilson's aesthetic seems to hover somewhere between [Samuel] Beckett's and [John] Cage's antithetical explorations of form, ambiguity, chance and rule." Offers a strong discussion of Wilson's collaboration with the East German playwright and follows this article by Arthur Holmberg's "conversation" with Wilson and Heiner Müller.

Thomas J. Taylor,
updated by Anne Fletcher

STANISŁAW IGNACY WITKIEWICZ

Born: Warsaw, Poland; February 24, 1885
Died: Jeziory, Poland (now in Ukraine); September
18, 1939

PRINCIPAL DRAMA

Mister Price: Czyli, Bzik tropikalny, wr. 1920, pr.
1926, pb. 1962 (*Mr. Price: Or, Tropical
Madness*, 1972)

Oni, wr. 1920, pb. 1962, pr. 1965 (*They*, 1968)

Straszliwy wychowawca, wr. 1920, pr., pb. 1935

Pragmatyści, pb. 1920, pr. 1921 (*The Pragmatists*,
1971)

Tumor Mózgowicz, pr., pb. 1921 (*Tumor
Brainiowicz*, 1980)

Metafizyka dwugłowego cielęcia, wr. 1921, pr.
1928, pb. 1962 (*Metaphysics of a Two-Headed
Calf*, 1972)

Gyubal Wahazar: Czyli, Na przełęczach bezsensu,
wr. 1921, pb. 1962, pr. 1966 (*Gyubal Wahazar:
Or, Along the Cliffs of the Absurd*, 1971)

Bezimienne dzieło, wr. 1921, pb. 1962, pr. 1967
(*The Anonymous Work*, 1974)

Kurka Wodna, pr. 1922, pb. 1962 (*The Water Hen*,
1968)

Nowe wyzwolenie, pb. 1922, pr. 1925

Nadobnisie i koczkodany: Czyli, Zielon pigułka,
wr. 1922, pb. 1962, pr. 1967 (*Dainty Shapes
and Hairy Apes: Or, The Green Pill*, 1980)

W małym dworku, pr. 1923, pb. 1948 (*Country
House*, 1997)

Mątwa: Czyli, Hyrkaniczny światopogląd, pb.
1923, pr. 1933 (*The Cuttlefish: Or, The
Hyrcanian Worldview*, 1970)

Szalona lokomotywa, wr. 1923, pb. 1962, pr. 1964
(*The Crazy Locomotive*, 1968)

Matka, wr. 1924, pb. 1962, pr. 1964 (*The Mother*,
1968)

*Wariat i zakonnica: Czyli, Nie ma złego, co by na
jeszcze gorsze nie wyszło*, pr. 1924, pb. 1925
(*The Madman and the Nun: Or, There Is
Nothing Bad Which Could Not Turn into
Something Worse*, 1966)

Jan Maciej Karol Wścieklica, pr. 1925, pb. 1962

*Sonata Belzebuba: Czyli, Prawdziwe zdarzenie w
Mordowarze*, wr. 1925, pb. 1938, pr. 1966 (*The
Beelzebub Sonata: Or, What Really Happened
at Mordowar*, 1980)

Szewcy, wr. 1934, pb. 1948, pr. 1957 (*The
Shoemakers*, 1968)

OTHER LITERARY FORMS

Although Stanisław Ignacy Witkiewicz's reputation rests primarily on his plays, he also produced important work in other forms. His first novel, *622 upadki Bunga: Czyli, Demoniczna kobieta* (1972; the 622 downfalls of Bungo: or, the demonic woman), written between 1910 and 1911 but published only posthumously, is a decadent, immature, autobiographical work that anticipates many of his later concerns. More significant is his second novel, *Poż egnanie jesieni* (1927; farewell to autumn), which ventures into the realm of political prophecy: A liberal revolution is soon overthrown by a more radical group of revolutionaries, and the increasingly repressive attempts at social engineering undertaken by the new regime serve only to foster boredom and inefficiency on a massive scale. The same anti-Utopian outlook manifests itself even more dramatically in Witkiewicz's most important novel, *Nienasycenie* (1930; *Insatiability: A Novel in Two Parts*, 1977). In this strangely prophetic work, a Chinese Communist Army, having subdued Soviet Russia, is encamped along the eastern frontiers of Poland and is about to launch a final assault against Western civilization. To weaken the resistance of their foes, the Chinese have disseminated a drug, in pill form, throughout the principal capitals of Europe. The pills are simply the organic counterpart of an ideology concocted by a Malayan-Chinese dialectician named Murti Bing: Anyone who ingests these pills is instantly converted to Murtibingism and thus perceives the futility of opposing the inevitable laws of history.

In addition to his fiction, Witkiewicz published a variety of other works that shed light on his drama and are of interest in their own right, including metaphysical studies of the arts, a formal philosophical treatise, and an account of his experiences with nicotine, alcohol, and other, more exotic drugs.

ACHIEVEMENTS

No play of Stanisław Ignacy Witkiewicz found any favor with either audiences or critics when performed during his lifetime. Three decades after his death, however, Witkiewicz won posthumous acclaim as a playwright who was a precursor of the Theater of the Absurd. It was Martin Esslin who coined this phrase in order to designate the common denominator linking the plays of such writers as Eugène Ionesco, Samuel Beckett, and Jean Genet. According to Esslin, playwrights who write in this mode subscribe to the thesis concerning the absurdity of human existence that was set forth by Albert Camus in *Le Mythe de Sisyphe* (1942; *The Myth of Sisyphus*, 1955). Esslin's *The Theatre of the Absurd*, when first published in 1961, made no mention of Witkiewicz. The revised, updated edition issued in 1969, however, includes new material in which Esslin duly recognizes the contribution made by Witkiewicz to the tradition of the Absurd (as well as that made by another Polish dramatist, Witold Gombrowicz). Even within Poland, Witkiewicz's plays were largely unknown before the cultural thaw that occurred in 1956. It was only in that year that Polish authorities rescinded the policy mandating the practice of Socialist Realism. This policy, imposed in 1950, precluded the possibility of performing or publishing "formalistic" plays of any kind. Since the liberalization, Witkiewicz's works have established themselves as a permanent part of the repertory offered by the modern Polish theater.

Starting in 1966, Witkiewicz's plays began to appear in English translation as a result of the efforts of Daniel Gerould. He and a number of dedicated co-workers began translating the twenty-three works that are included in the two-volume edition of Witkiewicz's plays that was published in Warsaw in 1962. Gerould has also written a perceptive analysis of Witkiewicz's entire literary œuvre in his full-length critical study entitled *Witkacy: Stanisław Ignacy Witkie-*

wicz as an Imaginative Writer (1981). Some literary critics, it should be noted, regard Witkiewicz's novels even more highly than they regard his plays. Despite the formidable linguistic difficulties in rendering any of these novels into another language, Louis Iribarne has succeeded in producing a lucid English translation of *Insatiability*. Published in 1977, this edition also contains an extensive introduction to Witkiewicz's life and work as well as a complete critical apparatus to accompany the novel itself. Witkiewicz has clearly been well served by the labors of Gerould and Iribarne on his behalf, and it is now possible for English-speaking readers to understand why he has become recognized as a major figure in the European avant-garde movement that flourished during the period between the two world wars. Although his work as a painter and graphic artist does not require the mediation of translators, Witkiewicz's achievement in the fine arts has not as yet received due recognition outside his native land.

BIOGRAPHY

While in his early thirties, Stanisław Ignacy Witkiewicz adopted the pseudonym "Witkacy" in order to distinguish himself from his famous father, Stanisław Witkiewicz (1851-1915). The elder Witkiewicz, whose family belonged to the landowning aristocracy of Lithuania, was a painter by profession; he was also highly influential as an aesthetic theorist. His most important book, a long treatise entitled *Sztuka i krytyka u nas* (1891; art and the critics in our country), argues that painting should be judged solely on the basis of formal criteria that are independent of religious, literary, or patriotic values. His own paintings were realistic in style, but he was at the same time a passionate admirer of the folk art and rustic architecture that were to be found among the mountaineers in the Tatra region of southern Poland. In 1883, he married Maria Pietrzkiewicz (1853-1931), a member of the petty gentry, who had been graduated from the Warsaw Conservatory in 1873 and taught music from time to time in order to supplement the income of the Witkiewicz family. Their only child was born in Warsaw on February 24, 1885. Five years later, the family moved to Zakopane, a village in the Tatra Mountains located sixty miles due south of Krakow. It was there that the child was baptized in 1891 in a ceremony in which the celebrated actress Helena Modjeska served as godmother.

By moving to Zakopane, the elder Witkiewicz sought to escape from the physical and spiritual miasma of the industrialized world. Convinced that formal schooling stifled creativity, he educated his son at home with the assistance of tutors. Under this enlightened tutelage, young Witkiewicz soon acquired a reputation as a child prodigy. He was taught the piano by his mother and the art of painting by his father. Somewhat to his parents' surprise, the boy displayed an inordinate fondness for reading plays and even wrote a few at the age of eight. The first of these was entitled *Karluchy* (1893; cockroaches), a work that depicts the invasion of a mythical kingdom by a horde of these vermin. Among the closest companions of his boyhood were Bronisław Malinowski and Leon Chwistek. Both these youths went on to become figures of international repute, Malinowski as an anthropologist and Chwistek as a philosopher. Between 1900 and 1905, Witkiewicz visited St. Petersburg, Munich, and Vienna as well as several cities in Italy. Such travels enabled him to keep abreast of the latest developments in the world of art. At age twenty, he decided to enroll in the Academy of Fine Arts in Krakow despite his father's heated objections that such training would lead to conformism and mediocrity. While the bohemian aspects of student life attracted the young man, the course of studies at the academy itself failed to interest him in any way. He therefore dropped out of the academy after about a year and returned home.

For the next few years, Witkiewicz led the life of a drifter. He painted bizarre pictures, wrote a novel, traveled abroad, and engaged in a number of serious love affairs. In 1913, owing to fears of impending madness, he sought treatment from a psychoanalyst who subscribed to the doctrines of Sigmund Freud. In the belief that marriage might be the best form of therapy, he also became engaged to Jadwiga Janczewska. His fiancé, however, committed suicide shortly thereafter because of a suspicion on her part that Witkiewicz was involved in a homosexual rela-

tionship with the composer Karol Szymanowski. Soon after this tragic event, Witkiewicz's mother decided that a prolonged stay abroad would do much to restore her son's equilibrium. She therefore made arrangements for him to accompany Malinowski on an anthropological expedition to the South Seas as private secretary and photographer. Things went well at first. He joined Malinowski in England, where his boyhood companion was then a postgraduate student at the London School of Economics, and they set out for Australia at once. En route, the ship stopped off at Ceylon, and Witkiewicz was enthralled by all the luxuriant vegetation and exotic clothing that he observed there. The island left such a lasting impression on him that many of the plays that he subsequently wrote in Poland were to have tropical settings. Once in Australia, he and Malinowski quarreled bitterly and severed their relationship permanently. Hence, he was left in Australia while his former friend continued on to New Guinea. By that time, however, war had broken out in Europe, and Witkiewicz resolved to become a participant.

Even though Zakopane and Krakow lay in the Austrian sector of partitioned Poland, Witkiewicz was a Russian citizen under the law because he had been born in Warsaw. He therefore went to St. Petersburg and enrolled in an elite military academy. As an only son, Witkiewicz might have exempted himself from military duty, but he chose not to claim this exemption. While his mother accepted the situation, his father was outraged. On graduation from officers' training school, Witkiewicz served as a lieutenant in the renowned Pavlovsky regiment. He was wounded in a battle fought near the Byelorussian city of Minsk in 1915 and subsequently received the Order of St. Anne for bravery under fire. While recuperating from his wounds in St. Petersburg, he availed himself of the opportunity to visit galleries where the works of many avant-garde artists were on display and developed a passionate admiration for the paintings of Pablo Picasso. Before long, St. Petersburg was in the throes of revolutionary violence. Witkiewicz not only managed to survive both the February and October revolutions, but he also was elected political commissar by his regiment. In June, 1918, the formerly czarist officer returned to his newly independent homeland.

Witkiewicz's father had died of tuberculosis in 1915 at Lovranno, a popular resort located near Rijeka (formerly Fiume) on the Adriatic seacoast of present-day Yugoslavia, where he had been in permanent residence since 1908 for reasons of health. His mother, however, had remained in Zakopane and operated a number of boardinghouses there until her death in 1931. Witkiewicz, for his part, was obliged to earn his own livelihood through painting. In 1924, he decided that he had nothing more to accomplish in this medium and henceforth concentrated on portrait painting for purely monetary reasons. To this end, he set up a so-called painting firm and went as far as to print a brochure outlining the rules under which the commissioned portraits would be executed. One of these rules flatly prohibited any kind of criticism on the part of the customer. Since he no longer took his artwork seriously, most of his creative energy went into the composition of plays and novels. Although he wrote several dozen plays during the 1920's, few of them were actually performed. Those that were staged, moreover, were dismissed as the by-products of a warped mind. It must be acknowledged that Witkiewicz did, in fact, use drugs in the mid-1920's in order to discover what effect they might have on creativity. These experiments were carefully controlled, however, and he never actually became addicted to any of these drugs, although he developed a lifelong dependence on alcohol and nicotine. Witkiewicz abandoned these experiments entirely once he concluded that the use of drugs did little to expand the scope of his artistic perception. He chronicled their debilitating effects in his treatise entitled *Nikotyna, alkohol, kokaina, peyotl, morfina, eter, + dodatek* (1932; nicotine, alcohol, cocaine, peyote, morphine, ether + appendix).

In 1923, Witkiewicz married a woman from Warsaw named Jadwiga Unrug in a modest ceremony that took place at Zakopane. The marriage was somewhat unconventional because she continued to reside in Warsaw while he spent most of his time staying with his mother in one of her boardinghouses in Zakopane. Those who knew the couple report that they had a genuine affection for each other. They did, however, remain childless. In 1929, Witkiewicz met Czesława Korzeniowska and soon began spending much more time in her company than was proper for a married man. During the 1930's, Witkiewicz's activity as a playwright was limited to finishing the script for *The Shoemakers* and to staging a few works that had been written in the previous decade. It was not until 1938 that he began a new play. Entitled *Tak zwana ludzkość w obłędzie* (so-called humanity gone mad), this play was completed in the following year. Unfortunately, the only parts that survive are the title page and the list of characters, which were published in 1972. It is known, however, that the content of the play was inspired by Witkiewicz's vision of the catastrophe about to be unleashed on humankind by the forces of Nazi Germany. When Germany attacked Poland on September 1, 1939, Witkiewicz dutifully reported for mobilization but was rejected on the grounds of age and poor health. As the Germans approached the outskirts of Warsaw, he and Korzeniowska joined a group of refugees fleeing eastward by train to Brześć. (This city, now called Brest and situated in Byelorussia, was designated as Brest-Litovsk while under the control of czarist Russia.) Soon after their arrival in Brześć, the city was bombed by German aircraft. They therefore decided to seek safety in the countryside and spent the next night in an open field outside the city. In the meantime, the Soviet army had crossed the Polish frontier and was advancing rapidly throughout all the eastern provinces. On September 18, 1939, only one day after the Soviet invasion, Witkiewicz committed suicide by slashing his wrists on a hillside near the village of Jeziora. His body, along with that of his semiconscious companion, was discovered the next day. Shortly thereafter, Witkiewicz was buried in a simple wooden coffin at an Orthodox cemetery located nearby.

ANALYSIS

It is essential to recognize that Stanisław Ignacy Witkiewicz devoted much effort to the development of a formal philosophical system. These endeavors in the sphere of philosophy culminated in the composition of an ambitious ontological treatise entitled

Pojęcia i twierdzenia implikowane przez pojęcie istnienia (1935; the concepts and principles implied by the concept of existence). Written between 1917 and 1932, this 180-page treatise was completely revised five times before publication. Despite its merits, only 20 of the 650 copies constituting the original printing were actually sold at the time. In this work, as his point of departure, Witkiewicz attempts to account for the particularity of existence. He then goes on to address the ultimate ontological question: Why does anything at all exist, when absolute nothing might just as well have prevailed? So as to elucidate the mystery of existence, Witkiewicz propounds a philosophical system that bears a distinct affinity with the doctrines set forth in Gottfried Wilhelm Leibniz's *Monadologie* (1714; *Monadology and Other Philosophical Essays*, 1898). Witkiewicz's treatise is, at the same time, a condemnation of such contemporary philosophies as Marxism, pragmatism, and logical positivism. As he sees it, these systems of thought are really dedicated to the task of refuting the validity of metaphysical problems rather than exploring them.

For Witkiewicz, retention of a "metaphysical feeling of the strangeness of existence" is of paramount importance. In a work entitled *Nowe formy w malarstwie i wynikające stąd nieporozumienia* (1919; new forms in painting and misunderstanding resulting therefrom), he discourses at length on the diminution of people's capacity to experience metaphysical mystery as a result of the evolution of society. Not only has scientific progress made life more comfortable for all strata of society, but it has also replaced religion as the ultimate explanation of reality. Witkiewicz concedes that religion still exists among the masses but only in a debased form that consists largely of perfunctory rituals. As religion declined, moreover, so did art. Whereas metaphysical wonder informed the work produced by the artists of ancient Greece and the Middle Ages, each of these epochs was succeeded by one in which verisimilitude to the external forms of nature took precedence over spirituality. Witkiewicz acknowledges that the French Impressionists performed a service by liberating color from the restraints imposed by the classicists, but he

also asserts that they failed to restore the metaphysical dimension to art in any meaningful way. The works of an artist such as Picasso, it may be assumed, do much more to evoke a metaphysical feeling of strangeness, in Witkiewicz's view. He insists, furthermore, that it is essential for art to perform this metaphysical function because religion and philosophy can no longer do so. Works of art such as those of Picasso, accordingly, serve as one of the last remaining buffers against the monstrous boredom of an increasingly mechanical and soulless society.

Witkiewicz applies these propositions specifically to the dramatic genre in his work called *Teatr: Wstęp do teorii czystej formy w teatrze* (1923; introduction to the theory of pure form in the theater). Here, the arts are classified on the basis of whether the aesthetic medium employed is "homogeneous" or "composite" in character. Music, which consists of sound, and painting, which consists of line and color, are homogeneous. Poetry and the theater, on the other hand, are both composite. Of all the arts, music is the freest because it is the least representational. Except when attempting to create program music, the composer works within the dimensions of what Witkiewicz termed Pure Form. The special status of music with respect to its independence from content had previously been underscored by the British writer Walter Pater. In an essay entitled "The School of Giorgione," which first appeared in the *Fortnightly Review* in 1877 and was later included in the third edition of his *Studies in the History of the Renaissance* (1888), Pater maintains that "all art constantly aspires to the condition of music." Although Witkiewicz foresaw the possibility of painting achieving the same freedom of form that characterizes music, it was not until the advent of abstract expressionism in the 1940's that this aesthetic ideal was realized in the nonobjective art produced by painters such as Jackson Pollock. While such freedom from representational content can never be attained in the world of the theater, Witkiewicz still urges playwrights to focus on Pure Form. In essence, he is proposing that plays be constructed on the basis of aesthetic principles analogous to those that inform the paintings of the Surrealists. What this amounts to in practice is the radical proposal that events in a play be exempt from the laws of natural science, that characters be free to act inconsistently, and that story lines be independent of psychological plausibility. Witkiewicz likens such devices to the axioms of non-Euclidean geometry, where parallel lines intersect and the shortest distance between two points is a curve.

THE WATER HEN

One of the best examples of Witkiewicz's concept of Pure Form may be found in the plot of his "spherical" tragedy in three acts entitled *The Water Hen*. As act 1 begins, a young man named Edgar Wałpor is preparing to shoot a woman known as the Water Hen at her own request. It is revealed that Edgar is the son of a retired sea captain who wishes him to become a great artist. Unfortunately, Edgar has no talent. The Water Hen, who is Edgar's mistress, believes that if he kills her, he will experience the mental anguish that leads to the creation of great art. When he finally discharges two shots from a rifle, she informs him that one of them missed her but the other went straight through her heart. She nevertheless keeps right on talking for another five minutes, as though nothing had happened. Immediately after these shots are fired, a ten-year-old boy named Tadzio enters the scene as though he had been summoned. The Water Hen instructs him to go to his father, and the boy goes up to Edgar without any hesitation. Edgar, however, is completely nonplussed, since he has never seen the boy before or even known of his existence. (The boy's true parentage, it should be noted, is to remain a mystery throughout the play.) When the Water Hen actually gets around to dying, her final words to Edgar consist of an exhortation for him to become great. Then, the setting switches magically from the open field where the shooting occurred to a location outside a barracks. Edgar's father and a number of guests arrive on the scene. After Edgar explains what happened to the Water Hen, her body is hauled away by some of his father's servants, and a table is set up for supper. Among the invited guests are the Duchess Alice of Nevermore and her gigolo. The father proposes marriage to the duchess on his son's behalf, and she accepts. Edgar also decides to adopt Tadzio and is looking forward to being both a husband and a father.

As related in act 2, life in the duchess's palace has its problems. Tadzio has withdrawn into a dreamlike trance, and the duchess continues to retain her gigolo. As for Edgar, he has now become a businessman and has invested most of his wife's money in an enterprise called the Theosophical Jam Company. One day, the Water Hen makes a sudden appearance just as dinner is about to be served. After determining the nature of Edgar's new circumstances, she concludes that her sacrifice on his behalf has been in vain. She then convinces Edgar that he needs to suffer physical pain if he is to fulfill his father's ambitions for him, and some servants thereupon wheel a medieval Spanish torture box into the room. Edgar is trapped inside and soon passes out. His torments are abruptly halted when his father arrives on the scene and orders his son's release. The Water Hen is then escorted out of the palace. Both the duchess and Tadzio are especially happy to see her leave. She had previously offended the duchess by claiming that the duchess's former husband, who had been devoured by a tiger in a Janjapara jungle, had been unfaithful to her. Tadzio had also been deeply hurt when the Water Hen denied that he was actually her son. Edgar, for his part, renounces art and resolves to forge closer bonds with his wife and son.

Act 3 takes place a decade later, and Tadzio has now become a student at the university in deference to his foster father's desire to turn him into a great scholar. While engrossed in study, Tadzio is surprised by a visit from the Water Hen. She appears more youthful and attractive than ever before, and he is completely captivated by her seductive maneuvers. He proposes marriage, and she accepts with alacrity. When Edgar returns to the palace and learns of their plans to marry, he enters strenuous objections. After failing to dissuade either of them, he kills the Water Hen a second time with the same rifle that he had used before. As she is about to expire, she proclaims that Edgar is her only love and that she was simply trying to make him jealous by marrying his son. Detectives who are looking for his wife's gigolo in connection with a criminal offense arrive on the scene and arrest the duchess for the murder of the Water Hen after the duchess implausibly claims to have perpetrated the deed out of love for the gigolo. She and the gigolo are led off, and Edgar thereupon shoots himself in the temple with a revolver. Before this domestic tragedy has run its course, a revolution breaks out, and the old order collapses. The gigolo turns out to have contacts with the revolutionaries, and he and the duchess are freed. In the meantime, Tadzio decides to abandon his studies so that he might become a scoundrel like the gigolo. As the play ends, Edgar's father and a few other representatives of the old order amuse themselves at a game of cards as they await slaughter at the hands of the revolutionary mob. Personal and social tragedy are thus linked in accordance with Witkiewicz's deeply ingrained sense of catastrophism.

No summary of a play by Witkiewicz can impart any idea of the stunning visual impact of an actual performance. Neither can it convey the richness of the dialogue in terms of witticisms and literary allusions. In the case of *The Water Hen*, its very title alludes to two dramatic masterworks of the nineteenth century: Henrik Ibsen's *Vildanden* (1884; *The Wild Duck*, 1891) and Anton Chekhov's *Chayka* (1896; *The Seagull*, 1909). In each of these plays, the shooting of a bird symbolizes the plight of the play's heroine. Since the Polish word for "hen" (*kurka*) sounds very similar to the term "whore" (*kurwa*), the title also contains an element of wordplay whose humor is completely lost in translation. Except for puns of this type that are predicated on an understanding of the Polish language, Witkiewicz's plays contain very little that is not accessible to readers or playgoers of other linguistic backgrounds.

The Shoemakers

The chief exception to the international character of Witkiewicz's dramatic œuvre is the work entitled *The Shoemakers*. Witkiewicz devoted more time to composing this play than he did to any other work for the theater. Written between the years 1927 and 1934, it is also the longest of Witkiewicz's plays. Although this ambitious work has established itself as a clear favorite among the public in Poland, there is little likelihood that it will ever meet with success elsewhere, owing to its presumption of a familiarity with Polish literature and history on the part of readers or

playgoers. In terms of content, it is very close to that of Witkiewicz's previously published novels and deals with the social stagnation and cultural boredom that follows the triumph of socialism. This theme has obviously struck a responsive chord among theatergoers in Poland. The play itself, however, manifests few characteristics associated with the concept of Pure Form.

The Madman and the Nun

Oddly enough, the same is true of the dramatic work of his that has enjoyed the greatest popularity in the United States: namely, *The Madman and the Nun*. "Dedicated to all the madmen of the world (including those on other planets)," this conventionally structured play is set in a lunatic asylum, where a young poet and drug addict is simultaneously undergoing treatment at the hands of three psychiatrists of conflicting theoretical persuasions. As the plot unfolds, the young poet seduces a beautiful nun who serves as his nurse and subsequently kills the Freudian psychiatrist whom he suspects of being his rival for the nun's affections.

There must have been many occasions during his lifetime when Witkiewicz saw himself in the role of the protagonist in *The Madman and the Nun*. His own works were frequently dismissed as the products of a deranged mind. Witkiewicz, however, never lost faith in the aesthetic viability of his plays and was certain that they would one day be accepted by the public and the critics alike. His judgment has now been vindicated by posterity, and many of his plays have achieved the status of classics in the repertory of avant-garde drama.

OTHER MAJOR WORKS

LONG FICTION: *Pożegnanie jesieni*, 1927; *Nienasycenie*, 1930 (*Insatiability: A Novel in Two Parts*, 1977); *Jedyne wyjście*, 1968; *622 upadki Bunga: Czyli, Demoniczna kobieta*, 1972.

NONFICTION: *Nowe formy w malarstwie i wynikające stąd nieporozumienia*, 1919; *Szkice estetyczne*, 1922; *Teatr: Wstęp do teorii czystej formy w teatrze*, 1923; *Nikotyna, alkohol, kokaina, peyotl, morfina, eter, + dodatek*, 1932; *Pojęcia i twierdzenia implikowane przez pojęcie istnienia*, 1935; *Niemyte dusze:*

Studia obyczajowe i społeczne, 1975; *Witkacy, malarz*, 1985 (*Witkacy, the Painter*, 1987); *Przeciw nicości: fotografie Stanisława Ignacego Witkiewicza*, 1986.

BIBLIOGRAPHY

Brandes, Philip. "A Wild Blend of Wit and the Macabre Fills *Madman and the Nun*." Review of *The Madman and the Nun*, by Stanisław Ignacy Witkiewicz. *Los Angeles Times*, April 2, 1999, p. 26. This review of a 1999 performance of *The Madman and the Nun* by the Buffalo Nights Theatre Company in Santa Monica, California, sheds some light on this absurdist play.

Esslin, Martin. *The Theatre of the Absurd*. 3d ed. New York: Penguin Books, 1991. The latest edition of a classic work on the Theater of the Absurd. Includes references to Witkiewicz. Bibliography and index.

Gerould, Daniel, ed. *Witkacy: Stanisław Ignacy Witkiewicz as an Imaginative Writer*. Seattle: University of Washington Press, 1981. Translator Gerould provides a biography of Witkiewicz that examines both his life and his writings. Bibliography and index.

Kiebuzinska, Christine Olga. *Revolutionaries in the Theater: Meyerhold, Brecht, and Witkiewicz*. Theater and Dramatic Studies 49. Ann Arbor, Mich.: UMI Research Press, 1988. A study of experimental theater, particularly the works of Witkiewicz, Bertolt Brecht, and V. E. Meierkhold. Bibliography and index.

Witkiewicz, Stanisław Ignacy. *Witkacy, Metaphysical Portraits: Photographs by Stanisław Ignacy Witkiewicz*. Leipzig" Connewitzer Verlag, 1997. This bilingual book contains essays along with selected photographs by Witkiewicz from an exhibition held in 1997 and 1998. The essays provide insight into his philosophy. Bibliography.

Victor Anthony Rudowski

FRIEDRICH WOLF

Born: Neuwied, Germany; December 23, 1888
Died: Lehnitz, East Germany; October 5, 1953

PRINCIPAL DRAMA
Mohammed, wr. 1917, pb. 1922, revised pb. 1960
Der Unbedingte, pb. 1919, pr. 1921
Das bist du, pr., pb. 1919
Der Löwe Gottes, pb. 1921
Die schwarze Sonne, pb. 1921, pr. 1924
Tamar, pr. 1922, pb. 1960
Die Schrankkomödie, wr. 1922, pb. 1955
Der arme Konrad, pr., pb. 1924
Kolonne Hund, pr., pb. 1927
Koritke: Oder, Die Zeche zahlt Koritke, pr., pb. 1927
Cyankali, Paragraph 218, pr., pb. 1929
Die Matrosen von Cattaro, pr., pb. 1930 (*The Sailors of Cattaro*, 1935)
Tai Yang erwacht, pr. 1931, pb. 1947
Die Jungens von Mons, pr. 1931, pb. 1952
Professor Mamlock, pr. 1934, pb. 1935 (English translation, 1935)
Florisdorf, pb. 1935, pr. 1936 (*Florisdorf: The Vienna Workers in Revolt*, 1935)
Laurencia: Oder, Die Schafsquelle, pr. 1937, pb. 1947 (adaptation of Lope de Vega Carpio's play *Fuenteovejuna*)
Das Trojanische Pferd, pr., pb. 1937
Peter kehrt heim: Oder, Bajonette, pr. in Russian 1937, pb. in German 1938
Das Schiff auf der Donau, wr. 1938, pr., pb. 1955
Beaumarchais: Oder, Die Geburt des Figaro, pb. 1941, pr. 1946
Patrioten, pb. 1943, pr. 1946
Doktor Wanner, pr., pb. 1944
Was der Mensch säet . . . , pb. 1945, pr. 1955

Die letzte Probe, pr. 1946, pb. 1947
Wie Tiere des Waldes, pr. 1948, pb. 1952
Bürgermeister Anna, pr. 1950, pb. 1952
*Thomas Münzer: Der Mann mit der
  Regenbogenfahne*, pr., pb. 1953

OTHER LITERARY FORMS

Friedrich Wolf is best known as a playwright and film writer, but he produced a considerable amount of long and short fiction, poetry, and nonfiction as well.

ACHIEVEMENTS

Friedrich Wolf was a remarkably prolific writer. After initial attempts in expressionism, he achieved extraordinary success and fame as a socialist playwright, an effective anti-Nazi agitprop writer, and an author of film exposés. Together with Bertolt Brecht, Wolf belongs to the pioneers of new directions in the development of dramatic art and stagecraft. When, between 1960 and 1968, Else Wolf and Walther Pollatschek prepared the collected works of the author, the large body of his literary corpus, much of which had been previously published in various forms, resulted in sixteen volumes of about four hundred pages each.

Many of Wolf's plays were translated into a number of foreign languages and performed in theaters in many countries, particularly in the Soviet Union. In the 1970's, his dramas remained in the repertoire of theaters in the German Democratic Republic, especially in Leipzig, Weimar, and Dresden. Works such as the anti-Fascist drama *Professor Mamlock* or the provocative tragedy *Cyankali, Paragraph 218* (cyanide, the abortion law) are still significant in the modern world.

BIOGRAPHY

Friedrich Wolf was born on December 23, 1888, in Neuwied on the Rhine, the son of a Jewish merchant. After completing elementary school, he continued his education in 1899 at the Königliche Gymnasium, a preparatory school in Neuwied. His lasting interests included the outdoors, sports, and later the youth movement Wandervogel. In 1903, he ran away from home, traveling to Holland as a cabin boy on

board a barge on the Rhine. His family succeeded, however, in persuading him to complete his high school education. Wolf was graduated in 1907, then briefly served in the military in Heidelberg. He then began to study painting in Munich but changed majors and continued to study philosophy and medicine at the universities of Tübingen, Bonn, and Berlin. His main interests were psychiatry, methods of natural healing, and public health policies. In 1912, Wolf completed his preliminary examinations and then wrote his dissertation on multiple sclerosis in children. He then spent a year practicing medicine in Meissen and in Jena. In 1913, he obtained his state license to practice medicine and became an assistant physician, at first at a hospital in Dresden, then in Bonn. In 1914, he became a naval doctor on an ocean liner with the Canada line of the *Norddeutscher Lloyd*. His earliest drama dates back to this time.

When World War I broke out, Wolf was drafted as a battalion medical officer on the western and eastern fronts. Having experienced the brutality of war and a number of personal hardships, he became a pacifist, although he was obligated to continue his service as a medical officer. In 1917, while trapped in the fierce combat in the trenches in Flanders, Wolf began to write his first significant dramatic work. In 1918, he became chief physician at a military hospital near Dresden; at this time, he joined the revolutionary workers' movement. During the November revolution in Germany that helped to bring World War I to an end, Wolf was a member of the Central Workers and Soldiers Council in Saxony. He also became a member of the Independent Socialist Party of Germany (USPD) and of the Socialist Group of Intellectual Workers in Dresden. In 1919, one of Wolf's plays was first produced on the stage.

In 1920, Wolf accepted the position of municipal medical official in Remscheid. His duties included—besides matters of public health and medical family practice—social work and family counseling and brought him into closer contact with the working class and the revolutionary labor leaders. When the reactionary "Kapp" uprising broke out, Wolf again became active in the workers' movement. In 1921, he joined the communal estate Barkenhoff, which was owned by the well-known artist and socialist Heinrich Vogeler and was located in Worpswede near Bremen; Vogeler had opened his estate to jobless workers and their families for communal settling and experimental living. Wolf served there as a physician and peat cutter. A more conventional situation was needed, however, for the care of his wife, daughter, and son, so he opened a private medical practice in the small Swabian town of Hechingen. Soon, however, his first marriage was dissolved by mutual agreement, and he married Else Dreibholz of Hechingen. Two sons resulted from this second marriage, Markus and Konrad; the latter was to become as famous as his father. A renowned filmmaker, Konrad Wolf served for many years as the president of the Academy of Arts of the German Democratic Republic; he died in 1982.

The medical practice did not keep Friedrich Wolf from his political activism. He had already been studying Marxism, Leninism, and the political goals of the Communist Party for a number of years. In 1926, he moved to Höllsteig, near Lake Constance, where he concentrated his efforts on completing a major medical work, *Die Natur als Arzt und Helfer* (1935; nature, your physician and helper), a sort of family medical guide. In 1925, he moved to Stuttgart, dedicating his medical practice to homeopathy and progressive methods of natural healing, a trend followed by a number of German physicians of that time.

The year 1928 marked a turning point in Wolf's life. He officially joined the Communist Party, became a member of the Arbeiter Theaterbund (workers' theater association), the Bund Proletarisch-Revolutionärer Schriftsteller (association of proletarian revolutionary writers), and the Arbeiter-Radio-Bund (workers' radio association). He was also a founding member of the Stuttgart Chapter of the Volksfilmverband (people's cinema association). In his famous address *Kunst ist Waffe* (1928; art is weapon), delivered at a convention of the Arbeiter Theaterbund Deutschlands (workers' theater association of Germany), Wolf set forth his ideas on contemporary drama. In 1931, he was questioned on a charge of abortion, but nationwide protests on his behalf prevented his being imprisoned. Wolf became more and

more involved in lecturing in favor of a revision of the abortion laws and similar matters of concern in public health policy. Later in 1931, Wolf visited the Soviet Union. In 1932, he began an association with the Spieltrupp Südwest, a socialist theater group, under the auspices of which he made his most important contributions to the agitprop movement. During this year, he paid his second visit to the Soviet Union, where Wolf attended the fifteenth anniversary celebrations of the October Revolution.

When Adolf Hitler seized power in Germany in 1933, Wolf emigrated to France via Austria and Switzerland. At the end of the year, he traveled once more to the Soviet Union. In 1934, he went to Warsaw in order to assist in the last stages of the production and to be present at the first night of the performance of his successful anti-Fascist drama *Professor Mamlock* in the Yiddish language. In the same year, he was delegated to the first Soviet Writers Congress. In 1935, he accepted an invitation to lecture on a tour through the United States and participated in the first American Writers Congress in New York City. A successful lecture tour through Scandinavia followed in 1936. Wolf traveled to France once more in 1938, planning to join the international Communist brigades in the Spanish Civil War, but he failed to get to Spain. When World War II broke out in 1939, Wolf was taken into custody by the French and detained at the French internment camp Le Vernet, later in two other camps in southern France. In 1941, Wolf was granted Soviet citizenship, for which he had applied earlier, and rescued from French detention by the Soviet authorities. In the Soviet Union, he was first employed in the Soviet anti-Fascist and information services; he later joined the Soviet army and was sent to the front lines, receiving the Red Star in 1943. One of the founders of the national committee of Freies Deutschland (free Germany), an organization of German emigrants, Wolf also participated in other organizational activities on behalf of Germans living in exile. He continued his anti-Fascist information and propaganda work in prisoner-of-war camps in the Soviet Union.

In 1945, after the end of the war, Wolf returned to Germany and settled in Berlin, where he immediately became one of the most prominent cultural leaders in the Soviet occupied zone (after 1949, the German Democratic Republic), working with the media, with various theaters, and with some of the publishing houses. He was the cofounder of the East German film company DEFA and of the newly organized Volksbühnen (Association of German Theater Workshops). During the immediate postwar years, Wolf was one of the most prolific contributors to the critical periodical *Ulenspiegel*, in which he published many satiric pieces. In 1948, he became the president of the Association of German Theater Workshops, chief editor of the important periodical *Volk und Kunst* (the people and art), and cofounder of the German PEN center. He participated in the International Peace Congress in Wroclaw, Poland, and received the honorary title of professor from the Government of Brandenburg. Toward the end of that year, he moved to a new home in Lehnitz near Oranienburg. In 1949, Wolf led the first German writers' delegation to Czechoslovakia; in that same year, after Germany was divided into the German Democratic Republic and the Federal Republic of Germany, Wolf was appointed by the former as ambassador to Poland. He also received the highest honor of the GDR, the Nationalpreis, for his most famous play, *Professor Mamlock*. In 1951, Wolf became a member of the German Academy of Arts, was elected to the executive committee of the German Writers Association, and again won the national prize for his film *Der Rat der Götter* (1950; the council of the gods). In failing health, Wolf asked to be relieved from his ambassadorial post. The Polish government bestowed on him the Polonia Restituta (with star), a medal of high honor. During the same year, Wolf was elected president of the Deutsch-Polnische Gesellschaft für Frieden und Gute Nachbarschaft (German-Polish society for peace and good neighborhood). In October, 1953, Wolf died of a heart attack. A museum and archives were established in his home in Lehnitz.

ANALYSIS

H. G. Wells described the early twentieth century as an "age of confusion." He was thinking of the political and social turmoil of the time, but considering the vast artistic output, the swift succession of aesthetic currents designated by so many "isms," the numerous contradictory theories existing side by side, and the fanaticism with which each movement set out to regenerate humankind, one would be inclined to extend Wells's statement to include literature and the arts. Friedrich Wolf's works, too, encompass some of these "isms." His early writings were strongly influenced by expressionism—in the visual and literary arts, a tendency that strives for the expression of subjective feelings and emotions rather than the objective depiction of reality or nature. When Wolf began his career as a playwright, this movement was at its peak, with plays such as Georg Kaiser's *Von Morgens bis Mitternachts* (pb. 1916, pr. 1917; *From Morn to Midnight*, 1920), Ernst Toller's *Masse-Mensch* (pr. 1920, pb. 1921; *Masses and Man*, 1924), Eugene O'Neill's *The Emperor Jones* (pr. 1920), and others. In a later period, expressionism was marked by the disillusionment of World War I, which prompted a new concern for social truths. In literary expressionism, the characters and scenes are presented in a stylized manner with the intent of producing an emotional shock, sometimes through grotesque humor. Expressionist drama also gave rise to a new approach to staging, scene design, and directing. The objective of prominent contemporary stage directors such as Erwin Piscator, for example, was to create a unified production as perceived by the audience, a legacy of German Romanticism. It is within this framework that Wolf wrote his early plays: *Mohammed* in 1917, *Das bist du* in 1918, *Der Unbedingte* in 1919, *Die schwarze Sonne* in 1920, and *Tamar* in 1921. The author later rejected expressionism and what it represented, and he rewrote some of his earlier plays in an attempt to adapt their structure and message to the principles of socialist realism.

DER LÖWE GOTTES

One of the few books which the army doctor Wolf carried in his backpack during his service in World War I was a German translation of the Qur'an. Amid the agonizing battles in the trenches of Flanders, Wolf wrote a typically expressionistic "scream play," *Der Löwe Gottes* (the lion of God). The work, specified as an "oratorium," consists of a succession of bold images, monologues, and dialogues; its key word is "heart." By means of a messianic figure, the author intended to depict the path of humankind. The play deals with the life of the Prophet Muhammad, the founder of Islam, until his flight from Mecca to Medina. Its focal point is the Prophet's vocation to action. The work has strongly pacifistic overtones, and Leo Tolstoy's "doctrine of nonviolence" forms an important element in the drama. In 1922, the play was published in K. Lorenz's book *Die rote Erde* (red earth), and again in 1924 under the title *Mohammed: Ein Schauspiel* (Muhammad: a play). When Wolf rewrote the play, he tried to concentrate the plot on the social issues in Mecca at the time of Muhammad's life and on the clashes between the ruling classes and the slaves. The new version, however, published in 1960 in the edition of the collected works, lacks the energy and immediacy of the original version, which Wolf had created "with the stroke of a pen." This should come as no surprise. Wolf had tried to adapt the play to the principles of socialist realism, which demand a faithful, concrete representation of historical truth in its revolutionary development—that is, as it should be according to Marxist doctrine—and these requirements are diametrically opposed to the expressionistic aesthetic that informed the original version.

DAS BIST DU

Although the expressionists believed that the decisive change in the life of modern people had to be accomplished by the individual, not by any social program, even in the original version of *Mohammed*, Wolf implicitly alluded to problems of his own time as well. This dimension is more clearly evident in *Das bist du* (that are you), produced in 1919, which was the first of a great number of Wolf's plays to be produced on the stage. The title refers to an ancient Indian saying. The prelude presents several as-yet-unformed "beings" in the process of metempsychosis. In the main action, they return as woman, youth, ax, cross, and bench, while the central characters, the Tolstoy-like figure of Andreas and the symbolic figure of evil, the blacksmith Lukas, have already experienced earthly incarnation. On earth, the "things" and "humans" meet. While the humans remain in a passive state, initially incapable of action, the things

(symbols of the antihuman) demand action: The ax wants to kill and seduce death; the cross, tired of the burden of love, wants to be an instrument of martyrdom again; and the bench wants to be a prop for the sinful deed.

The gardener, Andreas, lives in Utopia, a pure, Christian world of ideals, protected against temptation. Ruled by her desire, his wife, Martha, is a prisoner of her unquenched longing for love. The gardener's helper, Johannes, vacillates between the two of them, and the demoniac, evil nature of Lukas the blacksmith meets with no response from the woman. This state of human existence, devoid of all potential for development, remains eternally the same and is, therefore, sterile. Finally, however, it is transformed by willful action into tragedy: The wife seduces the youth, who in turn allows himself to be seduced. The blacksmith then pushes, tempts, and rouses the jealous husband, Andreas, to the bloody deed. The ax in Andreas's hand presses itself forward, and as Andreas sees his wife and the youth embracing on the bench, he fells the cross with the ax, and the falling cross strikes the youth dead.

In the epilogue, which is set on a glacier on another planet, the "humans" and "things" are transformed back into "beings" who find themselves in the next highest stage of metempsychosis. Now the "being" Andreas willingly chooses the woman, and with her, life. Johannes, who through his death has been purified, liberates the "beings" from the night of eternal sameness, a symbol for the rigid resistance of matter, and flares up into the radiant flame of the will, in which all beings merge and disappear: "We wanted to annihilate ourselves, but have been transformed." Elements of Indian and Christian religious philosophy, Arthur Schopenhauer's *Die Welt als Wille und Vorstellung* (1819; *The World as Will and Idea*, 1883-1886), and Wolf's own, still awkwardly articulated worldview are here compressed into a problematical transformation play. The primitive earthly action comes across much more effectively than the vague framework of reflection, abstract poetry, and thought.

DER ARME KONRAD

Most of Wolf's early plays carry strong autobiographical overtones and suggest ideas stemming from the Wandervogel youth movement. By the early 1920's, however, as the nationalist, conservative forces in Germany were growing more articulate, the left-wing writers felt the need to deal with problems of practical interest; they could no longer find their criteria in abstract aesthetics. Wolf, along with many left-wing writers, began to adopt a style associated with the so-called Neue Sachlichkeit (New Objectivity), frequently using material that was readily accessible in German life, past and present. *Der arme Konrad* (poor Konrad) illustrates this shift in Wolf's approach. A historical drama focusing on an episode from the year 1514 during the German peasants' uprisings, it is accompanied by extensive stage directions; Wolf had supplied his works with such annotations before, but in the case of *Der arme Konrad*, he added an afterward with information on his sources and extensive suggestions for the smaller theaters and drama workshops so popular with the socialists and Communists. A later edition carries a report by the author on former performances, specifically on open-air stages.

KOLONNE HUND

Kolonne Hund (Hund's troop) deals with Wolf's experiences of 1920 in Worpswede, where the artist Heinrich Vogeler had placed some land at the disposal of a group of former servicemen and unemployed workers. It was one of a number of similar veterans' rehabilitation colonies that sprang up all over postwar Germany, where these men and their families endeavored to overcome the economic difficulties bequeathed by the war. Though the government promised its support, the success of this venture depended on a favorable solution of the question of land reform. The play portrays the struggle of the settlers and the refusal of the government to give them the needed support and authority. The remarkable success of this drama in many parts of Germany shows that Wolf was dealing with a problem of wide and burning contemporary interest.

CYANKALI, PARAGRAPH 218

Cyankali, Paragraph 218 has never lost its appeal and significance. Wolf, who was developing his own version of a new theory of drama, especially in his famous speech (later printed as an essay) *Kunst ist Waffe*, wrote a special essay on *Cyankali, Paragraph 218*, which he updated several times. During his lifetime alone, the play was performed two hundred times at the Berlin Lessing-theater. The national radio network produced its own version, Twentieth Century-Fox made a film, and many other theaters in German and foreign cities such as Moscow, Amsterdam, Zurich, Copenhagen, Stockholm, Paris, Madrid, Warsaw, Tokyo, and Shanghai produced performances, some of which provoked a scandal. For example, in Stettin, Catholic youths stormed the stage with beer bottles and clubs, and in Basel, protestors threw tear-gas bombs on the stage and into the audience.

The theme of the controversial work harks back to similar themes from familiar earlier literature, such an Heinrich Leopold Wagner's *Die Kindermörderin* (child murderess), the Gretchen-theme in Johann Wolfgang von Goethe's *Faust: Eine Tragödie* (pb. 1808, pb. 1833; *The Tragedy of Faust*, 1823, 1828), Friedrich Hebbel's *Maria Magdalena* (pb. 1844; *Maria Magdalene*, 1935), Gerhart Hauptmann's *Rose Bernd* (pr., pb. 1903; English translation, 1913), and others. Paragraph 218 of the German Penal Code is the section forbidding a physician to perform an abortion, on pain of imprisonment. To Wolf, this problem appeared as a question directly involving the social realities of a capitalist society, rather than one of abstract morality. He felt that the effect of the regulation was to penalize the poor because those who had the necessary financial resources could always find the means to circumvent the law. It is the tragedy of Hete, the main protagonist in the drama, whose fiancé, Paul, is out on strike, that unable to pay the high fee demanded by doctors who were nevertheless willing to perform the operation, she feels forced to resort to unqualified quackery and dies of the consequences. Poverty and unemployment are the major reasons why she is compelled to prevent her child from being born. Set in the working-class milieu of Berlin and a large industrial conglomerate there, the play exposes the social and economic injustice tolerated by the government and the hypocrisy and corruption hidden, as the author sees it, behind the social respectability of a capitalist society.

THE SAILORS OF CATTARO

The Sailors of Cattaro, depicting in 1930 the events of 1917, was another very popular play. In the style of the New Objectivity, Wolf employed a historical incident—the revolt of sailors on an Austrian battleship in the Bay of Cattaro—to create a rousing piece of socialist agitation. In the text, Wolf incorporated one of Lenin's most telling statements, written on November 6, 1917, amid the Russian Revolution: "Once it starts you must follow it through to the end." The author researched the court-martial records and talked with some of the witnesses who had been in the Bay of Cattaro at the time of the mutiny. The names used in the drama are not fictitious but are the real names of those involved. The record reads: "On February 11, 1918, at 6 A.M. the following ringleaders of the naval revolt are to be shot in Skaljari near Cattaro, according to paragraph 156 of the Austrian Manual of War and the decision of the Court-Martial: Boatswain Mate Franz Rasch, Able Seaman Anton Grabar, Gunner's Mate Maté Jerko Sisgoric, and Gunner's Mate Bernicevic."

What led to this court-martial and the execution of these men? As Wolf sketches the scene, the crew, battle-weary and starving, are handing out the prohibited *Workers' Newspaper* from Vienna, which carries reports about worker unrest on the Continent. The Dalmatians and the Slovakians are suffering bitterly from ethnic discrimination. The revolt is finally triggered by an overzealous lieutenant's punitive drilling and his misappropriations in the officers' mess hall. Led by shipmate Franz Rasch and gunner Jerko Sisgoric, a sailors' council takes over the ship's command and takes the officers prisoner. The entire fleet joins the mutiny and hoists the red flag. After a few days, however, the uprising is undermined by disunity, egotism, intoxication with power, senseless excesses, and fear of court-martial, and it collapses under the fire of coastal regiments. The majority of the men turn over their leaders to receive the death penalty, thus buying their own rehabilitation. The play illuminates the aspirations of the rank and file, the men who must fight the world's wars. It insightfully depicts their officers as well. This antiwar play vividly recaptures the action behind the lines of the Central Powers. As early as 1935, it was translated into English and performed in New York City, where some of the witnesses of the events saw the play and reportedly wept and laughed, calling out, "Yes, that is what happened." East German critics consider this work to be the first significant drama of socialist realism in German literature.

PROFESSOR MAMLOCK

When Hitler seized power in Germany, Wolf emigrated and intensified his anti-Fascist struggle in his writings and stage productions in exile. *Professor Mamlock*, written in Switzerland and France at the beginning of Wolf's years in exile, is perhaps his most enduring work. It deals with the illusions of the Jewish surgeon Mamlock, who tries to remain detached from political life. His convictions, however, are shattered when, in the end, he is destroyed by the very forces that he had tolerated because he thought it no part of his job to bother with them. Under the pressure of events and the influence of his Communist son, who is active in the underground student movement, Mamlock discovers that duty requires him to take part in organized political resistance, but this insight comes too late for him.

The action of the play begins in 1932 and ends in 1933, the year in which Hitler seized power. Professor Mamlock, chief surgeon in a university hospital, a Jew by birth and at the same time a conservative German citizen who loves his country, is a veteran of World War I and votes for the war hero Paul von Hindenburg as president of the Republic. When fire destroys the Reichstag building and the anti-Semitic persecutions by the Nazis begin, Mamlock is told to leave his position as chief surgeon. Abandoned by his colleagues, he faces alone the powerful National Socialist party member and his successor in the clinic, Dr. Hellpach. Mamlock's insistence on a strict separation of professional life from politics provokes conflict in his own family. He naïvely believes the government's reports that the fire was an action of Communist terrorists and disagrees with his son Rolf, who has joined the underground movement of young dissidents. A new regulation permits Mamlock to return once more to his work as a surgeon but not as the department head. The new chief surgeon, Hellpach, pressures the clinic's personnel into opposing Mamlock's stay at the clinic. Finally Mamlock must face the truth. He exhorts his assistant, Dr. Inge Ruoff, who loves Rolf, to join his son in the political struggle. Feeling totally abandoned by both his colleagues and family, Mamlock commits suicide. Despite the tragic fate of the hero, there is some hope for the future in the figure of Dr. Inge Ruoff and her ethical commitment.

The playwright intended to entrust the first performance of this play to the well-known company of actors Truppe 31 under the leadership of Gustav von Wangenheim. The entire group and their director had emigrated to Switzerland, but, as a result of financial difficulties, the group was forced to dissolve. Therefore, Wolf sent the manuscript of *Professor Mamlock* to New York, where a progressive group of actors, the Theatre Union, took an interest in producing it. Again, however, to the deep disappointment of the author, the play was not produced, but another opportunity presented itself. The drama was translated into Yiddish and, in 1934, was performed in Poland at the Warsaw Kaminski Theater, with a prominent émigré, the German-Jewish actor Alexander Granach, in the title role. During the same year, the original German version of *Professor Mamlock* was performed in Zurich. This performance immediately gained international attention and marked the beginning of a very successful history of reception, with productions in many countries throughout the world. The work was first published in the exile press in Zurich and Moscow, and has been translated into a number of languages. It has been filmed twice, the second time in 1960 by Wolf's son Konrad Wolf.

The author reported that he and other refugees from the Hitler regime were often asked how the victory of the Nazis was possible in the country of Goethe and Friedrich Schiller, a highly developed culture, the "land of poets and thinkers." The plot of *Professor Mamlock* and its underlying meaning try to answer such questions, and more: Wolf also attempted to make visible the forces which eventually would be able to "wipe the brown disgrace from the face of the German nation." Three important topics of the 1930's are powerfully presented in *Professor Mamlock*: the

problem of the intellectual's life under an oppressive, authoritarian regime; the problem of the persecution of Jews, and, implicitly, discrimination against any minority group made scapegoat; and the beginning of the intensive anti-Fascist information and propaganda struggle by those exiled from Germany and even by small groups in Germany.

POSTWAR WORKS

In 1945, Wolf returned to a hungry, shivering, physically and mentally shattered, chaotic Germany occupied by foreign military forces. In the immediate postwar years, Wolf was occupied with the reconstruction of his nation, both in his writing and in his many other activities. He was particularly concerned with the condition of young people traumatized and disillusioned by the war, and it was to them that he dedicated the play *Wie Tiere des Waldes* (like animals in the forest). In this drama about the confusion, love, persecution, and death of young people, written right after the end of the war, Wolf already warned of the dangers of new wars. At the same time, he completed a drama that he had begun when he was still in Moscow. *Die letzte Probe* (the last rehearsal), the plot of which begins in Vienna, not only is a tragedy of love, but also was intended to be a tragedy of western emigration as seen by leftist political activists and writers. In *Bürgermeister Anna* (Mayor Anna), a comedy set in a village where the women manage affairs very well while the younger men are out fighting the war, Wolf exposes the nature of male gamesmanship in politics and the working world. The women, who focus their efforts on tasks for the common good, such as building a village school with their own hands and the help of a few cooperative men, gradually learn about those realities of the paternalistic working world. Under the leadership of their capable young mayor, Anna, however, they manage well in the end, when the new order of society is tested by the homecoming soldiers who, in turn, must also learn to adapt to the new ways.

THOMAS MÜNZER

Before his sudden, unexpected death, Wolf completed one more major drama. The theme of *Thomas Münzer: Der Mann mit der Regenbogenfahne* (Thomas Münzer, the man with the rainbow banner) was not new to the author, who for more than thirty years had maintained a keen interest in the history of the German peasant revolts during the sixteenth century. In his first historical drama written in the realistic style, *Der arme Konrad*, he had depicted one of the earliest peasant revolutionaries, and now, after more extensive studies on the subject, he chose as his main protagonist Thomas Münzer, a Thuringian theologian and leader of a group of rebellious peasants. There is, however, an important difference between the treatment of the two heroes in these plays on the German peasants' revolutions. In *Der arme Konrad*, the hero and main protagonist is in fact the people as a collective entity, which Konrad represents, but in *Thomas Münzer*, the complex leader figure is himself the main protagonist of the play. Wolf did not live to be present at the premiere of this, his last work for the stage.

OTHER MAJOR WORKS

LONG FICTION: *Der Sprung durch den Tod*, 1925; *Das Heldenepos des Alten Bundes*, 1925; *Kreatur*, 1925; *Kampf im Kohlenpott*, 1928; *Die Nacht von Béthinville*, 1936; *Zwei an der Grenze*, 1938; *Der Russenpelz*, 1942; *Heimkehr der Söhne*, 1944; *Bitte der Nächste: Dr. Isegrimms Rezeptfolgen*, 1948; *Die Unverlorenen*, 1951 (2 novels); *Menetekel: Oder, Die fliegenden Untertassen*, 1952.

SHORT FICTION: *KZ Vernet*, 1941; *Sieben Kämpfer vor Moskau*, 1942; *Märchen für grosse und kleine Kinder*, 1946; *Tiergeschichten für grosse und kleine Kinder*, 1952.

POETRY: *Fahrt*, 1922; *Lilo Herrmann: Ein biographisches Poem*, 1951; *Ausgewählte Gedichte*, 1954.

SCREENPLAYS: *Cyankali*, 1930; *SOS Eisberg*, 1933; *Professor Mamlock*, 1938 (in Russian); *Bürgermeister Anna*, 1949; *Der Rat der Götter*, 1950; *Thomas Münzer*, 1953.

NONFICTION: *Kunst ist Waffe*, 1928; *Die Natur als Arzt und Helfer*, 1935; *Zeitprobleme des deutschen Theaters*, 1947; *Goethe*, 1949; *Maxim Gorki*, 1953; *Aufsätze über das Theater*, 1957.

MISCELLANEOUS: *Gesammelte Werke*, 1960-1968 (16 volumes).

BIBLIOGRAPHY

Burns, Rob, ed. *German Cultural Studies: An Introduction*. Oxford, England: Oxford University Press, 1995. This general work on German culture in the late nineteenth century and the twentieth century covers Wolf in its discussion of socially critical art. Provides understanding of the world around Wolf.

Fetz, Gerald A. "From *Der arme Konrad* (1923) to *Thomas Münzer* (1953): Friedrich Wolf and the Development of the Socialist History Play in Germany." *German Studies Review* 10 (May, 1987): 255-272. A look at the development of the socialist history play in Germany through the works of Wolf.

Heizer, Donna K. *Jewish-German Identity in the Orientalist Literature of Else Lasker-Schüler, Friedrich Wolf, and Franz Werfel*. Columbia, S.C.: Camden House, 1996. Heizer compares and contrasts the works of Jewish writer Wolf with those of Else Lasker-Schüler and Franz Werfel. Bibliography and index.

Ingeborg H. Solbrig

WILLIAM WYCHERLEY

Born: Clive(?), near Shrewsbury, Shropshire, England; May 28, 1641(?)
Died: London, England; December 31, 1715

PRINCIPAL DRAMA

Love in a Wood: Or, St. James's Park, pr. 1671, pb. 1672

The Gentleman Dancing-Master, pr. 1672, pb. 1673
    (adaptation of Pedro Calderón de la Barca's
    play *El maestro de danzar*)
The Country Wife, pr., pb. 1675
The Plain-Dealer, pr. 1676, pb. 1677
Complete Plays, pb. 1967

Other literary forms

Although William Wycherley's reputation among modern readers rests entirely on his work as a playwright, he wrote poetry as well, most of it in his later years. Twenty-eight years after his last play, he published *Miscellany Poems: As Satyrs, Epistles, Love-Verses, Songs, Sonnets, Etc.* (1704), a collection of unremarkable pieces on a variety of subjects. The volume has lighter verses, songs of wine and women, but to the reader of the plays, there is matter of perhaps greater interest. Certain poems suggest that the dark vision of the later dramas continued to grow in Wycherley until he despaired of any hope for humanity.

Achievements

William Wycherley's dramatic canon consists of only four plays, and his stature in English letters depends almost entirely on a single work, *The Country Wife*. In his own day, *The Plain-Dealer* was his most popular comedy, but more recent criticism has called attention to certain problems with that play that have diminished its reputation. Interestingly, the play's flaws are a result of Wycherley's excessiveness in the very quality that makes his dramatic achievement unique. More than his contemporaries, Wycherley deals bluntly (some critics have said crudely) with the tendency of social conventions to corrupt natural human instincts. More specifically, he posits the need of men and women to come together in relationships of love and mutual respect, and he exposes the ills that result when that need is perverted by marriage for purely material reasons. As the real meaning for marriage, the strongest bond between two individuals, becomes infected and weakened by social concerns, so the more casual relationships between men and women suffer corruption as well. Finally, Wycherley's vision is a world of grotesques, moral cripples, through which a very few good people grope their way in search of honorable relationships.

Biography

It is not certain exactly where and when William Wycherley was born. The year may have been 1640 or 1641 and the place Clive in Shropshire or Basing House in Hampshire. His father, Daniel Wycherley, was serving as teller to the Exchequer at the time of William's birth; later, he served as chief steward to the marquis of Winchester and came under suspicion of embezzlement. In 1655, young Wycherley was sent for education to France, where he became a favorite of Madame de Montausier, who was instrumental in his conversion to Catholicism, although he returned to the Anglican Church in 1660. Wycherley stayed in France for four years, then returned to England and entered Queen's College at Oxford. He took no degree from Oxford and soon entered the Inner Temple. Law, however, was never a genuine interest for him. Court life held far greater appeal, and the ingratiating young man became a favorite of the duchess of Cleve-

William Wycherley (Hulton Archive by Getty Images)

land, King Charles II's mistress. It was to her that he dedicated his first play, *Love in a Wood*, which opened in 1671 at the Theatre Royal in Drury Lane. He wrote only three more plays, and his entire career as a playwright spanned only a relatively few years.

In 1678, as a result of ill health, Wycherley was sent to Montpellier for a rest at the expense of Charles II. When Wycherley returned, the king offered him the position of tutor to his son, the young duke of Richmond. The salary of fifteen hundred pounds a year, in addition to a pension when his services were no longer needed, was unusually generous. Unfortunately, Wycherley lost this fine opportunity and royal favor through a rash marriage. One day in 1679, he happened to meet a young woman in a London bookstore looking for a copy of *The Plain-Dealer*. Wycherley introduced himself to the young woman, who proved to be Countess Laetitia Isabella, daughter of the earl of Radnor and widow of the earl of Drogheda. Shortly after that meeting, they married in secret, but Charles and the duchess of Cleveland soon found out and, furious, banished him from the court.

Wycherley's new wife was ill-tempered and jealous, and her wealth was less than her debts. Their marriage was short-lived and ended with Isabella's death in 1681. Wycherley fell ever deeper into debt and in 1685 was confined to Fleet Prison, but the new king, James II, who believed that Manly, the protagonist of *The Plain-Dealer*, was a representation of himself, arranged for Wycherley's release and partial payment of his debts. The grateful author became a Catholic once more.

Wycherley's later years were rather uneventful. In 1704, he published his *Miscellany Poems* and began a correspondence with Alexander Pope, who was then only sixteen. In 1715, he married young Elizabeth Jackson, the intent apparently being to deny any inheritance to a despised nephew. "Manly" Wycherley, as he was known after his most popular character, died only eleven days after his wedding. He was buried in St. Paul's, Covent Garden.

ANALYSIS

When read in the sequence of their production on the stage, William Wycherley's four plays make an interesting study of a dramatist gaining mastery of his art. The early plays display a number of structural flaws and basic problems with dramatizing a story. Through what could only be deliberate experimentation, the several elements of drama are shaped, weighed, and positioned in a variety of ways until a near-perfect formula is achieved in *The Country Wife*.

LOVE IN A WOOD

The highest plot line of *Love in a Wood*, Wycherley's first play, concerns the adventures and trials of Valentine and Christina, idealized lovers who would seem more at home in a romance than a Restoration comedy of manners. Valentine, who had fled England for France after wounding a man in a duel, has secretly returned and is staying with his friend, Vincent. Ranger, another friend of Vincent, met Christina by chance while investigating the activities of his own mistress, Lydia. Through no fault of her own, Christina has now become the object of Ranger's desire, and this he has hastened to tell Vincent. Valentine concludes that Christina has been untrue, and five acts of the expected misunderstandings and confusions are needed to convince him that his jealousy is unfounded and to unite the pair in matrimony. A second level of the play concerns the adventures of Vincent and Ranger that do not directly involve Valentine. The fop, Dapperwit, also moves on this level, and together these three gallants generate the witty dialogue and bawdy action expected by a Restoration audience. The lowest level is occupied by an array of rogues and whores. Central are the efforts of the procuress, Mrs. Joyner, to match a mistress, a husband, and a particular suitor with the old usurer (Alderman Gripe), his sister, and his daughter, respectively.

Love in a Wood is much more complex than this simplified summary suggests. Minor characters and story lines clutter the action to such an extent that all but the most attentive viewers must, like the characters, find themselves lost in a wood. The play is obviously the work of a new playwright, one who is still learning the craft. Wycherley knew well all the things that might go into a drama. He knew Ben Jonson and the humors, and he understood his age's fondness for wit and was himself at least witty enough to satisfy that appetite. He was aware that ideal, romantic love could always find an audience, and he understood the importance of effective dialogue and could write it forcefully and naturally, if not elegantly. Unity, too, he was certain, was one of the several ingredients that a playwright should add to the pot.

Conscious attention to all of these elements can be seen in this first play, but also apparent is Wycherley's failure to understand that a cook need not empty his entire pantry to prepare one dish. *Love in a Wood* simply tries to do too much. There are too many characters, too many plots. Unity, which should be the natural effect of careful plotting and characterization, is lost in the stew. The rather artificial attempts to build in a kind of unity are obvious. For example, the play begins on the level of the low plot, with Mrs. Joyner being berated by Gripe's sister, Lady Flippant, for not finding her a rich husband. More low characters are added before the action shifts to the level of the wits, as Ranger and Vincent prepare to seek new love in St. James's Park. Ranger encounters Christina, and the audience is introduced to the high plot. In only two acts, Wycherley, in sequence from low to high, introduces his principals and plots, but there the neat if obvious organization ends as the action shifts among characters and levels quickly and too often without clear purpose.

Another and again only partially successful unifying device is the use of certain key characters as links between the three major plot levels. Both Vincent and Ranger serve to tie the world of Valentine and Christina to that of the wits; Ranger is actually the catalyst for the action involving the ideal lovers. Dapperwit exists in a limbo between the wits and the low characters. He does keep company with Vincent and Ranger but is clearly more fop than wit, and unlike them, his existence affects but little the world of Valentine and Christina. Dapperwit is much more at home with Mrs. Joyner and Lady Flippant, and on this level he does help to move the action. Thus, the low is directly linked to the middle and the middle to the high. There is still, however, a quite obvious gap between the high and the low; no single character links the extremes.

Construction and theme cannot be separated, and Wycherley's failure to achieve effective unity of de-

sign is reflected in his ambiguous message. Happy marriage based on ideal love appears possible. Valentine and Christina exist in the real world of Restoration London, and their love survives nicely in that world, but there, too, live Gripe, Flippant, and Dapperwit, and their message must leave the audience quite confused as to what ideal love is really all about.

THE GENTLEMAN DANCING-MASTER

Wycherley's second play, *The Gentleman Dancing-Master*, adapted from Pedro Calderón de la Barca's *El maestro de danzar* (wr. 1651), suggests that he was aware of the problems with *Love in a Wood*, but that he was unsure as to how to resolve them, for *The Gentleman Dancing-Master* is the pendulum at its opposite extreme. While *Love in a Wood* has three major plot levels and a host of minor intrigues and adventures, *The Gentleman Dancing-Master* has only one story to tell, and this it does with a cast of major characters only half the size of that of the first play. Hippolita, the fourteen-year-old daughter of Mr. Formal, is unhappily engaged to Mr. Paris, her cousin and an absurd Gallophile. Mr. Formal, almost as absurd in his devotion to Spanish manners and fashion, would do all in his power to preserve his daughter's virtue, and with the help of his widowed sister, Mrs. Caution, keeps her under careful watch. Hippolita, however, is smarter than the lot of them, and, with the unwitting help of Paris, she manages to conduct an affair with a young gallant, Mr. Gerrard, who at her suggestion poses as a dance instructor. The lovers plan an elopement, but Hippolita's doubts about Gerrard's motive—love or her money—and assorted other diversions postpone the nuptials until the end.

In his first play, Wycherley had aimed at too many targets. *The Gentleman Dancing-Master* aims at only one, a broad, comedic effect assisted by a large dose of farce. Wycherley himself was less than proud of this work as an indicator of his real literary skill, and critics have generally agreed that it has little to admire. First, there is the problem of the genre itself. Farce, while very popular with Restoration audiences, was held in low esteem by scholars. Truth to life was the principal criterion by which a play should be judged; so said most of the great English critics, including John Dryden, the leading dramatist, poet, and critic of the age. Believability is the least concern of a farce, for everything that contributes to a believable effect—fine characterization, realistic dialogue, tight plot development—must yield to the hilarity of the episode. Moreover, as farces go, *The Gentleman Dancing-Master* has been judged by many modern critics as especially uninventive.

To be sure, Wycherley's second play would never be studied as an example of Restoration comedy at its finest. Still, it is not without merit, and a brisk stage rendition reveals strengths that are lost in a reading. For example, the single plot line tends to hold together the broadly comic episodes, achieving a sense of unity that is most often lacking in farce. The play is about Hippolita's efforts to find a suitable husband, and a Hippolita well acted can keep that design always before the audience. Hippolita, certainly one of Wycherley's more interesting characters, is responsible for adding a rather larger dash of satire than is commonly found in farce, not so large a dash as to make the flavor noticeably bitter—after all, she does get her man—but still enough that the reader of Wycherley's later, darker comedies can look back to *The Gentleman Dancing-Master* and notice a hint of what was to come.

In this glimpse of Restoration society, a fourteen-year-old girl only recently returned home from boarding school is complete master of the revels. She rejects her father's choice of a husband, engineers her own courtship, and marries the man she wants, all under her father's roof and her aunt's close guard, and neither is aware of what has happened until the closing lines of the play. It is she who invents the dancing-master fiction and transforms a shallow young man, who is more interested in a dowry than a good marriage, into acceptable husband material. She displays the naïveté and frankness of a child and the insight and cleverness of a mature adult and can move between these extremes in a matter of a few lines. Yet all of this talent and effort is needed to obtain what ideally should be taken for granted: an assurance that the words of the wedding vow will be sincere, that her marriage will be based on mutual love, honesty, and respect. In Wycherley's world, however, such as-

surances are difficult to find. Even a child must be devious to accomplish what is right, when her own father and intended husband are themselves prime examples of misrepresentation.

Mr. Paris, who would be known as Monsieur de Paris, and Mr. Formal, who prefers to be called Don Diego, are as contemptible as they are absurd. Wycherley created the roles for James Nokes and Edward Angel, two of the most famous comic actors of the day. Indeed, Paris's part is the largest in the play, for it was doubtless Nokes as a French fool that the audience came to see. Both Formal and Paris have rejected what they are, Englishmen, to ape foreign manners: It is small wonder that they are so unaware of Hippolita's machinations. They have their own lies to live and would rather argue with each other as to whose lie is better than to see the reality of what is happening. That a fourteen-year-old girl with a sense of purpose can manipulate the adult world says little for that world. That the best husband available is a man so easily directed, a man who must be tested for sincerity before deemed acceptable, adds little reason for optimism, and finally that that fourteen-year-old is herself unsure of the true nature of her young man and is after all only adept at fooling fools must bring small reassurance. *The Gentleman Dancing-Master* is a comedy, a farce, but already the darker shadows have begun to fall.

THE COUNTRY WIFE

With his third effort, Wycherley brilliantly overcame the problems of his first two plays. *The Country Wife* is generally acknowledged as one of the finest comedies of the Restoration, and it is still frequently acted, not so much as a historical curiosity but because it is good theater. The plot is somewhat more complex than that of *The Gentleman Dancing-Master*, but it is tightly unified by linking characters who have real business in the variety of situations; there is none of the baffling confusion of *Love in a Wood*. The main action is moved by Horner—who, as his name suggests, delights in making cuckolds of the London husbands. To that end, he has caused the false rumor of his own impotence to be spread about the town; as expected, husbands who would never let their wives near Horner have foolishly relaxed their guard. Lady Fidget, Mrs. Dainty Fidget, and Mrs. Squeamish are among his willing conquests.

The adventures of Margery Pinchwife, the title character, form a second but closely related plot. Jack Pinchwife married his country wife because he was hopeful that such a woman would be ignorant of the fashions of the city and the promiscuity of the gallants and ladies. This decision, however, was not motivated by a sense of higher morality; indeed, Pinchwife may well be the most immoral character in the play, for, as his name suggests, his every action is directed by his intense fear of being made a cuckold and by a jealousy that can move him to viciousness. Despite her husband, Margery has learned of the way of the world and is anxious to sample it. She realizes that there are better relationships than that which she enjoys with Pinchwife and so cultivates an affair with Horner. The third plot does not relate quite so directly to the main plot, but the characters and action provide some obvious contrasts that serve to clarify and further comment on the play's theme. Alithea, Pinchwife's sister, is engaged to Sparkish. She is an intelligent woman of genuine honor; he is the usual ridiculous fop that so delighted Restoration audiences. Fully aware that her fiancé is a fool, she is resolved to go through with their arranged marriage, though in fact she loves Harcourt, a friend of Horner, and he loves her. At the last, Sparkish's misunderstanding of Alithea's part in the typically confusing episodes and intrigues that follow results in a broken engagement and a clear way to her union with Harcourt.

While Alithea's role is a relatively minor and unimpressive one on the stage, she does make a significant contribution to an understanding of Wycherley's message. Alithea stubbornly insists on behaving honorably in a world where there is no honor. She is obliged by custom and contract to go through with the marriage arranged by Pinchwife and respects that obligation, though the union must result in a life of misery and wasted talent for her and in material gain for men who neither need nor deserve it. In Alithea, the audience sees real virtue turned against itself by corrupt marital customs that not only make cuckolds of fools, which may not be so bad, but also make honorable people victims of their own honor, which is intolerable. Still, at the end, it is only Alithea who appears to have a chance for real happiness. Mrs. Pinchwife's unhappy fate is to return to her husband, while the husbands return to their fool's paradise, as Horner convincingly reaffirms the lie about his impotency.

Before concluding that Wycherley's message is to proclaim the inevitable rewards that come to virtue, one should remember that he had little choice but to inject some measure of happiness at the ending (the play is a comedy), and that Alithea's deliverance from Sparkish has nothing to do with the power of virtue. She is freed from the contract by Sparkish's stupidity and the chance outcome of the intrigues of the other characters. In the world of *The Country Wife*, honor is as impotent as Horner pretends to be, and if anything is temporarily set right, it is only because of luck.

The corruptive power of marriage without love is seen from a different perspective in the title character, Margery Pinchwife. Alithea shows the system's effect on honor; Margery shows its effect on innocence. She enters the world of fashion a complete ingenue, and so Pinchwife would keep her, but all that is said to her and all that she sees writes on the blank slate of her character. Her jealous husband foolishly describes the pleasures of city life, pleasures to be avoided, and thus awakens her interest in them; he takes her to a play dressed as a man, so that she will not draw the attention of other men, which gives her the inspiration to assume a disguise when she visits Horner. Yet it would not be altogether accurate to say that Margery is corrupted, for at the end of the play, her naïve belief that she can exchange Pinchwife for Horner as her husband and live a happily married life ever after shows a character who has really learned nothing of how the system works. She does, indeed, do things that conventional morality would deem wicked, but she is merely aping what she has seen: These are the proper city responses, written on the slate by the characters around her, and against the background of her innocence, their conduct is brought into sharp relief. Hers is rightly the title role, for through her the audience clearly sees the nature of the other characters and the world they have created.

There is no happy ending for Margery. Luck does not smile on her; she has not learned the true cunning of Horner that would allow her to make the best of the situation, and she is not one of the fools who can delude themselves with happy lies. She strikes a note at the end that is not quite comedy.

Mr. Harry Horner has been attacked by three hundred years of critics as one of the most immoral creations of the Restoration stage. In fact, there is no question of moral or immoral conduct in the high society in which he moves. The clearly moral alternative simply does not exist, and heroes are recognizable only by their superior wit and not at all by their deeds. Thus, though Horner does invent an obscene lie to help him bed other men's wives, his contempt for his victims manages to make him something more than simply another rake. He has honor of a sort, but certainly not Alithea's passive honor, not the honor of the martyr. Horner's honor allows him to use the weapons of the system against itself, and to him is the victory, for, with his lie still intact, he leaves the field strewn with cuckolds. That lie, however, is more than a tool for undoing fools; it is Wycherley's comment on the society. As the action moves the audience among various couples, it becomes increasingly clear that marriage has nothing to do with love or basic nature. It has become a thing arranged on paper and bought with money. Horner's impotence is a fiction. Ironically, the real sterility exists in the marriages of his victims.

THE PLAIN-DEALER

Wycherley's final and longest play, *The Plain-Dealer*, confirms what was apparent in *The Country Wife*: The author had learned well the lessons of plot construction and structural unity. It poses other problems of characterization, however, that make it less a masterpiece than his third effort. The story is simple. There are only two plots, and all the principal characters occupy the same social level and have occasion to interact, thus creating a sense of unity. Captain Manly, the title character, is described by the author as honest, surly, and good-humored. He believes firmly in plain dealing, and the shortage of others who share that belief has led him to misanthropy. After losing his ship in the Dutch wars, Manly has returned to London to seek another vessel. He soon discovers that his mistress, Olivia, thought to be a plain dealer like him, has married another man and appropriated the money Manly had left in her care. Torn between contempt and affection, Manly sends his young aide, Fidelia, to arrange a meeting with Olivia. Instead, Olivia develops a passion for Fidelia, who in fact is a wealthy young heiress disguised as a boy to be near Manly, whom she loves. Manly next discovers that Olivia's secret husband is Vernish, the only man he really trusted. At Olivia's home, Manly fights Vernish, takes back the money, and discovers that Fidelia, who lost her wig in the commotion, is really a young woman. He immediately decides that Fidelia is a more proper object for his affection, and together the couple plan their future in the West Indies.

In the second plot, Lieutenant Freeman, a young friend of Manly, attempts to marry the cantankerous old Widow Blackacre for her fortune. The widow, whose only delight is in controlling her own business and suing people, wants no part of such an arrangement. When Freeman convinces the widow's stupid son to accept him as his guardian with full power over his inheritance, Widow Blackacre retaliates by claiming that her son is a bastard and not a legal heir. Freeman, however, discovers this to be a lie, and in order to avoid a charge of perjury, the widow is forced to grant him a handsome annuity.

Captain Manly is perhaps the most puzzling character in Restoration drama, and the difficulty of the audience in interpreting him obscures the theme of the play. Like that other famous voyager, Lemuel Gulliver, Manly suffers from misanthropy, and the distorted judgment to which it leads him makes it difficult to judge how representative a spokesperson for the author he is intended to be. Certainly he has qualities to be admired. In relation to the collection of liars and frauds that surrounds him, his utter contempt is justified and his bluntness is refreshing. Still, he recognizes neither hypocrisy nor plain dealing when he sees them, and at times he is as willing to overlook or condone deliberate deception as he is at other times anxious to condemn it. Moreover, he is, like Horner, quite willing to practice a little deception of his own if it suits his purpose. Indeed, if Manly were not wrong and self-contradictory most of the time, there would be no play, for his mistakes move the plot. His greatest mistake is his choice of Olivia. She mouths the same philosophy of plain dealing as Manly but marries and steals in secret. Fidelia is the cause of another mistake; the plain dealer wanders through five acts unaware that his aide, the person with whom he plots revenge against Olivia, is a woman, and when her gender is discovered, he transfers his affection with embarrassing rapidity. Throughout those five acts, he has remained blind to the fact that Fidelia displays a faithfulness and devotion rare in a human being, and when he decides at last to love her, he is equally unconcerned that her disguise, while for a good purpose, was hardly consistent with plain dealing.

There is also the problem of Freeman. The lieutenant is really Manly's best friend, for Vernish turns out to be a villain. In fact, Freeman is the only character who deals plainly with Manly. He quite frankly tells his captain that truth is a handicap in the social world and honestly confesses his motives in the wooing of Widow Blackacre. Manly cannot tolerate the company of most dissemblers and hypocrites, but Freeman is an exception; apparently, honest hypocrites are acceptable.

Despite Manly's several mistakes and inconsistencies, he is still clearly the hero of the play, and Wycherley certainly intended the general audience response to be positive. After all, Manly does have the love of a good woman, who seems willing to suffer almost any humiliation for his sake, and he does have the sincere friendship of Freeman, something of a rogue, to be sure, but a likable rogue. The problems with Manly's philosophy of plain dealing are more apparent in a careful reading than they are in a lively performance, and his confusing behavior is in part a result of his being made to interact with Freeman and Fidelia, who have characterization problems of their own. Fidelia in almost any other play would present no difficulty. She is an idealized female who would be quite at home in a romance, but she seems strangely out of place in a world that requires a misanthrope for a hero. Moreover, her male disguise, which jars with Manly's love of plain dealing, is a conventional comedic device that would present no problem on another stage. Freeman, too, is a conventional figure, but confidant to Manly is not a proper job for a lovable rogue, and while Freeman would make an ideal friend for Horner, his role in *The Plain-Dealer* confuses the message.

Wycherley's final play, then, cannot be judged his best. It may well be, however, his darkest comment on society. Manly is certainly the closest thing to direct spokesperson that Wycherley ever created, and in *The Plain-Dealer* that spokesperson was finally allowed to comment openly on the world of knaves and fools and hypocrites and whores that had been presented with increasing pessimism in the three earlier plays. The problems with Manly may well be the inevitable culmination of Wycherley's vision: Society corrupts honor and innocence and infects with confusion even the best efforts of the best people. There is no firm ground on which a plain dealer can stand.

OTHER MAJOR WORK

POETRY: *Miscellany Poems: As Satyrs, Epistles, Love-Verses, Songs, Sonnets, Etc.*, 1704.

BIBLIOGRAPHY

Markley, Robert. *Two Edg'd Weapons: Style and Dialogue in the Comedies of Etherege, Wycherley, and Congreve.* New York: Oxford University Press, 1988. This study is concerned with the comic style and language of Sir George Etherege, Wycherley, and William Congreve as the rewriting or adaptation of systems of theatrical signification in predecessors, as the reflection of particular cultural codes of speech and behavior that would be accessible to their audience, and as a comment on the culture of which they and their audience were a part. Bibliography.

Marshall, W. Gerald. *A Great Stage of Fools: Theatricality and Madness in the Plays of William Wycherley.* New York: AMS Press, 1993. Marshall examines the concept of mental illness as it appears in the works of Wycherley. Bibliography and index.

Thompson, James. *Language in Wycherley's Plays: Seventeenth Century Language Theory and Drama.*

Tuscaloosa: University of Alabama Press, 1984. Thompson discusses how Wycherley used language in his dramas and relates his usage to the broader context. Bibliography and index.

Vance, John A. *William Wycherley and the Comedy of Fear*. Newark, N.J.: University of Delaware Press, 2000. An analysis of Wycherley and his works with the focus on his treatment of fear. Bibliography and index.

Young, Douglas M. *The Feminist Voices in Restoration Comedy: The Virtuous Women in the Play-Worlds of Etherege, Wycherley, and Congreve*. Lanham, Md.: University Press of America, 1997. A study of feminism and women in the works of Wycherley, George Etherege, and William Congreve. Bibliography and index.

William J. Heim,
updated by Genevieve Slomski

STANISŁAW WYSPIAŃSKI

Born: Krakow, Poland; January 15, 1869
Died: Krakow, Poland; November 28, 1907

PRINCIPAL DRAMA

Daniel, wr. 1893, pb. 1908, pr. 1927
Królowa polskiej korony, wr. 1893, pb. 1908, pr. 1919
Legenda, pb. 1898
Warszawianka, pr., pb. 1898
Lelewel, pr., pb. 1899
Meleager, pb. 1899, pr. 1908 (English translation, 1933)
Protesilas i Laodamia, pb. 1899, pr. 1903 (*Protesilaus and Laodamia*, 1933)
Klątwa, pb. 1899, pr. 1909
Legion, pb. 1900, pr. 1911
Wesele, pr., pb. 1901 (*The Wedding*, 1933)
Bolesław Śmiały, pr., pb. 1903
Wyzwolenie, pr., pb. 1903
Akropolis, pb. 1904, pr. 1916
Legenda II, pb. 1904, pr. 1905 (revision of *Legenda*)
Noc listopadowa, pb. 1904, pr. 1908
Powrót Odysa, pb. 1907, pr. 1917 (*The Return of Odysseus*, 1966)
Sędziowie, pr., pb. 1907
Skałka, pb. 1907, pr. 1958
Achilleis, pb. 1908, pr. 1925
Dzieła zebrane, pb. 1958-1971 (16 volumes)

OTHER LITERARY FORMS

Collaborating with Stanisław Przybyszewski on the periodical *Życie* (life), Stanisław Wyspiański contributed plays and essays in addition to serving as the magazine's art director. He began his career with paintings and pastels and was active as an interior designer, often designing sets for his own productions. Among his many architectural plans are a cycle of drawings of monuments, a project for a Polish acropolis, and an amphitheater. He also helped to renovate and rebuild the cathedral of the Wawel Castle in Krakow, designing stained glass and tapestries, some of which were unfinished at his death. Wyspiański translated and adapted the plays of others, including Pierre Corneille, Adam Mickiewicz, and William Shakespeare. He also wrote a few lyric poems called "rhapsodies," the majority of which reflect his love for Krakow, as well as his infatuation with Poland's past; some poems also served as studies that he later developed into dramas.

ACHIEVEMENTS

Wyspiański is regarded as the father of modern Polish drama. To appreciate his pioneering role, it is necessary to understand the state of Polish drama before he came on the scene. Throughout the nineteenth century, the Polish people had been subjected to the repressive policies of Prussia, Russia, and Austria, the three nations that partitioned Poland in the

1790's. The urban centers of Poland were not as developed as those of Western Europe, because many of the Polish gentry, who would normally be significant stimulus for cultural development, lived on isolated estates rather than in cities. It was thus difficult for Polish writers to maintain close contact with the theater, which thrived only in the larger cities and did not serve as an important literary vehicle before the turn of the twentieth century.

During the 1890's, the literary scene in Poland was undergoing a radical change. The positivist movement was no longer in vogue among young artists; the literary revolution that resulted in the acceptance of the Symbolists, decadents, impressionists, and other modernist groups was spreading rapidly from the West to the East. The intellectuals of Poland could no longer accept the theory that industrialization and scientific advancement would better the future of humankind. They believed that there must be something more to humanity, something more to the human soul that could not be grasped simply by the observation of natural phenomena. The modernist movement in Poland, known as Young Poland (Młoda Polska), turned to the mystical ideas of Polish Romanticism. Pessimism and fear were predominant characteristics of Polish modernism and of the *fin de siècle*. Young Poland believed that all arts should be unified in a "new" art: By intermingling characteristics and techniques belonging to the various art forms, an artist could produce new art forms with "colors" in music, "music" in literature, and "stories" in painting. The multitalented Wyspiański was uniquely qualified to help bring about this proposed unification of the art forms.

Wyspiański wrote his dramas in the style of Polish lyric poetry, a style that lent an operatic quality to his works. Concerned with the overall atmosphere generated by his works and the impression that would be left with the audience, the playwright concentrated on every aspect of his dramatic production. The Krakow Theater was quite prepared for the reforms Wyspiański was to introduce. Director Tadeusz Pawlikowski, in an attempt to create a sense of responsibility among the actors, taught that every single role, even the most minute, was of great importance to the staging of the play as a whole. No longer were fragmented individual roles the focal point of a play; the entire production was of artistic concern. In his dramas, Wyspiański explored specific moral, philosophical, or national problems. Because his goal was to create a "monumental theater," he did not present a piece-by-piece psychological analysis of certain characters and did not attempt objectively to represent historical incidents and persons.

Although Wyspiański was one of the key representatives of Young Poland, he did not cling to the program of Polish modernism, according to which "true" art ought not to deliver a political message. In his works, Wyspiański often examined political and historical questions concerning the tragic fate of Poland, emphasizing his own belief in the necessity of a strong Polish state. These nationalistic ideas inspired a number of Poles, reawakening the dream of the Romantics—to restore Poland to its proper place as a unified state in the history of Europe.

BIOGRAPHY

On January 15, 1869, Stanisław Mateusz Ignacy Wyspiański was born in Krakow, the old capital of Poland. His father, Franciszek, was a sculptor whose workshop was at the foot of Wawel Castle. There, as a young boy, Wyspiański had his first exposure to art and to the past of Poland, which could be said to be housed on the hill in Wawel Castle. It is quite clear from one of Wyspiański's poems, in which he recalls his father's atelier, that his visits to his father's shop left a lasting impression on him. His mother, Maria (neé Rogowska), was from an old Krakow family that strongly supported independence for Poland. She began teaching her son about the past greatness of his country and planted the seeds of Polish nationalism in him at an early age. She died when Wyspiański was only six years old, and his education continued in the household of his aunt, Joanna Stankiewiczowa.

Wyspiański attended Saint Anne's gymnasium from 1879 to 1887. From 1887 to 1890 he was under the guidance of Jan Matejko at the Academy of Fine Arts in Krakow while studying philosophy at the Jagiellonian University. Between the years of 1889 and 1890, he worked on the decoration of the

Mariacki church as an assistant to Jan Matejko. Matejko taught Wyspiański to be observant and to capture even the minutest details in the representation of a certain event. In Wyspiański's masterpiece, *The Wedding*, characters such as Stanczyk, Wernyhora, and Hetman were taken directly from the canvases of Matejko's monumental works.

Having completed this early phase of his studies, Wyspiański embarked on a journey that led him to many of the cultural centers of Europe. He visited Prague, and cities in Italy, Switzerland, Germany, and France. It was a golden opportunity, for Wyspiański's museum visits later served as the inspiration for his dramatic productions. While in Dresden and Munich, Wyspiański became acquainted with the works of Richard Wagner, whom he fervently admired and whose artistic style greatly influenced him.

Wyspiański spent almost three years in Paris at a time when Polish artists were not very familiar with European modernism. There he was introduced to new trends in paintings and drama; he attended avant-garde and naturalistic plays as well as productions of Shakespearean and classical Greek theater, and he became very interested in contemporary playwrights such as Maurice Maeterlinck, Gerhart Hauptmann, Henrik Ibsen, and August Strindberg. Contact with the already well-developed and strongly rooted modernist movement widened the young Wyspiański's perspectives and artistic goals. He rapidly evolved as a painter, writer, dramatist, and stage designer. It was in Paris, during the years from 1891 to 1893 that he wrote his first two plays, *Królowa polskiej korony* (the queen of the Polish crown) and *Daniel*.

When he returned to Krakow, Wyspiański was not yet convinced that his specific medium should be the theater, and he devoted most of his energies to his paintings and decorative work. In 1898, he was appointed as the art director of *Życie*, a magazine under the editorship of Przybyszewski, who was instrumental in forwarding the Young Poland movement. *Legenda* and *Warszawianka* were published in 1898, marking Wyspiański's literary debut. Wyspiański's most successful drama, *The Wedding*, premiered in Krakow on March 16, 1901. Suffering from syphilis, and aware that there was little or no hope of curing

the disease, he wrote his dramas hastily, often not refining them artistically. His literary career was short-lived, lasting only ten years. He died at the age of thirty-eight, on November 28, 1907, in Krakow.

ANALYSIS

Stanisław Wyspiański was not in total agreement with his fellow representatives of Young Poland, who believed that art should not contain a political message. He was convinced that the nationalistic and ideological functions of art were as important as their aesthetic functions. In his works, he presented personal views on Poland's political situation. According to the critic J. Z. Jakubowski, Wyspiański was convinced that contemporary Polish society was intellectually backward, totally unaware of contemporary art, and content with the country's political situation. Wyspiański believed that this backward, unaware condition caused the unfortunate political situation in which the Polish people found themselves. In an attempt to liberate the dreams of the Poles, Wyspiański satirized his own era in his dramas. He expounded a "monumental drama" that would contain an elemental moral evaluation of life and human actions. Influenced by the Greek theater, Wyspiański created key scenes designed to frighten the audience and arouse empathy. Using rhythm, music, and lighting effects, he was able to create a type of mass hypnosis in the audience. By creating such an atmosphere within the theater, he was able to place his viewer in a world on the border between realism and symbolism. In this manner, Wyspiański's theater became both the past and the present.

Wyspiański's dramas fit into distinct groups according to their thematic content. These classifications include dramas written in the classical Greek style (*The Return of Odysseus*, *Achilleis*), Krakow tradition tragedies (*Legenda*, *Bolesław Śmiały*), dramas based on Polish insurrections (*Noc listopadowa*, *Warszawianka*), and two satiric plays (*The Wedding*, *Wyzwolenie*).

In his dramas there is often a unification of two conflicting philosophical thoughts. Of interest in this respect is the dual-planed construction of several of Wyspiański's dramas. The technique that Wyspiański uses to "divide" the action into different planes has been called "live rocks" (*żywe kamienie*) or "live paintings" (*żywe obrazy*) by many critics. Monuments, historical figures, and characters from paintings come to life and add to the action of Wyspiański's dramas.

AKROPOLIS

Akropolis, a four-act play written in 1904, serves as a good example of Wyspiański's "living rock" technique. The action of the drama takes place after midnight on the eve of Easter Sunday. It is set among the monuments and other reminders of Poland's past in Wawel cathedral. On the main altar, the silver angels who hold the casket of Saint Stanislaw begin to move and speak to one another. They leave the casket behind and wander through the cathedral, bringing other statues to life, urging the monuments to live, to love, and even to forget their past. The culmination of act 1, and Wyspiański's message, is contained in the monologue of Clio, the muse of history, who exclaims that the souls of those buried at Wawel will return to earth after many years, after the cathedral is destroyed. Act 1 consists of a resounding cry of life over death: The statues are brought to life only after they forget the past.

As the play progresses, it becomes more and more fantastic. In this parable of death and resurrection, not only do statues move about and speak, but also figures from the past step down from old tapestries and begin to engage in discourse. Mythological deities, Greek heroes, and Polish historical figures come to life and communicate with one another. Act 2 thrusts the reader into the world of Homer's *Iliad* (c. 750 B.C.E.; English translation, 1611), and act 3, into the biblical story of Jacob.

Act 2 features scenes of courtship between Helen and Paris, as Hector prepares for battle. Wyspiański presents these two episodes in a paradoxical manner in order to emphasize the primary theme of the play: the victory of life over death. In *Akropolis*, the trite, almost silly actions of lovers Helen and Paris are seen as morally equivalent to the heroic deed of Hector, who loses his life in patriotic battle. Life and its pleasures are contrasted favorably with heroism and death; Wyspiański suggests that Hector's heroic

action ultimately had no effect on humankind's destiny.

The rivalry, in act 3, between the brothers Jacob and Esau again promotes the play's main theme. The biblical story of Jacob as presented in *Akropolis* tends to justify criminal actions in human beings' quest for power as long as life is lived to the fullest, echoing Friedrich Nietzsche's idea of the Superman, who is above judgment.

The action of *Akropolis* culminates in act 4 with the destruction of the cathedral and the triumphant entry of Christ, events on which the cult of life depends. Wyspiański was in apparent agreement with the anarchists of the nineteenth century, who believed that in order to build something new, one must destroy all of the old. Wyspiański believed that the Polish people were obsessed with their heroic past, and that this obsession led to an inability to act as a nation. The destruction of the cathedral is the destruction of a myth that prevented Poles from acting with resolve.

Akropolis was a bold experiment in which Wawel cathedral symbolizes the temple that houses the soul of humankind and from which it is freed at the end. By introducing different historical planes depicting moments of humanity's greatness and weakness at the same time, Wyspiański enables the reader to identify with the different symbols. He did not intend the transitions between the three different planes in *Akropolis* to be very smooth; the reader receives only a glimpse of the past, which is then destroyed.

THE WEDDING

In *The Wedding*, considered Wyspiański's masterpiece, the playwright chose to explore several contemporary issues that plagued his generation. For this work, which has been called one of the most distinguished and original works of Polish dramatic poetry, Wyspiański exploited the extreme populist ideas that then dominated the intellectual scene. The peasant, glorified by the intelligentsia, was considered to be the salvation of Poland, the backbone of the nation, and an integral part of any movement that would restore the country's autonomy. Wyspiański, as did several of his contemporaries, married a peasant girl in an attempt to ally himself with the class that would ultimately be his country's salvation. *The Wedding* is based on an actual event—the marriage of a fellow artist, Luejan Rydel, to a beautiful peasant girl in a village near Krakow. On a November evening in this village, guests from the intelligentsia meet with peasants who gather together to celebrate a wedding.

The setting is a room of the celebration house in which all the other guests are dancing and enjoying themselves. Here, several conversations between various guests take place. The dialogues are usually between two people, a characteristic of the *szopka*, traditional puppet theater staged in Krakow. The differences between the two social groups attending the wedding and the political atmosphere of the times are made apparent in the course of these conversations. Although the Polish gentry, especially those of the artistic community, have proclaimed that the peasant is essential to the development of a new Poland, they are not prepared to grant the peasant all those rights normally associated with freedom and a free country. The Editor, head of a conservative newspaper, in his conversation with Czepiec, a peasant, voices his opinion that the peasant has no need for any knowledge of the world outside his village. Throughout the evening, events follow a similar trend. Members of the gentry engage in conversation with members of the peasantry, and the differences between the two classes become more obvious. Even the Groom and the Bride do not communicate well. The Bride, after listening to the Groom's poetic confession of how much he loves her, can only exclaim that her shoes are uncomfortable. In these opening scenes, Wyspiański expresses the view that the unity of the two classes, so anxiously sought after in Poland at the turn of the century, was not a goal that could be soon realized. Wyspiański also informs the viewer through Czepiec's words that the peasants are ready to fight for Poland, as soon as their services are requested. The dialogues in act 1 quite clearly reflect that the peasants do not possess the knowledge necessary to interact fully with the upper class, but the peasants' desire for action and a free Poland make them more compatible with the gentry than the gentry might believe.

The realistic nature of act 1 begins to change with the entrance of Rachel, a young Jewish girl who claims to be *moderne*. The dialogues among the guests become more poetic, and the celebration in the house becomes more passionate. Near the close of the first act, Rachel entertains the idea of inviting to the wedding the symbolic Mulch (*Chochoł*, a rose bush wrapped in straw for the winter). The Poet, Bride, and Groom take up this idea and invite the Mulch and any one else the Mulch wishes to bring to the wedding.

The Wedding provides another example of Wyspiański's division of the action into different planes via "live paintings." The characters who visit the wedding seem to come from the painting that hangs above the Host's desk—a painting depicting a peasant uprising with Wernyhora, a semilegendary bard. Again, these characters are not human characters but inanimate objects that speak out for the Polish cause. Act 2 is effective because Wyspiański skillfully leads the characters of the play, the viewers, and the readers into this symbolic world. The atmosphere created by Wyspiański is of great importance to this smooth transition. Short flashes of action and dialogue against the background of a loud wedding create a hypnotic effect. The rhythm of the dialogue adds to the overall musical or operatic quality of the play. Colors on the stage change quite rapidly because the costumes of the nobles and the peasants contrast as much as the dialects in which the characters speak. The movement of the dialogues, the actors, and the scenes increases in intensity at the close of act 1 and provides the momentum leading into the wonderful fantasy of act 2.

The Mulch announces that there will be an abundance of guests at the celebration. Soon, the spirits of the past begin arriving, and they engage in conversation with one guest at a time. To the Poet appears the knight Zawisza Czarny, who fought the Prussians in the Battle of Grunwald. The Groom sees the ghost of Hetman, who earlier betrayed Poland's cause to Moscow. An old man at the wedding sees the spirit of Szela, who served the Austrian monarchy by exterminating the Polish nobility. Stanczyk, a court jester in 1540, appears to the Editor. Stanczyk is a very negative spirit, a voice of the unproductive past, and a reflection of the Editor himself. The Editor, like Stanczyk, is very pessimistic. He sees no future, choosing instead to look for the future in the past. On leaving the Editor, Stanczyk hands him his caduceus, instructing the Editor to muddy the waters with it. The name Stanczyk was also associated with a conservative Krakow political group of the nineteenth century. Wyspiański emphasizes in this scene that the conservative policies of the past, represented by the Stanczyk political party, have no place in Poland's future.

Perhaps the most important moment in act 2 is the appearance of Wernyhora, the semilegendary Ukrainian bard whose prophecies concerning Poland were utilized by several Polish writers. Adam Mickiewicz portrayed Wernyhora as a prophet of the resurrection of Poland. According to Juliusz Słowacki's *Beniowski* (1841), Wernyhora was to return in the future to point out the king of prophets. Wyspiański's Wernyhora comes atop a huge white stallion to visit the Host and hands him a golden horn with which the Host is to call the countryside to arms. Wernyhora instructs the Host to ride to Warsaw with the banner and call together the Sejm (a parliamentary assembly), thus leading the nation to insurrection. After Wernyhora leaves, the Host entrusts the golden horn, symbol of the insurrection, to a peasant at the wedding. The Host also instructs another peasant to call all peasants to arms; they are to gather at daybreak and wait for their orders.

These spirits are visions from the internal psyche of the characters taking on human, even superhuman, forms in order to engage in a polemic with their witnesses. The visions of act 2 thus become more real than reality itself. The monologues of the spirits more clearly reflect the convictions of the characters in the play who are representatives of contemporary Polish society. Act 2 also introduces a historical perspective to the play. The political situation in which Poland found itself at the time of *The Wedding* becomes clearer when compared to the historical periods that the spirits represent. The spirits symbolize deeds and persons, both heroic and cowardly. They also represent Poland's past glory. The interaction of these spirits with the other more realistic characters causes the border between the real and the supernatural to shift and disappear. Although the action is minimal, there is much dramatic tension as a result of this interplay between worlds.

In act 3, the apparitions disappear, and the viewer is returned to the wedding party. Some of the guests are drunk, and there is no mention of the activities that took place only moments earlier. It is as though the ghosts from Poland's past had never been there. One of the events that occurred during the unusual night is mentioned for the first time in act 3: The Bride dreamed that she was being taken through forests and villages by devils who told her that they were looking for Poland. Now, curious as to the meaning of this dream, she asks the Poet for his interpretation. He tells her that the Poland for which she is looking cannot be found anywhere on earth but that it exists in the heart.

The majority of the conversations among the guests in act 3 are very similar to those of act 1. The cold reality of the present seems to have returned. The peasants, who were instructed by the Host to gather at dawn and wait for their orders, clearly remember the strange happenings of the night. The city guests and the Host are quite surprised when they see the peasants gathering near the house before dawn. The Host is reminded of his night visitor, and, after some time, the events of the evening become somewhat more clear to him. The guests all wait for something to happen and are excited when they hear the sound of a horse's hooves. The peasant whose mission it was to blow the golden horn enters the yard, but the horn is lost. The symbol of insurrection is no longer in the people's hands. The play closes as the Mulch puts all the guests into a trance. He then leads them in a slow dance, reflecting the powerless nature of contemporary Polish thought.

Wyspiański the pessimist was very much like the nobility who wait for the miracle at the end of *The Wedding*: He entrusted the mission of leading Poland to freedom to fate. From *The Wedding* emerges a clear message: The gentry, after telling the peasants that they are to be the salvation of Poland and calling them to arms and action, are incapable of leading, unable to make the final, crucial call to arms. Like the Host, they are armed only with rhetoric and lack the confidence to be leaders. As the Host gave away the golden horn, so the gentry have abdicated their responsibility for true change in their country. Audiences at the turn of the century did not understand the satiric nature of Wyspiański's masterpiece; the true meaning of *The Wedding* was understood only after Wyspiański's death.

Having experienced European modernism in one of the key centers of "new" art, Paris, Wyspiański brought his knowledge and creativity to the theater of Krakow. His mastery of different artistic media enabled him to unify the different art forms, a key point in the many manifestos of the modernists. Wyspiański is not noted for developing the psychological side of characters in his works, but he did contribute to the growth of the Polish psychological drama. Through his two-leveled construction, Wyspiański was able to explore the inner feelings of his characters. In addition, this construction allowed him to make brilliant use of the space beyond the stage. Not only did Wyspiański propagate the ideas of the Polish modernist movement, but he also introduced a healthy argument against one of the principal theories of Przybyszewski.

According to the program of Young Poland, art should not concern itself with politics but rather constitute a revelation of the naked soul. Throughout *The Wedding* and many of his other works, Wyspiański accused the contemporary Polish artist of being unwilling to do battle with the foes of Poland. He ridiculed the artists of his generation for reaching into the past for heroic themes while remaining unable to perform heroic deeds themselves.

BIBLIOGRAPHY

Coates, Paul. "Revolutionary Spirits: The Wedding of Wajda and Wyspiański." *Literature/Film Quarterly* 20, no. 2 (1992): 127. Coates compares and contrasts Wyspiański's *The Wedding* with Andrzej Wajda's film version.

Kraszewski, Charles S. "Stanisław Wyspiański as Proselytising Translator: National Directioning in His Polonisations of *Hamlet* and *Le Cid*." *Canadian Slavonic Papers* 35, nos. 3-4 (September, 1993): 305. This study focuses on Wyspiański's translations into Polish of William Shakespeare's *Hamlet, Prince of Denmark* and Pierre Corneille's *Le Cid* and the strategy he pursued.

Romanowska, Marta. *Stanisław Wyspiański Museum: Branch of the National Museum in Cracow: A Guide Book*. Krakow: The National Museum, 1998. This guidebook to the museum for Wyspiański provides some insights into his life.

Terlecki, Tymon. *Stanisław Wyspiański*. Boston: Twayne, 1983. A general biography of Wyspiański that covers his life and works. Bibliography and index.

George A. Sumnik

Υ

WILLIAM BUTLER YEATS

Born: Sandymount, near Dublin, Ireland; June 13, 1865
Died: Cap Martin, France; January 28, 1939

PRINCIPAL DRAMA

The Countess Cathleen, pb. 1892, pr. 1899
The Land of Heart's Desire, pr., pb. 1894
Cathleen ni Houlihan, pr., pb. 1902
The Pot of Broth, pr. 1902, pb. 1903 (with Lady Augusta Gregory)
The Hour-Glass, pr. 1903, revised pr. 1912, pb. 1913
The King's Threshold, pr., pb. 1903 (with Lady Gregory)
On Baile's Strand, pr. 1904, pb. 1905
Deirdre, pr. 1906, pb. 1907 (with Lady Gregory)
The Shadowy Waters, pr. 1906, pb. 1907
The Unicorn from the Stars, pr. 1907, pb. 1908 (with Lady Gregory)
The Golden Helmet, pr., pb. 1908
The Green Helmet, pr., pb. 1910
At the Hawk's Well, pr. 1916, pb. 1917
The Player Queen, pr. 1919, pb. 1922
The Only Jealousy of Emer, pb. 1919, pr. 1922
The Dreaming of the Bones, pb. 1919, pr. 1931
Calvary, pb. 1921
Four Plays for Dancers, pb. 1921 (includes *Calvary*, *At the Hawk's Well*, *The Dreaming of the Bones*, *The Only Jealousy of Emer*)
The Cat and the Moon, pb. 1924, pr. 1931
The Resurrection, pb. 1927, pr. 1934
The Words upon the Window-Pane, pr. 1930, pb. 1934
The Collected Plays of W. B. Yeats, pb. 1934, 1952
The King of the Great Clock Tower, pr., pb. 1934
A Full Moon in March, pr. 1934, pb. 1935
The Herne's Egg, pb. 1938
Purgatory, pr. 1938, pb. 1939
The Death of Cuchulain, pb. 1939, pr. 1949
Variorum Edition of the Plays of W. B. Yeats, pb. 1966 (Russell K. Alspach, editor)

OTHER LITERARY FORMS

Throughout a literary career spanning a half century, William Butler Yeats distinguished himself principally by means of the production of some dozen volumes of lyric poems. His early work is most clearly indebted to the English Romantics, but his commitment to the cause of the Irish Literary Revival, of which he was the leader, and to the management of its showcase, the Abbey Theatre, gave him an increasingly public voice. The poetry of his last twenty years contains his most complex, modernist, and profound work and is often considered the highest achievement in that genre during the twentieth century.

Yeats was also the author of a considerable body of essays, reviews, and introductions during a career of literary journalism and theatrical management: *Essays and Introductions* (1961), *Explorations* (1962), and *Uncollected Prose by W. B. Yeats* (two volumes; 1970, 1976). He collected and edited writings and promoted the work of such collaborators as Lady Augusta Gregory and John Millington Synge. Yeats's early excursions into short fiction are collected in *Mythologies* (1959). Autobiographical fragments are found in *Autobiographies* (1926, 1955) and *Memoirs* (1972). *A Vision* (1925, 1937) sets forth a symbolic ordering of history and human character in a manner chiefly useful in explicating his poetry, while *The Senate Speeches of W. B. Yeats* (1960) gathers some of his public statements from the 1920's. The Yeats correspondence is partially collected in *The Letters of*

W. B. Yeats (1954) and in *Ah, Sweet Dancer: W. B. Yeats, Margot Ruddock—A Correspondence* (1970).

ACHIEVEMENTS

William Butler Yeats's reputation as one of the masters of modern literature rests mainly on his achievements in poetry, and his dramatic work has long been regarded less favorably as "poetry in the theater." This aspect of his œuvre has, however, been reassessed, and he has come to be regarded as one of the boldest and most original dramatists of the twentieth century. As one of the founders, first playwrights, and lifetime directors of the Abbey Theatre, Yeats was the central figure of the Irish Literary Renaissance. The example of efforts to develop a modern and national literature that drew on Celtic mythology, folklore, and the oral tradition of Ireland provided incentives for the latent talents of such dramatists as Lady Augusta Gregory, John Millington Synge, Padraic Colum, and Sean O'Casey.

Although Yeats experimented with several dramatic styles, including peasant realism, farce, and naturalism, his genius found its true métier in a highly sophisticated drama that combined poetry, dance, mask, and symbolic action to represent a world of ideals and pure passion. These plays, borrowed from the tradition of the Japanese Nō for their form and from Celtic heroic tales for their subjects, expressed Yeats's views of the primacy of imaginative or spiritual realities of which historical change and the differentiation of human character are emanations. Yeats was therefore at odds with modern realism and with its interest in individual character and social relations: An attitude of detachment and impersonality shaped his works into intensely ritualized expressions, having affinities both with religious drama and absurdism.

Yeats lived through revolutions in politics and sensibility. Most important, through a lifelong remaking of dramatic and lyric form and style, Yeats achieved a continuous renovation of his own spirit. Thus, he became one of those primarily responsible for the restoration to Ireland of its cultural heritage, at the same time forging an idiom that the modern world at large considers its own.

BIOGRAPHY

The eldest of the four children of John Butler Yeats, the painter, and his wife, Susan Pollexfen, William Butler Yeats was born in Sandymount, near Dublin. When he was nine years old, the family moved to London, where he attended the Godolphin School in Hammersmith, taking his holidays with his maternal grandparents in County Sligo in the rural west of Ireland. The Yeats family returned to Dublin in 1880, and the young Yeats thereafter completed his education at the high school and the Metropolitan Art School. During this time, from 1883 to 1886, he came under the influence of George Russell (Æ) and a circle of Dublin mystics, as well as John O'Leary, the aged Fenian leader.

These various influences turned the introverted boy from art to literature; from religious confusion (his mother was a Protestant, his father an agnostic) to Theosophy, the occult, and Rosicrucianism; and from the Oriental themes of his earliest literary efforts to Irish subjects. Yeats moved back to London in 1888. In 1890, he helped organize the Rhymers Club, where he made friends with many of the leading po-

William Butler Yeats (© The Nobel Foundation)

ets of the time, including Arthur Symons, William Morris, and Lionel Johnson, with whom he founded the Irish Literary Society in 1891.

In 1888, Yeats had met Maud Gonne, an actress and activist in behalf of Irish nationalism. A lifelong, unrequited obsession with her (she rejected marriage proposals in 1891 and again in 1916) accounts for the periodic intensification of his enthusiasm for nationalist politics, the subject of much of his poetry and two of his early plays, *The Countess Cathleen* and *Cathleen ni Houlihan.*

Yeats returned to Dublin in 1896, and in 1899, he collaborated with Edward Martyn and Lady Gregory in founding the Irish Literary Theatre, which in 1904 became the Abbey Theatre. The affairs of this theater—playwriting (peasant and Celtic themes), daily management, the promotion of playwrights with Irish subjects (Synge was the most notable)—were his preoccupations until about 1910.

After Ezra Pound introduced him to the Japanese Nō drama, Yeats wrote his *Four Plays for Dancers*: formal, symbolic, ritual plays based on Celtic, Irish, and Christian themes. He married Georgina Hyde-Lees in 1917 and, discovering her capacities as a medium, revived his interest in Spiritualism. With her assistance, he produced the systematized *A Vision*, which illuminates much of his mature drama and poetry. The couple lived in Dublin and at Thoor Ballylee, a restored Norman tower in County Galway, and had two children. During the last twenty-five years of his life, Yeats produced his most mature work in poetry, prose, and drama. He was appointed a member of the senate of the Irish Free State from 1922 to 1928, lectured widely in Europe and the United States, and received widespread recognition, including honorary doctorates and the Nobel Prize in Literature in 1923. In 1932, along with George Bernard Shaw and Æ, he founded the Irish Academy of Letters, and in 1936, he edited the controversial *Oxford Book of Modern Verse*. Failing health forced him to abandon Thoor Ballylee, and in the 1930's, he spent progressively more of each year in Italy and France. In 1939, shortly after completing his last play, *The Death of Cuchulain*, he died in the French Riviera and was temporarily buried there. His remains were returned to Drumcliff, County Sligo, his grandfather's parish, in 1948.

ANALYSIS

William Butler Yeats's reputation justly rests on his achievements in poetry, yet a considerable portion of that work is written for two or more voices and, therefore, is dramatic. Indeed, his first literary compositions were long dramatic poems, and throughout his life, he continued to publish his plays and poems side by side. Yeats believed that the language of poetry best represented imaginative reality, the life of the soul, or the introspective or subjective consciousness, as opposed to the spirit of science, the modern, extroverted age, the objective consciousness that draws its identity from external circumstances and that finds its appropriate expression in dramatic realism. Therefore, throughout a career as a dramatist consisting of four distinct phases, Yeats's sympathies remained mystical, Symbolist, and removed from the mainstream of popular drama. Nevertheless, he is one of the genuinely original dramatists of the twentieth century, with influences on verse drama and the work of Samuel Beckett.

THE COUNTESS CATHLEEN

When Yeats joined talents and ambitions with Lady Gregory and Edward Martyn to form the Irish Literary Theatre in 1899, his first contributions to the venture were *The Countess Cathleen* and *Cathleen ni Houlihan*. The former is a rather static verse drama in which a heroic native aristocrat sells her soul to merchant-demons in order to save the starving peasants. The play aroused controversy over its doctrinal content in Catholic Ireland, and its author's doughty defense of independence in artistic and patriotic self-expression established a pattern that was often to repeat itself.

CATHLEEN NI HOULIHAN

Yeats's most dramatically successful early work, however, is *Cathleen ni Houlihan*, one of several peasant plays that Yeats wrote. The play depicts in realistic terms the diversion of a young man's intentions from his impending marriage to a phase of the 1798 rebellion in Ireland. An anonymous old woman becomes a young queen because of the heroic commitment of Michael Gillane. Here is *The Land of Heart's Desire* rewritten in nationalist terms: The thrifty realism of the peasants gradually yields to the incantatory power of the old woman's lament, and the political allegory is triumphantly announced in the famous curtain line. With Maud Gonne in the title role reciting the credo of nationalist Ireland, Yeats was accused of producing unworthy propaganda. He protested that it came to him in a dream, but like the subject matter of all of his early work, its origins are demonstrably in the native folklore that Yeats had been collecting and studying since his conversion to the cause of Ireland's cultural distinctiveness. The theme of this particular play is, indeed, traceable through popular ballad to the Gaelic *aisling* (vision) convention and to the theme of the lady and the king found in medieval Irish literature. Its power on an Irish stage is therefore attributable to more than its last line. Yeats was to wonder, with some justification, how much this play contributed to the Easter Rebellion of 1916.

THE CUCHULAIN PLAYS

Before the heroism of that week burst on his and the nation's consciousness, Yeats was cultivating in himself and on the stage of the Abbey Theatre a renewed appreciation of the literature of ancient Ireland and its exaltation of heroic individualism, eloquence, aristocracy, and paganism. In the figure of Cuchulain, the hero of the Ulster Cycle, Yeats found the embodiment of these virtues, and he wrote a series of five plays dramatizing episodes from the hero's lone defense of Ulster, beginning with *On Baile's Strand*. Among Cuchulain's challengers is a young man in whom Cuchulain notes a resemblance to his abandoned wife, Aoife. Caught between his natural affinity for this image and his oath to King Conchubar to defend the province against intruders, Cuchulain is driven to combat. Too late, he discovers that the dead boy is his own son, and in his anguish, he rushes, sword in hand, into the waves until he drowns.

This play marks a significant advance in technique on Yeats's early dramatic efforts in its tight control and complexity of theme. The theme of conflicting loyalties operates at several levels simultaneously, so that Cuchulain's roles as loyal soldier, independent

hero, father, and son all conspire to bring on his tragic self-destruction. The framing device of the Fool and the Blind Man functions as an ironic lowlife commentary on the serious central action, while at the same time casting up counterpart images of Conchubar and Cuchulain as creatures guided by similarly fitful lights.

Yeats went on to write four other Cuchulain plays, *The Golden Helmet*, *At the Hawk's Well*, *The Only Jealousy of Emer*, and *The Death of Cuchulain*, as well as several others drawn from Celtic sources made available by translators such as Lady Gregory. His dissatisfaction with modern realism, however, with its focus on the drama of individual character, distanced him from the kind of work that made the Abbey Theatre popular. When Ezra Pound introduced Yeats in 1913 to the Nō theater of Japan, Yeats recognized the tradition which would enable him to shape his own ideas into a successful poetic drama.

THE DREAMING OF THE BONES

The Japanese Nō drama dates from the late Middle Ages, has strong Zen elements, and is highly stylized. It is a symbolic drama, developing the resources of mask, gesture, chanted dialogue, slow rhythmic dance, ornamental costume, chorus, and flute and drum to create an atmosphere of passionate reverie contained beneath an elegant repose. Yeats was attracted by the tone of gravity, detachment, mystery, grace, and nobility in these plays. His Spiritualist sympathies predisposed him to appreciate plays that featured figures in the process of "dreaming back" moments of extreme passion in their lives as they sought release from human desires and entrance into final peace. In his *Four Plays for Dancers*, especially *The Dreaming of the Bones* as well as in several later plays, these influences are evident. *The Dreaming of the Bones* is designed in two scenes joined by a choral interlude, according to the structure of a fantasy-style Nō such as *Nishikigi*. The Subordinate Player (here the Young Man) encounters the Main Players (here the Stranger and Young Girl) in a historical spot (the Abbey of Corcomroe) at a historical moment (1916). The Main Players tell the story of the place and ask for prayers and forgiveness of the Young Man, finally revealing themselves as the ghosts of

Diarmuid MacMorrough and Dervorgilla (the twelfth century couple whose marriage was instrumental in the Norman invasion of Ireland). Because the Young Man is a modern Irish patriot for whom that liaison was the original sexual-political transgression, he refuses, and the couple is left to continue their purgatorial "dreaming back" of their tragic sin. The various themes of the play—dream, war, resurrection, cyclic change—coalesce in the emblems of the birds in the Musicians' final chorus. Subsequent experiments with the Nō form demonstrate Yeats's greater facility in adapting it to the expression of his own views of the afterlife and his mythologization of the Irish past—especially in *The Only Jealousy of Emer, The Words upon the Window-pane*, and *Purgatory*.

The Words upon the Window-Pane

The Words upon the Window-Pane is a daringly successful combination of naturalism, Spiritualism, the "dreaming back" from the Nō, and Yeats's latter-day identification with eighteenth century Anglo-Ireland. In this dramatization of a Dublin séance, the tortured spirit of Jonathan Swift is invoked, though remaining unrecognized by any except the literary scholar John Corbet. Swift, the representative of intellectuality, classical ideals, and the natural aristocracy of Ireland, "dreams back" his rejection of the opportunity for fatherhood offered by Vanessa, thereby sharing Yeats's rejection of the "filthy modern tide" that would likely be their issue. In his management of middle-class character and dialogue, Yeats shows his capacities in the naturalistic style, but the dramatic coup here comes in the final scene, when these conventions are broken and the audience is left alone with an order of reality beyond the reach of skeptic or scholar.

Purgatory

In *Purgatory*, one of his last plays, Yeats achieved his most concentrated work for stage. The setting and action are symbolic, the language a brilliant fusion of colloquial and poetic idiom. The Old Man, the product of a marriage between a big house and a stable, lost his aristocratic mother at his birth and later murdered his drunken father. Now, accompanied by his son, the Old Man visits the scene of his parents' unfortunate wedding—unfortunate because it betrayed

class and because it produced him, a parricide. In an attempt to break the chain of evil, the Old Man stabs his son, but to no avail: The spirits of his parents are trapped in a perpetual repetition of their crime, unless God intervenes. Here, Yeats has devised a complex dramatic symbol for the demise of aristocratic Anglo-Ireland, the approach of global conflict, and the relationship between the living conscience and the stages of spiritual purgation to be encountered after death. The play is thus a summary exposition of Yeats's social and philosophical views in the later years of his life, drawing on the disciplines of language and construction that he had refined over a lifetime of experimentation.

Other major works

short fiction: *John Sherman and Dhoya*, 1891, 1969; *The Celtic Twilight*, 1893; *The Secret Rose*, 1897; *The Tables of Law; The Adoration of the Magi*, 1897; *Stories of Red Hanrahan*, 1904; *Mythologies*, 1959.

poetry: *Mosada: A Dramatic Poem*, 1886; *Crossways*, 1889; *The Wanderings of Oisin and Other Poems*, 1889; *The Countess Kathleen and Various Legends and Lyrics*, 1892; *The Rose*, 1893; *The Wind Among the Reeds*, 1899; *In the Seven Woods*, 1903; *The Poetical Works of William B. Yeats*, 1906, 1907 (2 volumes); *The Green Helmet and Other Poems*, 1910; *Responsibilities*, 1914; *Responsibilities and Other Poems*, 1916; *The Wild Swans at Coole*, 1917, 1919; *Michael Robartes and the Dancer*, 1920; *The Tower*, 1928; *Words for Music Perhaps and Other Poems*, 1932; *The Winding Stair and Other Poems*, 1933; *The Collected Poems of W. B. Yeats*, 1933, 1950; *The King of the Great Clock Tower*, 1934; *A Full Moon in March*, 1935; *Last Poems and Plays*, 1940; *The Poems of W. B. Yeats*, 1949 (2 volumes); *The Collected Poems of W. B. Yeats*, 1956; *Variorum Edition of the Poems of W. B. Yeats*, 1957 (P. Allt and R. K. Alspach, editors); *The Poems*, 1983; *The Poems: A New Edition*, 1984.

nonfiction: *Ideas of Good and Evil*, 1903; *The Cutting of an Agate*, 1912; *Per Amica Silentia Lunae*, 1918; *Essays*, 1924; *A Vision*, 1925, 1937; *Autobiographies*, 1926, 1955; *A Packet for Ezra Pound*, 1929;

Essays, 1931-1936, 1937; *The Autobiography of William Butler Yeats*, 1938; *On the Boiler*, 1939; *If I Were Four and Twenty*, 1940; *The Letters of W. B. Yeats*, 1954; *The Senate Speeches of W. B. Yeats*, 1960 (Donald R. Pearce, editor); *Essays and Introductions*, 1961; *Explorations*, 1962; *Ah, Sweet Dancer: W. B. Yeats, Margot Ruddock—A Correspondence*, 1970 (Roger McHugh, editor); *Uncollected Prose by W. B. Yeats*, 1970, 1976 (2 volumes); *Memoirs*, 1972; *The Collected Letters of William Butler Yeats: Volume I, 1865-1895*, 1986.

MISCELLANEOUS: *The Collected Works in Verse and Prose of William Butler Yeats*, 1908.

BIBLIOGRAPHY

Bornstein, George. *Material Modernism: The Politics of the Page.* New York: Cambridge University Press, 2001. A study of Modernism in Ireland, England, and the United States, focusing on Yeats and James Joyce. Bibliography and index.

Brown, Terence. *The Life of W. B. Yeats: A Critical Biography.* Malden, Mass.: Blackwell, 1999. A biography that examines the intellectual life of Yeats as well as his works. Bibliography and index.

Chaudhry, Yug Mohit. *Yeats, the Irish Literary Revival and the Politics of Print.* Cork, Ireland: Cork University Press, 2001. A study of Yeats's political and social views as well as a critique of his writings. Bibliography and index.

Holdridge, Jefferson. *Those Mingled Seas: The Poetry of W. B. Yeats, The Beautiful and the Sublime.* Dublin: University College Dublin Press, 2000. A study of Yeats's poetry that suspends it between the philosophies of both Kant and Burke, focusing on the source of the power of Yeats's mysticism.

Larrissy, Edward. *W. B. Yeats.* Plymouth, England: Northcote House in association with the British Council, 1998. A basic biography of Yeats that examines both his life and works. Bibliography and index.

Maddox, Brenda. *Yeats's Ghosts: The Secret Life of W. B. Yeats.* New York: HarperCollins, 1999. Maddox examines Yeats's connection to spiritualism and the occult. Bibliography and index.

Richman, David. *Passionate Action: Yeats's Mastery of Drama.* Newark, N.J.: University of Delaware Press, 2000. Richman examines the dramatic works of Yeats and discusses Irish literature. Bibliography and index.

Cóilín D. Owens,
updated by Peter C. Holloran

Z

YEVGENY ZAMYATIN

Born: Lebedyan, Russia; February 1, 1884
Died: Paris, France; March 10, 1937

PRINCIPAL DRAMA

Ogni Svyatogo Dominika, wr. 1920, pb. 1922 (*The Fires of St. Dominic*, 1971)

Blokha, pr. 1925, pb. 1926 (*The Flea*, 1971)

Obshchestvo pochetnikh zvonarei, pr. 1925, pb. 1926 (*The Society of Honorary Bell Ringers*, 1971)

Attila, wr. 1925-1927, pb. 1950 (English translation, 1971)

Afrikanskiy gost, wr. 1929-1930, pb. 1963 (*The African Guest*, 1971)

Five Plays, pb. 1971

OTHER LITERARY FORMS

Yevgeny Zamyatin is better known as a short-story writer and novelist than as a playwright. His main short stories (many of which are novellas) are *Uyezdnoye* (1913; *A Provincial Tale*, 1966), *Na kulichkakh* (1914; *A Godforsaken Hole*, 1988), *Ostrovityane* (1918; *The Islanders*, 1972), *Bol'shim detyam skazki* (1922; tales for grownup children), and *Nechestivye rasskazy* (1927; impious stories). His most famous short story, *Peshchera* ("The Cave"), is a sad story of an intellectual couple finding slow death in their frozen apartment in Petrograd during the revolution. Replete with allegories and metaphors, it presents reality in a highly structured and unreal fashion. Zamyatin would perfect that approach in his futuristic, anti-utopian novel *My* (wr. 1920-1921, 1927 [corrupt text], 1952; *We*, 1924). In a fictitious city, called the One State, a "benevolent" dictator holds a firm grip on all citizens, with the help of secret police. Through the eventual uprising and destruction of the One State, some characters undergo a metamorphosis that bodes well for a better future.

Zamyatin's other novel, the unfinished *Bich Bozhy* (1939; scourge of God), is a veiled reference to Joseph Stalin and his despotic rule. Zamyatin also wrote significant nonfiction, *Kak my pishem: Teoria literatury* (1930; how we write; a theory of literature), *Gerbert Uells* (1922; *H. G. Wells*, 1970), and *Litsa* (1955; *A Soviet Heretic*, 1970), in which he promulgates his views on literature.

ACHIEVEMENTS

Although Yevgeny Zamyatin was one of the most important Russian writers of the twentieth century, he did not receive official awards for his achievements, largely because of his ideological opposition to the communist regime in the Soviet Union. He was highly respected by his colleagues, especially by younger writers, a fact that brought Zamyatin at least some satisfaction. The direct persecution of Zamyatin by the authorities, who regarded him as a dangerous apostate, led to his exile and early death. The extent of this persecution can best be seen in the fact that only two of his plays, *The Flea* and *The Society of Honorary Bell Ringers*, were produced in the Soviet Union. Zamyatin's plays were warmly received by critics and the audience, as illustrated by the enormous popularity and numerous performances of *The Flea* before Zamyatin fell into complete disfavor with the authorities. Probably his two other plays, *The Fires of St. Dominic* and *Attila*, would have been just as popular, not only because of their allusions to and reflection of everyday life in the Soviet Union under the communist dictatorship but also because of Zamyatin's dexterity as a playwright.

BIOGRAPHY

Yevgeny Zamyatin was born in 1884 in the central Russian town of Lebedyan, in the Tambov province, south of Moscow. His father was a priest, who held strict religious and conservative views. After finishing high school in the nearby city of Voronezh, Zamyatin was graduated from the University of St. Petersburg with a degree in naval engineering. In 1905 he joined the Bolshevik Party and subsequently was arrested for his revolutionary activity and jailed briefly. He began to move toward a more liberal socialist view. Zamyatin published his first story in 1908, followed by his first exceptional story, *A Provincial Tale*, and by a satire about the army life in Vladivostok, *A Godforsaken Hole*, which established him as one of the best among the younger Russian writers.

As a naval engineer, Zamyatin was sent to England in 1916 to oversee the building of ice-breaker ships for the Russian government. There, he was able to observe the English way of life and English people. His experiences resulted in an impressive work, *The Islanders*, which advanced his status as a writer. Returning to Russia, he was engulfed in the Bolshevik Revolution of 1917. Even though he had once belonged to the Bolshevik Party and later to a leftist socialist party, he was highly critical of the way the revolution was carried out. When he criticized the barbarity and violence of the Bolsheviks, they began to view him with suspicion, a distrust that lasted until his death. At the same time, he was very active in literary circles, working closely with Maxim Gorky, a younger writer. Although young himself, Zamyatin had already acquired a reputation as an excellent stylist and was able to instruct younger, mostly proletarian writers in Petrograd who had no prior literary education. However, his heretical views, not only on literature but also on political matters, led to short imprisonments in 1919 and 1922. Finding it more and more difficult to publish his prose works, Zamyatin turned to writing plays, in the vain hope of getting them performed.

In 1921 Zamyatin wrote his most important work, *We*, which became the breaking point in his relationship with the authorities. He was unable to publish the novel in the Soviet Union, but its existence became well known, not only in literary circles but also through his public readings of the novel. When the novel was published in Russian by émigré writers in Czechoslovakia in 1927, the vilification of Zamyatin reached such level that he was forced to write a letter to Stalin, asking to be allowed to emigrate, with the somewhat wishful plea that he be allowed to return when the stringent conditions changed. To many people's surprise, Stalin gave his permission, and Zamyatin left for Czechoslovakia in 1931 and settled in France. It is believed that Gorky interceded for him with Stalin, thus sparing him further persecution, perhaps even death.

In France, Zamyatin led a secluded life, working on *Attila* (a veiled allusion to Stalin) and preparing his collected works for a publication. The difficulty of life in exile, away from his source of inspiration, and the need to make a living forced him to try his hand at writing film scenarios. His health began to deteriorate, and he died almost a forgotten man in 1937, having become better known abroad than in his homeland.

ANALYSIS

Yevgeny Zamyatin's reputation is likely to stand primarily on his short stories and novels, with his dramatic works, while significant in their own right, taking a secondary place. Although he was relatively free to write his plays, he was seriously limited in his ability to disseminate his works and stage his plays because of his ideological differences with the communist regime in the Soviet Union. The fact that two of his plays have never been staged in Russia (despite their receiving considerable approval abroad) may have contributed to the relative slighting of these works. An additional reason may be that most of his plays are somewhat dated, concerned as they are in one way or another with local matters. At the same time, three of his major plays are set outside of Russia and carry messages that concern all humankind. Zamyatin's ability to rise above local themes and give his plays universal meanings makes his plays worth reading and staging today.

THE FIRES OF ST. DOMINIC

The Fires of St. Dominic, a costume drama set in Seville, Spain, during the Inquisition in the second half of the sixteenth century, depicts the cruel role of the inquisitor Munebraga. Zamyatin lashes out not only at a doctrine of infallibility, at the suppression of heresy by ruthless means, but also at the weaklings who do not protest their loss of liberty. This historical drama was most likely inspired by Fyodor Dostoevsky's "Legend of the Grand Inquisitor" from *Bratya Karamazovy* (1879-1880; *The Brothers Karamazov*, 1912). Under this thin disguise, Zamyatin attacks the cruel behavior of the Bolsheviks and their leaders Vladimir Ilich Lenin and Joseph Stalin, who "were killing men to save mankind" in the first years of the revolution and later as well. Because of this attack on ideological conformity and the repressive mentality of the Bolsheviks, the play was never performed in Russia, although it has been staged by the Russian émigrés. Throughout his life, Zamyatin vigorously defended the right to heresy, there and elsewhere (for example, in the novel *We*). *The Fires of St. Dominic* transcends the borders of both Spain and Russia, while focusing on one of the most significant problems of societal behavior—the right to disagree.

THE FLEA

Zamyatin had a better luck, and success, with his second play, *The Flea*, a comedy. The play is based on Nikolai Leskov's story "Levsha" and bears the subtitle "The Story of Cross-eyed Lefty from Tula and the Steel Flea." It is basically a folk story about the craftsmen from Tula shoeing a flea. Zamyatin used the plot to demonstrate the natural intelligence and craftsmanship of common Russians, which would act as a force that would counteract the impact of intellectuals influenced by the ideas from abroad—a clear reference to the idea of communism. It is also one of the most optimistic works of Zamyatin, expressing his belief that Russian folk traditions will outlive the intrusion of foreign beliefs. A carnival atmosphere and a hefty dose of folk humor and popular speech added to the popularity of the play. Zamyatin wrote *The Flea* not as a simple folk tale but as a sophisticated rendition of a folk motif. The combination of this folk motif and the avoidance of direct allusions to contemporary political matters made it possible for the play not only to be staged but also to stay on the repertoire for four seasons and to enjoy an enthusiastic reception by the public.

THE SOCIETY OF HONORARY BELL RINGERS

This play is based on Zamyatin's *The Islanders*, which reflects his sojourn in England shortly before World War I. The characters are Englishmen, whom Zamyatin has mildly satirized in the novel. The new title, *The Society of Honorary Bell Ringers*, enhances the satire. Zamyatin pokes mild fun at the proverbial English obsession with punctuality and cleanliness, their reliance on things mechanic, and their somewhat loose morals concerning nudity. The play itself was first produced in 1925. It is the most innocuous of Zamyatin's plays in that, though it deals with a real life subject matter, it has little direct reference to Russia.

ATTILA

Written in 1927 in a mixture of prose and yrics, the tragedy *Attila*, Zamyatin's last play to be published and rehearsed, contains one of his cherished beliefs that revolution is permanent and that there is no final revolution, as the communists believe. In this sense, the play may be seen as criticism of Stalin and his belief that the Bolshevik Revolution was the last revolution. In essence, *Attila* depicts the clash between West and East, between the stale, moribund Roman society and the vigorous, barbaric hordes of the Huns. Attila is presented as a dynamic leader who is betrayed by the Princess of Burgundy and slain. The play had several rehearsals, but when it was ready for the stage, it was unexpectedly banned; by this time Zamyatin had become persona non grata. Unpublished and unperformed in his lifetime, the play served Zamyatin as a basis for the novel *Bich Bozhy* (scourge of God), which he wrote in France in the last years of his life and left unfinished. The new title makes it even clearer that Zamyatin has rejected the idea of a final revolution. It also points at Attila as the scourge of God, punishing a corrupt and decayed society such as that of the Roman Empire in its twilight years.

OTHER MAJOR WORKS

LONG FICTION: *My*, wr. 1920-1921, 1927 (corrupt text), 1952 (*We*, 1924); *Bich Bozhy*, 1939.

SHORT FICTION: *Uyezdnoye*, 1913 (*A Provincial Tale*, 1966); *Na kulichkakh*, 1914 (*A Godforsaken*

Hole, 1988); *Ostrovityane*, 1918 (*The Islanders*, 1972); *Bol'shim detyam skazki*, 1922; *Nechestivye rasskazy*, 1927; *Povesti i rasskazy*, 1963; *The Dragon: Fifteen Stories*, 1966.

SCREENPLAY: *Les Bas-fonds*, 1936 (*The Lower Depths*, 1937; adaptation of Maxim Gorky's novel *Na dne*).

NONFICTION: *Gerbert Uells*, 1922 (*H. G. Wells*, 1970); *Kak my pishem: Teoria literatury*, 1930; *Litsa*, 1955 (*A Soviet Heretic*, 1970).

MISCELLANEOUS: *Sobranie sochinenii*, 1929; *Sochineniia*, 1970-1972.

BIBLIOGRAPHY

Cavendish, Philip. *Mining the Jewels: Evgenii Zamiatin and the Literary Stylization of Rus'*. London: Maney, 2000. A thorough study of the folk-religious background of Zamyatin's sources of inspiration. It traces his attempts to reconcile the folkloric tradition and the vernacular through his artistic expression. In the process, drawing from the past and from the language of the people, he creates literature that is basically modernistic.

Collins, Christopher. *Evgenij Zamjatin: An Interpretative Study*. The Hague, the Netherlands: Mouton, 1973. Offers a rather complex interpretation of Zamyatin's works, mostly of *We*, on the basis of C. G. Jung's ideas of the conscious, unconscious, and individualism. It also discusses the artistic merits of individual works, including plays.

Richards, D. J. *Zamyatin, a Soviet Heretic*. New York: Hillary House, 1962. Overview of the main stages and issues in Zamyatin's life and works. Excellent, brief presentation of all facets of a very complex writer. Brief but pithy discussions of the plays, especially of *Attila*.

Shane, Alex M. *The Life and Works of Evgenij Zamjatin*. Berkeley: University of California Press, 1968. The most comprehensive overall study of Zamyatin in English. Shane covers Zamyatin's life and the most important features of his works, chronologically, in a scholarly but not dry fashion, and reaches his own conclusions. Pertinent discussion of plays. Extensive bibliographies.

Slonim, Mark. "Evgeny Zamyatin: The Ironic Dissident." In *Soviet Russian Literature: Writers and Problems, 1917-1977*. 2d ed. New York: Oxford University Press, 1977. A good portrait of Zamyatin as a leading literary figure of his time. Brief discussion of his plays within the framework of his entire opus. Excellent background details about his plays.

Vasa D. Mihailovich

ISRAEL ZANGWILL

Born: London, England; February 14, 1864
Died: Midhurst, West Sussex, England; August 1, 1926

PRINCIPAL DRAMA
The Great Demonstration, pr. 1892
Aladdin at Sea, pr. 1893
The Lady Journalist, pr. 1893
Six Persons, pr. 1893, pb. 1898
Threepenny Bits, pr. 1895
Children of the Ghetto, pr. 1899 (adaptation of his novel)
The Moment of Death, pr. 1900
The Revolted Daughter, pr. 1901
Merely Mary Ann, pr., pb. 1903 (adaptation of his short story)
The Serio-Comic Governess, pr., pb. 1904
Nurse Marjorie, pr., pb. 1906
The Melting-Pot, pr., pb. 1909
The War God, pr., pb. 1911
The Next Religion, pr., pb. 1912
Plaster Saints, pr., pb. 1914
The Moment Before, pr. 1916
Too Much Money, pr. 1918, pb. 1924

The Cockpit, pr., pb. 1921

The Forcing House: Or, The Cockpit Continued,
    pb. 1922, pr. 1926

We Moderns, pr. 1923, pb. 1925

The King of Schnorrers, pr. 1925 (adaptation of his
    novella)

Other literary forms

Israel Zangwill is better known for his novels and short stories than for his plays. His novel *Children of the Ghetto: Being Pictures of a Peculiar People* (1892) was an immediate critical and popular success. Its detailed portrayal of social and economic life in London's Jewish quarter presented believable characters, often torn between the traditional world of Eastern European Jewry and the new science and theology of the nineteenth century. Recent critics praise this novel, as well as the short stories in *Dreamers of the Ghetto* (1898) and *The King of Schnorrers: Grotesques and Fantasies* (1894), a series of comic vignettes, describing the adventures of a Sephardic Jew in eighteenth century London, whose wit and intelligence make him the king of beggars, or *schnorrers*. Essays in newspapers and journals, some collected into books, expressed Zangwill's ardent support for Zionism, women's suffrage, and pacifism.

Achievements

Israel Zangwill's only award was a five-pound prize granted him by *Society* magazine for a humorous short story in 1881. The story, "Professor Grimmer," was the first published work of its seventeen-year-old author.

Zangwill was proud of the favorable reception his ghetto novels and stories found among non-Jews. He believed his work countered traditional negative English literary stereotypes by creating positive images of England's Jewish immigrants as they struggled with life in London's slums. Zangwill was not the first person to use the melting-pot metaphor to envision the United States as a fusion of nationalities. However, his play helped popularize the image, which became a controversial topic in twentieth century debates over whether assimilation or multiculturalism was preferable for immigrants.

Biography

The child of immigrants from Latvia and Poland, Israel Zangwill grew up in the Whitechapel area of London. He was educated at the Jews' Free School, becoming a pupil-teacher there. Zangwill studied at night at London University, earning a B.A. with honors in 1884. In 1888, he resigned from the Free School because he opposed corporal punishment and began a career as a journalist, editing magazines and contributing regular columns, humorous stories, and essays to various publications. Zangwill soon became known as an outstanding writer of comic sketches. Collected in *The Bachelors' Club* (1891) and *The Old Maids' Club* (1892), they won him critical praise.

An 1889 essay on "English Judaism, a Criticism and a Classification" brought Zangwill to the attention of Judge Mayer Sulzberger, chairman of the publication committee of the newly founded Jewish Publication Society of America. In September, 1890,

Israel Zangwill in 1913. (Hulton Archive by Getty Images)

Sulzberger offered to have the society publish a novel on Jewish themes. Zangwill had already started thinking along those lines and, in seven months, produced a draft manuscript of *Children of the Ghetto*. The 1892 publication of the book established Zangwill as a major Jewish writer. Short stories collected in *Ghetto Tragedies* (1893), *The King of Schnorrers* (1894), and *Ghetto Comedies* (1907), helped establish Zangwill's reputation in England and in the United States as the leading English-language Jewish storyteller of his generation.

In the 1890's, several of Zangwill's plays had modest runs in London. The success of his 1899 adaptation of *Children of the Ghetto* in New York encouraged Zangwill to devote most of his later creative literary activity to the stage. He wrote fifteen plays between 1900 and his death in 1926. His greatest success came with *Merely Mary Ann*, adapted from an 1893 short story, which ran for 148 performances in New York City in 1903 before being staged in London and Vienna. The play was made into a movie three times. Zangwill earned more money from this play than from all his ghetto fiction combined.

When *The Melting-Pot* opened in Washington, D.C., in 1909, it received a warm reception led by President Theodore Roosevelt, who attended the first performance and applauded vigorously. Critics praised the production, and it drew enthusiastic audiences to theaters in Chicago and New York. *The Melting-Pot* did not open in London until 1914, where it was soon closed by the Foreign Office following the Russian government's objection to the play's references to Russia's persecution of Jews.

Zangwill expressed his hopes for peace in the unsuccessful *The War God* (1911), written in blank verse. The two plays in which Zangwill examined religious ideas were also disappointments. *The Next Religion* ran briefly in New York City in 1912, after the official censor banned it from the English stage considering it a derogatory portrait of Christianity. *Plaster Saints* opened in London in 1914 but met with little enthusiasm. Neither of Zangwill's political dramas, *The Cockpit*, produced in 1921, nor *The Forcing House*, staged shortly before Zangwill's death, succeeded.

In 1895, Zangwill met and fell in love with Edith Ayrton, a writer and ardent feminist. Although she was not Jewish, Zangwill married her in 1903; they had three children. After meeting Ayrton, Zangwill became an active speaker and writer for the women's suffrage movement. As World War I approached, he became an outspoken pacifist, but when war broke out, he supported Britain, despising Germany's autocratic militarism.

In 1895, Zangwill met the Zionist leader, Theodor Herzl, who converted him into an enthusiastic Zionist. Zangwill attended the First World Zionist Congress in 1897 and wrote vigorous essays expressing the pressing need for a Jewish homeland to which the persecuted Jews of Russia could flee. He joined Herzl in urging acceptance of the British government's offer of territory in East Africa. He was disappointed and angered when the Seventh Zionist Congress, insisting that only a Jewish homeland in Palestine was acceptable, rejected the British offer in 1905. Hoping to revive the East African plan, Zangwill resigned from the congress and formed the Jewish Territorial Organization for the Settlement of Jews Within the British Empire. Zangwill argued that Turkish control of Palestine made establishing a homeland there impossible, and the urgent needs of Russian Jews demanded an immediate solution. As president of the Jewish Territorial Organization, Zangwill devoted most of his time to the cause, writing numerous articles and unsuccessfully negotiating with the British government in pursuit of his dream.

Recognizing that his serious plays had been unsuccessful, Zangwill tried to revitalize his playwriting career with a satirical comedy. He had high hopes for *We Moderns* when it opened in the United States in 1923, with Helen Hayes in the leading role. However, reviews were devastating, and the play soon closed. A furious Zangwill blamed the production and decided to put on the play himself in London in 1925, where it again failed. Zangwill's mental and physical health deteriorated as he struggled with the play. He suffered a nervous breakdown and entered a nursing home, where he died unexpectedly at the age of sixty-two.

ANALYSIS

Although Israel Zangwill's fame rests on his fiction dealing with Jewish themes, just three of his twenty-one plays directly involve Jews. Two of the three (*Children of the Ghetto* and *The King of Schnorrers*) are based on previously published stories; only *The Melting-Pot*, dealing with religious and ethnic intermarriage, is an original work. Zangwill's early successes described the pathos and comedy of ghetto life. As he concentrated on playwriting, he became more didactic and turned to universal themes—his dramas now dealt with political problems, social and economic issues, war and peace, and the nature of true religion.

Despite the significance of the ideas he dramatized, few critics consider Zangwill a major playwright. Too often the plays deteriorate into sentimental melodramas, with stereotypical characters and unrealistic dialogue that detract from the serious themes he explored.

MERELY MARY ANN

Lancelot, a handsome and snobbish young composer, at first scorns a naïve but pretty serving girl, then begins to find her attractive, despite her coarse manners, and falls in love with her. When Mary Ann inherits a fortune from her brother in the United States, Lancelot decides he is not good enough for her, and the two part. The short story on which the play was based ended on this note, but for the stage version, Zangwill added a happy ending. Six years later, Lancelot, now a famous composer, returns to London and is reunited with his love. Despite the improbability of both the separation and reunion of the lovers, Zangwill's sentimental melodrama won praise from critics and attracted larger audiences than any of his serious plays.

THE MELTING-POT

David Quixano, an orphaned young Jewish immigrant composer whose parents were murdered in Russia during the Kishinev massacre of Jews, lives with his uncle and great-aunt in New York City. To the horror of his orthodox great-aunt, David no longer observes the Sabbath nor the rituals of Judaism. He hopes to write an American symphony celebrating the United States as God's crucible, welcoming all creeds and nationalities in order to blend them into a greater, all-inclusive humanity.

When David meets Vera Revendal, a Russian Christian, the two fall in love and plan to marry, despite the opposition of both their families. David's uncle, although himself no longer an observant Jew, turns him out of the house for proposing to marry outside the faith. Baron Revendal cannot believe his daughter could lower herself to marry a Jew. When David learns that Baron Revendal was responsible for the Kishinev massacre in which his parents perished, he calls off the marriage. However, after the successful presentation of David's American symphony, the two are reunited. At the end of the play, they are seen, hand in hand, contemplating the sunset and praising the United States as God's crucible, transforming all its people into a new human race.

Although audiences and many critics were enthusiastic, not everyone liked Zangwill's endorsement of religious and ethnic amalgamation. Jews objected to the idea that Judaism would be abandoned in the melting pot, and Christians did not agree that they needed to be fused with something else. Zangwill unconvincingly denied that the play celebrated intermarriage. He also found it difficult to answer those who wondered how he could reconcile the seeming contradiction between his celebration of the blending of nationalities in his play with his simultaneous fervor for Zionism and establishment of a Jewish national state.

THE NEXT RELIGION

Reverend Stephen Trame, an Anglican minister dissatisfied with traditional Christianity, proclaims the need for a new religion that will accept the revelations of modern science. As his religion develops and attracts converts, Trame adds ritual and dogma to please worshipers and monetary contributors. He urges devotees of the new religion to honor the memories of the three secular saints of his new church by following the ideals of brotherhood, reason, and love preached by Giuseppi Mazzini, Ralph Waldo Emerson, and Algernon Swinburne.

Some critics assume that because the trio of saints in the play are also people Zangwill admired, he therefore agreed with Trame's theology. However, because

Trame's religion becomes just as ritualistic and superstitious as the religion he rejected, Zangwill's drama is more an exposition of the difficulty involved in creating a replacement for the traditions of the past than an endorsement of a specific new religion.

Zangwill again tried writing about religious problems in *Plaster Saints*, in which he describes the dilemma of a clergyman who sins. He desires to atone for his sin but finds it difficult to do so without damaging his innocent family. Neither *The Next Religion* nor *Plaster Saints* pleased critics or attracted audiences.

THE COCKPIT AND THE FORCING HOUSE

The exiled heir to the throne of the fictional Balkan country of Valdania, who has grown up in New York, is recalled to her native country. There she hopes to improve schools and colleges and teach her people religious tolerance by molding the country into an imitation of the United States. Her dreams are shattered when the political leadership of Valdania leads the country into war with its neighbors, a socialist opponent of war is assassinated, and nationalist mobs riot in the streets.

The Forcing House is even more pessimistic about the possibility of realizing political ideals. Socialists ascend to power, promising universal equality and democracy. However, the government is taken over by opportunists who exploit the party's extremist propaganda to establish a fascist-style dictatorship that destroys existing political and social rights. Neither play attracted favorable responses, and both soon closed.

OTHER MAJOR WORKS

LONG FICTION: *The Premier and the Painter*, 1888 (with Louis Cowen, as J. Freeman Bell); *The Big Bow Mystery: The Perfect Crime*, 1892; *Children of the Ghetto: Being Pictures of a Peculiar People*, 1892; *Joseph the Dreamer*, 1895; *The Master*, 1895; *The People's Saviour*, 1898; *The Mantle of Elijah*, 1900; *Jinny the Carrier: A Folk Comedy of Rural England*, 1919.

SHORT FICTION: *The Bachelors' Club*, 1891; *The Old Maids' Club*, 1892; *Ghetto Tragedies*, 1893; *Merely Mary Ann*, 1893; *The King of Schnorrers: Grotesques and Fantasies*, 1894; *Dreamers of the Ghetto*, 1898; *The Celibate's Club: Being the United Stories of the Bachelors' Club and the Old Maids' Club*, 1898; *The Grey Wig: Stories and Novelettes*, 1903; *Ghetto Comedies*, 1907.

POETRY: *The Ballad of Moses*, 1892; *Blind Children*, 1903.

NONFICTION: *Motza Kleis*, 1882 (anonymously with Louis Cowen); *"A Doll's House" Repaired*, 1891 (with Eleanor Marx Aveling); *Hebrew, Jew, Israelite*, 1892; *The Position of Judaism*, 1895; *Without Prejudice*, 1896; *The People's Saviour*, 1898; *The East African Question: Zionism and England's Offer*, 1904; *What Is the ITO?*, 1905; *A Land of Refuge*, 1907; *Talked Out!*, 1907; *One and One Are Two*, 1907; *Old Fogeys and Old Bogeys*, 1909; *The Lock on the Ladies*, 1909; *Report on the Purpose of Jewish Settlement in Cyrenaica*, 1909; *Be Fruitful and Multiply*, 1909; *Italian Fantasies*, 1910; *Sword and Spirit*, 1910; *The Hithertos*, 1912; *The Problem of the Jewish Race*, 1912; *Report on the Jewish Settlement in Angora*, 1913; *The War and the Women*, 1915; *The War for the World*, 1916; *The Principle of Nationalities*, 1917; *The Service of the Synagogue*, 1917 (with Nina Davis Salaman and Elsie Davis); *Chosen Peoples: The Hebraic Ideal Versus the Teutonic*, 1918; *Hands off Russia*, 1919; *The Jewish Pogroms in the Ukraine*, 1919 (with others); *The Voice of Jerusalem*, 1920; *Watchman, What of the Night?*, 1923; *Is the Ku Klux Klan Constructive or Destructive? A Debate Between Imperial Wizard Evans, Israel Zangwill, and Others*, 1924; *Now and Forever: A Conversation with Mr. Israel Zangwill on the Jew and the Future*, 1925 (with Samuel Roth); *Our Own*, 1926; *Speeches, Articles, and Letters*, 1937; *Zangwill in the Melting-Pot: Selections*, n.d.

TRANSLATION: *Selected Religious Poems of Ibn Gabirol, Solomon ben Judah, Known as Avicebron, 1020?-1070?*, 1923.

BIBLIOGRAPHY

Adams, Elsie Bonita. *Israel Zangwill*. New York: Twayne, 1971. Along with a thorough critical analysis of Zangwill's literary works, Adams provides a brief biography, a chronology, and an annotated bibliography.

Leftwich, Joseph. *Israel Zangwill*. New York: T. Yoseloff, 1957. A memoir of Zangwill written by a follower. Leftwich describes personal reactions to his hero's life and works. He devotes a chapter to Zangwill's plays.

Udelson, Joseph H. *Dreamer of the Ghetto: The Life and Works of Israel Zangwill*. Tuscaloosa: University of Alabama Press, 1990. Udelson views Zangwill's works as a series of meditations on the nature of Jewish identity. He analyzes the contra-

dictory positions Zangwill entertained from time to time, noting readers' responses to them.

Wohlgelernter, Maurice. *Israel Zangwill: A Study*. New York: Columbia University Press, 1964. Concentrates on Zangwill's ideas regarding Zionism and religion, as well as art and politics. One chapter analyses the concept of ethnic amalgamation expressed in *The Melting-Pot*, along with reactions to the play.

Milton Berman

ZEAMI MOTOKIYO

Born: Near Nara, Japan; 1363
Died: Kyoto, Japan; 1443

PRINCIPAL DRAMA

Aridōshi

Ashikari (*The Reed Cutter*, 1970)

Atsumori (English translation, 1921)

Aya no tsuzumu (*The Damask Drum*, 1921)

Izutsu (*Well-curb*, 1955)

Kinuta (*The Clothbeating Block*, 1960)

Matsukaze (based on Kan'ami Kiyotsugu's play *Matsukaze and Murasame; The Wind in the Pines*, 1960)

Semimaru (English translation, 1970)

OTHER LITERARY FORMS

In addition to his plays, Zeami Motokiyo wrote a series of treatises on acting and playwriting, prepared for his family and his descendants, in which he discussed a wide range of topics, from styles of acting, singing, and gesture to matters concerning the philosophy of the theater and the complementary roles of playwright and actor in creating the sort of total theatrical experience he had in mind. The treatises do much to explain the aesthetics behind the individual dramas of Zeami that remain. In addition, he wrote a short essay on his life in exile, short verses (possibly sections of plays that are now lost), and a brief artistic reminiscence.

ACHIEVEMENTS

As a young man, Zeami Motokiyo took the popular theatrical forms available to him as an actor, and through his education, the force of his will, and his insight into the theatrical process, mastered a highly disciplined and poetic theatrical form, the Nō, which not only became the central focus for the highest traditions in the Japanese theater of his period but also the model and the touchstone for all the developments that followed in later centuries. In a very real way, Zeami and his dramas remained a source of inspiration for poets and playwrights up to the twentieth century. Not only did later writers of the Nō continue to emulate his methods of composing plays, but Kabuki and puppet dramatists from the seventeenth century onward borrowed plots, characters, and settings from Zeami's Nō dramas, often as a gesture of homage to the man whom they regarded as the greatest dramatist in the entire Japanese tradition. In the twentieth century as well, there was new interest in the work of Zeami. Modern Japanese dramatists such as Yukio Mishima have rewritten some of the old plays, finding in them the seeds of a contemporary consciousness, and Western writers and musicians from William Butler Yeats and Paul Claudel to Bertolt Brecht and Benjamin Britten have taken sustenance from these works to create their own modern versions of the Nō. For modern Western playwrights, Zeami, read in translation since the 1920's, seemed the first and perhaps the greatest exponent of a form of total theater that combined text, movement, gesture, dance, music, and chant into one transcendental unity. Other practitioners of the Nō, notably Zeami's father Kan'ami, began to approach this synthesis, but only Zeami fully attained it. For the modern Western reader, Zeami's dramas have a particular power in their concentrated poetic language that, even in translation, makes these plays uniquely able to suggest a dramatic movement from the world of everyday understanding to the realm of the ineffable. No other writer in the long Japanese tradition of the Nō possessed quite this power of language. In this aspect of his work, Zeami, however gifted as an actor, singer, and theoretician, was truly singular.

BIOGRAPHY

Despite the fact that Zeami Motokiyo was famous in his lifetime, relatively little is known about him. This is partially because, in his time, actors had very low social status. In fact, without the help of powerful patronage, Zeami might never have received the level of literary training one needed to learn the canons of Japanese poetry, which figure so heavily in the aesthetics of his dramaturgy.

Zeami began his career as a child actor in the troupe of his father Kan'ami (1333-1384), who took his troupe to shrines and temples for performances at festivals all over the country, staging his plays for a variety of local patrons. When Zeami was a boy of twelve, the shōgun Ashikaga Yoshimitsu (1358-1408), the political ruler of the nation and a powerful patron of the arts, saw his performance and was so captivated by the beauties of Zeami's technique as well as his person that he decided to patronize Kan'ami's troupe and have Zeami educated properly. It is clear from reading Zeami's treatises, written in his mature years, that he had become extremely well versed in the arts of poetry, literature, and philosophy, subjects to which a low-ranking person such as an actor could normally expect to have no access whatsoever.

Zeami's father died when the young actor was only twenty-two, and Zeami spent the rest of his career as head of the theatrical troupe his father had led,

serving as administrator, actor, playwright, and theoretician. As long as the patronage of Yoshimitsu continued, Zeami enjoyed high favor; when Yoshimitsu's successor Yoshimochi took power, however, Zeami began to lose favor in the court. In 1428, when Yoshimochi's younger brother Yoshinori became shōgun, Zeami and his family began to suffer real hardships. Eventually, at age seventy-two, Zeami was exiled to the remote island of Sado. Tradition has it that he was pardoned and permitted to return to the capital shortly before his death in 1443, but details concerning these matters are conflicting and obscure.

ANALYSIS

Zeami Motokiyo wrote a considerable number of plays. Many, but not all, of the texts survive. Because of Zeami's importance in the history of the Nō and of the homage always paid him, a large number of plays have been generously ascribed to his hand. Modern scholarship has lowered the number considerably. Judicious cross-referencing in the various treatises written by Zeami suggests a total of between forty and fifty plays that can safely be attributed to him.

It is also extremely difficult to date the individual texts because accurate performance records do not exist from that time and because his plays were often restaged, given new titles, and partially rewritten by Zeami himself. In his treatises, Zeami always recommended, in performance, a juxtaposition of the old and the new, in order to stimulate but not bewilder an audience, and he often adapted even his best plays to suit new circumstances of performance.

The dramatic form that Zeami perfected, Nō, differs considerably from any Western form of drama. Perhaps the closest Western analogy might be chamber opera, in which music and text intertwine, yet the parallel is inexact, since Nō involves masks and elaborate costuming, no scenery, only male actors, a few props, and a crucial use of dance. Even in musical terms, the score of a Nō play would be considered as partially improvised, with the orchestra and chorus following the lead of the chief performer. Thus, reading the text of a play by Zeami is a process similar to reading an opera libretto, which suggests, but does not re-create, the whole. Unlike many librettos, however, the Zeami texts reveal poetry of striking, synthetic beauty. For such modern Western writers as Yeats and Claudel, Zeami had achieved a form of poetic drama that seemed fully complete in itself.

Reading the text of a Zeami play, like looking over a libretto, may take only a few moments, but because the poetic concentration of the language is high, the full performance of one of his plays may take almost two hours. It has been conjectured that in Zeami's time, however, the pace was considerably quicker. At that time, a program of performances lasted all day, beginning with the performance of a slow and dignified play and concluding with a play of rapid tempo to end on a note of high excitement. After Zeami's time, the series was codified into a series of five groups; a normal program would include one of each, plus some comic interludes called *kyōgen*. It is by no means clear from Zeami's treatises, however, that he himself restricted his programs to an orderly sequence of god plays, warrior plays, woman plays, plays concerning madness, and demon plays. Even so, he did write plays that fit these later categories. Of the approximately fifty plays that he did compose, a majority have been translated, but a number of Nō plays by Zeami that were considered important in his time have still not been rendered into any Western language. Many of those plays are in the category of god plays, dealing with Buddhist and, more particularly, Shinto deities. Zeami's plays in the other categories are more familiar.

The form of a Nō play, as developed by Zeami and discussed at length in his treatises, uses a particular structure that is repeated (as are various musical and dramatic aspects found in traditional operatic form) in most of the plays. A Nō drama might best be described as a vision. The skill of the playwright lies in his ability to lead his audience into that vision. The figures presented and the poetic worlds conveyed may change, but the means by which the vision becomes possible on the stage must remain the same. Usually a particular play begins with the arrival of a priest or other traveler, who comes to a spot that has a history: a place where a famous person has lived or died, a crucial battle was fought, or a noted poet has

found inspiration. Opened to the experience of the place by his own knowledge and sympathy, the traveler next meets a person, often a rather mysterious one, who, through conversation, ascertains that the traveler is indeed one who has the ability and the sympathy to grasp the real meaning of what has happened there. Often this section of a Zeami play is couched in elegant and poetic language, so the first encounter is followed by an interlude in which a rustic or some other similar character repeats the nature of the incident; in this way, everyone in the audience can grasp the significance of the encounter. Then, in the final section of the play, the mysterious person whom the traveler first met reveals his or her true nature and describes in grand poetic language the event that happened on the spot, re-creating the moment also in dance, song, and mime. The play, which has begun slowly, reaches its highest pitch, then concludes as the vision fades and the newly enlightened priest or traveler, along with the audience, once again finds himself in the real world.

Although Zeami's plays vary in tonality and subject matter, they all have certain strong philosophical and emotional resemblances. The pain and chagrin of passion remembered, the growth of an understanding that salvation lies beyond and not in this world, and the saving power of a sincere emotion all link the dramas of Zeami to the sort of Buddhist philosophy prevalent in Japan during the difficult political period in which he lived. The confusions and disappointments of secular society at this time were such that a withdrawal in search of some transcendental understanding of reality became an important possibility for many people before, during, and after Zeami's generation. Such attitudes thus provided a logical point of departure for the characters that the playwright created for his audiences. Yet the kind of emotional self-consciousness that Zeami posited in those characters seems to make them accessible as well (though initially in radically different ways) to modern readers and audiences who may, for quite different social, political, and personal reasons, feel themselves alienated from society. It may be links such as these that make the work of Zeami seem strikingly contemporary. Even modern readers and spectators find that Zeami's work touches and justifies their most private feelings, showing by remote example something about the human condition that is wholly recognizable. In the end, Zeami's powerful belief in the efficacy of poetry, as Yeats was the first Westerner to observe, comes through as clearly today as when these dramas were first composed and performed.

THE WIND IN THE PINES

Zeami did not invent the form of the Nō play; indeed, he credited his father with the first high accomplishments in the genre. Nevertheless, it was in Zeami's hands that the potential of the form was fully realized, and in all five categories of Nō drama, Zeami's work constitutes an unsurpassed standard. Zeami often adapted plays by other writers; perhaps his greatest achievement is the reworking of a text presumably composed by his father; Zeami's play is entitled *The Wind in the Pines*. This piece is a "woman play" about the love of two fishergirls, Matsukaze and Murasame, for a courtier from the capital, Ariwara no Yukihira (818-893), who was exiled at Suma Beach, where the play takes place. In *The Wind in the Pines*, every element of Zeami's art combines to form a unified poetic whole.

Suma Beach by Zeami's time had a number of important literary associations, notably the fact that Prince Genji, the protagonist of the eleventh century novel *Genji monogatari* (*The Tale of Genji*, 1925-1933), had himself been exiled there. That fictional account in turn may well have been inspired by the actual exile of Yukihira, who left behind a famous thirty-one-syllable *waka* poem about the time he spent at Suma. Using this poem, Zeami brings his pilgrim-priest to Suma, where, as he is walking along, he notices a peculiar pine tree. Learning that the pine was planted on the graves of the two fishergirls, Matsukaze and Murasame, he is reminded that the tree, like their names, has lingered long after their deaths. He decides to stay and pray for them. Matsukaze and Murasame now enter, and Zeami creates for these two characters a highly poetic dialogue in which images of nature, in particular the moon (a symbol of Buddhist enlightenment), blend with a sense of their own evanescence as they dip into the

salt brine. The priest asks if he may stay the night in their humble shed, and as they agree, he comes to realize that he has encountered the ghosts of the two girls. In the brilliant climax of the play, Matsukaze reenacts her meeting with Yukihira, actually donning his cloak in a striking scene of remembered yearning. As the "dream of deluded passion" retreats, Matsukaze (whose name literally means "wind in the pines") and Murasame ("autumn rain") return to nature. Only the priest remains, with the sound of both in his ear. In this text, Zeami has captured with startling poetic power the Buddhist idea that each disparate person and thing is bound together in the all-encompassing Buddha nature. Like all of Zeami's plays, *The Wind in the Pines* reveals a deep knowledge of earlier classical Japanese literature, particularly poetry. The text is filled with a variety of quotations from numerous sources, skillfully woven into the individual lines, yet the intellectual pleasures of recognition for the audience are transcended by Zeami's own images growing out of those quotations, so that the poem of Yukihira serves as a seed from which Zeami's own gifts can blossom. All these images are combined by Zeami to create a sense of *aware*, that classic Japanese literary virtue that might best be described as a sense of the beauty and sadness that lie in one's intuitive understanding of the transience of all earthly things.

THE DAMASK DRUM

Another play by Zeami that deals with the pain of love is *The Damask Drum*, in which an old gardener, who has fallen in love with a lady of the court, is told that, despite the differences in their rank and age, if he can manage to make the sound of the drum that hangs by a garden pond reach her ears, she will allow him to see her again. The gardener, hoping for "an autumn of love" to close "the sequence of my years," attempts to beat the drum, only to find that it is covered not with leather but with damask and thus makes no sound. He then drowns himself in the pond, and the lady, possessed by his angry spirit, has a vision of the ghost of the gardener, who rises from the water to accuse her of her misdeeds. As with *The Wind in the Pines*, the play is filled with poetic images borrowed from poem collections, Chinese philosophical texts, and Japanese folk songs, each citation reinforcing the other to create the moral vision of a woman who bears the pain of the death that she has brought about. *The Damask Drum* is among the Nō plays adapted for modern actors by the celebrated modern novelist and playwright Yukio Mishima.

ATSUMORI

Among the warrior plays written by Zeami, none is more famous or more often performed than *Atsumori*. The drama is his adaption of a famous scene presented in the Japanese medieval war chronicles *Heike monogatari* (wr. 1190-1221, pb. c. 1240; *The Heike Monogatari*, 1918), which describes in detail the terrible civil wars in Kyoto in 1185 between the Minamoto and the Taira clans, wars that weakened the power of the central court and began the rise of military government in Japan. *The Heike Monogatari* deals more with human tragedy than political commentary, and Zeami's choice of the story of Atsumori illustrates well the sense of human loss inherent in the fall of the Taira. The story concerns the encounter between Kumagai, a warrior of the eventually victorious Minamoto clan, with the young courtier Atsumori, of the Taira clan. Kumagai himself is a rustic from the country, and he much admires the elegance and education of his putative enemies, the Taira. Riding down the beach, he meets an enemy soldier; pulling off the soldier's helmet, Kumagai finds the young Atsumori, a youth no older than his own son. Atsumori is, indeed, the very cultivated young man whose flute playing Kumagai had heard and admired just the night before coming from behind the enemy lines. Kumagai decides to spare Atsumori, who might well be his own son, but as he prepares to let him go, Kumagai is seen by other soldiers from his own clan. Atsumori realizes that he must die and asks simply that, because Kumagai is so understanding, it be by Kumagai's own hand. Kumagai is forced to behead the young man, and filled with sorrow over the meaninglessness of all earthly existence, he gives up his military career to become a Buddhist priest.

Zeami's dramatization begins many years later when Kumagai, now the priest Rensei, is on a pilgrimage. Returning to the scene of the battle to pray for the soul of Atsumori, he hears a young reaper playing the flute and is eventually rewarded with the knowledge that the reaper is the ghost of Atsumori himself, who now seeks the priest's prayers to gain salvation. Atsumori reenacts the scene of his death, and as the play ends, he asks that Rensei pray for him so that friend and foe alike may be born again on the same lotus in paradise. Like the woman play *The Wind in the Pines*, the warrior play *Atsumori* culminates in transcendence of earthly passion, but here the context and the language are altogether appropriate for the military subject. Zeami wrote in his treatises that a writer of Nō plays should choose for his subject a situation with which the audience will be at least somewhat familiar. In *Atsumori*, as in *The Wind in the Pines*, Zeami's originality and skill as a poet and dramatist lie not with the choice of subject matter but with the astonishing appropriateness of dramatic arrangement, movement, and diction.

ARIDŌSHI

In *Aridōshi*, a play about a Shinto god, the pilgrim himself is a poet. Ki no Tsurayuki (872-946), an excellent *waka* poet and writer of prose, and the first writer on Japanese aesthetics in Japanese literature, had become by Zeami's time a veritable god of composition. In the play, Tsurayuki travels to a famous Shinto shrine. As he arrives, night has fallen and he seeks light and a place to spend the night. He encounters the Shinto deity Aridōshi, who does not reveal his true nature at once but asks Tsurayuki why he is profaning the sacred space of the shrine. If he is really a great poet, Aridōshi continues, then he must offer up a poem to appease the god. Tsurayuki thereupon composes a fine poem, and the god, now convinced of the poet's sincerity, reveals his true nature and performs a ritual dance. The text ends with a paean to purity, poetry, dance, and song. The god disappears, and Tsurayuki, overwhelmed by his experience of the sacred, "continues his journey in the morning dawn." The structure of the play is quite like the others described, but in mood, musicality, and language, the effect is altogether unique.

THE CLOTHBEATING BLOCK AND SEMIMARU

Among Zeami's works, the plays dealing with mad characters (many of whom, because of their condition, are in touch with gods and spirits) are particularly effective as stage pieces. The circumstances giving rise to madness differ widely in the various plays of this category. *The Clothbeating Block*, for example, has as its main character a deserted wife who pines to death because she has been abandoned by her husband. In *Semimaru*, Zeami takes up the legend of the blind prince who was abandoned by his father the emperor and has lived as a recluse in a hut in the mountains, playing the lute. In Zeami's adaptation of the legend, the prince, Semimaru, accepts his abandonment by his father, saying that it was undertaken "to purge in this world my burden of the past, and spare me suffering in the world to come." He is joined in his solitude by his sister Sakagami, now half-crazed herself. Attracted by the sound of his music, she talks with him of their past and their affection for each other; yet eventually, she insists that she, too, must continue on with her own obscure pilgrimage, and Semimaru bids her a muted farewell as she disappears.

OTHER MAJOR WORKS

NONFICTION: *Kadensho*, 1400-1402 (English translation, 1968); *Kyakuraige*, 1433; *Kintōsho*, 1436; *On the Art of the Nō Drama: The Major Treatises of Zeami*, 1984.

BIBLIOGRAPHY

Hare, Thomas Blenman. *Zeami's Style: The Noh Plays of Zeami Motokiyo*. Stanford, Calif.: Stanford University Press, 1986. An examination of Zeami's life and his plays., Bibliography and index.

Keene, Donald. *Nō and Bunraku: Two Forms of Japanese Theatre*. 1965 and 1966. Reprint. New York: Columbia University Press, 1990. This work combines two separately published volumes on two early forms of Japanese theater, Nō and Bunraku (puppet theater). Zeami is included in the explanation of Nō theater. Bibliography and indexes.

_____. *Nō: The Classical Theatre of Japan*. Rev. ed. New York: Kodansha International, 1973. Keene's classic work on Nō retains its importance in understanding Zeami and this form of Japanese theater.

Keene, Donald, ed. *Twenty Plays of the Nō Theatre*. New York: Columbia University Press, 1970. This classic work contains translations of plays by Zeami and other major writers of Nō dramas. Also contains an explanation of the conventions of Nō theater.

Ortolani, Benito, and Samuel L. Leiter, eds. *Zeami and the Nō Theatre in the World*. New York: Graduate School and University Center of the City University of New York, 1998. A collection of the papers presented at the Zeami and the Nō Theatre in the World symposium, held in New York City in October, 1997.

Sekine, Masaru. *Ze-ami and His Theories of Noh Drama*. Gerrards Cross, England: C. Smythe, 1985. An examination of Zeami and his views about Nō drama. Index.

J. Thomas Rimer

PAUL ZINDEL

Born: Staten Island, New York; May 15, 1936

PRINCIPAL DRAMA
Dimensions of Peacocks, pr. 1959
Euthanasia and the Endless Hearts, pr. 1960
A Dream of Swallows, pr. 1964

The Effect of Gamma Rays on Man-in-the-Moon Marigolds, pr. 1965, pb. 1971
And Miss Reardon Drinks a Little, pr. 1967, pb. 1972
The Secret Affairs of Mildred Wild, pr. 1972, pb. 1973

The Ladies Should Be in Bed, pb. 1973
Ladies at the Alamo, pr. 1975, pb. 1977
A Destiny with Half Moon Street, pr. 1983
Amulets Against the Dragon Forces, pr., pb. 1989
Every Seventeen Minutes the Crowd Goes Crazy!,
    pr. 1995, pb. 1996

OTHER LITERARY FORMS

Paul Zindel once considered himself primarily a playwright, and in 1990 said, "basically, I'm a dramatist"; he has, however, enjoyed great success as a writer of novels for teenagers, and it is in this capacity that he is best known. His first such work, *The Pigman* (1968), has sold in the millions, and sequels such as *The Pigman's Legacy* (1980) have followed. A 1989 book, *A Begonia for Miss Applebaum*, was critically well received, and the autobiographical *The Pigman and Me* was published in 1992. Zindel's teen characters confront the pangs and thrills of young adult reality as they reach for friendship, for romantic love, for mature perspectives on sexuality, and for success or at least survival in school or work. In 1984, Zindel published his first novel for adults, *When a Darkness Falls*. During the 1990's Zindel began writing series chapter novels including comedy, mystery, and horror for pre-teen audiences.

Zindel has written screenplays for *Up the Sandbox* (1972), *Mame* (1974), *Runaway Train* (1983), and *Maria's Lovers* (1984), and a teleplay, *Let Me Hear You Whisper* (1966). He also writes for periodicals.

ACHIEVEMENTS

Paul Zindel's *The Effect of Gamma Rays on Man-in-the-Moon Marigolds* gained acceptance not only in the form of broadcasts on National Educational Television in New York but also through stage performances at the Alley Theatre in Houston, Texas. Zindel secured a Ford Foundation grant as a playwright-in-residence at the Alley in 1967. In 1970, the play opened in New York, Off-Broadway; then it moved to the New Theatre on Broadway. It closed on May 14, 1972, after 819 performances. *The Effect of Gamma Rays on Man-in-the-Moon Marigolds* received an Obie Award for the best Off-Broadway play in 1970. Also in 1970, Zindel won the New York Drama

Critics Circle Award for Best American Play and the Vernon Rice Drama Desk Award as the most promising playwright of the season. In 1971, he received an honorary doctorate from his alma mater, Wagner College, and a Pulitzer Prize in Drama.

The success of *The Effect of Gamma Rays on Man-in-the-Moon Marigolds* was followed in 1971 by a Broadway production of *And Miss Reardon Drinks a Little*, a play previously staged in Los Angeles in 1967. The Broadway production, starring Julie Harris, ran for 108 performances, and the play made the list of the ten best plays for the 1971 season. Zindel next brought a comedy to Broadway, *The Secret Affairs of Mildred Wild*, which lasted for only twenty-three performances.

Joining the Actors Studio in 1973, Zindel extensively revised earlier material to produce *Ladies at the Alamo*, which he himself directed at Actors Studio for a two-week run in 1975. He directed the same play in a brief Broadway run in 1977, as well as a New York revival of *The Effect of Gamma Rays on Man-in-the-Moon Marigolds* in 1978. The Coconut Grove Playhouse in Coconut Grove, Florida, premiered Zindel's *A Destiny with Half Moon Street* in its 1982-1983 repertory.

Zindel's plays have moved from little and regional theaters to Broadway and back. Critics say that his later plays have not fulfilled the expectations raised by his initial success. Still, Zindel's plays continue to be performed in high school, college, touring company, and regional repertory productions.

In 1998 Zindel was honored, along with forty-three other notable dramatists such as Edward Albee, by a walk-of-fame bronze star on the Playwrights' Sidewalk outside the Lortel Theater in Greenwich Village. In 2002 he also received the Margaret A. Edwards Award for his lifetime writing contribution to literature for young adults, an honor presented by the Young Adult Library Services Association.

BIOGRAPHY

Paul Zindel was born on May 15, 1936, in Staten Island, New York, to Paul and Betty (née Frank) Zindel. His father, a police officer, abandoned his wife and two small children, Paul and a sister. Betty

Zindel, a practical nurse, launched into numerous ventures, ranging from real estate to dog breeding, and sometimes took in terminally ill patients for board and care. The family moved almost annually.

This transient lifestyle and his mother's unwillingness, if not inability, to form meaningful relationships acquainted young Zindel with various forms of loss. Pets allowed at one home might be forbidden by the next landlord. Dogs raised for sale would eventually be sold. Board-and-care patients would sometimes die. The frequent moves, too, kept the boy, more often than not, in the role of newcomer in a neighborhood. It grew simpler to enjoy the worlds of imagination and, when possible, the manageable environments of aquaria and terraria.

In school, Zindel occasionally acted in plays and skits, some of which he wrote himself. At fifteen, he contracted tuberculosis and spent about eighteen months in a sanatorium, the sole youth in an otherwise adult community. He learned some parlor games and studied piano during his stay; more important, he became an interested observer of adult behavior. Returned to health and to high school, Zindel wrote a play for a contest sponsored by the American Cancer Society; it centered on a young pianist who recovers from a serious illness to play at Carnegie Hall. The play won for Zindel a Parker pen.

Zindel majored in chemistry at Wagner College in New York City. While completing his bachelor of science degree, he took a creative writing course with Edward Albee and wrote a play, *Dimensions of Peacocks*, during his senior year. Zindel was graduated in 1958, and after working briefly as a technical writer for a Manhattan chemical firm, he decided that he wanted to teach.

Completing a master of science degree at Wagner in 1959, Zindel began teaching chemistry and physics at Tottenville High School on Staten Island. His *Dimensions of Peacocks* received a minor staging; more significant, he attended his first professional theater production, Lillian Hellman's *Toys in the Attic* (pr., pb. 1960), and left with his appetite for theater whetted.

For the next several years, Zindel continued to teach and to write. A second play, *Euthanasia and the Endless Hearts*, had a brief coffeehouse production in 1960, and a third, *A Dream of Swallows*, managed a single performance Off-Broadway in 1964.

The Effect of Gamma Rays on Man-in-the-Moon Marigolds fared better. In 1965, it opened at the Alley Theatre in Houston, Texas. New York's National Educational Television ran four showings of its abridged teleplay format. Recognition grew, with the Ford Foundation underwriting Zindel as playwright-in-residence at the Alley in 1967. By 1969, Zindel felt sufficiently established in theater to resign from teaching. Playing in New York, *The Effect of Gamma Rays on Man-in-the-Moon Marigolds* accrued its various awards that prefaced the Pulitzer. From the New York plaudits, Zindel went to writing screenplays in California. Paul Newman produced and directed a movie version of *The Effect of Gamma Rays on Man-in-the-Moon Marigolds* in 1972, and Zindel wrote screenplays for *Up the Sandbox* and *Mame*.

When *The Effects of Gamma Rays on Man-in-the-Moon Marigolds* was on the rise, a publisher suggested that Zindel should write fiction for the teen market. His first teen novel, *The Pigman*, was both a critical and a popular success, as were several subsequent teen novels. Some critics have complained that while the argot of the young constantly changes, the teen dialogue in Zindel's later novels is indistinguishable from that found in his novels of the late 1960's and early 1970's. In other ways, too, Zindel has been accused of merely repeating a successful formula.

In 1973, following the year in California, Zindel made two major decisions. He married Bonnie Hildebrand, a screenwriter with whom he later had two children, Elizabeth and David, and he joined the Actors Studio in New York to learn the language of acting and directing as well as playwriting. At the same time, he resumed work on a manuscript that National Educational Television had turned down in 1970 as too explicit. In its earlier version, the play had centered on the exchanges and revelations of a group of women playing bridge and watching an exhibitionist in a building across the street. Zindel shifted the setting to a theater in Texas, and the conflict to a battle for control of the theater. To make the five characters more authentic, Zindel conducted in-depth interviews with five actresses from the Actors Studio. The result was *Ladies at the Alamo*.

Beginning in the mid-1970's, Zindel became more active as a novelist than as a dramatist, but he continued to be involved in the theater, producing new work as well as adaptations. He occasionally traveled to regional productions of his plays as part of publicity campaigns (as he did for the 1990 Cleveland Playhouse revival of *The Effect of Gamma Rays on Man-in-the-Moon Marigolds*), and to be active as a moderator for the Actors Studio West, in the Los Angeles Playwrights Unit. According to interviews, the process of filmmaking was destructive for him. His young adult novels are sometimes turned into plays; for example, *Confessions of a Teenage Baboon* (1977) began as a novel but became *Amulets Against the Dragon Forces*, produced at the Circle Repertory Theatre in 1989. Zindel's 1995 play *Every Seventeen Minutes the Crowd Goes Crazy!* was written on commission for the American Conservatory Theater's Young Conservatory in San Francisco. Zindel claims to have enjoyed the process of working with young actors in rehearsal. He intended that the play would address the most critical issue of the decade, the failure of parents to fulfill traditional roles. At the time, his own children had recently left home for college. Zindel wrote for a big cast, believing that young actors needed and deserved as much time onstage as possible.

ANALYSIS

Paul Zindel's plays closely follow his own life experience; certain features of his early years recur in his drama. His mother was bitter, transient, reclusive, and presumably uncertain of her place in life. Zindel's major plays commonly depict women struggling for identity and fulfillment, often damaged, if not destroyed, by betrayals or deaths of loved ones. These women in turn fail to provide the adequate care so desperately needed by the young people for whom they are left responsible. Another theme of Zindel's plays is the notion that modern society has replaced traditional religion with a secular faith of scientism accompanied by unbridled self-indulgence.

Zindel's marvelous storytelling ability has capti-

vated millions, and several of his works have been translated. His plays, certainly not as well accepted by critics or the public, still appeal. Zindel describes the drama form as one in which the players must shout the message of the work. In this vein, his characters and events exhibit unsettling qualities: the old people border on grotesque, shambling versions of death; events are capped by illogical and unpredictable outcomes; and character motivations result in bizarre behaviors. However, Zindel's repugnant misfits lay claim to the compassion, empathy, and integrity of the audience. As Zindel explains in commenting on his more recent prose works, humor and horror have much in common, and these qualities are readily apparent in a majority of his dramatic works.

THE EFFECT OF GAMMA RAYS ON MAN-IN-THE-MOON MARIGOLDS

The Effect of Gamma Rays on Man-in-the-Moon Marigolds opens to observers the lives of Beatrice Hunsdorfer and her two teenage daughters, Ruth and Tillie. Beatrice, overtly modeled after Zindel's mother, is a cynical, verbally abusive paranoid schizophrenic. Her untidy home was once her father's vegetable store. Her husband left her long ago and later died of a heart attack. For income, Beatrice boards an aged woman who needs a walker to creep slowly from bed to table to bathroom and back to bed.

Ruth, the elder daughter, is the more physically attractive yet is emotionally unstable and subject to convulsions in times of stress. Tillie, the younger, is bright and eager to learn. Beatrice, more concerned about her girls' looks and marriageability than about their intellectual growth, badgers both daughters but is most severe with Tillie.

Act 1 opens with Tillie, in darkness, marveling that the atoms in her hand may trace back to a cosmic tongue of fire predating the birth of the sun and the solar system. As lights rise on the home scene, Beatrice fields a telephone call from Mr. Goodman, Tillie's science teacher. He is concerned about Tillie's absences. Beatrice responds with several defenses. She thanks Mr. Goodman for giving Tillie a pet rabbit and compliments him on his looks. Claiming that Tillie does not always want to go to school, Beatrice says that she does not want to put too much pressure on Tillie, lest she turn convulsive, as Ruth has done. The phone call ended, Beatrice derides Tillie and Mr. Goodman, then orders Tillie to stay home. The girl is anxious to see a cloud-chamber experiment in science class. Beatrice threatens to kill the rabbit if Tillie goes. In contrast, Beatrice encourages Ruth to go to school, lets her rummage through mother's purse for lipstick, and gives her a cigarette on request. Ruth scratches Beatrice's back and gives negative reports on Tillie's activities at school. She also reveals that she has seen the school file on the family. It records the parents' divorce, the absent father's death, and Ruth's nervous breakdown.

The scene fades to darkness, and again Tillie speaks. She describes the fountain of atoms visible in the cloud chamber, a phenomenon that could go on for eternity. Rising lights reveal Tillie preparing to plant irradiated seeds. Beatrice, scanning realty advertisements, mixes conjecture on the potential of various properties with questions about Tillie's science project. Nanny, the aged boarder, begins the slow trek to the table as Tillie tries to explain the concept of atomic half-life to Beatrice. Beatrice disparages Nanny, her daughters, and herself through derisive double meanings for the term "half-life."

Beatrice phones Mr. Goodman, expressing concern that Tillie's seeds were irradiated, turning aside his explanations. After several other demonstrations of instability and cruelty, Beatrice shows another aspect of her character. During a thunderstorm at night, Ruth suffers another seizure. Beatrice orders Tillie back to bed in typically harsh fashion but cradles Ruth with genuine compassion and tells how her father, Ruth's grandfather, used to sell fruit and vegetables from a horse-drawn wagon. Beatrice's mother had died quite early, and her father fell seriously ill while Beatrice was still rather young. Anxious for her future, he urged her to marry for security's sake. She still sees her father's face in her nightmares.

The following scene shows Beatrice again lashing out at Tillie and Nanny until Ruth dashes in. She reports excitedly that Tillie is a finalist in the science fair. The principal calls to ask Beatrice to attend the final judging and awards. Beatrice is rude and evasive. Her first thought is that people will ridicule her.

Only after Tillie runs off in tears does Beatrice realize how her paranoiac response has hurt Tillie.

Act 2 opens with the Hunsdorfers about to leave for the final science fair presentations. Working as an attendance aide for Mr. Goodman, Ruth has overheard gossip about Beatrice, who used to be called "Betty the Loon." Ruth blackmails Tillie into giving her the rabbit by threatening to tell Beatrice the school gossip. Tillie concedes—she deeply wants her mother to share this one significant event in her life, even at the cost of her pet—but when Beatrice orders Ruth to stay home with Nanny, Ruth explodes with the epithet "Betty the Loon," and Beatrice crumbles emotionally. Ruth goes to school in Beatrice's place. In a scene change through a lighting shift, another science fair finalist, Janice Vickery, superficially explains the past, present, and future of her cat skeleton. Back at the Hunsdorfer home, Beatrice makes two phone calls. One is a bitter call to the high school. The other is to Nanny's daughter: Beatrice wants Nanny out of the house the next day. Finally, Beatrice heads upstairs with a bottle of chloroform.

In another shift by spotlight, Tillie cites the past, present, and future of her project. Lightly irradiated seeds produced normal plants. Moderately irradiated seeds produced various mutations. The heavily bombarded seeds either died or produced dwarfs. Knowing the range of effects, she believes some mutations will be good. She declares her faith in the strange, beautiful energy of the atom.

Beatrice is drunk when the girls get home. She has begun to refit the living room for a tea shop. Ruth brings the dead rabbit downstairs and goes into convulsions. The play closes with Tillie declaring her curiosity about the universe, her sense of place in the order of things, and her fascination with the atom.

The Effect of Gamma Rays on Man-in-the-Moon Marigolds presents a family, broken as Zindel's was, in financial straits, deriving income from a board-and-care patient, as Zindel's family had. Beatrice's unfinished real-estate and beauty classes mirror the varied attempts Zindel's mother made at supporting the family. The significance of Beatrice's preparation, in the last scene, for a tea shop is open to question. The move hints at growth in her character, yet she has killed the rabbit, the symbol of warmth and tenderness for the daughters. Tillie's success at least has stirred Beatrice to a new beginning.

Ruth has shifted from contempt for Tillie to pride in Tillie's achievement. That pride, however, seems rooted more in Ruth's concern for social status than in genuine understanding of either Tillie or the experiment. Tillie herself has not changed significantly in the play. At the outset, she speaks of her fascination with science. At the end, her success confirms her self-esteem and potential for growth in spite of the abuse from home.

Thus, the play relies on revelation of character more than on development of character in response to conflict. In a decade accustomed to "slice-of-life" literature and ambiguous if not bleak conclusions to many stories and plays, *The Effect of Gamma Rays on Man-in-the-Moon Marigolds* presents a positive faith in the future through science, and hope for one character in overcoming the emotional damage common in modern life.

AND MISS REARDON DRINKS A LITTLE

And Miss Reardon Drinks a Little offers a different constellation of women but still mirrors several aspects of Zindel's personal experience. The three Reardon sisters, Ceil, Catherine, and Anna, embody many of the ills of teachers long settled in the education system, ills well-known to Zindel and anyone else with some teaching experience.

Of the three sisters, Ceil has been the assertive one. She has taken the courses necessary to carry her from classroom to administrative work with the board of education. She took the chance of marrying Edward Adams, although Catherine dated him first. Ceil, too, arranged for their dead mother's estate to be settled seven months before the night of the play's action, and now Ceil is the one bringing papers for Anna's commitment for psychiatric care.

Act 1 begins with Mrs. Pentrano, the wife of the building superintendent, entering the Reardon sisters' apartment. She asks if the new lock has satisfied Anna and expresses concern for Anna's condition. A delivery boy brings groceries, including chopped meat, which Catherine arranges in a candy box. Untipped, the delivery boy exits with flippant sarcasm.

Mrs. Pentrano has been pressing Catherine for a cosmetics and toiletries order despite Catherine's objections. Ceil arrives and dismisses Mrs. Pentrano with little more than a greeting.

Catherine berates Ceil for making scant contact since their mother's death. She also complains that her fellow faculty members believe that Catherine's position as assistant principal is a consequence of Ceil's being on the board of education. Ceil cuts through the criticism with questions about Anna; she also expresses her concern for Catherine, who, people say, has taken to drinking. During their exchanges, Catherine eats raw meat from the candy box. Since her breakdown, Anna has turned vegetarian and wants no meat or animal byproducts in the apartment. Slaughter of animals is too reminiscent of human death.

Catherine explains to Ceil the development of Anna's condition. During a trip to Europe after their mother's death, Anna suffered a cat bite. She grew convinced that she had rabies. She demanded shots for the disease and thereafter was on tranquilizers so that she could return to teaching in September. Suffering harassment by students, however, Anna eventually broke down, committing some unspecified form of sexual indiscretion with a male student.

Anna enters. Groggy with medication, she had forgotten that Ceil was due for dinner. Catherine goes about preparing fruits and vegetables for their meal. Anna worries about the presence of Mother's old pistol in the apartment. Ceil assures her that Mother kept only blanks in the gun. Anna searches desk and bookcase until she locates the pistol in an album. Anna rambles about her condition, criticizes Ceil for taking Edward away from Catherine, then fires the pistol. Catherine tries to humor Anna, retrieves the pistol, and puts it back in the album, saying that Ceil can take it away later.

The second act opens with the sisters, still at dinner, interrupted by Fleur Stein. Fleur, an acting guidance teacher at the school where Catherine and Anna work, brings an official faculty get-well gift. Her husband, Bob, is getting the package from the car. Fleur says she debated whether the gift should be religious. Anna responds with a long story of losing religion because she saw a puppy hit by a truck. When Bob presents the gift, Anna loses control. They have brought her leather gloves. She throws them across the room. Ceil explains Anna's aversion to animal products, and Catherine belatedly introduces Ceil to the Steins. Fleur is counselor for the boy involved in Anna's case, and she pressures Ceil for help in securing her guidance teacher's licensure. In return, she will persuade the boy's parents not to sue for damages. Fleur downplays judgment on the incident, attributing a loss of traditional religious attitudes to modern acceptance of science. Bob Stein, given certain provocations, bluntly attributes Anna's breakdown to lack of male companionship. He offers to get Anna a date for the evening and drapes Fleur's fox fur stole over Anna's shoulders. She screams and kicks the stole away, deploring the cruelty of the fur trade. Bob reacts in anger, insulting all three sisters in turn. Catherine suggests that Anna show Bob their mother's album.

As the third act opens, Anna fires the pistol at Bob's face. Bob grabs the gun, telling Anna that she has real problems. Anna, in response to an earlier comment by Fleur, asks Bob why he never uses his own bathroom at home. He retorts that he hates the soaps and rough paper that Fleur steals from the school. Fleur attempts to smooth over Bob's irate exit, assuring Ceil that she will do her best to help. With the Steins gone, Ceil wants to discuss business with Catherine alone, but Anna insists on staying. She reminisces about an eccentric principal they once knew. Ceil brings out the commitment papers and tells Catherine to get Anna packed for travel the next day.

Catherine rebels at the order. Anna asks Ceil how Edward makes love to her. Furious, Ceil shoves meat from the candy box in Anna's face. She screams and runs off to wash. Ceil keeps Catherine from following Anna. Catherine finally admits that she hates the dominance in both their late mother and Ceil. In return, Ceil rebukes Catherine for leaving her choices in life to others. Ceil throws the commitment papers down and leaves. Catherine now must take responsibility for either keeping Anna home or committing her for psychiatric care.

Examining the lives of professional educators, Zindel presents a family with the occupational stability and social standing he himself experienced in his first career. The Misses Reardon, like Tillie and Ruth Hunsdorfer, have suffered from an unhealthy family situation: an absent father and a domineering mother. Ceil, assertive in her own right, made choices that carried her out of Mother Reardon's sphere of control and eventually to the top echelon of her profession. Her progress is a logical extension of the strength of character Tillie Hunsdorfer maintains despite Beatrice's dominance. Catherine and Anna, in contrast, show the effects of remaining under Mother's control to the end. Catherine shrinks from asserting herself: She cannot briskly dismiss Mrs. Pentrano as Ceil can; rather than cope with awkward comments by the Steins, she runs the blender; instead of confronting Anna with her own preference of diet, she sneaks meat into the house and eats it raw. Both Catherine's craving for raw meat and Anna's indiscretion represent inordinate reactions to unfulfilled needs.

In addition to the parallels in family dynamics, there is another link between *And Miss Reardon Drinks a Little* and its predecessor. Tillie Hunsdorfer's youthful faith in science has evolved, in Fleur Stein, into the laconic conclusion that science has supplanted religious faith in modern life. Anna, in contrast, cannot rationalize pain and suffering; she traces the loss of her religion to the death of a pup. Ceil makes no claims regarding religion. She does live by the premise, however, that a person must accept responsibility for choices in life and must seize opportunities for change and growth. At the close of the play, she leaves Catherine with the choice of compensating for Anna's incapacity at home or committing her for psychiatric care. Catherine seems, at last, ready to accept the responsibility.

AMULETS AGAINST THE DRAGON FORCES

Amulets Against the Dragon Forces, a revision of *A Destiny with Half Moon Street*, is exceptional for Zindel in that the protagonist and antagonist are both male; however, these characters also struggle with the issues of disappointment, inadequacy, and betrayal. A cycle of abuse is revealed as an old woman who had long ago attacked her son for his budding sexuality is brought home from the hospital to die. The son,

Floyd, is the antagonist of the play. He is now a nearly deranged adult and has a history of alcoholism and child abuse, one featuring the habitual use of young male prostitutes, a series of whom he has brought to the family home where he exchanges shelter for sexual favors. A divorced, itinerant practical nurse has been engaged to care for the dying mother, and she brings her own son, the protagonist Chris, into the household. Being the youngest and most innocent character, he retains some characteristics of childhood, including a hobby of creating balsa wood replicas of local landmarks populated by models he has carved. These "amulets" are mere charms and seem unlikely to stave off the "dragon forces" of the play's title. Chris uses the figures to represent characters in made-up stories. He hopes to become a writer—an ambition suggested to him by a mentally unstable teacher. For the near future, Chris plans to escape life with his kleptomaniac mother by going to Florida to live with his father, but the father refuses. Chris's mother does finally succeed in buying a home for herself and her son, barely completing the transaction before the old woman she is caring for dies. The play ends as Floyd suggests to Chris that the passage of time may someday allow the boy to accept his own disquieting sexual urges. Zindel has indicated that this is the last play he plans to write set in Staten Island and using events and factors influential in his own upbringing.

EVERY SEVENTEEN MINUTES THE CROWD GOES CRAZY!

Every Seventeen Minutes the Crowd Goes Crazy! portrays a family of teenage children recently abandoned by their parents, who communicate with the youngsters infrequently and then only via a fax machine. Written on commission for the American Conservatory Theater's Young Conservatory, the play addresses the breakdown of family life as caused by the societal ills of commercialism and hedonism. The parents prefer the thrill of the track, where the horse races finish "every seventeen minutes," and so have fled their failing careers and dependent offspring—children they find to be unbearable users. They express regret over leaving the youngest child, Ulie, who is only twelve years old, but predict his inability

to escape a future of self-centeredness. The older children plan various means of economic survival, including charging admission to regular keg parties, but they are meanwhile cleaning out any remaining cash advances available on their parents' credit cards. The overall effect is ironic and painful as the young protagonists bravely hide or perhaps even abandon their feelings of disappointment and longing for a return to a more normal life. A one-act play, the work begins and ends with the "Oprah-Speak Gap Chorus" chanting a jumble of slogans, ads, and *National Enquirer*-type headlines.

OTHER MAJOR WORKS

LONG FICTION: *When a Darkness Falls*, 1984.

SCREENPLAYS: *Up the Sandbox*, 1972; *Mame*, 1974; *Runaway Train*, 1983; *Maria's Lovers*, 1984.

TELEPLAYS: *Let Me Hear You Whisper*, 1966; *Alice in Wonderland*, 1985 (adaptation of the story by Lewis Carroll); *A Connecticut Yankee in King Arthur's Court*, 1989 (adaptation of the novel by Mark Twain).

CHILDREN'S LITERATURE: *The Pigman*, 1968; *My Darling, My Hamburger*, 1969; *I Never Loved Your Mind*, 1970; *I Love My Mother*, 1975; *Pardon Me, You're Stepping on My Eyeball!*, 1976; *Confessions of a Teenage Baboon*, 1977; *The Undertaker's Gone Bananas*, 1978; *A Star for the Latecomer*, 1980 (with Bonnie Zindel); *The Pigman's Legacy*, 1980; *The Girl Who Wanted a Boy*, 1981; *To Take a Dare*, 1982 (with Crescent Dragonwagon); *Harry and Hortense at Hormone High*, 1984; *The Amazing and Death-Defying Diary of Eugene Dingman*, 1987; *A Begonia for Miss Applebaum*, 1989; *The Pigman and Me*, 1992 (autobiography); *Attack of the Killer Fishsticks*, 1993; *David and Della*, 1993; *Fifth Grade Safari*, 1993; *Fright Party*, 1993; *Loch*, 1994; *The One Hundred Percent Laugh Riot*, 1994; *The Doom Stone*, 1995; *Raptor*, 1998; *Reef of Death*, 1998; *Rats*, 1999; *The Gadget*, 2001; *Night of the Bat*, 2001.

BIBLIOGRAPHY

Barnes, Clive. "Troubled Times for a Teen." Review of *Amulets Against the Dragon Forces*, by Paul Zindel. *New York Post*, April 7, 1989. Barnes finds a "commonplace honesty" beneath the play's pretentiousness in this review of the Circle Repertory Company's production. Barnes finds "the same quality of compassion" as in *The Effect of Gamma Rays on Man-in-the-Moon Marigolds.* Barnes states that the play has "the air of a work written to enable its author to get something off his chest."

DiGaetani, John L. *A Search for a Postmodern Theater: Interviews with Contemporary Playwrights.* New York: Greenwood Press, 1991. In one chapter, DiGaetani interviews Zindel about the influences of psychoanalysis on his work and the reasons for his gradual transition to young adult novels. Zindel's destructive relation with Hollywood is also discussed with considerable candor. Asked which playwrights Zindel admires, he replied, "I'm happy to say none."

Evett, Marianne. "'Moon-Marigolds' Author in Nostalgic Return Here." *Cleveland Plain Dealer,* November 4, 1990. This preview of Cleveland Playhouse's revival of *The Effect of Gamma Rays on Man-in-the-Moon Marigolds,* with Marlo Thomas in the role of Beatrice, includes a telephone interview with Zindel, who remembers the first productions and his "bubbly publicity agent (Bonnie Hildebrand). I ended up marrying her." He reports here that he "escaped East [from Hollywood] to keep my sanity intact."

Fischer, David Marc. "Paul Zindel: The Shouting Play, the Whispering Novel." *Writing* 24 (February/March, 2002): 20. Presents an interview with Zindel covering a discussion of his career as teacher and writer with emphasis on distinguishing between the style of language and writing appropriate for drama as opposed to the novel.

Forman, Jack Jacob. *Presenting Paul Zindel.* Boston: Twayne, 1988. A basic biography that includes criticism and interpretation focused primarily on Zindel's fiction. Useful indexes and bibliography.

Lesesne, Teri. "Humor, Bathos and Fear: An Interview with Paul Zindel." *Teacher Librarian* 27 (December, 1999): 60. Zindel discusses his thematic emphasis on teenage misfits in young-adult novels and drama, citing a scene from *The Effect of Gamma Rays on Man-in-the-Moon Marigolds* as an example of his best work.

Slaight, Craig, ed.. *New Plays from ACT's Young Conservatory.* Vol. 2. Lume, N.H.: Smith and Kraus, 1996. Contains the text of *Every Seventeen Minutes the Crowd Goes Crazy!* with commentary by Craig Slaight, Zindel, and student actors from the play.

Zindel, Paul. "Beyond Man-in-the-Moon Marigolds." Interview by Helen Dudar. *The New York Times,* April 2, 1989, p. B5. A long interview on the occasion of Zindel's later work, *Amulets Against the Dragon Forces,* twelve years after his last New York opening. He recaps his career, mostly in teen novels, and his sense of destructiveness in the maw of Hollywood. Good biographic profile, with a photograph.

*Ralph S. Carlson, updated by Thomas J. Taylor
and Margaret A. Dodson*

ÉMILE ZOLA

Born: Paris, France; April 2, 1840
Died: Paris, France; September 28, 1902

PRINCIPAL DRAMA
  Madeleine, wr. 1865, pb. 1878, pr. 1889

Thérèse Raquin, pr., pb. 1873 (adaptation of his novel; English translation, 1947)
Les Héritiers Rabourdin, pr., pb. 1874 (*The Rabourdin Heirs,* 1893)
Le Bouton de rose, pr., pb. 1878

Théâtre, pb. 1878

Renée, pr., pb. 1887 (adaptation of his novel *La Curée*)

Lazare, wr. 1893, pb. 1921 (libretto; music by Alfred Bruneau)

Violaine la chevelue, wr. 1897, pb. 1921

L'Ouragan, pr., pb. 1901 (libretto; music by Bruneau)

Sylvanire: Ou, Paris en amour, wr. 1902, pb. 1921, pr. 1924 (libretto; music by Robert Le Grand)

L'Enfant-Roi, pr. 1905, pb. 1921 (libretto; music by Bruneau)

Poèmes lyriques, pb. 1921

OTHER LITERARY FORMS

Émile Zola is known principally as a novelist and as the formulator of the literary movement known as naturalism, which proposed to examine the human species by observing scientifically, through the medium of a literary work, the effects of heredity and environment. Zola's first major novel was *Thérèse Raquin* (1867; English translation, 1881), followed by the twenty-novel cycle of *Les Rougon-Macquart* (1871-1893; *The Rougon-Macquart Novels*, 1885-1907), including such well-known novels as *Germinal* (1885; English translation, 1885), *L'Assommoir* (1876; English translation, 1879); and *Nana* (1880; English translation, 1880). Near the end of his life, he wrote two shorter series of novels, *Les Trois Villes* (1894-1898; *The Three Cities*, 1894-1898); and *Les Quatre Evangiles* (1899-1903; English translation, 1900-1903), which are both more visionary and idealistic than the realistic, earthy Rougon-Macquart novels. Less well known are his short stories, several of which were dramatized during Zola's lifetime. As a journalist and art critic, Zola was an early supporter of the Impressionist painters, but he dealt harshly with the popular playwrights of his day. In addition to his literary and critical works, Zola is remembered for his defense of Alfred Dreyfus in the famous newspaper article, "J'accuse" ("I Accuse"). Had Zola not so forcefully put his suspicions before the public, the case of the wrongfully convicted Dreyfus might never have been reopened nor the innocent man acquitted.

ACHIEVEMENTS

Émile Zola was never as skillful a dramatist as he was a novelist. In fact, none of his plays can be said to have achieved lasting success, although many of his novels and short stories have been successfully adapted for stage and film. His achievement in drama lies in the changes he was able to bring to the theater at a time when the stage was dominated by the *pièces à thèse* (problem plays) of Alexandre Dumas, *fils*, Victorien Sardou, and Émile Augier. The well-made play of the time was most often a neatly constructed illustration of a moral homily. Although these plays had once seemed modern and true to life, by comparison with the romantic plays of the early nineteenth century (such as those by Alexandre Dumas, *père*), they now seemed to Zola to be overly artificial and tritely idealized. By applying to the theater the force of his prestige as a novelist, Zola was able to insist on more lifelike scenes in costume, decor, and methods of acting. Instead of demonstrating a given "thesis," he developed his plays from the realities of everyday life. Through his own stage productions and dramatic criticism, he prepared the way for the innovative theater of André Antoine's Théâtre Libre, made possible the acceptance of Henry Becque, and encouraged Antoine to produce the plays of Henrik Ibsen and August Strindberg. Thus Zola's major contribution to the theater is found less in his own plays than in the new atmosphere of freedom and experimentation which he promoted and supported.

BIOGRAPHY

Émile-Edouard-Charles-Antoine Zola was born in Paris on April 2, 1840. His father, Francesco Antonio Zolla, the son of a Venetian family, came to Paris in 1830 seeking work as a civil engineer. After submitting a series of projects to the French government, he was received by King Louis Philippe, who accepted his proposal for the port of Marseilles. During his stay in Paris, François Zola (as he had then become) met Émilie-Aurélie Aubert, the daughter of a housepainter, Louis-Auguste Aubert. She was born in northern France, in Dourdan, near the great plain of the Beauce, and she was twenty-four years younger than François when they married in 1839.

Although Zola was born in Paris, his family moved south before he was one year old. After reaching an agreement with the city for an aqueduct, canal, and dam system to supply water to Aix, Zola's father seemed to have settled at last into a financially secure position. Unfortunately, he died of pleurisy in 1847, leaving his wife and seven-year-old son to manage as best they could in increasingly difficult circumstances.

Zola grew up, an only child doted on by his mother and her parents, living in working-class neighborhoods. He attended the Pension Notre-Dame and entered the Collège Bourbon at the age of twelve. It was here that he began his friendship with Paul Cézanne. Together with Jean-Baptistin Baille, they roamed the Provence countryside. Like Cézanne, Zola was never to lose his emotional attachment to Aix-en-Provence.

When his grandmother died in 1858, his mother moved the small household to Paris, where Zola was enrolled in the Lycée Saint-Louis. Homesick and somewhat behind his classmates, Zola did not do well and eventually failed his baccalaureate examinations.

Émile Zola (Library of Congress)

This failure prevented him from continuing to study for a profession. Thus he found himself at the age of nineteen, jobless and without professional qualifications, but determined to work by day and seek literary glory by night.

His first job was as a customs clerk, but in 1862 he became a clerk at the publishing firm of Hachette, eventually becoming head of the publicity department. This was the perfect place for him to meet publishers, authors, and critics. In 1864, his first book, the romantic *Contes à Ninon* (*Stories for Ninon*, 1895), appeared. After the publication of his second work, *La Confession de Claude* (1865; *Claude's Confession*, 1882), had attracted the attention of the public prosecutor, the Hachette publishing company gave Zola the choice of giving up his literary career or leaving his position at the publishing house. Thus, in 1866, Zola became a journalist, writing book reviews and literary news for *L'Événement*. It was through his newspaper columns that he also took up the defense of the Impressionist painters against the artistic establishment.

During those years when he was developing a reputation as a critic and writer, Zola was also setting up his own household. In 1864, Cézanne had introduced him to Gabrielle-Eléonore-Alexandrine Meley. Her background has remained something of a mystery, but it is known that her parents were not married and that her mother, who may have been a florist, died when she was ten. According to some, Gabrielle was a laundress when she met Zola; others believe that she, too, was a florist. In any case, they moved together in 1866 to an address near the Théâtre de l'Odéon. They were married in 1870, having earlier moved to a new apartment with Madame Zola. It is thought to have been Zola's mother who rechristened Gabrielle by her more properly middle-class name, Alexandrine.

The year 1867 marks the publication of *Thérèse Raquin*, Zola's first naturalist novel, in which he studied the effects of murderous passion and guilt on his two main characters. By this time, Zola's career as a journalist was established, and he was preparing to begin his twenty-novel cycle about the Rougon-Macquart family, set during the Second Empire. In preparation, he studied the theories of Charles Darwin and Hippolyte Taine and absorbed various scientific and medical studies of heredity and environment. Each setting in the series of novels was meticulously researched, each character conceived as an amalgam of genealogical and environmental influences.

In the 1880's, after a series of unsuccessful attempts to stage his own plays and after the phenomenal sensation created by his novel *L'Assommoir*, Zola agreed to have William Busnach adapt several of his novels to the stage. Although Zola's name is not included as the coauthor of the plays *L'Assommoir* (1879), *Nana* (1881), *Pot-bouille* (1883; piping hot), *Le Ventre de Paris* (1887; the belly of Paris), and *Germinal* (1885), it is known that he worked fairly closely with Busnach. The talents that made Zola a great novelist, however, did not transfer well to the stage. Busnach was apparently able to provide the dramatic impulse, transforming the thoroughly documented, epic sweep of Zola's novels into scenes for the stage.

In the meantime, Zola's reputation, even notoriety, as a novelist was growing, with the publication of *Nana*, *Germinal*, and *La Terre* (1887; *Earth*, 1888). *L'Œuvre* (1886; *The Masterpiece*, 1886) brought about a break in his friendship with the artists he had once defended, especially with Cézanne, who thought he recognized too much of himself in the artist Claude Lantier, the protagonist of the novel.

The year 1888 brought a transformation in Zola's personal life; he fell in love with a young seamstress, Jeanne Rozerot and eventually set her up in a second household near the Gare du Nord, where he was researching his novel on railroads, *La Bête humaine* (1890; *The Human Beast*, 1890). He and Jeanne were to have two children, Denise and Jacques. Alexandrine discovered the relationship shortly after the birth of Jacques and, although distraught at first, eventually was able to accept the existence of the young family. The absence of children in her marriage had long been a source of sorrow, and she took a kind and generous interest in Denise and Jacques, providing for their inheritance from their father and allowing them to adopt the surname Émile-Zola.

In the summer of 1893, *Le Docteur Pascal* (*Doctor Pascal*), the final volume of the Rougon-Macquart cycle, was published in both French and English. Zola had also been made an officer of the Legion of Honor. (Election to the French Academy would always elude him.) Naturalism as a strict formula for constructing a novel was behind him. The new literary movement was Symbolism, and Zola was preparing to embark on a new phase of visionary, symbolic writing. In his new series, *The Three Cities*, the characters are freer, much less products of their hereditary and environmental circumstances. The three novels of this cycle, *Lourdes* (1894; English translation, 1894), *Rome* (1896; English translation, 1896), and *Paris* (1898; English translation, 1898), represent a critical examination of religious faith, espousing instead a rational social philosophy that might bring about a better future for humankind; they are utopian in tone, expressing confidence in an idealistic socialism. (Needless to say, *Lourdes* was immediately placed on the Index.) Stylistically, however, none matches the life and energy of the Rougon-Macquart novels.

If *The Three Cities* focuses on truth and social justice, Zola's defense of Alfred Dreyfus was an application of his philosophy to real life. With the same meticulous research he had applied to his novels, Zola reconstructed the facts of the case, publishing them in *L'Aurore* as the famous essay, "I Accuse." Although he forced the government to reopen the case, Zola himself was brought to trial in 1898 and went into exile in England, where he began a new series of novels, "The Four Gospels." His exile ended in 1899 when the French court ordered a rehearing of the Dreyfus case. The sentence that had been passed on Zola the previous year was now ignored. Nevertheless, he had bravely called down on himself the hatred and abuse of the anti-Dreyfusard faction in France.

The Four Gospels was to be his spiritual testament, lyric hymns of praise to fecundity, work, truth, and justice. In the theater as well, Zola's interest was changing from naturalist to symbolic works. In this last decade of his life, Zola wrote six lyric dramas for the composer Alfred Bruneau, three of which were performed at the Opéra-Comique in Paris.

In the autumn of 1902, Zola and Alexandrine returned to Paris from their country house at Médan. Zola was sixty-two, ready to begin "Justice" and in the midst of work with Bruneau. As the nights were becoming cool in Paris, he had a fire lit in his bedroom. In the morning, he and Alexandrine were found collapsed in their room, asphyxiated by fumes from the fire. She regained consciousness and survived, but Zola died later that morning. The possibility exists that workmen deliberately blocked their chimney out of the dreadful hatred unleashed by Zola's role in the Dreyfus Affair, but it is equally likely that his death resulted accidentally from the dangerous custom of using coal fires to heat tightly closed rooms. His funeral oration was delivered by Anatole France; by the coffin stood Alfred Dreyfus. In 1908, under the presidency of Georges Clemenceau, the French government removed Zola's body to the Panthéon.

ANALYSIS

French writers seem to exhibit a need to write for the theater. It is as though seeing one's work performed onstage were a final imprimatur of success. Among the great nineteenth century novelists, both Stendhal and Honoré de Balzac attempted to write for the stage, but only Victor Hugo managed to achieve fame as a poet, novelist, and playwright. Zola attended regular dinners in Paris with a group that included Gustave Flaubert and Alphonse Daudet. These evenings were called the "dinners of the hissed authors" because everyone present had had a play hissed off the stage.

Nevertheless, Émile Zola remains important for the history of the theater because of his innovative dramatic theories. The artistic principle informing Zola's plays is the same as that of his novels—a desire to depict the truth. With his reformer's zeal, Zola set out to bring a greater measure of realism to a stage that was then dominated by the well-made play. He believed that these productions too often followed a standard formula well within the polite boundaries of social convention, portraying an idealized version of life. The public controlled the stage, he thought, by refusing to support any play that was not prettier than

life, with a happy, or at least a sweetly poignant, ending. The challenge Zola set for himself was to bring to the stage a measure of the stark, often sordid reality he described in his novels. As in his novels, naturalism in Zola's plays implied a scientific precision in observation combined with the artist's particular point of view. As always, special emphasis was placed on the effects of heredity and environment in shaping an individual destiny.

Even if Zola himself was unable to realize his vision of a new drama, he must be acknowledged as a revolutionary in theatrical history. It is his dramatic criticism and his experimentation in set design, costume, methods of acting, and subject matter that opened the way to twentieth century drama in France. It was he who had the vision to write in his 1875 preface to *Thérèse Raquin*, "Either drama will die, or drama will be modern and real."

MADELEINE

Zola's first full-length play, *Madeleine*, is a good example of his desire to apply scientific theory to a literary work. The story of Madeleine Férat proceeds from the hypothesis that a woman will always bear within her the indelible imprint of her first lover. It is impossible to escape one's past. In the play, Madeleine is a woman haunted by her questionable past. She had had a lover as a young woman in Paris, but he is presumed dead, and she is now respectably married to Francis, happy in her tranquil new life in a distant province. By malign coincidence, the lover, Jacques, returns, not for Madeleine, but to find his childhood friend Francis and to meet his friend's wife, whom he does not suspect is Madeleine. When she confesses her past to Francis, he is able to forgive her, but they flee from Jacques to regain their peace of mind alone. Unfortunately, they arrive at the very inn and are shown to the same room where Madeleine had spent a week with Jacques. Inevitably, old memories are rekindled, and Jacques himself appears. Madeleine realizes that she cannot escape her past without the forgiveness of her husband and mother-in-law. They return to seek the blessing of Francis's mother. Tragically, a stern and righteous family servant, seeking to punish Madeleine, convinces her that the mother will never forgive her. With her last hope of escaping the bondage of her past at an end, Madeleine poisons herself and dies. Through his portrayal of Madeleine, Zola demonstrates the force of the past in determining one's life. The play is not without its melodramatic moments, however, nor is the outcome inevitable.

The manager of the Théâtre du Gymnase rejected the play on the grounds that contemporary audiences would find it unacceptable, even offensive, thus confirming Zola's opinion that the theaters of his day deferred too quickly to their patrons. Indeed, Zola believed that theater management underestimated the public and that audiences were prepared to be challenged by greater realism than was then seen onstage in Paris. The fact remains, however, that *Madeleine* is too much a demonstration of a hypothesis to achieve dramatic success. The situations seem contrived, and the characters are too obviously subjects in an experiment whose outcome is preordained by the writer. The play did achieve a fair success in 1889 when produced by the Théâtre Libre as an example of Zola's early work.

THÉRÈSE RAQUIN

With very little change in plot and characterization, Zola expanded his play into the novel, *Madeleine Férat* (1868; English translation, 1880). As it happened, his first play to be staged was the dramatization of his first critically acclaimed novel, *Thérèse Raquin*. This novel adapted well to the stage because, unlike many of Zola's novels, with their epic crowd scenes, *Thérèse Raquin* is an intense domestic drama in which the conflict between the three principal characters entangles them with greater and greater constricting force. Even the setting is dark, dismal, and oppressive.

Thérèse Raquin has been reared from childhood by her aunt and has married her frail cousin and childhood companion, Camille. At the opening of the drama, they are living in Paris, as a household of three—mother, son, and daughter-in-law—in a small apartment above Mme Raquin's notion shop, which itself opens onto a dim enclosed passageway. The arrival of Laurent, a friend of Camille's youth, awakens Thérèse from her tranquil but somnolent existence. She and Laurent embark on a passionate love affair

even as Laurent is being welcomed into the family as a second son by the doting Mme Raquin.

Eventually, the force of their passion drives Thérèse and Laurent to plot the murder of Camille. While ostensibly on a summer picnic, they take him boating and drown him, feigning a tragic accident. Having disposed of the husband, they coolly suspend their relationship and play their parts so well that Mme Raquin and her friends actually urge the two to marry. Thus, Laurent takes Camille's place in the home of Mme Raquin. At this point, the play takes on the inexorable force of classic tragedy as Thérèse and Laurent are haunted by the specter of Camille's drowned corpse. As guilt increasingly poisons their relationship, Mme Raquin, who has become paralyzed and mute, comes to realize the truth about her son's murder. Driven mad by fear and remorse, their passion turned to hate, and confronted always by the unrelenting, accusing gaze of Mme Raquin, Thérèse and Laurent at last commit suicide at the feet of Mme Raquin, the silent, avenging fury.

Instead of offering his play to any of the established theaters in Paris, Zola took it to the struggling Théâtre de la Renaissance, where the manager was willing to gamble on the new play. The support of the well-known actress Marie Laurent, who was eager to play the part of Mme Raquin, encouraged the manager, who provided an excellent supporting cast. *Thérèse Raquin* thus had a short but fairly successful end-of-the-season run in 1873 and later toured in German and Scandinavian countries to favorable reviews. It has been noted that Thérèse is, in many ways, a precursor of Ibsen's strong-willed heroines, particularly in the play's intense conflict that can end only in catastrophe. Perhaps because of its emphasis on character analysis rather than on plot, *Thérèse Raquin* has fascinated modern audiences more often than any of Zola's other plays.

THE RABOURDIN HEIRS

Zola's next two plays were experiments in style. The first was a sardonic comedy, a sort of pastiche of Molière and Ben Jonson. In his preface to the play, Zola explains that again he wishes to set an example for modern writers of comedy and to protest the sorry state to which they have brought the proud heritage of

Molière. *The Rabourdin Heirs* represents an attempt to return to the source of modern comedy. As ever, Zola invokes the depiction of true and living types as the proper goal of the comic playwright.

The plot of *The Rabourdin Heirs* turns on the situation of a ruined merchant who not only pretends that his business is thriving but also pretends that he is dying. By means of this double ruse he not only extracts valuable gifts from those who expect to inherit a fortune but also discovers their true feelings as they reveal themselves around his "deathbed." Although the play does contain some amusing lines, Zola does not have a real gift for sustaining a comic sequence. Even when the truth is revealed, and the heirs realize that they will have to continue the ruse of Rabourdin's wealth to maintain their own credit, the moment is not played for its full ironic effect. Some, including Zola himself, have said that the play was unfairly attacked by critics, jealous of Zola's success as a novelist. There is some truth, though, in their main objections to the play: that it was not lively, that the characters were not sympathetic, and that the central situation never changed. These adverse reviews caused the play to close after seventeen performances.

LE BOUTON DE ROSE

With *Le Bouton de rose*, staged in 1878, Zola took a vacation from naturalism and wrote a light comedy at the request of the manager of the Théâtre du Palais-Royal. Zola had finished the novel *L'Assommoir* in 1876 and took the project as a form of relaxation. The publication of *L'Assommoir*, however, had made Zola a prominent personage. He was now the leader of the naturalist group of writers, and critics had no intention of letting him present a bit of farcical fluff onstage. The plot was inspired by one of the stories in Balzac's *Les Contes drôlatiques* (1832-1837; *Droll Stories*, 1874, 1891), in which a bridegroom who must leave his new wife asks his best friend to ensure his bride's fidelity in his absence. The wife, to reproach him for his lack of confidence, concocts an amusing ruse at the expense of both her husband and his friend. *Le Bouton de rose* merits mention only for its complete inversion of naturalist principles. Public and critics could not forgive Zola for what appeared to them to be total inconsistency

with his own philosophy of the stage, so vociferously argued in his theatrical criticism.

RENÉE

After the rout of *Le Bouton de rose*, Zola returned to his novels as the source of the one last play that would be entirely his own work. The novel he chose to dramatize was *La Curée* (1872; *The Kill*, 1886). This time he must have felt success was at hand in the form of Sarah Bernhardt, who was extremely eager to appear in what became the title role when the play was written as *Renée*. The play has been called a "Phaedra" in modern dress: The young wife of a wealthy Paris financier has an affair with her husband's son by an earlier marriage. Zola considered *Renée* to be an excellent vehicle for bringing naturalism to the stage. In the first place, the Phaedra theme was a classic subject, much admired by the French in Jean Racine's version, and the title role was one of Sarah Bernhardt's most successful roles. The Second Empire setting and the exposition of fierce passion dominating the main characters and leading to inevitable destruction were familiar to readers of naturalist novels. Instead of the Greek concept of fate, it would be heredity and environment that would betray the three main characters.

The play begins with the marriage of Aristide Saccard, an ambitious speculator, to Renée, the daughter of a well-to-do Parisian family. Renée feels that she is obliged to accept Saccard as her suitor because she has a past "tainted" by an earlier seduction. In order to tone down the implications of incest in the plot, Zola made the marriage between Saccard and Renée strictly one of convenience, a pure formality. The first act sets the terms of this relationship and also reveals that Renée has a hereditary flaw transmitted by her passionate mother, who was presumed to have died many years before but who in fact deserted her family for another man.

The following four acts take place ten years later as Renée discovers her love for Maxime, struggles briefly against her passion, then gives herself to him. In the meantime Saccard, who has grown rich in the corrupt, opulent economy of the Second Empire, has fallen in love with his wife and seeks to normalize their marital relations. Renée's passion flourishes in the sultry atmosphere of the Saccard hothouse, until, in a fury over Maxime's proposed marriage with a wholesome young Swedish girl, she reveals to Saccard that her lover is his son. Filled with disgust for both father and son, loathing herself as well, she puts an end to the family curse by committing suicide.

The extent of Zola's departure from established theatrical convention can be judged by the vehemence with which *Renée* was rejected by theater management. *Phaedra* was admirable; *Renée* was detestable. What the public would accept as a novel was intolerable onstage. In the meantime, Sarah Bernhardt had resigned from the Comédie-Française and was on tour in the United States. On her return, she felt unable to take part in such a controversial play. *Renée* was not staged, therefore, until 1887, when even Zola agreed that it had not been improved by the years of waiting in the wings.

The failure of *Renée* brought to an end Zola's dreams of staging a successful drama of his own. His particular writing talents—the evocative descriptive passages, the panoramic sweep of the crowd scenes, the epic grandeur of his novels—did not readily adapt to the stage. His meticulous method of research, which he thought of as constructing a novel like a grand edifice, was of limited value in writing a play. Moreover, he believed that the critics of his day resented his fame as a novelist, as if unwilling to allow success in both genres. Zola's own harsh and forthright criticisms of the theater made him especially vulnerable to attack when his own plays were produced.

Busnach and Zola

Thus, when Zola was approached by a dramatist named William Busnach, he agreed to allow the younger writer to adapt his current best-selling novel, *L'Assommoir*, for the stage. Because Zola's name appears nowhere on the scripts, the plays that Busnach created from his novels have normally not been included as part of Zola's work. It is known, however, from correspondence between the two men that Zola offered much advice and even wrote some of the dialogue. Many of the major departures from the plots of the novels were written at Zola's suggestion. The five plays resulting from the collaboration between Busnach and Zola are of interest, then, as examples of

Zola's naturalism brought to the stage, although Zola readily admitted that these plays represent a compromise between theatrical conventions of the time and his own notions of modern drama.

Busnach had previously been a writer of vaudeville, and he apparently had the dramatic flair necessary to appeal to contemporary audiences. He and Zola altered the plot structure of the novels to simplify and, in fact, to make them resemble typical popular melodramas. For example, *L'Assommoir*, the novel, is the story of Gervaise and Coupeau, their lives destroyed by the bad luck of an accidental injury to Coupeau and the subsequent disintegration of their lives as they succumb to the temptation of alcohol. In the play, however, a wicked rival of Gervaise deliberately causes Coupeau's fall at the construction site and thereafter reappears at crucial moments to ensure the complete destruction of the Coupeau family. Thus, the tragedy of Gervaise and Coupeau appears to result less from their own character and situation than from the purely malevolent intervention of another human being.

In spite of the fact that the novels were brought to the stage in somewhat lighter form, the plots still represent a greater measure of reality than had theretofore been seen in the theater. The scenes and costumes were taken from everyday life, and the actors avoided a declamatory style in favor of lifelike conversations. Worthy of mention are the realistic innovations in set design encouraged by Zola. For example, *L'Assommoir* featured real soap and hot water in Gervaise's laundry. In one riverside scene from *Nana*, a genuine stream flowed beneath cardboard trees bearing actual apples. Unfortunately the falling fruit distracted somewhat from the poetry of the love scene. The stage effects of *Germinal*, set in a coal mine, are said to have been spectacular, the gigantic machinery giving the same overpowering, menacing impression as the descriptive passages in the novel.

Germinal, however, was the last of Busnach's adaptations. Zola had become increasingly involved in the plays, insisting, this time against Busnach's advice, on presenting a scene of striking workers being fired on by the police. Zola had always maintained that Busnach's adaptations did not represent the theatrical revolution he envisioned. Nevertheless, *Germinal* was too revolutionary in its social message for the government, which refused to license the play. Perceiving that the licensing commission was one of the blocks in the way of theatrical progress, Zola made public his difficulties with the authorities. It took three years to put *Germinal* onstage, but Zola had struck a resounding blow on behalf of the theater against government censorship.

THÉÂTRE LIBRE

A more successful theatrical revolution was Zola's support of and involvement in André Antoine's Théâtre Libre, never a strictly naturalist creation, but instead a genuinely new direction in theater history. The program on opening night in 1887 included an adaptation by Léon Henneau of Zola's short story "Jacques Damour." Antoine always acknowledged his debt to Zola in launching and helping to establish his career as an innovative director. Thanks to Antoine and Zola, the plays of Henrik Ibsen and August Strindberg became known and appreciated in France.

BRUNEAU AND ZOLA

The year 1893 brought to a close the twenty-volume Rougon-Macquart cycle. Zola was ready for a new phase of his literary life. The novels of Zola's postnaturalist period are filled with lyric optimism for man's future, based on scientific progress and a rejuvenated France born out of the debacle of the Second Empire, with its humiliating defeat in the Franco-Prussian war. *Doctor Pascal*, the final volume of *Les Rougon-Macquart*, had ended with the birth of a child, humanity's hope for the future. Indeed, Zola's last novels were hymns of praise for work, truth, justice, and, above all, fecundity.

It is unsurprising then, that during the last decade of his life, Zola's interest in the theater should have turned toward the visionary, symbolic librettos that he composed for the opera with Alfred Bruneau. Bruneau had already performed a work adapted from *Le Rêve* (1888; *The Dream*, 1888), with lyrics by Louis Gallet. This was one of the first musical dramas staged in modern dress.

Encouraged by Bruneau's success, Zola himself wrote the libretto for a work entitled *Messidor*, which opened at the Paris Opera in 1897. As he had done

with the novel and dramatic play, Zola introduced several innovations in the operatic form that were startling to audiences of his time. First, *Messidor* was written in rhythmic prose rather than in verse. Furthermore, the plot of the opera turned on a strikingly modern conflict, that between industrial capitalism and the agrarian economy it disrupts. The title is intended to recall *Germinal*, both being names taken from the revolutionary calendar adopted in 1793. The two stories are similar in their sympathy for the miners and the peasants who are the victims of monopolistic business. In the opera, however, the people triumph in an idyllic and optimistic portrayal of the blessing of the fertile wheat fields. The social message of progress through fertility, of the people and of the land, was Zola's ever-present preoccupation during his last decade. *Messidor* enjoyed a successful run until the publication of "I Accuse" in 1898, after which riots outside the Paris opera caused performances to be discontinued.

The second libretto that Zola wrote for Bruneau was called *L'Ouragan* (the hurricane), for which the author had clearly drawn on the emotional turmoil of his personal life. Written just as Alexandrine was recovering from her trauma of discovering Zola's liaison with Jeanne Rozerot, *L'Ouragan* is set on an isolated island inhabited by two sisters from one family and two brothers from another. Both sisters love Richard, the elder brother; both brothers love Jeanine, the younger sister. Richard, who once sacrificed his love for Jeanine by leaving the island, returns accompanied by a young girl, Lulu. He discovers that his brother has been mistreating Jeanine. The tempest of destructive passions thus unleashed is symbolized by a hurricane that strikes the island, demolishing everything, but also preventing Marianne, the jealous older sister, from murdering Richard. As the sun shines cheerfully on the calm morning after the storm, the characters face the rebuilding of their devastated lives. The emotional hurricane, too, has blown itself out. With the dawn comes the possibility of a new order. Richard, the seeker of truth, sets sail with Lulu, the personification of hope.

In *L'Enfant-Roi*, his third libretto for Bruneau, Zola returned to the more realistic portrayal of a Parisian family, in this case, a baker and his wife. The plot again reflects Zola's own domestic situation, and it is also a reworking of *Madeleine* with a happy ending. The baker and his wife have been unable to have any children, but, unknown to the husband, the wife has had a child before her marriage by a cousin who was killed during the war. When the baker discovers his wife's secret visits to the boy, his jealousy nearly destroys their household and even their business, as malicious employees take advantage of his distraction to seize control of the bakery. In the end, peace is restored when the baker agrees to adopt the child for the sake of his wife's happiness. The virtues of honest labor and the joys of parenthood triumph over the darker forces of human nature. The symbolically fecund wheat fields of *Messidor* appear in this urban setting as the life-giving loaves of the baker's bread.

After Zola's death, Bruneau went on to compose music for three more lyric poems by Zola. *Violaine la chevelue* is a fairy-tale piece recalling the early *Stories for Ninon*; *Lazare* tells the story of a Lazarus who wishes to be left to his peaceful sleep; and *Sylvanire: Ou, Paris en amour* portrays a ballerina torn between her love and her art. This last work by Zola includes an elaborate symbolic ballet exalting the city of Paris.

OTHER MAJOR WORKS

LONG FICTION: *La Confession de Claude*, 1865 (*Claude's Confession*, 1882); *Le Vœu d'une morte*, 1866 (*A Dead Woman's Wish*, 1902); *Les Mystères de Marseille*, 1867 (*The Flower Girls of Marseilles*, 1888; also as *The Mysteries of Marseilles*, 1895); *Thérèse Raquin*, 1867 (English translation, 1881); *Madeleine Férat*, 1868 (English translation, 1880); *La Fortune des Rougon*, 1871 (*The Rougon-Macquart Novels*, 1879; also as *The Fortune of the Rougons*, 1886); *La Curée*, 1872 (*The Rush for the Spoil*, 1886; also as *The Kill*, 1895); *Le Ventre de Paris*, 1873 (*The Markets of Paris*, 1879; also as *Savage Paris*, 1955); *La Conquête de Plassans*, 1874 (*The Conquest of Plassans*, 1887; also as *A Priest in the House*, 1957); *La Faute de l'abbé Mouret*, 1875 (*Albine: Or, the Abbé's Temptation*, 1882; also as *Abbé Mouret's Transgression*, 1886); *Son Excellence*

Eugène Rougon, 1876 (*Clorinda: Or, The Rise and Reign of His Excellency Eugène Rougon*, 1880; also as *His Excellency*, 1897); *L'Assommoir*, 1877 (English translation, 1879; also as *The Dram-Shop*, 1897); *Une Page d'amour*, 1878 (*Hélène: A Love Episode*, 1878, also as *A Love Affair*, 1957); *Nana*, 1880 (English translation, 1880); *Pot-bouille*, 1882 (*Piping Hot*, 1924); *Au bonheur des dames*, 1883 (*The Bonheur des Dames*, 1883; also as *The Ladies' Paradise*, 1883); *La Joie de vivre*, 1884 (*Life's Joys*, 1884; also as *Zest for Life*, 1955); *Germinal*, 1885 (English translation, 1885); *L'Œuvre*, 1886 (*His Masterpiece*, 1886; also as *The Masterpiece*, 1946); *La Terre*, 1887 (*The Soil*, 1888; also as *Earth*, 1954); *Le Rêve*, 1888 (*The Dream*, 1888); *La Bête humaine*, 1890 (*Human Brutes*, 1890; also as *The Human Beast*, 1891); *L'Argent*, 1891 (*Money*, 1891); *La Débâcle*, 1892 (*The Downfall*, 1892); *Le Docteur Pascal*, 1893 (*Doctor Pascal*, 1893; previous 20 novels [*La Fortune des Rougon* through *Le Docteur Pascal*] collectively known as *Les Rougon-Macquart* [*The Rougon-Macquart Novels*]); *Lourdes*, 1894 (English translation, 1894); *Rome*, 1896 (English translation, 1896); *Paris*, 1898 (English translation, 1897, 1898; previous 3 novels collectively known as *Les Trois Villes*); *Fécondité*, 1899 (*Fruitfulness*, 1900); *Travail*, 1901 (*Work*, 1901); *Vérité*, 1903 (*Truth*, 1903; previous 3 novels collectively known as *Les Quatre Evangiles*).

SHORT FICTION: *Contes à Ninon*, 1864 (*Stories for Ninon*, 1895); *Esquisses parisiennes*, 1866; *Nouveaux Contes à Ninon*, 1874; *Le Capitaine Burle*, 1882 (*A Soldier's Honor and Other Stories*, 1888); *Naïs Micoulin*, 1884; *Contes et nouvelles*, 1928; *Madame Sourdis*, 1929.

POETRY: *L'Amoureuse Comédie*, wr. 1860 (in *Œuvres complètes*).

NONFICTION: *Mes haines*, 1866 (*My Hates*, 1893); *Le Roman expérimental*, 1880 (*The Experimental Novel*, 1893); *Documents littéraires*, 1881; *Le Naturalisme au théâtre*, 1881 (*Naturalism on the Stage*, 1893); *Nos auteurs dramatiques*, 1881; *Les Romanciers naturalistes*, 1881 (*The Naturalist Novel*, 1964); *Une Campagne*, 1882; *The Experimental Novel and Other Essays*, 1893 (includes *The Experimental Novel* and *Naturalism on the Stage*, better known as *Naturalism in the Theater*); *Nouvell Campagne*, 1897; *La Vérité en marche*, 1901.

MISCELLANEOUS: *Œuvres complètes*, 1966-1968 (15 volumes).

BIBLIOGRAPHY

Berg, William J., and Laurey K. Martin. *Émile Zola Revisited*. New York: Maxwell Macmillan International, 1992. A basic biography of Zola that covers his life and works. Bibliography and index.

Brown, Frederick. *Zola: A Life*. New York: Farrar Straus & Giroux, 1995. A comprehensive biography and literary discussion of the founder of naturalism, who became one of the nineteenth century's most influential literary figures. Bibliography and index.

Gallois, William. *Zola: The History of Capitalism*. New York: Peter Lang, 2000. An examination of how Zola depicted capitalism in his works. Bibliography and index.

Pollard, Patrick. *Émile Zola Centenary Colloquium*. London: Émile Zola Society, 1995. This collection of essays from a colloquium held by the Institute Français du Royaume-Uni and Birkbeck College, in London in September, 1993, examines various aspects of Zola's life and works.

Jan St. Martin

JOSÉ ZORRILLA Y MORAL

Born: Valladolid, Spain; February 21, 1817
Died: Madrid, Spain; January 23, 1893

PRINCIPAL DRAMA

Juan Dándolo, pb. 1830, pr. 1839 (with Antonio García Gutiérrez)

Vivir loco y morir más, pb. 1837

Cada cual con su razón, pr. 1839

Ganar perdiendo, pb. 1839 (adaptation of Lope de Vega Carpio's play *La noche de San Juan*)

Más vale llegar a tiempo que rondar un año, pb. 1839, pr. 1845

Apoteosis de don Pedro Calderón de la Barca, pb. 1840, pr. 1841 (verse drama)

Lealtad de una mujer: O, Aventuras de una noche, pr., pb. 1840

El zapatero y el rey, pr., pb. 1840 (part 1)

Un año y un día, pr., pb. 1842

Los dos virreyes, pr., pb. 1842 (adaptation of Pietro Angelo Fiorentino's novel *El virrey de Nápoles*)

El eco del torrente, pr., pb. 1842

Sancho García, pr., pb. 1842

El zapatero y el rey, pr., pb. 1842 (part 2)

El caballo del rey don Sancho, pr., pb. 1843

La mejor razón, la espada, pb. 1843, pr. 1849 (adaptation of Augustín Moreto y Cabaña's play *Las travesuras de Pantoja*)

El molino de Guadalajara, pr., pb. 1843

La oliva y el laurel, pr., pb. 1843

El puñal del godo, pr., pb. 1843 (*Dagger of the Goth*, 1929)

Sofronia, pr., pb. 1843

La copa de marfil, pr., pb. 1844

Don Juan Tenorio, pr., pb. 1844 (English translation, 1944)

El alcalde Ronquillo: O, El diablo en Valladolid, pr., pb. 1845

La calentura, pr., pb. 1847 (part 2 of *El puñal del godo*)

La reina y los favoritos, pr., pb. 1847

El rey loco, pr., pb. 1847

El excomulgado, pr., pb. 1848

Traidor, inconfeso y mártir, pr., pb. 1849

El cuento de las flores, pr., pb. 1864

El encapuchado, pr. 1866, pb. 1870

Don Juan Tenorio, pr. 1877 (operatic version; music by Nicolás Manent)

Pilatos, pr., pb. 1877

Other literary forms

José Zorrilla y Moral first achieved fame and popularity with his lyric and narrative poetry, which exceeds in quantity, if not in quality, his dramatic writings. Most of these poems were inspired by the history and lore of Spain, as were his plays. They are outstanding manifestations of the poet's creative capabilities; his vivid imagination, his facility in versification, and the musical qualities of his verses give life to old Spanish legends and traditions. Many of these same legends became the subjects of his plays.

His autobiography, while not always a reliable source of information, is an excellent example of controlled prose, free of the stylistic exaggerations to be found in much Romantic writing. The book is an excellent self-portrait of Zorrilla y Moral: the artist, totally dedicated to his craft, and the man, humble and good.

Achievements

José Zorrilla y Moral achieved at an early age and maintained throughout his life a degree of popularity comparable only to that of Lope de Vega Carpio in the seventeenth century and for similar reasons. His lively and at times extravagant imagination, his awesome facility with versification, his skill in creating scenes of great dramatic effect, were all at work in the dramatization of legends and historical events and characters long dear to Spanish audiences. They were his favorite subject matter, although he succeeded in writing a tragedy following classical models, *La copa de marfil* (the ivory cup), that was perfect in form but somewhat cold and unappealing. He also wrote two allegorical works, *Apoteosis de don Pedro Calderón de la Barca* (apotheosis of Pedro Calderón de la Barca) and *La oliva y el laurel* (the olive and the laurel). It was in the first part of *El zapatero y el rey* (the cobbler and the king), however, that Zorrilla y Moral revealed his brilliance in the drama. The play deals with some incidents in the life of King Pedro I (1320-1367), known to some as "the Cruel," to others as "the Just." Zorrilla y Moral emphasizes the latter quality, portraying the king as defender of the people against the nobility and the clergy. He is a character of great dramatic appeal, brave, just, and far superior to his enemies.

Some critics consider *El zapatero y el rey*, part 1, to be Zorrilla y Moral's best piece. It probably is not, but the reasons for its success are clear. The play shares characteristics with his best later works—namely, subject matter familiar to his audience, emphasis on some trait in a character that presents the character in a new light, a series of scenes of sure dramatic effect, and a richness and variety of versification that had and still has a spellbinding power on audiences. His other plays were more or less successful in direct relation to the presence in them of one or more of the above elements. In his *Don Juan Tenorio*, for example, the protagonist experiences a deep and genuine Christian conversion, but even before this, he is brave, daring, gallant, generous, and extremely appealing—indeed, a character of heroic dimensions, perhaps initially roguish, but ultimately noble. As in others of Zorrilla y Moral's better works, here, too, everything contributes to the portrayal of the main protagonist, including the supporting character Doña Inés, who is so lyrically portrayed by the author.

Don Juan Tenorio is not a perfect work, but it continues to be the author's best-known. According to critical consensus, Zorrilla y Moral's true masterpiece is *Traidor, inconfeso y mártir* (traitor, unconfessed and martyr). The work shows him to be both an excellent poet and a first-rate dramatist who knows the theater. The play is based on the old legend of the baker from Madrigal who claimed to be King Sebastian of Portugal (who had disappeared in a war). From the opening scenes, the attention is centered on the protagonist, and the pace of the action is maintained to give the main character true heroic dimensions. The playwright's discourse and poetic descriptions are beautiful, and the suspense, mystery, heroism, and passion that Zorrilla y Moral created are fascinating to spectators and readers alike.

Zorrilla y Moral surpassed his contemporaries in the use of Spanish folklore. He saw himself in the tradition of the great dramatists of the Golden Age, such as Lope de Vega, Tirso de Molina, Pedro Calderón de la Barca, and Agustín Moreto y Cabaña. They, like he, felt deeply the beauty, richness, and endless dramatic possibilities within the cultural tradition of Spain. He had the good fortune of coming on the theatrical scene after such Romantic authors as Ángel de Saavedra, Juan Eugenio Hartzenbusch, and Antonio García Gutiérrez, and was thus able to avoid the declamatory style, excessive sentimentality, and reliance on incredible coincidences that mar so many of these writers' plays. In a sense, Zorrilla y Moral represents a reaction against those authors, inspired in part by his desire to remain close to the playwrights of the Siglo de Oro.

A modern perspective reveals that Zorrilla y Moral's plays transcend the tenets of Romanticism as a historical literary movement, while on the other hand they show a close similiarity to those aspects that one may call romantic in the works of authors such as Homer, Dante, William Shakespeare, Lope de Vega, Miguel de Cervantes, and others.

BIOGRAPHY

José Zorrilla y Moral left an unparalleled chronicle of his life in his works, his letters, and his autobiography. If to these sources is added the information provided by contemporary newspaper accounts of the productions of his plays and of the many public readings he gave of his poetry, it is possible that more is known of him than of any other Spanish author of his time.

He was born in Valladolid, Spain, in 1817, into a middle-class family. His father was a lawyer who worked for the government in different capacities, and the young Zorrilla y Moral moved with his family first to Seville in 1826, then to Madrid in 1827. In both cities, the boy was enrolled in prestigious schools but was not a good student. A hyperactive imagination, sensitive personality, and precocious capacity for versifying drove him to write and to recite verses at twelve years old. He began the study of law in Toledo in 1833 but experienced little interest and even less success in the field. Two years later, he published both his first poem and short story. It was then that his very strict father decided to take direct control of Zorrilla y Moral's life, and as a result, the young poet fled to Madrid without a cent. This obscure existence would soon change, however, and for an unusual reason: After attending the burial of the great satirist José de Larra y Sánchez de Castro, the young Zorrilla y Moral stepped forward and read with trembling voice a deeply expressive poem much in the spirit of Larra's work. Some of the writers present at the funeral offered him work in literary magazines and solicited his collaboration.

Zorrilla y Moral soon enjoyed the friendship of the most important writers of the day, and in 1837, he published one of his his first plays, *Vivir loco y morir más* (to live crazy and die crazier). In 1839, he was married to Florentina O'Reilly, a woman several years his senior, who brought him a son from a previous marriage. The same year, he began a highly prolific period of writing, and his fame and popularity grew accordingly. His works touched a responsive chord in his readers and spectators, who were already familiar with the traditions and legends he used in his writing and who appreciated the musicality of his verse. Zorrilla y Moral was soon considered to be the national poet of Spain and was the recipient of many official honors. In 1843, the government bestowed on him the Cross of Carlos III, and in 1848, he was offered membership in the Royal Spanish Academy, although at that time he refused. In 1844, he wrote and produced what was to become his most famous work, *Don Juan Tenorio*, and in 1846, he left for France, where he contracted with editor Fréderic Baudry for the publication of his complete works (*Obras de Don José Zorrilla*, 1847). During his stay in Paris, he met the most important French writers of the day. In 1849, he produced and published his masterpiece *Traidor, inconfeso y mártir*, acclaimed by both the critics and the general public. This play marks the high point of his dramatic production, though he continued to write narrative and lyric poems of arresting beauty.

In 1855, Zorrilla y Moral sailed for America, where he spent eleven years in Mexico and Cuba. Everywhere he went, he was accorded great honors. On his return to Spain in 1866, he was welcomed with delirious enthusiasm in every city he visited. The poet himself contributed to this excitement by giving emotional public readings of his old and new poems. On several of these occasions, his plays were restaged in his honor in the city he happened to be visiting.

Commissioned by the Spanish government, Zorrilla y Moral traveled to Italy in 1871 to find

Spanish properties in Italian libraries. The task was neither suitable nor appealing to him, however, and he soon abandoned the mission and went to France. Five years later, he returned to Spain and tried his hand again at drama. The results were two notable failures: *Pilatos* (Pilate), and the libretto for a new *Don Juan Tenorio* set to music. His fame, however, was not diminished nor was the affection, admiration, and gratitude of his countrymen. In 1885, he was offered again, and accepted, membership in the Royal Spanish Academy.

The greatest tribute the poet received was his coronation as the national poet in Granada in 1889. It was fitting homage to a true and great poet, as well as a humble and exemplary citizen, who had given poignant and masterful literary form to so many elements of Spanish history and civilization. The triumphant scenes of this coronation had their counterpart in the outpouring of grief and in the deep sense of loss felt throughout the Spanish-speaking world when the poet died in Madrid in 1893.

ANALYSIS

After the opening night performance of *Cada cual con su razón* (1839), José Zorrilla y Moral told the applauding audience that he was not sure whether his play was good or bad—but that he knew that it was *Spanish*. He went on to say that he loved his country and he did not want to borrow anything from the literary traditions of France. The statement is important as it indicates clearly the direction his dramatic activity would take on all but a few occasions. Spanish history and traditions from the Visigothic period to the seventeenth century were the most important sources of his inspiration, as the playwright approached historical figures and events looking for ideal character models—personifications of positive qualities that the author endeavored to explore and develop to the fullest in his art. In Zorrilla y Moral's plays, the positive and noble triumphs over the negative and destructive, though his idealized characters are never presented in the abstract, but rather in the historical context in which they lived. Exercising poetic license, Zorrilla y Moral added some details of character and omitted others to bring out positive

traits that he felt would be instructive to audiences. Like the best Spanish dramatists of the seventeenth century, Zorrilla y Moral saw certain historical figures as heroic, a view still relevant today.

Zorrilla y Moral is unquestionably the best Spanish dramatist of the Romantic period, although changing tastes and the author's own criticisms of some of his works have unjustly emphasized the least positive aspects of his plays. More reflective and balanced critics have called attention to the enduring merits of Zorrilla y Moral's theater. Though it is true that his easy facility with Spanish verse and his preference for imagery of sound and color can at times detract from character development and dramatic effect, there is no dearth of positive values in his plays, and in his best works a perfect balance of lyrical richness and dramatic moments creates truly memorable theater. The subject matter of most of his works is Spanish and Catholic, a fact that may limit their appeal to Spanish-speaking audiences. Nevertheless, the virtues, vices, and ideals that are beautifully, forcefully, and convincingly presented in Zorrilla y Moral's plays are of universal significance and deserving of a wider audience.

EL ZAPATERO Y EL REY, PART I

After a few faltering, initial steps, Zorrilla y Moral achieved his first play based on a historical subject, with almost complete artistic success: *El zapatero y el rey*, part 1. The piece deals with certain events in the life of King Pedro I of Castile, mainly as they relate to a legend in which the cleric Colmenares either kills the father of the shoemaker Blas Pérez or kidnaps his wife, depending on the version of the story. The cleric bribes the judges trying his case, who merely condemn the cleric not to attend choir for six months (though he will continue to receive his salary). Blas Pérez takes justice into his own hands and fatally stabs Colmenares during a religious procession presided over by the king himself. King Pedro then administers justice for the murder of Colmenares, condemning Blas Pérez not to make any shoes for a year and giving him a purse of gold coins.

The character of the king is beautifully presented in scenes of great dramatic effect. He cares for his humble subjects, walks among them, talks to them, and dispenses justice evenhandedly. As in many of Zorrilla y Moral's later plays, the protagonist clearly dominates the work, enhanced and illuminated by the subordinate characters. Colmenares acts as the king's extraordinary double, a device frequently used in Zorrilla y Moral's plays with excellent results, for it serves well to give added prominence to the main character. In contrast to Colmenares, who represents the clergy, King Pedro I appears as a more complete, human person: Though he is certainly a king, and a heroic one at that, he acts as a father-figure to his subjects. *El zapatero y el rey*, part 1, was well written, very well received, and clearly showed its author to be a genuine and powerful new dramatic voice.

For Zorrilla y Moral, as perhaps for every artist, aesthetic verisimilitude is far more important than historical fact. In *El zapatero y el rey*, as well as in others of his plays, he shows little concern for depicting an accurate biography or chronology. Although he includes many details that have a semblance of historical truth, he departs from the historical sources. Zorrilla y Moral's King Pedro I, presented as an embodiment of justice, appears to be quite different from the fourteenth century tyrant who first bore that character's name. Thus the playwright seems to challenge the conventional truth of history, or rather, of historians, preferring the perspective of popular legends and traditions.

EL ZAPATERO Y EL REY, PART 2

In 1842, the second part of *El zapatero y el rey* was produced with even greater success than the first. It is in actuality a new play, a dramatization of King Pedro I's final years, particularly of his death at the hands of his half-brother, the future King Enrique. The work has terrifying and somber moments. Two of the better wrought scenes are, in act 2, the description of the conspiracy to assassinate the king, and, in act 3, King Pedro's monologue. The dialogue is especially well written, and the verses, always fluid and robust, have a musical quality that captivates the audience. Some critics argue that this *El zapatero y el rey* is even better than the first.

SANCHO GARCÍA

Sancho García, which bore the subtitle "Tragedy in Three Acts and in a Variety of Verses," dramatizes another famous legend from the early days of the country of Castile: A countess is having an affair with a Moorish nobleman named Muza. Her son, Sancho García, finds out about the affair from his page Sancho Montero; Muza thus convinces the countess to poison her son. She sends her maid Estrella with the poison, but Estrella tells her lover—Sancho Montero—about her task, and the loyal page immediately warns Sancho García. During a banquet, Sancho García forces his mother to drink the poison, and Muza is killed by Sancho Montero. In Zorrilla y Moral's play, the countess is not killed but is imprisoned.

All the elements of high drama are present in the legend of Sancho García. In Zorrilla y Moral's play, the title character is portrayed as the hero who, through his bravery and courage, rids the nascent country of Castile of the evils that would soon destroy it: a treacherous Moor who, under false promises of peace, has been welcomed to the countess's bedroom, and a countess who, too eager to please her lover, tries to get rid of her son and heir. Sancho García's confrontation with his mother and with the Moor are poetically forceful, as the main protagonist appears as an appealing hero who brings honor and freedom to his subjects.

DAGGER OF THE GOTH

The one-act play *Dagger of the Goth* is, in its brevity, one of Zorrilla y Moral's most beautiful compositions. This is because of the famous story it dramatizes—as well as the creation and development of the characters, the profound passions that animate it, and the perfect dramatic situations created by the author. Probably because of its brevity, the tension of the action never fails, and the intensity of its poetic vigor is undiminished throughout.

EL CABALLO DEL REY DON SANCHO

Another work produced in 1843 which deserves mention is *El caballo del rey don Sancho* (King Sancho's horse), published the same year. The horse of the title is poetically portrayed in a skillful manner as a symbol of royal power; Zorrilla y Moral's stage directions call for a real horse to make its appearance onstage.

DON JUAN TENORIO

The play that gave Zorrilla y Moral lasting recognition, *Don Juan Tenorio*, was apparently written in twenty-one days. It was produced in 1844, with no more than moderate critical success. Several scenes were praised for their excellent theatrical effect, and the variety of its versification was applauded. Some incongruities were criticized, and the staging of the final moments was considered somewhat childish. Don Juan's salvation—Zorrilla y Moral's new twist to the legend—was unacceptable to the critics as they found it poorly prepared and somehow offensive to the concept of a God who is merciful but also just. By deciding to rewrite the legend of Don Juan, however, Zorrilla y Moral knew that he was taking on a challenge of incredible proportions. Tirso de Molina, the seventeenth century dramatist, had given the legend of Don Juan its first dramatic form in a powerful, although not perfect play, a work essentially religious and moralistic in intent, in which divine justice is finally meted out to Don Juan, that scourge of women, society, and religion. Later versions of the myth had given more attention to the don's sexual exploits, but had remained basically faithful to Tirso de Molina's model and its denouement.

Zorrilla y Moral set out to portray a very different Don Juan. In his version, Don Juan is saved from damnation by the love he feels for Doña Inés. This proposition could sound almost blasphemous to persons of religious sensibility who are familiar with the traditional ending of the myth, yet it was the element of which the author remained most proud. With it he claimed he had corrected Tirso de Molina, Molière, and George Gordon, Lord Byron (the other major authors who, by that time, had treated the Don Juan story) by being more Christian than they in presenting true Christian love. Zorrilla y Moral was thus proposing a new and daring theological resolution to the Don Juan legend: salvation through repentance and regenerative love. The doctrine is valid, its presentation in the text is sufficiently explicit and credible, yet in the first performances of the play the actors portraying Don Juan lacked the necessary degree of sensitivity to make the don's difficult process of conversion believable. Don Juan's change of heart was therefore criticized as arbitrary, unmotivated, and highly unsatisfactory. Indeed, the play demands an exceptional director and excellent acting to make this conversion, and other scenes, work.

Don Juan Tenorio, then, is not a perfect piece, and no one has criticized its defects more harshly than did Zorrilla y Moral himself. For example, he justly observed that the passage of time in his play is so confusing that at times neither the characters nor the audience knows what time of day it is. Subsequent critics, however, have been much more sympathetic to the play. They have convincingly demonstrated its many elements of unity, as evidenced by the numerous parallelisms between the two parts of the play. Critics have shown how the other characters in the story contribute to enhancing the qualities of courage, daring, nobility, and mystery in the hero, Don Juan. They have praised the character of Doña Inés, with which the author was also pleased. Additionally, they have defended the confusion of the passage of time in act 1 as perfectly plausible, since the corresponding scenes take place during Carnival, when the normal course of time is suspended.

What has seldom been questioned in criticism of *Don Juan Tenorio* is the tremendous appeal of the central character, which overshadows whatever defects the play may otherwise have. This appeal resides in the poetic presentation of the heroic Don Juan, both before and after his conversion. He makes an indelible impression on the spectators. The play also has marvelous scenes and beautiful poetic passages of mysterious and irresistible charm. *Don Juan Tenorio* continues to be the most popular play in the Spanish-speaking world, and every year it is successfully staged in innumerable places on or near All Souls' Day. The play is not well-known elsewhere, perhaps because of the deeply Spanish qualities of Don Juan, and perhaps also because the brilliant verse and lyrical tone of the text do not fare well in translation.

TRAIDOR, INCONFESO Y MÁRTIR

The defects that the author and critics found in *Don Juan Tenorio* are totally absent in *Traidor, inconfeso y mártir*, published and produced in 1849. From its first performance, author and critics alike considered it his best work, and it continues to be so regarded. The play dramatizes one version of the legend of King Sebastian of Portugal, who disappeared in war, causing several impostors to try to take his place. In the play, Gabriel de Espinosa and his "daughter" Aurora arrive at an inn in Valladolid. The mayor has them jailed, and soon thereafter the mayor's son César falls in love with Aurora. Gabriel de Espinosa claims to be a baker, but his jailers see in his sword Portugal's coat of arms. They ask the king of Spain to execute the "impostor" and to set Aurora free. After the sentence is carried out, some papers are found that prove that Gabriel de Espinosa was indeed King Sebastian of Portugal and Aurora the natural daughter of the mayor of Valladolid.

The general structure of the play, the creation of brilliant and effective moments, the most appropriate use of colorful and beautiful poetry, show the dramatist at his best, putting all his gifts at the service of good drama, expressing his art with conciseness and impressive skill. The exuberance of style often associated with Romantic works is absent. The small number of characters, all male, except Aurora, are excellently drawn. From the beginning the plot is full of intrigue and suspense, as Zorrilla y Moral's verse flows with hypnotic effect. King Sebastian is noble, generous, and brave; Aurora is a model of tenderness and loving passion; the denouement of the story has all the ingredients of high tragedy and drama. The work is balanced, sober, and controlled, and has passion, mystery, intrigue, suspense, and beautiful poetry throughout. Nevertheless, though *Traidor, inconfeso y mártir* is undoubtedly superior to *Don Juan Tenorio*, it never attained equal popularity and appeal.

Later works

After *Traidor, inconfeso y mártir*, there is very little of Zorrilla y Moral's work that deserves critical examination. The author's second rendering of the legend of Don Juan, this time set to music by Nicolás Manent, was a failure, as was his play *Pilatos*.

Other major works

POETRY: *Poesías de don José Zorrilla*, 1837-1839 (6 volumes); *Cantos del trovador*, 1840-1841 (3 vol-

umes); *Vigilias del estío*, 1842; *Flores perdidas*, 1843; *Recuerdos y fantasías*, 1844; *La azucena silvestre*, 1845; *El desafío del diablo*, 1845; *Un testigo de bronce*, 1845; *María*, 1850; *Un cuento de amores*, 1850 (with José Heriberto García de Quevedo); *Granada*, 1852 (2 volumes); *Al-Hamar, el Nazarita, rey de Granada*, 1853; *La flor de los recuerdos*, 1855-1859 (2 volumes); *El drama del alma*, 1867; *La leyenda del Cid*, 1882; *¡Granada mía!*, 1885; *Gnomos y mujeres*, 1886; *El cantar del romero*, 1886; *¡A escape y al vuelo!*, 1888; *De Murcia al cielo*, 1888; *Mi última breca*, 1888.

NONFICTION: *Recuerdos del tiempo viejo*, 1880-1883 (3 volumes).

MISCELLANEOUS: *Obras de Don José Zorrilla*, 1847; *Obras completas*, 1943 (2 volumes).

BIBLIOGRAPHY

Arias, Judith H. "The Devil at Heaven's Door: Metaphysical Desire in *Don Juan Tenorio*." *Hispanic Review* 61, no. 1 (Winter, 1993): 15. A discussion of the boundary between the real and fiction in *Don Juan Tenorio*.

Cardwell, Richard A., and Ricardo Landeira, eds. *José de Zorrilla: Centennial Readings*. Nottingham, England: University of Nottingham, 1993. These essays honoring the one-hundred-year anniversary of Zorrilla y Moral's death discuss his life and works. Bibliographical references.

Schurlknight, Donald E. *Spanish Romanticism in Context: Of Subversion, Contradiction, and Politics: Espronceda, Larra, Rivas, Zorrilla*. Lanham, Md.: University Press of America, 1998. A study of the role of politics in Spanish Romanticism that examines the works of Zorrilla y Moral, José de Espronceda, Mariano José de Larra, and Angel de Saavedra (Rivas). Bibliography and index.

Ter Horst, Robert. "Epic Descent: The Filiations of Don Juan." *MLN* 111, no. 2 (March, 1996): 255. The author compares and contrasts Zorrilla y Moral's *Don Juan Tenorio* with Tirso de Molina's *El burlador de Sevilla*.

Ricardo Arias

CARL ZUCKMAYER

Born: Nackenheim, Germany; December 27, 1896
Died: Visp, Switzerland; January 18, 1977

PRINCIPAL DRAMA

Kreuzweg, pr. 1920, pb. 1921

Pankraz erwacht, pr. 1925

Der fröhliche Weinberg, pr., pb. 1925

Schinderhannes, pr., pb. 1927

Katharina Knie, pr. 1928, pb. 1929

Der Hauptmann von Köpenick, pr., pb. 1931 (*The Captain of Köpenick*, 1932)

Der Schelm von Bergen, pr., pb. 1934

Bellman, pr. 1938

Des Teufels General, pr., pb. 1946 (*The Devil's General*, 1962)

Barbara Blomberg, pr., pb. 1949

Der Gesang im Feuerofen, pr., pb. 1950

Ulla Winblad, pr., pb. 1953 (revision of Zuckmayer's drama *Bellman*)

Das kalte Licht, pr., pb. 1955

Die Uhr schlägt eins, pr., pb. 1961

Das Leben des Horace A. W. Tabor, pr., pb. 1964

Kranichtanz, pb. 1966, pr. 1967

Der Rattenfänger, pb. 1975

OTHER LITERARY FORMS

Carl Zuckmayer's collected works, *Werkausgabe in zehn Bänden, 1920-1975* (1976), consists of ten volumes. In addition to his plays, Zuckmayer's works include the novel *Salwàre* (1936; *The Moon in the South*, 1937), numerous short stories and poems, as well as two volumes of an autobiographical nature— *Pro Domo* (1938) and *Als wärs ein Stück von mir* (1969; *A Part of Myself: Portrait of an Epoch*, 1970). He also wrote several film scripts and adaptations of American plays for the German stage.

ACHIEVEMENTS

The mention of Carl Zuckmayer's name among reasonably educated people in the German-speaking countries invariably conjures up a number of major dramatic characters, as well as the names of great actors and actresses who embodied these characters on the stage and on the screen. People think of Curt Jürgens as Schinderhannes and as the Devil's General, of Werner Krauss as the Captain of Köpenick, and of Paula Wessely as Barbara Blomberg. Zuckmayer's major plays had a tremendous popular appeal. He created a dramatic universe that has become part of the cultural consciousness of generations of German-speaking people. His dramatic œuvre depicts at least three distinct periods of twentieth century German history: the end of the Wilhelminian Empire, the Weimar Republic, and the Third Reich. In addition to mirroring the modern age in Germany, he has written a number of remarkable historical plays that have their settings in other centuries and in other countries. Zuckmayer's autobiographical work *A Part of Myself* is appropriately subtitled: It is indeed a fascinating "Portrait of an Epoch."

BIOGRAPHY

Carl Zuckmayer was born on December 27, 1896, in the village of Nackenheim in the Rhenish Hesse district, where his father owned and operated a small factory. In 1900, his family moved to Mainz, a city that then had some eighty-four thousand inhabitants. Zuckmayer attended the Humanistische Gymnasium (academic high school) there from 1903 to 1914. When World War I broke out, he enlisted as a volunteer and attained the rank of lieutenant by the end of the war. The war years were of paramount importance for his development as a man and as an artist. His fellow soldiers came from all regions of Germany and from all social classes. The future writer of realistic dramas took careful note of their various dialects and modes of expression. He also had time to read widely. This reading, together with his firsthand experience of the war, led him to adopt an idealistic, pacifist worldview. In 1917, he published several poems in *Die Aktion*, a pacifist-socialist weekly.

After the war, he served briefly on the Workers' and Soldiers' Council in Mainz and on the Revolutionary Students' Council of the University of Frankfurt. During 1919 and 1920, he studied economics, philosophy, botany, and biology at the universities of Frankfurt and Heidelberg. While in Frankfurt, he was in contact with young socialists and pacifists, notably with Carlo Mierendorff, who was the editor of *Das Tribunal*, a periodical that advocated comprehensive social reforms. Zuckmayer joined such writers as Kasimir Edschmid and Theodor Däubler in contributing to *Das Tribunal*. At the same time, he became acquainted with the expressionist dramas of Fritz von Unruh and Walter Hasenclever, which were then performed in Frankfurt. Zuckmayer's political and philosophical thinking was influenced by his socialist and pacifist friends, and in his writing he emulated the practitioners of expressionism. In 1920, his first drama, entitled *Kreuzweg*, had its premiere in Berlin. It consisted of a series of expressionistic outpourings about love and death that were poorly related to a sort of plot involving some peasants who revolt against their feudal lord. The play was lambasted by the critics and closed after three performances; for a while Zuckmayer was forced to eke out a living as a freelance writer and as a singer in cabarets, along with a variety of other jobs.

In 1922, Zuckmayer's friend Kurt Elwenspoek, the newly appointed director of the theater in Kiel, offered him a job as *Dramaturg* (literary adviser). The two friends shocked and infuriated the conservative burghers of Kiel by staging plays by such avant garde authors as Georg Büchner, Ernst Barlach, August Strindberg, and Frank Wedekind. When they presented Terence's erotic comedy *Eunuchus* (161 B.C.E.; *The Eunuch*, 1598) in a daring and provocative adaptation by Zuckmayer, both he and Elwenspoek were fired on the spot, and the theater was closed by the police. During the 1924-1925 season, Zuckmayer and Bertolt Brecht were employed as *Dramaturgen* by the prestigious Deutsches Theater in Berlin. At that time, Zuckmayer was more concerned with society and politics than was Brecht, who was then in his expressionist phase and had become known for such plays as *Baal* (wr. 1918, pb. 1922; English translation, 1963) and *Im Dickicht der Städte* (pr. 1923; *In the Jungle of Cities*, 1961). It was partly under

Carl Zuckmayer in 1976. (AP/Wide World Photos)

Brecht's influence that Zuckmayer wrote his second play in an expressionist vein, entitled *Pankraz erwacht*. It was also a failure, and the eminent critic Alfred Kerr suggested that both the play and its author ought to be forgotten. Fortunately, Kerr was quite wrong about the second part of his suggestion, because in the very same year, 1925, Zuckmayer's comedy *Der fröhliche Weinberg* had its premiere in Berlin. It was a tremendous success and was shortly afterward performed in more than one hundred theaters. Also in 1925, Zuckmayer married the actress Alice Frank, née von Herdan. During the next several years, Zuckmayer enjoyed huge artistic and financial successes with his plays *Schinderhannes* (also based on Terence's *Eunuchus*), *Katharina Knie*, and *The Captain of Köpenick*.

The latter also provoked numerous diatribes in the Nazi press, and in 1933 (the year that Adolf Hitler assumed power in Germany), Zuckmayer moved to Austria, where he had purchased a country house in 1926. In 1938, when the Germans annexed Austria, Zuckmayer emigrated to Switzerland. His plays and books having been banned in Germany and Austria, his financial situation became precarious. In 1939, he was deprived of his German citizenship, and he moved to the United States. He was first a scriptwriter in Hollywood, then a lecturer at the dramatic workshop of the New School in New York, and starting in 1941, a farmer near Barnard, Vermont. Zuckmayer's years in exile were difficult ones: He was cut off from his linguistic milieu and forced to devote most of his time to his chores as a farmer, and his literary output diminished to a trickle. It was precisely during this time of hardship and isolation, however, that he created one of his masterpieces: *The Devil's General* was written during the period of 1943 to 1945 and had its premiere in Zurich in 1946.

Beginning after the play's German premiere in 1947, Zuckmayer participated in numerous discussions with German students and other young people about the issues raised in the play. During the next ten years or so, he lived alternately in the United States and in Europe. In 1958, he took up permanent residence in Saas-Fee, Switzerland. During the last twenty years of his life, Zuckmayer wrote a number of plays and prose works, and he was showered with prizes and honors, including the Great Cross of Merit of the Federal Republic of Germany and the Great Austrian State Prize. He died in Visp, Switzerland, on January 18, 1977.

ANALYSIS

Carl Zuckmayer's apprenticeship in the theater during the early 1920's and particularly the failure of *Pankraz erwacht* eventually led him to an important insight:

> For the first time I recognized my limits. . . . I had neither the gift, nor intention of founding a new literary epoch, a new theatrical style, a new direction in art. . . . But I knew that a revitalized impact and revitalized values (*eine neue Lebendigkeit der Wirkung und der Werte*) can be achieved by human artistic means which transcend the limitations of time, which will never become obsolete. . . . I wanted to approach nature, life, and truth, without distancing myself from the demands of the day, from the burning subject-matter of my time.

Although Zuckmayer said that this statement was not intended as a "program" for his future dramatic production, the fact is that after *Pankraz erwacht*, he wrote only "realistic" dramas with plots structured according to Aristotelian principles, intended to inspire "pity and fear" in the audiences of serious dramas and to celebrate life with all its folly in comedies. One of the most important touchstones for the success or failure of a drama is the question of characterization and audience identification with the protagonists. Those plays that contain a fairly large number of full-bodied, "round" characters have the greatest effect on the audience. In Zuckmayer's case, such characters are usually firmly rooted in regions he knew well, and they speak languages or dialects he knew well.

DER FRÖHLICHE WEINBERG

A case in point is *Der fröhliche Weinberg*. This rollicking comedy is set in Rhenish Hesse, Zuckmayer's home district. The time of the action is the fall of 1921 during the grape harvest. Jean Baptiste Gunderloch, a rich winegrower (and a widower), has resolved to give half of his vineyard and half of his other possessions to his daughter Klärchen as a dowry, to auction off the other half, and to live from the proceeds during his retirement. Klärchen is being wooed by a student named Knuzius, but she really loves Jochen Most, the owner of a freighter plying the Rhine. Gunderloch has set a condition that must be met before he will consent to Klärchen's marriage to anyone: She must be pregnant by the man in question, and she must be involved in the matter "voluntarily and with pleasure." In other words, Gunderloch wants to be sure of having a grandchild, and he wants his daughter to have a happy sex life. Klärchen confesses to Annemarie, her father's housekeeper, who is Jochen's sister, that she does not love Knuzius, that he "has no talent for love," and that she believes he is only after her dowry. Her major problem is how to rid herself of Knuzius's assiduous attentions long enough to be able to see Jochen and clear things up with him. Annemarie advises Klärchen to tell Knuzius that she is pregnant. In this way she will be able to plead sickness and absent herself from the party to be held that night. When Klärchen does make her "confession" to Knuzius at the end of act 1, his first and only reaction is to shout "Hey! Gunderloch! Father-in-law!" Her suspicions are thus confirmed.

The entire act 2 is devoted to a big party in the village inn. The party is given by Gunderloch for this season's wine buyers, for the prospective bidders at the auction to be held the following morning, and for his friends in the village. As the richest vintner in the region, he is also obliged by custom to provide free cider for a group of veterans who have formed a choir. The party is very boisterous, the wine flows in streams, and there is dancing and singing. While Knuzius dances with Babettchen, the innkeeper's daughter, Klärchen tries to explain to Jochen that she is not engaged to Knuzius and that she is not pregnant, but he stubbornly refuses to listen to her; all he wants is to beat Knuzius to a pulp. He soon gets his chance because the bleating "singing" of the veterans so infuriates Gunderloch that he wants to throw them out of the room. There ensues a monumental general brawl that Gunderloch survives as the sole victor. Act 3 takes place before sunrise in the courtyard of the inn. It consists of a series of declarations of love and offstage lovemaking. First, Gunderloch realizes that he is far too young and full of vitality to retire and to live alone. He and Annemarie (who has loved him secretly for a long time) quickly reach an understanding, and their love is consummated in an arbor in the garden. Then Knuzius, who is totally drunk, declares his love to Babettchen and denounces Gunderloch and Klärchen. Babettchen tells him to sleep off his inebriation, but she intimates that she might be interested in him. Next, Jochen and Klärchen are finally able to communicate and to clear up the misunderstanding between them. They also make love immediately. Finally, one of the wine buyers and the daughter of one of the prospective buyers of the vineyard enter the courtyard, only to disappear quickly thereafter in the barn. The play ends as Gunderloch announces that he will not sell any of his possessions and that he and Annemarie, and Jochen and Klärchen will marry. Babettchen will marry Knuzius, and the wine buyer will marry the girl he seduced during that memorable night.

The main characters of *Der fröhliche Weinberg* consist of several stock characters in folk comedy, such as a country girl who is mistakenly attracted to an educated or upper-class man from the city, a dowry hunter, and a kindhearted but clever confidante. Zuckmayer used these stock characters to construct an effective comic plot. Beyond that, he imbued his main characters with an aura of contemporaneity, and he surrounded them with an entourage of secondary characters designed to accentuate this aura. For example, when Knuzius asks for Babettchen's hand in marriage, he uses the anti-Semitic language and concepts typical of the Nazis: "As I ask for her hand . . . I am not only striving for the fulfillment of personal wishes, but also for the restoration of our nation's health in view of its virtue, its fitness for military service, its cleanliness, its loyalty, and its racial purity." While these words are met by laughter and applause, their meaning is surely undercut by the fact that they are spoken by the impecunious dowry hunter who, according to Klärchen, has no talent for love. It is also noteworthy that Knuzius spends the night sleeping on a pile of manure while the other protagonists are making love. Similarly, when some of the veterans and the teacher direct anti-Semitic remarks at the Jewish wine buyers, these remarks are consistently rejected and proved nonsensical by other characters. Incorporating these topical concerns in his comedy seemed to be Zuckmayer's way of achieving his goal of not "distancing [himself] from the demands of the day." Indeed, these topical allusions, and particularly the characterization of Knuzius, prompted several protests against the play from right-wing groups. The most important aspect of the play, however, is its joyful affirmation of life. This affirmation is expressed in the almost ritualistic rash of marriages at the end of the play, in the unabashed sensuality of the four protagonists, and in several instances of vivid nature imagery. When Gunderloch, Annemarie, Jochen, and Klärchen meet in the morning, for example, they notice that the vineyards are steaming, that the trees are laden with fruit, and that the fragrance of blossoms is rising from the soil. Nature's bounty and human love become fused in Annemarie's words, "now everything is growing for our happiness." Plot construction, characterization, the finely nuanced use of language, and the splendid nature imagery—all these elements combine to make *Der fröhliche Weinberg* into a first-rate comedy.

THE CAPTAIN OF KÖPENICK

Zuckmayer's undisputed masterpiece is *The Captain of Köpenick*. Although this "German fairy tale," as it is subtitled, consists of twenty-one scenes and includes seventy-three characters, its basic plot (based on an actual incident that occurred in 1906) is quite simple: Wilhelm Voigt, a cobbler, has recently been released from jail, where he spent fifteen years for a minor offense. His native village has struck his name from its lists and now refuses to give him a residence permit. In order to get employment elsewhere, he needs a residence permit, and in order to obtain that, he must furnish proof that he is employed. In an attempt to end this impossible situation, he breaks into a police station to obtain the necessary forms, stamps, and papers with which he could forge a passport. He is caught and sentenced to a new jail term. After his release, the vicious cycle regarding residence permit and employment repeats itself. This time, however, Voigt decides on a radical cure for his problem. He purchases a captain's uniform in a pawnshop, puts it on in a public toilet, and orders a group of soldiers to accompany him to Köpenick, a suburb of Berlin, where he arrests the mayor and confiscates all the money in the town hall. He finds out too late that there is no passport office (and thus no forms and stamps) in Köpenick. He sends the mayor to Berlin under military escort, dismisses the soldiers, and goes to live in a hotel. For the next few days, all the newspapers are full of the exploits of the "Captain of Köpenick," and the police are embarrassed by their inability to find the impostor. Eventually Voigt turns himself in at police headquarters but not without first striking a bargain to the effect that after his third jail sentence he will be given proper papers.

Parallel to this main action runs a secondary action involving the uniform that Voigt eventually purchases. During the first scene, Captain von Schlettow, who has recently been promoted to that rank, tries on the uniform. Shortly afterward he has to resign from

the Prussian army because he gets into a brawl in an establishment that is off-limits to soldiers. The uniform is returned to the store and is next purchased by a lieutenant of the reserves. When he becomes too fat to wear it, it is used at a costume ball, and it finally ends up in the pawnshop where Voigt finds it. The uniform thus becomes a leitmotif in the play, a symbol of authority that commands blind obedience, while the person who wears it means very little. It is significant that von Schlettow's misfortune in the ill-reputed establishment arises from the fact that he acts in the authoritarian manner of an officer while wearing civilian clothes. Similarly, when the mayor of Köpenick asks the "captain" for identity papers, Voigt simply points to a bayonet held by one of "his" soldiers and asks whether "that does not suffice." The mayor then meekly accepts his arrest. The butt of Zuckmayer's irony in this play is the unquestioning deference to authority (indeed to the mere trappings of authority) at the expense of humanness and common sense. Although this point is repeatedly made throughout the play, the ingenious device of the ubiquitous uniform also enables the playwright to present a kaleidoscopic view of all the social strata of Wilhelminian Germany. His mastery of the nuances of language (ranging from low-class Berlin dialect, to military jargon, to standard German) is a sheer delight. Although this linguistic differentiation is difficult to translate into other languages, the utter theatricality of *The Captain of Köpenick* prompted an English translation that was performed at the prestigious National Theatre in London.

THE DEVIL'S GENERAL

In December, 1941, Zuckmayer read a newspaper report that the renowned flying ace Ernst Udet had fatally crashed while testing a new type of plane. Zuckmayer knew Udet from World War I, and he knew that Udet was opposed to the Nazi regime. Udet became the model for General Harras, the protagonist of Zuckmayer's *The Devil's General*. The principal action of the play concerns Harras's development from an unenthusiastic, even unwilling collaborator with the Nazi regime to an opponent who eventually atones for his service to the "devil" (Hitler) with his death. During act 1, a group of air force officers, high government officials, three actresses, the wife of one of the officers, and her sister are assembled around General Harras in a private dining room of a fashionable Berlin restaurant. He is giving a party to honor Colonel Eilers, a fighter pilot who has recently shot down his fiftieth enemy plane.

During the party, the various characters reveal their reasons for supporting the Nazi regime. The spectrum ranges from honest belief in the purer and better world advocated by the Nazi ideology, to political opportunism (the adherents of which see Nazism as a bulwark against communism), to sheer egotism professed by those who have enriched themselves at the expense of Jews or whose careers have been furthered by the Nazis. In a sense, Harras belongs to the last category: The one thing he loves most in life is flying, and the air force has allowed him to indulge his passion. He also likes high living, as illustrated by the expensive delicacies and wines he serves at his party at a time when food is severely rationed for the average German citizen. At the same time, he is not a member of the Nazi party, and he particularly despises the regime's narrow-minded and foolish racial policies. One of the most moving texts that Zuckmayer ever wrote is Harras's description of the ethnic and cultural mixture that makes up the population of the Rhine Valley—a pithy and brilliant refutation of the Nazi doctrine of racial purity.

During one of the conversations in act 1, the specific problem that will lead to Harras's downfall is mentioned. He is in charge of quality control of new fighter planes and cannot find out why some of them crash when they are first put into service. Act 2 takes place in Harras's apartment. He has just been released from Gestapo headquarters, where he has been interrogated for two weeks. He is given a period of ten days to find out why some of the planes are crashing. This act contains two important turning points in Harras's development. First, he receives a letter of thanks and farewell from a Jewish surgeon whom he planned to help escape. The surgeon has been tortured in a concentration camp for six months, and he simply has no strength left and cannot face life in a foreign country. By the time Harras receives his letter, he and his wife have already com-

mitted suicide. On reading this letter, Harras realizes his guilt:

> Everyone has his conscience Jew, or several, so that he can sleep at night. But one cannot buy off one's guilt with that. That is self-deception. We are still guilty of that which is happening to thousands of others whom we do not know and whom we do not help. We are guilty and damned to all eternity. To permit villainy to occur is worse than perpetrating it.

After this insight, it appears for a short while that Harras might flee and build a new life for himself with the young actress Diddo, but then the second turning point occurs. The evening paper carries a report that Harras's friend Eilers has crashed in one of the new planes, just above the airfield. Harras decides to ascertain the cause for this and all the other crashes.

Act 3 takes place in Harras's office at the military airfield, on the last day of the period of grace that had been granted to him. In spite of a meticulous investigation, he has not been able to determine why some of the planes are defective. Toward the end of the play, Oderbruch, the chief engineer of the plant where the planes are made and Harras's close friend of twelve years' standing, confesses to him that he and other members of the resistance movement have been sabotaging the aircraft. In a poignant personal statement, Oderbruch explains his motivation:

> No brother of mine died in a concentration camp. I did not love a Jewess. No friend of mine was chased out of the country. I did not know anyone who died in action on June 30. But one day—I was ashamed of being a German. Since then I have not been able to rest until— until it is over.

With Oderbruch's confession and with SS guards at the main gate, the moment of decision for Harras has come: If he exposes Oderbruch and his resistance operation, he will be completely rehabilitated and will continue to enjoy the prestige and luxurious life of an air force general. If Harras accepts Oderbruch's advice to fly abroad (a small plane is standing by, ready for takeoff), he can work actively against the Nazi regime. Harras chooses neither of these alternatives. He takes up one of the fighter planes he knows to be defective and promptly crashes. The government orders a state funeral for him. The profoundly ambivalent decision taken by Harras mirrored the ambivalent moral position of many spectators, as became evident in Zuckmayer's discussions with German audiences and in the heated debate that raged in the press. Harras is a most effective protagonist in terms of Aristotelian drama: He certainly inspires pity and fear, and he allows the audience to identify emotionally with him. Many of the young people in the audiences identified more with Lieutenant Hartmann, however, a secondary character whose development from an idealistic supporter of the regime to a morally outraged opponent is one of the subsidiary actions of the play. During the last few scenes of the play, Hartmann becomes a sort of idealistic extension of Harras. He will be able to do what Harras could not do. As Oderbruch and Hartmann join in the Lord's Prayer while Harras's plane crashes, the drama ends on a note of atonement and faint hope.

The three plays discussed in this essay are generally considered to be Zuckmayer's best. They are sometimes grouped together and called his "German trilogy." The plays that Zuckmayer wrote after World War II (mostly historical dramas) did not grow from the author's emotional essence; their characters and plots are rather obvious intellectual constructs. Thus, none of these later plays projects the aura of reality (albeit poetic reality) that distinguishes the earlier ones.

OTHER MAJOR WORKS

LONG FICTION: *Salwàre*, 1936 (*The Moon in the South*, 1937; also as *The Moons Ride Over*, 1937).

SHORT FICTION: "Die Affenhochzeit," 1932 ("Monkey Wedding," 1938); *Herr über Leben und Tod*, 1938; *Der Seelenbräu*, 1945; *Engele von Löwen*, 1955; *Die Fastnachtsbeichte*, 1959 (*Carnival Confession*, 1961).

POETRY: *Der Baum*, 1926.

SCREENPLAY: *Der blaue Engel*, 1930 (*The Blue Angel*, 1968).

NONFICTION: *Pro Domo*, 1938; "Aufrufzum Leben," 1942 ("Appeal to the Living," 1942); *Die Brüder Grimm*, 1947; *Die langen Wege*, 1952; *Als wärs ein Stück von mir*, 1969 (*A Part of Myself: Portrait of an Epoch*, 1970); *Einmal wenn alles vorüber ist: Briefe an Kurt Grell*, 1981.

MISCELLANEOUS: *Werkausgabe in zehn Bänden, 1920-1975*, 1976 (10 volumes).

BIBLIOGRAPHY

Finke, Margot. *Carl Zuckmayer's Germany*. Frankfurt, Germany: Haag and Herchen, 1990. A biography of Zuckmayer that focuses on the Germany of his time. Bibliography and index.

Grange, William. *Partnership in the German Theatre: Zuckmayer and Hilpert, 1925-1961*. New York: Peter Lang, 1991. This study examines the close relationship between Zuckmayer and his principal director, Heinz Hilpert, in the staging and production of German drama. Bibliography and index.

Mews, Siegfried. *Carl Zuckmayer*. Boston: Twayne, 1981. A basic biography of Zuckmayer that examines his life and works. Bibliography and index.

Wagener, Hans. *Carl Zuckmayer Criticism: Tracing Endangered Fame*. Columbia, S.C.: Camden House, 1995. Wagener expresses his distress at the declining amount of scholarship involving Zuckmayer and his gradually fading reputation among scholars.

Franz P. Haberl

ARNOLD ZWEIG

Born: Gross-Glogau, Silesia (now Głogów, Poland); November 10, 1887
Died: Berlin, East Germany; November 26, 1968

PRINCIPAL DRAMA

Abigail und Nabal: Tragödie in drei Akten, pr., pb. 1913, revised pb. 1920

Ritualmord in Ungarn: Jüdische Tragödie in fünf Aufzügen, pr., pb. 1914, revised pb. 1918 (as *Die Sendung Semaels*)

Die Lucilla, wr. 1921

Die Umkehr des Abtrünnigen, pb. 1925

Das Spiel vom Sergeanten Grischa, pb. 1929, pr. 1930

Die Aufrichtung der Menorah: Entwurf einer Pantomime, pb. 1930

Laubheu und keine Bleibe: Schicksalscomödie, pb. 1930

Bonaparte in Jaffa: Historisches Schauspiel, pb. 1949

Soldatenspiele: Drei dramatische Historien, pb. 1956

OTHER LITERARY FORMS

Arnold Zweig's numerous novels and collections of short stories or novellas have assured his place in literary history. The publication of *Der Streit um den Sergeanten Grischa* (1927; *The Case of Sergeant Grischa*, 1928), a novel adapted from his play for which he could find neither a publisher nor, until 1930, a producer, brought Zweig his first major success, although his earlier novel, *Die Novellen um Claudia* (1912; *Claudia*, 1930), was well received. Zweig published three volumes of poetry between 1910 and 1958. His essays and letters appear in ten volumes published between 1920 and 1968.

ACHIEVEMENTS

In 1915, Arnold Zweig was awarded the Kleist Prize for his drama *Ritualmord in Ungarn*. World War I and the rise of Nazi Germany intervened before he again received such public recognition. In 1939, however, he attended a meeting of the PEN Club in New York City, where he was warmly received by such personages as Albert Einstein and Thomas Mann, both, like Zweig, exiles from Nazi Germany. In that year, President Franklin D. Roosevelt received Zweig in the White House.

Living as an exile in Palestine from 1933 until 1948, Zweig, stripped of his German citizenship in 1935, returned to Berlin by official invitation in 1948. The next year, he was elected to the Volkskammer, the parliament of the recently formed German Democratic Republic. As a member of the World Peace Council, he was a delegate in 1949 to the World Peace Conference in Paris. In 1950, he received Germany's National Prize for Literature and was elected president of the German Academy of the Arts. The University of Leipzig awarded him an honorary doctorate in 1952. Zweig received his most prestigious international award, the Lenin Peace Prize, in 1958.

BIOGRAPHY

Arnold Zweig, the eldest of Adolf and Bianca van Spandow Zweig's three children, experienced anti-Semitism early in his life. Nine years after his birth on November 10, 1887, Zweig's family, prosperous grocers who supplied members of the military with food, was abruptly robbed of its livelihood when the Prussian ministry of war forebade Jews from supplying food to the military.

Stripped of their means of making a living, the Zweigs moved to Kattowitz (now Katowice, Poland) in 1896. So strained were their finances that nine-year-old Arnold went to work in a bookstore. He completed his secondary education in 1907, then pursued studies in literature, languages, art, and philosophy at universities in Breslau (1907-1908), Munich (1908-1909 and 1913-1914), Berlin (1909-1911), Göttingen (1911-1912), and Rostock (1912-1913). German students frequently moved from university to university, studying with the professors who most interested them.

Zweig, who planned to teach modern languages, began a doctoral dissertation on Paul Jakob Rudnick but abandoned it. He published his first major fiction, *Aufzeichnungen über eine Familie Klopfer* (notes about the Klopfer family) in 1911 and followed it with *Claudia*, which enjoyed considerable success.

His first drama, *Ritualmord in Ungarn*, a tragedy written in 1912 and published in 1914, was banned by the censors, although it brought Zweig the Kleist Prize in 1915. Zweig was conscripted to serve in the German army in April of that year and served until the armistice in November, 1918. Meanwhile, on July 5, 1916, during a leave from the army, he married his cousin, Beatrice Zweig, an artist, with whom he had two sons.

Arnold Zweig in 1949. (AP/Wide World Photos)

During his final year of military service, Zweig contracted tuberculosis of the eyes, which severely limited his vision. He was assigned to the press corps of the Ober-Ost division in Lithuania and Russia. Poor vision plagued him for the rest of his life. On discharge, he resumed his university studies at Tübingen, studying literature and sociology, but he soon dropped these studies for a career as a freelance writer.

By 1924, Zweig had moved to Berlin, where he became editor of *Jüdische Rundschau*, a Zionist publication, and of *Die Weltbühne*. His socialist views and idealistic Zionism dominated his writing. He demanded humane treatment of Jews coming to Germany from Eastern Europe. His reading of Sigmund Freud resulted in his writing *Caliban: Oder, Politik und Leidenschaft* (1927; Caliban; or politics and passion), a psychoanalytical study of anti-Semitism. Zweig sent Freud a copy of his book, beginning a friendship and extensive correspondence between the two that continued until Freud's death in 1939.

As Nazi Germany grew increasingly inhospitable to Jews, Zweig made a scouting trip to Palestine in 1932. In March, 1933, he fled from Berlin with his family, traveling to the south of France, a refuge for German Jewish writers. In December, 1933, the Zweigs moved to Haifa in Palestine, remaining there until 1948. After Germany revoked Zweig's citizenship in 1935, Palestine in 1936 granted him a passport, enabling him to make annual trips to Europe and to attend the PEN Club meeting in New York City in 1939.

After the war, the Zweigs returned to Berlin in 1948, living in the eastern part of the city. There Zweig was welcomed as a significant literary figure. He entered politics and served as president of the German Academy of the Arts. He and his family remained in East Berlin until his death on November 26, 1968.

ANALYSIS

Arnold Zweig was an antimilitarist whose experiences during World War I colored a great deal of his writing. Although he had written *Abigail und Nabal*, a biblically based drama, and *Ritualmord in Ungarn*, based on a famous trial in Hungary, before the war, it was not until 1917 that he planned two works, *Die Lucilla* and *Das Spiel vom Sergeanten Grischa*, in both of which he attempted to analyze the causes of war, which he considered an inevitable result of Germany's overall social posture.

Zweig lived through the 1920's in a Germany in which social democrats struggled against Marxist revolutionaries, toward whom Zweig was sympathetic. Anti-Semitism had long existed in Germany, but during the economically devastating years following World War I, many Germans became more stridently anti-Jewish. Zweig's response to this prejudice was to produce *Juden auf der deutschen Bühne* (1927; Jews on the German stage), in which he emphasizes the contributions German Jews made to their country.

His early interest in psychology was intensified by his reading of Freud and by his subsequent extended correspondence with him as well as by his personal exposure to psychoanalysis as a patient. In his novella *Pont und Anna* (first published in 1925 in *Regenbogen*), Zweig explores Germany's repression of memories of war as well as Freud's theory of how shock affects memory. This novel reflects the new morality that pervades Zweig's later writing.

After his resettlement in Palestine, Zweig wrote little drama. His *Soldatenspiele: Drei dramatische Historien* contains his *Austreibung 1744 oder das Weihnachtswunder*, *Bonaparte in Jaffa*, and *Das Spiel vom Sergeanten Grischa*. It met with little popular success because the dialogue was stilted and too ideologically heavy for the stage. Zweig knew that the stage was a medium through which he could reach and influence large audiences of all social classes, as such dramatists as Ernst Toller and Gerhart Hauptmann were doing. Drama, however, was not Zweig's most effective genre. It is in his short stories and novels that he wrote most naturally and effectively.

RITUALMORD IN UNGARN

This play records the events of a trial that took place in 1882-1883 in Hungary. Referred to as the Tisza-Eszlar affair after the place in which it took place, the trial focuses on the aftermath of the disappearance of fourteen-year-old Esther Solymossi from her peasant mother's home in April, 1882. Two politicians suggested that Jews had abducted Esther and killed her to obtain blood for use in the Passover service. Their strident accusations cause Esther's widowed mother to charge the Jews in town with abduction and murder.

Judge Bary comes to town as the investigating judge. He and the two politicians who initially raised the question torture fourteen-year-old Moritz Scharf, son of the caretaker of the synagogue, so painfully that he confesses to the offense and incriminates others. A long trial ensues. In the course of it, Judge Bary's chicanery is brought to light and on August 3, 1883, the twenty-nine Jewish defendants are acquitted.

A revised version of the play *Die Sendung Semaels* was published in 1918 and performed the following year. In both plays, the characters are generally portrayed as either wholly good or wholly evil. Moritz is too pure and innocent to be believable, whereas the prosecutors are depicted as being unbelievably evil. Even when members of the Jewish community confess to greed and indifference to the poor during a Passover service, Zweig fails to demonstrate the motives for such behavior.

DAS SPIEL VOM SERGEANTEN GRISCHA

The novel that brought Zweig his earliest recognition began as a play based on an experience Zweig had as a German soldier in Belgium during World War I. He conceived of writing this ironic tale in dramatic form late in 1917 after he had been told the story by a noncommissioned officer. A Russian prisoner of war, as the tale was told, had escaped and assumed the identity of a Russian deserter. He was recaptured behind German lines and, for purely political reasons, was ordered executed by General Schieffenzahn, quite in violation of the rules governing the treatment of prisoners of war.

After his capture, Grischa's true identity is uncovered. He is clearly innocent of any charges that would, under the rules of war, justify his execution. Despite this, General Schieffenzahn, who has issued an order that all deserters be executed, demands Grischa's execution both as a morale builder for the German soldiers under his command and as an example to those who might consider deserting as the war winds down. Before he learned of this event, Zweig was convinced of the fairness and humanity with which the German army administered law. Grischa's execution robbed him of this idealistic view and produced the ironies that pervade this play.

BONAPARTE IN JAFFA

Composing this play between 1934 and 1938, Zweig, newly exiled to Palestine, found many parallels between Napoleon Bonaparte's cruel massacre of more than three thousand Turks in Jaffa and the Holocaust that was developing in Nazi Germany. The Turkish prisoners of war could not be transported and there were no provisions to feed them, so Napoleon ordered them executed as he prepared to march on Acre.

Desgenettes, the army's surgeon general, appalled by Napoleon's decision, proclaims that the army consists of soldiers, not butchers. Grosjean, Desgenettes's assistant, tries to justify the massacre, but when he finally comes on the fields of decaying Turks, he is appalled and realizes that he is supporting a shameful dictator, not the liberator he supposed Napoleon to be. Grosjean was, in Zweig's mind, like those Germans whose opposition to Hitler came too late to prevent the Holocaust.

OTHER MAJOR WORKS

LONG FICTION: *Die Novellen um Claudia*, 1912 (*Claudia*, 1930); *Der Streit um den Sergeanten Grischa*, 1927 (*The Case of Sergeant Grischa*, 1928); *Junge Frau von 1914*, 1931 (*Young Woman of 1914*, 1932); *De Vriendt kehrt heim*, 1932 (*De Vriendt Goes Home*, 1933); *Erziehung vor Verdun*, 1935 (*Education Before Verdun*, 1936); *Einsetzung eines Königs*, 1937 (*The Crowning of a King*, 1938); *Versunkene Tage*, 1938; *Das Beil von Wandsbek*, 1947 (*The Axe of Wandsbek*, 1947); *Die Feuerpause*, 1954; *Die Zeit ist reif*, 1957 (*The Time Is Ripe*, 1962); *Traum ist teuer*, 1962.

SHORT FICTION: *Aufzeichnungen über eine Familie Klopfer*, 1911; *Die Bestie*, 1914; *Geschichtenbuch*, 1916; *Bennarone*, 1918; *Drei Erzählungen*, 1920; *Gerufene Schatten*, 1923; *Söhne: Das zweite Geschichtenbuch*, 1923; *Frühe Fährten*, 1925; *Regenbogen*, 1925; *Der Spiegel des grossen Kaisers*, 1926; *Knaben und Männer*, 1931; *Mädchen und Frauen*, 1931; *Spielzeug der Zeit*, 1933 (*Playthings of Time*, 1935); *Stufen: Fünf Erzählungen*, 1949; *Über den Nebeln*, 1950; *Der Elfenbeinfächer*, 1952; *Westlandsaga: Erzählung*, 1952; *Der Regenbogen*, 1955; *A Bit of Blood and Other Stories*, 1959.

POETRY: *Der Englishche Garten*, 1910; *Entrückung und Aufruhr*, 1920; *Fünf Romanzen*, 1958.

NONFICTION: *Das ostjüdische Antlitz*, 1920; *Das neue Kanaan*, 1925; *Lessing-Kleist-Büchner*, 1925; *Caliban: Oder, Politik und Leidenschaft*, 1927; *Juden auf der deutschen Bühne*, 1928; *Herkunft und Zukunft: Zwei Essays zum Schicksal eines Volkes*, 1929; *Bilanz der deutschen Judenheit 1933*, 1934 (*Insulted and Exiled: The Truth About the German Jews*, 1937); *Der Früchtekorb*, 1956; *Literatur und Theater*, 1959; *Über Schriftsteller*, 1967; *Sigmund Freud-Arnold Zweig Briefwechsel*, 1968 (*The Letters of Sigmund Freud and Arnold Zweig*, 1970).

BIBLIOGRAPHY

Kahn, Lothar. "Arnold Zweig: From Zionism to Marxism." In *Mirrors of the Jewish Mind*. New York: T. Yoseloff, 1968. Kahn traces the political turmoil that a sensitive Jew in Nazi Germany experienced in the period before World War II. This turmoil is reflected in Zweig's later dramas, even when he is dealing with historical subjects quite removed from the 1930's.

Pfeiler, William K. "Arnold Zweig." In *War and the German Mind*. New York: Columbia University Press, 1941. Published a number of years after Zweig's forced departure from Germany, this assessment shows how living in exile affected his writing and his thinking. A valuable assessment written even as Zweig's literary and intellectual development were undergoing substantial changes.

Salamon, George. *Arnold Zweig*. Boston: Twayne, 1975. This is the only full-length study of Zweig in English. It is thorough and dependable, although it emphasizes the author's prose fiction considerably more than his dramas. Salamon's insights into how the dramas influenced some of Zweig's most notable prose fiction are valuable.

R. Baird Shuman

AMERICAN DRAMA

AMERICAN DRAMA

Until the post-World War I era, American drama, confronted with religious hostility and then by economic necessity and academic indifference, struggled to come into its own as a respected literary genre at home and as a force that made itself felt on foreign stages. A commonplace of American literary history is that the plays of Eugene O'Neill, in Walter J. Meserve's words, marked "America's full-scale arrival into the modern drama of western civilization."

In an article in a 1907 issue of *Atlantic Monthly*, John Corbin quoted Edmund Stedman, who proclaimed a literary declaration of independence for American drama: "Quote boldly, then, I prophesy the dawn of the American drama; and quite confidently, too, for the drama has already dawned." Decrying the exhaustion of the European-influenced melodrama, Corbin applauded dramas by William Vaughn Moody and Percy MacKaye as plays "which challenge comparison with the best work of the modern stage in any country." Moody's *The Great Divide* (pr. 1906) and MacKaye's *Jeanne d'Arc* (pr. 1906) are hardly plays for which modern historians and critics would claim such eminence, but Corbin expressed an optimism about American drama that would become a reality in the post-World War I era in the dramas of O'Neill.

Kenneth Macgowan claims, in his introduction to *Famous American Plays of the 1920's* (1959), that the book might have been titled "The American Drama Comes of Age." When American drama finally came into its own, each decade thereafter left its unique mark on stage history. In the 1920's, Eugene O'Neill's stylistic experiments initiated a period of explosive growth and rich variety. In the 1930's, the social protest dramas of Clifford Odets and his contemporaries dramatized the personal conflicts of individuals and families at odds with themselves and with the conditions in the country. In the 1940's, Tennessee Williams and Arthur Miller emerged at the forefront of post-World War II writers concerned with psychological and moral dilemmas of individuals in a society readjusting to a peacetime economy and Cold War diplomacy. Their mood continued into

the 1950's in the Beckettian plays of Edward Albee, with his bleak vision of American culture and its alienated or dismembered characters. Albee, Miller, and Williams continued into the following decades, while social-protest dramatists flourished in Off-Broadway and Off-Off-Broadway theaters such as the Open Theatre, the Living Theatre, Café La Mama, the American Place Theatre, and the Public Theatre. Although the latter decades of the twentieth century witnessed some gains in minority theater by gay, feminist, and black dramatists, it was Sam Shepard, with his expressionistic utilization of the cowboy myth, and David Mamet, described by Ruby Cohn as the writer with "the most concentrated American stage speech since Edward Albee," who captured critical attention as playwrights with the potential to join the ranks of O'Neill, Williams, Miller, and Albee.

A latecomer to literary history, American drama had its beginnings in the two preceding centuries, during which it slowly developed from plays modeled on foreign subjects and on the prevailing English and European styles of sentimental comedy and tragedy to those derived from native experience and characterized by a realism and literary quality that gained respectability domestically and internationally.

There was strong hostility from religious groups in colonial times, a carryover from the Puritan closing of the English theaters from 1642 to 1660. Except for the Southern states, where Episcopalians settled, the theater was considered frivolous. Puritan New England, Huguenot New York, and Quaker Philadelphia, where the American drama eventually took root, rallied against the theater. Their religious opposition was strengthened by the country's preoccupation with the Revolutionary War. The high value placed on the thrifty use of time and money further consolidated opposition to such "trivial" pursuits as the theater. Yet even in earliest times, formal functions such as commencements featured quasi-theatrical performances at the College of William and Mary, the College of Pennsylvania (now the University of Pennsylvania), and Princeton. These performances took the form of recitations of odes and, occasionally, masques. A "pastoral colloquy" at the College of William and Mary in 1702 may well have been the first college dramatic performance in America.

Over the years, still another division developed, that between "theater" and "drama," caused by purely commercial considerations. As popular entertainment, theater relied on traditional audience tastes for its survival. Theater managers and producers could not risk plays by new authors experimenting with subject matter and style. Consequently, these writers turned to the small, noncommercial theaters. Much of their success was a result of their association with groups such as the Provincetown Players and the Theatre Guild. Later, the Group Theatre and the Actors Studio strengthened the importance of the little theater movement. The inheritors of this tradition are to be found in cities and campuses across the country and in New York in Off-Broadway and Off-Off-Broadway theaters and theater clubs such as the Manhattan Theatre Club, the Hudson Guild Theatre, the American Place Theatre, the Public Theatre, and Theatre Row, along West Forty-second Street. Some of these, such as the Public Theatre, have nurtured dramatists-in-residence. David Rabe and Lanford Wilson are but two dramatists who have had their plays steadily produced in resident theaters. Such regional theaters as the Goodman and Steppenwolf theaters in Chicago, the Actors' Theatre of Louisville, and the Long Wharf in Connecticut are among groups that continue a vital tradition that began with the Provincetown Players and the Theatre Guild in the 1920's.

On Broadway, indigenous musicals have enjoyed the financial successes denied much of the time to "serious" drama. Occasional dramatic imports such as those brought over by the Royal Shakespeare Company of London have enjoyed success with their limited runs. Serious plays by O'Neill, Williams, Miller, Albee, and others have enjoyed some financial success, but these are the exception rather than the rule.

The commercial division between theater and drama frequently has been carried over to the university level, where drama as literature is taught in English departments and plays are produced by theater departments. Until the end of the second decade of the twentieth century, the literary ambitions of the drama took a backseat to theatrical stageability and popular demand. This tardiness contrasts markedly with the national identity that native poetry and fiction enjoyed in the 1850's with the outpouring of literature by major writers such as Walt Whitman, Nathaniel Hawthorne, and Herman Melville. Not until seventy years later was American drama to experience such acceptance.

Yet in the time since, international recognition of major American plays and playwrights has come swiftly. O'Neill received the Nobel Prize in Literature in 1936, and his play *More Stately Mansions* (pb. 1964) was premiered posthumously in Stockholm in 1967. Sir Laurence Olivier played the father in *Long Day's Journey into Night* (pr. 1956) at the Old Vic in London in 1972. Miller directed—or helped direct—*Death of a Salesman* (pr. 1949) in China in 1983. Even the plays of later playwrights—Shepard's *Curse of the Starving Class* (pb. 1976) and Mamet's *Glengarry Glen Ross* (pr. 1983)—received their premieres at two of London's prestigious theaters, the Royal Court and the National, respectively.

A second major commonplace about American drama is its derivative nature. During the eighteenth and nineteenth centuries, the plays of William Shakespeare, Richard Brinsley Sheridan, and a host of lesser dramatists, both English and Continental, were popular on the American stage. As will be discussed later, the subject matter and styles of foreign dramatists influenced the American dramatists of the time. Even in the twentieth century, the influences of Aeschylus, Sophocles, Henrik Ibsen, August Strindberg, Anton Chekhov, George Bernard Shaw, Bertolt Brecht, and Samuel Beckett, among foreign dramatists, are evident in the plays of O'Neill and others. Miller's *All My Sons* (pr. 1947), for example, is an adaptation of Ibsen's *Samfundets støtter* (pr. 1877; *The Pillars of Society*, 1880) that is placed in a contemporary American setting.

Only in musical theater has the United States contributed innovatively to the history of world drama. The musical drama is, indeed, so indigenous that its transplantation to a foreign stage sometimes seems unnatural. Its unique Whitmanesque paradoxical qualities of idealism and energetic brashness are inimitably American. Not until the 1980's did imported musicals such as the English *Cats* (pr. 1981) compete with native musicals on the New York stage.

Singular moments in American dramatic history when theater and drama coalesced to produce luminous moments on the stage must include Pauline Lord's appearance in Sidney Howard's *They Knew What They Wanted* (pr. 1924) and O'Neill's *Anna Christie* (pr. 1921); Alfred Lunt and Lynn Fontanne in Robert E. Sherwood's *Idiot's Delight* (pr. 1936); Laurette Taylor as Amanda Wingfield in Tennessee Williams's *The Glass Menagerie* (pr. 1944); Lee J. Cobb as Willy Loman in the 1949 production of Miller's *Death of a Salesman*; Jessica Tandy as Blanche DuBois in Williams's *A Streetcar Named Desire* (pr. 1947); and Colleen Dewhurst and Jason Robards (quintessentially O'Neillian actors) in the 1973 production of *A Moon for the Misbegotten* (pr. 1947).

Special events also mark stage history, such as the 1984 production of *Death of a Salesman*, with a jaunty Dustin Hoffman as Willy Loman, contrasting vividly with the defeated Willy of Cobb's portrayal. In an interesting coincidence, a new play about salesmen of another sort—this time, real estate salesmen—appeared in tandem, as it were, with the Miller drama. *Glengarry Glen Ross* dramatizes the distinctively American confidence game that has been the subject of many dramatists since the 1920's. Hailed by critics as an updated sequel to *Death of a Salesman*, Mamet's drama is a hard-hitting, brilliant verbal choreography of a basic American myth. Rather than focusing conventionally on the causes and consequences of the conflicts created by the betrayal of ideals, Mamet transforms the disillusionment into an energetic poetry that takes on a life of its own. Like Williams before him, Mamet transforms even the harshest American realities into a celebration of the vitality and energy that are usually the domain of the musical. He brings the dynamic of Carl Sandburg's poetry to the stage. (It is an interesting coincidence that, like Sandburg, Mamet hails from Chicago.) The

dapper Willy Loman of Hoffman, then, is, at least in part, akin to the spirit of Mamet's salesmen.

EARLY AMERICAN DRAMA

The beginnings of American drama date back to April 30, 1598, near El Paso, Texas, when a comedy about soldiers on a march, written by a Captain Marcos Farfan de los Godos, was performed. Spanish-speaking areas, for the most part, were more congenial to theatrical entertainments than were those colonized by the English and Dutch.

Among other "firsts" on the American theater scene was a play by Virginia landowner William Darby. His *Ye Bare and Ye Cubb* (pr. 1665), "the first record of a play in English," resulted in a lawsuit against the author brought by an Edward Martin. Darby was found not guilty.

The "first play written by a native American to be performed by a professional company," reports the historian of drama Arthur Hobson Quinn, was performed "on the stage of the Southwark Theatre in Philadelphia in 1767." That play was *The Prince of Parthia*, a heroic tragedy by Thomas Godfrey. The Southwark Theatre, which replaced an earlier one built outside the limits of Philadelphia (like Shakespeare's on London's South Bank) and torn down after protests from religious groups, became the first permanent theater in America.

Written in blank verse and depicting historical events in a foreign country, *The Prince of Parthia* was influenced by many plays, including William Shakespeare's *Hamlet, Prince of Denmark* (pr. c. 1600-1601), *Macbeth* (pr. c. 1606), *Richard III* (pr. c. 1592-1593), *Julius Caesar* (pr. c. 1599-1600), and *Romeo and Juliet* (pr. c. 1595-1596) ; Francis Beaumont and John Fletcher's *The Maid's Tragedy* (pr. 1610-1611); John Dryden's *Aureng-Zebe* (pr. 1675); and Nicholas Rowe's *Tamerlane* (pr. 1701), among others. The traditional tragic passions of love, jealousy, loyalty, and revenge motivate the action, involving two brothers, one of whom returns in triumph to Parthia from a military victory, and Evanthe, the maiden for whose hand the two brothers compete. Personal and political passions eventually lead to Evanthe's suicide by poison, as well as the suicide of Arsaces (the brother whom she loves). Order is restored to the kingdom by Gotarzes, a younger brother, who, like Fortinbras in *Hamlet, Prince of Denmark*, is a figure outside the main action of the play. Although lacking in a native subject, the play is significant, as Quinn observes, as "the only play of American origin that was actually performed on a native stage during this period, before the Revolution." (Having died at an early age, Godfrey himself did not live to see his play performed or published.)

The history of the Southwark Theatre, at which *The Prince of Parthia* was produced, involves the beginning of the actor-manager tradition in colonial times. A number of British plays—such as Shakespeare's *Richard III*, William Congreve's *Love for Love* (pr. 1695), Dryden's *The Spanish Friar: Or, The Double Discovery* (pr. 1680), Joseph Addison's *Cato* (pr. 1713), Thomas Otway's *The Orphan: Or, The Unhappy Marriage* (pr. 1680)—were brought to America by an English actor-manager named Lewis Hallam. With his company, which included members of his family, Hallam began American theatrical history in prerevolutionary Williamsburg, New York, and Philadelphia. Contending with opposition from religious groups, he finally left for Jamaica, where he died, leaving a widow and a son to return to the United States to resume their theatrical activity. Mrs. Hallam's second husband, David Douglass, became manager of what was probably the first "American Company," the actual name that the performing group assumed. Douglass built the Southwark Theatre in Philadelphia, and his first and very long season included the production of Godfrey's *The Prince of Parthia*.

When war broke out, pursuits such as the theater, already strongly opposed on moral and economic grounds, were outlawed by an unenforceable resolution passed by the Continental Congress in 1774, which reads as follows:

> We will in our several stations encourage frugality, economy and industry, and promote agriculture, arts, and the manufactures of this country, especially that of wool; and will discountenance and discourage every species of extravagance and dissipation, especially all

horse-racing and all kinds of gaming, cockfighting, exhibitions of shews, plays, and other expensive diversions and entertainments.

Douglass and his company left voluntarily for the West Indies, and the prerevolutionary period in American drama came to a close. During the war, however, the lean beginnings of drama took on a decidedly native turn in the many satires directed against the British. Just as the prerevolutionary drama was associated with the names of Hallam, Douglass, and Godfrey, that of the war period belongs to political satirists such as Mrs. Mercey (née Otis) Warren of Massachusetts, where patriotic plays thrived. Characters, frequently military and political figures of the time, were taken from real life, and the settings were real places such as Faneuil Hall in Boston. In addition to the satiric writers, dramatists such as Hugh Henry Breckenridge portrayed generals on both sides with dignity, mostly in long speeches of blank verse.

The stern prohibitions of the Continental Congress in 1774 did not entirely prevent theatrical entertainments. Young Lewis Hallam, son of the British theatrical entrepreneur, and John Henry reestablished the American Company, and when Pennsylvania repealed the prohibition of theaters in 1789, moral opposition lessened and increasing emphasis was placed on dramatic quality.

If *The Prince of Parthia* can lay claim to being the first tragedy by a native performed in the first professional American theater, *The Contrast* (pr. 1787), produced by the American Company at the John Street Theatre in New York on April 16, 1787, was the first such comedy. Its author was Boston-born, Harvard-educated Royall Tyler, and his play met with success in New York, Baltimore, Philadelphia, Boston, Charleston, and Richmond. Like the author of *The Prince of Parthia*, Tyler had seen much British drama, and it is not surprising that *The Contrast* (advertised in Boston as "A Moral Lecture in five parts") is an American adaptation of England's memorable eighteenth century comedy of manners, Sheridan's *The School for Scandal* (pr. 1777).

In *The Contrast*, a servant, Jonathan, provides an interesting insight into contemporary attitudes toward the theater. Having purchased a ticket to an entertainment where "they play *hocus pocus* tricks," he was mistakenly directed to a "play-house," "where the devil hangs out the vanities of the world upon the tenter-hooks of temptation." In the narration of his adventure to a fellow servant, Jenny, Jonathan describes the reaction of the people sitting near him: "[they] set up such a hissing—hiss—like so many mad cats; and then they went thump, thump, thump, just like our Peleg threshing wheat and stampt away, just like the nation." When Jonathan finishes his tale, Jenny concludes that he was surely at a playhouse, whereupon Jonathan admits to having demanded a refund of his money and having been told that he had been watching not the sights he thought he had paid to see but something called the "School for Scandalization." Popular audience identification with or rejection of characters and action on the stage commonly expressed itself in strong reactions such as those described by Jonathan.

THE NINETEENTH CENTURY

The second comedy by a native American to be performed on the professional stage was William Dunlap's *The Father: Or, American Shandyism* (pr. 1789), a play influenced by another English work, Laurence Sterne's novel *The Life and Opinions of Tristram Shandy, Gent.* (1759-1767). *The Father* also holds the distinction of being the first professionally produced comedy of an American author to be published.

Dunlap, born in New Jersey, was also America's first major playwright-producer. A man of many interests, he seems to have been the Samuel Johnson of the late eighteenth and early nineteenth century American stage. Among his varied publications, the first chronicle of the American stage, *A History of American Theatre* (1832), stands out. Drama criticism had begun, and Dunlap records the formation of groups that gathered to support and stimulate interest in the theater by reviews in the magazines.

Especially important during the Dunlap era was his long-standing association with August von Kotzebue, a German dramatist whose domestic melodramas were very popular on the American stage. Amer-

icans during the early nineteenth century were enjoying the same kind of melodramatic fare that was popular on the English stage.

Two other major figures in nineteenth century stage history merit mention here. James Nelson Barker wrote the first surviving drama about Pocahontas, *The Indian Princess: Or, La Belle Sauvage* (pr. 1808). Taken from John Smith's *The Generall Historie of Virginia, New England, and the Summer Isles* (1624), the play used native history. Although remembered primarily for his romantic dramatizations of native subjects, Barker also wrote plays that featured exotic foreign settings. John Howard Payne, author of more than sixty plays, was known for his adaptations of foreign plays. Payne's exotic, gothic melodramas, such as *Ali Pacha: Or, The Signet Ring* (pb. 1823), entertained American audiences, as did his domestic melodramas.

Hastily and cleverly written for performances, melodramas—domestic and exotic, drawn from sources as varied as Shakespeare, Charles Dickens, Sir Walter Scott, Kotzebue, and Guilbert de Pixérécourt—fulfilled the expectations of early nineteenth century audiences. Major authors such as Dickens were popularized for audiences who demanded sheer spectacle, heroines saved from villains, and strong musical reinforcement of emotions.

It was in this period that the Scribean well-made play, featuring a formulaic plot fleshed out with much action and stage business, reached its peak. Victorien Sardou, Alexandre Dumas, *père*, and their countryman Eugène Scribe were the major figures grinding out such formula plays, to which the European dramatists of the latter half of the nineteenth century reacted in their realistic and psychological plays. Ibsen, Strindberg, Shaw, and Chekhov began the modern period of drama with plays in which ideas and complex characterizations replaced the melodrama that dominated the stages earlier in the century.

With beginnings, then, in Godfrey, Tyler, Dunlap, and Barker, drama had taken hold in the United States, its directions influenced by religious, economic, and historical forces.

During the Civil War period, George H. Boker, educated at the College of New Jersey, wrote tragedy in blank verse that is distinguished by its literary quality. His *Francesca da Rimini* (pr. 1855) was the first play in English to be based on the story of Dante's famous pair of lovers, Francesca and Paolo. Irish-born Dion Boucicault, who had spent some time in France before emigrating to the United States, found American culture a rich source of dramatic material. His *The Octoroon: Or, Life in Louisiana* (pr. 1859), based on Mayne Reid's novel *The Quadroon: Or, A Lover's Adventures in Louisiana* (1856), is about interracial romance. Boucicault wrote sympathetically about the poor. He was also important for his efforts (with Boker) to bring about the passage of the first copyright law in 1856. The legislation, however, came too late to give Harriet Beecher Stowe the right to have a voice in the stage adaptation of *Uncle Tom's Cabin: Or, Life Among the Lowly* (1852). Her novel was adapted with little success by Charles Western Taylor and with much success by George L. Aiken, both stage versions having been produced in 1852, the same year that the novel was published.

Other late nineteenth century dramatists provide important links in the historical development of American drama. Their interest in the realism of character and events was part of a reaction (conscious or not) against the superficiality and predictability of the prevailing melodrama. In contrast to the outsized passions of melodrama, Quinn observes, James Herne's *Margaret Fleming* (pr. 1880) and *The Reverend Griffith Davenport* (pr. 1899) deal with "less obvious material and the finer subtlety of motive." William Gillette's *Secret Service* (pr. 1895) moved the drama a step further in the realism of action. Had the author not invoked an improbable ending in regard to the fate of the hero, a Civil War spy, he might have "created a tragedy of uncommon power." Even so, Quinn concludes, *Secret Service* is a "melodrama of a high order."

Clyde Fitch also produced a prodigious output of plays and earned for himself an international reputation, especially with *The Truth* (pr. 1906), a drama about a promiscuous wife, sympathetically drawn, who, in spite of her wayward nature, loves her husband devotedly. Fitch's *Beau Brummell* (pr. 1890), drawn from the novel by William Jesse and the stage adaptation of Blanchard Jerrold, features a hero-philanderer who also demonstrates heroic goodness. Fitch's sympathetic heroes and heroines constitute the melodrama's counterpart to Ben Jonson's biting studies of "humours"; Fitch's characters, Quinn notes, are "endowed with a shining virtue or possessed by one absorbing vice." Like Gillette, Fitch also wrote spy dramas, among them *Nathan Hale* (pr. 1898) and *Major André* (pr. 1903).

EARLY TWENTIETH CENTURY

At the turn of the twentieth century, theater continued to depend on foreign influences in both style and subject matter, despite efforts to create serious native drama. The much-needed catalyst for change was provided in 1913, with the beginning of Workshop 47, the famous playwright course at Harvard taught by George Pierce Baker. O'Neill became Baker's most distinguished student; among the many other enrollees in Baker's classes, those who were most influential in shaping the course of American drama include Sherwood, S. N. Behrman, George Abbott, Philip Barry, and Sidney Howard. Baker's influence extended to those involved in the production aspects of the theater and to critics as well, including Heywood Broun, Brooks Atkinson, and John Mason Brown. When Baker moved to Yale, he numbered among his protégés Elia Kazan, important for his work in the Group Theatre and the Actors Studio and for his direction of Williams's *A Streetcar Named Desire* and Miller's *Death of a Salesman* in the late 1940's. The effect of Baker's classes was eventually felt not only throughout the United States but also internationally.

At the time that Baker started Workshop 47, William Vaughn Moody, himself a Harvard graduate, had already left his Harvard teaching post to write his own poetic dramas. Others, such as Percy Mackaye, also of Harvard, had formed a band of serious writers who worked for changes in the drama. Yet even as these efforts for change were under way, financial problems continued to plague the stage, especially in New York, where the twenty theaters of 1903 had grown to eighty in 1927 and the tastes of popular audiences had to be satisfied. The demands of the "fabulous invalid," as Broadway has been labeled, created a two-tier stage system.

The earliest impetus to modern American drama came from the Provincetown Players, housed in the Wharf Theatre in Provincetown, Massachusetts. There, O'Neill's *Bound East for Cardiff* (pr. 1916) and *Thirst* (pr. 1914) were staged, and O'Neill himself played the part of the black man in the latter. In 1916, the group moved to New York's Macdougal Street, and by 1925, Quinn records, the Players had put on "ninety-three new plays by forty-seven playwrights, practically all American." It was, indeed, a playwright's theater in the sense that financial considerations were not paramount. The company was fueled by a zeal to provide opportunity to writers who would otherwise lack a forum for new ideas in the theater. As noted above, beginning with these innovations of the post-World War I years, each decade has had its own little theater movement.

THE 1920'S

The decade of the 1920's proved important to modern American theater. The distinction between the dramatists of the 1920's and their predecessors was twofold. First, the dramatists of the 1920's achieved a genuine breakthrough in their freedom to treat every aspect of human reality. Second, they introduced a range of styles and forms that gave the American theater an unprecedented vitality.

Earlier dramatists such as James Herne and William Vaughn Moody, who had attempted to bring change to the worn-out comedies, farces, and melodramas of their time, had succeeded only partially. Herne's *Margaret Fleming* and Moody's *The Great Divide*, although inching closer to genuine realism in dialogue and plot, were still characterized by emotional excess and by the artificially theatrical big speech. Then, in one decade, the long gestation period of American drama came to an end, its birth characterized by honesty and naturalness in language and plot.

Nowhere is the phenomenon more strikingly illustrated than in three plays that were staged in the fall of 1924: Maxwell Anderson and Laurence Stallings's *What Price Glory?*, Sidney Howard's *They Knew*

What They Wanted, and O'Neill's *Desire Under the Elms*. *What Price Glory?* is a realistic comedy about the futility of war. Stallings had lost a leg in World War I, and Anderson, at the time, was a committed pacifist. Like many writers of the 1920's, they shunned any romanticism about love and war in their characterizations of the two main characters, Captain Flagg and Sergeant Quirt. Whether fighting each other (over women) or the enemy in trenches, the men experience disillusionment in a fast-moving, hilarious series of events.

In Howard's Pulitzer Prize-winning *They Knew What They Wanted*, a folk drama later adapted to the musical stage as *The Most Happy Fella* (pr. 1956), Tony, an Italian immigrant grape grower, employs deception to win a girl much younger than he, sending her a photograph of his handsome young hired hand instead of one of himself. The trick backfires when Tony's bride is seduced by the hired hand, by whom she has a son. In the end, Tony overcomes his murderous rage, seeing the girl's mistake as one of the head, not of the heart.

The third play of this remarkable season, O'Neill's *Desire Under the Elms*, is, like Howard's, a drama about an older man and a young wife. Here, however, the illegitimate father is the youngest son of the old man, and the setting is a rockbound New England farm. The child is murdered by the mother as a demonstration of her love for its father, and the couple, as the play ends, is imprisoned.

O'Neill transcended his contemporaries in the tragic dimensions with which he endowed his characters. The young couple, struggling in the knowledge of events that they cannot overcome, acquire a moral wisdom in what Quinn calls their "conflict with something—fate, circumstance, moral and social law—which hampers or crushes" them. As in Greek tragedy, the wisdom comes too late. In its departure from the "virtue conquers all" endings of earlier American plays, O'Neill's Oedipal-based drama marks an important development in dramatic history. A few years later, in *Mourning Becomes Electra* (pr. 1931), O'Neill expanded the sense of tragedy in an Aeschylean attempt to trace through several generations the destiny of a guilt-haunted New England family. This tragic sense permeates O'Neill's works, despite their diversity of style, unifying the early lyric sea plays; the expressionistic plays such as *The Emperor Jones* (pr. 1920), *The Great God Brown* (pr. 1926), and *Dynamo* (pr. 1929); the naturalistic *The Iceman Cometh* (pr. 1946); and the unfinished autobiographical cycle of plays, of which *Long Day's Journey into Night* is his masterpiece.

O'Neill fused theater and drama, putting compelling theatricality at the service of psychological insight. What Nathaniel Hawthorne, Herman Melville, and Walt Whitman are to American fiction and poetry, O'Neill is to its drama. In the anguished search of his characters for something to which to belong, O'Neill joins the tradition of Ralph Waldo Emerson and Henry David Thoreau. The necessity of people to claim or reclaim something of their most primitive selves is the force that drives O'Neill's characters.

O'Neill's ambitious stagecraft, his attempts—not always successful—to combine conflicting psychological, sociological, and moral forces in the personal lives of his characters, place him in the company of such major figures in world drama as Ibsen and Strindberg. Quinn's estimate of O'Neill still holds: that "he is a great dramatist because he is more than a dramatist," for "he will be finally estimated by . . . his profound imaginative interpretation of aspiring humanity, struggling upward, even through sin and shame, toward the light." On a worldwide scale, O'Neill's dramas continue to be performed in a steady stream of productions. On the national level, his major successors have carried on his traditions, although in narrower ranges. Miller in his sociomoral plays, Williams in his psychological and poetic explorations of neurotic characters, and Albee in his highly stylized concern with the moral wasteland that the American Dream has become—all have assumed in part the mantle of O'Neill.

If the emergence of three remarkable plays within a few months of one another—a ribald comedy, a realistic folk drama, and a tragedy—stands out as a phenomenon of 1924, they are only three of a large number of dramas that vitalized the stage during that decade. Sherwood and Anderson began writing at this time, even though their major dramas were writ-

ten later. Thornton Wilder wrote novels and a few one-act plays and, much later, *Our Town* (pr. 1938), *The Skin of Our Teeth* (pr. 1942), and *The Matchmaker* (pr. 1954). Elmer Rice's *Street Scene* (pr. 1947) dramatized tenement life on the streets of New York, and DuBose Heyward and Dorothy Heyward's *Porgy* (pr. 1927) did the same for the blacks of Charleston, South Carolina. George S. Kaufman and Marc Connelly, one of the most successful of many playwriting teams of the decade, were responsible for a prolific output of satires on the American success story, the most famous of which is *Beggar on Horseback* (pr. 1924). Kaufman also collaborated with Edna Ferber on *The Royal Family* (pr. 1927) and with Ring Lardner on *June Moon* (pr. 1929), and staged John Steinbeck's novel *Of Mice and Men* (pr. 1937). The decade also included bright comedies about upper-class society by Philip Barry, whose urbane wit in *Holiday* (pr. 1928) saves the play from the sentimental moralizing to which it quite easily might have descended. The 1920's were indeed a brave new world for the American stage.

THE 1930'S

If the playwrights of the 1920's were bold in their treatment of subject matter and dramatic form, those of the 1930's were more self-confident in their social and political commitment and, in their topicality, perhaps more brave. Their leading voice was Clifford Odets, whose *Awake and Sing!* (pr. 1935) continues as a stage favorite, despite its label as a period piece. Odets and his contemporaries—William Saroyan, Sherwood, Anderson, and Lillian Hellman—wrote their major dramas during the Great Depression. This was the era of the Federal Theatre Project (1935-1939), which made live theater available to a general public for the first time. As the first government-subsidized theater in the United States, the project provided Orson Welles with his first directorial experience, one result of which was the formation of the Mercury Theatre by Welles and John Houseman.

A second very important development of the time was the establishment of the Group Theatre, the 1930's version of the Provincetown Theatre and Theatre Guild, which had nurtured the dramatists of the 1920's. Out of the Group Theatre emerged some of the most productive theater figures of the twentieth century: Stella Adler, Luther Adler, Harold Clurman, Lee J. Cobb, Morris Carnovsky, Elia Kazan, and Franchot Tone, among others.

The protest drama and its depressed milieu enjoyed a close relationship in the 1930's, perhaps as in no other time. Many dramatists, consequently, became the targets of criticism from conservative groups. Characterized as radical, left-wing, and tinged with various shades of "pink," some continued to be criticized for the rest of their lives, as in the case of Hellman.

The protest plays were direct descendants of the plays of the 1920's. Social, political, and moral problems, although a part of the fabric of earlier dramas, became more pronounced in the very late 1920's and throughout the 1930's. Because of their narrower thematic focus, the dramatists of the 1930's fall into the shadow of O'Neill, much as Ben Jonson and Christopher Marlowe are overshadowed by William Shakespeare. However, they form an important group, and they provide a connection between the two war eras. Indeed, the tradition of the social-problem drama, whether handled satirically, realistically, or tragically, has been the point of departure for the plays of Miller, Williams, Albee, and most American dramatists since the 1930's.

Three important plays produced in 1935 stand out as representative of the 1930's. Sherwood's *The Petrified Forest* carries its weight of social criticism, but in a melodramatic style. The setting, an isolated filling station on the edge of a desert; the plot, with its roots in the crime drama or thriller; and the use of stock characters, such as an impoverished writer, an American Legionnaire, and a banker, provide the ingredients that make for an evening of conventional theater. The requisite touch of sentimentality is provided when a gangster listens to the writer's request to shoot him so that his insurance money may go to the station owner's daughter, whom he has made his beneficiary. The play, which also became a successful film, powerfully evokes the moral bankruptcy against which the socially committed dramatists of the 1930's were reacting.

Anderson's *Winterset*, a second noteworthy play produced in 1935, dramatizes the tragedy of a modern Electra and Orestes: a sister and a brother through whom the truth is brought to light concerning a crime for which an innocent Italian immigrant was convicted and executed. With his blank-verse exploration of the complex issue of crime, punishment, and their accompanying guilts, Anderson—whose reputation in the 1930's was much higher than in subsequent years—was acclaimed as a major writer of tragedy. Based loosely on the famous Sacco-Vanzetti case, *Winterset* was preceded by *Gods of the Lightning* (pr. 1928), a social-protest play about the factual aspects of the same case, which Anderson had written in collaboration with Gerald Hickerson.

A third important play of 1935, Clifford Odets's *Awake and Sing!*, concerns an extended Jewish family fighting against poverty. Conflicts occur between the young and the old, the liberal and the conservative, the practical mother and the aging but still passionately Marxist grandfather—and between the characters' dreams and the realities that they all must face. Odets developed his characters within a deliberately loose plot, focusing primarily on the strong characterizations of each member of the family. Like Rice in *Street Scene* and like the Heywards in *Porgy*, Odets painted his antiheroic characters with broad strokes of dignity and compassion. In spite of its period flavor, the play is frequently produced and seems to enjoy a popularity denied by contemporary audiences to the other two plays of 1935 discussed above.

Hellman, another important writer of the era of social protest, wrote steadily until her death in 1984 and is one of America's major female dramatists. From her plays of the 1930's, *The Children's Hour* (pr. 1934) and *The Little Foxes* (pr. 1939), to her World War II drama *Watch on the Rhine* (pr. 1941), an admonitory play set in the United States, Hellman assumed a clear anticapitalist and anti-Fascist stance, yet she also made individual morality a strong issue. Often criticized for her dependence on melodramatic components and on the conventions of the well-made play, Hellman was praised for her powerful characterizations. Her characters seem driven by psychological and biological forces beyond their control.

Fascinated by the darker side of experience, she dramatized such subjects as malice in children and greed in adults. Villains triumph over characters who are good but weak. Throughout her career, Hellman fought against the evil that for her became symbolized in the activities of the House Committee on Un-American Activities investigations of the 1950's.

THE 1940'S

If the 1930's represent, at least in retrospect, some cohesion in the use of drama as a vehicle for social protest, the 1940's seem far removed from any such unity. Thus, it is fitting that Wilder's *The Skin of Our Teeth* should be regarded by many critics as the most memorable play of the first half of the decade. An expressionistic, farcical drama of epic events that span human history from the Ice Age to the present, the play proclaims that there is no order, no cause-effect relationship in events, and, consequently, no explanation of the catastrophic events that humankind has survived from earliest times. Therefore, one can learn little or nothing from history. What pleasure or even comfort human beings can hope for is to be found in the little events of life. Wilder had said much the same thing in his realistic-sentimental play of the late 1930's, *Our Town*. Later, in the 1950's, his conventionally constructed farce, *The Matchmaker*, about two apprentices and their employer and their antics on the town, dramatized the same views.

During World War II, only two decades after an earlier war that was supposed to end all wars, the theater, like the country in general, was especially in need of optimism. Escape from the problems of the time was provided in the plethora of musicals, and muted optimism appeared in Saroyan's *The Time of Your Life* (pr. 1939). Even some musicals, however, were tinged with social issues; Anderson's *Lost in the Stars* (pr. 1949), for example, was based on Alan Paton's novel about apartheid in South Africa, *Cry, the Beloved Country* (1948).

With the war's end, the American theater entered a period of extraordinary achievement, equaled perhaps only by the 1920's. Three major plays, Williams's *The Glass Menagerie* and *A Streetcar Named Desire* and Miller's *Death of a Salesman*, stand out among many fine plays of the era; the last two were directed by Kazan of the Actors Studio. In the decades since these three plays first appeared, the names of Amanda, Laura, and Tom Wingfield; Stanley Kowalski and Blanche DuBois; and Willy, Biff, and Linda Loman have become household names on the world stage. The original productions of these plays provided audiences with unforgettable performances by Laurette Taylor, Jessica Tandy, Marlon Brando, Lee J. Cobb, and Mildred Dunnock.

Criticized for writing exclusively about the weak and fragile in a society that is dominated by the strong, Williams became America's major poet of the theater. Similarly, Miller, attacked by the Right for being too negative about the American capitalistic system and by the Left for not being critical enough, has shown that artistic integrity and social commitment are not mutually exclusive.

In the plays of both Williams and Miller, the influence of European dramatic traditions is evident. In particular, Williams often recalls Strindberg, while Miller has close ties to Ibsen. Like Miss Julie in Strindberg's play of the same title, Williams's heroines are trapped by social conventions. Blanche DuBois is torn between the gentility of an Old South upbringing and the harsh realities of the lower classes into which her sister has married. Laura Wingfield is the victim of a well-intentioned, practical mother of that same Southern background and of the poet-brother who needs to escape. Like Strindberg's and O'Neill's characters, those of Williams find themselves trapped between their illusions and reality. Tom Wingfield, as character and narrator in *The Glass Menagerie*, tells his audience: "Yes, I have tricks in my pocket, I have things up my sleeve. But I am the opposite of a stage magician. He gives you illusion that has the appearance of truth. I give you truth in the pleasant disguise of illusion." Like O'Neill's, Williams's characters are haunted by a sense of doom, and, indeed, they are doomed. As misfits in society, they are neurotic, their very neuroticism striking a deep chord in the American psyche and providing their author with a rich vein of poetic drama.

In his January, 1985, review of Olof Lagercrantz's biography of Strindberg, Miller writes of Strindberg's influence on English-speaking playwrights: "Strindberg struck strongly into Eugene O'Neill, is quite directly mirrored in Samuel Beckett and Harold Pinter, in Tennessee Williams and Edward Albee." He refers to these playwrights' concern with the "world of the subconscious, where the sexual encounter especially was a fight to the death, a world where the mother did not nurture but suffocated and destroyed her offspring, a world where domination (usually female) was the key to life." In O'Neill's *Desire Under the Elms* and Albee's *The American Dream* (pr. 1961), the fight is to the death, and in Williams's *The Glass Menagerie*, the emotional suffocation is total.

Miller, on the other hand, is an artistic descendant of Ibsen. In the latter's *The Pillars of Society*, a father builds a defective ship, only to have his son embark on that ship and go down with it. In Miller's *All My Sons*, a father who is engaged in the manufacture of airplane parts is guilty of similar negligence, resulting in unnecessary deaths during World War II.

Miller also adapted Ibsen's *En folkefiende* (pr. 1883; *An Enemy of the People*, 1890), a strong condemnation of civic-minded leaders who eventually turn an entire community against an idealist who exposes water pollution, an exposure that threatens the financial health of the town, since its baths provide income for the owners and workers. The pitting of moral values against financial gain constitutes the conflict in a number of Miller's plays.

It was in *Death of a Salesman*, however, that Miller redefined tragedy and began a debate among critics and scholars. The question on which the debate turns is whether the antihero of contemporary literature can achieve tragic stature. Purists hold that since Willy Loman, Miller's protagonist, never achieves the dignity that results from wisdom gained through experience, he is not a tragic hero. To the end, Willy lacks wisdom, clinging to the illusion that his insurance money will provide his son Biff with an opportunity for a new start. Thus, Willy's death, by suicide, is tainted by incompetence: It is the last act of a loser.

Charley, Willy's old friend, comments at the funeral that no one dares blame Willy: "A salesman is got to dream, boy. It comes with the territory." Linda,

sobbing at the funeral, cannot understand Willy's suicide, especially since the last payment on their home was made that day. Only Biff, the more disillusioned of the two sons, has known the truth all along: "He [Willy] never knew who he was."

The American Dream of success is exposed for the illusion that it can become when challenged by certain realities of life. The pipe dreams of O'Neill's characters and the dreams that haunt Williams's heroines find a sharp focus in the Loman family. Indeed, as noted above, selling and salesmen are at the heart of the American success story and are thus of recurring significance in American drama: Willy's brothers exist in Hickey of *The Iceman Cometh* and in the real estate salesmen of Mamet's *Glengarry Glen Ross*. This trilogy of salesmen—Willy, Hickey, and Roma—embodies the rapidly deteriorating morality of the confidence game at the very heart of the American Dream success story.

The importance of Kazan's productions has already been noted in connection with the emergence of Williams and Miller. Kazan was one of three important figures from the Group Theatre of the 1930's—the others were Lee Strasberg and Cheryl Crawford—who, in the 1940's, formed the Actors Studio. They and their graduates strongly influenced the course of American drama, as Baker had done earlier in the century at Harvard and at Yale.

THE 1950'S

During the 1950's, the old lines between "theater" and "drama" were redrawn, sending the "serious" and new dramatists, producers, directors, and actors scurrying to the small theaters of Off-Broadway and to the even smaller ones of Off-Off-Broadway. The Antoinette Perry Awards (or Tonys, as they came to be known on Broadway) were supplemented by the Off-Broadway selections for best plays and productions (or Obies). Regional theaters and arts complexes sprang up in the major metropolitan areas, Lincoln Center in New York being the most prominent.

The times were troubled by the Washington investigations conducted by the House Committee on Un-American Activities, which called various artists in for questioning. Miller's *The Crucible* (pr. 1953), an allegorical drama about witch-hunting in colonial Salem, dramatizes the mood of the 1950's. It was the decade of blacklisting in California, as a result of which a large number of left-wing writers, directors, and actors were unable to find work.

Writers from earlier decades experimented with new styles. Hellman, for example, wrote a loosely plotted drama in the Chekhovian style, *The Autumn Garden* (pr. 1951), while Williams, departing from the naturalistic poetry of *A Streetcar Named Desire* and *The Glass Menagerie*, wrote the expressionistic *Camino Real* (pr. 1953).

A group of writers, some of them new, wrote social-problem plays, among them Robert Anderson, Arthur Laurents, and William Inge—labeled by critic Gerald Weales as "the new [Arthur Wing] Pineros." In support of this judgment, Weales quotes Shaw, who observed that a certain class of writers conquered "the public by the exquisite flattery of giving them plays that they really liked, whilst persuading them that such appreciation was only possible from persons of great culture and intellectual acuteness."

Another important group of writers are those whom Weales calls "the video boys," who wrote for television, almost as training for the stage. Their stage writing frequently reflects film and television technique in the fluidity realized by lighting and multiple stage sets. In subject matter, these playwrights— among them Paddy Chayefsky (*Marty*, pr. 1953) and William Gibson (*The Miracle Worker*, pr. 1956, 1959)—resemble the new Pineros.

Poets and academics also left their mark on the stage of the 1950's. Archibald MacLeish (*J. B.: A Play in Verse*, pr. 1958) and Robinson Jeffers (*The Cretan Woman*, pr. 1954, and, earlier, *Medea*, pr. 1947) took up the mantle of Maxwell Anderson, and they, in turn, were followed in the 1960's by Robert Lowell, whose *Old Glory* trilogy (pb. 1965) is an adaptation of stories by Hawthorne and Melville. Lowell's dramas, which deal with ideological conflicts in colonial times, also carry on the tradition of social protest.

Strasberg sees the 1950's as a time of "numerous playwrights, yet fewer important plays." The decade "inspires the feeling of having hit bottom, yet produces the greatest play of our time—O'Neill's *Long Day's Journey into Night*." The posthumous production of this major drama—written, it should be noted, well before the 1950's—occurred during a time that saw the successful production of two other O'Neill plays that had not fared well earlier: *The Iceman Cometh* and *A Moon for the Misbegotten* (pr. 1947). The role of Hickey in *The Iceman Cometh* gave Jason Robards prominence in a career that was distinguished by many O'Neill roles. O'Neill's *A Touch of the Poet* (pr. 1957) and *Hughie* (pr. 1958) also were given successful productions.

THE 1960's

The 1950's were not to close, however, without the emergence of a major new voice on the American stage, that of Edward Albee, whose pessimism about American cultural values seemed an exorcism of the general malaise of the time. Optimism regarding the American Dream, closely scrutinized or questioned in earlier plays and still insisted on by popular audiences, collapses under its own weight in Albee's early plays. In no other American dramatist and in no other Albee play is this collapse so total as it is in *The American Dream*. A searing comedy, the play probes the psychological dismemberment of a child by its parents and by the social institutions whose ostensible purpose it is to nurture the young. The play catapulted Albee into fame as America's own absurdist dramatist. *The American Dream* was preceded by Albee's trio of short plays, *The Zoo Story* (pr. 1959), *The Death of Bessie Smith* (pr. 1960), and *The Sandbox* (pr. 1960), the first of which remains one of his most frequently produced plays.

The Zoo Story premiered in Berlin, Germany, in 1959, produced by the Schiller Theater Werkstatt. In a historical coincidence, its first American staging took place in 1960 at the Provincetown Playhouse, a name inextricably linked with O'Neill and the coming of age of American drama. In this strikingly accomplished debut, Albee presented a life-and-death struggle in the guise of a fight over a park bench. The combatants are a successful publishing executive and a social failure who has spent the day walking up to Central Park from Greenwich Village; their struggle is actually a desperate attempt on the part of the failure, Jerry, to attempt some human communication with the executive, Peter. The themes for the brilliant Albee dramas to follow, among them *Who's Afraid of Virginia Woolf?* (pr. 1962), are established in this first play.

As an inheritor of the mantle of O'Neill and Williams, Albee explores the dark, complex psychological and sociological forces that have shaped his characters and their worlds. O'Neill's characters search for something larger than themselves, something to which they can belong; those of Williams and Miller at least maintain tenuous links with the human family; Albee's, consciously or unconsciously, find themselves alienated from one another and from their universe. *Who's Afraid of Virginia Woolf?*, a Strindbergian battle of the sexes, presents a fascinating study in which long-repressed conflicts and guilts are exorcised, leaving both major characters, a history professor and his wife, exhausted at the end. The play enjoyed a successful initial run on Broadway and has been revived frequently, attracting major talents of the time, from the clawing, naturalistic film performances of Elizabeth Taylor and Richard Burton to the more subdued later Broadway version, directed by Albee himself and featuring Colleen Dewhurst and Ben Gazzara in beautifully and classically balanced interpretations of their roles.

Following the emergence of Albee as the United States' fourth major dramatist, the Off-Broadway, Off-Off-Broadway, and university and regional theaters, which had begun as independent and frequently isolated efforts appealing only to small audiences, initiated a second coming-of-age of American drama. Beginning around 1960, Broadway prices began a steady and unprecedented escalation, so that by 1985, tickets for Harvey Fierstein's *La Cage aux Folles* (pr. 1983) on New Year's Eve were bringing in seventy-five dollars apiece. Although an extreme example of the financial stranglehold in which Broadway found itself, *La Cage aux Folles* illustrates a phenomenon that has affected even the straight dramas of the day.

In *New Broadways: Theatre Across America* (1996), Gerald Berkowitz traces the growth of the small theaters that began springing up independently all across the country, partly in response to the prohibitive cost of Broadway productions. In 1967, the Ford Foundation began a generous program of theater subsidy. The Alley Theatre of Houston, the Arena Stage of Washington, and the Mummers Theatre of Oklahoma City were among the major recipients. Benefiting from subsidies as well were the American Place Theatre in New York, the Center Stage in Baltimore, the Hartford Stage Company, the Seattle Rep, the Stage/West of West Springfield, Massachusetts, the Actors Studio in New York, the American Shakespeare Festival, and the Guthrie Theatre of Minneapolis. The Ford Foundation not only subsidized writers and actors but also built new theaters for the Alley and the Mummers and bought and renovated theaters for the American Conservatory Theatre and the Actors' Theatre of Louisville. Other foundations followed with their own subsidies, but Ford has remained the most active. Additional impetus to theaters across the country was provided by the National Endowment for the Arts, which began in 1966. Even Broadway became the recipient of subsidies, by means of the Theatre Development Fund, jointly established by the Twentieth Century Fund, the Rockefeller Brothers Fund, and the National Endowment for the Arts. The Fund, Berkowitz explains, "began by buying up blocks of tickets to forthcoming plays of artistic merit but uncertain commercial strength and reselling them at a discount to students and similar groups, thereby encouraging new audiences while giving the productions a financial buffer." Among the notable plays produced as a result were Lanford Wilson's *The Hot l Baltimore* (pr. 1973), Jason Miller's *That Championship Season* (pr. 1972), and Arthur Kopit's *Wings* (pr. 1978).

Finally, the greatest of all financial boosters for both Broadway and Off-Broadway theatergoers, the half-price tickets booth on Duffy Square (called TKTS), opened in 1973, a boon sponsored by the Theatre Development Fund. Discount vouchers for Off-Off-Broadway productions supplemented the half-price sales at the TKTS booth. The impact of the Theatre Development Fund was felt across the country, and the influence of the half-price idea carried as far as London's Leicester Square, where the English implemented a similar arrangement. Ironically, the prices of theater tickets in London, already low, because many of the English theaters were subsidized, were cut in half by the English borrowing of the American half-price idea.

In time, Off-Broadway became in its way a minor Broadway as it underwent its own institutionalizing. Prominent among the theater groups in this transitional period were Joseph Papp's Public Theatre, Lynn Meadow's Manhattan Theatre Club, the Hudson Guild Theatre, the American Place Theatre, and the Roundabout Theatre. Financial pressures exerted their influence here, as they had on Broadway, and smaller groups sprouted, such as Ellen Stewart's Café La Mama. Off-Off-Broadway also enjoyed a groundswell in the 1960's.

As a result of this minor but flourishing stage renaissance, many dramatists were provided with opportunities to write and to have their plays produced, opportunities that would not have existed without the subsidies. Both the established Off-Broadway theater and the Off-Off-Broadway efforts can be seen as the offspring of the theater of the 1920's, when the Provincetown Players figured so importantly in bringing about the United States' coming of age in drama, but without subsidies or a tradition behind them.

Among the newcomers to the stage scene in the 1960's were a number of African American dramatists. When Lorraine Hansberry wrote plays in the late 1950's, blacks were still referred to as "negroes," and her play *A Raisin in the Sun* (pr. 1959) evokes the period flavor of her time. Amiri Baraka (LeRoi Jones) opposed the merging of blacks into the mainstream of white drama, and his *Dutchman* (pr. 1964) has earned for itself a place in the John Gassner and Bernard F. Dukore anthology, *A Treasury of the Theatre* (1970). Ed Bullins also writes outside the mainstream theater; like O'Neill before him, Bullins has attempted an ambitious cycle of plays. His first volume of plays, published in 1969, includes *Goin' a Buffalo* (pr. 1968), *A Son, Come Home* (pr. 1968), and *The Electronic Nigger* (pr. 1968), all three of which were produced at the American Place Theatre. In the 1975 season, *The Taking of Miss Janie* won the New York Drama Critics Circle Award. The strong black

movement was associated with the Negro Ensemble Company, and small theaters devoted to black populations sprang up across the country, particularly in cities with large black populations.

Another group of dramatists became vocal during the 1960's, a group that still finds itself the least accepted of minority movements on the stage. Explicitly homosexual or gay and lesbian drama found expression in groups such as the Ridiculous Theatrical Company. For them, the main mode of dramatizing the homosexual experience is farce or, at least, a farcical tone, even when psychological realism and poignant emotion are central to the play. Laughter seems to be the means by which uncomfortable subjects gain some measure of acceptance on the stage. Writers, producers, and actors such as Martin Duberman, Robert Patrick, Charles Ludlam, Ronald Tavel, and Kenneth Bernard are important figures in the development of gay drama in this narrow sense.

The 1960's also saw the emergence of a number of women dramatists, most of whom were writing within the traditions of the contemporary feminist movement. The consciousness-raising function of the movement tended to limit the appeal and, some maintain, the quality of the drama thus produced. Among the groups founded to encourage women dramatists are the Womanspace Theatre in New York, the Circle of the Witch in Minneapolis, the Washington Area Feminist Theatre in Washington, and Interart Theatre in New York. As a group, the feminist playwrights were more loosely organized and more diverse in both content and style than were other minority dramatists. These women appear in Honor Moore's 1977 anthology, *The New Women's Theatre: Ten Plays by Contemporary American Women*, which includes plays by Corinne Jacker, Joanna Russ, Ursule Molinaro, Tina Howe, Honor Moore, Alice Childress, Ruth Wolff, Joanna Kraus, and Myrna Lamb and a stage arrangement by Eve Merriam, Paula Wagner, and Jack Hoffsiss.

Two women dramatists whose plays were brought to the national scene in the late 1970's and early 1980's through the Actors' Theatre of Louisville are Marsha Norman, whose *'Night, Mother* (pr. 1981), her fifth play, won for her both critical acclaim (including a Pulitzer Prize in 1983) and commercial success, and Mississippi-bred Beth Henley, whose bizarre comedies about middle-class life in the South (most notably *Crimes of the Heart*, pr. 1979, which won a Pulitzer Prize in 1981), enjoyed performances across the country as well as in New York.

THE 1970'S

All three minority movements discussed above (black, gay, female) were part of a larger new wave of American dramatists from which emerged several particularly promising playwrights. In this new wave, two interesting phenomena developed: one involving a popular playwright who wrote steadily for Broadway and for film, Neil Simon, and the other involving a quartet of dramatists who started their careers in small theaters and who have continued to develop steadily: David Rabe, Wilson, Mamet, and Shepard. The last two have demonstrated a uniqueness of style that sets them apart as writers with the potential to join the ranks of O'Neill, Miller, Williams, and Albee.

Simon began his career as a writer for television comedians such as Sid Caesar. On the stage, Simon became famous for his play *The Odd Couple* (pr. 1965). Having made a reputation with his jokes (particularly his one-liners) and with his technical mastery of the television-style situation comedy, he enjoys popularity among middle-class audiences. According to Berkowitz, Simon is—"in purely financial terms—the most successful playwright in the history of the world, with (among other records) more Broadway performances of his plays in the 1960's than Williams, Miller, Albee, Inge, Pinter, [John] Osborne and [Richard] Rodgers put together." Jewish and New York-born, Simon stems from the tradition of Odets and Chayefsky in his concern with the little man who has big dreams and for whom his dreams are the only escape from a dull existence. Another recurring concern is the mismatched couple, whether they be roommates, husband and wife, or lovers. Like the British playwright Sir Alan Ayckbourn, with whom he is frequently compared, Simon is capable of a Chekhovian brand of humor that challenges his reputation as merely an exceptionally slick writer of

popular plays. His autobiographical trilogy, *Brighton Beach* (pr. 1982), *Biloxi Blues* (pr. 1984), and *Broadway Bound* (pr. 1986), amply illustrates his ability to sustain a seriousness that tones down his predilection for gag lines.

Wilson arrived in New York from the Midwest and West and provided the Caffé Cino, a major Off-Off-Broadway enterprise, with its first success, *The Madness of Lady Bright* (pr. 1964). He helped establish the Circle Theatre Company and became a resident playwright at a time when Off-Broadway productions were beginning to find their way uptown. Wilson's *The Hot l Baltimore*, still his best-known play, and his Missouri trilogy about the Talley family, consisting of *Fifth of July* (pr. 1978), *A Tale Told* (pr. 1981), and *Talley's Folly* (pr. 1979), are deeply rooted in American social consciousness. An early play, *Balm in Gilead* (pr. 1965), enjoyed unusual success when revived in 1984; the play is set in a rundown New York café, and its assortment of characters recalls O'Neill's *The Iceman Cometh*.

Also establishing himself by means of Off-Broadway residency (the Public Theatre of Joseph Papp), Rabe, a Vietnam veteran, continued the tradition of *What Price Glory?* in a trilogy of plays about the Vietnam experience: *The Basic Training of Pavlo Hummel* (pr. 1971), *Sticks and Bones* (pr. 1969), and *Streamers* (pr. 1976). During a time of civil unrest and heightened protest, *Sticks and Bones*, which concerns the return of a blind veteran to an America that does not understand him, won a Tony Award. Rabe's *The Basic Training of Pavlo Hummel* has been likened to Brecht's *Man Is Man* (pr. 1926) for its expressionistic style.

Like Wilson and Rabe, Mamet has a career closely tied to the small theaters. His *A Life in the Theatre* (pr. 1977) and *American Buffalo* (pr. 1975) were staged at the Goodman Theatre in Chicago, and *Sexual Perversity in Chicago* (pr. 1974) premiered at the student-founded Organic Theatre Company. Mamet himself helped found a series of small theaters in the Chicago area.

Lean in language, character, and plot, Mamet's theater has affinities with the minimalism of Pinter, and like Pinter, Mamet, more than any other American dramatist, employs characters and situations that are dominated by, indeed created by, language and language rhythms. *American Buffalo* is a play in which nothing much happens except that three very limited and inarticulate would-be petty thieves hatch a plan that is never implemented. The thrust and parry of the dialogue constitutes the action of the play; the tightly controlled speech rhythms and the elemental human situations—security, threat, intrusion, and dispossession—are compelling. The same elements can be found in *A Life in the Theatre*, about a pair of actors, one aging and one young, and in *Duck Variations* (pr. 1972), a conversation between two old men on a park bench. *Glengarry Glen Ross*, about real estate salesmen in Florida selling land that does not exist, spins out a similar situation in a more complexly plotted play. Both *American Buffalo* and *Glengarry Glen Ross* were successful Broadway productions, the latter appearing during the same season in which a production of *Death of a Salesman*, as noted above, featured Hoffman's perky, energetic Willy Loman. Without the social morality of Miller as a dominant idea, but with a devastating linguistic hilarity, Mamet brilliantly accomplishes by a different means what Miller achieved in his classic play. *Speed-the-Plow* (pr. 1988), complementing *American Buffalo* and *Glengarry Glen Ross*, extends the selling myth in an even more scathingly comic satire on the dark undergirdings of American culture.

Shepard, having written more than forty plays, built a solid reputation among critics and scholars. The reputation rests on his archetypical view of America, in which folklore (cowboy and desperado) and fantasy blend with a high theatricality of style that is inimitably his. The heroic cowboy psyche struts through his contemporary characters in the persons of the faded rock star Hoss in *The Tooth of Crime* (pr. 1972) and of Slim and Shadow in *Back Bog Beast Bait* (pr. 1971), two Jesse James-like characters who wander in search of people with enemies. *True West* (pr. 1980) pits a slick Hollywood writer against an uncouth brother; by the end of the play, the two have reversed roles. Elemental forces are released in the conflict between a man and a woman in *Fool for Love* (pr. 1983). Like the Gary Cooper figure

of *High Noon* (1952), the cowboy and the hired gun search for scores to settle, knowing that one day they themselves will become victims. In Shepard's family plays, *Curse of the Starving Class* and *Buried Child* (pr. 1978), the effects of the American myth are seen in the familial lives of the characters, while *Operation Sidewinder* (pr. 1970) demonstrates the myth at work in the area of technology. *A Lie of the Mind* (pr. 1985), more encompassing than either of its predecessors (*Curse of the Starving Class* and *Buried Child*), rounds out what constitutes a trilogy of Shepard's family plays. Shepard represents graphically the split between the commercial and the small theaters. Like Lanford Wilson, Rabe, and Mamet, Shepard has his roots in the Off-Off Broadway and Off-Broadway movement, his first play, *Cowboys* (pr. 1964), having been staged at Theatre Genesis.

Shepard's plays, mythical and fantastic, require visceral performances in which Jungian levels of American consciousness in all of their violence are explored. His unique re-creation of the American myth recalls O'Neill's concern with pipe dreams, Williams's with the strain of Puritanism, Miller's with conscience, and Albee's with a moral wasteland.

Both Shepard and Mamet have been produced frequently in London. *Curse of the Starving Class* and *Glengarry Glen Ross* were given premiere productions at London's prestigious Royal Court Theatre and National Theatre of Great Britain, respectively. These two playwrights, with their distinctive voices, appear to be the inheritors of the tradition carried forward by O'Neill, Williams, Miller, and Albee.

THE 1980's AND 1990's

Since Shepard and Mamet, no dramatist has appeared with the innovative impact of either of these two writers. Instead, a number of traditional dramatists who began writing plays in the 1970's (and even earlier) have made their mark in the Off-Broadway theaters in New York. A. R. Gurney, John Guare, and Romulus Linney, with roots in the academic-literary tradition, have assumed increasing prominence. Incorporating some elements of the prevailing Beckettian or Brechtian theater, each in his unique way has reinvented themes and styles of earlier writers.

An example is Gurney's *The Cocktail Hour* (pr. 1988), which not only plays on T. S. Eliot's themes in *The Cocktail Party* but also is replete with literary allusions. A central theme in most of Gurney's dramas is the fading tradition of the middle-class, white Anglo-Saxon, Protestant (WASP) ethic in the United States. A striking illustration is *The Dining Room* (pr. 1982), about a family, depicted as each generation adheres to, or departs from, the attitudes and values of the preceding generation. The title *The Old Boy* (pr. 1991) speaks for itself. *Who Killed Richard Cory?* (pr. 1976), a reference to a character from a poem by Edwin Arlington Robinson, and *The Perfect Party* (pr. 1985) are among the nearly twenty dramas in which the rituals of the dominant WASP class are analyzed with a mixture of poignancy, humor, and criticism.

Influenced by Chekhov, Ibsen, and Shaw, Guare, best known for *The House of Blue Leaves* (pr. 1971), *Six Degrees of Separation* (pr. 1990), and *Four Baboons Adoring the Sun* (pr. 1992), explores the American Dream myth. *Six Degrees of Separation*, a play based on an actual event reported in *The New York Times*, focuses on an ingenious youthful impostor who finds his way into the intimate lives of the affluent. Utilizing at times, as in *The House of Blue Leaves*, elements of absurdist techniques, Guare has said that he writes about those whose dreams "of the future and outside the house were greater than their ability to enjoy what was right there in the house." In *Four Baboons Adoring the Sun*, a couple, with children from previous marriages, realize their dreams, but at the expense of the death of one of their many children. The Greek sense of tragedy slowly evolves to a climax involving the interfering jealousy of the gods in a twentieth century re-creation of the Icarus myth.

Linney, the most academic of the three playwrights, roots his dramas in political, social, and historical matters. Influenced by O'Neill, Friedrich Dürrenmatt, Albee, and Pinter, he has written about historical and literary figures, relating these to contemporary situations and attitudes: *The Sorrows of Frederick* (pb. 1966), about a father-son relationship; *The Love Suicide at Schofield Barracks* (pr. 1972), about Vietnam War issues; *Childe Byron* (pr. 1977),

about a father-daughter relationship; and *Three Poets* (pr. 1989), three one-act plays, each about a female poet.

August Wilson, an African American dramatist, developed a solid reputation in one decade with *Ma Rainey's Black Bottom* (pr. 1984), *Fences* (pr. 1985), *Joe Turner's Come and Gone* (pr. 1986), and *The Piano Lesson* (pr. 1988). All were first produced at the Yale Repertory Theater and then moved to New York. His play *Two Trains Running* (pr. 1990), Wilson has said, is yet another illustration of his interest in the folkloric aspects of black culture. An important new black voice as well as an inheritor of the Langston Hughes tradition, he updates humorously and poignantly themes to be found in earlier black writers.

Along with Gurney, Guare, Linney, and August Wilson, the direction toward traditionalism includes other articulate, critically applauded writers, the youngest of these being Jon Robin Baitz (*The Substance of Fire*, pr. 1991 and *The End of the Day*, pr. 1992). Scott McPherson, whose *Marvin's Room* swept nearly all the Off-Broadway awards in 1992, joins, among others, Christopher Durang, Craig Lucas, Herb Gardner, and Donald Margulies in a postmodern era, a term loosely designating a time of consolidation of tradition and innovation.

BIBLIOGRAPHY

Bigsby, Christopher W. *Modern American Drama: 1945-2000*. New York: Cambridge University Press, 2001. Surveys major figures in latter-twentieth century drama, including Eugene O'Neill, David Mamet, Arthur Miller, Edward Albee, Tennessee Williams, and Sam Shepard.

Bloom, Clive. *American Drama*. New York: St. Martin's Press, 1995. Explores the coming of age of American drama through chapter essays on prominent playwrights, and a final essay on contemporary feminist theater.

Brietzke, Zander. *Aesthetics of Failure: Dynamic Structure in the Plays of Eugene O'Neill*. Jefferson, N.C.: McFarland, 2002. Provides an analysis of the conflicts in O'Neill's plays, with particular attention paid to genre, language, characters, space, and action. Also gives some biographical details and a chronological listing of his fifty plays that includes the plays' production history, principle characters, and brief commentary.

Demastes, William W. W., Thomas P. Adler, and Judith E. Barlow. *Realism and the American Dramatic Tradition*. Tuscaloosa: University of Alabama Press, 1996. Explores the development of realism in the American drama from James Herne to modern-day playwrights such as Sam Shepard, David Mamet, and Marsha Norman. Specific topics include the Provincetown Players' experiments with realism, feminist realists of the Harlem Renaissance, and the personal lyricism of Tennessee Williams.

Fleche, Anne. *Mimetic Disillusion: Eugene O'Neill, Tennessee Williams, and U.S. Dramatic Realism.* Tuscaloosa: University of Alabama Press, 1996. Focuses on the ways in which mid-twentieth century drama in the United States shifted away from representational theater and toward a poststructuralist "disillusionment" with mimesis. Provides new readings of O'Neill's and Williams's major works of the 1930's and 1940's.

Matlaw, Myron, ed. *Nineteenth Century American Plays*. New York: Applause Theater Book Publishers, 2001. A reprint of a 1967 edition, this collection brings together seven nineteenth century plays by dramatists such as Anna Cora Mowatt, Dion Boucicault, Joseph Jefferson, and Bronson Howard. Matlaw's introduction provides a survey of the development of American drama up through the nineteenth century, and prefaces to each play provide historical context for the work.

Murphy, Brenda. *American Realism and American Drama: 1800-1940*. New York: Cambridge University Press, 1987. Explores the early and important connection between literary realism and stage realism. Clifford Odets, Lillian Hellman, William Dean Howells, and Eugene O' Neill are particularly surveyed, and the author includes a discussion on the impact of Freud on drama.

Shiach, David. *American Drama: 1900-1990*. New York: Cambridge University Press, 2000. Emphasizes key periods, topics, themes, and comparisons in literature, rather than on individual authors or plays, thus calling attention to important literary, historical, and social contexts of the twentieth century.

Susan Rusinko

CONTEMPORARY AMERICAN DRAMA

If the greatest challenge of theater has been to make illusion seem real, the greatest challenge of American theater has been to create theater that is in kind or degree peculiarly American. Among those twentieth century American playwrights who successfully met this challenge are Eugene O'Neill and Arthur Miller, who addressed something peculiarly American in their works; Tennessee Williams and Horton Foote, who found in one of the country's regions something that spoke to its national character; and many others who found in the shortcomings of America's national myths something telling in its national experience. These national myths came into question particularly during the 1990's as matters of race, gender, and sexual preference were brought into particularly high relief.

Perhaps five aspects of American theater were particularly notable during the 1990's: First, the staying power of voices in American theater that had first been heard twenty-five or even fifty years before; second, the vitality and courage with which American theater led the way in exploring the degree to which one's sexual preferences defined—for better or worse—one's place in the American experience; third, the ever-increasing importance of women playwrights on the American stage; fourth, the continued decline of racial and ethnic barriers; and fifth, the depth and breadth of young authorial talent that seemed to be emerging, and emerging with aplomb.

RESONANT AMERICAN VOICES

First produced in 1946, the revival of O'Neill's *The Iceman Cometh* was one of the most sought-after tickets of the 1998-1999 Broadway season, and that same season, the revival of Miller's 1948 classic *Death of a Salesman* earned a Tony Award for Brian Dennehy for his portrayal of the beleaguered title character Willy Loman and a Tony nomination for Kevin Anderson for his portrayal of Willy's eldest son Biff.

New works by such long-declared masters of American theater as Miller, Williams, and Foote were also being performed. To commemorate his 1944 Broadway debut, Miller opened a new play, *Last Yankee* (pr. 1993), doing so nearly fifty years after the day of his first Broadway production, *The Man Who Had All the Luck* (pr. 1944). Not surprisingly, that play was revived in 2002.

The master of the southern gothic genre, Williams proved that a great playwright's work quite literally survives its author when Williams's *Not About Nightingales* (wr. 1939) was given its Broadway premier in 1998, fifteen years after Williams's death. Fellow southerner Foote also had new work mounted on the American stage during this period, including *The Carpetbaggers Children* (pr. 2001), and he was richly rewarded when he won a Pulitzer Prize in 1995 for his *The Young Man from Atlanta* (pr. 1995). For nearly half a century, Foote's writing had explored family life and its assorted dynamics, reminding his audiences that the middle-class nuclear family is—at once—the strongest and weakest of our social constructs.

This focus on family life also proved to be an ongoing concern of Sam Shepard. Shepard extended the familial theme of *True West* (pr. 1980) and his Pulitzer Prize-winning *Buried Child* (1979; pr. 1978) with yet another play set in the Southwestern desert, *The Late Henry Moss* (pr. 2000), a play distinctive for giving the missing father figure of Shepard's earlier works a presence on the stage, as two brothers tried to lay to rest a father to whom neither was close.

Christopher Durang and John Guare, both of whom twenty years earlier established themselves as forces to be reckoned with in American comedy, returned in force to the New York stage during the 1990's: Durang's six one-acts *Durang/Durang* (pr. 1994) and then *Sex and Longing* (pr. 1996) were produced, and Guare, perhaps still best known for his *The House of Blue Leaves* (pr. 1971), returned with *Six Degrees of Separation* (pr. 1990) and *Four Baboons Adoring the Sun* (pr. 1992).

David Mamet's *Oleana* (pr. 1992) reminded Mamet's critics and admirers alike of how long power had been a concern of his work and of how long his characters had been struggling to better one another through the use of the spoken word. This was evidenced once again by the 1994-1995 production of the aptly named *The Cryptogram* (pr. 1994), in which Mamet's heroine brutalized others as she sought a tongue in which to express her own pain.

Once the *enfant terrible* of the American stage, Edward Albee won a 2002 Tony Award for his play *The Goat: Or, Who Is Sylvia?* In 1994, he had won a Pulitzer Prize in Drama, his third, for *Three Tall Women* (pr. 1991). Running in the 1993-1994 season, *Three Tall Women* took its place amid Albee's more openly autobiographical works, and it was this fact on which the critics focused. His three principle characters, dubbed A, B, and C, were a thinly veiled treatment of his adoptive mother at various stages in her life.

For audiences who had followed Albee's career from the late 1950's and his New York City production of *The Zoo Story* (pr. 1959), *Three Tall Women* served as a delightful coda. If *The Zoo Story* had established what would become one of Albee's central interests as a playwright—among them all the ways in which people find to isolate themselves from one another—*Three Tall Women* showcased a woman at three stages of her life, finally demonstrating that the greatest tragedy was not how isolated she was from others, but rather how fully isolated Albee's protagonist was from herself.

Albee went on to appreciative reviews when his *The Play About the Baby* (pr. 1998), starring Marian Seldes and Brian Murray, opened in the United States during the 1999-2000 season, the success of which opened doors for his *The Goat*, his first proper Broadway debut in the nearly twenty years that had passed since *The Man Who Had Three Arms* (pr. 1982). *The Goat* is a four-character play that follows the protagonist, Martin, through a family dilemma that he had not anticipated. At mid-life, Martin's skyrocketing career and his stable marriage are threatened by his entering into a sexual relationship with a goat, a sexual practice considered unacceptable by the culture at large. Although Albee's concern with bestiality garnered critical attention, Albee's greater interest was

in exploring at what point one's right to sexual preference ends and deviant sexual behavior begins. When considered in this light, it becomes clear that Albee's play follows a thematic preoccupation of the stage in the 1990's.

HOMOSEXUALITY AND AIDS

Tony Kushner's *Angels in America: A Gay Fantasia on National Themes*, first produced in 1991 in San Francisco, was a seven-hour play so epic in vision and so operatic in production that it had to be mounted over a pair of theatrical seasons. It came to Broadway in two lengthy installments, with *Part One: Millennium Approaches* brought to the stage in 1992-1993 by director George C. Wolfe, and *Part Two: Perestroika* staged the following season. Each play garnered a Tony Award for Best Play, in 1993 and 1994 respectively. So successful were Kushner's Pulitzer Prize-winning *Angels in America* plays that *Angels in America* has become the signature treatment of what it means to be gay in the United States.

This is understandable, given its scope and execution. However, *Angels in America* was hardly alone in dealing with gay and lesbian life in the 1990's. There were door-openers at the beginning of the decade such as Terrence McNally's *Lips Together, Teeth Apart* (pr. 1991). A deceptively simple comedy, *Lips Together, Teeth Apart* takes place over a Fourth of July weekend on New York's Fire Island. Act by act, for three full acts, a pair of heterosexual couples reveal their preconceptions, misunderstandings, and ultimately their anxieties about homosexuality, perhaps their anxieties most of all. Larry Kramer's *The Normal Heart* (pr. 1985) and *The Destiny of Me* (pr. 1992) offered life partners first acknowledging and then solemnly confronting the acquired immunodeficiency syndrome (AIDS) epidemic, while in Paul Rudnick's *Jeffrey* (pr. 1993), solemnity about AIDS is little more than a passing mood, for the protagonist finds he is surprisingly ready to throw caution to the wind when he meets the man of his dream. McNally's *Kiss of the Spider Woman* (pr. 1993) was a surreal, sometimes labyrinthine examination of two cellmates in a South American dungeon for whom sexual preference was only one delimiting factor among many, and Paula Vogel's *The Baltimore Waltz* (pr. 1992) and *And Baby Makes Seven* (pr. 1986) were less interested in one's sexual preference than in how it limited one's options. Moises Kauffman's *Gross Indecency* (pr. 1998) followed Oscar Wilde through a gauntlet of Victorian prejudice, homophobia disguised as jurisprudence, and literary censorship, focusing on the relationship between art and the life choices of the artist.

WOMEN'S INCREASING VISIBILITY

During the 1990's, the American stage did much to open a discussion about homosexuality and AIDS and kept that discussion underway from a variety of viewpoints. There was not one voice, but many, and something similar might be said in regard to Wendy Wasserstein, Beth Henley, Margaret Edson, Vogel, and other women playwrights. Women playwrights who came to prominence in the 1980's and 1990's on the high tides of feminism proved to have longevity and to speak in many voices rather than a few.

Wasserstein first achieved widespread attention with her *The Sisters Rosensweig* (pr. 1992), a sendup of Anton Chekhov's *Tri sestry* (pr. 1901; *The Three Sisters*, 1920) that earned her an Outer Critics Circle Award as well as a faithful following, and as the decade moved to its conclusion, her *An American Daughter* (pr. 1997) suggested that she deserved the warm reception.

Best known for her plays of the 1980's set in the deep South, Beth Henley established herself with *Crimes of the Heart* (pr. 1979), *The Miss Firecracker Contest* (pr. 1980), and *The Debutante Ball* (pr. 1985), all wicked comedies in which the honey of her southern belles was sure to be laced with venom. Although Henley might well have continued writing in this mode, she opted instead to challenge herself and her audience by moving from comic realism into expressionist theater with *Control Freaks* (pr. 1992), exploring the powers of nonlinear narrative in *L-Play* (pr. 1996), and updating the nineteenth century's "play of manners" with the very mannered construction of *Impossible Marriage* (pr. 1998).

Vogel proved that her two earlier plays, *The Baltimore Waltz* and *And Baby Makes Seven* were but delightful finger exercises leading up to her tour-de-force examination of incest, *How I Learned to Drive* (pr. 1997), a play that won the New York Drama Critics Award, the Lucille Lortel Award, and the 1998 Pulitzer Prize, among others.

Edson's first play, *Wit* (pr. 1999) won the 1999 Pulitzer Prize in Drama, the New York Drama Critics Award, the Lucille Lortel Award, the Drama Desk Award, and the Outer Critics' Circle Award.

The dramatic monologue enjoyed a certain panache in the 1990's, and if there was one area in which the talents of women seemed particularly to shine, it was this. The monologue came to the stage in many variations, including versions of forms better known in print, such as the newspaper column (Kathryn Grody's *A Mom's Life*; pr. 1990, rev. 1999), the memoir (Lynn Redgrave's *Shakespeare for My Father*; pr. 1993), or letters (Eileen Atkins's *Vita and Virginia*; pr. 1993, a dramatization of the correspondence between Virginia Woolf and Vita Sackville-West). Perhaps no stage monologue had quite the impact of Eve Ensler's *The Vagina Monologues* (pr. 1997). *The Vagina Monologues* swept the country, often playing to audiences consisting mostly of women. Putting together transcriptions of what women had reported about their genitalia and offering it as "readers theater," the play was as near to a tribal rite as American theater had known since *Hair* in 1968. Each night on stages throughout the country, a trio of actresses perched on plain stools read from manuscripts they held in their hands. The play was more celebration than production. Often they changed actresses mid-run, which was much in keeping with what the readings had to offer. It was simply understood: The stars of the evening were not the actresses on stage but rather women who only now were being given a voice.

RACIAL AND ETHNIC BARRIERS

Anna Deveare Smith composes in something of the same spirit as Ensler. First in *Fires in the Mirror* (pr. 1992), then in *Twilight: Los Angeles, 1992* (pr. 1993), and finally in *House Arrest*, presented at the Joseph Papp Public Theatre in 2000, Deveare Smith's authorial method has been to transcribe accounts of those involved in major cultural events, then bring their testimony to the stage verbatim, playing each of the characters herself, using their words, the arrhythmia of their voices, a strategy that would raise issues about what it means to call one's self a "playwright."

Deveare Smith's favorite subject matter is the calumnies reported nightly on the television news broadcasts. *Fires in the Mirror*, for instance, deals with an incident in Crown Heights, Brooklyn, an area where lower middle-class African Americans live side by side with affluent Hasidic Jews, with one group doing its best to ignore the presence of the others. Specifically, the play focuses on what happened when an esteemed Hasidic "rebbie" took the life of a black youth in a traffic incident, and in return, as an act of vengeance, a gang of twenty blacks murdered a young Talmudic scholar, putting the area on the brink of social collapse.

A chronicle of how divided the United States remains as a multicultural country, Deveare Smith's work focuses on realities that belie the melting-pot myths of the country, for rarely do her characters envision a truly "united states" of America. What her characters speak of instead are the walls that separate one America from another. Deveare Smith is only one of the playwrights of color whose work has contributed both in form and content to the American stage of late, and while it is tempting to pigeonhole her as a minority playwright with an interest in giving voice to minority issues, the truth is that Deveare Smith writes very much about America itself. This is true once again of August Wilson, whose work deals with the disparity between the American Dream and the daily grind of American life for most of its citizens.

Wilson's noted play from this period is *Jitney* (pr. 2000), an examination of being black in the 1970's as seen through the eyes of a trio of nonunion taxicab drivers in Pittsburgh who find themselves struggling to make a living at a time when the United States seems headed for unbridled prosperity. To fully appreciate what the playwright is about, however, one must see this work in the context of a playwriting project Wilson had underway for nearly a quarter of a century. Each new play addresses one particular period in America's recent history: *Joe Turner's Come and Gone* (pr. 1986) is set in 1911; *Ma Rainey's Black Bottom* (pr. 1984) is set in the 1920's and was winner of the New York Drama Critics Circle Award for Best Play; *The Piano Lesson* (pr. 1987) is set in the 1930's; *Seven Guitars* (pr. 1995) is set in the 1940's; *Fences* (pr. 1985), winner of the Drama Desk Award, the New York Drama Critics Circle Award, and the Pulitzer Prize, is set in the 1950's; *Two Trains Running* (pr. 1990) is set in the 1960's; and *King Hedley II* (pr. 2001) is set in the 1980's. The race of his characters aside, Wilson has become for many one of the foremost chroniclers of the myths and realities of upward mobility in this country.

Some of these same myths and realities are chronicled in Suzan-Lori Parks's *Topdog/Underdog*, for which she won the 2002 Pulitzer Prize. Her characters are brothers, named as a joke by their father "Lincoln" and "Booth." Fate puts them together under the same roof when Lincoln leaves his wife and moves into Booth's tenement apartment. Living in such close proximity, the pair at first discover how different they are from one another as men and later how lethally similar. What they share most of all are a cardsharp's skills. Each is masterful at three-card monte. It is only through this game of sleight of hand played on the streets of New York City that either can envision a better life than they have already known, a freedom from the shackles of poverty and race. Early in the play, Lincoln comes on stage dressed as his namesake; to make ends meet he has taken a job in "white face" at a local arcade dressed as Abraham Lincoln. There he is a target for would-be assassins trying to win a stuffed animal. This is one of the play's most moving dramatic moments, but more important, it effectively dramatizes its theme: the emancipation with which President Lincoln is identified in history also carries with it its own demise.

YOUNG TALENT

Parks is to be counted among the many vital, important young playwrights in the United States who showed promise early in the decade, then went on to fulfill it. After several years of absence following the success of *Angels in America*, Kushner mounted *Homebody/Kabul* (pr. 2001), the first significant production to deal with life in Afghanistan following the September 11, 2001, terrorist attacks on the World Trade Center and the Pentagon, and Rudnick mounted *Rude Entertainment* (pr. 2001; includes three one-act plays: *Mr. Charles, Currently of Palm Beach*; *Very Special Needs*; and *On the Fence*), three comic one-acts dealing with flamboyantly gay life and its place in American culture. Donald Margulies, whose *Dinner with Friends* (pr. 1998) won a Pulitzer Prize and the Lucille Lortel Award, found success earlier in the decade with plays about dysfunctional families such as *The Loman Family Picnic* (pr. 1989) and about the trials of cultural identity such as *Sight Unseen* (pr. 1991), featuring a Jewish artist who thinks of himself as defying and exceeding both those labels.

However, the work of a still younger generation of playwrights was emerging at the same time. For instance, *Proof* (pr. 2000), which won for David Auburn a Pulitzer Prize, was his first important production for the stage. This was true also of Warren Leight's *Side Man* (pr. 1998), a play set in the twilight of the jazz era about the failing marriage of an able musician. David Lindsay-Abaire, whose bizarre comedy *Wonder of the World* (pr. 2000) played to large audiences and general acclaim, had only one earlier New York success to his credit, *Fuddy Meers* (pr. 1999), a comedy about human dysfunction with a stroke victim as its central character.

At the turn of the second millennium, the United States' younger important playwrights such as Kushner or Parks were no longer its youngest. This was promising indeed for the future of American theater. Perhaps never before had American theater known such a wonderful mix of talents from so many generations of writers nor had it ever embraced such a mix with such joy. Clearly there was room on the American stage for such masters as O'Neill, Williams, Miller, Foote, Albee, and their theatrical kin, room for Mamet, Shepard, and the like, and room for still younger playwrights.

BIBLIOGRAPHY

Bigsby, Christopher W. *Contemporary American Playwrights*. Cambridge, England: Cambridge University Press, 2000. Details the decades from the 1970's through the 1990's, examining how playwrights such as Wendy Wasserstein, John Guare, Paula Vogel, and Tony Kushner redefined the American experience and the politics of gender and sexuality.

Bloom, Harold, ed. *Edward Albee*. New York: Chelsea House, 1987. Though dated, this collection of work on Albee's plays is still the best primer for anyone coming to the playwright's work for the first time.

Clum, John M., ed. *Staging Gay Lives: An Anthology of Contemporary Gay Theater*. New York: HarperCollins, 1995. Begins with an excellent introduction to the subject by Tony Kushner, and presents ten plays that examine AIDS, homophobia, and the politics of being gay.

Kolin, Philip C., and Colby H. Cullman, eds. *Speaking on Stage: Interviews with Contemporary American Playwrights*. Tuscaloosa: University of Alabama, 1996. Offers interviews with twenty-seven prominent modern-day playwrights, including Terrence McNally, Ntozake Shange, Edward Albee, Beth Henley, and David Mamet, with topic-driven sections that include "Anxiety and Alienation" and "Celebrating Difference."

McDonough, Carla J. *Staging Masculinity: Male Identity in Contemporary American Drama*. Jefferson, N.C.: McFarland, 1996. Using a postmodern, gender-studies approach, McDonough explores the portrayal of manhood in plays by such dramatists as Sam Shepard, David Mamet, August Wilson, and Arthur Miller.

McNamara, Brooks, ed. *Plays from the Contemporary American Theater*. New York: New American Library, 2002. Introduction to the subject by McNamara and several plays from late twentieth century dramatists, including August Wilson, Beth Henley, Christopher Durang, and John Guare.

Roudane, Matthew C., ed. *Public Issues, Private Tensions: Contemporary American Drama*. New

York: AMS Press, 1993. Critically explores the thematic centrality of public issues and private tensions in American theater since 1945. Playwrights discussed include David Mamet, Arthur Miller, Sam Shepard, and Edward Albee.

Wolfe, Peter. *August Wilson*. New York: Twayne, 1999. Provides an overview of the life and works of August Wilson.

Jay Boyer

AFRICAN AMERICAN DRAMA

Seeking to extricate the power of African American music and dance from the stereotypes and trivializations of minstrelsy in its various forms, African American dramatists struggled during the twentieth century to locate or create an audience receptive to the full range of their thematic and theatrical concerns. The attempt to develop an autonomous style without sacrificing all access to production confronts African American playwrights, collectively and individually, with a paradoxical situation in which they must first demonstrate their mastery of traditionally European American themes and techniques to dispel stereotypes concerning African American ability and character.

Faced with tensions between their African and European American audiences, and with class tensions within the black audience, African American dramatists have followed three distinct paths. Some, concentrating on commercial success in the predominantly white mainstream American theater, have contributed to Broadway-style revues only tangentially concerned with challenging inherited conceptions of African American experience. More self-consciously literary playwrights, usually working on the margins of the commercial theater, have occasionally achieved some commercial success with plays designed to increase white awareness of the variety and complexities of the African American experience. Increasingly, however, serious African American dramatists have sought to address directly an African American audience, frequently but, given the cultural and economic realities of the United States, by no means exclusively in theaters located in the black communities.

HISTORICAL DEVELOPMENT

Ed Bullins, a major figure in both contemporary and African American drama, describes this historical development and contemporary direction in a statement that has exerted a substantial impact on the subsequent development of the tradition:

> With the present Black Writers turned away from addressing an anticipated white readership and appealing

the plight of Blackness in America to their masochistic delight, the literature has changed from a social-protest oriented form to one of a dialectical nature among Black people—Black dialectics—and this new thrust has two main branches—the dialectic of change and the dialectic of experience. The writers are attempting to answer questions concerning Black survival and future, one group through confronting the Black/white reality of America, the other, by heightening the dreadful white reality of being a modern Black captive and victim. These two major branches in the mainstream of the new Black creativity, the dialectic of change (once called protest writing, surely, when confronting whites directly and angrily, then altered to what was called Black revolutionary writing when it shifted . . . away from a white audience to a Black) and the dialectic of experience (or being), sometimes merge, but *variety* and *power* in the overall work are the general rule.

As Bullins suggests, early African American dramatists and performers did in fact anticipate a white audience or, in the rare case where the plays were published, a white readership. Complicating matters was that audience's familiarity with the minstrel shows, such as that of Thomas Rice, which developed in the South as early as the 1830's and enjoyed a vogue well into the twentieth century. Originally performed by whites in blackface imitating songs and dances they had witnessed in slave communities, the minstrel shows rapidly developed into travesties with no direct relationship to any actual African American culture. By the time blacks formed their own troupes after the Civil War, the minstrel stereotypes were so firmly established that black performers were forced to add the familiar blackface makeup if they wished to attract an audience.

Despite this pressure to correspond to preconceived stage images, however, several black dramatists, and especially black performers, established serious reputations during the nineteenth century. Actors such as Ira Aldridge and Victor Séjour, who performed primarily in Europe, also wrote plays on racial themes, as did William Wells Brown, whose abolitionist play *The Escape: Or, A Leap for Freedom* (pr. 1858) is generally credited as the first work of African American dramatic literature. Paul Laurence Dunbar, who frequently performed his own dialect poetry for white audiences grounded in the neo-minstrel stereotypes of the plantation tradition, collaborated with Will Marion Cook on *Clorindy: Or, The Origin of the Cakewalk* (pr. 1898), the first African American play to receive a full-scale commercial production. Although Bob Cole's *A Trip to Coontown* (pr. 1898) was produced by blacks, it was not until 1916 that a serious play written, acted, and produced by blacks was performed in the United States. Sponsored by the National Association for the Advancement of Colored People, Angelina Grimke's *Rachel* (pr. 1916), while addressed primarily to a white audience, did not pander to the stereotypes of tragic mulatto, black beast, or comic darky.

THE HARLEM RENAISSANCE

The movement in African American drama from an exclusive address to the white audience toward Bullins's black dialectics began during the Harlem Renaissance of the 1920's. Responding to the growth of sizable African American communities in northern urban centers, black playwrights seriously envisioned for the first time a theater not predicated entirely on white expectations. Companies such as Cleveland's Karamu House and Gilpin Players (named after Charles Gilpin, one of the first black actors to earn a major reputation as an actor on American stages), Philadelphia's Dunbar Theatre, and New York's influential Lafayette Players, along with the Krigwa Little Theatre movement, which under the sponsorship of W. E. B. DuBois established theaters in many large cities, provided proving ground for black actors and playwrights. At about the same time, plays by European American dramatists, especially Ridgley Torrence (*The Rider of Dreams*, pr. 1917), DuBose and Dorothy Heyward (*Porgy*, pr. 1927), Paul Green (the Pulitzer Prize-winning *In Abraham's Bosom*, pr. 1926), Marc Connelly (*The Green Pastures: A Fable*, pb. 1929), and Eugene O'Neill (*The Emperor Jones*, pr. 1920, and *All God's Chillun Got Wings*,

pr. 1924), began to treat African American characters and themes more seriously than had their predecessors. The presence of a black-oriented, if not yet predominantly black, audience, accompanied by the partial abatement of minstrel stereotypes, encouraged a significant number of African American playwrights to begin working during the 1920's and 1930's.

Many, including Zora Neale Hurston (*Great Day*, pr. 1937), Wallace Thurman (*Harlem*, pr. 1929), Countée Cullen and Arna Bontemps (*God Sends Sunday*, pr. 1931), Georgia Douglas Johnson (*Plumes*, pb. 1927), Jean Toomer, and Langston Hughes, had previously worked and remain best known as poets and novelists. Others, including Frank Wilson (*Walk Together, Chillun*, pr. 1936), Hall Johnson (*Run Little Chillun*, pr. 1933), and especially Willis Richardson, established their reputations primarily as dramatists. Whatever their primary literary focus, however, the playwrights of the Harlem Renaissance responded to the call sounded by James Weldon Johnson in the preface to *The Book of American Negro Poetry* (1922) for a new type of artist who would do for African Americans "what [John Millington] Synge did for the Irish; he needs to find a form that will express the racial spirit by symbols from within rather than by symbols from without."

As Sterling Brown observed in *Negro Poetry and Drama* (1937), the plays written in response to this call were of two distinct types: the problem play, which extended the "political" tradition of Grimke and William Wells Brown, and the folk-life play, which to some extent attempted to reconstruct the materials that had been trivialized in the minstrel tradition. Among the most successful playwrights to work with both approaches was Richardson, who wrote a half-dozen plays of lasting interest, including *The Broken Banjo* (pr. 1925) and *The Chip Woman's Fortune* (pr. 1923), the first play by an African American produced on Broadway. More powerful as literature, Toomer's complex philosophical character study "Kabnis," published as section 3 of *Cane* (pb. 1923), a work incorporating prose and poetry as well as drama, presented insurmountable staging problems given the generic conventions of the era.

DEPRESSION ERA

As the excitement of the Harlem Renaissance gave way to the political determination of African American writing of the Great Depression era, attention gradually shifted away from the optimistic aesthetics of the influential critic Alain Locke, cofounder along with Montgomery Gregory of the Howard University Players, whose anthology *Plays of Negro Life* (1927) included work by both black and white writers. Supported by programs such as the Federal Theatre Project, playwrights such as Hughes and Theodore Ward, whose *Big White Fog* (pr. 1938) is widely considered the most powerful African American play of the decade, contributed to the proletarian theater exemplified by European American dramatists such as Clifford Odets. Despite the shift away from mainstream political positions, much pressure remained on black playwrights to align their views with those of their radical white contemporaries. Hughes, who began writing plays in the 1920's and had the first Broadway hit by an African American playwright in *Mulatto*, which ran from 1935 to 1937, supported leftist political causes in plays such as *Scottsboro Limited* (pr. 1932), as did novelist Richard Wright, whose *Native Son* (1940) was a commercial success in a dramatic adaptation by Wright and white playwright Paul Green. Although best known as a poet, Hughes continued to work in theater throughout his career, although he abandoned the explicitly political focus in later plays such as *Simply Heavenly* (pr. 1957) and *Tambourines to Glory* (pr. 1963).

POSTWAR DEVELOPMENTS

The transition from a drama addressed to an anticipated white audience to Bullins's black dialectics accelerated after World War II, proceeding in two major phases. The first phase, involving recognition of serious African American drama from a mainstream white audience, centered on the commercial and artistic success of a sequence of plays reinforcing the premises of the nonviolent Civil Rights movement of the 1950's and early 1960's. The second, heralded by Amiri Baraka's stunning *Dutchman* (pr. 1964) and culminating in the community theater movement frequently associated with black nationalist politics, re-directed attention to the internal concerns of the African American community. By no means devoid of assertive political commitment, the plays of the first phase typically endorsed an integrationist philosophy, partially in deference to the anticipated white audience and partially as a result of the early successes and promise of Martin Luther King, Jr.'s interracial strategies. The first major success of the period, Louis Peterson's *Take a Giant Step* (pr. 1953), was followed rapidly by William Branch's *In Splendid Error* (pr. 1954), Alice Childress's *Trouble in Mind* (pr. 1955), and Ossie Davis's *Purlie Victorious* (pr. 1961).

The most significant plays of this phase were Lorraine Hansberry's *A Raisin in the Sun* (pr. 1959) and James Baldwin's *Blues for Mister Charlie* (pr. 1964). Although Baldwin's play drew substantial critical and political attention largely as a result of his position as a novelist and community spokesperson, *A Raisin in the Sun* is unarguably the first major contribution of an African American playwright to the dramatic literature of the United States. Focusing on the tensions between the members of an African American family seeking to realize their individual conceptions of the American Dream, the play possesses a variety and power equal to that of any play written in the dominant realistic mode of the mainstream stage of the 1950's.

Although *Blues for Mister Charlie* failed to match the 530-performance run of *A Raisin in the Sun*, which won the New York Drama Critics Circle Award for 1958-1959, the two plays established a lasting African American presence in American drama on Broadway, Off-Broadway, and Off-Off-Broadway as well as on community and regional stages previously devoted almost entirely to European American drama. Douglas Turner Ward's Negro Ensemble Company has maintained a continuing presence Off-Broadway with productions such as Ward's own *Day of Absence* (pr. 1965) and Charles Fuller's *A Soldier's Play* (pr. 1982), which was the second Pulitzer Prize-winning play by an African American dramatist. The first, Charles Gordone's brilliant absurdist work *No Place to Be Somebody* (pr. 1969), produced by leading Off-Broadway producer Joseph

Papp, reflects the developing avant-garde tradition in black theater. Several plays by Baraka, Bullins, and Adrienne Kennedy (*Funnyhouse of a Negro*, pr. 1964, and *A Rat's Mass*, pr. 1966) had substantial influence on experimental dramatists outside the African American community. Reflecting the continuing interaction of African and European American avant-garde theaters, *The Gospel at Collonus* (pr. 1983), an adaptation of Sophocles' work written by prominent white experimental playwright Lee Breuer but given its emotional power by the improvisational performance style of the all-black cast, followed *Dutchman* and several of Bullins's plays as winner of the Obie Award for best play. Other plays by African American dramatists that have made a notable impact on mainstream audiences during the 1960's and 1970's include Lonne Elder's *Ceremonies in Dark Old Men* (pr. 1969) and Joseph Walker's *The River Niger* (pr. 1972).

COMMUNITY THEATER MOVEMENT

Although these playwrights have made an impact in the mainstream theatrical world, the energy of African American drama since the mid-1960's derives in large part from the community theater movement spearheaded by Baraka and Bullins. Repudiating not only the focus on the white audience but also the emphasis of many earlier playwrights on the problems of the black middle class, these dramatists oriented their work toward the entire black community. In part, this shift can be attributed to the growing influence of the separatist philosophy of Malcolm X as the Civil Rights movement confronted a new set of problems in the North.

Baraka's *Dutchman* marked the major transition point in African American theater, emphasizing the common position of all blacks, however fully assimilated into the mainstream. The climactic murder of the articulate black protagonist by a white woman, who has manipulated his complex self-consciousness, provided a symbol that exerted a major impact on younger playwrights such as Ron Milner, Jimmy Garrett, Richard Wesley, Marvin X, Sonia Sanchez, and Ben Caldwell. Working in community theaters such as Baraka's Spirit House of Newark, Bullins's

and Robert MacBeth's New Lafayette Theater and Woodie King, Jr.'s New Federal Theatre of New York, John O'Neal's Free Southern Theatre of Mississippi and New Orleans, Val Gray Ward's Kuumba Theatre of Chicago, and the Black Arts/West of San Francisco, these playwrights struggled to create a theater designed specifically to reach an audience unlikely to attend traditional theatrical events.

Drawing heavily on traditions of African and African American music and dance, many of their plays, including Milner's *Who's Got His Own* (pr. 1966), Garrett's *And We Own the Night* (pr. 1967), and Wesley's *The Last Street Play* (pr. 1977), redirected "protests" intended for whites when presented in mainstream theaters toward the revolutionary, usually nationalist vision that Bullins associates with the "dialectic of change." Particularly in his Obie Award-winning *The Taking of Miss Janie* (pr. 1975) and in the plays from his Twentieth Century Cycle (most notably *In New England Winter*, pb. 1969, and *In the Wine Time*, pr. 1968), Bullins demonstrated a thematic power and technical versatility matched in American drama only by O'Neill.

Perhaps the best of the plays by Bullins is *The Taking of Miss Janie*, a play about racial tensions in the 1960's. The audience learns about the characters from the dramatization of the action (for example, at the party of lead character Monty) and from the characters themselves, who speak directly to the audience, sharing their thoughts. Monty, a black college student who writes poetry, wants to have sex with—and actually control—the beautiful white woman named Janie. He calls her Miss Janie, a joke that she seems unable to comprehend. To Monty, Janie, because she is a very attractive young white woman, represents the privileged and the fortunate. He realizes that she wants to be friends with him, yet he resents her, believing that she considers herself superior because of her skin color. He therefore calls her Miss Janie, seemingly calling attention to a perceived master-slave relationship. Janie enjoys his poetry, even though it is quite pessimistic and dark, and she wants desperately to be friends with him, but he doubts her sincerity, thinking that she is using him and merely wants the novelty of having a black friend. Monty doubts Janie's sincerity because she refuses to have sex with him; he considers her refusal proof that she is using him, yet Janie believes that sex hinders the opportunity for a man and woman to be friends. It is difficult to discern how truthful the characters are with the audience, with each other, and with themselves. Monty maintains a friendship with Janie, waiting patiently for his opportunity to have sex with her, which represents his ultimate goal. In the end, because she proves unwilling to have sex with him, he rapes her. The rape is not an act of sex, but rather one that exhibits power and dominance. The black man thus controls and dominates the white woman, a female whom he believes symbolizes superiority and perhaps even slave owners.

The racial tensions are complicated further in *The Taking of Miss Janie* by the presence of several other characters. Rick and Peggy are African American characters who clearly manifest hatred for whites, referring to them as devils. Their hatred for white people is returned by the prejudice toward blacks by white characters Mort Silberstein and Lonnie, Janie's jazz-playing boyfriend, both of whom make racist remarks. Rick becomes upset when meeting Lonnie because he believes that Lonnie is a usurper—a white man playing black music. Bullins clearly disapproves of Silberstein and Lonnie for their anti-African American attitudes, but his black characters such as Peggy, Monty, Rick, and Flossy do not appear to be benevolent or wholesome people either. Rather they are characters who hate white people and who are just as racist as the white characters. However, they are portrayed as more honest about their feelings than the white characters. Rick makes it clear to all the white people whom he meets that he believes that they are devils. Peggy also hates white people and blames them for the failure of her marriage to Monty. She then marries a white person. After that marriage does not work out, she decides to try being a lesbian. The characters seem to be searching for themselves, confused about their lives, and preoccupied with race.

Although the community theater movement underwent substantial changes as racial issues assumed a less prominent position in public debate during the late 1970's and 1980's, its impact is evident in the works of dramatists who have chosen to work closer to the American mainstream. Although African American dramatists continue to confront pressure to orient their work toward a white audience, most of the simplistic stereotypes have been called into question to the extent that new playwrights, building on the achievements of Bullins and Baraka even while working from sharply differing political premises, are able to employ the power and beauty of the African American performance traditions without needing to compromise their vision of the complexity of African American life.

DRAMATIZING ASSIMILATION

In the mid-1980's, African American drama began de-emphasizing the revolutionary and recolonization aspects of the political platform, searching instead for a strong dramatic voice to tell the story of African American assimilation into mainstream American ideals. That voice was found in the work of August Wilson, whose series of plays, each based on a decade in the history of African American family life, have been developed in cooperation with the Yale Repertory Theatre and the O'Neill Center, officially known as the National Playwrights' Conference. The plays have moved successfully from the League of Resident Theatres (LORT) circuit onto Broadway, with a new play appearing about every two years. The link between the two not-for-profit institutions is Lloyd Richards, until 1992 the artistic director of the Yale Repertory and the institutional director of the O'Neill Center. He has guided Wilson's plays through the play development process, at the O'Neill Center in staged reading format, and at the Yale Repertory in their first professional productions, many of which moved to other LORT theaters before attempting a Broadway run.

Wilson's preeminence as an African American playwright is evident in his output of notable plays, which focus on separation, migration, and reunion to depict the physical and psychological journeys of African Americans in the twentieth century. These thematic explorations are heightened with his use of African American musical traditions and the depiction of the conflict between a Christian tradition and African folklore and heritage. His plays *Jitney* (pr. 2000), *Seven Guitars* (pr. 1995), *Two Trains Running* (pr. 1990), *The Piano Lesson* (pr. 1987), *Joe Turner's Come and Gone* (pr. 1986), *Fences* (pr. 1985), and *Ma Rainey's Black Bottom* (pr. 1984), which won the third Pulitzer Prize received by an African American, have all been produced to wide acclaim.

Fences tells the story of Troy Maxson, his son, Cory, and his wife, Rose. Bitter because he was too old to play major league baseball when Jackie Robinson broke the color barrier, Troy resorts to hauling garbage in order to make a living. Cory shares Troy's athletic abilities, yet the father refuses to allow his son to play sports. Troy asserts that he refuses to allow Cory to waste his life playing sports when white people, who control sports and academic scholarships, will not permit African Americans to get ahead. Cory, stung by his father's refusal, becomes bitter and correctly asserts that Troy is actually jealous because Cory enjoys opportunities that were denied his father. Wilson indicates that although racism still exists, times have changed and that it is actually the father's jealousy and bitterness, not prejudice, that inhibits Cory from attending college on a football scholarship. The play focuses on the patriarchal African American family, particularly the relationships between Troy and Cory, and between Troy and Rose. When Troy impregnates Alberta, Rose becomes furious, causing permanent scars in their marriage. Troy's adultery renders him subjugated to his wife, making Cory feel that his father no longer rules the Maxson family; he subsequently challenges his father's authority, which results in Cory being forced to leave the house, never to return in his father's lifetime (he comes back for Troy's funeral). Cory had attempted to supplant his father, yet he finds that he, himself, is supplanted, being replaced by Troy's new daughter, a product of his affair with Alberta. When Cory is thrown out of the home by his father, which is part of a rite of passage and, unfortunately, a family tradition (Troy's father had thrown him out a generation before), Troy throws his belongings over the fence. Troy believes that fences are meant to keep intruders out, yet Rose believes, according to Troy's friend Bono, that fences are designed to keep families in, to maintain the family unit.

Ma Rainey's Black Bottom dramatizes a story about the legendary blues singer Ma Rainey and her band. The play demonstrates the racism that Rainey and other African Americans encountered. For example, Rainey purchases a new car, yet a police officer questions her about the automobile, doubting that an African American could buy such a nice car and believing that she must have stolen it. Furthermore, her musicians must insist on being paid in cash because no business is willing to cash checks from African Americans. Ma Rainey has an attitude problem, causing her to be habitually late and disrespectful to the record company producers, yet Wilson implies that there is a reason for her behavior. She realizes that the record producer has no respect for her and is using her to make a substantial profit. She compares herself to a prostitute: After the producer has captured her voice on tape, he has no use for her, just as a male customer has no use for a prostitute after he has satisfied his lust. Thus, she prolongs the recording session as much as possible to earn a semblance of respect.

The Piano Lesson concerns a man, Boy Willie, who comes to sell his sister's piano, a family heirloom because it has images of their family members engraved on it. Although Berniece refuses to play the piano, she does not want to part with it because her uncles Doaker and Wining Boy, along with her father, Boy Charles, took it from the house of Sutter, the slave owner, believing that it belonged to them because of the family history engraved on it. During the removal of the piano, Boy Charles was killed; thus, Berniece cannot part with it. Boy Willie wants to sell the piano so that he can use the money to purchase land from Sutter's brother. Wilson thus creates a fascinating dilemma: Selling the piano is tantamount to betraying the family history, yet selling the piano can allow the family to thrive and to own the land on which the family was previously owned as slaves, thus reclaiming family history. Berniece looks back to the past, while Boy Willie focuses on the future.

Wilson's *Seven Guitars* debuted in 1995. Set in the 1940's, it tells the tragic story of blues guitarist

Floyd Barton, whose funeral opens the play. The action flashes back to recreate the events of Floyd's last week of life. Floyd had arrived in Pittsburgh to try to get his guitar out of the pawn shop and to convince his former lover, Vera, to return with him to Chicago. A record he made years earlier has suddenly gained popularity, and he has been offered the opportunity to record more songs at a studio in Chicago.

The play's central conflicts are Floyd's struggle to move forward in his musical career and his personal strife with Vera and his band mates. A subplot centers on Floyd's friend Hedley and his deteriorating physical and mental health as his friends attempt to place him in a tuberculosis sanitarium. The play contains some of Wilson's familiar character types, including the mentally aberrant Hedley; the troubled-by-the-law young black male protagonist, Floyd; the capable and independent woman, Louise; and the more needy, younger woman, Ruby. It also contains elements of music, dance, storytelling, violence, and food.

The 2000 play *Jitney* is about a gypsy cab service operated by Becker, a good man whose son, Booster, has just been released from prison after serving a long sentence for murdering a white woman, his girlfriend. The woman falsely accused Booster of rape after her father caught her having sex with him. While out on bail and awaiting the trial, Booster gets revenge by shooting her to death. Becker cannot forgive his son because Booster's imprisonment has caused his wife to be so unhappy that she dies; Becker thus blames his son for his wife's demise, permanently straining the father-son relationship. Wilson manifests again his skill in dramatizing poignant familial relationships. Another character, Youngblood, is falsely accused of sleeping around on his wife Rena, when actually he is saving money and surprising his wife by looking for—and purchasing—a house. When the cab company goes out of business because of Becker's accidental death, the audience realizes that Youngblood is the only one there who has a bright future. As his name implies, he is a new kind of person, an ambitious family man who thus distinguishes himself from the other characters, such as Fielding and Turnbo, whose lives are going nowhere.

INFLUENTIAL WOMEN PLAYWRIGHTS

The death of Baldwin in 1987 took away one of the most effective African American talents from the stage. Political activists such as Baraka became less active in the theater in the 1990's but vocal in other cultural affairs. The void left by Baldwin and the relative absence of prominent male African American playwrights in the late 1980's and 1990's opened the door for a new direction in African American theater: plays by women dramatists. Female African American playwrights, in the last decades of the twentieth century, gained attention for plays that expanded theatrical boundaries and created theater that offered unforgettable images in culturally resonant, historically significant, and deeply personal plays.

A novelist, poet, and playwright, Ntozake Shange has aptly labeled her creations "choreopoems" for their blend of poetry, drama, prose, and autobiography. Her works, labeled "militant feminism" by some critics for their portrayal of violence and their contentious relationship with black men, also display a youthful spirit, a flair with language, and a lyricism that carries them to startling and radical conclusions. Her contradictory style, such as the use of both black English and the erudite vocabulary of the educated, is at the heart of her drama. She is best known for her 1976 play *for colored girls who have considered suicide/ when the rainbow is enuf*, which was honored in that year by the Outer Critics Circle and won Obie and Audelco Awards as well as Tony and Grammy award nominations in 1977. The play is a recital, individually and in chorus, of the lives and growth of seven different black women, named according to their dress colors. The term "colored girls" in the title evokes a stereotype of black women yet also contains a germ of hope for the future (the "rainbow," both of color and of eventual salvation). These figures are representative voices of black women that express fury at their oppression both as women and as blacks. The scenes are often somber, portraying rape, abuse, city dangers, and abortion, reflecting the recurrent motif of the thwarting of dreams and aspirations for a decent life by forces beyond one's control: war, poverty, and ignorance. Yet a saving grace appears toward the end of the play, when the seven women fall into a tighter circle of mutual support, much like a religious "laying on of hands" ceremony, in which they say, "i found god in myself/ & i loved her/ i loved her fiercely." Their bitter pain, shown throughout the dramatic episodes, turns into a possibility of regeneration.

Suzan-Lori Parks gained the mainstream limelight in 2002 when she became the first African American woman to win a Pulitzer Prize in Drama and earned rave reviews for her play *Topdog/Underdog* (pr. 2001). Yet Parks's career also was rewarded generously during the 1980's and 1990's. *The New York Times* called her the "year's most promising playwright" in 1989, her work was supported by grants from the Rockefeller and Ford foundations and the National Endowment for the Arts, and she received a MacArthur Award in 1986.

Parks's plays are marked by a unique use of language and speech, an approach that forefronts the vernacular in an attempt to reproduce speech both as it is spoken and as her audience assumes it may be spoken. She seeks a hypnotic and musical emphasis of words, a technique that accounts for much of the repetitive patterns in her work. Although she strives to dissect the black experience as it intersects with a white society, she often leaves room for a playfulness: As one critic noted, "(W)ith humor and insight, (she) wriggles free of political straitjackets and thumbs her nose at real racisms, too." Her early short plays include *The Sinners' Place* (pr. 1984) and *Betting on the Dust Commander* (pr. 1987). Her full-length play *Imperceptible Mutabilities in the Third Kingdom* (pr. 1989) won the Obie Award for the best play of 1990. One section of *Imperceptible Mutabilities in the Third Kingdom* takes place on the day of emancipation in 1865 and is played in whiteface by African American actors. *Venus* (pr. 1996) focuses on the life of a "sideshow freak," a black woman brought to England as the Venus Hottentot and put on public display because of her ugly figure that contradicted European notions of beauty.

Topdog/Underdog combines elements of a hip-hop riff and a Greek tragedy. The protagonist brothers, named whimsically by their father Lincoln and Booth, have been forged in a matrix of deprivation

that has left them with meager family ties, little education, and few opportunities. They express their frustrations in rhythmic poetry, enhanced by a self-deprecating sense of humor. They act out their misfortunes, each dependent on the other and resentful, protective, and menacing.

Pearl Cleage is another female playwright who rose to prominence in the 1990's. She uses the written word as a journalist, poet, and novelist to explore blacks' experiences on the American landscape, often employing historically accurate African American experiences and cultural lessons. Self-described as a third-generation black nationalist feminist, Cleage's works examine the relationships and the impacts of racism and sexism. She gained fame in 1992 with her production of *Flyin' West*, which portrayed sisters Sophie and Fannie, who, after nearly twenty years of arduous labor, are now wheat farmers and rising leaders in their community. The setting is post-emancipation Kansas, a landscape that serves as a metaphor for home, where black residents can experience a newly defined freedom as landowners. Like thousands of blacks who left Tennessee, Mississippi, and Kentucky during the Kansas Exodus of 1879, the sisters are captivated by the "free land" being given out by the American government. Cleage has said of her characters that by flying West "they were no longer the creature of another's will." The themes of *Flyin' West* include the power of memory—the sisters' recollections of the brutal South—and of imagination—their hopes for the freedom to be found in the West. Other plays by Cleage include *Hospice* (pr. 1983), *Blues for an Alabama Sky* (pr. 1994), and *Bourbon at the Border* (pr. 1997).

Playwright and performance artist Anna Deveare Smith uses a unique blend of journalistic technique—interviewing subjects from all walks of life—with the art of re-creating their words in performance, ultimately presenting controversial events from multiple points of view. In doing so, she has successfully explored issues of racial tensions, community, and character in the United States, most notably in *Twilight: Los Angeles, 1992* (pr. 1993). *Twilight* examined the 1992 Los Angeles riots and became the first play in her continuing series *On the Road: A Search for the*

American Character. Fires in the Mirror (pr. 1995) followed, a play that explored the 1991 Crown Heights riots in Brooklyn that erupted after a Hasidic man's car jumped a curb, killing a six-year-old black child, and the subsequent retaliatory killing of a Hasidic rabbinical student. The play is drawn verbatim from a series of more than fifty interviews with Crown Heights residents, politicians, activists, religious leaders, gang members, street dwellers, victims, and perpetrators. *House Arrest*, the 2000 installment of the series, explores the mythic role of the presidency in American society.

Adrienne Kennedy favors a surrealistic and expressionistic form, her plays capturing the irrational quality of dreams while offering insight into the nature of the self and being. Most of her works are complex character studies in which a given figure may have several selves or roles. In this multidimensional presentation lies Kennedy's forte—the unraveling of the individual consciousness. Her plays grow out of her own experiences as a sensitive and gifted black American who grew up in the Midwest. While there is often little plot in Kennedy's plays, there exists a wealth of symbolism concerning the inherent tensions of the African American experience. Some of her best known plays include *Funnyhouse of a Negro* (pr. 1962), *The Owl Answers* (pr. 1963), *A Rat's Mass* (pr. 1966), *A Movie Star Has to Star in Black and White* (pr. 1976), *June and Jean in Concert* (pr. 1995), and *Sleep Deprivation Chamber* (pr. 1996). Kennedy's daring break from a realistic style in theatrical writing and her bold exploration of her own family history, cultural experience, and identity have arguably laid a foundation for Parks, Shange, Cleage, and Deveare Smith in their own dramatic approaches and explorations of similar topics.

BIBLIOGRAPHY

Bean, Annemarie, ed. *Sourcebook on African American Performance: Plays, People, Movements.* New York: Routledge, 1999. A series of articles explores the period between the Black Arts Movement of the 1960's and the New Black Renaissance of the 1990's. Topics include the professional, revolutionary, and college stages; concert dance; community activism; step shows; and performance art.

Elam, Harry Justin, and David Krasner, eds. *African American Performance and Theater History: A Critical Reader.* London: Oxford University Press, 2000. An anthology of critical writings that explores the intersections of race, theater, and performance in the United States. Chronicles every nonmusical African American play produced from 1969 to 2000, providing an overview comment, a summary, an actor comment, and a statement about critical reception for each play.

Gavin, Christy, ed. *African American Women Playwrights: A Research Guide.* New York: Garland, 1999. A comprehensive guide to African American drama by female playwrights, helpful to scholars and students studying gender and feminist issues in African American drama.

Hill, Errol. *The Theater of Black Americans.* New York: Applause Theater Book Publishers, 1990. Traces the origins of African American theater, beginning with the Negro spiritual and the birth of the Harlem Renaissance to the emergence of a national black theater movement in the 1960's.

Krasner, David. *Resistance, Parody, and Double Consciousness in African American Theater, 1895-1910.* New York: St. Martin's Press, 1998. Using the fields of history, black literary theory, cultural studies, performance studies, and postcolonial theory, Krasner examines several major productions near the turn of the twentieth century, arguing that the period was replete with moments of resistance to racism, parodies of the minstrel tradition, and double consciousness on the part of performers.

Okur, Nilgun Anadolu. *Contemporary African American Theater: Afrocentricity in the Works of Larry Neal, Amiri Baraka, and Charles Fuller.* New York: Garland, 1997. Explores the dramatic imagination of African American playwrights during the turbulent years of the Civil Rights and Black Power movements, focusing on three playwrights in particular to reveal the roots of an Afrocentric approach to the theater.

Craig Werner, updated by Thomas J. Taylor and Eric Sterling

ASIAN AMERICAN DRAMA

Asian American drama emerged from the identity politics and student radicalism of the 1960's and 1970's. The term "Asian American" was coined in the 1960's as a replacement for "Oriental," a term that many considered a demeaning colonialist description that exoticized all individuals to whom it was attached. By contrast, the term "Asian American," implying a coalition or strategic alliance of peoples from widely dispersed geographical regions, became a political identifier, a verbal banner under which immigrants from Asian countries and their descendants could unite in the struggle against racism, ethnic profiling, economic discrimination, and invisibility.

Many Asian American playwrights feel that their work, because of their cultural heritage and their ethnic identities, can be regarded as Asian American drama. Despite the fact that their audiences make certain assumptions about any work thus labeled—that the work must be Asian inflected and must represent the total experience of an ethnic minority—Asian American playwrights emphasize the diversity of theme, the fluidity of genre, and the universality of emotion in their dramatic creations.

Although in form, structure, and focus, Asian American drama varies as widely as does any body of art, plays and performance pieces by artists of Asian descent often share common concerns: the search for identity and self-definition, the complexities of a life lived on cultural borders, the effects of racism, and the excavation of buried cultural histories. Moreover, the plays typically raise similar questions: What constitutes an authentic Asian American experience? Is there an Asian American cultural identity?

HISTORY

Theatrical activity has always been an integral component of Asian American communities. Historically, "Chinatowns" in California cities, in New York, and in Seattle mounted productions of traditional Cantonese operas and dramatized folk tales, and Japanese immigrant communities performed their versions of the Kabuki and Nō dramas of their homeland. These performances were re-creations of cultural traditions imported from immigrants' native countries, rather than plays that attempted to re-create and re-enact the performers' current lives and situations.

During the nineteenth century and the first half of the twentieth century, Asian characters onstage existed primarily as caricatures, as two-dimensional stereotypes: the evil Oriental (Fu Manchu and Ming the Merciless); the loyal domesticated Charlie Chan with his agreeable "Ah so"; the geisha; the dragon lady; and the shrinking lotus blossom beauty who walks three paces behind her man. Moreover, these characters were generally played by white actors, and production handbooks of the period gave explicit instructions for makeup that could turn a Caucasian into an exaggerated Oriental. Meanwhile, with rare exception, Asian performers were limited to traditional dramatic forms such as Chinese opera, or they performed on the "Chop Suey" vaudeville circuit. Very occasionally, an actor of Asian descent had the opportunity to perform in main stage productions such as Oscar Hammerstein II and Richard Rogers's *Flower Drum Song* (pr. 1958), yet even in that venue, the Asian characters were thinly disguised stereotypes. The situation would not change dramatically until the emergence in the late 1960's of student strikes worldwide, which in turn fostered a radical political climate that gave rise to the Asian American movement.

Hawaii arguably served as the birthplace of what would later be called Asian American drama. The earliest immigrants from the Asian countries—mainly China and Japan—brought with them a variety of forms of traditional theater, folk drama, pageants, and festivals that involved role playing. These popular modes of performance would ultimately find their way into more structured and self-consciously artistic forms of theater. In 1928, Gladys Li's play, *The Submission of Rose Moy*—about a young woman who must decide between the traditional ways of her immigrant parents and the seductive freedoms of the

West—was produced at the University of Hawaii; nearly twenty years later in 1947, the University of Hawaii's Theater Group put on a production of Bessie Toshigawa's *Reunion*, a play about the return of World War II veterans who fought with the Japanese American 442nd regimental combat unit. Like the Asian American plays that would follow—in Hawaii and on the United States mainland—in the coming decades, *The Submission of Rose Moy* and *Reunion* raised questions about assimilation, identity, and racism in their portrayal of the tensions growing from the chasm between East and West. Reflective plays such as these found a formal outlet in 1955 when the Honolulu Theatre for Youth was created.

1960's and 1970's

In the United States of the 1960's, the Asian American community consisted of immigrants from a handful of countries, and the defining label encompassed primarily those whose heritage was Chinese or Japanese (the earliest immigrants), and to a lesser extent, Philippine, Korean, or Indian (the second wave) immigrants. Therefore, the earliest theatrical productions that bore the Asian American stamp examined the viewpoint and experience of those cultures in the majority. With the 1952 reforms in immigration law, immigrants from other Asian and Pacific nations began to make their home in the United States, changing the composition of the Asian American community. In particular, the end of the Vietnam War saw an increase in Vietnamese, Cambodian, and Hmong immigrants, and the Asian American experience onstage expanded to reflect the lives, dreams, and concerns of the newest arrivals.

Asian American drama grew out of the frustration felt by Asian-descent actors who felt marginalized, deprived of all but stereotypical roles on the American stage and screen. In response, the first Asian American theater company, East West Players, was established in Los Angeles in 1965 under the artistic direction of the famed actor, Mako. With the help of Ford Foundation funding, East West Players sponsored a playwriting contest for Asian American writers in 1968 and thus launched the careers of the first generation of Asian American dramatists, including

Wakako Yamauchi, Frank Chin, and Momoko Iko. In the next decade, other theater companies emerged: LaMama Chinatown in New York; Kumu Kahua, or "Original Stage," in Honolulu; the San Francisco-based Asian American Theatre Company; the Northwest Asian Theatre Company in Seattle; and New York's Pan Asian Repertory (which grew out of LaMama Chinatown in 1977). These theaters, along with Joseph Papp and the Public Theatre in New York City, nurtured a second generation of Asian American playwrights: Jeannie Barroga, Philip Kan Gotanda, Jessica Hagedorn, Velina Hasu Houston, David Henry Hwang, Genny Lim, and Elizabeth Wong.

Late twentieth century

In the 1970's, most Asian American theatrical activity was confined to the West Coast or New York. The 1980's and 1990's saw the establishment elsewhere in the United States of a number of significant theater companies, including Theatre Mu in Minneapolis and Angel Island Theatre Company in Chicago. These ethnic theater companies began to produce the work of playwrights from Asian immigrant communities founded after the 1960's. In New York, the Ma-Yi Theatre focuses mainly on productions by Filipino American playwrights, the National Asian American Theatre Company mounts productions of classic plays—such as works by Eugene O'Neill and Molière—with Asian actors; and the Yangtze Repertory Theatre brings together traditional Chinese theater with Asian American theater. San Francisco's theater scene is enriched by the Filipino American Teatro Ng Tanan ("the people's theater").

Mainstream stages also have noticed Asian American writers and performers. In particular, New York's Public Theatre—responsible for bringing Hwang and Hagedorn to the notice of New York theater audiences—stages at least one Asian American work each season, and the Mark Taper Forum in Los Angeles sponsors the Asian American Theatre Workshop. Two popular Asian American novels—Maxine Hong Kingston's *The Woman Warrior* (1976) and Amy Tan's *The Joy Luck Club* (1989) have been adapted for the stage with productions by, respectively, the Berkeley Repertory Theatre in 1994 and the Long Wharf Theatre in Connecticut in 1997.

The growing number of playwriting competitions aimed at the ethnic community has fueled the rapid growth of Asian American drama. Among the most significant of these competitions are The Seattle Group Theatre's annual Multicultural Playwrights Festival, and the biannual Ruby Schaar Yoshino Playwright Award sponsored by the National Japanese American Citizens' League.

Some of the American theater's most interesting experimental work has come from playwrights and performers of Asian descent. Perhaps because so many of these artists are forced by birth and circumstance to straddle cultural and personal boundaries, Asian American playwrights often employ untraditional staging that privileges unusual interpretations of space and time. Among those who have done notable experimental work are Ping Chong and Hagedorn, as well as Han Ong, Amy Hill, and the troupe Peeling the Banana, among the younger generation of theater artists. Slant Performance Group, which consists of three actor-musician-dancers, pushes the boundaries of performance art through its dramatizations of contemporary life in the Asian American community and its celebration of life on the borders.

BIBLIOGRAPHY

Berman, Misha, ed. *Between Worlds: Contemporary Asian-American Plays.* New York: Theatre Communications Group, 1990. The first anthology of plays by Asian American dramatists, this collection introduced American readers to an entire body of theatrical writing that stages the Asian American experience. Although most of the selections are short pieces—not necessarily the playwrights' most significant work—the anthology as a whole represents the range and scope of Asian American drama at the beginning of the 1990's.

Eng, Alvin, ed. *Tokens? The NYC Asian American Experience on Stage.* New York: Asian American Writers' Workshop, 1999. Includes ten plays and performance pieces to provide "a great visceral snapshot of what Asian American theater was like in New York City in the 1990's." Also includes a

section, "The Verbal Mural," that identifies New York as a crucial site for the performance of Asian American identity and commentary by using interviews with sixteen noted Asian American theater artists.

Houston, Velina Hasu, ed. *But Still Like Air, I'll Rise: New Asian American Plays.* Philadelphia, Pa.: Temple University Press, 1997. This collection of eleven plays represents a wide range of Asian-descent American playwrights living and working in the United States. Included are plays by both established and new playwrights.

Lee, Josephine. *Performing Asian America: Race and Ethnicity on the Contemporary Stage.* Philadelphia, Pa.: Temple University Press, 1997. A critical study of Asian American drama, this volume offers a wide-ranging analysis of the history and development of Asian American theater and the emergence of "a newer pan-Asian sensibility." Comments on seventeen plays and performance pieces by a dozen of the most significant Asian American theater artists.

Nelson, Brian, ed. *Asian American Drama: Nine Plays from the Multiethnic Landscape.* New York: Applause Books, 1997. Many of the nine plays in this collection are the work of "Third Wave" playwrights. Together, the plays represent a new awareness that identity politics must take into account a variety of non-Asian elements—gender, mixed-race concerns, and European cultures.

Uno, Roberta, ed. *Unbroken Thread: An Anthology of Plays by Asian American Women.* Amherst: University of Massachusetts Press, 1993. A collection of six plays by Genny Lim, Wakako Yamauchi, Momoko Iko, Velina Hasu Houston, Jeannie Barroga, and Elizabeth Wong, this volume also includes a very useful detailed appendix listing plays (and first production dates) by Asian American women. The chosen plays are landmarks in Asian American theater, and are essential reading for a thorough understanding of the contributions of Asian American playwrights to the American stage.

E. D. Huntley

LATINO DRAMA

Identity—that is, one's connection to heritage and search for autonomous existence—has been the leading theme throughout the history of Latino drama in the United States. According to Elizabeth C. Ramírez's *Chicanas/Latinas in American Theatre* (2000), "in earlier decades (primarily during the [Richard] Nixon administration) there was a concerted effort to combine all Spanish-speaking groups in the United States into one, designating the term 'Hispanic' for this massive population." Yet, the term "Hispanic" speaks of a collective, homogeneous Latino experience and ignores the diversity of each single culture that contributes to it. Among the numerous groups that belong to Latino culture in the United States, the three largest are Mexican Americans or Chicanos (American-born Mexicans), Puerto Ricans or Nuyoricans (New Ricans), and Cuban Americans, whose modern theater has acquired several names, including Cuban American and Cuban exile theater. The multitude of terms signify an acute awareness of Latino origins within—and in opposition to—the mainstream culture, a postmodern political consciousness of "the other" as both outsider and insider. "There are many subject positions one must inhabit; one is not just one being," wrote literary critic Gayatri Spivak. "That is when a political consciousness comes in."

Poet and novelist Lois Griffith's writing, as an outcome of such political consciousness, was a political activity. She writes in *Action: The Nuyorican Poets Cafe Theater Festival* (1997), "My cityscape is painted in spit, blood, and curses that depict the devil as the uninformed accomplice in the murder of innocence. Theater captures life's intent from moments when we confront our motives for action." This poet's words demonstrate the very modern, Antonin Artaud-like mission of theater to imitate life. Because modern Latino consciousness is arguably always political consciousness, modern Latino theater as its mirror is always political theater.

ORIGINS

Noted scholar in Latino history Nicolás Kanellos gives the beginning of the nineteenth century, when Mexican and Spanish troupes toured the cities of northern Mexico, as the origin of Latino theater. After the Mexican War (1846-1848), when the United States gained the land constituting the modern-day states of California, Arizona, New Mexico, Nevada, Utah, and Colorado, theatrical culture grew steadily. In Southern and Northern California, the number of theater houses and professional touring companies continued to increase. However, it was not until the beginning of the twentieth century that the first generations of Chicano playwrights emerged, inspired by the events of the Mexican Revolution (1910-1920). Identity and immigration became the thematic orientation of their work. The end of the nineteenth century also witnessed the roots of Cuban American theater. According to Kanellos, the first Cuban American theaters were established by tobacco entrepreneurs who relocated to the coast of Florida because of the turbulent events of the Spanish-American War (1898). The first half of the twentieth century saw a variety of developments and disappointments for Latinos.

The Great Depression devastated Latino theater, and through the 1950's most amateur and professional theaters produced Spanish plays or translated American plays. In the meantime, exciting developments were happening on the international stage. Influential Mexican artists such as Xavier Villaurrutia, co-founder of Teatro de Ulises and Teatro de Orientación, and playwright and political critic Rodolfo Usigli studied drama at Yale University as Rockefeller Fellows.

During the 1940's, one of the most sophisticated national theatrical traditions was developed in Puerto Rico, when many independent theaters emerged. One of these was Emilio S. Belaval's Areyto Drama Society, which produced political plays in the tradition of social realism. Immigrating Puerto Rican artists brought their theatrical expertise to their new home nation. According to Puerto Rican scholar John V. Antush, "not in any of the arts, not even in the novel, has *puertorriqueñidad* emigrated to the United States more effectively than in the drama."

One figure central to this transition was René Marqués. His *La carreta* (pr. 1953; *The Oxcart*, 1969) dealt with the topic of Puerto Rican immigration, thematically grounded in the issues of the psychological impacts of lost and reconstructed identity, disappointment in the motherland, and the prospect of returning home. When *The Oxcart* was first produced by director Roberto Rodríguez Suárez in 1953, it launched the Puerto Rican theater movement in New York. The production was a success and served as an example of political drama for future generations of Puerto Rican playwrights and poets.

In the meantime, events in international theater continued to inspire modern playwrights worldwide. Modernism gave birth to masterminds such as Henrik Ibsen, George Bernard Shaw, Eugene O'Neill, Bertolt Brecht, and Artaud and introduced movements such as realism, expressionism, Surrealism, Theater of the Absurd, and Theater of Cruelty. Social realism, as a philosophical movement that raised political consciousness of the working classes and criticized governments and regimes, was particularly popular in Latin American countries, which had been convulsed by a series of repressive governments and revolutionary upheaval by the beginning of the twentieth century. Social realism became the leading philosophy of the first generations of Latino immigrants, who were also occupied with topics of social justice as well as émigré identity.

1950's AND 1960's

One of the most exciting events in the adolescence of Chicano theater was the founding of El Teatro Campesino by Luis Miguel Valdez in 1965. Born and educated in the United States, playwright Valdez remained involved in the field of Latino theater through activism, writing, and teaching. One of his plays, *Los vendidos* (pr. 1967), gives examples of the ideological apparatus of American-born Latin artists. His cast, consisting of Mexican and Mexican American stereotypes (farmworker, urban Johnny, *revolucionario*) confronts the most uncomfortable myths about the people of Mexican heritage in both Anglo American and Latino cultures. Valdez's El Teatro Campesino produced the newest, most experimental, often most

confrontational works by Latino playwrights, thus starting an official phase in Latino theater that continued to awaken political consciousness in American-born Latino descendants.

Unlike Valdez's Chicano theater, Cuban American independent artists concentrated, during the 1950's and 1960's, on their pasts rather than their futures. The Cuban exile drama of Omar Torres, Julio Matas, José Cid Pérez, Leopoldo Hernández, José Sánchez-Boudy, Celedonio González, Raúl de Cárdenas, and Matías Montes-Huidobro was based on a rich literary heritage of a mother-tongue that was transferred as a "frozen culture" to the new land. The group's dramatic themes were drawn from social difficulties in Cuba, rather than the impact of the culture shock experienced in the United States.

In New York, Roberto Rodríguez Suárez, who directed the successful original production of *The Oxcart* by Marqués, founded Nuevo Círculo Dramático, an important Latino theater on the East Coast, which also served as a professional school for actors, directors, and playwrights. In 1967, Miriam Colón, an actor as well as Rodríguez Suárez's apprentice and collaborator, founded Puerto Rican Traveling Theatre (PRTT) as "a bilingual theatrical organization which would emphasize the dramatic literature of Puerto Rico and Latin America, highlighting the contributions of Hispanic dramatists in the United States, and . . . mak[ing] these theatrical presentations accessible to people." Along with Colón's group, the Ensemble Theatre Studio, the Manhattan Theatre Club, and Circle Rep—all still in existence—provided an arena for experimental Latino theater. In the 1960's the Judson Poets Theater, El Teatro Repertorio Español, Nuestro Teatro, La Mama Experimental Theater Club, and Caffè Cino also proved to be important venues in supporting early Latino drama. Other companies that existed for a shorter term because of the lack of financial stability included the Latin American Theater Ensemble (LATE), Tremont Art Group, and Centro Cultural Cubano.

THE NUYORICAN POETS CAFE

The Nuyorican Poets Cafe, one of the most influential intellectual groups in the history of Latino theater, launched the avant-garde generation of Puerto Rican artists. In 1974, the cafe was founded by Miguel Algarín and provided a space, physical and intellectual, for the development of new work. Playwrights, poets, actors, and directors of different races and heritages, including Miguel Piñero, Wesley Brown, Rome Neal, Lois Elaine Griffith, and Lucky Cienfuegos, joined this collective experience of theater that sought to mirror real life. In *Action: The Nuyorican Poets Cafe Theater Festival*, founder Algarín summarized the mission:

> The Nuyrican Poets Cafe was started so that all actors of all color could drop the bandanas wrapped around their heads, pull the razors out of their pockets and the knives from their jackets, and just act. At the Cafe they auditioned for roles that had substance, knowing they would not be stereotyped into the familiar urban guerilla war front image. We looked to portray the life characterized by urban decay, but after first locating the real pulse of the street. We looked for where the street drama was and who could write about it. Truth first, then theater. Actors benefitted from this process, because they were never asked to devalue their experience and backgrounds by playing *West Side Story* over and over. We looked for theatrical language that realistically portrayed life on Avenues D, C, B, and A, unlike the Hollywood versions epitomized by *Kojak* or *Baretta*. It worked as theater, but it also gave us the means to exorcize the pain in our lives. Theater as catharsis.

The much-celebrated playwright and poet Miguel Piñero became a member of the cafe and a mentor and friend to his colleagues. Piñero began writing under the mentorship of Marvin Felis Camillo while serving his five-year sentence for armed robbery at the prison in Ossining, New York (Sing Sing). There, Camillo's drama workshop grew into an acting company of former convicts called The Family. The Family members cast the original production of Piñero's *Short Eyes: The Killing of a Sex Offender by the Inmates of the House of Detention Awaiting Trial* (pr. 1974), which won the Obie and the New York Drama Critics Award for Best American Play of 1973-1974. *Short Eyes* is set in a house of detention where most of the prisoners are of American minority groups.

Isolated, silenced, hardened by discrimination and the animal conditions of the detention facility, the inmates struggle in search of their true identity and justice in a white man's world. "I feel nothing," says Paco, a Puerto Rican prisoner, "mistake, it happens, *eso pasa*. Someday I'll be in the streets walking, minding my own business, and then boom-boom, I'll be shot down by a police, who will say it's a mistake, I accept it, as part of my *destino*." In the play, innocence and truth rarely survive, according to the *destino* of Paco's people.

Other Latino organizations included the Latin Insomniacs, El Teatro Ambulante, the Rican Organization for Self Advancement, and Teatro Otra Cosa. The WOW Café, Dixon Place, San Diego's Sushi Gallery, and Los Angeles's Highways were spaces of gatherings, work development, and performances as well. These small, antitheatrical, antimainstream performance spaces inspired more than a few future playwrights, including Carmen Rivera, Eduardo Iván López, Reuben Gonzalez, Fred Valle, Yolanda Rodríguez, Eva López, and José Rivera.

"WAVES" OF PLAYWRIGHTS AND THEMES

The decades of 1970's and 1980's offered opportunities and increasing financial support from the government and corporations for experimental work by Latino playwrights. The founding of Cuban playwright and artist Maria Irene Fornes's Lab at INTAR Hispanic American Arts Center in New York marked another important stage in the development of Latino theater, with playwrights such as Eduardo Machado, Cherrie Moraga, and Milcha Sanchez Scott paving the road as the Lab's first generation. Playwright Caridad Svich distinguished the Lab as the beginning of the actual "first wave" in the history of Latino theater, "following the singular presences of Fornes, Piñero, and Valdez." This first wave generation now spoke volumes about the search for Latino identity.

Following the footsteps of Fornes, whose dramatic themes include sexism, class systems, ageism, and other discrimination, Moraga examines ideologies that influence and separate generations. Medea, the heroine of Moraga's *The Hungry Woman* (2001), is a victim of such ideologies. Her life as a warrior woman is torn between the old myths and traditions of the Mexican Indians and the belief systems and freedoms of the American land, creating a place in Medea's mind that is beautiful and magical, yet taxing and self-destructive. An innovative theme that *The Hungry Woman* deals with is homosexuality. "My private parts," says Luna's lesbian lover, "are a battleground. I see struggle there before I see beauty." Like Fornes, Moraga examines the body of a woman as a mother, a lover, a wife, and an object, while inviting the audience to consider homosexuality and homophobia as aspects of Chicano and Anglo culture.

Carmen Rivera, in *Julia de Burgos: Child of Water* (pr. 1999), brings up another crucial theme in Latino experience—literacy. The heroine, Julia Duran, struggles with her inability to read, despite a passionate desire to learn. While a young girl in Puerto Rico, she is inspired by poetess Julia de Burgos but is prevented by her living conditions from receiving the education she craves. Julia experiences immigration, assimilation, marriage, and motherhood. Not until the later years of her life does she learn to read and write, celebrating her accomplishment with her first poem, a symbolic return to the de Burgos poem that inspired her. For Rivera's heroine, empowerment by language and knowledge is one of the goals of the feminist movement and the most important part of one's struggle for independence.

The second wave of Latino playwrights included Migdalia Cruz, Coco Fusco, Nao Bustamante, Carmelita Tropicana, and Mac Wellman. According to Svich, these playwrights were concerned with introducing their identity to the Anglo culture through "a more realistic and more metaphorical kind of representation, one that could exist outside of the imposed 'ghetto' of 'Latino' theater." Cruz's play *Fur* (pr. 1997), for example, deals with the universal topics of beauty, love, and the female body. The play revolves around what seems to be a typical love triangle. The plot achieves absurdity when one of the female characters is seen and described by two others as a furry carnivorous beast that is kept in a cage. The elements of the absurdist theater serve as metaphorical representation of the misogynist objectification of the female body and its imprisonment, or rape, by the male

gaze. The plot amplifies the psychology of lust, jealousy, obsession, and love.

The playwrights in the third wave of Latino theater are united by their goal to strengthen the collective and individual voices of the culture, despite the discomfort of their marginality. Diverse characters, settings, and themes introduce and deconstruct myths and stereotypes about Latino people in order to conduct a common, universal discourse. Some of the Latino playwrights that belong to the third wave are Nilo Cruz, Luis Alfaro, and Naomi Iizuka. Playwright, performer, writer, and journalist Luis Alfaro, in his play *Straight as a Line* (pr. 1994), draws on his role as an AIDS (acquired immunodeficiency syndrome) activist. His only two characters are Mum, a Las Vegas prostitute who abandoned her son, and Paulie, a young homosexual man who worked as a prostitute in New York until contracting AIDS. In this dysfunctional family, the themes of the comedic dialogue deal with survival, body and identity politics, psychoanalysis of family and nation, victimization, and the redemptive pathos of a postmodern lifetime.

The three waves of Latino theater have created new themes and sparked unique artistic discussions. According to Lee A. Jacobus, "gay, lesbian, African American, Hispanic American, and Native American groups have been virtually ignored by commercial theater." Bound together through the common theme of otherness, these groups searched for a language that could not be ignored any longer. Besides the question of national and individual identity, Latino dramatists are now discussing universal questions of class, gender, and sexuality.

Miguel Algarín notes, "(w)hen a people are oppressed, the only way to hold their cultural space is to start talking. Language is inherently biased against people of color—I mean literally how the nouns, adjectives, and verbs work internally to show people their space in society. What language communicates to people who have already been put down is how society regards them; in their case, often with little respect." Speaking through theater, Latino artists have increased their influence on the mainstream culture, advocating not homogeneity and assimilation, but multiculturalism, individualism, and transgression.

BIBLIOGRAPHY

Algarín, Miguel, and Lois Griffith, eds. *Action: The Nuyorican Poets Cafe Theater Festival.* New York: Touchstone, 1997. Provides an overview of the history of the Nuyorican Poets Cafe by the founder.

Arrizon, Alicia. *Latina Performance: Traversing the Stage.* Bloomington: Indiana University Press, 1999. Begins an examination of Latina performance by focusing on early twentieth century oral traditions and theatrical personalities, then traces the subsequent emergence of Latina dramatic aesthetics in its position of "in-betweenness."

Garza, Roberto J., ed. *Contemporary Chicano Theatre.* Notre Dame, Ind.: University of Notre Dame Press, 1976. Traces the development of Mexican American theater in the twentieth century.

Harasym, Sarah, ed. *The Post-Colonial Critic: Interviews, Strategies, Dialogues.* New York: Routledge, 1990. A seminal work that influenced the postcolonial and identity politics movements.

Huerta, Jorge. *Chicano Drama: Performance, Society, and Myth.* New York: Cambridge University Press, 2001. Explores Chicano theater and how it presents its community and identity while caught between the United States and Mexico. Gives biographies of playwrights and analyses of their plays.

Kanellos, Nicolás. *A History of Hispanic Theatre in the United States: Origins to 1940.* Austin: University of Texas Press, 1990. Traces the origins and development of Latino theater in the United States.

Ramírez, Elizabeth C. *Chicanas/Latinas in American Theatre: A History of Performance.* Bloomington: Indiana University Press, 2000. A feminist critical source on playwrights in Latino theater.

Svich, Caridad, and María Teresa Marrero, eds. *Out of the Fringe: Contemporary Latina/Latino Theatre and Performance.* New York: Theatre Communications Group, 2000. Traces three distinct stages in contemporary Latino theater and examines their trends and themes.

Vera V. Chernysheva

NATIVE AMERICAN DRAMA

Native American drama is both contemporary and lost in time, readily accessible and nearly irretrievable, familiar in form and uncharted in contour. This double aspect of what can be considered the drama of Native Americans comes from two separate bodies of work: one, an ethnic drama that flourished in the last three decades of the twentieth century and continues to flourish; the other, a living art form tied to religion, ritual, and dance that began to perish at the end of the nineteenth century with the increasing removal of Indian peoples to reservations and that is now all but lost as a vibrant form.

HISTORICAL BACKGROUND

Contemporary Native American drama, like the drama of other American minority groups, was born in the cultural revolution of the late 1960's and early 1970's as the success of the Civil Rights movement and the failure of the Vietnam War became apparent to most Americans. As the viewpoint of a single dominant racial group loosened its hold on the culture, the validity of other viewpoints was considered. Drama was a powerful tool in this cultural revolution. Black playwright Lorraine Hansberry's *A Raisin in the Sun* (pr. 1959) gave Americans an unforgettable glimpse of the dignity and self-defined agency of an African American family. Frank Chin and other Asian American playwrights established a theater group that would educate the United States about issues such as the atrocities of Angel Island, the heroism of workers on the transcontinental railroad, and the unnecessary humiliation of the Japanese American internment camps.

The American Indian Theatre Ensemble, founded in 1972 and changed to the Native American Theatre Ensemble in 1973, took on the tremendous and exhilarating task of presenting, through drama, Native Americans in their own terms. The figure of the Indian in American literature, as in popular literature and culture of several centuries, was a misrepresentation, skewered between the misbegotten poles of the uncivilized "savage" and the romantic keeper of nature's secrets. In a labor no less Herculean than that of African American dramatists, Native American playwrights tried to shake themselves free of centuries of stereotypes to create realistic characters conceived from their own personal experiences. The American Indian Theater Ensemble resolved not only to rectify the cultural image of the Native American but also to produce a body of drama intended primarily for the Indian community.

HANAY GEIOGAMAH

A key figure in the history of contemporary Native American drama is playwright Hanay Geiogamah. His work is well represented in two anthologies of Native American drama: *Seventh Generation: An Anthology of Native American Plays* (1999) and *Stories of Our Way: An Anthology of American Indian Plays* (1999). Of Kiowa and Delaware background, Geiogamah was active in the crucial founding years of the American Indian Theatre Ensemble, which produced his one-act play *Body Indian* (pr. 1972).

Body Indian is a difficult play and demonstrates the problems Native American playwrights face in creating a new, realistic drama based on contemporary Native American life. At first reading, the play seems to be about alcoholism (a disease that has disproportionately plagued Native Americans since early European settlers used alcohol as an item of trade), and its realism is intense and shocking. Bobby, in his thirties, is alcoholic; he has lost a leg in a drunken stupor on the railroad tracks. As the play begins, he arrives at his Indian "uncle's" apartment with two of his aunts. The group gathered there has been drinking for some time, as have Bobby and his aunts. There is some socializing and more drinking. Then Bobby, who has hidden in his artificial leg some money he plans to use to enter a detoxification program, passes out. The group of friends and relatives move toward him, intent on finding some cash to restock the dwindling wine supply. Before the play ends, Bobby has been robbed a half dozen times; his money is gone, and his uncle is about to leave the apartment to pawn Bobby's artificial leg.

The problem for a mainstream audience is the tone of the play: The intense realism seems to be the tool of social tragedy. In an interview in a special "Ethnic Theater" issue (1989-1990) of the multicultural literary journal *Melus* celebrating the first ten years of the New WORLD Theater, Geiogamah himself admits to being unsure of the play's tone before he took it to a Native American audience. That audience's reaction to the humorous side of the play made the playwright realize he had created a tragicomedy, one that not only successfully brought a social problem into the light of community attention but also emphasized the indigenous communities' ability to survive the most hopeless of situations. The "sardonic smile" that the stage directions indicate Bobby is wearing as he surveys his final state in the play has been linked to the Coyote/Trickster character in Native American mythology: Have we been tricked into overlooking the humor of the play?

The play also functions at a symbolic level, as the title *Body Indian* suggests: Bobby represents the impoverished Native American population, bled of vitality to a level at which victims begin to victimize each other. Sound effects of drum and rattles compete with the sound of an approaching train and train whistle; stage directions indicate that the cast freezes at this symbolic annunciation of European modernity, the soulless culture that has terrorized the Native American population as it displaced them from their homelands.

Another play by Geiogamah is *49* (pr. 1975). This upbeat play deals with the kind of social gathering of primarily young Native Americans called the "49." The event begins after midnight and lasts through the night; it is a social, sexual, and spiritual event during which young Native Americans discard their apathy toward tradition and sing the songs of the tribe. The vitality of a whole people flows back into them, and they actively resist police efforts to break up their gathering. The pace of the play is quick as scenes alternate between the choruslike prophecies of Night Walker, the ceremonial leader, and the looming confrontation between the young group and the police.

The tone of the play is the polar opposite of *Body Indian*; the resistance and hope of the young people in the play reflect the increasing optimism and activism of the mid-1970's.

WILLIAM S. YELLOW ROBE, JR.

Another influential and prolific playwright is William S. Yellow Robe, Jr., an Assiniboine Sioux from the Fort Peck reservation in Montana. He has been associated with the Sante Fe Institute of American Indian Arts (IAIA), where he taught playwriting for three years beginning in 1993. The IAIA had been running a training program in indigenous theater for several years at the time Yellow Robe joined the faculty. Like Geiogamah, Yellow Robe employs a social realism in his plays that is tempered with the moderating influence of memory and tradition.

Yellow Robe's *The Independence of Eddie Rose* (pr. 1991) depicts a few days in the life of a dysfunctional Native American family. Eddie, sixteen, is torn between a desire to flee the reservation and a need to protect his younger sister from the threat of sexual abuse from his mother's current boyfriend. Help and guidance are provided by his aunt Thelma, who retains the healing ways of the community. Eddie, only a teenager himself, forces his mother to sign papers documenting her boyfriend's sexual abuse and signing over custody of his sister to his aunt before he leaves home. Eddie's vitality and instinctive turning to healing ways mark a turning away from an attitude of helpless victimization.

Yellow Robe has been an articulate spokesperson for Native American theater. Interviewed for the special "Ethnic Theater" issue of *Melus* by Roberta Uno, an Asian American playwright and then artistic director of New WORLD Theater, the Montana writer spoke out on differing expectations of mainstream and minority playwrights. Although mainstream writers are seen as possessing individual voices, minority authors are seen as spokespersons for their people, he asserted. Commenting on his own choice to work on the East Coast rather than the West Coast, Yellow Robe pointed out that, for many Westerners, the idea of paying money to see Indians perform onstage is totally alien.

In his one-act play *Sneaky* (pr. 1987), Yellow Robe constructs a rebellion against the meaninglessness of modernity. The three Rose brothers, all in their thirties, steal their mother's body from a funeral parlor in order to give her a traditional funeral and send her back to her people properly. A good deal of comedy ensues as Frank, the oldest and the mastermind of the plan, tries to convince the others while supervising Kermit, the youngest, who is in an alcoholic haze. The act pulls the three brothers together; in the final scene, their mother's body is placed in a tree and, searching for an Indian way to pray, they create an "Our Father" prayer that deconstructs modernity.

OTHER MODERN PLAYWRIGHTS

Like every form of minority drama, Native American drama has to fight against indifference and lack of knowledge on the part of some mainstream audiences. The playwright must be aware that he or she is also writing for audiences who may not be aware that Indians still exist. This creates a double burden of the need to educate as well as to create vibrant drama, a heavy load for any playwright to incorporate into a single play.

Roxy Gordon and Leanne Howe, both Choctaws, demonstrated in their *Indian Radio Days* (pr. 1993) just how light that burden could appear to be. The play is structured as a radio show, with the narrator interviewing a flotsam of characters involved in key historical events, pseudo-events, or the fabrication of the many stereotypes surrounding American indigenous citizens. The pace of the play is light and fast, and the tone is bracingly ironic, building as the stranger-than-fiction events of Native American history race by. Performances of the play gain spontaneity as bingo cards are distributed to the audience, who play periodically and listen to the "Rez" (reservation) gossip of a Bingo Lady.

Other representative playwrights include the three Miguel sisters, founders in 1975 of Spiderwoman Theater, whose drama has done much to reincarnate the figures and themes of traditional native legends, and Diane Glancey, whose *The Woman Who Was a Red Deer Dressed for the Deer Dance* (pr. 1995) ex-

plores the theme of intergenerational conflict and the transmission of traditional values. As more anthologies of contemporary Native American drama are published, the astounding variety and creativity of the contemporary scene become more apparent.

RECONSTRUCTING A LOST DRAMA

If history is examined beyond the removal and displacement of native peoples, the outlines of a living culture in which dance and drama were an integral part of a way of life can be glimpsed. Hints of what this drama was like can be found in the records of anthropology and in a few extraordinary documents such as *Black Elk Speaks: Being the Life Story of a Holy Man of the Oglala Sioux*, an account of the Oglala Sioux Horse Dance performed in the 1870's by the nonnative poet John G. Neihardt that was first published in 1932. The story of this performance was told to Neihardt by Black Elk, the young visionary who transformed a private vision-dream into a healing performance for his nation.

Neihardt's book contains an account of both the vision that Black Elk had as a nine-year-old boy and an account of the performance event that was informed by this vision, an event that took place when the visionary was seventeen years old. Neihardt's rendering of Black Elk's account offers students of Native American drama a rare opportunity to study the connection between private vision and community performance. It also poses a challenge to the typical European understanding of what drama is: The portrait of a hero or heroine struggling against society and its conventions is a product of nineteenth and twentieth century forces of modernity, forces that have increasingly focused on the individual and have seemingly exiled the spirit world from creative performance.

To understand the Oglala Sioux performance of the Horse Dance as described in Neihardt's account, it is important to imagine a dramatized version of *Piers Plowman*, the medieval poem in which the dream-vision of a young man helps him construct a way of healing for his people. Here the focus is not on the individual but on the communal; the imaginative act of the visionary becomes the treasured road that will redeem his people from annihilation.

Because the language used to describe theater performance is tied to the conventions of European drama, there are no categorical terms to describe the kind of performance Black Elk describes; "pageant" may be close to the reality of the enormous communal effort, one that took place outside in a space approximately the size of a football field. At the center of the field is the Rainbow Tipi, the site of the drama's beginning when the young visionary enters the tent and encounters the Six Elders, who present him with gifts for his journey.

Outside the tent, at the four corners of the compass, teams of horsemen wait, mounted, for the slow, clockwise rotation around the tent that enacts the events of the vision. In the tipi, the Elders draw a sacred circle on the ground and paint on it to show a red road from north to south and a black road from east to west. They beat their drums and sing verses about each group of horses, which rotate with the chanting.

It becomes increasingly clear in the narrative of the performance the extent to which the horse is at the center of the pageant; this is an important point, for the Horse Dance is a celebration of the horse during which human beings cross over the border of creaturehood and dwell in the skin of the horse, seeing creation with the eyes of a fellow creature.

The Japanese writer Yuko Tsushima has commented on the narrative art of the Ainu people, the indigenous hunters displaced from Japan's main island by agricultural immigrants from Korea some thirteen hundred years ago, praising their narratives for an unusual shifting of point of view: In the tale of the bear, the bear is the first-person narrator. This very quality, which Tsushima prizes in Ainu tales, is at the center of the Horse Dance; at the moment of the shifting point of view, humankind is back under the skin of grace. At the point of the shift, Black Elk reports the neighing response of the horses as he sees again in the sky the vision that had troubled him as a child.

The procession of horses and riders makes a complete revolution around the field. As the second revolution starts, spectators join in the procession, both on horseback and walking. At the end of the procession,

the sacred circle in the Rainbow Tipi is examined; the earth there now shows the marks of tiny horse hooves. Right relation has been restored by crossing over into the creaturehood of another being. Tales of healing begin to pour in to Black Elk.

Although Neihardt's record presents an unusual opportunity to participate imaginatively in a lost form of Native American drama, it is not the only such source. Works like *Cherokee Dance and Drama* by Frank G. Speck, Leonard Broom, and Will West Long (1951) also reconstruct some of the drama-pageants of Native Americans, most of which involve a similar crossing over to an animal point of view.

Exploring the records of the lost drama-pageants heightens appreciation of contemporary Native American drama and other genres. Spiderwoman Theater's *Power Pipes* (pr. 1992) is a modern dance-drama featuring characters such as Wind Horse Spirit Warrior and Owl Messenger; the play is performed on the borders of myth and reality. Such an investigation also deepens understanding of the dramatic narratives of Leslie Marmon Silko: *Ceremony* (1977) and *Storyteller* (1981) exist at the moment of crossing over from the modern to the mythic, from the fragmentation of the contemporary to the wholeness under the skin of creation.

BIBLIOGRAPHY

Black Elk, Nicholas, and John G. Neihardt. *Black Elk Speaks: Being the Life Story of a Holy Man of the Oglala Sioux*. 1932. Reprint. Lincoln: University of Nebraska Press, 2000. A key work for penetrating beyond the loss and erosion of Native American culture to recapture part of the mystery and power of the pageant-drama. Contains helpful illustrations.

Geiogamah, Hanay, and Jaye T. Darby, eds. *Stories of Our Way: An Anthology of American Indian Plays*. Los Angeles: University of California, Los Angeles American Indian Studies Center, 1999. Geiogamah has written an informative introduction for this anthology that outlines the history of Native American playwriting since 1970. Contains a wide variety of representative Native American plays from the last three decades of the twentieth century as well as the text of Lynn Riggs's *Cherokee Nights* (pb. 1936).

Gisolfi, Mimi, ed. *Seventh Generation: An Anthology of Native American Plays*. New York: Theatre Communications Group, 1999. This pioneering anthology brings together many of the best plays from representative Native American playwrights. Valuable information is included about each playwright and the production history of each play. A useful introduction invites comparison between indigenous sand paintings and Italian sawdust paintings, symbols of an art that is destroyed to give a sense of healing.

Speck, Frank G., and Leonard Broom, in collaboration with Will West Long. *Cherokee Dance and Drama*. Berkeley: University of California Press, 1951. This work preserves many of the seasonal dance-dramas of the Cherokee. It succeeds in placing the drama within the context of Cherokee life. Diagrams of dance patterns are included as well as photographs of dance masks.

Hideyuki Kasuga

AMERICAN REGIONAL THEATER

"Regional theater" has always been an uncomfortable term for the network of professional nonprofit theaters that are found throughout the United States. One of the movement's pioneers, Nina Vance, said the term made them sound second-class, and although many agree with her, no one has coined a better term. Some theaters tried the term "resident theater," but that implied a resident company that they did not have. "Repertory theater" was tried as well, but performing plays in repertory means alternating the same shows throughout the season, and most of the theaters were not doing that. As uneasily as the title fits, "regional theater" has become the catch-all term for most theaters outside New York City that use professional personnel but operate as not-for-profit businesses. Other theaters outside New York City include community, college/university, or professional commercial theaters such as dinner, touring, and outdoor theaters.

Hundreds of fine regional theaters exist across the United States, producing interesting revivals of the classics as well as provocative new plays and experimental works. Most regional theaters owe much to the communities that support them, and in return they offer an array of services such as school performances and tours, training for young people, and other educational programs. Like the city ballet and orchestra, the regional theater now enjoys a foothold in the cultural landscape of most American cities and of many smaller towns and rural areas. Unfortunately, however, this was not always the case. It has taken nearly one hundred years and the efforts of some very determined artists for professional theater to spread its wings and escape the confines of the commercial theater district of Broadway to earn the reputation it enjoys today.

EARLY TWENTIETH CENTURY ROOTS

At the turn of the twentieth century, American theater was very much a commercial venture. It had evolved from the colonial days of British touring companies into a network of theater "circuits" that were controlled and operated, at first, by prominent family companies. Early pioneers of American theater brought the English tradition of a resident company to the shores of the United States in the early 1800's. Throughout the nineteenth century those companies concentrated their performances in certain areas of the eastern United States. These circuits relied on a series of theaters in towns of close proximity, and the companies would perform on a regular basis in the theaters, moving from town to town. By the mid- to late nineteenth century, the theater had become a prominent social gathering place. Theatergoers often cared less about the play and more about seeing certain actors, thus giving rise to the American "star system." By the end of the century, resident companies were a thing of the past and managers were casting star players to tour the circuits for a purely commercial audience. These circuits were eventually taken over by an unofficial "family" of powerful theatrical producers who came to be known as New York's theatrical "Syndicate," a cartel of sorts that controlled first-class theatrical production in the United States for a period of time.

Meanwhile, European theater experienced an artistic revolution during this period. Norwegian playwright Henrik Ibsen introduced a new kind of play genre known as "realism," in which actors had to behave more naturalistically onstage. Punctuated by themes of social significance and psychological depth, this new approach inspired directors like Konstantin Stanislavsky, who formed the Moscow Art Theatre with writer Anton Chekhov in the late 1890's. Stanislavsky realized that realist plays required a new kind of actor, and over a period of several decades, he developed his "method" of teaching actors, which evolved into standard practice in Europe and in the United States. It was the touring of Stanislavsky's "independent" art theater company (and others like his) in the United States that inspired the movement toward artistic theater in America.

THE RISE OF THE "LITTLE THEATER"

Around the time of World War I, the United States' commercial theater experienced a decline. The advent of film excited mainstream audiences, and many flocked to each new release, leaving conventional theater behind. The Syndicate dissolved, and instead of theater circuits and live performances, "moving pictures" were appearing in most of the old theaters. Theater artists who witnessed the touring performances of the European companies became enthusiastic about this new kind of theater, and the Little Theater movement was born. In emulation of the European independent art theaters, more than fifty groups formed their own "little theaters" across the country—notably in Chicago, New York, Detroit, and Provincetown, Massachusetts. From 1912 until 1920, members of the Little Theater movement studied and reproduced new drama and production methods and contributed greatly to the artistic life of American theater.

A need for funding eventually dampened the artistic goals of most of these theaters until they came to be known as "community theaters," relying on recent Broadway hits and pageantry to survive. On the positive side, however, the Little Theater movement introduced the idea of producing professional theater outside of Broadway's commercial companies, and by 1925, there were almost two thousand community theaters registered with the Drama League of America, a group started in 1910 that supported and encouraged local development of theater.

Former members of the Little Theater groups, especially the Washington Square Players and the Provincetown Players, went on to lend their extraordinary talents to developing several resident or repertory theaters. After the Washington Square Players split up, some members formed the Theatre Guild, a highly respected group dedicated to producing professional theater without regard to commercial value. The Provincetown Players began in 1916 in Massachusetts and soon moved to New York City, becoming a highly prolific company in the following decade. Although the Provincetown Players, the Theatre Guild, and groups others like them finally succumbed to financial pressures and either turned to commercial ventures or completely disbanded by the late 1920's, they made valuable contributions to the revolution toward artistic theater in the United States.

THE FEDERAL THEATRE PROJECT

Another important contribution to the American theater revolution came from an unlikely source—the government. With the United States suffering through a long economic depression in the 1930's, President Franklin D. Roosevelt instituted the Works Progress Administration (WPA), a national program to revitalize the country's economy by putting Americans to work on federal projects. One of the most remarkable sections of the WPA was the Federal Theatre Project (FTP). Centered in New York and headed by a college drama professor named Hallie Flanagan, the FTP initiated a tremendous number of programs throughout the country. It ran training programs for directors, playwrights, and actors; created new theaters dedicated to ethnic groups and minorities; and encouraged theaters to be established in odd places such as warehouses, high school auditoriums, and outdoor parks. Although it lasted only four years, the impact of the FTP on American theater, especially the regional theater movement, is undeniable. Without these new theaters and theater artists who gained their training and experience in an FTP theater, the future of the noncommercial theater would have been an uncertain one. Many of those inspired by Flanagan and the FTP soon became directly responsible for making regional theater a reality.

REGIONAL THEATER PIONEERS

By the end of the 1930's, drama curriculum was being offered in colleges and universities, nearly every large township had a community theater, and the American public had been introduced to many new forms of drama and production techniques. However, the best theater, the professional venue, remained in New York City on Broadway or in professional touring companies that emanated from it. It would take the efforts of three adventurous women to begin a serious movement toward decentralizing American professional theater.

Although an organization known as the American National Theatre and Academy (ANTA) was chartered by Congress in 1935 to help establish theaters outside New York City and an academy to train theatrical personnel, it received very little funding and became, instead, a center for networking news and information about the American theater. Yet ANTA stalled after the FTP took the lead in theater matters and, later, as World War II occurred. A woman named Margo Jones, however, picked up the torch in 1947 and opened the country's first professional arena theater (theater-in-the-round) in her native Dallas, Texas. She had served as assistant director for the Houston Federal Theatre, which failed to succeed but initiated an adult performing group started in 1936 called the Houston Community Players. Jones eventually made the theater her full-time job. It was with this group that she introduced the arena staging method, which, along with being recognized as the mother of regional theater, would become her "claim to fame." In 1944, she received a grant from the Rockefeller Foundation to develop her plan for a professional nonprofit theater in her hometown of Dallas.

In June, 1947, she opened Theatre '47, a name that changed each year (Theatre '48, Theatre '49). The theater closed four years after her untimely death in 1955. Her book, *Theatre-in-the-Round* (1951), outlined her ideas about arena staging as well as her strategies for creating and maintaining a professional theater. It became a noted reference to those interested in the movement and for those who chose to follow in her footsteps.

Another important step in the revolution was taken by a woman who had worked with Jones and the Houston Community Players and who began her own independent theater in Houston in 1947. Nina Vance met with a group of interested people, thirty-seven of whom donated a small sum each to begin a season of plays and the Alley Theatre was born. Though completely amateur through its first few years, Vance struggled with the problems of finding and relying on volunteer personnel. In the early 1950's, she persuaded the board of directors to allow payment to a few "semiprofessional" actors. Al-

though this did not sit well with the community volunteers who had worked so hard to make the Alley a success, it was the best decision for the survival of Vance's dream. In 1954, the Alley became a fully professional theater, hiring only Equity actors (Actors' Equity is the union that all professional theater actors join to be labeled as "professional") and granting professional experience to talented rising actors, directors, and designers. In 1960, the Alley Theatre became one of the first regional theaters to receive a major grant from the Ford Foundation. The three-year promise of $156,000 would enable the theater to attract better-known actors who would work in Houston for the $200-a-week salary for more than forty weeks in a season. This nearly quadrupled the usual salary of $57.50 and put the Alley Theatre on the road to permanence and national recognition. In 1962 the Alley Theatre received another substantial grant, enabling it to construct its permanent home, a structure completed in 1968 and opened with national press attention. The Alley Theatre remains one of the most prestigious and successful regional theaters in the country.

A few years after the founding of Theatre '47 and the Alley Theater, Zelda Fichandler opened the Arena Stage in Washington, D.C., in 1950. Like Vance before her, Fichandler received important grants from the Ford Foundation to support her company, hold actor training, and obtain a permanent theater building. Fichandler's company, unlike Vance's, began as a professional venture with Equity actors. Her seasons introduced revivals of popular American plays such as Tennessee Williams's *The Glass Menagerie* (pr. 1944) along with the classics and new plays by established writers like Arthur Miller and Agatha Christie. Fichandler's theater soon became the most recognized and highly respected regional theater in the country and the acknowledged capital of arena staging. Its premiere of *The Great White Hope* in 1967 marked a major turning point in the history of regional theater. Howard Sackler's play, based on the life of black boxing champion Jack Johnson, played to such an enthusiastic reception from audiences and critics alike that it became a film and moved to Broadway. It garnered many awards, including the

1969 Pulitzer Prize. This type of recognition for an original play that premiered in regional theater was a new phenomenon and sparked the interest of a national audience in the value of regional theaters and their place in developing new drama.

THE ACTORS' WORKSHOP

A theatrical revolution had clearly begun, and other groups sprang up across the country, emulating the style, format, and function of the Alley Theatre and the Arena Stage, but each with its own distinct leader and vision. Some of the most notable include the Milwaukee Repertory Theater, The Charles Playhouse in New England, and the Actors' Workshop of San Francisco. The latter deserves special mention in any overview of the early days of regional theater. Founded by two college professors, Herbert Blau and Jules Irving in 1952, the Actors' Workshop held the dream of many for becoming a "national theater," something that still eludes American society. Notably, it was the first company outside New York to sign an Off-Broadway contract with Actors' Equity, and although important historically, this was not a force of stability for the actors, whose salaries were extremely low. With their first grant from the Ford Foundation, however, the Actors' Workshop became financially viable and in 1960 started rotating its repertory. This was a risky move for that era, but the Actors' Workshop was making history with its approach.

Although the Actors' Workshop did interesting experimental work and maintained its professional status, it never formed a true bond with its community. While other regional theaters were finding ways to give back to their cities through educational programs aimed toward cultural enrichment, the Actors' Workshop made no effort to compromise, serve, or break down the wall of apathy apparent in its audience. In 1965, Blau and Irving were invited to head the Repertory Theater of Lincoln Center in New York City. Perhaps they saw this as a chance to finally establish a national theater, but Blau soon discovered he was unsuited to management and left Irving to carry on. Irving left the Repertory Theater in 1972, abandoning the dream that he and Blau had pinned their hopes on years earlier.

THE GUTHRIE THEATER

The 1963 opening of the Guthrie Theater in Minneapolis, Minnesota, signaled the significant evolution of regional theater. The Guthrie was founded by Sir Tyrone Guthrie, Oliver Rea, and Peter Zeisler, all of whom left behind prosperous theatrical careers because of a growing dissatisfaction with their work in London and New York. Instead of relying on their hometowns, the trio did an exhaustive search for the right locale in which to situate their theater. They decided Minneapolis had the right cultural climate to support a theater that focused on revivals of classic plays. The three men, however, demanded that most of the money needed would have to be committed up front before they would take residence in the city. The locals came through with more than $2 million plus a grant from the Walker Foundation for the land and money for construction. Unlike Vance, Fichandler, Blau, and Irving, who started theaters using unorthodox locales such as a beer factory or judo academy, the Guthrie founders created their own complex. A volunteer organization sold thousands of subscriptions and secured an audience of nearly 200,000 for the inaugural season. The Guthrie's opening is thought by some to have been a defining moment in the history of regional theater. The idea of a classical repertory of plays done in a new facility with the brightest of professional theater's talents had an undeniable impact on theater in the United States.

One of the Guthrie Theater's major impacts came in the area of actor training. Before the Guthrie introduced performances of such demanding literature, there was little attempt to help actors understand the psychological nuances of contemporary plays such as those by Williams and Edward Albee. Very little, if any, training was offered in voice production or movement. Because of the physical demands of plays by William Shakespeare, Molière, Sophocles, and others, new actor training programs recognized the need for a more comprehensive curriculum in preparing the actors' instruments of voice and body for the stage. Since its opening, the Guthrie has enjoyed a prestigious reputation, critical success, and audience support. It remains one of the foremost regional theaters in the United States.

REGIONAL THEATER COMES OF AGE

Although the regional theater movement has seemed at times like a disparate band of independent thinkers chasing their own visions of the perfect theater, several of the original objectives held by Jones, Vance, and Fichandler have remained the same. The first, and probably most important, vision was to create an atmosphere in which quality professional theater could flourish outside Broadway's commercial enterprises. The idea that good theater is for everyone and should not be confined to one area of the country stayed central to the movement in all stages of its development. This philosophy helped give birth to a number of theaters that meet the needs of a diverse, multicultural American community. Independently, many regional theaters continued the efforts of the Federal Theatre Project in supporting and encouraging the expansion of theater with the inclusion of ethnic and minority groups. The decentralization of American professional theater was a move away not just from the bright lights of Broadway but from the largely white, upper-middle-class audiences who patronized it.

The other dominant objective for regional theater has been to offer completely professional theater in a noncommercial venue. The opportunity to take risks and not to serve the whims of the popular audience has been, perhaps, regional theater's second-greatest accomplishment. Thanks to the generous funding of many foundations, such as the Ford, Rockefeller, and Doris Duke foundations, regional theaters have been able to remain financially solvent while exploring the artistic boundaries of theater. Government funding from the National Endowment for the Arts (NEA) has also been instrumental in furthering the progress of educational programs offered to the communities the theaters serve.

The final sustaining goal of the regional theater movement has been to remain independent in vision and mission. In the early days, the passionate pioneers focused all their energy toward creating a theater free from the restrictions and censorship prevalent in commercial theater. Each had a vision of how theater could or should be. It is the dream of nearly every theater entrepreneur to have a company of actors who can explore and stretch the boundaries of drama and production methods according to their own philosophies. This drive toward independence has led to a rich diversity in contemporary regional theaters. There are theaters that focus solely on Shakespeare, the classics, developing new plays, European drama, minority drama, women's issues, experimental work, and many other avenues. There is no rule that says a regional theater has to work with any one kind of drama, staging method, actor, or theatrical space.

SUPPORT AND ADVOCACY

The League of Resident Theatres (LORT) was established in the mid-1960's by Peter Zeisler of the Guthrie Theater, Thomas Fichandler from the Arena Stage, and a lawyer, Morris Kaplan, to serve as a trade organization for resident theaters. It negotiates contracts with the various theater unions and serves as the main regulating body for the country's network of professional nonprofit theaters. LORT's objectives are to promote the general welfare of resident theaters in the United States, to encourage community interest and effective communication between theaters and the public, to assist resident theaters in dealing with labor relations and legal activities, and to inform government agencies of theaters' needs. The membership requirements are minimal but include provisions for the following: that all member theaters be incorporated as nonprofit Internal Revenue Service-approved organizations, that each self-produced production be rehearsed for a minimum of three weeks, that the theater have a playing season of twelve weeks or more, and that the theater operate under a LORT-Equity contract. As of 2001, LORT boasted a membership of seventy-five theaters spread across the United States, including the Arena Stage, the Alley Theatre, the Guthrie Theater, and the Milwaukee Repertory Theatre, as well as other prominent theaters such as the Long Wharf Theatre, the Mark Taper Forum, and the Goodman Theatre.

Another organization that has given support, encouragement, and advocacy to the United States' professional nonprofit theaters is the Theatre Communications Group (TCG), which began in the early 1970's to serve the broader needs of the country's professional nonprofit theaters. Its list of board members over the years has featured prominent personalities of the American theater scene. Past presidents include Nina Vance and Oliver Rea. At the turn of the twenty-first century, TCG had more than four hundred member theaters and seventeen thousand individual members. It offers an employment search network, legal advice, and lobbying power in Washington D.C.; publishes *American Theatre* magazine; and supports workshops, new plays, conferences, and all other services pertaining to the support of regional theater.

UNIVERSITY PROGRAMS

One final aspect of contemporary American regional theater is its support of university training programs for theater artists. The FTP of the 1930's encouraged the development of university drama programs, but it was not until the emergence of prominent regional theaters that training took a more professional direction. The availability of professional theater jobs outside New York City created a new demand for more professional degrees to be offered in the university setting. The combination of university training programs with regional theaters was a natural marriage of convenience during the last quarter of the twentieth century. Degrees such as the bachelor of fine arts (BFA) and master's of fine arts (MFA) are now offered in every aspect of theater—acting, directing, designing—by most theater departments in the United States' major universities. Many have a direct association with a regional theater or have a nonprofit professional theater on or near the campus. Students train in the classroom and then provide valuable services to the regional theater working as assistants, apprentices, ushers, and so forth. The association with the theater gives students an opportunity to witness professional theater in action while providing them with valuable theater experience for their résumés.

BIBLIOGRAPHY

Beeson, William, ed. *Thresholds: The Story of Nina Vance's Alley Theatre*. Houston: Wall, 1968. An account of the founding and development of the Alley Theatre in Houston. A good reference for those wanting details of the earliest regional theater development.

Berkowitz, Gerald M. *New Broadways: Theatre Across America, Approaching a New Millennium*. Rev. ed. New York: Applause Theatre Book Publishers, 1996. Traces the development of American theater since 1950 with special attention to Off-Broadway and the rise and spread of regional theater.

Blau, Herbert. *The Impossible Theatre: A Manifesto*. New York: Macmillan, 1964. Cofounder of the Actors' Workshop in San Francisco, Blau shares his personal philosophies concerning theater. Sometimes esoteric and hard to follow, his book is nonetheless a valuable resource for any student of the early days of American regional theater.

Cohen, Leah Hager. *The Stuff of Dreams: Behind the Scenes of an American Community Theater*. New York: Viking Penguin, 2001. Chronicles "a year in the life" of a small theater near Boston, Massachusetts, focusing specifically on four parallel story lines as the theater sets out to produce David Henry Hwang's *M. Butterfly*. Enlightening for its glimpse into contemporary community theater production.

Flanagan, Hallie. *Arena*. New York: Duell, Sloan, and Pearce, 1940. Hallie Flanagan's personal account of the Federal Theatre Project is interesting and important reading for any student of American theater. She details the program from its beginnings until its end.

Guthrie, Tyrone. *A Life in the Theatre*. New York: McGraw-Hill, 1959. Sir Tyrone's personal account of his prestigious theatrical career, including his founding and directorship of the Guthrie Theater in Minneapolis.

Hewitt, Barnard. *Theatre U.S.A., 1665-1957*. New York: McGraw-Hill, 1959. Hewitt's book is an important source of information on the history of American theater from its colonial beginnings to the mid-twentieth century. He covers the Little Theater movement and Federal Theatre Project quite well.

Jones, Margo. *Theatre-in-the-Round*. New York: McGraw-Hill, 1951. Margo Jones, the mother of the regional theater movement, tells her own story of the founding and operation of Theatre '47 in Dallas, Texas.

Zeigler, Joseph Wesley. *Regional Theatre: The Revolutionary Stage*. New York: Da Capo Press, 1977. Zeigler's undisputed bible of the American regional theater movement covers the earliest days to the beginning of its golden era in the mid-1970's. A comprehensive, personal, and helpful account of the story of regional theater in the United States.

Jill Stapleton-Bergeron

NEW YORK THEATER: ON AND OFF-BROADWAY

New York City and professional theater in the United States are such natural associations that it takes an effort of the historical imagination to recall that, in the days before sound movies came along, virtually every city had a theater for visiting performances and larger cities had resident stock companies of their own. Early in the nineteenth century, however, New York City established its centrality in the nation's theatrical activity, and with time came the preeminence of Broadway as a theater district and as an international entertainment icon. Even now, after many economic and artistic vicissitudes, Broadway is to theater what Hollywood is to movies—the mainstream, the standard setter. If Broadway signifies mainstream, Off-Broadway (and its 1960's sibling Off-Off-Broadway) means experiment, unorthodoxy, and quite often outrageous provocation.

EIGHTEENTH AND NINETEENTH CENTURIES

Theater in New York City long predates the emergence of Times Square as its geographical and symbolic center. As it did everywhere in the United States, the theater had a slow and uncertain early development in New York. The historical record shows no true professional theatrical activity in the city before approximately 1750, when Englishmen Walter Murray and Thomas Kean presented William Shakespeare's *Richard III* (pr. c. 1592-1593) in the Nassau Street Theatre, a venue used before only for amateur theatricals. Another British group, the Hallam Brothers' London Company of Comedians (later renamed the American Company), successfully promoted the construction of three new theaters, the main one being at John Street in lower Manhattan. The repertory of these pioneer troupes was entirely British, including *Richard III*, Shakespeare's *The Merchant of Venice* (pr. c. 1596-1597), and Joseph Addison's *Cato* (pr. 1713).

The American Revolution (1776-1783) put a temporary end to professional theatrical activity in New York City, but when the theaters reopened there were American playwrights and American plays to join the previous repertoire of British imports. Royall Tyler's historically important *The Contrast* was presented at the John Street Theater in April, 1787, and 1789 saw the debut (also at the John Street Theater) of William Dunlap's *The Father: Or, American Shandyism.* Dunlap's busy and prolific career in theater would earn him the unofficial title of Father of American Drama.

When the John Street Theater closed in 1798, New York's center of theatrical activity became the Park Theatre, which was also managed by the versatile Dunlap. For the next quarter century, the Park was the leading theatrical venue in the city, serving as the American performing home to leading performers from England and helping to develop native-born acting talent such as Edwin Forrest, J. H. Hackett, and Charlotte Cushman.

Well into the nineteenth century, the United States remained culturally dependent on England and Europe. Thus, throughout the eighteenth and nineteenth centuries, Shakespeare remained the most frequently acted playwright in New York. American subjects for the stage did emerge, however. Besides Tyler and Dunlap, the list of American playwrights who successfully staged American situations and themes includes John Augustus Stone (*Metamora: Or, The Last of the Wampanoags*, pr. 1829). Though not the first American play to put the figure of the Native American at its center, *Metamora* was certainly the most popular of the era. Other notable plays on the New York stage included Anna Cora Mowatt's *Fashion* (pr. 1845); Benjamin A. Baker's *A Glance at New York* (pr. 1848) with its street-tough fireman Mose, a part that generated countless imitations; Dion Boucicault's *The Octoroon: Or, Life in Louisiana* (pr. 1859, 1861); Frank Murdoch's *Davy Crockett* (pr. 1872); and, most important of all, George L. Aiken's adaptation of Harriet Beecher Stowe's abolitionist classic *Uncle Tom's Cabin: Or, Life Among the Lowly* (pr. 1852).

As the nineteenth century came to an end, New York City was firmly established as the national center of American theater, but the theater district known today as Broadway was still a work in progress. In the 1850's, New York theater meant Greenwich Village. During the 1870's and 1880's, the theaters had moved farther uptown, but it was not until the 1900-1930 period that the Longacre (now Times) Square area became the Broadway of theater history and legend.

1900-1945

Between 1900 and 1928, approximately eighty theaters were built between Thirty-ninth and Fifty-fourth streets within a block or two of Broadway. Many of these, having undergone much transformation and renovation, still function as theatrical venues today. New names emerged in the creative ranks of New York and Broadway theater. The popular musical theater, which had begun in various forms of revues on other nonnarrative formats, began to crystallize as a storytelling mode with the popularity in the United States of W. S. Gilbert and Sir Arthur Sullivan and the development of the homegrown operetta of Sigmund Romberg and Victor Herbert.

The modern drama of England and the European continent began to have its impact on New York playwrights and audiences, introducing uncharacteristically realistic content and style into this entertainment world. Melodramas gave way to the influence of Henrik Ibsen and George Bernard Shaw. The American playwrights who most exemplified the new realism include Clyde Fitch, Bronson Howard, James A. Herne, and William Vaughn Moody.

In the area of straight (nonmusical) drama, the 1920's and early 1930's might be called the Age of O'Neill. Eugene O'Neill, the introverted, serious son of flamboyant nineteenth century star of the stage melodrama James O'Neill, saw his first play produced on Cape Cod by the Provincetown Players. This group moved to New York and in 1916 launched O'Neill's New York career with *Bound East for Cardiff* (in tandem with Susan Glaspell's *Trifles*, pr. 1916). In 1920, *Beyond the Horizon* won O'Neill his first of four Pulitzer Prizes in Drama; *Anna Christie* (pr. 1921) won him his second. Other powerful dramas from O'Neill during the 1920's and 1930's in-

clude *The Emperor Jones* (pr. 1920), *The Hairy Ape* (pr. 1922), *All God's Chillun Got Wings* (pr. 1924), *Desire Under the Elms* (pr. 1924), *Strange Interlude* (pr. 1928), *Mourning Becomes Electra* (pr. 1931), *Ah, Wilderness!* (pr. 1933), and *The Iceman Cometh* (pr. 1946). O'Neill won the Nobel Prize in Literature in 1936, but his influence declined, beginning in the late 1930's, until a posthumous production of *Long Day's Journey into Night* (pr. 1956) reestablished his position as the leading American playwright of the first half of the twentieth century.

The American theater produced many other fine playwrights during this period, many of whom deserve to be better known. A concise list would include Sidney Howard, Philip Barry, Elmer Rice, Maxwell Anderson, Clifford Odets, Thornton Wilder, and Lillian Hellman. Their work embraced the whole range of genres from sophisticated comedy to social realism and various forms of experimental theater.

The story of the drama of the era was not only its important playwrights. Orson Welles and John Houseman contributed monumentally to the vitality of the New York stage in their work with the Federal Theatre Project (1935-1939) and their own Mercury Theatre. Also worth remembering are the Living Newspaper productions of the Federal Theatre Project, and a number of significant novels that were adapted into striking theatrical successes, including Richard Wright's *Native Son* (pr. 1941), Erskine Caldwell's *Tobacco Road* (pr. 1933), and Sinclair Lewis's *It Can't Happen Here* (pr. 1936).

1945 AND AFTER

Despite all this creativity, the popularity of the live stage was slowly but steadily being undermined by the rising competition for audiences from sound movies. In the years after World War II, it would be the work of a new generation of strong playwrights, the re-invention of the Broadway musical, and the development of a lively and adventurous experimental theater Off-Broadway that would keep the theater alive in New York.

The first of the new generation of playwrights was Tennessee Williams. His first Broadway success came in 1945, when *The Glass Menagerie* (first produced a year earlier) opened at the Playhouse Theatre on Broadway. The play's lyricism, sensitive exploration of family relationships, loneliness, and power of memory have had a lasting impact on the American theater. Williams's next play, *A Streetcar Named Desire* (pr. 1947), dropped lyricism in favor of a tough, sexually charged naturalism, both in action and in speech. Elia Kazan directed Marlon Brando, Kim Stanley, Karl Malden, and Jessica Tandy in the first Broadway production. Other powerful plays of sexual passion and repression followed, the most notable including *Cat on a Hot Tin Roof* (pr. 1955), *Sweet Bird of Youth* (pr. 1959), and *The Night of the Iguana* (pr. 1961).

Williams's primary rival for greatness between the late 1940's and the early 1960's was Arthur Miller. With *All My Sons* (pr. 1947) and *Death of a Salesman* (pr. 1949), Miller established himself as a powerful dramatist of the family, but also one with a strong political point of view. Not as lyrical as Williams, Miller used the stage to challenge the American national conscience about its private and public values. In no play of his is this aspect more clearly exposed than in *The Crucible* (pr. 1953), which uses the infamous Salem witch trials to expose and attack the political inquisitions of Senator Joseph McCarthy during the 1950's. Other fine work followed with *A View from the Bridge* (pr. 1955), *After the Fall* (pr. 1964), *Incident at Vichy* (pr. 1964), and *The Price* (pr. 1968).

Williams and Miller were not the only interesting playwrights in the postwar years. Midwesterner William Inge emerged in 1950 with *Come Back, Little Sheba* to challenge Williams and Miller for Broadway supremacy. He followed *Come Back, Little Sheba* with *Picnic* (pr. 1953), *Bus Stop* (pr. 1955), and *The Dark at the Top of the Stairs* (pr. 1959). Sympathetically drawn characterizations and a gift for natural, quietly poetic dialogue marked his work. Other thoughtful, popular playwrights on Broadway in the 1950's include George Axelrod (*The Seven Year Itch*, pr. 1952), Robert Anderson (*Tea and Sympathy*, pr. 1953), Jerome Lawrence and Robert E. Lee (*Inherit the Wind*, pr. 1955), Dore Schary (*Sunrise at Campobello*, pr. 1958), William Gibson (*Two for the Seesaw*, pr. 1958, and *The Miracle Worker*, stage pr.

1959), and Lorraine Hansberry (*A Raisin in the Sun*, pr. 1959).

A new generation of Broadway playwrights arrived in the 1960's. Edward Albee followed a series of strikingly original absurdist Off-Broadway one-acts with the electrifying mainstream hit *Who's Afraid of Virginia Woolf?* (pr. 1962). No single Albee play since has had a corresponding impact, but the playwright fashioned a distinguished career both on and off Broadway with plays like *A Delicate Balance* (pr. 1966), *Seascape* (pr. 1975), and *Three Tall Women* (pr. 1991), all Pulitzer Prize winners.

Come Blow Your Horn (pr. 1960) was Neil Simon's debut, and he went on to be the most commercially successful Broadway playwright in the postwar years. After 1960, hardly a year passed without a Simon comedy on the stage, and in many years he had two or more running simultaneously. Since the 1960's, Simon's laugh-filled domestic comedies have kept audiences filling the theaters for hits like *The Odd Couple* (pr. 1965), *Chapter Two* (pr. 1977), *Broadway Bound* (pr. 1986), and *Lost in Yonkers* (pr. 1991). After the run of *Brighton Beach Memoirs* (pr. 1982) at the classic Alvin Theatre, its owners, the Nederlander organization, renamed the theater the Neil Simon Theatre in 1983, as high an unofficial honor as Broadway has for its notables.

Since the 1970's, playwrights who have moved back and forth between Off-Broadway and Broadway include David Mamet, John Guare, Beth Henley, Terence McNally, and August Wilson.

MUSICAL THEATER

On the musical front, the popularity of Richard Rodgers and Oscar Hammerstein II's *Oklahoma!* (pr. 1943) did for the musical theater what *A Streetcar Named Desire* and *Death of a Salesman* had done for the straight play. It set an example of inventiveness and energy that raised the bar for its successors and made "Broadway musical" a household word, not just for New Yorkers but for city visitors for whom a ticket to a popular Broadway musical became an inseparable part of a trip to New York City.

The 1940's and 1950's saw the team of Rodgers and Hammerstein succeed with *Carousel* (pr. 1949),

South Pacific (pr. 1949), *The King and I* (pr. 1951), and *The Sound of Music* (pr. 1959), all of which went on to Hollywood film adaptations and, over the years, to road tours and revivals. Some other successful musicals during these years were *The Pajama Game* (pr. 1954), *Damn Yankees* (pr. 1955), *My Fair Lady* (pr. 1956), and *West Side Story* (pr. 1957).

In the 1960's and 1970's, musical theater became more aggressive in its selection of subject matter and, in particular, its expression of sexuality onstage. Hal Prince's *Cabaret* (pr. 1966) led the way with its outrageous Kit-Kat Club girls and a slyly salacious performance by Joel Grey as the Emcee. In 1968, the rock musical *Hair* brought Age of Aquarius nudity to Broadway.

Key figures in the new musical were producer director Prince and choreographer-directors Bob Fosse (*Pippin*, pr. 1972; *Chicago*, pr. 1975; and *Dancin'*, pr. 1978) and Michael Bennett, whose *A Chorus Line* (pr. 1975) built its book from the personal experiences of members of its original cast and became one of the longest-running musicals of its era. If the art of the dance drove the work of Fosse and Bennett, score and lyrics set the work of Stephen Sondheim apart from anyone else. Working with Prince, Sondheim produced the most consistently innovative and distinguished musicals of the second half of the twentieth century, including *Company* (pr. 1970), *A Little Night Music* (pr. 1973), *Pacific Overtures* (pr. 1976), *Sweeney Todd* (pr. 1979), and, with James Lapine, *Sunday in the Park with George* (pr. 1983) and *Into the Woods* (pr. 1987).

In the 1990's, the Broadway musical was sustained by the expensive, long-running, heavily toured "mega-musical." Andrew Lloyd Webber's *Cats* (pr. 1982) and *The Phantom of the Opera* (pr. 1988) were the exemplars, but the Disney corporation stepped in strongly, completely renovating the classic New Amsterdam Theatre on Forty-second Street and opening it with the spectacular *The Lion King* (pr. 1997), directed by Julie Taymor.

OFF-BROADWAY AND OFF-OFF-BROADWAY

The term "Broadway" became both a specific location along Broadway (the Times Square area) and a representative of commercialism in American theater. For good or ill, it became a high-stakes, high-pressure zone where (some felt) money talked more loudly than art.

The first Off-Broadway was a reaction to Broadway commercialism. Long before the term "Off-Broadway" was coined in the 1950's, a number of small, independent theaters had been developed, mainly, but not exclusively, in lower Manhattan. These included the Neighborhood Playhouse School of the Theatre (began 1915) on the lower East Side, the Provincetown Players (begun in Cape Cod, Massachusetts, in 1916, later moving to New York City), and the Group Theatre, formed by Harold Clurman, Lee Strasberg, and Cheryl Crawford to promote the Konstantin Stanislavsky method of actor training and new playwrights with strong political foci.

The Off-Broadway known today came into being in the early 1950's when director José Quintero reestablished lower Manhattan as a theatrical center with the Circle in the Square Theatre. Other notable Off-Broadway companies include the Living Theatre of Judith Malina and Julian Beck, which started in Greenwich Village and found audiences for its radical theater in venues around the world, and the New York Shakespeare Festival, headed by Off-Broadway impresario Joseph Papp—arguably the most important single figure in the Off-Broadway movement. Papp fought City Hall to bring free Shakespeare to Central Park and to ghetto neighborhoods, and he orchestrated an expansion into the East Village scene with the New York Public Theatre.

Variety, more than anything, typified Off-Broadway theater. Tom Jones and Harvey Schmidt opened *The Fantasticks* (pr. 1960) for what would become a lyrical four-decade run, while at the St. Mark's Playhouse, Gene Frankel presented *The Blacks* (pr. 1961) with a high-powered and outspoken cast of African American actors that included James Earl Jones, Cicely Tyson, Godfrey Cambridge, and Lou Gossett, Jr. The St. Mark's Playhouse also became home to the Negro Ensemble Company formed by Robert Hooks, Gerald Krone, and Douglas Turner Ward. With new plays by playwrights such as Edward Albee and LeRoi Jones (Amiri Baraka), Off-Broadway soon began to outproduce Broadway in both numbers of productions and variety and innovation.

The line between Off-Broadway and Off-Off-Broadway is a fine one, because geographically they intermingle, particularly in lower Manhattan. The Actors' Equity Association made one functional distinction by allowing Equity actors to work out of Equity pay scale in theater spaces of fewer than one hundred seats for limited runs. This allowed small theater operations located in churches, coffeehouses, and other small venues to stay alive as Off-Broadway itself began to enjoy commercial success and attract uptown money. At a philosophical level, Off-Off-Broadway came to define a theater where the performance of radical politics, sexualities, and theatrical practices could be indulged with a freedom that began to make Off-Broadway look conservative. Pioneers in this movement include Joe Cino's Caffe Cino, the Performance Group, and the Judson Poet's Theater. Venues like these fostered the early work of Ed Bullins, Adrienne Kennedy, Megan Terry, Sam Shepard, and other talented playwrights and performers. Gradually, the term Off-Off-Broadway expanded to include a variety of group theaters (including the Theatre for the New City, the Wooster Group, Mabou Mines, Charles Ludlam's Ridiculous Theatre Company, and Playwrights Horizons) and individual performance artists.

While New York theater (Broadway in particular) often comes under fire for commercial opportunism and artistic timidity, it has remained alive by an interesting balancing act of compromise and experiment. Ultimately, there is still nothing quite like the social experience of going to a New York theater to share a show with live performers, a lively animated audience, and a city which has made live theater a part of its core identity. Each show, no matter how transient, reconnects every audience to a shared cultural activity as old as the most ancient sacred ritual and as contemporary as today's *The Village Voice* or *The New York Times*.

BIBLIOGRAPHY

Eliot, Marc. *Down Forty-second Street: Sex, Money, Culture, and Politics at the Crossroads of the World*. New York: Warner Books, 2001. Chronicles the evolution of Forty-second Street from a hotbed of prostitution and other illicit activities in the early twentieth century to a commercialized, successful theater district. A fascinating social and political history of the rise of New York City's most visible neighborhood.

Frommer, M. Katz, Myrna Frommer, and Harvey Frommer. *It Happened on Broadway: An Oral History of the Great White Way*. New York: Harcourt, 1998. Broadway insiders—playwrights, directors, actors, composers, choreographers, and many more—tell their stories, bringing to the public anecdotes and legends that elucidate the rise of Broadway theater.

Henderson, Mary C. *Theater in America: Two Hundred Fifty Years of Plays, Players, and Productions*. New York: Harry N. Abrams, 1996. A wonderful topically and historically organized overview with the beautiful illustrations of a fine art book and an authoritative scholarly text.

Little, Stuart W. *Off-Broadway: The Prophetic Theater*. New York: Coward, McCann and Geoghegan, 1972. A lively and readable account of the personalities and events that brought Off- and Off-Off-Broadway into being. Plenty of insider details and interesting anecdotes.

Wilmeth, Don B., and Christopher Bigsby, eds. *The Cambridge History of American Theater*. 3 vols. Cambridge, England: Cambridge University Press, 1998. An indispensable guide to American theater from its beginnings to the end of the twentieth century. Each volume has informative period and thematic articles, comprehensive bibliographies, and a helpful time line of theatrical activity in context.

Roger J. Stilling

OBIE AWARDS

When *The Village Voice* Obie Awards were instituted during the 1955-1956 theatrical season, they recognized for the first time the important and significant dramatic activities that flourished Off-Broadway in the dozens of small theaters, church auditoriums, and public meeting halls that were used for the presentation of plays that could not, for various reasons, be performed on Broadway.

The venues in which these plays were presented were smaller than Broadway theaters, thereby limiting the size of audiences and the revenues of such productions. Likewise, the tickets were not expensive, further limiting the profitability of such presentations. No one associated with Off-Broadway theater was in it for profit. Indeed, it was a rare Off-Broadway production that did not lose money. The salaries of those associated with such plays were considerably lower than those of their counterparts on Broadway.

Jerry Tallmer, drama critic for *The Village Voice*, an avant-garde newspaper that appeared weekly in New York City's Greenwich Village starting in 1955 and soon attracted a national audience, established *The Village Voice* Obie Awards in 1956. He and his colleagues at *The Village Voice* realized that Off-Broadway theater served two fundamental purposes. For one thing, it made possible the production of significant older plays that were not being brought to Broadway. While this conservation function of Off-Broadway theater was of the utmost importance, more important still was the opportunity that Off-Broadway theater provided for the promotion of innovative theater. Off-Broadway theater produced plays that were too far outside the mainstream to be considered suitable for production by the profit-driven Broadway theaters because of their high overhead and complex financial structure.

Over and above these functions, Off-Broadway theater served as a proving ground for young talent, not only for young actors, but also for fledgling playwrights, directors, set designers, and all manner of people involved in the production of plays. Tallmer envisioned an awards program that would honor people in every aspect of play production and would also encourage small acting companies. As a result, the Obies recognize a much broader field of play production than many comparable awards.

THE EARLY OBIES

The Obie Awards are the highest honor paid to Off-Broadway productions. They have been compared to the Tony Awards given by the American Theatre Wing in recognition of major contributions to theater, although their scope is narrower, limited to productions on Off-Broadway stages in New York City.

The Obie Awards were from the outset not tightly bound by structured and immutable categories. They were designed to celebrate every aspect of dramatic production. The first Obie Awards in 1956 recognized achievement in the following categories: best new play, best production, best actress, best actor, best director, best musical, distinguished performances by actresses, distinguished performances by actors, sets (including lighting and costumes), and special citations given to theaters or acting companies.

From year to year, some categories were added while others were dropped, although what was included varied with every new group of awards the judges bestowed. In 1958, for example, when there was no prize for best director, four new categories appeared: best adaptation, best revival, best comedy, and best one-act play. These categories did not appear the following year, although in that year a new category, best revue, was added.

In 1969, all the categories that had been in place since 1956 were dropped. In that year individuals were simply recognized with a play title following their name: No accolade such as "distinguished play" or "best actress" was provided. These awards were all grouped under the heading "General Citations for Outstanding Achievement." In that year, several theater companies, notably Theatre Genesis, the Open

Theater, OM Theater, and the Performance Group, were recognized, Theatre Genesis for "sustained excellence" and the others for specific productions.

In 1971, the former groups of categories were resurrected and included "best foreign play" and "distinguished plays." Both of those categories had occurred from time to time in previous years, along with the more typical plays honoring specific performers, directors, and designers.

The Obies are unique in that they do not limit the number of honorees in any category, so that in a particularly good year, true excellence can be recognized. This is quite unlike the problem posed in the annual awarding of Pulitzer Prizes, in which there is one prize in each category. In a particularly fruitful year, three or four plays may very well be deserving of Pulitzer Prizes, but, according to the rules governing the Pulitzer Prizes, only one award can be given. Of course, it must be remembered that individuals receiving Obies are given a simple plaque in recognition of their achievement rather than a large monetary award. Even the monetary awards given to acting companies are relatively modest.

OFF-OFF-BROADWAY PRODUCTIONS

In 1964, the Obie Awards were expanded to include a recent phenomenon that was making an impact on theater, Off-Off-Broadway. Whereas Off-Broadway theater preserved traditional theater and encouraged innovation among new playwrights, Off-Off-Broadway was what Ross Wetzsteon called a "third stage . . .[a] revolution against the revolutionaries."

By the mid-1960's, Off-Broadway was becoming somewhat mainstream. Compared with Off-Off-Broadway, which was a revolutionary type of theater, Off-Broadway seemed almost conventional. Off-Off-Broadway plays dealt directly and often harshly with the social problems of the 1960's: racial tensions, the Vietnam War, and social and political conditions that resulted in the string of high-profile assassinations before the decade was over. The sheer energy and sincerity of such productions made them worthy of a recognition that they could not gain from conventional sources. It was at this point that the Obies

could serve to encourage a wholly new approach, albeit a quite disturbing one, to American theater. The output of those writing for Off-Off-Broadway was astounding.

Some companies staged as many as fifty new plays a year, working with minimal props, performing in whatever space they could find either free of charge or for small sums of money. They priced tickets so that most theatergoers could easily afford them. Perhaps the most influential of these Off-Off-Broadway venues was Ellen Stewart's Café La Mama, a few blocks south of St. Mark's Place, where at any given time between Thursday and Sunday, two plays might be going on simultaneously, one upstairs and another in one of the "piggyback theaters" in the basement.

SELECTING THE WINNERS

The process for choosing Obie recipients is as informal as the kinds of theater the awards honor. The judges, members of *The Village Voice* drama staff, along with two guest critics whom *The Village Voice* selects—usually critics from New York City daily newspapers or national weekly news magazines—meet once a month throughout the year. They discuss Off-Broadway and Off-Off-Broadway productions and, over time, produce a master list of possible honorees. In the early days this list consisted of seventy to one hundred entries from which some twenty winners would finally be selected at the last meeting of the judges in May.

As time went on, however, the lists grew in size. By 1993, more than thirty Obies were awarded. This number grew to nearly forty in 1999 and was back at thirty-four the following year. In the first decade and a half of the Obie Awards, the typical number of prizes given was about twenty, considering that the awards for distinguished performances and for distinguished direction typically had more than one recipient—often as many as nine or ten, collectively.

Perhaps the strongest factor in ensuring the breadth and value of the Obies is that there are no formal nominations for them. The judges consider the entire field for the season in question, including plays that may have run for only two or three week-ends in a church basement, in the back room of a bar, or in an isolated loft somewhere in lower Manhattan.

When he accepted an Obie Award for his 1975-1976 performance in David Mamet's *American Buffalo* (pr. 1975), Mike Kellin remarked, surely hyperbolically, that only ten people saw the show but fortunately seven of them were Obie judges. Edward Albee revealed his respect for the Obie Awards in his statement that seven out of ten times, the award for the best play goes to what actually turns out to be the best play.

THE OBIE AS A FIRST AWARD

Many—indeed, probably most—of the recipients of Obie Awards receive their first national recognition as actors, playwrights, or directors when they receive this award. Edward Albee, for example, was virtually unknown when *The Zoo Story* (pr. 1959) brought him an Obie as one of three distinguished plays receiving the 1960 award. In this year, also, Samuel Beckett, whose name was not familiar to most playgoers, received an Obie for *Krapp's Last Tape* (pr. 1958).

Beckett, recipient of the 1969 Nobel Prize in Literature, went on to receive a second Obie for *Happy Days* (pr. 1961) in 1962 and a third for *Play* (pr. 1963; English translation, 1964) in 1964. Whereas Albee's recognition for winning the Obie paved the way for him to stage his subsequent productions on Broadway (later in his career he returned to Off-Broadway with *Three Tall Women*, pr. 1991), Beckett continued to write Off-Broadway productions long after his first award. LeRoi Jones (later known as Amiri Baraka) was little known in 1964 when he received an Obie for *Dutchman* (pr. 1964). In the same year, three more of his plays were produced Off-Broadway, *The Baptism*, *The Slave*, and *The Toilet*, perhaps spurred on by the recognition *Dutchman* had received.

Lanford Wilson and Mamet both won their first major dramatic awards when they were given Obies, Wilson for *The Hot l Baltimore* (pr. 1973) in 1973 and Mamet for *American Buffalo* in 1975. *American Buffalo* went on to win the New York Drama Critics

Circle Award. Wilson and Mamet have since been acknowledged as being among the United States' leading playwrights.

Among actors who received Obies when they were still largely unknown to theater audiences were such luminaries as Dustin Hoffman, George C. Scott, Jason Robards, Jr., Colleen Dewhurst, Zero Mostel, Eileen Brennan, Nancy Marchand, Anne Meacham, Barbara Harris, Olympia Dukakis, James Earl Jones, Al Pacino, Rue McClanahan, Hector Elizondo, and Stacy Keach. Although most of these performers went on to make names for themselves in Hollywood or on Broadway, many of them relished opportunities to return to Lower Manhattan to perform Off-Broadway for a pittance of what they were paid elsewhere. Dewhurst once said that returning to Off-Broadway was like returning home, echoing the sentiments of many Obie winners who had graduated to distinguished careers in acting.

THE ROSS WETZSTEON GRANT

When the Obie Awards chairperson, Ross Wetzsteon, died in 1998, *The Village Voice* established special annual awards of two thousand dollars in his memory. These awards are designed to help struggling Off-Broadway or Off-Off-Broadway theatrical companies meet their expenses. The grant recognizes that in some cases, such companies, accustomed to economizing in every possible way, can be kept afloat simply by receiving relatively small sums to help them meet their expenses.

The Ross Wetzsteon Grant for the 1999-2000 season went to The Foundry, with three other Obie Grants going to the Big Dance Theater, Circus Amok, and Five Myles. These grants have become a significant factor in helping to sustain companies that stage innovative dramas but that struggle from year to year on stringent budgets.

BIBLIOGRAPHY

Berkowitz, Gerald M. *New Broadways: Theatre Across America, Approaching a New Millennium.* New York: Applause Theatre Book Publishers, 1996. Surveys American professional theater since 1950, with a thirty-page chapter devoted to

Off-Broadway and a substantial part of another chapter to Off-Off-Broadway.

Brantley, Ben. *The New York Times Book of Broadway: On the Aisle for the Best Plays of the Last Century.* New York: St. Martin's Press, 2001. Offers a comprehensive look at the twenty-five most influential Broadway and Off-Broadway plays of the twentieth century, as well as one hundred additional "memorable" plays. Each play entry has the original *New York Times* review, theater and length of run, and vintage production photographs.

Horn, Barbara Lee. *Ellen Stewart and La Mama: A Bio-Bibliography.* Westport, Conn.: Greenwood Press, 1993. Chronicles the life and career of Ellen Stewart and her Café La Mama, an influential experimental theater that greatly impacted the rise of Off-Off-Broadway. Includes annotated bibliography and a listing of La Mama's plays and Stewart's awards.

Little, Stuart W. *Off-Broadway: The Prophetic Theater.* New York: Coward, McCann and Geoghegan, 1972. A worthwhile assessment of Off-Broadway and Off-Off-Broadway theater, defining clearly the differences between the two. The appendix, "Off-Broadway Award Winners—1955-1971," lists all of the Obie Awards for those years, along with the Vernon Rice Awards, and the Drama Desk-Vernon Rice Awards.

Wetzsteon, Ross, ed. *The Obie Winners: The Best of Off-Broadway.* Garden City, N.J.: Doubleday, 1980. This anthology is valuable for its excellent introduction by the late Ross Wetzsteon, former chairperson of the Obie Awards, who discusses the history of these awards briefly but cogently.

R. Baird Shuman

PULITZER PRIZES

In 1903 Joseph Pulitzer, journalist and owner of two major newspapers, St. Louis's *Post-Dispatch* and New York City's *The New York World*, decided to make a gift of two million dollars to New York's Columbia University. His will, dated April 16, 1904, stipulated that $550,000 of that sum be reserved to fund prizes in journalism, letters, and music. It created an Advisory Board of the School of Journalism to administer the prizes. This board, originally formed in 1912, consisted of thirteen members but by the mid-1990's had increased to seventeen members. The name was changed, first in 1950 to the Advisory Board on the Pulitzer Prizes, then in 1979 to the Pulitzer Prize Board.

THE DRAMA AWARD

Pulitzer specified the terms that would govern the awarding of the Pulitzer Prizes, and the Advisory Boards through the years have done their best to stay within the boundaries the donor originally set. Pulitzer stipulated that the final approval of all awards rested with the president of Columbia University, who was given the power to veto any recommendations made by the Advisory Board and the various juries.

In the case of the drama award, a play could be considered only if it had been performed in New York during the twelve months between March 2 of a given year and March 1 of the following year, and only if it represented the educational value and power of the stage in raising the standard of good morals, good taste, and good manners. Plays original in their sources and that dealt with American life were given preference.

THE CHANGING SCENE IN AMERICAN DRAMA

American drama did not come into its own until the 1920's, when the first truly significant American playwright, Eugene O'Neill, emerged. In 1920, he received the second Pulitzer Prize awarded in drama, for *Beyond the Horizon* (pr. 1920). The first Pulitzer Prize in the field had gone to Jesse Lynch Williams for a relatively innocuous play, *Why Marry?* (pb. 1918). The prize was withheld in 1919, as it had been in 1917. O'Neill's *Anna Christie* (pr. 1921) brought him his second Pulitzer Prize in 1922, and by the end of the decade, in 1928, he had received yet another Pulitzer Prize for *Strange Interlude* (pr. 1928). He was not to receive his fourth Pulitzer Prize until twenty-nine years later, in 1957, for *Long Day's Journey into Night* (pr. 1956).

One may wonder why such O'Neill plays as *Mourning Becomes Electra* (pr. 1931), *Ah, Wilderness!* (pr. 1933), *The Iceman Cometh* (pr. 1946), and *A Moon for the Misbegotten* (pr. 1947) were passed over. Certainly *Mourning Becomes Electra* and *The Iceman Cometh* seem worthy of the highest recognition from a literary standpoint. They did not, however, conform to the guidelines Pulitzer had established in his will, under the terms of which an author's best work might well be passed over while works of less literary significance might receive the award if they were considered "uplifting."

Such was the case in the heated controversy over Edward Albee's *Who's Afraid of Virginia Woolf?* (pr. 1962). The Drama Jury, on which John Mason Brown and John Gassner served, recommended the play for a Pulitzer Prize. In a year when Broadway's offerings were marginal at best, the Albee play loomed above any of its competitors. The Advisory Board, however, reversed the Drama Jury, pointing out that *Who's Afraid of Virginia Woolf?* did not meet the so-called "uplift" provision of Joseph Pulitzer's guidelines. Their action caused Brown and Gassner to resign from the Drama Jury, stating that such an action was making a farce out of the drama award.

The upshot was that no award in drama was made for 1963. When Albee's *A Delicate Balance* (pr. 1966), certainly not of the caliber of *Who's Afraid of Virginia Woolf?*, was awarded a Pulitzer Prize in 1967, Albee considered declining the award. He reconsidered, however, accepting the prize after making a formal protest suggesting that the Pulitzer Prize in Drama had ceased to be an honor at all.

Albee justified accepting the award by saying that were he to refuse it, he would not feel as free to criticize it as he would having accepted it. He also feared that if he refused the award, others designated to receive Pulitzer Prizes in that year might decline their awards in support of him. He acknowledged that although the Pulitzer Prize is an honor in decline, it is, nevertheless, an honor. Albee received a second Pulitzer Prize in 1975 for *Seascape* (pr. 1975), ironically another play of not nearly the literary quality of *Who's Afraid of Virginia Woolf?* He received a third Pulitzer Prize in 1994 for *Three Tall Women* (pr. 1991), a play of considerable literary quality.

ALTERING THE GUIDELINES

Partly as a result of the controversy that the rejection of *Who's Afraid of Virginia Woolf?* engendered, a special committee of the Drama Award in 1964 recommended that the "uplift" clause be expunged from the guidelines. The whole fabric of American life was drastically changing, and any searching drama would necessarily reflect such changes, the depiction of which would not necessarily be uplifting.

There was little serious, deeply searching American drama at the time the awards were established. Subsequent noteworthy drama often offended delicate sensibilities but brought to center stage social problems and conditions that required venting. Also, it was noted that the 1955 award, somewhat inconsistently, had gone to Tennessee Williams for *Cat on a Hot Tin Roof* (pr. 1955), a play of great literary importance that clearly did not conform to the "uplift" standard articulated in the Pulitzer guidelines.

Cat on a Hot Tin Roof likely would have been rejected had Benjamin McKelway of the Washington *Evening Star*, a member of the Advisory Board, not absented himself from the meeting in which the 1955 recommendations were made. McKelway had not seen *Who's Afraid of Virginia Woolf?* but nevertheless argued strenuously against giving the award to Albee for the play, citing the "uplift" provision in his successful attempt to scuttle the play's chances. At the 1964 meeting, Barry Bingham of the Louisville Courier-Journal suggested that anyone who had not read a book or seen a play being considered for the

prize abstain from passing judgment on the work in question.

WITHHOLDING THE PRIZE

It is possible to withhold a Pulitzer Prize in any category if, in the eyes of the Advisory Board, no work in a given year meets the standards established for the prize in that category. In the period from 1917 to 2001, eighty-four Pulitzer Prizes in Drama might have been awarded. As it turned out, the prize in drama was withheld fourteen times during this period, in 1917, 1919, 1942, 1944, 1947, 1951, 1963, 1964, 1966, 1968, 1972, 1974, 1986, and 1997.

Pulitzer awards were disrupted in the early 1940's because of World War II, but the withholding of the prize six times between 1963 and 1974 is particularly telling. This was a time of considerable social unrest in the United States. The most important plays of the period reflected the social upheaval that characterized the era. Plays that employed coarse language, sexual situations, sexual deviation, and other elements offensive to some who served on the Advisory Board were at a distinct disadvantage, regardless of any literary excellence they might possess.

THE HALCYON YEARS

The award was not withheld once in the twenty-one years from 1920 to 1941. The United States was bristling with dramatic activity during that period, during which the Theatre Guild and the Group Theatre were both flourishing. Awards were given to some of the more searching social dramas of the period such as Paul Green's *In Abraham's Bosom* (pr. 1926), Elmer Rice's *Street Scene* (pr. 1929), Marc Connelly's *The Green Pastures: A Fable* (pr. 1929), Maxwell Anderson's *Both Your Houses* (pr. 1933), Sidney Kingsley's *Men in White* (pr. 1933), and Robert E. Sherwood's *Abe Lincoln in Illinois* (pr. 1938) and *There Shall Be No Night* (pr. 1940).

Thornton Wilder received two Pulitzer Prizes in the 1930's and 1940's, one for the nostalgic, reflective play *Our Town* (pr. 1938) and one for his comedy, *The Skin of Our Teeth* (pr. 1942). Moss Hart and George S. Kaufman shared the 1937 award for their comedy *You Can't Take It with You* (pr. 1936). Other comedies were awarded the prize through the year 1945, notably Zona Gale's *Miss Lulu Bett* (pr. 1920) in 1921; in 1925, Sidney Howard's *They Knew What They Wanted* (pr. 1924); Sherwood's *Idiot's Delight* (pr. 1936) in 1936; and in 1945, Mary Coyle Chase's *Harvey* (pr. 1945).

Perhaps no play met the Pulitzer guidelines more closely than William Saroyan's *The Time of Your Life* (pr. 1939), which was awarded the prize in 1940. This loosely structured play was about the inherent goodness of humankind. Saroyan, however, returned the check to the Advisory Board that he received as a prizewinner, apparently without rancor. The board advised him that the play had already received the prize and would be recorded as the winner in the permanent annals of the organization. The check that Saroyan returned went into the Pulitzer Fund.

"CATCH-UP" AWARDS

In some instances, notably in the cases of Albee and Lillian Hellman, the playwright's best play literarily was not deemed suitable for the award, usually because of the "uplift" clause. Hellman's most celebrated play, *The Children's Hour* (pr. 1934), had homosexual overtones that probably precluded it from receiving the 1935 award. The Drama Jury attempted to honor Hellman by awarding her the prize in 1960. The Advisory Board, however, balked, and the award was not made. Albee certainly received "catch-up" awards after the controversy over *Who's Afraid of Virginia Woolf?*

An attempt was also made to honor Clifford Odets, who had been passed over for such plays as *Awake and Sing!* (pr. 1935), *Paradise Lost* (pr. 1935), and *Golden Boy* (pr. 1937). The Drama Jury in the years in question had such an array of strong plays to choose from that Odets lost out to Zoë Atkins, whose *The Old Maid* (pr. 1934) won the prize in 1935, to Sherwood, whose *Idiot's Delight* took the 1936 award, and to Hart and Kaufman, whose *You Can't Take It with You* was the winner in 1937. Finally Odets's *The Flowering Peach* (pr. 1954), a redaction of the story of Noah and the flood, would have won the 1955 award save for a technicality.

Many of the plays that received recognition in the

1980's and 1990's would not have met the "uplift" requirement in effect earlier. They dealt openly with such controversial topics as race relations (notably August Wilson's *Fences*, pr. 1985, and *The Piano Lesson*, pr. 1987, and Alfred Uhry's *Driving Miss Daisy*, pr. 1987); homosexuality (notably Tony Kushner's *Angels in America: A Gay Fantasia on National Themes, Part One: Millennium Approaches*, pr. 1991, and Jonathan Larson's *Rent*, pr. 1996); and feminism (notably Wendy Wasserstein's *The Heidi Chronicles*, pr. 1988). They did not deal with the "smiling" aspects of American life but rather focused upon the provocative social problems that reflected modern America in the throes of realistically working through the more challenging and enigmatic dilemmas that faced people in the waning years of the twentieth century.

BIBLIOGRAPHY

Adler, Thomas P. *Mirror on the Stage: The Pulitzer Plays as an Approach to American Drama.* West Lafayette, Ind.: Purdue University Press, 1987. Adler succeeds in demonstrating that one way of assessing the course of American drama during the twentieth century is by examining the plays that won Pulitzer Prizes. This intriguing book is essentially a social history.

Bates, Douglas. *The Pulitzer Prize: The Inside Story of America's Most Prestigious Award.* New York: Carol Publishing Group, 1991. Bates presents interesting anecdotal material about Pulitzer Prizes in the various fields in which they are awarded. A solid overview of the prizes and of the man who established them. Helpful bibliography.

Hohenberg, John. *Diaries: Inside America's Greatest Prize.* Syracuse, N.Y.: Syracuse University Press, 1996. Private record of Hohenberg's tenure (1954-1976) as administrator of the Pulitzer Prizes, offering intimate insight into the controversies and decision-making of this period.

_____. *The Pulitzer Prizes: A History of the Awards in Books, Drama, Music, and Journalism, Based on the Private Files over Six Decades.* New York: Columbia University Press, 1974. This comprehensive and thorough study of the awards from 1917 to 1974 is an invaluable resource, limited only by the fact that it is a quarter of a century old. For the years that it covers, it is indispensable.

Toohey, John L. *A History of the Pulitzer Prize Plays.* New York: Citadel Press, 1967. Like Hohenberg's aforementioned book, this valuable resource needs updating. For the period it covers, it provides a brief rundown of each winning play, including a synopsis of the play, a list of actors and their roles, and a sampling of contemporary criticism of the play. Excellent illustrations.

Whitelaw, Nancy. *Joseph Pulitzer and the New York World.* Greensboro, N.C.: Morgan Reynolds, 2000. A biography of Pulitzer, offering a glimpse into the New York literary scene at the turn of the twentieth century. Black-and-white photographs throughout.

R. Baird Shuman

TONY AWARDS

The American Theatre Wing's Antoinette Perry Awards, popularly known as the Tony Awards, have been presented for distinguished achievement in the theater since 1947. They have since become the most prestigious awards for live, professional theater in the United States.

THE AMERICAN THEATRE WING

The process that led to the Tony Awards began in 1917 when Rachel Crothers, one of the leading American women playwrights, and six of her colleagues rallied professional theater workers to form an organization to aid war relief. By the end of World War I, the Stage Women's War Relief represented every segment of the New York professional theater. Together they collected food and clothing, set up servicemen "canteens" on Broadway, and sold millions of dollars worth of Liberty Bonds. Subsequently, during the Great Depression, Crothers organized the United Theatre Relief, continuing her humanitarian work and demonstrating her belief that theater professionals could serve society in more ways than merely entertainment.

In 1939, Crothers again rallied theater professionals to provide war relief for American allies. The Stage Women's War Relief became a branch of the British War Relief Society and was soon known as the American Theatre Wing War Service. A men's division was established with Gilbert Miller serving as chairman. When the United States entered World War II after the bombing of Pearl Harbor on December 7, 1941, the American Theatre Wing separated from the British War Relief Society. Antoinette Perry, an actress and one of the United States' first successful women directors, was chosen president and secretary of the American Theatre Wing, which by this point encompassed the women's and men's organizations. Between 1941 and 1945, theater professionals continued the humanitarian projects begun during World War I. Under Perry's progressive leadership, the Wing continually expanded its operations, eventually sponsoring fifty-four separate projects. The most well known of these were the Stage Door Canteens, offering servicemen a place to have a sandwich and a soft drink (no alcohol was served), to be entertained by volunteer performers, to meet theater stars, and to dance with chorus girls.

At the conclusion of the war, the American Theatre Wing remained an active organization but turned its humanitarian efforts to serving the civilian population. In 1946 the American Theatre Wing founded its Professional Training School under the G.I. Bill and trained thousands of returning military personnel for careers in all aspects of the professional theater.

ESTABLISHMENT OF THE TONY AWARD

After five years spending most of her waking hours and personal fortune as the visionary leader of the American Theatre Wing, Perry died of a heart attack on June 28, 1946. Jacob Wilk, an executive at Warner Bros., suggested to Broadway producer John Golden that a memorial should be established to recognize Perry's humanitarian work and leadership. The Wing established a committee chaired by Brock Pemberton, one of Perry's closest friends and associates, to consider the proposal. Recalling the many Wing projects created by Perry, the committee's members decided that an appropriate commemoration should be a project that encouraged improvement in the theater arts. This notion was combined with a growing dissatisfaction with theater awards given by "outsiders." The Pemberton Committee announced that a self-renewing memorial in the form of annual awards, given by theater professionals for theater professionals, be established in Perry's name to honor innovative and distinguished achievement in the Broadway theater. The Antoinette Perry Award was not to be like Academy Awards that pitted professionals against each other in a competition for a single "best" award in each category. The committee also decided that a simple scroll, together with an engraved compact for the women and a cigarette case for the men, would be more appropriate than any kind of statue.

Early award ceremonies

There was no voting to determine the recipients of early Tony Awards. Instead, a fifteen-member panel met in secret to determine who the recipients should be. It was announced that specific award categories would not be permanent and that nominees would not be revealed. In order to maintain complete confidentiality and to eliminate competition, no records were kept of those early deliberations. The first Tony Awards were presented April 6, 1947, in the grand ballroom of the Waldorf Astoria Hotel. Presentations are held on Sunday because that is the day most Broadway theaters are dark. Vera Allen, the new chairwoman of the Wing, presided over the festivities, which included dinner, dancing, and entertainment provided by Mickey Rooney, Ethel Waters, David Wayne, and Herb Shriner.

There were only nine categories in 1947, but some included multiple award recipients. Awards for outstanding performances were presented to Ingrid Bergman, Helen Hayes, José Ferrer, and Fredric March. Outstanding debut performance went to Patricia Neal, and outstanding musical performance went to David Wayne. Kurt Weill received an award for outstanding score. *All My Sons* (pr. 1947) was honored with awards for Arthur Miller, playwright, and Elia Kazan, director. Two awards were given for choreography. Outstanding technical awards were presented for scenic and costume design. The first "special awards" were presented to P. A. McDonald for set construction, Burns Mantle for the annual publication of *The Ten Best Plays*, Jules J. Leventhal for the season's most prolific backer and producer, and Dora Chamberlain for courtesy as the treasurer of the Martin Beck Theatre. The final special awards were presented to Ira and Rita Katzenberg for being enthusiastic first-nighters, and Vincent Sardi for his theater-oriented restaurant.

Award categories

Tony Award categories have changed through the years. Best play awards were not given until 1948, while separate awards for straight and musical plays began in the same year and continued to expand through the years until a complete suite of parallel awards were presented. Some awards reflect their times and pay tribute to the willingness of the Wing to experiment with categories. In 1948, for example, Mary Martin and Joe E. Brown received Tony Awards for "spreading theater to the country while the originals perform in New York." Stage technicians were honored most years until their category was eliminated in 1964. Orchestra conductors received awards from 1948 through 1957. In the late 1960's separate awards were given for music and lyrics, but these categories were combined again in the early 1970's. By 2001, the number of categories numbered twenty-five, including best play, best musical, book of a musical, original score, choreography, scenic design, costume design, lighting design, director of a play, director of a musical, revival of a play, and revival of a musical. The Performance Awards include leading actor in a play, leading actress in a play, featured actor in a play, featured actress in a play, leading actor in a musical, leading actress in a musical, featured actor in a musical, and featured actress in a musical.

The award matures

After the awards presentation in 1948, the Wing decided that a more formal award should be presented together with the scroll. The United Scenic Artists sponsored a design contest won by Herman Rosse for his three-inch-diameter silver medallion with a profile of Perry on the obverse and the masks of comedy and tragedy on the reverse. The medallion was first presented in a velvet-lined box but since 1968 has been mounted on a black lucite stand with a metal armature and engraved with individual winners' names.

The Tony Award presentation was carried on WOR radio and broadcast nationally over the Mutual Radio Network beginning in 1947, the award's first year. In 1956 the Tony Awards presentation was first broadcast on local New York City television by the Du Mont network. In order to make the television awards presentation more exciting, the award nominees were made public for the first time.

In 1967, the American Theatre Wing aligned with the League of New York Theatres (now the League of American Theatres and Producers), thus joining the humanitarian and professional arms of Broadway Theater in the presentation of the Tony Awards. The location for the presentations moved from various hotel ballrooms to the Shubert Theatre in 1967 in preparation for the first national televised broadcasting of the Tony Awards on the Columbia Broadcasting System (CBS). In 1997 the Public Broadcasting Service (PBS) joined with CBS in televising the awards show to improve ratings. The less popular technical awards are presented during the first hour on PBS; then CBS takes over for the more popular performance and best show awards.

NOMINATIONS AND VOTING

To be eligible for a Tony Award, a play must have opened during the current Broadway season in a Broadway theater with a minimum of 499 seats. (Theaters with fewer than 499 seats are considered Off-Broadway theaters regardless of their location.) The listing of eligible productions is given to a thirty-member nominating committee, composed of actors, directors, producers, publicists, administrators, designers, and educators. This committee must select between three and six nominees in each category. If there are insufficient nominees in any one category, it is eliminated for that year. Nominees are announced publicly the first Monday after the official cut-off date of each year's Broadway season.

Ballots are then mailed to approximately 710 eligible theater professionals encompassing the board of directors of the American Theatre Wing, members of the governing boards of Actors' Equity Association, the Dramatists Guild, the Society of Stage Directors and Choreographers, United Scenic Artists, and the Association of Theatrical Press Agents and Managers, as well as critics whose names appear on the first night press list. All those eligible to vote are required to see as many Broadway productions as possible during the season and may vote only in categories for which they have seen all nominees. Ballots are mailed to an accounting firm, which tallies the votes and prepares the "winner envelopes" to be opened live during the Tony Award presentation. Names of winners are never announced in advance. However, those receiving the Regional Theatre Award and other special awards are confidentially notified in advance so they can attend the presentation.

IMPACT AND TRENDS

Winning a Tony Award can mean the difference between failure and success for a Broadway play. In 1985, *Big River* (pr. 1984) a musical based on Mark Twain's *Adventures of Huckleberry Finn* (1884) and written by William Hauptman, opened with no stars, almost no advance ticket sales, and less than enthusiastic reviews. It had been developed in one of America's regional theaters with music by country and western singer Roger Miller. It struggled to remain open until it won seven Tony Awards, including outstanding musical, consequently going on to run for more than one thousand performances. Winning a Tony Award is even more important for plays, which often are only able to sustain a run and earn a profit if they win a Tony Award.

Predicting theater trends proves less than easy because it is difficult to gauge what play an audience will embrace. Sometimes plays that enjoyed great success in regional or foreign theaters fail miserably on Broadway. *Quilters*, by Molly Newman and Barbara Damashek, was the most successful musical in regional theaters throughout the United States during the 1980's. Its Broadway run in 1985 lasted less than one week. Some Tony Award winning plays seem to prepare the audience for future productions. Yasima Reza's *Art* (pr. 1994; English translation, 1996) created an audience for Michael Frayn's *Copenhagen* (pr. 1998). Both of these plays had profitable runs that likely gave producers the courage to back other dramatic "intellectual exercises." Moreover, the Wing has never fallen into set patterns of recognizing only the known and familiar. Throughout its history it has recognized theatrical innovation, whether it be in new technologies or dramatic forms. That recognition ensures support for experimentation and new artistic visions.

The significance of the impact of the Tony Awards can be best illustrated by *The Producers, The New Mel Brooks Musical* (pr. 2001), the 2001 musical comedy by Mel Brooks and Tom Meehan, which was proclaimed the most successful production in Broadway history, not because it made the most money or because it had the longest run but because it won twelve Tony Awards out of fifteen nominations, the most ever for a single production.

BIBLIOGRAPHY

Jewell, James C. *Broadway and the Tony Awards: The First Three Decades, 1947-1977*. Washington, D.C.: University Press of America, 1977. Traces the early evolution of the awards and Broadway theater.

Lindroth, Colette. *Rachel Crothers: A Research and Production Sourcebook*. Westport, Conn.: Greenwood Press, 1995. Chronicles the life and times of Rachel Crothers, a prominent actress and director credited with founding the organizations that led to Antoinette Perry's involvement in the theater.

Morrow, Lee Alan. *The Tony Award Book: Four Decades of Great American Theater*. New York: Abbeville Press, 1987. Lavishly illustrated with photos, posters, and *Playbill* covers, this oversized volume includes a history of the American Theater Wing, description of the major awards, and hundreds of brief biographies of the most famous winners in each category. This includes the usual listing of nominees and winners (through 1987). It is the only source that includes citations for all Special Tony Awards.

Stevenson, Isabelle, and Roy A. Somlyo, eds. *The Tony Award*. New York: Crown Publishers, 2001. This is the official guide of the American Theatre Wing, providing a brief history of the organization and listings of winners (since 1947) and nominees (since 1956) in all categories. The achievements recognized by special awards are not described. The volume, first issued in 1987, is updated periodically.

Gerald S. Argetsinger

BRITISH DRAMA

British Medieval Drama

In England, as on the Continent, theater in the classical sense virtually disappeared after the sixth century. With the decline of the study of Greek, classical tragedy lost its cultural currency and was almost entirely forgotten. Fortunately for later ages, some copies of Greek tragedies were preserved, notably in Irish monasteries. Roman comedy seems to have had at least a minimal existence, surviving in the *histriones* and *ioculatores* of medieval entertainment. The single example of classical comedy in the Middle Ages is found in the adaptations of Terence by the tenth century Benedictine nun Hroswitha of Gandersheim. Her plays on the saints, however, seem to have been confined to her native Saxony and therefore did not affect the development of English drama.

Liturgical drama

It was through religious ceremonies that drama was reborn in Europe in the tenth century. The simplest form of such liturgical drama was the trope, an amplification of a passage in the Mass or Divine Office. The best-known writer of tropes was Tutilo, of the Abbey of Saint Gall. Tropes were known in England, for a Winchester troper (a medieval book containing tropes) dates from the late tenth century. Tropes were often expanded into lengthy poems, sometimes in dialogue form, known as "sequences" or "prose," which became universal in the Christian liturgy. Some of them, such as Saint Thomas Aquinas's *Lauda Sion* (1265), are still in use today.

The first notable development of tropes into drama occurred in the famous *Quem quaeritis*, a dialogue between two sides of the choir, one side representing the women at the empty tomb of Christ on Easter Day, the other side representing the angel who tells them that Christ is risen. It was to become the most famous of all medieval liturgical plays, eventually developing into more elaborate Resurrection plays. These dialogues were at first exclusively in Latin and were performed within the Mass and, later, during the Divine Office, predominantly by clerics.

The prototype of the *Quem quaeritis*, again from the Abbey of Saint Gall, dates from about 950.

The *Quem quaeritis* was undoubtedly very popular in England. It is described in great detail in the manuscript *Regularis Concordia*, dating from about 970. The document was drawn up by bishops, abbots, and abbesses of England on the suggestion of King Edgar. It is now ascribed with relative certainty to Aethelwold, bishop of Winchester, as part of a book of customs relating to the Benedictine observances. It gives detailed directions for the dramatization of the *Quem quaeritis* and insists on the instructive aspect of the representation. The same manuscript also contains directions for a *Depositio Crucis* on Holy Thursday.

The development of liturgical drama in medieval Europe knew no national boundaries. The universal use of Latin and the numbers of *clerici vagantes*, or wandering clerics, made borrowings an ordinary occurrence. Thus, the growth of the *Quem quaeritis* play into a more elaborate *Visitatio sepulchri*, with more characters, many nonbiblical, followed a pattern that was evident throughout Europe. The incorporation of Peter and John, along with congregational participation, began in the twelfth century and continued well into the fourteenth. The only English manuscript of this type comes from the Church of Saint John the Evangelist in Dublin, a fifteenth century manuscript of a fourteenth century text.

Nativity plays, which were never quite as popular as the Easter cycle, began around the eleventh century and followed the same pattern of development as that of the Resurrection plays. Later Nativity plays centered on the shepherds (*pastores*) who were nearby at Jesus's birth and the three kings (*reges*), or wisemen, who came from the East to pay tribute to him. Simple stage props and costumes were used in such productions.

That Christmas and Easter liturgical texts in Latin existed in England is evident primarily from secondary sources because many manuscripts were destroyed during the Reformation in the sixteenth century. With the exception of the *Regularis Concordia*, the Winchester troper, the Dublin *Quem quaeritis* of the fourteenth century, and a manuscript from the Nunnery of Barking, there are no extant texts of Latin Easter plays. The last-named manuscript probably dates from about 1363-1376 and is ascribed to Katherine of Sutton, who may have been the adapter. The text contains several standard liturgical dramas: *Quem quaeritis*, a *Visitatio Sepulchri Depositio Crucis*, and an *Elevatio Crucis*.

There is no extant text of a Latin Christmas play, but such a *representatio* is referred to in a Salisbury inventory of 1222, and similar references occur in the York statutes of 1255. Both Christmas and Easter plays are mentioned in the thirteenth or fourteenth century statutes at Lichfield Cathedral, which provide for representations of *Pastores*, a *Resurrectio*, and a *Peregrini* (depicting the disciples on their way to Emmaus, traditionally performed on Easter Monday). There are references to Latin liturgical plays at Lincoln in 1317, and a fifteenth century Cornish manuscript, with a text dating from about 1300-1325, contains an *Origo Mundi*, a *Passio Domini Nostri Jesu Christi*, and a *Resurrectio*. Numerous manuscripts indicate that such Latin liturgical plays continued to be performed until well into the sixteenth century.

VERNACULAR RELIGIOUS DRAMA

By the thirteenth century, drama began to move gradually into the vernacular, and plays were performed outside the church. At the beginning, both Latin and the vernacular were used side by side. The earliest English documents are the twelfth century Anglo-Norman *Ordo representacionis Adae*, with the prophecies in Latin and in Norman French, which were probably played to French audiences, and the so-called Shrewsbury Fragments, a fifteenth century manuscript with a text dating from the late thirteenth to the early fifteenth century, with the role of one shepherd and the third Mary in English.

Although clerical objections are frequently given as an important reason for the development of the vernacular drama, critics such as Karl Young, E. K. Chambers, and A. P. Rossiter see such prohibitions as directed more toward secular drama. The most fa-

mous of these clerical prohibitions was made by Robert Grosseteste, chancellor of the University of Oxford and bishop of Lincoln, who in 1244 called on clerics to end participation in miracle plays and mystery plays. (Mystery plays, or mysteries, dramatized biblical stories and apocryphal narratives featuring biblical figures; miracle plays, or miracles, as the name implies, centered on miraculous incidents, frequently presented as episodes in the lives of well-known saints or martyrs.) Grosseteste's main thrust, however, seems to have been against May games and other forms of popular entertainment. A book titled *Manuel des Pechiez* (c. 1300), by William of Wadington, translated into English verse by Robert Mannyng and titled *Handlyng Synne* (1303), approved reverent religious drama and verse but condemned outdoor mysteries and miracles.

By the thirteenth century, few of the faithful understood Latin, so that the transition to the vernacular was natural and appropriate. The elaborate ceremonies made an outdoor presentation more appropriate than an indoor one, and some roles were more suited to secular actors than clerical. The development of a truly vernacular English theater was hampered in its early stages by the fact that many educated people spoke French, whereas English dialects were the language of ordinary people. By the late fourteenth or early fifteenth century, however, a vernacular tradition had been firmly established.

The first English mystery play extant is a thirteenth century dialogue called *The Harrowing of Hell*; inferior to similar contemporary French manuscripts, it is written in a rather primitive thirteenth century East Midland dialect. The play portrays a wily, bargaining Satan and ends with the overthrow of his power—a very popular theme in the liturgical drama of the Middle Ages. There are few records of English vernacular plays on the great Christmas and Easter cycles, but from the existing manuscripts one can infer that their development was similar to that of vernacular drama on the Continent. Records tell of an Easter play performed about 1220 outside a Beverley minster, in a churchyard, and even include details of a "miracle" strikingly similar to that described in Acts, chapter 20: A child who fell from a window while watching the play, it is alleged, was miraculously unhurt.

In the South of England, the Passion play was very popular in the fourteenth and fifteenth centuries, as it was in France. At Christmas in 1378, the minor clergy of Saint Paul's presented *The History of the Old Testament*; in 1384, a mystery play at Skinner's Well, lasting five days, told how "God created Heaven and Earth out of nothing, and how he created Adam and so on to the Day of Judgement." It is not known whether these plays were associated with the Corpus Christi and with the performances of the trade guilds. Records indicate that London had its Corpus Christi procession and that the guilds marched in order of preference.

The institution of the Corpus Christi procession in the second quarter of the fourteenth century had a great impact on the mystery plays. Another important factor was the so-called *Northern Passion*, a simple poem in Northern English, translated from French, that told the story of Christ's public life, Passion, death, and burial. It seems to have been very popular, particularly influencing the York-Towneley cycle of plays. A poetic translation of the apocryphal *Gospel of Nicodemus* into Northern English was also very popular and influenced the various mystery plays. One of the best-known episodes is the Harrowing of Hell, present in almost every cycle and generally providing the occasion for the most dramatic creativity. In fact, such vernacular sources seem to have had greater influence on the English plays than did Latin documents.

The great English mystery plays were popular for about 250 years, from the beginning of the fourteenth until slightly after the middle of the sixteenth century. At first, the mysteries were little more than translations or paraphrases of the Latin liturgical dramas, written in simple meters or stanzas. Among the most popular verse forms were octosyllabic couplets and quatrains, not always regular in rhyme or in the number of metric feet to the line. Some plays, such as those in the Chester Cycle, use the eight-line ballad stanza. As the mystery plays developed, they increasingly deviated from the Latin originals, adding apocryphal, legendary, and folk characters, much like the

plays on the Continent, as well as humorous and popular elements.

The most famous English mystery plays center on the celebration of the feast of Corpus Christi. The Corpus Christi cycle may have been established in Chester as early as 1327-1328, although according to Chambers and others, this date is questionable, because no further mention of the celebration occurs until about a century later. The pageants consisted of cycles of plays performed by the various guilds in competition with one another; each guild was assigned a play related to the craft or trade of its members, so that bakers performed the Last Supper at Beverley, Chester, and York; cooks performed the Harrowing of Hell (Beverley and Chester), supposedly because of their tolerance for fire; watermen reenacted the flood; and so on. Because this was an event that included the entire town, the plays were given outdoors, with the players and their scenes transported on wagons to a given station, in the street or the public square, where the audience assembled to view them.

Although the origin of such plays at the festival of Corpus Christi has provoked much controversy among scholars, it is generally acknowledged that they fit logically into this feast. As a celebration of the Eucharist, Corpus Christi points to the origin of liturgical drama in the ceremony of the Mass. Aside from symbolic considerations, late springtime was the logical season for such performances in England's damp, cold climate; indeed, the Corpus Christi cycles seem to have been a phenomenon of northern Europe, while in southern Europe such pageants were more likely to take place during Holy Week, culminating in Christ's Passion.

Although records of the Corpus Christi plays are plentiful, mainly from the documents and account books of the guilds, few cycles have been preserved completely. There are only four complete extant cycles: the Chester Cycle; the York Cycle, first mentioned in 1387, and which may be the oldest if the Chester date of 1327-1328 is not accurate; the Wakefield Cycle, of about 1425-1450; and the N-town Cycle (also known as the *Ludus Coventriae*), the origin of which has not been established. There are also fragments of cycles from Norwich, Newcastle upon Tyne, and Coventry. Independent plays, which have not been proved to be parts of the Corpus Christi cycle, include *Abraham and Isaac*, the Digby plays, a mid-fifteenth century *Burial and Resurrection* (preserved in Bodleian manuscript), and the fifteenth century Croxton *Play of the Sacrament*. From these plays, one can infer something of the scope and nature of religious drama in medieval England.

The city of Chester was independent and prosperous from the fourteenth to the sixteenth centuries. Its guilds showed pride in their successful business skills, yet they remained unspoiled by modernity. Accordingly, their plays remain among the simplest and the most religious of the period. The plays in the Chester Cycle were enacted in heavy vehicles that traveled from one station to another. There were twenty-four pageants in the series, and two sets of banns, or public announcements, of which only five are extant.

Among the surviving cycles, the Chester Cycle bears the greatest resemblance to the French mystery plays. *Abraham and Melchisedek*, though popular in the French plays, is found in England only in the Chester Cycle. *Octavian and the Sybil* also resembles the French plays. Other plays unique to the Chester Cycle are *The Woman Taken in Adultery*, *The Healing of the Blind Man at Siloam*, and *Christ in the House of Simon the Leper*. Although most of the plays show great fidelity to Scripture, the treatment of Lucifer in the first play of the cycle, like many other contemporary accounts, goes well beyond the biblical text. The fourth play of the cycle, *Abraham and Isaac*, is noteworthy for its dramatic development, while the seventh play, an Adoration of the Shepherds titled *The Shepherds' Offering*, has a degree of complexity evident nowhere else in the cycles. The latter features a clownish figure, the shepherd Gartius, who, though introducing humor, does not interrupt the reverent atmosphere of the cycle. The plays on the ministry and the Passion of Christ are very different from the others in their simplicity and lack of adornment. The Chester plays persisted until after 1570 and are best preserved in a late sixteenth century manuscript.

The York and Wakefield Cycles are linked in various ways that suggest a special relationship not found between other cycles. They are both preserved in incomplete manuscripts, in the dialect of fifteenth century Yorkshire.

The manuscript of the York Cycle is clearer and gives a fuller picture of its place of origin. York was the center of the earliest British Christianity and the birthplace of Alcuin, who brought scholarship to Charlemagne's empire through his palace school. By 1415, the period of the city's greatest growth and expansion, York was large and rich, with numerous trading companies. The York manuscript contains forty-eight plays, all of them quite short, although there seem to have been fifty-one in the complete cycle, according to a list prepared and signed in 1415 by Roger Burton, city clerk of York; a later list includes fifty-seven plays. Documents from 1399 and 1417 refer to twelve playing places, although later there were sixteen; there are many records of the plays among the regulations of the municipality. The York Cycle enjoyed a long and celebrated history: As early as 1397, King Richard I visited York to witness the plays, and they had their last performance as late as 1584.

The York Cycle has led scholars to conjecture a precyclic state of the Old Testament plays, probably without the influence of a previous Passion play. Thirteen of the York plays—the group from the Conspiracy to the Burial—are written in alliterative verse. These are excellent works, probably composed by one author of great talent. As at Chester, there were significant revisions among the various plays during their long performance history; some of the York plays were borrowed directly by Wakefield.

The Wakefield plays are known through a single manuscript that fell into the possession of John Towneley by the early nineteenth century; hence, they are also called the Towneley plays. The manuscript contains thirty-two plays that were performed by craft guilds at Wakefield, although no Wakefield records tell of such pageants. Critics hypothesize that the York plays were taken over by Wakefield at a given stage of development, after which the two cycles evolved independently of each other, because six of the plays that the cycles have in common are almost identical while thirteen of the plays that they have in common were revised at York but not at Wakefield. The York sponsors probably supplied the wagons to Wakefield after the merger of the plays. Four Wakefield plays—Isaac, Jacob, *Prophetae*, and Octavian—do not appear in the York Cycle. Several plays from the Wakefield Cycle, including those depicting Paradise, the events immediately following the Resurrection, Pentecost, and *The Assumption and Coronation of the Virgin*, have not survived.

The most significant aspect of the cycle is the work of the so-called Wakefield Master (c. 1420-c. 1450), unique in Middle English, with his clever, complicated style and wit. He uses many local allusions and colloquial idioms and adapts secular material for comic purposes. Along with the well-known *Secunda Pastorum* (commonly known as *The Second Shepherds' Play*), this anonymous dramatist was the author of *Mactacio Abel* (commonly known as *The Killing of Abel*), *Processus Noe cum Filiis* (commonly known as *Noah*), *Magnus Herodes* (commonly known as *Herod the Great*), and *Coliphizacio* (commonly known as *The Buffeting*). The Wakefield Cycle is unique in its presentation of two shepherds' plays, the second of which, as noted above, is one of the most popular of all medieval plays. *The Second Shepherds' Play* combines the liturgical *Officium pastorum* with a folktale of a pseudo-Nativity. Mak steals a sheep from three shepherds and hides it in the cradle prepared for the child that he and his wife are expecting. When the suspicious shepherds come to find their stolen sheep, Mak and his wife claim that their newborn child is in the cradle and refuse to allow the shepherds to enter. The play shifts from witty farce to serious drama as the angels announce the birth of Christ and the shepherds go to adore him. It is not known what guild performed this play, but Wakefield was the center of a prosperous wool industry in the fifteenth century, which probably accounts for the popularity of the shepherd theme.

The last complete cycle is preserved in what is known as the Hegge manuscript, Cotton Vespasian D. VIII. Because the town to which it refers has not been identified (it had been erroneously ascribed to Coventry), the cycle is often referred to as N-town, taken

from the banns (that is, the official proclamation listing the plays and their subjects) that accompany it. Many scholars believe that this cycle was performed by touring players because there is nothing to associate it with the guilds. The banns indicate thirty-nine plays, constituting a complete Corpus Christi cycle. The N-town Cycle is notable for its strong Marian orientation; for this reason, as well as because of its dialect, Hardin Craig, Chambers, and several other critics assign the cycle to Lincoln. Lincoln was a cathedral city—at the time, one of the largest in England—with a collegiate establishment and a center of ecclesiastical study. It was a center of Marian devotion, with special honor paid to Saint Anne, the mother of the Virgin Mary, as early as 1383. (Indeed, Craig associates the N-town plays with Saint Anne's Day, July 26, rather than Corpus Christi.) Lincoln also seems to have been a center of ecclesiastical drama for many years; Robert Grosseteste was bishop of Lincoln when he denounced abuses in Church plays.

Because the banns do not agree with the existing plays, it is supposed that considerable revision occurred. At the heart of the cycle are quatrains of four feet, although some plays use the ballad-type stanza, characteristic of the Chester plays. The plays with a Marian orientation include *The Barrenness of Anna*, *The Presentation of Mary in the Temple*, *The Betrothal of Mary*, *The Salutation and Conception*, and *Mary's Visit to Elizabeth*. There is also a complete Passion cycle in two parts—introduced, as in the Marian cycle, by a special prologue called *Contemplacio*. The most conspicuous play of the N-town Cycle is a very elaborate one on the Assumption, full of great learning and theology and based in part on the popular *Legenda Aurea* (Golden Legend). On the whole, the plays of this cycle differ from those of the York and Chester Cycles in their unity, in their learned quality, and in their greater use of liturgical Latin.

Other towns had elaborate Corpus Christi plays, which were known mainly from records rather than the plays, for with the exception of the four cycles discussed above, only fragments remain. The most important are the Coventry plays; they were so popular that the term "Coventry play" became synonymous with a Corpus Christi play. The number of participating guilds at Coventry seems to have been smaller than elsewhere. There is no evidence of Old Testament subjects, although Craig insists that they must have existed. There are only two surviving plays: the Shearmen and Taylors' play and the Weavers' play. The first shows the tendency of the Coventry plays to combine many topics into one play, for it comprises a prologue by Isaiah, an Annunciation, a Doubt of Joseph, a Journey to Bethlehem, a Nativity, a Visit of the Shepherds, a Herod and the Magi, a Visit of the Magi, and a Slaughter of the Innocents. Craig connects this play with the shearers because their guild seal shows Jesus in the arms of Mary receiving the gifts of the Magi. The Weavers' Pageant is the scene of Christ's Disputation with the Doctors and contains elements linking it to plays in the other cycles. In general, the Coventry plays are very simple, close to the Latin originals, and free from comedy. They maintain the reverent tone of the liturgical dramas, yet they constitute the least learned of the cycles. They exhibit little clerical influence, revealing the simplicity and naïve religious faith of the people.

A very important fragment comes from the Digby manuscripts, which are of uncertain origin and authorship. This fragment contains four plays: *Conversio Beati Pauli* (*The Conversion of Saint Paul*, 1976), a Mary Magdalen play, a Slaughter of the Innocents and Purification, and a morality play known as *Mind, Will, and Understanding*. They seem never to have been parts of a Corpus Christi cycle, but rather of smaller cycles, belonging perhaps to the East Midlands. *The Conversion of Saint Paul*, probably destined for an outdoor performance in a small town, is rather verbose and pompous. The Mary Magdalen play is the most ambitious of all surviving English mystery plays; it was probably enacted on a circular stationary stage, with spectators viewing it from all sides. It also has a sensational and widely extended course of action, which calls for a great many scenes and seems to suggest a very extravagant performance. The play borrows allegorical figures from the morality and *Paternoster* plays—namely, the

Seven Deadly Sins—and thus may have been a transitional work.

Although the importance of mystery plays in medieval English drama is well documented, the place of miracle plays is less certain. Some scholars argue that miracle plays in England were related to folk plays centering on Saint George, which belong more properly to the comic theater. There are more records of miracle plays in Scotland than in England, particularly on obscure saints and topics. Because so few plays have survived, there is no conclusive study of miracle plays in English, and critical theories concerning the genre must rely on conjecture.

One of the earliest recorded miracle plays is a life of Saint Catherine. It was written by 1119 by a Frenchman, Geoffrey de Gorham, who, before becoming abbot of Saint Albans, settled at Dunstable, where he composed the play. Unfortunately, the manuscript was lost in a fire. English scholars include the dramas of Hilarius, an Englishman, in their history of the miracle play because he wrote the semiliturgical plays *Suscitatio Lazari* (*The Raising of Lazarus*, 1975), *Danielis Ludi* (*The Play of Daniel*, 1959), and *Iconia Sancti Nicolai* (c. 1120-1130; *The Image of Saint Nicholas*, 1976). These works are in Latin and French and were probably performed for French audiences. From the life of Saint Thomas à Beckett, it is clear that miracles based on the lives of confessors (that is, believers who gave heroic evidence of their faith but were not obliged to suffer martyrdom) were performed in London in the twelfth century. References to lost mid-fifteenth century miracles include a Saint Laurence and a Saint Susannah, both of Lincoln; a Saint Dionysius from York; a Saint Clara at Lincoln; and a Saint George at Kent. In the early sixteenth century, plays of Saint Swithin, Saint Andrew, and Saint Eustace were acted in Braintree, Essex. Nothing, however, is known concerning the content of these works.

The only surviving example in English of a full-fledged miracle play is the Croxton *Play of the Sacrament*, found in Trinity College, Dublin, in the latter half of the fifteenth century, although it seems to have originated in Suffolk. The play resembles a French miracle, *La Sainte Hostie*; indeed, its anti-Semitic treatment of the central character, a Jewish merchant, had its counterparts in medieval drama throughout Western Europe. *Dux Moraud* (c. 1300-1325) is a fragment that contains the part of one actor only; it tells the story of an incestuous daughter who kills her mother and her child, born of her union with her father, and then tries to kill the father, who miraculously repents on his deathbed. On the whole it is similar to the French miracles of the Virgin, although she is not mentioned here.

One of the most important forms of medieval English drama was the morality play (or morality), a kind of dramatic allegory in which personified vices (such as Sloth and Envy) contend with personified virtues (such as Perseverance and Mercy) for man's soul. In addition to the vices and virtues, other personified abstractions (most notably, Death) enter the fray. The recurring theme of the English morality plays is the certainty of death and the desire of human beings to justify themselves before God. Moralities have a serious tone and were often performed in church, in the manner of liturgical plays, with appropriate costumes. The character representing Death was robed as a skeleton, and there was usually a dramatic spectacle in which the Dance of Death was played. There was a door or sepulcher into which the victims of Death disappeared, and a pulpit from which the priest admonished the congregation.

The Castle of Perseverance (c. 1440) is one of the earliest extant moralities, as well as one of the most extensive and learned. It follows Mankind (Humanum Genus) from infancy to old age. The World, the Flesh, and the Devil proclaim their intention to destroy him, and in his youth they tempt him, along with the Seven Deadly Sins. At the age of forty, he takes refuge in the Castle of Perseverance, but, after a raging battle, he is overcome by Covetousness. His old age is given to ill-humor and hoarding, and by the time Death claims him, Mankind has been deserted by all of his friends. In Heaven, Justice and Truth debate his fate with Peace and Mercy. God awards the judgment to the latter, and Mankind is admitted to Heaven.

The two most inspiring moralities on the theme of death are *Everyman* and *The Pride of Life*. The latter was found in a Dublin manuscript copied in the fifteenth century but thought to be much earlier in origin. It is the story of the King of Life, who defies Death and calls in both Health and Strength to aid him in the combat. Death wins, but the intervention of the Virgin saves the King of Life from eternal destruction. The play ends with a debate between the Body and the Soul. Although the play contains some references to the idea of personal sin, it recalls the motif of the Dance of Death in its portrayal of Death as the impersonal victor over all.

The best known of all medieval moralities is *Everyman*. Although it is dated from the early sixteenth century, it may have appeared much earlier. It closely resembles the Flemish *Elckerlijk*, first printed in 1495, and it is debatable which is the earlier; one may be a translation of the other. The play is remarkable for its classical simplicity and the concreteness of its allegorical characters. It begins with God, weary of human offenses, summoning Death to bring him the soul of Everyman. Everyman is surprised by Death's arrival and asks for time to find a companion for the journey. He first addresses Fellowship, who is interested in the adventure but turns back when he discovers the nature of the trip; Kindred does the same. Good Deeds wants to come along but cannot stand, weighed down by the heaviness of Everyman's sins. Knowledge then leads Everyman to Confession and Repentance, after which Good Deeds is able to accompany him. Beauty, Strength, Discretion, and Five Wits accompany him to the grave, where they all bid him farewell, and he commends his soul to God as Good Deeds promises to speak for him.

After 1500, very few new moralities appeared. The best known of these are *Mundus et Infans*, or *The World and the Child* (c. 1508-1522), a compressed life-cycle play dealing with the Seven Ages of Man; *Hickscorner*, or *Hick Scorner* (c. 1513), important because it was the first morality to use a comic figure for its principal character; and *Youth* (c. 1513), resembling *Hickscorner* but limited to the problems of youth. After this, most moralities passed into the genre known as the interlude.

Although most English plays seem to have had their origin on the Continent, especially in France, it appears that the English morality was unique in introducing the theme of death. Moralities developed into many other dramatic forms, such as the *sottie* in France, and in England exerted great influence on the Tudor drama.

Closely related to moralities are the *Paternoster* plays. The earliest reference to this genre dates from the third quarter of the fourteenth century: John Wycliffe speaks of *Paternoster* plays at York and elsewhere. In 1399, the *Paternoster* Guild of York performed a *Ludum Accidie*, or play on Sloth. From the records at Beverley, it is evident that all seven sins were presented in eight pageants, which were given at stations in the city. The *Paternoster* plays at York spanned two centuries, from the late fourteenth century to 1572, while there are records of eight performances at Lincoln during the period from 1397-1398 to 1521-1522. Unfortunately, all of these texts are lost, and conjecture concerning the genre must rely on contemporary descriptions of the plays and on the extant Mary Magdalen play (mentioned above), dating from the last half of the fifteenth century, in which there are elements of the *Paternoster* plays. Related to the *Paternoster* plays is the Creed play, which was performed at York every ten years around August 1, from about 1446, and perhaps persisting into the sixteenth century. The text of this play, unfortunately, is also lost.

COMEDY

Although the development of liturgical drama can be traced in some detail, the origin of comedy in medieval Europe is much more difficult to document with any certainty. Comedy was popular in the ancient world, and although there is no record of dramatic performances in the early Middle Ages, the institutions of minstrels, *ioculatores*, and *histriones* kept the comic spirit alive. That the comic tradition survived is evident from the many clerical pronouncements against it. As early as 679 C.E., the English clergy was admonished by the Council of Rome that the practice of maintaining musicians and of countenancing *iocos vel ludos* should be discontinued. In the ninth century, King Edgar chided the monks for taking part in mimes and dancing in the streets.

Among the folk customs associated with comedy is the Feast of Fools, which was celebrated around January 1. This feast was especially popular in France toward the end of the twelfth century, where a *Missel des Fous*, in Sens, dates from the thirteenth century and contains the well-known parody *Prose of the Ass*. The Feast of Fools provoked clerical interdictions throughout the Continent; in England, where this feast was least prevalent, it seems to have been strongest in Lincoln and Beverley. It was condemned by Robert Grosseteste in 1236 and, much later, by William of Courtney, archbishop of Canterbury, who found the custom still alive in Lincoln in 1390. The custom of naming an *archiepiscopus puerorum*, or Boy Bishop, observed around the feast of the Holy Innocents, December 28, was extremely popular in England. The first mention of the custom is in an inventory of a church in Salisbury, in 1222, which calls for a ring for the Boy Bishop. Surviving accounts indicate that the ceremony was quite elaborate: The arrival of the Boy Bishop at court was accompanied by carols, New Year's gifts, jousts, tournaments, and, in the fourteenth century, by *ludi* or *larvae*, for which the common name was mummings.

Mummings were first mentioned in 1377, in a Stowe manuscript. Mummings, which were played at Christmas time and involved much gaiety and pageantry, were originally "dumb" shows in which players, disguised as emperor, pope, knight, and so on, arrived on horseback, invited notables to a game of dice, and, at the end of the game (which the notables always won), accepted refreshments and performed dances. The first author known to employ dramatic effects in mummings was John Lydgate, a monk of the cultural center of Bury St. Edmunds: His *Mumming at Hertford* (1427-1430) involved the king himself in the action and included dialogue.

Other folk festivals that may have given rise to comedy include May Day, associated with Robin Hood plays, and Plough Monday, the Monday after Twelfth Night, which gave rise to the Saint George plays. Robin Hood is mentioned in William Langland's *The Vision of William, Concerning Piers the Plowman* (1362). The first extant ballad on this theme, *A Lytell Geste of Robyn Hoode*, dates from

1500, and the earliest Robin Hood play dates from 1475. Titled *Robin Hood and the Sheriff of Nottingham*, it may be the play referred to in Sir John Paston's letter of 1473, in which he speaks of an unruly servant whom he kept with him to play Robin Hood and Saint George.

The Saint George plays were performed throughout England, Wales, Ireland, and Scotland, sometimes with another saint or hero but always with the same basic story. The first act is a prologue; the second act features a fight, in which George (Saint or Prince) is killed; and in the third and final act, the slain hero is revived by a doctor. The play's central action is the fight and resurrection, and the doctor is a comic figure. Ridings (or processions) were also added to the celebration. The fullest account of these plays comes from the Norwich riding, established by 1408. In 1537, the character of Saint Margaret was added to the story. The Saint George Guild survived the Reformation, and dumb shows, ridings, and pageants on the Saint George theme continued to be performed long afterward.

The earliest piece of English comedy is known as the Cambridge prologue, dated not later than 1300. A fragment, it consists of twenty-two lines of French followed by twenty-two lines of English, presenting a request for silence made by the herald of a pagan emperor who swears by "Mahum" (Mahomet). The Rickinghall fragment, from the late thirteenth or early fourteenth century, tells of a boastful king who summons his nobles into his presence; it consists of two stanzas of French followed by nine lines of English. A farcial dialogue of the *fabliau* type, *Interludium de Clerico et Puella*, dating from the end of the thirteenth century, features a procuress named Eloise, suggesting an Anglo-Norman origin. *Dame Sirith*, also of the thirteenth century, is the only surviving Middle English *fabliau* outside of Geoffrey Chaucer's work. It tells how a reluctant girl, Margeri, is persuaded to accept the advances of the clerk Wilicken through a coarse folk motif known as the "weeping bitch." The use of English so early suggests a popular audience.

The farce as such is not a form indigenous to English comedy; like many other forms in English literature, the farce developed from French models. *La Farce de maître Pierre Pathelin* (wr. c. 1469; *The Farce of Master Pierre Pathelin*, 1905) was well known in England by 1535, and French actors had visited England in 1494 and 1495. Six "Minstrels of France" came to England in 1509, and it is supposed that they produced some of their farces in England.

The first English playwright who made extensive use of the element of farce was John Heywood, who believed that drama was intended to entertain and not to teach. He did not have a highly developed dramatic technique, but he excelled at farce. His *The Play of the Weather* (pb. 1533), though cast in the style of a morality in the character of Merry Report, a humorous vice, is actually a pleasing comedy. Jupiter sends Merry Report to several people to learn their preferences about the weather. They all differ, so he decides that things shall remain as they are, and all will have their turns. Heywood's most important comedy is *Johan Johan the Husband, Tyb His Wife, and Sir Johan the Priest* (pb. 1533; commonly known as *Johan Johan*), which has no connection with any religious play. The French original for this farce, *Farce nouvelle et fort joyeuse du pasté*, was discovered only in 1949. The story concerns a jealous husband, Johan, who intends to beat his wife, Tyb, because she is visiting Sir John too long and too often. Tyb dupes her husband into inviting the priest, and when Sir John arrives, Tyb sends her husband to fetch water in a pail with a hole in it. When he finally returns, he interrupts their lovemaking, only to be sent away to mend the pail. At the end of his patience, he finally pursues the fleeing priest and Tyb. Other plays by Heywood include *The Pardoner and the Friar* (pb. 1533), *The Four P.P.* (pb. 1541-1547), and *Witty and Witless* (pb. 1846, abridged; pb. 1909).

The study of the Latin classics during the Renaissance introduced Plautus and Terence into the curriculum beginning about 1510. Original Latin and French plays were often performed in schools and universities, beginning with *Miles Gloriosus* (*The Braggart Warrior*, 1767) in 1522. Schoolmasters frequently wrote imitations and adaptations for their students. One of the best of these was done by Nicholas Udall, when he was headmaster at Eaton. Udall's

Ralph Roister Doister (pr. c. 1522), the first of the Roman-type comedies, tells with considerable wit the classic story of the braggart and the parasite. *Gammer Gurton's Needle* (pr. c. 1562), by "W. S." (William Stevenson?), is also among the best of the plays written for the schools and universities; it is distinguished by a perfect accommodation of the academic to the popular.

Like the serious theater, comedy was indebted to Italian sources. George Gascoigne's *Supposes*, a well-shaped comedy of intrigue, is the best example of this type. Primarily a translation from Ludovico Ariosto's *I suppositi* (pr. 1509; *The Pretenders*, 1566), it was first performed at Gray's Inn in 1566. Romantic comedy was popular in the decade from 1570 to 1580. The subjects were taken mostly from chivalry and Arthurian romances. Unfortunately, few of these plays have survived, though their loss is to be regretted more by the literary historians than by theatergoers. It seems that the children's companies preferred to enact plays from classical history and legend, whereas the romantic comedies were usually played by adult troupes.

Comic elements are present in many serious dramas of the sixteenth century, and the distinction between genres is frequently blurred. The influence of the morality continued to dominate, and even Heywood's farces, except *Johan Johan* and *The Pardoner and the Friar*, end with a lesson. It is therefore difficult to isolate a comic genre at this time. Even in the Middle Ages, religious drama had its comic elements, as in *Secunda Pastorum* (fifteenth century; commonly known as *The Second Shepherds' Play*) by the Wakefield Master. By the end of the sixteenth century, elements of the medieval farce, though not absent, were subordinated to classical characteristics, if not themes, and the stage was set for the Elizabethan drama.

INTERLUDES AND THE TUDOR DRAMA

As the thirteenth century witnessed the development of the vernacular theater from the liturgical Latin plays, so the sixteenth witnessed a similar change. Plays moved outdoors in the thirteenth century to accommodate broader spectacle and secular

actors. At the end of the fifteenth century, and particularly during the sixteenth, English plays moved back indoors—to the Court, to the Great Hall of Palaces, to the Inns of Court, and to schools and universities. Acting became a specialized profession, with companies of men, usually four in number, and boys, generally from ten to twelve in a troupe, performing plays expressly written for their company. Because the companies were relatively small, parts were often doubled. The most famous early company of adult actors was the Court Interluders, which existed from 1493 to 1559. Among the prominent boys' groups were Paul's Boys, from the choir school of St. Paul's Cathedral, and the Children of Windsor. The division between professional and amateur and between men's and boy's companies was not absolute because a given troupe sometimes included both.

Plays performed in this context—indoors, to cultivated audiences, often by professional actors—were known as interludes. These plays, generally short and featuring only a few characters, may have begun as short pieces between the acts of religious dramas, but by the sixteenth century they had developed into an independent genre with its own distinctive conventions. Thus, the interludes provided a transition between the religious drama of the Middle Ages and the full flowering of secular drama in the Elizabethan theater.

The development of interludes was influenced by mummings and similar genres and by the elaborate pageants for the Tudor court. The first mention of a proto-interlude comes from Thomas de Cabham, who died in 1313. Other early forms of the interlude include John Lydgate's *Mumming at Hertford*, performed as part of the Christmas entertainment for the king, and Benedict Burgh's *A Christmas Game* (late fifteenth century), a solemn work comprising twelve stanzas addressed by a presenter to the Apostles.

The first important writer of interludes was Henry Medwall, whose *Nature* dates from about 1500. Medwall was chaplain to John Morton, cardinal archbishop of Canterbury, and was of the household of Sir Thomas More. Medwall's sister, Elizabeth, married John Rastell, a lawyer, printer, and playwright. Their daughter, Medwall's niece, Elizabeth Rastell, married

John Heywood, whose plays were printed by William Rastell, Elizabeth's brother. Finally, Heywood's daughter married the poet John Donne. This illustrious family was to play a leading role in English dramatic history in the sixteenth century. Medwall's *Nature*, despite its lofty morality theme of sensuality as unreason, contains much comedy, seasoned with tavern talk and allusions to contemporary London. It is for *Fulgens and Lucres* (pr. c. 1497) that Medwall is best known. This interlude had the distinction of being the first purely secular drama in English; in the style of a *débat*, it deals with the question of nobility of lineage versus nobility of soul.

Medwall's brother-in-law, John Rastell, is also noted for a nature interlude, *The Nature of the Four Elements* (pr. c. 1517), the only play ascribed with certainty to him. Not unlike Medwall's play, this one depicts humanity as struggling between Studious Desire and Sensual Appetite. Rastell also has his hero listening to lectures on astronomy and geography; these lectures are given by Experience, a great traveler who speaks of newfound lands. *The Nature of the Four Elements* was the first English work to name America and the earliest printed attempt to teach astronomy in the vernacular. *Calisto and Meliboea* (pr. c. 1527) is often ascribed to Rastell, and certainly was printed by him. Called "a new comedy in English in the manner of an interlude," it was the first English work to call itself a comedy. *Calisto and Meliboea* is based on the Spanish novel *La Celestina* (c. 1502) and concludes a seduction story with the heroine's repentance, including the lustful details preceding it.

John Heywood's interludes, especially *Johan Johan*, belong more properly to farce and the comic theater. John Redford's interlude *Wit and Science* (pr. c. 1530), written for the acting company Paul's Boys, is an allegory of the undergraduate life. Wyt woos Miss Science, the daughter of Dr. Reason and his wife, Experience, yet falls into many errors before he finally achieves his goal. This play, one of the purest allegories among the interludes, is also among the wittiest; it has very good speakable parts and is still performed today. The same theme is repeated in the anonymous *The Marriage of Wit and Science* (pr. c. 1568), although with less brilliance.

One of the most notable interludes of this period is John Skelton's *Magnyfycence* (pb. 1516), a morality with the familiar Renaissance theme of moderation. Potter sees the originality of this play in the way that Skelton uses linguistic devices, such as alliteration, repetition, and long lists of names, to illustrate lack of measure. The play is said to have addressed the lack of measure in contemporary events, especially the growing power of Cardinal Wolsey and the extravagance of King Henry VIII.

One of the most important factors in the changing character of sixteenth century drama was the Reformation. Writers began to use the theater as a tool for propaganda purposes, to which the morality and the interlude were well suited. At the same time, the government worked to eliminate religious drama—especially the miracle plays, because of their association with the Roman Catholic Church. Moralities survived better than mysteries. The first steps in this direction were taken under Henry VIII in 1543, although some of the mystery cycles had ceased to be performed even before this time. In 1547, Edward VI repealed Henry's statute and allowed moralities to be performed, but Corpus Christi was suppressed as a feast of the English Church in 1548, thus dealing a death blow to the famous mystery cycles. Elizabeth made no effort to root out the plays, but local authorities did. Although there are records of mysteries in extreme northwestern counties as late as 1612, by the end of the third quarter of the sixteenth century, the Corpus Christi play was no longer the center of theatrical activities.

Moral interludes at first took up the Protestant cause. The most zealous Reformation writer was John Bale. In the 1530's he wrote a cycle of plays based on the life of Christ, anti-Catholic moralities, and anti-Catholic history plays. Only five of his twenty-odd plays have survived. *Three Laws* is the first Protestant morality, as well as the first play divided into five acts. The plays on the life of Christ are devoid of all imagination in an attempt to follow Scripture exactly, and thus they lack the charm that made the mystery plays so attractive. Bale's best play is the historical drama *King Johan* (pr. c. 1539). Johan (John) becomes an idealized Christian hero, the noble champion of an England widowed of her husband, God, by false religions. *King Johan* is original in the choice of a historical theme for political morality.

Among other Protestant moralities and interludes, less vehement than Bale's, one of the most notable is David Lindsay's *A Pleasant Satire of the Three Estates* (pr. 1540), an excellent example of Scottish drama. The character of John o' the Commonweal approaches the memorable creations of Elizabethan and Jacobean comedy. Richard Wever's *Lusty Juventus* (wr. 1550) treats the popular prodigal son theme, which is also found in Thomas Ingelund's *The Disobedient Child* (wr. 1560) and Gascoigne's *The Glasse of Government* (pb. 1575). This theme probably came from German sources; in the Protestant moralities, indoctrination rather than education of youth becomes uppermost. The only extant Catholic morality is the anonymous *Respublica* (wr. 1553). Because the counterattack is less vehement than the anti-Catholicism that prompted it, *Respublica* is superior to most plays in the genre, with widely differentiated characters in contemporary society and witty comic elements.

Although the discovery of Plautus and Terence marked the interlude with a comic thrust, the Renaissance interest in Seneca turned serious drama away from the religious themes to secular and even tragic ones. In 1559, 1560, and 1561, Seneca's tragedies appeared in Jasper Heywood's translations, and the first notable product of the Senecan influence was also the only example of strict classical tragedy in Tudor England: Thomas Norton and Thomas Sackville's *Gorboduc* (pr. 1561; also as *The Tragedy of Ferrex and Porrex*, pb. 1570). The play is divided into five acts and into scenes within the acts. There is absolutely no comedy, and all the principal protagonists are killed. Following the morality tradition, the play becomes an apology for the divine right of kings. This type of drama, however, did not prevail in England; more influential was a mixture of tragedy and comedy.

The first play in the tragicomic vein was Richard Edwards's *Damon and Pithias* (pr. 1564), performed at Elizabeth's court by the boys of the Chapel Royal. Edwards's prologue is the first statement of dramatic

principles in English. The play has classical sources both in comedy and in tragedy; at the same time, it includes references to its contemporary audience. Not totally emancipated from the morality tradition, court tragicomedies maintained a Vice character. They also regularly featured king and counselor scenes and episodes of conflict and violence. Another typical play of this type is John Pickering's *A New Interlude of Vice, Containing the History of Horestes* (pb. 1567), wherein the Vice character is Revenge disguised as Courage.

The court tragicomedy was generally characterized by lengthy scenes and melodrama. Thomas Preston's *Cambises*, played at court during the Christmas season of 1560-1561, is a typical example. Based on Herodotus, with many accretions along the way, it features a Vice character, Ambidexter, who is both a double-dealer and a slapstick clown. "R. B." (probably Richard Bower), the author of *Apius and Virginia* (pr. 1567), presented an idealized melodrama of a seduction scene and a father who kills his daughter to save her honor. The Italian influence, along with the classical, was strong in such plays, as in Robert Wilmot's *Gismond of Salerne* (pr. 1565), based on Giovanni Boccaccio's *Decameron*, a fine play that is able to be staged even in modern times.

Although none of these plays is great, they represent certain important tendencies. One is the allegorical legacy of the moralities, which profoundly influenced William Shakespeare. Another is the fusion of genres, tragedy and comedy, which was to characterize mature English drama, in contrast to the strict separation of comedy and tragedy in the French theater. Finally, these plays point to the almost complete secularization of drama, which made possible a fully developed national theater.

BIBLIOGRAPHY

Alford, John A., ed. *From Page to Performance: Essays in Early English Drama*. East Lansing: Michigan State University Press, 1995. Twelve essays explore the role of performance in English drama from the twelfth to the seventeenth centuries. Focuses on moralities, university drama, and interludes.

Davidson, Clifford, et al., eds. *The Drama of the Middle Ages: Comparative and Critical Essays.* New York: AMS Press, 1982. Provides a general overview and interpretive criticism of medieval drama.

Gassner, John. *Medieval and Tudor Drama: Twenty-four Plays.* New York: Applause Theater Book Publishers, 1990. Offers several mystery and miracle plays from the medieval era, including Everyman, Tudor interludes and comedies, and some useful source materials.

Kastan, David, and John D. Cox, eds. *A New History of Early English Drama.* New York: Columbia University Press, 1997. Rather than an emphasis on individual playwrights and play titles, the twenty-six original essays of this work focus on the socioeconomic and historical contexts that gave rise to early English drama and the contextual effects on performance and physical space. Bibliography and index.

Kipling, Gordon. *Enter the King: Theatre, Liturgy, and Ritual in the Medieval Civic Triumph.* New York: Oxford University Press, 1997. Traces the importance of rites and ceremonies in medieval civilization and their translation into theatrical performances.

Moore, E. Hamilton. *English Miracle Plays and Moralities.* 1907. Reprint. New York: AMS Press, 1969. Provides history and criticism of early Christian dramas in England.

Tydeman, William, Louise M. Haywood, Michael J. Anderson, et al., eds. *Medieval European Stage, 500-1500.* Cambridge, England: Cambridge University Press, 2001. The editors bring together a comprehensive selection of documents and analyses to elucidate the survival of classical tradition and development of the liturgical drama, the growth of popular religious drama in the vernacular, and the pastimes and customs of the people.

Irma M. Kashuba

Elizabethan and Jacobean Drama

The rich intellectual life in England during the late sixteenth and early seventeenth centuries is reflected in literary works of the period. The Renaissance, with its accompanying movements, the new Humanism and the Reformation, brought with it a consciousness of artistic beauty and a love of learning little known since the days of classical Greece and Rome. From the days of Geoffrey Chaucer (c. 1343-1400), poetry bloomed in this favorable climate—a poetry different in mood and subject from that of the earlier medieval poets. Prose fiction, too, took tentative steps toward the novel as the stories people had to tell began to expand beyond the boundaries of rhyme and meter, but it was drama that overshadowed all other literary forms from the beginning to the end of the Renaissance.

The rebirth of arts and learning that came to England during the Renaissance brought with it the great drama of classical Greece and Rome. The guidance of Aristotle and the models of Sophocles, Aristophanes, Seneca, Plautus, Terence, and others brought to the Renaissance Englishman a view of humankind, of the world, and of human beings' relationship with the world in many respects different from the medieval view. Long before the introduction of classical drama into England, the citizens of cities and villages were acquainted with drama associated with the Church. The transition from native English mystery, morality, and folk plays to what is generally called "regular" English drama came about slowly from approximately the middle of the sixteenth century. The happy marriage of classical and native English drama gave birth to a hybrid type of literature.

Classical influence was strong during the Renaissance. In the early sixteenth century, Seneca's tragedies were translated into English and served as a model for regular English tragedy. The five-act structure; the observance of the unities of time, place, and action; the emphasis on character; and the use of the ghost were Senecan devices employed by English Renaissance writers of tragedy. For comedy, the works of the Roman dramatists Plautus and Terence, with their clear plot development, wit, use of prov-erbs, and natural dialogue, served as models. Elizabethan dramatists adopted the five-act structure almost completely, but they did not slavishly follow classical models in observing the dramatic unities. Native English settings and humor remained dominant in drama, but they were regularized and modified somewhat by the classical models.

A PERIOD OF TRANSITION

The period from about 1550 to 1580 may be thought of as a period of transition from mystery, morality, folk plays, and interludes to regular English drama. Classical influence was strong during this period, because those scholars who were writing and producing the plays were the same scholars who had introduced the literary works of classical Greece and Rome into England. Nicholas Udall, for example, who wrote the first regular English comedy, *Ralph Roister Doister* (pr. c. 1552), was an Oxford scholar and headmaster at Eton who studied and translated Terence. Seneca's tragedies had been translated into English by 1580 and served as an example for English tragedy.

One can see in *Jack Juggler* (pr. c. 1553-1558), perhaps by Udall, an excellent example of how Plautus was used in an English setting. The English dramatist takes the opening scene of Plautus's *Amphitruo* (186 B.C.E.; *Amphitryon*, 1694) and transforms it into London farce. *Jack Juggler*, however, is not a full comedy, only an interlude. Not until *Ralph Roister Doister* does one see a full English comedy composed according to the classical rules. It is divided into acts and scenes and has a consistent plot with a beginning, middle, and end. The characters Ralph Roister Doister and Matthew Merrygreek are patterned after the Roman *miles gloriosus* and parasite, respectively. Although the pattern is classical, the setting is English. The play depicts middle-class life in London, with Dame Christian Custance and her English servants replacing the Roman courtesan and her entourage.

Another English comedy of this period is *Gammer Gurton's Needle* (pr. c. 1562), probably by the Cambridge scholar William Stevenson. Like *Ralph Rois-*

ter *Doister*, *Gammer Gurton's Needle* is divided into acts and scenes and has a well-conceived, complex plot in the classical manner, but although the pattern is classical, the substance of the play is native English. Even Diccon, the most Roman of the characters, reminiscent of the intriguing slave of Roman comedy, is transformed into a distinctively English character. Whereas the setting of *Ralph Roister Doister* is urban, *Gammer Gurton's Needle* is set in a village. The dialogue, full of dialect and earthy language, helps to make the play more realistically English than any other early regular English drama. Its author was clearly a scholar of Roman comedy, but he was writing about and for English people.

One of the better Italian adaptations of Plautus and Terence, Ludovico Ariosto's *I suppositi* (pr. 1509; *The Pretenders*, 1566), was translated into English as *Supposes* and presented at Gray's Inn by George Gascoigne in 1566. Best known as a source for William Shakespeare's Lucentio-Bianca plot in *The Taming of the Shrew* (pr. c. 1593-1594), Gascoigne's translation is also important for having made available in English a comedy that, while modeled on the major Roman comedy writers, eliminated the classical characters of the slave, courtesan, and pander and built the plot around a love story, as though the inspiration for the play were more from Giovanni Boccaccio or Chaucer than from Plautus or Terence.

The influence of classical tragedy can also be seen in early sixteenth century England. *Gorboduc* (pr. 1561; also as *The Tragedy of Ferrex and Porrex*, pb. 1570), by Thomas Norton and Thomas Sackville, the first regular English tragedy, is directly modeled on Senecan tragedy. It has five acts, observes the unities, avoids comic situations, and employs a chorus. Violence, and indeed almost all the action, takes place offstage, as in classical models, but even here the theme is English, not Greek or Roman. The play's didactic purpose is to warn Queen Elizabeth of the dangers of leaving the kingdom without an heir to rule. Taking as its plot the story from legendary British history of old King Gorboduc, who, like the legendary King Lear, divided the kingdom between his two offspring, the play would presumably offer the potential for exciting stage action involving murder, intrigue, revenge,

revolution, and love. In fact, little occurs onstage except long reports of offstage action, inexplicable dumb shows, and almost endless, dull speeches. Although the play may strike the modern reader as tedious, its historical importance cannot be overstated. Not only does *Gorboduc* set the form for later Renaissance tragedy but also, and more important, the play is written in blank verse, a meter introduced into English some few years earlier by Henry Howard, earl of Surrey. The meter was used with good results by Thomas Kyd, refined by Christopher Marlowe into the "mighty line," and immortalized by Shakespeare.

Other adaptations of classical tragedy in English include *Jocasta* (pr. 1566) and *The Misfortunes of Arthur* (pr. 1588). *Jocasta* is a tragedy in blank verse in the Senecan style, adapted by Gascoigne and Francis Kinwelmershe from Lodovico Dolce's *Giocasta* (wr. 1549, an adaptation of a Latin translation of Euripides' *Phoinissai*, c. 410 B.C.E.; *The Phoenician Women*, 1781). *Jocasta* offered nothing new to English tragedy. The same can be said of *The Misfortunes of Arthur*, by Thomas Hughes, also written in blank verse and exhibiting a marked Senecan influence. Hughes based his plot on ancient British legends from Geoffrey of Monmouth and Sir Thomas Mallory.

Another type of play introduced during the period of transition is the chronicle, or history, play. The plays in this category drew their subject matter, as did much of the prose and both folk and street ballads of the period, from the English chronicles. John Bale's *King Johan* (pr. c. 1539) showed future dramatists the way to move from morality plays to more modern ideological history plays. The play features such allegorical characters as Sedition, Dissimulation, Private Wealth, and Usurped Power, conspirators against the righteous monarch, Johan. The allegorical character Imperial Majesty (representing the Protestant monarch Henry VIII) finally sets things right. *Richardus Tertius* (pr. 1579), by Thomas Legge, although a Latin play, is noteworthy as a transitional play because it uses recent English history. *The Famous Victories of Henry V* (pr. c. 1588) also uses recent national history as its subject. It neglects classical models almost completely, patterning its form more on the medieval miracle play. It is the earliest example of a play based on a popular rather than a scholarly view of history. In introducing Sir John Oldcastle (the prototype of Shakespeare's Sir John Falstaff) and many episodes involving Prince Hal in his madcap days, the anonymous playwright provided in rough form the material Shakespeare was later to use in creating his famous political plays involving Henry IV and Henry V.

Other chronicle plays that may be called transitional in the sense that they showed the way for later, better representatives of the type are *The Troublesome Raigne of John King of England* (pr. c. 1591), *King Leir and His Three Daughters* (pr. c. 1594), *The Lamentable Tragedy of Locrine* (pb. 1595), and *The First Part of the Tragical Raigne of Selimus* (pr. 1594). *The Troublesome Raigne of John King of England*, perhaps written by George Peele or Christopher Marlowe, is a rather loosely constructed play written at the height of anti-Catholic sentiment. It served as the primary source for Shakespeare's *King John* (pr. c. 1596-1597). *King Leir and His Three Daughters* is more nearly a dramatic presentation of the story taken from Raphael Holinshed's *Chronicles of England, Scotland, and Ireland* (1577) than it is a Senecan tragedy. Shakespeare's later treatment of the Lear legend has overshadowed the considerable value of its predecessor, but although the anonymous playwright provides neither the panorama nor many of the specific, sensual elements of Shakespeare's greater work, *King Leir and His Three Daughters* is a well-written and moving chronicle play. *The Lamentable Tragedy of Locrine* (by "W. S.", perhaps William Stevenson) combines both Senecan machinery and rather crude English humor in a history play. *The First Part of the Tragical Raigne of Selimus* echoes many lines from *The Lamentable Tragedy of Locrine* and uses many of the same sensational devices introduced by Seneca, but similarities end there. *The First Part of the Tragical Raigne of Selimus* takes its plot from Turkish, not British, history and features extravagant passions presumably calculated to appeal to unsophisticated theatergoers.

THE RISE OF ELIZABETHAN DRAMA

During the latter part of the sixteenth century, the popularity of dramatic productions increased among all segments of the English population, from the rustics, who, as Hamlet tells the players, "for the most part are capable of nothing but inexplicable dumb shows and noise," to the educated middle class to the nobility. Plays on almost every conceivable subject were written to appeal to some segment of the population, and a few were able to include something for everyone. What had begun in the Church and developed in the schools had now become so popular that both the writing and the acting of drama became a business enterprise. Tropes (passages or sequences for parsing the Mass) had expanded into medieval mystery and morality plays, and those, in turn, given the stimulus of classical thought and forms, had evolved into school drama. So successful had drama been in delighting audiences while teaching them Christian morality and Humanistic concepts that the next logical step in development was into the public realm.

In religious drama, the choir as stage had given way to the nave, the porch, and the churchyard; the churchyard, in turn, had given way to the open field; and the field, to the flatbed wagons on which players performed at different locations. In secular drama there was a centuries-long period of evolution, similarly, culminating in the construction of public theaters expressly designed for the production of plays. In 1576, James Burbage (father of the renowned Elizabethan actor Richard Burbage) built The Theatre just outside the city boundaries of London. Although some evidence, in the form of municipal records, exists to indicate that an earlier public theater had been built and used, Burbage's theater is generally considered to be the first major effort to establish a place where professional actors could practice their trade. The location of the public theater in Shoreditch, a name that adequately describes the area, allowed the acting companies to escape the jurisdiction of the unfriendly London authorities. When its lease ran out in 1596, The Theatre closed. The Curtain, built in the same general area, opened around 1577. From about 1592, when the Rose was refurbished there (it had been built in 1587), the Bankside, an area south of the Thames, just opposite the City but in the county of Surrey, became the "theater district" for London: The

Swan was erected there around 1596, the Globe in 1599, and the Fortune in 1600.

These public theaters were built primarily for the production of plays, but they were all nevertheless built on the plan of the innyard. The roofless auditorium offered only standing room for the mob, or the "groundlings," and seats in the roofed galleries for those who could pay more. These theaters were three stories high and either round or octagonal. The front of the stage extended out into the pit. Above the stage, beginning about half way back, was a balcony supported by two columns. Above this, set back somewhat, was a second balcony. Under the first balcony and in line with the second balcony was an upper stage, and behind that was a curtained-off inner stage.

Theaters built inside London had to claim that they were "private" playhouses catering to a special clientele, usually a wealthy and influential one. The first attempt to open a theater in London, in the Blackfriars district, was made in 1596 by the same man who had built the original Theatre, James Burbage, but after much time and expense, the city authorities refused Burbage permission to open the Blackfriars. The second attempt to open the Blackfriars, in 1600, was successful, but not without great difficulty. Private theaters in Stuart times, however, proliferated because of the comfortable seating, artificial lighting, and elaborate stage machinery.

The actors in early religious plays had been amateurs, controlled first by the Church and later by the trade guilds, and even after troupes of professional actors began touring England presenting interludes in the houses and castles of great families, much drama was being performed by child actors, both in school drama and in the homes of nobility. That child actors were serious rivals to the adult acting companies is illustrated by Hamlet's referring to them as "an aery of children, little eyases, that cry out on the top of question, and are most tyrannically clapped for 't." In 1574, a royal permit was given to Lord Leicester's Men, allowing them to act throughout the realm, but not until 1576, when Burbage built the first public theater, did professional companies have a place especially established for them to present their plays. Given the generally medieval view of morality of the

time, the acting companies were composed entirely of men and boys, with women's roles being taken by the boys.

There were two prominent adult professional acting companies during the latter part of the sixteenth century and the early seventeenth century: Lord Leicester's Men and the Admiral's Men. The latter group was headed by the notable Elizabethan financier Philip Henslowe, whose diary is an invaluable aid to scholars as a window to the daily operations of early theater management. Henslowe's son-in-law, the great actor Edward Alleyn, was co-owner. The company, which gained its name and reputation from its patron, the Lord High Admiral, owned two theaters, the Fortune and the Hope. The company was later known as the Earl of Worcester's Men, then as the Queen's Men, and then as the Prince's Men.

The second company was considerably more famous, having as one of its members William Shakespeare. Lord Leicester's Men, managed by Richard Burbage, took its name from the patron Robert Dudley, earl of Leicester. Its theaters were The Theatre, the Globe, and Blackfriars. At the death of Dudley, the company came under the patronage of Lord Strange, becoming Lord Strange's Men and later, when he became Lord Derby, Derby's Men. The company went on to have more patrons and therefore different names: Lord Hunsdon's Men, the Lord Chamberlain's Men, and then, in 1603, the King's Men.

UNIVERSITY WITS

Elizabethan drama evolved quite naturally from the intellectual climate of the times and was accompanied by the growth of acting as a profession. The increasing popularity of drama led to acting companies, special theaters, and the need for new material to enact. The new playwrights were not the Church scholars of medieval times or the schoolmasters of the middle sixteenth century. Rather, a new occupation developed, that of the professional playwright. Educated young men from Oxford and Cambridge, passionate young minds excited by the Humanistic spirit who had no inheritance or patrons to support their literary efforts, found in drama a way to mold language and ideas into a form that would support them. This group of educated young men, known as the University Wits, included John Lyly, Robert Greene, George Peele, Thomas Lodge, Thomas Kyd, Thomas Nashe, and Christopher Marlowe. Because these men not only were familiar with classical models but also were trendsetters in developing a distinctively English literature, they lent to the evolving drama both a form and dignity borrowed from the Aristotelian mold and an immediacy in language and idea sparked by an awareness of the political, social, moral, and economic problems of sixteenth century England.

Others in the new profession of acting learned from the University Wits and, in some notable cases, improved on them. Often the acting companies, both adult and children's companies, contracted with a professional dramatist to have a play written, but so hungry for material were the companies that their members, individually or in cooperation with others, would revise old plays to suit present needs or would fashion plots from old plays, poems, or tales into new dramas. These practical dramatists could often create works that combined the best of Humanistic ideas with the most practical dramatic techniques.

The predecessors of Shakespeare, therefore, built a tradition of excellence that would have given the Elizabethan age a luster had Shakespeare himself never written a word. Lyly, although he wrote not for professional adult companies but for children's companies, nevertheless had considerable influence on later playwrights. He carried the extravagant language of his *Euphues, the Anatomy of Wit* (1578) over into his drama with an effect thoroughly new in English drama. Many modern audiences find Lyly's style tedious and almost unreadable, marked as it is by heavy use of alliteration, antithesis, and elaborate similes and catalogs of fictitious authority to support insignificant arguments. Lyly's work is nevertheless a landmark in the history of English literature, setting a standard that showed the age that the English language was capable of art and grace. Shakespeare mocked the excesses of the euphuistic style in such works as *Love's Labour's Lost* (pr. c. 1594-1595), *Henry IV, Part I* (pr. c.1597-1598), and *King Lear* (pr. c. 1605-1606), but his plays reveal the devotion to style, the confidence in the resources of the language, that informed Lyly's works. Excessive as Lyly's rhetoric was, he illustrated the richness of English.

Through his witty dialogue, Lyly emphasized the intellectual comedy of wit rather than farcical comedy of situation. Lyly's best play is *Endymion, the Man in the Moon* (pr. 1588), an allegory praising Queen Elizabeth and the earl of Leicester. Elizabeth is portrayed as Cynthia, the chaste huntress, and Leicester is the faithful lover Endymion. Other plays by Lyly are *Campaspe* (pr. 1584), a prose comedy based on the classical story of Alexander, the beautiful Campaspe, and her artist-lover Apelles. In *Sapho and Phao* (pr. 1584) and *Midas* (pr. c. 1589), Lyly uses the old allegorical devices, while in *Galathea* (pr. c. 1585) and *Love's Metamorphosis* (pr. c. 1589), he employs pastoral elements. *Mother Bombie* (pr. c. 1589) is fashioned on the style of Plautus, with mistaken identity serving as its complication; *The Woman in the Moon* (pr. c. 1593), written in blank verse, satirizes women. All are pretty plays but slender in plot and significant ideas. As pieces of highly ornamental lace, Lyly's plays did not stand up well on the vigorous Elizabethan stage, but they served as models for the greatest drama the world has known.

If Lyly's plays are overly refined, those of Thomas Kyd are frank, often bombastic, full of blood and thunder. Although Kyd's sensationalism often overpowers the more truly tragic elements of his plays, his realism in language and action nevertheless gave a vigor to drama theretofore unknown on such a large scale. Lyly may have showed Marlowe and Shakespeare the way to delicate artistry, but Kyd showed them how to use raw power to grab the attention of the audience. Strongly influenced by Seneca, Kyd introduced revenge tragedy to English drama. Most scholars believe that Kyd wrote an early version of *Hamlet*, called the *Ur-Hamlet* (from the German *Ur*, "origin" or "source"). His reputation, however, rests on *The Spanish Tragedy* (pr. c. 1585-1589), the quintessential revenge tragedy. Here, Kyd introduces a ghost, insanity, and a play-within-the-play—all elements employed by Shakespeare in *Hamlet*—and, unlike the authors of *Gorboduc*, he presents violent action on the stage.

Greene is perhaps as well known for his prose as for his drama; like most of the professional writers of the age, Greene tried his hand at almost every type of writing that might bring him income. Educated at Cambridge, Greene expected to acquire fame as well as fortune, but both eluded him during his lifetime, and posterity has been only slightly kinder. Because he was not an actor himself, he merely wrote for others, a task that he did not entirely enjoy. In *Greene's Groatsworth of Wit Bought with a Million of Repentance* (1592), he calls actors "apes," "peasants," "painted monsters," and puppets "that speak from our mouths." Shakespeare is "an upstart crow, beautified with our feathers." He advises his fellow University Wits—probably Marlowe, Nashe, and Peele—to stop writing for actors, "for it is a pity men of such rate wits should be subject to the pleasure of such rude grooms."

Nevertheless, Greene wrote drama. *A Looking Glass for London and England* (pr. c. 1588-1589), written in collaboration with Lodge, resembles earlier religious drama rather than the secular drama of its own time. *Orlando furioso* (pr. c. 1588), based on Ariosto's work of the same title, is a play of lighter tone, but not completely successful. *James IV* (pr. c. 1591), not a history play but a serious comedy taken from a story by the Italian writer Giambattista Giraldi Cinthio, is perhaps most important for introducing Oberon, king of the fairies, to the English stage. Greene's best play is *Friar Bacon and Friar Bungay* (pr. c. 1589), a romantic comedy. The play draws on the legends that had grown around the thirteenth century philosopher and scientist Roger Bacon, whose thinking was so far in advance of his time that he was credited with magical powers. Greene shows that the magic of love is as inexplicable as the "magic" of Friar Bacon.

Friar Bacon and Friar Bungay was the first full romantic comedy on a pattern that Shakespeare was soon to immortalize—a pattern that was to be followed by all later writers of romantic comedy. The character of Margaret sets the ideal of the Renaissance woman: Greene's Margaret is a bright, vivacious, virtuous, and charming woman who can hold her own in dealing with any man. Whether Greene in-

tended to help show the way to "apes" and "puppets," he did so anyway.

As another of the University Wits, Peele wrote poetry and drama in a vain attempt to earn a living by his literary skills. Although some scholars have suggested that Peele spent some time as an actor, little evidence exists to support this contention; indeed, Peele's plays show scant knowledge of how to combine plot and character with ideas in a manner attractive to an audience. Those plays usually attributed to Peele are *The Arraignment of Paris* (pr. c. 1584), *The Battle of Alcazar* (pr. c. 1589), *David and Bethsabe* (pr. c. 1593-1594), *Edward I* (pr. c. 1590-1591), and *The Old Wives' Tale* (pr. c. 1591-1594). His contribution to the development of English drama is to be found in the verse employed in his plays: He softens without destroying the mighty line of Marlowe's blank verse and makes it fit for romantic drama.

The contribution of Lodge to drama is much less than to prose romance. Along with his poems and pamphlets, Lodge wrote the pleasant prose romance *Rosalynde: Or, Euphues Golden Legacy* (1590) used by Shakespeare as a source for *As You Like It* (pr. c. 1599-1600). Like the other University Wits, Lodge extended his literary experiments into drama. He collaborated with Greene in *A Looking Glass for London and England* and wrote at least one play independently, *The Wounds of Civill War* (pr. c. 1586), dealing with the civil strife between the Romans Marius and Sulla. Although the play is interesting as an early treatment of Roman history on the English stage, it suffers from ponderous speeches and a confused plot.

Nashe is best known for a series of pamphlets written during the famous Martin Marprelate controversy and for his anti-romantic prose narrative *The Unfortunate Traveller: Or, The Life of Jack Wilton* (1594), a precursor of the English novel. In *The Isle of Dogs* (pr. 1597), Nashe collaborated with Ben Jonson on a comedy that so pointedly portrayed the abuses of the state that Jonson was sent to jail. Nashe's only complete extant play is *Summer's Last Will and Testament* (pr. 1592), a play of courtly compliment that includes some of Nashe's characteristic satiric thrusts. The play has very little plot or action, but it has some vigorous moments and some surprisingly good poetry.

MARLOWE

Marlowe, Shakespeare's famous contemporary, is remembered not only for his poetry and drama but also for his colorful, often violent life and his mysterious death in a tavern brawl. In contrast to his fellow University Wits, he seemed less interested in establishing his reputation as a writer or in earning a living than in pushing life and ideas to the limits. In particular, the philosophical and political ideas of Niccolò Machiavelli fascinated Marlowe, and in his plays, he takes those ideas to their logical conclusion.

Marlowe's skepticism concerning the reigning medieval conception of human beings' place in the cosmos is implicit in his obsessive preoccupation with the nature of power. Some critics believe that Marlowe's skepticism is ultimately resolved on the testing ground of the plays; in their view, Marlowe should be read as a Christian Humanist. Other critics argue that Marlowe (who was accused of atheism by fellow playwright Thomas Kyd, with whom he had been living) clearly rejected the Christian worldview; according to their reading of the plays, Marlowe identifies with his proud, defiant, overreaching protagonists.

Marlowe's *Tamburlaine the Great* (*Part I*, pr. c. 1587; *Part II*, pr. 1587), based on the story of the Tartar king Timur Lenk, examines the nature of power as exhibited in the title character, Tamburlaine, who, as a young shepherd enamored of the riches and trappings of power, sets out to rule the world. This intoxication with power leads him to overcome all earthly adversaries, and he becomes an absolute monarch. The young Tamburlaine ignores the medieval concepts of divine intervention into worldly affairs and sets out to be his own god by becoming king; as his follower Theridamas says, "A god is not so glorious as a king." When the ruler's captive, the Turkish emperor Bajazeth, whom Tamburlaine wants to control absolutely, takes his own life, the man who would be god discovers that a power greater than his exists. Although he can take or spare life, he cannot, after all, control life and death. In the second part of the play, after defying the gods, Mahomet, and the Koran (Qur'an), the great Tamburlaine dies.

In *Doctor Faustus* (pr. c. 1588, pb. 1604), Marlowe analyzes yet another search for power, perhaps the most universal of human desires. Like Marlowe himself, Faustus is an educated man, a master of philosophy, medicine, law, and theology, but he is "still Faustus, and a man," still unresolved of the ambiguities of life. Finding no absolute answers in traditional studies, Faustus decides to try his brains "to gain a deity." He turns to magic, some scholars say to science, as humankind's way to know all things; as Faustus says, "A sound magician is a mighty god." Faustus finds, as did Tamburlaine earlier and as does Macbeth later, that no activity of humankind is infinite. Although he learns a number of fascinating tricks, Faustus is still merely a human being.

The Jew of Malta (pr. c. 1589) provides another Machiavellian character, at least as the Elizabethans generally understood Machiavelli. Barabas the Jew seeks power and wealth with no regard for values that might be dictated by a morally ordered universe. Because Barabas is so outrageous in his ideas and actions, so much so that Machiavelli himself would doubtless have detested him, his characterization often descends to bathos.

In *Edward II* (pr. c. 1592), however, the protagonist is a more convincing figure. Marlowe's Edward, unlike the typical Marlovian protagonist, is a weak and vacillating man. As Edward's power decreases, the audience's sympathy for him increases, and as young Mortimer's power increases, the audience's sympathy for him decreases, much as in Shakespeare's treatment of the weak Richard II and the strong Bolingbroke in *Richard II* (pr. c. 1595-1596). In *Edward II*, Marlowe created a complex, well-crafted tragedy based on an application of Aristotelian principles to English history rather than on the Senecan model. Shakespeare was to use and build on Marlowe's model in the plays of his second tetralogy.

Although the themes and forms of Marlowe's drama were widely influential, it was the poetry of his plays that had the greatest impact. The "mighty line" that Ben Jonson and all succeeding critics saw in the blank verse of *Tamburlaine the Great* set the standard poetic form for the majestic speeches characteristic of Renaissance drama. To speculate on what Marlowe might have achieved had he lived past his twenties is irresistible but ultimately futile. This much, however, is certain: No dramatist other than Shakespeare has shown more promise in his early works.

SHAKESPEARE

With Marlowe, the foundations of great Elizabethan drama had been laid—or rather, with Marlowe and the early works of Shakespeare, for in his early works Shakespeare was learning the trade of playwright. By 1595, the marriage of classical ideas and forms with native English literature and culture was consummated and secure.

Shakespeare, from the village of Stratford-upon-Avon, learned his craft not from studies at Oxford or Cambridge but from his own reading of classical literature, from earlier English dramatists and poets, from his connection with the professional theater as an actor, and from his extraordinary perception of human nature.

Shakespeare has been justly praised for his perception of human motivations and for the genius that allowed him to mirror these amazing perceptions in dramatic works of unparalleled power and linguistic virtuosity. Still, Shakespeare was not a dramatist who descended fully developed from Mount Olympus. He was a working dramatist of the professional theater as it was taking shape in Elizabethan England. He was, without question, the greatest dramatic poet of his time, but he was also the heir of a tradition of great poetry.

It is likely that Shakespeare saw himself primarily as a working dramatist who wrote drama because his company needed plays to act, for he made no great effort to protect his plays for posterity. Sixteen texts of his plays appeared in quarto form during his lifetime, but Shakespeare himself appears not to have been involved in their publication. The result is that such quartos are of uneven quality. Some are from the author's foul papers (the texts actors used for actual performance of the plays), considered "good" quartos even though they have the kinds of errors one might expect to find in a copy when the author does not read and correct galley proofs. Other quarto publications were pirated in one way or another and show the kind of corruption of text one might expect from such "bad" quartos. Many of Shakespeare's plays remained unpublished until seven years after his death, when two of his fellow actors, John Heminge and Henry Condell, collected his dramatic works (with the exception of *Pericles, Prince of Tyre*, pr. c. 1607-1608) in 1623 and published them in folio form. Of the thirty-six plays in this 1623 First Folio, eighteen had never been printed before. Even in the case of Shakespeare's 154 sonnets, although the poet had promised his patron in Sonnet 18, "So long as men can breathe or eyes can see,/ So long lives this, and this gives life to thee," the poems were not published until 1609, and some question exists about whether Shakespeare authorized the publication.

Since 1623, scholars have busied themselves with finding internal and external evidence to use in dating Shakespeare's plays. Once a chronology was established (insofar as any scholarly question concerning Shakespeare is ever "established"), certain patterns of the development of Shakespeare as a dramatist began to emerge. His plays may be categorized into four periods for the purpose of highlighting certain elements of his artistic development. Shakespeare did not so categorize his plays, nor did Heminge and Condell, and scholars can find fault with any attempt at categorization. The problems of the literary historian are compounded by the fact that Shakespeare did not limit himself to any single dramatic genre during any period of his career; he wrote comedies, histories, tragedies, and combinations and variations throughout his literary life. With these caveats posted, one may reasonably discuss Shakespeare's dramatic works in four periods of development.

The first period covers about five years, from 1590 to 1594, when, in order to supply his company with material to perform, Shakespeare began to adapt the plots and devices of earlier dramatists. He borrowed from Plautus, Terence, Lodge, Peele, Greene, Marlowe, and others; his purpose seems to have been to provide his fellows with a well-structured script that dealt with a subject already approved by audiences. During this time, Shakespeare was learning his craft, experimenting with presenting plot exposition in dialogue, with problems of characterization, with language, and with all that his predecessors had taught him. Although this first period was a time of experimentation and imitation, the plays nevertheless reveal glimpses of Shakespeare's poetic genius and his clear perception of human behavior and motivation.

To this first period also belong the poems *Venus and Adonis* (1593), which the author called "the first heir of my invention," and the more mature *The Rape of Lucrece* (1594). Some of the sonnets were at this time being circulated in manuscript form, but it is not certain which ones or when they were written. The plays of the first period represent all the popular types—comedy, history, and tragedy—and they are imitative and flawed.

Which play is Shakespeare's first has been the subject of much conjecture, but evidence is inadequate to lead to any secure conclusion. *Titus Andronicus* (pr. 1594) was certainly one of Shakespeare's first plays and clearly a melodrama. It is a bloody play, closer to Senecan tragedy than is Kyd's *The Spanish Tragedy*. The motif of eating human flesh, for example, derives from act 4 of Seneca's *Thyestes* (English translation, 1581). Because the play includes such horrors as rape, mutilation, murder, and cannibalism, some critics want to deny that Shakespeare wrote it, but in fact *Titus Andronicus* shows a great talent for effective presentation of plot so as to achieve suspense and an acceptable conclusion. Shakespeare's purpose in this early attempt at tragedy was almost certainly to provide for his company a play that would capitalize on the public's taste for sensational material presented with some degree of realism on the stage, and the play accomplishes that limited purpose, but in delivering a popular play to his company, Shakespeare also improved on his source.

The comedies in this first period are reflections of what Shakespeare had seen and read in the academic theater influenced by Plautus and Terence, the courtly drama of Lyly, and the popular comedy of Greene and Peele. *The Comedy of Errors* (pr. c. 1592-1594), which was an adaptation of Plautus's *Menaechmi* (of the late third or early second century B.C.E.; *The Twin Menaechmi*, 1595), is a farce involving two sets of identical twins separated at an early age and brought together by chance as adults. Shakespeare's play,

though a farce, has a structure more complicated than and superior to that of Plautus, and although dialogue irrelevant to the plot and emotive speeches unprepared for in characterization detract from the play's artistic unity and coherence, this early comedy presents in the marital conflict between Antipholus of Ephesus and Adriana, his wife, a good analysis of the intricacies of human relationships. In *Love's Labour's Lost*, the influence of Lyly is more clearly seen than in any other play of the period. The source of the comedy is not known, but the play at once uses and satirizes the romantic subjects and euphuistic style of Lyly. Beneath the witty dialogue and jests, however, is the serious contrast of nature with the artificiality of society. *The Two Gentlemen of Verona* (pr. c. 1594-1595) presents a love story that is less contrived than that of *Love's Labour's Lost*, and the characters are less caricatured, but Shakespeare's attempt to make his characters more individualized and more believable causes some problems, because the plot itself is not realistic but romantic.

The history plays of this early period were doubtless written to capitalize on the great spirit of nationalism that flourished after the English defeat of the powerful Spanish Armada in 1588. Only three authentic chronicle plays had been written before 1590, but soon history, especially English history, was to become an important subject for all types of literature. Shakespeare's early efforts at historical drama presented the story much as he found it in his sources, with characterization being subordinate to plot, but under the influence of Marlowe and prompted by his own interest in individual psychology, Shakespeare soon learned to use the stories and characters he found in history to write plays analyzing politics, love, hate, revenge, and other elements of the human condition.

The three parts of *Henry VI* (pr. c. 1590-1592) are uneven, lacking unity and coherence, but with the last play in the tetralogy, *Richard III*, Shakespeare had learned to escape the dramatic problems of episodic history by concentrating on a single character and a single theme, complex though they both might be. Here, the clash between the ideas of divine and Machiavellian power that so fascinated Marlowe is taken up and analyzed minutely and realistically; as in *Tamburlaine the Great*, the Machiavellian Richard runs afoul of the natural order and is defeated. In *King John*, Shakespeare continues his movement away from mere episodic history to concentration on theme—here, the theme of patriotism. Some scholars see this play as a rewrite, commissioned by his acting company, of an earlier play perhaps by Marlowe or Peele, *The Troublesome Raigne of John King of England*, but Shakespeare's treatment of the story is more than a mere rewrite. Here, he personalizes history, analyzing contemporary political concepts, an exercise he was to develop more fully in his history plays of the second period.

In his second period, from about 1595 to 1600, Shakespeare was no longer an apprentice dramatist imitating the work of others to produce plays for his company; rather, he had become a journeyman, able to plan his own work and create artistic works based on his understanding of his material, his audience, and his perceptions of human behavior. The plays of his second tetralogy derive from Raphael Holinshed's *Chronicles of England, Scotland, and Ireland* and from an earlier drama, *The Famous Victories of Henry V* (pr. c. 1588), but these sources serve merely as a vehicle for exploring the major question of political theory: whether power derives from divine right or from military power. To serve his purpose, Shakespeare felt free to change the historical age of Richard II's queen from that of a child to that of a mature woman, of Prince Hal from a boy of fifteen to a young warrior, of Hotspur from a man of about forty-five to one about the same age as Hal. The playwright moves armies about to suit his dramatic purposes and introduces pumps, gunpowder, and cannons into early fifteenth century England, where these devices were not yet in use.

In *Richard II*, Shakespeare continues his inquiry into the nature of kingship, showing the political folly of one who depends wholly on divine power to protect his authority: "Not all the water in the rough rude sea," Richard shouts, "can wash the balm off from an anointed king," yet he discovers that vaporous angels are no match for Bolingbroke's army. The play ends with Richard's descent from monarchical power and

high-flown illusions (exquisitely mirrored in the play's language and imagery) as Bolingbroke, now Henry IV, takes his place and the cycle of rise and fall begins anew.

The two parts of *Henry IV* (pr. c. 1597-1598) center on the political troubles of King Henry IV, who depends on military strength to attain and keep the crown, and the political development of Prince Hal (the future Henry V), whose grasp of the Machiavellian principle of situational ethics eventually surpasses that of his father. Indeed, the two plays focus less on their title character than they do on Hal and his personal and political maturation. This development culminates in *Henry V* (pr. c. 1598-1599), which concerns the reign of England's most successful king up to the time of Elizabeth. Having learned much about human nature and the requirements of kingship through the negative examples of the profligate rogue Falstaff and the hotheaded young nobleman Hotspur (in the plays about Henry IV), Hal uses Hotspur and Falstaff as Marlowe's Tamburlaine used Bajazeth—as steps to the throne—and then rids himself of them when they are of no more political use. Unlike Tamburlaine, however, Hal acts on the basis of a mature comprehension of his place as the representative, rather than the embodiment, of divine will. His understanding of his central role as monarch in the Elizabethan hierarchy of being—responsible both to the people of his nation and to God—makes him in many ways Shakespeare's ideal ruler.

The second period of Shakespeare's dramatic development contains more festive comedies than any other type of play. *The Taming of the Shrew* (pr. c. 1593-1594) derives from George Gascoigne's *Supposes*, from an old tale in a medieval English jestbook, and perhaps from a comedy of about the same time as Shakespeare's, with an almost identical title, *The Taming of a Shrew*. Shakespeare builds on his analysis of male-female relationships begun in *The Comedy of Errors* by contrasting the love affair of the romantic young lovers Lucentio and Bianca with that of the more mature Petruchio and Katherina. Here Shakespeare turns the farcical elements he found in his sources into a carefully drawn comedy in which Kate (as she is called in the play) learns what love is. *A*

Midsummer Night's Dream (pr. c. 1595-1596), written for private presentation rather than for the public theater, continues the theme of love. The five plots taken from various sources are carefully woven into a unified masterpiece showing that "the course of true love never did run smooth"—primarily because, as Puck remarks, "Lord, what fools these mortals be."

In *The Merchant of Venice* (pr. c. 1596-1597), *Much Ado About Nothing* (pr. c. 1598-1599), *As You Like It* (pr. c. 1599-1600), and *Twelfth Night: Or, What You Will* (pr. c. 1600-1602), Shakespeare's technical talents, clear perception of human relationships, and humor are developed to the point of mastery. All these plays treat love as the noblest of human attributes and reveal an optimistic view of humankind's ability to work through conflicts to the natural harmony that love brings to human beings.

In *The Merchant of Venice*, Shakespeare contrasts the honorable friendships between Antonio and Bassanio, Bassiano and Portia, and several other pairs of lovers with the unnatural hatred of the Jewish moneylender Shylock—a figure suggested by Marlowe's Barabas. Shakespeare's villain, however, is no unmotivated monster; rather, he is a man poorly treated by the Christian characters in the play, a man who does not understand the natural model of mercy or love. The play is dominated by the clever Portia, who does understand the model and who has the intelligence and force of personality to establish it in the midst of conflict.

Much Ado About Nothing continues the optimistic spirit of romantic comedy and again features a witty woman who helps to bring natural order to chaotic situations. The relationship between Benedick and the witty Beatrice is contrasted to that between Claudio and Hero. When the two major characters learn that they love each other, they combine to make right the evil engineered by the hateful Don John. Beatrice, aware of the benefits of love and justice, leads the successful efforts to reestablish harmony among members of society; all, one is given to understand, live happily ever after.

In *As You Like It*, a wise young woman again leads the way through conflict to order. Shakespeare borrowed the plot from Thomas Lodge's prose romance *Rosalynde: Or, Euphues Golden Legacy*, but the play uses only Lodge's names and settings, not his characterization. Once again, the villains, whose greed brings suffering and hardship, are pitted against a discerning young woman who orchestrates the return to order. Shakespeare's Rosalind understands that the courtly love tradition is mere nonsense and that secure love comes not from glandular secretion but from trust won by understanding.

In *Twelfth Night*, it is young Viola, shipwrecked on the shores of the fictive kingdom of Illyria, who teaches the lovesick Orsino and the morbid Olivia what love is and what it can do. There are no villains here, except for the puritanical Malvolio, who is more churl than villain, but there are clowns aplenty, as in the other comedies. Sir Toby Belch and Sir Andrew Aguecheek are buffoons in the tradition of Bottom, Launcelot Gobbo, Dogberry, and Touchstone—the play's true clowns—whereas the ostensible clown, Feste, who "wears not motley in his brain," anticipates the wise fool of *King Lear* in his position as truthteller by means of parody.

Although common themes and similar devices run through all of these comedies, each play has its own flavor and emphasis. They are all examples of "high comedy," plays in which the situations, wit, humor, and developments are generated from the characters rather than the other way around. Taking traditional devices from others and adding his own understanding of human nature and of the theater, Shakespeare created romantic comedy of unsurpassed quality.

Another play of this period, *The Merry Wives of Windsor* (pr. 1597), is different in many respects from the other comedies written at about the same time, as are the characters it borrows from the second-period history plays. Legend has it that Shakespeare wrote this comedy at the request of Queen Elizabeth, who wanted to see a dramatic presentation of Falstaff in love, but because Falstaff was created specifically to fulfill a thematic purpose in the last three plays of the second tetralogy, he is in most respects a different character. The result is a low comedy, producing much fun but little of the serious thought of the other comedies of the period.

The only tragedy of the second period is different from both earlier and later tragedies. In his *Romeo and Juliet* (pr. c. 1595-1596), Shakespeare presents the story of two young people who discover the glory of honest, natural love. The English interest in romance can be deduced from the popularity of the many prose romances and from the hundreds of love poems of the period, including the source of Shakespeare's play, the poem *The Tragicall Historye of Romeus and Iuliet* (1562), by Arthur Brooke. Here, Shakespeare shuns the vagueness of sentimental courtly love to dramatize the discovery of true love that he was to use as the theme in his great romantic comedies of the second period, as well as in the sonnets and many of the tragedies and comedies of later periods. The love of Romeo and Juliet is contrasted throughout the play to other concepts of love and marriage: the youthful infatuation that Romeo had for the aloof Rosaline; the effeminate emotion that Mercutio scorns; the proper alliance between families that old Capulet seeks to arrange; the essence of decorum that Paris desires; and the sexual satisfaction that the earthy nurse believes love to be. When Friar Lawrence chides Romeo for loving Rosaline one day and Juliet the next, Romeo explains to him the difference: Juliet loves him back, honestly and without reservation. Their love is celebrated in magnificent poetry; the sonnet, epithalamium, and aubade express the couple's love in the clearest possible terms. The young lovers are impetuous and overhasty in their relationship, and they are sometimes unthinking; their immaturity is displayed not in their love for each other but in their reactions to events not of their making. The play does not indict their relationship; on the contrary, their love, because it is so natural and honest, is perhaps too pure to survive in a flawed world, and thus they must die. Nevertheless, the deaths of the "star-cross'd lovers" result in a sense of pathos rather than the sense of fear and awe that the later tragedies evoke.

The third period of Shakespeare's development, from 1600 to about 1608, is commonly referred to as his "great period," his "tragic period," or his "bitter period." The great tragedies and dark comedies written during this period analyze the most difficult problems concerning humankind, the cosmos, and human beings' relationship with the cosmos; they show the greatness of people in constant conflict with their darker nature.

The comedies of this period begin with *All's Well That Ends Well* (pr. c. 1602-1603), a play that ends with Bertram promising to love and cherish his wife, Helena, but this comic ending has been reached by a tortuous path. Bertram, forced by the King of France to marry Helena, promptly leaves his bride with this contemptuous message: "When thou canst get the ring upon my finger which never shall come off, and show me a child begotten of thy body that I am father to, than call me husband. . . ." Instead of appealing to the kind of love Benedick has for Beatrice or Orlando has for Rosalind, Helena must rely on trickery to fulfill the requirements of her husband. Taking the place of Bertram's new mistress, Diana, in her husband's bed, she gets the ring and gets a child. The order of marriage is preserved by the so-called bed trick rather than by the dignity of human love. There is no purifying Forest of Arden here, no musical Illyria.

Neither is the world of *Measure for Measure* (pr. 1604) a happy place. The unyielding justice sought by Shylock in *The Merchant of Venice* becomes here the driving force of the play. The rule of Vienna is left by Duke Vincentio to his deputy, Angelo, who seeks by puritanical law to force morality on immoral man. He orders Claudio, a young gentleman, to be executed for seducing his betrothed, Juliet, yet when Claudio's sister, Isabella, appeals to the deputy to be merciful to her brother, Angelo agrees to do so only if Isabella will yield her body to him. Isabella, as extreme in her prudishness as Angelo is in his hypocrisy, refuses to give up her maidenhead to save the life of her brother, much to Claudio's distress. The play is saved as a comedy only when the rampant immorality of the citizens of Vienna is controlled by Vincentio, who has been observing the situation disguised as a friar.

The third comedy of the period, *Troilus and Cressida* (pr. c. 1601-1602), is perhaps the most bitter of all, so much so that scholars have for years been undecided whether to call it a comedy or a tragedy. In the 1623 folio, Heminge and Condell gave it the title

The Tragedy of Troilus and Cressida, but in most surviving copies of that collection the play is placed without pagination between *Henry VIII* (pr. 1613), the last of the histories, and *Coriolanus* (pr. c. 1607-1608), the first in the section of tragedies. There is a love story here, that of Troilus and Cressida, but Troilus is a lovesick young fool in the Petrarchan tradition, and Cressida is little better than a prostitute. The story of the Trojan War offers material to present humankind's nobility, but Shakespeare's treatment is anything but ennobling. Homer's great story is set in the mire, amid the petty squabbling of the Greeks and the irrationality and immorality of the Trojans. Hector is the most likely candidate to represent noble man, but after delivering a clear and rational argument to his brothers Paris and Troilus on why they should seek the high moral ground by returning Helen to the Greeks and thus end the bloodshed, he abruptly tosses godlike reason aside and agrees to continue the war. The deformed and scurrilous Thersites best expresses the theme of the play in his several remarks on what motivates man: "Lechery, lechery! still wars and lechery! Nothing else holds fashion."

Shakespeare's analysis of human beings' darker nature finds its greatest expression in the tragedies of the period. Political power, a subject that he had analyzed from a historical point of view in the second tetralogy, is presented darkly in the tragedies of this period. *Julius Caesar* (pr. c. 1599-1600), based on Sir Thomas North's translation of Plutarch's *Bioi paralleloi* (c. 105-115 C.E.; *Parallel Lives*, 1579), continues to use the chronicles as a source, as do many of Shakespeare's later tragedies, but here the emphasis is on individual human tragedy rather than history or politics, as is the case with *Richard III*, *Richard II*, and the other history plays with tragic overtones.

What A. C. Bradley calls "the four principal tragedies of Shakespeare" belong to this third period: *Hamlet, Prince of Denmark* (pr. c. 1600-1601), *Othello, the Moor of Venice* (pr. 1604), *King Lear*, and *Macbeth* (pr. 1606). In each of these plays, Shakespeare shows how the private virtues of great characters are, in the political and social contexts of the action, flaws leading to great suffering.

Hamlet, like the biblical character Job, finds that his expectation of a morally ordered universe causes him to hesitate to act when faced with the horror of insensitivity and injustice surrounding him in Denmark. Only late in the play does he decide that "there's a divinity that shapes our ends" regardless of the chaos existing in society, at which time he acts as a minister of heaven to restore order, but such action in the midst of evil destroys this good man as well.

The life and death of the great general Othello follows a similar pattern. Because he is a man "who thinks men honest that but seem to be so," he is easy prey to the brilliant villain Iago, who seems to be honest but is not so. The innocence of both Othello and Desdemona in an evil plot concocted by Iago causes their virtues to work against them. Desdemona's desire to help her husband and their friend Cassio contributes circumstantial evidence to aid in persuading Othello that she is indeed the whore that Iago suggests that she is. Othello's idealistic desire to protect the order of the cosmos then leads him paradoxically to contribute to the chaos of evil manufactured by Iago: He kills his beloved Desdemona. When, at the end of the play, Othello learns of the duplicity that led him to murder the one he held most dear, he also gains insight into the aspects of his personality that made him vulnerable to such duplicity. He is, as he recognizes before taking his own life, "one who loved not wisely, but too well."

King Lear, too, is an essentially good man who learns that he lives in a world in which love and virtue can be aped by mere words used by Machiavellian characters to further their own selfish ends. Two of Lear's three daughters, Goneril and Regan, "love" him only when he has power: When he gives up his power (by parceling out a third of his kingdom to each), they turn him out into the storm. He and, to a lesser extent, the earl of Gloucester learn that power in society comes not from virtue but from soldiers. Lear is, indeed, a man "more sinn'd against than sinning," but "sin" has no real meaning for those who do not recognize a moral order. Nevertheless, Shakespeare in this play offers a tribute to the power and supremacy of love in the person of Cordelia, Lear's third daughter, who, at the play's beginning, had refused to substitute the "letter" of her love and respect for her father with the "spirit," as expressed in her refusal to flatter her father with appropriate but empty words (as had her sisters) in order to gain her third share of his kingdom. Enraged by her unwillingness to bow to his authority and astounded by the truths she expresses instead, Lear disowns the only one of his offspring who truly loves him. At the play's end, a much battered, maddened, yet wiser Lear acknowledges his wrong, and father and daughter are reconciled in one of the most touching and humanly true scenes of Shakespeare's entire canon.

The consequences of flouting the moral order are further examined in *Macbeth*, but the pattern is somewhat different, for here good and evil coexist in the same characters. Macbeth fully understands the implications of disorder in the lives of men, as he demonstrates when he tells King Duncan that "the service and loyalty I owe,/ In doing it pays itself" and again when he tells Lady Macbeth, "I dare do all that may become a man./ Who dares do more is none," but his and his lady's lust for power eclipses his understanding, and they murder Duncan in order to gain the throne. Like Marlowe's Tamburlaine and Doctor Faustus, Macbeth becomes less than a man by trying to be more than a man; like Hamlet, Othello, and Lear, Macbeth and Lady Macbeth are tragically aware of the consequences of their actions. Lady Macbeth's conscience catches up with her, and Macbeth knows that in an ordered existence, he should have "honor, love, obedience, troops of friends," whereas through his unnatural deed he has gained only "curses" and "mouth honor" in their stead. Macduff, in killing Macbeth, executes the inexorable fate due to those who deny the universal order.

The fabric of these great tragedies is so rich and varied that no literary historian can do more than select a few generalities of many to indicate the importance of these works in Western culture. They show one of the greatest minds of all time analyzing philosophical problems that all thinking people consider at some time during their intellectual development, and they present these ideas in the finest dramatic poetry the world has to offer. Shakespeare's view of human-

ity is not always pleasant, but it is accurate, and dark though the tones and settings of the plays may be, in every case the worth and dignity of humankind is affirmed at the conclusion of the play.

The other three tragedies belonging to this period have never been accepted by scholars as of the same intellectual and artistic quality as the four principal tragedies described above. Perhaps they show the beginnings of Shakespeare's period of experimentation, but they are close enough to the great tragedies to warrant considering them alongside the others. *Antony and Cleopatra* (pr. c. 1606-1607) contains neither the horror of the proportions presented in earlier tragedies nor any hero of the stature of Hamlet, Othello, Lear, or Macbeth. Some scholars have a difficult time seeing Antony and Cleopatra as heroes at all, for, as Antony's soldiers believe, Antony is here in his "dotage" and Cleopatra is revealed as merely a capricious woman. Nevertheless, they are noble characters in conflict with others who are less noble. Antony is no Hamlet, nor was he meant to be, but neither is he merely an attendant lord. The play's only villain—and that is too strong a word—is Octavius Caesar, whose villainy consists in his wanting to be landlord of the world, a desire shared by much of the world's population. Antony and Cleopatra have discovered that "the nobleness of life" lies not in building an empire but in love, and in their struggle to live in a world that does not understand such a nonmaterialistic goal, they die.

In *Coriolanus*, a similar idea is presented. Coriolanus is an idealistic man of great talents, a nonpolitical man lured into the political world described by Machiavelli. Because he shuns the situational ethics required by anyone who operates in such an arena, he is destroyed. Similarly, Timon in *Timon of Athens* (pr. c. 1607-1608) is a generous man forced to flee society because of the greed and ingratitude of other people. Timon dies hating all humankind, but Alcibiades, who was also banished by the ungrateful leaders of Athens, returns to conquer Athens and restore order to society. Shakespeare's "bitter period," thus, appears from this perspective to reflect a realistic view of human beings' actions coupled with an optimistic belief in human beings' potential.

The plays of the fourth period, from about 1608 to 1613, appear to be experimental works. Shakespeare had left London for Stratford sometime in 1611, but even before that time he seems to have left the harshness of reality for the more pleasant realm of romance. Indeed, four plays of his final period are romances. These late plays still contain evil, guilt, and suffering, but mythology and magic are ever present to set things right in a way that does not occur in reality. Some scholars have suggested that the late romances indicate that Shakespeare had found a new faith in the goodness of humankind, but in fact the darkness in humankind presented in these plays is not neutralized by rational action, as it is in the plays of the third period, but by magic or improbable chance. In *Pericles, Prince of Tyre*, *Cymbeline* (pr. c. 1609-1610), *The Winter's Tale* (pr. c. 1610-1611), and *The Tempest* (pr. 1611), evil is transcended rather than confronted.

In *The Tempest*, the best of the late plays, the Machiavellian concept of life is represented by Antonio, the usurping duke of Milan, and Sebastian, his brother, who will murder their own kin to further their ambitions. No moral values guide their actions; as Antonio says, "I feel not/ This deity in my bosom." On another level of the action, there is a counterpoint between the bestial Caliban and the airy spirit Ariel. The action is controlled by Prospero, the rightful duke of Milan, exiled by his usurping brother, Antonio. Prospero, who can call up spirits to do his bidding, is generally regarded as a figure for the artist; his genial magic suggests the prevailing tone of the late plays.

In the last years of his life, Shakespeare wrote no plays by himself, but on two occasions he did lend his talents to plays by his friend John Fletcher. Shakespeare's contribution to *The Two Noble Kinsmen* (pr. c. 1612-1613) appears to have been limited to a few scenes, which Fletcher reworked and placed into the play in appropriate places. In *Henry VIII*, Shakespeare's part is largely a matter of conjecture, but the largest part has been attributed to Fletcher. Scholars believe, on the other hand, that the character of Queen Katherine, who is the best developed character in the play, is Shakespeare's.

The place of Shakespeare's plays in the history of Elizabethan drama is, therefore, at the peak. He was clearly influenced by his predecessors, who gave him the tools to practice his craft, but he sharpened the tools and created from the material of life works of art that have never been surpassed. As Shakespeare's famous contemporary Ben Jonson said of him, "He was not of an age, but for all time."

JONSON

Jonson is second only to Shakespeare as a giant of the period. The two were in many ways very different kinds of dramatists. In his *An Essay of Dramatic Poesy* (1668), John Dryden said of Jonson, "If I would compare him with Shakespeare, I must acknowledge him the more correct poet, but Shakespeare the greater wit. . . . I admire him, but I love Shakespeare," a view not uncommon among later scholars.

Jonson's best plays are his comedies, created, in the tradition of Plautus and Terence, to ridicule human foibles. If Shakespeare presented the mystery and complexity of human life, Jonson concentrated on human folly. His *Every Man in His Humour* (pr. 1598), with its well-constructed plot, stands as the first important comedy of humors on the English stage. In this genre, of which Jonson was the major exponent, human foibles are examined as a product of excessive personality traits (which, in medieval times, had been thought to result from an imbalance in the four bodily humors), concentrated in individual characters. A companion play, *Every Man Out of His Humour* (pr. 1599), has a more complex plot and suggests that humors are cured by their own excesses. Other early Jonson comedies are allegorical and satiric. *The Case Is Altered* (pr. 1597), based on a plot by Plautus, is a rather romantic comedy set in modern Italy, but the two other early comedies contain much more satire: *Cynthia's Revels: Or, The Fountain of Self-Love* (pr. c. 1600-1601) is a complex allegory praising Queen Elizabeth and satirizing some of Jonson's contemporaries, while *Poetaster: Or, His Arraignment* (pr. 1601) has a Roman setting and contains scathing attacks on the dramatist's adversaries.

The comedies written between about 1605 and 1614 are generally considered to be Jonson's best, most mature comedies. *Volpone: Or, The Fox* (pr. 1605), perhaps the greatest satiric comedy in English, shows the effects of greed on individual characters and society in general. *Epicœne: Or, The Silent Woman* (pr. 1609), thought by Samuel Taylor Coleridge to be the most entertaining of Jonson's comedies, is not so biting in its satire of humanity generally as *Volpone*; the gulling of the old recluse Morose is all in a kind of fun in which no one gets hurt. Greed and other human foibles are again satirized in *The Alchemist* (pr. 1610), a play relying on the medieval belief in alchemy to show how the human desire to solve complex problems with quick, simple answers makes people susceptible to quackery. *Bartholomew Fair* (pr. 1614) uses a rather simple, though well-ordered, plot to present a realistic pageant of colorful London characters—a veritable circus of pickpockets, mountebanks, confidence men, religious hypocrites, ballad mongers, puppetmasters, and many others. The good fun ends with all characters being forgiven their transgressions.

The late comedies return to the allegorical and satiric form of some of Jonson's earlier plays, with limited success. To this group belong *The Devil Is an Ass* (pr. 1616), *The Staple of News* (pr. 1626), *The New Inn: Or, The Light Heart* (pr. 1629), *The Magnetic Lady: Or, Humours Reconciled* (pr. 1632), and *A Tale of a Tub* (pr. 1633). The plots continue to be developed along the lines of classical comedy and are imaginatively drawn, but the characters remain mere emblems.

Jonson's two tragedies, both on Roman themes, are different in several respects from those of Shakespeare. Jonson, perhaps to display his superior knowledge of classical history, chose as his subjects minor incidents from Roman history; he also took as his sources the original Latin works rather than English translations or dramatic adaptations. *Sejanus His Fall* (pr. 1603), which derives from Tacitus, stretches the unity of time; the play depicts the destruction of the powerful Sejanus by the Emperor Tiberius. The psychological analysis of the tyrant's mind is well done both dramatically and intellectually, leading to the creation of Jonson's great comic character Volpone. *Catiline His Conspiracy* (pr. 1611) uses classical sources and dramatic devices, including a ghost and chorus, to show how humankind's bestial nature shapes political history. Characterization here, however, is weaker than in *Sejanus His Fall*.

Jonson wrote two pastoral plays, one of which, *The Sad Shepherd: Or, A Tale of Robin Hood* (pb. 1640), employs exquisite poetry in a mixture of pastoral and realistic traditions. The play exists only as a fragment; Jonson's other pastoral, "The May Lord," is now lost.

Jonson's poetical ability as a dramatist can be seen in the pastoral fragment *The Sad Shepherd*, but it is developed fully in his many masques written throughout his career. The masque is a highly ornamental type of drama written to provide entertainment at courtly functions and celebrations and different from the drama written for the public theater, for the companies of child actors, and for academic purposes. Jonson was the principal writer of masques during the reign of James I, and in these elaborate productions he replaced his satiric wit with his talent for writing carefully crafted poetry. Among the many masques he wrote for production at the court of James I are *The Satyr* (pr. 1603), *The Penates* (pr. 1604), *The Masque of Blacknesse* (pr. 1605), *Hymenaei* (pr. 1606), *The Masque of Beauty* (pr. 1608), *Hue and Cry After Cupid* (pr. 1608), *The Masque of Queens* (pr. 1609), *Oberon* (pr. 1611), *The Golden Age Restored* (pr. 1616), and *Gypsies Metamorphosed* (pr. 1621). These plays contain neither great character development nor profound ideas, for the purpose of masques was to provide not social commentary but courtly entertainment. What they do show is another side to this prolific and complex writer.

Like many of his colleagues, Jonson collaborated with other dramatists in writing plays. He had gone to jail for his part in writing *The Isle of Dogs* (pr. 1597) with Nashe, a play now lost. He had better luck with *Eastward Ho!* (pr. 1605), written in collaboration with George Chapman and John Marston. Scholars have been unable to determine with certainty which parts were written by which authors, for the play contains none of the biting satire of Jonson, the psychological analysis of Chapman, or the bitterness of Marston. The plot is realistic, presenting the virtues and pettiness in the lives of common tradesmen. The moral, if it can be taken at face value, is rather mundane, but the play is a pleasant comedy that presents middle-class London life in the style of Thomas Deloney or Thomas Dekker.

DRAMA AFTER JONSON

Had Shakespeare and Jonson never written drama, the history of the theater during the Renaissance would appear as a continuum from the late Elizabethan period through the early Jacobean period, or almost so. The tradition developed by the University Wits was continued by George Chapman, Thomas Dekker, Thomas Middleton, John Webster, John Ford, Francis Beaumont, and John Fletcher. These men, individually or in collaboration, wrote plays superior to any written for two hundred years or more thereafter. Their relative obscurity is caused simply by their proximity to the greatest dramatists in our culture. Others, such as John Marston, Thomas Heywood, Philip Massinger, Cyril Tourneur, and James Shirley, were good dramatists whose works lie even deeper in the shadows of Shakespeare and Jonson.

CHAPMAN

Chapman, perhaps best known in the twentieth century as the translator of Homer who impressed the English Romantic poet John Keats, was a leading literary figure in his day. He contributed both comedies and tragedies in response to the growing demand in London for new plays. His plots are generally more episodic than dramatic and are often exaggerated; his characters are distinctive and sometimes powerful, but seldom are their motives carefully analyzed. His comedies include *The Blind Beggar of Alexandria* (pr. 1596), *An Humourous Day's Mirth* (pr. 1597), *The Gentleman Usher* (pr. c. 1602), *All Fools* (pr. 1604), *Monsieur d'Olive* (pr. 1604), *The Widow's Tears* (pr. c. 1605), and *May Day* (pr. c. 1609). Three others were written in collaboration: *Eastward Ho!* with Jonson and Marston, and *The Ball* (pr. 1632) and

Chabot, Admiral of France (pr. 1635) with James Shirley. The comedies develop interesting characters in usually improbable plots. The vulgarity of some of the subplots in *May Day* seems strange coming from the moral Chapman, but certainly the play offers a realistic treatment of its subject.

Chapman's five tragedies offer an interesting study of the Renaissance view of Stoicism. Drawing primarily on French history rather than English, Chapman created strong heroes placed in stories of political intrigue. The protagonist of *Bussy d'Ambois* (pr. 1604), the best of his tragedies, is a character much like Shakespeare's Hotspur in *Henry IV, Part I*, Othello, Kent in *King Lear*, and Coriolanus. Bussy is a tested soldier out of place in the world of courtly intrigue. His tragedy is as much a result of his surprising passion for a married woman as of political intrigue. In *The Revenge of Bussy d'Ambois* (pr. c. 1610), Bussy's brother Clermont, more of the detached stoic character than Bussy, philosophizes with himself on the subject of morality, revenges the murder of his brother, and dies by his own hand. *The Conspiracy and Tragedy of Charles, Duke of Byron* (pr. 1608) returns to the theme of *Bussy d'Ambois* to show a strong character whose passions lead to his destruction. Chapman's last two tragedies, *The Wars of Caesar and Pompey* (pr. c. 1613) and *Chabot, Admiral of France*, both present heroes who react stoically to the problems that beset them. Chapman's purpose throughout seems to be to use drama to present psychological studies of characters in the manner of Shakespeare before him and Webster after, and although his dramatic structure is often faulted by scholars, he was one of the most popular of the Jacobean dramatists.

DEKKER

Another important dramatist of the late Renaissance is Dekker, a man whose love of life is reflected in his comedies. He took part in the "war of the theaters" that erupted between Jonson and Marston, writing the comedy *Satiromastix: Or, The Untrussing of the Humourous Poet* (pr. 1601)—the humorous poet being Jonson. Dekker's attack was not vitriolic, but Jonson soon realized that he was far too easy a target and withdrew from the "war." Dekker is best known for *The Shoemaker's Holiday: Or, The Gentle Craft* (pr. 1600), a pleasant comedy using a plot and characters borrowed from Thomas Deloney's prose romance *The Gentle Craft* (1597). Other comedies by Dekker are *The Whole History of Fortunatus* (pr. 1599; commonly known as *Old Fortunatus*), the two parts of *The Honest Whore* (pr. 1604 and c. 1605 respectively), *The Whore of Babylon* (pr. c. 1606-1607), *If This Be Not a Good Play, the Devil Is in It* (pr. c. 1610-1612; also as *If It Be Not Good, the Devil Is in It*), *Match Me in London* (pr. c. 1611-1612), and *The Wonder of a Kingdom* (pr. c. 1623). In addition, Dekker collaborated with other writers. His comedies are remarkable for their realistic portrayal of contemporary life and customs in essentially romantic plots. He excelled at the creation of individual scenes, although connections between the scenes are not always adequately provided.

MIDDLETON

A dramatist known to have collaborated with Dekker is Middleton who probably had a hand in writing *The Honest Whore* with Dekker. Middleton's portrayal of London citizens in a decidedly unromantic manner is an interesting cross between Dekker and Jonson. His most important comedies among the many he wrote are *The Phoenix* (pr. 1604), *Michaelmas Term* (pr. c. 1606), *A Trick to Catch the Old One* (pr. c. 1605-1606), *The Old Law: Or, A New Way to Please You* (pr. c. 1618), and *A Game at Chess* (pr. 1624). Generally considered to be his best plays are *A Trick to Catch the Old One* and *A Game at Chess*. His comedies present life as he found it, in all of its coarseness, but his fine poetry and mastery of language attracted the attention of audiences during his day and of scholars since. Middleton also collaborated with Dekker on *The Roaring Girl: Or, Moll Cutpurse* (pr. c. 1610) and probably with Jonson and Fletcher on *The Widow* (pr. c. 1616). He wrote two tragedies in collaboration with William Rowley: *A Fair Quarrel* (pr. c. 1615-1617) and his best, *The Changeling* (pr. 1622), plays that contain good ideas well dramatized but that are marred by highly sensational, bloody scenes.

WEBSTER

The plays of Webster are second only to those of Shakespeare in their analysis of the psychology of evil. Scholars have long admired the magnificence of Webster's villains but condemned their motivations as obscure. Modern scholarship has argued that the characterizations in Webster's two best plays, *The White Devil* (pr. c. 1609-1612) and *The Duchess of Malfi* (pr. 1614), are in fact complex, virtually clinical analyses of psychological disorders. The horrors visited on the virtuous Duchess of Malfi by her brother Ferdinand, for example, can be traced to the same source as his lycanthropy: his incestuous love for his sister and his inability to achieve his desires or even to admit them to himself.

Webster wrote only two other plays but collaborated on several others. *Appius and Virginia* (pr. c. 1634; with Thomas Heywood) is a Roman tragedy that lacks the analysis of horror found in his other tragedies. *The Devil's Law-Case* (pr. c. 1619-1622) is a romantic comedy that illustrates Webster's grasp of comic satire. Both plays have been neglected by scholars because they do not contain the startling portrayal of horror long thought to be Webster's forte; they deserve to be reexamined in the light of modern scholarship. Webster collaborated on two plays with Rowley, *A Cure for a Cuckold* (pr. c. 1624-1625) and *The Thracian Wonder* (pr. c. 1617); he also collaborated with Dekker, notably on *Westward Ho!* (pr. 1604).

FORD

Ford, like Webster, is known for his use of sensationalism. He explores frustrated love, as many of his colleagues did, but the problems that lead to the frustration are not the usual ones. Complex plots, as in *The Broken Heart* (pr. c. 1627-1631), lead the audience through a maze of sympathies and emphases. The play begins with a love triangle involving the unhappy heroine, Penthea; moves its focus to her brother, who is murdered by her lover; and ends by concentrating on Princess Calantha, who stoically receives the news of the death of her two friends and of her father the king long enough to set her affairs and those of the state in order before dying of a broken heart. In his best play, *'Tis Pity She's a Whore* (pr.

c. 1629-1633), Ford uses the theme of incest, as Webster did in *The Duchess of Malfi*, but in Ford's play incest is much more central to the plot and more explicitly treated. Indeed, so sympathetic is Ford's treatment of the brother and sister, Giovanni and Annabella, whose incestuous love leads to their tragic deaths, that some critics have seen a conflict between the play's apparently moral conclusion (sin is punished) and its inner logic.

Among Ford's other contributions to drama are *Perkin Warbeck* (pr. c. 1622-1632), *The Fancies Chast and Noble* (pr. c. 1631), and *The Lady's Trial* (pr. 1638). All the plays show clear construction and often scenes of intense passion and emotion. *Perkin Warbeck* is generally considered to be the best history play written after those of Marlowe and Shakespeare. Ford also collaborated with Dekker and Rowley on *The Witch of Edmonton* (pr. 1621) and with Webster on *The Late Murther of the Son upon the Mother* (pr. 1624). Several plays known to be by Ford are no longer extant.

BEAUMONT AND FLETCHER

The names of Beaumont (c. 1584-1616) and Fletcher, while they both wrote plays individually and Fletcher collaborated with several other dramatists, are almost always mentioned together because of the great success of the plays that they wrote in collaboration. The one play sometimes assigned solely to Beaumont is *The Woman Hater* (pr. c. 1606), a kind of burlesque comedy; some modern scholars believe that Beaumont was also the sole author of the mock-heroic satiric comedy *The Knight of the Burning Pestle* (pr. 1607). About twenty plays are usually assigned to Fletcher alone, including the pastoral *The Faithful Shepherdess* (pr. c. 1608-1609), a play of excellent poetry and rich imagery. Fletcher collaborated on many other plays with such dramatists as Massinger, Rowley, Middleton, and perhaps even Shakespeare.

The best works of Beaumont and Fletcher, however, are to be found among the plays jointly written by them rather than in their solo efforts. *Philaster: Or, Love Lies A-Bleeding* (pr. c. 1609), one of the finest plays of its day, is a tragicomedy that achieves genuine pathos. The play was acted often during the

seventeenth century and returned to the stage well into the nineteenth century. *The Maid's Tragedy* (pr. c. 1611) suffers from sensationalism and sentimentality, but its well-constructed plot and vivid characterization made it a popular play during its day. Both Beaumont and Fletcher were men of good family and good education, giving them a familiarity with men and women of high social standing and a certain contempt for the common person. They were able to write interesting and successful plays that often achieve brilliant effects, but they seldom explored the basic questions of human psychology with the intensity of Marlowe, Shakespeare, Jonson, or Webster.

OTHER JACOBEANS

Marston, Heywood, Massinger, Tourneur, and Shirley are usually ranked somewhat lower than the Jacobean dramatists discussed above, although some noteworthy critics would disagree with this ranking in a given case. Marston began his literary career as a poet, turned playwright, and then gave it all up to become a priest. He entered the war of the theaters against Jonson with his *Histriomastix: Or, The Player Whipt* (pr. 1599) and was held up to ridicule as the character Crispinus in Jonson's *Poetaster*, but the battle ended quickly, and Marston collaborated with Jonson and Chapman in *Eastward Ho!* in 1605. He even dedicated to Jonson his most famous play, *The Malcontent* (pr. 1604), the story of a virtuoso cynic. The deposed Duke Altofronto, disguised as the jester Malevole, roams the court commenting on immorality and injustice. In *The Malcontent*, however, as in Marston's other plays, the characters' motivations are often lost in the vigor of the action.

Heywood is usually listed as a major Jacobean dramatist on the strength of volume alone, for he wrote more than two hundred plays wholly or in part, many of which are no longer extant. His plays include histories, romantic comedies, realistic comedies, allegorical plays, and a number of pageants. The best of his plays are the domestic dramas, the ones in which specific elements of private life are dealt with interestingly and without undue sensationalism. Charles Lamb's description of Heywood as a "prose Shakespeare" is certainly hyperbolic; Heywood was a professional writer turning out plays for actors on proven themes. His best play is *A Woman Killed with Kindness* (pr. 1603), a kind of domestic tragedy on the order of Shakespeare's *Othello, the Moor of Venice*. In Heywood's play, the woman is guilty of adultery but repentant; her husband, controlling his rage and jealousy as Othello does not, banishes his wife to a manor "seven mile off," there to live out her life. When she is near death, he goes to her side and forgives her. *The English Traveler* (pr. c. 1627) presents a similar theme of seduction, repentance, and death from shame. Most of Heywood's plays present the same kind of delicate, thoughtful reactions to sin and a kind of quiet morality. Neither the sin, if that is what it is, nor the morality, if such exists, is analyzed as in the plays of Marlowe, Shakespeare, and others.

Massinger, who spent his dramatic apprenticeship in collaboration with Fletcher and such other dramatists as Dekker and Rowley, wrote comedies, tragicomedies, and tragedies. His plot construction is skillful and his characterization competent, but his prejudice in favor of the nobility causes his characters to have a kind of irritating predictability. His best play is *A New Way to Pay Old Debts* (pr. c. 1621-1622), with its interesting presentation of the political and financial kingmaker Sir Giles Overreach. Sir Giles is not uncommon as an overreacher—a rather usual character type in drama of the Renaissance—but Massinger presents in Sir Giles a more subtle type of empire builder than is usually analyzed. Massinger's overreacher does not aspire to be ruler, a position dangerous because of its high profile; rather, he seeks to place others in position of power and wealth so as to secure his own position without the dangers faced by those in the forefront. So strict is the morality of Massinger's plays that Sir Giles is caught in a trap created by his own greed, and he pays for his sins. *The City Madam* (pr. c. 1632), a play on a similar theme, is almost as lively and skillful, but its villain, Luke Frugal, does not quite measure up to Sir Giles in consistency and motive. Here again, the distrust that the noble audience of the private theater had of the middle class is at the heart of the plot.

Two plays are usually credited to Tourneur, a poet and dramatist about whose life little is known. *The Revenger's Tragedy* (pr. 1606-1607), regarded by some critics as one of the masterpieces of Jacobean drama, shows the corrupting power of revenge. Vindice, the protagonist, like his predecessor Hamlet, begins the play as a moral man caught up in a plot of lust and murder; unlike Hamlet, however, Tourneur's revenger acts not as a minister of heaven but as a man who learns to plot and murder with glee. Vindice recognizes at the end of the play that he has been corrupted when he says, "'Tis time to die when we're ourselves our foes." Tourneur's other play (if indeed he wrote either one—there is some question) is also a revenge tragedy, *The Atheist's Tragedy: Or, The Honest Man's Revenge* (pr. c. 1607). As in the earlier play, the dramatist here uses the revenge theme to express Christian virtues. A ghost is employed, as in many earlier revenge tragedies, but this time the ghost does not appear to direct revenge but to urge that revenge be left to God. The play thus offers an interesting addition to the usual revenge theme, but the idea is marred by the rather unrealistic application of reward for a moral life. Because he trusts in the moral order to set things right rather than taking the law into his own hands, Charlemont is rewarded with the same kind of material gain that has caused the villainy in the play. Interesting in the play is the presentation of the new materialism that came to late sixteenth century England.

One of the last dramatists of the period is Shirley, a professional playwright of whose works more than thirty plays are extant—more than any playwright of the period except Shakespeare and Fletcher. Shirley's plays are consistently competent in structure and characterization, drawing as he did on the models of his contemporaries over a wide range of themes and plots. Of his six tragedies, *The Cardinal* (pr. 1641) is the best. It has all the trappings of revenge tragedy sensationally displayed, as they had been presented by Kyd and the great writers of revenge tragedy who followed him. There are echoes here of Webster's *The Duchess of Malfi*, but Shirley is content to present the action without psychological probing. He wrote many more comedies than tragedies, the best being *Hyde Park* (pr. 1632) and *The Lady of Pleasure* (pr. 1635). The former is an early comedy of manners that looks forward to the drama of the Restoration. Shirley provides no hint that the pleasures of the aristocracy presented in this comedy would lead to the 1642 Civil War, only a few years away. The latter play presents a similar picture of an aristocracy for whom life is defined by their own pleasures and trivial concerns. The characters play at love in a sensual London, and the morality that is reaffirmed at the end of the play is little more than a witty refusal to sink completely into the mire.

Shirley was at the height of his career when, on September 2, 1642, the ruling Puritan administration proclaimed that "public stage-plays will cease and be foreborne," thus putting an end to the greatest period of English drama the world has known. It had its origins in the ideas and structures of Greek and Roman drama and in the realism of native English drama and life. It was able to grow to maturity because the intellectual and social climate of England was such that citizens were free politically and economically to pursue those ideas wherever they led. That persons of rare genius such as Shakespeare and Jonson happened along during the development of drama elevated the achievement to a level that has enthralled succeeding generations, but even without their contributions, the high reputation of Elizabethan and Jacobean drama would be secure. Rarely before or since has literature of any type held such a clear mirror up to nature, and never with such consistency.

BIBLIOGRAPHY

Braunmuller, A. R., and Michael Hattaway, eds. *The Cambridge Companion to English Renaissance Drama*. Cambridge, England: Cambridge University Press, 1995. Ten well-known scholars from Britain and North America contribute informative studies about the principal theaters, playwrights, and plays of the period between 1580 and 1642.

Dollimore, Jonathan. *Radical Tragedy: Religion, Ideology, and Power in the Drama of Shakespeare and His Contemporaries*. 1984. Reprint. Durham, N.C.: Duke University Press, 1994. This work still stands as a major reinterpretation of Renaissance drama and a pioneering critical work.

Egendorf, Laura K., and Chris Smith. *Elizabethan Drama*. Farmington Hills, Mich.: Gale Group, 2000. Twenty essays devoted to elucidating the historical events and social circumstances that defined this era and affected theater. The book is divided into five sections: "A Historical Overview of Elizabethan Drama," "The Characteristics of Elizabethan Drama," "Elizabethan Drama as a Reflection of Elizabethan Society," "An Examination of William Shakespeare," and "Assessing Elizabethan Drama."

Kastan, David Scott, and Peter Stallybrass, eds. *Staging the Renaissance: Reinterpretations of Elizabethan and Jacobean Drama*. London: Routledge, 1990. Argues, in a number of essays by notable Renaissance critics, that the Elizabethan stage was an intersection for numerous cultural forces, which defined and redefined social meanings.

Leggatt, Alexander. *Introduction to English Renaissance Comedy*. Manchester, England: Manchester University Press, 1999. Provides history and criticism of England's theatrical comedies.

Neill, Michael. *Issues of Death: Mortality and Identity in English Renaissance Tragedy*. New York: Oxford University Press, 1998. In the Elizabethan era, tragedy was one of the principal instruments through which people could imagine their mortality. This collection of essays looks at death in this era through three lenses: a trope of apocalypse, the psychological and affective consequences, and the conventions and motifs borrowed from the funeral arts. Examines *Othello, the Moor of Venice*, *Hamlet, Prince of Denmark*, and *The Duchess of Malfi*.

Wiggins, Martin. *Shakespeare and the Drama of His Time*. London: Oxford University Press, 2000. Traces the intimate connection of Shakespeare's plays with those of this contemporaries, including Christopher Marlowe, Thomas Kyd, Ben Jonson, and John Fletcher. Describes the principal audience fashions, artistic conventions, and professional circumstances that defined, and enabled, Shakespeare's plays and those of his colleagues.

Eugene P. Wright

RESTORATION DRAMA

The term "restoration" in Restoration drama refers to the return of the monarchy to England after something more than a decade of Puritan rule. Yet the term might with equal justice be applied to the stage itself, for during the Commonwealth interregnum, Puritan authorities repeatedly endeavored, though with limited success, to banish public performances of plays. From September 2, 1642, when Parliament proclaimed that "while these sad causes and set times of humiliation do continue, public stage-plays shall cease, and be forborne," until August 21, 1660, when King Charles II granted patents to Thomas Killigrew and Sir William Davenant to establish theaters, drama in England led a precarious existence.

Late seventeenth century British drama enjoyed a restoration in more than a political sense. As the political structure of the country returned to an older form, so, too, the drama, at least initially, looked back to pre-Commonwealth days to find its conventions, plots, characters, and themes. Indeed, in 1660 no new plays were available when the theaters reopened. Furthermore, both Davenant and Killigrew were products of the earlier period, having acted and written during the reign of Charles I, and most of the surviving actors—many had been killed fighting for the king in the Civil War—knew only the older dramatic conventions. During the Restoration period, about 175 pre-Commonwealth plays were revived, and among plays acted frequently over the years, about half date from before 1660.

Over the next forty years, however, English drama took on a voice peculiar to the age. The period's major contributions were the comedy of manners or wit and the heroic tragedy, both of which emerged rather quickly and endured throughout the era. Alongside these predominant forms, other types of comic and serious plays coexisted on the stage. Among the former were burlesques and farces, political satires, and comedies of intrigue; among the latter, operas and pastorals. Toward the end of the century, domestic or pathetic tragedy offered some variety to the theater-going public.

As these plays drew from the stagecraft and literature of the Jacobean and Carolinian drama, so the plays of the eighteenth century drew from the Restoration. John Gay's *The Beggar's Opera* (pr. 1728) and Henry Fielding's *Tom Thumb: A Tragedy* (pr. 1730) differ little from George Villiers's *The Rehearsal* (pr. 1671) or Joseph Arrowsmith's *The Reformation* (pr. 1673), which satirize the vogue for heroic tragedy. Charles Goring's *Irene* and Lewis Theobald's *The Persian Princess*, first performed in February and May, 1708, respectively, rely on the same kind of exotic settings that John Dryden was using four decades earlier for his heroic tragedies; as late as 1749, Samuel Johnson's *Irene: A Tragedy* (pr. 1749) provided viewers with the same conflict between love and honor, as well as exotic settings and elevated diction, that Restoration audiences had found in the tragedies of Nathaniel Lee. Furthermore, late seventeenth century plays retained their popularity well into the next century. William Congreve's *The Old Bachelor* (pr. 1693) was acted six times in 1724-1725, whereas Charles Shadwell's *The Fair Quaker of Deal* (pr. 1710) was performed only three times that season. Sir Richard Steele's *The Tender Husband: Or, The Accomplished Fools* (pr. 1705) was performed no more frequently than Sir George Etherege's *The Man of Mode: Or, Sir Fopling Flutter* (pr. 1676) in that period. The persistent popularity of this last piece, which may be viewed as the epitome of the Restoration comedy of wit, so troubled Steele that in the epilogue of a revival of William Shakespeare's *Measure for Measure* (pr. 1604), he sharply criticized audiences' admiration for the play's hero:

> The perjur'd Dorimant the beaux admire;
> Gay perjur'd Dorimant the belles desire:
> With fellow-feeling, and well conscious gust,
> Each sex applauds inexorable lust.
> For shame, for shame, ye men of sense begin,
> And scorn the base captivity of sin.

Restoration drama thus does not end abruptly with the end of the seventeenth century. Nevertheless, one finds a change in both playwrights and plays. By 1700, virtually every major Restoration dramatist had died or retired from the stage. Dryden died in 1700; in the same year, Congreve, following the failure of *The Way of the World* (pr. 1700), abandoned the theater. Thomas Shadwell had died in 1692, Sir John Vanbrugh turned to architecture, and William Wycherley, though he lived until 1715, did not write a play after 1676. The new generation of dramatists confronted an audience more bourgeois, devoted to at least the trappings of a newer, stricter morality, interested in sentiment and domesticity rather than wit and heroics. Not until the late eighteenth century, with the comedies of Richard Brinsley Sheridan and Oliver Goldsmith, did witty comedy revive, and even then the revival was only partial and sporadic. The world of the Restoration passed away, taking with it the world of its drama.

FOREIGN INFLUENCES

Many of the playwrights of the Restoration would fit easily into that category that Alexander Pope described as "the mob of gentlemen who wrote with ease." Among the dramatists were two dukes, four earls, a viscount, a baron, fifteen knights and baronets, and dozens of gentlemen. During Oliver Cromwell's regime, a number of these men lived in exile; as a result, they became familiar with the Continental drama of the period. Killigrew wrote *The Princess* (pr. c. 1636) in Naples, *Bellamira Her Dream* (pb. 1664) in Venice, *Claracilla* (pr. c. 1636) in Rome, *The Parson's Wedding* (pr. c. 1640) in Basle, *Cecilia and Clorinda* (pb. 1664) in Turin, and *The Pilgrim* (pb. 1664) in Paris. *The Parson's Wedding* was revived in 1664, the same year in which the other plays were published. The patentee of one of London's two theaters was obviously well versed in foreign drama. Etherege, to cite another example, lived in Paris when Molière was producing his works and drew from them for his own plays.

Molière was in fact the most influential foreign dramatist in the period; his plays served as sources for numerous Restoration comedies. *L'École des maris* (pr. 1661; *The School for Husbands*, 1732) was the basis of at least part of Sir Charles Sedley's *The Mulberry-Garden* (pr. 1668) and Thomas Shadwell's *The Squire of Alsatia* (pr. 1688). John Caryll's *Sir Salomon* (pr. 1669) derives from *L'École des femmes* (pr. 1662; *The School for Wives*, 1732). *Le Misanthrope* (pr. 1666; *The Misanthrope*, 1709) gives much to William Wycherley's *The Plain-Dealer* (pr. 1676) and Shadwell's *The Sullen Lovers: Or, The Impertinents* (pr. 1668). *L'Avare* (pr. 1668; *The Miser*, 1672) became Shadwell's *The Miser* (pr. 1672) and the fourth act of *The Squire of Alsatia*. *Les Fourberies de Scapin* (pr. 1671; *The Cheats of Scapin*, 1701) was the basis of Thomas Otway's *The Cheats of Scapin* (pr. 1676).

Other French writers also influenced their English counterparts. Pierre Corneille's rhymed tragedies probably helped determine the metrical form of heroic tragedy, and the French romances provided plots for a number of these plays. Dryden borrowed from Madeleine de Scudéry's novel *Le Grand Cyrus* for *Secret Love: Or, The Maiden Queen* (pr. 1667) and *The Conquest of Granada by the Spaniards* (pr. 1670-1671). Lee's *The Princess of Cleve* (pr. 1680?, pb. 1689) owes much to Gautheir de Costes de La Calprenède's novel of that title, and *Cassandre* (1644-1650) provided material for Lee's *The Rival Queens: Or, The Death of Alexander the Great* (pr. 1677) and John Banks's *The Rival Kings* (pr. 1677). From France, too, came the new convention of using women rather than boys to fill female roles; without this innovation, the comedy of wit—with its strong emphasis on sex—would have been impossible.

Other countries also contributed to the Restoration repertoire. King Charles himself asked Sir Samuel Tuke to translate Pedro Calderón de la Barca's *Los empeños de seis horas*, which became the popular *The Adventures of Five Hours* (pr. 1663), a play that started a vogue for comedies that featured Spanish settings and characters, swordplay, and also a strict code of honor. Agustín Moreto y Cabaña's *No puede ser: O, No puede ser guardar una mujer* (pb. 1661) was the basis of John Crowne's *Sir Courtly Nice: Or, It Cannot Be* (pr., pb. 1685), also adapted at the request of the king, and Sir Thomas St. Serfe's *Tarugo's Wiles: Or, The Coffee House* (pr. 1667). Wycherley's *The Gentleman Dancing-Master* (pr. 1672) is a loose adaptation of Calderón's *El maestro de danzar* (pr.

c. 1652), and George Digby, earl of Bristol, turned Calderón's *No siempre lo peor es cierto* (pb. 1652) into his play *Elvira* (pr. 1664).

The Italian *commedia dell'arte* provided yet another source for Restoration drama, particularly the farce and burlesque. On May 29, 1673, and September 29, 1675, the diarist John Evelyn records seeing a troupe of Italian actors, led by Tiberio Fiorilli, who performed in England frequently during the next decade. Edward Ravenscroft sought to capitalize on the popularity of the *commedia dell'arte* with his *Scaramouch, a Philosopher, Harlequin, a School-Boy, Bravo, Merchant and Magician: A Comedy After the Italian Manner* (pr. 1677), and the actor William Mountfort turned Christopher Marlowe's *Doctor Faustus* (pr. c. 1588) into a farce, *The Life and Death of Doctor Faustus* (pr. 1685), introducing both Harlequin and Scaramouch into the piece. Part of the vogue for opera also came from the Italians; on October 22, 1660, Guilo Gentileschi received a patent to build a theater for Italian opera that provided a model for English extravaganzas.

ELIZABETHAN AND JACOBEAN INFLUENCE

Yet while foreign influences were important, they were less significant than the earlier English drama in determining the form and the content of Restoration plays. In *An Essay of Dramatic Poesy* (1668), Dryden wrote,

We have borrowed nothing from [the French]; our plots are weaved in English looms; we endeavour therein to follow the variety and greatness of characters, which are derived to us from Shakespeare and Fletcher, the copiousness and well-knitting of the intrigues we have from Jonson, and for the verse itself we have English precedents of elder date than any of Corneille's plays.

Dryden claimed too much in denying any foreign debt at all, but he was correct in noting how much the Restoration drew from Elizabethan and Jacobean literature.

Ben Jonson was not especially popular during the Restoration: Of all of his plays, only *The Alchemist* (pr. 1610), *Epicœne: Or, The Silent Woman* (pr.

1609), and *Volpone: Or, The Fox* (pr. 1605) were performed with any regularity during the period. Yet his influence, particularly on comedy, was far from negligible. His insistence on realistic rather than romantic comedy helped steer Restoration dramatists in that direction; their comedies share Jonson's claim, in the prologue to *Every Man in His Humour* (pr. 1598), to portray "deeds and language such as men do use." Shadwell, at least in his earlier works, sought to write Jonsonian comedies of humors rather than the newer comedies of wit, claiming that the latter were immoral. His characters, like Jonson's, are obsessed with some peculiarity that causes them to act in an unusual and therefore comical way. The *dramatis personae* of *The Sullen Lovers: Or, The Impertinents* (pr. 1668) describes Stanford as "a morose, melancholy man, tormented beyond measure with the impertinence of people, and resolved to leave the world to be quit of them." Emilia is "of the same humour with Stanford." Minor characters in the play include the cowardly bully Huffe; Lady Vaine, a whore who pretends to be a lady; and Sir Positive At-all, a pretender to universal knowledge. As the title to Shadwell's third play, *The Humorists* (pr. 1670), indicates, this work, too, is in the Jonsonian tradition. His characters such as Sneak, Crazy, and Briske, their names describing their particular "humors," are closely related to Zeal-of-the-Land Busy and Adam Overdo from Jonson's *Bartholomew Fair* (pr. 1614).

Wycherley, too, drew on the humors tradition. In *The Plain-Dealer*, a number of minor figures are humors characters: Novel, "an admirer of novelties"; Lord Plausible, "a ceremonious, supple, commending coxcomb"; Major Oldfox, "an old, impertinent fop." Even Manly, the main character, is described in Jonsonian terms as "of an honest, surly, nice humor." Lesser dramatists also relied on Jonson, as indicated by such titles as *The Humourous Lovers* (pr. 1667) and *The Triumphant Widow: Or, The Medley of Humours* (pr. 1674), by William Cavendish, Duke of Newcastle, and Nevil Payne's *The Morning Ramble: Or, The Town Humours* (pr. 1672).

Even after Shadwell abandoned the comedy of humors, the tradition continued in the minor characters of many comedies of wit. Sir Joseph Wittol and Captain Bluffe in Congreve's *The Old Bachelor* are like Matthew and Bobadil in Jonson's *Every Man in His Humour*, Wittol foolishly admiring his supposedly brave companion, Bluffe claiming, like Bobadil, to be the greatest hero ever but tamely submitting to a beating. The one-dimensional nature of humors characters makes them particularly suitable to farce, where they provided the bulk of the *dramatis personae*, and even in the comedies of wit the names of the chief characters—Wildair, Sparkish, Horner (that is, cuckolder), Ranger, Valentine, Sir Fopling Flutter, Lord Foppington—rely on the humors tradition.

Like Jonson, Thomas Middleton in his city comedies provided a precedent for realism. Again like Jonson, Middleton drew his characters from the lower ranks of society—they are much better acquainted with Cheapside than Hyde Park—yet they are not always content with their social status. Hoard aspires to be a country gentleman in *A Trick to Catch the Old One* (pr. c. 1605-1606), Yellowhammer stresses his Oxfordshire connections and seeks to improve his status through aristocratic marriages for his children in *A Chaste Maid in Cheapside* (pr. 1611), and Quomodo envisions his progress toward a rich country estate that he hopes to get from Easy in *Michaelmas Term* (pr. c. 1606). These characters are pretenders, the forerunners of the Witwouds of Restoration comedy, who would claim a code of behavior and style of life not their own.

Richard Brome, writing shortly after Middleton, presented similar would-be aristocrats. Widgine reflects on Sir Paul Squelch in *The Northern Lass* (pr. 1629): "I have heard Sir Paul Squelch protest he was a Gentleman, and might quarter a coat by his wife's side. Yet I know he was but a Grasier when he left the country; and my lord his father whistled to a team of horses. . . . But now he is Right Worshipful." Mistress Fichow in the same play seeks to marry someone who will make her a lady. Brome also introduces a forerunner of the Restoration heroine, the sexually liberated woman. Rebecca in *The Sparagus Garden* (pr. 1635) observes, "I see what shift soever a woman makes with her husband at home, a friend does best abroad." Alicia, from *The City Wit: Or, The Woman Wears the Breeches* (pr. c. 1629) also seeks to supple-

ment her husband with a lover. The spirit of the age was not ready, though, for their intrigues to succeed.

Brome, like Middleton and Jonson, deals with the lower and the lower-middle classes. James Shirley applied their realism to the world of leisure, contrasting those who would belong to the fashionable world with those who truly do. The silly and affected Lady Bornwell in *The Lady of Pleasure* (pr. 1635) tries to pose as a socialite; against her pretensions, Shirley juxtaposes the polished Celestina. While the play's moralizing marks it as pre-Restoration, the characterization foreshadows Etherege and Congreve.

The wife of Charles I, Queen Henrietta Maria, introduced to the court the doctrines of Platonic love. The love in Restoration comedy is anything but Platonic; the tragedies, on the other hand, borrow heavily from this tradition. The high-flown rhetoric of heroic tragedy, for example, follows the convention that refined diction is the only kind suitable for lovers. Such Platonic notions generated a strong realistic backlash, however, reflected in the poetry of the Cavaliers and in such plays as *The Country Captain* (pr. c. 1639), by Cavendish, in which Sir Francis, a polished courtier, seduces Lady Huntlove. At the end of the play, Sir Francis reforms and urges his mistress to do likewise, but Lady Huntlove is neither condemned nor punished.

By the outbreak of the Civil War, then, English drama had developed a number of elements utilized by Restoration playwrights. Despite Puritan efforts to suppress the drama after 1642, plays were published and rather regularly produced: Under the Commonwealth, there were fourteen editions of *Mucedorus* (pb. 1598); eight of Marlowe's *Doctor Faustus*; six editions of Francis Beaumont and John Fletcher's *Philaster: Or, Love Lies A-Bleeding* (pr. c. 1609), *A King and No King* (pr. 1611), *The Maid's Tragedy* (pr. c. 1611), and George Chapman's *The Revenge of Bussy d'Ambois* (pr. c. 1610). One bookseller advertised more than five hundred plays. A major publishing event of the period was the appearance of the Beaumont and Fletcher folio in 1647; their plays were immensely popular in the latter half of the seventeenth century, when thirty-nine were definitely performed and three others may have been performed. In

1668-1669 alone, eleven Beaumont and Fletcher plays were revived, compared with six by Shakespeare. Not only were these plays perennial favorites, but also their emphasis on genteel romance influenced comic writers, while their exotic settings and tragicomic plots were taken up by writers of serious plays. Publication thus helped keep alive the English dramatic traditions. As Sir Aston Cokain observed in the preface to Brome's *Five New Plays* (1653), "though we may/ Not them in their full glories yet display,/ Yet we may please ourselves by reading them."

In fact, it was possible to see a number of plays in their full glory. *The Kingdom's Weekly Intelligencer* for January 18-25, 1648, noted, "It is very observable, that on Sunday January 23 there were ten Coaches to hear Doctor Usher at Lincoln's Inn, but there were above sixscore coaches on the last Thursday in Golden Lane to hear the players at the Fortune." John Evelyn attended a performance at the Cockpit on February 5, 1648, and even after the Parliament issued another ordinance against acting, it was informed in September "that stage-plays were duly acted, either at the Bull or Fortune, or the private house at Salisbury Court." On New Year's Day, 1649, soldiers broke up performances at the Cockpit and Salisbury Court. Raids occurred repeatedly at these theaters over the next several years, indicating that plays continued to be produced. Sir Daniel Fleming, on a visit to London, reported spending twopence to see a play in 1653; during the next two years, he spent a shilling and fourpence at the theater. Parliament was no more successful in suppressing plays in the provinces. The historian Anthony Wood records seeing plays at the Blue Anchor tavern, Oxford, on July 6, 1657, at the Cross Inn on July 17, 1658, and at the Roebuck on July 8, 1659. Though English actors performed "by stealth," they nevertheless performed.

Occasionally, new plays were performed, too, among them Davenant's *The Unfortunate Lovers* (pr. 1638) and *Love and Honour* (pr. 1634), the latter summarizing in its title the basic conflict of Restoration heroic tragedy. Davenant's *The Siege of Rhodes, Part I* (pr. 1656) and *Part II* (pr. 1659), may be regarded as the progenitor of this genre. Abraham Cowley's *The Guardian* (pr. 1650) received several

private performances and was revised in 1661 as *The Cutter of Coleman Street*. This work was but one of several leveled against the Puritans: Samuel Sheppard's *The Committee-Man Curried* (pr. 1647), *The Cuckow's Nest at Westminster* (pr. 1648), and *Craftie Cromwell* (pr. 1648) as well as John Capon's *The Disease of the House* (pr. 1649) began a tradition that continued after the Restoration with such plays as John Tatham's *The Rump* (pr. 1660), Robert Howard's *The Committee* (pr. 1662), and John Lacy's *The Old Troop* (pr. c. 1664).

Etherege's *The Comical Revenge: Or, Love in a Tub* (pr. 1664) provides a good illustration of the viability of these older dramatic traditions. The serious lovers, Beaufort and Graciana, Bruce and Amelia, speak in heroic couplets that express Platonic sentiments. The witty Sir Frederick, with his epigrams, is an early version of the Restoration truewit, but his widow-chasing recalls Fletcher. Cully is a Jonsonian coward, and his gulling is reminiscent of Easy's in *Michaelmas Term*. Cully is also a Puritan; the satire against him suggests the anti-Puritan plays of the interregnum. Dufoy, the French valet, is similar to Monsieur le Frisk in Shirley's *The Ball* (pr. 1632), to Galliard in Cavendish's *The Varietie* (pr. 1641), and to Monsieur Raggou in Lacy's *The Old Troop*.

Restoration drama thus drew from earlier literary traditions; it also relied on its social and political milieu. In his defense of Restoration comedy against charges of immorality, Charles Lamb claimed that the plays were inoffensive because "they are a world of themselves almost as much as fairyland." The characters "have got out of Christendom into the land—what shall I call it?—of cuckoldry—the Utopia of gallantry, where pleasure is duty, and the manners perfect freedom. It is altogether a speculative scene of things, which has no reference whatever to the world that is."

Nothing could be further from the truth. John Stafford wrote in the epilogue to Thomas Southerne's *The Disappointment* (pr. 1684):

> In Comedy your little selves you meet,
> 'Tis Covent Garden drawn in Bridges-Street.
> Smile on our author then, if he has shown
> A jolly nut-brown bastard of your own.

> Ah! Happy you, with ease and with delight,
> Who act those follies, poets toil to write.

Wycherley's prologue to *The Plain-Dealer* states that the author "displays you, as you are," and, at the end of the period, Vanbrugh's *The Provok'd Wife* (pr. 1697) makes a similar claim:

> 'Tis the Intent and Business of the Stage,
> To Copy out the Follies of the Age;
> To hold to every Man a Faithful Glass,
> And shew him of what Species he's an Ass.

The Character of a Coffee-House (pr. 1673) describes the company as composed of "a town wit, a silly fop and a worshipful justice—a worthy lawyer and an errant pickpocket, a reverend nonconformist and a canting mountebank, all blended together to compose an oglio of impertinence." That grouping could easily serve as the male cast of a Restoration comedy. So much a reflection of the times are these plays that when Etherege was serving as ambassador in Ratisbon (in Bavaria), he wrote back to England, "Pray let Will Richards send me Mr. Shadwell's [play] when it is printed, that I may learn what follies are in fashion." Etherege himself was accused by Captain Alexander Radcliffe of a lack of invention, of merely transcribing what he heard at the coffee-houses: "So what he writes is but translation/ From Dog and Partridge conversation." Gerard Langbaine at the end of the century declared in *An Account of the English Dramatic Poets* (1691) that Etherege's *The Man of Mode* was "as true comedy, and the characters drawn to the life as any play that has been acted since the restoration of the English stage." Sir Richard Steele, no admirer of Restoration comedy, conceded in *Tatler* #3 that, in the character of Horner, Wycherley had provided "a good representation of the age in which that comedy was written; at which time love and wenching were the business of life, and the gallant manners of pursuing women was the best recommendation at court."

Dryden's *The Kind Keeper: Or, Mr. Limberham* (pr. 1678) needed no literary precedents to satirize the practice of keeping a mistress. The vice was so ingrained that a group of powerful keepers suppressed the play after a three-day run. So fashionable was the practice that Lord Chamberlain North was advised to keep a mistress because he was ill-regarded for not doing so. By the same token, the character Foresight, through whom Congreve satirizes belief in astrology in *Love for Love* (pr. 1695), might owe something to Calderón's *El astrólogo fingido* (pb. 1633) and the humors tradition, but Dryden, the earl of Shaftesbury, and the famous John Partridge, whom Jonathan Swift satirized, all believed in this pseudoscience. Lord Nonsuch in Dryden's *The Wild Gallant* (pr. 1663) believes that he is pregnant; this farfetched situation is based on a story that circulated about Dr. Pelling, chaplain to Charles II, who so imagined himself.

Political controversies also inspired the drama. As noted above, Puritans were frequently satirized in the years immediately following the return of the monarchy, and during the panic caused by the supposed Popish Plot, another spate of political plays appeared. Even Otway's *Venice Preserved: Or, A Plot Discovered* (pr. 1682), though much more than a representation of partisan political concerns, drew on this atmosphere of fear, and plays such as Crowne's *City Politiques* (pr. 1683) depict the period's factional strife.

Not only real situations but also real people served as models. Sir Positive At-all in Shadwell's *The Sullen Lovers* is a humors character, but he was based on Sir Robert Howard. Robert Hooke, curator of the Royal Society, was portrayed as Nicholas Gimcrack in Shadwell's *The Virtuoso* (pr. 1676). Hooke, who attended a performance, noted in his diary that the likeness was readily observed: "Damned dogs! *Vindica me Deus*. People almost pointed." Joseph Arrowsmith lampooned Dryden as Tutor in *The Reformation*, and Villiers satirized him as Bayes in *The Rehearsal*. William Chamberlayne attacked two other contemporary dramatists, Elkanah Settle and Edward Ravenscroft, as Sir Symon Credulous and Sir Joseph Simpleton in *Wits Led by the Nose* (pr. 1677). The earl of Shaftesbury was a popular butt, especially around 1680. Sir Fopling Flutter in *The Man of Mode* was based on the notorious fop Beau Hewitt, Dorimant was modeled on John Wilmot, earl of Rochester, and Medley—as even his name suggests—was clearly modeled on Sir Charles Sedley. Vanbrugh's

The Relapse: Or, Virtue in Danger (pr., pb. 1696) portrayed Beau Fielding as Lord Foppington, even including the duel in which Fielding received a minor wound. The drama thus held up a mirror in which the age could see itself.

COMEDY

This mirror was selective, though, in what it reflected. In his preface to *An Evening's Love: Or, The Mock Astrologer* (pr. 1668), Dryden wrote, "Comedy consists, though of low persons, yet of natural actions, and characters; I mean such humours, adventures, and designs, as are to be found and met with in the world," but the world of Restoration comedy is a limited one indeed. Of eighty-five successful comedies in the period, seventy are set in England, sixty-four of them in London. The characters, like the setting, reflect a restricted social environment; all but fourteen of the plays set in England treat the upper-middle class.

This limited outlook is not surprising, for, as already noted, many of the playwrights were themselves from the upper classes. Further, as Samuel Johnson noted in the next century, "The drama's laws the drama's patrons give,/ And we who live to please must please to live." The Restoration theater, especially in the first two decades of the period, attracted a much more restricted audience than did the Elizabethan or Jacobean stage. In 1642, London was able to support its seven theaters—Salisbury Court, Blackfriars, the Globe, the Fortune, the Red Bull, the Drury Lane Cockpit, and the Hope. Twenty years later, it had to struggle to support two; when one house was full, the other was likely to be empty. For example, when *Tarugo's Wiles* opened at the Duke's Theatre on October 5, 1667, Killigrew tried to counter with a revival of one of his plays. Samuel Pepys noted that the older play did not attract many viewers: "To see how Nell [Eleanor Gwyn] cursed, for having so few people in the pit, was pretty." Two year later, when Shadwell's *The Royal Shepherdess* (pr. 1669) was doing well, Killigrew again had difficulties. "Lord, what an empty house," Pepys wrote in his diary (February 26, 1669). In 1682, the two companies were forced to merge. Competition resumed in 1695, but with the same disastrous consequences, so that in 1707 a second merger was necessary.

In part, this situation resulted from the higher prices. Whereas an Elizabethan could see a play for a penny, a Restoration playgoer had to pay at least a shilling. The newer theaters were small, and they employed elaborate—hence expensive—scenery; prices reflected these circumstances. Also, there remained a strong bias against stage plays. Shadwell claims in the epilogue to *The Lancashire Witches, and Tegue O Divelly the Irish Priest* (pr. 1681),

> The City neither likes us nor our wit,
> They say their wives learn ogling in the pit;
> They're from the boxes taught to make advances,
> To answer stolen sighs and naughty glances.

Not only was the fare on the stage regarded by many as improper, but also the presence of prostitutes and rakes in the audience deterred many of the puritanically inclined.

The drama's patrons were therefore drawn from an educated, upper-class coterie. Literary men attended regularly: Sir Charles Sedley, Etherege, George Villiers, Shadwell, Dryden, Killigrew, and Davenant. Among the royalty and the nobility, Charles II and the duke and duchess of York were frequently in the audience. So, too, were Prince Rupert, the dukes of Ormond, Norfolk, and Albemarle, Lady Castlemagne, Lady Dorset, and Lady Elizabeth Bodvile. Pepys does occasionally record "The house was full of citizens" (January 1, 1663) or "The house full of Parliamentmen" (November 2, 1667), but the very fact that he mentions this element indicates how unusual it was to find them in the theater in any number.

Although the comedies of the period reflect this upper-class London world, they are not mere reportage. The dramatists used situations and characters from real life, but they molded that material, imposing on it a structure and outlook. What gives Restoration comedy its peculiar flavor is the ethos that informs the writing.

Chief among the beliefs expressed in Restoration comedy is the importance of being natural. Hence, the heroes of these comedies shun affectation, while the less admirable characters are pretenders, whether to wit, morality, or bravery. In Etherege's *She Would If She Could* (pr. 1668), Lady Cockwood pretends to conventional morality but tries to commit adultery. The truewit Gatty, on the other hand, hates to dissemble. Lady Fidget in Wycherley's *The Country Wife* (pr. 1675) objects to Horner's very name as well as to the word "naked" in "naked truth." Actually, it is the truth that she dislikes. She is willing enough to go to bed with Horner; she seeks only the reputation of honor, not the thing itself. In this regard, she is the antithesis of the truewit Horner, who does not care what others think of him provided he can have what he truly seeks, pleasure.

The motto of the truewit might read, "To be rather than to seem." In *The Man of Mode*, Harriet, the heroine, objects to plain women who present themselves as beauties and to dull men who try to be wits. She also criticizes the diversions at Hyde Park because she regards the supposed politeness there as mere show. When characters act in a manner that is contrary to nature—when, for example, Old Bellair in *The Man of Mode* seeks to rival his son for the hand of Emilia, when Sir Sampson Legend seeks to marry Angelica in Congreve's *Love for Love* even though he is fifty and she is less than half his age, when Lady Wishfort offers herself as a rival to her niece Millamant in *The Way of the World*—they are certain to be ridiculed and defeated. As George Savile, Marquess of Halifax, wrote in *The Lady's New Year's Gift: Or, Advice to a Daughter* (1688), "Unnatural things carry a deformity in them never to be disguised; the liveliness of youth in a riper age, looketh like a new patch upon an old gown; so that a gay matron, a cheerful old fool may be reasonably put into the list of the tamer sort of monsters." Or, as Congreve wrote in "Of Pleasing,"

> All Rules of pleasing in this one unite,
> Affect not any thing in Nature's spight . . .
> None are, for being what they are, in fault,
> But for not being what they wou'd be thought.

Perhaps Horner in *The Country Wife* best summarizes this attitude: "A pox on 'em, and all that force nature and would be still what she forbids 'em! Affectation is her greatest monster."

Because they shun affectation, the truewits avoid excess in dress and speech. Dorimant in *The Man of Mode* objects when Handy spends too much time dressing him, exclaiming, "That a man's excellency should be in the neatly tying of a ribbon or a cravat!" Sir Fopling, as affected in his dress as in every other aspect of his behavior, notes that Dorimant's cravats never are handsome. Harriet in *The Man of Mode* also does not care for elaborate dress, again showing herself the female equivalent of Dorimant. Isabella in Aphra Behn's *Sir Patient Fancy* (pr. 1678) objects when her maid spends too much time fixing her hair; she is, of course, a truewit.

The vanity of fops is symbolized by their over-attention to appearance, often expressed by their fondness for admiring their images in mirrors. Mock-mode in George Farquhar's *Love and a Bottle* (pr. 1698) or Sir Philip Mode-love in Mrs. Susannah Centlivre's *A Bold Stroke for a Wife* (pr. 1718) are but two of the fops and fools who spend their time before a glass. Sir Courtly is so engrossed in his own reflection that he proposes to the wrong woman. Martha rejects Dapperwit in Wycherley's *Love in a Wood: Or, St. James's Park* (pr. 1671) because he is already wedded to himself.

Truewits, as the name indicates, speak well, but they do so naturally. The Witwouds, on the other hand, lack this natural ability, and their various attempts to compensate for their deficiency render them ridiculous. Melantha in Dryden's *Marriage à la Mode* (pr. 1672) cannot go visiting until her maid Philotis furnishes her with her daily quota of French words. Witwoud in *The Way of the World* trusts to his memory rather than his invention for clever comments and lards his conversation with an excess of similes. Puny in Abraham 6's *The Cutter of Coleman Street* (pr. 1661) "scorns to speak anything that's common," and Sir Mannerly Shallow in Crowne's *The Country Wit* (pb. 1675) seeks farfetched metaphors.

As speech should not be overdone, neither should it be too unpolished. Mere railing is not wit, a fact that Novel and Manly in *The Plain-Dealer*, Brisk in Congreve's *The Double Dealer* (pr. 1693), and Petulant in *The Way of the World* fail to understand. Scandal and Ben in *Love for Love* are honest and likable, but they both fail the test of the truewit because their speech is inappropriate: Scandal is too willing to rail, while Ben uses jargon. Language serves as a key to character. In *The Man of Mode*, Old Bellair rambles and fills his talk with such uncouth phrases as "a dad," "out a pize," and "a pize on 'em." Sir Fopling speaks aimlessly, and Mrs. Loveit exaggerates, sounding like a tragic heroine. These mannerisms instantly reveal the characters as flawed.

This concern with the natural helps explain the sexual freedom of the plays and of the age. When Mrs. Loveit urges Dorimant to be faithful to her, he replies, "Constancy at my years! 'Tis not a virtue in season. You might as well expect the fruit of autumn ripens i' the spring. . . . Youth has a long journey to go, Madam; shou'd I have set up my rest at the first inn I lodg'd at, I shou'd never have arriv'd at the happiness I now enjoy." Restoration comedy recognizes the sexual impulse. As Dorimant says when he keeps a tryst with Bellinda at the same time that he is wooing Harriet, "I am not so foppishly in love here to forget I am flesh and blood yet." Valentine in Southerne's *Sir Anthony Love: Or, The Rambling Lady* (pr. 1690) also acknowledges the frailty of the flesh: "I may be a lover, but I must be a man."

Sexual appetite is natural in the young, both men and women; what is not natural, and hence deserving of ridicule, is prudishness. In fact, about half the prudes yield to men. Olivia in *The Plain-Dealer* claims to hate the very thought of a lover, and she objects to the immorality of Wycherley's "china" scene in *The Country Wife*. Typically, she is exposed as deceitful and unchaste. It is a flaw to deny one's sexuality; yet virtually every heroine remains chaste. A woman who goes to bed with a truewit will be well provided for and perhaps even married off to someone but not to the hero. Dorimant sleeps with Mrs. Loveit and Bellinda, but he marries Harriet, who has not yielded to him. Mirabell has slept with Mrs. Fainall; she is married to another, and Mirabell marries Millamant in *The Way of the World*. Valentine gives money to his former mistress, Margery, by whom he has had a child, but he marries Angelica in *Love for Love*.

Like the prude, the fools and fops deny their sexuality. Because they affect virtue and are hypocritical,

they are fit subjects for satire. Smuggler in Farquhar's *The Constant Couple: Or, A Trip to the Jubilee* (pr. 1699) belongs to the Society for the Reformation of Manners, yet he offers to pay Lady Lovewell to sleep with him. Alderman Gripe, "a bellows of zeal," seeks to seduce a young girl in *Love in a Wood*. In John Crown's *Sir Courtly Nice* (pr. 1685), Testimony excuses his attempted rape by observing that despite his actions he has a sense of sin. It is not religion these plays attack, it is pretense.

This concern for natural behavior does not extend to an admiration for scenic nature. Restoration drama is social in its concerns, exploring the ways that people ought to interact with one another. The countryside is rejected because in the rural world social activity is limited. Furthermore, audiences were urban, and the plays demonstrate that bias. As previously noted, the majority of successful Restoration comedies are set in London, and rustic characters in the plays are almost always presented as foolish. Harriet tests Dorimant's love by insisting at the end of *The Man of Mode* that he follow her into the country; she can imagine no greater sign of devotion. To Alithea in *The Country Wife*, being sent down into the country is the worst fate that can befall a woman; it is the equivalent of death. Horner in that play finds that being away from the city for any length of time has a deleterious effect on a person's behavior. As Horner says to Pinchwife, "I see a little time in the country makes a man turn wild and unsociable, and only fit to converse with his horses, dogs, and his herds." In *The Way of the World* Millamant tells her rustic would-be suitor Sir Wilfull Witwould, "I nauseate walking; 'tis a country diversion. I loathe the country and everything that relates to it." In Colley Cibber's *The Provok'd Husband: Or, A Journey to London* (pr. 1728)—the tradition lingered into the next century—Sir Francis, Lady Wronghead, and Squire Richard have been reared in the country and are consequently shown as foolish and imperceptive, as is the hoyden Prue in Congreve's *Love for Love*.

The "natural" man in the Restoration is urban; he is also unselfish. The truewit seeks pleasure, but he is not the slave of lust. Characters who are driven by their appetites, such as Surly in *Sir Courtly Nice*,

Heartwell in *The Old Bachelor*, and Blunt in Behn's *The Rover: Or, The Banished Cavaliers* (*Part I*, pr., pb. 1677; *Part II*, pr., pb. 1681), are all punished for their unbridled lechery. Surly is gulled and then beaten off the stage, Heartwell falls in love with a whore, and Blunt is gulled by a prostitute. No Restoration truewit would use force against a woman to have his way with her.

Indeed the truewit scrupulously adheres to a code of honor. Horner enjoys sex, but he does not pursue Alithea, whom he regards as the province of a fellow truewit. The wives of fools are fair game, chiefly because they are willing, but not the mistress of a friend. When Horner thinks that Harcourt has lost Alithea to Sparkish, he is truly sorry; and when the arrival of friends prevents Margery Pinchwife from leaving his room, he is careful to guard her reputation. So, too, Dorimant protects Bellinda's image. As she says, "He's tender of my honor though he's cruel to my love." Bevil lies to protect his mistress in Shadwell's *Epsom-Wells* (pr. 1672), and Roebuck is careful about what he says because "the tongue is the only member that can hurt a lady's honor" (*Love and a Bottle*). Etherege summarizes this code when he writes, "A friend that bravely ventures his life in the field to serve me deserves but equally with a mistress that kindly exposes her honor to oblige me, especially when she does it as generously too, and with as little ceremony" (*She Would If She Could*).

Restoration comic heroes marry well, an important consideration in an age when a gentleman could attain wealth only through inheritance or marriage, but their primary aim is pleasure, not wealth—they are not mercenary. Ranger in *Love in a Wood* is sorry that the lady he loves is an heiress, because her wealth may lead others to suspect him of having selfish motives in pursuing her. Valentine in *Love for Love* wants money, but only so he may woo Angelica; once he thinks that she intends to marry another, he is ready to sign over his inheritance for her. Like their male counterparts, the female truewits are generous. Pleasant in *The Parson's Wedding* will marry a man of "wit and honor though he has nothing but a sword at his side." Lucia, too, prefers wit and honor

to money, rejecting a rich suitor who is foolish in *Epsom-Wells*. Christina in *Love in a Wood* is willing to marry Valentine despite his poverty.

When people do marry for money, they are destined for unhappiness. Mrs. Brittle of Thomas Betterton's *The Amorous Widow* (pr. 1670) is ready to commit adultery because she is unhappy in her mercantile marriage. Lady Brute in *The Provok'd Wife* has engineered a financially successful marriage, but she is miserable. Lady Dunce in Otway's *The Soldier's Fortune* (pr. 1680) summarizes the lot of these women:

> Curst be the memory, nay double curst,
> Of her that wedded age for interest first;
> Though worn with years, with fruitless wishes full,
> 'Tis all day troublesome and all night dull.

Restoration comedy thus seeks to demonstrate the proper way to behave, rewarding those who abide by its social code, ridiculing and punishing those who violate it. Throughout the period, the plays stress this moral purpose. The dedication to Behn's *The Lucky Chance: Or, An Alderman's Bargain* (pr. 1686) can serve as a representative of dozens of similar statements, from Cowley's *The Cutter of Coleman Street* in 1661 to Congreve's *The Way of the World* in 1700. Behn states that plays "are secret instructions to the people, in things that 'tis impossible to insinuate into them any other way. . . . 'Tis example alone that inspires morality, and best establishes virtue." The examples held up for admiration are the characters who are true to their own natures, sincere, generous, clever, unaffected. The vices are hypocrisy, selfishness, pretension.

Seen in this light, Restoration comedy hardly seems immoral, but as the eighteenth century approached, the audiences' and critics' attitudes toward what was natural changed. Steele provides a measure of that shift in his attack on *The Man of Mode* in *Spectator* #65, dated May 15, 1711:

> A fine gentleman should be honest in his actions, and refined in his language. Instead of this, our hero, in this piece, is a direct knave in his designs and a clown in his language. . . . This whole celebrated piece is a per-

fect contradiction to good manners, good sense, and common honesty. . . . There is nothing in it but what is built upon the ruin of virtue and innocence. . . . I allow it to be nature, but it is nature in its utmost corruption and degeneracy.

Good manners, good sense, common honesty, and nature—these are the very terms Etherege would have used. For Etherege, though, Dorimant is the embodiment, not the antithesis, of these qualities. Jeremy Collier, whose *A Short View of the Immorality and Profaneness of the English Stage* (1698) epitomized the new taste in drama, also spoke in the same terms as the playwrights he was attacking; it is his definition of those terms that differs from theirs. Thus, in criticizing the Restoration portrayal of women, he writes,

Now to bring women under such misbehavior is violence to their native modesty, and a misrepresentation of their sex. For Modesty, as Mr. Rapin observes, is the character of women. To represent them without this quality, is to make monsters of them, and throw them out of their kind.

To Etherege, Wycherley, Dryden, and their fellow playwrights, the prude, the one who denies her sexuality, is the monster. They recognized and accepted human frailty and appreciated human pleasures. One reason that the dramatists who responded to Collier failed to persuade him or his adherents is that the two sides could not understand each other: They used the same words but meant opposite things by them. To cite but one example, Farquhar in "A Discourse upon Comedy" (1702) claims that *The Old Bachelor* is moral because, through the character of Fondlewife, Congreve shows the folly of an old man's marrying a young woman. Such a moral was not what Steele and Collier had in mind, though; they were seeking absolute virtue, not social proprieties.

This shift in the understanding of what is natural, and hence what is moral, affected the plays of the 1690's. As early as 1668, Shadwell had criticized the moral tone of the comedies of wit, but Shadwell's was a lone voice in the 1660's, and he was sufficiently aware of his singularity to conform to the ethos of the period in his later plays. By the time Col-

lier was writing, the world of the Restoration had yielded to the more bourgeois, mercantile forces that were increasingly prominent after the Glorious Revolution.

Representative of this new mood was the Society for the Reformation of Manners, which in 1694 published a "Black Roll," listing several hundred people whom it had prosecuted for immorality, and "Proposals for a National Reformation" that urged, among other measures, "that the public play-houses may be suppressed." Members of the society were forbidden to attend the theater. One can understand why Farquhar makes the hypocritical Smuggler a member of this society. By 1734, it claimed to have prosecuted almost one hundred thousand people for such offenses as whoring, cursing, drunkenness, and Sabbath breaking. In 1699, Nahum Tate proposed bowdlerizing all plays, and John Dennis reported in 1721 that at the turn of the century there was much sentiment in favor of closing the theaters. Grand juries brought indictments against Congreve for *The Double Dealer* and Thomas D'Urfey for *The Comical History of Quixote* (pr. 1694), and a London grand jury sought the prohibition of the posting of playbills on the grounds that they encouraged vice. On March 4, 1699, Dryden wrote to Elizabeth Steward, "This day was played a revised comedy of Mr. Congreve's called *The Double Dealer*, which was never very taking; in the playbill was printed—'Written by Mr. Congreve, with several expressions omitted!': what kind of expressions these were you may easily guess, if you have seen the Monday's Gazette, wherein is the King's order for the reformation on the stage."

Even in the plays of Congreve, who had no qualms about Restoration morality, one sees a change from the comedies of the 1660's and 1670's. Valentine in *Love for Love* had a mistress before the play begins, but he has given up wenching. Mirabell in *The Way of the World* also had a mistress, but he has forsworn gallantry before the first scene; he will not even allow himself to be seduced. The play that generally marks the real break with Restoration comedy, though, is Cibber's *Love's Last Shift: Or, The Fool in Fashion* (pr. 1696), which antedates Collier's attack on the stage and so suggests that even without such criticism dramatists detected and were responding to new audience demands. Loveless, a rake, has wasted the fortune of his wife, Amanda, and then fled. On his return to England, Amanda seduces him and then reveals her identity to him. Loveless repents of his former sins and promises "never-ceasing tears of penitence." Cibber conceded that for most of its length the play espouses Restoration values, but when Restoration rakes marry, neither do they promise, nor do their brides expect, fidelity. Cibber had correctly gauged the mood of his audience; Tom Davies described the reaction:

> The joy of unexpected reconcilement, from Loveless's remorse and penitence, spread such an uncommon rapture of pleasure in the audience, that never were spectators more happy in easing their minds by uncommon and repeated plaudits. The honest tears shed by the audience at this interview conveyed a strong reproach to our licentious poets, and was to Cibber the highest mark of honor.

Vanbrugh satirized *Love's Last Shift* in *The Relapse*: In Vanbrugh's "sequel," Loveless returns to his rakish ways and carries off his wife's cousin to bed while she cries, "Help! Help!"—but she does so "very softly." Vanbrugh, however, allows no cuckolding in his plays. John Dryden, Jr., in *The Husband His Own Cuckold* (pr. 1695), presents two cuckolding attempts; both fail. In Mrs. Manley's *The Lost Lover* (pr. 1696), Olivia has been forced to marry Smyrna, a rich old merchant, though she loves Wildman. In 1676, she would have yielded to him and everyone would have been happy; now she remains faithful to her husband. Belira does yield to her lover, who subsequently mistreats her, thus offering a moralistic warning. By 1709, Mrs. Centlivre was writing a play in which the heroes are named Faithful, Lovely, and Constant instead of Ranger, Wildair, Careless, or Horner (*The Man's Bewitch'd: Or, The Devil to Do About Her*, pr. 1709).

The older tradition did not vanish at once. William Burnaby's *The Modish Husband* (pr. 1702) harks back to the heyday of witty comedy when Lord Promise persuades his friend Lionel to court Lady Promise so that he (Lord Promise) may pursue Lady Cringe. The play failed because it was too risqué for the time. Mrs. Mary Pix's *The Deceiver Deceived* (pr. 1697) allows the heroine one chance at adultery before she reforms and gives up her lover, Count Andrew, for her husband.

Farquhar's *The Beaux' Stratagem* (pr. 1707) indicates how playwrights still sympathetic to the ethos of Restoration comedy felt obliged to cope with altered audience expectations. The wits win, but they do so morally rather than cleverly. Archer cannot seduce Mrs. Sullen but must wait for her to get a divorce so that he can marry her. Aimwell seeks to deceive the rich Dorinda into marriage by impersonating his titled brother. At the last minute, though, he repents and abandons his design in a sentimental speech: "Such goodness who could injure; I find myself unequal to the task of villain; she has gain'd my soul, and made it honest like her own; I cannot, cannot hurt her." Dorinda is so impressed that she agrees to marry him anyway. Happily, Sir Charles Freeman then enters and announces that Aimwell's brother has died, making Aimwell the viscount after all. Chastity and prudence have replaced wit and daring as the key virtues, and the plays now focus on moralistic examples of how one should act rather than on satiric portraits of how one should not act.

HEROIC TRAGEDY

It is difficult to imagine that the same dramatists who penned witty Restoration comedies often also wrote the heroic tragedies of the age or that audiences who appreciated the realistic portrait of a Dorimant or a Horner would endure the bombast and whining of the period's tragic heroes. Indeed, there is evidence that audiences did not appreciate the tragedies, for though more tragedies than comedies were written, a higher percentage of them failed, nor did they always elicit the expected response. When Morat in Dryden's *Aureng-Zebe* (pr. 1675) announced, "I'll do't to shew my arbitrary power," Cibber claims that the audience laughed. Dryden's Lisideus says, "I have observed that, in all our tragedies, the audience cannot forbear laughing when the actors are to die; 'tis the most comic part of the whole play.' Pepys records a fine example of the response high-flying speeches might get. On October 4, 1664, Pepys attended a performance of Roger Boyle, earl of Orrery's heroic play *The Generall* (pr. 1663). Sedley, according to Pepys,

> did at every line take notice of the dullness of the poet and badness of the action, that most pertinently, which I was mightily taken with; and among others where by Altemuri's command Clarimont, the general, is commanded to rescue his rival, . . . he, after a great deal of demur, broke out, "well, I'll save my rival and make her confess, that I deserve, while he do but possess." "Why, what, pox," says Sir Charles Sedley, "would he have him have more, or what is there more to be had of a woman than the possessing her?"

In many ways, the tragedies of the period seem the antithesis of the comedies. Heroes in Restoration tragedy speak of virtue and honor, the catchwords of hypocrites in Restoration comedy. In Restoration tragedy, children are supposed to obey their parents regardless of consequences; in the comedy of the period, children do as they please. Marriage is the culmination of love in the tragedies; in the comedies, it is only the beginning of a new set of problems— hence the oft-repeated proviso scene in which lovers try to avoid at least some of the pitfalls that they foresee in the wedded state.

Such opposites are Restoration comedy and tragedy that the speeches of the heroes in the one are those of the villains in the other. The following speech could be that of Dorimant or Horner:

> Marriage, thou curse of love, and snare of life,
> That first debas'd a mistress to a wife!
> Love, like a scene, at distance should appear;
> But marriage views the gross-daub'd landscape near.

In fact, it is spoken by the evil King of Grenada in the second part of Dryden's *The Conquest of Granada by the Spaniards*. In *The Man of Mode*, Dorimant tells Mrs. Loveit, "What we swear at such a time may be a certain proof of a present passion, but to say truth, in love there is no security to be given for the future." Maximin expresses a similar sentiment in Dryden's tragedy *Tyrannic Love: Or, The Royal Martyr* (pr. 1669):

> If to new persons I my love apply,
> The stars and nature are in fault, not I. . . .
> I can no more make passion come or go,
> Than you can bid your Nilus ebb or flow.

A witty, rakish speech, this, but Maximin is a villain.

Whereas the comedies seek to present a realistic portrait of the age, Restoration tragedy attempts to present the ideal. Dryden, whose criticism and example helped set the tone of the genre, declared in his essay "Of Heroic Plays":

> An heroic poet is not tied to a bare representation of what is true, or exceeding probable: but . . . he may let himself loose to visionary objects, and to the representation of such things as depending not on sense, and therefore not to be comprehended by knowledge, may give him a freer scope for imagination.

Commenting on this lack of realism, Mrs. John Evelyn wrote to Ralph de Bohun in 1671, "Love is made so pure, and valour so nice, that one would imagine it designed for an Utopia rather than our stage." While she was referring specifically to Dryden's *The Conquest of Granada by the Spaniards*, she might have been describing virtually any heroic tragedy.

The setting of these plays suggests their focus on the unreal; they are remote in time and space from modern England. Instead, they are placed in ancient Greece or Rome, Moorish Spain, sixteenth century Latin America, medieval Turkey, or Morocco.

In language, too, these tragedies differ markedly from the comedies. Dryden compared heroic drama to the epic; this analogy with poetry prompted tragic playwrights to turn to the heroic couplet for their dialogue. Pepys found that Dryden's *The Indian Queen* (pr. 1664) was "spoiled by the rhyme, which breaks the sense," and John Milton had rejected the use of rhyme for the epic. The debate over whether rhyme was in fact appropriate to tragedy was a heated one. In his dedication to *The Rival Ladies* (pr. 1664), Dryden defended the practice. Sir Robert Howard criticized it in his preface to *Four New Plays* (1665)— although he, too, employed couplets "not to appear singular"—and Dryden replied in *An Essay of Dramatic Poesy* (1668), calling heroic couplets "the noblest kind of modern verse" and hence best suited to the elevated form of tragedy. Prose was too realistic for the genre. Not every dramatist agreed; Thomas Porter's *The Villain* (pr. 1662), modeled in part on Shakespeare's *Othello, the Moor of Venice* (pr. 1604), is in prose and also contains some comic business, a practice shunned in heroic tragedy. John Wilson's *Andronicus Commenius* (pr. 1664) utilizes the exotic setting of heroic tragedy, in this case the Constantinople of 1185, but the play is unrhymed, as is Nevil Payne's *The Siege of Constantinople* (pr. 1674). Still, the majority of the tragedies written before 1676 are rhymed, and Dryden wrote confidently in "Of Heroic Plays: An Essay" (1672) that unrhymed tragedy would fail on the stage.

Yet, by 1677, Elkanah Settle felt obliged to apologize for using rhyme in *Ibrahim* (pr. 1676). Even Dryden abandoned the practice as unnatural after *Aureng-Zebe*. Between 1660 and 1680, forty-two plays in rhymed couplets were staged; during the next two decades, only five were. The rejection of rhyming did not, however, signal a shift to prose. Instead, dramatists turned to blank verse, which frequently had end-stopped rather than run-on lines and thus resembled the rhymed couplet it superseded.

Not only is the language of Restoration tragedy unnatural in its form but its content is exaggerated. Maximin in Dryden's *Tyrannic Love* (pr. 1669) declares that he can love more fervently than the gods. Caesario in Lee's *Gloriana: Or, The Court of Augustus Caesar* (pr. 1676) declares, "E'en in my childhood I was more than man." The imagery in the speeches is also marred by this penchant for hyperbole. Lee's *Sophonisba: Or, Hannibal's Overthrow* (pr. 1675) likens Hannibal to a whale, and the villain in Crowne's *The Ambitious Statesman: Or, The Loyal Favorite* (pr. 1679) compares himself to the same animal. When Ascanio is poisoned in Lee's *Caesar Borgia: Son of Pope Alexander the Sixth* (pr. 1679), he rants, "I burn, I burn, I toast, I roast, and my guts fry,/ They blaze, they snap, they bound like squibs/ And crackers. I am all fire." Roxana in Lee's *The Rival Queens* (pr. 1677) declares, "My brain is burst, debate and reason quenched,/ The storm is up, and my hot bleeding heart/ Splits with the rack, while

passions, like the winds,/ Rise up to heaven and put out all the stars." Not to be outdone, Alexander in the same play claims, "I'll strike my spear into the reeling globe/ To let it blood, set Babylon in a blaze,/ And drive this god of flames [Cupid] with more consuming fire."

The characters who utter such speeches are larger than life. When a character in Settle's *The Conquest of China* (pr. 1675) defeats a "few millions" at the outset of the play, he regards that action as mere prologue to serious battle. Thomazo in *The Siege of Constantinople* defeats the Turks practically single-handed. Drawcansir (*The Rehearsal*) gives an accurate, though satiric, portrait of these tragic heroes:

> Others may boast a single man to kill;
> But I, the blood of thousands, daily spill.
> Let petty Kings the name of Party know:
> Where e'er I come, I slay both friend and foe.

The plots of these tragedies tend to be all of a piece. A virtuous hero falls in love with an equally virtuous heroine. She, however, is loved by another to whom the hero owes allegiance and respect—a father, a prince, and sometimes, as in *Aureng-Zebe*, both at once. The hero thus faces a conflict between love and honor. In *Sophonisba*, Massinissa must choose between his love for the heroine and his loyalty to Scipio. Antony in *All for Love* must choose between duty (Rome and Octavia) and love (Cleopatra). Titus in Lee's *Lucius Junius Brutus: Father of His Country* (pr. 1680) must choose between Teraminla (love) and Brutus (duty). Another female, a villainess, may further complicate the situation by falling in love with the hero, as Nourmahal, the lecherous stepmother of Aureng-Zebe, falls in love with him. The hero generally chooses the path of honor, but the conflict is happily resolved at the end of the play through the deaths of the evil blocking characters and the marriage of the virtuous couple; less often, it is settled by the deaths of all the principals.

As this description implies, Restoration tragedy is gory. In Settle's *Fatal Love* (pr. 1680), every character ends up dead except for Lysandra, preserved perhaps so that someone may deliver the epilogue. The stage direction at the end of *The Conquest of China* calls for everyone to die. Payne's *The Siege of Constantinople* ends with "a great number of dead and dying men in several manners of deaths. The Chancellor, Lorenzo, and Michael empal'd." In *The Fatal Jealousy* (pr. 1672), eleven of thirteen named characters are dead at the end of the play. Even *Titus Andronicus* (pr. 1594), the bloodiest of Shakespeare's plays, was made more violent in the Restoration version (pr. 1687), and one of Dryden's objections to *Troilus and Cressida* is that the two leading characters are left alive at the end of the piece.

Tutor in Arrowsmith's *The Reformation* (pr. 1672) provides a good summary of these features of Restoration tragedy. He explains that he begins with an exotic situation and noble characters. Then, he says,

> you must always have two ladies in love with one man, or two men in love with one woman; if you make them the father and the son, or two brothers or two friends, 'twill do the better. . . . Then, sir, you must have a hero that shall fight with all the world; yes, i' gad, and beat them too, and half the gods into the bargain if occasion serves. Last of all . . . put your story into rhyme, and kill enough at the end of the play, and *probatum est*, your business is done for a tragedy.

Heroic tragedy, so remote in many ways from the comedies, nevertheless resembles them in its concern for strict poetic justice. In the comedies, the truewit gets the girl and the estate, while the Witwouds and fools are exposed and often punished. Similarly, in the tragedies the good characters almost always survive to attain thrones and spouses, while the evil characters are killed. This insistence on meting out rewards and punishment restricted the scope of tragedy, which could not present good people struggling against forces greater than themselves or otherwise noble figures fatally flawed and so effecting their own destruction. The Nahum Tate revision of *The History of King Lear* (pr. 1681) demonstrates the consequences of this outlook: Tate's King Lear remains alive, and Cordelia marries Edgar; good characters should be rewarded. By the same logic, Dryden kills off Troilus and Cressida because they are bad and so must be punished. When Dryden presents the destruction of heroic virtue in *Cleomenes, the Spar-*

tan Hero (pr. 1692), he feels obliged to explain this unusual practice.

This strict adherence to poetic justice explains part of the attraction of heroic tragedy. Further, because the age offered little heroism in real life, it enjoyed seeing such actions on the stage even as it laughed at the unreality of the representation. Nor can one dismiss the transmuting magic of the stage. The work that seems dull or ludicrous on the page can become compelling in the theater. The operas of Richard Wagner and Giuseppe Verdi appear bombastic and absurd in the reading, but in performance the effect is powerful. In the theater, one suspends disbelief, and a good actor can do much with the poorest of texts. Cibber, himself a talented actor who began his career during the last years of the Restoration, emphasized this point in *An Apology for the Life of Colley Cibber* (1740):

> There can be no stronger proof of the charms of harmonious elocution, than the many even unnatural scenes and flights of the false sublime it has lifted into applause. In what raptures have I seen the audience at the furious fustian and turgid rants in Nat Lee's *Alexander the Great*! When these flowing numbers came from the mouth of a Betterton, the multitude no more desired sense to them than our musical connoisseurs think it essential in the celebrated airs of an Italian opera.

Finally, there was the spectacle, intended to attract the audience. As Richard Flecknoe noted in 1664, "Our theaters now for cost and ornament are arrived to the height of magnificence." Lee in *The Rival Queens* presented the spectacle of a bird fight in midair. His *Sophonisba* called for a heaven of blood, two suns, a battle between armies of spirits, and arrows flying through the air. So elaborate and expensive were the sets that they were often reused. Dryden's *The Indian Emperor: Or, The Conquest of Mexico by the Spaniards* (pr. 1665) was a sequel to his *The Indian Queen* in costuming and stage sets more than in characters, only two of whom had survived the first piece. In the prologue, Dryden apologized for recycling the scenery and outfits, but later dramatists also used them. The prison reappeared in Settle's *The Fe-*

male Prelate (pr. 1679) and *Fatal Love* (pr. 1680) and in Joseph Harris's *The Mistakes* (pr. 1690); the grotto was used again in Lee's *Sophonisba* and D'Urfey's *Commonwealth of Women* (pr. 1685).

OTHER FORMS

While heroic tragedy was the age's chief contribution to serious drama, other forms did appear on the stage. Among the most popular was opera. Davenant's *The Siege of Rhodes*, originally performed during the Commonwealth period but revived after the Restoration, provides an early example. In 1661, Charles II paid a French opera company under Jean Channoveau three hundred pounds for a production of *The Descent of Orpheus into Hell* (pr. 1661). *The Tempest: Or, The Enchanted Island* (pr. 1667), by Davenant and Dryden, and *Macbeth* (pr. 1663), by Davenant—operatic adaptations of Shakespeare's plays—are full of stage machinery and sound effects. Like the heroic tragedies, these plays are far removed from reality; in many cases, the characters in Restoration opera do not even pretend to be human. In the preface to *Albion and Albanius* (pr. 1685), Dryden notes that "the suppos'd persons are generally supernatural, as gods and goddesses, and heroes which at least are descended from them, and are in due time to be adopted into their number." These operas attracted large audiences, but they were very expensive to stage and hence not often produced. Shadwell's *Psyche* (pr. 1675), for example, cost eight hundred pounds, and Dryden's *The State of Innocence, and Fall of Man* (pb. 1677), a dramatization of Milton's *Paradise Lost* (1667, 1674), was never acted because it would have been too expensive. *The Fairy Queen: An Opera* (pr. 1692; possibly by Settle, music by Henry Purcell), an adaptation of Shakespeare's *A Midsummer Night's Dream* (pr. c. 1595-1596), cost three thousand pounds; despite its popularity, it lost money.

The pastoral was another alternative to the heroic. Whereas the latter stressed bravery and duty, the pastoral tragedy praised rural retirement. During periods of political crisis, drama mirrored popular concerns. In the early 1680's, when the Popish Plot and the succession weighed heavily on people's minds, about half the serious plays were political.

The most enduring rival to the heroic was, however, the domestic tragedy. Otway's *The Orphan: Or, The Unhappy Marriage* (pr. 1680) revolves around the love of two brothers for the orphan of the title, Monimia. The setting—Moorish Spain—and the rivalry of the two brothers are both heroic elements, but the play is not concerned with affairs of state. *Venice Preserved*, perhaps the most popular tragedy of the period, again is largely domestic in its interests. The background is a plot to overthrow the Venetian government, so the play may be read as an anti-Whig fable. Jaffier faces a choice between love for his wife and loyalty to his fellow conspirators—the standard heroic dilemma. Where the protagonist of heroic drama chooses duty, though, Jaffier chooses love, betraying his comrades after one of the plotters tries to rape Belvidera. This emphasis on the domestic rather than the public sphere also characterizes John Banks's *The Unhappy Favorite* (pr. 1681) and *Vertue Betray'd* (pr. 1682); the latter dwells on the love of Piercy and Anna Bullen and on young Elizabeth's affection for her mother. The political, public world supplies only the setting.

As the comedy of wit yielded to a more moralistic, sentimental form, so heroic tragedy was replaced by a more middle-class variety. In his prologue to *The Fair Penitent* (pr. 1703), Nicholas Rowe observed that "we ne'er can pity what we ne'er can share" and so rejected the presentation of kings and queens for "a melancholy tale of private woe." On the stage as in real life, the aristocratic Tory forms of the Restoration yielded to the bourgeois, Whig concerns of the next century.

BIBLIOGRAPHY

Birdsall, Virginia Ogden. *Wild Civility: The English Comic Spirit on the Restoration Stage*. Bloomington: Indiana University Press, 1970. Provides close readings of eleven Restoration comedies by such dramatists as Etherege, Wycherley, and Congreve. Stresses the attempt of the rake-hero to create "an elegant lifestyle in which the passions are not denied but accommodated as vital forces for extending and enriching experience."

Brown, John Russell, and Bernard Harris, eds. *Resto-*

ration Theatre. Stratford-Upon-Avon Studies 6. New York: St. Martin's Press, 1965. A collection of ten essays exploring various aspects of the subject, including the language of the plays, Molière's influence on English dramatists of the period, and Restoration acting.

Fisk, Deborah Payne, ed. *The Cambridge Companion to English Restoration Theatre.* Cambridge, England: Cambridge University Press, 2000. Brings together a chronology of texts and major events, short biographies, and extensive bibliographies for nearly fifty dramatists with analysis from noted American and British critics. Dryden, Wycherly, and Congreve are among those discussed, and explorations of minor playwrights and the first women dramatists are also included.

Gill, Pat. *Interpreting Ladies: Women, Wit, and Morality in the Restoration Comedy of Manners.* Athens: University of Georgia Press, 1994. Gill claims that these plays interpret women, and for Gill the plays do so based on how women interpret the jokes that men direct at them. If women understand the witty sexual allusions, then those women are morally suspect, whether the females are on stage or in the audience. Gill maintains that Etherege, Wycherley, and Congreve exhibit a misogynism absent from the works of Aphra Behn, for whom "women's interpretive knowledge and skill are always a given and never an issue."

Hughes, Derek. *English Drama, 1660-1700.* New York: Oxford University Press, 1996. An ambitious survey of more than four hundred plays written in this period. Examines the way that language operates in these works, including how women respond to male linguistic authority. Sees a shift from a "drama of hierarchy" in the 1660's to a "drama of dislocation" in the 1690's.

Kewes, Paulina. *Authorship and Appropriation: Writing for the Stage in England, 1660-1710.* London: Oxford University Press, 1998. A full-length study of the cultural and economic status of playwriting in the Restoration era, arguing that the period was a decisive one in the transition from Renaissance conceptions of authorship toward modern ones.

Lynch, Kathleen M. *The Social Mode of Restoration Comedy.* New York: Macmillan, 1926. A classic study. Begins by looking at the debt that Restoration comedy owed to the Caroline stage, thus demonstrating the Englishness of the plays she examines. She sees a strong Platonic influence lingering from the court of Henrietta Maria in the period before the English Civil War.

McMillin, Scott. *Restoration and Eighteenth Century Comedy: A Norton Critical Edition.* 2d ed. New York: W. W. Norton and Company, 1996. Provides history and criticism of the eighteenth century comedy.

Owen, Susan J. *Restoration Theatre and Crisis.* London: Oxford University Press, 1997. Places Restoration drama into a larger historical context, exploring how political partisanship in the theater was a result of political processes at large. Also examines the arena of sexual politics, examining the political significance of themes such as disharmony in the family.

_____, ed. *Companion to Restoration Drama.* Malden, Mass.: Blackwell Publishers, 2002. Provides a comprehensive overview to the contextual history of Restoration drama. Explores a multitude of topics with chapters like "The Restoration Actress," "Libertinism and Sexuality," "Masculinity in Restoration Drama," "Heroic Drama and Tragicomedy," while also closely examining the noted playwrights of the period.

Young, Douglas M. *The Feminist Voices in Restoration Comedy: The Virtuous Women in the Play-Worlds of Etherege, Wycherley, and Congreve.* Lanham, Md.: University Press of America, 1997. Examines the unique portrayal of women in several plays by these noted Restoration dramatists. While seventeenth century marriage was a bargaining process for property and women were treated as men's property, these dramatists brought forth female characters who demanded independence and equality.

Joseph Rosenblum

Eighteenth Century British Drama

Most histories of the drama in Britain during the eighteenth century maintain implicitly or explicitly that the course of the development of the drama during this period was determined not so much by the playwrights as by the performers and theater managers and that the more managers and playwrights strove to please and succeeded in pleasing their audiences, the more the quality of the drama declined. Whereas during the Restoration, plays were composed by, for, and about members of the aristocracy, by the beginning of the eighteenth century, the theater had widened its appeal to include the middle class, and a higher percentage of women—especially "respectable" women—attended the theater. By mid-century, middle-class morality, tastes, and interests had gradually become the dominant shaping force in the development of the drama. As the eighteenth century theater drew to a close, audiences also included members of the lower class, for whom the cost of Restoration and early eighteenth century theater had been prohibitive. The more bourgeois was the orientation of the theater, however, the more that members of the aristocracy turned elsewhere for their entertainment and the more that gifted writers abandoned the drama to express themselves in other genres. Although theatergoers of all ranks had always considered drama more a form of entertainment than one of artistic expression, never before the end of the eighteenth century had the rift been so great between drama and literature.

THE PLAYWRIGHTS

Whatever its artistic shortcomings, however, during the eighteenth century, drama proved immensely attractive to writers as well as to the general public. As a result of the greatly increased size of audiences and the consequent increased demand for entertainment, for the first time since the age of William Shakespeare, it was once again possible to make a living as a playwright. Generally, playwrights would sell the copyright to their plays to theater managers for an amount somewhere between one hundred and two hundred pounds. Although playwrights would receive additional revenue based on attendance, they would get nothing for revivals. Moreover, unlike the drama of the previous century, which was dominated by a dozen or so masters, almost all of whom were male, the drama of the eighteenth century abounded with playwrights of both sexes, many of whom wrote only a single play or published their plays anonymously. Playwrights had the opportunity to work in a much wider variety of theatrical genres than had been available during the seventeenth century, as a typical evening's entertainment at the theater included, in addition to the full-length play that served as the main feature, a prologue and an epilogue, *entr'actes* of music and dancing, and finally an afterpiece of brief comedy, farce, burlesque, or pantomime. Thus, on a single evening, an audience might see both humorous and serious pieces. Usually, playwrights who attempted to write more than one dramatic work did not restrict themselves to the confines of a single dramatic genre but extended their talents as widely as they could in order to cater to the eclectic tastes of the eighteenth century audience. Aaron Hill, for example, wrote pseudoclassical tragedy, heroic tragedy, domestic tragedy, opera, and farce, as well as translations and adaptations of the plays of Voltaire. Prominent literary figures who are more important to critics for their contributions to other genres—Joseph Addison, Sir Richard Steele, Henry Fielding, James Thomson, Edward Young, and Samuel Johnson—also tried their hands at drama, with various degrees of success. Indeed, of the most famous writers in eighteenth century literary history, only Jonathan Swift and Alexander Pope chose not to pursue playwriting.

THE PLAYS

As one might expect, this wide variety of talents and diffusion of interests among playwrights occasioned a corresponding variation in the quality of the drama produced during the eighteenth century. The absence of dominant figures to direct the development of the drama, as John Dryden had done in the previous century, afforded the dramatists of the age unprecedented latitude in their choice of genre and theme. One might expect these circumstances to have generated highly individualized expression and much experimentation in drama, but such was not the case. The effect of this lack of dominant figures was almost wholly negative. Particularly in the latter half of the century, the tragedy lacked purpose and direction, and the comedy became formulaic and sentimental. During the Restoration, generic distinctions had been relatively clearly drawn, and writers had tried to vary and perfect forms whose conventions the masters had established. In the eighteenth century, however, playwrights composing tragedy struggled to find satisfactory new forms by combining various elements from existing tragedies.

Most of the original tragedies written during this period merely synthesized elements extracted from earlier English and Continental plays. Throughout the century, playwrights borrowed plots, character types, rhetorical modes, and themes from classical, Elizabethan, Shakespearean, Restoration, and, later, early eighteenth century drama, as well as from French and Italian drama (especially from mid-century on) and from German drama (particularly during the final years of the century). On the whole, the comedy of this age is of better quality than is its awkwardly derivative tragedy, largely because the comic playwright generally had to choose between composing "laughing" comedy or "weeping" comedy. Unquestionably, the playwright's reliance on recombination of familiar elements contributed to the stultification of the drama. Although there was some experimentation, very little that was composed was fresh or original. Only one form that originated during this period ultimately proved lasting and significant—domestic tragedy, which was refined on the Continent but only rarely attempted in England.

A cultural movement of the eighteenth century that was reflected in and shaped by the drama was sentimentalism, which became, from the second decade of the century, an increasingly pervasive influence on both tragedy and comedy. Sentimentalism brought to the theater a new emphasis on benevo-

lence and pity and a new goal for the playwright, the eliciting of pathos. One's heart rather than one's reason became the guide as well as the measure of one's worth. The popularity of Jean-Jacques Rousseau's social criticism fostered the development of a humanitarian concern bred by sentimentalism, which emphasized the dignity and worth of the lives of ordinary men and women. The problems of women, especially of married women, also became serious topics for tragedy (most obviously in Nicholas Rowe's she-tragedies) and comedy alike (see, for example, George Farquhar's *The Beaux' Stratagem*, pr. 1707, and Sir John Vanbrugh's *The Provok'd Wife*, pr. 1697). Although the fully emancipated woman remained an object of satiric attack, the drama afforded greater recognition of the problems of being a woman.

As the shift in the makeup of the audience was reflected in the more sympathetic presentation of women, so, too, was this change reflected in the presentation of members of the mercantile class. Traditional butts of ridicule in the Elizabethan and Restoration comedy, merchants were presented during the eighteenth century with dignity and respect. Merchants are, for example, openly praised in two of the most successful and influential comedies of the century, by the character Sealand in Steele's play *The Conscious Lovers* (pr. 1722) and by the character Stockwell in Richard Cumberland's play *The West Indian* (pr. 1771). So, too, are they presented sympathetically in tragedy, most obviously in George Lillo's *The London Merchant: Or, The History of George Barnwell* (pr. 1731), in which Thorowgood eulogizes the dignity and worthiness of the merchant's trade in order to emphasize the tragic dimension of the protagonist's fall.

In the eighteenth century, as in every period since the beginnings of public drama, the success or failure of the plays did not depend wholly on their aesthetic or ethical merits. The fate of a play might depend, for example, on the political sentiments it expressed or was perceived as expressing. A playwright's political allegiances could boost the success or ensure the failure of a play irrespective of its intrinsic merits. The enthusiastic reception afforded Rowe's *Tamerlane* (pr. 1701), for example, was augmented by the obvious analogies Rowe drew between his hero and King William III and between his villain and King Louis XIV. Addison's *Cato* (pr. 1713) was also extraordinarily successful because of the contemporary political allusions the audience recognized. Yet politics could damn a play as well as promote it. John Home's *The Fatal Discovery* (pr. 1769), for example, was successful only until the audience became aware of Home's allegiance to Lord Bute. Similarly, Hugh Kelly's *A Word to the Wise* (pr. 1770) met with so much opposition because of his politics that Kelly had his next play, *Clementina* (pr. 1771), produced anonymously. Even at the very close of the century, because of his well-known sympathies with William Blake and Thomas Paine, Thomas Holcroft also produced many of his plays anonymously. Although politics remained a vital force in English drama throughout the century, the nature of the political allusions shifted noticeably. Whereas political allusions in drama during the first half of the century were generally faction- or party-oriented, those that followed the outbreak of the French Revolution in 1789 were generally nationalistic. During the final years of the century, largely in response to the French Revolution, occasional pieces such as Frederick Pilon's *The Battle of the Nile* (pr. 1799) were composed to express English nationalistic sentiment. Despite their exuberant patriotism, plays such as these are of little literary value.

LICENSING ACT OF 1737

Another political factor contributing to the decline in quality of eighteenth century theater was the Licensing Act of 1737. Sir Robert Walpole advanced the act ostensibly to help maintain order in London but actually to deter satiric attacks against him and his party, especially those leveled by Fielding. The Licensing Act decreed that all play scripts were subject to the censorship of the Lord Chamberlain and that only the Drury Lane and Covent Garden theaters would be permitted to perform plays. This act was a particularly repressive measure, since, for the first time in one hundred years, there were five playhouses simultaneously offering plays in London. In addition

to decreasing the accessibility of the theater to the audience, the Licensing Act effectively crushed the artistically stimulating competition between playhouses and vastly decreased the likelihood of playwrights and managers offering new, untried, and hence riskier plays. At first, the managers of the unlicensed theaters circumvented the law by advertising musical performances and staging plays during what purported to be the intermissions. Eager to boost their profits by eliminating their competition, however, the managers of the Covent Garden and Drury Lane theaters assisted the authorities in exposing and suppressing such practices, so that by mid-century virtually no such renegade productions were offered. Subsequent licensing acts, passed in 1756 and 1788, extended licensing from London to all of England, and the act was not officially withdrawn until 1968. The hold of the monopolies over London theaters remained unshaken until 1766, when Samuel Foote assumed the management of the Little Theatre at the Haymarket, and slowly but gradually offered the main theaters competition. At first his performances were billed as "entertainments" and staged in early afternoon, primarily during the summer season. Later the theater was given official sanction and became the third patent theater.

The Licensing Act also strongly influenced the tone and the content of plays performed after 1737. At first, only selected passages were altered, but gradually the form and content of entire plays were affected. Because self-consciously moral plays were more likely to obtain the censor's approval, these were more frequently submitted for approval, were approved, and were performed more than were plays laden with controversial matter such as sex, religion, and politics. Thus, the Licensing Act reinforced in the drama the expression of middle-class tastes and the movement toward the avoidance of controversial (and thus significant and intellectually oriented) subject matter. The effects of the act were not entirely negative, however, for in the search for plays that would be inoffensive to the censor and successful with the public, the theater managers, particularly David Garrick, began performing Shakespearean drama much more frequently than they had before.

Though William Shakespeare had never disappeared from the stage, a number of his plays had not been performed in many years: *Antony and Cleopatra* (pr. c. 1606-1607), *Cymbeline* (pr. c. 1609-1610), and *Coriolanus* (pr. c. 1607-1608), for example. These Garrick revived. Largely as the result of his efforts, by mid-century, Shakespeare's romantic comedies had again become popular. Garrick himself adapted *A Midsummer Night's Dream* (pr. c. 1595-1596) as *The Fairies* (pr. 1755). Later, Adam Smith transformed *As You Like It* (pr. c. 1599-1600) into *The Noble Foresters* (pb. 1776), and John Philip Kemble, in 1780, altered *The Comedy of Errors* (pr. c. 1592-1594) and, in 1790, *The Two Gentlemen of Verona* (pr. c. 1594-1595). Garrick thus sparked the great revival of interest in Shakespeare that would be continued by Kemble and that would greatly influence the subsequent development of drama both in England and on the Continent. Garrick is also important in the history of the production of Shakespeare for his insistence on using more reliable texts for performance than had previously been employed.

THE AUDIENCES

Whether in original or adapted form, the plays of Shakespeare attracted large audiences. Though by no means as docile as the audience of today, the audiences of even the early years of the century were considerably better behaved than were their Elizabethan and Restoration counterparts. Nevertheless, at the beginning of the century, players still faced an audience whose members were often drunk and rowdy and who shouted catcalls during the performances, and playwrights still felt the need to "pack" the audience with friends and hirelings to combat "first nighters" determined to ensure the play's failure. As the drama grew more decorous over the course of the century, however, the audience, too, became increasingly self-restrained—and increasingly prudish. Perhaps because they were not as well educated and as intellectually oriented as were members of the Restoration audience, the members of the eighteenth century audience wanted their drama to be emotional, sentimental, and didactic rather than intellectually stimulating. They longed to hear effusive declarations of sentiment rather than clever repartee. Loud or open laughter they believed, reflected a distinctly unattractive lack of breeding as well as insensitivity, at a time when a tender heart and a refined mien were the most desirable traits.

As the drama became increasingly dominated by the bourgeoisie, its two traditional sustainers, the aristocrats and the artists, gradually dissociated themselves from the theater. Among the aristocrats, the French fashion of holding private theatricals became popular during the last two decades of the century. In private theaters on their own estates, they performed plays for one another. Blenheim, the home of the duke of Marlborough, was noted for such productions, as was Richmond House. In France, where the private theatrical had arisen earlier, these plays were referred to as *scènes princières* and were given by Madame de Pompadour, Marie Antoinette, and the duc d'Orléans. During the 1770's, Charles Collé was renowned for his productions of these dramas. By diverting aristocratic and artistic interests from the public theater, however, the fashion of the private theatrical only augmented the domination of the middle class and the mediocre over both the French and British drama. In England, the decline in the quality of the drama was also encouraged by the popularity of the "little theaters." Although only Drury Lane and Covent Garden were permitted to put on full-length plays, the little theaters were allowed to present brief entertainments, such as pantomimes, burlesques, farces, spectacles, and animal acts. Such productions, which were extremely popular with audiences, diverted the attention of both audience and playwright from legitimate theater.

THE THEATERS

Substantial architectural as well as aesthetic changes also occurred in the theater during the eighteenth century. In the beginning of the century, new playhouses were built to accommodate the expansion of the audience. In 1705, the famous playwright-architect Sir John Vanbrugh designed the Queen's Theatre in the Haymarket, where the French House was also erected, and in 1732, the Theatre Royal was erected in the Covent Garden. The Little Theatre in

Lincoln's Inn Fields also thrived, serving as the home for Fielding's great comedies. The early years of the century also witnessed great interest in the theater outside London. Already well established, the theater in Dublin was prospering, and new theaters sprang up in Bath, in Tunbridge Wells, and in the provinces. This growth in the construction of theaters was abruptly checked by the Licensing Act of 1737. After 1737, the widespread interest in the drama that had been generated prior to 1737 had so greatly expanded the number of theatergoers that the Drury Lane and Covent Garden theaters were insufficiently large to accommodate all who wished to attend plays. Even before the Licensing Act, so much interest had developed in the theater that the Haymarket had expanded its maximum seating capacity from nine hundred in 1705 to thirteen hundred in 1735. Drury Lane was thus remodeled in 1762, and continuing expansion of the audience necessitated additional remodeling in 1780 and complete rebuilding in 1793. Covent Garden, too, was remodeled in 1782 and eventually rebuilt in 1792. Great theaters were built on the Continent as well. In France, for example, the two main theaters were the Comédie-Française and the Comédie-Italienne, the latter the less traditional and the more innovative of the two theaters. The Opéra Comique, which was founded in 1713, joined with the Comédie-Italienne in 1762, while the Théâtre de la Foire offered popular pieces, such as farces, vaudevilles, and *comédies à ariettes* (light musical comedies), to French audiences.

In addition to the expansion of seating capacity, there were other physical changes within the theater. As in the previous century, would-be wits and critics continued to habituate the pit, but the more fashionable members of the audience left the first gallery to the middle class. For a substantial fee, wealthy members of the audience could still obtain seats onstage during performances until 1763, when Garrick, the manager of the Drury Lane Theatre, refused to allow this disruptive practice to continue. This restriction was not innovative on Garrick's part, for onstage seating had been banned at the Comédie-Française in Paris four years earlier. During the eighteenth century, the shape of the stage also changed: The apron

grew smaller, with the performing area shrinking gradually into the familiar picture-frame stage. Thus, physically as well as spiritually, the theater was receding from the flesh-and-blood world of its audience.

Although remodeling made it possible for increasing numbers of people to attend the theater, the ultimate effect of the enlargement was to accelerate the decline in the quality of the productions and to discourage the writing of plays of depth and subtlety. Given the relatively primitive state of stage lighting in the eighteenth century, the increased distance of the audience from the stage made it more difficult to see the facial expressions and gestures of the actors. Moreover, the enlarged theaters were, as a rule, acoustically poor: The Haymarket, for example, had acoustics so dreadful that it was impossible to perform plays there, and its stage had to be given over entirely to the production of opera. Actors who wished to avoid having their words garbled into incomprehensibility or swallowed up in space were compelled to speak lines in inappropriate (albeit audible) pitches and monotonous tones. Thus, it became impossible for an actor to give a performance that had much subtlety or naturalness.

Such physical problems in the theater encouraged theater managers and audiences to become visually rather than aurally oriented and thus to prefer tragedies that relied not on great verse but on spectacle and comedies that relied on farce rather than on incisive dialogue. To ensure substantial profits, theater managers included animal acts, pantomimes, and dances in addition to the full-length play. Visual elements were incorporated into virtually every production, sometimes in very curious ways. In a revival of Rowe's grim tragedy of pathos *The Tragedy of Jane Shore* (pr. 1714), for example, a rope dance was included in the fifth act. By mid-century, audiences were drawn at least as much by afterpieces and by the dramatic periphery and spectacle as they were by the full-length play itself. Thomas Morton's *Columbus: Or, A World Discovered* (pr. 1792), for example, was well attended largely because of the startling realism of its stage effects, which included swirling clouds, thunder, lightning, a volcanic eruption, and trees being uprooted by the wind. By the end of the century, effect came to be what mattered most. Thus, when Matthew Gregory ("Monk") Lewis included black servants as characters in a play set in Wales, he explained in the preface to the play that he did so in order to make possible greater variety in the costumes. These productions lacked originality as well as literary excellence, for much as television networks reduplicate the basic formulas behind one another's successful shows, Drury Lane and Covent Garden each frantically copied the successful shows of the other rather than attempting to develop something new. Thus, in 1750, for many weeks, two productions of Shakespeare's *Romeo and Juliet* (pr. c. 1595-1596) were offered simultaneously, Drury Lane's featuring Garrick and George Anne Bellamy, and Covent Garden's featuring Spranger Barry and Susannah Cibber.

Responding to and accelerating the orientation of the drama to spectacle were several very important developments in stagecraft. In 1765, Garrick adapted from the French a greatly improved technique for lighting the stage. During the first half of the century, as during the Restoration, lighting had been supplied by footlights and by chandeliers suspended over the stage in plain view of the audience. Garrick replaced the latter with "direct sidelighting," candles arranged in pyramid-shaped forms set in the wings out of the sight of the audience. In addition to being far less distracting than older methods of lighting, the new form could, with the use of colored screens, be made to shed colored light, thus providing effects that would enhance the appeal of plays dependent on visual elements.

Toward the close of the century, substantial innovations were also made in scenery, replacing the painted palaces, tombs, temples, prisons, and gardens that had served as settings. In the 1770's, under the auspices of Garrick, Philip James de Loutherbourg developed a new type of scenery for the Drury Lane Theatre. Using transparent dye, Loutherbourg painted two different scenes, one on each side of a sheet of sheer cloth. Because only the illuminated side would be visible to the audience, scenes could be changed easily and rapidly by a simple shift in lighting. Loutherbourg was also famous for his innovative "roman-

tic" landscapes, which presented not the symmetrical, formal scenes of past years but rugged, irregular natural shapes. Another important current in the development of scenery was also initiated at Drury Lane, under the auspices of Garrick's successor, Kemble. When Kemble hired William Capon to design scenery, Capon tried to produce scenery accurate to the most minute historical detail. This new interest in historical accuracy was also reflected in the costuming of the last quarter of the century. It was considered very innovative when, in 1764, Shakespeare's *Richard III* (pr. c. 1592-1593) was presented in period costume, as it was in 1773 when the famous actor Charles Macklin performed *Macbeth* (pr. 1606) in Scots dress. Perhaps because their success depended heavily on their reputations as beauties, the actresses of the period did not adopt historical costumes but continued to wear contemporary, fashionable dress until 1790, except for the occasional "breeches parts," which afforded them the opportunity to display their legs.

ACTORS

Unquestionably, the actors of the century exercised great influence over the development of the drama. They encouraged playwrights to compose specific parts with them in mind, and the dramatists, eager to have plays produced, would write dramas as vehicles for famous actors' and actresses' dramatic specialities—Farquhar, for example, composed *Sir Harry Wildair, Being the Sequel of a Trip to the Jubilee* (pr. 1701) especially for Robert Wilks. As a result, plays tended to rely on the same types rather than introducing fresh and innovative characters. Another obstacle to the development of high-quality drama was the lack of discipline with which actors approached their trade. Richard Brinsley Sheridan's *The Rivals* (pr. 1775), for example, failed miserably on its opening night largely because several principal actors did not know their lines well. Often while onstage, when not delivering their own lines, actors and actresses fell out of character entirely, even engaging in conversation with members of the audience while other actors were speaking. Actors also adopted a similarly casual attitude toward rehearsals, from which many members of the cast were absent or, if present, were inattentive. The famous tragic actress Sarah Siddons once remarked that she had played Belvidera, the female lead in Thomas Otway's *Venice Preserved: Or, A Plot Discovered* (pr. 1682), without benefit of a single rehearsal. This lack of rehearsal also encouraged actors to engage in the common practice of freely ad-libbing lines rather than adhering strictly to the script penned by the playwright, a tendency very likely encouraged by the popularity of the *commedia dell'arte*, which relied extensively on improvisation. Nevertheless, the eighteenth century witnessed an abundance of excellent actors, the most famous of whom include Colley Cibber, Booth, Wilks, James Quin, Barry, Macklin, Garrick, Kemble, Ann Bracegirdle, Kitty Clive, Peg Woffington, and Siddons.

Curiously, as the drama grew less literary, its performers and performances became more self-consciously professional. The eighteenth century also saw great changes in acting style, again largely as a result of the efforts of Garrick. Actors such as Quin, who adhered to the older style, strode out onto the apron and declaimed in a highly formal manner. Garrick and his rival Macklin, however, strove for greater realism and subtlety in performance. Macklin became famous for his natural rendering of Shylock in 1741, the same year Garrick debuted in *Richard III*. Garrick insisted on the need to display emotion to make the drama effective. Thus, he employed facial expression and gesture to enliven his performance and, rather than adhering rigidly to the versification in the plays, used stresses and pauses to heighten the effect of the dialogue. During his visit to Paris in 1763, Garrick was asked by Denis Diderot to illustrate in practice the theory of acting presented in Diderot's *Paradoxe sur le comédien* (wr. 1773).

As theater manager as well as actor and playwright, Garrick exerted great influence over the drama. Unlike the theater managers of the previous century, those during the eighteenth century were not courtiers but were, like Garrick, professional theater people. Among the more famous managers of Drury Lane Theatre were Cibber, Steele, Garrick, Kemble, and Sheridan, and the most famous manager of the

Little Theatre in the Haymarket was Fielding. Theater managers were often criticized for their rude and whimsical treatment of playwrights as well as for their tendency to make financial considerations rather than artistic merit their primary criterion in selecting plays to produce. Garrick, for example, was attacked by Arthur Murphy in the preface to *Alzuma* (pr. 1773), as was Kemble by George Colman the Younger in the preface to *The Iron Chest* (pr. 1796). Because of Sheridan's erratic vacillation between irresponsibility and tyranny, Kemble resigned his Drury Lane partnership and became manager of Covent Garden. The Continent, too, had its share of famous playwright-managers. Two of the most famous German theater managers were Johann Wolfgang von Goethe, who managed the ducal theater in Weimar from 1791 until he resigned in 1817, and August Wilhelm Iffland, who directed the Mannheim National Theatre and who, like Garrick, was also the foremost actor of his day.

Thus, a variety of forces contributed simultaneously to the widening of the audience and to the decline of quality in the drama: the encouragement of mediocrity and the discouragement of the controversial stemming from the Licensing Act, the artificiality of sentimentalism, the popularity and excellence of drama from the past and from the Continent, the lack of real competition between the playhouses, the temptation offered to playwright and theater manager alike of easy labor and certain profit in the production of drama other than the full-length play, the "star system," and technological advances and architectural alterations within the playhouse itself. Nevertheless, the drama of the eighteenth century is worthy of study—when not for its intrinsic literary merits, for its reflection of the age and for its influence on subsequent drama.

COMEDY

Although the British comedy of the eighteenth century shares the eclecticism of the tragedy of the period in its recombination and synthesis of a wide variety of earlier forms, these plays typically adhere more to one than to the other of two theoretical positions concerning comedy—to "laughing comedy," that which is designed primarily to amuse, or to "weeping" or, more commonly, "sentimental comedy," with its overt didacticism, exemplary characters, and exaltation of pathos. When considering the comedy of this period, it is perhaps most important to remember that there was no great struggle for preeminence between the comedy of manners, the predominant comic form of the previous age, and sentimentalism, which became an increasingly pervasive influence on drama during the eighteenth century. Although sentimentality eventually dominated eighteenth century comedy, initially it merely colored scenes, character types, or dialogue rather than manifesting itself as an independent comic genre. In fact, very few sentimental comedies, as such, appeared during the first half of the century. Most new comedies written before 1750 relied heavily on the traditions of the comedy of manners, of intrigue, and of humors, as well as on the farce, burlesque, and, after 1728, the ballad opera. Of these forms, during the first half of the century, the Restoration comedies of manners (especially those by Dryden, William Wycherley, Sir George Etherege, and William Congreve) and the transitional plays of Vanbrugh and Farquhar were the regular comedies most frequently offered. Although sentimentalism clearly dominated the stage during the latter half of the century, the comedy of manners and other species of laughing comedy continued to thrive in abbreviated form as afterpieces.

The two main comic trends of the eighteenth century are observable in its opening decade, in the laughing comedies of Vanbrugh and Farquhar and in the more obviously moralistic comedies of Cibber and Steele. Although relying heavily on the tradition of the Restoration comedy of manners, Cibber's *Love's Last Shift: Or, The Fool in Fashion* (pr. 1696) broke with this form in its sympathetic and somewhat serious consideration of a wife's concern over her spouse's adultery as well as with the last-act repentance of her rake-husband. Cibber's impetus in writing such a play was likely more pragmatic than moralistic. He seems to have been responding to the disdain of the contemporary audience for the cynicism and immorality of Restoration comedy, to perceptions reflected by Jeremy Collier's *A Short View*

of the Immorality and Profaneness of the English Stage (pr. 1698). Cibber's *The Careless Husband* (pr. 1704) similarly employs the sudden reformation of its hero and the serious consideration of the problems within marriage.

The plays of Farquhar and Vanbrugh also exemplify the movement away from both the style and the spirit of the Restoration comedy of manners. Though both playwrights satirize vice, their satire is gentler and less cynical than that of their predecessors. Farquhar's masterpieces, *The Recruiting Officer* (pr. 1706) and *The Beaux' Stratagem*, are set not in London but in the country and are peopled by coarser and more realistic characters than those in the comedy of manners. Much of the humor in these plays arises from physical movement and situation rather than from witty dialogue. *The Beaux' Stratagem* also departs from the comedy-of-manners tradition in its occasionally serious attitude toward marriage and in its emphasis on virtue as well as wit as an essential characteristic of a hero. Vanbrugh offers an even more serious consideration of the problems within marriage in *The Relapse: Or, Virtue in Danger* (pr. 1696), which he wrote in response to the facile reformation at the conclusion of Cibber's *Love's Last Shift*, and in *The Provok'd Wife*. Overt moralizing, however, characteristic of sentimental comedy, is absent from these plays.

It was with the later comedies of Steele that "genteel" or "reformed" comedy (which presents the comedy of manners form in the sentimental spirit) really seized hold on the theater. In his comedies as in his essays, Steele's purpose was the advancement of good breeding and virtue. He sought to eliminate coarseness but not wit from the comedy of manners, to transform the comedy-of-manners conception of the hero as rake into the hero as moral exemplar. Like Cibber's, Steele's early comedies largely consist of a comedy-of-manners plot with a reformation in the final act. Such is the case in his first comedy, *The Funeral: Or, Grief à-la-Mode* (pr. 1701), and in the unsuccessful *The Lying Lover: Or, The Ladies' Friendship* (pr. 1703), whose purpose, Steele declared, was to elicit "generous Pity" rather than laughter, and which, he felt, was "dam'd for its piety."

Again, however, like those of Cibber and Vanbrugh, Steele's early comedies depart from the comedy-of-manners tradition by focusing seriously and sympathetically on domestic issues. Whereas the sentimentality of Steele's early comedies resides largely in their conclusions, his later plays are increasingly permeated by sentimentality; his *The Conscious Lovers* was the first (and, for more than forty years, the finest) English sentimental comedy.

The Conscious Lovers, like subsequent sentimental comedies, was intended to elicit an emotional more than an intellectual response from the audience, to stir up pity and admiration (emotions more traditionally associated with tragedy) for an exemplary pair of lovers in distress. In *The Conscious Lovers*, as in subsequent comedies of this subgenre, the focal characters are middle-class lovers who are unashamed of their devotion to each other. Marriage is presented as an ideal goal, the attraction between the lovers based on the virtue rather than the wit or wealth of the potential spouse. The hero, with whom the audience is intended to sympathize, is not a cynical rake but is, like his beloved, an intensely benevolent and sensitive soul who is given not to witty repartee but to prolonged, rapturous pronouncements about love and virtue. Such plays consider not the manners but the fundamental nature of humankind, which, they optimistically assume, is inherently good and perfectible. In his preface to *The Conscious Lovers*, Steele declares that he wishes his drama to "chasten wit, and moralize the stage," to inspire in the audience "a Joy too exquisite for Laughter." Whereas Restoration comedy typically satirized vice, the principal purpose of sentimental comedy was to advance the cause of virtue and morality. Dependent as it is on the moral aphorism, the dialogue of sentimental comedy is unrealistic and formulaic, as are the plots typical of this genre. Inevitably, poetic justice triumphs, and virtue is unexpectedly and improbably rewarded, usually in tangible as well as in intangible terms. Although these plays are concerned with moral questions in social contexts, rarely do their playwrights espouse revolutionary political or social positions; the morality they advocate is wholly conventional and middle-class. Sentimental comedy is free from indelicacy and vice—and, often, from humor, for the moralistic emphasis and the rigid conception of decorum rendered many of these plays tedious and somewhat grim fare.

The sentimental comedy established by Cibber and Steele was widely imitated both at home and on the Continent. During the first half of the century, for example, sentimental comedy was written in England by the Reverend James Miller, Thomas Baker, William Burnaby, Charles Johnson, and Robert Dodsley. One of the better sentimental comedies of this period is *The Foundling* (pr. 1748), by Edward Moore, who is more commonly remembered for his tragedy *The Gamester* (pr. 1753). James Dance's *Pamela* (pb. 1741), a dramatization of Samuel Richardson's sentimental novel *Pamela: Or, Virtue Rewarded* (1740-1741), is also worthy of note in that it inaugurates the eighteenth century fashion of rendering popular novels into dramatic form.

During the decade of the 1750's, no new comedies were offered, but sentimental comedies continued to appear in subsequent decades. The foremost writers of sentimental comedy after 1750 were Kelly and Cumberland. Kelly is remembered most for his *False Delicacy* (pr. 1768), with which Garrick hoped to undermine the success of Oliver Goldsmith's *The Good-Natured Man* (pr. 1768). The conflict in *False Delicacy* arises from the characters' extreme consideration for one another's feelings, but the conclusion of the play ultimately applauds rather than criticizes the characters for their excessive sensibilities. Cumberland's play *The Brothers* (pr. 1769) is more typical of sentimental comedy than is Kelly's *False Delicacy*, but it is for his second play, *The West Indian*, that Cumberland is best remembered. In writing *The West Indian*, Cumberland was determined to present in an extremely positive light characters drawn from groups who were the victims of prejudice, traditional butts of ridicule. Such are the Irishman O'Flaherty and the West Indian Belcourt, the latter a typical hero of sentimental comedy. Belcourt is also significant as a reflection of the influence of Jean-Jacques Rousseau's conception of the "child of Nature." So successful was Cumberland in elevating the stature of the Irishman through this play that Sheridan's use of a comic Irishman in the original version of *The Rivals* elicited hostility rather than laughter from the play's audience. Cumberland again defended the oppressed in *The Fashionable Lover* (pr. 1772), in which he served as an advocate for the Scots, and in *The Jew* (pr. 1794). In concert with Garrick and George Colman the Elder, he also wrote another very successful comedy, *The Clandestine Marriage* (pr. 1766). Other sentimental comedies of the latter half of the century include William Whitehead's *School for Lovers* (pr. 1762), Frances Sheridan's *The Discovery* (pr. 1763) and *The Dupe* (pr. 1763), Isaac Bickerstaffe's *The Maid of the Mill* (pr. 1765), George Colman the Elder's *The English Merchant* (pr. 1767), Hannah Cowley's *Which Is the Man?* (pr. 1782), Lieutenant-General John Burgoyne's *The Heiress* (pr. 1786), and Macklin's *The Man of the World* (pr. 1781).

At the close of the century, the most prominent writers of sentimental comedy were Elizabeth Inchbald and Holcroft, who were also participants in the humanitarian movement in literature. Inchbald's attitudes toward drama—views that are representative of her age—are reflected in her prefaces to the plays in *The British Theater* (1806), the collection that she edited. Inchbald believed that artistic success depended on "scrupulous purity of character and refinement of sensation" and that laughter should be confined to the lower forms of comedy, such as farce and burlesque, because, in her view, the primary purpose of high comedy was to educate and edify. Her own plays offer much social criticism—*Such Things Are* (pr. 1787), for example, is based on the experiences of the prison reformer John Howard. This play is also of interest in its reflection of Rousseau's conception of the noble savage in the characterization of Zedan. Whereas Inchbald's views were expressed quite openly in her dramas, Holcroft's highly controversial political opinions were not. Holcroft's comedies are much like those of Cumberland, except that Holcroft relies more heavily on sensational and tragic elements. *The Road to Ruin* (pr. 1792), a sentimental comedy about the problems of gambling, is his most famous play.

Thus, in England, sentimental comedy gradually increased its emphasis on pathos and at the same time degenerated into a simplistic conception of the relationship between virtue and reward. Over the course of the century, English sentimental comedy neither enlarged the scope of emotions to which it appealed nor explored fresher, larger issues. The form constituted a lengthy dramatic experiment that was sustained by a belief in (and a desire to augment) the fundamental benevolence of humankind. Sentimental comedy was, however, an experiment that succeeded more in commercial than in aesthetic terms.

FRENCH COMEDIES

The sentimental comedies of Cibber and Steele were also imitated successfully in France, where playwrights came to place even greater emphasis on the pathetic and on philosophical and ethical declamation. Because of its pronounced emphasis on pathos, the sentimental comedy of France is designated *comédie larmoyante* ("weeping comedy"). Like English sentimental comedies, plays in the tradition of the *comédie larmoyante* employ bourgeois characters and are highly moralistic and overtly didactic. In France, at the opening of the century, the most popular comic playwrights were those following in the tradition of Molière, among them Florent Carton Dancourt, from whom Vanbrugh and Foote both borrowed extensively, and Alain-René Lesage, who was extraordinarily prolific as a playwright, although he is best remembered for his four-volume novel *Histoire de Gil Blas de Santillane* (1715-1735; *The History of Gil Blas of Santillane*, 1716, 1735; better known as *Gil Blas*, 1749). Jean-François Regnard's *Le Légataire universel* (pr. 1708; *The Universal Legatee*, 1796), a comedy of intrigue satirizing vice in Molièrian manner, also anticipates the *comédie larmoyante* in its theme and style. Other important approximations of the form are *Le Philosophe marié* (pr. 1727), by Philippe Néricault Destouches, which John Kelly translated into English in 1732 as *The Married Philosopher* and which Inchbald later adapted as *The Married Man* (pr. 1789), and Destouches's *Le Glorieux* (pr. 1732; *The Conceited Count*, 1923). Although Pierre-Claude Nivelle de La Chaussée is typically credited with producing the first actual *comédie larmoyante* with his *La Fausse Antipathie* (pr. 1733), the most famous dramatist of this movement was Marivaux. In an amusing rather than a satiric manner, Marivaux's plays offer a minute exploration of the sentiments of lovers, especially women. The polished dialogue he employs in scenes offering such psychological exploration and revelation led to the coinage of the literary term *marivaudage*. Two of his plays that exerted the greatest influence on French comedy are *Arlequin poli par l'amour* (pr. 1720; *Robin, Bachelor of Love*, 1968) and *Le Jeu de l'amour et du hasard* (pr. 1730; *The Game of Love and Chance*, 1907).

German comedy

The French *comédie larmoyante* was introduced in Germany by Christian Fürchtegott Gellert's *Das Los in der Lotterie* (1747). Although many literary historians identify Gotthold Ephraim Lessing's *Minna von Barnhelm: Oder, Das Soldatenglück* (pr. 1767; *Minna von Barnhelm: Or, The Soldier's Fortune*, 1786) as the finest German sentimental comedy, significantly more popular both in Germany and in England were the artistically inferior plays of August von Kotzebue. Kotzebue adapted Friedrich Schiller's type of drama, which appealed primarily to the elite, to suit popular taste. Audiences were drawn to his plays not merely because of their sentimental and humanitarian emphasis, however, but also because of their sensationalistic plots. Thirty-six of Kotzebue's plays were translated into English, and twenty of these were performed on the English stage between 1796 and 1801. In 1799, for example, translations and adaptations of *Die Spanier in Peru: Oder, Rollas Tod* (pr. 1794; *The Spaniards in Peru: Or, Rolla's Death*, 1799) were done by Anne Plumptre, Matthew Gregory Lewis, Richard Brinsley Sheridan, Thomas Dutton, Robert Heron, and Matthew West, and another version was produced by Benjamin Thompson the following year. In England, the most popular adaptations of Kotzebue's plays were A. Schink and George Papendick's rendering of *Menschenhass und Reue* (pr. 1789) as *The Stranger: Or, Misanthropy and Repentance* (pb. 1798) and Sheridan's *Pizarro: A Tragedy in Five Acts* (pr. 1799). *Menschenhass und Reue* was again reworked in 1799 as *The Noble Lie* by Maria Geisweiler. Kotzebue's plays did not meet with unanimous praise, how-

ever, as is evident in Jane Austen's novel *Mansfield Park* (1814), in which the characters debate the degree of immorality and offensiveness to be found in Kotzebue's dramas.

Italian comedy

In Italy during the eighteenth century, comedy developed along a substantially different course as a result of the pervasiveness and persistence of the influence of the *commedia dell'arte*. A species of improvisational comedy based on the stock characters Harlequin, Columbine, and Scaramouche, the *commedia dell'arte* ("comedy of the profession") originated during the mid-sixteenth century with the rise of the first regular Italian theatrical companies. Despite the efforts of a number of dramatists, the influence of the *commedia dell'arte* remained apparent in Italian comedy throughout the century. One of the first to attempt to break from this tradition and develop a higher form of Italian comedy was Carlo Goldoni. Of Goldoni's approximately three hundred plays, almost half are prose comedies, many of which are derived from the comedy of manners and sentimental comedy and which thus place greater emphasis on character development and dialogue than did traditional Italian comedy. Although he exposes human folly, Goldoni's tone is typically one of warm humor rather than of harsh satire. His comedies are highly moralistic, and the morality they espouse is distinctly middle-class. His masterpieces, which were produced between 1757 and 1762, are *I rusteghi* (pr. 1760; *The Boors*, 1961) and *Le baruffe chizzotte* (pr. 1762; *The Squabbles of Chioggia*, 1914). Opposing the changes instituted by Goldoni was Carlo Gozzi, whose most famous play is *L'amore delle tre melarance* (pr. 1761; *The Love of the Three Oranges*, 1921). An advocate of the tradition of the *commedia dell'arte*, Gozzi was especially successful with the production of his nine *fiabe* ("fantastic plays"), which appeared between 1761 and 1765. Based on Asian tales or on fairy tales, the *fiabe* were translated into German in 1777 and 1778 and exerted a strong influence on Goethe, Schiller, Lessing, and August Wilhelm Schlegel.

French drame

As the result of the efforts of Denis Diderot in

France, yet another dramatic form developed at the same time as the *comédie larmoyante*—the *drame*. A *drame* is a serious but not tragic play that focuses on the concerns of middle-class characters. Although this form has comic potential in its concentration on middle-class characters and tragic potential in the seriousness with which it addresses their concerns, the tone of the *drame* does not alternate between comic and tragic but remains consistently serious. As in the sentimental comedy, the eliciting of emotion for and identification with the characters are prime considerations of the playwright. Deliberately trying to shape the development of the *drame*, Diderot published his critical theory of the drama along with his plays. Thus, the unsuccessful play *Le Fils naturel; Ou, Les Épreuves de la vertu* (pr. 1757; *Dorval: Or, The Test of Virtue*, 1767) was published with the theoretical work *Entretiens sur "Le Fils naturel"* in 1757, and the successful play *Le Père de famille* (pr. 1761; *The Father of the Family*, 1770; also as *The Family Picture*, 1871) was published with *Discours sur la poésie dramatique* in 1758. Among Diderot's many followers and imitators in the *drame* were Louis-Sébastien Mercier's *La Brouette du vinaigrier* (pr. 1775) and Michel Jean Sedaine's *Le Philosophe sans le savoir* (pr. 1765), the latter perhaps the finest *drame* produced during the century. Sedaine did not confine his playwriting to this sober genre but also wrote plays belonging to another genre of French drama, the vaudeville, variety shows employing music, dance, and spectacle. Still another famous follower of Diderot was Pierre-Augustin Caron de Beaumarchais, whose *Essai sur le genre dramatique sérieux* (1767; *Essays on Serious Drama*, 1974) both echoes and modifies the ideas of Diderot. Beaumarchais is best remembered for the trilogy that comprises *La Folle Journée: Ou, Le Mariage de Figaro* (pr. 1784; *The Marriage of Figaro*, 1784), in which he attempted to review laughing comedy; *Le Barbier de Séville: Ou, La Précaution inutile* (pr. 1775; *The Barber of Seville: Or, The Useless Precaution*, 1776), which blends the comedy of humors and of intrigue with social and political satire; and *L'Autre Tartuffe: Ou, La Mère coupable* (pr. 1792; *Frailty and Hypocrisy*, 1804).

LATE CENTURY COMEDY

Despite its overwhelming popularity both in England and on the Continent, the sentimental comedy never met with universal approbation; from the time of its inception, many critics found fault with it. In "A Defense of Sir Fopling Flutter" (1723), for example, the famous critic John Dennis argues that Steele, with his "Joy too exquisite for Laughter," "knows nothing of the rules of comedy, the purpose of which is not to set up patterns of perfection but to picture existing follies which we are to despise." Indeed, so pervasive was the obsession with morality in the comedy that Garrick jokingly suggested that a steeple should be placed atop the playhouse. Perhaps the most famous criticism of the sentimental comedy is that offered by Goldsmith in his *Essay on the Theatre: Or, A Comparison Between Sentimental and Laughing Comedy* (1773), in which Goldsmith condemned the genre as "bastard tragedy," an infelicitous mingling of genres that produced unnatural, pompous plays. Goldsmith's own plays, *The Good-Natured Man* and *She Stoops to Conquer: Or, The Mistakes of a Night* (pr. 1773), aptly illustrate his views. His comedies are replete with warm humor, and though they employ low comedy, they are never coarse or obscene. He shares the sentimentalists' benevolent view of human beings but not their overt didacticism. Though Goldsmith eschewed weeping comedy, he neither advocated nor attempted a return to the comedy of manners of Congreve. Goldsmith's own dramas are *sui generis*; they set no fashion, and he had no direct imitators.

The tradition of the laughing comedy, with its roots largely in the Restoration comedy of manners, continued throughout the century, generally incorporating some sentimental elements. Early examples of such comedies include Burnaby's *The Reform'd Wife* (pr. 1700) and *The Ladies' Visiting Day* (pr. 1701), unusual for its Restoration-style cynical wit; Charles Johnson's *The Masquerade* (pr. 1719); Mrs. Susannah Centlivre's *A Bold Stroke for a Wife* (pr. 1718); Arthur Murphy's *The Way to Keep Him* (pr. 1760) and *Know Your Own Mind* (pr. 1777); and Colman the Elder's *The Jealous Wife* (pr. 1761) and *The Clandestine Marriage* (pr. 1766), the latter written in collaboration with Garrick and Cumberland.

The finest eighteenth century comedy of manners after Congreve is unquestionably that produced by Sheridan—indeed, until Sheridan, no writer after Congreve had successfully attempted a full-length comedy of manners. Voicing his dramatic theory in the *Prologue* [to *The Rivals*] *Spoken on the Tenth Night* (pr. 1775), Sheridan condemned the didacticism of sentimental comedy as well as its fusion of comic with tragic elements. Sheridan's plays are primarily comedies of manners with some reliance on "humours" characters. As in the plays of Cumberland and Goldsmith, the hero is a good-hearted prodigal. Sheridan shares the benevolence but not the pathos of sentimentalism, and the wit but not the profundity of Congreve. The object of his satire in his most famous plays, *The Rivals* and *The School for Scandal* (pr. 1777), is sentimentality, "The Goddess of the woeful countenance—/ The sentimental Muse," as Sheridan describes her. Sheridan does not disagree with the basic morals and assumptions of his society, only with their corruption and distortion. Another writer in this tradition was Mrs. Hannah Cowley, who is more often remembered for her comedies of intrigue derived from Behn and Mrs. Centlivre. Like Sheridan, Cowley blended the comedy-of-manners tradition with sentimental elements in *The Belle's Stratagem* (pr. 1780), *Which Is the Man?*, and *A Bold Stroke for a Husband* (pr. 1783), as did Inchbald in *I'll Tell You What* (pr. 1785) and *Every One Has His Fault* (pr. 1793).

Contemporary laughing comedy did not serve as the sole alternative to the sentimental comedy, however, for the comedy of previous ages still appeared on the stage. Philip Massinger's *A New Way to Pay Old Debts* (pr. c. 1621-1622) was revived in 1748, as was Ben Jonson, George Chapman, and John Marston's *Eastward Ho!* (pr. 1605) in 1752, and the coffin scene in Steele's *The Funeral* is indebted to Francis Beaumont's *The Knight of the Burning Pestle* (pr. 1607). Garrick adapted Jonson's *Every Man in His Humour* (pr. 1598) in 1751 as well as *The Alchemist* (pr. 1610) in 1774, and versions of his *Epicœne: Or, The Silent Woman* (pr. 1609) were produced by both Francis Gentleman (in 1771) and Colman the Elder (in 1776). Of the Elizabethan comedies, how-ever, as with the tragedies, those by Shakespeare were unquestionably the most frequently performed and the most influential. Indeed, one might attribute some of the impetus behind the development of senti-mental comedy to the revival and popularization of Shakespeare's romantic comedies, adaptations of which were written by George Granville, Burnaby, and Charles Johnson, among others, beginning in the 1730's. In 1756, Garrick furthered the trend toward the presentation of distressed virtue and more imagi-native drama by bringing Shakespeare's *The Tempest* (pr. 1611) and *The Winter's Tale* (pr. c. 1610-1611) back to the stage.

Despite their ostensibly distasteful immorality, the comedies of the Restoration also retained their popu-larity. Though performed in an essentially unaltered form during the first half of the century, in later years these comedies appeared only in bowdlerized and moralized adaptations or in condensed versions, as afterpieces. Congreve and Dryden were frequently re-vived, Etherege occasionally, and Wycherley only rarely until Garrick produced his emasculated adapta-tion of *The Country Wife* (pr. 1675) as *The Country Girl* in 1776, the same year Bickerstaffe's adaptation of *The Plain-Dealer* (pr. 1676) appeared. Perhaps the profusion of excellent comedies already available di-minished the desire of the audience for new comedies or discouraged playwrights from attempting forms that appeared already to have been perfected.

Both the comedy of intrigue and the comedy of humors, which had been very popular during the Res-toration, disappeared as independent forms during the eighteenth century. A number of new comedies of intrigue did, however, appear at the opening of the century, including Francis Manning's *All for the Better: Or, The Infallible Cure* (pr. c. 1702), Cibber's *She Wou'd and She Wou'd Not: Or, The Kind Impos-ter* (pr. 1702), Christopher Bullock's *Woman Is a Rid-dle* (pr. 1716), and Richard Savage's *Love in a Veil* (pr. 1718). Unquestionably, the best comedies of in-trigue were those produced by Mrs. Centlivre, who adroitly blended intrigue with sentimentalism in *The Gamester* (pr. 1705) and *The Busie Body* (pr. 1709). The format of these comedies of intrigue had re-mained essentially the same as that employed during the Restoration, except, perhaps, that the newer plays relied more heavily on farce. By 1730, however, the comedy of intrigue as a genre unto itself virtually ceased, perhaps because its atmosphere of trickery and deceit seemed antithetical to sentimentality. Traces of the comedy of intrigue persisted, however, in many plays, such as Bickerstaffe's *'Tis Well It's No Worse* (a 1770 rendering of a work by Pedro Calderón de la Barca), Joseph Atkinson's *The Mutual Deception* (pr. 1785), and Cowley's *A School for Greybeards: Or, The Mourning Bride* (pr. 1786). Similarly, though few attempted the comedy of humors as a form in itself, numerous sentimental and laughing comedies include humors characters. One of the few who did attempt to sustain the form was Charles Shadwell, the son of the famous Restoration humors playwright Thomas Shadwell; the younger Shadwell met with little success in his attempt to follow in his father's generic footsteps. Typical of his works is *The Fair Quaker of Deal: Or, The Humors of the Navy* (pr. 1710). Another comedy of humors is Thomas Baker's *Tunbridge Walks: Or, The Yeoman of Kent* (pr. 1703). Around 1730, the form seems to have experienced something of a brief revival with the appearance in that year of both Miller's *The Humours of Oxford* and Fielding's *Rape upon Rape: Or, The Justice Caught in His Own Trap* (pr. 1730).

THE AFTERPIECE

Rather than devote their talents to high comedy, playwrights attempting original laughing comedies usually turned to the composition of the afterpiece, the drama that usually followed the main entertainment. Typically, the afterpiece was a farce, ballad opera, burlesque, or pantomime. Not only were such forms easier to compose than a full-length play, but also these afterpieces were often much more popular with the audience and were offered for many more performances. Although on the whole the literary merit of afterpieces is inferior to that of the longer plays, many have genuine comic appeal, and the form demands consideration in any history of eighteenth century drama as a reflection of the taste of the age.

An extremely popular form for the afterpiece was farce, which draws its humor from situation rather than from character or dialogue. Having no uniform set of characteristics, farce allowed the artist much greater latitude than did the longer play. Some of the most prominent dramatists of the century composed farces, and this form reached its pinnacle of popularity and quality during the eighteenth century. Vanbrugh, Cibber, and Rowe, for example, wrote farces during the first decade of the eighteenth century, and Mrs. Centlivre, Bickerstaffe, Bullock, and Charles Johnson did so during the second. A number of popular farces were written by Garrick also, whose best received farce was *The Lying Valet* (pr. 1741). Garrick's talent lay not in creating new characters and scenes but in heightening the humor of the old by condensing and accelerating the action. During the second half of the century, Colman the Elder, Murphy, and Sheridan also dabbled in this form. Colman's *Polly Honeycombe* (pr. 1760), which satirizes romantic novels, is a farce, as is his *The Deuce Is in Him* (pr. 1763), in which he again attacks sentimentality. Murphy's *The Citizen* (pr. 1761) and *Three Weeks After Marriage: Or, What We Must All Come To* (pr. 1776) were both very successful, as was Macklin's *Love à la Mode* (pr. 1759) and Inchbald's *Appearance Is Against Them* (pr. 1785). Less successful was Sheridan's *St. Patrick's Day: Or, The Scheming Lieutenant* (pr. 1775). The form did not change much over the course of the century, except that in later years it incorporated material from the pantomime. A unique species of farce was that offered by Foote between 1747 and 1777. Foote's farces depended on the mimicry of contemporary public figures, both public and private, including their physical defects. In *The Minor* (pr. 1760), for example, he caricatured the Methodist George Whitefield. Devoid of literary or aesthetic value, performances of Foote's plays were nevertheless enormously popular. His best piece, *Taste* (pr. 1752), satirizes virtuosi (that is, pretentious connoisseurs). Another extremely popular—and controversial—farce was James Townley's *High Life Below Stairs* (pr. 1759), which satirized the pretentiousness and dishonesty of servants. So strongly did footmen object to the depiction of servants in the play that they almost rioted during the second performance.

Without question, however, it was Henry Fielding who composed the finest farces of the eighteenth century. Fielding's farces employ political, social, and dramatic satire, though his best satires of contemporary drama are more appropriately designated burlesques. Among his finest farces are *The Letter-Writers: Or, A New Way to Keep A Wife at Home* (pr. 1731), *The Author's Farce, and The Pleasures of the Town* (pr. 1730), *Pasquin: Or, A Dramatic Satire on the Times* (pr. 1736), and *The Historical Register for the Year 1736* (pr. 1737). Though "farce" is the term most appropriate to designate these works, they include elements drawn from the comedy of manners, of intrigue, of humors, and burlesque, and most also include songs. Using farce as a vehicle for satire, Fielding expanded the scope of the form to include themes such as a country election and a state lottery.

Another form of afterpiece at which Fielding excelled is the burlesque; in this genre, only John Gay is his equal. Probably the most famous burlesque of the eighteenth century is Fielding's *Tom Thumb: A Tragedy* (pr. 1730); more farcical than Gay's burlesque, the targets of Fielding's satire are not merely heroic dramas but also, as the mock annotations suggest, pompous critics, editors, and readers. Many eighteenth century burlesques are the "rehearsal plays" that follow the example of George Villiers, duke of Buckingham's *The Rehearsal* (pr. 1671). Such are Clive's *The Rehearsal: Or, Bays in Petticoats* (pr. 1750), which satirizes female dramatists; Garrick's *A Peep Behind the Curtain: Or, The New Rehearsal* (pr. 1767); and Sheridan's *The Critic: Or, A Tragedy Rehearsed* (pr. 1779). Henry Carey's *The Tragedy of Chrononhotonthologos* (pr. 1734) satirizes tragedy, while his *The Dragon of Wantley* (pr. 1737) satirizes opera. Gay's main contribution to this genre is *The Mohocks* (pb. 1712), burlesquing Dennis's tragedy *Appius and Virginia* (pr. 1709).

A form of burlesque perfected by John Gay is the ballad opera, of which his *The Beggar's Opera* (pr. 1728) is the most influential example. *The Beggar's Opera* simultaneously satirizes both Italian opera and sentimentality, parodies Shakespeare, Dryden, and Otway, and elicits genuine concern for its characters as well as laughter. For contemporary audiences,

much of the play's humor derived from Gay's parodies of well-known songs. The great success of *The Beggar's Opera* stimulated a barrage of imitations, including Charles Johnson's *The Village Opera* (pr. 1729), Charles Coffey's *The Beggar's Wedding* (pr. 1729), Essex Hawker's *The Wedding* (pr. 1729), and George Lillo's *Silvia: Or, The Country Burial* (pr. 1730). Satiric, sentimental, realistic, and pastoral imitations of *The Beggar's Opera* were all produced, but none approached Gay's success. The heyday of the ballad opera was from 1728 to 1738, but the genre was revived later in the century by Bickerstaffe's *Love in a Village* (pr. 1762). Other writers who attempted the form in the later years of the century were John O'Keeffe, Charles Dibdin, and Sheridan, whose highly successful *The Duenna: Or, The Double Elopement* (pr. 1775) was based on Wycherley's *The Country Wife*.

Perhaps the most profitable and popular form of afterpiece from midcentury on was the pantomime, a form believed to have been developed for the English stage during the 1720's by John Weaver, a dancing master at Drury Lane. So popular was the pantomime that admission prices for it were frequently twice the amount of those for other kinds of entertainment. In developing this form, Weaver drew on a variety of traditions, primarily on English farce and satire, on classical mythology, and on the stock characters found in the Italian *commedia dell'arte*. The story line of the pantomime focuses on the adventures of Harlequin, which were presented through dance, acrobatics, and gesture rather than through dialogue. The titles of these pieces reflect their curious mixture of sources and subjects: *The Loves of Mars and Venus* (Weaver, pr. 1717), *Harlequin Turned Judge* (Weaver, pr. 1717), *The Jealous Doctors* (John Rich, or "Lun," pr. 1717), *Harlequin Doctor Faustus* and *Harlequin Shepherd* (both by Thurmond, pr. 1723 and pr. 1724, respectively). Pantomime remained popular throughout the latter half of the century, as playwrights expanded the subject matter to include historical spectacle, current events, Asian tales, and popular literature. Later pantomimes include Henry Woodward's *Harlequin Ranger* (pr. 1751) and *Queen Mab* (pr. 1750); Dance's *The Witches: Or, Harlequin Cher-*

okee (pr. 1762) and *The Rites of Hecate: Or, Harlequin from the Moon* (pr. 1763); John O'Keeffe's *Harlequin Teague: Or, The Giant's Causeway* (pr. 1782); and Garrick's self-parodic *Harlequin Invasion* (pr. 1759). The form was satirized by Fielding in *The Author's Farce*, as well as by Kelly in *The Plot* (pr. 1735) and in the anonymous *The British Stage* (pr. 1724), *The English Stage Italianized* (pr. 1727), *Harlequin Horace* (pr. 1731), and *Harlequin Student* (pr. 1741).

TRAGEDY

In Britain during the eighteenth century, tragedy was by no means as popular as was comedy, constituting but a small percentage of the number of plays performed. Although several dramatists made significant contributions to this genre—most notably, Addison, Nicholas Rowe, Don DeLillo, and Home—their influence was not nearly as pervasive or powerful on either their contemporaries or their successors as was that of Dryden and Otway on other tragic playwrights of the previous century. Generally, those playwrights who wrote tragedies did not attempt to specialize in the form but exercised their talents—or limitations—in other genres as well.

If one calculates a play's popularity according to the number of performances given, the most popular tragedies of the century were, by far, those by Shakespeare. His works were edited during the eighteenth century by Rowe (1709), Pope (1723-1725), Lewis Theobald (1733), Thomas Hanmer (1743-1744), William Warburton (1747), Samuel Johnson (1765), Edward Capell (1767-1768), George Steevens (1773), Edmond Malone (1790), and Isaac Reed (1785), and Shakespeare was universally praised as a natural genius; nevertheless, his tragedies were often revised substantially to render them more compatible with contemporary sensibilities. Even the great Johnson, whose preface to his edition of Shakespeare is a landmark in the history of literary criticism, preferred Nahum Tate's 1681 adaptation of *King Lear* to the original. Garrick also adapted *King Lear* (in 1756), as did Colman the Elder (in 1768) and Kemble (in 1788). Although modern literary critics might tend to dismiss such adaptations as worthless, it is worth-

while to note that the film script for the famous production of *Richard III*, in which Sir Laurence Olivier plays the title role, is based on Tate's version of the play.

Other Elizabethan and Jacobean tragedies were also revived and adapted during the eighteenth century. Rowe's *The Fair Penitent* (pr. 1703) is based on Philip Massinger's *The Fatal Dowry* (pr. c. 1616-1619); Lillo reworked *Arden of Feversham* (pr. 1759), and Colman the Elder adapted Fletcher's *Philaster: Or, Love Lies A-Bleeding* (pr. c. 1609) in 1763. Jonson's *Sejanus His Fall* (pr. 1603) was adapted by Francis Gentleman (in 1752) and anonymously as *The Favourite* (in 1770). More popular than the Elizabethan tragedies, however, were the heroic dramas of the Restoration, those by Dryden, Elkanah Settle, and Nathaniel Lee in particular, and the pathetic tragedies of the late seventeenth century, especially those written by Otway, Thomas Southerne, and John Banks. Thus William Addington developed Dryden's play *Aureng-Zebe* (pr. 1675) into *The Prince of Agra* (pr. 1774), while Bickerstaffe transformed *Don Sebastian, King of Portugal* (pr. 1689) into *The Captive* (pr. 1769). Southerne's *The Fatal Marriage* (pr. 1694) became Garrick's *Isabella* (pr. 1757), while *Oroonoko: Or, The Royal Slave* (pr. 1695), Southerne's adaptation of Behn's novel, underwent various transformations in the hands of John Hawkesworth (in 1759), Francis Gentleman (in 1760), and John Ferrar (in 1788).

It is not surprising that such earlier tragedy surpassed the popularity of contemporary eighteenth century tragedy, for many contemporary plays suffered from serious weaknesses in dialogue, character development, plot structure, and form. The dialogue, for example, is often bombastic or woodenly formal in plays derived from heroic drama or, as the century progresses, is laden with sentimental *sententiae* or pre-Romantic hyperbole. The atmosphere of many of these tragedies lacks the tragic aura of malign and inexorable fate. Many plots rely excessively on anagnorisis (recognition or discovery) to create dramatic tension, as is done successfully in John Home's *Douglas* (pr. 1756) and, less felicitously, in William Whitehead's *Creusa, Queen of Athens* (pr. 1754), Arthur Murphy's *The Orphan of China* (pr. 1759), and Cumberland's *The Carmelite* (pr. 1784).

Perhaps the most damning flaw of these tragedies, however, is their uncertainty of generic identity: The bulk of the original tragedies written in Britain during the eighteenth century consist of a patchwork of elements drawn from other tragedies, from tragedies old and new, domestic and foreign. The plots of these plays are generally drawn from three sources—from classical themes (such as Addison's *Cato* and Whitehead's *The Roman Father*, pr. 1750) or from Asian tales (such as John Hughes's *The Siege of Damascus*, pr. 1720; and Hill's *The Tragedy of Zara*, pr. 1736, and *Merope*, pr. 1749, both derived from Voltaire) or from English history, especially of the medieval period (such as Hill's *Elfrid: Or, The Fair Inconstant*, pr. 1710, and Ambrose Philips's *The Briton*, pr. 1722). Over the course of the century, though the structure of most tragedies remained essentially classical, the subject matter became increasingly Romantic, but never did a single coherent form predominate, developed and perfected by masters and imitated by those striving to be such. Within the confines of a single scene, pathos derived from Otway, Southerne, or later from Rowe, diction derived from Dryden (if elevated) or from Shakespeare (if "natural"), and characters derived from classical drama may cohabit uneasily.

Because of their lack of fixed form, the more polymorphous tragedies of the eighteenth century are usually referred to simply as Augustan tragedies. Those that do offer a coherent sense of form may usually be classified as belonging to the subgenres of pseudoclassical tragedy, she-tragedy, domestic tragedy, or Romantic tragedy. These categories, however, are overlapping and artificial, and do not reflect the entirely of each play, only its prevailing mode. Even those tragedies that may reasonably be assigned to specific genres incorporate diverse elements from diverse sources.

Pseudoclassical tragedy is a subgenre of particular interest to the literary historian in that it reflects one of the strongest critical currents of the age, the belief, maintained by the "ancients," in the necessity of adhering to classical rules to produce the finest tragedy.

Based on a misreading of Aristotle, the Rules had dominated the French drama written in the seventeenth century and had exerted a profound influence on that of Germany, Italy, and Britain. During the early decades of the eighteenth century, critics both in England and on the Continent persisted in admonishing playwrights for violating the Rules, especially those concerning the unities of time, place, and action. Thomas Rymer, Dennis, and Charles Gildon were the most influential British advocates of the Rules, and it is to their encouragement that historians owe the persistence of attempts to popularize pseudoclassical tragedy in England. Pseudoclassical plays rely heavily on classical drama for their plots, characters, structure, and themes; Dennis himself, for example, employed classical subjects as the bases for his unsuccessful tragedies *Iphigenia* (pr. 1699) and *Appius and Virginia*.

Perhaps the most important force in the development of pseudoclassical tragedy was the seventeenth century French playwright Jean Racine, who during the eighteenth century remained a force to be imitated or resisted. Charles Johnson's pseudoclassical tragedy *The Victim* (pr. 1714), for example, is based on Racine's *Iphigénie* (pr. 1674; *Iphigenia in Aulis*, 1700). Similarly, Philips's aesthetically and financially successful tragedy *The Distrest Mother* (pr. 1712), for which Steele wrote the prologue and Addison the epilogue, owes much to Racine's *Andromaque* (pr. 1667; *Andromache*, 1674).

Philips's tragedy is important in literary history as an example of an artistically and financially successful pseudoclassical tragedy and as an early example and progenitor of the she-tragedy. Most important, however, it was the positive reception afforded this pseudoclassical tragedy that convinced Addison to complete one of his own after a ten-year delay and to offer on the stage what would prove to be the foremost English pseudoclassical tragedy, *Cato*. Greeted with virtually universal critical approbation, *Cato* generated a legion of pamphlets and was translated into French, German, Italian, and Polish. More than any other tragedy during the first half of this century, *Cato* elevated the esteem in which English drama was held by the literati of the Continent.

Although Addison's *Cato* is unquestionably an example of a successful pseudoclassical tragedy, the play also illustrates the limitations of the genre. Strive though he does to adhere to the Rules, Addison nevertheless violates them with his inclusion of a subplot and his somewhat broad interpretation of the unities. A more serious and symptomatic defect in *Cato* is that, despite the sincerity of the sentiments this tragedy expresses, the play lacks emotional force and psychological depth. The pseudoclassical emphasis on decorum renders this tragedy, like other pseudoclassical tragedies, overly restrained and passionless; its characters are admirable but distant and unapproachable. Indeed, the best scenes of plays of this type are those that are least "classical" and that rely most on the heroic or the pathetic. Although contemporary critics praised pseudoclassical tragedy, the public, on the whole, shunned it; indeed, most historians of the theater agree that the success of *Cato* derived at least as much from its allusions to contemporary politics as from its exemplification of critical theory or its intrinsic merit as a drama. So artfully written was Addison's tragedy that the opposing political factions in the audience all claimed that Addison was a spokesman for their position.

Although the production of pseudoclassical tragedy declined in the 1720's, other playwrights continued to equal Addison's success during the century. Among these playwrights are James Thomson (who is more renowned for his poem *The Seasons*), in his *The Tragedy of Sophonisba* (pr. 1730); Samuel Johnson, in *Irene: A Tragedy* (pr. 1749); Whitehead, in *The Roman Father* and *Crëusa, Queen of Athens*; Murphy, in *Alzuma*, based on Sophocles' play *Electra*; and John Delan, in *The Royal Suppliants* (pr. 1781), which blends Euripides' *Hērakleidai* (c. 430 B.C.E.; *The Children of Heracles*, 1781) with Aeschylus' *Hiketides* (c. 463 B.C.E.; *The Suppliants*, 1777).

Pseudoclassical tragedy was popular on the Continent as well as in Britain. In Italy, the foremost composer of pseudoclassical tragedy was Francesco Scipione Maffei, whose *Merope* (pr. 1713) was one of very few Italian tragedies to be performed on the English stage during the eighteenth century. *Merope* was lauded by Goldsmith, both praised and condemned by Voltaire (who produced his own version in 1743), and carefully examined by Goethe and Lessing. In Germany, the most important force in the pseudoclassical movement in drama was Johann Christoph Gottsched, who tried to model German pseudoclassical tragedy on the French as part of his effort to reunite the German drama with literature. Gottsched's most famous play is the very successful *Der sterbende Cato* (pr. 1732), which is essentially a translation of François Michel Crétien Deschamps's *Caton d'Utique* (pr. 1715), with Addison's conclusion substituted for Deschamps's. Gottsched was also influential in the history of German theatrical production as well as the composition of plays, being one of the first to demand that actors adhere strictly to the script and to pursue historical accuracy in costuming, and he produced a bibliography of German drama that scholars still find useful today, titled *Nötiger Vorratzur Geschichte der deutschen dramatischen Dichtkunst* (1757-1765).

Subsequent leaders in the German pseudoclassical movement rejected French classicism, believing that the French had misinterpreted Aristotle, and insisted on returning to the Greek texts themselves for their models. The most famous of the German dramatists advocating this Greek-oriented pseudoclassicism were Lessing, Goethe, and Schiller—the latter two more famous for their contribution to the Sturm und Drang movement. Lessing believed that the Rules were not "rules" per se but merely suggestions. In *Kritische Briefe, die neueste deutsche Literatur betreffend* (1759-1760) and *Hamburgische Dramaturgie* (1767-1769; *Hamburg Dramaturgy*, 1889), Lessing enunciates his critical position, condemning the tragedies of Gottsched, Pierre Corneille, Racine, and Voltaire for their lack of action and praising Shakespeare as the greatest modern dramatist. Lessing even asserts that Shakespeare adhered to Aristotle's actual principles more closely than did Corneille. The ideal tragedy, Lessing believed, would blend Shakespearean characterization and incident with Sophoclean restraint of form, principles that Lessing incorporated in the composition of his extremely influential tragedy *Emilia Galotti* (pr. 1772; English translation, 1786).

In France, the predominant force in the shaping of tragedy was Voltaire. Like the German tragedians, Voltaire found the old models no longer satisfactory, but he offered an alternative solution. Voltaire enunciated his theories partly in response to his chief rival, Prosper Jolyot de Crébillon, whose innovation in the drama consisted of the exploitation of the horrific, as is evident in his *Atrée et Thyeste* (pr. 1707) and Voltaire's *Œdipe* (pr. 1718; *Oedipus*, 1761). Though an admirer of Racine and fundamentally a classicist who believed in clear generic distinction, decorum, and the unities, Voltaire was inspired by Shakespeare to initiate a number of significant innovations in the drama. Rather than turn back to the Greeks, Voltaire modernized and renewed classicism by placing a new emphasis on the emotions, especially on pathos, and by extending the range of characters and settings used in tragedy to include the Oriental and the exotic, as in *Mahomet* (pr. 1742; *Mahomet the Prophet*, 1744) and *Alzire, l'Orphelin de la Chine*, (pr. 1755; *The Orphan of China*, 1756). Voltaire also wrote philosophical tragedies focusing on subjects other than love. *Alzire* and *Mahomet*, for example, center on religious conflict. Voltaire violated the Rules by presenting violence onstage, and he also expanded the use of spectacle. The performance of *Adélaïde du Guesclin* (pr. 1734), for example, included a riot, thunder, and the firing of a cannon. Voltaire's dramas and ideas were widely imitated and adapted: In England, Hill's *The Tragedy of Zara* was based on Voltaire's *Zaïre* (pr. 1732; English translation, 1736), which was, in turn, derived from Shakespeare's *Othello, the Moor of Venice* (pr. 1604), and Murphy's *The Chinese Orphan* and *Alzuma* are also adaptations of plays by Voltaire. Voltaire's movement away from rigid classicism is sometimes regarded as a significant step toward the beginning of Romantic tragedy.

Besides pseudoclassicism, another influential force in the development of tragedy during the early part of the century was the heroic drama, with its standardized characters (great souls struggling in love), plots (bold exploits and contemptible betrayals), settings (temples, tombs, palaces, prisons, gardens), and bombastic dialogue. The plays of Racine, Dryden, and Lord Orrery were most frequently imitated by playwrights attempting to make use of this tradition. Although the eighteenth century witnessed the production of relatively few new heroic dramas, heroic elements recur in a variety of tragic genres throughout the century. This influence is evident, for example, in the popularity of Asian motifs, as in John Mottley's *The Imperial Captives* (pr. 1720), Gay's *The Captives* (pr. 1724), Charles Marsh's *Amasis, King of Egypt* (pr. 1738), Miller's *Mahomet the Imposter* (pr. 1744), and Lillo's *Elmerick: Or, Justice Triumphant* (pr. 1740). A catalog of contemporary heroic drama would include Cibber's *Xerxes* (pr. 1699), Gildon's *Love's Victim: Or, The Royal Queen of Wales* (pr. 1701), and Charles Johnson's *The Sultaness* (pr. 1717), based on Racine's *Bajazet* (pr. 1672; English translation, 1717).

DOMESTIC TRAGEDY AND SHE-TRAGEDY

Whereas the pseudoclassical and the heroic drama both attempted to elicit admiration for their heroes, the pathetic and domestic tragedies were more designed to arouse warmer emotions, particularly sympathy. Playwrights composing pathetic and domestic tragedies during the eighteenth century turned to Shakespeare, to Otway, and to Southerne for direction, as did Rowe, one of the most famous and most influential dramatists of the eighteenth century. Although he designated Shakespeare as his guide, Rowe's concern with cultivating pathos for admirable but distressed women is more reminiscent of Otway than it is of Shakespeare. Precedents for his violation of poetic justice are, however, evident in both of his models. Although Rowe achieved success with his early political tragedy *Tamerlane*, his most influential works were his she-tragedies, especially *The Fair Penitent* (a 1703 adaptation of Massinger's *The Fatal Dowry*) and *The Tragedy of Jane Shore*. Rowe himself coined the term "she-tragedy," which refers to those tragedies whose primary purpose is to elicit pathos for the unjust suffering of a woman. Although Rowe did not initiate the form—Banks is usually credited with having done so in the previous century—it was Rowe who popularized it. Also included in this category are Rowe's unsuccessful *The Tragedy of Lady Jane Gray* (pr. 1715), Philips's *The Distrest Mother*, Thomson's *The Tragedy of Sophonisba*,

Samuel Johnson's *Irene*, and Charles Johnson's *Caelia: Or, The Perjured Lover* (pr. 1732), which, with Rowe's *The Fair Penitent*, served as one of Richardson's main sources for his multivolume novelistic tragedy *Clarissa: Or, The History of a Young Lady* (1747-1748).

Rowe's efforts in developing the she-tragedy did not please everyone: The classical critics, for example, feared that Rowe's emphasis on love would accelerate the decline of tragedy. Such fears were not without basis, for aside from Jane Shore, even Rowe's female characters elicit only pathos and lack tragic grandeur. Nevertheless, Rowe's plays are very important in the history of British drama, for in them one can observe the beginnings of the development of domestic tragedy. Although Rowe's characters are not middle-class, neither are they royalty, and though his tragedies center on historical figures who shaped the destiny of their nation, Rowe's most memorable scenes are those focusing on the characters' private, domestic concerns. Rowe's emphasis on pity and suffering and the occasional aphoristic bent of his dialogue are also interesting reflections of the growth of sentimentalism.

THEORIES OF TRAGEDY

Fueled by an increasing emphasis on the eliciting of emotion in the interest of advancing didactic intentions, by mid-century literary critics had turned from a preoccupation with formalistic concerns (such as the Rules) to explore the psychological sources of tragic pleasure. The focus in criticism thus shifted during the eighteenth century from the text and aesthetic concerns to the emotional response of the audience. In France during the seventeenth century, René Descartes had maintained that the stimulation of the emotion was in itself pleasurable, while his English contemporary, Thomas Hobbes, had argued that the viewer derives pleasure from tragedy as the result of remarking the contrast between others' misfortune and the viewer's own comparatively happy circumstances, a view similar to that later advanced by the pseudoclassical dramatist and critic Johann Elias Schlegel in *Von der Unähnlichkeit im Nachahmen* (pb. 1764). In the eighteenth century, two rival explanations for tragic pleasure predominated. In "Of

Tragedy" (1757), David Hume asserted that the pleasure obtained from tragedy is aesthetic and that this pleasure is enjoyed only so long as the beauty of the tragedy is not overbalanced by its horror. An even more influential explanation, however, was that offered disparately by Anthony Ashley Cooper, the third earl of Shaftesbury, by Francis Hutcheson, and by Edmund Burke, each of whom maintained that the pleasure comes from exercising sympathy for the distressed characters. Thus, during the eighteenth century, audiences and critics alike reinforced dramatists' inclination to relegate aesthetic concerns to the second rank and to concentrate instead on emotional stimulation and response.

Such an emphasis on drama's mechanical rather than aesthetic essence is reflected by Lillo's *The London Merchant*, the first successful domestic tragedy in England. In his dedication to the play, Lillo asserts the importance of having a "moral" to his tragedy that will prove "useful." Its author himself a member of the merchant class, *The London Merchant* focuses on the concerns of the middle-class people, as eighteenth century comedies and the periodical essays of Addison and Steele had already done for some time. Lillo was not the first to attempt domestic tragedy in English: The anonymous Elizabethan play *A Yorkshire Tragedy* (pr. 1608) and Thomas Heywood's *A Woman Killed with Kindness* (pr. 1603) also focus on middle-class characters, as does Hill's *The Fatal Extravagance* (pr. 1721), which was based on *A Yorkshire Tragedy*. Unlike the Elizabethan domestic tragedies, however, Lillo employs the middle class for more than setting, and unlike Hill's tragedy, Lillo's was successful on the stage. Although self-indulgent in its bid for an emotional response and dogged in its didacticism, *The London Merchant* offered its audience a recognizable and convincing sense of tragic fate. Lillo was also innovative in his use of prose for his tragedy as well as in his employment of a British rather than a classical or exotic Eastern setting. Curiously, however, despite the play's overwhelming and century-long success onstage, few English tragedies were modeled on it. Neither was Lillo's other domestic tragedy, the blank-verse *Guilt Its Own Punishment: Or, Fatal Curiosity* (pr. 1736), widely imitated, though it did spawn two adaptations, one by Colman the Elder, in 1782, and another by the novelist Henry Mackenzie, in 1784. Indeed, the only other eighteenth century English domestic tragedies of note are Charles Johnson's unsuccessful _Caelia_, Moore's _The Gamester_ (which Diderot translated into French), Home's _Douglas_, and Cumberland's _The Mysterious Husband_ (pr. 1783). Though comparatively well written, _Caelia_ failed because of what was considered the indelicate realism of Johnson's depiction of a brothel. From the failure of _Caelia_, one may deduce a partial explanation for the paucity of fine tragedy in this period: Overly concerned with propriety and insistent in their demand for facile moralizing, the eighteenth century audience would not accept the indecorousness of realistic suffering onstage.

GERMAN TRAGEDY

Lillo's domestic tragedies were, however, received enthusiastically and imitated widely on the Continent, particularly in Germany. The first German _bürgerliches Trauerspiel_, or "bourgeois tragedy," was Lessing's _Miss Sara Sampson_ (pr. 1755; English translation, 1933), which owes much not only to Lillo but also to Johnson's _Caelia_ and to Richardson's tragic sentimental novel _Clarissa_. Lessing's later tragedy, _Emilia Galotti_, also a _bürgerliches Trauerspiel_, is important because it anticipates the type of drama produced by those involved in the Sturm und Drang movement. Goethe's _Clavigo_ (pr. 1774; English translation, 1798, 1897) and _Stella_ (pr. 1776; English translation, 1798) are also domestic dramas in the tradition of _Emilia Galotti_. German bourgeois tragedies would be translated into English and would then stimulate the development of English melodrama and Romantic tragedy. Lillo's _Guilt Its Own Punishment_ also inspired the rise of another form of tragedy in Germany, the _Schicksalstragödie_, or "tragedy of fate." Such tragedies focus on a family doomed by a curse that is fated to strike at a specific time and through a specific symbolic instrument. Although Moritz adapted _Guilt Its Own Punishment_ for the German stage in 1781, the first _Schicksalstragödie_ did not appear until _Der vierundzwanzigste Februar_ (pr. 1810) by the Romantic playwright Zacharias Werner. His later, more famous play, _Die Schuld_

(pr. 1813), affords another example of the _Schicksalstragödie_.

One of the most important movements in German intellectual and literary history was the Sturm und Drang movement, led by young writers hostile to the artificiality and cynicism of French classicism. At its strongest between 1760 and 1785, the major proponents of the Sturm und Drang were Johann Gottfried Herder, who is generally credited with being its founder, Jakob Michael Reinhold Lenz, Friedrich Maximilian Klinger, Heinrich Leopold Wagner, Schiller, and Goethe. It was from a tragedy by Klinger, _Der Wirrwarr: Oder, Sturm und Drang_ (pr. 1776; _Storm and Stress_, 1978), that the name for the movement was derived. Inspired by the ideas of Rousseau, the unconventionality of Shakespeare (as interpreted by Herder), and the realism of Mercier and Diderot, the proponents of this pre-Romantic movement found classicism stifling and drama that adhered to classical principles lacking in nature, originality, and passion. Fired by nationalism, they exuberantly lauded and drew on the folk literature of Germany, sharing the spirit with which the English turned to James Macpherson's Ossianic tales. Two professors from Zurich, Johann Jakob Bodmer and Johann Jakob Breitinger, together produced a collection of medieval literature, _Sammlung von Minnesingern_ (1758-1759), as their contribution to the revolt against the classicism exemplified by Gottsched. The drama of the Sturm und Drang often presented the theme of resistance to tyranny, glorified the Middle Ages, and exalted relentless individualism in its heroes, who were frequently misfits in their society (see, for example, the protagonists in the plays of Goethe and Schiller). Character rather than social consciousness, however, was the more important concern of the Sturm und Drang drama. Among the finest literary works produced by the movement are Goethe's _Götz von Berlichingen mit der eisernen Hand_ (pr. 1774; _Götz von Berlichingen with the Iron Hand_, 1799) and his masterpiece, _Faust: Eine Tragödie_ (pr. 1829; _The Tragedy of Faust_, 1823). Though not published until 1808, _Faust_ was begun and published as a fragment in the 1790's at the height of the Sturm und Drang, as Goethe's glorification of the ardent individualism of *Faust* suggests. Of the plays of Schiller, who succeeded Goethe as the leader of the Sturm und Drang movement, *Die Räuber* (pb. 1781; *The Robbers*, 1792) had a great influence on both Lewis's *The Castle Spectre* (pr. 1797) and Richard Cumberland's *Don Pedro* (pr. 1797). Schiller's *Kabale und Liebe* (pr. 1784) inspired an anonymous English adaptation titled *Cabal and Love* (pr. 1795) as well as a rendering by Lewis as *The Minister* (pb. 1797). Other important Sturm und Drang dramas include Klinger's *Die Zwillinge* (pr. 1776) and Lenz's *Die Soldaten* (pb. 1776; *The Soldiers*, 1972).

By the 1780's, however, the Sturm und Drang movement had largely spent its force, and its historical tragedies evolved (or devolved) into the formulaic, pseudomedieval *Ritterdrama* produced by Klinger, Graf von Torring, and Joseph Babo. The best of the *Ritterdramen* is one of the earliest examples of the form, Klinger's *Otto* (pb. 1775). From approximately 1780 until 1805, Goethe and Schiller turned from the Sturm und Drang ethos back to classicism and attempted to synthesize the best elements of Romanticism and classicism. During this period, Goethe produced his excellent tragedy *Iphigenie auf Tauris* (pr. 1800; *Iphigenia in Tauris*, 1793), and he also shaped the development of the drama from a different perspective as the manager of the ducal theater in Weimar (from 1791 until 1817). Schiller, too, contributed several superb tragedies to German drama: *Don Carlos, Infant von Spanien* (pr. 1787; *Don Carlos, Infante of Spain*, 1798), *Wallenstein* (pr. 1799), which was translated into English the following year by Coleridge, and *Maria Stuart* (pr. 1800; *Mary Stuart*, 1801), his most popular play.

In Italy, Vittorio Alfieri also composed tragedies full of passion that were based on historical themes, but Alfieri adhered strictly to the unities as part of his efforts to achieve highly intense, concentrated effects with his drama. Among his finest tragedies are *Filippo* (wr. 1775; *Phillip*, 1815), *Don Garzia* (wr. 1779; English translation, 1815)—which offers an interesting contrast with Schiller's play of the same title and approximate date of composition—*Saul* (pr. 1794; English translation, 1815), and *Mirra* (pr.

1819; *Myrrha*, 1815). The characters in Alfieri's best dramas are drawn from ancient, biblical, and European history, and, like the protagonists of Sturm und Drang tragedy, they are often presented as opponents of tyranny.

In both England and Germany, interest in the national past was accelerated by the "translation" and dissemination of the fraudulent *The Poems of Ossian* (1765), which purported to be translations of Gaelic poems by the legendary Ossian that were "discovered" by James Macpherson, as well as by Thomas Percy's *Reliques of Ancient English Poetry* (1765). Translated into German during the Sturm und Drang era, the English Ossianic poems kindled in German intellectuals the desire to explore their own primitive literature. In Germany, the most outstanding figure involved in this bardic movement in the drama was Friedrich Gottlob Klopstock. Of Klopstock's six plays, three of them focus on biblical subjects: *Der Tod Adams* (pb. 1757; *The Death of Adam*, 1763) *Salomo* (pb. 1764; *Solomon: A Sacred Drama*, 1809) and *David* (pb. 1772), and three form a trilogy centering on the exploits of the national hero Hermann: *Hermanns Schlacht* (pb. 1769), *Hermann und die Fürsten* (pb. 1784), and *Hermanns Tod* (pb. 1787). Stressing the inspiration behind the latter group of plays, Klopstock referred to the plays of the trilogy as *Bardiete*. Also important in the bardic movement in the German drama was Heinrich Wilhelm von Gerstenberg, whose tragedy *Ugolino* (pr. 1769) allows the reader to observe much anguish but little action.

ENGLISH ROMANTICISM

A pre-Romantic concern with national history and folk literature similar to that in Germany was also a dominant force in the development of English romantic tragedy. Henry Brooke's *The Earl of Essex* (pr. 1750), Richard Glover's *Boadicea* (pr. 1753), and Hannah More's *Percy* (pr. 1777), for example, all focus on figures derived from British history. Initially, tragedies continued to manifest the imprint of classicism at the same time that they exhibited pre-Romantic tendencies. Thus, despite its setting in primitive Britain, William Mason's *Elfrida* (pb. 1752) includes a chorus similar to that found in Greek tragedy, and though Home's *Douglas* adheres to the neoclassical Rules and also to the concept of decorum, the characters are placed in a wild, ancient setting that seems to reflect their psychological turmoil.

In England, the influence of Ossian was felt most profoundly in romantic tragedy. Home's *The Fatal Discovery* (pr. 1769), for example, is based directly on one of the Ossian tales. Concentrating on arousing the emotions and exciting the imagination, romantic tragedies are fixed in ancient, picturesque settings. The hero is typically one whose true worth is not recognized by those around him, and the whole world seems to echo his inner turmoil. As the century progressed, romantic tragedies increasingly employed fantastic costuming, scenery, and staging to heighten their dramatic effect, concentrating increasingly on spectacle rather than formalistic or aesthetic concerns.

During the final years of the eighteenth century, romantic tragedy blended with sentimental comedy to produce two overlapping forms, the melodrama and the gothic drama. Melodrama of the last decade of the eighteenth century employed the simplistic character delineation, moralistic didacticism, and facile poetic justice evident in lesser examples of sentimental comedy but placed a greater emphasis on sensationalism. On the whole, these early melodramas are weakly constructed, with much action but little or no attention given to providing the characters with psychological complexity or realistic motivation. The first play explicitly termed a "melo-drama" was Holcroft's *A Tale of Mystery* (pr. 1802), but included in the genre are earlier plays, such as Cumberland's *The Wheel of Fortune* (pr. 1795) and Thomas Morton's *Columbus*, which is based on Guilbert de Pixérécourt's *Cœlina: Ou, L'Enfant du mystère* (pr. 1800; *The Tale of Mystery*, 1802). In France, the most famous melodramatic playwright was Pixérécourt. Best remembered for his melodrama *Sélico: Ou, Les Nègres généreux* (pr. 1793), Pixérécourt specialized in adapting popular novels with sensational plots.

Closely akin to the melodrama is the gothic drama, which employs complex plots replete with hidden chambers, dire curses, and mysterious apparitions. Among the more successful plays in the genre are Colman the Younger's *The Iron Chest*, Lewis's *The Castle Spectre*, and Cumberland's *The Carmelite*. Curiously, one of the most influential plays in the development of gothic drama was never offered on the stage—Horace Walpole's *The Mysterious Mother* (pb. 1768), which was circulated in manuscript form and which provided many dramatists with suggestions for characters and plot. The influence of *The Mysterious Mother* is especially apparent in Cumberland's *The Mysterious Husband*.

Neither melodrama nor gothic drama constitutes either comedy or tragedy proper, for though both elicit pity and fear, they almost invariably conclude happily. Both forms of drama are nevertheless worthy of attention as illustrations of the divorce that occurred between theater and literature during the latter half of the eighteenth century. The composition of literary tragedy and comedy persisted at the century's end, in the form of plays designed not for presentation in the theater but for reading in the study. These "closet dramas" are typically lacking in theatrical technique as well as vitality—exits and entrances are omitted, the characters appearing and disappearing, speaking and remaining silent, without any apparent reason. Closet dramas tend to be abstract and philosophical, far removed from the realm of ordinary human passions. Joanna Baillie offered some of the better examples of this form in *A Series of Plays* (pb. 1798-1812), which includes her tragedies *Count Basil: A Tragedy* (pb. 1798) and *De Montfort: A Tragedy* (pr. 1800) as well as her comedy *The Tryal: A Comedy* (pb. 1798). Among the most popular closet dramas were German plays in translation, perhaps because these plays offered readers the genuine tragic spirit that their own contemporary tragedy no longer afforded. Benjamin Thompson's *The German Theater* (1800) was the most popular collection of German plays in translation, though many editions of translations of individual work were also available.

Although patterns of decline in both the tragedy and the comedy of eighteenth century drama have been identified in this study, it should be noted that historians of drama regard this period as a time of germination, a period preceding and thus necessarily less mature and attractive than an age of flowering.

What was engendered in the eighteenth century in the theater was something fine and new, an unquestioning affirmation of the dignity and importance of the human spirit, whatever the birthright of the container in which that spirit resides. Rowe and Lillo paved the way for the plays of Henrik Ibsen, August Strindberg, and Arthur Miller; Steele and Sheridan ushered in the plays of Oscar Wilde and George Bernard Shaw. The sin to which the dramatists of the age freely gave themselves, that of pleasing the audience at the expense of artistic concerns, is one from which no age is free. One can only hope that the playwrights of succeeding generations will draw as much profit from the drama of the present age as the present has derived from that of the eighteenth century.

BIBLIOGRAPHY

Backscheider, Paula R. *Spectacular Politics: Theatrical Power and Mass Culture in Early Modern England*. Baltimore, Md.: Johns Hopkins University Press, 1993. Explores the formation of a politically involved and informed public in seventeenth and eighteenth century England and the way in which it impacted British drama.

Brewer, John. *The Pleasures of the Imagination: English Culture in the Eighteenth Century*. Chicago: University of Chicago Press, 2000. Details the movement of high culture out of the court and into diverse spaces in London in the late seventeenth century, thus transforming the following one hundred years into a vibrant, dynamic national culture. Explores the contextual linkages between literature, painting, music, and the theater with a public eager for exposure to the arts.

Finburg, Melinda C. *Eighteenth Century Women Dramatists*. London: Oxford University Press, 2001. Brings together four plays by noted female playwrights Susanna Centlivre, Hannah Crowley, Mary Pix, and Elizabeth Griffith. Also provides a critical introduction, comprehensive annotation, and informative bibliography.

Kavenik, Frances M. *British Drama, 1660-1789: A Critical History*. New York: Twayne, 1995. Using a popular-culture perspective, Kavenik argues that the drama produced in these years was the most innovative since Shakespeare's time, giving rise to such forms as the musical and the situation comedy. The first chapter is comprehensive in its description of theaters, stage apparatus, playwrights, performers, audiences, and critics of the period, and it is followed by four chronologically arranged chapters that detail key developments during designated sub-periods.

Kinservik, Matthew J. *Disciplining Satire: The Censorship of Satiric Comedy on the Eighteenth Century Stage*. Lewisburg, Pa.: Bucknell University Press, 2002. Explores the effects of the Stage Licensing Act of 1737 on its main target, satiric comedy, by focusing on the careers of dramatists such as Henry Fielding, Samuel Foote, and Charles Macklin.

McMillan, Scott, ed. *Restoration and Eighteenth Century Comedy: A Norton Critical Edition*. New York: W. W. Norton and Company, 1996. Chronicles the development of eighteenth century comedy and provides critical interpretation.

Woodfield, Ian. *Opera and Drama in Eighteenth Century London: The King's Theatre, Garrick, and the Business of Performance*. Cambridge, England: Cambridge University Press, 2001. Explores the emerging manager-actor-audience relationships in eighteenth century London, examining specifically topics such as "The New Managers Take Control," "Recruitment Procedures and Artistic Policy," and "The King's Theatre Flourishes."

Laurie P. Morrow

Nineteenth Century British Drama

Modern stereotypes of nineteenth century British drama call to mind heartless, mustachioed, black-caped villains; helpless, innocent, poverty-stricken heroines; clean-cut, upright, there-in-the-nick-of-time heroes; and "curses, foiled again." Such are the elements that make up the popular conception of melodrama, for a popular conception holds that the melodrama was virtually the only form of drama to hold the boards in the nineteenth century theater. Although melodrama was certainly popular and influential, the age also produced Romantic verse drama, high tragedy, sophisticated comedy, and plays of ideas. In addition, numerous extravaganzas, burlettas, farces, and comic operas satisfied audience demands for novelty and variety. Poets, such as George Gordon, Lord Byron and Percy Bysshe Shelley, novelists, such as Charles Dickens, and playwrights, such as W. S. Gilbert and Oscar Wilde, wrote for this stage and its players. John Philip Kemble, Edmund Kean, William Charles Macready, Samuel Phelps, Charles Mathews, and Lucia Elizabeth Bartolozzi (Madame Vestris) are but a sampling of the nineteenth century theater's stars. Those who acted toward the beginning of the period were illuminated by candlelight; those who succeeded them were illuminated by limelight, then by gaslight, and finally by electricity. This technological transition was only one among many other theatrical and dramatic developments of the period. While the importance of these developments cannot be slighted, it is equally important to consider the nineteenth century theater as more than merely the product of a transitional period.

Playhouses

Shortly after King Charles II was restored to the British throne in 1660, he reopened the theaters, which had been closed at the outbreak of the English Civil War in 1642. Charles II granted patents (licenses that could be sold or willed to heirs like other kinds of property) to two of his courtiers, Thomas Killigrew and Sir William Davenant. The theaters that they established and those of their successors enjoyed a veritable monopoly that was not abolished until the Theatre Regulation Act of 1843.

During the eighteenth century, this monopoly had been strengthened by the Licensing Act of 1737—a measure aimed at controlling the unlicensed playhouses that had been built during a period when the government's enforcement of the theatrical patents had been lax. Because these unlicensed playhouses had also been hotbeds of antigovernment satire, the Licensing Act further required that all dramatic manuscripts be submitted to the Lord Chamberlain for censorship. The practical effect of this legislation was that by the beginning of the nineteenth century, there were two classes of theaters: the two patent houses, Drury Lane and Covent Garden, and the more numerous minor (that is, nonpatent) theaters, such as the Olympic and the Adelphi. The acting of "legitimate" drama (five-act tragedies and comedies) was restricted to the patent houses, while "illegitimate" drama (melodramas, extravaganzas, burlettas, hippodramas, pantomimes, and spectacles) was the province of the "minors." This division of theatrical labor persisted until it was abolished by the aforementioned Theatre Regulation Act of 1843. The Lord Chamberlain's censorship powers, however, remained in force until 1968.

Theater architecture

The rather intimate eighteenth century theater auditorium had been divided into pit, box, and gallery. The pit, at ground level, consisted of rows of backless benches; the rowdier elements of the audience tended to congregate there. One level up, around the sides of the theater, were the boxes—the location preferred by the fashionable. At the upper level were one or more galleries: The first gallery attracted the middle classes, while the second was often frequented by servants and apprentices.

By the beginning of the nineteenth century, the population of London had grown substantially, increasing the number of potential theatergoers, especially among the working classes. In 1792 and 1793, Covent Garden's seating capacity was increased to three thousand, while in 1794 Drury Lane's was increased to thirty-six hundred. In 1828, the King's Theatre converted some of the pit benches into seats with backs. The Haymarket followed suit in 1843, replacing these primitive "stalls" with upholstered seats in 1863. At first, only a few rows of pit benches were removed, but by the 1880's the pit had vanished entirely in favor of the stalls. With the stalls came the practice of reserved seating.

The boxes were retained except for those at the pit level, which were removed to allow expansion of the pit and subsequently of the stalls. The number of galleries was increased from one or two to as many as four or five. New methods of theater design eventually removed the pillars dividing various sections of the galleries, thus turning them into modern balconies.

After 1860, there was a tendency to reduce theater size. The Criterion Theatre, for example, built in 1874, seated 660, and few theaters remained with a seating capacity above fifteen hundred. Smaller theaters meant fewer galleries, or balconies, so the boxes were also converted to balconies and renamed the Dress Circle. What had been the first gallery was renamed the Upper Circle, while the second gallery simply remained the Gallery. The customary horseshoe-shaped auditorium was gradually replaced by a fan-shaped one that afforded better sightlines for the new staging techniques that were being developed.

THE STAGE AND STAGECRAFT

The nineteenth century theater had inherited from its eighteenth century predecessor a shallow stage framed by a large proscenium arch. Jutting out from this arch was a large apron, on which most of the acting was done, the shallow backstage being reserved for scenery, which was changed by the pushing and pulling of painted flats and wings along wooden grooves. On either side of the proscenium arch were the proscenium doors, used for entrances and exits. (Performers normally did not enter or exit through the wings or through any other part of the scenery.)

Throughout most of the eighteenth century, scenery, though sometimes spectacular, was used primarily to suggest a general atmosphere. Under the influence of the Romantics, the nineteenth century theater began to use scenery to suggest particular places—often in minute detail. For example, when Drury Lane was enlarged in 1794, the dimensions of its stage measured eighty-five feet wide by ninety-two feet deep—sufficient to allow use of a remarkably detailed Gothic-cathedral set. Indeed, the theater's concern with architectural accuracy even went so far as the consulting of an archaeologist, Sir Lawrence Alma-Tadema, whom Sir Henry Irving hired to design scenery for his productions of William Shakespeare's *Cymbeline* (pr. c. 1609-1610) in 1896 and *Coriolanus* (pr. c. 1607-1608) in 1901.

The larger auditoriums and stages also allowed theater managers to satisfy a growing demand by the audience for spectacle. Indeed, the large auditoriums encouraged this taste because they made subtle, intimate scenes and actions difficult both to see and to hear. Sadler's Wells Theatre, for example, featured a water tank that enabled it to stage sea battles. Astley's Amphitheatre boasted a circus ring in front of its stage, which was used for the presentation of equestrian dramas.

Various staging devices also contributed to spectacular effects. Among the best known were the "vampire trap," which allowed an actor seemingly to walk through a wall, and the more complicated "ghost glide," which made an actor seem to rise mysteriously from the earth.

Alongside the grand-scale Romantic dramas, with their often spectacular sets, were smaller-scale dramas of everyday life. The box set, popularized by Madame Vestris during her management of the Olympic Theatre, was first used there in 1832. This set completely enclosed the acting area and gave the illusion of watching the action inside one or more rooms with their fourth walls removed. Thus, all the acting took place behind the proscenium arch instead of spilling over onto the stage apron. Indeed, this apron shrank considerably throughout the nineteenth century as actors began more and more to move through the scenery instead of merely using it as a backdrop while they declaimed their lines from the apron.

As the illusion of reality came to be more important, managers began to emphasize productions that integrated acting, scenery, and costuming. In 1823, James Robinson Planché persuaded Charles Kemble, manager of Covent Garden, to stage Shakespeare's *King John* (pr. c. 1596-1597) with historically accurate costuming, thus beginning a vogue of theatrical antiquarianism. Planché himself extensively researched ancient modes of dress. In 1834, he published his *History of British Costume*; it remained the definitive work on theatrical costuming throughout most of the nineteenth century. Planché also encouraged Madame Vestris to devote equal care to the costuming of the "minor" drama. Thus, at the Olympic Theatre, the exaggerated costumes that had characterized comedy and burlesque gave way to clothes more like those worn in everyday life.

LIGHTING

The illusion of reality was further enhanced by the development of new stage-lighting techniques. The eighteenth century theater had used candles and oil lamps. Varying the lighting levels, either onstage or in the auditorium, was nearly impossible. Limelight, invented by Thomas Drummond in 1816, used a mixture of hydrogen and oxygen, which heated a column of lime until it glowed. Covered with a lens, this light acted much like a spotlight and was also used for special effects. Gaslights became popular in the 1840's, making it possible to control lighting intensity better than ever before. In 1881, the Savoy Theatre was totally illuminated by a new power source, electricity, and by 1900 almost all the London theaters had followed suit. With both gas and electricity, the lighting levels in the auditorium could also be controlled, so that the lights could be dimmed during performances, if the manager desired.

The use of the curtain also changed during the nineteenth century. It had been customary to raise the curtain at the beginning of a play and not to lower it until the end. Scene changes were accomplished in full view of the audience. Thus, the curtain usually was not used to mask scene changes or indicate the end of an act. As the penchant for the illusion of reality grew stronger, theater managers believed that such scene changes detracted from the effect they desired and so began to use the curtain to hide the process and to preserve the illusion.

This illusion was further enhanced by the use of three-rather than two-dimensional scenery. The old grooves eventually disappeared as newer methods of setting up and removing scenery were developed. Actors thus could make the most integrated use of scenery possible.

ACTORS, MANAGERS, AND PLAYWRIGHTS

Although nineteenth century actors used a wide variety of techniques, three important styles can be readily identified. The first is the classic style, popularized by John Philip Kemble and Sarah Kemble Siddons. This style demanded that an actor catch the essence of a character and express it with dignity, grace, declamation, and stately poses. Naturalness resided in the catching, rather than in the expressing, of this essence. The art of the actor was not to be concealed but rather to be revealed and admired.

The second style, the Romantic, sought naturalness through emphasizing a character's passions—a stark contrast to the reasonableness of the classic style's interpretation. Actors achieved their effects chiefly through exaggeration of, and sometimes through rapid changes among, the various emotions they sought to portray. Edmund Kean helped to establish this style, though his critics judged both his acting and his personality to be somewhat erratic.

The realistic style was encouraged by Charles Fechter. Fechter, an actor, managed successively the Princess's Theatre and the Lyceum Theatre, both in London. His emphasis on the box set and his interest in creating an illusion of reality led him to demand that his actors move and speak more like persons in everyday life. Fechter's enthusiasm for this style was not limited to contemporary drama but was extended to the classics as well.

Actor-managers such as Fechter were not uncommon. For example, in 1788, Kemble succeeded Richard Brinsley Sheridan as manager of Drury Lane before moving to Covent Garden in 1803. One of the best-known managers was William Charles Macready. An actor who combined the best of the classic and Romantic styles (with a touch of realism thrown in), Macready was dissatisfied with current theatrical practices and saw managing as a way to effect reforms. He managed Covent Garden from 1837 to 1839 and Drury Lane from 1841 to 1843. Macready emphasized the importance of rehearsals, which had previously been perfunctory—the star often not bothering about them in order to conserve strength for the actual performance. Furthermore, he insisted on dictating where his actors were to stand instead of allowing them to choose the positions that were personally most advantageous. All in all, Macready strove for a unified effect that also extended to his sets and costumes, which were designed with great concern for their historical accuracy.

Among Macready's acting company was Samuel Phelps, who, as eventual manager of the run-down Sadler's Wells Theatre, attracted large audiences by offering a bill consisting almost exclusively of poetic drama. Phelps acted in his own productions and, like Macready, took great pains to achieve historical accuracy. In 1862, he left Sadler's Wells to tour, but later in the decade his productions of Shakespeare's plays revived the sagging fortunes of Drury Lane.

Madame Vestris's work at the Olympic has already been mentioned, especially her use of the box set and her insistence on more realistic costuming for the "minor" drama. She herself was famous for her roles in light comedy. Her second husband, Charles Mathews, was well known for the same types of roles. (Her first husband, Armand Vestris, had been a dancer.) Vestris and Mathews combined their managerial talents, first at Covent Garden, from 1839 to 1842, and then at the Lyceum, from 1847 to 1856.

One of the most influential actor-managers was Charles Kean, son of the more famous Edmund Kean. Never the actor his father was, Charles gave up acting in favor of managing the Princess's Theatre in 1850. He was assisted by his wife and leading lady, Ellen Tree. He was also Master of the Revels—an appointment granted him by Queen Victoria. Kean managed to attract a fashionable audience by setting his curtain time and arranging his theatrical bill to cater to upper-class tastes. He presented chiefly Shakespeare and melodramas, using long runs to offset the cost of his productions, which had escalated in response to Kean's demands for historical accuracy.

John Baldwin Buckstone was a comedian-turned-manager of the Haymarket from 1853 to 1876. He was also the author of numerous plays, including the successful melodrama *Luke the Labourer; Or, The Lost Son* (pr. 1826). Planché twice satirized both Buckstone and his entertainments, in *Mr. Buckstone's Ascent of Mount Parnassus* (pr. 1853) and in *Mr. Buckstone's Voyage Round the Globe in Leicester Square* (pr. 1854). Buckstone's melodramas, however, found their home at the Adelphi, managed by Benjamin Webster—a former actor from Madame Vestris's company. He was also Buckstone's predecessor at the Haymarket Theatre, which he managed from 1837 to 1853, the year Buckstone took over.

Marie Wilton Bancroft, an actress in the "minor" theaters, and her husband, Squire Bancroft, a provincial actor, acquired a run-down theater, which they remodeled and reopened as the Prince of Wales's Theatre in 1865. The Bancrofts were especially successful at staging the contemporary dramas of Thomas William Robertson—plays that demanded realistic settings, though not always totally realistic acting. Among the Bancrofts' most important contributions to the theater were their reduction of the theater bill to a single play, their adoption of regular matinee performances, their refinement of the box set, and their extension of the proscenium arch across the floor of the stage, which confined all the acting behind the imaginary "fourth wall," enhancing the pictorial effect.

Sir Henry Irving gained his acting fame in melodramas. His leading lady was the equally famous Ellen Terry, who excelled in Shakespearean roles as well. Irving managed the Lyceum Theatre from 1878 to 1898. He was a proponent of pictorial realism. It was Irving who, in 1881, removed the grooves that had been used to shift scenery, thus opening the way for increased use of three-dimensional sets. He also extended historical accuracy of costume to include those of the minor characters, who had previously been neglected in favor of the major characters. Stage lighting received the same care, and Irving experimented with color as well as with intensity of lighting. It was for his acting, however, that Irving was knighted in 1895. He was the first English actor to be so honored. Two years later, Squire Bancroft followed in his footsteps.

Herbert Beerbohm Tree managed the Haymarket Theatre from 1887 until he built Her Majesty's Theatre in 1897. Although he often acted in his own productions, his fame rests chiefly on his establishment of an annual Shakespeare festival and also on his acting school, which eventually became the Royal Academy of Dramatic Art.

Another important manager was the nonacting Richard D'Oyly Carte, who brought into partnership the playwright W. S. Gilbert and the composer Sir Arthur Sullivan. In 1881, D'Oyly Carte built the Savoy Theatre especially for the production of Gilbert and Sullivan's comic operas. There, his managerial skills were needed not only to get the operas staged but also to get them written because the stormy partnership between Gilbert and Sullivan often threatened the success of his enterprise. Gilbert insisted on supervising every detail of rehearsals, while Sullivan sulked and complained that his music had been reduced to a mere accompaniment for Gilbert's lyrics. Were it not for D'Oyly Carte's diplomatic persuasiveness, far fewer of the Savoy operas would exist to delight today's audiences.

If Gilbert and Sullivan were to some extent prima donnas, so also were some of the nineteenth century's greatest actors. The nineteenth century theater produced the star system. In the eighteenth century, actors had been engaged by a manager for an entire season, and they were hired for a particular "line of business," which meant for a particular type of part, such as tragic hero, romantic hero, or low comedian. Playwrights customarily fashioned their works to match the talents of a particular company, which offered plays on a short-run, repertory basis. In the nineteenth century, the staggering costs of mounting new productions (because of more elaborate sets and costumes) and the great popularity of leading actors and actresses (which could be used to fill the large theaters and help managers recoup their production costs) led to the hiring of a leading actor or actress only for the run of a specific play, not for the entire season. Moreover, the repertory system was generally abandoned in favor of the long run. Furthermore, ensemble acting was subordinated to the showcasing of the star, the rest of the cast sometimes being used for little more than feeding lines or enhancing atmosphere. Stars also commanded enormous salaries that sometimes forced theatrical managers into bankruptcy. The Romantic drama, with its emphasis on the hero, encouraged the star system. The more realistic drama, such as that of Robertson, favored a return to ensemble playing, though not necessarily to the repertory system itself.

The repertory system had enabled the eighteenth century theater to sustain itself with the support of fewer audience members because it relied on attracting the same people over and over again. As the population of London grew, so did the potential audience, enabling a theater to sustain a long run by attracting different people each night. As the eighteenth century aristocratic influence began to wane, that of the nineteenth century working classes began to assert itself both in the pit, where rowdyism was frequent, and on the stage, where the escapism of spectacle and the familiarity of realism were both indulged. The melodrama, with its simple, clear-cut morality, its appeal to emotion, and its ability, depending on whether it was a gothic thriller or a domestic drama, to provide both escapism and realism, was the staple of this kind of audience and the salvation of theater managers. The coarse behavior of the working-class audiences also had the effect, however, of keeping a large part of the sober middle classes away from the theater. Charles Kean's reforms at the Princess's Theatre helped to change that pattern. By timing his curtain to coincide with more fashionable dining habits and by banishing some of the more objectionable incidental entertainments to the music halls, he was able to attract Queen Victoria herself to his theater. Her presence and patronage began to confer respectability on theatergoing. Replacing the pit with the stalls also helped to change the makeup of the audience to that of a more middle- and upper-class mixture. Such works as the Savoy operas of Gilbert and Sullivan were especially designed to attract and not offend this more desirable type of theatergoer.

THE BUSINESS OF PLAYWRITING

The playwrights who wrote for the nineteenth century theater faced substantial challenges. They had to gain the attention of audiences sometimes more intent on being seen than on seeing the entertainment: While plays were being performed, theater patrons chatted socially, arranged an assignation or two, commented on the performance, often with hisses and catcalls, and purchased refreshments from vendors. Occasionally there were riots. Furthermore, the managerial practice of allowing people to enter the theater after the performance was half over for half price created further disturbances. The gradual removal of the pit and the attracting of a better-educated, more restrained audience produced a group of theatergoers who by the end of the century watched in relative silence the stage action going on behind the fourth wall.

During the first years of the century, playwrights did not grow especially rich from their works. They might receive the benefits from the third, sixth, and ninth night's performances. Additionally, they might sell their copyright for several hundred pounds. After that, they received nothing, no matter how popular their plays might prove. Planché's popular historical drama *Charles XII: Or, The Siege of Stralsund* (pr. 1828) is a case in point. After an unauthorized performance of this work in 1828 netted Planché nothing, he sought legal remedy. Five years later, in 1833, Planché's friend Edward Bulwer Lytton was instrumental in getting Parliament to pass the Dramatic Authors Act, which vested copyright with the author for his lifetime plus twenty-five years and provided fines for unauthorized performances.

Shortly after mid-century, the prolific playwright Dion Boucicault successfully exploited the royalty system to earn more than sixty-five hundred pounds from his play *The Colleen Bawn* (pr. 1860). Before the Dramatic Authors Act, the same play would have netted its author only about one one-hundredth of that amount. A similar reform, which was again prompted by Planché, resulted in royalties being paid to the writers of lyrics for operettas. Previously, they had received only a very small payment, royalties being reserved for the composers of the music. All in all, the more lucrative royalty system served to attract more talented writers to the theater, so that by the end of the century, high-caliber plays were more than occasional phenomena.

This copyright protection was not extended to foreign plays until 1852, when copyright was granted to these works for five years. This copyright applied only to translations, not to adaptations, so managers seeking to evade payment for foreign dramas made minor changes in the foreign works and produced them. French plays were their favorite source, and playwrights such as Planché and Boucicault supplied the theaters with numerous adaptations. These plays coincided well with the tastes of working-class audiences. Shortly before his death, however, Planché proposed the establishment of an English art theater, in which commercialism would be subordinated to aesthetic considerations.

Better known writers than Planché also discussed the state of English drama, often with a keen interest in its past. For example, Samuel Taylor Coleridge, writing "On the Characteristics of Shakespeare's Plays" (1836), maintained that Shakespeare's judgment was equal to his genius. William Hazlitt, in "On Wit and Humour" (1819), extended the eighteenth century discussion of this topic. Charles Lamb, in "On the Artificial Comedy of the Last Century" (1822), tried to reassess Restoration comedy using other than moral criteria. Thomas Babington Macaulay, in "Comic Dramatists of the Restoration" (1841), argued that Restoration comedy does present a moral standard—a very bad one. George Meredith, in *An Essay on Comedy* (1877, 1897), asserted that comedy requires a cultivated society since its aim is intellectual as well as emotional. Finally, Oscar Wilde, in "The Decay of Lying" (1889), emphasized the beauty of the drama's artifices (its lies) and claimed that life copies art more often than art copies life.

PLAYS

In the first half of the nineteenth century, theaters presented varied bills that usually lasted five or six hours and might include two full-length plays and several other entertainments. These productions began between six and six-thirty in the evening and ended between one and two in the morning. Madame Vestris at the Olympic Theatre reduced the number of pieces offered, so that her theater let out by eleven o'clock. Charles Kean provided only a short curtain raiser and main play. By the end of the century, most managers had eliminated even the curtain raiser, presenting only the main play.

Variety was certainly not lacking among the types of nineteenth century plays. There were the Romantic verse drama, the melodrama, the comedy of manners, the problem play, the comic opera, and numerous farces, burlettas, and extravaganzas. Revivals of Shakespeare's plays were popular, especially if they starred Edmund Kean or if they featured historically accurate sets and costumes. In addition, adaptations of French plays could always be counted on to fill out a theatrical bill of fare. Many plays were adapted from novels, especially those of Sir Walter Scott and Charles Dickens. Mary Shelley's *Frankenstein* (1818) was also very popular.

The Romantics

The Romantic dramatists emphasized the primacy of passion over reason. Joanna Baillie, for example, was noted for writing plays in which a single passion predominated. Her *Plays of the Passions*, published between 1798 and 1812, filled three volumes. Percy Bysshe Shelley, in his preface to *The Cenci* (pb. 1819), even went so far as to assert that "the highest moral purpose . . . of the drama, is the teaching of the human heart." Shelley's play, however, had a little too much passion. Count Cenci's thoroughgoing dedication to evil and his incest with his daughter Beatrice kept the play off the boards until it was finally produced by the Shelley Society in 1886.

Both heroes and villains fascinated Romantic writers. Shelley's Count Cenci pursues his own will at all costs, even that of his own life. He both repels and fascinates the viewer, who recoils from his evil but envies his freedom and power. His villainy is straight out of Jacobean drama, but his liberty, however perverted, marks him as a creature of the nineteenth century, which admired rebels of whatever stripe. Shelley's Prometheus, the hero of *Prometheus Unbound: A Lyrical Drama in Four Acts* (pb. 1820), is a rebel, but with a noble cause. In stealing fire from the gods, he reaps great benefits for humankind and great suffering for himself. The Romantic heroes and villains eventually found their way into the melodrama, though with their stature much diminished.

Horror and the supernatural also intrigued the Romantic dramatists, whose gothic dramas inspired terror by evoking evil, supernatural forces at work in an eerie setting, such as a ruined church or a medieval castle. This genre had become established by the end of the eighteenth century, as exemplified by Matthew Gregory ("Monk") Lewis's *The Castle Spectre* (pr. 1797). Perhaps the nineteenth century's most famous example of the gothic drama is Charles Robert Maturin's *Bertram: Or, The Castle of St. Aldobrand* (pr. 1816). Its settings include a castle and a monastery; its special effects call for ferocious storms and midnight processions; and its villain displays a passion close to frenzy, a role tailor-made for Edmund Kean, who produced and starred in the play. Coleridge's *Remorse* (pr. 1813) also belongs in this category.

Shakespeare's history plays were much admired by Romantic dramatists, who attempted to imitate their predecessor in plays whose heroes and villains could make passionate speeches, often about liberty and tyranny. James Sheridan Knowles's *Virginius: Or, The Liberation of Rome* (pr. 1820) popularized this type of play, but it was epitomized in Bulwer-Lytton's *Richelieu: Or, The Conspiracy* (pr. 1839). Bulwer-Lytton played fast and loose with historical data in order to create a magnificent, but unhappy, Richelieu who is ennobled by a grand passion for France. Robert Browning's *Strafford* (pr. 1837) and Alfred, Lord Tennyson's *Queen Mary* (pr. 1876) and *Becket* (pr. 1893) were also written in imitation of Shakespeare.

Such lofty subjects, however, also coexisted with the less exalted ones of domestic drama, frequently centered on conflict between social caste and a romantic love that leaps the barrier of rank; the claims of filial duty often complicate matters. Bulwer-Lytton's *The Lady of Lyons: Or, Love and Pride* (pr. 1838) and John Westland Marston's *The Patrician's Daughter* (pr. 1842) illustrate the type, to which may be added Browning's *A Blot in the 'Scutcheon* (pr. 1843).

Some of the most famous Romantic poets, such as William Wordsworth and John Keats, were not successful in writing stageable plays. In part, their failure resulted from their overemphasis on text at the expense of staging and from their skeptical, if not contemptuous, attitude toward the ability of the theater's mass audiences to appreciate the refined poetry of their plays. Their solution was to write "closet drama"—poems in dramatic form that were not intended to be staged. Shelley's *Prometheus Unbound*, Browning's *Pippa Passes* (pb. 1841), and Algernon Charles Swinburne's *Atalanta in Calydon* (pb. 1865) might be called "closet dramas" because they were intended to be read but not acted. Only Byron wrote at all successfully for the stage, giving it the "Byronic hero"—a combination of hero and villain, often a rebel, motivated by deep passions and given to introspection. Byron's tenure on the governing committee of Drury Lane certainly gave him the practical theatrical knowledge that his Romantic counterparts lacked. Although only *Marino Faliero, Doge of Venice* (pr. 1821) was acted in Byron's lifetime, most of his remaining plays were eventually performed, including *Manfred*, published in 1817 and finally staged at Covent Garden in 1834.

MELODRAMA

The melodrama shared many elements with the Romantic verse drama, chiefly its emphasis on emotion, its archvillains, its heroes, and its sensationalism. The *mélodrame* originated in France. Originally, the term simply meant a three-act play accompanied by music. Such an arrangement was perfectly suited to nineteenth century British theatrical conditions. Because the minor theaters were not allowed to produce five-act plays and because their productions had to contain a specified number of songs, the melodramatic form was ideal. In fact, desirable five-act plays were often simply redivided and the requisite music added. Even *Othello* was not immune from this treatment. As the century progressed, however, the amount of music diminished until it was sometimes little more than the occasional striking of a chord in observance of the letter, if not the spirit, of the law.

The melodrama, like the medieval morality play, depicted the conflict between virtue and vice, with virtue almost always triumphant after either the defeat or the conversion of the villain. Most often, an innocent heroine (frequently an orphan) is the victim of the moral tug-of-war, but she is eventually rescued from disaster either by the hero or by an unexpected turn of events. The setting for a melodrama might be gothic, domestic, or more specialized—nautical, for example: Douglas William Jerrold's *Blackeyed Susan* (pr. 1829) is liberally laced with the language of the sea. Indeed, stock characters from the nautical melodrama, particularly the "jolly jack tar" and the chorus of sailors, eventually reappeared in Gilbert and Sullivan's nautical operetta *H.M.S. Pinafore: Or, The Lass That Loved a Sailor* (pr. 1878).

Thomas Holcroft's *A Tale of Mystery* (pr. 1802) is commonly considered to be the first British melodrama, even though it was merely an adaptation of a French play by Guilbert de Pixérécourt, *Cœlina: Ou, L'Enfant du mystère* (pr. 1800; *The Tale of Mystery*, 1802). Holcroft's stage directions reveal his use of music to enhance mood. They also reveal his use of highly stylized acting, especially the striking of poses or attitudes.

Buckstone's *Luke the Labourer* was a domestic melodrama, notable for its use of two heroes and two villains and for its social protest against the injustice of debtors' prisons. Jerrold's *The Rent Day* (pr. 1832) protested the injurious system of farm rents that had to be paid no matter how ruinous payment might be to the farmer. Boucicault's *After Dark: A Tale of London Life* (pr. 1868) was set in the London underworld and included a thrilling rescue in the depths of London's newly opened subway system. More sentimental was *East Lynne* (pr. 1874), adapted by T. A. Palmer from Mrs. Henry Wood's 1861 novel of the same title. The heroine abandons her husband and children to live with her villainous seducer; her sufferings end only after a tearful deathbed scene. Leopold David Lewis's *The Bells* (pr. 1871) was one of the most popular melodramas of the period. The role of Matthias, a murderer who has concealed his crime for years, was one of Sir Henry Irving's favorite parts. A less spectacular play, but one often called the finest of the melodramas, is Henry Arthur Jones's *The Silver King* (pr. 1882). Its hero mistakenly thinks he has killed a man and flees to the western United States, where he makes a fortune in silver mining. He returns to England just in time to keep his poverty-stricken wife and sick child from being evicted. Detectivelike, the hero finally manages to clear his name and send the real murderer to jail.

PROBLEM PLAYS

Refinements of the melodrama eventually resulted in the social problem play. As the term suggests, a social problem was presented, with varying degrees of realism. The playwright might suggest a resolution or leave the question open. Thomas William Robertson wrote a series of such plays, produced by the Bancrofts and each sporting one-word titles and dealing with a particular social problem: *Society* (pr. 1865), *Play* (pr. 1868), *Home* (pr. 1869), *School* (pr. 1869), *War* (pr. 1871), and *Caste* (pr. 1867). The latter is perhaps his best-known work; it deals with the complications of marrying above or beneath one's station. Limited movement between classes is finally condoned, while the retention of class distinctions is supported. The aristocratic George D'Alroy marries Esther Eccles, a former dancer with a theatrical company. The entire Eccles family, including the drunken father, is depicted with compassionate good humor. The play's elaborate stage directions, which called for practicable scenery—that is, real chairs, tables, teacups and saucers, and bread and butter—gave rise to the term "cup-and-saucer drama." Robertson carefully constructed his dialogue for ensemble acting—the lines and actions would not otherwise make sense. The play's most obvious elements of melodrama are its sentimentalism, Mr. Eccles's attempted villainy, and the use of tableaux (picturesque poses struck and maintained by the cast).

WELL-MADE PLAYS

Arthur Wing Pinero and Henry Arthur Jones further developed the social problem play, taking advantage of the conventions of the well-made play in the process. The well-made play was originally a French product—the *pièce bien faite*. It gained prominence through the numerous plays of Eugène Scribe, Victorien Sardou, Eugène Labiche, and Georges Feydeau. Its basic formula is a well-told story, full of complications and coincidences and designed to hold the audience's attention from moment to moment. All in all, this type of play was blatantly theatrical, its artifices often barely concealed or sometimes not concealed at all.

In their use of the conventions of the well-made play, Pinero and Jones attempted to achieve greater verisimilitude than had their French counterparts, even though the former's works often seem artificial to modern theatergoers. Among contemporary reviewers, George Bernard Shaw criticized the clumsiness of the exposition in Pinero's *The Second Mrs. Tanqueray* (pr. 1893). The production of Henrik Ibsen's *Gengangere* (pb. 1881; *Ghosts*, 1885) in London in 1891 caused a sensation because, among other things, the play featured a woman with a past. Pinero did likewise: Aubrey Tanqueray's marriage to a woman with a past leads inevitably to his own social isolation and to her suicide. Pinero's play helped to popularize Ibsenism in England; indeed, by the end of the decade, the critic William Archer had translated most of Ibsen's plays.

A woman with a past also causes catastrophe in Jones's *Michael and His Lost Angel* (pr. 1896). She seduces a man of the cloth to their mutual destruction. A woman with a present, however, the notorious Mrs. Ebbsmith, is the main character in Pinero's 1895 play of the same title. Agnes Ebbsmith is an example of the new woman, but she enjoys liberation from conventions only to be defeated by those conventions at the end of the play. Despite her unconventional relationship with Lucas Cleeve and her throwing of a Bible into the fire, she discovers that she is not the leader she thought she was. Although Shaw's plays are beyond the scope of this essay, many of them also dealt with social problems, often suggesting unconventional solutions.

COMEDIES OF MANNERS

The eighteenth century comedy of manners continued into the nineteenth century, which elevated the comedy's moral tone by banishing much of the witty sexual innuendo that had long characterized the genre. The setting is usually the drawing room, in which the social games being played are exposed for the audience's amusement as well as for its admiration, the latter being reserved for characters who can best play the game. Boucicault's *London Assurance* (pr. 1841) illustrates the type. Sir Harcourt Courtly is the ridiculous superannuated beau; his son Charles, the rakish but reformable man-about-town; and Grace Harkaway, the witty, sprightly young woman whom Charles contrives to win. The drawing room of Squire Harkaway's house provides ample space for plots and counterplots, with the best gamesters eventually winning. The most striking character in the play, however, is Lady Gay Spanker, who spends most of her life riding to hounds and dominating her husband Adolphus (Dolly). She, too, takes part in the romantic games and almost loses her husband, whom as she discovers in the process, she truly loves. Witwouds, witlings, and truewits can all be found, but even the latter seem to be at the mercy of fortune's vicissitudes in a world whose workings they do not ultimately understand. Only barefaced "London assurance" carries them through.

A year earlier, Bulwer-Lytton's comedy *Money* (pr. 1840) had depicted a different kind of game playing. In order to discover how his friends and relatives truly feel about him, the rich Sir John Vesey pretends to have lost all of his money. Sir John gets the knowledge he seeks, repudiates all the sycophants, and marries Clara, who has loved him faithfully, even without his fortune.

Toward the end of the century, Oscar Wilde's plays continued in the comedy-of-manners tradition. More than *Lady Windermere's Fan* (pr. 1892) or *A Woman of No Importance* (pr. 1893) or *An Ideal Husband* (pr. 1895), *The Importance of Being Earnest: A Trivial Comedy for Serious People* (pr. 1895) developed the form to its utmost by subordinating considerations of theme and character to those of style. In the play's several drawing rooms, Algernon, Jack, Gwendolyn, and Cecily play the social games that will allow them to be properly paired before the final curtain. To achieve his effects, Wilde used mistaken identities, preposterous situations, witty remarks, and the pun on Ernest/earnest. In the process, however, Wilde's witty epigrams and artifices seem to hint at a reality not successfully approached by the more serious melodrama, whose conventions this play burlesques.

The Importance of Being Earnest was indebted to Gilbert's *Engaged* (pr. 1877). In this play, Gilbert turned upside down and inside out the conventions of the melodrama. His aim was to expose the mercantile morality that underlay much of Victorian sentimentality. Gilbert was to use this technique again in the Savoy operas. In *The Pirates of Penzance: Or, The Slave of Duty* (pr. 1879), for example, Gilbert uses a chorus of orphans—pirates, that is—whose king forces himself to get through much "dirty work" in the name of business. In *H.M.S. Pinafore*, the notion of caste is turned upside down as seaman Ralph Rackstraw exchanges rank with Captain Corcoran, while Sir Joseph Porter, who is engaged to the captain's daughter Josephine, resigns her hand, observing that love does indeed level ranks, but not that much. In *The Mikado: Or, The Town of Titipu* (pr. 1885), however, almost all ranks are leveled in the person of the aristocratic, bureaucratic Pooh-Bah, who among his other roles is Chancellor of the Exchequer, Archbishop of Titipu, and Lord-High-Everything-Else.

BURLETTAS AND BURLESQUES

The Savoy operas were among the most popular entertainments of their era. The burletta was equally popular. It, too, was a form of comic opera, only it consisted of a play of no more than three acts with at least five songs interspersed with the dialogue. This form was especially suited to the needs of the minor theaters and offered them a chance to adapt regular plays to fit the requirements of the Licensing Act. The burlesque, on the other hand, was a play that treated a serious subject humorously. (It did not feature strippers and off-color humor, as the terms' later usage, particularly in the United States, came to suggest.) The extravaganza relied on spectacle and whimsy to tell a story—often an adaptation of a fairy tale. Planché wrote a number of these fairy tales, many of them adapted from the French. The hippodrama used horses, either onstage or, more often, in a special ring constructed in front of the stage on the floor of the pit. Pantomimes, especially Christmas ones, were also popular. Finally, vaudeville and the music halls offered a mixture of songs, dances, dramatic sketches, acrobatic stunts, and other kinds of entertainment. Nineteenth century audiences were certainly not without a wide choice of theatrical diversions.

PERSPECTIVE

Nineteenth century audiences were not so very different from either their predecessors or their successors. They sought to escape from their everyday lives by going to the theater, while at the same time they enjoyed seeing themselves portrayed onstage. Despite the growing pressure toward realism, these audiences were keenly aware of theatrical artifice—so much so, in fact, that writers who considered the text of their plays to be more important than their staging had a difficult time succeeding in the theater. Although these audiences were often sentimental and sententious, they were surprisingly responsive to experimentation, even at the expense of the shocking of their sensibilities.

To see nineteenth century theater only as a transition between that of two other centuries is to look at it with a far too limited vision. Indeed, the theaters of all periods are transitional to some extent. The nineteenth century theater was exactly that: the *nineteenth century* theater, a product, as well as a reflection, of its era—an era of both artificiality and realism, whose creative tensions produced some bad theater but overall much more that was good.

BIBLIOGRAPHY

Bratton, J. S., Breandan Gregory, Michael Pickering, et al. *Acts of Supremacy: The British Empire and the Stage, 1790-1930.* New York: St. Martin's Press, 1991. Analyzes the way in which British drama reflected and reinforced British imperialism.

Burroughs, Catherine. *Women in British Romantic Theater: Drama, Performance, and Society, 1790-1840.* New York: Cambridge University Press, 2000. Eleven essays by leading scholars examine the contribution of women playwrights, actors, translators, critics, and managers who worked in British theater during the Romantic period.

Hoagwood, Terence Allan, and Daniel P. Watkins, eds. *British Romantic Drama: Historical and Critical Essays.* Teaneck, N.J.: Fairleigh Dickinson University Press, 1998. Provides a historical context for nineteenth century drama by examining lesser-known playwrights from the period and the theme of revolution in plays.

Hudston, Sara. *Victorian Theatricals.* London: Methuen, 2001. Acts as a critical anthology and brings together extensive introductions, notes, and chronologies as well as drawings and photographs of theatrical ephemera, with works from 1800 to 1895, and sets them in their social and historical context.

Jenkins, Anthony. *The Making of Victorian Drama.* Cambridge, England: Cambridge University Press, 1991. Examines seven Victorian playwrights who, despite their own ideals and prejudices and the theater's conservatism, tried to come to terms with such important subjects as the status of women, chivalry, and the allure of money.

Powell, Kerry. *Women and Victorian Theatre.* Cambridge, England: Cambridge University Press, 1998. Chronicles the development of women's roles in theater as playwrights, actresses, and managers and explores the interconnections of Victorian gender and playwriting of the period.

Stephens, John Russell. *Profession of the Playwright: British Theater, 1800-1900.* Cambridge, England: Cambridge University Press, 1992. Discusses the working world of the playwright in nineteenth century Britain by focusing on several major and minor authors, including James Robinson Planché, Dion Boucicault, Albert Wing Pinero, W. S. Gilbert, Alfred, Lord Tennyson, Henry Arthur Jones, and George Bernard Shaw.

Wagner-Lawlor, Jennifer A., ed. *The Victorian Comic Spirit: New Perspectives.* Brookfield, Vt.: Ashgate, 2000. Twelve essays explore such topics as "Laughing at the Almighty: Freethinking Lampoon, Satire, and Parody in Victorian England," "Dickens's Dystopian Metacomedy: Hard Times, Morals, and Religion," and "The Laugh of the New Woman."

Valerie C. Rudolph

TWENTIETH CENTURY BRITISH DRAMA

Although George Bernard Shaw is frequently lauded as the dramatic heir of the great Norwegian realist Henrik Ibsen and, consequently, as the father of modern British drama, any attempt to survey the modern movement also reveals a variety of short-lived movements and individual experiments. From the chronicle dramas of John Drinkwater to the absurdist plays of Harold Pinter, the essence of modernism seems to inhere in experimentation, in change itself. To be sure, criticism of societal values is hardly reserved for the twentieth century playwright alone, yet the nagging suspicion that all values are relative, that existence is merely a series of personal compromises, is characteristic of the new wave.

As a result, twentieth century plays, taken in the aggregate, suggest a worldview far different from that of the nineteenth century. Pinter's dark comedies may seem unrelated to the lighthearted, whimsical operettas of W. S. Gilbert and Sir Arthur Sullivan, just as John Osborne's bitter Angry Young Men dramas differ radically from the farces and sentimental social comedies of Arthur Wing Pinero or Henry Arthur Jones. Both literary and historical facts—the impact of the realist Ibsen, on one hand, and World War I, on the other—hedge the revival of British drama, as does a complicated interplay among the demise of old forms of entertainment and their administration, increasing urbanization and leisure time, technological advancement, and a new, independent dramatic spirit.

FORCES OF CHANGE

Historians of the theater stress the confusion that opened the twentieth century, when the actor-manager system changed, repertories grew, and music halls and motion pictures influenced the legitimate stage. Although powerful figures such as Sir Herbert Beerbohm Tree, Forbes Robertson, and Charles Frohman did provide commercial viability for the theater, they were criticized for arranging showcases primarily for their own talents. Ironically, criticism of the actor-managers was transferred almost verbatim

to the music-hall managers, who offered huge salaries for cameo appearances of serious actors and who also lured promising authors by incessant demands for dramatic sketches, often presented in a triple or quadruple bill. In addition, the threat of music-hall mergers sparked the trade union movement, the effect of which was felt in 1906 when the Variety Artists' Federation called the first theatrical strike.

An important part of the revival was the transformation of dramatic form, staging, and definition—a transformation caused, in part, by increasing internationalism. Not only did the growth of the publishing industry bring an increasing number of foreign plays into the public's hands but also a large number of foreign companies on tour presented works in their original languages. Evidence of such ferment may be seen in William Butler Yeats's experimentation with Japanese Nō plays, as well as in the presence of actresses Etelka Gerster and Helena Modjeska; the latter had begun her career by introducing William Shakespeare to her native Poland.

In addition, both Ibsen's use of fewer acts in his well-made problem plays and the ever-present demand for one-act sketches for the music halls affected dramatic structure. An entire generation of new playwrights, lured by good remuneration, became skilled in the short play—prologue, central action, epilogue—rather than in the classical five-act structure. Another force on dramatic structure was the increasingly popular motion picture, which had been silent until the early 1920's and was initially welcomed as a force to counteract the attraction of music and variety halls. Like the music-hall playlet, the motion picture, with its episodic structure, found itself mimicked onstage; wordless vignettes and brief scenes became acceptable dramatic techniques.

Staging also changed as nineteenth century display gave way to twentieth century reductionism. The heavy sets with wings and backdrops favored by the provincial playhouses, as well as the intricate stage machinery (sometimes complete with panoramic effects) that were used in the spectacles, were replaced by more movable sets. Gordon Craig, who used lighting as if it were paint, revolutionized stage design, as did his contemporaries, the Swiss Adolphe Appia and the Austrian Max Reinhardt. The efforts of other, more modest experimenters are evident today: William Poel, for example, founder of the Elizabethan Stage Society (1894), moved against then current practice by employing a "modern" open stage with little scenery for his Shakespearean productions.

Undeniably, the commercial inroads made by the music halls on the legitimate theater are in part to blame for the virtual disappearance of tragedy during the first three decades of the twentieth century: Plays, farces, comedies, and sketches abounded, but the audience presented with a drama was almost certain to see melodrama, not tragedy. The overcommercialization of the stage also may be seen, however, as a positive force, encouraging by indirection the development of numerous private theatrical societies and regional theaters for the production of literary or social plays unlikely to make a profit in London's West End.

The first years of the twentieth century are memorable, then, not only for such changes but also for the advent of several giants of the age as well as important regional movements. Shaw changed the course of drama with his "plays of ideas," which mixed serious social commentary with comedy, while the whimsy of Sir James Barrie is still revived today in *Peter Pan: Or, The Boy Who Wouldn't Grow Up* (pr. 1904). Literary dramatists appeared as well, including the poet laureate John Masefield, the novelist Thomas Hardy, and such writers as Fiona MacLeod (pseudonym of William Sharp), whose works were performed at the Glastonbury Festival. Of all the regional movements, the Celtic revival in Ireland had the most profound effect. The establishment of the Abbey Theatre provided a showcase for authors such as William Butler Yeats, John Millington Synge, and Sean O'Casey, whose use of folk legends and speech patterns and whose experiments with verse and form influenced later dramatists. In addition, among the provincial repertory theaters, the Manchester deserves special credit for encouraging the production of serious social plays that appealed to the working classes.

The course of modern British drama was also shaped by the two world wars, which not only changed the physical face of London and the expectations of the audience but also decimated almost an entire generation of young men. In the city itself, no new theaters were built between 1914 and 1959, when the Mermaid Theatre opened. World War I, during which audiences escaped to farces, comic revues, and thrillers, exacerbated the split between the commercial and the literary theater. To be sure, the British Drama League began in 1919 to offer classes and other resources, and the Stage Society continued until 1930 to offer plays by Shaw and other influential writers such as Maxim Gorky, Luigi Pirandello, and Jean Cocteau. Theatrical clubs such as Ashley Dukes' Mercury Theatre appeared, and left-wing organizations such as the Unity Theatre Club offered political plays. Personalities recognized today as leading proponents of the classical style—Dame Sybil Thorndike, Sir Laurence Olivier, Sir John Gielgud, Sir Alec Guinness, and Charles Laughton among them—dominated the acting scene, while Tyrone Guthrie directed the Old Vic Theatre not only in 1933 and 1936 but also during World War II, when it was bombed and the company moved to the New Theatre.

In the aftermath of World War II, the distance between the commercial and literary theater became greater: American musicals were popular, and impresarios such as Prince Littler controlled both London and provincial stages. Interest in serious drama was widespread, however, as the actor-manager system was revived, with Gielgud at the Haymarket Theatre from 1944 to 1945, and with Olivier at the St. James Theatre from 1950 to 1951. Aided by subsidies from the Arts Council of Great Britain, provincial repertories revived, and Shakespearean seasons were presented at the Old Vic and at Stratford-upon-Avon. Traditionalists and experimentalists alike found interest in the revival of poetic drama and the conservative plays of T. S. Eliot, on the one hand, and, on the other, in the performances of Paul Scofield at theaters such as the Unity Theatre and the Arts Theatre, or the productions of the new "plays of ideas" by Terence Rattigan and John Whiting. The increasingly experimental nature of plays that looked to Dadaism and the language of gesture helped to force the end of censorship by the Lord Chamberlain in 1968. Perhaps not surprisingly, tragedy, a disappearing genre at the turn of the century, did not resurface, and playwrights moved to highlight social and political commentary with absurdist techniques.

MELODRAMA IN THE FIRST TWO DECADES

The popular conception of melodrama that features a weeping heroine in peril of "a fate worse than death," a double-dyed villain in a sweeping cloak, and a handsome, energetic hero who arrives in the nick of time is probably derived more from nineteenth century provincial performances than from fashionable West End productions. In fact, by the turn of the century, melodrama no longer incorporated music and song with sensational incident but rather focused on the sensation itself: The evocation of powerful emotions that culminated in a happy ending was the formula. Another change was evident: Melodrama became a democratic medium, not confined to well-known, sometimes "literary" authors, but open to thousands of unremembered playwrights whose works are not likely to be revived. One example is that of the owner-managers of the Standard Theatre at the turn of the century, Walter and Frederick Melville, who wrote the plays they themselves produced. While the works of their Victorian predecessors were often published, the plays of these and such authors as Charles Darrell, Emma Litchfield, and Royce Carleton exist only in manuscript, if at all. Further confusing the record is the fact that even commercial successes were likely to have premiered in the provinces under a variety of titles.

Although in many cases the works of these forgotten playwrights are marred by stilted diction and superficial plots, they were above all sincere, and to that their success may be attributed. Writing with an equal belief in his endeavor was Sir Hall Caine, whose popular novels, among them *The Manxman* (1894) and *The Christian* (1897), delighted Victorian readers. Caine collaborated on a stage version of the former with the melodramatic actor Wilson Barrett; an adaptation of the latter opened to wide critical acclaim at

the Lyceum Theatre in 1907. Caine himself stressed the depth of his own agreement with the "social propaganda" that he propounded in this latter play. Similarly, his revision and intensification of melodramatic patterns in *The Manxman* resulted in *Pete*, produced at the Lyceum Theatre the next year. Caine mingled melodrama with domestic, social, and religious themes, but his other triumphs resulted from his grandness of conception and his choice of exotic settings: Iceland in *The Prodigal Son* (pr. 1904), an adaptation of his 1904 novel, and the Isle of Man in *The Bondman* (pr. 1906), which was an adaptation of his 1890 novel of the same title.

Caine was not the only well-known novelist to venture into melodrama. W. Somerset Maugham produced a number of melodramas—from *The Tenth Man*, produced in 1910, to *The Sacred Flame*, produced and published in 1928—that were considerably less successful than his society plays, such as *The Circle* (pr. 1921), about romantic love, and *The Constant Wife* (pr. 1926), about adultery. More surprisingly, William Archer, the pioneering translator of Ibsen and proponent of realism, achieved instant popularity with his play *The Green Goddess* (pr. 1921). Indeed, until the 1920's, audiences enjoyed revivals as well as new versions of such romantic melodramas as Charles Hannan's *A Cigarette-Maker's Romance* (pr. 1901), and Montagu Barstow and Baroness Orczy's *The Scarlet Pimpernel* (pr. 1903), as well as the historical romance *Henry of Navarre* (pr. 1908), by William Devereux. As the decades passed, however, the realistic spirit affected melodrama in such a way that chronicle plays began to replace those that had subsisted primarily on the strength of their beautiful period costumes.

Another popular movement produced the crime drama, or thriller. Perhaps the first of this genre was William Gillette and Arthur Conan Doyle's *Sherlock Holmes* (pr. 1899), a remarkably well-bred exercise in detection when compared with the increasingly sensational productions that followed. As the genre developed, the hero-detective gave way to the hero-crook; the crook to the murderer; and, finally, to balance the score, the murderer to the lawyer. George Pleydell's *The Ware Case* (pr. 1915) is typical of the trial plays; *Sexton Blake, Detective* (pr. 1908), of the theme plays, this one both written and produced by John M. East and Brian Daly, who formed The Melodramatic Productions Syndicate to market their series. Arnold Ridley's long-running cult play *The Ghost Train* (pr. 1925) was more substantial than the host of plays to employ a series of tricks and thrills as a replacement for plot. Ghost plays enjoyed a vogue; *A Murder Has Been Arranged* (pr. 1930), by the Welshman Emlyn Williams, is representative of this genre. Also notable in the development of the crime drama or thriller is Williams's *Night Must Fall* (pr. 1935), a compelling and perennially revived dramatic portrait of a psychotic killer. Although Williams's play typifies the psychological thriller, another kind of thriller developed in the line of the 1921 and 1922 "Grand Guignol" theater seasons, featuring plays whose emphasis on realistically depicted physical torment and hair-raising suspense, treated with a certain artificiality, gave "Grand Guignolism" its notoriety.

NONCOMMERCIAL THEATER IN THE
FIRST TWO DECADES

While managers of music halls and theaters were engaged in a struggle for economic survival, noncommercial, or "minority," drama proliferated. Plays of propaganda, religion, and fantasy as well as village and children's theater became popular. Regional drama and repertory companies such as the Abbey Theatre in Dublin and the Gaiety Theatre in Manchester were important parts of the dramatic revival. Political diatribe in dramatic form and problem plays were a novelty during the first decades of the new century; on the opposite end of the intellectual spectrum from the popular comedies in the commercial theater, they were frequently privately performed and dealt with topics such as women's suffrage, socialism, and evolution. A typical, and initially popular, example is Guy du Maurier's *An Englishman's Home* (pr. 1909), treating the astonishment of a British homeowner at a (presumed) Russian invasion.

Another movement that stressed simplicity of approach and sincerity of performance in contrast to commercial spectacle was the village drama movement, whose proponents, harking back to the Roman-

tic belief in primitivism and the noble savage, suggested the hope that local actors, untutored by all but nature, would express their homespun philosophy about the worth of life in an influential way.

The power shift among the variety and music halls, the cinema, and the legitimate theater was complemented by the rise not only of dramatic festivals and private acting societies but also of repertory theaters throughout Britain. Some, like the St. Pancras People's Theatre, were innovative in acquiring civic funding; others, such as the Gate Theatre Studio, were private clubs formed to evade the censorship of the Lord Chamberlain, who licensed publicly performed plays. Major pageants and festivals involved well-known playwrights: The August, 1929, Malvern Festival, for example, by Barry Jackson, was dedicated to Shaw, who wrote *The Apple Cart* (pr. 1929)—political discussion masquerading as moral drama—for the occasion; Bishop George Bell inaugurated the Canterbury Festival with Masefield's *The Coming of Christ* (pb. 1928).

A number of lesser-known societies provided the foundation for the more successful repertories. Because typical nineteenth century scenery was both heavy and expensive, producers were unwilling to invest in the untried playwright; hence, such organizations as Poel's Elizabethan Stage Society and the Pilgrim Players (begun in 1904) in Birmingham came into existence. Of these, the best known is the Independent Theatre, which was set up by J. T. Grein in 1891: This association, which produced noncommercial plays by such figures as George Meredith and Thomas Hardy, is noted for introducing both Ibsen and Shaw to its members.

Although Grein's theatrical association did not develop into a national theater, the movement was under way. In London, John Eugene Vedrenne and Harley Granville-Barker collaborated at the Royal Court Theatre to initiate a series of three "seasons" beginning on October 24, 1904, in which matinees were given in repertory. As some theater historians point out, these were primarily "social" events and hardly the way to introduce plays that appealed to the intellect, although John Galsworthy, famous for *The Forsyte Saga* (1922), entered the theater with his *The*

Silver Box (pr. 1906). Indeed, because more than two-thirds of the 788 performances were devoted to plays by Shaw, the Court seasons are sometimes seen more as a vehicle for Shavian ambition than as a disinterested effort to introduce the repertory. Granville-Barker himself was more successful as an actor and producer than as a playwright, although he wrote in a variety of genres, from the fantastic in *Prunella: Or, Love in a Dutch Garden* (pr. 1904) to the political in *His Majesty* (pb. 1928).

Although other managers held seasons at such theaters as the Savoy, Haymarket, Bijou, St. Martin's, and Fortune, none seemed appropriate for a national theater except the Old Vic, whose history, beginning in 1818, identifies it as a house of melodrama, a music hall, a temperance coffeehouse, a cinema palace, an opera stage, and finally, in 1914, a Shakespearean theater. In 1963, the National Theatre of Great Britain opened its first season at the Old Vic with a production of *Hamlet*. In addition, the Stratford Memorial Theatre held annual festivals from 1879. Today, the Arts Council of Great Britain subsidizes the Royal Shakespeare Company, the National Theatre, and the English Stage Company.

IRISH LITERARY RENAISSANCE

Outside London, nationalism provided the catalyst for new theatrical interest. Although Welsh efforts proved unsubstantial, the Scottish National Theatre Society arose in 1922, after a number of similarly named patriotic efforts, and in 1927, Sir James Barrie and others began the touring Masque Theatre. Indeed, these efforts mimicked the success of the Abbey Theatre, rooted initially in the revolutionist Maud Gonne's political/theatrical group "The Daughters of Ireland" and brought to life by the efforts of Yeats, Lady Augusta Gregory, and Edward Martyn to create an independent theater to preserve Gaelic literary heritage.

The Abbey Theatre, housed in the Mechanics' Institute and funded by Annie Horniman, opened in 1904 with Yeats's *On Baile's Strand* and Lady Gregory's *Spreading the News*. In 1910, however, Miss Horniman withdrew from the project. In 1924, the Abbey became state-subsidized; in 1951, the company moved to the Queen's Theatre and, fifteen years later, to its own house. With B. Iden Payne and Lewis Casson, Horniman in 1908 acquired the Gaiety Theatre for the Manchester Playgoers' Association, which encouraged new playwrights such as Allan Monkhouse, Stanley Houghton, and Elizabeth Baker to explore themes of interest to the working class; interestingly enough, such plays were less concerned with jobs and living conditions than with family problems, as in Houghton's *Hindle Wakes* (pr. 1912), a sympathetic treatment of the new woman's sexual rights, or in Harold Brighouse's *Hobson's Choice* (pr. 1915).

The Abbey Theatre, however, became known worldwide as the heart of the Celtic revival with productions such as Lady Gregory's *The Travelling Man* (pb. 1909), which invokes the mystical figure of the unconventional tramp; Rutherford Mayne's *The Turn of the Road* (pr. 1910), Padraic Colum's *Thomas Muskerry* (pr. 1910), and St. John Ervine's *Mixed Marriage* (pr. 1911) deal with the despair of the young under the domination of the old. Other plays critical of the Celtic mythos, such as those by Synge or O'Casey, evoked patriotic riots or indifference.

Distinctively Celtic elements have defined the modern sense of drama, including plays by Yeats, remembered for his lyricism and symbolism; by Synge, for his Celtic linguistic patterns and ethos; and by O'Casey, for his prodigious experimentation. The Abbey also enriched the one-act play form, which in Ireland became the vehicle for expressing elemental human aspirations in such plays as Synge's *Riders to the Sea* (pb. 1903). Also to the Abbey's credit, or, rather, primarily to Yeats's, is the successful production of the verse play.

Yeats's development from the idea, in *The Countess Cathleen* (pb. 1892) and *Cathleen ni Houlihan* (pr. 1902), that reform comes through changing social institutions to the idea that the artist's concern must be with symbols representing spiritual understanding derives from his interest in the intensely ritualistic Nō drama, incorporating stylized gestures and language. Indeed, he eventually couples violence with formalism in a Sophoclean manner: To participate in violence vicariously is, in the long run, less destructive than looting and burning.

Yeats's success influenced Synge to produce *Riders to the Sea*, in which the combination of Maeterlinckian symbolism and lyric dialogue produces almost pure tragic action. Synge's best-known play, *The Playboy of the Western World* (pr. 1907), examines the Irish propensity for belief in myths of their own making. While Synge's achievements in *Riders to the Sea* and *The Playboy of the Western World* are universally acknowledged, his last play, *Deirdre of the Sorrows* (pr. 1910), has not received the recognition it deserves. Produced posthumously by Yeats, this unfinished masterpiece incorporates Irish legend and Celtic lyricism. More influential than Synge, O'Casey, self-educated hod-carrier-turned-playwright, can be seen as a symbol of modern man, able to cross class lines and to rewrite history, treating the 1916 Easter Rising in *The Plough and the Stars* (pr. 1926), the 1920 resistance in *The Shadow of a Gunman* (pr. 1923), and the new Irish Republic in *Juno and the Paycock* (pr. 1924). His experimentation is well shown in the morality play *Within the Gates* (pr. 1934), in *Red Roses for Me* (pr. 1943), a support for the transport workers' strike, and in *Purple Dust* (pr. 1944), a burlesque of the British. His later *Cock-a-Doodle Dandy* (pr. 1949), with its magnificently crested magical rooster, representing the vitalism underlying puritanical repression, is far removed from his early slice-of-life works.

MODERN RELIGIOUS AND VERSE DRAMA

Like the plays of the Irish Literary Renaissance, religious drama eventually bridged the gap between private and commercial theater. The successful dramas of T. S. Eliot and Christopher Fry, however, were preceded by many private productions. Censored on the stage and not allowed within the Church, even centuries-old morality plays such as the fifteenth century *Everyman* had difficulty finding a performance venue. In 1904, however, a modern morality play for Christmas, *Eager Heart*, by Alice Buckton, was a wildly popular nonprofit production that eventually gave rise to the Incorporated Company of Eager Heart to honor the impoverished child who gave shelter to the Holy Family. Other groups, such as the Morality Play Society, founded in 1911 by Mabel Dearmer, were established to give performances, frequently without pay, of plays with religious themes. Such productions were far removed from both commercially successful spectacles such as Wilson Barrett's *Sign of the Cross* (pr. 1896) and revisionist versions such as D. H. Lawrence's *David* (pb. 1926), yet they did contribute to the popular and critical climate that allowed Eliot's series of modern moralities, including *The Cocktail Party* (pr. 1949) and *The Elder Statesman* (pr. 1958), to be performed.

Similarly, the climate of interest generated by such private performances provided welcoming as well to quasi-religious and fantasy plays. Barrie's *Peter Pan*, for example, in its own way paved the way to A. A. Milne's *Mr. Pym Passes By* (pr. 1919) and the adaptation of Kenneth Grahame's children's book *The Wind in the Willows* (1908) as the play *Toad of Toad Hall* (pr. 1929). Jerome K. Jerome's *The Passing of the Third Floor Back* (pr. 1908), a work that makes use of an impoverished boarder as a catalyst for good, and Vane Sutton-Vane's *Outward Bound* (pr. 1923), in which a cruise ship provides, in fact, passage to Heaven or Hell, are further examples, as is Laurence Housman's *Little Plays of St. Francis* (pr. 1922), a collection of short plays reminiscent of *Eager Heart* in their simplicity.

The flourishing of religious drama in private, noncommercial theatrical clubs and associations and the production of religious spectacle plays constitute, however, only two-thirds of the story: Serious religious drama composed in twentieth century idiom and attractive to commercial ventures is perhaps a peculiarly modern manifestation. To be sure, the success of the *Eager Heart* nonprofit venture was phenomenal, but by that time managers had already learned the value of mounting lavish productions of such spectacles as Barrett's *Quo Vadis* (pr. 1900), based on the novel of the same title by Henryk Sienkiewicz, and Caine's *The Christian*. Even the medieval morality play *Everyman* was modernized and presented at the Drury Lane by the American Walter Brown as *Everywoman* (pr. 1911).

T. S. Eliot's own brand of liturgical drama is different, however, in that it partakes less of the spectacle and more of the comedy of manners, with the exception of *Murder in the Cathedral* (pr. 1935), composed for the 1935 Canterbury Festival. Even that play, however, written for an audience predisposed not only to understanding but also to participating in the tale of the martyrdom of Thomas à Beckett, is closer to the classical Greek definition of spectacle, with its choral movements and sonorous poetry, than to the profitable ventures of Drury Lane. Indeed, Eliot seems to have possessed the very divided consciousness that is depicted as the bane of modern humanity in such poems as "The Love Song of J. Alfred Prufrock" and *The Waste Land* (1922). Although he was drawn to create a new poetic idiom within the superficial comedy of manners that appeals to modern audiences, he was also deeply convinced that modern materialism and worldliness are spiritual dead ends. Somewhat like the seventeenth century French playwright Molière, who prefaced his play *Tartuffe: Ou, L'Imposteur* (pr. 1664; *Tartuffe*, 1732) with the statement that moral lessons in a comic drama were more effective than sermons, Eliot employed the comedy of manners as an overlay to his more serious message.

To a modernist, Eliot appears as a reactionary. In contrast to the expansive optimism of Shaw's drama, Eliot's plays purvey a narrow asceticism far removed from the realist's call to social action. In fact, Eliot's stated intention to "redeem society" has a distinctly liturgical flavor, emphasizing individual rather than social salvation. In his plays, only the saints, such as Beckett, or Cecilia in *The Cocktail Party*, seem to be fully human; the others, even the "guardians" who have come to some sort of rapprochement with a moral system, suffer from shallowness. His light society dialogue, which at times is more polished than that of Noël Coward, the modern master of the comedy of manners, has affinities not only with Yeats's formal lyric verse but also with Synge's and O'Casey's use of dialect. Like them, as well, Eliot drew on legend or myth, reaching to Anglican traditions as well as to Greek formalism and to Aristophanes' black humor. In addition, he made extensive use of popular rhythms: Vaudeville airs, children's rhymes, and journalistic phrases are all evident, even in his first dramatic experiment, *Sweeney Agonistes* (pr. 1933).

Whether Eliot was indeed rebel or reactionary is, however, a matter of some critical debate. In his experimentation with language and in his radical attempt to align religion and life, he seems the former; in his opposition to the Liberal cause, his evident assumption that social action is placebo, not cure, and his insistence that redemption inheres in reaching the still point of the cosmic design, he seems the latter. His characters are clearly not part of a social structure larger than, perhaps, that of the family or a social circle, unlike those in O'Casey's plays; in fact, when Eliot's characters come to some measure of understanding their guilt, they become further isolated. Lord Harry Monchensey in *The Family Reunion* (pr. 1939), for example, after understanding that his sense of guilt, his harassment by the Furies, is a transference of his father's murderous wishes, gives up the family estate as well as the comfort of remarriage. Likewise, Colby in *The Confidential Clerk* (pr. 1953) retreats from a newfound family to be a church organist, and Lord Claverton, guilty of financial chicanery and murder in *The Elder Statesman*, withdraws to die after confessing his misdeeds to his daughter.

In comparison with the more exuberantly poetic Christopher Fry, Eliot seems to have taken the *via dolorosa*, or the negative way, of the mystic Saint John of the Cross; nevertheless, his deliberate attempt to impose poetic language on a naturalistic setting and to suggest thereby another level of meaning is important to the development of religious drama. Fry's language alone poses a contrast to Eliot's work; in fact, the same criticism is made of him that was made of O'Casey, that he is carried away by the sheer poetic freight of words. Like O'Casey, too, his plays are broader in scope than Eliot's, tending to give the effect of panorama rather than of drawing-room comedy. Critics have compared Fry's dramatic structure to that of such eighteenth century writers as Richard Brinsley Sheridan, Fry's witty persiflage to that of Oscar Wilde, and his eye for absurdity to that of Pirandello and Jean Anouilh.

What Fry provides that Eliot does not is a worldly, albeit Christianity-based, optimism that finds its focus in the compassion and humanity of his characters. His theme, like Eliot's, is conversion, yet Eliot's conversions are either otherworldly or isolating, whereas Fry's are centered on life, a focus that seems to show his indebtedness to Shakespeare. In *The Lady's Not for Burning* (pr. 1948), for example, the plot is about witchcraft and the absurdity of a legal system, yet the theme is the conflict between life and death. The hero, Thomas Mendip, with logic reminiscent of Wilde's, argues for the validity of death in a society full of shortcomings, in a world that shows in its deceptiveness no evidence of God. The supposed witch, Jennet Jourdemain, argues for life, like a heroine from one of Shaw's plays. Each to some extent convinces the other. In Fry's plays, female characters typically stand at the center of perception, their higher love allowing them to help their male counterparts transfuse earthiness into sublimity.

The list of those devoted to increasing the popularity of poetic drama is long, and it includes a series of loose associations. Certainly Yeats and his associates were influential, although some critics consider their influence to have been negative: While Yeats was master of the form he developed from the Nō play, such minor lights as Gordon Bottomley and Lascelles Abercrombie were led in the direction of increasing idiosyncrasy. In *Stonefolds* (pr. 1907) and other plays dealing with the life of the worker, Wilfred Gibson combined the Manchester School approach with poetry.

Although Yeats, Eliot, and Fry may therefore be seen as the twentieth century high points in a long tradition of verse drama, a subsidiary pool of less important dramatists did contribute to public expectations of the form. Many are scarcely remembered, such as Stephen Phillips, whose *Herod* (pr. 1900) and *Paolo and Francesca* (pr. 1902) caused him to be compared by contemporary critics to John Milton and Dante. Others were noted in other genres: The scholar John Middleton Murry, for example, ventured into satire with the play *Cinnamon and Angelica* (pb. 1920). Even those hailed, with some reason, as the precursors of a new poetic drama, such as James Elroy Flecker, whose *Hassan* (pr. 1923) ran for nearly three hundred performances, have fallen into disregard. Others are better remembered. Sir Gilbert Murray, known for his classical translations, is one:

His *Oedipus Rex* (pr. 1912) was directed by Reinhardt, and his *Alcestis* was produced at Covent Garden in 1924. Masefield, named poet laureate in 1930, is another. Influenced like Eliot by Christian themes, like Yeats by Nō drama, and like Murray by classical tragedy, he wrote such plays as *The Tragedy of Pompey the Great* (pr. 1910) and *The Trial of Jesus* (pb. 1925), as well as ringing denunciations of injustice and its effects on the innocent, as in *The Tragedy of Nan* (pr. 1908).

Between the two world wars, verse drama and political drama converged in the works of Stephen Spender, W. H. Auden, and Christopher Isherwood. Spender, for example, openly castigates Nazi fascism in his verse play *Trial of a Judge* (pr. 1938), while the others experimented with a variety of other themes. Auden and Isherwood collaborated on such plays as the symbolic *The Ascent of F6* (pr. 1937), written in both verse and prose. Auden is especially noted for his experimentation with popular verse forms and his Brechtian expressionism. His Group Theatre, in which, along with Rupert Doone and Robert Medley, he produced innovative, noncommercial drama, sponsored Spender's play as well as others, including Eliot's *Sweeney Agonistes*. A similar convergence of verse drama and religious drama affords speculation for the critic, for much of the verse drama that is revived today achieved its popularity by attaching itself to universal themes, from Yeats's Celtic quasi-mysticism to Eliot's Anglicanism. Much must be attributed to the quality of the verse as well; while many of the unremembered playwrights of the past produced their turgid dramas with little understanding of dramatic structure and less of verse music, both Eliot and Yeats began as poets, as did Dylan Thomas, whose autobiographical *Under Milk Wood: A Play for Voices* (pr. 1956) was both a radio and a stage success.

SHAPERS OF THE AGE

To consider as a pair the two playwrights who together shaped the twentieth century idea of comedy—George Bernard Shaw and Noël Coward—is to look at different facets of the genre in which the British, despite the havoc of two world wars and concomitant economic woes, have gained ascendency. Shaw was a philosophical realist whose ready wit was based on his faith in the creative evolution to which he refers in his prefaces and afterwords, as in "The Revolutionist's Handbook," appended to *Man and Superman* (pb. 1903). Coward, on the other hand, was a comedic realist of a different stamp; his comedies of manners reproduce glittering cocktail conversation in a way that proves him the heir of the epigrammatic Wilde. As playwrights, Shaw and Coward have this in common: They are witty and take a humorist's joy in frustrating expectations, Shaw by relentlessly following the logic in the problem he poses and Coward by providing neat twists in his plots. There the similarity ends.

Unlike Coward, Shaw brought to his work as a playwright experience as a novelist, political polemicist, and critic. While to some he seemed a philosophical butterfly, sampling major theories as they became current, in fact his constant experimentation from 1885 to 1950 was firmly grounded in a belief in human perfectibility. To begin with, his interest in Karl Marx and his role in founding the Fabian Society, where he was friendly with Beatrice and Sidney Webb, dated from the early 1880's and was a reaction against the antihumanitarian society that supra-individualism seemed to encourage. Again, his attachment both to "evolutionary socialism" and "revolutionary socialism" superseded his brief attachment to Carlylian hero-worship, which paled in the light of twentieth century totalitarianism. Finally, although he postulated the existence of a "Life Force" that moves even bumbling human efforts in the direction of "creative evolution," his belief in perfectibility, dependent as it was on the operation of human will informed by moral passion, was unallied with fatalism.

In his early years, Shaw not only espoused but also revolutionized the play of ideas movement with his serious comedies collected as *Plays Unpleasant* (pb. 1898). These deal with poverty, war, prostitution, women's rights, and other ethical questions, rather than with what he labeled "romantic follies," which he satirizes in *Plays Pleasant* (pb. 1898). *Candida: A Mystery* (pr. 1897), for example, is Ibsen's *Et dukkehjem* (pr. 1879; *A Doll's House*, 1880) turned

upside down; rather than choosing to leave an apparently fruitless marriage, Candida chooses the less obviously "weaker" of her two admirers—her clergyman husband, rather than the poet Marchbanks.

Similarly, Shaw attacks the melodramatic mode in his *Three Plays for Puritans* (pb. 1901), so named because of G. K. Chesterton's attack on the playwright's sermonizing. Typically, Shaw not only subverts a popular form into comedy but also takes a generally accepted formula—in *The Devil's Disciple* (pr. 1897), for example, the exhortation that one should love one's neighbor as oneself—and applies it with inexorable logic. Hence, Dick, the black sheep of the Dudgeon family, offers his life for the minister. The minister discovers that his vocation is war, not peace, but his wife cannot understand that Dick is dying for principle, not for love of her.

Illuminated by wit and a pursuance of logic to unexpected ends, Shaw's more mature plays go beyond Ibsen. *Major Barbara* (pr. 1905) illustrates Shaw's method well: Taking as his text that "the root of evil is poverty," he gives us Undershaft, whose munitions factory has enabled him to set up a thriving socialist community, much to the horror of his daughter, who is a major in the Salvation Army. For Shaw, religion is a mere bandage that obscures the truth that only those aware of hard economic fact can indeed do good. Again, in *Saint Joan* (pr. 1923), which, next to *Man and Superman*, critics agree to be one of his greatest plays, Shaw attacks conventional religiosity as he depicts the visionary whose unconventional perceptions cause her destruction by those who in more ordinary terms are "good." In *Man and Superman*, Shaw explores the nature of good. Based on the Don Juan legend, the play illustrates the idea that the Life Force is all conquering: Although the central plot is superficially romantic, centered on the pursuit of Jack Tanner by Anne Whitfield, the dream sequence that features an argument between the Devil and Tanner on the nature of Heaven and Hell is the philosophical heart of the play. That Heaven is a state of action is underscored by the characterization of "Ricky-Ticky-Tavy," a poetic hero whom Anne rejects because his incapacity to deal realistically with life would make him an inadequate husband and father. Tanner expresses Shaw's own distaste for aestheticism as well as for the false romantic fervor that passes for moral passion.

One of Shaw's later plays, *Back to Methuselah* (pb. 1921)—a long account of human history—reaffirms his belief, somewhat sobered by World War I, that only through the eventual evolution of the Superman can the human race be salvaged. He foresees a Utopia in which those who achieve lengthy life spans evolve into pure thought. While Shaw's growing pessimism about the achievement of a present-day Utopia through socialistic means is evident, the play does demonstrate his continuing optimism about the creative evolution of humanity.

An examination of Sir James Barrie and Noël Coward is helpful in ascertaining the special genius of Shaw, whose plays, because of their undergirding in social and intellectual movements, have proved perdurable. In Barrie, intellect such as Shaw's is expressed as wisdom about human nature; in Coward, it is expressed as worldliness, savvy about human beings as social animals. Shaw's brilliance of wit is whimsy in Barrie, glittering dialogue in Coward. If Shaw is master of the mind and Barrie of the heart, Coward is neither; he is, rather, a master of repartee. Shaw's relentless logic leads to a moral imperative; Barrie and Coward, on the other hand, deal with everyday complexities, the former in terms of feelings, the latter in terms of social complications.

Coward is best known for shaping the form of the comedy of manners to twentieth century demands and expectations. He finds wit, which has sometimes been called "brittle," in diverse and intricate relations between the sexes. Typical is his first successful comedy, *Hay Fever* (pr. 1925), which, supposedly based on a biographical incident, features sprightly quarrels and a round-robin exchange of partners during a weekend visit. His *Tonight at 8:30* (pr. 1935-1936) is a collection of short plays written with himself and Gertrude Lawrence in mind as stars. His most commercially fruitful alliance with Lawrence was, however, *Blithe Spirit* (pr. 1941), in which Spiritualism is both burlesqued and made the *raison d'être* of the plot: During a séance, Elvira, Charles Condomine's first wife, mistakenly kills Ruth, his second wife,

and, exorcism failing, Charles leaves on vacation while the two spirits destructively take possession of his living room. To be sure, Coward also wrote more serious drama. His *Still Life* (pr. 1936), about a love affair, became the film *Brief Encounter* (1946).

To move from the sophisticated comedies of Coward to Barrie's whimsical plays may seem to be to travel from the adult's to the child's world, especially because Barrie is most famous for *Peter Pan*. Like the introductions and stage directions written by Shaw, those by Barrie go beyond the matter at hand, exploring the motives of the characters as well as the orientation of the playwright; to this degree, the plays are really readers' plays. Barrie's comedy reached its height in *The Admirable Crichton* (pr. 1902), in which he posits an impossible, albeit delightful, situation—the marooning of a well-to-do family on a desert island to demonstrate the butler Crichton's insistence that human nature makes true equality an impossible goal. Even in an unstructured situation, someone, in this case the resourceful Crichton, is a leader.

More prolific than Barrie, yet touched with the same type of fantastical humor, was James Bridie, a Scottish playwright whose reputation has suffered because of the unevenness of his work. Concentrating primarily on biblical themes, Bridie, both early and late, as in *Tobias and the Angel* (pr. 1930) and *The Baikie Charivari: Or, The Seven Prophets* (pr. 1952), provides a Shavian twist to his plots. In the first play, the blind Tobias thwarts the Devil with the help of the angel Raphael in disguise; in the second, a group of villagers are both ordinary folk and characters in a Punch-and-Judy scenario that is manned by the Devil himself. The framework gives rise to discussions about the search for truth through theoretical and practical means.

POSTWAR MODERNISM

Although certain major playwrights, such as Eliot, Shaw, and Coward, seem to define much of the twentieth century, perspective is more difficult to gain on contemporary writers, not only because of their proximity in time but also because audiences still feel the implicit effects of, for example, World War II and the economic recessions that shaped a new theatrical style. Postwar playwrights faced a world in which even ultimate values seemed meaningless. Not only did faith in God seem groundless, but faith in human nature was likewise questioned, especially in the light of the concentration camps, with their suggestion of international complicity in human suffering. As some critics note, even the Nuremburg war-crimes trials affected the question of universal values, for there the question of the conflict between a nation's laws and its moral imperatives was as much on trial as were those who engaged in wartime atrocities.

The role of the mass media in publicizing details about the war and its aftermath cannot be ignored: In effect, television, with its graphic pictures and instant analysis, contributed to a general decline of the sort of optimism that Shaw espoused. Other influences were important as well, most notably the works of Jean-Paul Sartre and Albert Camus, who introduced British playwrights and playgoers to existentialism.

Both Sartre, whose *L'Être et le néant* (1943; *Being and Nothingness*, 1956) defined the new stance, and Camus, the father of the absurdists, viewed the human condition as illogical. Unlike their followers, however, they insisted on the ability of the individual human being to choose to act in an ultimately meaningless world: Free of all codified moral imperatives, one might initially feel anguish or despair, but one can choose to create for oneself the standards by which one will live. Camus finds absurdity in the search for clarity in a chaotic world, in the search for answers in an ungrounded universe. His early characters in, for example, *Caligula* (pr. 1945; English translation, 1948), can overcome absurdity only by refusing to recognize it; in a later play, *Les Justes* (pr. 1949; *The Just Assassins*, 1958), however, they substitute action for denial and demonstrate the working of responsibility.

Although Camus and Sartre were particularly important philosophically, Bertolt Brecht was an important influence theatrically. With his state-supported Berliner Ensemble, which incorporated not only a corps of actors but also all the other artistic and managerial personnel necessary for production, he pro-

foundly influenced the antirealistic trend of contemporary theater.

In England, changing political and philosophical winds resulted in much theatrical experimentation. Indeed, the fragmentation of the theater at this point in the century seems to reflect the common person's schizophrenia in a war-torn society, especially since those who followed both Camus and Sartre pushed absurdity to its extreme in denying even the possibility of creative action. Samuel Beckett is important in this regard. Born in Ireland but eventually residing in France, where his friendship with James Joyce developed, Beckett, like Yeats, experimented with static drama but developed it into an existential statement about the essential futility of action. His *En attendant Godot* (pr. 1953; *Waiting for Godot*, 1954), for example, presents two tramps, Vladimir and Estragon, who wait endlessly and inexplicably for Godot. "It's awful," they agree; nothing happens, except that Pozzo trails by with his slave Lucky, whose talents include a stream-of-consciousness monologue. At the end of the play, Pozzo and Lucky have gone blind and dumb, respectively, and Godot has not arrived. In another depiction of futility, *Fin de partie: Suivi de Acte sans paroles* (pr. 1957; *Endgame*, 1958) presents characters waiting, but this time each is as visibly deformed as the ruined world outside his room. While Clov cannot rest, the blind Hamm cannot move; Hamm's legless and senescent parents are stowed in dustbins. All await death, paralyzed in an irrational world. The silence, the isolation, the endless boredom that underscore the futility of action are nevertheless balanced by the persistent survival of even the most internally ravaged of Beckett's characters.

Absurdists such as Beckett transformed the sort of stage familiar to the playgoer at the turn of the century in a number of ways. Heavy plotting went the way of heavy scenery; in addition, as the focus on existence itself intensified, plays were stripped of realistic props as well as of a linear time frame and realistic characterization and setting. Language, often grotesquely simplified, was no longer an aesthetic medium to be enjoyed for its diction or wordplay but rather an emblem of the futility of communicating, even in the most basic terms. In short, playwrights such as Beckett attempted to eliminate all that distracts from contemplation of the human condition, at times, perhaps, achieving a modern parable, the characters of which are not unrelated to the archetypes of, for example, John Bunyan, but the plots of which reflect the illogic of the postwar era.

The absurdist worldview influenced several groups of playwrights whose interest lay primarily in social issues and whose names are associated with two important theaters. Both the English Stage Company, from 1956 to 1965 under the leadership of George Devine and his assistant Tony Richardson, and the Theatre Workshop, headed by Joan Littlewood, had profound effects, not only in encouraging new playwrights but also in providing a voice for new audiences.

Perhaps the best-known products of the English Stage Company are John Osborne and John Arden, although others contributed to the absurdist movement. Norman Simpson, for example, whose *A Resounding Tinkle* (pr. 1956) was a Royal Court Theatre prizewinner, is distinguished by his attempt to forge absurdism to fantasy. The English Stage Company, in residence at the Royal Court Theatre, featured Osborne's *Look Back in Anger* (pr. 1956) as its third new production. Influenced by the absurdist interpretation of the human condition—that one is at the mercy of an irrational, chaotic world and, by extension, of one's own unexamined impulses—Osborne nevertheless suggests that one can alleviate existential despair by attempting to change the political and social system. His characters are therefore considerably more vital and active than Beckett's Hamm or Lucky, for example, in attempting to counter such forces, if only through resounding diatribes against what cannot be helped. Jimmy Porter in *Look Back in Anger* is the original "angry young man": Disillusioned, frustrated, lashing out against the hypocrisy of social conventions, he expresses his anger against the universe by verbally lacerating his wife, who retorts through nonresponse. Among the plays that followed, both *The Entertainer* (pr. 1957) and *Inadmissible Evidence* (pr. 1964) take declining public figures—the first, a vaudeville entertainer; the second, a lawyer, himself on trial—as their spokespeople

and analyze the "evidence" behind the façade. In *The Entertainer*, Osborne takes as his symbol of despair an aging music-hall entrepreneur who, through a series of monologues, verbalizes his progressive decay. Episodic in structure, the play shows the influence of Brecht: The entertainer has an abortive affair, fails to stage a financial trick, and finally is unable to arrange any star performances. More than a British version of Arthur Miller's *Death of a Salesman* (pr. 1949), *The Entertainer* is also a parable about the successive decay of Britain from strength to indifference.

Another successful Royal Court playwright who also reinterpreted the absurdist philosophy is John Arden, whose objective pose between the elements of chaos and order and conventionality and revolt forces the audience to participate by examining their own worldviews. While *Live Like Pigs* (pr. 1958) was generally considered inconclusive, *Serjeant Musgrave's Dance: An Unhistorical Parable* (pr. 1959) seemed to espouse a pacifistic stance, suggesting that war is only one form of violence, the imposition of ideas another. Similarly, in his other plays—*The Happy Haven* (pr. 1960), written in collaboration with Margaretta D'Arcy, for example, or *Armstrong's Last Goodnight: An Exercise in Diplomacy* (pr. 1964)—Arden seems interested primarily in the balance between opposites rather than in their resolution. In this sense, he seems to follow, but only conceptually, the Strindbergian notion that life is strife, and unresolvable strife at that.

Like the Royal Court Theatre, the Theatre Workshop attempted to win the allegiance of the working class to the theater by adopting some of the methods of popular entertainment. Littlewood's group, which toured from 1945 to 1953, when it settled in East London, relied on Brechtian methods and improvisation; in a departure from traditional practices, it generated plays through the cooperative efforts of actor and playwright, including, for example, Frank Norman and Lionel Bart's *Fings Ain't Wot They Used t'Be* (pr. 1959). After 1961, when Littlewood retired, the group lost much of its direct influence but remained a force in theater education. Many modern playwrights owe their subject matter and style to Littlewood's group. Henry Livings, for example, trained there as an actor, but his realistic and bitter works, such as *Big Soft Nellie* (pr. 1961) and *Nil Carborundum* (pr. 1962), display Littlewood's emphasis on the deleterious effects of work on humanity; similarly, Bernard Kops, although much different from Livings in his emotional freight, exhibits in such works as *Change for the Angel* (pr. 1960) the experimentation with language that Littlewood encouraged.

Both Shelagh Delaney and Brendan Behan were showcased by Littlewood. Delaney's one major success, *A Taste of Honey* (pr. 1958), treats illegitimacy, abuse, and homosexuality with close observation and empathy. Behan, on the other hand, produced two plays that were hailed as the Theatre Workshop's answer to Osborne's *Look Back in Anger*. Like O'Casey, Behan examines the human cost of revolution, in *The Quare Fellow* (pr. 1954) and in *The Hostage* (pr. 1958); also like O'Casey, he experiments with a variety of approaches. Perhaps Littlewood's best-known playwright was the self-taught Arnold Wesker, whose early plays demonstrate his political interests and his suggestion that the working class is oppressed because it is incapable of vision. His trilogy comprising *Chicken Soup with Barley* (pr. 1958), *Roots* (pr. 1959), and *I'm Talking About Jerusalem* (pr. 1960) traces the fortunes of the Kahn family from the strongly socialistic mother to the disillusioned children, who eventually discover that neither escapism nor self-reliance is the answer. Like Osborne, Wesker suggests that the political and social system is awry; further, he looks to collaborative efforts to solve the problem. Another play, *The Kitchen* (pr. 1959), suggests that implicit and explicit brutality stems from the adverse effects of environment on workers. *Chips with Everything* (pr. 1962) treats a similar theme within the context of the military, in which the enlisted men are equivalent to the workers in their deprivations. To encourage an active interest in theater among the working classes, Wesker founded Centre 42—which, however, eventually became a haven for the avant-garde rather than performing its intended function.

Among the host of playwrights influenced by absurdism and the new theater movements, Harold Pinter emerges as the most important. Others, to be

sure, made their marks with one or two significant contributions. John Whiting and Robert Bolt, for example, were seen as serious rivals to Pinter. From Whiting's early *Saint's Day* (pr. 1951) to his later *The Devils* (pr. 1961), his vision was uncompromising and generally bleak; his career was cut short by his premature death. Although Whiting's *The Devils*, a play in which demoniac possession is explored as sexual neuroticism, achieved success in its Royal Shakespeare Company production, Bolt's plays have appealed more consistently to the West End audience. His well-known study of Sir Thomas More, *A Man for All Seasons* (pr. 1960), has more of a connection with Drinkwater's early epics than with the social commentary of the mainstream absurdists. Again, such writers as Ann Jellicoe, who wrote *The Sport of My Mad Mother* (pr. 1958) and *The Knack* (pr. 1961), as well as Nigel Dennis, author of *The Making of Moo* (pr. 1957), have won recognition, as has David Storey, whose *In Celebration* (pr. 1969) and *The Contractor* (pr. 1969) illustrate his idea that the class system has isolated workers from their spiritual legacy.

Pinter's consistent output defines the human condition in the 1950's and 1960's. Influenced by Beckett in his absurdist plots and simplistic language, Pinter evokes in his early plays a nameless sense of menace, as with the inexplicable darkness in *The Room* (pr. 1957). Later, the menace, existentially grounded in the human condition, is seen to emanate from the characters themselves. In *The Birthday Party* (pr. 1958), Stanley is abducted by two strangers whose motive appears to be to harangue him with meaningless questions. Similarly, in *The Dumb Waiter* (pr. 1960), the gunman Ben shoots his companion Gus on orders from an unseen "boss." Finally, in *The Homecoming* (pr. 1965), the characters' self-brutalization is evident as Teddy's wife, Ruth, panders to the various needs of the all-male family she has joined, becoming mother and sister, whore and homemaker, at the same time.

Osborne and Pinter may be seen as the prototypes of two complementary branches of postwar drama. On the one hand, the mood was absurdist: Characters faced with a relativistic world found inaction or escape their only means of survival. On the other hand, it was political: Angry Young Men such as Osborne waged verbal war against the political and social abuses they believed could be rectified. As some critics suggest, the mood of the 1960's was a combination of these two elements. Playwrights seemed to see absurdity in the past and hope in the future, the end to be achieved through an angry response to what was dehumanizing. From this mood arose several important theaters as well as playwrights such as Peter Shaffer and Tom Stoppard.

In the 1960's, government subsidies became especially important to support the theatrical troupes responsible for the postwar dramatic renaissance. The National Theatre, for example, whose first director was Sir Laurence Olivier, began in 1963 to present a wide range of productions under the aegis of visiting directors and a permanent company. Considerably less conservative than the National Theatre, the Royal Shakespeare Company, chartered in 1961, broadened its scope not only to include absurdist plays but also to sponsor avant-garde experiments. In 1963, for example, the troupe presented such playwrights as Antonin Artaud and Jean Genet in a Theater of Cruelty from which emanated Peter Brook's memorable production of *Die Verfolgung und Ermordung Jean Paul Marats, dargestellt durch die Schauspielgruppe des Hospizes zu Charenton unter der Anleitung des Herrn de Sade* (pr. 1964; *The Persecution and Assassination of Jean-Paul Marat as Performed by the Inmates of the Asylum of Charenton Under the Direction of the Marquis de Sade*, 1965; better known as *Marat/Sade*) the next year. Although beset by subsidy problems, the Royal Shakespeare Company is best known for the modern interpretations given to Shakespeare's works by Brook, who intended less to present the original texts than to focus on, for example, elements stressed by the Theater of Cruelty or on psychological motifs. Other groups were important as well, not only in encouraging new playwrights but also in forcing the repeal of censorship. The English Stage Company continued its policy by opening the Theatre Upstairs; other subsidized groups ranged from the Mermaid, which has presented Elizabethan and eighteenth century drama, to the National Youth Theatre, established in 1956 under Michael Croft,

which has presented such works as Peter Terson's *Zigger Zagger* (pr. 1967) and *Fuzz* (pr. 1969).

Outside London, provincial repertories doubled in number; one of the most important, the 69 Theatre Company, was housed in the Royal Exchange Theatre in Manchester. The company, which was fathered by the 59 Theatre Company that played at the Lyric Theatre, began its productions in 1968 at the Manchester University theater and eventually built its own theater-in-the-round, a model of innovative modern architecture. The company's best-known director, Michael Elliott, directed premieres of Ronald Harwood's plays—*The Ordeal of Gilbert Pinfold* (pr. 1977), *A Family* (pr. 1978), featuring Paul Scofield, and *The Dresser* (pr. 1980), featuring Tom Courtenay.

Although government and private subsidies played an important role in the burgeoning theatrical activity, the Theatres Act of 1968 paved the way for further experimentation. For 231 years, every play produced publicly had to be licensed by the Lord Chamberlain; the 1968 act abolished the office and allowed for greater freedom not only in the commercial theater but also in such underground groups as Charles Marowitz's Open Space theater and Ed Berman's Inter-Action street theater. The drive for complete freedom of expression is evident in the works of playwrights such as Edward Bond, whose *Saved*, notorious because of a scene in which a baby is stoned to death, had to be performed privately in 1965; in 1968, his *Narrow Road to the Deep North*, which explores the way in which weakness of will leads to violence, was performed publicly.

Among the most promising of the new playwrights of the 1960's were Peter Shaffer and Tom Stoppard. Shaffer, in particular, ventured into a variety of theatrical genres, from his *Five Finger Exercise* (pr., pb. 1958), about the domestic power brokering that a private tutor engenders, to *The Royal Hunt of the Sun* (pr. 1964), a historical drama about the communion between the powerful and the vanquished, between Pizarro and the Inca Atahuallpa. *Black Comedy* (pr. 1965) and *The Battle of Shrivings* (pr. 1970), an argument about the perfectibility of human beings, were less successful. Unlike Shaffer, Stoppard followed both Pinter and Beckett, especially in *Rosen-*

crantz and Guildenstern Are Dead (pr. 1966), whose absurdist vision is incorporated in two minor characters from *Hamlet* who can make little sense of the events transpiring around them.

THE LAST THREE DECADES

British drama of the 1970's, 1980's, and 1990's features a mixture of old and new artists. Many playwrights who began their careers in the 1950's and 1960's continued to produce new dramatic works that developed their original preoccupations. For example, Beckett persisted in presenting the silence and isolation that he perceived in the modern world in plays such as *Waiting for Godot* by producing works that became briefer and briefer: *Breath* (pr. 1970) contains 120 words and lasts approximately thirty-five seconds, while *Not I* (pr. 1972) runs no more than sixteen minutes, and *That Time* (pr. 1976) no more than half an hour. Other dramatists even returned to the same characters and situations they had presented in earlier works; in *Déjàvu* (pr. 1992), Osborne picks up the life of Jimmy Porter, his protagonist in *Look Back in Anger* (pr. 1956), thirty-six years later. Unfortunately for Jimmy, the situation in England has not significantly improved since 1956.

Although some playwrights stayed on essentially the same course during this period, others took slightly different directions. In the 1970's, for example, Arden, collaborating with his wife, Irish activist and actress Margaretta D'Arcy, focused his drama more explicitly on Irish questions in plays such as *The Non-Stop Connolly Show* (pr. 1975), *The Little Gray Home in the West* (pr. 1978), and *Vandaleur's Folly: An Anglo-Irish Melodrama* (pr. 1978). Pinter also pursued a more overtly political direction. His later works often show the silencing of either an entire people, as in *Mountain Language* (pr. 1988), or an individual, as in *The New World Order* (pr. 1991), by an oppressive political power.

Two of the most promising playwrights of the 1960's—Shaffer and Stoppard—continued to mount successful productions in the 1970's and 1980's. Shaffer produced and published two of his most well-received plays in the 1970's—*Equus* in 1973 and *Amadeus* in 1979 (published in 1980). He structured both works around seemingly antagonistic characters—the psychiatrist and his patient in *Equus* and Wolfgang Amadeus Mozart and Antonio Salieri in *Amadeus*—and then showed how this seeming opposition actually masked a greater number of similarities. His later work *Lettice and Lovage* (pr. 1987) also revolves around this same kind of opposition. Stoppard also enjoyed continued success during this period. Plays such as *Jumpers* (pr. 1972), *Travesties* (pr. 1974), *Night and Day* (pr. 1978), *The Real Thing* (pr. 1982), and *Hapgood* (pr. 1988) combine his characteristic wit and dazzling wordplay with an exploration of more philosophical concerns.

These earlier playwrights have been joined by a number of dramatists who emerged during the 1960's and 1970's. These writers were linked by their desire to critique contemporary British life through comedy, direct political attacks, or a mixture of both. The most successful (and prolific) playwright of domestic comedies is undoubtedly Sir Alan Ayckbourn. He began mounting West End productions in 1967 with *Relatively Speaking*, which was modeled on Oscar Wilde's *The Importance of Being Earnest: A Trivial Comedy for Serious People* (pr. 1895). In the early 1970's, Ayckbourn began producing one play per year at his home theater in Scarborough before moving it to London. His plays are often distinguished by their technical innovation. For example, the marital farce of *How the Other Half Loves* (pr. 1969) is intensified by having the living-dining areas of the two principal couples occupy the same physical space, while in *Taking Steps* (pr. 1979), the comic mishaps are heightened by presenting three stories of an English country house—downstairs living room, upstairs bedroom, and attic—on one level. Ayckbourn's technical innovation has also been accompanied by experiments in form and narrative structure. For example, in his trilogy *The Norman Conquests* (pr. 1973), he created a series of plays meant to be seen on three successive nights, with the onstage action in one play becoming offstage action in the other two. In *Sisterly Feelings* (pr. 1979), some of the middle scenes may vary from performance to performance depending on an actress' spur-of-the-moment decision or a coin toss. *The Revengers' Comedies* (pr.

1989) takes a classic British form—the revenge play—and puts it in a modern context; the performance itself spans two evenings. Although Ayckbourn's plays have often been criticized as lightweight compared to the more overtly political concerns of his contemporaries, his later plays show the darker undertones of contemporary domestic life. *Woman in Mind* (pr. 1985) revolves around Susan, an unhappy woman who escapes the realities of her present life by creating a more congenial dream family, while *A Small Family Business* (pr. 1987) illustrates the corruption that begins at home.

Social concerns paired with innovative staging and style also characterize the work of Caryl Churchill, one of Great Britain's most successful female dramatists. In *Cloud Nine* (pr. 1979), whose first act is set in colonial Africa during the Victorian era and whose second act is set in present-day London, Churchill comments on sexual repression and imperialism by linking them with economic repression and political imperialism. To illustrate the role conditioning present in society, Churchill uses unusual casting, including males playing female roles (and vice versa), white people playing black roles, and adults playing children. The Royal Court's first resident woman dramatist, Churchill deals with feminist themes in some of her works such as *Top Girls* (pr. 1982), where a number of historical female figures dine with Marlene, the owner of the Top Girls employment agency. The play illustrates the sacrifices women must make in order to succeed in a male-dominated world. Churchill, however, is not solely concerned with women's issues. In *Serious Money* (pr. 1987), she creates a "city comedy" in the tradition of Ben Jonson, John Marston, and Thomas Middleton that critiques the London financial world; she even writes the play in rhymed couplets. In *Mad Forest: A Play from Romania* (pr. 1990), she depicts the political repression in Romania and the overthrow of the Ceauşescus.

Churchill is one of many female dramatists who actively produced works during the last decades of the twentieth century. While a number of these playwrights have presented so-called women's issues in their plays, these are not their only concern. Some of the most notable of these writers are Nell Dunn (*Steaming*, pr. 1981), Pam Gems (*Dusa, Fish, Stas, and Vi*, pr. 1976; *Piaf*, pr. 1978; *Camille*, pr. 1985; and *The Blue Angel*, pr. 1991), Sarah Daniels (*The Devil's Gateway*, pr. 1983; *Masterpieces*, pr. 1983; *Byrthrite*, pr. 1986; and *Gut Girls*, pr. 1988), and Timberlake Wertenbaker (*The Grace of Mary Traverse*, pr. 1985; *The Love of the Nightingale*, pr. 1988; *Our Country's Good*, pr. 1988; and *Three Birds Alighting on a Field*, pr. 1991).

Irish drama has also undergone a resurgence during this period, led, to some extent, by Brian Friel, who began producing plays as early as 1964 with *Philadelphia, Here I Come!*, a memory play in which Gareth O'Donnell lives through his last hours in Ireland before immigrating to the United States. Friel's plays tend to be driven by character and setting; often, characters find themselves caught in the conflict between traditional Irish life and modern-day realities. For example, in *Aristocrats* (pr. 1979), Friel shows the decline of the O'Donnell family, who must eventually leave their home, Ballybeg Hall. *Dancing at Lughnasa* (pr. 1990) returns to the form of the memory play as the narrator, Michael, recalls an important fortnight in his family's life that occurred in 1936. Friel has also greatly aided the production of new Irish drama when he cofounded, with actor Stephen Rea, Field Day Productions, a theater company dedicated to bringing professional theater to cities throughout Ireland. Its first production was Friel's own play *Translations* (pr. 1980).

One of Great Britain's most explicitly political playwrights is David Hare, whose dramas demonstrate the failures of contemporary England. He illustrates this theme in *Plenty* (pr. 1978), depicting twenty years in the life of Susan Traherne, who never adjusts to "normal" life after her experiences as a courier for the French Resistance during World War II. Hare has also played an important role in the contemporary theater as a founder of fringe companies—including the Portable Theatre in 1968 and Joint Stock in 1974—and as a director of the work of other political dramatists, including David Edgar, Trevor Griffiths, Stephen Poliakoff, Howard Brenton, Snoo Wilson, and Howard Barker. Hare even cowrote *Pravda: A Fleet Street Comedy* (pr. 1985), a satire of Fleet Street, with

Brenton. His plays of the late twentieth century look closely at the decline of established British institutions such as the family (*The Secret Rapture*, pr. 1988), the Church of England (*Racing Demon*, pr. 1990), and the legal system (*Murmuring Judges*, pr. 1991).

Although British drama of the twentieth century has moved from Shaw's evolutionary optimism to Beckett's absurdism, from solutions to questions, it is, on the whole, strong in a serious comic spirit. As the nineteenth century's penchant for melodrama and spectacle seems to modern eyes to suggest escapism, so the witty dialogue in the comedy of manners, the fantasy, and the exuberant Shavian denouements seem to provide relief, not resolution. The perceptive audience may suspect that the comedy is really a cover for a pressing problem, the inability of the individual human being to cope with an intractable universe. The newer playwrights exhibit a theatrical vitality that belies the bleakness of their philosophical views. Indeed, every depiction of a random, ominous universe is in itself a violation of that universe, for even an unstructured play presents some sense of form. At the end of a century in which dramatists have traveled from realism to absurdism, from integrated dramatic structure to the episodic structure of Brechtian epic theater, from poetry to naturalistic speech and to the language of gesture, the critic thus looks for a playwright to create a new tragedy as well as a new comedy, to model a brave new world onstage as well as to reflect the old one, to show what lies beyond wordlessness and the impossibility of action.

BIBLIOGRAPHY

Griffiths, Trevor R., and Margaret Llewellyn-Jones. *British and Irish Women Dramatists Since 1956: A Critical Handbook*. London: Taylor and Francis, 1993. Provides a sweeping overview of the renaissance of British drama since the 1950's and women's role within it. Covers fringe companies, well-known playwrights, black and lesbian dramatists, and also looks at women's contributions from Wales, Scotland, and Ireland.

Innes, Christopher D. *Modern British Drama, 1890-1990*. Cambridge, England: Cambridge University Press, 1992. A comprehensive overview of the trends and developments of British theater in the twentieth century. Includes subjects such as social themes and realistic formula, the comic mirror, poetic drama, and feminist theater.

Lacey, Stephen. *British Realist Theatre: The New Wave in its Context, 1956-1965*. London: Routledge, 1995. Analyzes the way in which a defining period in modern British drama was related to other developments in postwar culture and politics, including social science, the novel, and cinema.

Reinelt, Janelle G. *After Brecht*. Ann Arbor: University of Michigan Press, 1996. Examines the legacy of German playwright Bertolt Brecht in the work of contemporary British playwrights' Howard Brenton, Edward Bond, Caryl Churchill, David Hare, Trevor Griffiths, and John McGrath. Explores these playwrights work with the National Theatre, the Royal Shakespeare Company, and fringe companies such as Foco Novo, Joint Stock, and Portable Theatre.

Smith, Leslie M. *Modern British Farce: A Selective Study of British Farce from Pinero to the Present Day*. Rowman and Littlefield, 1989. Examines the role of farce in twentieth century drama, with chapters such as "The Nature of Farce," "A.W. Pinero and the Court Farces," and "Farce and Contemporary Drama." Includes appendix, chronological list of plays, notes, bibliography, and index.

Zeifman, Hersh, and Cynthia Zimmerman. *Contemporary British Drama, 1970-1990*. Toronto: University of Toronto Press, 1993. Nearly two dozen essays examine the range of British drama between 1970 and 1990 by focusing on the work of fourteen playwrights, including Harold Pinter, Peter Schaffer, Edward Bond, and Tom Stoppard. Bibliography.

Patricia Marks,
updated by Sharon L. Gravett

CONTEMPORARY BRITISH DRAMA

Contemporary drama in Britain reinforces a lengthy and strong theatrical tradition, while employing innovative strategies and themes that reflect recent developments in British society and culture. Many of those dramatists who achieved success in the 1960's and 1970's continue to produce remarkable work. At the same time, a number of historical factors have influenced the work of a new generation of playwrights. British drama throughout the twentieth century frequently challenged social norms, but the political and cultural impact of Prime Minister Margaret Thatcher's conservative government, which dominated the 1980's, continued to be felt in the years following her tenure. The entrepreneurship, unemployment, economic upheaval, dismantling of the welfare state, and Thatcher's seeming insistence on "Victorian values" generated explicitly political drama in the 1980's, much of which criticized the prevailing values of radical conservatism. This is evidenced most obviously in the plays of David Hare and Howard Brenton.

In the 1990's, the aftershocks from the preceding decade were felt in the form of attacks on the new consumerism encouraged by Thatcher and on the "political correctness" response emanating from the Left. At the same time, tensions in Northern Ireland continued to confront Britain, and a number of new Irish playwrights emerged not only to address these issues but also to consider the condition of Ireland as a whole. One of the most significant developments of the contemporary era in Britain has been the "coming-of-age" of second- and third-generation immigrants from former colonies. Representatives of "Black Britain"—a term appropriated by Britons whose ethnic origins lie in the West Indies, Africa, and the Indian subcontinent—have invigorated all of the arts in Britain, including drama. Taken as a whole, British drama of the late twentieth and early twenty-first centuries reflects mainstream traditions and fringe elements while introducing a variety of new concerns and techniques.

Despite cuts in government funding for the arts throughout the 1980's, new and innovative dramatists found a number of theatrical companies and outlets willing to encourage their work in the last decades of the twentieth century. Outside of London, these include the Hull Truck Theatre; Sheffield's Forced Entertainment (notable for employing digital and video media to dissolve boundaries of theater, performance art, and installation art); Out of Joint, established in 1993, which presents the work of new British playwrights throughout the country and in continental Europe; and the Paines Plough, which is largely responsible for supporting the work of "angry young dramatists" such as Mark Ravenhill and Sarah Kane. Provincial theaters such as Edinburgh's Traverse Theatre, Manchester's Royal Exchange Theatre, and Leeds's West Yorkshire Playhouse, built in 1990, brought new drama to large audiences. At the same time, the Royal Court Theatre reinvigorated its commitment to discovering and supporting many new playwrights during the period 1992-1998 at the insistence of its artistic director, Stephen Daldry. Moreover, the establishment of Channel Four as another British television channel at the end of 1982 proved a boon for dramatists. Unlike its American counterparts, Channel Four was not bound by "standards and practices," and its subsidiary, FilmFour, commissions, broadcasts, and distributes a range of plays and screenplays from contemporary writers and independent filmmakers.

CONTINUITY IN DRAMATISTS

British playwrights whose names were already well established continued to produce some of the most remarkable plays of the twentieth century's last decade. Harold Pinter's highly political absurdist impulse underscores his *The New World Order* (pr. 1991), which implicates the promotion of democracy in acts of political torture. *Ashes to Ashes* (pb. 1996) exemplifies Pinter's abiding concern for uncertainty and, in typically Pinteresque fashion, portrays two characters whose superficial exchanges merely emphasize the silence of that which is unsaid. *Celebration* (pr. 2000) returns to the familiar territory of his *The Room* (pr. 1957), in which the menacing and the banal merge in sinister comedy. Tom Stoppard's own brand of absurdism, his passion for the metahistorical and the metatheatrical, and his phenomenally playful and intelligent linguistic agility all find expression in *Arcadia* (pr. 1993), which alternates between the early nineteenth century and the present, and in *The Invention of Love* (pr. 1997), which imagines the afterlife of poet A. E. Housman as he confronts the River Styx. Stoppard reached an even wider audience with his screenplay, cowritten with Marc Norman, for the academy award-winning *Shakespeare in Love* (1998), an invigorating and imaginative portrait of Shakespeare's life in London, full of witty dialogue and comic anachronism.

Britain's foremost female playwright, Caryl Churchill, has continued to examine feminist and other political issues. *Mad Forest: A Play from Romania* (pr. 1990) emerged from her experiences with Romanian acting students in exploring the fall of ruthless dictator Nicolai Ceauşescu. The themes of devastation, repression, and transformation examined in this play are explored in a less realistic vein in *Skriker* (pr. 1993), a surreal drama focusing on the constant metamorphoses of the title character, a mythical Celtic figure who haunts two young women as they travel to urban London. Of particular interest in this play is Churchill's Joycean linguistic profusion of puns and allusions.

Although their sheer numbers preclude further consideration, many other notable and long-established playwrights, from Sir Alan Ayckbourn to David Hare, from Pam Gems to Peter Shaffer, have continued to produce diverse and successful works of drama for the contemporary British stage.

A THEATER OF SHOCK

Undoubtedly, one of the most significant developments on the British stage in the 1990's was also the most controversial: that which Alex Sierz and others have called "in-yer-face theater." Determined to challenge directly audience expectations and sensibilities, as Samuel Beckett had done two generations earlier, the work of a number of young British dramatists suggested that nothing was "obscene" or unsuitable for the stage. Among this group, the most significant

are Mark Ravenhill, Anthony Neilson, Martin McDonagh, and Sarah Kane.

The plays of these dramatists transgress taboos of all kinds and refuse the audience the position of the detached spectator, aiming willfully—and judging from various reviews, successfully—to offend. Clearly a response to a certain tendency toward nostalgia and revivals in the British theater, as well to the heavy emphasis on morality on one side of British politics in the 1980's and the knee-jerk political correctness on the other, "in-yer-face" theater must be seen in this contextual light.

Ravenhill's body of work, which includes *Shopping and Fucking* (pr. 1996), *Faust Is Dead* (pr. 1997), *Some Explicit Polaroids* (pr. 1999), and *Mother Clap's Molly House* (pr. 2001), is calculated to attack social conventions and consumerism with shocking and explicit stage imagery. Neilson is the most confrontational exponent of what has been termed "experiential theater," in which the audience is not invited but forced to experience brutal emotions represented on the stage. In plays such as *Normal* (pr. 1991), *Penetrator* (pr. 1993), and *The Censor* (pr. 1997), Neilson offers perhaps the most explicit portrayals of sexual fantasy and violence ever seen in the British theater.

The controversial Anglo-Irish playwright Martin McDonagh offers vicious and comic portraits of rural Irish life, even though he has never lived in the country. His *The Beauty Queen of Leenane* (pr. 1996), the first play of *The Leenane Trilogy* (also known as the *Connemara Trilogy*), portrays the distilled relationship of mother and daughter, whose deep bitterness toward one another is matched only by their mutual dependence. *The Lieutenant of Inishmore* (pr. 2001) is equally dark and equally cruel. McDonagh is as successful as he has been controversial, emerging from obscurity in the mid-1990's to become resident playwright at the Royal National Theatre and to see four of his plays running simultaneously in London's West End theaters.

Sarah Kane achieved even greater notoriety than her male counterparts. She provoked audiences with horrific scenes of rape, torture, and mental illness in such plays as *Blasted* (pr. 1995), *Phaedra's Love* (pr.

1996), and *Cleansed* (pr. 1998). Her last work, *4.48 Psychosis* (pr. 2000) takes its title from that time in the morning when most suicides occur. Sadly, Kane herself committed suicide before seeing it produced, at the age of twenty-eight. Although Kane's work was attacked vigorously by many critics, it has been defended and praised by such luminaries as Edward Bond and Pinter.

WOMEN DRAMATISTS

Kane's success hinted at a broader truth: To a degree greater than at any time during its history, modern-day theater in Britain features the work of women playwrights. In addition to Churchill and Gems, a new generation of female writers has produced highly successful and influential drama. Their numbers abound and between them they have placed feminist issues firmly at the center of the contemporary British stage. Among the most important are Sarah Daniels, Debbie Isitt, and Judy Upton, each of whom presents feminist issues with varying degrees of frankness.

Daniels's powerful and complex female characters respond to the demands and the traps of a male-centered culture. In 1983's *Masterpieces*, the representation of women in the media is examined: A woman who has just viewed graphic images of sex and torture at the cinema is approached by a man in the subway; acting instinctively, she pushes him to his death on the tracks. *Neaptide* (pr. 1986) portrays a lesbian mother forced to conceal her sexual identity to keep her job as a schoolteacher and to protect her daughter, while *Head-Rot Holiday* (pr. 1992) examines the impact of prison life on young mothers. The title of Isitt's *The Woman Who Cooked Her Husband* (pr. 1991) offers a clue to the consequences of a middle-aged man's philandering. Isitt's hallmark is her keen eye for suburban bitterness and her biting humor. She founded the Snarling Beasties company and often acts in and directs productions of her own plays, including both the theatrical and the cinematic versions of *Nasty Neighbours* (pr. 1995, 2000). Upton most fully belongs to the "in-yer-face" spirit of the turn of the twenty-first century in portraying angry and powerful young women whose language and behavior

conventionally are deemed outrageous; in other words, her characters are often "girlz," to borrow the title of one of her plays (*The Girlz*, pr. 1998). From *Ashes and Sand* (pr. 1992) to *Sliding with Suzanne* (pr. 2001), Upton offers brutally honest and highly successful portraits of marginalization and exploitation and, in doing so, exposes a great deal of social hypocrisy.

DRAMA IN TWO IRELANDS

No writer in Northern Ireland can escape what are somewhat euphemistically called "the Troubles," but if the Troubles are largely seen from a male point of view, Christina Reid's plays offer a valuable corrective. Reid combines an obviously strong dramatic tradition in Ireland with a concern for the ever-present dangers of life in the North. Her first play, *Did You Hear the One About the Irishman?* (pr. 1982), takes its title from the typical opening line of jokes about the stupidity of the Irish. The joke here, though, is less the improbably idealistic relationship between a Catholic and a Protestant, neither of whom can comprehend the dangers they face. Rather, it is the backdrop to this naïveté: Representatives from both of their families have suffered imprisonment and death because of the endless cycle of violence. The juxtaposition is typical of Reid's dark humor. Subsequent plays, including the gritty and grimly realistic *Joyriders* (pr. 1986) and *The Belle of Belfast City* (pr. 1989), explore the poverty and misery faced by the inhabitants of Belfast as a result of the political conflicts.

Among the many Irish playwrights to emerge from the Irish Republic, one of the most celebrated is Conor McPherson, whose Olivier Award-winning and internationally acclaimed *The Weir* (pr. 1998) is a worthy successor to the great dramatic tradition in Ireland. Set entirely in the local pub of a rural village, the play turns on the arrival of Valerie, an educated and attractive outsider who generates awkward and futile sexual interest among the regulars. Soon the men turn to ghost stories in a bid to impress the newcomer, and Valerie herself reveals that the house she has purchased is haunted. The ghosts and hallucinations in these stories become an emblem of rural Ireland, which, McPherson suggests, is also haunted by its past and its isolation.

DRAMA IN A MULTICULTURAL AGE

Large-scale immigration to Britain began after World War II and continued as former colonies gained their independence. First-generation immigrant playwrights such as Michael Abbensetts and Mustapha Matura established reputations in the 1970's. Abbensetts's work for the theater and television is notable for its realistic representation of the black experience in Britain. His most important play, *Alterations* (pr. 1978), offers a microcosm of the immigrant condition in Britain, portraying a West Indian tailor struggling to complete an order that will allow him to acquire his own shop and a measure of independence. Matura, who immigrated from Trinidad in 1961, uses Britain as a geographic and artistic vantage point to explore Trinidadian life and culture in such plays as *Rum an' Coca Cola* (pr. 1976) and *Independence* (pr. 1979). His early works documenting the West Indian immigrant experience in Britain were groundbreaking, and in the 1980's, his ebullient *The Playboy of the West Indies* (pr. 1984) and *The Trinidad Sisters* (pr. 1988) transformed canonical plays by John Millington Synge and Anton Chekhov, respectively, by setting them in Trinidad and employing the locutions of the Caribbean.

Caryl Phillips, who arrived in England from the West Indies before he was a year old, examines the sense of geographical and cultural dislocation deriving from migration. *Strange Fruit* (pr. 1980) focuses on the children of a single immigrant mother who are drawn, despite their English education, to the culture of the West Indies. *The Shelter* (pr. 1983) addresses one of the most abiding racial and sexual taboos; here, the growing relationship between a shipwrecked black former slave and a white widow in the eighteenth century is balanced by the subsequent exploration of a relationship between a black immigrant and a white Englishwoman in 1950's London.

As first-generation immigrants established families, their British children began to explore through drama the complex racial and cultural issues faced by West Indian and South Asian communities. Winsome

Pinnock, one of the few black women playwrights whose work is regularly performed on the contemporary British stage, takes up Phillips's taboo theme of interracial relationships in *Talking in Tongues* (pr. 1991), which explores the sexual tensions at a New Year's Eve gathering of black and white co-workers. In *Leave Taking* (pr. 1989), too, the British-born Pinnock draws on her Caribbean heritage in exploring the intermingling of languages and cultures in contemporary Britain. Primarily realistic in vein, Pinnock's work is notable for confronting issues generally avoided by her white compatriots.

The same is true of Hanif Kureishi and Ayub Khan-Din, both born of a white English mother and a South Asian immigrant father. Both writers established reputations at the Royal Court Theatre and both have produced successful screenplays. Kureishi's drama, like his novels, employs comic reversals and unexpected juxtapositions to explore questions about personal, cultural, and national identity. *Borderline* (pr. 1981) portrays the parodoxical position in which the South Asian community in Britain finds itself: The characters, threatened verbally and physically, nevertheless find a measure of freedom and opportunity in their adopted land. However, these possibilities undermine all attempts by first-generation immigrant characters to assert and maintain a South Asian way of life. Kureishi's screenplay *My Beautiful Laundrette* (1985) focuses on the homosexual relationship between a young entrepreneurial son of an immigrant Pakistani socialist and his employee, a white former schoolmate with a history of participating in anti-immigration demonstrations in Thatcher's Britain.

Similar themes are represented in Khan-Din's *East Is East* (pr. 1997), a riotous comedy set in 1970's Lancashire against the backdrop of the racism exemplified by British politician Enoch Powell's notorious 1968 "Rivers of Blood" speech. *East Is East* explores the futile attempts of an immigrant Pakistani father to impose his Muslim traditions and values on his secular English children. Strict obedience, circumcisions, and arranged marriages are demanded by their father, but the children, with tacit support from their English mother, find ways to subvert their father. Khan-Din followed *East Is East* with *Last Dance at Dum Dum* (pr. 1999), a portrait of an Anglo-Indian family in Calcutta in the 1980's, a time of increasing religious and political tensions in India. These "British" characters represent the last futile gesture of the empire; their Hindi landlord seeks to evict them from their decaying colonial house, an obvious emblem of the fading illusion of British imperial influence. The work of each of these writers is central to contemporary British theater, not only for its own merits but also because it represents, often far more fully than that of their white counterparts, the multicultural reality of contemporary British life.

BIBLIOGRAPHY

Berney, K. A., ed. *Contemporary British Dramatists.* Detroit, Mich.: St. James Press, 1994. This collection offers brief analyses of more than 150 writers for the stage, radio, and television, and of thirty-four of the most influential and representative plays of the mid- to late-twentieth century. Drama critic Michael Billington offers a useful general introduction.

Boireau, Nicole, ed. *Drama on Drama: Dimensions of Theatricality on the Contemporary British Stage.* New York: St. Martin's, 1997. Boireau's compilation of critical essays share a common theme: the self-reflexivity of contemporary British theater as exemplified in the work of Beckett, Stoppard, Pinter, Timberlake Wertenbaker, and others. Early essays provide a historical context for the metatheatrical technique of the play-within-a-play, and the bulk of the collection examines the postmodernist use of the technique in the work of selected British playwrights.

Palmer, Richard H. *The Contemporary British History Play.* Westport, Conn.: Greenwood, 1998. Palmer investigates the influence of new historicism—a theoretical approach centered on the notion that history is constructed, not simply "uncovered"—on more than fifty of Britain's most prominent playwrights of the contemporary age. Palmer points out the ways in which recent history plays by such writers as Bond, Churchill, Brenton, and Shaffer express a new conception of history that rejects the "great man" biographical dramas of the past in favor of an interest in how history itself is produced.

Shank, Theodore, ed. *Contemporary British Theatre.* London: Macmillan, 1994. A broad and extremely useful collection, covering such topics as Welsh and Scottish drama, the revision of Greek drama on the contemporary stage, technical innovations in direction and set design, and the influence of electronic media on the British stage.

Sierz, Aleks. *In Yer Face Theatre: British Drama Today.* London: Faber and Faber, 2001. Examines in-yer-face drama with one eye on public and critical reactions and the other on its place within mainstream and fringe British theatrical tradition. Sierz argues that plays by Ravenhill, Kane, McDonagh, Upton, and others, far from being calculated simply to shock, offer an important critique of the prevailing values and hypocrisies of contemporary British life. Well written and highly accessible.

John L. Marsden

IRISH DRAMA

"Let us learn construction from the masters and language from ourselves," William Butler Yeats, one of the founders of the Abbey Theatre, advised aspiring playwrights. Indeed, an aptitude for language and humor was a distinctive feature of drama written by Irish authors, but not until the establishment of the Abbey Theatre at the beginning of the twentieth century was it possible for Irish playwrights to draw on indigenous precedents, distinct from those supplied by England's literary tradition. Since the seventeenth century, as Irish dramatists looked toward London for their audiences, Irish drama had taken British theatrical conventions for its own. As the central arena of the cultural-political movement known as the Irish Literary Renaissance, the Abbey Theatre placed the island's resources of myth, social custom, folklore, and language at the service of a generation of dramatists whose work is recognizably Irish. The success of this national theater continued, with some qualifications, through the years, but by the 1920's, a reaction to the preoccupations with national history and identity, rural mores, and religion led to the internationalization of theater in Ireland. As a result of these developments, dramatic writing in Ireland began to produce works of various characters: either provincially British, discretely national, or Continental. Similarly, a historical account of Irish drama falls into three main phases: Anglo-Irish, Irish-national, and contemporary drama.

ANGLO-IRISH PRECEDENTS

Through most of the nineteenth century, Ireland retained some regional vestiges of mumming, a traditional folk drama that ritually reenacted significant events in the memory of the community, but it was not until the early seventeenth century that literary drama set its first roots in Irish soil with the founding of a small theater on Werburgh Street in Dublin in 1637, followed later in the century by the Smock Alley Theatre. Thereafter, the city had a continuous theatrical presence, and many provincial centers had seasonal houses. From its beginnings to the end of the nineteenth century, however, Irish drama was primarily of colonial character, only in minor ways distinct from what could be seen on the stages of London or provincial England. With the collapse of the Gaelic social and political order at the beginning of the seventeenth century, the cultural traditions of Ireland were abandoned, and no Irish institutions remained to graft that inheritance to the life of the cities and the new institution of the stage. Until the end of the nineteenth century, the only contacts with the ancient civilization available to the serious artist were relatively inaccessible relics in the folklore of the countryside and in the manuscript rooms of the museums and academies. These repositories held a rich lode of heroic, romantic, and folk legends that bore witness to a sophisticated, indigenous Celtic civilization.

It is not surprising, therefore, that although many of the most distinguished dramatists writing in English between 1700 and 1900 were born in Ireland, their works were written according to the idiom and conventions of the English stage. Neither the spirit of the times nor the conditions in Ireland were conducive to reflections on what were considered accidents of birth. Scions of the Anglo-Irish Protestant ascendancy, these writers typically attended an Irish grammar school and Trinity College, Dublin, before emigrating to London to pursue professional or theatrical careers. Many of them were Grub Street hacks, writing sentimental commercial comedy, melodrama, or farce, as the commercial market demanded, but the most distinguished of them were the pioneers of new developments in English drama. Two of the earliest Irish-born dramatists were the seventeenth century's Nahum Tate and Thomas Southerne, best known, respectively, for their popular adaptations of William Shakespeare's plays and Aphra Behn's novels. William Congreve, whose *Love for Love* (pr. 1695) is the masterpiece of the comedy of manners, and George Farquhar, author of the genial and entertaining comedies *The Recruiting Officer* (pr. 1706) and *The Beaux' Stratagem* (pr. 1707), perhaps derived from their Irish birth some of the detachment and humor that enabled them to develop a satiric style. The sentimental comedy of the eighteenth century had its chief exponents in two Irishmen, Sir Richard Steele and Hugh Kelly, before the arrival of Oliver Goldsmith. In his 1773 "An Essay on Theatre" and his classic laughing comedy *She Stoops to Conquer; Or, The Mistakes of a Night* (pr. 1773), Goldsmith put an end to sentimental comedy's effete mélange of tragedy and comedy by purifying once again the springs of humor. This refreshing departure in English comic style was continued by Richard Brinsley Sheridan in *The Rivals* (pr. 1775) and his classic *The School for Scandal* (pr. 1777).

During all of this period and until the nineteenth century, the most visible Irish feature of the drama was the convention of the stage Irishman: a humorous character, either gentleman or peasant, whose distinctive features were his outrageous dialect, proclivity to "Irish bulls" (blunders in speech or logic), and pugnacious disposition. This endearing caricature has many variants (soldier, priest, gentleman, fortune hunter, servant) and can be found in the English theater from Tudor times—notably in Farquhar's Roebuck (*Love and a Bottle*, pr. 1698) and Sheridan's Sir Lucius O'Trigger (*The Rivals*), evolving in the nineteenth century into the Conn (*The Shaughraun*, pr. 1874) of Dion Boucicault. Boucicault was the most prolific and successful Irish dramatist of the nineteenth century, especially with *London Assurance* (pr. 1841), a comedy of manners, and several Irish melodramas, including *The Shaughraun*. By the 1890's, two other Anglo-Dubliners had begun to establish themselves in the tradition of stage comedy established by their forebears: George Bernard Shaw and Oscar Wilde. Shaw soon became the leading social satirist and comedian of ideas in the modern British theater, and Wilde, by virtue of his brilliantly witty comedies, especially *The Importance of Being Earnest: A Trivial Comedy for Serious People* (pr. 1895), was the most celebrated—and infamous—of the Decadents. The Irish origins of these dramatists enabled them, like so many Anglo-Irish writers before them, to view with some dispassion the English class system, English social customs, and habits of feeling and speech, and their own socially indeterminate position (as outsid-

ers in Ireland as well as England) gave them a sense of independence and contributed to the skepticism with which they treated their English materials. On the other hand, with the exception of Shaw's *John Bull's Other Island* (pr. 1904), neither made explicit use of distinctively Irish themes.

IRISH-NATIONAL DRAMA

By the late nineteenth century, however, the Irish Literary Renaissance had introduced to the stage the resources of Ireland's long-neglected cultural tradition. The father of this movement was the poet William Butler Yeats. Under the influence of John O'Leary, an aging revolutionary and *littérateur*, the young Yeats turned from a career begun in the spirit of late Victorian English letters to the folklore of the west of Ireland and the heroic legends of Celtic literature that were, by the end of the nineteenth century, becoming available in contemporary English translation. In the company of Lady Augusta Gregory, a folklorist and folk dramatist, and Edward Martyn, a landed gentleman with strong affinities for Henrik Ibsen's social, symbolic drama, Yeats founded the Irish Literary Theatre in 1899, which within several seasons became the showpiece of the national literary movement: Dublin's Abbey Theatre.

The founders of this theater took their cue from the presence of several European precursors: Ole Bull's in Norway (established in 1850), André Antoine's Théâtre Libre in Paris (1887), Germany's Freie Bühne Theater (1889), J. T. Grein's Independent Theatre in London (1891), and the Moscow Arts Theatre (1897). In contrast with these antecedents, however, Yeats, Lady Gregory, and Martyn were beginning as pioneers. Although this group had a diversity of talents, sensibilities, and inclinations, they agreed on the necessity to replace the caricature of Irish life on the stage with serious and authentic drama, drama that would be at once popular yet not ruled by political orthodoxies, and they committed themselves to experimentation with an imaginative and poetic drama that would harness heroic legend to the demands of the modern stage. Yeats developed his dramas from indigenous folk and mythic materials, the French Symbolists, Ibsen's poetic dramas, and, later, Japanese No drama; Martyn modeled his work on the more social and realistic of Ibsen's works; and Lady Gregory drew on folklore, local history, and heroic sources that she herself collected or translated, shaping these materials with the techniques of French comedy.

The Irish Literary Theatre opened in May, 1899, with Yeats's poetic play *The Countess Cathleen* (pr. 1899) and Martyn's problem play *The Heather Field* (pr. 1899). This initial double bill was to foreshadow the character of the Irish theater's repertoire during the ensuing decades. The low-key naturalistic acting style of the company, led by William and Frank Fay, and the financial patronage of Annie Horniman soon won for the Irish Literary Theatre a solid reputation. By 1904, it had found a permanent home on Abbey Street (thus the name Abbey Theatre), and the dramatic movement was attracting many talents in the rising generation, including John Millington Synge, George Fitzmaurice, and Padraic Colum. Meanwhile, under Bulmer Hobson, the Ulster Literary Theatre was providing in Belfast what the Abbey Theatre had begun in Dublin.

Yeats himself experimented with several dramatic styles, including peasant realism, farce, and modern naturalism, but his genius found its true métier in a highly sophisticated drama that combined poetry, dance, mask, and symbolic action to represent a world of ideals and pure passion. These plays borrowed from the Japanese Nō for their form, from Celtic heroic tales for their subjects, and expressed Yeats's view of the primacy of imaginative or spiritual realities of which historical change and the differentiation of humanity are emanations. In all of his work, but most comprehensively in his plays for masks, Yeats's enmity against modern realism can be seen. An attitude of detachment and impersonality shapes his works into intensely ritualized expressions, having affinities with both ancient religious drama and modern absurdism.

In Cuchulain, the central figure of the Ulster Cycle of Celtic tales, Yeats found a symbolic conjunction of the virtues of heroic individualism, eloquence, aristocracy, and pagan self-realization—values that he sought to insinuate into the character of modern Ireland. In his *Four Plays for Dancers* (pb. 1921), and especially in *The Only Jealousy of Emer* (pr. 1922), the convergence of Japanese technique and Celtic subject is most evident. Beyond the plays themselves, with their masterful fusion of private passion and public vision, Yeats's legacy to Irish drama consists of haughty artistic independence and a heightened awareness of the possibilities for verse drama in a hostile age. Following his example, verse drama has had a small but persistent tradition in Ireland, notably in the works of the poet Austin Clarke and Donagh MacDonagh and in the productions of the Lyric Players Theatre, Belfast.

Before long, however, the Abbey Theatre had developed its own distinctive blend of naturalism, romanticism, and poetry, as exemplified principally by the plays of John Millington Synge during the first decade of the twentieth century and of Sean O'Casey during the 1920's. Synge was the first Irish dramatist to combine successfully the influences of Molière's design and humor, Jean Racine's musicality, Irish myth and folklore, and the extravagant dialect of English to be found in the remote regions of Ireland. Synge was the first major success of the Abbey Theatre, in terms of both the realization of its theoretical objectives and its becoming the focus of consciousness for the emerging nation. Synge's reputation rests on the output of the last seven years of his brief life: six plays, two of which, *Riders to the Sea* (pb. 1903) and *The Playboy of the Western World* (pr. 1907), are masterpieces. These plays in particular exhibit the characteristic qualities of intense, lyric speech drawn from the native language and dialects of Ireland, romantic characterization in primitive settings, and dramatic construction after the classics of European drama. Three central themes dominate Synge's work: the enmity between romantic dreams and life's hard necessities, the relationship between human beings and the natural world, and the mutability of all things. The production of some of his plays, notably *The Playboy of the Western World*, aroused public controversy, provoking riots and a bitter public debate over the play and over freedom of expression on the stage. In retrospect, *The Playboy of the Western World* is universally acclaimed as one of the classics of dramatic comedy and marks the zenith of the Abbey Theatre's early years. Synge had considerable influence in shaping the style and theme of subsequent Irish drama, as exemplified by the works of Fitzmaurice, Michael J. Molloy, and John B. Keane, and some influence outside Ireland, most notably in the work of Federico García Lorca and Eugene O'Neill.

Although Synge's work was the most accomplished transmutation of Irish rural life into lyric realism, other dramatists in the literary movement made worthy contributions to the style that was to become the hallmark of the Abbey Theatre: Lady Gregory's many comedies based on folklife rendered in humorous and colorful "Kiltartan" dialect, Colum's realistic tragedies of peasant life set in the midlands, Fitzmaurice's fantasies and realistic tragedies set in his native Kerry. These writers had many inferior imitators, and the Abbey Theatre went into a decline. That decline was arrested, however, by the arrival of O'Casey in 1923.

In many ways Synge's city equivalent, O'Casey brought the language, the humor, and the sufferings of the Dublin poor to the stage, especially in his three "Dublin plays": *The Shadow of a Gunman* (pr. 1923), *Juno and the Paycock* (pr. 1924), and *The Plough and the Stars* (pr. 1926). In these works—set against the political struggles of the previous decade—he showed himself a master of tragicomedy and a trenchant critic of personal and national self-deception. When he submitted his play *The Silver Tassie* (pr. 1929) to the Abbey Theatre, codirectors Yeats and Lady Gregory rejected it for what they considered an ill-conceived expressionist second act; an acrimonious public exchange followed, and O'Casey severed his relationship with the Abbey Theatre. His later plays are marked by a more strident Marxism and by less certainty in the handling of the Irish materials that he continued to employ throughout his long remove to the south of England.

During the 1920's, the talented "second generation" of Abbey playwrights emerged: T. C. Murray, Lennox Robinson, and Brinsley MacNamara. These dramatists helped establish domestic realism as the hallmark of the Abbey Theatre, a preference relayed in Belfast by the Ulster Group Theatre in the 1940's.

Murray's work is stark tragedy, Robinson's ranges from farce to historical treatments of the decline of the Anglo-Irish class, and MacNamara wrote many popular comedies of small-town life. As the official state theater, the Abbey benefited from a modest subvention but suffered from some restrictions. A fire in 1951 caused a temporary move, remedied in 1966 with the building of the new Abbey Theatre on the same site and realizing Yeats and Lady Gregory's plans for a large, commercial auditorium along with a pocket theater, The Peacock, for poetic and experimental works.

It was not entirely a coincidence that in the same year as O'Casey's falling out with the Abbey directorate, Dublin got its second serious theater: the Gate Theatre. Founded by Hilton Edwards and Micheál MacLiammóir, the Gate Theatre set out to bring European and international classic theater to Ireland, in contrast to the perceived introversion of the Abbey Theatre. Almost immediately, with Denis Johnston's sensational expressionist play about Irish nationalism, *The Old Lady Says No!* (pr. 1929), the Gate Theatre began its signal service to Irish audiences in importing contemporary European and American drama as well as encouraging much of the best experimental work by Irish playwrights.

During the 1950's, three dramatists emerged who represented quite different traditions and social sectors: Brendan Behan, a political dramatist from Dublin's working class; John B. Keane, author of many popularly successful folk melodramas; and Dubliner Samuel Beckett, whose inimitable theatrical genius blends some Anglo-Irish coloration into his dramas of persistence in the face of dissolution and death (most notably in *All That Fall*, pr. 1957). Behan, whose two plays *The Quare Fellow* (pr. 1954) and *The Hostage* (pr. 1958) were produced by Joan Littlewood at the Theatre Royal, London, gained an international reputation of spirited tragicomedy.

CONTEMPORARY IRISH DRAMA

Irish drama in the last decades of the twentieth century was healthier than in any other period since the 1920's, despite commercial demands and the counterattractions of other media. The annual Dublin

Theatre Festival, state subventions to the Gate Theatre and individual dramatists, and local amateur dramatic societies encouraged potential writers for the stage. Although there were regular complaints about excessive accommodation to the tourist trade in theatrical offerings by the main theaters, new dramatists found outlets at the Peacock and many smaller independent and provincial theaters and the national television network (RTE). A significant development has been the appearance of a considerable body of work for the stage by dramatists from Northern Ireland whose work reflects both the social disruption caused by the political violence and the questions of political and cultural identity provoked by the physical confrontations on the streets.

The three senior dramatists in the last decades of the twentieth century were Brian Friel, Hugh Leonard, and Tom Murphy. In Friel's œuvre of impressive range, from his early success, *Philadelphia, Here I Come!* (pr. 1964) to his large successes, *Translations* (pr. 1980) and *Dancing at Lughnasa* (pr. 1990), his central preoccupation has been the relationship of Ireland's communitarian past to its present circumstances of social and political change. The dominant mood of his plays is bittersweet, while technically he applies various nonrealistic techniques to realistic situations. In *The Freedom of the City* (pr. 1973) he has written one of the best plays on the conflict in Northern Ireland. Friel also founded the Field Day Theatre to develop new plays and playwrights and to accomplish on a larger scale what his plays try to do individually. Besides the encouragement to new playwrights, however, the most important contribution of the Field Day Theatre has not been a theater piece but a series of pamphlets, somewhat in the manner of fellow-Irishman Jonathan Swift in the eighteenth century. These pamphlets deal in particular with the development of theater in Ireland and with Irish problems in general. They are grouped as published, under separate titles: The first six pamphlets are collected as *Ireland's Field Day* (1985); the next three as *The Protestant Idea of Liberty* (1985); and the next three as *The Apparatus of Repression: Emergency Legislation* (1986).

Leonard's eye, on the other hand, focuses on Ireland's recent economic prosperity; he is primarily a witty social satirist of considerable technical virtuosity (refined through much commercial television work). His most accomplished play in this vein is *The Patrick Pearse Motel* (pr. 1971), a brilliant farce. His greatest critical success, however, has been the autobiographical *Da* (pr. 1973). A poignant portrait of the complex relations between a gifted young man and his adoptive parents, it is invested with more feeling than his broader social satires. Tom Murphy writes with more force and less nostalgia of the dysfunctional family, the de-racination of Irish emigrants, and the decline of religious belief in an impressive œuvre from *A Whistle in the Dark* (pr. 1961) to *Bailegangaire* (pr. 1985). His stark and surreal dramas were only belatedly recognized in Ireland.

The leading dramatists in contemporary Ireland are Frank McGuinness, Sebastian Barry, and Martin McDonagh. Two of the most original and powerful plays in the late twentieth century were McGuinness's *Observe the Sons of Ulster Marching Towards the Somme* (pb. 1985) and Barry's *The Steward of Christendom* (pr. 1995). Set on the western front on the eve of the infamous battle (July 1, 1916), McGuinness's play examines the ideological cul-de-sac of Ulster loyalism, in its inability to reach an accommodation with Irish nationalism or with an evolved British imperialism.

Barry's is a memory play that depicts the plight of the Catholic loyalists marginalized by history during the Dublin Lock-Out of 1913. Through the recollections of an aged man confined to a mental hospital, it contrasts the complacency of Victorian Ireland with the ethos of the Irish Catholic nationalist state that was to replace it. McDonagh burst on the scene with great flourish in his series *The Leenane Trilogy* (includes *The Beauty Queen of Leenane*, pr. 1996; *A Skull in Connemara*, pr. 1997; *The Lonesome West*, pr. 1997) while *The Aran Trilogy* (includes *The Cripple of Inishmaan*, pr. 1997; *The Lieutenant of Inishmore*, pr. 2001; *The Banshees of Inisheer*, not produced) was sensational in its application of Pinteresque technique to Irish settings. Other plays of considerable note in their analysis of Irish identity are Thomas Kilroy's *Double Cross* (pr. 1986), and Stewart Parker's *Pentecost* (pr. 1987), and Marina Carr's *The Mai* (pr. 1994), while other late twentieth century playwrights of note are Thomas Kilroy (*Double Cross*, performed in 1986 at the Field Day Theatre), Anne Devlin (whose *Ourselves Alone*, *The Long March*, and *A Woman Calling* were produced and published together in 1986), Bernard Farrell (*All the Way Back*, pr. 1985, pb. 1988), and Tom MacIntyre (*Dance for Your Daddy*, pr. 1987).

Irish activist and actress Margaretta D'Arcy, best known for her collaborations with John Arden, is a noted Dublin-born playwright active in examining and dramatizing the political questions of the country. Long productions (sometimes as long as twenty-six hours) revolving loosely around the life and activities of James Connolly (the six-part *The Non-Stop Connolly Show* was produced through the 1970's but was published in full in 1986) have set her work apart even from the more radical Irish theater. Her plays have been described by Michael Etherton as emphasizing "the central and unresolved conflict between revolution and reform: the relationship of socialism to republicanism in the context of north and south, and the issue of land in Ireland that continues to underscore the struggle today; their particular depiction of women; the emblematic theatre that they have recreated and its antecedents in carnival and the Corpus Christi cycle of the medieval theatre."

BIBLIOGRAPHY

Clark, William Smith. *The Early Irish Stage: The Beginnings to 1720*. Westport, Conn.: Greenwood, 1955. A pioneering study of Irish dramatic traditions from folk plays to the growth of Dublin theaters after the Restoration.

Etherton, Michael. *Contemporary Irish Dramatists*. New York: St. Martin's Press, 1989. With sections on Belfast, Dublin, and the provincial theaters, a general and easy-to-read survey of Irish drama between 1960 and 1987.

Fitz-Simon, Christopher. *The Irish Theatre*. New York: Thames and Hudson, 1983. A well-illustrated and encyclopedic survey from miracle plays to modern times presented from the point of view of a stage director.

McDonald, Ronan. *Tragedy and Irish Writing: Synge, O'Casey, Beckett*. New York: Palgrave, 2001. Analyzes the development and evolution of Irish tragedy via the works of three preeminent Irish writers.

Mahony, Christina Hunt. *Contemporary Irish Literature: Transforming Tradition*. New York: St. Martin's Press, 1998. Contains an eighty-page survey of the representation of Irish life onstage between 1960 and the 1990's.

Murray, Christopher. *Twentieth Century Irish Drama: Mirror up to Nation*. Manchester, England: Manchester University Press, 1997. A wide-ranging survey of the relationship between Irish drama and the public scene from Yeats to the mid-1990's.

Owens, Cóilín, and Joan Radner, eds. *Irish Drama, 1900-1980*. Washington, D.C.: The Catholic University of America Press, 1991. An anthology of eighteen representative plays with individual introductions, detailed annotations, and bibliographies.

Roche, Anthony. *Contemporary Irish Drama: From Beckett to McGuinness*. New York: St. Martin's Press, 1994. An intensive academic study of Beckett's relationships with Yeats and Behan, but also surveying the work of Friel, Murphy, McGuinness, and the Field Day Group.

Watson, George J. *Irish Identity and the Literary Revival: Synge, Yeats, Joyce, and O'Casey*. Washington, D.C.: Catholic University of America Press, 1994. Traces the development of a true Irish presence in the literary world by examining the contributions of four noted literary figures.

Cóilín D. Owens,
updated by Thomas J. Taylor